# Risk Management and Insurance: Perspectives in a Global Economy

To Dinah

*Harold D. Skipper*


To my dear parents and Jeannie, my wife

*W. Jean Kwon*

# Risk Management and Insurance

## Perspectives in a Global Economy

Harold D. Skipper and W. Jean Kwon

Blackwell
Publishing

BLACKWELL PUBLISHING
350 Main Street, Malden, MA 02148-5020, USA
9600 Garsington Road, Oxford OX4 2DQ, UK
550 Swanston Street, Carlton, Victoria 3053, Australia

First published 2007 by Blackwell Publishing Ltd

1    2007

*Library of Congress Cataloging-in-Publication Data*

Skipper, Harold D.
    Risk management and insurance : perspectives in a global economy / Harold D. Skipper and
W. Jean Kwon.
       p. cm.
  Includes bibliographical references and index.
  ISBN 978-1-4051-2541-3 (hardcover : alk. paper)
  1.  Risk management. 2.  Insurance.  I. Kwon, W. Jean. II. Title.
  HD61.K86 2007
  368—dc22

                                                                           2007002718

A catalogue record for this title is available from the British Library.

Set in 10.5/12 Times
by Charon Tec Ltd (A Macmillan Company), Chennai, India
www.charontec.com
Printed and bound in the United States
by Sheridan Books, Inc.

For further information on
Blackwell Publishing, visit our website:
www.blackwellpublishing.com

# Contents

# Preface

Risk lies at the core of all human endeavors. We humans spend a great deal of time, effort and money in coping with risks' downsides. This coping is perhaps most obvious at the societal level where our taxes fund governments – the world's largest entities and whose *raison d'etre* is risk management. Businesses too must manage their risks efficiently and effectively if they are to succeed. Of course, individuals and families cope with risks daily, relying on government and businesses to assist in the process. We have attempted to craft this book with these ideas in mind while recognizing the impossibility of addressing their full panoply.

## AIM AND APPROACH

Our aim is to provide students and practitioners who have an interest in the profession of risk management (and, therefore, insurance) with the fundamentals necessary to embark on mastery of the subject. The book's underlying premise is that we can understand risk and insurance only if we understand their underlying principles and the factors that give rise to risk. This approach differs from the more traditional textbooks in that (1) our orientation is the world, not a single nation's market, (2) we focus on underlying principles, avoiding much institutional detail that is best learned through training and (3) we seek to instill in the reader an appreciation for the great importance of understanding the factors that shape risk in the world.

We build naturally on students' other academic subjects, including economics and the other social sciences, finance, marketing, law and management to demonstrate how risk management and insurance are integral to business operations. Students often have difficulty mastering the interrelationships between subjects. It is too easy for them to lose sight of the logic that drives decision-making under conditions of uncertainty.

We also seek to synthesize the material in a way that is directly relevant for the person who is not necessarily interested in becoming a risk and insurance specialist. The nonspecialist seeks mastery of three things: (1) concepts that will prove useful in decision-making in later life, (2) an understanding of the broad elements of the subject and (3) the risk-related issues confronting society. Risk and insurance problems encountered later in life rarely match the typical textbook presentation, with the result that students find themselves unprepared to abstract from what they have learned. We attempt to present the student with a cohesive, integrated perspective from which future problems can be analyzed and solved.

Thus, our approach is to instill an intuitive appreciation for risk. We do this primarily through examples that simultaneously illustrate the economic building blocks of risk. We return time and again throughout the book to market imperfections and their critical role in shaping how society, businesses and individuals deal with risk. We believe that students of risk and insurance who master these few, common-sense economic principles will carry into their future work a way of thinking about risk that will serve them well for decades to come. Because of the book's international orientation, we include in Part I a chapter on the economics of international trade as being similarly necessary.

In Part II, we offer a series of chapters that explore the factors that shape the risk environment internationally. In this respect, our approach differs from other introductory risk and insurance textbooks that largely omit this critically important aspect of mastery of the subject matter. Our mission is to sensitize readers to the underlying demographic, cultural, technological, physical and other global trends influencing societal risk and security perceptions and responses. We use this foundation to explore the appropriate role and nature of both the private sector and government in the provision of economic security. In doing this, we rely chiefly on the economic concepts of market imperfections. This chapter series is *not* about lists of risks. Rather, we attempt to inculcate within the reader an understanding of why society should concern itself with some risks, but not others.

Part III of the book explores corporate risk management. With the increasing role of multinational corporations (MNCs) worldwide and a dearth of relevant material about their risk management, we emphasize risk management for MNCs. Of course, the principles and the great majority of the practices apply equally for purely national entities. As we adopt an enterprise-wide approach to corporate risk management (ERM), we introduce relevant principles and explore some of the practical aspects of both organizational and financial risk management in this part. By emphasizing certain elements of MNC risk management, we seek to both deepen and broaden the student's understanding of ERM.

As insurance is of critical importance in managing societal, organizational and family risks, Part IV of the book examines insurance and insurance markets worldwide. As with the other parts of the book, our focus is international with a strong emphasis on economic principles.

We close the book with what we hope is a thought-provoking discussion of the future of risk. Because today's students will live and work in a future characterized by rates of change unprecedented in history, we take the position that our responsibility as authors extends to causing them critically to examine their own "official view of the future."

## HOW TO USE THE BOOK

As implied in the preceding discussion, the book first establishes essential principles, terminology and background upon which later material relies. With these fundamentals, we next set a societal risk context through our examination of the factors shaping risk internationally. Readers are then prepared to extend these fundamentals and contexts to corporate risk management and the study of insurance in a global economy.

We are mindful that some professors and others will face time and other constraints that perhaps do not allow sufficient time to cover the entire book. While the book has been assembled as a cohesive whole that can be covered within a typical semester-long course, we have attempted simultaneously to construct it such that portions can be used separately. For example, professors wishing to emphasize societal risk management issues will find that Parts III and IV perhaps can be omitted. Similarly, those wishing to emphasize corporate risk management could omit much of Part II, picking only those portions applicable directly to ERM. Of course, other combinations are possible through judicious selection of chapters and portions of chapters.

## FEATURES

Liberal use has been made of figures and tables and especially of what we call *Insights*. *Insights* amplify the text material itself by offering insight through additional key information or interesting vignettes from newspapers, books and other publications.

All key terms are defined. To draw attention to them, all appear in boldface font when defined. Italicized terms indicate emphasis or are the names of laws, regulations, treaties, etc. Of course, a fully glossary of all key terms is included, along with a listing of all abbreviations we use frequently in this book.

## SUPPLEMENTS

We make presentation files containing all figures in this textbook that professors and lecturers may download from the website managed by us. We also offer at the same webpage updated information and data (sources) as and when they become available. The URL of the webpage is: http://facpub.stjohns.edu/kwonw

## THANKS

So very many people deserve our thanks for their help in developing this book. First, we must acknowledge with our thanks the pioneering work done by so many of the authors who prepared chapters for Harold D. Skipper's 1998 book, *International Risk and Insurance: An Environmental-Managerial Approach*, which is out of print. This book likely was the first true university-level textbook on the subject, and, as is evidenced by appropriate footnotes, we have drawn from some of its chapters in crafting our own chapters in this book. Authors of those chapters include Samuel H. Cox, William S. Custer, William R. Feldhaus, Larry D. Gaunt, Martin F. Grace, Ellwood F. Oakley III, Bruce A. Palmer and Richard D. Phillips all of Georgia State University; Patrick L. Brockett of the University of Texas; Helen I. Doerpinghaus of the University of South Carolina; H. Felix Kloman then of *Risk Management Reports*; Brian McGreevy then of the Life Office Management Association; Frederick Schroath from Kent State University; Tara C. Skipper then of Southern Methodist University; James P. Tenny of Leahey & Johnson, P.C.; and Marc M. Tract of Rosenman & Colin, LLP.

We also express our appreciation to the many academics who reviewed earlier versions of chapters, including Dan Jones of the University of Houston; George Krempley of Ohio State University; Donghui Li of the University of New South Wales, Australia; and Michael Powers of Temple University. Our thanks also go to Conrad Ciccotello, William R. Feldhaus, Martin F. Grace, Robert W. Klein and Richard D. Phillips who critiqued chapters that are included in whole or part in this book and were originally drafted for an earlier book. Special appreciation goes to Ismael Rivera-Sierra, Richard Waller, Galina Spicehandler and Andrew Seville all of the Kathryn & Shelby Cullom Davis

Library, the School of Risk Management, St. John's University; to George Lobell, Laura Stearns, Desiree Zicko, Simon Eckley, and Lisa Eaton, all of Blackwell Publishing; and to Charon Tec Ltd (A Macmillan Company) and its team.

Of course, none of these individuals is responsible for errors, omissions or opinions contained in this book. They remain the sole responsibility of the authors.

Harold D. Skipper                                    W. Jean Kwon
Atlanta                                                   New York

The authors and publisher gratefully acknowledge the permission granted to reproduce the copyright material in this book. Every effort has been made to trace copyright holders and to obtain their permission for the use of copyright material. The publisher apologizes for any errors or omissions and would be grateful if notified of any corrections that should be incorporated in future reprints or editions of this book.

# Part I

# Introduction

# Chapter 1

# Introduction to Risk Management and Insurance

## INTRODUCTION

Humans have always sought to reduce uncertainty.[1] This innate risk-reduction drive motivated the earliest formations of clans, tribes and other groups. Group mechanisms ensured a less volatile source of life's necessities than that which atomized humans and families could provide. The group provided greater physical security and helped their less fortunate members in times of crises.

People today continue their quest to achieve security and reduce uncertainty. We still engage in activities and rely on groups to help reduce the variability of income required to obtain life's necessities and to protect acquired wealth. The group may be our employer, the government, or an insurance firm, but the concept is the same. In some ways, however, we are more vulnerable than our ancestors. The physical and economic security formerly provided by the tribe or extended family diminishes with industrialization. Our income-dependent, wealth-acquiring lifestyles render us and our families more vulnerable to societal and environmental changes over which we have little control. Contemporary individuals are in need of more formalized means to mitigate the adverse consequences of unemployment, loss of health, old age, death, lawsuits and loss of wealth.

As extensions of human activity, businesses are similarly vulnerable. Every firm faces the possibility of losing a key employee due to premature death or loss of health, damage or destruction of its property caused by a natural or man-made calamity and being held responsible for the economic loss suffered by others because of the firm's actions. With increasing concentrations of property and people and with increasingly complex servicing, manufacturing and industrial processes, businesses have come to appreciate that they today are exposed to greater risk than ever.

Risk is universal and lies at the heart of all economic activities of individuals, businesses and governments. Through effective use of risk management techniques, we attempt to use our limited economic resources – land, capital and labor – efficiently to further our economic wellbeing. Scientific, technological and managerial developments have afforded us the ability of dealing with many of those risks. True, the frequency of loss has been decreasing for many technologically sophisticated processes and activities, but the adverse consequences of losses that do occur have increased. For example, the combined effect of a growth in

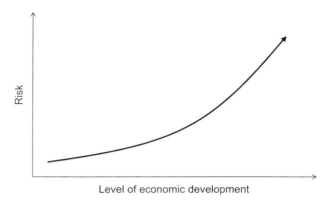

**Figure 1.1**    Risk and Economic Development

population, a rise in property density and value, and expanded interactions among people across national boundaries have resulted in higher frequency and severity of catastrophic losses. A Swiss Re (2006) study indicates that the number of human-made catastrophes worldwide has risen from around 60 in 1970 to 248 in 2005. The number of natural catastrophes has also risen from around 30 to nearly 150 cases over the same period. Further, we face possibilities of unprecedented harm, as whole societies continue to grow economically. Figure 1.1 suggests a stylized version of this phenomenon.

With economic development, risks that formerly could be managed effectively within families, tribes, or small enterprises became too large for such internalization. Indeed, many of the world's contemporary risks are now managed at the national and, in some instances, the international level.

Merely agreeing that the effective management of risks is likely to become more critical with economic development fails to inform us about how they affect and are affected by economic development. A better understanding of risks would allow individuals, governments and businesses to make more informed decisions about the issues relevant to them.

## THE IMPORTANCE OF AN INTERNATIONAL PERSPECTIVE

Decisions about how to deal with some risky activities and processes have become incredibly complex. The consequences of wrong decisions or just plain bad luck can have profoundly adverse effects, not only on decision-makers, but also on employees, customers, suppliers and citizens. Increasingly, adverse effects can spill across industries and even national borders, causing grave harm to the innocent and uninvolved. For these reasons, the study of the management of risk in a global context is more important than ever.

The cliché that the "world is getting smaller" is indeed accurate. Advances in transportation, telecommunication and information technology truly have combined to render the remotest corners of the globe accessible. Real-time coverage by mass media via satellite and through the Internet permits us to be first-hand witnesses to the world's unfolding economic and political events. An increasing number of companies no longer perceives their markets as purely

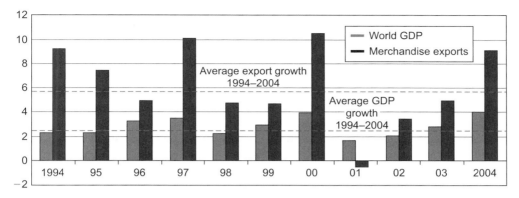

**Figure 1.2**   Growth in the Volume of World Merchandise Trade and GDP, 1994–2004 (Annual Percentage Change). *Source*: WTPO.

national. Some multinational enterprises conduct such extensive international operations that no particular country can claim to be their "home." Microsoft is everywhere. BP Amoco operates in more than 24 countries and owns 38 chemicals sites worldwide. Toyota operates 52 manufacturing companies in 27 countries. Coca Cola owns more than 400 brands in excess of 200 countries.

In most markets, a significant proportion of goods and services competes directly or indirectly with those of other countries. The proportion of cross-border trade continues to grow worldwide. For example, the world exchanged merchandise valued at US$6.2 trillion in 2000. This is in addition to exports of commercial services amounting to US$1.4 trillion during the same year. As Figure 1.2 shows, the growth rate of world merchandise trade routinely exceeds that of overall national output.

To think of globalization primarily in terms of trade, however, is wrong. **Foreign direct investment** (FDI) – investment by foreigners in domestic businesses – has grown at a faster rate than world trade. The annual publication of the United Nations Conference on Trade and Development (UNCTAD), *World Investment Report*, shows that FDI inflows tend to grow at rates greater than merchandise trade. This impressive growth is in part a result of advancement in technology and the internationalization of production – intra-firm, cross-border trade in components, parts and business services. Products from airplanes to pencils contain elements manufactured, assembled, designed, or financed in multiple countries.

In today's economy, distinguishing "domestic" from "foreign" products and services (and risks) is increasingly difficult. Financial services in general and insurance in particular are being globalized in even more subtle ways. Such foreign investments and operations connote additional and more complex risks.

In a global economy, competitiveness is heightened as price differentiation becomes a less feasible alternative to improved operating efficiency. The continuing worldwide activity by businesses through reengineering, outsourcing, downsizing, or flattening the organizational structure attests to the correctness of this view. Given that 80 percent of the value added to goods and services is attributable to people – human capital – efficiency gains can be more easily achieved through enhanced knowledge. In such an environment, knowledge moves businesses and entire national economies forward. This assertion applies equally to knowledge about risk and its management. Today, and even more so in the future, the business or country that fails to seek out and exploit knowledge wherever it may be found, that believes it can produce and rely exclusively on nationally generated knowledge or processes, or that believes it has little to learn from competing firms or countries internationally, eventually will find itself in economic decline.

The above observations apply to the management of risk in another sense. Firms not directly involved in international activities often believe that understanding risk management practices and issues of other cultures is of little relevance to them. This view is myopic.

True, the way risk is dealt with naturally differs to suit each country's sociocultural, demographic, political and economic circumstances. Although these circumstances can vary dramatically, business operations throughout the world, including the management of risk, have innumerable features and challenges in common. By exchanging ideas on how to meet these challenges, businesses can benefit themselves and their markets. Thus, electrical utilities in many nations could learn much from the way that the French effectively and efficiently manage risks of nuclear power generation. The *bancassurance* movement in the Spain offers lessons for its successful introduction in other countries.

# RISK MANAGEMENT AND ECONOMIC GROWTH

Risk management entails the process by which risks are identified and evaluated, and decisions then made and implemented for the most effective and efficient means of managing the risks. Economists argue that the more pervasive and extensive the use of risk management, the more sustainable will be economic growth and development. Here we explore why we believe that risk management will be increasingly important in the future and its role in economic growth.

## The Growing Importance of Risk Management

Historically, economic development and growth have meant concentration of economic resources and increased specialization in production. Villages became towns, which became cities. Many "mom-and-pop" operations became small corporations, some of which became national corporations, with some of these becoming multinational corporations.

Concentration has increased not only in terms of value, with a consequent heightened possibility of catastrophic loss, but also through forward and backward linkages, such as dependencies on suppliers of raw materials, equipment, services and technology. This result carries the possibility of business interruption, not only for the individual business, but also for its customers and its suppliers in the vertical or horizontal production chain.

Developing countries and economies in transition have witnessed a trend toward large-scale construction and manufacturing projects with associated high values that loom large as a proportion of the country's total exposure to loss. A loss could leave the business and even the national economy in dire difficulties. The destruction of a large-scale industrial complex in Zimbabwe could put the nation's economy into difficulty, whereas the destruction of a similar complex in Japan would not.

**High-value (highly protected) risks** – complex and highly integrated industrial properties that use the latest technology in construction, property maintenance, and production process – are becoming common worldwide. Offshore oil refineries, mega-size hydraulic dams, nuclear power plants, high-rise commercial buildings, and other human-made high-value risks sprout across the world. The potential for harmful spillover effects on innocent individuals, businesses and even the government grows. In some instances, the attendant exposures have exceeded the experience of local specialists and state authorities in managing them, thus aggravating the potential for significant harm to workers, business viability and even the national economy.

Resource concentration occurring in countries or regions with substantial exposures to natural disasters magnifies the need for effective risk management. Destruction from floods, droughts, tropical cyclones, earthquakes, tsunamis and a host of other natural calamities seems regularly to thwart the best efforts of humans to mitigate attendant damages, especially among the least developed countries. Increasingly, human-made catastrophes, whether intentional such as terrorism, or unintentional such a financial crisis, seem regularly to occupy the headlines. Of course, economic development often aggravates the exposure to and leads to natural disasters. Building in flood or earthquake-prone areas and clearing of the rain forests in Brazil and Indonesia are but two examples. Good risk management practice, which is also good economics, arguably is more important today than ever before because of these situations.

The trend toward resource concentration, the increasing effects of natural and human-made events, and changing consumer attitudes and expectations play a central role in explaining why risk management has become such an important topic globally. The public in many countries has developed a sense of risk consciousness and has become more sensitive to the dangers resulting from highly complex technologies. The 1984 industrial accident at a Union Carbide plant in Bhopal, India, which resulted in more than 2,500 deaths and thousands more permanently disabled, focused world attention on the great potential for harm caused by economic development. The explosion and near meltdown at the nuclear power-generating facility at Chernobyl, Ukraine, in 1986 resulted in enormous direct and indirect property damages, many deaths and thousands of individuals exposed to life-shortening amounts of radiation. The September 11, 2001 terrorist attacks in the U.S. and their aftermath further solidified the public's view of a world full of uncertainty.

Economic development often carries another menacing externality: pollution. The short-term and long-term effects of air, water and land pollution are of great concern worldwide. Risk management principles applied at the level of the corporation can mitigate some of the adverse effects of pollution. However, so long as the full marginal costs of pollution are not internalized to the polluters, economic incentives are to produce more rather than less pollution. Driven by consumer pressure to deal effectively with pollution, we can expect governments themselves increasingly to look to risk management to address this issue.

These and hundreds of other, less-newsworthy calamities worldwide have heightened the public's sensitivity to the potential for harm inherent in contemporary society. This heightened sensitivity has merely augmented an already emerging consumerist view that events, processes, products and services should deliver value and performance as expected and with little or no potential harm. Legislative enactments and judicial decisions in many countries have given substance to this view.

Finally, risk management has assumed greater importance as its scope continues to expand. In the past, its application was thought of as being limited mainly to operational (e.g., manufacturing, marketing) issues. Today, it finds application in minimizing financial risks to business and in helping governments resolve public policy issues.

## The Role of Risk Management in Economic Growth

A more extensive application of risk management principles and processes offers benefits to individuals and businesses and, thereby to national economies. By reducing long-term financial variability, risk management can render firms more competitive. Their products and services will offer better value, and shareholder value can be enhanced through a reduction in cash flow volatility. Risk management can facilitate more adequate and efficient risk financing and leads to a reduction in a firm's risk-related costs. Also, because businesses with effective risk management programs are more creditworthy, their cost of capital might be lower than otherwise.

From a macroeconomic standpoint, risk management techniques can reduce the number of commercial and industrial enterprises that would otherwise become insolvent. This reduction in uncertainty leads to an expansion of the domestic credit and capital markets, thus aiding in the development of domestic commerce and enterprise.

The most apparent benefit of effective risk management results from loss control. Effective loss control measures can reduce the frequency and severity of work-related injuries and illnesses, work interruption and other causes of economic losses. The number of off-job injuries and illnesses from industrial accidents, pollution, flood, motor accidents and other adverse events can also be reduced when effective loss control programs are in place.

Risk management offers numerous, albeit less apparent, benefits to individuals. It can reduce production costs, which in turn can make goods and services available to consumers at lower cost. A reduction in the number and severity of injuries should reduce the drain on supporting families, the need for welfare programs for injured persons and their families, and taxes needed for their support.

By reducing costs, risk management helps new businesses develop and renders existing businesses to be better able to compete in domestic and foreign markets. The reduction in risk can make it easier for exporters to obtain the financing and insurance required for successful export marketing.

# THE LANGUAGE OF RISK AND INSURANCE INTERNATIONALLY

The mastery of any subject requires mastery of its terminology. The study of risk and insurance in its international context is no different. This section introduces such terminology.

The terms **international risk** and **international insurance** most commonly refer to (1) unintended outcomes and (2) insurance transactions, respectively, that transcend or cross national boundaries. International risk can also flow from the consequences of international business activities. For example, a corporation is exposed to a foreign exchange risk when it transacts business in a currency other than that of its domiciliary country. Similarly, the possibility of a typhoon roaring across the Far East and causing property damage and human casualties in several countries is an international loss exposure.

Other definitions of international risk and international insurance flow from the comparative study of organizations and practices of different countries. If we explore the different types of risks to which purely national corporations in Morocco are exposed and compare them with risks faced by purely domestic corporations in Columbia, we are engaging in a comparative study of international risks. Comparative studies widen our horizons and provide insight into our own culture and practices. This book examines international risk and international insurance on both a cross-border and comparative basis.

## Country Classifications

Any discussion of risk and insurance in a global context is facilitated by use of common country terminology. As anyone who has done international work or study knows, however, national economic data are not always reliable and no universally accepted country classification scheme exists. The United Nations (UN) has one approach, the International Monetary Fund (IMF) and the World Bank another.[2] For purposes of this book, we classify countries based on the stage of their economic development and by their membership in intergovernmental organizations.

### By stage of economic development

We classify countries by their stage of economic development broadly into:

- *Developed market economies*: This classification includes countries that are generally democratic, have market-oriented economies, and usually have high per capita gross domestic product (GDP) (e.g., above US$10,000). Market economies rely predominately on the private sector for resource allocation and production decisions. Prices in the economies are determined by voluntary exchanges between producers and consumers, and between workers and the owners of the factors of production. Market economies are characterized by decentralized decision-making and, usually, a system of private ownership of the means of production.

  Market economies include Organization for Economic Cooperation and Development countries, several other developed economies and mini-states like Andorra and Liechtenstein. This classification is also sometimes called variously **high-income countries**, **advanced countries**, **economically advanced countries**, **industrialized countries**, the **north** and the **first world**.

  One special category of developed market economies is **newly industrialized economies**, also known as newly industrialized countries (NIEs), which are countries experiencing rapid industrialization and economic development. Included in this category are the Four Tigers – Hong Kong, Korea, Singapore and Taiwan.

- *Developing Economies*. Countries falling within this classification generally are characterized as having a relatively low per capita GDP (e.g., less than US$5,000) and comparatively low levels of output, living standards and technology. Important exceptions exist. Some major oil exporting countries, such as certain members of the **Organization of Petroleum Exporting Countries (OPEC)** – Kuwait, Qatar and the United Arab Emirates-have high per capita incomes, but a skewed income distribution and a paucity of selected services to certain population segments.

  Developing countries are also sometimes referred to as **underdeveloped countries**, **undeveloped countries**, **low-** (or **middle-**) **income countries**, the **south** and the **third world**. The poorest developing countries (per capita income below US$500) are classified as **least developed countries (LCDs)**. About 90 countries have per capital GDP at or below US$5,000.

  There are two special types of developing economies: emerging markets and economies in transition:

  1. *Emerging markets* are economies that are moving towards market-oriented systems, and grow at a rate faster than the growth rate of the global economy as a whole.
  2. *Economies in transition* are nation states that are adopting market-oriented economic policies and that generally are becoming more democratic. This grouping

**Table 1.1**    World's Distribution of GDP, Trade and Population (Rounded)

|  | GDP (%) | Exports of Goods and Services (%) | Population (%) |
|---|---|---|---|
| *Advanced economies* | **56.3** | **75.1** | **15.4** |
| United States | 21.4 | 13.6 | 4.6 |
| European Union | 19.9 | 37.7 | 6.2 |
| Japan | 7.3 | 6.0 | 2.1 |
| Asia | 3.3 | 9.4 | 1.3 |
| Other | 4.4 | 8.4 | 1.2 |
| *Developing countries* | **37.6** | **20.3** | **78.0** |
| Africa | 3.2 | 2.0 | 12.5 |
| Asia | 22.2 | 9.3 | 52.2 |
| Middle East and Turkey | 4.0 | 4.2 | 5.0 |
| Western Hemisphere | 8.2 | 4.7 | 8.4 |
| *Economies in transition* | **6.2** | **4.7** | **6.6** |
| Central and Eastern Europe | 2.3 | 2.4 | 1.9 |
| CIS and Mongolia | 3.8 | 2.2 | 4.7 |
| Total | **100.0** | **100.0** | **100.0** |

*Source*: International Monetary Fund (2002).

includes almost all of the nations of Central and Eastern Europe. This classification is sometimes called **previously centrally planned economies**.

- *Centrally planned economies.* This term applies mainly to traditionally Communist countries where resource allocation, production and pricing decisions are made by an economic planning body – typically the government – not by market forces. With the collapse of the Soviet Union, most of the states formerly closely identified with it are evolving toward more democratic and market-oriented systems. The major remaining centrally planned economies are principally in Asia (e.g., Cambodia, North Korea, Laos and Mongolia), Cuba and several African states. This classification is also sometimes called variously **planned economies**, **Communist countries** and the **second world**. Several of the formerly centrally planned economies, particularly China, have adopted more liberal economic policies, thus having become major economies in transition.

Table 1.1 shows the distribution of world GDP (in purchasing power parities) in terms of some of the above economic and intergovernmental classifications.

## By membership in intergovernmental organizations

Intergovernmental organizations have addressed global and regional market concerns for many decades. More recent international trade agreements explicitly promote market liberalization. This section reviews some of the better known such organizations and agreements. Some of these organizations have broad, international mandates while others have a regional focus. The informed student of any economics-based subject would wish to be familiar with these entities.

*Global intergovernmental organizations*

Membership in what we term global intergovernmental organizations is open to virtually all nations. Here we discuss five such organizations.

*The United Nations*

Created in 1945, the mandate of the **United Nations** (UN) [www.un.org] is broad – all relating to risk management for society as a whole. It is charged with maintaining peace and security; facilitating friendly relations among nations; cooperating to solve international economic, social, cultural and humanitarian problems and promoting respect for human rights and fundamental freedoms; and serving as the center for harmonizing actions among nations to attain these ends. These mandates are carried out through its five principal organs:

- *The General Assembly* is the main UN deliberative body composed of 192 nations, with each holding one vote. It has authority over the UN budget and is a forum for discussion of major issues such as war, hunger, pollution, human rights and disease. Decisions are made by two-thirds majority vote on important matters, such as peace and security, otherwise a simple majority rules.
- *The Security Council* is a 15 member council with authority in areas of peace and security. Five members are permanent: China, France, Russia, the U.K. and the U.S. The other 10 members are elected by the General Assembly. Decisions require majority vote but with no permanent member veto.
- *The Economic and Social Council* is the principal organ for coordinating economic and social work and UN specialized agencies. The council has 54 members elected by the General Assembly for 3-year rotating terms.
- *The International Court of Justices*, a panel of 15 judges elected by the General Assembly, is charged with settling international disputes (such as border controversies) and investigating human rights violations.
- *The Secretariat*, the staff for the UN, is composed of about 14,000 employees worldwide. It headquarters in New York City. Other important offices are located in Geneva and Vienna. The UN Secretariat is headed by a Secretary-General elected by members for a five year term.

In addition to the above UN bodies, the UN works closely with a range of other intergovernmental organizations including the International Monetary Fund, the World Bank and the World Health Organization collectively considered as the UN Family of Organizations. Figure 1.3 shows the scope of this cooperation.

*The International Monetary Fund*

The **International Monetary Fund** (IMF) [www.imf.org] was created in 1945 to help promote the health of the world economy. Headquartered in Washington, DC, it is governed by and accountable to the governments of its 184 member countries. The IMF and the World Bank (see the next section) were conceived at a UN conference convened in Bretton Woods, U.S., in 1944. The 45 governments represented at that conference sought to build a framework for economic cooperation that would avoid a repetition of the disastrous economic policies that had contributed to the Great Depression of the 1930s.[3]

# The United Nations System

**Principal Organs**

## Trusteeship Council

## Security Council

**Subsidiary Bodies**

- Military Staff Committee
- Standing Committee and ad hoc bodies
- International Criminal Tribunal for the former Yugoslavia (ICTY)
- International Criminal Tribunal for Rwanda (ICTR)
- UN Monitoring, Verification, and Inspection Commission (Iraq) (UNMOVIC)
- United Nations Compensation Commission
- Peacekeeping Operations and Missions

## General Assembly

**Subsidiary Bodies**

- Main committees
- Human Rights Council
- Others sessional committees
- Standing committees and ad hoc bodies
- Other subsidiary organs

**Advisory Subsidiary Body**

- United Nations Peacebuilding Commission

**Programmes and Funds**

- **UNCTAD** United Nations Conference on Trade and Development
  - **ITC** International Trade Centre (UNCTAD/WTO)
- **UNDCP[1]** United Nations Drug Control Programme
- **UNEP** United Nations Environment Programme
- **UNICEF** United Nations Children's Fund
- **UNDP** United Nations Development Programme
  - **UNIFEM** United Nations Development Fund for Women
  - **UNV** United Nations Volunteers
  - **UNCDF** United Nations Capital Development Fund
- **UNFPA** United Nations Population Fund
- **UNHCR** Office of the United Nations High Commissioner for Refugees
- **WFP** World Food Programme
- **UNRWA[2]** United Nations Relief and Works Agency for Palestine Refugees in the Near East
- **UN-HABITAT** United Nations Human Settlements Programme

**Research and Training Institutes**

- **UNICRI** United Nations Interregional Crime and Justice Research Institute
- **UNITAR** United Nations Institute for Training and Research
- **UNRISD** United Nations Research Institute for Social Development
- **UNIDIR[2]** United Nations Institute for Disarmament Research
- **INSTRAW** International Research and Training Institute for the Advancement of Women
- **UNU** United Nations University
- **UNSSC** United Nations System Staff College

**Other UN Entities**

- **OHCHR** Office of the United Nations High Commissioner for Human Rights
- **UNOPS** United Nations Office for Project Services
- **UNAIDS** Joint United Nations Programme on HIV/AIDS

## Economic and Social Council

**Functional Commissions**

Commissions on:
- Human Rights
- Narcotic Drugs
- Crime Prevention and Criminal Justice
- Science and Technology for Development
- Sustainable Development
- Status of Women
- Population and Development
- Commission for Social Development
- Statistical Commission

**Regional Commissions**

- Economic Commission for Africa (ECA)
- Economic Commission for Europe (ECE)
- Economic Commission for Latin America and the Caribbean (ECLAC)
- Economic and Social Commission for Asia and the Pacific (ESCAP)
- Economic and Social Commission for Western Asia (ESCWA)

**Other Bodies**

- Permanent Forum on Indigenous Issues (PFII)
- United Nations Forum on Forests
- Sessional and standing committees
- Expert, ad hoc and related bodies

**Related Organizations**

- **WTO** World Trade Organization
- **IAEA[4]** International Atomic Energy Agency
- **CTBTO Prep.Com[5]** PrepCom for the Nuclear-Test-Ban-Treaty Organization
- **OPCW[5]** Organization for the Prohibition of Chemical Weapons

## International Court of Justice

**Specialized Agencies[6]**

- **ILO** International Labour Organization
- **FAO** Food and Agriculture Organization of the United Nations
- **UNESCO** United Nations Educational, Scientific and Cultural Organization
- **WHO** World Health Organization
- **World Bank Group**
  - **IBRD** International Bank for Reconstruction and Development
  - **IDA** International Development Association
  - **IFC** International Finance Corporation
  - **MIGA** Multilateral Investment Guarantee Agency
  - **ICSID** International Centre for Settlement of Investment Disputes
- **IMF** International Monetary Fund
- **ICAO** International Civil Aviation Organization
- **IMO** International Maritime Organization
- **ITU** International Telecommunication Union
- **UPU** Universal Postal Union
- **WMO** World Meteorological Organization
- **WIPO** World Intellectual Property Organization
- **IFAD** International Fund for Agricultural Development
- **UNIDO** United Nations Industrial Development Organization
- **UNWTO** World Tourism Organization

## Secretariat

**Departments and Offices**

- **OSG[3]** Office of the Secretary-General
- **OIOS** Office of Internal Oversight Services
- **OLA** Office of Legal Affairs
- **DPA** Department of Political Affairs
- **DDA** Department for Disarmament Affairs
- **DPKO** Department of Peacekeeping Operations
- **OCHA** Office for the Coordination of Humanitarian Affairs
- **DESA** Department of Economic and Social Affairs
- **DGACM** Department for General Assembly and Conference Management
- **DPI** Department of Public Information
- **DM** Department of Management
- **OHRLLS** Office of the High Representative for the Least Developed Countries, Landlocked Developing Countries and Small Island Developing States
- **DSS** Department of Safety and Security
- **UNODC** United Nations Office on Drugs and Crime
- **UNOG** UN Office at Geneva
- **UNOV** UN Office at Vienna
- **UNON** UN Office at Nairobi

Published by the United Nations Department of Public Information DPI/2431—August 2006

**Notes:** Solid lines from a Principal Organ indicate a direct reporting relationship; dashes indicate a non-subsidiary relationship.
1 The UN Drug Control Programme is part of the UN Office on Drugs and Crime.
2 UNRWA and UNIDIR report only to the GA.
3 The United Nations Ethics Office and the United Nations Ombudsman's Office report directly to the Secretary-General
4 IAEA reports to the Security Council and the General Assembly (GA).
5 The CTBTO Prep.Com and OPCW report to the GA.
6 Specialized agencies are autonomous organizations working with the UN and each other through the coordinating machinery of the ECOSOC at the intergovernmental level, and through the Chief Executives Board for coordination (CEB) at the inter-secretariat level.

**Figure 1.3** The UN System

The IMF's main responsibilities include:

- promoting international monetary cooperation;
- facilitating the expansion and balanced growth of international trade;
- promoting exchange stability;
- assisting in the establishment of a multilateral system of payments;
- making its resources available (under adequate safeguards) to members experiencing balance of payments difficulties.

More generally, the IMF is responsible for ensuring the stability of the international monetary and financial system – the system of international payments and exchange rates among national currencies that enables trade to take place between countries. It seeks to promote economic stability and prevent crises, to help resolve crises when they do occur, and to promote growth and alleviate poverty. It employs three main functions – surveillance, technical assistance and lending – to meet these objectives.

The IMF works to promote global growth and economic stability – and thereby prevent economic crisis – by encouraging countries to adopt sound economic policies. Surveillance is the regular dialog and policy advice that the IMF offers to each of its members. Generally once a year, the IMF conducts in-depth appraisals of each member country's economic situation. It discusses with the country's authorities the policies that are most conducive to stable exchange rates and a growing and prosperous economy. Members have the option to publish the IMF's assessment, and the overwhelming majority of countries opt to do so.

Technical assistance and training are offered – mostly free of charge – to help member countries strengthen their capacity to design and implement effective policies. Technical assistance is offered in several areas, including fiscal policy, monetary and exchange rate policies, banking and financial system supervision and regulation, and statistics.

If member countries experience difficulties financing their balance of payments, the IMF is also a fund that can be tapped to help in recovery. Such financial assistance is available to give member countries the breathing room they need to correct balance of payments problems. A policy program supported by IMF financing is designed by the national authorities in close cooperation with the IMF, and continued financial support is conditional on effective implementation of this program.

*The World Bank*

The mission of the **World Bank** [www.worldbank.org], established in 1944 and also located in Washington, DC, is to reduce poverty and improve living standards worldwide.[4] It is not a bank in the common sense of the word. Rather, it is made up of two development institutions owned by its 184 member countries: the International Bank for Reconstruction and Development (IBRD) and the International Development Association (IDA). The IBRD focuses on middle-income and creditworthy-poor countries, while the IDA focuses on the poorest countries. They assist these countries through a range of programs designed to:

- build capacity by strengthening their government and educating government officials;
- create infrastructure by promoting judicial and legal systems that encourage business, protect individual and property rights, and honor contracts;
- develop robust financial systems to underpin economic development, including financial intermediaries such as banks and insurers;
- combat corruption (otherwise the above three goals can be thwarted).

They support these programs by providing low-interest loans, interest-free credit and grants for education, health, infrastructure, communications and other development-related purposes.

The World Bank group is composed of two important subsidiary organizations designed to support the bank's mission through non-governmental means:

- *The International Finance Corporation* (IFC) promotes sustainable private-sector investment in developing countries, thus helping them reduce poverty and improve people's lives. The IFC provides loans, equity, structured finance and risk management products, and advisory services to build the private sector in developing countries.
- *The Multilateral Investment Guarantee Agency* (MIGA) promotes FDI in developing countries to support economic growth, reduce poverty, and improve citizen's lives. Concerns about investment environments and negative perceptions of political risk often discourage FDI. MIGA addresses these concerns by providing political risk insurance, technical assistance and dispute mediation services.

*The World Trade Organization*

The **World Trade Organization** (WTO) [www.wto.org], established in 1995 in Geneva, Switzerland, is the only global intergovernmental organization that deals with the rules of trade between nations.[5] With 149 member states, its objective is to ensure that trade in both goods and services flows as smoothly, predictably, and freely as possible. If trading systems function in this way, consumers and producers know that they can enjoy secure supplies and greater choice of products, components, raw materials and services that they use. Producers and exporters know that foreign markets will remain open to them. The result should be a more prosperous, peaceful and accountable economic world.

Virtually all decisions in the WTO are taken by consensus among all member countries, and they are ratified by members' congressional or other deliberative bodies. Trade friction is channeled into the WTO's dispute settlement process where the focus is on interpreting agreements and commitments and how to ensure that countries' trade policies conform with them. The risk of disputes spilling over into political or military conflict is, thereby, reduced. By lowering trade barriers, the WTO's system also breaks down other barriers between peoples and nations.

At the heart of the system – known as the multilateral trading system – are the WTO's agreements, negotiated and signed by a large majority of the world's trading nations. These agreements are the legal ground rules for international commerce. Essentially, they are contracts, guaranteeing member countries important trade rights. They also bind governments to keep their trade policies within agreed limits to everybody's benefit. The agreements were negotiated and signed by governments, but their purpose is to help producers of goods and services, exporters and importers conduct their business.

Of particular relevance to this book is the **General Agreement on Trade in Services** (GATS) that sets up a multilateral framework of principles and rules for trade in services as distinct from trade in goods. GATS binds signatory countries to support liberal markets in services, including financial services, through a series of commitments. Each country makes market access and other commitments as to how it will treat foreign service providers. These commitments are negotiated with other member states through the so-called "trade rounds" and are subject to dispute settlement procedures in the event of disagreement among states.

There is no inherent obligation for members to continue liberalization outside of their commitments. Negotiations end when, through an offer and acceptance process, all countries agree to accept the offers of all other countries; that is, when a balance of commitments is achieved. Future progress depends on future trade rounds and the balance of commitments achievable in those rounds.

### The World Health Organization

The **World Health Organization** (WHO) [www.who.int] is the UN specialized agency for health, headquartered in Geneva. Established in 1948, WHO's objective is the attainment by all peoples of the highest possible level of health. **Health** is defined in WHO's Constitution as a state of complete physical, mental and social wellbeing and not merely the absence of disease or infirmity.

WHO is governed by its 193 member states through the **World Health Assembly**, composed of representatives from member states. The main tasks of the World Health Assembly are to approve the WHO program and the budget for the following biennium and to decide major policy questions.

WHO is tasked with a wide range of responsibilities and activities, from responding to natural and human-made disasters, such as the 2004 tsunami in the Indian Ocean that killed 255,000 individuals, to working with national health agencies to ensure clean water for human consumption, to responding immediately and coordinating the world's response to the next major outbreak of contagious diseases, such as the avian flu.

### Regional intergovernmental organizations

Numerous regional and specialized intergovernmental organizations exist worldwide. Here we discuss a few of those most relevant to this book.

### The Organization for Economic Cooperation and Development

The period following World War II saw the need to reduce tariffs and other restrictions on trade and international transactions. The IMF and the **General Agreement on Tariffs and Trade** (GATT) – the predecessor organization to the WTO – were the first and most important multilateral institutions created to address these needs. The **Organization for Economic Cooperation and Development** (OECD) [www.oecd.org] and its predecessor organization advanced these efforts among developed market-economy countries.

All 30 OECD countries are market economies. Table 1.2 shows OECD member countries.

OECD member countries account for about three-quarters of the world's production of all goods and services, but only 24 OECD countries fall into the World Bank's high-income group. The Czech Republic, Hungary, Mexico, Poland, Slovakia and Turkey are middle income. The OECD works closely with 70 other non-member countries.

The mission of the OECD is to promote the liberalization of international trade in goods and services as well as the progressive freeing of capital movements. These goals are fostered through the requirements of the two OECD liberalization codes – the Code of Liberalization of Current Invisible Operations and the Code of Liberalization of Capital Movements – and, to a limited extent, in the National Treatment Instrument (NTI). The Invisibles Operations Code not only promotes the liberalization of current payments and transfers (as does the IMF), it also seeks to address restrictions on underlying service sector transactions that may be hindered by legal or administrative regulations or practices.

The Capital Movements Code is the only multilateral instrument outside the European Union that promotes liberalization of capital movements including foreign establishment via direct investment. It addresses transactions in various service sectors such as insurance

**Table 1.2**   OECD Member Countries

| *European Union countries* | *European Free Trade Association countries* |
|---|---|
| Austria | Iceland |
| Belgium | Norway |
| Czech Republic | Switzerland |
| Denmark | |
| Finland | *North American Free Trade Association countries* |
| France | Canada |
| Germany | Mexico |
| Greece | United States |
| Hungary | |
| Ireland | |
| Italy | *Other countries* |
| Luxembourg | Australia |
| The Netherlands | Japan |
| Poland | Korea |
| Portugal | New Zealand |
| Slovakia | Turkey |
| Spain | |
| Sweden | |
| United Kingdom | |

and transportation, or specific types of transactions such as real estate and financial credits, thus improving access to each other's markets for services and investment. Complementing this code, the NTI provides protection for foreign investment and establishment; essentially, OECD members must treat investment from other member countries on a basis that is no less favorable than that afforded to residents.

The OECD and its codes provide an institutional framework to gauge progress toward liberalization based on notification, examination and consultation among members and to deal with measures taken that are inconsistent with the codes. The OECD codes are legally binding instruments for members, but no formal enforcement mechanism is in place to ensure member compliance. The codes establish a standard of liberalization to which members (and non-members) aspire. Member countries may take reservations to the codes for measures in their countries that are inconsistent with the codes. Members are then encouraged to liberalize their markets by removing or limiting these reservations over time. Once a reservation is removed, it cannot be reinstated, thus promoting progressive liberalization and preventing the erection of new barriers.

*The European Union*
Formerly known as the European Community, the **European Union** (EU) [www.europa.eu] is an economic union composed of 27 European countries (see Table 1.3). The EU is run by five institutions: the European Parliament, Council of Ministers, European Commission (EC), European Court of Justice and Court of Auditors. These institutions can render binding orders – the most important of which is the directive – not only on member states, but on their citizens as well. In addition, the following four other bodies are part of the institutional system: European Economic and Social Committee, Committee of the Regions, European Investment Bank and European Central Bank.

**Table 1.3**  EU Members and Applicant States

| Initial member states | | | | |
|---|---|---|---|---|
| Austria | Belgium | Denmark | Germany | Greece |
| Finland | France | Ireland | Italy | Luxembourg |
| The Netherlands | Portugal | Spain | Sweden | United Kingdom |

| Member states admitted in May 2004 | | | | |
|---|---|---|---|---|
| Cyprus | Czech Republic | Estonia | Hungary | Latvia |
| Lithuania | Malta | Poland | Slovenia | Slovakia |

| Member states admitted in 2007 | |
|---|---|
| Bulgaria | Romania |

| Applicant states as of January 2007 | | |
|---|---|---|
| Croatia | Turkey | Former Yugoslav Republic of Macedonia |

*Source*: EU.

The EC has the primary responsibility for proposing and administering directives and orders. It is given the power to negotiate trade agreements and take trade-related actions with non-member countries for areas within its competence. Proposed directives are reviewed and commented upon by the European Parliament. The Council of Ministers officially issues directives. A **directive** is an order that requires member countries to enact new national laws or alter existing laws to come into compliance with the directive's provisions. Directives are meant to establish minimum harmonization of essential regulation throughout the EU They are the principal means by which the EU is creating its single market. The European Court of Justice adjudicates disputes between member states or between the EU and member states.

The EU's principal objectives include establishing European citizenship, promoting economic and social progress, and asserting Europe's role in the world. The EU continues toward its goal of unifying its member countries into a single market of goods, services, investment and people. This includes seeking collaboration with intergovernmental organizations sharing similar objectives which it has done.

Since early in the history of the European Economic Community (EEC), the EU has attempted to create a single market in financial services using the EEC Treaty provisions requiring freedom of establishment, freedom of services, and freedom of capital movements. The goal was to allow EU financial firms to establish or provide services anywhere in the EU without restrictions on the transactions.

Specific to insurance, the EC has issued a series of directives to foster the freedoms mentioned above. In general, these directives have established a single license system. The system allows insurance firms authorized by the member state where their head office is located (the **home country**) to operate both via establishment and via freedom of services throughout the EU In general, an insurer needs only a single authorization and is subject only to the supervision, rules and practices of its home country. These directives also have provided that citizens in one EU state have a right to purchase insurance from insurers domiciled in other member states.

EU member states retain much authority in the insurance sector. For example, the latest directives – the so-called Third Generation Directives – prohibit national requirements for the prior approval of rates and forms except for compulsory insurance. Member states, however, still can require rates and technical reserves to be based on local actuarial requirements. The member states also retain authority for market conduct oversight, contract law and insurance taxation.

Several upcoming and unresolved issues affecting the EU insurance sector remain, all of which have implications for international insurance markets. This includes pension reform issues and the privatization of pension schemes in some countries; environmental liabilities as the cleanup of waste sites grows in significance; solvency regulation, especially for financial conglomerates; and standardization of insurance accounting.

*The North American Free Trade Agreement*
Canada, Mexico and the U.S. created the **North American Free Trade Agreement** (NAFTA) [www.nafta-sec-alena.org] in 1994. Its primary objective is to create a free trade area throughout North America by, over time, removing trade and investment barriers between member countries. Discussion is underway to expand NAFTA throughout the Americas, thus creating the **Free Trade Agreement of the Americas** (FTAA) [www.ftaa-alca.org].

NAFTA contains specific provisions that help member countries establish a comprehensive set of rules and principles governing trade and investment in financial services. The following summarizes key NAFTA principles and provisions governing financial services, including insurance:

*   *Commercial presence*: Financial services firms from one member country have the right to establish operations in other NAFTA countries, although they may be required to form subsidiaries for the operations. Member countries guarantee the current level of access to their markets.
*   *Cross-border trade in financial services*: Consumers from one NAFTA country must have the freedom to purchase financial services in the territory of another NAFTA country. A country may not impose new restrictions on the ability of financial services firms to provide cross-border services. Each government, however, may require registration of firms and financial instruments involved in cross-border transactions.
*   *National treatment*: Each NAFTA country must treat financial services firms of another NAFTA country no less favorably than it treats its own firms. Specifically, this principle requires each U.S. state to treat Canadian and Mexican insurance firms like in-state insurance firms. However, a U.S. state may treat Canadian or Mexican firms located in another U.S. state in the manner that it treats U.S. insurance firms located in that other state.
*   *Most-favored-nation treatment*: One NAFTA country may not treat financial services firms from another NAFTA country less favorably than it treats similarly situated financial services firms from any other country, including non-NAFTA countries. However, a NAFTA country is not prevented from applying different treatments where the difference is based on valid regulatory harmonization or recognition of home-country regulation in a particular country.
*   *New financial services and data processing*: Each NAFTA country must allow financial services firms from other NAFTA countries to offer new products permitted under domestic law. The member country must also allow the firms to transfer data from one NAFTA country to another for processing.
*   *Regulatory transparency*: Each NAFTA government is required to provide its draft financial services laws and regulations to interested persons before putting them into effect and to allow them to comment on the drafts. In addition, each government's regulatory

authorities must provide information on the status of an application for business and to act on the application expeditiously.

- *Prudential carve-out*: NAFTA does not prevent any country from maintaining or taking prudential measures to protect investors and policyholders or to maintain the soundness of financial institutions and the financial system, even if the measures are inconsistent with other NAFTA provisions. This is similar to the prudential carve-out in the GATS.
- *Dispute settlement*: NAFTA established a Financial Services Committee to administer its provisions and to participate in dispute settlement procedures. With limited exceptions for certain investments, private investors cannot bring disputes under NAFTA; only member countries can.

NAFTA specifically prohibits any increase in barriers to trade and investment, while imposing no constraints on member countries' ability to lower barriers to non-members. Indeed, Mexico has since entered into preferential trade arrangements with several non-NAFTA countries, although services and insurance have not been covered in these.

*Association of Southeast Asian Nations*
Founded in 1967 by five nations – Indonesia, Malaysia, the Philippines, Singapore and Thailand – **Association of Southeast Asian Nations** (ASEAN) [www.aseansec.org] promotes regional peace and stability. It also promotes economic, social and cultural developments among member countries by coordinating policies in agriculture, trade, communication, transportation, science, finance and culture. It has over the years added five new members, namely Brunei, Cambodia, Laos, Myanmar and Vietnam.

ASEAN member countries adopted the Hanoi Plan of Action in 1998. The plan includes several proposals for financial services market reform: developing liquid markets, adopting standards of disclosure and dissemination of economic and financial information, intensifying deregulation of the financial services industry, and intensifying negotiations of financial services sector liberalization under the ASEAN Framework Agreement on Services (AFAS). Member countries also agreed to accelerate the implementation of the ASEAN Free Trade Area (AFTA) and implement the framework agreement on ASEAN Investment Area (AIA).

*Asia-Pacific Economic Cooperation*
Founded in 1989, **Asia-Pacific Economic Cooperation** (APEC) [www.apecsec.org.sg] has grown into a means to promote open trade and economic cooperation in the Asia-Pacific region that accounts for more than one-half the world's GDP. It has 21 member economies including most ASEAN member states, all three NAFTA member countries and Russia.

APEC is the only intergovernmental organization operating on the basis of non-binding commitments. Unlike the WTO, the OECD and other multilateral trade bodies, APEC entails no treaty obligations, with decisions made on a consensus basis and undertaken voluntarily.

In 1994, APEC's members adopted the goal of free and open trade and investment in Asia-Pacific. The developed member states intend to reach the goal by the year 2010, with developing states reaching it by 2020. It remains to be seen how successful this attempt will be and how it will affect trade in general and financial services in particular. Any progress in APEC helps shape the world's largest regional financial services market.

*Southern Cone Common Market*
Argentina, Brazil, Paraguay and Uruguay created The Southern Cone Common Market, better known as MERCOSUR (*Mercado Comun del Cono Sur*) [www.mercosur.org.uy], in

1991. Member countries aim to achieve, through integration, free trade among themselves, and to establish common economic policies and external tariffs. Although none of the member countries ranks among the world's largest, Argentina and Brazil already account for more than one-half of Latin American GDP. MERCOSUR has worked closely with the EU in recent years.

*Common Market for Eastern and Southern Africa*

**The Common Market for Eastern and Southern Africa** (COMESA) [www.comesa.int] was established in 1994 to take advantage of a larger market size, to share the region's common heritage and destiny, and to allow greater social and economic cooperation among member countries. Its ultimate objective is creating an economic community. In 2001, nine of the member countries – Djibouti, Egypt, Kenya, Madagascar, Malawi, Mauritius, Sudan, Zambia and Zimbabwe – created the COMESA Free Trade Area, within which member countries are not subject to tariffs on goods that conform to COMESA rules of origin.[6] Today, COMESA has a total of 20 member states.

COMESA has created several institutions. They include COMESA Trade and Development Bank, PTA Reinsurance Company (ZEP-Re) and African Trade Insurance Agency, all operating from Nairobi, Kenya. The Africa Trade Insurance Agency, supported by the World Bank, underwrites political and credit risks for firms in COMESA member states.

*Other regional organizations*

Many other regional economic trade groups exist, which include the **Central American Common Market** with five member countries, the **Andean Group** comprising five countries in northern South America and the **Caribbean Community and Common Market** in the Americas. The **Economic Community of West African States** and **Southern African Development Community** are two such organizations in Africa. The **Arab League** having several Arab countries of Northern Africa and East Asia as members offers similar intergovernmental services in the Middle East. Most exist to promote economic and other spheres of cooperation among like-minded countries.

## Risk Classifications

Individuals and businesses sometimes analyze risk subjectively and based only on their experiences or feelings at the time. Risk managers and insurance professionals do not rely on this non-scientific approach. Rather, they view risk as deviations from the expected. We follow this approach and define **risk** as the relative variation of actual from expected outcomes.

The term risk is often used in insurance to mean loss exposure. **Loss exposure** is a thing or person subject to the possibility of a loss (e.g., an automobile, a house, a business, or a life). Insurance professionals often use the term peril interchangeably with risk, although the precise meaning of **peril** is the cause of a loss. Examples of perils are fire, windstorm, flood, and terrorism.

Historically, a distinction has been drawn between managing hazard risks and managing other risks. A **hazard** is a condition that increases the likelihood of loss. For example, a **physical hazard** refers to the poor physical condition of a property increasing the likelihood of a loss (e.g., poorly lit business premises increasing the likelihood of an accident). **Moral hazard** refers to a change in human attitude increasing the likelihood of a loss.

A hazard risk is sometimes called a **pure risk** – a risk where the range of outcomes involves only no loss or a loss. Traditionally, both insurers and corporate risk managers have concerned themselves primarily with hazard risk management, with other intermediaries, such as banks, and corporate Chief Financial Officers (CFOs), concerning themselves with managing other risks. This less focused means of managing corporate risks continues to change, as businesses increasingly try to implement seamless enterprise-wide risk management strategies. We adopt this enterprise risk management approach in this book.

It will prove convenient, however, to define and analyze risks by broad category, as different techniques are available for different types of risk. For discussion purposes throughout this book, we classify risks as being primarily (1) financial, (2) operational and (3) strategic.

## Financial risks

**Financial risk** arises from an individual's or organization's ownership or use of financial instruments. Financial risks can arise from numerous sources, including interest rate changes, foreign currency transactions, extensions of credit, issuance of stock, and use of derivatives. Thus, businesses that extend credit to their customers run the financial risk that some will default. Individuals incur financial risk when they borrow money to buy a car or house and when they make investments. Financial risks are mainly external to the individual and business and, therefore, less subject to direct control except through careful selection or by not owning or using them. Financial risks can be further categorized as market risk, credit risk and price risk:

- *Market risk* is the potential change in asset value arising from changes in the values of underlying financial instruments. Often, firms and individuals are most concerned with losses associated with market risk. Such losses can result from inflation, fluctuations in interest rates or exchange rates, or other adverse developments in capital markets. Market risk includes asset liquidity risk – the ease with which invested assets can be converted into cash or cash equivalents. The terms **interest rate risk** and **exchange rate risk** refer to exposure to changes in interest rates and foreign exchange rates, respectively. Because market risks affect society or the economy as a whole, they are also called **systematic risks**. Risks that are unique to a firm (or individual) and which, therefore, often can be controlled by the firm (or individual) are called **nonsystematic risks**.

- *Credit risk*, also known as **counterparty risk**, is the uncertainty surrounding whether a counterparty to a transaction will perform its financial obligations in full and on time. Examples of this risk include the failure of a debtor to repay a loan, a failure to receive payment for the product or service that a firm has provided, or a failure of a derivative guarantor to meet its obligations. In insurance, it refers to uncertainty whether an insurer (or reinsurer) will meet its claims obligations at the time of loss.

- *Price risk* means the potential loss in revenue arising from product mispricing. For example, insurance companies are vulnerable to price risk because they must establish a price (premium) before the actual costs of production (claims and expenses) are known. All other firms are subject to varying degrees of price risk.

## Operational risk

**Operational (internal) risks** include those risks that arise from the existence and activities of an individual or from the operations of an organization. For organizations, the risk is associated with human errors, system failures, and inadequate procedures and controls.

These risks can be thought of as largely internal to the individual or organization and as deriving directly from personal, business, or other activities or from the physical or mental condition of individuals. As such, the individual or organization usually can exercise some control over them. Examples of this class would be uncertainty about legal liability arising from faulty products or automobile accidents, damage to and loss of use of property arising from a fire, loss of health because of cancer, and employee work stoppages and strikes.

Hazard risks are an important type of operational risk. Such risks can be further classified, according to the generic nature of the exposure, to the following categories:

- *Personal risk* is uncertainty related to loss of health, incapacity, death and outliving one's financial resources.
- *Personnel risk* is uncertainty related to the loss to a firm due to death, incapacity, loss of health, prospect of harm to or unexpected departure of key employees.
- *Property risk* is uncertainty related to loss of wealth due to damage or destruction of property.
- *Liability risk* is uncertainty related to financial responsibility arising from bodily injury (including death) or loss of wealth that a person or an entity causes to others.

Not surprisingly, hazard risks are commonly the subject matter of insurance. Other operational risks exist. When the cause of loss is the firm's concentration of business or property in a narrow sector or territory, it is termed as **concentration risk**. When uncertainty is associated with a firm's good reputation being sullied with the result that it suffers decreased revenues, increased expenses, or both because of some event that damages its reputation such as accounting fraud or product recall, it is often termed as **reputational risk**.

### Strategic risk

The third classification includes strategic risk which that stem from macroeconomic and other broad societal influences and trends. These risks encompass demographic, economic, political and technological factors that can touch every organization and individual. It includes such matters as the legal and regulatory environment, consumer preferences, terrorism and global warming. This class of risk is external to the organization. While these risks are not directly controllable, actions can be taken to plan for and often to mitigate their adverse effects. Of course, new strategic risks continue to evolve.

## The Risk Management Process

All individuals, businesses and governments must deal with risk. Existing risk management practices, whether exercised by an individual, a firm, or a government agency, seem to follow rather standardized steps. These steps are known as the **risk management pro-cess** and involve:

- *risk analysis* for the identification and evaluation of the possible outcomes associated with events or activities;
- *risk control* for the exploration of techniques to control adverse outcomes;
- *risk financing* to decide how to finance the costs of adverse outcomes that occur.

Historically, risk management has been concerned mainly with situations whose outcomes involve losses, without the possibility of gain. As noted above, this view of risk management is changing as corporate executives and government officials realize that a fragmented approach to the management of risk is less effective and efficient than an integrated approach that involves all the risks to which an entity is exposed.

Most large businesses and governments have departments dedicated to risk management. We explore risk management in detail in Part III of this book.

## Insurance Classifications

Insurance is an important risk management tool. In a typical insurance arrangement, the insurer promises, in return for a premium, to fulfill its contractual obligations upon the occurrence of some event, often a qualified loss. Insurance can be viewed as a risk transfer arrangement from the viewpoint of contract law. Insurance can also be viewed as a risk financing arrangement, because the promise that the insurer gives is contingent capital that the insured secures for future use, subject to the terms and conditions of the contract. This risk transfer/financing arrangement helps the insured to be subject to less cash flow volatility.

The entire scheme of insurance functions if the insurer can insure a sufficient quantity of similar loss exposures such that its overall claims experience is reasonably predictable. The greater the number of insureds that are independently exposed to loss, the more predictable the insurer's experience.

As further described in Chapter 19, this comfortably predictable experience does not always materialize. The independence criterion is often violated because of the catastrophic nature of certain natural and human-made disasters. For example, Hurricane Andrew that smashed through the U.S. state of Florida in 1992 ultimately caused the failure of 11 insurance firms and the weakening of dozens more. The financial hit to insurers worldwide from the September 11, 2001 attacks was more devastating.

Unforeseen environmental changes can wreck insurers' pricing assumptions. Life and health insurers did not anticipate the additional AIDS claims that emerged years ago. Liability insurers still do not know how much environmental impairment losses will cost them – perils they never intended to cover. In spite of these and a host of other unforeseen operational risks, the world's insurers and reinsurers are largely profitable, stable financial institutions.

Insurance can be classified in many ways. To provide the reader with a framework to aid understanding, we offer four classifications:

- social versus private;
- life versus nonlife;
- personal versus commercial;
- direct insurance versus reinsurance.

### *Social versus private insurance*

Governments have determined that they, not the private sector, should provide some types of insurance (see Chapter 9). In fact, most countries have extensive social security schemes that provide survivor, retirement, disability, health and unemployment benefits to qualified citizens.

Social insurance is provided by government and possesses several characteristics. First, participation is compulsory and financing relies on government-mandated premiums (i.e., taxes). Second, income security is provided for well-defined risks (e.g., unemployment, retirement), and the recipient is not subject to an economic needs test. Finally, it emphasizes social equity (i.e., income redistribution), a characteristic that distinguishes it from private insurance that emphasizes individual actuarial equity.

Private insurance is offered by insurance firms in the private sector. Its purchase may be compulsory, as with auto-liability insurance, but need not be. Premiums reflect insureds' expected losses.

This book covers both classes of insurance, although private insurance is emphasized. Also, we make no distinction in this book whether state-owned insurers are monopolists or compete with private insurers.

### Life versus nonlife insurance

The insurance business has historically divided itself between companies that sell insurance on the person, known as **life insurance**, and those that sell insurance to protect property, referred to as **nonlife insurance**. This classification is not completely satisfactory, as overlaps and variations exist, yet will serve our purposes.

Nonlife insurance is also known as **general insurance** in Commonwealth countries and as **property-casualty** or **property-liability insurance** in North America and certain other markets. The nonlife branch includes insurance to cover the following types of loss exposures:

- property (e.g., damage to or destruction of homes, automobiles, businesses, or aircraft);
- liability (e.g., payments to third parties due to negligent operation of an automobile, professional negligence and product defects);
- workers' compensation and health insurance payments in some countries.

The life branch – also known as **life assurance** – includes insurance that pays benefits on a person's:

- death (life insurance or assurance);
- living a certain period (endowments, annuities and pensions);
- incapacity (disability and long-term care insurance);
- injury or incurring a disease (health insurance), in countries not classifying such insurance in the nonlife category.

The life and nonlife branches of insurance perceive themselves differently, with some justification. Many countries prohibit **composite insurance** operations – a single corporation selling both life and nonlife insurance products, although joint production via holding companies and affiliates usually is permitted. Life and nonlife insurance markets are covered in Chapters 21 and 22, respectively.

### Personal versus commercial insurance

We can classify insurance based on the target group of insurance purchasers. As such, **personal insurance** is any insurance designed for individual consumers. This can include individual life and health insurance, homeowner's (householder's) insurance, and family automobile (motor) insurance.[7] **Commercial insurance** is any insurance designed for organizations, such as business property insurance, general (public) liability insurance, business interruption (loss of income) insurance, professional liability (errors and omissions) insurance and so forth.[8] In some markets, insurance purchased by commercial organizations, especially manufacturing firms, is termed **industrial insurance**.

The EU uses another classification. It defines **large risks** as firms that have met at least two of the following conditions: assets greater than €6.2 million, sales over €12.8 million, and 250 or more employees. Conversely, **mass risks** in the EU are insureds not meeting the above conditions, including individuals.

As will be made clear in Chapters 8 and 9, government oversight is more stringent in personal insurance than in commercial insurance because of greater information asymmetry problems in personal insurance. This book covers both personal and commercial insurance.

### Direct insurance versus reinsurance

Insurance sold to the public at large is classified as **direct insurance**. Insurers selling such insurance are called **direct (writing) insurers** or **primary insurers**, and attendant premiums are **direct premiums**.

As further discussed in Chapter 23, insurance firms usually hedge their own portfolios of risks through the purchase of insurance on these portfolios, which is called **reinsurance**. They do so to hedge themselves against volatilities in their insurance portfolios, to minimize undue potential loss concentrations, to secure greater underwriting capacity, to stabilize overall financial results, and to take advantage of special expertise of specialized insurance firms. Reinsurance typically involves large exposures to loss, often those with a catastrophic loss potential.

**Reinsurance** is a contractual arrangement between a direct insurer (that initially underwrites exposure) and another insurer. The party that assumes risk from a direct insurer is called the **reinsurer** or the **assuming company**, and the attendant premium is called a **reinsurance premium**. In the reinsurance market, the direct insurer is also termed the **cedant**, the **ceding company**, and the **reinsured**. Reinsurance is available from **professional reinsurers** whose primary function is accepting risks from direct insurers, from other direct insurers that sell reinsurance through their own reinsurance departments and in Lloyd's markets.

As a means of risk management, reinsurers typically seek their own reinsurance. We use the term **retrocession** to distinguish this type of reinsurance from that purchased by direct companies. The insurance company assuming retroceded risks is termed a **retrocessionaire**. No firms specialize in retrocession business only, and we include retrocession in reinsurance for data collection and regulation.

In the reinsurance market, both the buyer and the seller are knowledgeable participants. As a result, government intervention into the reinsurance transaction has historically been kept to a minimum. In recent years, however, governments have begun to impose more regulation on reinsurance firms. Governments also share data and information about cross-border reinsurance transactions. This book covers both direct insurance and reinsurance.

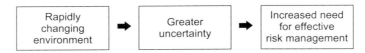

**Figure 1.4**   The Changing Environment and Risk Management

# THE ENVIRONMENT FOR RISK AND INSURANCE INTERNATIONALLY

The setting for this book is the world, for mastery of the study of risk and insurance demands an international perspective. While the authors explore the different dimensions of risk, risk management and insurance, the reader should be attuned to their less direct but more valuable messages. Peoples and governments have different resources, attitudes and values, and so use different means to solve similar problems. No single way is necessarily the "right" way or necessarily better than others. If we develop an appreciation within each of us for this simple idea, we free ourselves and the organizations that we manage to a degree from the tyranny of our own biases bred from ethnocentricity. We broaden our horizons, thereby making ourselves better, more tolerant world citizens, and more valuable and insightful employees and employers. This book seeks to instill these values.

This book also is about change. The world is characterized by accelerated rates of changes as we hear, read about, and see every day. To be successful in this new millennium, individuals, businesses, and governments must be adaptable. Educational materials, such as this book, should seek to prepare the reader for a life and career as divorced as feasible from our own ethnocentricity. To understand change, we must appreciate the economic, social, political and other forces that drive change. Most of the forces for change are now blind to national borders. This book explores these forces, and attempts to suggest how risk management and insurance practices have been and will be shaped by them.

That the pace of change in societies worldwide is at an unprecedented level makes environmental monitoring more important than ever. Simultaneously, the greater the pace of change, the greater is the need for effective risk management, as depicted in Figure 1.4.

Environmental factors are not subject to our direct control. Just as the sailor has no control over the wind and, with experience and knowledge, sets his or her sails in anticipation of how it will blow, so too should we carefully consider how the "winds of change" might blow to determine our appropriate strategy.

We classify these environmental forces broadly as follows: catastrophes, demographics, politics, law, and sociocultural. Of course, environmental forces do not lend themselves to such precise-seeming categorization. Overlap is inevitable, and our listing is not all-inclusive. Nonetheless, we believe that this approach will aid comprehension.

# THE STRUCTURE OF THIS BOOK

This book is structured as follows. Part I, composed of this and two other chapters, provides an introduction to the subject and presents the economic theory of risk from the individual's, business's and society's perspectives. It also sets out the theory of international trade. Part II explores the factors that shape the risk environment internationally. Part III is composed of a series of chapters that explore corporate risk management from a broad perspective. Part IV explores the international dimensions of insurance. This book concludes with a chapter intended to help the reader contemplate the future of risk and insurance.

## DISCUSSION QUESTIONS

1.  Is an appreciation for international events important to students of risk management and insurance, even if they intend to work exclusively for domestic firms with no international operations? Explain carefully.
2.  Is the study of risk management becoming more or less important in your country? Why?
3.  What special risks would you expect multinational corporations to encounter that purely national firms ordinarily would not encounter? Speculate about some of the ways of dealing with such special risks.
4.  Randomly select one economically developed country and one developing country, and compare classification of insurance between the two countries.
5.  What do you think are the prerequisites for the development of insurance in economically underdeveloped countries?

## NOTES

1.  This chapter draws from Skipper (1998), Chapters 1 and 3.
2.  In 2003, for example, the World Bank classified a total of 208 countries into the following categories: 56 high-income (OECD and non-OECD) countries, 34 upper middle-income countries, 54 lower middle-income countries27 and 64 low-income countries.
3.  This section draws from www.imf.org.
4.  This section draws from www.worldbank.org.
5.  This section draws from www.wto.org.
6.  As of January 2007, Burundi and Rwanda are also members of the free trade area.
7.  In the U.S. and some other countries, the term **personal** *lines* **insurance** refers exclusively to nonlife insurance purchased by individuals.
8.  In the U.S. and some other countries, the term **commercial** *lines* **insurance** refers exclusively to nonlife insurance purchased by organizations.

## REFERENCES

International Monetary Fund (IMF) (2002). *World Economic Outlook* (September). Washington, DC: IMF.

Skipper Jr., H.D., ed. (1998). *International Risk and Insurance: An Environmental/Managerial Approach*. Boston, MA: Irwin/McGraw-Hill.

Swiss Re (2006). "Natural Catastrophes and Man-Made Disasters 2005," *Sigma* 2. Zurich: Swiss Re.

United Nations Conference on Trade and Development (UNCTAD) (Annual). *World Investment Report*.

# Chapter 2

# Risk Perceptions and Reactions

## INTRODUCTION

The presence of risk and uncertainty complicates decision-making. We explore in this chapter why this is true by examining decision-making under uncertainty by individuals, businesses and society.

We begin the examination with a discussion of the expected value rule and the expected utility rule as well as their relationships to decision-making by individuals. We then discuss corporate reactions to risk and their decision-making under uncertainty. Finally, we examine economic efficiency as a social goal, imperfections in capital markets, externalities, and societal decision-making under uncertainty.

## INDIVIDUAL DECISION-MAKING UNDER UNCERTAINTY

Decisions about how to deal with risk are all about tradeoffs. We weigh an activity's benefits against its costs. In principle, we undertake risky activities whose benefits we perceive to be greater than their costs. Conversely, we try to avoid or otherwise mitigate the adverse effects of harmful conditions if we perceive that the costs of doing so are "reasonable." But what is a reasonable price to pay to mitigate the effects of undesirable, uncertain conditions?[1]

### Risky Decisions and the Expected Value Rule

We explore this important question through a simple example. Consider the decision that John must make concerning an inheritance of $10,000 from an uncle. He is unsure of what to do with the money, so he asks his friend Bill the banker for advice. Bill suggests that John either store the money in a safe or invest the money in a 1-year certificate of deposit (CD) issued by a government-insured bank and guaranteed to earn 7 percent per year. The two possibilities are shown below.

| Option | | Payoff |
|---|---|---|
| ❶ Store the money in a safe | ⇨ | $10,000 |
| ❷ Invest in CD | ⇨ | $10,700 |

John's decision is trivial. If he decides to store the money in a safe, he knows for certain that he will have $10,000 in 1 year. If John decides to purchase the CD, he knows for certain that he will have $10,700 in 1 year's time. Unsurprisingly, John rationally decides to invest in the CD.

Suppose Bill offers a third alternative. John could invest the $10,000 in a new type of mutual fund. The payoff on this mutual fund in 1 year depends upon a coin flip at yearend. If the coin comes up heads, John earns 30 percent on his investment for the year – a handsome return. If the coin comes up tails, John loses 15 percent.

John now faces a more complex decision. As shown in the payoff table below, the choice between options ❶ and ❷ is still a decision based on certainty, and John clearly prefers option ❷ to option ❶. The choice between options ❷ and ❸ is not so simple. Option ❸ offers a 50 percent chance of an additional $2,300 payoff over the option ❷ payoff. Likewise, the 50 percent chance of tails means that he would be left with only $8,500.

| Option | | Probability | Payoff |
|---|---|---|---|
| ❶ Store the money in a safe | ⇨ | 1.0 | $10,000 |
| ❷ Invest in CD | ⇨ | 1.0 | $10,700 |
| ❸ Invest in mutual fund | ⇨ | ⎰0.5 | $13,000 |
| | | ⎱0.5 | $8,500 |

To help John, we introduce a simple statistical concept. That is, the **expected value** (EV) of a set of $n$ possible outcomes equals the sum of these outcomes, each weighted by the probability of its occurrence; that is,

$$EV = \sum_i p_i x_i \tag{2.1}$$

where $p_i$ is the probability of a particular outcome $x_i$.

Intuitively, the expected value is the value that prevails *on average*. In our example, the expected value of the mutual fund is the average value that John could expect if he invested $10,000 into the fund over many years. Therefore, the expected value option ❸ is the weighted average of two possible outcomes (heads or tails) that John could expect if he invested $10,000 into the investment fund, or:

$$EV_3 = 0.5 \times \$13,000 + 0.5 \times \$8,500 = \$10,750$$

The expected values of options ❶ and ❷ are $10,000 and $10,700, respectively, as each is a certainty.

How does John proceed to decide among the alternatives? Some people suggest that he select the alternative with the highest expected value – doing so is referred to as following the **expected value rule** in making decisions. Under this rule, John picks option ❸.

## Risky Decisions and the Expected Utility Rule

The expected value rule is a logical means of deciding among alternatives, but it ignores risk – something that is important to individuals, although less so to corporations as we will see. In fact, most people are averse to risk and willing to forego some return to minimize risk, as we demonstrate next.

### *The Paradox posed by Bernoulli*

To explore individual risk aversion, consider the following gamble. A coin is flipped until the first tail appears. Two dollars are won if a tail appears on the first toss, $4 if it appears on the second, $8 if it appears on the third, and $2^n$ if it appears on the $n$th toss. In other words, the possible winnings double with each successful toss. How much would you be willing to pay to play this game, recognizing that you could win billions of dollars?

Let's begin our analysis by calculating the gamble's expected value:

$$EV = \sum_{1}^{\infty} \frac{1}{2}^{i} \times \$2^{i}$$
$$= 1 + 1 + 1 + \dots$$
$$= \infty$$

The gamble has an infinite expected value! Would you be willing to pay everything that you own to play this game? If you followed the expected value rule, you would and would be happy to do so! In reality, few individuals seem willing to pay more than $10 to play it, even with the enormous expected value of the payoff!

This experiment, known as the **St. Petersburg Paradox**, was suggested in an essay published in 1738 by the famous Swiss mathematician Daniel Bernoulli. This essay is considered by Peter Bernstein to be ". . . one of the most profound documents ever written, not just on the subject of risk but on human behavior as well."[2] Bernoulli argued that different people ascribe different values to risk. We have but to think about whether all passengers in an airplane during turbulence suffer equal anxiety. Certainly they do not.

It is good that all of us do not value risk in precisely the same way. If we did, thousands of uncertain business ventures, investments and other activities would be avoided. Some of us, after all, are more venturesome than others. As Bernstein observes: "think of what life would be like if everyone were phobic about lightning, flying in airplanes or investing in start-up companies. We are indeed fortunate that human beings differ in their appetite for risk."[3]

Bernoulli not only correctly noted that we value risk differently, but he also suggested a systematic relationship between risk and wealth. He observed that the satisfaction or utility derived from small increases in wealth was inversely related to the quantity of goods previously possessed. "For the first time in history Bernoulli [applied] . . . measurement to something that *cannot be counted*. He has acted as go-between in the wedding of intuition and measurement."[4]

Bernoulli established that the expected value rule is violated because it ignores the uncertainty inherent in risky outcomes. Recall the example of our friend John. Although the choice with the highest expected value is option ❸, John still may prefer option ❷ to ❸ because the former entails no uncertainty. To put it another way, the potential reward for taking on the risk of option ❸ may not be high enough to induce John to pick ❸ instead of ❷.

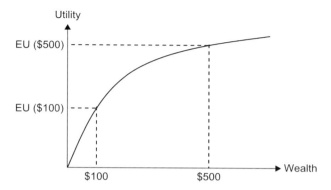

**Figure 2.1**    Sample Risk-Averse Utility Function

We have benefit of Bernoulli's insights, but how do we now operationalize his inverse relationship? This brings us to the notion of utility and risk aversion.

## *The expected utility rule*

Economists have taken Bernoulli's ideas further by modeling frameworks intended to describe how individuals make decisions under conditions of uncertainty. We begin our examination of this important work by defining key terms. We use **utility** to mean an index of satisfaction derived from economic goods. A **utility function** maps a particular wealth level to a corresponding level of satisfaction for an individual. Such a function is useful as it translates an individual's attitudes toward wealth and risk into a mathematical form that can be used in quantifying the individual's wealth and risk preferences. As such, it provides a way of systematically answering questions about the benefits and costs associated with an individual's risky decisions.

A utility function for a risk-averse person exhibits two characteristics:

* Increasing wealth leads to increasing levels of satisfaction.
* The marginal utility of wealth decreases as wealth increases.

Thus, suppose a risk-averse person, walking down the street, finds $100. By the first assumption, we know that she feels better because her wealth has increased. As she continues to walk down the street, she finds a second $100. Her satisfaction level increases again because of the second $100, but, by assumption two, it does not increase quite as much as it did when she found the first $100. This second assumption is known as the **law of diminishing marginal utility**. An example of a utility function that satisfies these two assumptions is shown in Figure 2.1.

As a practical matter, hardly any of us knows our utility functions. Even so, the theory is useful. For example, if different utility functions prescribe similar behavior, we can infer that reasonable individuals, including investors, might be wise to follow those prescriptions, even if they do not know their individual utility functions. Also, we could conduct analysis using different utility functions, say from those representing extreme risk aversion to those representing risk neutrality, and use those mappings as a means of assessing our own behavior in risky situations.

Return, again, to our example with John. This time we use the expected utility rule to predict whether John will choose option ❷ or ❸. The **expected utility rule** states that risk-averse individuals will select the option with the highest expected utility. Just as the expected value rule was a tool used to predict behavior under uncertainty, the expected utility rule can be used to predict the choices people make when faced with uncertainty.

The **expected utility** (E.U.) of a set of risky outcomes equals the sum of the utility levels of each outcome weighted by the probability of its occurrence; thus,

$$EU = \sum_i p_i \times U(x_i) \tag{2.2}$$

where $p_i$ is the probability of outcome $i$ and $U(x_i)$ is the utility derived from wealth level $x_i$.

With this tool in hand, where should John invest his money? Assume that it has been determined that John's utility function is the natural logarithm of wealth.[5] The resulting expected utilities of all three options are:

$$EU_1 = 1.0 \times U(10{,}000) = 1.0 \times \ln(10{,}000) = 9.21$$

$$EU_2 = 1.0 \times U(10{,}750) = 1.0 \times \ln(10{,}750) = 9.28$$

$$EU_3 = 0.5 \times U(13{,}000) + 0.5 \times U(8{,}500)$$
$$= 0.5 \times \ln(13{,}000) + 0.5 \times \ln(8{,}500) = 9.26$$

Using the expected utility rule, we now predict that John will choose option ❷ over option ❸ as he receives 9.28 units of utility for option ❸ and only 9.26 units for option ❷. The reward for taking on the risk of option ❸ is inadequate compared with the riskless CD investment.

Let us return to the St. Petersburg Paradox. Assuming a risk-averse person's utility function is again $U(x) = \ln(x)$, we can determine how much this person would pay to undertake the coin flipping game. Recall that the expected value of the game is infinite. Using the earlier equation we can calculate the expected utility of this game as follows:

$$EU = \sum_i p_i \times U(x_i)$$
$$= \sum_{i=1}^{\infty} \left(\frac{1}{2}\right)^i \times U(2^i)$$
$$= \sum_{i=1}^{\infty} \left(\frac{1}{2}\right)^i \times \ln(2^i)$$
$$= \ln(2) \sum_{i=1}^{\infty} \left(\frac{1}{2}\right)^i \times (i)$$
$$= \ln(2) \times 2 = \ln(2^2) = 4$$

Therefore, a risk-averse person with logarithmic utility would be willing to bet only \$4.00 to partake in the game.

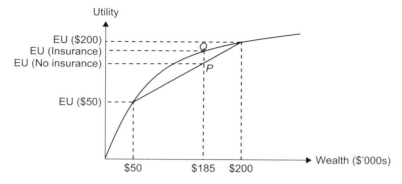

**Figure 2.2**   Maria's Expected Utility with Insurance: Actuarially Fair Premium

*Expected utility and the demand for insurance*

So far, we have considered risk only in the context of investments, and certainly this is relevant for individuals. The expected utility framework, however, can be useful also in determining whether an individual will purchase insurance as a means of minimizing uncertainty.

Insurance involves the transfer of a risky possibility to an insurance company in exchange for a certain amount of money (wealth) known as a premium. Above, we were trying to decide whether John should choose the risky or the riskless investment. We can use the same expected utility framework to decide whether a person should pay a premium to transfer the financial consequences of a risky outcome.

Suppose Maria owns a home worth $150,000 in the Philippines, and she has $50,000 in other assets. The probability of an earthquake in any year is 10 percent and, in case of a quake, the home will be totally destroyed. Maria can purchase insurance from XYZ Insurance Company that, in the event of a loss, would fully indemnify her. XYZ charges a premium equal to the expected value of the loss – called the **actuarially fair premium**.[6] Using equation (2.1) we determine the actuarially fair premium to be:

$$EV = 0.1 \times \$150,000 + 0.9 \times \$0 = \$15,000$$

Should Maria purchase the insurance? First, assume that she is risk averse. Now consider Figure 2.2. Maria's choices are (1) pay $15,000 for homeowner's insurance and transfer any risk of loss to XYZ or (2) not insure and subject herself to the possibility of a total loss of the property. If Maria chooses to insure her home, her wealth at the end of the year is $185,000 ($150,000 + $50,000 − $15,000), no matter whether an earthquake strikes during the year. Therefore, her expected utility will be:

$$EU_{\text{Insurance}} = 0.1 \times U(185,000) + 0.9 \times U(185,000) = U(185,000)$$

If Maria chooses not to purchase the insurance, her end-of-year wealth will be either $200,000 (with no loss) or $50,000 (with total loss). Her expected utility, therefore, is:

$$EU_{\text{No insurance}} = 0.1 \times U(50,000) + 0.9 \times U(200,000)$$

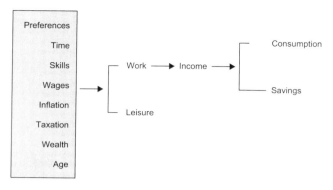

**Figure 2.3**   Work or Leisure

Note that the expected utility with insurance is greater than the expected utility without insurance as shown in Figure 2.2. Thus, she would purchase the insurance. The straight line between the two alternative utility positions when Maria chooses not to insure represents all linear combinations of those two points and is called the **expected utility line**. The intersection of the expected utility line and the expected wealth represents the expected utility of not insuring. This result occurs because the weights used to calculate the expected utility and the expected wealth are the same. For example, the expected utility of insuring is greater at point Q than the expected utility of not insuring at point P. In fact, whenever insurance is offered at an actuarially fair premium, the expected utility for risk-averse individuals of insuring is always greater than the expected utility of not insuring – a result often referred to as the **Bernoulli Principle** in recognition of the contributions of Daniel Bernoulli.

*Insurance demand and lifetime utility maximization*

What does economics have to say about how individuals might make decisions regarding their personal risk exposures taken over their entire lifetimes? We begin by noting that individuals occupy their time either in activities that produce income (or its equivalent) or in those that do not. For the sake of simplicity, we label these two states as work and leisure. Our investment in ourselves – in human capital – plus our preferences, time, wealth, income and a host of other factors, influences how we divide our time between work and leisure. As Figure 2.3 illustrates, work gives rise to income which in turn is spent on consumption or is saved.

Economic theories of consumption seek to explain consumer consumption and saving behavior over one's lifetime. With this in mind, it will prove insightful to examine briefly such theories that seek to explain the purchase of insurance against personal loss exposures.

*Economic theories of consumption*

Economic theories of consumption begin with the assumption that rational consumers seek to maximize their *lifetime* utilities. The maximization of lifetime utility involves attempts by us to allocate our incomes in such a way as to achieve an optimum lifetime pattern of consumption. This means planning for the future and not living only for today. This concept is rational, but on what basis would we expect individuals to make income allocations

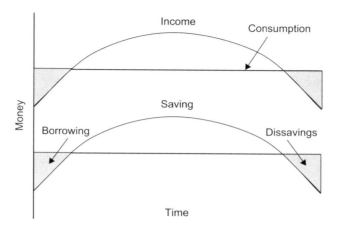

**Figure 2.4**    The Life Cycle of Consumption and Saving

between now and the future or, stated differently, between consumption now and consumption (saving) for the future?

The most widely accepted hypothesis explaining this allocation is the **life cycle hypothesis**. Under this hypothesis, the typical individual's income will be (1) low in the beginning and end stages of life and (2) high during the middle stage of life. In spite of these life cycle changes in income, however, the individual can be expected to maintain a constant or increasing level of consumption. Figure 2.4 is a presentation of a life cycle of income and consumption. The shaded areas in early and later life represent periods when consumption exceeds income (i.e., periods of dissaving).

In early life, expenditures exceed incomes which, except for the occasional child star, are typically zero. Our families cover these deficits. As we enter the workforce, our incomes increase. Ideally, incomes continue to increase throughout most of our working lifetimes, with their exceeding expenditures to allow for saving, as shown in the lower portion of Figure 2.4. The area above the consumption line and enclosed by the income curve represents periods of savings during which any earlier debts are repaid and amounts accumulated for retirement. At retirement, our incomes cease or at least typically diminish, with our entering a period of dissavings as we draw down our retirement savings.

*Consumption theories and insurance*
We showed above that risk-averse individuals can increase their satisfaction (utility) by the purchase of insurance. How does this result change if we include the life cycle model of consumption and the possibility of dying in our analysis? We similarly can show that risk-averse individuals will increase their expected *lifetime* utility by the purchase of life insurance to provide payments on death and of annuities to provide payments during retirement.[7] Conceptually, the same consumption pattern – as illustrated by the upper horizontal line in the figure – could be achieved through the appropriate use of personal insurance as could be achieved if the time of death were known with certainty. Without life insurance, the lifetime consumption pattern would be different and involve less enjoyment.

Research has shown that highly risk-averse individuals guard against a failure to have sufficient income later in life, so they save more than individuals who are less risk averse, and they would be expected to purchase more insurance. The degree of individual risk aversion, therefore, is an important determinant of individual consumption (and saving) patterns, as well as of aggregate national savings and insurance consumption.

The preceding economic findings probably come as no particular surprise to thoughtful students of risk management. This observation, however, in no way diminishes the importance of the research. Practical, real-world problems, and consumer decision-making can appear bewildering and confusing in the absence of a systematic theory to put them into some intellectual order. Theories lead to models that lead to tests that confirm, refute or cause modification of the models or theories. In so doing, we learn more about consumer preferences and choice. Better-suited products and services offering good value often result.

## Sounds Great, But . . .

Utility theory offers a logical, consistent means for making rational decisions in the face of uncertainty. But psychologists and behavioral economists note that humans do not always behave in a logical, consistent manner, nor do they always make what economists would define as rational decisions. As an article in *Fortune* magazine stated, perhaps only somewhat facetiously: ". . . when it comes to sorting out complicated stuff like our own financial affairs, we are actually foolish, sentimental, illogical, and badly flawed."[8] We humans suffer two problems not fully accommodated by utility theory: (1) we sometimes act on emotions rather than the pure logic of the original *Star Trek*'s Mr. Spock and (2) we sometimes experience *cognitive difficulties* – meaning that we do not understand the significance and limitations of the information that we have at our disposal.

Much of our knowledge about these two problems stems from the work of Amos Tversky and Daniel Kahneman whose theory we explore below. These and other researchers have shown that we humans routinely make decision-making errors when compared to the economically rational person, but often the errors are reasonably predictable.

Although considered by many economists to be much less important than utility theory, prospect theory continues to gain adherents. A *prospect* means a lottery. **Prospect theory** is similar to utility theory in that individuals seek to maximize their expected (weighted) utility. It differs, however, in two key respects. First, instead of a utility function, a so-called value function is hypothesized. Second, instead of true underlying probabilities, a revised probability weighting function is used.

### Prospect theory: loss aversion and the value function

Experiments have suggested that we humans actually make decisions regarding the possibility of gains and those involving the possibility of losses in different ways, contrary to the smooth, concave utility function hypothesized earlier. This finding has vitally important implications for how we deal with uncertainty.

Kahneman and Tversky hypothesized that each of us has a personal **value function** that reflects our degree of satisfaction derived from gains and losses from some reference point. The **reference point** is each individual's point of comparison or standard against which risky decisions are contrasted. This point is not static and can vary for the same individual depending on how the choices are framed or presented to the individual. The reference point might be wealth but often is not. It can be lives saved, credits earned or anything else valued by the individual. Because the reference point can vary, it is subject to manipulation, for example, through advertisements and on how an inquirer asks a question.

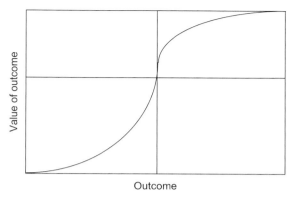

**Figure 2.5** Illustrative Prospect Theory Value Function

An experiment reported by Richard Thaler illustrates this point. Thaler told one class of students that they had just won $30. He then offered them the following options: (1) a coin toss gamble in which they would win an additional $9 for a total of $39 if heads and they lose $9 of the initial $30 if tails or (2) no gamble (i.e., keep the $30). Seventy percent of the class elected the gamble, even though its expected value was zero; that is, the same as the no gamble option. To another class, Thaler did not offer the initial $30 winnings. Instead he offered them a choice between (1) a coin toss gamble in which they would win $39 if heads and win $21 if tails or (2) $30 for certain. Only 43 percent elected the gamble. Of course, the choices offered to the two classes were identical. The difference was in how the choice was framed.

The Kahneman-Tversky value function is assumed to be concave in gains, as with a utility function, but convex in losses, as Figure 2.5 illustrates.[9] As shown, the value function has a positive slope throughout the range with a kink at the reference point. At that point, the slope abruptly changes.

Kahneman and Tversky report on an experiment that illustrates this asymmetry.[10] Subjects first chose between (1) a gamble involving an 80 percent chance of winning $4,000 and a 20 percent chance of winning nothing and (2) $3,000 with certainty. Note that the gamble has the higher expected value ($3,200). However, 80 percent of their subjects chose the $3,000 certain. People were risk averse, as utility theory suggests. Bernoulli would be happy!

The researchers then restated the choice in the negative. They asked subjects to choose between (1) a gamble involving an 80 percent chance of losing $4,000 and a 20 percent chance of losing nothing and (2) a $3,000 loss with certainty. Note that now the gamble, whose expected value is *minus* $3,200, results in less wealth on average than the $3,000 certain loss. Risk aversion suggests that people should elect the $3,000 certain loss. Yet, Kahneman and Tversky report that 92 percent of the subjects opted for the gamble. People were risk seekers when the choice involved losses exclusively. Bernoulli would be unhappy!

So which is it? Tversky answers: "It is not so much that people hate uncertainty – but rather, they hate losing." They are willing to undertake even an unfair gamble to avoid a certain loss. In other words, *loss aversion*, not *risk aversion*, is important in decision-making. This pattern reveals itself in numerous uncertain situations. Consider the following coin toss gamble: if a head appears, you pay $1,000; if a tail appears, you receive an agreed

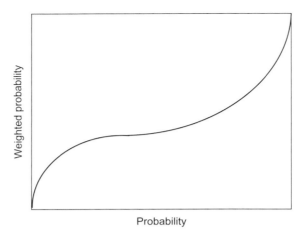

**Figure 2.6**   Probability Weighting Function. *Source*: David Laibson and Richard Zeckhauser, "Amos Tversky and the Ascent of Behavioral Economics." *Journal of Risk and Uncertainty*, (1998) 16, p. 14.

amount. What amount of money must be offered to you to engage in the gamble? For most people, the answer is about $2,000 – twice the amount of a fair gamble.

In fact, through numerous simulations, Richard Thaler has determined that "losing money feels twice as bad as making money feels good."[11] A value function captures this loss aversion if it has a slope ratio of 2:1 at the reference point.

The second major component of prospect theory is the probability weighting function. Kahneman and Tversky's findings, supported by other psychological research, suggest that people routinely overestimate the probability of unlikely events and underestimate the likelihood of more frequently occurring events. We believe that flying really is dangerous and that smoking really is not as bad as health experts suggest. Thus, in making decisions about unlikely or highly likely events, we overweight the former and underweigh the latter.

This result led Kahneman and Tversky to hypothesize an S-shaped curve that, like the value function, exhibits diminishing marginal sensitivity. Figure 2.6 illustrates such a curve. We show a 45 degree line representing the actual probabilities for reference. Thus, as the curve shows, we accord a weight of zero to events whose probabilities of occurrence are zero or exceptionally close to zero. As we move from completely or extremely improbable to merely highly improbable events, we overestimate the likelihood of their occurring, with the degree of overestimation diminishing with increasingly likely but still improbable events.

Similarly, we accord a weight of one to events that are certain or almost certain to occur. Thus, the curve shows that as we move from certain or extremely probable to merely highly probable events, we underestimate the likelihood of their occurring, with the degree of underestimation diminishing with less likely but still probable events. Hence, as we move away from the end-points, the weighting function flattens. Experimental results suggest that the curve lies mostly below the 45 degree line.

The shape of the weighting curve allows prospect theory to explain observations that are inconsistent with utility theory. If we substitute the weights for probabilities to derive expected utilities, we might explain why people purchase low-probability, high-reward lottery tickets. They substantially overweight the probability of winning. It might also explain why people purchase flight insurance![12]

### Other anomalies

Behavioral economics offers us several other explanations for financial behavior that seems inconsistent with utility theory. Here we introduce briefly the concepts of decision regret, mental accounting, and the endowment effect.

- *Decision Regret*: Loss aversion means that people hate to lose more than they like to win. As a consequence, humans often suffer **decision regret**, meaning that we feel far worse about having made bad choices than we do about our failures to have made smart choices. This phenomenon means that we will often delay making decisions about risk because we might regret them. Better to hold onto a loser stock than sell it!

- *Mental Accounting*: A dollar is a dollar. Right? Wrong, at least for many of us. Thus, investors often consider dividends differently from the equivalent stock-value appreciation, even ignoring different tax treatment. Money won from gambling often is available for further gambling or simply to "blow" on fun whereas the other money in our pocket may be off limits. When we do this, and most of us do, we engage in what is called **mental accounting**, which means that we tend to separate a whole into components. Instead of looking at the big picture and making decisions related to it, as utility theory would suggest, we consider individual small decisions separately. Mental accounting may be behind the decision of individuals and businesses often to make insurance purchase decisions on a case-by-case basis, rather than considering their entire financial and risk portfolios.

- *Endowment Effect*: We come lastly to Thaler's **endowment effect** – the tendency to set a higher price to sell that which we already own than what we would be willing to pay to purchase the identical item if we did not own it. Thaler was led to this conclusion after his studies on the value of a human life. He asked two questions of his subjects. First, how much would they be willing to pay to eliminate a one-in-a-thousand chance of their immediate death? Second, how much would they have to be paid to accept an additional one-in-a-thousand chance of their immediate death? He found "astounding" differences between the answers to the two questions. People often would pay no more than $200 to eliminate an existing 0.001 chance, but they would require $50,000 to accept an additional 0.001 chance of death. The endowment effect has been found in numerous investment decisions as well, confounding the rational investor model.

## Conclusion

So where does all of this disagreement leave us? Prospect theory and its offshoots, as mentioned, continue to gain followers. At the same time, however, problems lurk for its adherents. Much of its experimental support relies on contrived experiments, not real-world experiences. Importantly, somewhat of an apples-and-oranges situation exists in comparing utility theory with prospect theory. Economic models of behavior based on utility theory usually provide complete mathematical representations of behavior and, therefore, are subject to generalizability, testing and possibly useful forecasting. Prospect theory is mostly linguistically based and, therefore, less subject to mathematical precision and attendant benefits. The importance of these differences at present is unknown.

## BUSINESS DECISION-MAKING UNDER UNCERTAINTY

Now that we have an understanding of individual decision-making under uncertainty, we turn next to how businesses make such decisions. Are they risk (loss?) averse, just like individuals? The answer depends on what we mean by a business.

### Types of Businesses

Businesses worldwide generally come in one of three basic forms: sole proprietorships, partnerships or corporations. A **sole proprietorship** is a business owned by an individual. The owner holds title to the assets and is responsible for the liabilities. A **partnership** is a business owned by two or more individuals. Business assets are owned by the partnership. Under the typical partnership arrangement, **general partners** are fully responsible for the partnership's liabilities, and limited **partners** are responsible only to the extent of their investment in the partnership.

A **corporation** is a business separate and distinct from its owners and possesses three features:

- limited liability of its owners (they can lose only what they have invested);
- easy transfer of ownership (owners merely sell their shares of stock, assuming buyers can be found);
- continuity of existence (its continued existence is unrelated to whether its owners are alive).

Most corporations are **closely held corporations** meaning that they are owned by a small number of investors, usually a family, with their stock not sold on any organized exchanges. Typically, the managers have an ownership interest in the business.

### Sole Proprietorship and Partnership Reactions to Risk

Being indistinguishable from the individual who owns it, the sole proprietorship's risk perception and behavior logically will be that of its owner. As such, business decisions directly reflect the degree of risk aversion of the owner.

The same principle applies generally to the partnership form – its risk perception and behavior reflect some combination of the owners' degrees of risk aversion. An exception to this generality can occur if the partnership interest is held by many partners, has a ready market or is a small portion of the partners' overall investment portfolio, or if the partners have a sound understanding of how the value of their partnership interest changes with changes in the value of other investments. In practice, very few partnerships exhibit even one of these exceptions. You will understand why we include these limited exceptions after we explore the risk reactions of corporations.

### Corporate Reactions to Risk

The corporation's expected reaction to risk comes as a surprise to many students. As a separate legal entity from its owners, the corporation must be operated by managers hired by the owners. As individuals are risk averse, it seems reasonable to conclude that the owners of the corporation would want their managers to reflect this risk aversion and to reduce the risks of the firm. However, this is not invariably so. To understand this important point, we first remind the reader of some important corporate finance fundamentals.

### The goal of the firm and owner risk profiles

The objective of any business is to maximize the value of its owners' interests in the firm. They do this by undertaking only those projects whose net present values are positive. Stated differently, managers should maximize the firm's net positive cash flow.

Of course, the separation of ownership and management is a practical necessity for large firms today. We know that owners want to maximize their wealth, but each also has unique risk and liquidity preferences for lifetime consumption. If management is to act in the best interest of the firm's owners, how can it balance these conflicting owner objectives? The good news is that managers, at least in theory, need concern themselves only with maximizing owners' wealth and need not concern themselves with other owner objectives and preferences.

By assembling their own portfolio of financial assets, owners can determine their own consumption and risk profiles. They do not need management's help to do this. In fact, owners would not ordinarily want management to take their lifetime liquidity and risk preference goals into consideration. They want managers simply to maximize net present values, acting as *risk-neutral* agents for the owners and undertaking every project whose net present value is positive, irrespective of its risk.

### Why corporations should be risk neutral?

The corporate finance literature argues that, under reasonable assumptions, investors in corporations generally will require higher returns only for those risks that they are unable to diversify in capital markets, the so-called systematic risks. Under the capital asset pricing model (CAPM), systematic risk is measured as the sensitivity of the firm's stock price to movements in the general stock market. Stockholders generally are unconcerned about risks (i.e., cash flow volatility) that are unique to the business. By diversifying their individual investment portfolios, they can virtually eliminate this unsystematic risk – the risk that is unique to the business and not caused by general economic and other factors external to the firm.

This means that corporate managers should not take their owners' risk preferences into consideration as the owners will adjust their personal portfolios to their individual risk preferences. Rather, managers should make decisions as if the owners are risk neutral and not risk averse. A **risk-neutral utility function** is based on the following two assumptions:

- Increasing wealth leads to increasing levels of satisfaction.
- The marginal utility of wealth is constant as wealth increases.

The first assumption is the same as with risk-averse utility functions. The second is different. Unlike a risk-averse person, a risk-neutral person gains the same incremental satisfaction with increasing increments in wealth. A risk-neutral entity recognizes a risky situation, but does not alter its decision-making processes over any change of its wealth. An example of a utility function that satisfies the two assumptions of risk neutrality is shown in

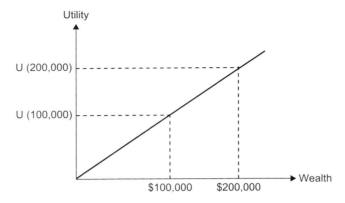

**Figure 2.7**    Sample Risk-Neutral Utility Function

Figure 2.7. A consequence of risk neutrality is that the entity would engage only in those risk-management practices whose net present values were positive, meaning that the firm would never pay a risk premium. We can see this result graphically in Figure 2.7 as there is no curvature in the utility function.

### *Why do corporations manage risks?*

In practice, we know that corporations devote considerable effort to managing their risks, and they undertake actions, such as buying insurance, that suggest that they do not behave as risk-neutral decision-makers. Four general reasons have been offered for this result:[13]

*   managerial self-interest;
*   corporate taxation;
*   cost of financial distress;
*   capital market imperfections.

#### *Managerial self-interest*

A potential **principal-agent** relationship exists whenever one person (called the agent) acts for another (called the principal). When the agent's and the principal's interests do not coincide (diverge), we have what is referred to by economists as a potential **principal-agent problem**. One such common problem occurs when managers (agents) do not always work in the best interests of the business's owners (principals). Thus, managers may attempt to benefit themselves, from terms of salary and perquisites, at the expense of the owners. They may not work as diligently as they would if they owned the firm, or they might not exclude riskiness from their decisions.

Of course, the board of directors (the owners' agent) could fire management for failure to maximize the firm's value. In theory, owners select the members of the board to look after their interests and to engage managers who will do likewise. In practice, it is not unusual for management to suggest directors sympathetic to *their* interests and for such directors to have a stronger allegiance to management than to owners.

The solution to this problem is to establish a system to monitor management and to try to seek a better alignment of management and owner interests. Managers can be monitored through audits, appropriate financial reporting and other means, although these activities are not foolproof – as the massive failure of Enron Corporation in 2002 reminds us. A better alignment of management-owner interests can be attained through offering management appropriate stock options, bonuses and perquisites that are directly related to how closely management's actions benefit owners, although these are not foolproof either. The threat of an actual takeover by outside interests of the firm also encourages management to work for the interests of existing owners, for a takeover could mean a loss of their jobs.

Besides the above management-self-interest problems, the concentration of managers' wealth (stock holdings and capitalized career earnings) in the firm they manage may afford them little ability to diversify their personal wealth. This fact gives them an interest in avoiding volatility since, other things being equal, stability improves their own situation. This logic applies especially to family-owned and other closely held business firms.

*Corporate taxation*

Under a progressive tax structure (i.e., the corporate tax rate increases with increasing taxable income), corporations have an incentive to smooth their net income streams to reduce tax liabilities. Activities that reduce the volatility of reported earnings may actually enhance shareholder value. Thus, a firm might be willing to pay a tax-deductible risk premium to purchase insurance if it might reduce its taxes in the long run.

*Costs of financial distress*

The third reason offered for risk management by firms is the avoidance of the costs of financial distress. Financial distress derives from the threat of bankruptcy. Financial distress can lead to costs being imposed by the courts that require various audits and accountings and place great demands on management time. Additionally, bankruptcy itself can be costly. Direct costs include payments for legal, accounting and other external advice as well as management's distraction and time. Further, numerous indirect costs are incurred, such as loss of a market dominant position, customers canceling their business and a falloff in new business. For these reasons, firms may choose lower-risk strategies than if the costs of financial distress were minimal. In the process, they are actually maximizing owner value.

Thus, the purchase of insurance, even at actuarially unfair rates, may be value enhancing if the insurance costs less than the expected costs of the buyer becoming financially distressed. For example, consider a furniture manufacturer that does not wish to purchase insurance on its assembly plant. The plant houses all operations and is subject to the possibility of a fire. As all operations are at one location, a fire would be particularly devastating. The company could either finance any potential losses caused by fire by purchasing insurance or make plans to borrow money in the debt market to rebuild the plant after a fire. Assume, based upon the company's balance sheet and earnings potential, it can currently borrow money at 8 percent. The question is, would it be able to borrow at 8 percent if it suffered a total loss of the plant due to a fire? The answer is "probably not." A total loss would not only adversely affect the company's balance sheet, but it would also severely affect its future cash flow, as the company would be unable to build and sell any furniture until a new plant was built.

*Capital market imperfections*

As long as a firm can finance positive net present value projects from internal funds, it need not rely on external finance. However, external funds will be necessary at times if the firm is to take advantage of all appropriate projects. At such times, the cost of external finance may be higher than the cost of internal finance because of (1) high transaction costs associated with external finance, (2) imperfect information about firm riskiness by those who might provide the external finance, or (3) the high cost of financial distress. This results in under-investment. Thus, volatility may cause the firm to forego some investments if it is forced to seek external funds. Because of this, the firm may logically seek to reduce volatility (e.g., purchase insurance), thereby enhancing owner value.

## Conclusion

There are circumstances under which even widely held corporations might not strictly follow the expected value rule. They might allow expected cash flow volatility (risk) to influence their decisions, opting for projects with less risk, and avoiding those that impose high risk on the firm. In general, however, we expect owners of widely held corporations to prefer their managers to ignore volatility unless it increases taxes, might bankrupt the firm, or forces the firm to seek external finance.

Remember, however, that the vast majority of businesses are *not* widely held corporations. They are sole proprietorships, partnerships and small or closely held corporations. We expect these businesses to take risk into consideration in their decisions, in similar, if not identical, ways as their individual owners.

# SOCIETAL DECISION-MAKING UNDER UNCERTAINTY

Having explored how individuals and businesses make decisions under conditions of uncertainty, we now examine how society makes such decisions. Our examination is necessarily limited, with, for example, our omitting important topics related to political science and analysis of voting and concepts of social justice.

## Economic Efficiency As a Social Goal

Just as individuals seek to maximize their welfare (i.e., their individual utilities), so too do societies want to maximize their welfare. The problem is that what you believe to be good for society (e.g., motorcycle riders should be required to wear helmets) and what your neighbor believes (e.g., wearing a helmet interferes with her enjoyment of bike riding and her individual rights) often differ. Because of these types of differences in individual preferences (coupled with other reasons discussed below), there is no such thing as a *societal* utility function. Economics offers an alternative, however.

Economics is concerned with the efficient allocation of resources. A fundamental economic principle is that individuals and businesses should undertake risk management (and all other) actions so long as the marginal (i.e., additional) benefit is greater than the marginal cost. We should undertake no actions whose marginal costs exceed their marginal benefits, because such actions cost more than they give us in benefits. We could agree, in principle, that society should also adopt this logical concept in dealing with risk.

Economists measure benefits based on the concept of "willingness to pay." Willingness to pay (WTP) generally relies on market prices. Are you willing to pay the $100 price of a concert ticket? If you are, presumably you have concluded that the benefits of attending the concert exceed the ticket price. If not, the price is "too high" considering the benefits. On its face, this approach seems reasonable. However, two issues arise.

### Even if it's efficient, is it fair?

*First*, we face the issue of fairness and social justice. For example, what if you are a poor student for whom $100 spent on the ticket means that you must bread and peanut butter for a week? You might find the price to be too high and not attend the concert. To your rich cousin and his obnoxious, wealthy older friends, the price is low. Hence, only rich people attend the concert! Is it "fair" to ration concert tickets based on the WTP doctrine? Maybe you say "Well, I don't much like it, but it's not unfair." But what if, instead of concert tickets, it is healthcare or education that is being rationed based on the WTP doctrine? Should only rich people have access to healthcare and education?

Competitive markets, relying on the WTP doctrine, result in an efficient allocation of society's resources. Efficiency in this context – called **Pareto efficiency** – means that society's scarce resources are allocated such that no one in society can be made better off without making someone else worse off. However, society may not necessarily prefer a Pareto efficient allocation of its resources if it results in some people having no access to education, healthcare or food. Concepts of fairness and of taking care of the less fortunate are universally pursued. A society, therefore, may support universal health insurance, public education, public assistance and other such programs because of fairness, social justice and compassion.

Economics has little to say about these issues except as they involve externalities (see below). True, people generally agree that extreme inequality of income, wealth, or opportunity is unfair and efforts should be made to rectify such extremes. Nonetheless, there is much less agreement as to what constitutes "fairness" and the extent to which greater equality of income, wealth and opportunity should be pursued for its own sake. Such issues are particularly complex because they are intertwined with social values and culture. Resolving them is more the province of philosophy, political science, and cultural anthropology than economics.

### Even if it's fair, is it efficient?

The *second* problem with relying exclusively on the efficiency model in making societal risk management decisions relates to the rigorous conditions required of the model. We mentioned earlier that economics is all about tradeoffs. We evaluate tradeoffs using the concept of opportunity cost. The **opportunity cost** of any action is the value of the most desirable foregone alternative action in that situation. Opportunity costs arise whenever resources available to meet wants are limited so that all wants cannot be satisfied. Money spent for one good is unavailable to spend on another. Should I spend $100 for the concert ticket, $100 for movie tickets and fast food with my girlfriend, or $100 to eat decently for a week? The market says, in effect, that each of the three options has equal value; that is, the cost to society of each option is identical.

But is this really correct? What if the concert organizers managed to secure permission to hold the event in a field that is in the middle of an ecologically sensitive wilderness area? The concert will result in the destruction of delicate wildlife and the pollution of the grounds and nearby streams. Also, several tenant families will be displaced, leaving them destitute and homeless. The $100 price of the concert ticket does not include these costs.

In other words, the opportunity cost of the ticket is higher than its price. Besides the direct costs incurred by the concert organizers, they also are imposing costs on other people and society for which they pay nothing.

Such cost shifting occurs whenever direct or accounting costs are reduced by measures that impose costs on other persons, including the community at large or even future generations. In other words, it exists whenever the *economist's* definition of costs and the *accountant's* definition of costs are not the same. In such instances, the market price of the good fails to capture all resource costs and, therefore, is actually below what it would be if all opportunity costs were included. With price too low, more will be produced and sold, hence imposing even more costs on others and society and using more of society's scarce resources than justified.

Thus, market prices do not always equal opportunity costs. In fact, they rarely are so wonderfully aligned, in part because competitors work hard to avoid doing so, as we will see. As a result, resources will be allocated inefficiently to various degrees. Even imperfectly competitive markets typically allocate resources better in most cases than any other systems yet created.

## Imperfections in Markets

The failure of a market to allocate resources efficiently means that some goods or services may be unavailable or available only in some suboptimal way (e.g., at prices higher than those prevailing in a perfectly competitive market).[14] We term market-based (as contrasted with government-driven) situations causing an inefficient allocation of resources as **market imperfections** or **market failures**. Market imperfections reduce societal welfare. An understanding of these imperfections is important because they can greatly affect the quality of the decisions that society makes about risk and security.

Let us first be clear about the conditions under which *no* imperfections exist. Insight 2.1 offers a "microeconomics 101" refresher. If a market has no imperfections (i.e., it is the so-called **perfectly competitive market**) societal welfare, as defined by economists, is maximized. Thus, except for concerns about fairness and compassion which society addresses via its political processes, we want markets to be as competitive as possible.

We discuss market imperfections by grouping them around four general classes of problems:

- market power;
- externalities;
- free rider problems;
- information problems.

### Market power

The first assumption within the competitive model means that a sufficiently large number of buyers and sellers compete such that none is large enough to influence price. In fact, most sellers and some buyers can influence price, at least to some degree. The ability of one or a few sellers or buyers to influence the price of a product or service is called **market power**.

Several conditions can give rise to market power, including: (1) governmentally created barriers to entry, (2) economies of scale, and (3) product differentiation/price discrimination.

---

## INSIGHT 2.1: CONDITIONS FOR A PERFECTLY COMPETITIVE INSURANCE MARKET

The following conditions are necessary for perfectly competitive markets.

- *A sufficiently large number of buyers and sellers are present such that no one buyer or seller nor any group of them can influence the market.* This condition means that all buyers and sellers are **price takers** – none can influence the price of the product as determined by its supply and demand. Underlying this assumption is that neither sellers nor buyers engage in collusive behavior.

- *Sellers have freedom of entry into and exit from the market.* This condition means that new competitors can enter the market if they see that existing firms are making *excess* profits. Firms must not only respond to rivals after they enter the business, but they also must anticipate new competitors. Thus, if competitors know that entry barriers are low, they will tend automatically to hold the line on price increases even if no new competitors actually enter the market. The mere threat of new entry can be sufficient to ensure that firms will make only *normal* profits. Conversely, competitors will exit a market if they cannot make normal profits or if they can make greater profits elsewhere.

- *Sellers produce identical products.* This condition means that no seller can differentiate its products from those of its rivals. Hence, buyers have no incentive to pay more than the market price for any firm's products.

- *Buyers and sellers are well informed about the products.* This condition means that all firms and consumers possess full knowledge about the product or service under consideration and that none has knowledge unknown to others.

---

*Governmentally created barriers to entry*

Market power arises when a market has entry or exit barriers and few sellers. Varying degrees of market power are found within markets worldwide. Most such market power is created or facilitated by government as opposed to non-government actions. As such, they could be alleviated by reducing government intervention. Thus, business sectors in several countries are monopolistic, and many others sectors are oligopolistic. A **monopoly** exists when there is only one supplier of a product or service. An **oligopoly** exists when there are only a few suppliers, and they can exercise market power (often because of entry barriers).

National tax regimes can lead to the creation of market power. Some countries assess higher taxes on the local business of foreign companies than they do on the local business of domestic companies. Such practices are analogous to trade tariffs and can be expected to have similar adverse economic consequences (see Chapter 3).

In financial services, national licensing requirements technically are entry barriers, although they may be justified on consumer protection grounds. Licensing requirements include minimum capitalization, fitness qualifications and, in some jurisdictions, detailed operating plans.

*Economies of scale*

Economies of scale, another type of entry barrier, can afford a firm market power. **Economies of scale** exist when a firm's output increases at a rate faster than attendant increases in its production costs. In industries that enjoy economies of scale, the larger the firm the more efficiently it can operate, thus putting new entrants at an immediate competitive advantage.

Firms typically achieve a certain size – called the **minimum efficient scale** (MES) – at which long-run average costs are at a minimum; further growth yields no additional efficiencies. If further growth neither adds nor detracts from efficiency (i.e., average costs are constant), the firm is operating at **constant returns to scale**. If further growth diminishes efficiency (i.e., average costs increase), the firm is operating at **decreasing returns to scale**. If, however, efficiency increases (i.e., average costs decrease) over an industry's entire relevant output range, then the MES is so large relative to market size that only one firm can operate efficiently – a so-called **natural monopoly**.

Whether a firm possesses market power from scale economies depends, of course, on its size relative to its market rather than its absolute size. A small firm in a tiny market may wield monopoly power. A large multinational corporation in an international market may have little such power. Also, even a monopolist or oligopolist may be unable to exercise market power if the market is **contestable**, meaning that entry barriers are low and exit is easy. In such instances, the mere threat of competition from possible new entrants may be sufficient to cause existing firms to behave as if the market were competitive.

*Product differentiation and price discrimination*

The pure competitive model assumes **product homogeneity** – meaning that products are perfect substitutes in the minds of buyers. The competitive model also assumes that all suppliers charge the same price for these products. **Product differentiation** occurs when, because of product quality, service, location, reputation or other attributes, one firm's products are preferred by some buyers over rivals' products. When a large number of firms produce similar but not identical products, they are engaged in **monopolistic competition** which gives the firms an element of monopoly power (i.e., the ability to influence price). **Price discrimination** occurs when firms offer identical products at different prices to different groups of customers.

Companies routinely seek to differentiate their products from those of their competitors. Some products are more difficult to differentiate than others. Additionally, companies sometimes practice price discrimination. Extreme price discrimination can, in theory, lead to **predatory pricing** – lowering prices to unprofitable levels to weaken or eliminate competition with the idea of raising prices after competitors are driven from the market. If practiced on an international basis, predatory pricing is called **dumping** (see Chapter 3). Although theoretically possible, we have no evidence of widespread predatory pricing generally or dumping in particular. Predation is a viable strategy only if reentry barriers are high, which generally is not the case in competitive markets.

## *Externalities*

We noted above that opportunity costs do not always equal market prices because of cost shifting. In other words, producers can impose spillover effects on others. A manufacturing facility that pollutes the surrounding air, water or land imposes costs on the neighboring population in terms of a less pleasant environment, poorer health and lower property values. Conversely, if a new business opens in an economically depressed area, its providing additional jobs may decrease the incentive for some people to resort to criminal activities, thereby providing a beneficial spillover effect to the local community.

These are examples of **externalities** – benefits or costs that occur when a firm's production or an individual's consumption has direct and uncompensated effects on others. If others benefit, we have a **positive externality**. If costs are imposed on others, we have a **negative externality**. Societal risk management is particularly concerned about negative externalities.

### *The nature of externalities*

The purely competitive economic model does not accommodate externalities easily, because the market prices of goods and services that carry externalities fail to reflect their true (opportunity) costs. With the polluting manufacturing facility, its direct costs of production as measured by its accounting expenses for labor, machinery, transportation, etc., fail to capture the firm's true economic costs of production, because the business imposes uncompensated costs on the surrounding community. This means that its production costs are understated, that the firm's prices are lower than they should be, and, therefore, that more of the firm's products will be manufactured than is socially desirable – further contributing to pollution. If the facility were forced to compensate the community for its lessened enjoyment, poorer health and lower property values, its direct costs of production would align more closely to its true economic costs.

Herein lies the problem with allowing competitive markets to deal freely with goods and services that carry externalities. With negative externalities, too much of the good or service will be produced or consumed, the price will be too low, and too little effort and resources will be devoted to correcting or reducing the externality. Conversely, with positive externalities, too little of the good or service will be produced, its price will be too high, and too little effort will be devoted to enhancing the externality.

### *The importance of property rights*

Negative externalities such as pollution can persist in competitive markets because the persons adversely affected by the negative spillovers have poorly defined, dispersed or no property rights. This odd-sounding statement can be understood by two simple examples. First, imagine that a mining operation allows its tailings to wash onto your property, ruining your fishing lake. You sue the company for the value of the ruined lake. You win because your property rights were clearly infringed upon by the mining company. The mining company's costs rise because it must compensate you (and others similarly affected) in an amount equal to the costs that it attempted unsuccessfully to impose on you. This brings its accounting costs into closer alignment with its true, economic costs.

Now consider the same mining operation except that the tailings now wash into the ocean. No one "owns" the ocean or, stated differently, we all have an interest in the ocean but cannot necessarily support a legal claim that our *personal* property rights have been violated. Even if each of us could actually claim a proportionate ownership of the ocean, how could the owners successfully assert their claims. Why should I incur the costs to do so if I can simply sit on the sidelines and benefit from others' legal actions, but without having to pay anything? Everyone has an incentive to be a "free rider" on everyone else, so no one does anything!

Thus, the mining company succeeds in imposing uncompensated costs on society. Because its production costs exclude these societal costs, the accounting costs are lower than the true economic costs. Consequently, the company's prices are lower than they should be, so too much is sold and pollution is correspondingly greater than it would be in the first situation.

There are important problems in trying to curb pollution. Too often, property rights are not well established or they are widely dispersed, thus precluding meaningful actions by private citizens against the polluter. Government action is required, as we explore in Chapter 4.

### Free rider problems

Some collectively consumed goods and services that are desired by the public – called **public goods** – carry extensive positive externalities. Examples include public education, lighthouses, regulation, police and fire protection services, basic research and development, and national defense. When such goods and services are available to others at low or zero cost, they can cause a **free rider problem**. Thus, the shipowner who operates a lighthouse cannot exclude other ships from using it. By contrast, a **private good** is one in which one person's consumption precludes it being consumed by another. A public good is characterized by **non-rival consumption** – meaning that one person's consumption of the good or service does not reduce its availability to others.

The problem with public goods is that, left to itself, a competitive market is unlikely to provide as much of them as society really wants. Each shipowner has an incentive to encourage other shipowners to build the lighthouse, but each might wait for the others to do so, anticipating a "free ride." Consequently, governments generally provide public goods, and they are appropriately financed by societal revenues (i.e., taxes). Indeed, the existence of public goods is one of the primary justifications for having a tax system.

### Information problems

An important assumption of the perfectly competitive model is that both buyers and sellers are well informed. Information problems occur when buyers (or sellers) lack sufficient information to make an informed purchase (or sales) decision. Thus, when we buy an automobile, an insurance policy, investments, medical services and a host of other goods and services, we do so largely on faith. We are not truly informed buyers. We hope that some agency (usually the government) is there to protect our interests and to ensure that the seller does not take unfair advantage of us.

Markets that suffer such information asymmetries often are regulated if the goods or services involved are important elements of our lives or the economy. Even so, all of us can recall stories where some seller took advantage of our ignorance or even misrepresented a product or service. Conversely, some of us probably can recall where we took perhaps unfair advantage of some seller!

Information problems are of two types: (1) asymmetric information and (2) non-existent information. We discuss each.

*Asymmetric information: problems and solutions*

**Asymmetric information** problems arise when one party to a transaction has relevant information that the other does not have. Asymmetry information problems can be classified as those relating primarily to the buyer and those relating primarily to the seller. The first two below relate primarily to the buyer whereas the last two relate primarily to the seller.

- A so-called "**lemons" problem** exists when the buyer knows less than the seller about the seller's products. (A "lemon" is a slang term used in the U.S. automobile business to connote an automobile that appears sound but, in fact, is defective in some way.) Thus, the typical insurance buyer is unsure about the suitability and price of insurance policies as well as about the solidity of insurers backing the policies. Is he or she buying a "lemon?" Is the insurer (or its agent) taking advantage of the consumer's poor knowledge about insurance?

- A **principal-agent (or agency) problem** exists when the buyer of services knows less about its agent's actions than does the agent. The term agent is used here in a generic sense meaning any person acting for another person (its principal). Thus, the interests of company managers (the "agents") may not always align with the interests of the company owners (their "principal"). Managers may be more interested in making money for themselves than in making profits for the firm's owners. Also, the typical company cannot always depend upon its salespeople (agents) being completely forthcoming in sales situations; after all, many salespeople are interested in making the sale to secure a commission. In these and a host of other situations, inefficiencies can arise when the interests of the agent and the interests of the principal diverge.

- *Adverse selection* exists when the seller knows less than the buyer about the buyer's situation. The typical bank cannot be completely sure that the loan applicant is disclosing all relevant information. Is the individual withholding or misrepresenting important credit-related information?

- *Moral hazard* is the propensity of individuals to alter their behavior when risk is transferred to a third party. For example, insureds have a tendency to alter their behavior – to be less careful – because of the existence of insurance. (This problem is explored in depth in Chapter 20.)

In each of the above instances, the adversely affected party can obtain more information to reduce the adverse consequences of the information asymmetry. The ill-informed buyer can engage in deeper research about the quality and prices of potential purchases, to reduce the chances of making a poor decision. The bank considering the issuance of a loan can request additional information about the applicant. The board of directors (representing the interests of the owners) can establish a stricter system of monitoring managers, and managers can tighten supervision of salespeople. Insurers can undertake deeper claims investigations to root out fraudulent or exaggerated claims.

Why don't the parties simply obtain more information – indeed, simply secure as much information as they believe they need to make well-informed decisions? Contrary to the costless information assumption of the competitive model, securing more thorough information raises costs – either to the consumer (e.g., increased search costs) or to the seller (e.g., securing information from other sources). Tradeoffs are inevitable between (1) the additional expenses incurred to become better informed and (2) the additional costs inherent in making decisions with less information.

### Non-existent information

In many instances, neither the buyer nor the seller has complete information because desired information simply does not exist. If individuals do not have complete knowledge about the consequences of their present and future choices, they face uncertainty. This uncertainty leads them to take ameliorating actions intended to reduce their risk exposure. These offsetting actions require the expenditure of additional resources, thus decreasing overall benefits to society.

Environmental factors – such as the economy, inflation, new laws and regulations, and changing consumer attitudes and preferences – present great uncertainty to both buyers and sellers, thus rendering decision-making suboptimal. These and other like situations are addressed through actions such as diversification and creation by governments of various "safety nets" for its citizens, such as deposit insurance.

Non-existent and asymmetric information problems mean that some individuals are so completely ill informed that they are unable to know their own best interests. One of the premises for social insurance programs is that individuals will not or cannot fully arrange for their own financial security, so government must force them to do so.

## CONCLUSION

We can imagine that market imperfections can and do result in prices not measuring opportunity costs accurately. In turn, this means no society should rely exclusively on competition to ensure adequate levels of risk assessment, control and financing. We have employee health and safety laws and regulations, environmental pollution standards and oversight, product liability laws, banking regulation and literally hundreds of other laws, regulations and standards, the purposes of which are to ameliorate for market imperfections.

But societies also have government and private "safety nets" such as welfare, public housing, indigent medical care, charitable services and a host of other programs that might seem remote from the economics of imperfect markets. They seem to spring from a societal sense of fairness, compassion, ethics or other non-economic fountain. How society makes these calls stems from the culture of the people, the nature of the political system and the level of economic development. Rich countries can do more to help their poor people than can poor countries. A democracy provides a means for making political decisions on these important issues.

As long as a voluntary but risky decision by an informed business or individual is an exclusively private matter, with the benefits and the costs of the decision inuring only to that business or individual and imposing no costs on anyone else, we would argue that society should have no voice in the decision. Of course, the individual or business might be poorly informed. Moreover, many risky decisions do impose costs on others, especially through the public safety and healthcare services that must respond to adverse outcomes. Social benefits and costs often do not align with private benefits and costs. When this misalignment is substantial, society has economic justification for interfering in private decisions.

Several techniques exist by which these societal risk management decisions can be evaluated and made. These are explored in this book, with all relying on some form of benefit–cost comparison.

## DISCUSSION QUESTIONS

1. "If individuals were not risk averse, insurance would not exist." Do you agree with this statement? Justify your answer.
2. "If individuals were not risk averse, risk management would not exist." Do you agree with this statement? Justify your answer.
3. Why would we ordinarily expect corporations whose shares were widely held to be risk neutral?
4. Even corporations whose shares are widely held often seem to be risk averse. (a) Offer some sound economic reasons for such corporate behavior. (b) Offer some practical reasons for such corporate behavior.
5. Justify the following statement: "If externalities did not exist, society would have no worry about pollution."
6. "If a market is operating with reasonable efficiency, government should leave it alone." Under what circumstances would you (a) agree and (b) disagree with this contention?

## NOTES

1. This section draws from Phillips (1998).
2. Bernstein (1996), p. 100.
3. Id., p. 105.
4. Id., p. 106.
5. Utility functions commonly used for descriptive purposes are based on the log of wealth or the square root of wealth. Both of these mathematical functions have shapes similar to that shown in Figure 2.1. Of course, neither function necessarily represents a particular individual's utility function.
6. This is the economist's term to mean that the premium equals the expected value of the insurance benefit with no allowance for expenses, etc. It does not mean that any other premium is "unfair." The term carries no judgment value. Actuaries use the term "pure premium" to denote the same concept.
7. Yaari (1965) and Pissarides (1980).
8. O'Reilly (1998).
9. Laibson and Zeckhauser (1998).
10. Kahneman and Tversky (1979).
11. As quoted in O'Reilly (1998), p. 174.
12. Flight insurance is usually priced well above the actuarially fair premium. Further, the probability of dying in an airplane crash is slim. Generally, individuals who buy flight insurance are either exceedingly risk averse or greatly overestimate the probability of airplane accidents.
13. This section draws from Santomero and Babbel (1997).
14. This section draws in part from Skipper (1998), Chapter 10.

## REFERENCES

Bernstein, P.L. (1996). *Against the Gods: The Remarkable Story of Risk*. New York: John Wiley & Sons.

Kahneman, D. and Tversky, A. (1979). "Prospect Theory: An Analysis of Decisions Under Risk." *Econometrica*, 47 (2): 263–272.

Laibson, D. and Zeckhauser, R. (1998). "Amos Tversky and the Ascent of Behavioral Economics." *Journal of Risk and Uncertainty*, 16: 7–47.

O'Reilly, B. (1998). "Why Johnny Can't Invest." *Fortune* (November 9): 173.

Phillips, R.D. (1998). "The Economics of Risk and Insurance: A Conceptual Discussion," Chapter 2, in H.D. Skipper Jr., ed., *International Risk and Insurance: An Environmental-Managerial Approach*. Boston, MA: Irwin/McGraw-Hill.

Pissarides, C.A. (1980). "The Wealth-Age Relation with Life Insurance." *Economica*, 47 (November): 451–457.

Santomero, A.M. and Babbel, D.F. (1997). "Financial Risk Management by Insurers: An Analysis of the Process." *The Journal of Risk and Insurance*, 64 (2): 233–234.

Skipper Jr. H.D. (1998). "Rationales for Government Intervention into Insurance Markets," in H.D. Skipper Jr., ed., *International Risk and Insurance: An Environmental-Managerial Approach*. Boston, MA: Irwin/McGraw-Hill.

Yaari, M. (1965). "Uncertain Lifetime, Life Insurance, and the Theory of the Consumer." *Review of Economic Studies*, 32 (April): 137–150.

# Chapter 3

# The Economics of International Trade

This chapter explores the economics and policy underlying international trade.[1] The term "international trade" carries with it some notion of the flow of funds internationally, either cross-border or through local establishment of a foreign-owned presence. The question examined here is whether such trade is logical and beneficial, and, if so, to whom it is beneficial.

We explore the question by setting out the economic principles underlying international trade. We next examine the traditional methods by which international trade is restricted and the classical arguments used in their support. Shifting our emphasis to the practical aspects of international trade negotiation, we then set out several widely accepted fair trade concepts and illustrate how they are applied. We conclude with a discussion about deregulation and liberalization of markets.

## THE ECONOMIC THEORY OF TRADE

The notions of free trade can be traced to Adam Smith's *The Wealth of Nations* (1776). At the time Smith wrote his book, the dominant trade philosophy held that trade amounted to a zero-sum transaction; that is, if one nation wins other nations must lose and vice versa. This trade theory, called **mercantilism**, contended that, by restricting imports and promoting exports through government subsidies or other preferential treatments, a nation could become richer because increased exports required increased payments from other nations. The greater the payments, the richer one's own country became.

Smith proposed a radically different philosophy, which became part of the broader **classical economic theory**, based on the premise of trade gains to both parties. Smith believed that the goal of economic activity should be to satisfy consumers' demand for goods and services. The wealth of a nation was not the size of its gold stock but the productive ability of its labor, land and capital. By producing goods and trading them with others, a country could increase its wealth. According to Smith, significant gains could be made by production specialization. This view contrasted directly with those of the mercantilists, who would have their countries compete in every industry and not necessarily just those where they were most efficient.

*These differences are fundamentally important*, yet not fully appreciated. Even today, perhaps the majority of the world's citizens adhere to a mercantilist concept (e.g., witness some unions' demands for protection). The critical flaw in this now defunct concept was the mercantilist failure to understand the role of specialization and to distinguish between absolute and comparative advantage.

## Absolute and Comparative Advantage

Smith's notion of specialization led David Ricardo (1817), another economist, to develop the notions of comparative advantage and absolute advantage. Thus, a firm (or country) has an **absolute advantage** over another firm (country) if it can produce the same output as the other firm (country) at less *absolute* cost. A firm (country) has a **comparative advantage** over another firm (country) if it can produce the same output as the other firm (country) at less *relative* or *opportunity* cost.

As noted in Chapter 2, **opportunity cost** is a measure of the cost of foregoing one activity to engage in another requiring the same amount of resources. As resources are limited, they should be allocated for optimal productivity. If a resource is used in a sub-optimal way, society suffers a relative loss equal to the value lost because of the failure to use the resource in the more productive way.

The following example illustrates the essential differences between absolute and comparative advantage. Suppose that the world comprises two countries only, East and West, and that each produces only two goods: wine and cheese. Table 3.1 gives the number of worker-hours required in each country to produce one bottle of wine and one kilogram of cheese. West requires 3 hours to produce a bottle of wine, while East can produce a bottle in only 1 hour. In West, 7 hours are required to produce one kilogram of cheese, while in East, only 5 hours are required. Both wine and cheese are more costly to produce in West. Hence, East has an *absolute advantage* over West in the production of both goods.

To the mercantilist, this situation would suggest that no gains from trade are possible as Western goods are absolutely more expensive than Eastern goods. Moreover, to the mercantilist – and also to many individuals today – East would eventually make everything in the world and West's people would languish forever in poverty, never being able to compete because of East's greater efficiency.

This view is wrong. We are mistaken if we allow decisions to be based on the total cost differentials between the countries. Rather, they should flow from the *comparative* cost differentials of each country.

The next to last column of Table 3.1 shows the relative cost of wine as measured by the amount of cheese production that must be foregone to produce an additional bottle of wine. This relative cost is calculated as the hours needed to produce each bottle of wine divided by the hours required to produce each kilogram of cheese. This column shows that a bottle of wine costs 0.43 kilogram of cheese in West but only 0.20 kilogram of cheese in East. Thus, wine is relatively less expensive in East than in West.

The last column of the table shows the relative cost of cheese as measured by the amount of wine production that must be foregone to produce each additional kilogram of cheese. It takes only 2.33 bottles of wine to buy a kilogram of cheese in West, while five bottles are required in East.

This relative production cost analysis reveals that East has a comparative advantage in wine production, and West has a comparative advantage in cheese production. Thus, trade

**Table 3.1**   Production Costs for East and West in Terms of Wine and Cheese

| | For Absolute Advantage | | For Comparative Advantage | |
| --- | --- | --- | --- | --- |
| | Work required to produce one bottle of of wine (hours) | Work required to produce one kilogram of cheese (hours) | Production cost of wine in units of cheese | Production cost of cheese in units of wine |
| West | 3 | 7 | 0.43 | 2.33 |
| East | 1 | 5 | 0.20 | 5.00 |

is beneficial to East if it buys West's relatively less expensive cheese, and trade is beneficial to West if it buys East's relatively less expensive wine.

The example in Table 3.1 illustrates why the mercantilists are wrong. Trade is not a zero-sum game. The combination of specialization and trade benefits both countries. Eastern wine producers can buy one kilogram of cheese for five bottles of wine in East. If we allow trade with West, Eastern wine producers can purchase 2.15 kilograms of cheese with the same five bottles of wine (5 $\times$ 0.43). Thus, Eastern producers gain an extra 1.15 kilograms of cheese by selling their wine in the West.

A similar story applies to Western cheese producers. They could receive more wine per kilogram of cheese by selling to Eastern consumers. Thus, each country gains by exporting the commodity in which it holds a *comparative* advantage and importing the good where it is comparatively disadvantaged.

Misconceptions about international trade abound. Insight 3.1 sets out three such common misconceptions. Each in some way focuses on the notion of opportunity cost. By understanding opportunity cost and the benefits of exploiting comparative advantage, we can understand how trade restrictions increase opportunity costs to an economy and thereby penalize economic growth. A country cannot purchase from the lowest opportunity cost provider if trade is restricted, and the welfare of its citizens suffers as a result.

The comparative advantage in the Table 3.1 example is determined by differences in labor resources needed to make wine and cheese. Not all comparative advantages, however, arise from labor productivity differences. A country may have a comparative advantage because of land, natural resources, or simple abundances of other productive inputs. It may have a comparative advantage because of capital or entrepreneurial ability.

In financial services, many production inputs may lead to an absolute or comparative advantage. Financial intermediaries with easy access to highly developed capital markets would be expected to have an advantage over those operating in countries with under-developed capital markets. This advantage can be an absolute advantage – because the *total cost* of capital may be lower – and a comparative advantage – because the *opportunity cost* of capital versus labor is lower – of firms domiciled in those economically advanced countries. Again, although the total cost of capital may be lower in a country with access to a highly developed capital market, it is the relative or comparative advantage that is important.

Understanding opportunity cost and comparative advantage is fundamental to understanding the gains from trade. Adam Smith's notion of specialization and David Ricardo's ideas about comparative advantage revolutionized the way 19th-century England and ultimately the world understood and conducted trade.

A concerted effort has been made since World War II to reduce barriers to international trade. For the most part, countries with a developed market-economy have been the

## INSIGHT 3.1: COMMON MISCONCEPTIONS ABOUT TRADE

*Myth 1: Free trade is beneficial only for efficient producers. Some countries are inefficient at producing everything and therefore would always lose.*

This misconception is based on a belief that absolute advantage drives trade. Our example showed that East had an absolute advantage in both wine and cheese production, but there were still gains from trade! These gains were due to the *relative* efficiency of each country in producing wine and cheese. Thus, East had a comparative advantage in wine and West in cheese. Remember, if another country can produce an identical item less expensively than one's own country, why not purchase the less expensive item and have more money to spend on other things?

*Myth 2: Low-wage foreign competitors always will take jobs away from higher-wage markets.*

This misconception is sometimes referred to as the sweatshop labor argument and is a particular favorite of labor unions arguing for protection from foreign competition. Domestic labor, it is argued, should be protected against low-wage foreign workers. In our example, West has less efficient workers than East (as it takes more time to make the same amount of cheese and wine). West, therefore, will have lower wages. This is immaterial as it is not the absolute cost of labor, but its relative cost that is important. If it is cheaper to import than to produce, then a country should do so. Low wages or low productivity is not a reason to restrict trade, because we do not compare costs or productivity across countries, only just the relative cost or relative productivity.

*Myth 3: Trade exploits a country and makes it worse off. This is especially true if the country uses more labor to produce the goods it exports than other countries use to produce the goods it receives in return.*

This myth has its roots in the Marxist notion that the value of a country's production is created solely by its labor. If a country employs more labor relative to other factors of production and relative to other countries, its labor is being "exploited" because of unequal exchange. Unequal exchange does not mean a poor country loses from trade. What does it matter if one country gains more than another if *both* are better off from trade? Policies restricting trade between rich and poor countries make poor countries poorer by denying them the gains from trade and forcing them to spend resources unproductively to produce their own goods.

*Source*: Adapted from Krugman and Obstfeld (1994). © Reprinted with permission of Addison-Wesley Educational Publishers, Inc.

20th-century advocates of free trade. These countries engaged in a pattern of multilateral tariff reduction treaties known as the GATT. As a result of a series of negotiations known as **trade rounds** – trade negotiations conducted under the auspices of the WTO or, in the past, the GATT – the average worldwide tariff on manufactured goods was reduced from 40 percent in 1947 to less than 10 percent by the mid-1970s. The average tariff worldwide has since fallen to 5 percent. Because of trade liberalization, worldwide economic growth

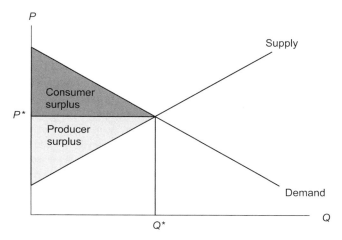

**Figure 3.1**  Consumer and Producer Surpluses

increased. With the introduction of the WTO and the expansion of its role in the global economy, the world is experiencing a greater expansion than ever in international trade.

## Static Welfare Analysis of International Trade

We now consider the economics of international trade more analytically. We first examine the static effect, that is, at one point in time. Dynamic gains and losses are discussed next.

We must introduce the concepts of consumer surplus, producer surplus, and deadweight loss. **Consumer surplus** can be thought of as the difference between what a consumer is willing to pay for a good and the actual price of the good. Many consumers would be willing to pay more than the market price, and the total of all such differences yields total consumer surplus. Likewise, **producer surplus** can be thought of as the difference between the actual market price for a good and the price at which a supplier would be willing to sell the good. Many suppliers would be willing to sell their production at prices below those dictated by the market.

Figure 3.1 illustrates consumer and producer surplus. $P^*$ is the equilibrium market price for, say, automobile insurance of equilibrium quantity $Q^*$. The area below the demand curve and above $P^*$ measures consumer surplus. The area above the supply curve and below the equilibrium price $P^*$ measures producer surplus.

### Pareto improvements

We can agree that any action that increases consumer surplus but does not decrease producer surplus benefits society in an economic sense and with all else being equal. We can also agree that any action that increases producer surplus and does not decrease consumer surplus also is beneficial for society, all else being the same. Finally, we can agree that any action that increases both consumer and producer surplus is desirable, other things being

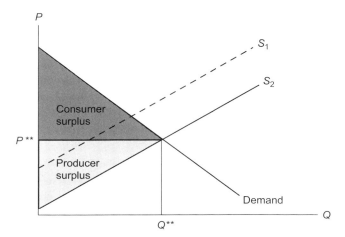

**Figure 3.2**   Effect of an Increase in Supply on Consumer and Producer Surpluses

the same. Each of these three outcomes is referred to as a **Pareto improvement**, meaning that at least one person is better off and no one is worse off.

Such an improvement is illustrated in Figure 3.2. Producers have achieved greater efficiency in production because of, say, technology and can now offer a greater supply of goods at every price. This result can be seen by the shift in the supply curve from $S_1$ to $S_2$. We see that producer surplus has increased; that is, the area above the supply curve and below the new equilibrium price $P^{**}$ is larger than before. In addition, consumer surplus also has increased; that is, the area below the demand curve and above the new equilibrium price is larger. As the total area (producer and consumer surpluses) has increased, overall welfare is enhanced.

### Deadweight societal losses due to trade restriction

We now investigate the static effects of trade restrictions on global trade through an example. Figure 3.3 shows the demand and supply conditions for a country for a particular good. The world price ($P_w$) is $10 and the domestic price ($P_d$) is $17.50 for the good. This domestic market is a candidate for imports because the world price is lower than the domestic price, but domestic producers would lose market share and strong profits. They lobby the government for tariff protection, arguing that unfettered imports would result in job losses.

Suppose the government falls for their arguments and proposes a tariff ($T$) of $5 on the good, but first requests a study of the anticipated economic effects of the tariff. Using basic trade economics and knowing the characteristics of the item's supply and demand, you determine that imposition of the tariff can be expected to bring about the following results:

- *Rise in producer surplus*: By the imposition of the tariff, the import price rises to $15 ($P_w + T$) from $10 ($P_w$). This price increase benefits domestic producers. The gain in producer surplus is shown as the area ABDC: that is, the area above the domestic supply curve and below the old price that is gained by producers. This means that, at a given quantity, the producer obtains more than its opportunity cost of production. Producer surplus in Figure 3.3 amounts to $37.50 ($5 \times 5 + \frac{1}{2} \times 5 \times 5$).

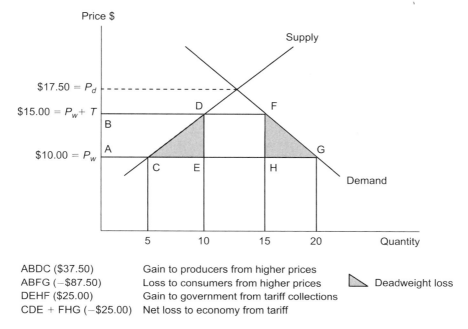

ABDC ($37.50)        Gain to producers from higher prices
ABFG (−$87.50)       Loss to consumers from higher prices        ◺ Deadweight loss
DEHF ($25.00)        Gain to government from tariff collections
CDE + FHG (−$25.00)  Net loss to economy from tariff

**Figure 3.3**   Welfare Effects of Trade Restrictions

- *Loss of consumer surplus*: Consumers suffer from the price increase. This loss in consumer surplus is $87.50 and is depicted by the area ABFG; that is, the area below the
  demand curve and above the old price that is now lost to consumers.

- *Gain in government surplus*: Government gains from imposition of a tariff by the
  amount of the tariff collected. Here it is measured by the area EDFH, which is $25.

- *Deadweight loss for society*: The net gain (or loss) to the economy from imposing a tariff can be measured as the sum of producer, consumer and government gains. The loss to
  consumers is greater than the gains to producers and the government by $25 ($37.50 +
  $25 − 87.50), depicted by the areas of triangles CDE and HFG. In other words, the
  economy will have suffered what is known as a **deadweight loss** – the loss of benefit
  that consumers would have enjoyed under free trade, but that was transferred neither to
  the producer nor to the government and simply evaporated because of the imposition of
  the trade barrier.

The more sensitive demand is to price (i.e., the more price elastic), the flatter will be the
demand curve and the smaller consumer losses from trade restrictions, other things being
equal. Conversely, the lower the price sensitivity (the less price elastic), the greater will be
consumer and deadweight losses, *ceteris paribus*. Thus, tariffs on necessities are likely to
have higher deadweight losses than tariffs on goods that have many substitutes.

Increased trade benefits an economy. Free trade brings an increase in jobs in industries for
which the country has a comparative advantage and a corresponding loss of jobs in industries for which the country has a comparative disadvantage. In general, the value of the new
jobs in industries with a comparative advantage is greater than the value of the job loss in
disadvantaged industries, because transferring workers to the industry with the comparative

advantage increases the wealth of the country. If protection is maintained, the cost of keeping jobs in inefficient industries can be high and overall national prosperity hindered.

A legitimate role for government could be the subsidization of labor relocation and retraining to take advantage of a country's comparative advantages. The amount of the subsidies necessary for retraining labor and refocusing capital to take advantage of a country's comparative advantage can be relatively small compared with the loss of consumer surplus from trade restrictions. The essential distinction here is between social and private benefits; often what is beneficial to society as a whole can cause private harm.

## Dynamic Welfare Analysis of International Trade

A static welfare analysis fails to factor in the additional benefits resulting from the effects of trade on future efficiency. The dynamic trade model considers these additional sources of societal benefits.

A stylized, parochial case helps make the point. As a result of the increased quality and quantity of Japanese imports, the U.S. automobile industry began to suffer a decline in its combined market share in the late 1970s. Until then, the U.S. industry acted in an oligopolistic fashion and sold mainly large, fuel inefficient cars. Competition from Japanese imports caused tremendous dislocations in the U.S. automobile industry. Many workers were laid off and numerous operations reengineered.

With stronger competition from Japanese auto makers, the U.S. industry had no choice but to compete on cost and quality. Inefficiencies were wrung from the industry and greater attention accorded consumer preferences and improved customer service. Consumers benefited from higher-quality U.S.-manufactured automobiles. In fact, consumers in other developed and developing economies now have a greater choice of styles, quality, performance and fuel economy for their choice of car. This benefit is dynamic, accruing over time due to the existence of competition.

An important economic explanation for the existence of protectionism relies on the theory of rent seeking. In the economic sense, **rents** are benefits that are greater than the opportunity costs of production that are captured by private entities (or individuals) as a result of government action. Economists object to this use of governmental power to benefit private entities at the public's expense. Concerning international trade, rent seeking was recognized early as a reason for trade restrictions.

> Trade by its very nature is free, finds its own channel, and best direct[s] its own course: and all laws to give it rules and direction, and to limit and circumscribe it, may serve the particular ends of private men, but are seldom advantageous to the public. (D'Avenant, 1700)

This quotation clearly describes rent seeking and its consequences. Industries can obtain rents in various ways, such as securing tax breaks, lobbying for laws or taxes (e.g., tariffs) that increase costs to competitors, or seeking outright grants of governmental resources. Not only does rent seeking lead to deadweight losses, it also wastes resources spent on rent-seeking activities. Rent seeking adds no productive value to an economy.

Rent seeking is a directly unproductive, profit-seeking activity. In the absence of some worthwhile social objective (e.g., providing for the disadvantaged in society), taking money from one party and giving it to another party does not increase social wealth, because the total amount of wealth does not change while the infrastructure necessary for this transfer process can be expensive.

A further cost to society from trade restriction is often hidden. Figure 3.3 showed what is called a partial equilibrium result; that is, only the market directly affected is analyzed. This methodology understates the cost of trade restriction because indirect effects are ignored. For example, suppose a country's premium tax rate on foreign insurers is twice that on domestic insurers. This discriminatory tax acts as a tariff and can be expected to (1) make insurance more expensive, (2) transfer consumer surplus to domestic insurers, (3) provide the government with some additional tax revenue, and (4) create deadweight losses to society.

Higher insurance prices lower the quantity demanded. In turn, insurers do not need as many employees. Other markets are also affected. As an input to other businesses, insurance now is more expensive, making the products sold by domestic enterprises somewhat more expensive or profits lower. This can cause domestic enterprises to be somewhat less competitive in the world market, and local consumers to pay somewhat higher prices. These and other secondary effects can be as important as the direct effects and are an additional cost of protectionism.

## Common Trade Restricting Techniques

International trade is constrained in numerous ways. Some difficulties in conducting trade – such as coping with different languages, cultures and customs – are inherent in the process. Other restrictions are deliberately imposed by government and are rationalized on one or more of several bases. In this chapter, we explore the four traditional means by which governments restrict trade: (1) tariffs, (2) quotas, (3) subsidies, and (4) government procurement practices.

### Tariffs

A **tariff** is a tax levied on imported goods. The economic effects of a tariff are illustrated in Figure 3.4, where $P_w$ denotes the world price, and $P_d$ is the domestic price without free trade. Because the world price is lower than the domestic price, the good should be imported. Under free trade, domestic producers would supply quantity $Q_1$, with imports supplying the balance, $Q_2 - Q_1$, demanded by consumers. If a tariff ($T$) is imposed, the price increases to $P_w + T$, and imports decrease to $Q_4 - Q_3$.

Tariffs reduce imports, increase domestic prices and, thereby, reduce consumer surplus and provide rents to the protected domestic industry. Recall from Figure 3.3 that tariffs increase producer surplus and government revenues, but their *net* effect is negative because consumer surplus loss is greater than the gains from the tariff.

Few explicit examples of tariffs per se are found in financial services trade. Differential tax treatment between local and foreign insurance firms is one.

### Quotas

Governments also use quotas to restrict international trade. **Quotas** are limitations on the quantity of goods produced or purchased. **Import quotas** restrict the quantity of imports into a market, whereas **export quotas** restrict exports from a market.

The economic effects of a quota are illustrated in Figure 3.5. Under free trade, the world price is $P_w$, and $Q_4 - Q_1$ units are imported. If no imports were allowed, the price in the domestic market would be $P_d$ and the output sold (exclusively by domestic producers)

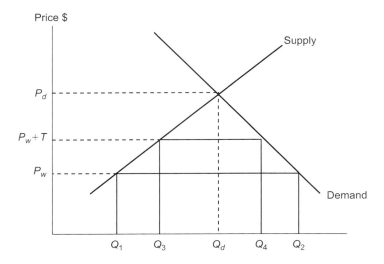

$P_dQ_d$ is the domestic price-quantity equilibrium
$Q_2-Q_1$ = imports in a free-trade regime
$Q_4-Q_3$ = imports with a tariff

**Figure 3.4**    Effects on Price and Quantity of a Tariff

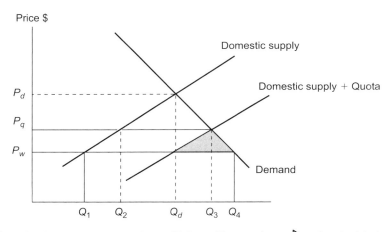

$P_dQ_d$ is the domestic price-quantity equilibrium with no trade        Deadweight loss
$Q_4-Q_1$ = imports in a free-trade regime
$Q_3-Q_2$ = imports with a quota

**Figure 3.5**    Welfare Effects of a Quota

would be $Q_d$. By contrast, with a quota of a fixed number of units, the domestic market supply curve shifts to the right by the number of units allowed under the quota. Price rises from $P_w$ to $P_q$, and imports are now $Q_3 - Q_2$. Again, the loss of consumer surplus is greater than the gain to producers, because quotas impose deadweight losses.

Quotas raise prices just as tariffs do. Unlike tariffs, however, quotas commonly produce no revenue for the governments imposing them. The quota license holder – the entity with the right to import or export a good or service – benefits as it receives a **quota** rent, which is a return than that which the licensee would earn without the license. When the government provides an import license to a foreign firm (or another government), the economic effect is to transfer wealth abroad. This fact makes the cost of the quota higher to the domestic economy than the cost of an equivalent tariff.[2]

The direct and indirect economic effects of quotas can be illustrated by the Japanese imposition of a voluntary export restraint (VER) on automobile exports in the 1980s. Pressure from U.S. and U.K. automobile manufacturers on their governments resulted in the Japanese automobile industry agreeing to limit car exports to both countries. The effect was to restrict supply and thereby to raise the price of Japanese-made automobiles, as predicted by international trade theory. In the process, U.S. and U.K. automobile manufacturers were protected.

The indirect effects of the VER were different than expected. Although Japanese exporters experienced a fall in the number of cars sold, their profit per car rose as they began to make items standard that previously had been options and to manufacture and export more high-profit cars. The VER resulted in windfall profits for the Japanese manufacturers, higher prices for U.S. and U.K. consumers, and some increased profits for U.S. and U.K. automobile manufacturers, but a deadweight loss to the U.S. and U.K. economies.

VERs have been a favorite form of restricting international trade by developed countries as, on the surface, they appear to be purely voluntary on the part of the exporting country, painless to consumers, and helpful to local producers. We know otherwise. WTO members agreed in 1994 to phase out then existing VERs and ban their future use.

Taiwan provides an example of a quota being applied to insurance. Its insurance market was briefly open to new insurers, including a few foreign firms, during the early 1960s. No new insurers were admitted for the next quarter century or so. With pressure from foreign governments, the Taiwanese government changed its policy and gave U.S. insurers exclusive access in the form of branch operations in 1987. The entry limit was much like a quota. Ordinarily a quota can be thought of as a fixed number of units of, say, automobiles, but, for insurance, a quota can be a fixed amount of insurer capacity. The Taiwan insurance market was fully opened to new domestic and foreign insurers with Taiwan's entry into the WTO in 2001.

## Subsidies

**Subsidies** are governmental actions that lower the cost of products to individuals. Subsidies can take the form of tax rebates (credits), preferential tax rates or deductions, or outright grants. They make domestic products less expensive than foreign products, thus affording domestic producers a government-provided competitive advantage. All governments subsidize purchases of some products. If a subsidy is based solely on the nationality of the producer, it is a barrier to trade.

Figure 3.6 illustrates the welfare effects of a subsidy. Without a subsidy, the market price and output level are $P_1$ and $Q_1$. If the government offers a subsidy, the effect is to increase supply to "Domestic supply + Subsidy," thereby leading to an increase in output to $Q_2$ and lowering of the price to $P_2$. Consumer surplus increases by area $P_1ECP_2$. However, the resource cost of producing this product (including the subsidy) is area $ABCEP_1$, which is greater than the gains to consumers by the area BEC. BEC represents the deadweight loss to society of this policy.

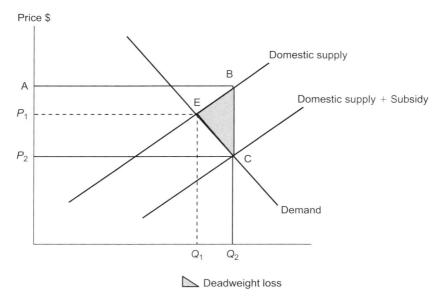

**Figure 3.6**   Welfare Effects of a Subsidy

Subsidies exist in insurance, although they are often difficult to be identified as such. Some governments (e.g., Switzerland) allow their domestic insurers to establish tax-deductible contingency reserves against uncertain future catastrophes. Other countries (e.g., the U.S. and Canada) do not. These tax deductions have the economic effect of a subsidy.

### *Government procurement*

Governments typically are required by their own laws to buy from local producers. For example, the U.S. government is required to buy certain goods and services from local producers if the domestic price is no more than 12 percent higher than the foreign price. In fact, government procurement was explicitly excluded from the key national treatment obligations under the GATT as well as from the main commitments of the GATS.

Government procurement allows domestic producers to charge the government – thus taxpayers – more than they charge other buyers. This policy costs taxpayers more than it benefits them unless economies of scale or other market failures exist. Countries also do this to make available larger markets for their domestic producers. On average, government procurement represents about 10–15 percent of a nation's GDP.

As for insurance, many countries mandate that the government and its contractors purchase insurance from domestic insurers even if less expensive and higher-quality coverage is available elsewhere. By design, all are subject to government procurement in a monopolistic market serviced by a government-owned or local private entity.

Some WTO members voluntarily entered into the Agreement on Government Procurement (AGP), effective in 1996, thereby placing certain limits on government procurement practices that favored national producers. The AGP covers mainly general rules and obligations concerning tendering procedures based on the principle of non-discrimination.

# FAIR TRADE CONCEPTS

Many international trade strategies have evolved over time, the purposes of which are to encourage the growth of free trade. These strategies, collectively termed as **fair trade principles**, are the guiding precepts intended to ensure that international trade between and among nations is "fair." These precepts include the following:

- *Market access* means the right of a foreign firm to enter a country's market. Access can be via establishment or cross-border, with the mode of access giving rise to different public policy considerations. A right of market access obviously is fundamental to the principle of free trade, yet perhaps no country permits foreigners completely unrestrained market access.

- *Non-discrimination (or most-favored-nation (MFN) treatment)* means that no country's firms obtain better market access than any other country's firms do. Thus, an MFN trading partner's businesses enjoy the best possible – that is, the *most* favorable – market access. In combination with reciprocity (discussed below), non-discrimination can lead to dramatic liberalization. Thus, if two large economies strike a certain liberalized market access bargain with each other, the MFN principle requires them to extend the same bargain to small economies as well – economies that may not enjoy much bargaining clout. By a combination of these principles, a little trade liberalization can be expanded and increased.

- *Transparency* requires that regulatory and other legal requirements regarding market access and domestic operation should be clearly set out and easily available. Another dimension of transparency requires the **tariffication** of trade barriers – the replacement of non-tariff trade barriers (e.g., import quotas) with tariffs. Many trade agreements further require signatory countries to **bind the tariff**; that is, to promise not to raise tariffs. Tariffication renders the cost of protectionism more transparent and can facilitate further negotiation to reduce protectionism. Non-tariff barriers generally do more economic harm than do tariffs.

- *National treatment* requires governments to enact and administer domestic laws and regulations such that foreign products and services are accorded treatment no less favorable than that accorded domestic producers in similar circumstances. National treatment can be thought of as another type of non-discrimination standard applied to domestic operations after a foreign firm has secured market access. It is thus intended to ensure equality of competitive opportunity for foreign entrants.

- *Reciprocity* denotes the response in kind by one or more governments to trading actions taken by another government. This definition can take on several interpretations, from positive ("you lower your trade barriers, and I will lower mine") to negative ("you restrict my companies doing business in your market, and I will restrict your companies doing business in my market"). As a trade liberalization and negotiation tool, reciprocity insists that trade "concessions" by one country should be matched in kind by its trading partner countries. For example, if a country lowers its tariffs, its trading partners should lower their tariffs in response. If the trading countries follow the MFN principle, such reductions will apply to all of their trading partners.

These are not economic principles but rather constitute a means of making it easier to identify and ultimately lower trade barriers. They are part of accepted international trade negotiation and are embedded in many trade agreements.

# INTERNATIONAL TRADE IN INSURANCE: ECONOMICS AND POLICY

This section explores the economics and policy underlying international trade in insurance. The phrase "international trade in insurance" most often carries with it some notion of cross-border funds flow, via either direct cross-border insurance or delivery through local establishment of a foreign-owned entity such as a subsidiary or agency. We begin by juxtaposing actual government policy in insurance against the preceding fair trade concepts. We then examine the arguments advanced for restricting international insurance trade. The section closes with an overview of deregulation and liberalization in insurance.

## An Analysis of Fair Trade in Insurance

While the worldwide trend is toward freer markets in insurance and fewer governments supporting policies inconsistent with the fair trade precepts, problems nonetheless persist. An overview of these problems follows, arrayed around the preceding fair trade concepts.

### Market access difficulties

No country permits foreign insurers completely unrestrained market access. This is because of the great potential for consumer abuse that exists when no market entry standards are imposed.

Free-trade advocates acknowledge the need for protecting consumers from possible harm that could arise from unbridled foreign (and domestic) insurer market access. At the same time, they note that many countries impose entry barriers that are seemingly unrelated to consumer protection. The extreme in market access denial occurs in countries with monopolist insurers such as Cuba, Iran, Myanmar and North Korea. Other countries may flatly deny access to all foreign insurers or limit their access through indirect means through one or more of the following policies:

- *Localization of ownership requirement*: The government requires the majority, if not the totality, of insurer ownership to be held by nationals of the country.

- *Domestication requirement*: The local government permits foreign insurers in the domestic market only via local establishment of a subsidiary – a costly means of conducting insurance trade in many circumstances. For example, the Malaysian government ordered all branches of foreign insurance firms to be domesticated by 1998.

- *Localization of insurance requirement*: Often coupled with a domestication requirement, this requirement stipulates that certain or all lines of insurance covering property or lives situated within a country or liability related thereto must be placed with locally licensed insurers only. A common variation of the localization of insurance requirement, often found in developing countries, is a regulation or law that insists that imports (and exports in some instances) must be insured in the local market.

- *(Economic) needs test*: The government permits foreign insurance firms to conduct operations only if equivalent products are unavailable from local insurance firms or if their operations are judged by local authorities to result in substantial benefit to the local economy.

- *Mandatory cessions*: This policy requires that licensed insurers, often only in nonlife lines, must reinsure certain percentages of their direct business with the national or regional reinsurer commonly on a proportional basis. The avowed purposes of mandatory cessions are to increase local retention capacity and for the reinsurer to be able to negotiate better reinsurance terms internationally. Their effect is to limit other reinsurers' access to the national reinsurance market. Mandatory cessions are still found in Africa and sporadically in Asia and South America.

### Non-discrimination problems

MFN problems in insurance are less prevalent than market access, transparency and national treatment problems. One reason stems from the technical interpretation of MFN. This principle states nothing about whether market access is granted or about the nature of that access. It addresses only the narrow element of whether the host country treats foreigners similarly, which can mean that the country treats all foreigners equally bad or good! Thus, a country that prevented all foreign insurers from entering its market would be treating all foreign firms equally.

### Transparency issues

Transparency problems are common in insurance. Insurance laws and regulations in several countries are not clearly set out and readily available. Foreign firms encounter transparency problems in countries where insurance authorities have broad discretionary powers, as foreign insurers may have no clear understanding of the market or operational and market conduct requirements. Those countries whose insurance markets have historically been relatively closed may have unclear or nonexistent due process. In this case, foreign and even domestic insurers may not fully understand either their rights to appeal regulatory decisions or the process by which an appeal is launched. In Japan, lack of transparency in license or product approval had been an issue among foreign insurers operating or wishing to operate in the country until the government issued its version of a financial big bang in the early 1990s.

### National treatment inconsistencies

The national treatment standard seems eminently fair and reasonable at first, but many countries fail to observe it in insurance. Also, its strict application does not always result in equality of competitive opportunity. National treatment problems exist in several markets. Differences between countries in rules regarding permissible activities of financial services firms can create trade barriers. Some countries have different initial capital or deposit requirements for foreign insurers than for domestic ones. Many countries assess higher taxes on foreign than on domestic insurers. Some countries deny or restrict foreign insurer membership in local trade associations, thus denying them equivalent access to domestic statistics, research and lobbying.

Denial of equality of competitive opportunity can take on more subtle forms. Countries that have stringent pricing and product form regulations or that prohibit use of certain distribution channels (e.g., independent agency, brokerage or e-insurance) may not be violating a strict interpretation of the national treatment standard. Nevertheless, their actions constitute hindrances to new entrants. Such strict regulation affords already-established firms a competitive advantage over new entrants, whether foreign or domestic.

In general, firms from different countries may not enjoy comparable levels of market access under a national treatment standard. This is especially likely to be true the greater the asymmetry of regulation – particularly in regulation-intensive industries such as insurance. One obvious solution to this problem is regulatory harmonization. Another is to use mutual recognition with home country control of each country's competitive advantage. Mutual recognition can mean better treatment for foreign firms than does national treatment if the home country's rules are superior to those of the host country. Permitting such regulatory competition could set in motion a continuous process of regulatory Darwinism, leading to market-driven regulatory convergence.

### *Reciprocity issues*

Conceptually, reciprocity can result in treatment more favorable than national treatment. Its application, however, has most often resulted in less favorable treatment. So-called **mirror-image reciprocity** holds that trading partners will "mirror" the market access and other conditions followed by each other: that is, one or more trading partners imposing or impose or offer identical market access and other conditions to the other(s). Suppose, for example, that country X permits banks to sell insurance but country Y does not. Under a national treatment standard and without reciprocity, banks from country Y doing business in country X would be permitted by country X to sell insurance, and banks from country X doing business in country Y would not be allowed by country Y to sell insurance.

Country X might contend that it provides better treatment to foreign banks than other countries, specifically country Y, provide to its banks. Country X then adopts reciprocity rather than national treatment as its policy toward foreign firms. This means that country X would accord Y's banks the same (mirror-image) market access and other treatment as country Y extended to X's banks. Thus, country Y's banks would be barred from selling insurance in country X because country Y prohibits banks from selling insurance. Of course, country X's intent is to encourage country Y to change (liberalize) its laws but the practical effect can be to restrict rather than liberalize trade.[3]

Outcomes from reciprocity-based liberalization are uncertain, largely because reciprocity is a negotiation, not an economic, concept. Reciprocity-based liberalization potentially requires industry-specific and country-specific analyses. Such analyses call for a substantial bureaucratic structure and a great potential for conflict with an accompanying need for dispute resolution mechanisms. Also, the process is exceedingly time consuming.

One type of reciprocity is intended to punish or discourage "bad" behavior. **Retaliation** occurs when a jurisdiction in some way restricts access to its market in response to a trading partner's restricting access or failure to lower existing trade barriers to that partner's market.

The threat of retaliation can lead to liberalization. If one country believes another is engaging in practices that restrict trade unduly, it might threaten to retaliate unless the offending country eliminates or loosens the restrictions. Such a threat by a major trading partner typically carries great weight. Retaliation, however, is a risky trade weapon. If one country increases protection against imports, its trading partners may do likewise. The effect can result in trade wars of the type that contributed to the Great Depression of the 1930s.

# Arguments for Restricting Trade in Insurance

Because of the apparent success of some countries' industrial policies (or joint governmental and industrial cooperation), economists have reevaluated their models of free trade and their underlying assumptions. The traditional trade model assumes perfectly competitive markets with all industries experiencing constant returns to scale and with no externalities present. This, however, may not be the case and arguments have been developed to justify government intervention or trade restrictions. The financial services area has seen many such rationales for trade restrictions. We examine this issue with a focus on international insurance trade.

Within insurance, trade restrictions almost always revolve around arguments as to why a greater foreign insurer involvement in the domestic insurance market should be avoided. The arguments are as old as those related to international trade itself, for they spring from the same concerns. Although the arguments individually are numerous, we present some of the more common ones around the following four themes:

- Foreign insurers will dominate the domestic market.
- The insurance industry should remain locally owned for strategic reasons.
- Foreign insurers will provoke a greater foreign exchange outflow.
- Trade restrictions are necessary for market development and consumer protection.

## *Foreign insurers' dominance*

Proponents of constraining international trade in insurance argue that foreign insurers could dominate or destabilize the domestic market. Three bases for this view are (1) economies of scale and scope, (2) price and market distortion, and (3) infant industry protection.

### *Economies of scale and scope*

Because multinational firms tend to be large and operate in several countries, they could enjoy substantial economies of scale and scope as well as dynamic efficiency:

- As noted in Chapter 2, economies of scale exist when the value of a firm's output increases at a rate faster than attendant increases in its production costs; in other words, when the marginal benefit from producing one more unit is greater than its marginal cost.

- Economies of scope exist when a firm realizes efficiencies from the joint production of products or services. **Economies of scope in production** when multiple products can be produced at less cost than the sum of the costs of producing each separately. Similarly, **geography-based economies of scope** exist when a single firm can operate in multiple markets at less cost than can multiple firms each for a single market.

- Economies of scale and scope are static efficiency concepts, and reflect size and product mix cost effects for a given time frame. **Dynamic efficiency** involves promptness in incorporating product and process innovations and other operational efficiencies (also called X-efficiencies) into production, for example, a firm's ability to more quickly develop products in response to changing technological or market conditions.

Global insurance firms could enjoy substantial such economies. These scale and scope economies could allow foreign-owned insurers to operate at lower cost and to offer lower prices than locally owned insurers in a domestic market. The result could be that many locally owned insurers could not compete and would cease operations, thus eventually leading to foreign insurers' dominance in the domestic market.

Fairly extensive research exists on economies of scale in insurance. The studies generally find that scale economies exist for smaller and mid-sized insurers, but not for very large insurers. In fact, several studies find scale *diseconomies* for large or very large insurers. Evidence on the existence of product scope economies is more limited. The studies are uniform in finding only limited or no product-based scope economies for insurers.

These scale and scope studies in insurance suggest that, while possible in selected cases, multinational insurance firms are unlikely to be able to use their large-size and multi-product production abilities to "take over" a country's insurance market. What they do suggest is that markets with relatively small firms can benefit from the lower costs of more efficient, larger insurers competing in the market. Also, even if foreign firms could and did dominate the market, the question arises as to why government should care. If citizens and businesses can secure lower-cost, higher-quality insurance through foreign-owned insurers, the economy is better served and overall social welfare enhanced. The nationality of the firm's owners should be irrelevant.

*Price and market distortion*

Even if multinational insurance firms do not enjoy economies of scale, their large size could permit them to exercise much greater economic clout than smaller, locally owned domestic insurers. Foreign firms may use technology better and possess greater management skills than locally owned insurers.[4] Under either scenario, foreign insurers could charge lower prices than locally owned firms. Thus, admission of foreign insurers could cause such incredible pressure on prices that all insurers would be forced to engage in a so-called "cut throat" price competition. Weaker, locally owned insurers could not compete in the longer term and could become insolvent.

Others could contend that a small market, especially that of a developing economy, may be able to support only a limited number of producers. The entry of one or more strong foreign firms to the market could result in market distortion, and the weaker local insurers would presumably fail. The foreign firms – having weathered the intense competition because of superior financial resources or greater efficiency – would then emerge with a dominant market position.

*Political dimensions*

The market domination concern has both political and economic dimensions. When analyzing it purely as a political issue, we cannot dismiss the market domination concern completely.[5] Each nation has the right to organize its internal market as it wishes. If a nation wants to exclude foreigners in whole or in part, that is its affair. These types of policies may have little concern with economics and may flow from political ideology, a desire to protect local culture or a host of other non-economic concerns. Nevertheless, government and citizens should understand fully the consequences of such policies. The economic consequences of isolation generally will be depressed economic growth. Moreover, such governments and citizens need to investigate whether a vested interest group is using non-economic arguments to support policies that enrich them at the expense of the general public.

*Economic dimensions*

Analyzed purely as an economic issue, the market domination concern seems largely unjustified. It is probably true that many multinational corporations enjoy sufficient financial resources and efficiencies with which they could dominate some emerging markets. The question is less whether they could do so; it is more whether they would want to engage in such activities. Available evidence in insurance markets suggests that they would not for a number of reasons, including the following:

- *Local control*: Few insurance markets internationally are dominated by foreign-owned insurance firms. Most markets that permit foreign involvement have a blend of ownership arrangements, but local citizens often hold control through a majority ownership interest.

- *Adverse effects*: The presence of foreign entities is undesirable if the national economy suffers some detriment resulting from foreign firms' abuse of their dominant role, e.g., setting price, quantity and quality of products or services. Examination should be conducted whether markets with foreign-owned firms having substantial market shares have, in fact, experienced any such adverse effects. Markets with a substantial or growing foreign presence are largely those with a reputation for offering individuals and businesses high-quality services at low prices. Anecdotal evidence from markets that have or are gaining a substantial foreign presence (e.g., Argentina, Australia, Austria, Canada, Chile, China, Denmark, Hong Kong, Mexico, Poland, the Netherlands, the U.K. and the U.S.) seems to support this view. In particular, Chile's market opening and resultant efficiency gains are legend.

  This economic concern may be more apparent than real for other reasons. The establishment of a new insurance firm is no speedy process under the best of circumstances. Staff must be hired and trained. Policies must be designed and priced. Distribution networks must be established. Achieving break-even often takes many few years.

  New insurers must build a local image and often gain market share slowly. For example, the aggregate market share – measured in direct premiums – of all foreign nonlife insurance firms in Korea, which opened its doors to foreign insurers in the 1980s, was still less than 5 percent of the local market in 2002. Besides, locally owned insurers often have substantial advantages over their new rivals. They typically have many years of experience and a deep understanding of the local culture. They understand the local market and have established relationships with customers and other stakeholders. As in Mexico and Vietnam, local insurance firms faced with efficient foreign insurers can exploit these competitive advantages while improving efficiency.

- *Dumping and under-pricing*: Concern exists that foreign firms could engage in dumping which, as noted in Chapter 2, is selling products or services at less than their cost of production to gain market share. The rationale for dumping is to gain a dominant market position by driving competitors from the market. Once accomplished, the firm could safely raise prices, realizing monopolistic profits. At the first sign of any new upstart firm, the dominant firm could temporarily lower prices to thwart the potential competitor in an attempt to hold its monopolistic position in the market.

  In insurance markets, locally and foreign-owned firms occasionally price insurance at less than the cost of production. The practice may be because of optimistic loss forecasts or a desire to avoid losing market share. The inherent slowness of establishing an insurance firm, coupled with increasing pressures by shareholders on managers to improve firm value, argue against the contention that insurers deliberately offer coverage at a loss, at least for a sustained time. It is doubtful that any single insurer has the market power successfully to carry out a plan of market domination by means of dumping. In fact, the greater the foreign involvement within a country's insurance market, the less likely that even a giant foreign insurer could sustain such a plan.

Even if a foreign insurer attempted to gain market dominance by dumping, the effects seem more likely to be positive than negative for the local economy. Economically, selling insurance at a loss amounts to a subsidy from the foreign insurer to the host country. More importantly, if a market is reasonably competitive with no substantial economies of scale, such predatory pricing would not result in market dominance but in lower-cost insurance for consumers.

Economic theory also suggests that, if a market is profitable enough to attract foreign competitors that ultimately drive out weak, local firms, the foreign firms would not be able to raise prices without attracting other entrants. Thus, dumping is unprofitable in the long run because attempts to recoup losses through higher future prices would attract competitors, which in turn would drive down prices.

• *Competition regulation*: Finally, attempts by locally or foreign-owned insurers to dominate a market are best addressed through competition regulation, as discussed in Chapter 24. To the extent that policymakers have a legitimate basis for concerns about restraints on competition, the first-best remedy is regulation that goes directly to the offense. Limits on market access run counter to the goal of competition regulation.

In summary, the best *insurance* against any adverse effects of any possible market dominance by foreign insurers may be for government to encourage greater competition. A greater foreign presence within a market is an important means of doing so.

### Infant industry basis

The **infant industry argument** contends that government should shelter certain "infant" industries from the fullness of foreign competition until the industries are sufficiently mature to be able to compete with foreign firms on a reasonably equal basis. The argument is centuries old and superficially appealing.

Its efficacy remains questionable, however First, a competitive market should not need protection because small or inexperienced local entrepreneurs, despite temporary disadvantages, would still have incentives to enter the market in the expectation that returns over the longer term should make good any short-term losses. Second, if government nonetheless insisted on aiding an infant industry, more efficient and less welfare-reducing means exist (e.g., a production subsidy) than trade barriers.

Ignoring the theoretical deficiencies of the argument, we have the experience of developing countries, as Kenen (1994, p. 281) observes:

> The histories of developing countries that have used infant-industry protection teach us three lessons. First, it is hard to choose the right industries [to shelter from competition]. If protection is granted very freely, some of it will go to industries that cannot reap economies of scale or experience. Second, firms obtaining infant-industry protection are reluctant to give it up. They do not want to suffer cuts in output. . .and they frequently acquire enough political influence to block trade liberalization. Third, infant-industry protection can hurt other industries, even when it is confined to promising candidates.

Applying these general lessons to insurance, we draw the following inferences:

- *Insurance may not enjoy a comparative advantage*: The infant industry argument is predicated on the protected industry enjoying a comparative advantage; otherwise the "infant" can never forgo protection if it is to survive. Many have questioned whether most emerging markets can reasonably expect a comparative advantage to exist for their domestic insurance industries in regional and global competition.

- *Protection has already been extended for decades*: Infant industry protection has already been granted to the insurance industries in most developing countries for decades. Enough time has passed for local firms in those countries to have achieved the necessary economies, if they are ever to achieve them.

- *Protection causes higher price or inferior quality*: Insurance services are an input in business production. To the extent that local producers pay higher-than-world prices for insurance or receive inferior services from local insurers, their goods and services are less competitive in open markets. Even in closed markets, consumers suffer higher prices and lower consumer surplus for the consumption of all goods and services where insurance is used as an input.

### Keep insurance local for strategic reasons

Another rationale for insurance-related trade restrictions revolves around protecting a country's strategic interests. Two proffered reasons relate to (1) national security and (2) national economic diversification.

#### National security

Two commonly cited examples of the tie between insurance and national security involve the London market. In creating two large Arab insurance groups during the late 1970s and early 1980s, investors cited the desire to reduce the region's vulnerability to the London market's withdrawal of marine insurance capacity in time of conflict. During the Falkland Islands' conflict of 1982 between the U.K. and Argentina, U.K. insurers and reinsurers put the Argentine transportation industry into difficulty by suspending coverage on Argentine cargo, ships and aircraft.

Two observations seem relevant to these examples. First, the relevant capacity withdrawn in each instance above was via cross-border insurance trade. At that time, neither the Arab countries concerned nor Argentina permitted local establishment of foreign-owned insurers. They discouraged creation of more national insurance capacity that, at least conceptually, could have reduced their dependence on cross-border insurance. Of course, foreign-owned domestic insurance firms might withdraw capacity during any conflict between the host and home countries. However, domestic firms, whatever their ownership, remain fully subject to domestic government oversight, unlike the situation with cross-border insurance.

Second and more importantly, if a country is concerned about possible harm to the economy from a withdrawal of foreign insurance or reinsurance capacity, it should encourage good risk management practices in the local economy. For example, local insurance firms and businesses should avoid becoming highly dependent on insurance carriers from a single country, and spread their insurance placements with carriers of various nationalities.

Such diversification probably offers greater economic promise of stability than limitations on foreign insurer involvement.

### National economic diversification

Another cited strategic reason for restricting international insurance trade is the desire for national economic diversification. Too great a concentration of national resources in a handful of agricultural, manufacturing or other commercial operations could subject the national economy to undesirable volatility as the world market imposes prices and other conditions on local producers. To avoid this situation, policymakers may encourage diversification of national production across a range of industries. Insurance is sometimes earmarked as one of those industries whose local production is both feasible and desirable.

Two observations seem relevant here. First, a question arises whether government truly can identify the "right" industries that warrant favored treatment. In this sense, the concern here is identical to that of the infant industry debate. The competitive model argues for allowing entrepreneurs and investors to make their own decisions. In the absence of failure of an important market, government should establish a neutral position with respect to such decisions.

Second, even if policymakers decide to encourage the creation or expansion of national insurance capacity, nothing in the diversification argument suggests that the local capacity need be exclusively or even primarily locally owned. Foreign direct investment can be a great assistance in diversifying a national economy.

### Preservation of foreign exchange reserves

Policymakers from developing countries have long expressed concern that foreign operations can adversely affect their countries' balance of payments. Indeed, this concern has been one of the driving forces behind the desire of policymakers to develop indigenous insurance capacity. The theory is to reduce insurance-related foreign exchange outflow by having local insurers provide the bulk of the national insurance supply.

While fewer governments today are persuaded by this argument than in past times, we still observe such actions. For example, Cambodia's 2000 enactment of its insurance law provided that all risks situated in the country must be insured locally. It is said to have added this provision to the law because of concerns about foreign exchange outflow.

### Import substitution

In the past, numerous developing countries adopted a so-called **import substitution** policy under which the government promoted and protected those local industries that competed directly with imports. In this way, so went the theory, scarce foreign exchange funds could be reserved for other foreign goods and services whose purchase was deemed essential to local economic development or social welfare.

The chief problem with this idea was that governments had to decide among potentially thousands of industries claiming to be logical candidates for import substitution protection. Even if governments had made optimal decisions, the economic effects still could have been harmful to the economy in the long run. Import substitution requires the diversion of an economy's scarce resources to import-competing sectors. By doing so, the export-competing sectors are handicapped because of having to pay more for inputs, including insurance. They must pay more because (1) they are discriminated against the national competition for resources and (2) they have to purchase inputs from the protected import-competing sectors with all their inherent inefficiencies and attendant higher costs. Consequently, exports become less competitive and the import substitution policy may deplete foreign exchange reserves. Because of these shortcomings, most governments have largely abandoned import substitution policies as hindrances to economic growth, perhaps the most well known being India which, for decades, inhibited its own economic growth by adhering to this ill-fated policy.

### The nature of insurance-related trade flows

Insurance-related foreign exchange transactions attach to both cross-border and establishment trade in international insurance services. With cross-border trade and agency-establishment trade, premiums paid by domestic insureds (or ceding insurers) flow directly to foreign insurers (or reinsurers). These remittances are offset to a greater or lesser degree by commissions paid and claims payments. These flows are all current account items. In a given year, outflows could exceed inflows or vice versa. Over the long run, however, outflows could be expected to exceed inflows.

With foreign-owned subsidiaries and most branch offices, premiums paid by domestic insureds (or primary insurers) to those foreign-owned insurance firms are purely national transactions. They do not enter international current account flows. The same is true for commissions and claims paid. In contrast, the funds spent to establish the subsidiary or branch are capital account inflows. Profits retained represent additional capital infusions. Profits remitted to the head office represent current account outflows. Further outflows can emanate from payments for reinsurance and services from the parent. Thus, with establishment insurance trade, the host country initially could expect a large foreign exchange inflow, followed by likely outflows in the future.

The twin arguments of import substitution and infant industry protection in insurance led to the creation of a locally owned, national insurance industry in virtually every developing country. Even in countries where insurance had been available initially from private entities, governments decided to nationalize the industry (e.g., Bangladesh and India).[6] Because local underwriting capacity often was inadequate, domestic insurers placed heavy reliance on foreign reinsurers. In the process, an indirect foreign exchange outflow was sometimes substituted for a direct outflow, with little net difference to the country.

One aspect of the import substitution policy is supportable. Additional national insurance capacity can reduce insurance-related foreign exchange outflows. That additional capacity, however, need not be locally owned, and government need not try to "pick winners." Locally established, foreign-owned insurers bring additional risk financing capacity to the market, which helps the domestic industry increase retention and the economy reduce foreign exchange outflows. In addition, insureds that formerly placed their risks offshore could have an incentive to bring them into the domestic market.

Nonetheless, emerging markets are likely to realize a net foreign exchange outflow from insurance. Most countries worldwide are net importers of insurance and reinsurance. It is critically important to realize, however, that drawing policy inferences from any such outflow is exceedingly risky. Indirect effects should be carefully considered. For example, assume that a national market is a net importer of insurance and that this result is partially attributable to recent liberalization moves by the government. A liberalized market will offer lower prices and better value than a protected market, other things being equal.

As a production input, insurance affects prices charged for other goods and services produced in the economy. The more competitive the economies' goods and services, the greater the foreign exchange inflow will be. Thus, foreign-provided insurance may offer better value but constitute a foreign exchange drain. As a lower-cost production input, however, it helps in export promotion. Also, goods and services sold exclusively domestically can become more competitive with imports, thereby resulting in less foreign exchange outflow.

It is true that foreign involvement in the insurance markets of emerging economies can lead to a net insurance-related foreign exchange outflow over the long term. We cannot conclude, however, that a country's overall balance of payments will be adversely affected. Potentially important indirect effects should be considered.

### Market development and consumer protection concerns

In an ideal world, complete freedom would be extended to insurers and reinsurers to provide cross-border insurance services and to customers to purchase insurance from whomever they wanted. The logic supporting this position stems from the very foundation of competition: the greater the competition, the greater will be customer choice and value, other things being the same. In other words, consumers in this idealized, liberalized insurance world would enjoy lower premium rates for equivalent coverage as well as product innovations otherwise unavailable from domestic insurers. In addition, domestic market capacity could be protected from undesirable risk concentrations and possible disruptions to the local economy. Finally, anticompetitive practices, such as local cartel behavior, would be less likely with complete freedom of cross-border insurance trade.

The economic logic for the above position would be unassailable if insurance markets exhibited fully the traits of the perfectly competitive model. In practice, however, two sets of problems argue against the position: (1) the macroeconomic effects on the national economy and (2) protection of ill-informed buyers.

#### Macroeconomic effects on the national economy

Many countries, particularly developing countries, have argued that cross-border insurance trade has negative macroeconomic effects for the national economy. In contrast to insurance purchases from locally established insurance firms that invest funds locally to secure their insurance obligations – thus aiding economic development – cross-border insurance purchases usually result in little or no investment in the country where the risk is situated. Rather, foreign insurance firms are likely to invest the funds in their domiciliary countries. Also, in contrast to establishment insurance trade by foreign firms, cross-border trade might not result in creation of local insurance expertise or technology transfer to the local market and, hence, is less beneficial in terms of human resource development to the country.

In isolation and with other things being the same, the above macroeconomic concerns are valid. The issue, however, is more complex than the above simple analysis suggests. We should consider important secondary effects. If the national market fails to offer desired coverage because of insufficient local capacity or problems of pricing or product availability, forcing customers to purchase inferior coverage locally may be self-defeating in the longer term. An inadequate local capacity or limiting spread of risk can endanger the very foundation of the insurance market and thereby wreak havoc on individuals and industries within the economy that rely on insurance. If this danger is to be avoided, domestic insurers must rely on international reinsurance, thereby substituting indirect cross-border insurance (reinsurance) for direct cross-border insurance and inserting another expense component in the process.

Even if capacity and spread of risk are not problems, forcing consumers to purchase higher priced or more limited coverage locally means they have inferior coverage or pay more for the coverage than consumers elsewhere in the world. This can result in depriving local consumers of some economic security. With continuing liberalization and internationalization of national markets, national and international competition intensifies. In such an intensively competitive world, differences in the quality and price of production inputs, such as insurance, potentially can mean the difference between success and failure.

### Protection of ill-informed buyers

The second argument against complete freedom for cross-border insurance trade revolves around the concept that government has an obligation to protect ill-informed buyers. This argument finds concrete support in both economic theory and fact. Because of the close tie that insurance has with the overall public interest and its quasi-fiduciary nature, governments worldwide have been reluctant to ignore the natural information imbalance in positions between certain insurance buyers and sellers. In fact, the insurance laws in numerous countries prescribe the protection of policyholders' interests as a key objective of insurance regulation and supervision.

A critical assumption in the competitive market model is that buyers are well informed about the products they purchase and the companies from which they purchase them. Sophisticated insurance buyers, such as large corporations, have reasonable opportunity to become well informed, to avoid incompetent or financially weak insurers' and to make sound policy purchase decisions. The need for government oversight is correspondingly diminished. The same logic applies to insurance transactions between insurance firms; that is, reinsurance and retrocession.

The situation with individual consumers and small businesses is different. They easily can be misled. They may not know enough even to make appropriate inquiries as they negotiate for insurance. They can be notoriously easy prey for the unscrupulous insurance seller. Thus, the logic for restricting pure cross-border insurance trade with respect to individuals and other poorly informed buyers is sound. An exception can occur when a reciprocal agreement exists between two jurisdictions. A **reciprocal agreement** is a formal recognition between two nations – or between two U.S. states – that the consumer protections to one country's (state's) citizens are guaranteed also to the citizens of the other country (state) who purchase insurance from an insurer domiciled in the first country (state). This mutual recognition approach underpins the E.U.'s Single Market Program.

The logic in favor of restriction is less compelling with insureds' own-initiative cross-border insurance trade. Consumers who voluntarily initiate insurance purchases with unlicensed foreign insurers effectively forfeit the regulatory protection otherwise afforded by their home country. The regulations of many countries, including those of OECD member countries, are generally consistent with this view, although several countries discourage cross-border purchases through a denial of favorable tax treatment.

## Deregulation and Liberalization of Insurance Markets

Risk management and insurance providers offer cross-national services on a routine basis. Technological changes, product innovations and global financial integration change the nature of risk management and risk financing worldwide. Hence, the challenge for governments is to adopt policies that recognize changes in the global market, while maintaining fundamental consumer protection standards as well as financial and operational soundness in the local market.

Local markets are being privatized at unprecedented speeds. Private entities in developing economies now manage many formerly government-run enterprises. Local economies, especially the financial services sector, are being deregulated as well. **Deregulation** is the process of reducing regulation to that which is minimally necessary to achieve its goal and, in the process, placing greater reliance on market forces to ensure consumer protection.

Liberalization efforts often move in tandem with deregulation. **Liberalization** is the process of breaking down government and artificial barriers for international trade and investment. Market liberalization policies are commonly pursued bilaterally and multilaterally by asserting that foreign firms should have a right to enter a country's market and compete with domestic firms on a non-discriminatory basis. Consumer protection and consumer confidence in private institutions and products are the basis for sound markets. Liberalization can be enhanced with greater cooperation and understanding by policymakers to common consumer protection issues.

Liberalization and deregulation efforts, however, may dictate the need for stronger regulatory oversight in some areas. Greater competition means that competitors may seek to mislead or otherwise withhold information that could be deemed harmful to making the sale. In other words, the conduct of competitors in the market may suffer without strong regulatory vigilance. Additionally, with greater competition, businesses have stronger incentives to try to minimize the challenges of having to compete and seek to restrain competition, as businesses did in the 19th and 20th centuries. Thus, competition regulation has becomes more, not less, important with greater competition. Finally, with greater competition, firms have incentives to operate with the minimum possible capital base. While this is not a major problem with most firms, it can be disastrous for financial services firms – or more accurately, their customers who rely on a future promise in exchange for money today.

Governments can do much to promote competition within their markets. A pro-competitive policy involves liberalization and deregulation. The most pro-competitive market access approach is to allow foreign undertakings into the market and to allow foreign entrants to decide their own mode of access. If access is via establishment of a subsidiary or joint venture, the national treatment principle historically has been considered the most liberal.

This view is not always correct, however, as we discussed earlier in this chapter. If access is cross-border or by agency or branch office, the most liberal approach is home country control with complete freedom for foreign suppliers to solicit domestic customers and for domestic customers freely to seek coverage from foreign firms. Whatever the mode of market access, regulatory transparency is critically important to ensure a competitive market.

## CONCLUSION

The arguments in support of a liberalized international insurance trading system are compelling, subject to the caveat that governments should undertake measures to minimize harm to consumers. The world's national insurance markets continue to move away from their historically insular positions, toward acceptance of the view that their overall national economic interests are better served through greater competition and that greater competition from foreign insurance firms is beneficial.

The challenges for insurance firms domiciled in previously highly protected and highly regulated markets that are now being deregulated and liberalized are enormous. The dislocations created by government "changing the rules of the game" will continue to result in mergers, acquisitions and some failures. Modern pricing, reserving, underwriting, marketing and management techniques must be incorporated into operations in record time if existing insurers have any hope of competing successfully with new entrants. The static and dynamic benefits of a more liberal global insurance market promise exciting times for all participants.

## DISCUSSION QUESTIONS

1. What are the pros and cons of allowing foreign insurer entry into developing markets? Is your answer different if you are considering a developed economy?
2. "Infant industry protection is the only way to ensure that insurance firms in emerging markets can survive, and a national insurance industry is essential to economic growth and vitality." Analyze this quote.
3. Explain carefully the differences between tariffs, quotas and voluntary restraints. Who benefits from each of these methods to restrict trade?
4. What is the most common rationale for restricting international trade in insurance for your country? Evaluate that position based on the mercantilist philosophy, the free-trade philosophy and the managed trade philosophy.

## NOTES

1. This Chapter draws from Grace and Skipper (1998).
2. When the right is assigned to a foreign government, that government can allocate the quotas any way it desires. A rational method of allocation is an auction whereby the foreign government receives a direct benefit from the auctioning of the import rights. Thus, trade restrictions in one country can make the governments of other countries better off!
3. The second generation of banking and insurance directives of the EU contains reciprocity provisions. A great concern of EU trading partners at the time of their promulgation was that the provisions would be interpreted to require mirror-image reciprocity. The EU, however, did not adopt this interpretation.
4. The underlying theory of and studies on economies of scale assume that every firm has access to the same technology and managerial talent pool.

5. Indeed, a historical problem interfering with political efforts to promote freer trade between developed countries and developing countries relates to the exploitation of many developing countries when they were colonies or newly independent states. In such times, private property rights were ill defined for the masses, democracy was largely nonexistent, and an elite few dominated economic activity. In such conditions, the benefits of international trade were said to inure chiefly to the elite not to the average man or woman.
6. The insurance markets in Bangladesh and India are now reopened to the local private sector. The Indian market is partially open to foreign insurance firms as well, while Bangladesh still does not permit foreign insurers' access to its market, with the exception of American Life Insurance Company that has long offered insurance to selected segments of the population.

# REFERENCES

D'Avenant, C. (ca. 1700). *An Essay on East India Trade.*

Grace, M.F. and Skipper, H.D. (1998). "International Trade in Insurance," Chapter 5, in H.D. Skipper Jr., ed., *International Risk and Insurance: An Environmental-Managerial Approach.* Boston, MA: Irwin/McGraw Hill.

Kenen, P.F. (1994). *The International Economy*, 3rd edn. Cambridge: Cambridge University Press.

Krugman, P. and Obstfeld, M. (1994). *International Economics: Theory and Policy.* New York: Edison-Wesley Educational Publishers.

Ricardo, D. (ca. 1817). *The Principles of Political Economy and Taxation.*

Smith, A. (ca. 1776). *The Wealth of Nations.*

*Wall Street Journal* (1989). Trade restriction and the great depression, (date xxx).{AQ2}

# Part II

# Factors Shaping the Risk Environment Internationally

# Chapter 4

# Societal Risk Assessment and Control: Theory and Practice

## INTRODUCTION

The terrorist attacks in the U.S. on September 11, 2001 shocked and horrified the civilized world. Human and economic losses were enormous. Perhaps as important to U.S. citizens and their government was the signal value of the events. The world was forever changed. Society was seen suddenly as being incredibly vulnerable. Citizens wanted to know how their governments, in the future, would better identify and assess this terrible threat and prevent further occurrences. In other words, what enhanced societal risk management activities would be undertaken? Simultaneously, we want policymakers to weigh economic and social costs (e.g., diminished civil liberties) against societal benefits of greater national security.

This chapter begins our exploration of how society should and does manage risks. How do we determine acceptable levels of societal risk – terrorism and otherwise – and what tools do and should governments employ to cope with them? What societal risk management decisions are best left to individuals and businesses? Which ones require governmental responses and what should the responses be? The purpose of addressing these and related issues is both to help us understand the role and functioning of government in risk management and to provide context for latter discussions in this book dealing with the role and functioning of multinational corporations in risk management. Issues covered in this section are not subject to direct control by corporate risk managers, although it is crucial that these risk managers understand the potential impact of societal risk on their firms and react accordingly.

This chapter explores the risk assessment and control aspects of societal risk management. We first establish the rationale for why government intervention is sometimes desirable. We then explain alternative means available to government to control the risks faced by its citizens. Finally, we explore the social theory of risk.

## THE ROLE OF GOVERNMENT IN SOCIETAL RISK MANAGEMENT

Governments exist to operationalize the collective will of their citizens – at least in theory. In general, democracies should be better at reflecting societal will, including those decisions relating to risk management, than are other forms of government. In economic terms, a democracy should have fewer principal (citizens)-agent (government) problems, at least in the long run.

In a market economy, we argue that government intervention should be limited to those circumstances for which market outcomes are, for some reason, unacceptable. This principle applies to all activities, including those relating to societal risk management. Thus, many aspects of societal risk management are best left to individuals and businesses. This dimension of societal risk management is explored in the two latter parts of this book. Government, however, has a critically important role when market outcomes are hindered by imperfections or fail to capture societal notions of fairness. The ultimate objective of such government intervention is to influence health, safety and environmental outcomes.[1] We emphasize this governmental role here.

## The Inevitability of Tradeoffs

Every human activity involves risk. We incur at least some risks when we eat, walk, exercise, drive a car, work, mow the lawn and engage in every other activity in life. The idea of a risk-free society is meaningless. At the same time, no one intentionally puts his or her life, health or property at risk unless there is some reason – some benefit – in doing so. In other words, we inevitably make tradeoffs, as risk cannot be eliminated.

When we drive a 20-year-old sub-compact car, we are more likely to be injured or killed in an accident than if we drove a new, full-size luxury car with an array of the latest safety features. We perhaps drive the old, riskier small car in preference to the luxury car because new cars cost too much. We are unwilling or unable to spend such a large share of our money for a luxury car. In each instance, we are trading off safety for money or, more precisely, that which the money not spent on the luxury car would buy; that is, its opportunity cost.

In a societal risk management context, the existence of tradeoffs means that resources used to identify, assess and control one hazard could have been used in other ways, including the management of other exposures. As such, societal risk management programs should carefully consider these alternative uses (opportunity cost) of resources, otherwise society risks wasting them.

For example, should government be able to intervene into the decision as to the type of vehicle that you can drive, even if some vehicles are riskier than others? Most of us probably say "no" within reason. What if the decision is between tap water and bottled water? Again, most probably say "no." What if the tap water contains high levels of lead? What if citizens don't know that the levels are high or don't know what is "high" or don't know that lead is harmful? Should government intervene in these situations? If so, is government's role solely to inform the citizenry or should it take some positive action to eliminate the lead?

In principle, governmental intervention – when justified – should reflect the level of risk reduction that society desires. This contention begs two questions:

*   How do we determine society's risk-reduction preferences?
*   Under what circumstances is intervention justified?

## Societal Risk-Reduction Preferences

The answer to the first question turns on the value that society places on incremental risk reduction, such as saving an additional life. In answering this question, we need to be clear about two important matters. *First*, we are concerned with what we might term "statistical lives" not with the lives of identified, specific individuals. Thus, we do not have to answer such questions as "how much effort (money) are we willing to expend to save the life of 2-year-old Suzy who swallowed a dozen aspirin tablets." Rather, we answer questions such as "how much are we as a society willing to spend to reduce from an estimated 100 to 50 the number of children who die each year from swallowing aspirin."

*Second*, societal risk management typically is concerned with marginal or incremental reductions in the likelihood of death, injury, damage by flood and other perils rather than changes that eliminate all possibility of injury, death and damage. Thus, society cannot eliminate the possibility of child poisoning by aspirin unless we are willing to forego aspirin altogether – an unacceptable result because of the many benefits of aspirin.

Assume that the current level of fatal aspirin poisoning of children under the age of 5 is 0.5 per million. How much are we willing to pay to reduce that rate to 0.1 per million? Would each of us be willing to pay an additional $1.00 per 100 aspirin for this incremental reduction? What about $100 per 100? What affect will higher aspirin costs have on the elderly and those prone to heart attack, many of whom rely on aspirin to prevent cardiovascular diseases?

To make such societal risk management decisions, we are effectively placing an economic value on lives (or injuries or damage). What are we willing to pay – in the above example – to save the lives of four additional children out of 10,000,000? We might be uncomfortable thinking about the issue in monetary terms, but we have no alternative if we are to utilize our societal risk-reduction resources in ways that save the most lives for a given cost. Societal risk control – as with individual and organizational risk control – is all about tradeoffs! So long as living involves activities that can cause harm, we inevitably make tradeoffs.

In thinking about this economic valuation of life concept, we should be clear about why we want to establish this value. In wrongful death lawsuits, courts rely on similar approaches – all built on valuing human capital. In such instances, the valuation of life relates directly to individual earnings. Variations of the human capital approach, however, are inappropriate for societal risk management decisions because they fail to capture benefits accruing to society as a whole from saving an additional life. Rather, the appropriate valuation approach is based on the concept of willingness to pay (WTP) to achieve certain levels of risk reduction.[2]

The WTP approach to establishing a value of risk reduction is economically the same as that which we follow in other contexts. Thus, if we are trying to determine whether it makes economic sense to build a new public parking garage, we would inquire as to what users would be willing to pay to use it. If the sum of the individual WTP amounts exceeds the costs and no other opportunity offers a higher return for the risks, building the new garage makes economic sense and is a good use of societal resources. We use the same logic when assessing the benefits of risk control.

A short example will illustrate the concept. A landfill is gradually contaminating the drinking water of our city of 1,000,000 inhabitants. Scientists estimate that relocating the landfill would reduce the annual average fatality rate from drinking the water by two lives. Suppose that each citizen is willing to pay $5 per year for this level of overall risk reduction but no more. After all, the odds of any given citizen being the unlucky one is exceptionally small – less than being killed in an automobile accident. In total, therefore, the city's residents are willing to pay $5.0 million ($5 $\times$ 1,000,000) per annum for the two expected lives saved. Thus, to these citizens, the economic value of one expected life saved is $2.5 million.

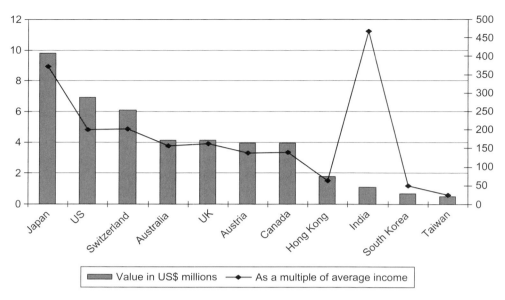

**Figure 4.1**    Implied Value of Worker Life (2002 GDP Per Capita in Purchasing Power Parities). *Sources*: "Living Dangerously", 2004, p. 7 citing Viscusi and *The Economist*

These tradeoffs reflect attitudes about small probabilities of harm. They do not imply that anyone would accept certain death for $2.5 million. Additionally, these WTP amounts do not measure what our survivors should be willing to accept in a wrongful death case or in the purchase of life insurance. Note that these amounts are not set by government or other external observers. Rather, this approach provides society with a logical *theoretical* basis for designing safety, environmental and other public policy initiatives that reflect how much individuals themselves value a particular risk reduction.

A practical challenge in implementing this approach occurs in estimating costs and, especially, benefits. For example, as discussed in Chapter 6, little agreement exists on the long-term benefit to society of reductions in greenhouse gases. One researcher who examined what workers were willing to pay to reduce the risk of employment-related death found enormous variations internationally (see Figure 4.1). In general, as countries get richer, the WTP amounts increase, with a 10 percent increase in income per capita leading to a 5–6 percent WTP increase.[3]

## When is Government Intervention Justified?

Individuals and businesses should continue to undertake safety and other risk control activities as long as the marginal private benefit exceeds the marginal private cost. In the same vein, society should continue to undertake risk control activities as long as the marginal social benefit exceeds the marginal social cost. In a world of perfect competition, the sum of the private benefits and costs equals social benefits and costs, and no government intervention is needed. This world does not exist. Even matters that seem to be purely private can have social consequences; i.e., carry externalities, as Insight 4.1 illustrates.

Various imperfections distort resource allocation. Consequently, private benefits and costs do not sum to social benefits and costs. Moreover, even if they did, society values things other

INSIGHT 4.1: INDIVIDUAL FREEDOM AND SOCIAL
CONSEQUENCES: MOTORCYCLE HELMET LAWS

Those in the U.S. who oppose laws requiring motorcyclists to wear helmets typically argue that the cyclist should be free to decide for him/herself. Many economists
agree, assuming the cyclist is a well-informed, rational decision-maker and assuming
the benefits and costs of the choice are "purely private;" that is, enjoyed and incurred
only by the individual making the decision. If these assumptions were true, helmet
laws would be paternalistic and inefficient. Let us suppose that the first assumption
is reasonable and proceed to the second.

Motorcycle accidents actually entail many costs to society. State police and emergency medical crews and facilities are taxpayer funded. Some hospitals are private, but
society ends up paying many medical bills. The opportunity costs of motorcycle accidents also include the social and economic losses to family and friends and to the larger
community if the accident victim was a productive, contributing worker and citizen.

If helmets substantially reduce these social costs, then paternalistic helmet laws
may actually be economical. That is, the overall benefits of helmets (measured by
the avoided medical and morgue costs, avoided pain and suffering, and higher economic production) may outweigh the overall costs of helmets (measured by the value
of resources used to produce helmets and the value of discomfort and reduced riding pleasure incurred in wearing them). Helmet laws may be (socially) efficient, even
though many cyclists may choose to ride without a helmet. The point is that few risk-
reduction decisions are purely private: individual choices typically have significant
social consequences.

*Source*: Swaney (1997). © from "The Basic Economics of Risk analysis," in V. Molak, ed., *Fundamentals of
Risk Analysis and Risk Management.* Reproduced by permission of Routledge/Taylor & Francis
Group, LLC.

than efficiency. In this section, we explain why society cannot rely exclusively on competition to ensure adequate social risk control. The discussion builds on the market imperfections introduced in Chapter 2.

### Public goods

The existence of public goods provides a rationale for government risk management actions.
Recall that, with public goods, social benefits exceed private benefits, so the market will
produce too few of the affected goods because of the free rider problem. Having government provide the public good improves efficiency.

National defense and police protection are classic examples of public goods. The military protects everyone, even those who pay no taxes. Police do likewise and help preserve
order in society, which is essential to efficient markets. The law and its fair interpretation
by courts also are essential public goods, especially as they establish clear and enforceable
property rights. This reduces uncertainty, providing an environment conducive to economic
prosperity. When rules are transparent and enforced impartially, transactions and monitoring costs can be kept low.

Loss control resources often have elements of public goods. Reducing the likelihood of flooding for one person by appropriate water management practices reduces the risk for others in a flood plain. Indeed, numerous aspects of community disaster preparedness have elements of public goods.

When many people face similar hazards, risk assessment and information dissemination often are public goods. Thus, if government provides risk management information only to one member within a group, other members can benefit at little or no additional cost. Without government involvement in risk information dissemination, too little would be produced. Having discovered adverse side effects of a drug (assessment), the national drug oversight agency incurs about the same cost in publicizing its finding for the benefit of the public whether a dozen or a million people read about it.

### Information problems

Another important rationale for government intervention into societal risk management revolves around the information problems that individuals encounter in attempting to make informed decisions about risk. In numerous instances, individuals either (1) do not have access to relevant risk-related information or (2) are unable to interpret or evaluate the information.

Concerning access, firms often know more about the riskiness of their products and manufacturing processes than do citizens, customers and rank-and-file employees; that is, the market suffers from information asymmetry. Firms may have insufficient incentives to disclose adverse information voluntarily. Doing so could hurt sales or cause employees to demand higher, risk-adjusted wages. One has but to recall the decades-long claims by some cigarette manufacturers that smoking cigarettes was not proven harmful to health, even though, as we learned later, they possessed evidence of such harm.

Government may conclude that the best course of action is to ensure that citizens have sufficient information to make informed risk assessments. Government may require manufacturers to provide hazard warnings, as is the situation with cigarettes, alcoholic beverages, drugs, pesticides, workplace safety and certain consumer goods.

Alternatively, government could conclude that hazard warnings are insufficient, because individuals are unlikely to fully comprehend the information or are unsure as to how to use it. This is the reason for requiring prescriptions for potentially dangerous drugs. Additionally, we have evidence that consumers can easily suffer information overload, in which case even otherwise reasonable disclosure may not have the desired effect. Less, not more information is needed. Thus, in the face of imperfect information, government may be in a better position to assess tradeoffs than are individuals. Economies of scale in research and experimentation may strengthen this position.

Information problems are particularly daunting for policymakers because of some seemingly anomalies. Recall from Chapter 2, for example, that individual evaluation of low-probability, high-severity events poses especially difficult issues. These and other seemingly irrational reactions by individuals complicate societal risk management by causing a diversion of resources toward hazards that evoke fear and dread and whose technology is not well understood even though those exposures may involve less objective risk than better known hazards. Thus, the likelihood of death per mile traveled is much greater with automobiles than with airplanes. Yet, society spends far more to avoid an additional air fatality than a traffic fatality.

When hazards are reasonably homogeneous across large population segments, citizens may be especially interested in having government experts establish and enforce safety standards.

This is the logic for much health and safety regulation at the governmental level. When government assumes the role of certifying the safety of products, activities or processes, consumers naturally come to rely on government to protect them. In turn, consumers may take fewer precautions themselves, thus weakening market discipline. For example, during the 1980s, many U.S. savings institutions engaged in risky behavior by offering interest rates on deposits that were higher than they could earn on the invested funds. Customers did not worry much about the possibility of these institutions becoming insolvent – and there were hundreds – because they knew that their deposits were guaranteed by an agency of the U.S. federal government. Because consumers expect to be protected, it can be difficult for government to withdraw from this role.

## Externalities

Most environmental problems involve externalities; that is, social costs exceed private costs. While it is easy to recall pollution that was accidental, such as the sinking and massive pollution of the Prestige oil tanker off the coast of Spain and the Chernobyl nuclear power plant explosion, most environmental impairments are the result of mining and manufacturing operations.

### Why externalities exist

Negative externalities are byproducts of industrialization. Businesses succeed by providing a good or service for which people are willing to pay. Businesses seek to maximize revenue and minimize costs. A mining operation, therefore, might seek government permission (a property right) to extract and sell ore, but, if it can, it prefers to avoid the high costs of land reclamation and of disposal of tailings. This is because the natural incentives are asymmetrical: a market economy encourages businesses (and individuals) to capture benefits but it fails to encourage the capture of all costs. Indeed, as costs are equivalent to negative revenue, the incentive is to avoid costs if possible.

Before industrialization, failure to consider the negative effects of human activity on the land, water or air was probably "no big deal." Natural processes could be counted upon to break down these comparatively small, isolated byproducts. With industrialization and ever-larger populations, what formerly were isolated "bads" that affected few people, now degrade many others' lives and property rights.

With externalities of this sort, one party – usually a business – successfully imposes costs on others. This cost shifting means that the private (accounting) costs of production are understated – because not all production costs are internalized to the firm – and, therefore, resulting prices are lower than they should be. Because prices are lower than they should be, more of the offending products are sold than if prices reflected all costs of production (i.e., both private costs and the costs shifted to others).

Figure 4.2 illustrates this concept. Supply curve $S'$ reflects the private production costs of steel with increasing quantity produced. Demand curve $D$ reflects the societal demand for steel. The market will clear at price $P'$ and quantity $Q'$. Assume, however, that costs in the amount of $C$ are imposed on citizens from higher healthcare costs, because the production process pollutes the air. If the social costs (i.e., both private and shifted costs) of production were taken fully into consideration, the supply curve would be higher by $C$. It should be $S''$. The new equilibrium would be at $P''$ and $Q''$. Thus, with negative externalities, prices are lower than they should be and, therefore, more of the product giving rise to

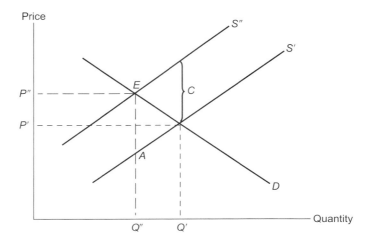

**Figure 4.2**   Private versus Social Costs

the externality will be produced – resulting in still more pollution – than would occur if the pricing were correct.

*The importance of property rights*

As introduced in Chapter 2, the fundamental problem with externalities turns on property rights and their enforcement. By **property rights**, we mean any stream of benefits inuring to a person or business and that is subject to government protection. The value of a piece of land reflects the present value of future benefits from owning the land. When we own property, it means that the government recognizes and will protect our rights in something – be it land, loan repayments, a contract, income, our life or our health.

Imagine, for example, that the citizens in Figure 4.2 illustration sued the steel manufacturers to recover their medical costs. Assume that they were able to establish that the pollution was the proximate cause of their poor health and that they won a judgment that reflected precisely the economic value of their losses. The steel manufacturers would then be required to pay the amount *EA* to citizens. In this situation, private production costs would increase by *EA*, resulting in a new supply curve *S″*. Private production costs now equal societal production costs, with the appropriate equilibrium. Prices now include all production costs, so less is produced and pollution is reduced.

Note that pollution is not eliminated. It is reduced to that which society finds appropriate. It is appropriate because the marginal social costs associated with the manufacture of steel equals the marginal social benefits. Society is unwilling to "pay the price" for even less pollution. The "price" could be a mandate by government for further reductions in pollution, which would cause production costs to rise further. True, society would realize health improvements, but it would mean still higher steel prices and, therefore, less steel output. In turn, this would lead to more expensive cars, appliances and other goods containing steel. Society's demand curve incorporates society's current WTP for this risk reduction, and it would prefer a somewhat less healthy society and somewhat less pricey goods to the opposite situation.[4]

**Table 4.1**   Illustration of Coase Theorem: The Rancher and the Farmer

| Number of Cows (1) | Total Rancher Benefits ($) (2) | Marginal Rancher Benefits ($) (3) | Total Farmer Harm ($) (4) | Marginal Farmer Harm ($) (5) | Net Social Benefits ($) (2)−(4) |
|---|---|---|---|---|---|
| 0 | 0 | 0 | 0 | 0 | 0 |
| 1 | 60 | 60 | 10 | 10 | 50 |
| 2 | 110 | 50 | 32 | 22 | 78 |
| 3 | 150 | 40 | 71 | 39 | 79 |
| 4 | 180 | 30 | 130 | 59 | 50 |
| 5 | 200 | 20 | 201 | 71 | −1 |
| 6 | 210 | 10 | 301 | 100 | −91 |
| 7 | 190 | −20 | 421 | 120 | −231 |

The key to achievement of this desirable new equilibrium was the ability of victims successfully to assert a violation of their property rights. In fact, as we show below, an efficient societal outcome is possible even if the victims are unable to assert a violation of their property rights, provided that all parties' rights are unambiguous and certain other conditions are present.

*Coase's theorem*

Ronald H. Coase of the University of Chicago *Law* School won a Nobel Prize in *Economics* for his insights into negative externalities and the importance of property rights. Before Coase, economic analysis maintained that a market of decentralized decision-making would fail to achieve an optimal solution when an externality was involved, because self-interested actors (e.g., steel manufacturers) would fail to take into account the harm imposed on others. Coase turned this notion on its head by proving that, irrespective of whether someone is liable for damages that she creates, in a regime of zero transaction costs, the result is the same. An example will help make this seeming contradiction clear.

Assume that our "society" consists of a rancher and a farmer. The rancher benefits from having her cattle graze on the farmer's crops, but the farmer realizes losses. Table 4.1 shows the net benefits to the rancher and the net costs to the farmer arising from each additional cow. It also shows the net benefits to society – the simple difference between total social benefits and total social costs.

Table 4.1 shows that, if the rancher buys one cow and allows it to graze in the farmer's fields, she realizes a marginal gain of $60. The farmer suffers $10 in harm to his crops. Society is better off by $50 from this event, so, from a social point of view, it is desirable for the rancher to buy this cow. The benefit to the rancher from the second cow is somewhat less at $50, making the rancher's total benefit $110. The additional cost imposed on the farmer is even more harm to crops at $22, for a total harm of $32 from both cows. However, society is better off with two than with one cow.

With the third cow, again we find that society is better off, although the farmer at this point probably is not too happy about the result. Society is not better off, however, if the rancher buys the fourth cow, because it costs the farmer more than the rancher benefits. Thus, we see that, from society's point of view, the optimum number of cows is three. If we ignore costs, however, the maximum benefit to the rancher occurs at six cows. Conversely, if we ignore benefits, the minimum cost to the farmer occurs at zero cows.

So, what will be the outcome? We now introduce property rights. There are three possibilities: (1) the rancher is unambiguously liable for any damage done to the farmer's crops (i.e., the farmer holds the rights), (2) the rancher is unambiguously not liable (i.e., the rancher holds the rights), or (3) the law is ambiguous as to whether the rancher is liable.

Under the first scenario, the rancher is liable for damage caused by her cows. How many cows will the rancher buy? Zero? No. The rancher will buy the first cow, as she realizes a benefit of $60 and then can compensate the farmer at least $10 for the damage inflicted by her cow. She will also buy the second cow, because the benefit to the rancher ($50) exceeds what she would have to pay to the farmer (at least $22). The same is true for the third cow.

The fourth cow inflicts damage of $59 and the rancher realizes a marginal benefit of only $30. The rancher, being an astute businessperson, will not buy the fourth cow. Thus, when the farmer holds the property rights, the efficient number of cows in this private transaction is three – the same number as that which we found from society's point of view. So, when the property rights are held by the intended "victim," we achieve the societal optimum outcome.[5]

Let's explore the second scenario wherein the rancher is not liable for any damage that her cows inflict on the farmer's crops. How many cows will the rancher buy now? Six? No. The farmer suffers harm of $301 at six cows and society's net benefit is a loss of $91 – not a good result. If the farmer bargained with the rancher, he would pay at least $10 – the marginal rancher benefit for the sixth cow – for the rancher not to acquire the sixth cow. The economically rational rancher would accept the offer. In fact, the farmer would pay up to $100 – the marginal farmer harm for the sixth cow – to discourage the rancher from buying the sixth cow.

Similarly, the farmer will bargain and would pay up to $71 to entice the rancher not to acquire the fifth cow, and the rancher would accept it because her marginal benefit from the fifth cow is only $20. The same logic applies to the fourth cow. The farmer would pay up to $59 for the rancher not to acquire the fourth cow and the rancher would agree, as the marginal benefit is less ($30).

The most the farmer would pay the rancher not to acquire the third cow is $39. The rancher would not agree to this arrangement, as her benefit from the third cow is $40. Thus, the efficient number of cows under this second private scenario is three – the same as for scenario one and the same as we found optimal for society. So, even when the victim has no property rights, we achieve the societal optimum outcome![6]

What about scenario three where property rights are not clear? In this situation, presumably both the farmer and the rancher consult attorneys who advise each that the law is unclear. Perhaps the farmer decides to sue but for an uncertain outcome. The rancher decides to fight the suit, with each incurring large legal expenses. The farmer says that he wants no cows grazing on his land, and the rancher wants six cows grazing. Of course, we cannot say what the outcome of this litigation would be, as the rights of the respective parties are unclear. Whatever the outcome, it is unlikely to be optimal, unless the judge "splits the difference" and allows three cows to graze!

This example illustrates the famous **Coase Theorem** – when property rights are unambiguous and there are no transactions costs, markets will generate efficient outcomes, even with externalities. This result suggests that government's role is to ensure that property rights are unambiguous and to help minimize transaction costs. If this happens, government need not concern itself with pollution or any other negative externality – at least from a societal efficiency standpoint. Individual self-interest will lead us to an efficient outcome.

*Limitations on the application of coase bargaining*

Regrettably, Coasian bargaining solutions have proven elusive in practice for several reasons. First, in many instances, property rights are not well defined, especially for environmental media. No property rights attach generally to outer space, the atmosphere, the oceans, rivers, large lakes and land without clear title (as exists in dozens of countries worldwide). Moreover, even where property rights are well defined, transactions costs can be so great as to thwart action. Such often is the situation with environmental risks whose effects are widely dispersed across a large population. Coasian bargaining may be impossible because of high costs.

Moreover, why should I undertake the expense of defending a property right (e.g., a clean river) when I can rely on others to do so? The defense of communally owned property through private costs lends itself to free rider problems – resulting in no action.

Additionally, injury often is not as clear as that which we saw with our farmer and rancher. The adverse effects of some environmental risks remain hidden to us, and others take such long periods to manifest themselves that the enterprise causing the damage may have long ago vanished, making bargaining impossible. Similarly, bargaining is impossible where external effects cross generations – as with climate change – since future generations have no voice.

### Market power

As alluded to above, businesses strive to keep production costs low, thereby maximizing profits. While they want to ensure a safe working environment, they evaluate safety aspects as they do any other projects. Is the net present value positive? In making this analysis, the costs of new safety equipment or procedures are usually clear. The benefits include fewer worker days lost, fewer lawsuits, fewer and smaller workers' compensation claims, and fewer bottlenecks because key employees are unable to work. However, what if the employer is effectively the "only game in town," as is true in many areas? It is in a superior position relative to employees and can enjoy market power in terms of purchasing labor. Part of this market power might materialize as lower wages than otherwise. It just as easily can manifest itself in reduced levels of employee safety – which is the economic equivalent of lower wages. The same logic could be applied to a company's ability to impose negative externalities on the small community in which it is located. In such situations, worker safety and community pollution may be substandard.

Market power also can result when companies secure preferential treatment – rents – from government. Companies are not keen on government intervention that might raise production costs. Therefore, businesses often oppose imposition of standards or regulations that lead to cost increases. Indeed, according to one theory, government regulation is often "captured" by the affected industry and protects the industry more than the public (see Chapter 8). Of course, this type of market power comes about because of the failure of government to do its job, not from market failure. In other words, we have a principal (citizens)-agent (government) problem. The solution is having higher standards for the representatives of the people.

### Other problems with the market

Society encounters other difficulties in trying to rely exclusively on the market in decisions about risk management. Markets allocate "voice" by the ability and WTP by those who demand products and services, including risk management services. The more money a person or business controls, the more powerful the voice. Those controlling little or no money have correspondingly less input if societal risk management decisions are determined exclusively by the interaction of demand and supply forces. The result is that the poor, future generations and other species may have little or no voice on matters relating to societal risk control. Do we consider outcomes derived in this manner to be "fair," "just" or "ethical" even if they are efficient?

Moreover, how should we make informed decisions about matters that may be irreversible? Of course, this issue is relevant at the individual level, as adverse health and safety outcomes occasioned by employment or other injury can be irreversible; for example, death! At the societal level, the issue of irreversibility finds particular relevance for many environmental risks. What is it worth to society to avoid causing the extinction of a species? Conflicts arise regularly between protecting jobs and protecting animals and plants such as the snail darter fish, the spotted owl and the beach mouse.

Possibly permanent adverse ecological effects are associated with ozone depletion; biotechnological processes (e.g., genetic engineering); nuclear, biological, and chemical warfare and accidents; deforestation; and global warming. The possibility of irreversible effects enormously complicates policy decision-making – after all, recovery from irreversible adverse effects is impossible. Many argue that societal benefits of risk reduction should be greater with irreversible than with reversible events, but how should we measure them? There is no easy answer.

# ALTERNATIVE APPROACHES TO SOCIETAL RISK MANAGEMENT

It should be clear from the preceding discussion that governments have a range of approaches that they can take in addressing societal risk issues. These approaches generally fall into five generic categories:[7]

- privatization of risk reduction;
- provision of economic incentives;
- regulation of risk-related activities;
- establishing legal liability for damages;
- creating victim compensation funds.

## Privatization of Risk Reduction

One response to societal risk issues is that individuals and organizations are capable of making their own decisions and should do so, provided that they have sufficient information and that property rights are clear. With this philosophy, government's role is limited to ensuring that risk-related information is disclosed and that property rights are unambiguous and related transactions costs are low. We discussed the property rights issue earlier, so we need not repeat the discussion here. With information disclosure, there may be requirements to warn of hazards and to suggest loss control strategies.

The appropriateness of this approach depends on the nature of the risk involved. Government provision of risk-related information is clearly appropriate if generation of the information is a public good. Risk-related information is likely to have public good characteristics for many environmental risks, as individuals within given groups tend to face similar risks.

Also, greater information may spur appropriate private responses for risks that carry few negative externalities and for which the individual has reasonable loss reduction or insurance opportunities. Thus, reducing the level of radon gas in your house does not affect the radon risks faced in his neighbors' houses – no opportunity for free riders. You can undertake effective loss control measures by, say, installing radon filters.

If a person can be made aware that certain products are dangerous, she can avoid purchasing them. The same logic applies for certain jobs. She need not take them or can demand appropriate risk-adjusted wages.

## Economic Incentives

Another approach is to provide economic incentives that encourage a reduction in harmful activities by risk generators. Common instruments usually proposed are Pigovian taxes, refundable deposits and fees, and tradeable emission rights. With Pigovian taxes, named for the famous English economist A.C. Pigou, the activities causing negative externalities, such as pollution, are taxed. Conceptually, the tax is set at an amount that precisely equals the costs shifted to society and not embedded within the risk-generating firms' private costs of production. In Figure 4.2, the tax should equal *EA*. Pollution would be reduced because private costs now equal social costs. Implementation of such a tax has complexities, not the least of which is determining what to tax, how to tax it, and the correct level of taxation.

Refundable deposits are amounts paid by consumers, beyond the price, that are returned to the consumer if the expended product or container is recycled appropriately. For example, deposits on hazardous waste materials such as automobile batteries encourage proper disposal, and waste disposal fees encourage recycling and waste reduction.

An alternative to taxation is to sell rights to pollute, which themselves can be traded. With this approach, governments determine an allowable pollution level and then sell the rights to pollute.[8] The market for pollution rights functions as any other market. Firms that value the rights most, pay the most for them. Firms decide whether it is more economical to buy these rights or to undertake pollution-control activities. While the use of pollution rights suffers from some of the same complexities as Pigovian taxation, there are now viable markets in them in some countries (as discussed later) and optimism for even greater reliance on them in the future.

With economic-incentive approaches, government does not tell firms how to achieve a desirable societal goal, but rather lets them decide. In this way, acceptable levels of environmental risk and other negative externalities should be achieved at the least cost. The potential for the use of such *ex ante* economic incentives to manage risk depends on the type of risk involved. Deposits and fees can reduce the environmental risks of waste disposal. Pigovian taxes at point of emission of air or water pollutants encourage emission reductions, which reduce the risks from polluted air or water. Similar taxes on combustion of fossil fuels or use of chlorofluorocarbons can reduce the risks of global warming or ozone depletion. As these emissions and uses are continual and predictable, they are amenable to such taxation.

The same is not true for risks that are discrete and stochastic (i.e., accidents). Examples include chemical spills or releases, unintended releases of genetically modified organisms, and outbreaks of food contamination. There appears to be limited potential for using stand-ard *ex ante* economic-incentive mechanisms for managing accident-type risks.

When accidents are covered by insurance, however, some economic incentive to reduce risks can be created through the use of experience rating – use of past loss experience to price risk during the current period. A primary function of experience rating is to reduce the moral hazard problems generally associated with insurance. Experience rating is used, for example, in workers' compensation programs to encourage large employers to improve workplace safety. While evidence on effectiveness is mixed, experience rating remains, in theory, an effective means to reduce the costs of accidents.

## Regulation of Risk-Related Activities

Historically, the most common means by which government has sought to control external-ities, such as pollution, and establish acceptable levels of safety is through direct regulation. Such regulation typically has consisted of detailed rules and standards. With regulation, behavior is mandated rather than encouraged through the use of economic incentives. It is the antithesis of reliance on pricing incentives. Regulation can be directed toward loss prevention by reducing the probability of an accident or toward loss mitigation by reducing the magnitude of damages if an accident should occur. For example, regulation of landfill operation is designed to reduce the risk of contamination by reducing the probability of leaching. Regulation of the workplace environment is intended to reduce the probability of work-related accidents. Alternatively, regulation can be used to mandate the steps that must be taken when an accident occurs so as to contain the resulting damage.

While regulation has been used in many areas of public policy, its application to the control of health, safety and environmental risks has a particularly challenging component, namely, the setting of safety goals. The value of life concept discussed earlier in this chapter is becoming the most widely used approach, although other approaches exist. For example, using labor market data, Viscusi observes that the price that Americans put on the value of a life is around $7.0 million.[9] This contrasts to the costs, shown in Table 4.2, of various risk-reducing regulations in the U.S.

Table 4.2 shows regulations that pass and fail the $7.0 million threshold. Note the extreme variations, from $0.1 million per life saved for regulation of "child-proof" lighters and three others, to $100 billion per life saved for regulations dealing with landfill restric-tions. If societal risk management is all about tradeoffs, we cannot conclude that U.S. gov-ernment is spending its citizens' money in ways that achieve maximum safety enhancement for the costs! (Other governments likely are doing no better.)

For the regulatory approach to be an appropriate means of risk management, the risk must have several characteristics:

- *The actions that determine the level of risk must be observable at reasonable cost.* If they are not, then monitoring is not possible and violations of the regulation cannot be detected, making regulation ineffective.
- *Those actions should be somewhat standardized.* As it is generally impractical to specify different behavior for each person or firm, regulations must apply to groups of individuals or firms.
- *The regulatory body should have better information about the risk than those whose actions generate it.* With the information, the regulatory body will be in a better posi-tion to determine the most cost-effective means of risk reduction.

**Table 4.2**   Estimated Costs per Life Saved for Selected U.S. Risk Regulations (in 2002 U.S. dollars)

| Regulation | Years Issued | Cost per Life Saved |
|---|---|---|
| Child-proof lighters | 1993 | 100,000 |
| Respiratory protection | 1998 | 100,000 |
| Logging safety rules | 1998 | 100,000 |
| Electrical safety rules | 1990 | 100,000 |
| Steering column standards | 1967 | 200,000 |
| Hazardous waste disposal | 1998 | 1,100,000,000 |
| Hazardous waste disposal | 1994 | 2,600,000,000 |
| Drinking water quality | 1992 | 19,000,000,000 |
| Formaldehyde exposure | 1987 | 78,000,000,000 |
| Landfill restrictions | 1991 | 100,000,000,000 |

*Source*: "Living Dangerously" (2004), p. 7 citing Morrall.

Unfortunately, as the discussion in Insight 4.2 highlights, seemingly reasonable regulatory requirements do not always have the desired results because people change their behaviors.

While the above characteristics provide the possibility for cost-effective regulation, the main argument in favor of regulation is that, if complied with, its effects are more certain than those of indirect economic incentives. Some governments have concluded that strict regulation is appropriate for environmental risks when it is better to be safe than sorry – even if such regulation is not completely cost effective, as explained later.

## Legal Liability for Damages

Legal liability is an alternative to the use of *a priori* regulation. Liability is generally thought to serve two purposes. First, it provides an incentive for risk generators to undertake risk-reducing activities. Second, liability compensates victims who suffer damages, thereby protecting them from the negative effects of others' actions.

The effectiveness of liability in reducing risks and providing compensation depends on both how the legal rule applies and the nature of the risk. An important difference between the use of liability and regulation is that liability allows those whose actions generate risks to decide on the most appropriate way to reduce those risks. In this sense, the *ex ante* effect of liability is similar to economic incentives. Also, liability has an advantage over regulation when actions taken to reduce risks are not easily observable and thus not easily subject to monitoring and compliance verification.

The incentive effects of liability are directly related to the probability that a risk generator will be held liable for the full amount of damages. Herein lie some problems. The liability of the injurer may be uncertain – hence, payments to victims are uncertain. Liability may be uncertain because of the successful assertion of defenses. The injury may not manifest itself for many years. Even when it appears, the linkage between a firm's risky activities and the injury may be difficult to establish, particularly if multiple causes exist. The firm may be out of business or the value of the liability may exceed firm value plus insurance, making full recovery impossible. Hence, while legal liability has its place in social risk management, it cannot be a substitute for all other policy approaches.[10]

INSIGHT 4.2: CONSUMER BEHAVIOR AND REGULATION: THE LULLING EFFECT

To reduce the risk of child poisoning, the Food and Drug Administration in 1972 imposed a protective bottle cap requirement on aspirin and other selected drugs. The strategy was to design caps that made opening containers of hazardous substances more difficult. Such protective packaging requirements and other safety standards can, however, reduce precautionary behavior – what Viscusi calls the **lulling effect**. First, regulation can lead to a reduction in safety related efforts for the affected product. Parents may leave protective caps off bottles because they are difficult to open. Second, regulation may produce misperceptions that lead consumers to reduce their safety precautions because they overestimate the product's safety. Parents may increase children's access to bottles because they are supposedly "childproof." Finally, regulation may induce consumers to lower their safety precautions with regard to unregulated products. Parents may no longer believe it necessary to keep all medicines in a locked drawer because some are deemed to be "safer," thereby increasing access to unregulated products. These effects are quite general and are not restricted to the case of protective bottle caps.

The economic mechanism generating this effect is similar to that which produces moral hazard problems in insurance. As one reduces either the probability of a loss or the size of the loss, individual incentives to take precautionary actions are reduced. Regulations function much like insurance in this regard, with the only difference being that one need not pay an insurance premium.

Ignoring the inconvenience imposed on individuals with no children, such as the elderly with arthritis, who found the caps difficult to open, one would expect that the impact on safety should be favorable if consumer behavior remained unchanged. In practice, consumer behavior often does not remain the same. The introduction of seatbelts and antilock brakes in automobiles, for example, diminished drivers' incentive to exercise care.

Indeed, Viscusi found the net effect of the safety cap requirements on aspirin and analgesic poisoning rates to be adverse. The overall behavior pattern was consistent with what would occur if safety caps led to a decrease in parental caution. He observed that the more general ramification of these results is that technological solutions to safety problems may induce a lulling effect on consumer behavior. The safety benefits will be muted and perhaps more than offset by the effect of the decreased efficacy of safety precautions, misperceptions regarding the risk-reducing impact of the regulation, and spillover effects of reduced precautions with other products.
*Source*: Viscusi (1992), pp. 224–242.

## Victim Compensation Funds

A final policy approach to societal risk management is to create victim compensation funds. Such funds often are intended to make available compensation or indemnification to the injured without incurring the high transaction costs and being subject to uncertainty of the tort system. Under this approach, taxpayers or employers typically contribute money to build a fund from which victims' claims are paid, in whole or part. In the U.S., such funds have been established for asbestos victims, workers' compensation, black lung disease, and, more recently, victims of the September 11 attacks.

These funds are essentially a form of third-party insurance. They carry the same advantages and disadvantages of all insurance including the moral hazard problem of dulling risk-reduction efforts by insureds. Insurance is more effective with monetary than with non-monetary losses (such as pain and suffering), but does not always function well for injuries resulting from prolonged exposure. Insurance funds can be useful for some societal risks but are of limited use for other risks such as environmental.

## Conclusion

In designing an appropriate risk management policy, it is essential that the nature of the risk be identified and the goal of the policy be specified. Alternative approaches vary in their ability to achieve efficient risk reduction, efficient risk spreading, and appropriate allocation of the costs of risk-generating activities, with policies achieving some goals at the expense of others. No single approach dominates for all types of risks and all goals. Because societal risk management has multiple goals that cannot be achieved generally with a single policy instrument, appropriate policy requires a combination of approaches.

# UNDERSTANDING SOCIETAL RISK PERCEPTIONS AND DECISION-MAKING

Humans have always conscientiously and innovatively coped with life's uncertainties.[11] Surely, commonalities exist among them. If we can discover these commonalities, we not only gain greater insight into ourselves, but we also might be better able to understand and predict how individuals and groups may react to and, ultimately, best control certain risky situations. Should authorities allow construction of a new nuclear power generating facility? If so, where and under what geological and other physical conditions? What minimum level of safety must be engineered into the project and who decides? These are the types of contemporary questions with which societies wrestle.

Social theories of risk fall into two categories: individualist and contextualist. **Individualist risk theories** focus on the behavior of individuals when faced with risky conditions, from which generalizations about group risk behavior may be inferred. The two most fully developed individualist risk theories are grounded in the social sciences of psychology and economics. We cover both below, with particular attention to the former, given the extensive discussion of economics in Chapter 2.

**Contextualist risk theories** begin with the context in which risk-based decisions are made (e.g., culture, affinity group, organization, lifestyle), drawing inferences about group and then possibly individual risk behavior. An anthropological culture-based theory of risk is the most developed contextualist theory, and is covered below. According to many authorities (e.g., Renn, 1992), sociology offers no consistent theory of risk perception, so none is presented here.

**Table 4.3**    Hazard Descriptions for Low- and High-Risk Events

| Risk Factor | Low Risk | High Risk |
| --- | --- | --- |
| Dread | Controllable | Uncontrollable |
| | Low dread | Dread |
| | Not global catastrophic | Global catastrophic |
| | Consequences not fatal | Consequences fatal |
| | Equitable | Not equitable |
| | Individual | Catastrophic |
| | Low risk to future generations | High risk to future generations |
| | Easily reduced | Not easily reduced |
| | Risk decreasing | Risk increasing |
| | Voluntary | Involuntary |
| Unknown | Observable | Not Observable |
| | Known to those exposed | Unknown to those exposed |
| | Old risk | New risk |
| | Risk known to science | Risk unknown to science |

*Source*: © by Slovic (1992). Reproduced with permission of Greenwood Publishing Group, Inc., Westport, CT

## The Fallacy of Objective Risk: The Contribution of Psychology

The **psychological** (or **psychometric**) **theory of risk perception** contends that risk is inherently subjective, and our perceptions of risk are influenced by innumerable social, political, cultural, psychological and other factors. As such, the so-called "objective risks" do not truly exist but are themselves only perceptions derived under human-made assumptions, models or formula. Humans perceive various features of decision problems and this, in turn, leads to feelings of risk. Our perception of risk generates these feelings.

Risk-based applied research by psychologists has enhanced our understanding of the dynamics of risk perception and of individuals' cognitive limitations in processing risk information. Such research has been the basis for much of what is now labeled behavioral economics, suggesting that individuals overestimate the likelihood of occurrence of infrequent catastrophic events and underestimate the likelihood of some more frequently occurring events.

### Risk perception, dread, and the unknown

Perhaps the most important finding from the psychological literature on risk perception is that people take into consideration many factors – such as catastrophic potential, voluntariness, familiarity and dread – in evaluating the seriousness of a risk. Using factor analysis, psychologists find that individual risk perception has two basic dimensions. The first and more important, labeled *dread*, concerns the extent to which the consequences of an event are potentially catastrophic and uncontrollable. The second relates to the extent to which the risk is *unknown*. Most readers recognize these two factors in their own risk perceptions, for example, in concerns about climate change and genetic engineering. Hazards considered "voluntary" tend to be rated "controllable" and "well known." Table 4.3 shows how typical hazard descriptors are sorted on these two factors.

Especially interesting and relevant for policymakers is that experts' risk perceptions are often not closely related to any of the various risk characteristics. Experts seem to base their perceptions primarily on expected annual mortality rates. Consequently, much of the public debate between experts (focusing on statistics) and lay people (influenced by feelings of dread) is unlikely to alter either group's position – putting policymakers in the middle and unable to please both groups. As the public at large has more votes than do scientists, it should come as no surprise that policies on safety may be based more on risk perception than on science.

Research also suggests that risk selection, perception and concerns vary by the way that risk information is presented to research subjects and by the methods used to analyze the information. While these findings are unsettling at one level, researchers suggest that this shows that people have no unitary mental representation of risks and that the representation they construct depends critically on the questions asked.

### Understanding the effects of harmful events

Psychologists have been in the forefront of questioning the use of traditional risk analysis to model the effects of unfortunate events. The impact of an unfortunate event may extend far beyond its direct harmful effects. Sometimes, the event affects all companies in an industry, no matter which company was responsible for the mishap. In extreme cases, the indirect costs of a mishap extend past industry boundaries, affecting companies, industries, and agencies whose business is minimally related to the initial event.

Consider the 1979 Three Mile Island nuclear reactor accident in the U.S. The accident involved no deaths and few, if any, latent cancer fatalities, but the total social costs were enormous. Besides the direct impact on the electric utility that owned the facility, the accident led to increased costs to society because of stricter regulation, reduced reactor operations worldwide, greater public opposition to nuclear power, reliance on more expensive energy sources, and increased costs of reactor construction and operation. Traditional economic risk analyses tend to neglect these higher-order impacts, thereby potentially underestimating the costs of certain mishaps (Slovic, 1992).

Because of the potentially severe indirect consequences of high profile unfortunate events, psychological research has accorded great attention to what such events signal or portend. An event's **signal value** reflects the perception that the event provides new information about the likelihood of similar or more destructive future mishaps. Thus, accidents that involve many deaths may produce little *social* disturbance if they are part of familiar and well-understood systems (e.g., automobile wrecks). By contrast, even small accidents in poorly understood systems (e.g., nuclear reactor) might have great social consequences because of what it is perceived as portending. According to Slovic, an important implication of this idea is that the effort and expense, beyond that suggested by a cost-benefit analysis, might be warranted to reduce the possibility of "high-signal accidents."

## Economic Theories of Risk Perception

Economics provides the most fully articulated and tested theory of individual risk perception. As discussed in Chapter 2, utility theory offers a consistent, logical framework for decision-making under conditions of uncertainty. Utility theory is conceptually capable of subsuming psychological, cultural and all other influences on individual risky decisions. It allows comparisons between the risks and benefits of different options through a single measure (unit or the monetary equivalent). However, decisions must be made by individuals (versus a group), and all consequences must be internalized with the individual. Economics offers theories of group decision-making, but they are not well developed. Economic theory includes externalities but cannot yet cope with them fully in decision-making.

The economic model relies on the assumptions of rationality in economic behavior (e.g., consistency) and a utilitarian ethic. In fact, as demonstrated in Chapter 2, the rapidly growing area of behavioral economics, founded by psychologists studying risk, provides new insight into how individuals make decisions respecting risk and how, in traditional economic terms, these decisions seem irrational. Economics offers few insights into poorly understood, complex processes, especially with low frequency high severity catastrophic events or into activities that inspire fear, terror, and distrust among the public. Economists have yet to deal effectively with the paradox of why the marginal cost of saving an additional life varies greatly across different ways of dying.

## Risk Perception is Selective: The Contribution of Anthropology

Cultural anthropologists assert that the appropriate starting point for examination of risk perceptions is the group, not the individual. Douglas (1966) deduced from her work that each group emphasizes that which reinforces the moral, political or religious order that holds the group together. From this early work, she and other anthropologists have developed a topology of social structure and views of nature.

### *The importance of social processes in risk perception*

Anthropologists believe risk perception stems from a social process that we can understand only through social and cultural analysis. Each group highlights some risks and downplays others, and each devises means for coping with some risks but not others. Risks chosen for attention reflect the group's **worldview** – the deeply held beliefs about the environment (nature) and its organization and shared values. The chosen risks may not be the most dangerous, and the danger inherent in the risks chosen may be exaggerated or minimized because of the social, cultural and moral worth of the risk-causing activity.

Selective risk perception is natural, as humans cannot possibly focus attention on all risks. Under this theory, selective attention corresponds to **cultural biases** that justify different ways of behaving; that is, worldviews (shared values and beliefs) corresponding to different patterns of social relations.

### *Social relations and the group–grid topology*

Social relations are described using two variables: group and grid. The **group** variable represents the degree to which the individual is incorporated into a social unit. It answers the question "who am I?" Where group is weak, repetitive interactions between individuals are infrequent and limited to specific undertakings. Hence, weak-group individuals rely on themselves and tend to be competitive. Strong-group individuals interact frequently and in a wide range of activities. The sense of group is stronger than the sense of self. They depend on each other, which promotes values of solidarity rather than competitiveness.

The **grid** variable represents the degree to which members of a social grouping are constrained by internally or externally imposed classifications. It answers the question "what may I do?" Common classifications are profession, kinship, race, gender, age, nationality and so on. With high grid, social classifications severely circumscribe individuals' social

| Grid | Strong | **Stratified Individuals**<br>Life is a lottery,<br>risks are out of our control,<br>and safety is a matter of luck. | **Hierarchists**<br>Risks are acceptable if institutions have<br>the routines to control them. |
|---|---|---|---|
| | Weak | **Individualists**<br>Risks offer opportunities and should be<br>accepted in exchange for benefits. | **Egalitarians**<br>Risks should be avoided unless they are<br>inevitable to protect the public good. |
| | | Weak | Strong |
| | | Group | |

**Figure 4.3**    Anthropology's Grid-Group Topology. *Sources*: © by Slovic (1992). Reproduced with permission of Greenwood Publishing Group, Inc., Westport, CT

activities. With low grid, an egalitarian state of affairs exists where no one is precluded from social activities because they are not members of some preferred classification, for example, because they are the wrong sex, are too old, or do not hold certain jobs.

As independent variables, grid and group typically are represented in two-dimensional space. For simplicity purposes, each variable may be separated into low and high, thus producing four prototype social relations – individualists, stratified individuals (fatalists), hierarchicalists and egalitarians – as illustrated in Figure 4.3.

Rayner (1992) describes the characteristics of each quadrant. For individualists, the absence of restrictions on social behavior arising from rules or from the prior claims of others leads to a competitive social environment. American entrepreneurs are a familiar example.

As we move toward the upper right, individualism and competition may not be entirely absent, but more control will be vested in formal systems until, at the extreme top right corner, hierarchical authority strictly controls all aspects of social life. That authority may be in the form of religious beliefs, a state bureaucracy or, on a smaller scale, a patriarchal family head.

At the bottom right of the continuum between competition and find a collectivist egalitarian framework (strong-group/weak-grid), such as maintained within many religious sects, revolutionary political groups, and some segments of the antinuclear movement and other environmentalists. Finally, in the upper left sector (weak-group/strong-grid) is the category of stratified, often alienated individuals. Hierarchical systems exclude these people from the ladders of power. Often, these are people who have the fewest or the least socially valued skills.

A continuum exists between high and low group and high and low grid. Also, the group-grid topology is not intended to relegate individuals or social organizations to certain categories for all purposes. Thus, an individual may take on egalitarian characteristics in her church, hierarchists characteristics with her young children, and individualist characteristics in her business.

### *Risk perception and social relations*

Wildavsky and Dake (1990) suggest further what would be expected in terms of risk perceptions of these social relations patterns. They observe that individualist cultures (e.g., the U.S.)

would be expected to support self-regulation, including the freedom to bid and bargain as the means for addressing risk. The labyrinth of normative constraints and controls on behavior valued in hierarchies (e.g., Japan) would more likely be perceived as threats to the autonomy of individualists who prefer to negotiate for themselves. Social deviance is a threat to individualists only when it limits freedom to contract or when it is disruptive of market relationships.

Egalitarians would claim that nature is fragile to justify sharing the earth's limited resources. This is a discomforting position to individualists who claim that nature is "cornucopian." If we will but release people from artificial constraints (e.g., excessive environmental regulations), we will have abundance for all and, by that, more than compensate for any environmental damage.

Hierarchists and individualists have something in common. Hierarchists approve of technological processes and products, provided their experts have given the appropriate safety certifications and the applicable rules and regulations are followed. In hierarchical culture, good comes if they follow their experts' rules; bad if they do not.

People who hold egalitarian biases (i.e., who value diminishing distinctions among peoples) would perceive technological dangers to be great and benefits to be small. They believe that an inegalitarian society is likely to insult the environment, just as it exploits poor people. They also would rate social deviance risk to be low. Egalitarians perceive the risk of war to be low to moderate. They are likely to mistrust the military – a prototypical hierarchy.

Cultural theory's predictions for the individualist bias are the opposite. Its adherents perceive technological dangers as small, in part because they trust their institutions to control or compensate for untoward events. These same predictions hold for hierarchists. Thus, both are technologically optimistic; individualists because they see technology as a vehicle for unlimited individual enterprise and hierarchists because they believe that technology endorsed by their experts will improve the quality of life.

The anthropological theory of risk perception is relevant for decision-making at the level of nation-states. Hofstede (1995) notes that Anglo countries such as Australia, Canada, New Zealand, the U.K. and the U.S. tend to be more *individualistic* (low-group/low-grid) whereas Denmark, Finland, the Netherlands, Norway and Sweden tend to value *solidarity* more. Austria, Germany, Italy and Switzerland are more individualist whereas Belgium, France and Spain "take a middle position."

Low-group countries depend more on the market to deal with risk. High-group countries expect government to have a larger role in risk mitigation and the provision of economic security, especially for social security and catastrophic insurance. In fact, these generalizations mostly hold, based on Hofstede's country classifications.

### Applications of cultural risk theory

Empirical studies of the cultural theory of risk perception generally have shown results consistent with the theory (Dake, 1992). Moreover, studies of contrasting theories of group risk perception consistently find the cultural component to be a most important factor (Wildavsky and Dake, 1990). An important and consistent finding in the anthropological literature is that the most powerful factor for predicting risk perceptions is trust in institutions or ideology (worldview), which is largely about which institutions can be trusted.

An especially relevant application of cultural risk theory relates to the fragility (or lack thereof) of nature. Ecologists manage our natural resources. They, naturally, are concerned about how to improve their effectiveness. Thompson (1983) and others found that ecologists'

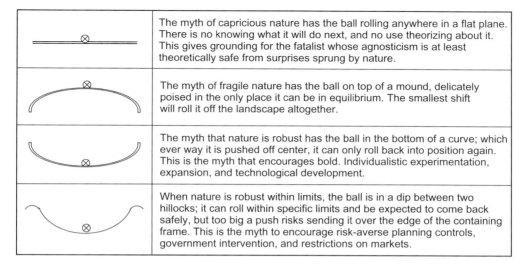

| | The myth of capricious nature has the ball rolling anywhere in a flat plane. There is no knowing what it will do next, and no use theorizing about it. This gives grounding for the fatalist whose agnosticism is at least theoretically safe from surprises sprung by nature. |
|---|---|
| | The myth of fragile nature has the ball on top of a mound, delicately poised in the only place it can be in equilibrium. The smallest shift will roll it off the landscape altogether. |
| | The myth that nature is robust has the ball in the bottom of a curve; which ever way it is pushed off center, it can only roll back into position again. This is the myth that encourages bold. Individualistic experimentation, expansion, and technological development. |
| | When nature is robust within limits, the ball is in a dip between two hillocks; it can roll within specific limits and be expected to come back safely, but too big a push risks sending it over the edge of the containing frame. This is the myth to encourage risk-averse planning controls, government intervention, and restrictions on markets. |

**Figure 4.4**    Four Anthropological Myths Concerning Nature's Robustness. *Source*: A Credible Biosphere," a chapter in Risk and Blame: Essays in Cultural Theory, Mary Douglas. © 1992 and Routledge. Reproduced by permission of Taylor & Francis Books, U.K.

views can be characterized as falling into one of four categories. Each of these categories corresponds to one of the four prototypes within the group-grid format, as follows:

- Nature is fragile (egalitarians).
- Nature is capricious (fatalists).
- Nature is robust (individualists).
- Nature is only robust within limits (hierarchists).

Each of these categories can be represented by a ball in a landscape, as shown in Figure 4.4. For each category, individuals holding that particular view tend to seek information that reinforces their worldview and reject contrary information. Hence, those who believe that nature is fragile will have been reducing their demands on nature while beseeching others to do likewise; the hierarchists will have been trying to plan and control; the entrepreneurial individualists will have gone on with their expansionist policies; while the fatalists stand back and mock all others' futile efforts (Douglas, 1992).

More precise information about the relationships between social relation patterns and risk perceptions concerning the above issue as well as countless others could permit more reasoned policy debates and decisions. Consistent with the view that objective risk is a fiction, risk communication perhaps should focus less on facts and statistics and more on institutional confidence and credibility of hazard information.

## CONCLUSION: THE ULTIMATE RISK BEARER

We note the obvious: government risk assessment and control activities are neither always efficient nor effective. We need only recall that just as there are market imperfections, so too are there government imperfections. Indeed, the consequences of poor government risk assessment and control can be devastating. Such failures could literally mean the end of humankind. September 11 represents one such failure, but hundreds of others exist – some larger (e.g., the 2004 Indian Ocean tsunami), most smaller.

Even so, governments are the ultimate insurers for all societal risks, including those for which no formal program exist. If a societal loss is sufficiently grave, government will provide financing. To take two extreme examples, the U.S. government would certainly provide funds to hasten recovery if terrorists detonated a nuclear device in a major U.S. city. Also, governments would step in to guarantee the financial soundness of their banking systems were they to come into question (as recently occurred in Japan and Korea, among other countries). A common example of government being the ultimate insurer plays out any time a hurricane, tornado or other severe natural catastrophe wreaks havoc and government makes a special allocation of resources to the affected area.

In these and countless other examples, government usually is performing the role expected of it by citizens – restoring or preserving order. Of course, moral hazard problems are created by some of these payments, but, in many instances, the negative externalities created by disorder justify the intervention. In such circumstances, we can consider government as functioning as a mutual insurer with citizens as the obligatory insureds-owners. Tax payments are the "premiums," but they bear no relationship to insureds' risks.

The enormous size of governments' societal risk assessment and control responsibilities means that bureaucratic inefficiencies and failures are inevitable. The concept of government operating under a true integrated risk management approach remains even further removed than that which we observe for business.

## DISCUSSION QUESTIONS

1.  Assume that it has been determined that certain enhanced crumple zones on cars would reduce fatality rates by 1/100,000. Automobile manufacturers estimate that production costs would increase by $150 per car to include this new design:
    (a)  Analyze whether the marginal benefit is reasonable in light of the marginal cost.
    (b)  Might your answer in part (a) differ between rich and poor countries? Is this "fair?"
    (c)  Speculate about why the expected fatality rate reduction might not be realized even if the new crumple zones were added to cars.
2.  Critically analyze the following quote: "Attempts to place a monetary valuation on life are morally repugnant."
3.  Explain how taxes can be used to achieve a socially acceptable level of pollution. Could fines for pollution accomplish the same goal? Explain.
4.  Is pollution always a negative externality? Explain.
5.  Argue both the pros and cons of the following: "Government has no right to discourage smoking."

## NOTES

1.  This section draws in parts from Viscusi (1992).
2.  If we are called upon (or forced) to take on additional risk, the analysis shifts from WTP for added safety to that which we are willing to accept for taking on the additional risk. For small changes in risk, the willingness-to-pay and willingness-to-accept amounts should be approximately equal. As we learned in Chapter 2, however, in practice the willingness-to-accept amounts often are multiples of the WTP amounts.
3.  "Living Dangerously" (2004), p. 7, citing Viscusi.
4.  Of course, it is reasonable to believe that demand differs from society to society; thus, not all curves are the same. Thus, citizens of Switzerland, being

richer, might prefer even less pollution (and higher steel prices) than might citizens of Ghana. It is for this reason that attempts to establish international pollution standards are resisted by many developing countries. They believe that such standards would retard their economic development and, therefore, hinder growth in personal income. We know that better health is associated with higher income. We also know that higher incomes mean greater economic freedom. So, is it better to have less pollution but lower incomes or more pollution and higher incomes? Developing countries, too, must consider the opportunity costs (tradeoffs), just as richer countries must. But richer countries, such as the U.S. and Japan, can more easily afford the luxury of greater safety.

5. Of course, the same optimum societal result would occur by the farmer successfully asserting a viola-

tion of his property rights in court, winning a judgment equalling his economic loss.

6. But is it fair to the farmer? Perhaps not, but it is government's role to define and protect property rights. What if the farmer is a "squatter" and does not actually own the land?

7. This discussion draws from Segerson (1992).

8. We have another example here of how the framing of a risk issue affects perception. Politicians have resisted the notion of tradeable pollution rights but have found acceptable the equivalent notion of tradeable pollution reduction credits.

9. "Living Dangerously" (2004), p. 7.

10. Another problem with liability is that aggressive rules and court interpretations can cause some products to be removed from the market due to liability concerns rather than true economic cost concerns.

11. This section draws on Skipper and Skipper (1998).

# REFERENCES

Dake, K. (1992). "Myths of Nature: Culture and the Social Construction of Risk." *Journal of Social Issues*, 48 (4): 21–37.

Douglas, M. (1966). *Purity and Danger: Concepts of Pollution and Taboo*. London: Routledge and Kegan Paul.

Douglas, M. (1992). "A Credible Biosphere," in *Risk and Blame: Essays in Cultural Theory*. London: Routledge.

Hofstede, G. (1995). "Insurance as a Product of National Values." *The Geneva Papers on Risk and Insurance*, 20 (77): 423–429.

"Living Dangerously" (2004). *The Economist*, 370 (January 24): 3–5.

Rayner, S. (1992). "Cultural Theory and Risk Analysis," in S. Krimsky and D. Golding, eds., *Social Theories of Risk*. Westport, Connecticut: Praeger.

Renn, O. (1992). "Concepts of Risk: A Classification," in S. Krimsky and D. Golding, eds., *Social Theories of Risk*. Westport, Connecticut: Praeger.

Skipper, H.D. and Skipper, T. (1998). "The Sociocultural Environment for Risk and Insurance," Chapter 16, in H.D. Skipper, ed., *International Risk and Insurance: An Environmental-Managerial Approach*. Boston: Irwin/McGraw-Hill.

Segerson, K. (1992). "The Policy Response to Risk and Risk Perceptions," in D.W. Bromley and K. Segerson, eds., *The Social Response to Environmental Risk*. Boston: Kluwer Academic Publishers.

Slovic, P. (1992). "Perceptions of Risk: Reflections on the Psychometric Paradigm," in S. Krimsky and D. Golding, eds., *Social Theories of Risk*. Westport, Connecticut: Praeger.

Swaney, J.A. (1997). "The Basic Economics of Risk Analysis," in V. Molak, ed., *Fundamentals of Risk Analysis and Risk Management*. Boca Raton: Lewis Publishers.

Thompson, M. (1983). "A Cultural Basis for Comparison" in H. Kunreuther and J. Linnerooth, eds., *Risk Analysis and Decision Process: The Siting of Liquefied Energy Gas Facilities in Four Countries*. Berlin: Springer-Verlag.

Viscusi, W.K. (1992). *Fatal Tradeoffs: Public and Private Responsibilities for Risk*. New York: Oxford University Press.

Wildavsky, A. and Dake, K. (1990). "Theories of Risk Perception: Who Fears What and Why?" *Daidalus*, 229 (4): 41–60.

# Chapter 5

# Catastrophe Risk Assessment: Natural Hazards

## INTRODUCTION

Hurricane Katrina's 2005 devastation of the U.S. city of New Orleans – not to mention the catastrophic floods in Bangladesh and earthquakes along the Pacific Rim during the year violently reminded us that the world is a risky place. Not that we needed reminding: humans worldwide already had an increased feeling of peril thanks to increasing numbers of natural and human-made catastrophes besieging us every year. Despite a two-thirds increase in life expectancy during the previous century, unparallel health and healthcare for most citizens, decreasing rates of industrial accidents, lower transportation accident rates and a host of other data indicating enhanced safety, the perception is that life is getting riskier. Portions of this perception match objective reality – the opportunity for major catastrophes has grown with increasing industrial sophistication, the advent of genetic and other new technologies, growing coastal populations, an increasingly networked society, and greater political and social unrest. At the same time, our perceptions are selective, if not distorted, as we explored in the preceding chapter. The result is that society fails to utilize its limited risk control resources to maximum effectiveness.

This chapter examines some of the natural factors that have led to concern about catastrophes attendant to them and the need for governments' responses to them. The next chapter examines some of the human-made hazards that hold catastrophic potential. All such exposures have the potential for imposing substantial negative externalities on society. In an interconnected, globalized world, catastrophic events increasingly respect no national boundaries and should not be considered solely matters of national sovereignty.

## CATASTROPHIC EVENTS: DEFINITION AND TRENDS

No universal definition of a catastrophic event exists. The U.S.-based Insurance Information Institute defines catastrophe as any event causing US$25 million or more in insured losses. At least one U.S. state government classifies an event as catastrophic when resultant damage exceeds US$25 million. Swiss Re classifies events as catastrophic using a three-prong approach that considers the amount of insured losses, total damage and human casualties. The values are changed each year. For its 2006 study, it classified a loss as catastrophic if it reached or exceeded any one of the following values:

|  |  | *Amount* |
| --- | --- | --- |
| Insured losses | Shipping | US$15.6 million |
|  | Aviation | US$31.2 million |
|  | Other losses | US$38.7 million |
| *or* total damage |  | US$77.5 million |
| *or* casualties | Death or missing | 20 |
|  | Injured | 50 |
|  | Homeless | 2,000 |

Another major reinsurance, Munich Re, classifies all natural events by the degree of severity with class 3–6 events being catastrophic as defined using minimum numbers of fatalities and value of property damage. Munich Re's most recent classification is as follows:

| Class | Descriptions | Overall Losses in U.S. dollars | | |
| --- | --- | --- | --- | --- |
|  |  | *2000–2005* | *1990s* | *1980s* |
| 0 Natural event | No property damage (e.g., forest fire with no damage to buildings) | | | |
| 1 Small-scale loss event | 1–9 fatalities and/or hardly any damage | | | |
| 2 Moderate loss event | 10–19 fatalities and/or damage to buildings and other property | | | |
| 3 Severe catastrophe | 20+ fatalities | >50 million | >40 million | >25 million |
| 4 Major catastrophe | 100+ fatalities | > 200 million | > 160 million | > 85 million |
| 5 Devastating catastrophe | 500+ fatalities | > 500 million | > 400 million | > 275 million |
| 6 Great natural catastrophe | Thousands of fatalities, economy severely affected, extreme insured losses | | | |

The number of natural and human-made catastrophes has risen continuously, as Figure 5.1 illustrates. Swiss Re recorded a total of 397 catastrophes in 2005 comprised of 149 natural and 248 human-made disasters. These numbers represent a significant increase from the 2004 result.

The severity of property damage associated with catastrophic loss events has displayed dramatic increases recently. Most of the increase and volatility is attributable to what are termed great natural catastrophes with an exception of the losses resulting from the September 11, 2001 terrorist acts. **Great natural disasters**, as defined by the UN (and

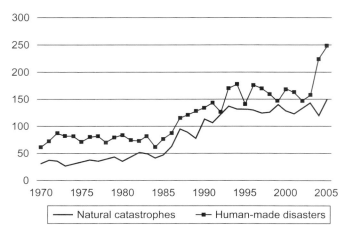

**Figure 5.1**    Frequency of Catastrophes: 1970–2005. *Source*: Swiss Re, Sigma No. 2/2006

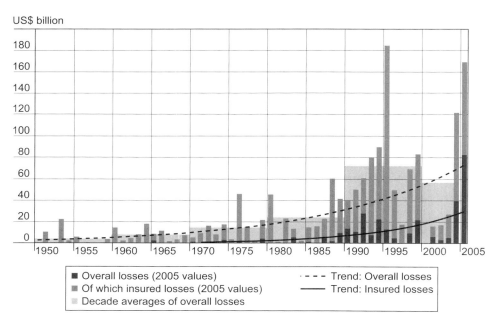

**Figure 5.2**    Overall and Insured Losses: 1950–2005 (Adjusted to Present Values). *Source*: Munich Re (2006)

Munich Re), are catastrophes of such magnitude that the affected region's capabilities to respond effectively are clearly overstretched and supra-regional or international assistance is required. In general, this means that fatalities number in the thousands, hundreds of thousands of people are made homeless, or economic losses reach exceptional orders of magnitude – depending on the economic circumstances of the countries concerned.

Figure 5.2 illustrates this trend.[1] It shows yearly economic and insured losses from great natural catastrophes, along with trend lines for each. Note that both the number and magnitude of great natural catastrophes have increased. While many scientists believe that global warming contributes to this trend, the primary reason is the increasing concentration of people and property in areas most exposed to such events.

The increasing concentration of people in hazardous areas and the concurrent increase in the amount and value of property in those areas are caused by several factors. First, *population increases* in many countries mean that people often have little choice but to settle in high-hazard areas. As population density increases, more and more land areas must be used. Consider the developing world's many mega-cities wherein people build houses and shanties on steep slopes, close to dangerous manufacturing or mining operations, or on waste dumps prone to landslides and susceptible to massive loss of life from earthquakes.

Second, *economic reasons* explain much of the concentration trend. Because of economies of scale or scope, many businesses marshal factors of production in close proximity. Production and distribution often take on a mega-scale: expensive power plants, expansive distribution centers, giant oil tankers and jumbo jets. All of these may make economic sense, but they create enormous target risks in the physical environment.

Additionally, people are drawn to areas that hold potential for greater economic prosperity, such as cities. Already, more than 40 percent of the world's population lives in large cities, twice the proportion of 40 years earlier. The proportion is projected to increase to 60 percent in another 40 years. The adverse effects of natural (and human-made) disasters in resulting mega-cities are multiplied. Not only is the potential for extensive loss of life and property destruction enormous, but also the thousands or even millions of displaced citizens becoming refugees exacerbate an already awful situation.

Third, *personal reasons* explain this concentration trend. People want to live in pleasant locations, particularly when they retire or become more affluent and can afford second homes. Coastal areas continue to experience substantial population gains, with the need for additional and more expensive housing, more extensive infrastructure and attendant commerce to support the population base. This means that other citizens are drawn there for economic reasons.

For example, more than one-third of the U.S. population of 300 million lives in the 330 counties (or equivalent) bordering the Atlantic and Pacific Oceans, the Gulf of Mexico and the Great Lakes. This number represents a 13.3 percent increase from 1990. Projections are for increases of another 11 percent in only 6 years. Population density in these areas is triple the density of non-coastal counties, and the ratio is growing.

This increasing concentration not only creates greater exposures to national catastrophes, it also endangers coastal ecosystems, resulting in shrinking habitats, greater pesticide and fertilizer runoffs, and greater pollution from industrial, commercial and personal activities. Developed countries can afford to deal effectively with these problems if the political will exists to do so. Developing countries face a much more daunting challenge.

## TYPES OF NATURAL DISASTERS

Our understanding of the causes and effects of natural catastrophes has improved measurably over the past two decades. This knowledge has allowed improved maps of natural hazards, building codes, construction standards and emergency preparedness. Additionally, scientists continue to refine mathematical models that attempt both to simulate and predict frequency and severity of natural catastrophes, but with only limited success.[2]

Many types of natural disasters exist. Figure 5.3 is a reproduction of a global map of natural hazards that highlights regions susceptible to various natural disasters. We examine four as holding the greatest routine catastrophic potential: earthquakes, storms, volcanic activity and floods.

## Earthquakes

Earthquakes are among nature's most destructive forces. Either directly or indirectly, they have accounted for the greatest loss of life over recorded history.

### Nature and locations

Earthquakes are caused by friction between moving tectonic plates. Earthquakes originate at fairly well-defined **faults**, which are plate boundaries, making some geographic locations more likely to experience adverse effects from these periodic events. Unfortunately, the boundaries between continental and oceanic plates are often close to coastlines, resulting in coastal areas being susceptible to earthquakes as well as storm and flood damage.

The Pacific Rim is especially prone to earthquake activity due to the thinner Pacific plate being forced beneath the thicker continental land mass. This so-called "Ring of Fire," shown in Figure 5.4, contains a 40,000-kilometer band of seismic activity that extends along the west coast of South and North America, across Alaska and the Aleutians, Japan, and China, then to the Philippines, Indonesia, the South Pacific islands and New Zealand. It extends separately through northern India, Iran and much of southern Europe. The potential damage from earthquakes has been growing because of increased urban development and aging buildings more vulnerable to damage.

Over the centuries, earthquakes in this ring have claimed millions of lives. The most recent devastating earthquake occurred in October 2005 in Kashmir, in Pakistan. The tremors lasted 50 seconds but caused the razing of entire towns and villages. A generation of young people was almost completely wiped out when hundreds of schools collapsed, killing thousands. Construction methods ill suited for earthquakes resulted in some 200,000 houses being destroyed, mostly when their walls collapsed allowing the heavy roofs to crush occupants.[3] With 88,000 fatalities, approximately 200,000 injured and more than 3 million homeless, the Kashmir quake ranks second only to the December 2004 tsunami (see below) as the worst natural catastrophe of the past decade.

Other major disasters created by earthquakes include the 1976 Tangshan earthquake that hit 160 kilometers east of Beijing, taking 240,000 lives and destroying 180,000 buildings. The previous major disaster in the ring took place in 1923 in Tokyo, leaving 142,000 dead. The 1995 Kobe earthquake in Japan, lasting only 14 seconds, claimed 5,000 lives and caused more than US$100 billion in economic loss. A 2003 Iranian earthquake leveled the city of Bam, with 41,000 lives lost. For the U.S., some 84 percent of annual economic loss from earthquakes occurs in California along the Ring of Fire.

### Frequency and severity

Earthquake frequency has so far proved impossible to predict, in spite of an enormous amount of research. The severity of an earthquake relates to the amount of seismic energy released at the earthquake's hypocenter, the area of the fault where the sudden rupture takes place. The magnitude is commonly measured using the open-ended **Richter scale**,

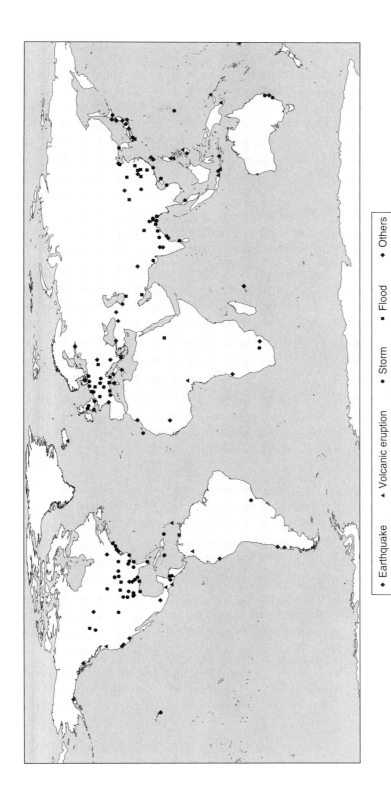

**Figure 5.3** World Map of Natural Hazards. *Source*: World of Natural Hazards (2000). © Munich Re

♦ Earthquake    ▲ Volcanic eruption    ● Storm    ■ Flood    ♦ Others

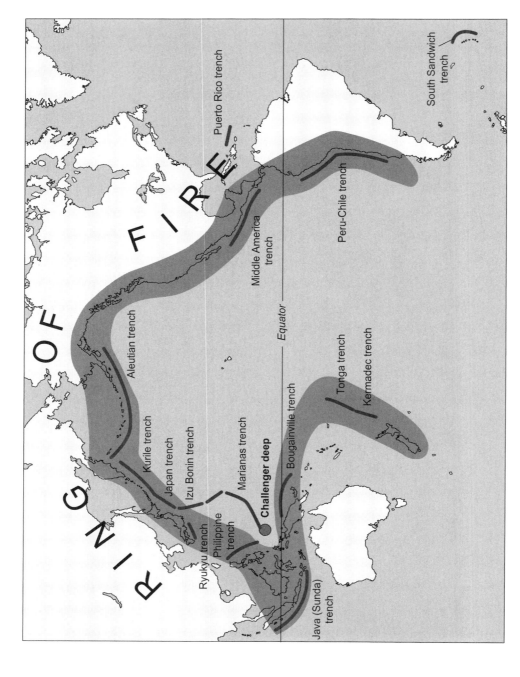

**Figure 5.4** Ring of Fire. *Source:* U.S. Geological Survey (www.usgs.gov, 2004)

a logarithmic scale starting at 0 but with no theoretical upper limit. Each whole number increase in magnitude represents a 10-fold increase in energy.[4] Earthquakes of magnitude 7.0 and higher are considered to be "major." The most severe earthquake in recorded history occurred in Chile in 1960 and registered 9.5.

The extent of destruction following an earthquake depends on much more than its severity alone. The quality of construction, nature of the soil, and the proximity of significant concentrations of people and property to major earthquake faults all influence results. Indeed, some alarming loss estimates result from assuming worst-case earthquake scenarios, especially in high-density areas such as Japan and California.

### Tsunamis and earthquakes

**Tsunamis** are large, rapidly moving ocean waves produced by the displacement of water caused by earthquakes, landslides, volcanic eruptions or even a sufficiently large meteorite impact. As most tsunamis are caused by underwater earthquakes, we discuss them in this section.

Tsunamis are sometimes incorrectly referred to as tidal waves, but they have no relation to tides. The word is Japanese and means "harbor wave" because of the devastating effects these waves have had on low-lying Japanese coastal communities. A tsunami is actually a series of waves that can travel at speeds averaging 725 (and up to 1,000) kilometers per hour in the open ocean.

In the morning of December 26, 2004, the most devastating tsunami in recorded history and one of history's most deadly of all catastrophes was created by an earthquake centered in the Indian Ocean, west of the Indonesian island of Sumatra, and within the Ring of Fire. At 9.0, the earthquake was the third most severe ever recorded and caused the loss of 255,000 lives.[5] The affected area was huge, extending thousands of kilometers – from Thailand and Malaysia in the east through Sri Lanka, India and the Maldives and as far as Kenya and Somalia in the west. Even Somalia, some 5,000 kilometers from the epicenter, suffered 300 fatalities. Hundreds of villages and towns throughout the region were obliterated.

The earthquake created a 3–4 meter upward movement of the ocean floor over a 1,000 kilometers distance consequently lifting the overlying water column. The size of a tsunami depends on the strength of the earthquake, the height of the water column above the epicenter, and the speed and direction of the crust rupture. In this case, the tsunami was probably made up of three or four high waves approximately 200 kilometers long, each a little more than a meter in height on the open sea. Tsunami waves are quite different from all other waves. They are much longer and stretch along the entire water column. They travel very fast without losing much energy.

Tsunamis are hardly perceptible on the open sea and pose no danger there. It is only when they slow down in shallow water that they become dangerous. At this point, they "run up;" that is, they become shorter and slower and drop to a speed of 30 kilometers per hour at a water depth of 10 meters, with their heights increasing accordingly. Suddenly a wall of water 5–10 meters high and in extreme cases, higher, towers up near the shoreline. Unlike waves that are generated by storms, the height of the original wave is not the most important factor as far as its destructive power is concerned; this is determined by the flow velocity, the topography of the coast, and direction the tsunami takes and its path.

One particularly malicious feature of tsunamis is that the sea recedes before the first wave lands. This unusual phenomenon makes the uninformed curious, often with their walking out onto the newly created, wider beach, only to be swept away by the oncoming massive wave.

INSIGHT 5.1: THE FUTURE CANARY ISLANDS
TSUNAMI

One group of scientists believes that conditions are ideal for a tsunami-producing landslide on the island of La Palma in the Canaries. The western flank of the island's active volcano has the potential to give way in a future eruption. If it did, a huge mass of rock weighing 500 billion tons would fall into the Atlantic Ocean. Experts in Switzerland have simulated the potential effects of such a collapse. The resulting tsunami would cause massive destruction along the coasts of the U.S., the U.K., and many African countries, within a matter of hours. Their model shows that it could generate a wave capable of engulfing every port on the east coast of the U.S., which they believe may have happened during a similar tsunami 120,000 years ago.
*Source*: www.pbs.org/wgbh/nova/tsunami/once-nf.html

With warning systems in place in the Pacific Ocean, bordering countries can have from as little as 15 minutes to several hours' advance warning of the onslaught of a tsunami. The Indian Ocean had no such system, nor do the other susceptible regions worldwide. While complaining about complacency, experts point out that tsunamis more destructive than the Sumatra tsunami are feasible in parts of the world that may think themselves relatively immune (see Insight 5.1).

## Storms

The storm risk consists of a variety of potentially catastrophic events that collectively have represented the most significant of all the natural hazards.[6] Scientists define storms by wind speed and locations. The **Beaufort scale**, shown in Table 5.1, is used to measure the velocity of a storm's wind speed.

The generic term for low-pressure systems that usually form in the tropics is a **tropical cyclone**. They are accompanied by powerful thunderstorms. Once a tropical cyclone achieves sustained winds speed of at least 39 miles per hour (Beaufort 8 level), it becomes a **tropical storm** and receives a name. Once a tropical cyclone's winds exceed the Beaufort 11 level, it is designated a **hurricane** if it originates in the North Atlantic Ocean, the Northeast Pacific Ocean east of the dateline, or the South Pacific Ocean east of 169E. This same severe tropical cyclone originating in other regions carries the following names:

- **typhoon** in the Northwest Pacific Ocean west of the dateline;
- **severe tropical cyclone** in the Southwest Pacific Ocean west of 160E or Southeast Indian Ocean east of 90E;
- **severe cyclonic storm** in the North Indian Ocean;
- **tropical cyclone** in the Southwest Indian Ocean.

Tropical cyclones are formed in the atmosphere over warm ocean areas, in which wind blows in a large spiral around a relatively calm center or "eye." Circulation is counterclockwise in the Northern Hemisphere and clockwise in the Southern Hemisphere. Tropical cyclones

**Table 5.1**    The Beaufort Scale of Wind Velocity

| Number | Descriptive Term | Wind Speed (Miles per Hour) |
|---|---|---|
| 0 | Calm | 0–1 |
| 1 | Light air | 1–3 |
| 2 | Light breeze | 4–7 |
| 3 | Gentle breeze | 8–12 |
| 4 | Moderate breeze | 13–18 |
| 5 | Fresh breeze | 19–24 |
| 6 | Strong breeze | 25–31 |
| 7 | Weak gale | 32–38 |
| 8 | Gale | 39–46 |
| 9 | Strong gale | 47–54 |
| 10 | Storm | 55–63 |
| 11 | Violent storm | 64–72 |
| 12 | Hurricane | 73+ |

**Table 5.2**    Saffir–Simpson Scale

| Category | Wind Speed (per Hour) | | Storm Surge Height | |
|---|---|---|---|---|
| | (Miles) | (Kilometers) | (Feet) | (Meters) |
| 1 | 74–95 | 119–153 | 3–5 | 1.0–1.7 |
| 2 | 96–110 | 154–177 | 6–8 | 1.8–2.6 |
| 3 | 111–130 | 178–209 | 9–12 | 2.7–3.8 |
| 4 | 131–155 | 210–249 | 13–18 | 3.9–5.5 |
| 5 | >155 | >250 | >18 | >5.6 |

*Source*: Swiss Re, *Sigma* No. 1/2005, and others.

are further rated using the **Saffir–Simpson scale**, shown in Table 5.2 along with the approximate storm surge. This scale ranges from categories 1 (weakest) to 5 (strongest), which corresponds with potential property damage and flooding expected along the coast. Categories 3–5 are considered "major hurricanes."

Tropical storms and cyclones occur wherever conditions are favorable, in whatever large body of water. The earth has averaged 91.1 such cyclones per year over the period 1945–2005. Figure 5.5 gives the breakdown of these occurrences by major region over this period. The most active region has been the Western Pacific Basin, with an average of 28.1 per year. The Eastern Pacific area and the Australian region have averaged 13.8 and 12.3 per year, followed by the Atlantic Basin's annual average of 10.6.

### The 2005 hurricane season

With insured losses of US$30 billion from Atlantic tropical cyclones, the 2004 hurricane season was considered exceptional.[7] This new record did not last long, being more than doubled to US$80 billion in 2005. The 2005 hurricane season witnessed a list of unusual

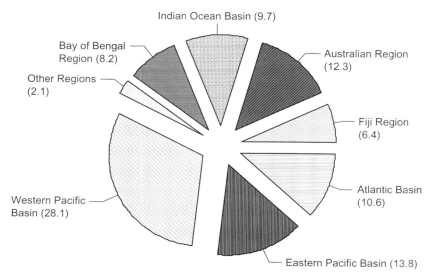

**Figure 5.5**    Average Number of Tropical Storms and Hurricanes per Year by Region. *Source*: Reprinted with permission by Hurricane Alley

events, many of which have not been observed since weather recordings in the Atlantic began on a systematic basis in 1851.[8] The events can be summarized as follows:

- *A highly active start to the season*: The year 2005 witnessed seven tropical storms in June and July versus a maximum of five such storms in the past during these months (1887, 1933, 1936, 1959, 1966, 1995 and 1997).

- *Peak intensity values*: Three of the 10 strongest hurricanes ever recorded occurred in 2005.

- *Lowest central pressure ever recorded*: The 2005 season recorded the lowest central pressure in the Atlantic (Hurricane Wilma) and, hence, probably the highest ever wind speeds.

- *Record number of named tropical cyclones*: The 27 named tropical cyclones in 2005 (15 of which reached hurricane force) broke all past records: 21 tropical storms in 1933 and 12 hurricanes in 1969. As a result, the list of 21 names chosen by the World Meteorological Organization (WMO) was not long enough for the first time ever. The last six cyclones were, therefore, named after the first six letters in the Greek alphabet: Alpha, Beta, Gamma, Delta, Epsilon and Zeta.

- *New areas affected – Europe and Africa*: At the beginning of October, Hurricane Vince formed near the island of Madeira, to become the most easterly and northerly tropical cyclone ever to occur in the Atlantic. At the end of November, Tropical Storm Delta passed over the Canary Islands and continued toward the Moroccan coast. It was the first tropical cyclone ever in this region.

### Hurricane Katrina

During this season, Hurricane Katrina laid waste to much of the Louisiana and Mississippi Gulfcoasts of the U.S., flooding the city of New Orleans (see Insight 5.2). The storm

## INSIGHT 5.2: HURRICANE KATRINA AND A FAILURE OF GOVERNMENT

It started as a tropical depression on August 23, 2005, some 200 miles southeast of Nassau. Its birth and growth were monitored closely by the U.S. National Weather Service (NWS), which issued advisories at regular intervals. Some six days later, it roared onto the southeast corner of Louisiana, almost exactly where the NWS had predicted more than a day earlier. It would prove to be both the most costly disaster in U.S. history and perhaps the most ineptly ever handled by government officials whose jobs were to minimize death and destruction.

*The storm and the warnings*: Two days after its formation, a weak Hurricane Katrina (category 1) hit southern Florida, to emerge into the eastern Gulf of Mexico on August 26. At 10:00 on August 27, the U.S. National Hurricane Center (NHC) issued a hurricane watch for southeastern Louisiana, including New Orleans, which was extended to Mississippi and Alabama later that afternoon. That evening, some 35 hours before landfall, the director of the NHC telephoned to officials in Louisiana, Mississippi and Alabama, including the mayor of New Orleans, to inform them of the storm's intensity and its potential to be devastating and catastrophic.

Upon passing over a deep layer of 90°F water (which was some 2–5°F warmer than the long-term average), Katrina strengthened significantly, reaching category 5 intensity on August 28, with maximum sustained winds of 175 miles per hour. The NWS advisory that morning characterized Katrina as a "potentially catastrophic" storm, predicting an impact on Louisiana resulting in "human suffering incredible by modern standards," with "most of the area . . . uninhabitable for weeks . . . perhaps longer." The NWS field office in New Orleans was more pointed. Its morning bulletin predicted catastrophic damage to New Orleans, including partial destruction of one-half of the well-constructed houses in the city; severe damage to most industrial buildings rendering them inoperable; the creation of a huge debris field of trees, telephone poles, cars and collapsed buildings; and a lack of clean water. Unfortunately, the NWS and NHC proved remarkably accurate in capturing Katrina's eventual wrath and destruction.

*The impact*: With intense winds and a massive storm surge, the effect of Hurricane Katrina on southeast Louisiana was indeed catastrophic. After 11:00 on August 29, several sections of the levee system in New Orleans were breached, and 80 percent of the city was under water at peak flooding, which in some places was 20-feet deep, requiring emergency evacuation of tens of thousands of residents who had not left prior to the storm. They were lifted off roofs by helicopters or carried to safety in boats. Indeed, stranded survivors dotted the tops of houses citywide. Many others were trapped inside attics, unable to escape. Some chopped their way to their roofs with hatchets and sledgehammers which residents had been urged to keep in their attics in case of such events.

Survivors were taken to the Superdome, the Convention Center, a piece of high ground known as the Cloverleaf and other dry spots in the city. At these locations, they were subjected to unbearable conditions: limited light, air and sewage facilities in the Superdome; the blistering heat of the sun; and in many cases, limited food and water. They feared for their safety and survival – and the survival of their city. Seemingly no one was in charge. Outside government help would take days to arrive and, interestingly, the first to arrive was from Canada (a specialized urban search and rescue team from Vancouver). Many big businesses were the main sources of local help (much of it provided for free), with many stores being back in operation days before the Red Cross or FEMA the U.S. Federal Emergency Management Agency arrived, including Home Depot (23 of its 33 stores in Katrina's impact zone re-opened the next day), Wal-Mart (113 of its 126 stores in the impact zone were re-opened within a bit more than two weeks), and FedEx (five days after impact, brought in 125 desperately needed walkie-talkies for rescuers) (*Fortune*, 2005, pp. 50–84).

From the marshes of Louisiana's Plaquemines Parish to the urban center of New Orleans to the coastal communities of Mississippi and Alabama, Katrina cut an enormous swath of physical destruction, environmental devastation, and human suffering. At least 1,100 Louisianans and 200 Mississippians died as a result of Katrina.

Mississippi experienced a different storm than Louisiana – in essence, a massive, blender-like storm surge versus the New Orleans flooding caused by breached and overtopped levees. By the end of the day on August 29, due largely to a storm surge that reached 34 feet in the western parts of the state – and extended inland as far as 10 miles – more than one-half of Mississippi was without power and had suffered serious wind and water damage. In addition to the surge, high winds and tornadoes left thousands of homes damaged and destroyed, and as many as 66,000 Mississippians were displaced from their homes.

The economic, environmental and political ramifications of Katrina have been widespread and could in some respects be long-lasting due to effects on large population and tourism centers, the oil and gas industry, and transportation. The hurricane severely damaged or destroyed workplaces in New Orleans and other heavily populated areas of the northern Gulf coast, resulting in thousands of lost jobs and millions of dollars in lost tax revenues for the affected communities. The proximate cause of these problems was the hurricane, but the ultimate failure was that of government, which was continuing as this book was going to press (*Fortune*, 2006).

*Sources*: www.nhc.noaa.gov/ and *Failure of Initiative* (2006).

---

highlighted not just the great forces of nature but also the incredible failure of government. Interestingly, the risk to the New Orleans area from hurricanes had been widely known for decades. Much of the area is below sea level and remained dry only because of an elaborate, ancient pumping system and levees that were designed and built decades earlier. It was widely known that these levees were not designed to withstand severe hurricanes and their strong storm surges. As was said: that New Orleans would someday be inundated was a question of "when" not "if. "[9] Nevertheless, comparatively little had been done to update the system over many years, with requests for adequate funding either not forthcoming or diverted for other uses.

## *Has something fundamental changed?*

We know that hurricane frequency and intensity in the North Atlantic have increased substantially during the preceding 10 years in comparison to the period 1900–2005. Climatologists believe that some of the increase is due to a natural climate cycle – called the **Atlantic multidecadal oscillation** (AMO) – that occurs in this region every 60–80 years. The latest warm portion of this cycle is believed to have begun in 1995. Warm cycles last up to 30 years. Thus, we could witness a higher than average number of hurricanes for some years.[10]

At the same time, intensity has increased as well. Category 4 and 5 hurricanes accounted for 21 and 10 percent, respectively, of all hurricanes since 1995, compared with 14 and 6 percent, respectively, since 1900. Weaker hurricanes (categories 1 and 2) have been less frequent in the current phase.

While researchers agree that warming waters fuel hurricane intensity, there has been less agreement on as to whether the Atlantic waters have heated up because of the AMO or because of global warming. Increasingly, evidence supports the view that a combination of the natural cycle and global warming explains the increase in hurricane activity. For example, one study found that during much of the 2005 hurricane season, sea-surface temperatures across the tropical Atlantic where many Atlantic hurricanes originate were a record 1.7°F above the 1901–1970 average.[11] By analyzing worldwide data on sea-surface temperatures since the early 20th century, researchers were able to calculate the causes of the increased temperatures in the tropical North Atlantic. Their conclusion was that global warming explained about one-half (0.8°F) of this rise. After effects from the 2004 to 2005, El Nino accounted for another 0.4°F and the AMO explained less than 0.2°F of the rise. The remainder was due to year-to-year variability in temperatures.

That the number of strong hurricanes increased from 2.6 to 4.1 per year from the previous warm phase to the current warm phase is consistent with this study's findings. Additionally, the change in the level of activity also influences the number of landfalls and, hence, the amount of damage and loss of life. In the case of major hurricanes, the annual average number of landfalls in the U.S. has increased by about 230 percent – from 0.3 to 1.0, compared with the last cold phase (approximately 1971–1994) – and by about 70 percent – from 0.6 to 1.0, compared with the last warm phase (approximately 1926–1970).

Of course, global warming does not guarantee that each year will set records for hurricanes. However, long-term ocean warming is expected to raise the baseline of hurricane activity.[12]

## Floods

**Flood** refers to partial or complete inundation of a normally dry land area caused by an overflow of tidal, river, or lake water or after a heavy rain. In the field of risk management and insurance, the likelihood of flooding in a given area often is given by the estimate of how often the area floods. For example, a **100-year flood** means that the area is expected to flood, on average, every 100 years. Thus, the likelihood of flooding in any 1 year is 1 percent.

Flood damage can result from a single event, such as a hurricane or thunderstorm. However, floods also occur due to repeated exposure to rainfall. Property located near major bodies of water is most susceptible to flood loss. However, property located elsewhere is not immune. For example, in 1995, Hurricane Opal stagnated over a section of the U.S. land for almost 2 weeks. The long duration of steady rain caused significant flooding in areas not considered to be flood prone.

## Volcanism

The term **volcano** refers both to the vents in the earth's crust through which gases, molten rock or lava, and solid fragments are discharged and to the conical shaped mountains or hills produced by the lava and other erupted material around the vent.[13] **Lava** refers to molten material that has erupted onto the surface, while **magma** is molten material that can erupt from volcanic activity. Volcanoes may be either dormant (having no activity), active (currently erupting) or extinct (no longer active at all). Most volcanoes are located along the boundaries of more than a dozen of the earth's enormous 80-kilometer deep plates, and erupt when they collide or spread apart such that magma pushes upward. Thus, the Ring of Fire is home to dozens of volcanoes, but volcanic eruptions also occur in other areas known as hotspots.

### Volcanic hazard assessment

Volcanic eruptions are one of earth's most dramatic and violent agents of change. Not only can powerful explosive eruptions drastically alter land and water for tens of kilometers around a volcano, but tiny liquid droplets of sulfuric acid erupted into the stratosphere can also change our planet's climate temporarily. Eruptions often force people living near volcanoes to abandon their land and homes, sometimes forever. Those living farther away are likely to avoid complete destruction, but their cities and towns, crops, industrial plants, transportation systems and electrical grids can still be damaged by tephra (solid matter ejected into the air), lahar (debris flows), and flooding.

Volcanic activity since 1700 AD has killed more than 260,000 people, destroyed entire cities and forests, and severely disrupted local economies for months to years. Even with our improved ability to identify hazardous areas and warn of impending eruptions, increasing numbers of people face certain danger. An estimated 500 million of the world's inhabitants are at risk from volcanoes.

The record of past eruptions, interpreted from geological mapping and dating of a volcano's deposits, provides the only practical guide to most likely future hazards and the frequency of their recurrence. Hazard-zone maps and associated analyses provide an essential basis for design of monitoring networks, long-term eruption forecasts, land-use planning and short-term emergency plans. During an eruption, real-time monitoring observations are combined with analysis of the volcano's past activity to evaluate the most likely hazards on an hour-to-hour basis during the course of the eruption.

### Climate change and volcanism

Mighty volcanic eruptions can severely interfere with the global climate and influence it for many years.[14] This was illustrated very strikingly by the eruption of Mt. Tambora in Indonesia on April 11, 1815. In this mammoth event, a total of 50 cubic kilometers of tephra and ash particles were blown into the atmosphere within a few days. The effects were global, with the year 1816 going down in history as the year without a summer. Mean temperatures for that year in Europe and eastern parts of the U.S. were much lower than in any of the previous 200 years. These low temperatures were accompanied by excessive rainfall in Europe and unusually dry weather in New England, leading to substantial crop failures and famine. The monsoon cycle in India was severely disrupted, which had negative repercussions on farming and the food situation.

The effects on the global climate generated by even a gigantic eruption like that of Mt. Tambora last only for a few years. The temperature fluctuation caused by eruptions of such dimensions barely exceeds 1°C. This transient phenomenon is not generally regarded as climate change, but much larger eruptions have occurred in the geological past. The most dramatic of these must have been the eruption of Mt. Toba on Sumatra (Indonesia) about 73,500 years ago. Estimates of the ejecta volume range from 2,000 to 6,000 cubic kilometers, compared to the 50 cubic kilometers by Tambora. The Toba eruption produced a caldera – a collapsed crater – measuring 100 by 30 kilometers, which today is known as Lake Toba. The volume ejected would have been sufficient to cover the whole of India with a layer of ash 1 meter thick.

With the aid of ice cores, it is possible to reconstruct the amount of ejected gases and the length of time they remained in the atmosphere. According to these investigations, such large amounts of sulfur gases were ejected that up to 5 billion tons of sulfuric acid aerosols were formed. Compare this with the "mere" 150 million tons ejected by Mt. Tambora. At least 90 percent of the sun's radiation was blocked out, producing an estimated drop in the mean global temperature of between 5°C and 6°C – as much as 15°C in tropical latitudes – which lasted for at least 6 years. Such a drop in temperature would have resulted in ice age conditions, and must have had a grave impact on the human population of the time by reducing photosynthesis and the availability of food.

With the aid of DNA analyses, evolution research has shown that humanity went through a critical phase at this time, at the end of which only a few thousand humans are thought to have survived. Although there is no conclusive proof, there seems to be a connection between this evolution crisis and the Toba eruption.

## CONCLUSION

We have explored some of the natural factors that seem to hold among the greatest potential for doing extensive harm. Our discussion is incomplete, for example, omitting altogether threats that many experts say receive far too little attention yet are capable of massive and even worldwide destruction. Insight 5.3 offers an overview of such "Gee Gees."

While smart policymakers will enlist the market's powerful assistance when it makes sense, ultimately societal risk management is the responsibility of national governments and the intergovernmental organizations to which these governments cede responsibility and authority. Natural catastrophes cannot be prevented, so governmental action centers on better forecasting and loss mitigation. Government often has a role also in loss financing.

## DISCUSSION QUESTIONS

1. Is your country of birth or residence immune from natural catastrophe? If not, find the records of recent natural events that caused human casualty, property damage or both. Do they meet the definition of catastrophe by an international organization or insurer?
2. Discuss why tsunamis are closely related to earthquakes.
3. What are the possible factors affecting the rise of natural catastrophes in modern society? Describe the factors also reflecting the environments in the region with which you are familiar (e.g., the Caribbean, northern European or South Pacific).

INSIGHT 5.3: MANKIND'S GREATEST THREATS: "GEE GEES"

A news item by the BBC noted that scientists claim that giant tsunamis, super volcanoes and earthquakes could pose enormous threats to societies. Global Geophysical Events or "Gee Gees" are not being taken seriously enough, it noted, with the result that monitoring and strategic actions are insufficient.

While governments worldwide are ratcheting up security against terrorism, the question arises as to whether we are simultaneously affording too little attention to even graver risks: giant walls of water that can devastate coastal cities, volcanoes so big that their ashes crush houses 932 miles away, giant earthquakes, and asteroid impacts. These are very rare events and, if we are lucky, nothing like them will happen in our lifetimes, but they could.

Volcanoes and earthquakes are relatively common occurrences, but Gee Gees are altogether on an different scale. As discussed in this chapter, a "super volcano" erupted in 1815, when Mt. Tambora in Indonesia exploded violently, in the largest eruption in recorded history, killing 92,000. Yet, far larger earthquakes have occurred, with far more severe consequences – and they will occur again.

Governments are not entirely ignoring the threat of Gee Gees. The greatest danger to humanity comes from asteroids, potentially the most deadly forms of the so-called near earth objects (NEOs). The U.S. and European space agencies are planning missions to test how the course of asteroids and comets can be altered, but it will be many years before humankind will have any such ability. According to some scientists, the threat of cosmic mega disasters could be essentially abolished within 30 years. In 1995, scientists knew of about 300 large NEOs. Today, about 3,000 have been identified, and within 20 years, it is said that we could be aware of 90 percent of all NEOs 1 kilometer or larger in size – so-called "earth killers". Other scientists are not so confident, guessing that large NEOs pass close to earth, undetected, every year. They also observe that NEOs smaller than 1 kilometer can inflict catastrophic damage.

We know that NEOs, usually in the form of meteorites, regularly hit the earth, with the 20th century witnessing them at the rate of about one per year. The largest, estimated to have been 60 meters in diameter, crashed in Siberia on June 30, 1908, causing massive damage and leveling forests for hundreds of miles. Had it hit a city, the effects would have been devastating. Fortunately, comparatively few humans lived there. A large NEO came within about 300,000 miles of the earth on March 8, 2002. As if to confirm the skepticism of some scientists, this asteroid was not detected until 4 days *after* it had passed the earth.

*Source*: news.bbc.co.uk/2/hi/science/nature/3549812.stm and www.space.com/scienceastronomy/solarsystem/asteroid_fears_020326-1.html

4.  Investigate the process of recovery from Hurricane Katrina (U.S.), the 2004 tsunami (Indian Ocean), or any major natural catastrophe in recent years. Examine the scale, scope and speed of the process to estimate how long it will take to complete it.

# NOTES

1. Munich Re (2005), p. 13.
2. This section draws in part from Feldhaus (1998).
3. The fracture was caused by the Indian subcontinent drifting northward and colliding with Eurasia and is frequently the location of extreme earthquakes. The last major quake in this region was in 1555. Since then, an enormous amount of seismic energy has built up, of which no more than 10–20 percent was released in this most recent quake. Seismologists expect even more destructive earthquakes to occur. Munich Re (2006), p. 31.
4. Another measure – the **Modified Mercalli Intensity scale** – is based on the effects of ground shaking on people, buildings and landscape, and consists of a series of responses ranging from mild disturbances to total destruction. The lower intensity numbers generally deal with the manner in which an earthquake is felt, while the higher numbers are based on observed structural damage.
5. This discussion draws from Munich Re (2005), pp. 26–30.
6. A class of storms not discussed here is severe thunderstorms. They include tornadoes, hail storms and straight-line wind gusts. They are not considered here because their effects, while potentially severe, tend to be localized. Severe thunderstorms attract comparatively less attention than hurricanes but have done more insured damage than any other natural catastrophe during the preceding two decades.
7. **Hurricane season** refers to that portion of the year that has a relatively high incidence of tropical storms and hurricanes. The hurricane season in the Atlantic, Caribbean and Gulf of Mexico is June 1 to November 30. In the Eastern Pacific Basin, it runs from May 15 to November 30. The season for the Central Pacific Basin is June 1–November 30.
8. This discussion draws from Munich Re (2006).
9. Although it did not happen in 2006, hurricane experts expect a relatively busy hurricane season in 2007.
10. The chance of a levee breech in any year had been estimated at between 1-in-200 and 1-in-300. In contrast, the Dutch systems to control flooding from storms are engineered to 1-in-10,000 events.
11. Trenberth and Shea (2006).
12. Ibid.
13. This discussion draws from volcanoes.usgs.gov/.
14. This discussion draws from Smolka (2005).

# REFERENCES

*A Failure of Initiative* (2006). Final Report of the Select Bipartisan Committee to Investigate the Preparation for and Response to Hurricane Katrina at www.gpoacess.gov/congress/index.html

Feldhaus, W.R. (1998). "The Physical Environment for Risk and Insurance," Chapter 17, in H.D. Skipper, ed., *International Risk and Insurance: An Environmental-Managerial Approach.* Boston, MA: Irwin/McGraw-Hill.

*Fortune* (2005). "A Meditation on Risk." *Fortune*, 152 (October 3): 50–62.

*Fortune* (2006). "The Long, Strange Resurrection of New Orleans." *Fortune*, 154 (August 21): 86–109.

Munich Re (2005). *Annual Review: Natural Catastrophes 2004.* Munich: Munich Re.

Munich Re (2006). *Annual Review: Natural Catastrophes 2005* at www.munichre.com/

Smolka, A. (2005). *Weather Catastrophes and Climate Change – Is there Still Hope for Us?* Munich: Munich Re.

Swiss Re (2006). *Natural Catastrophes and Man-made Disasters 2005.* Zurich: Swiss Re.

Trenberth, K. and Shea, D. (2006). "Atlantic Hurricanes and Natural Variability in 2005." *Geophysical Research Letters*, 33 (June 27).

# Chapter 6

# Catastrophe Risk Assessment: Human Factors

## INTRODUCTION

As discussed in the preceding chapter, human-made catastrophes now compete with those provided by nature. Technological developments and advances offer new opportunities for things to go wrong in big ways. Dense population and property concentration in urban areas internationally exacerbates human-made disasters. This chapter explores selected areas of human endeavor that carry a catastrophe potential. We begin with a discussion of the risks presented by terrorism. We then explore risks associated with critical infrastructure. Finally, we examine three dimensions of environmental risk: climate change, genetic engineering and nuclear power.

## TERRORISM

Many consider the tragic events of September 11, 2001 to have been one of the U.S. government's greatest risk management failures. Insight 6.1 offers the narrative from *The National Commission on Terrorist Attacks Upon the United States* that describes these events.

Terrorism is not new, but its magnitude is. In fact, the Center for Terrorism Risk Management Policy at RAND (U.S.) shows that 777 different groups caused 19,856 terrorism-related events globally between January 1968 and January 2005.[1] Those events took 25,595 lives, with 66,665 injured. The Revolutionary Armed Forces of Colombia, Basque Fatherland and Liberty, the National Liberation Army of Colombia, Hamas, the Communist Party of Nepal, Hezbollah, al-Fatah, the Taliban, the Irish Republican Army and al Qaeda are just some of the more widely recognized terrorist groups identified by the Center. Combating terrorism – referred to as non-conventional or asymmetric warfare – is an enormously complex task, given its characteristics, particularly its non-state, amorphous nature and typically non-military objectives. Insight 6.2 highlights key characteristics of terrorism.

Terrorism is solidly also a world problem, as attacks carried out in many countries, including in Russia, Spain and the U.K., attest. It is beyond the scope of this book to explore the reasons behind terrorism, but the *9/11 Commission's* detailed report does so and recommends a risk management strategy for dealing with them. Terrorism represents one of

## INSIGHT 6.1: A NATION TRANSFORMED

At 8:46 on the morning of September 11, 2001, the U.S. became a nation transformed.

An airliner traveling at hundreds of miles per hour and carrying some 10,000 gallons of jet fuel plowed into the North Tower of the World Trade Center in Lower Manhattan. At 9:03, a second airliner hit the South Tower. Fire and smoke billowed upward. Steel, glass, ash and bodies fell below. The Twin Towers, where up to 50,000 people worked each day, both collapsed less than 90 minutes later.

At 9:37 that same morning, a third airliner slammed into the western face of the Pentagon. At 10:03, a fourth airliner crashed in a field in southern Pennsylvania. It had been aimed at the U.S. Capitol or the White House and was forced down by heroic passengers armed with the knowledge that America was under attack.

More than 2,600 people died at the World Trade Center, 125 died at the Pentagon, 256 died on the four planes. The death toll surpassed that at Pearl Harbor in December 1941 . . . . This immeasurable pain was inflected by 19 young Arabs acting at the behest of Islamist extremists headquartered in distant Afghanistan. Some had been in the U.S. for more than a year, mixing with the rest of the population. Though four had training as pilots, most were not well educated. Most spoke English poorly; some hardly at all. In groups of four or five, carrying with them only small knives, box cutters and cans of Mace or pepper spray, they had hijacked the four planes and turned them into deadly guided missiles.

Why did they do this? How was the attack planned and conceived? How did the U.S. government fail to anticipate and prevent it? What can we do in the future to prevent similar acts of terrorism?

*Source*: "Executive Summary," *The 9/11 Report* (2004), p. 1.

## INSIGHT 6.2: WHAT IS TERRORISM?

General agreement exists that terrorism exhibits five characteristics:

- involves violence or its threat against people (as opposed to property),
- the violence is not an end in itself but rather is aimed at instilling fear or having a deep psychological impact on others (which means attacking national symbols shows the terrorists' power),
- perpetrated to accomplish political goals,
- civilians or non-combatants are targeted (usually those who are identified with the government or offense as perceived by terrorists), and
- perpetrated by non-governmental actors or at least governments of questionable legitimacy.

Thus, we define terrorism as any act by non-governmental players involving violence or the threat of violence against civilians for the purpose of intimidating a population or compelling a government to do or abstain from doing some act. Literally hundreds of definitions terrorism exist worldwide, so the one offered here will not be universally accepted. Agreeing on a definition of terrorism is important, because it facilitates cooperation among law enforcement officials nationally and internationally and helps define counter-terrorism policy.

the greatest human-made societal threats, aside from convention war.[2] We explore the four aspects that have given rise to the greatest concerns: terrorists' use of nuclear, biological, chemical, or conventional explosives.

## Use of Nuclear Weapons

The greatest concern by U.S. policymakers is the possibility of terrorists securing and detonating a nuclear weapon in a major U.S. city. If this were to occur, the effects on society, the economy, and financial markets would be profound. Severe retaliation by the U.S. military would follow which could lead to incalculable disruption to the global economy.

### Building conventional nuclear weapons

To put the potential into context: it is said that as many as 200,000 individuals could die from the detonation of a relatively small nuclear weapon in Manhattan, with every building in the Wall Street financial area destroyed. Luckily, construction of a conventional nuclear weapon is not easy. In fact, few individuals worldwide possess the required expertise. The construction of a fission-type bomb requires years of work by teams of individuals trained in building and assembling the components. Consequently, the likelihood of terrorists building conventional nuclear weapons without some form of state sponsorship is considered quite remote.

Buying or stealing an operable nuclear weapon or key components seems a far more attractive alternative. The *9/11 Commission* cited an incident in which al Qaeda paid US$1.5 million to a Sudanese military officer for what it believed was weapons-grade uranium (*The 9/11 Report*, 2004). The cylinder turned out to be bogus, but the episode demonstrates what the terrorists hoped to do or, as one al Qaeda operative explained, "it's easy to kill more people with uranium."

Russian nuclear weapons are stored at more than 100 sites, and experts express concern about their security. The U.S. and Russia combined have around 26,000 nuclear weapons, although less than one-half are considered "active." Besides the U.S. and Russia, other states possessing nuclear weapons and that have signed the Nuclear Non-Proliferation Treaty (NNPT) – intended to limit the spread of nuclear weapons – include the U.K., France and China. India, Pakistan and North Korea have conducted nuclear tests, but are not NNPT signatories, with each country said to possess nuclear weapons. Israel is believed also to have nuclear weapons, and concern exits that Iran is developing them. North Korea, in particular, is known to have a brisk business in international arms sales, including missiles, with many observers concerned about the likelihood of the government selling a nuclear weapon to al Queda.

### Building unconventional nuclear weapons

Experts express more concern about the possibility of terrorists building and detonating a so-called **dirty bomb** that consists of nuclear waste by-products wrapped or mixed with conventional explosives. The explosion of such a weapon would spread radioactive materials widely, contaminating property and people.

The detonation of a dirty bomb in downtown Manhattan at noon would kill thousands with many thousands more suffering radiation poisoning. Decontamination of important and expensive buildings and property would be exceptionally time-consuming and costly. Indeed, some properties might require permanent abandonment, as happened after the Chernobyl, Ukraine, disaster.

### Methods of controlling the nuclear weapons risk

No national or global network exists that integrates all of the technological pieces together to form a comprehensive resource against terrorism. Indeed, as late as 2007 and despite spending billions to enhance homeland security, the U.S. government still had failed to integrate its various terrorist databases.

Increased public attentiveness is considered to be an important component of societal risk control of terrorist acts. Suspicious activities are more likely to be reported by citizens to government authorities. Naturally, governments have significantly increased their vigilance to reduce the possibility of a nuclear event, with many efforts said to be comprehensive, extensive and logically designed. Questions remain, however, whether sufficient financial, technological and human resources are being devoted to carry them out for optimum effectiveness. For example, many of the *9/11 Commission's* recommendations for enhanced effectiveness have yet to be implemented. In other words, the likelihood of government failure remains.

## Use of Biological Agents

**Bioterrorism** – the threat of biological weapons use by terrorists – is considered by many as more serious than the nuclear threat, because it is easier to accomplish and can kill thousands. Biological weapons are easier to manufacture than are nuclear weapons, because many rely on the use of substances found in nature. Already, terrorists have used such weapons, such as the nerve gas attack in a Tokyo subway. Both anthrax and ricin have been mailed to U.S. public figures.

### Categories and dispersion of biological warfare agents

The two categories of biological warfare agents are those that are contagious (can be spread from individual to individual) and those that are not. For example, smallpox is contagious, and anthrax is not. The heating or air conditioning system of a building or other enclosed area such as a subway car would be the most likely method of distributing a biological agent.

Luckily, isolating and producing large quantities of virulent strains of a given biological agent are difficult tasks believed to be beyond the current knowledge and capabilities of terrorists groups. Biological agents are extremely sensitive to a wide variety of factors such as sunlight, humidity and temperature that can easily kill the microbes.

### Preventing and detecting a bioterrorism attack

One of the problems in combating bio-terrorism is the limited number of methods available to prevent and control attacks. Smallpox vaccinations ceased to be given routinely in many countries decades ago when the disease was thought to have been eradicated. Their reintroduction into the health system has been suggested in light of the terrorist threat.

With contagious agents, quarantines of infected individuals, as was done in 2003 with the SARS epidemic, can also be used to limit deaths and injuries. Drugs can reduce death rates in some situations. High-efficiency air filters with positive pressure systems can protect occupants of buildings and other enclosed areas.

Efforts are underway to develop portable devices that can immediately detect biological attacks. Various types of databases involving medical facilities linked with analytical programs that can detect a biological attack are also under development.

## Use of Chemical Weapons

The knowledge to make chemical weapons has been known for decades. The equipment and ingredients are readily available, as they are used in many common commercial applications.

### Types and dispersal of chemical weapons

Mustard gas and other types of chemical weapons have existed since World War I. The manufacture of chemical weapons is difficult, however. Their production is dangerous, often involving highly volatile and corrosive chemicals. Moreover, the danger increases with the amounts necessary to inflict mass casualties. Finally, quantities sufficient to cause a catastrophic event would be subject to a high probability of detection.

Even so, highly toxic chemicals could be used to contaminate food or water supplies. Water supplies in most cities are continually tested for contaminants. Commercial sprayers could be mounted on aircraft or other vehicles; however, 90 percent of the agent likely would dissipate. The consensus view is that effective delivery of large quantities of chemical weapons would prove difficult.

### Detecting and controlling damage from a chemical attack

A chemical weapons attack probably would be evident quickly because reactions by affected individuals would be obvious. The sarin attack in Japan resulted in almost immediate reactions from individuals in the subway trains.

However, many first responders – police, firefighters and emergency medical technicians – are said to be inadequately trained and poorly equipped to deal with the injuries from a chemical weapons (or other weapons of mass destruction) attack, with shortages persisting in radios, breathing apparatuses and safety gear. Most emergency medical personnel lack the tools to determine the nature of the chemical (or biological) agent used and there remains a dearth of government response teams trained to deal with large attacks.

## Use of Conventional Explosives

As the 1995 Oklahoma City (U.S.) bombing of a government office building that killed 168 demonstrated, the use of conventional explosives can cause enormous damage. If such an explosion occurred at a facility for the storage or production of toxic chemicals, damage to nearby countryside, workers and residents could be significant. For example, of the more than 60,000 chemical plants in the U.S., 124 present special risks to large numbers of individuals because of their location and the nature of the chemicals that they process. Other nations have similar exposures.

Even with the obviously enhanced security attendant with airplane travel, airplanes remain a potentially significant terrorist threat. Two widely recognized possibilities include (1) foreign passenger airlines unknowingly training pilots who turn out to be terrorists and (2) use of cargo or private aircraft which undergo less scrutiny. Nations undoubtedly have plans in place to shoot down aircraft believed to threaten national security, but identifying them in time to take action remains a challenge.

All other modes of transportation also can be used to deliver explosives that cause catastrophic damage. Explosive-laden ships could destroy bridges and other structures, including petrochemical storage facilities in port cities. Train and truck shipments similarly could be the mode of destructive delivery, including destruction of key dams that could cause significant loss of life and property and disruption of water supplies.

Conventional explosives are delivered by both vehicles and suicide bombers in the Middle East and, increasingly, in other regions as well. The best defense against such attacks involves barriers that keep individuals and vehicles away from buildings, bridges, dams and other major targets.

## Conclusion

Terrorism is not likely to be defeated completely in the near future, if ever. The reasons are multifold. First, the root causes of terrorism seem a long way from being addressed sufficiently. Second, terrorism is simply too cheap. The *9/11 Commission* estimated that the 9/11 attacks cost less than $500,000 – an amount that the U.S. spends every three or four minutes to fight the war in Iraq. This asymmetric warfare is expensive only for those defending against it. Additionally, many nations, including the U.S., can never make their borders completely secure – except as the nation decides to withdraw from the world stage entirely.

Concerns about terrorism likely will remain for many years. What is required, therefore, is that everyday citizens develop both the maturity to live with it and the willingness to invest in reasonable measures to mitigate the risk. Today's terrorist masterminds know that the main consequences of their attacks are not the immediate damage inflicted, but the collateral consequences of eroding the public's trust in the institutions and services on which it depends.

The direct economic costs of 9/11, for example, were dwarfed by indirect costs in terms of massive stock market losses, hits to economic growth, higher unemployment, and airline industry losses. Because societal behavior resulting from the signal value of an attack can have economic consequences far greater than the attack itself, policymakers must consider this aspect along with any direct affect.

Certainly, the fight against terrorism must continue and be financed. Certainly, also, the consequences of another large terrorist attack could be profound. Nevertheless, society should not lose sight of the opportunity costs of the fight. To put but one dimension into perspective for a single year, 2003, a total of 625 people – including 35 Americans – were killed in terrorist attacks worldwide. At the same time, more than 43,000 were killed in automobile accidents in the U.S., and three million died worldwide from AIDS.

# CRITICAL INFRASTRUCTURE RISKS

Modern economies are built on the ability to move goods, people and information safely, efficiently and reliably – all of which rely on a country's infrastructures.[3] Consequently, it is of the utmost importance to government, business and the public that the flow of services provided by critical infrastructures continues unimpeded in the face of natural and human-made hazards. **Critical infrastructures** are systems whose incapacity or destruction would have a debilitating impact on the defense or economic security of a nation. They include communications, electrical power systems, gas and oil, banking and finance, transportation, water supply systems, and government and emergency services.

Although the infrastructure hardware (i.e., the highways, pipelines, transmission lines, communication satellites and network servers) initially is the focus of discussions, the services that these systems provide are the real value to the public. Therefore, high among the concerns in protecting these systems from harm is ensuring the continuity (or at least the rapid restoration) of service.

## Causes and Consequences of Infrastructure Failures

Over their lifetime, infrastructure systems must resist a formidable array of threats and insults. In the natural realm, earthquakes, extreme winds, floods, snow and ice, volcanic activity, landslides, tsunamis and wildfires all pose risk. To this list must be added terrorist and other malicious acts, design faults, excessively prolonged service lives, aging materials and inadequate maintenance. Analysis of past events, improved prediction and forecasting methods, and better engineering design and construction have enhanced the ability of infrastructure systems to withstand all types of hazards, yet crippling failures continue to occur.

The consequences of infrastructure failure can range from the benign to the catastrophic. Fires following earthquakes are obvious examples of how a single hazard event can have consequences far beyond the initial damage as demonstrated in San Francisco, U.S. in 1906 and in Kobe, Japan in 1995. Hazard mitigation for such lifeline infrastructures as water, electricity and communications has generally focused on first-order effects – designing the systems to resist the loads imparted by extreme natural events, and more recently, malevolent acts such as sabotage and terrorism. However, as these systems become increasingly complex and interdependent, hazard mitigation must also be concerned with the secondary and tertiary failure effects. Of even greater significance is the impact of complex infrastructure system failures on social, economic and political institutions.

## Complex Systems and Self-Organized Criticality

Mitigating damage to critical infrastructure and ensuring continuity of service is complicated by the interdependent nature of these systems. **Interdependent effects** occur when a disruption spreads beyond itself to cause appreciable impact on other systems, which in turn cause more effects on still other systems.

The interdependency problem is further compounded by the increasing dependence of physical infrastructure on information technology systems. Communication and information technologies have had a significant impact on infrastructure system design, construction, maintenance, operations and control, and more change is inevitable. Although the coupling of physical infrastructure with information technology promises improved reliability and efficiency at reduced cost, surprisingly little is known about the behavior of these coupled systems and, thus, their potential for cataclysmic failure. Software is fragile by nature, and experience has shown that the software element of control and data acquisition systems is usually the least robust part of an integrated system.

In his book, *Normal Accidents*, Perrow (1999) describes numerous failures of what he terms "tightly coupled, complex systems." Such accidents occur when systems are sufficiently complex to allow unexpected interactions of failures; safety systems are defeated and sufficiently tightly coupled to allow a cascade of increasingly serious failures ending in disaster. A particularly troubling characteristic of these tightly coupled, complex systems is that they predictably fail but in unpredictable ways. Similar chains of events do not always produce the same phenomena, but system level or "normal" accidents of major consequence continuously recur. Perrow contends that, in our search for speed, volume, efficiency and the ability to operate in hostile environments, we are prone to neglect those system designs that are inherently more reliable and safe.

Complexity is associated with the concept of self-organization, a concept developed by Dutch physicist Per Bak. **Self-organization** implies that systems are under no direct control but, like Adam Smith's "invisible hand," realize uncoordinated results greater than the sum of individual parts. Complex self-organizing systems tend to balance at a point where a small incremental change can push the system toward a new equilibrium or to total collapse. While controversial at the time, self-organized criticality has now been used to explain the behaviors of traffic jams, volcanoes, earthquakes, evolution and mass extinction, avalanches, forest fires, economic markets, the spread of epidemics and how the brain works. Things do not always move along smoothly at a steady pace but are subject to occasional, sudden catastrophic events that cause the system to either rebalance at a new equilibrium or, in the worst case, break down entirely.

Self-organized criticality is probably a more powerful tool than a probability model for the study of cascading infrastructure failures. It is because the tails of the frequency distributions of many extreme events behave in accordance with so-called power laws – rather than the more commonly known normal or bell-shaped distribution – that relate the number of events of different sizes by a constant proportion. Thus, the catastrophic system failures that Perrow calls normal accidents cannot be dismissed as statistical anomalies – unique intersections of very rare and random events – but rather as the expected behavior of complex, self-ordering and closely coupled systems. Taken together, the work of Perrow and Bak supports a discomforting premise that, although it may not be possible to predict the precise nature of the next Chernobyl or Bhopal, a cascading failure of similar consequence is to be expected if we continue to rely on the types of critical-state systems that seem to be the root causes of these disasters.

Adam Smith's invisible hand and Bak's self-organizing complexity need to be considered together for their relevance to business and society. On the one hand, we have self-organized systems as demonstrated by competitive markets that exhibit higher efficiency than centrally controlled or managed systems. On the other hand, while self-organized systems are more efficient, they are also on the verge of criticality and, therefore, can be more vulnerable to widespread failure. Centrally managed systems, such as large government monopolies, are less efficient, but may exhibit higher reliability. Most human-made systems are not entirely self-organized or completely managed, but lie between the two extremes. On the one end, we have highly efficient but less reliable self-organized systems. On the other, we have highly managed, reliable but less efficient systems. Figure 6.1 illustrates this relationship.

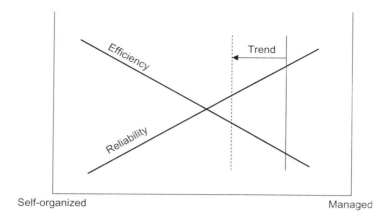

**Figure 6.1**    Relationship between Efficiency and Reliability in Systems. *Source*: Koubatis and Schönberger, 2004, p. 25. Reproduced with permission by The Geneva Association

The extent to which systems operate near their capacity is a factor in determining their reliability. Having spare capacity, however defined – whether for individuals, holding lots of cash; for businesses, extra inventory; or for society, making bridges 5 times stronger than required – means that the system is better able to absorb unexpected shocks. From an economic perspective, however, this spare capacity comes at a price that typically means reduced efficiency.

While systems are rarely at either extreme of the spectrum, today's competitive economic environment pushes businesses and governments from a state of spare capacity (and greater reliability) toward the state of maximizing expected economic benefit and efficiency. Moves to liberalize markets, deregulate industries and privatize governmental and social benefit schemes all are examples of this trend. Such trends pose no difficulties when the risks are identified, understood, accepted and managed effectively. The problem is that too often all such risks are not identified (and in self-organizing complex systems, they cannot be fully identified) and, therefore, cannot be fully understood, accepted or managed effectively.

## Understanding How Complex Systems Behave

Understanding how complex, interconnected systems behave when subjected to the external stresses of natural and technological hazards presents enormous challenges, but deepening this understanding is essential to minimizing failures in complex national infrastructure systems. Such systems operate at the edge of stability, where the environment is constantly changing, and the systems must continuously adapt to the situation and each other.

Three key processes relevant to this discussion are as follows:

- *Variation* in an interactive system, as in a biological community, reduces the vulnerability to single-point failures. The reduced efficiency brought about by independent elements (or evolutionary paths) is balanced by increased robustness of the system. By studying how interactive communities adapt, thrive, or perish, there is much to learn regarding what types of systems are inherently safer in practice.

- *Interactions* between members of the same group or social framework, while enhancing communication and simplifying information transfer, can have disastrous consequences if the jointly held information is wrong.

- *Selection* deals with choosing successful strategies and rejecting those that lead to failure.

The key here is learned behavior that will enable participants to survive in a complex, evolving environment. In the absence of actual conditions in which to learn adaptive behavior (such as warfare for the military), there is a need to train the participants by other means (e.g., gaming or simulation).

Three Mile Island and Chernobyl, for example, provide insights for understanding how systems might be designed to lessen the frequency and impact of cascading failures. In both cases, the intersection of concurrent reinforcing technological and human failures led to disaster. Neither the technological failures (which were relatively straightforward) nor the operator errors alone would have produced the ultimate outcomes. At both Three Mile Island and Chernobyl, the operators' commonly held views of the situation were uniformly wrong and ultimately contributed to the system breakdowns. Fortunately, in the case of Three Mile Island, an outside agent who had not been influenced by observing the emerging events, intervened just before the system failure. None of the workers at Three Mile Island had been trained to expect anything resembling the types of problems that they actually confronted. They had no successful patterns or strategies to call upon and were unable to adapt to the rapidly changing conditions.

Much knowledge has been gained and advances made in such forensic engineering – the study of engineering failures. However, concerns persist that commonly used forensic techniques often fail to capture adequately the influence of all contributing factors, not merely the obvious or easy. This concern is illustrated clearly in the Institute of Medicine's (2000) study of errors in the healthcare industry:

> The complex coincidences that cause systems to fail could rarely have been foreseen by the people involved. As a result, they are reviewed only in hindsight; however, knowing the outcome of an event influences how we assess past events. **Hindsight bias** means that things that were not seen or understood at the time of the accident seem obvious in retrospect. Hindsight bias also misleads a reviewer into simplifying the causes of an accident, highlighting a single element as the cause and overlooking its multiple contributing factors. Given that the information about an accident is spread over many participants, none of whom may have complete information, hindsight bias makes it easy to arrive at a simple solution or to blame an individual, but difficult to determine what really went wrong.

## Conclusion

Our critical infrastructure systems are at risk from threats that we may not yet foresee. Potential failure nodes are repeatedly created at the intersections of tightly coupled, highly sophisticated transportation, electric power and communications systems, and are compounded by their reliance on information systems and software. As Little (2003) asserts, we need a better understanding of the "vulnerability of complexity." More research can yield a better understanding of networks and interconnections; the effects of deregulation, privatization and globalization; and better software and system designs. Some research approaches may be fairly simple and call for the reinstitution of "shock absorbers and circuit breakers"

INSIGHT 6.3: TOO LITTLE, TOO LATE FOR MANY OF THE WORLD'S INHABITANTS

Every year in developing countries, a million people die from urban air pollution and twice that number from exposure to stove smoke inside their homes. Another 3 million inhabitants die prematurely every year from water-related diseases. All told, premature deaths and illnesses arising from environmental factors account for about a fifth of all diseases in poor countries, bigger than any other preventable factor, including malnutrition. In environments such as these, concern about global warming is a remote, rich country issue.

*Source*: "How Many Planets?" (2002), p. 11.

in both a physical and operational sense to increase the resilience and reliability of infrastructure systems. Others will be more esoteric and call for the application of sophisticated analytical, modeling and forecasting tools to improve understanding of the systems and the modes and consequences of failure. Still others may focus on the conflicts inherent in increased economic efficiency through capacity shedding, outsourcing and just-in-time operational systems versus resilience through redundancy.

## ENVIRONMENTAL RISKS

The term **environmental risk** can take on many meanings but, for purposes of this chapter, it refers to risks to the environment resulting from human activities. Again, our concern is with those risks that carry the potential for substantial and pervasive negative externalities. This focus is not meant to detract from some of the world's more fundamental environmental problems, as Insight 6.3 reminds us. In this section, we provide overviews of three such risks:

- climate change;
- genetic engineering;
- nuclear-generated electrical energy.

### Climate Change

The world's climate results from the vertical and horizontal transportation of energy through the atmosphere.[4] The atmosphere consists of 78 percent nitrogen, 21 percent oxygen, 1 percent argon, and other trace gases including carbon dioxide, ozone and methane. Without these "greenhouse" gases (GHGs) to trap heat, the earth's average temperature would be a lifeless 30°C or so colder. GHGs are increasing due to growing consumption of fossil fuels, resulting in a greater retention of thermal radiation on the earth's surface.

#### *The problem*

According to the UN's Intergovernmental Panel on Climate Change (IPCC) – the world's most authoritative body of scientists working on this issue – global temperatures have

---

INSIGHT 6.4: EVIDENCE THAT EARTH WARMEST IN AT LEAST 400 YEARS

**Washington** – there is sufficient evidence from tree rings, boreholes, retreating glaciers, and other "proxies" of past surface temperatures to say with a high level of confidence that the last few decades of the 20th century were warmer than any comparable period in the last 400 years, according to a new report from the National Research Council. Less confidence can be placed in proxy-based reconstructions of surface temperatures for 900–1600 AD, said the committee that wrote the report, although the available proxy evidence does indicate that many locations were warmer during the past 25 years than during any other 25-year period since 900.

The committee pointed out that surface temperature reconstructions for periods before the Industrial Revolution – when levels of atmospheric greenhouse gases were much lower – are only one of multiple lines of evidence supporting the conclusion that current warming is occurring in response to human activities, and they are not the primary evidence.

The National Research Council is the principal operating arm of the National Academy of Sciences and the National Academy of Engineering. It is a private, non-profit institution that provides science and technology advice under a (U.S.) congressional charter.

*Source*: National Academy of Engineering at www8.nationalacademies.org/onpinews/newsitem.aspx?RecordID=11676.

---

risen about 0.6°C since the 19th century and human activity has contributed to this result. A study released in 2006 by the U.S.-based National Research Council (NRC) effectively supported this conclusion but further concluded that the last few decades of the 20th century were the hottest in at least 400 years and possibly much longer. Insight 6.4 highlights elements of the NRC press release.

Global temperatures have risen by about 0.6°C since the 19th century. Other measures of climate bolster the theory that the world is getting warmer: satellite measurements suggest that spring arrives about a week earlier now than in the late 1970s, for example, and records show that migratory birds fly to higher latitudes earlier in the season and stay later. According to the UN's IPCC – by far the most authoritative body of scientists working on this issue – humans are probably not responsible for all the measured warming. But the trend is undoubtedly due in large part to substantial increases in carbon dioxide emissions from human activity. Since the middle of the 19th century, the average concentration of carbon dioxide – a so-called GHG – in the world's atmosphere has risen from some 280 parts per million (ppm) to around 370 ppm. Burning fossil fuels account for about three-quarters of human emissions, with deforestation and changes in land use (mainly in the tropics) accounting for the rest.

We also know that the trend of increasing global temperatures has continued into the 21st century, as the accompanying chart to Figure 6.2 showing the hottest years on record highlights. We also know that, since the Industrial Revolution, human activities have contributed significantly to the so-called greenhouse effect. Atmospheric concentrations of GHGs have risen from around 280 ppm two centuries ago to around 370 ppm today.

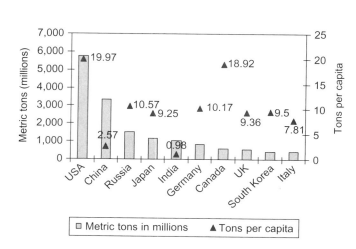

**Figure 6.2**   Top 10 Countries in Carbon Dioxide Emissions from Fossil Fuels

Burning fossil fuels accounts for about three-fourths of human emissions, with defor-estation and changes in land use accounting for the rest. Total worldwide carbon dioxide emissions from the consumption of petroleum, natural gas, coal and the flaring of natu-ral gas amount to about 25 billion metric tons per year. This averages to about 4 tons per human per year. Figure 6.2 shows the top 10 countries in carbon dioxide emissions from fossil fuels.[5] Collectively, they account for almost two-thirds of the world total, with the U.S. alone accounting for almost one-fourth of the world total.

There are good reasons to believe that global temperatures will continue rising. The worry is that rapid rises will lead to climate changes that could be devastating for many (although not all) parts of the world. Central America, most of Africa, much of south Asia, and northern China could all be hit by droughts, storms, and floods, and otherwise made miserable. The Amazon rain forest could become depleted, decreasing the production of oxygen and releasing huge volumes of carbon. Rising ocean levels could devastate coasts worldwide – where increasing proportions of populations live. Because the tropics would be hit so hard and because most people there are poor, those most likely to be affected will be least able to adapt.

The colder parts of the world may benefit from warming, but they too face perils. One is the conceivable collapse of the Atlantic "conveyor belt," a system of currents that gives much of Europe its relatively mild climate; if temperatures climb too high, the system may undergo radical changes that damage both Europe and America. That points to the biggest fear: warming may trigger irreversible changes that transform the earth into a largely unin-habitable environment.

Addressing climate change issues has proven difficult for two reasons. First, carbon diox-ide has a long-life span. It remains in the atmosphere for centuries. This fact makes this an intergenerational issue. Second, carbon dioxide in the atmosphere can be reduced only on a global basis. Emissions do not respect national borders.

Beyond these facts, however, the issue becomes less clear. For example, it is impossible to predict with any confidence how quickly future emissions of carbon dioxide and other GHGs will rise. The reason for this lack of sufficient modeling is that we cannot predict future economic growth rates many years into the future, nor can we know the effect that new technology will have on the issue. Moreover, in spite of ever-improving models, we still cannot predict with great confidence the effect on climate of increasing concentrations of GHGs. Consider but one unknown: how the world's carbon cycle will respond. If the world's climate gets warmer, the earth might become greener. In turn, this additional lushness could lead to more carbon dioxide being sucked from the atmosphere. Alternatively, some scientists worry that the earth could be so stressed that natural processes for removing carbon dioxide could become less efficient. Numerous other variables, such as aerosol particles, the effects of clouds, and cosmic radiation, will affect future climate patterns, but linking these variable to climatic changes will remain a daunting challenge.

The IPCC contends that, in the absence of corrective action, carbon dioxide concentrations will rise by 2050 to between 450 and 550 ppm. This increase is estimated to cause average temperatures to rise by between 0.5°C and 2.5°C over this same time period.

There is general agreement that global warming will almost certainly cause the sea level to rise. Indeed, recent photographic and other evidence already points to massive melting of glaciers and warmer water. The most widely accepted projections would have the world's oceans rise by from 5 to 32 centimeters by 2050. While this amount may, at first, seem modest, it must be realized that miles of beaches and wetlands would be inundated by a water level increased of just a few tens of centimeters.

### *The options*

While little debate exists among scientists today as to whether human activities are meaningfully contributing to global warming, less agreement exists about its ultimate effects and what should be done – in large measure because actions require more of a political than a scientific solution. The worst effects might not be felt for a century, but the costs of tackling the problem starts immediately. That is the dilemma. It is asking a great deal of politicians who are subject to elections every 2–6 years to agree to undertake potentially costly activities today but whose benefits might not be felt for decades – a combination of the free rider and agency problems – for the future is a constituency who do not vote today.

One strategy accepted by many governments and experts is to ensure that any increase in the world's temperature is limited to between 2°C and 3°C above the current level over time. This goal would require limiting $CO_2$ atmospheric concentrations to between 500 and 550 ppm over the next century.[6] The cost of achieving this goal would be high, based on known technology.  Of course, technology of a type not now even imagined could lower this cost, perhaps substantially. For example, new technology has allowed the costs of deep-water oil and gas development to fall to one-third of its level just 15 years ago.

Also, the nature of the problem may change. The overwhelming pollution problem more than a century ago was horse manure clogging city streets; a century hence, many of today's problems could seem equally irrelevant. The challenge, of course, is knowing today what is the equivalent of the 1890 horse manure problem.

In the short run, efforts need to ensure that developed countries use energy much more efficiently and figure out how to make profits from the very problem of global warming. For example, BP reached it target of a 10 percent reductions in emissions below its 1990 levels without any net cost to the firm. Indeed, BP asserts that it saved its shareholders around US$650 million by using energy more efficiently and reducing leaks and waste. Yet achieving the above goals will require emission reductions beyond those attained from efficiency improvements. Some widely discussed options include:

- In power generation, which accounts for about 35 percent of total emissions, options include switching from coal to less-carbon-intensive natural gas, greater reliance on nuclear power (along with viable safety), use of coal made free of carbon and greater use of non-carbon sources such as windmills, solar energy, and the like.

- In the domestic and commercial sectors, which account for 25 percent, buildings can be made more efficient, electrical appliances can be made ultra-efficient, and power grids can be digitally controlled to operate closer to optimum potential.

- In transportation, which accounts for 20 percent, engines can be made ultra-efficient, innovative advanced injection techniques can be developed, hybrid electric-gasoline vehicles are already helping, and opportunities exist for emission reduction in aircraft.

### The role of the market

Economists contend that the gains achieved in emission reduction through government mandates come at a needlessly high price. That is because technology mandates and bureaucratic rules stifle innovation and ignore local realities, such as varying costs of abatement. They also fail to use cost–benefit analysis to assess trade-offs. Formerly, environmentalists generally were unconvinced. This is changing.

Harnessing the market's potential to reduce GHGs holds great promise. As discussed in Chapter 4, governments have several options in this respect. Emission trading ranks highly for its potential, as discussed earlier. Sweden's sulfur tax, introduced more than a decade ago, resulted in a 50 percent drop below legal requirements in the sulfur content of fuels. U.S. policymakers have adopted similar approaches that do not cripple the market or impose high costs.[7] The European emission trading system, started on a trial basis in 2005, is to be fully operational by 2008. It is said to be the most advanced market-based example addressing $CO_2$ emissions.

The idea, of course, is to ensure that production costs include attendant negative externalities. Externalities are only part of the battle, however, in fixing market distortions. The other half involves scrapping environmentally harmful subsidies. These range from prices below market levels for electricity and water to cash handouts for industries such as coal. The OECD estimates that removing such subsidies, along with introducing taxes on carbon-based fuels and chemicals use, would result in dramatically lower emissions by 2020 than current policies would be able to achieve.

Such subsidies do double damage, by distorting markets and by encouraging behavior that harms the environment. For example, the subsidies extended by EU countries to their fishing fleets have so encouraged overfishing as to have caused near collapse of many North Atlanta fishing grounds. As *The Economist* notes, "fishing is an example of the 'tragedy of the commons,' which pops up frequently in the environmental debate. A resource such as the ocean is common to many, but an individual 'free rider' can benefit from plundering that commons or dumping waste into it, knowing that the costs of his actions will probably be distributed among many neighbors."

Unfortunately, markets currently are not very good at appreciating and valuing environmental goods, although as we have noted earlier, important efforts are underway to harness their great power. For example, consider that forests exhibit positive externalities in the form of carbon storage and watershed protection for which their owners are not compensated. Innovators are trying to develop markets for some of these long-ignored "co-benefits," thereby producing new revenue flows for forest owners and giving them incentives to avoid and even reverse further deforestation.

Many economists note that prices are also distorted because conventional economic measures (e.g., gross domestic products, GDP) measure wealth creation improperly, as they ignore the effects of environmental degradation. For example, its logging industry's output is included in China's GDP, yet the billions of dollars worth of damage from devastating floods caused by over-logging is ignored. More comprehensive measures are needed.

Markets, even if they got everything right, must yield to public discourse and government policy. As we learned in Chapter 2, markets are efficient but not always fair. Also, applying cost–benefit analysis to climate change is more complex than to most other public policy issues. Aside from the uncertainty of the future costs and benefits, benefits will not be realized for decades or centuries whereas much of the abatement costs will be incurred today. The analysis therefore turns greatly on the discount rate used. A typical discount rate of, say, 3–6 percent, commonly used in short-term public policy issues, would result in the virtual elimination from consideration of benefits (and costs) incurred 100 or so years hence.

## Genetic Engineering

The genetic revolution likely will be to the 21st century what the information revolution was to the 20th century.[8] Less than 50 years have passed since the first structural model of DNA was put forward. In the early 1970s, molecular biologists learned to exchange genes between unrelated organisms with the help of genetic engineering methods. The market for genetically engineered drugs was born. When human DNA was decoded in 2000 in the Human Genome Project, this young technology and its seemingly infinite possibilities became a subject for debate not only among scientists, but also in society at large. In the coming decades, genetic engineering will have a decisive influence on both economies and society as a whole and will also open up a wealth of otherwise inconceivable opportunities and, possibly, risks.

### What is it?

Genetic engineering is a branch of biotechnology, which is a discipline that encompasses all innovative methods, techniques, processes and products using living organisms or their cellular constituents. It is not new. Microorganisms have been used for centuries to make cheese, wine and bread. Likewise, plants and animals have been selectively bred for centuries. One of the most significant innovations of genetic engineering as opposed to these classical biotechnology methods is the ability to "cross species barriers" using genetic recombination.

Genetic engineering now makes it possible to introduce a trait or a gene coding for a trait into an organism in a form formerly unknown in the species, including the transfer of one plant's properties to another plant species. The long-term consequences of being able to cross species barriers by means of genetic recombination are profound. Genetic engineering already has influenced many market segments, such as drugs, vaccines, medical products, diagnostics, plant breeding, renewable resources, novel foods, enzymes for food production and in detergents, fine chemicals, environmental biotechnology, and analytical services.

## The debate

Genetic engineering probably evokes more controversy and public debate than any other new technology. After all, this science intervenes in life processes in fundamental ways and can influence the way that we view ourselves.

On the one hand, the benefits from genetically engineered drugs – such as the development of new vaccines against such infectious diseases as Ebola or AIDS, cancer treatments, and drugs with fewer side effects – are easily conveyed to the general public and widely accepted. The prospect of better health oils the wheels of public acceptance. On the other hand, a fierce ethical debate is raging in borderline areas, such as research using embryos and the "right of ignorance" in conjunction with gene diagnostics. Attitudes about biotechnology in general and genetics in particular often are intimately linked to individuals' ethical standards and fundamental beliefs; science may have no place in shaping the opinions of such individuals. On balance, the scientific-industrial complex as a whole seems pleased with the overall acceptance of genetic engineering in the medical and pharmaceutical arena.

The situation in the food industry is different. Users of genetic engineering have yet to communicate convincingly the agricultural benefits of the new technology, due, among other things, to the fact that such benefits are largely intangible to the average consumer. Food safety is politically sensitive and has had a considerable impact on policy decisions affecting biotechnology.

A large majority of the public – especially in Europe – still has considerable uncertainty, which is further reinforced by a highly polarized public debate in the media and general public ignorance of the subject. Uncertainty about residual risks, which greets every new technology, is particularly widespread in developed economies that place high value on health and safety. Fears concentrate essentially on abuse of the technology and possible uncontrollable consequences for humans and the environment. Surveys also have shown that the public has little confidence in politicians' abilities effectively to steer and control genetic engineering for the benefit of all – as opposed to being for the benefit of politically well-connected multinational corporations.

## Assessing public concerns

The debate over genetically modified food differs from other technologically based debates in that it has taken the traditional perception of risks into two directions. First, this debate focuses on hypothetical or speculative risks. Do any such risks even exist? As public perception focuses on perceived risks and dangers and as the personal benefits of genetically modified food are not immediately tangible, the question is: "Why accept any potential risks – whether proven or not?" Advocates point out the dilemma of trying to develop tests to disprove a speculative negative. Tests and experience to date show no evidence of damage or losses attributable to genetic engineering. But, counter the skeptics, this is not conclusive proof of no risk – just of none found so far.

Second, the debate does not concentrate solely on risks specific to genetic engineering, but has raised social, ethical, cultural, political and economic arguments against use of the technology. According to many observers, the debate is in reality fueled by a combination of fear of the unknown (and possibly unknowable) health hazards and environmental risks, misgivings about manipulating nature and possibly losing biological diversity, and finally political resistance against excessive influence of multinational corporations.

Avoiding societal risk is indisputably the responsibility of the state. Potential risks attributable to genetic engineering must be controlled whenever they arise. It is today easy to politicize risks that evoke fear of the unknown and dread, particularly as the fears cannot

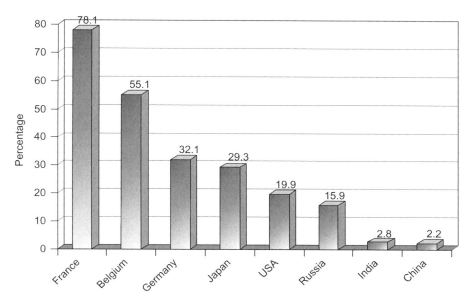

**Figure 6.3**    Electrical Power from Nuclear Generation for Selected Countries (2005). *Source*: U.S. Energy Information Administration

be entirely dispelled with scientific data. This is especially true of the hypothetical and speculative risks associated with genetic engineering that dominate both the public and the political debate.

It is axiomatic that today's research findings can prove to be tomorrow's mistake. Yet, there is no evidence that genetic engineering, in itself, involves any special risks at all as compared to conventional agriculture. Indeed, argue advocates, as most traditional foods have never been tested for toxicity, current scrutiny of genetically modified food is far more stringent than is applied to conventionally bred food organisms.

Currently the debate is concentrated on the control, labeling and monitoring of genetically modified products as well as on the liability for such products. The lack of mandatory labeling for such products and constituents has caused public unrest. Clearly, there is a need to develop and implement a strategy to address public concerns. Public communication programs have been effective in some countries. The factors found to be successful in developing communication strategies are:

- public education;
- consultation with all relevant parties;
- provision of a transparent, scrupulously independent, regulatory system.

## Nuclear-Generated Electrical Energy

Some 441 commercial nuclear power reactors operate in 31 countries, with about one-fourth in the U.S. nuclear power generates about 17 percent of the world's electricity, with country proportions varying greatly, as Figure 6.3 shows. It relies on fission (splitting of atoms) of uranium to generate heat that produces steam that turns turbines connected to generators that produce electricity. Reactor fuel is in the form of small ceramic pellets containing uranium that are then encased in metal rods. These rods are assembled into bundles and inserted into a reactor that is encased in a steel vessel that is housed in a concrete and steel containment building. Control rods composed of boron or other material are inserted to absorb neutrons given off by the fuel rods, thereby controlling the fission process. The rods must be cooled, which is accomplished in many reactors through water circulation around the rods.

At the time nuclear power was introduced more than 50 years ago, it was broadly supported by scientists and the public. It was hailed as being more efficient and cost effective than alternative means of electrical generation, such as coal-fired plants. Importantly, it also was "clean" because it produces no GHGs, thus ultimately leading to a healthier environment. The 1979 accident at Three Mile Island altered both the economics of nuclear power and this consensus.

### Operational safety

The big fear in nuclear power is a **core-melt accident** – an event that results in the melting of part of the fuel in a reactor core. It can occur if the fuel rods are exposed to air because of a loss of both primary and emergency cooling. A nuclear meltdown is known in North

### INSIGHT 6.5: THE CHERNOBYL DISASTER REVISITED: A GLOBAL WARNING

#### Background

Sometime after midnight on April 26, 1986, the operators of Chernobyl Unit 4 in the Ukraine in what was then the Soviet Union were testing the plant's capacity to cope with a loss of off-site power. The power fell to a level far greater than anticipated and the operators were obliged to disconnect several safety systems to stabilize the plant and continue the tests. Shortly thereafter the reactor went into "prompt critical" condition, an uncontrollable, runaway situation. The power level went to about 500 times normal, and the reactor exploded from the pressures that were generated. The force blew off the 1,000-ton steel and cement radiation shield, part of the containment structure, as well as the 350-ton refueling gear over the reactor, severing pressure tubes and connecting pipes. The reactor core was exposed to the atmosphere. The graphite moderator promptly caught fire. Large quantities of radioactivity escaped and were borne away by the wind.

It took until May 6 to stabilize the damaged reactor and halt continuing releases of core radioactivity. The reactor had, finally, to be entombed, initially using several thousand tons of sand, lead, clay and boron brought in and dropped from the air and, after radiation levels had decreased, with steel and concrete.

**The 20th Anniversary** (*excerpts from remarks to the UN General Assembly by Kemal Derviş, UN Coordinator of International Cooperation on Chernobyl*)

"There is no question that Chernobyl was a shattering tragedy. Hundreds of emergency workers risked their lives in responding to the accident, and some sadly perished. Hundreds of thousands of "liquidators" labored to build the sarcophagus around the damaged reactor. More than 330,000 people were uprooted from their native towns and villages; 5,000 people who were children at the time of the accident contracted thyroid cancer. Millions in the region were left traumatized by lingering fears about their health.

The region's mostly rural economy was devastated. Livelihoods lost 20 years ago have not yet been recovered. Farming villages have struggled to overcome the stigma of living in "contaminated" regions. Many communities have sunk into resignation, apathy, or even fatalism.

In recounting the enormous human cost of the Chernobyl tragedy, however, it's important to remember that this is a very sad anniversary – but *not* a hopeless one. Much has been done to cope with the legacy of Chernobyl.

Granted, the initial Soviet silence on the accident was reprehensible, and most Soviet citizens as well as the international community remained unaware for days that an accident had happened. This "original sin" of Chernobyl endangered millions, and has left a deep legacy of mistrust among those who were denied timely, credible information.

That said, both the Soviet government and, after 1991, the newly independent states of Belarus, the Russian Federation, and Ukraine have devoted vast resources and great ingenuity to protecting the population from the effects of radiation and to mitigating the consequences of the accident. These efforts have been largely successful.

As the UN solemnly marks the 20th anniversary of the Chernobyl disaster, we stand in solidarity with those affected by the tragedy and renew our commitment to assisting communities in their recovery. Today, while the anniversary is tinged with sadness, we also acknowledge that this is a time for hope, as we move forward in building a better future for all those whose lives have been changed by this tragedy."

*Sources*: United Nations at chernobyl.undp.org/english/; and Kendall, H.W. (1991). "The Failure of Nuclear Power," in M. Shubik, ed., *Risk, Organizations, and Society*. Originally published by Boston, MA: Kluwer Academic Publishers. With kind permission of Springer Science and Business Media.

America as the **China syndrome**, from the exaggerated notion that molten reactor material could burrow to China, as popularized by the 1979 film of the same name. The only large civilian nuclear meltdown was the 1986 Chernobyl accident, as Insight 6.5 explains. Additionally, several partial core meltdowns have occurred elsewhere, and several Russian and U.S. nuclear submarines have experienced catastrophic nuclear meltdowns. Of course, a nuclear power facility is a classic example of a critical infrastructure risk exhibiting self-organized criticality.

No one is certain of what happens with meltdowns. Of course, a reactor **scram** – the sudden shutting down of a nuclear reactor usually by rapid insertion of control rods either automatically or manually – may suffice, but it also may not. If it does not suffice, resultant heat could melt through the steel-walled reactor vessel, in which case, some 200 tons of molten uranium and fission product spills onto the concrete floor of the containment building. The worst-case scenario would have the 1,200–2,500°C molten soup burn through the floor and hit ground water, resulting in a chemical explosion blasting radioactive material over a large area. The best-case scenario would have the containment building successfully holding the fiery soup.

According to the U.S. Nuclear Regulatory Commission (NRC), the likelihood of a nuclear power plant accident that results in release of significant radioactivity is "very small."[9] To prevent the accidental release of radioactive material, nuclear power plants are constructed with several barriers between the radioactive material and the surrounding environment. The first barrier arises from the cladding (the sealed metal rods encasing the fuel). The second barrier is the 9–12 inch steel walls of the vessel encasing the reactor. The third barrier is the containment building, a heavily reinforced structure of concrete and steel several feet thick that surrounds the reactor vessel and is designed to contain radioactivity that might be released from the reactor system in the event of a serious accident.

An adequate supply of water must be provided for cooling the fuel at all times. The NRC notes that diverse and multiple safety systems can provide the necessary cooling water. In addition, operators are required to maintain plants within specified operating limits and under strict conditions.

### High-level wastes

A second major concern cited by critics relates to the high-level wastes produced by nuclear power plants (and also from making nuclear weapons). After some time in use, fuel rods become inefficient in generating power and must be removed and replaced. At this point, they are highly radioactive and exceptionally hot, thus requiring remote handling and substantial shielding. Such high-level wastes produce radiation capable of causing death within short periods of direct exposure.

For example, a dose of 500 rem received all at once is fatal.[10] Even 10 years after removal from a reactor, a typical spent fuel assembly still produces more than 10,000 rem per hour. Further, if constituents of these high-level wastes were to enter ground waters or rivers, they would enter the food chain, creating the potential for large-scale harm.

The only way radioactive wastes finally become harmless is through decay, which can take hundreds of thousands of years for some isotopes. Plutonium-239 has a half-life of 24,000 years. Thus, for society to feel confident that such wastes will not cause harm, they must be either reprocessed to render them harmless or stored safely in facilities that will not break, leak or deteriorate for thousands of years. Reprocessing has proven a path for some countries, although it also produces wastes, but smaller amounts. It is quite expensive. Presently, the world has no storage facilities, with Finland and the U.S. the only countries constructing them at present.

In 2002, after years of study by scientists, the U.S. President approved the first U.S. development of a long-term geological repository site at Yucca Mountain, Nevada, 90 miles northwest of Las Vegas.[11] The Governor of Nevada notified the U.S. Congress of his state's objection to the proposed repository, but Congress voted to override the objection.

The site will be designed to house 77,000 metric tons of wastes. The earliest operational year is 2010. Full storage will require 24 years, with the facility to be effectively sealed in 2035. Critics question whether such sites can ever be completely stable geologically over thousands of years and whether the storage cylinders and underground buildings themselves can be expected to survive intact such long periods.

Advocates point out that, while nothing is completely safe, the Yucca Mountain area has remained virtually unchanged geologically for millions of years. Numerous studies conducted of Yucca Mountain's physical characteristics and the potential waste containers and underground facilities suggest that the repository is highly unlikely ever to experience volcanoes, erosion or other geological processes and disruptive events. In addition, by locating the repository in solid rock about 1,000 feet underground and on average 1,000 feet above the water table, the waste should be protected from the impacts of earthquakes.

Just within the U.S., some 40,000 metric tons of spent fuel are stored temporarily in large water-cooled pools and dry storage casks at 72 plant sites in 36 states. Additionally, it is estimated that more than 100 million gallons of highly radioactive waste and 2,500 metric tons of spent fuel from the development of nuclear weapons and research are stored temporarily on U.S. military establishments.

Critics observe that thousands of tons of this deadly nuclear waste are accorded comparatively low levels of physical protection. While containment buildings are designed to withstand the impact of small aircraft, no such protection is accorded the exposed storage pools, making a potentially tempting target for terrorists. Additionally, an NRC study examining the risks of a spent fuel fire concluded that while the fire risk was low – that is, the spent fuel would have to be left out of water for several hours – the consequences "could be comparable to those for a severe reactor accident."

Finally, critics point to the danger inherent in transporting nuclear waste to Yucca Mountain, noting that crashes are inevitable (the U.S. Department of Energy estimates at least 50) and attacks cannot be ruled out. Such events could threaten the health and safety of millions near targeted interstate highways and rail lines. Moving wastes to the repository will require thousands of highly radioactive shipments through 44 states. Proponents counter that the shipping casks containing the wastes have been designed and tested to withstand accidents and fire, so the actual risk is minimal.

### *The future of nuclear power*

The future of nuclear power will be determined by three interrelated factors:

- *Safety:* The public must believe that existing and especially future power plants are safe. New plant designs promise not only greater efficiency and longer useful lives, but also reduce the opportunity of human error through superior design. Already nine new reactor designs are in the advanced planning stages.

- *Economics:* The second factor determining the future of nuclear power is economics. Governments continue to deregulate their power industries worldwide, resulting in more competition that, in turn, forces greater operational efficiency. As we know from the earlier discussion on critical infrastructure risks, this can run counter to safety, so balance will be essential.

- *Politics:* Ultimately, in democracies, the future of any science is determined by society's perceptions as manifested in political choices. Pollution and global climate change are important societal risks that must be managed appropriately. Nuclear power, operated safely, can help mitigate the growth in GHGs. Power companies and nuclear plant builders and their advocates can be expected to make this point ever more forcefully with time, provided we witness no further major accidents. Also, as memories of Three Mile Island and Chernobyl continue to fade (and assuming no further accidents), opponents might slowly lose these tragedies for their cause. Advocates of nuclear power will continue to argue that it is the only effective future alternative to fossil fuels and that it is safe, economical and clean.

These technical arguments seem to be taking root as nuclear power seems to be making a comeback. Already, some 32 reactors are being built worldwide, mostly in India, China and neighboring countries. These so-called "third-generation" reactors are more advanced than previous designs and are said to be less accident prone. Finland, France, Japan, Korea and Russia have new plants under construction or consideration. An unlikely alliance between the nuclear industry and many "greens" is emerging as a growing number of these environmentalists come to believe that nuclear energy has a substantial role in controlling carbon emissions.

# THE ROLE OF THE PRECAUTIONARY PRINCIPLE

We noted earlier in this book that the economic-based approach to making societal risk-related decisions would have policymakers rely on cost-benefit analyses, focused on willingness to pay. Many governments, scientists and others find this approach unacceptable in assessing technology for which questions exist about whether it could materially harm the environment or human health. Instead, they urge the application of the **precautionary principle**, which holds that, where there are threats of serious or irreversible damage, lackof full scientific certainty about whether damage could ensue should not be used as a reason for postponing cost-effective measures to prevent environmental (or other) damage. The adoption of this principle by policymakers has the effect of shifting the burden of proof from those who oppose the activity to those who advocate it; in other words, to err on the side of caution, by some definitions, even when there is little or no evidence of harm, as alluded to in the discussion above about geneticallymodified food.

The principle is said to have originated in Germany in the early 1970s. Since then, it has been embedded into some international environmental agreements. It was formally adopted by E.U. countries in the Treaty of Maastricht in 1992. It has been extended from environmental issues to developments related to human health. Its adoption as Principle 15 by world leaders at the 1992 *UN Conference on Environment and Development* in Rio de Janeiro is said to have marked a turning point in advocating its widespread international application. With controversy, it was adopted as well into the *Framework Convention on Climate Change*, *UN Biodiversity Convention* and *the Biosafety Protocol*. Recently, the European Commission expanded application of the principle to ban foods that the public perceives as a health risk, even in the absence of scientific evidence of such a risk.

Its legal underpinnings are said to be "elusive and difficult to define," and the principle remains controversial. As one can quickly deduce from the anthropological theory of risk (group-grid), the principle is a culturally framed concept. Unsurprisingly, the high-group E.U. and low-group U.S. cultures hold different viewpoints on its application.

Critics of the principle point out that there really is nothing uniquely new or risky in present technology that, in many ways, did not exist with prior technology. They assert that society simply is becoming more risk adverse and, in the process, denying itself and, more importantly, the world's poorest the many benefits of scientific advancements. Moreover, they point out that, while there are indeed societal risks in a failure to restrict certain developments, there also are societal risks in overly restricting them. As Brunton (1995) has noted, the risks in permitting certain things to go ahead "tend to be much more visible and politically threatening." For example, "approving a new medicinal drug which turns out to have harmful side effects – such as thalidomide – can produce highly visible victims, heart-rendering news stories, and very damaging political fallout. But incorrectly delaying the introduction of a drug produces victims who are essentially invisible." Would government employees charged with being guardians of a nation's health exercise such "excessive" caution? The careful reader will recognize the behavioral economist's concept of *decision regret* at play here (see Chapter 2).

Proponents are equally vocal in arguing that this "better safe than sorry" principle is nothing more than common sense applied to societal risk management. They contend that the technology of today (e.g., genetically modified organisms, environmental pollutants, beef hormones) is potentially more harmful than in times past, and when the potential for adverse effects is irreversible, we are foolish to fail to take extra precautions. The careful reader will recognize the psychologist's concepts of "unknown" and "dread" inherent in proponents' arguments.

## CONCLUSION

Human-made catastrophes, including terrorism and other loss-causing anti-social behavior, can, in theory, be prevented. We also know, however, that human-made self-organized complex systems will continue to fail; after all, they are designed, made, and managed by imperfect humans. Yet, governmental efforts at loss prevention with respect to all human-made catastrophes can be expected to be at least partially effective, given sufficient resources and commitment.

Science also has a major role to play with respect to technologically related risks such as pollution and genetics, but sometimes has itself become suspect as more scientific research is conducted or funded by corporations that have a vested interest in the outcome. For example, the tobacco industry was able for decades to engage scientists to exploit to the industry's financial advantage the very small amount of residual uncertainty over the risks of smoking in fending off regulation. There seems to be an increasing risk of science becoming debased in the process.

As noted in Chapter 4, government's role extends to warnings and other disclosures of potential or impending harm. Yet this role cannot be divorced from an equally important role of ensuring that citizens have sufficient education to understand the disclosure and enough resources to act on the information. At the same time, government must recognize that people often respond to risks in seemingly irrational ways and must craft its efforts to accommodate the receivers' perceptions or risk.

## DISCUSSION QUESTIONS

1. Describe the precautionary principle and relate its differing degrees of support in the U.S. and the E.U. to the cultural theory of risk.
2. Little disagreement exists today as to whether humans are contributing to global warming. Disagreement persists, however, about how important the consequences will be and what, if anything, to do about it now. Explain the pros and cons of this disagreement.
3. Some students were debating the issue of the "greenhouse effect" and its impact on the planet. (a) One student argues that the greenhouse effect was actually beneficial to the earth's inhabitants. Do you agree? Explain. (b) Increases in the greenhouse effect attributable primarily to an increase in trace gases in the atmosphere have been linked to global warming. Discuss the impact of global warming on the physical environment.

4.   What effect, if any, would you expect changing demographics, as discussed in Chapter 7, to have on (a) losses from hurricanes, (b) the risk of terrorism, (c) social views about climate change, and (d) social views about genetically modified food?

## NOTES

1.   MIPT Knowledge Base at db.mipt.org/Incident TargetModule.jsp.
2.   This section draws from Forbes (2004).
3.   This section draws heavily from Little (2003) © 2003 ieee and Koubatis and Schönberger (2004), pp. 11–26.
4.   This section draws heavily from Brown (2004) and "How Many Planets?" (2002).
5.   Data from http://www.eia.doe.gov/emeu/international/carbondioxide.html.
6.   While many people believe that the 500–550 ppm goal would help avoid the worst calamities, we should recognize that this is a judgment informed by current knowledge, rather than a confirmed conclusion.
7.   At the time this measure was proposed, it was hugely controversial. The U.S. power industry insisted the cuts were prohibitively costly, while nearly every green group decried the measure as a sham.
8.   This section draws heavily from Munich Re (2003).
9.   This discussion draws from *Fact Sheet on Nuclear Reactor Risk* at www.nrc.gov/reading-rm/doc-collections/fact-sheets/reactor-risk.html.
10.  Roentgen Equivalent Man or "rem" is a measure of the amount of damage to human tissue from a dose of radiation.
11.  This discussion draws from "Why Yucca Mountain?" at www.ocrwm.doe.gov/ymp/about/why.shtml.

## REFERENCES

Brown, J. (2004). "Beyond Kyoto." *Foreign Affairs*, 83 (4): 20–32.

Brunton, R. (1995). "The Perils of he Precautionary Principle," *Australasian Biotechnology*. 5(4): 236–238.

*Executive Summary of 9/11 Report* (2004). *The National Commission on Terrorist Attacks Upon the United States*. Washington, DC: Government Printing Office.

Feldhaus, W.R. (1998). "The Physical Environment for Risk and Insurance," Chapter 17, in H.D. Skipper, ed., *International Risk and Insurance: An Environmental–Managerial Approach*. Boston, MA: Irwin/McGraw-Hill.

Forbes, S.W. (2004). *The New World of Risk*. Atlanta, GA: Life Office Management Association.

"How Many Planets? A Survey of the Global Environment" (2002). *The Economist*, July 4.

Institute of Medicine (2000). *To Err Is Human: Building A Safer Health System*. Washington, DC: National Academy Press.

Kendall, H.W. (1991). "The Failure of Nuclear Power," in M. Shubik, ed., *Risk, Organizations, and Society*. Boston, MA: Kluwer Academic Publishers.

Koubatis, A. and Schönberger, J.Y. (2004). *Vulnerabilities and Criticalities of Technical and Organisational Systems in the New Services Economy*. (Etudes et Dossiers No. 280), Zurich: The Geneva Association.

Little, R.G. (2003). "Toward More Robust Infrastructure: Observations on Improving the Resilience and Reliability of Critical Systems" at csdl.computer.org/comp/proceedings/hicss/2003/1874/02/187420058a.pdf.

Munich Re (2003). *Genetic Engineering: A Challenge for the Insurance Industry*. Munich: Munich Re.

Perrow, C. (1999). *Normal Accidents: Living with High-Risk Technologies*. Princeton, NJ: Princeton University Press.

*The 9/11 Report* (2004). *The National Commission on Terrorist Attacks Upon the United States*. Washington, DC: Government Printing Office.

# Chapter 7

# Societal Risk Management and Changing Demographics

## INTRODUCTION

Demographer Richard Easterlin famously observed that "demography is destiny."[1] By this he meant that a society's demographic profile today – especially in terms of population size and age and sex composition – profoundly affects what that society's demographic profile will be in the future, for today's babies are tomorrow's students, then workers, then retirees. In turn, tomorrow's demographic profile profoundly affects that society's employment opportunities and economic growth prospects as well as its relative importance in the world as measured by its economic, social and political power.

The risks that societies – countries – face today are both numerous and potentially grave, ranging from global warming to terrorism. None, however, is as certain or as likely to have as enduring an effect as the world's forthcoming demographic changes in general and what has been labeled as "global aging" in particular. For almost the entirety of human history, the elderly represented a tiny portion of the world's population – never more than 3 percent. Today, more than 15 percent of the population in developed economies is elderly, and that share is projected to reach 25 percent by 2030 and to increase still further thereafter. While the elderly proportions are not as high in developing economies, their proportions too will increase over the next few decades.

The coming demographic transformation will affect almost every dimension of both the public and private sectors and economies. The effects will underlie the greatest risk management challenges facing nations. The enormous fiscal costs, arising from supporting the public pension and health benefits systems in developed economies, are the most discussed challenge. Other effects, however, could prove of even greater importance. Population aging could cause economic growth to slow dramatically, at the same time that tomorrow's families were compelled to cope with numerous frail elders and tomorrow's businesses were compelled to cope with a dearth of young consumers. Globally, the entire geopolitical order could be rearranged in profound ways, as the developed countries' proportion of total world output shrinks and the political balance of power shifts.

This chapter explores some of the more important potential consequences of the forthcoming demographic transformation and the means for dealing with these consequences.

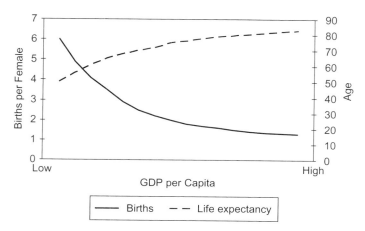

**Figure 7.1**    Relationship Between Life Expectancy and Fertility and Income

We begin with an exploration of the demographic changes taking place worldwide. We next explore the various effects that aging might have worldwide, including those related to fiscal balance, economic growth and labor market challenges, financial markets, and international economic and political stability.

## THE DEMOGRAPHIC TRANSFORMATION

This century's demographic transformation is causing **population aging**, which results from the combination of rising longevity and falling fertility rates. Increasing longevity increases the relative number of elderly, and decreasing fertility rates decrease the relative number of young. Both greater longevity and falling fertility rates are associated with economic development. In general, increasing personal incomes means that people have access to better healthcare, live in safer conditions, and have fewer children because of urbanization and a lesser need to have many children to attend to elder parents. Figure 7.1 offers a stylized version of this evolution that has been observed to varying degrees in every country whose citizens achieve greater income.

The world's population was comparatively young in 1950, with a median age of 23.6. The median age rose to 26.4 at the beginning of this millennium and is expected to rise to 36.8 by 2050. The United Nations (2003) reports that people aged 80 years or over in five countries will account for 54 percent of the oldest people globally. The countries are China (98 million), India (47 million), the U.S. (29 million), Japan (17 million) and Brazil (13 million). Cohen (2003, p. 1172) offers his concerns:

> By 2050, the human population will probably be larger by 2 to 4 billion people [to 8.9 billion], more slowly growing . . ., more urban, especially in less developed regions, and older than in the 20th century. Two major demographic uncertainties in the next 50 years concern international migration and the structure of families. Economies, nonhuman environments and cultures (including values, religions and politics) strongly influence demographic changes. Hence human choices, individual and collective, will have demographic effects, intentional or otherwise.

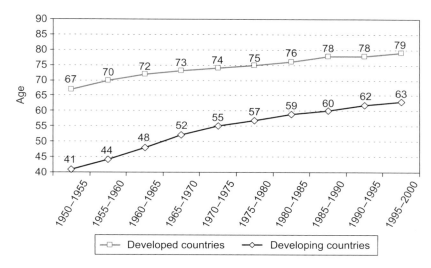

**Figure 7.2**    Trends in Life Expectancy at Birth for Developed and Developing Countries. *Source*: The United Nations

## Increasing Life Expectancies

**Life expectancy** is the average number of total years that humans of a given age live. For example, life expectancy for the typical child born in the U.S. in 2000 was about 76.5 years. Life expectancy for a typical 65-year old in 2000 was about 17.5 (or to age 82.5).

Worldwide, life expectancy at birth rose dramatically during the 20th century. Gains during the century exceeded such gains achieved over the previous 50 centuries. Figure 7.2 shows the trajectory of these gains for developed and developing countries during the second half of the 20th century.[2]

For the U.S., females born in 1900 could, on average, expect to live to age 48 (males to age 46). Females born at mid-century could expect to live to age 71 (males, 65), an enormous gain of 23 years over only 50 year. Females born at the end of the last century could expect to live to 80 (males, 74), a 9 year gain over the 1950 number. The dramatic improvements during the first half of the 20th century were due primarily to the pervasive positive externalities of improved sanitation, better personal hygiene because of greater understanding of its importance, and a healthier and more stable food supply. The gains during the latter half-century were due more to improved healthcare.

Differences in life expectancy are observed by sex and socioeconomic status. The gap between female and male life expectancies grew for most of the 20th century, but has declined over the past 10 or so years, perhaps due to the greater rate of smoking cessation among males than females – although greater proportions of males than females still smoke.[3] We also know that wealthier people, on average, live longer than poorer people, because the rich usually have access to better healthcare and tend to be more knowledgeable about the importance of lifestyle on health.

## Decreasing Fertility Rates

As Figure 7.1 suggests, increasing incomes are associated with decreasing fertility rates. The world, on average, has experienced higher incomes and greater health than in times past.

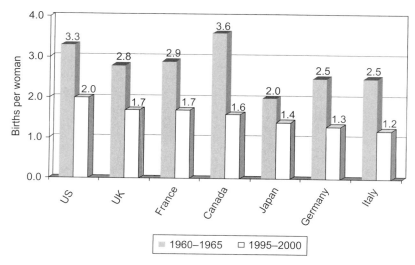

**Figure 7.3**    Fertility Rates in the G7 Countries. *Source*: The United Nations

Worldwide **fertility rates** – the average number of lifetime births per woman – have fallen from 5.0 births in the mid-1960s to 2.8 births today.[4] The rates for every developed country in the mid-1960s were above the **replacement rate** of 2.1 births – the birth rate needed to maintain a stable population over time, ignoring immigration. Today, fertility rates are below replacement rates in 61 countries (including every developed country) and substantially below in many of the countries. Figure 7.3 highlights fertility rates for the Group of Seven (G7) economies.

## Population Aging

This combined effect of increasing life expectancy and decreasing fertility causes population aging. Figure 7.4 shows the proportion of population in the developed and developing world at age 65 and over for the 100-year span of 1950–2050. Clearly, the proportion of elderly is growing worldwide. Figure 7.5 compares the proportion of people at age 65 or older for the year 2000, and offers projections to year 2050 for the G7 countries. Note that Germany, Italy and Japan are expected to have particularly large age 65+ segments, whereas the U.K. and the U.S. will have larger but comparatively smaller segments.

## IMPLICATIONS FOR FISCAL BALANCE

The problems of economic insecurity and resulting social unrest occasioned by ever-expanding populations of involuntarily unemployed dominated social thinking in developed countries during much of the 20th century. The resulting solutions to this problem of societal risk were labor laws that often sacrificed efficiency for stable employment, especially in Europe, and substantial social insurance programs such as in the U.S. Social Security system.

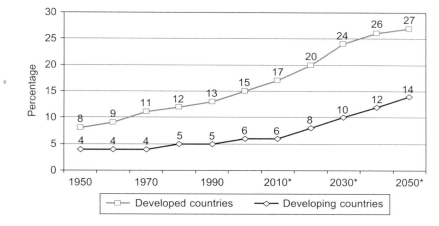

**Figure 7.4**   Percentage of World's Population Aged 65 and Over (* Projection). *Source*: The United Nations

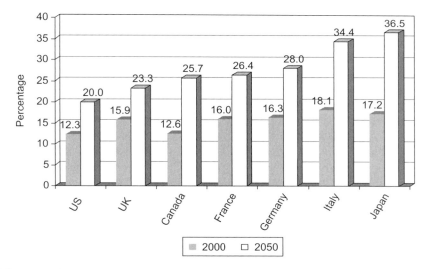

**Figure 7.5**   Proportions of Populations Aged 65 and over in G7 Countries: 2000 and 2050. *Source*: The United Nations

When 20th-century governments in the developed countries decided to expand public pensions – the most expensive component of social welfare programs – they decided to fund them on a pay-as-you-go (paygo) basis. The paygo model was attractive compared to a "fully funded" basis for at least two reasons. First, paygo appeared to be affordable, as it did not require pre-funding for those who had already retired and were eligible for pension benefits. Second, at program inception, the number of retired beneficiaries was comparatively small and the number of contributing workers was large. This relationship seemed likely to continue to expand indefinitely. With time, these original expectations proved illusory.

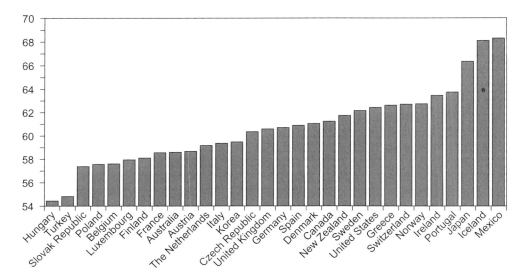

**Figure 7.6**    Estimated Effective Retirement Ages of Males in OECD Countries (2000). *Source*: OECD

Changes in life expectancy affect public pension programs. For example, when the U.S. Social Security system was founded in 1935, the typical worker who reached the system's normal retirement age of 65 was expected to live another 12 years. Today, system retirees can expect to live another 18 years. If the normal retirement age had been indexed proportionally to longevity since 1935, today's retirees would have to wait until age 72 to receive full Social Security benefits.

Workers in the developed countries, however, are retiring earlier, not later, thereby compounding the impact of rising longevity on pensions costs. For example, during the mid-1960s, the average age of actual retirement within the G7 economies was 66; today it is 62 and falling. Figure 7.6 offers estimates of actual retirement ages for the OECD countries as of the year 2000.

## Effect on Public Budgets

Demography is indeed destiny, especially for public budgets. Population aging translates directly into a lower ratio of taxpaying workers to retired beneficiaries that, in turn, translates into greater demands on public budgets. The UN projects that the ratio of working-age adults (aged 15–64) to elderly (aged 65 and greater) in the developed world will drop from 4.5 to 1 today to 2.2 to 1 in 2050. The actual ratio of contributing workers to retired beneficiaries is lower and is due to drop further, because not all younger adults work and many retire before 65. According to estimates by the IMF, this support ratio will fall by 2050 to 2.3 in the U.S., 1.5 to 1 in Japan, 1.4 to 1 in France and 1.2 to 1 in Germany. In Italy, it may sink below 1 to 1 by the year 2050, meaning that more people would be collecting benefits than are paying taxes. Figure 7.7 shows recent and projected future support ratios for the G7 countries.

The European Commission and the OECD published a long-term projection of the possible impact of global aging on public budgets. According to their estimates, spending on public pensions in the typical developed country could grow from 8.8 percent to 13.2 percent

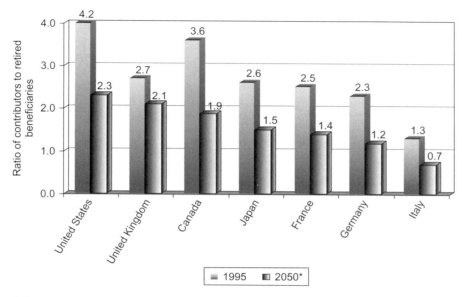

**Figure 7.7**    Ratio of Contributors to Retired Beneficiaries in the G7 Public Pension Systems (* Projection).
*Source*: The IMF

of GDP by 2050. This represents a 50 percent increase in public budgets. Even so, many knowledgeable observers believe that this projection may be a serious underestimate. They argue that official projections are derived from a set of assumptions about future economic and demographic developments that are overly optimistic and unlikely to be realized.

Researchers at the Global Aging Initiative at the Center for Strategic and International Studies (CSIS) are among the skeptics. They devised their own projections by adjusting key assumptions within the official projection to more closely reflect historical trends. The CSIS models suggest that the total portion of national output dedicated to public pensions in the typical developed country grows from 8.8 percent to 15.8 percent of GDP by 2050, almost twice the growth rate estimated by the European Commission and the OECD.

The magnitude of the extra fiscal burden to fund public pensions varies greatly among the developed countries. Some are aging more rapidly than others. Some have earlier retirement ages and more generous benefits than others. Figure 7.8 shows the revised CSIS projections based on historical trends for each of the G7 countries.

Irrespective of the accuracy of the long-term projections, we know that, in the absence of substantial and unanticipated changes, pension costs in almost every country will begin an inexorable rise around 2010 and continue climbing rapidly for two to three decades thereafter before slowing or plateauing at a much higher level than at present. Global aging represents a permanent shift in the age structure of the developed world's population and will put permanent and substantial pressure on public budgets.

Pensions are not the only public costs projected to grow as societies age. Healthcare for the elderly will also constitute a large burden. In developed countries, each elder on average consumes 3–5 times more healthcare than a younger adult. Moreover, the older the elders, the more costly their care becomes. In the U.S., the overall per capita ratio of public healthcare spending on the "old old" (aged 85 and greater) to spending on the "young old" (aged 65–74) is roughly 3 to 1. For nursing home care, the ratio is roughly 20 to 1.

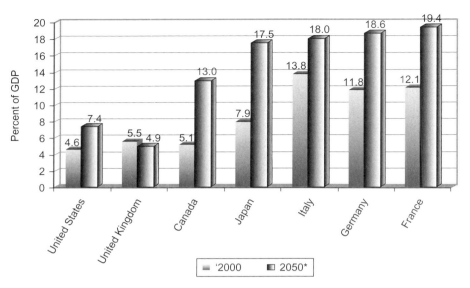

**Figure 7.8**    Spending on Public Pensions as a Percentage of GDP for the G7 Countries (* Projection). *Source*: EC-OECD and CSIS

What makes these differentials so ominous is that the population of the "old old" is expected to grow the fastest. The UN projects that the number of elderly aged 65–74 in the developed world will grow by roughly 50 percent between now and 2050, while the number aged 85 and over will grow by nearly 300 percent. Today, just one in 10 elders in the developed world is 85 or older. By mid-century, this share will be one in five.

According to the CSIS, these demographic multipliers threaten to interact explosively with the rising trend in healthcare costs. Due mostly to the introduction and diffusion of new technologies in the healthcare industry, per capita public healthcare spending in developed countries has grown 1.2 percent per annum faster than per capita GDP over the past 30 years.

The official projections assume that future per capita spending will grow at the same rate as per capita GDP growth. Even so, the European Commission and the OECD project that public health benefits for the elderly will more than double – from 2.1 percent of GDP today to 4.6 percent by 2050. By comparison, the CSIS projects that healthcare spending will continue to grow 1 percentage point faster than per capita GDP. Under the CSIS projection, public healthcare spending on the elderly in the typical developed country will increase by 7.3 percent of GDP between now and 2050, more than twice the growth rate of official projection. The CSIS projection indicates that public retirement spending in the typical developed country could grow from 11 to 23 percent of GDP by 2050.

## Solutions

To stabilize spending as a share of GDP, public pension benefits in almost every developed country would eventually have to be cut by 30 to 6tt0 percent. Yet in almost every country, workers remain highly dependent on public pensions and are unprepared for and likely unwilling to accept large benefit reductions. Even in the U.S., where public pension benefits are modest by developed-country standards, Social Security income accounts for roughly

60 percent of the total income of average-income retirees. In France, Germany and Sweden, public pensions account for roughly 80 percent. Among lower-income retirees, the dependence is even greater.

Only a handful of countries, most of them in the English-speaking world, have *funded private* pension systems that cover one-half or more of the workforce. Just three countries – Japan, the U.K. and the U.S – account for more than 80 percent of the entire world's funded pension assets.

As societies scale back public pension promises, they must develop new means of supporting the elderly that do not overburden the economy, overtax the young, or lead to public turmoil. Although the generosity of today's paygo systems will inevitably be reduced, retirement security can be strengthened, although the challenge of global aging leaves no painless options.

## Traditional strategies

Over the past few decades, governments have paid for the growth in retirement benefits by raising taxes, cutting other programs, or borrowing from the public. These traditional strategies alone likely will be of limited use in the future. The reasons are as follows:

*   *Tax rates already high*: Taxes in most developed economies are already high. In the E.U., total taxes average 45 percent of GDP. In many European countries, tax rates to support social welfare programs already exceed 30 percent. If the CSIS projections are on target, payroll taxes would have to be raised by another 30 percent to equal the projected GDP growth of 12 percent. Such enormous increases probably are impossible politically. Even if feasible, such high tax rates would slow economic growth rates, exacerbate already high rates of structural unemployment, and push more workers into the growing "informal" economy. Therefore, few countries will be able to raise taxes enough to cover the projected growth in retirement benefits, and many may not be able to raise them much at all.

*   *Reducing other government expenditures likely insufficient*: Cutting other government expenditures may help. The projected growth in retirement spending, however, is so large that some governments could eliminate all general purpose funding – from defense and infrastructure to police and schools – and still incur budget deficits for the next 25 years. Even for the U.S., with its *comparative* young population and less expensive public pension systems, the crowding out strategy may already have run its course.

*   *Borrowing additional money likely infeasible*: Borrowing to cover the rise in public pension costs is not an option for the developed world as a whole. Within a few decades, widening government deficits would exhaust worldwide savings. If the rise in pension costs were temporary, individual countries might be able to borrow to meet it. Unfortunately, the rise will be permanent, and any country trying to borrow its way out of the problem likely risks economic ruin.

## New strategies

Successful reform relies on some combination of traditional and new approaches. In broad terms, recommended strategies rely on three avenues: (1) reduction of pension costs, (2) substitution of funded retirement savings, and (3) stimulation of economic development and workforce productivity. We summarize each avenue below in this section.

### Reduction of pension costs

The cost of existing public pension systems can be reduced. Although the details for how to accomplish this vary, all reform plans ultimately achieve their cost reduction in one or more of the following four ways:

*   reducing the generosity of new pensions (e.g., changing the benefit formula);
*   reducing the generosity of current pensions (e.g., providing less generous cost of living increases or taxing benefits);
*   restricting pension eligibility (e.g., raising the minimum retirement age or economic-means testing benefit eligibility);
*   changing retirement incentives (e.g., allowing elderly workers to continue to accrue benefits).

### Funded retirement savings

The second avenue is to substitute funded retirement savings, in whole or part, for today's paygo promises. This funding strategy has advantages, including higher national savings and the potential for higher returns on contributions. Funding also decouples retirement security from the ups and downs of demographics and, to the extent that foreign investment is allowed, from the ups and downs of national economic performance as well.

Ideally, this funding strategy should allow workers and retirees in the aging developed world to benefit from the growth possibilities of the younger developing world. In designing funded systems, however, governments face several important issues and choices, including:

*   Is the funding mechanism held in the public or private sector?
*   How are the transition costs from paygo to a funded system handled?
*   Should the system rely on partial or full funding?
*   Is participation mandatory or voluntary and, if the former, will it be so for all workers or only for younger and new workers?

### Economic development and workforce productivity

The third avenue is to ease the future fiscal burden, hence the need for benefit reductions, through broader strategies that boost the size and productivity of tomorrow's economy and workforce. These strategies apply to areas of the economy beyond fiscal balances and are discussed in the next section.

## ECONOMIC GROWTH AND LABOR MARKET CHALLENGES

Public debate about the effects of the coming demographic transformation on public pension and health systems is well underway, even if meaningful action has yet to be taken in

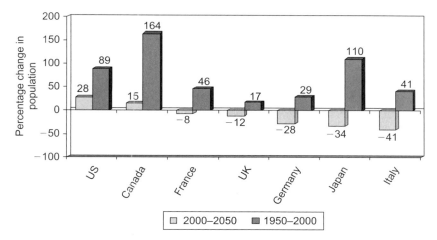

**Figure 7.9**    Percentage Change in Working-Age Populations (Aged 15–64) in the G7 Countries. *Source*:
The United Nations

most developed countries. An unavoidable and much needed corresponding debate about
its effects on labor markets and economic growth is just emerging.[5]

## Expected Decline in Labor Force

The coming era of unprecedented population decline in developed countries promises profound effects on labor supply as well as on national and global economic growth. In the past,
governments worried about overpopulation. Today, most worry about depopulation.

Already, the working-age population of several countries, including Italy and Japan, is
shrinking. By 2010, the UN projects that working-age (aged 15–64) populations of most developed countries will be in decline, the only exceptions being Australia, Canada, Ireland, New
Zealand and the U.S. Europe's population under age 15 is already 23 percent smaller than it was
in 1970. Japan's is 25 percent smaller. The population in Europe peaked in 1997 at 729 million
and began declining for the first time in modern memory. In 2007, Japan's population began to
shrink as well. By 2030, the populations of most developing countries also are projected to be
falling.

In the most rapidly aging countries, population losses will be dramatic. The UN projects that,
by mid-century, there will be 28 percent fewer working-age Germans, 36 percent fewer working-
age Japanese, and 42 percent fewer working-age Italians. Because of relatively higher fertility
rates and strong immigration, the Canadian and U.S. situations are more favorable, as Figure
7.9 suggests.

## The Economics of National Output and Growth

A nation's total output – its GDP – is the simple product of the number of workers times
the average wage. Thus, a nation's GDP will increase if the number of workers, average
wage or both increases. Since the Industrial Revolution, increasing populations and labor
forces have fueled world growth. At the same time, average wages rose because worker

productivity increased thanks to workers becoming more knowledgeable and efficient. Additionally, physical capital has been employed more intensively. During the last decades of the 20th century, population growth in developed countries accounted for one-half to two-thirds of the rise in each country's GDP. The remainder came from gains in labor and capital efficiency. What about the future?

Standard economic growth models indicate that a shrinking labor force does not necessarily lead to economic stagnation. A decline in the size of the labor force can be offset by an increase in worker productivity. Worker productivity can be enhanced through greater use of physical capital, particularly technology, and other techniques such as worker education and training and improved processes. Theoretically, it is possible to achieve positive economic growth despite a shrinking labor force if productivity increases at a meaningfully higher rate than the shrinkages in the labor force.

This happy result seems unlikely to materialize for two reasons. First, economic theory teaches that productivity improvements diminish as more of a given production factor is employed. Thus, as more workers have to be replaced by physical capital such as machines and computers, the smaller the degree to which production can be increased through the use of this additional physical capital – for example, by adding an additional unit of machinery. Second, it is doubtful that labor productivity can be substantially enhanced when workers, on average, are getting older. Much depends on whether productivity can be increased through technological progress. Might this happen?

The larger the drop in the labor supply, the faster productivity growth must rise if the real economic growth rate is to be sustained. In recent decades, productivity growth among the developed countries has averaged about 1.4 percent per annum. The three major economic powers – the E.U., Japan and the U.S. – would need *additional* productivity growth of about 1 percent per year or more if their national products are to continue to expand at the same rates as in the past. This might materialize but seems unlikely.

## Savings and Investment in Aging Populations

Some economists believe that the growing labor shortage of the coming decades will lead to marked wage increases. If so, that would create incentives to substitute physical capital for the missing human capital. A further increase in the capital intensity of production, therefore, could be one important answer to the demographic distortions expected in the labor market.

It is questionable, however, whether, in a real world of aging populations, the substitution process would take place without major frictions. Investment is necessary to increase capital intensity. This leads to the complex subject of savings and investment. Even in normal times with no major upsets, their development is rarely smooth or equal.

Declining populations may go hand in hand with a drop in investment because of weakening demand. Families without young children have a lower propensity to consume than those with children. Government spending is also conditional on demographic trends, because expenditure on education and infrastructure is dependent on population size and density. If this conjecture holds, we would expect a fall in investment, especially as enterprises operating in stagnating or even shrinking sales markets would run a higher risk of misplaced investment.

A much greater risk is that savings may not be as high as necessary. Both theory and experience show that individual propensity to save depends on age. Young adults have, as a rule, high consumption requirements and, therefore, save little. In middle age, propensity to save is very high, especially as saving for retirement takes on greater importance. Retirees generally save only for their heirs, if at all. If one assumes that propensity to save takes such a hump-shaped path over the life cycle (as depicted in Figure 2.4), then propensity to save in the triad regions will still be high in the coming years, but will fall steeply as the baby boom generation enters retirement.

## Population Aging and Technical Progress

The strategy of compensating for a growing labor shortage by injecting more capital will lead to sustained growth only if the decline in marginal productivity, which accompanies rising factor input, can be slowed or even reversed through technological progress. These technological aids also must be continuously enhanced; that is, they must become ever more productive.

To have continuous productivity growth, there must be a continuous stream of innovation – inventions that are exploited economically in new production processes and new products as well as in new markets. There is considerable evidence that countries with young, growing populations are more innovative than countries in which the average age of the labor force is rising toward 50 and young workers are scarce. Most advances in technological research are made by young people.

Young people contribute greatly to the dissemination of new knowledge throughout the economy. Young workers have had up-to-date training. They are geographically mobile and flexible in their choices of jobs. Moreover, acceptance of technical innovations is probably highest among this age group. The importance of these characteristics can hardly be overrated.

Individual physical and mental capacities generally decline with age. The older the workers, the longer it takes to nurture such capacities, and the more the knowledge acquired during their training diminishes in value. Of course, experience acquired over the working life increases at the same time. In view of the faster pace of structural change in the 21st century, however, this factor could count for less and less. The growing depreciation of job-specific knowledge and skills represents a considerable threat to the development of productivity in aging populations.

Young people are generally more prepared to accept risks than their elders. Not only does a higher remaining life expectancy enable young people to derive greater benefit from successful investments, they also show greater resilience in the event of poor decisions. Put differently, aging societies could run short of entrepreneurs, especially dynamic and pioneering innovators. A recent survey of 21 nations shows that, in all cases, the 25–44-year olds are the most active group in entrepreneurship and that entrepreneurial activities are highly correlated to economic growth (Reynolds et al., 2000).

This perception tallies with the thinking behind the **theory of endogenous growth** that is based on the belief that a positive correlation exists between the development of productivity and economic growth. This theory holds that the emergence and dissemination of new knowledge triggers self-propelling processes, disseminated in network structures. Experts engaged in research and development drive technological progress in close contact with experts from other enterprises. Information is exchanged through many channels, as when experts move from one entity to another. The productivity of an economy then rises in line with the density of the networks and the intensity of communication. Countries with large numbers of scientific and technological elites or large pools of highly qualified workers have an advantage. This theory, therefore, suggests achieving such high growth rates will be even more challenging for most developed countries.

## Solutions

Opportunities to strengthen economic growth in the triad regions exist. (Again, see Figure 2.4.) These include the general areas of increasing efficiency (i.e., better use of resources) and of importing resources. Measures to increase efficiency include the following:

- removing obstacles to work by adopting strategies to persuade those who do not work to get jobs and those with jobs to work more (some examples include: (1) making disability and unemployment benefits less generous in countries in which their generosity provides little incentive for recipients to return to work; (2) encouraging employers to provide benefits, such as daycare and eldercare, that make it easier for employees with dependents to work; and (3) ensuing equal pay for equal work, thus drawing more females into the work force);
- emphasizing improvements in education and training at all age levels;
- raising productivity growth by altering regulatory and tax policies that discourage entrepreneurship (e.g., long delays and high costs of new business startup) or promote capital misallocation (e.g., by differential taxing of savings and investment);
- rewarding child rearing through public funding of family allowances and other prenatal incentives;
- increasing immigration.

The importation of resources also has an important role to play, for the problems of population aging cannot be solved solely in a national context. The labor markets in most emerging economies will be in surplus for some decades. The situation is reversed with regard to capital. Emerging markets are short of capital, whereas developed countries will potentially continue to accumulate high savings for many years to come. Under these circumstances, the transfer of resources would seem to be in the interests of both.

Migration of workers from emerging economies is one logical but controversial solution, particularly in Europe, and increasingly in the U.S. as well, where opinion is divided over whether and to what extent migration may be helpful in dealing with their demographic problems. The debate is often emotional. Many take the erroneous view that migration can prevent population aging. The UN estimates that the elder dependency ratio in Europe can be kept constant until 2050 only with extremely high net immigration of 25 million people per year. A comprehensive adoption of this policy will result in 75 percent of Europeans being immigrants or their descendants by the end of the 21st century. Migration on this scale seems highly unlikely for social and political reasons. Even though migration is not a remedy for all ills, it can help, but this can happen only if the bulk of the migration is to labor markets, not to welfare systems, as is often the case today.

## THE CHALLENGES TO FINANCIAL MARKETS ——————

Population trends could affect the stability of global financial markets.[6] Fiscal crises resulting from budget deficits could undermine saving rates, and, in extreme cases, provoke fears of default of sovereign bonds and currency shocks. Even in the absence of fiscal crisis, financial markets could be significantly affected as burgeoning populations of aged, retired workers across the developed world spend down their life savings, more or less in unison.

World savings must equal world investment since the world is a closed system. If investment demand in the developed world does not fall commensurately with the decline in saving, the result could be dramatic swings in interest rates and equity returns. In turn, this could result in capital outflows as investors seek better yields abroad. Such outflows could adversely affect productivity growth, which could further lessen the chances of productivity improvements in the developed world.

Further, smaller young cohorts could cause a steep contraction in housing demand. This contraction could undermine real estate values at the household level, which, in turn, could weaken the balance sheets of financial institutions that hold mortgages and mortgage-backed assets.

Potentially adverse financial trends in developed countries could be reinforced by population aging in Eastern Europe and in East and Southeast Asia. The nations in Asia also could experience declining saving rates just as deficit pressures are peaking in developed nations. For example, modeling by the IMF suggests that these nations, too, will experience declining saving rates as their populations age. Even so, developing nations are likely to have higher saving rates and be the source of much of the world's capital in the long run.

Cost is not the only reason public pensions need to be reformed. Most economists believe that *unfunded* pension benefits substitute for genuine savings and thereby reduce capital formation and economic growth. When government promises citizens future income, they need not save as much for their retirement. In most countries, retirement rules and benefit formulas penalize continued work, once minimum eligibility ages or service requirements are met. The establishment of funded social security schemes and employer-sponsored private pension systems in developed and developing countries could mitigate the downward pressures on aggregate global saving.

## IMPLICATIONS FOR INTERNATIONAL RELATIONS AND STABILITY

The demographics-is-destiny thesis carries over easily to countries' relative position in the world political and military power structure.[7] Two general theories seem relevant here.

- **Political power theory** suggests that, other things being equal, countries with large populations are more powerful politically than are countries with small populations. This is traditionally so because large countries can field large military establishments with their large populations and probably large national budgets.

- The second theory concerns rising and declining population bases. In general terms, **economic power theory** offers that deteriorating population bases mean declining economic strength, which, in turn, invites other countries to expand into that space. For countries with rising populations, the theory breaks into two sub-themes. Countries with rapidly rising populations of young that cannot be accommodated internally are believed to be destabilizing forces on the world political stage. The other sub-theme holds that creative management of an expanding population base amplifies national power on the international stage.

## The Global Generation Gap

As we know, during the past half-century, a global generation gap has emerged in which the richest countries have aged much more than the poorest. This trend will continue and has enormous geopolitical implications.

At one extreme of this generation gap are the aging developed economies. As we have discussed, these countries face the twin challenges of unsustainable old-age benefit promises and potentially weakened economies because of labor shortages and shrinking numbers of consumers.

In the middle is a group of emerging economies that are aging rapidly amidst the throes of industrialization and urbanization. Fertility rates for many of these countries, including China, Korea, Sri Lanka, Taiwan and Thailand are already below replacement rates, and birthrates are falling rapidly in countries such as Mexico, Brazil, India and Iran. Increasingly, this group of countries must carry the burden of global growth. It is critical that crises in the very young countries not be allowed to disrupt their progress.

At the other extreme is a group of countries, mainly in the Islamic world and Africa, that will remain very young and continue to experience high birthrates for at least the next 20 years and possibly beyond. In the youngest countries, populations have doubled during the past 18 years, and, in some, populations are likely to double again during the next 20 years. Living standards can rise only if a country's economy grows faster than its population; that is, only if productivity increases. Living conditions in several of these countries have grown increasingly harsh and unforgiving in recent decades, and they could grow still harsher and less forgiving in the years to come.

## The Global Challenge

Exploding child dependency is causing a decline in living standards and fostering resentments in ultra-youthful societies. The median ages in Afghanistan, Iraq, Pakistan, Saudi Arabia and Syria are all under 19. The typical Palestinian and Yemeni is barely 15. In 1950, Saudi Arabia had just over 3 million citizens. By 2050, it is projected to be at 120 million at current birth rates.

This is a problem and issue of enormous significance. Exploding populations are occurring in societies that generate few opportunities for jobs, offer only limited avenues for political expression, have comparatively low educational levels or opportunities, and usually afford women (mothers) even fewer educational and occupational opportunities. During the past 20 years, politics in many such societies has become seriously radicalized. Unfortunately, prospects for meaningful improvement in the years to come seem remote. Unemployment and hopelessness combined with the impetuousness of youth are a dangerous mix.

Ultra-youthful societies also are characterized by high levels of social violence. Of the world's 25 youngest countries (most in central Africa), 16 have experienced major civil conflicts since 1995. The worst of this violence has been perpetrated by rag-tag armies of machete-wielding teenagers, some of them as young as 12. Iran's median age was 17 at the time of its 1978 revolution, and China's was 19 when its Cultural Revolution shook the world. Any comprehensive theory of global conflict will reflect that the 20th century's bloodiest upheavals, from Europe's wars to Cambodia's holocaust, began with surpluses of teenagers.

Contrast these observations with the E.U. after World War II. Europe adopted a sophisticated and elaborate set of social and economic policies to minimize future social tensions.

## INSIGHT 7.1: WILL NATO BE TOO OLD TO FIGHT?

The North Atlantic Treaty Organization (NATO) was formed more than 50 years ago in response to the threats posed by the then Soviet Union. The rapid aging of Europe will only deepen the age and military disparity within the NATO allies on both sides of the Atlantic. The shrinking of the alliance's domestic work forces is now a demographic certainty, and competition from the private sector will make military recruitment harder than ever before. Countries with manpower shortages may prove unwilling to commit to military confrontations, instead relying on ad hoc diplomacy and outright appeasement.

There will also be no money in European budgets for militaries. Their social welfare systems are heavily mortgaged to cover pension and health expenditures for their rapidly aging populations. Generous welfare state commitments will divert revenue from maintaining military preparedness, and many European allies are likely to allow their armed forces to continue aging into obsolescence. Under current trends, Europe will lack the ability and the motivation to influence international security.

Meanwhile, the yawning generation gap with the third world poses grave problems for the West. A report released by the CIA points out that "youth bulges" often accompany political instability, ethnic wars, revolutions and anti-regime activities. Young men with few economic opportunities are easily recruited into radical causes.

In much of the volatile Middle East, exploding birthrates have created ultra-young societies. Unemployment, already a serious problem in these countries, is likely to get much worse in coming decades. A lack of economic prospects and fewer opportunities to emigrate, a byproduct of anti-terrorism, is quickly turning the region into a pressure cooker. If it explodes, will the developed world be too old to contend with it?

*Source*: Romm (2002).

---

The great lesson of the first half of the 20th century was that mass unemployment and poverty had provided the kindling for class warfare and ultimately the tragedy of two world wars and wasted resources and lives. This realization led every industrial country to establish generous welfare states, although many in the U.S. do not think of the social insurance system in this way. Of course, these policies now produce a burden on European economies and national budgets and have significant implications for national power. Insight 7.1 offers one expert's views on this important issue. We know that social spending in the developed world continues to expand. Will social spending so crowd out military spending in the future that some developed countries will be unable or unwilling to meet their own national security needs? If so, what, if anything, will other countries – particularly the U.S. – do about challenges to such countries' national sovereignty?

Already, spending on national defense by the developed countries has been in decline for several years, as measured by its proportion of GDP. See Figure 7.10. The demise of the Cold War certainly explains part of this decline, but the massive increase in social welfare spending – also shown in Figure 7.10 – has been an important factor in governments' budget reallocations and promises to be even more important in the future.

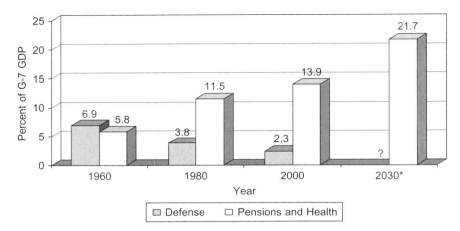

**Figure 7.10**   Defense and Social Welfare Spending as Percentage of GDP for the G7 Countries (* Projection). *Source*: CSIS, CIA (U.S.), OECD, and OMB (U.S.) (various years)

**Table 7.1**   Twelve Largest Countries Ranked by Population

| Rank | 1950 | 2000 | 2050* |
|---|---|---|---|
| 1 | China | China | India |
| 2 | Soviet Union | India | China |
| 3 | India | U.S. | U.S. |
| 4 | U.S. | Indonesia | Pakistan |
| 5 | Japan | Brazil | Indonesia |
| 6 | Indonesia | Russia | Nigeria |
| 7 | Germany | Pakistan | Bangladesh |
| 8 | Brazil | Bangladesh | Brazil |
| 9 | U.K. | Japan | Congo |
| 10 | Italy | Nigeria | Ethiopia |
| 11 | France | Mexico | Mexico |
| 12 | Bangladesh | Germany | Philippines |

*Projection.
*Sources*: CSIS and UN.

Developing countries seem destined to play an ever-larger role in the geopolitical calculus. Fifty years ago, six of the world's 12 most populous nations were developed countries. Today, just three are developed – Germany, Japan and the U.S. Fifty years from now, only the U.S. will remain on the list, as Table 7.1 projections suggest.

Many of the middle group of developing countries discussed above face a double challenge. They too will face population aging – just later – and they are not yet "rich." Mexico is projected to age more during the next 40 years than America did in the past 120. China's age structure is projected to be older than America's by 2025. If the UN's projections are correct, India and the U.S. will have markedly similar age structures at mid-century. All face the prospect of growing old before they grow rich. Motivated by this sobering reality, more and more political leaders are racing to make their countries as rich as they can and as fast as they can. In the process, they continue to place greater reliance on the market-economy model while recognizing that liberal international trade policies benefit all.

## CONCLUSION

The casual observer might be forgiven for regarding the above trends and issues with something less than alarm. After all, projections many decades into the future are notoriously unreliable, and much of the above analyses are based on assumptions about the nature of a future that no one can know. Clearly, the question is not whether the future will prove the assumptions wrong, but by how much and in what direction. While little can be done in the short term about the forthcoming demographic transformation, the plain fact is that we cannot know what options the future may hold for productivity increases, immigration policy, market openness and transparency, world peace, and dozens of other issues that bear directly on the effects of the demographic transformation on labor markets, economic growth, financial markets and international stability.[8]

Good risk management calls for the identification and assessment of risks using the best tools and techniques available at the time of the assessment. If this process reveals exposures whose occurrence could meaningfully disrupt the organization, the logical next step is some combination of risk control and financing measures. We do not fail to take action because of the possibility that the assessment might, in hindsight, prove wrong. Societal risk management issues are no different.

Under a plausible worst-case scenario, collapsing global growth in the rich and middle-income countries would usher in an economic dark age from which no welfare state could emerge intact. The last time such a disaster occurred was in the 1930s' Great Depression. The overriding need to prevent such a meltdown defines the geopolitical imperative of the next several decades.

Developing economies are particularly vulnerable. Their social safety nets are modest. Thus, social peace in these nations likely will depend to a great extent on the state of the global economy. China estimates that its GDP must expand by at least 8 percent per year to prevent rising unemployment. If a chain reaction of global economic shocks were to undermine China's growth rate, it might be unable to contain the ensuing social unrest. Of course, soaring unemployment and misery would not be limited to China. The youngest societies could be expected to experience even greater instability.

Another scenario holds that global aging is creating important opportunities. The wise and graceful aging of the industrial world could prove a boon to global prosperity and social stability. Aging and declining populations seem almost certain to slow GDP growth in the rich countries. As suggested earlier, this, in turn, could reduce the number of profitable investment opportunities in their domestic economies. In response, managers of capital increasingly would look to the developing world for more lucrative investment opportunities.

If risks can be contained, a river of capital could flow to developing nations, whose large labor forces and low productivity hold the promise of high returns. In this win-win scenario, rich country retirees reap high rates of return on their savings while helping to accelerate economic development in the developing regions of the world.

Realizing this potential will require a historic expansion of global trade and investment alongside fundamental structural reforms in both the developed and developing regions. For their part, the developing countries must create the physical, educational, financial and legal infrastructure needed to become safer, more productive places to invest. The rich countries need to place more of the retirement burden on saving – for example, by expanding *private pensions* – to ensure that they remain capital exporters. Further, as has been suggested, they should act decisively to avert fiscal and economic crisis by lengthening work lives, accepting more immigrants, and taking steps to boost productivity.

Finally, the developed economies must actively intervene to strengthen the moderate elements in the world's ultra-youthful societies. The sooner today's youthful countries begin to age, the more peaceful and prosperous we will all become. The era ahead will be one of great danger, but one of great opportunities.

## DISCUSSION QUESTIONS

1. In the context of the several demographic factors that affect the insurance industry worldwide, why is the aging of societies an especially significant factor?
2. Is tampering with the aging process desirable? Explain.
3. How do the demographic profiles of the U.S., Japan and Europe differ? (a) What might be the implications for economic growth and labor markets of these differences? (b) What might be the implications for world security of these differences?
4. Could you envision the forthcoming worldwide demographic transformation as causing the U.S. to become more isolationist? Why or why not?
5. What could thwart the realization of the supposed forthcoming demographic transformation?

## NOTES

1. This chapter draws heavily from Jackson (2002) and Jackson and Howe (2003).
2. While dramatic improvements have been made in life expectancy, no such improvements have been made in the **human life span** – the maximum number of years that humans can live. It is believed to be around 120 years and is said to have remained unchanged for the past 100,000 years. Whereas substantial resources are expended on research into diseases that afflict the elderly, comparatively little is expended on research on the aging process itself. See Hayflick (2000).
3. Smoking reduces typical life expectancy by 7–10 years. Thus, a typical female who smokes will not live as long as a typical male who does not smoke.
4. Of course, the general worldwide relationship between income and fertility rates does not apply universally. For example, Docquier (2004) observes that the relationship between income and fertility varies depending on how income is distributed within the population and on the private cost of education.
5. This section draws heavily from Walter (2001).
6. This section draws heavily from *Meeting the Challenge of Global Aging* (2002), pp. 17–22.
7. This section draws heavily from Hamre (2003).
8. Shriver (2003) contends that population projections may induce fears of population excess in some and fears of cultural extinction in others.

## REFERENCES

Cohen, J. (2003). "Human Population: The Next Half Century." *Science* 302: 1172–1175.

Docquier, F. (2004). "Income Distribution, Non-convexities and the Fertility-Income Relationship." *Economica*, 71 (May): 161–174.

Hamre, J.J. (2003). "The Geopolitical Implications of Global Ageing in the Industrial Countries." *The Economic and Budgetary Impacts of Global Ageing*, March 4.

Hayflick, L. (2000). "The Future of Ageing." *Nature*, 408 (Nov 9): 37–39.

Jackson, R. (2002). *The Global Retirement Crisis.* Washington DC: Center for Strategic and International Studies.

Jackson, R. and Howe, N. (2003). *The 2003 Aging Vulnerability Index.* Washington DC: Center for Strategic and International Studies.

*Meeting the Challenge of Global Aging* (2002). Washington, DC: Center for Strategic and International Studies.

Reynolds, P., et al. (2000). Global *Entrepreneurship Monitor: 2000 Executive Report*, p. 9.

Romm, C. (2002)."NATO in the 21st Century: Defeated by Demography?" *The San Diego Union Tribune*, October 4.

Shriver, L. (2003). "Population in Literature." *Population Development Review*, 29: 153–162.

United Nations (2003). World Population Prospects: The 2002 Revision. New York: United Nations, Population Division, Department for Economic and Social Information and Policy Analysis, UN Secretariat.

Walter, N. (2001). "Is Slow Growth Conducive to Rising Productivity?" *Aging and the Global Economy.* Third Plenary of the Commission on Global Aging, Tokyo, August 28.

# Chapter 8

# Regulation of Private-Sector Financial Services

## INTRODUCTION

Previous chapters explored several important societal risk assessment and control concepts and explained when government intervention seems justified and how. The emphasis chiefly related to health, safety and environmental outcomes – what has been called **social regulation**. This and the following chapter complete the analysis of government intervention relating to risk management by emphasizing the financing and legal dimensions of societal risk management – what has been called **economic regulation**.

Of course, risk financing (financial security) can be pursued through either the private or public sector. Government has roles in both. First, government may have an important role in minimizing the chances that the economy or consumers of private-sector financial services are harmed because of market imperfections. Usually, this role manifests itself in financial services regulation, which is the topic of this chapter.

Second, because the private market will not provide financial security against all risky circumstances faced by citizens (and businesses), society determines that government should provide or facilitate certain levels of financial security for all citizens or selected cohorts of them. The best-known example is social insurance that, along with other public-sector financial services, is covered in the following chapter. We maintain the principle that government intervention should be limited to those circumstances under which market outcomes are, for some reason, unacceptable.

## PRIVATE-SECTOR FINANCIAL SERVICES

The economic security services provided by private financial institutions are essential to contemporary societies. Simultaneously, they pose risks to consumers and the entire economy. Government's response to the management of these risks typically is regulation. In exploring financial services regulation, we first should be clear about the scope, role and types of financial intermediaries that provide financial security services.

## The Scope and Role of Financial Services

**Financial intermediaries** are firms or other entities that bring together providers and users of funds. Their "products" are financial services offered through the financial intermediation process. Ancillary services such as financial advice, credit cards, brokerage and trust management also may be included. A financial intermediary may not actually manufacture (underwrite) all of the financial services it sells. Some sell the services of other firms, as when a bank sells an insurance company's policies.

Depository institutions (banks, credit unions, savings banks, and savings and loan associations), insurers and securities firms comprise the three major classes of financial intermediaries. More specialized, large intermediaries include mutual funds and pension funds. In many markets, there also exists a range of other, usually smaller specialized intermediaries such as finance companies, real estate investment trusts and mortgage companies.

Financial intermediation of all types matches savers with investors, thus obviating the need for savers to locate investors directly and vice versa. All financial intermediaries issue their own claims, whether in the form of savings accounts, insurance policies, certificates of deposit, mutual fund shares, etc., to individuals and businesses and receive funds for doing so. These funds are then invested in bonds, mortgages, stocks and other financial instruments. By doing so, investment is not confined to the sector in which the saving takes place. Funds can flow to the most productive sectors in an economy, which in turn implies the possibility of larger productivity gains.

Financial intermediaries would not exist if competition were perfect. Firms and households, each with perfect information and incurring no transactions costs, would deal directly with each other, avoiding the transaction costs of and having no need for the information services of intermediaries. The real world, of course, affords less-than-perfect information and transactions are not costless.

In fact, customers do not have the time, resources or ability to gather complete and adequate information about each possible financial transaction; that is, information asymmetries exist. Financial intermediaries help solve these problems. Moreover, owner–investors cannot be certain that managers of their firms will always work in the owners' best interests; that is, agency problems exist. Financial intermediaries can both help monitor the management of firms in which they invest and conduct research to help investors make informed decisions. Furthermore, complete, frictionless markets do not exist in which individuals can trade all possible financial claims among themselves to achieve their preferred mix of risk and liquidity. Financial intermediaries and financial markets enable individuals and businesses to change their existing risk and liquidity profiles.

In this transformation process, financial intermediaries' price risk, a necessity for competitive market success. While this activity is perhaps most commonly associated with insurers, commercial and investment banks also price risk when they make loans and underwrite securities. What distinguishes insurers from most other financial intermediaries in this regard is that insurers' underwriting processes are usually more complex because of greater possibilities of adverse selection and moral hazard.

## Types of Financial Intermediaries

Financial services traditionally have been delivered through financial institutions dedicated primarily to one of the three sectors mentioned above. We cover these three as well as mutual funds and pension funds below. More recently, financial conglomerates offering multi-sector products have evolved.

### Depository institutions

**Depository institutions** are financial intermediaries that take in funds principally as short-term deposits and make them available as personal and commercial loans. The most common form of depository institution is the commercial bank. Of the world's 50 largest banks based on revenues in 2004, 30 were European, eight North American, four each in China and Japan, and two each in Australia and Brazil.[1] Banks offer a range of services for business use (e.g., export finance, letters of credit, payroll services and sometimes securities underwriting) and for personal use (e.g., credit cards and trust and brokerage services).

Commercial banks are critical to the implementation of a country's macroeconomic policy through the central bank that controls monetary policy (see later in this chapter). For this reason, their activities have important spillover effects in an economy.

### Securities firms

**Securities firms**, also called **investment banks**, are financial intermediaries that bring together the issuers of securities with investors. Four firms dominate this concentrated market, each located in the U.S. They are involved more with direct intermediation (sales between firms and investors) than with portfolio intermediation (management of security portfolios).

Securities firms perform five key functions: underwriting, investing, market making, trading and custodial servicing. The underwriting function involves both the packaging and pricing of new debt or equity issues for clients. Once packaged, the securities are sold to investors via a public or private offering. The investment function entails managing assets for institutional or private investors.

The market making and trading functions are similar in that both involve transactions on the secondary market. While market making, the firm acts as either agent or principal. Acting as an agent, the firm is a conduit of a trade, receiving fees or commissions for the service. When a securities firm assumes the role of the principal, it holds an inventory position in an underlying security. This is an important distinction from a risk management standpoint, because the firm bears the risk of future price fluctuations. Securities firms have been reducing their emphasis on trading and market making, largely because of concern about risk.

The custodial function includes services in connection with mergers and acquisitions as well as research and settlement facilities. Many firms' retail subsidiaries (brokerage houses) service clients through a network of stockbrokers.

### Insurance companies

As we already know, insurance companies are financial intermediaries that specialize in allowing individuals and businesses to purchase contingent claim contracts that are payable to the contract holders (or designees) upon the occurrence of enumerated events (usually losses). Life insurance offers payment assurance of a fixed or variable sum in the event of death, incapacity or loss of health. Life insurance includes saving products that are important means of providing retirement income. Nonlife insurance offers indemnification against losses caused by damage or destruction to property and liability resulting from negligent acts. Of the world's 48 largest insurers based on 2004 revenues, North America claims 22, Europe hosts 15, Asia has 10, and Australia has one.

## Mutual funds

**Mutual funds** are pools of managed assets offering investors convenient access to the securities markets. In the U.S., funds are sold predominately through securities brokers or directly to the public at no sales commission charges. In Europe, funds are sold predominately through banks. The number of mutual funds worldwide continues to grow rapidly, as do assets under management. The world's largest mutual funds are stand-alone firms – most in the U.S. – and generally are not managed by other financial intermediaries. Exceptions are found in Europe.

## Pension funds

Private **pension funds** specialize in managing diversified portfolios of assets dedicated to providing retirement income to plan participants. Pension plans may be established by employers to provide retirement income for their workers or by individuals, with the former dominating worldwide. Pension fund assets might be managed by the fund itself or any other financial intermediary or by the individual. Most pension assets are subsumed within the total assets of their managing intermediary, be it a bank, mutual fund or life insurer. The U.S. is home to the world's greatest concentration of pension assets. Pension funds generally are considered parts of corporations or government agencies – that is, they are not separate entities – so do not appear in listings of large financial intermediaries worldwide. Nonetheless, we know that the growth in private pension funds worldwide has been enormous, fueled by aging, more affluent populations, favorable tax treatment, and revenue-starved public pension plans.

## Financial conglomerates

Financial conglomerates are increasingly common. A **financial conglomerate** is any group of companies under common control whose predominant activities consist of providing significant services in at least two of the three sectors: depository services, securities and insurance. This definition embraces either or both production and distribution of financial services. Terms such as *bancassurance*, *allfinanz*, universal banking and financial conglomerates are all used to convey some notion of financial services convergence or integration. Typically, a non-operational holding company owns all or most of the shares in separately incorporated, capitalized sectoral subsidiaries.

Financial services integration occurs when firms in one sector create and sell products containing significant elements traditionally associated with products of another sector. We call this **product integration**. Thus, unit-linked annuities and variable life insurance combine elements of insurance and securities. The securitization of banks' asset cash flows (e.g., mortgages, credit card balances and other debt portfolios) combines important elements of investment and commercial banking. Alternative risk transfer techniques such as catastrophe options and bonds, standby letters of credit, and finite risk transfer mechanisms offer other examples. Money market mutual funds, offered by investment banking firms, are effectively demand deposit accounts. This product convergence trend can be expected to continue, thereby complicating regulation.

Finally, financial services integration can occur at the level of the advisor, without necessarily any supply-side integration or even cooperation. We term this **advisory integration**. Thus, personal financial planners, accountants, attorneys, risk management consultants, agents and brokers often effectively integrate financial services for their clients. They may sell products themselves or direct the client's purchasing behavior based on an integrated financial or risk management program. Integration also occurs when employers or affinity groups offer a range of financial products to employees or group members, as, for example, when an employer offers a cafeteria of employee benefits that may be self-funded or not. This type of integration also complicates regulation.

# GOVERNMENT'S ROLE IN REGULATING PRIVATE-SECTOR FINANCIAL SERVICES

This section presents the economic rationale for government regulation of private financial markets. We then introduce the various theories underlying government intervention into markets as well. We close this section with a short discussion of government imperfections.

## Why Governments Regulate Financial Services

The financial intermediation process is ripe with market imperfections that justify concern by consumers and government. Most of these market imperfections were set out in Chapter 2. It is sufficient here to illustrate three of the market problems: (1) information asymmetry, (2) market power and (3) negative externalities.

Because buyers of many financial services are not as well informed as the sellers, it is often comparatively easy for buyers to be misled or to make decisions on incomplete or inaccurate information – in other words, they may not understand their purchases or the intermediary's financial solidity. This information asymmetry – the lemons problem – is the basis for most securities and insurance regulation and, to a lesser extent, for banking regulation.[2]

As noted earlier, market power exists when the seller (or buyer) can exercise meaningful control over price. Firms seek to create market power, and thus enhance profitability, through market segmentation and product differentiation strategies. Market power can result also from increasing returns to scale and from concerted practices among competitors that restrain competition, such as market sharing arrangements, pricing collusion, or exclusive dealings. Thus, another justification for government regulation of financial services is to help ensure competitive markets and minimize abuses arising from market power.[3]

Finally, as we know, negative externalities exist when a firm's activities impose uncompensated costs on others. The most important negative externality in private-sector financial services stems from the possibility of systemic risks. As discussed in Chapter 2, systemic risks exist because the difficulties of financial intermediaries can cause harm elsewhere within an economy. There are two types of systemic risks:

• Risk of **cascading failure** exists when the failure of one financial institution is the proximate cause of the failure of others. This can occur, for example, if a bank's default on its short-term credit obligations to other banks precipitates other bank failures – ultimately causing harm to other businesses and economic activities. Much of bank regulation and, to a lesser extent, securities and insurance regulation are designed to minimize cascading failures.

- The second type of systemic risk are in which many depositors (or other creditors) demand their money at once. Runs are caused by a loss of confidence in the financial institution, often precipitated by a real or imagined fear of insolvency. The regulation of banks and the creation of government deposit insurance find justification because of concerns about this systemic risk.

Different approaches have been followed by government in responding to these market imperfections in the provision of private-sector financial services. In each case, regulation can be justified if the market itself cannot rectify the problem and, importantly, government can ameliorate the harm.

## Theories of Regulation

Several theories attempt to explain why regulation exists. These theories apply also to social regulation of the types discussed in the preceding chapters.

### *Public interest theory of regulation*

Under the **public interest theory of regulation**, regulation exists to serve the public interest by protecting consumers from abuse. This regulatory theory flows directly from the goal of government seeking to rectify market imperfections. The objective is to maximize economic efficiency, including preventing or making right significant societal or consumer harm that results from market imperfections. The premise that government can rectify or ameliorate market imperfections presumes that government can correctly identify the market failure, will function for the overall public good, and will be indifferent to conflicts of interest in general and special interest group pressures. The theory has its detractors who posit less noble purposes for regulation.

### *Private interest theories of regulation*

Under **private interest theories of regulation**, regulation exists to promote the interests of private parties. Thus, Peltzman (1976) suggests that self-interested regulators engage in regulatory activities consistent with maximizing their political support. Under this theory, regulators might exhibit pro-industry biases to gain industry financial and other backing. Conversely, regulators might engage in activities that appeal to consumers (voters) such as price suppression to gain their support, even if the long-term effects were detrimental.

Meier (1988) asserts that regulation will be shaped by a type of bargaining that occurs between private interest groups within the existing political and administrative structure. Interest groups include consumers, the regulator, political elites (courts and the legislative body), and the regulated industry. Political resources, saliency and complexity of regulatory issues determine interest group influence. These groups are not homogeneous, so bargaining outcomes vary from issue to issue.

The best-known private interest theory is the **capture theory of regulation** in which regulation is "captured" by and operated for the benefit of the regulated industry. Stigler (1971) and others contend that special interest groups, being well organized and well financed, influence legislation and regulation for their own benefit. Special interest groups in financial services include all financial intermediaries, agents, brokers and the firms that provide services to these industry participants. Thus, for example, U.S. banks complained for decades about being prohibited from selling insurance, because agents opposed to banks selling insurance influenced legislators and regulators.

Consumers, being widely dispersed, ill organized, poorly financed and, on a given issue, not as well informed as special interest groups, may be ineffective in comparison with the regulated industry. Regulation unduly influenced by special interests could be expected to result in:

- restrictions on entry of new domestic and especially foreign entrants;
- suppression of price and product competition;
- control of inter-industry competition from those selling similar or complementary products.

Each of these phenomena is found in financial markets to varying degrees and, under appropriate conditions, can be justified under the public interest theory. Government's difficult task is to recognize when an interest group's public interest arguments mask self-interest, private motivations.

## Government Imperfections

When governments intervene into private markets, policymakers assert the need to correct or prevent some perceived harm; that is, to help rectify imperfections in the market and, thereby, to move the market toward greater efficiency and enhanced social welfare. Of course, policymakers are unlikely to use the economists' terminology in justifying intervention, but behind their words, lurk (or, rather, *should* lurk) sound economic justification. If financial markets were *perfectly* competitive, regulation would be unnecessary.

### *When intervention is justified*

Thus, within a competitive market, we deem government intervention for economic purposes desirable only if all of the following three conditions exist:

- Actual or potential market imperfections exist.
- The market imperfections do or could lead to meaningful economic inefficiency or inequity.
- Government action can ameliorate the inefficiency or inequity.

Conversely, if at least one of the three conditions is not met, no government intervention is warranted. No intervention is justified into financial services markets that exhibit no market imperfections, or where imperfections exist but they do not lead to important inefficiencies or inequities. Even if market imperfections exist and they are judged to be meaningful, no intervention is justified if government's actions could not ameliorate the imperfection. After all, there is no guarantee that government intervention will be successful (or that government's assessment of the imperfection is accurate). Indeed, government intervention can make matters worse. Sometimes, the best governmental reaction is no action, even for inefficient markets.

### Government failures

Just as there is no perfect competition, there is no perfect regulation. Just as *market* failures exist, so do *government* failures. Government failures can occur for many reasons (White, 1996):

- *Difficulty in identification and formulation.* Policymakers can have difficulty in formulating and implementing otherwise laudable goals. To do so, they must first identify the problems that are to be solved – a challenging task. Moreover, the hoped-for solutions themselves sometimes create more problems than they solve. Information problems also exist for governments.

- *Principal-agent problems.* Government employees may have little or no direct incentive to carry out laws and regulations fully and fairly. In other words, principal-agent problems exist with government employees who are agents for the public (the principal). Couple this problem with the fact that many countries compensate civil servants poorly, and opportunities sometimes exist for laxity and even abuse (e.g., bribery)!

- *Rent-seeking behavior.* Regulation can lead to behavior that is inconsistent with the competitive model. The regulated will often engage in **rent-seeking behavior**; that is, they will seek to influence regulation in a way that gives economic benefit for themselves.[4] Such activity is, in itself, non-productive and decreases market efficiency. It can distort the marketplace and further decrease social welfare. In other words, producer surplus is accorded undue weight in comparison with consumer surplus. Of course, the opposite also can occur, as when regulators who control prices refuse to approve economically justifiable increases, thereby according undue weight to consumer surplus.

- *The problem of capture.* Finally, and related to rent-seeking behavior, is the problem of capture. As discussed in the preceding section, the regulated are usually well informed and have substantial interest in the nature and quality of regulation, whereas consumers typically have diverse interests and are not well organized or informed. This situation can cause the regulator, because of its self-interest or ignorance, to favor the producer's perspective instead of the consumer's. Moreover, some civil servants either are or hope to be closely allied with industry interests because of having or anticipating employment in the industry after their regulatory stint. This so-called "revolving door" problem is associated with capture.

## OVERVIEW OF FINANCIAL SERVICES REGULATION

Generally, regulatory intervention falls into three categories: prudential, market conduct and competition policy:

- **Prudential regulation** is concerned with the financial condition of the financial intermediary.

- **Market conduct regulation** refers to government prescribed rules establishing inappropriate marketing practices.
- **Competition policy (antitrust) regulation** is concerned with actions of the intermediary that substantially lessen competition.

Prudential regulation evolved primarily because of information problems and negative externalities (especially for banking). Market conduct regulation evolved primarily because of information problems. Competition policy regulation evolved because of market power concerns. Prudential regulation remains the most critical element in government oversight of financial intermediaries.

## Commercial Banking Regulation

Commercial banks are subject to oversight in every national market. To establish a bank, a national or sub-national authority must grant a charter but only upon satisfactory demonstration that the applicant has met all financial, personnel and other conditions. The U.S. has a dual banking system under which banks may be either federally (called national banks) or state chartered.

Every major market provides for some type of deposit insurance on the savings of customers. Deposit insurance exists not so much to protect individual banking customers as to protect the integrity of the entire banking system, thereby protecting an entire economy; in other words, the objective is to minimize the possibility of systemic risk, particularly bank runs. Banks typically are required to participate in the deposit insurance scheme.

Banks are subject to oversight by the nation's central bank and usually a banking regulator. The focus on both is on bank solvency. The central bank provides risk management for a nation's entire economy through its control of monetary policy. The objective is to provide a stable economy by controlling reserve requirements and the discount rate and by providing payment system guarantees and access to needed funds. These and other activities also minimize the likelihood of cascading failures in the banking system.

Key elements of banking supervision internationally are supported by and coordinated through the **Basel Committee on Banking Supervision** (BCBS), better known as the **Basel Committee** [www.bis.org/bcbs] from its location in Basel, Switzerland.[5] It was established by the Group of Ten (G10) countries in 1974. Today, 13 central banks and monetary authorities are members of the Basel Committee. The BCBS does not possess any formal intergovernmental supervisory authority. It sets broad supervisory standards and guidelines and recommends statements of best practice that national authorities may implement in their local markets.

Since 1975, the BCBS has been promoting two principles: (1) no foreign banking establishment should escape supervision and (2) supervision should be adequate. In 1988, it introduced a capital measurement system known as the **Basel Capital Accord**. This system – a banking credit risk management framework with a minimum capital standard of 8 percent – has been adopted by, not only BCBS member countries, but also in almost all other countries with active multinational banks. The BCBS proposed a new Capital Adequacy Framework in 1998, which has since been adopted. This framework – known informally as **Basel II** – comprises three pillars: (1) minimum capital requirements, (2) supervisory review of an institution's internal assessment process and capital adequacy, and (3) effective use of disclosure to strengthen market discipline as a complement to supervisory efforts. Insight 8.1 is taken

---

**INSIGHT 8.1: NEW INTERNATIONAL BANK SOLVENCY STANDARDS** ⎯⎯⎯⎯⎯⎯⎯⎯⎯⎯⎯⎯⎯⎯⎯

As banks get bigger, they also become smarter. That, at any rate, is the theory underpinning a new set of rules on risks and capital for banks around the world, formally called the "International Convergence of Capital Measures and Capital Standards" and informally "Basel II." The code has been drafted by the Basal Committee on Banking Supervision, an offshoot of the Bank of International Settlements (BIS), which supports and coordinates the work of the leading central banks around the world. It is a gentlemen's agreement among leading regulators which all countries with international banks are encouraged to adopt, but which relies on national law for its implementation.

One striking feature of Basel II is its principle that banks should have the option to decide for themselves where they think their big and little risks lie, and then allocate their capital accordingly, subject to national regulators' rules and national laws. Another feature is that it will probably allow many big banks to reduce the capital needed for their current balance sheets, in some cases quite sharply.

Europeans, by and large, are keen to get on with it. The European Union has passed legislation to implement Basel II next year (2007). Americans, by contrast, are worried on three accounts. First, they think the rules are too slack. . . . Second, they reckon that American banks will not be able to implement the rules reliably without at least another four years' practice, if ever. Third, they fear that the rules will give the biggest banks too much of an advantage over small banks.

Those worries have persuaded America to adopt Basel II later and more gradually.

*Source*: A Survey of International Banking (2006) appearing at www.economist.com/surveys/displaystory.cfm?story_id=6908488.

---

from one of the surveys of *The Economist* magazine about the efforts to establish international solvency standards in banking.

## Securities Regulation

Securities regulation focuses on both the new and secondary issues markets, mandating certain disclosures to prospective purchasers about the securities. Penalties apply for fraud or misrepresentation. Secondary market regulation often also requires registration of national exchanges, brokers and dealers. The objective of securities regulation, is to rectify buyers' information asymmetry problems by ensuring that they have adequate information to make informed decisions.

Following U.S. corporate scandals in 2001 and 2002 involving Enron, WorldCom, Arthur Andersen and others, a new law – the *Sarbanes-Oxley Act* – was introduced in the U.S. in an attempt to restore investor confidence. Many observers contend that the act constitutes the most sweeping corporate reform within any major economy in recent decades. The act overhauled governance requirements for publicly held companies by introducing more rigorous financial reporting requirements, enhanced the role and independence of the audit committees of corporations' boards of directors, provided for regulation of auditing firms, and established new crimes and enhanced penalties for corporate misconduct. Given that U.S. capital markets trade securities issued by publicly held firms worldwide, the act also has influenced the ways local corporations are regulated in many countries.

National securities regulatory agencies' activities are coordinated through the **International Organization of Securities Commissions** (IOSCO). Established in 1983, IOSCO [www. iosco.org] is a cooperative forum whose members regulate over 90 percent of the securities transactions worldwide. IOSCO adopted *Objectives and Principles of Securities Regulation* (IOSCO Principles) in 1998. It approved ISOCO Assessment Methodologies in 2003, which is expected to enable an objective assessment of the implementation of the IOSCO principles.

IOSCO maintains two important working groups: the Technical Committee and the Emerging Markets Committee. The Technical Committee examines issues related to multinational disclosure and accounting, regulation of secondary markets, regulation of market intermediaries, enforcement and the exchange of information, and investment management in the securities markets worldwide. The Emerging Markets Committee establishes principles and minimum standards for, offers training programs to, and facilitates exchange of information and transfer of technology in emerging markets.

## Insurance Regulation

Insurance regulation, like banking regulation, is focused chiefly on monitoring and preventing insolvencies. However, unlike banking regulatory solvency monitoring that aims to prevent systemic risks, insurance regulatory solvency monitoring is aimed more at protecting policyholders from losses occasioned by insurer insolvency. As with banking, every nation has an agency charged with overseeing and supervising its insurance marketplace. We take up the details of insurance regulation in Chapter 24.

The task of coordinating the work of national insurance regulators falls to the **International Association of Insurance Supervisors** (IAIS) [www.iaisweb.org], formed in 1993. Recognizing the increasing international character of insurance markets, the IAIS seeks to promote cooperation among insurance supervisors, to set international standards for insurance regulation and supervision, to provide training for members, and to coordinate work with other financial services sector regulators and intergovernmental organizations. The IAIS represents more than 100 jurisdictions, with more than 70 observers – including industry associations and insurance companies – representing the financial services industry.

The IAIS issues principles, standards and guidance papers on issues related to insurance supervision. Its Executive Committee, which runs the association, is supported by three key committees – namely, the Technical Committee, the Emerging Markets Committee and the Budget Committee – and several subcommittees (e.g., Enhanced Disclosure Subcommittee and Financial Conglomerate Subcommittee). The IAIS meets annually, but various committees meet more frequently to pursue IAIS work. Annual meetings also serve as a means to exchange information and views on common issues such as intermediation, reinsurance, AIDS, financial integration, cross-border insurance and trade liberalization efforts.

## Financial Conglomerate Regulation

Details of financial institution regulation vary not only from country to country but from financial sector to financial sector. This observation applies particularly to prudential regulation. Nonetheless, some generalizations can be drawn in the extent of overall regulation and the activities that governments permit within a financial conglomerate.

## Permissible activities

In a survey of 54 of the world's major financial centers, the Institute of International Bankers (2002) finds that the majority, especially the largest centers, permit financial conglomerates to undertake banking, insurance and security activities.[6] The survey does not speak to the important issue of consistency of prudential oversight across financial services sectors.

Table 8.1 gives a summary of the survey. It shows that the overwhelming majority of countries allow joint banking and securities activities, with most permitting banks to undertake securities activities within the bank itself. Several others require some or all securities activities to be undertaken through subsidiaries or affiliates. Of the countries surveyed, only China prohibits any joint undertakings.[7]

The situation with insurance is somewhat different. It appears that few, if any, countries permit insurance underwriting within a bank. The majority allows joint arrangements, through subsidiaries or affiliates. Several countries prohibit any affiliation between insurance and banking, with a few others prohibiting banks from owning insurers but allowing them to act as agents or brokers for unaffiliated insurers.

## The joint forum

The barriers among and distinctions between the main financial services sectors – insurance, banking and securities – have begun to erode. (We discuss this in more detail in Chapter 25.) This financial services integration raises questions whether it introduces additional or more complex market imperfections and, therefore, whether different or additional regulation is needed. These questions are limited neither by national boundaries nor to a single sector. With the continued globalization of financial services, it was recognized that an international approach was desirable.

At the initiative of the Basel Committee, an informal group of banking, securities, and insurance regulators was formed in 1993 to examine issues relating to supervision of financial conglomerates. The Tripartite Group established in 1995 was the first to address cross-sectoral issues on an international level associated with integration.

A more formal approach emerged with the creation of the **Joint Forum on Financial Conglomerates** [www.bis.org/bcbs/jointforum.htm] in 1996, which was charged with taking forward the work of the Tripartite Group. Better known as the **Joint Forum**, it consists of an equal number of senior banks, securities, and insurance supervisors representing the Basel Committee, IOSCO, and the IAIS. Representatives from 13 countries have participated in the forum. The European Commission attends in an observer capacity. The Joint Forum's primary responsibility today is examining the common interests of the three financial services industries – including financial conglomerates operating across industries – and developing principles and identifying international best practices. The common interests include:

* risk assessment and management, including internal control and capital issues;
* use of the audit and actuarial functions in the supervision of regulated entities and corporate groups containing regulated entities;
* corporate governance and fit-and-proper tests;
* outsourcing of functions and activities by regulated firms;
* different definitions of banking, insurance, and securities activities (e.g., risk and capital definitions) and the potential that they may lead to regulatory arbitrage;
* identifying the core principles of the banking, insurance and securities sectors that are common as well as understanding the differences where they arise.

**Table 8.1** Permissible Activities for Banking Organizations in Various Centers (2002)

| Securities | | | Insurance | |
|---|---|---|---|---|
| *Permitted Through the Same Legal Entity* | *Permitted Through Subsidiaries or Affiliates* | *Not Permitted* | *Permitted Through Subsidiaries or Affiliates Only* | *Not Permitted* |
| Argentina | Brazil | China[e] | Australia[b] | Colombia |
| Australia | Canada | | Austria[b] | India |
| Austria | Colombia | | Bahrain[c] | Israel |
| Bahrain | Egypt | | Belgium[b] | Pakistan |
| Belgium | Greece | | Bermuda[b] | Panama |
| Bermuda | India | | Bolivia[b] | Peru |
| Bolivia | Indonesia | | Brazil[b] | Russia |
| Cayman Islands | Israel | | Canada[b] | |
| Chile | Japan | | Cayman Islands | |
| Czech Republic | Korea | | Chile[c] | |
| Denmark | Mexico | | Czech Republic[b] | |
| Estonia | Panama | | Denmark[b] | |
| Finland | Philippines | | Egypt[b] | |
| France | Poland | | Estonia[b] | |
| Germany | Romania | | Finland[c] | |
| Hong Kong | Singapore | | France[b] | |
| Ireland | United States | | Germany[b] | |
| Italy | | | Greece[a] | |
| Latvia | | | Hong Kong[a] | |
| Luxembourg | | | Japan[b] | |
| New Zealand | | | Indonesia[b] | |
| The Netherlands | | | Ireland[b] | |
| Nigeria | | | Italy[a] | |
| Norway | | | Korea[b] | |
| Pakistan | | | Latvia[b] | |
| Peru | | | Luxembourg[b] | |
| Portugal | | | Mexico[b] | |
| Russia | | | The Netherlands[b] | |
| South Africa | | | New Zealand[b] | |
| Spain | | | Nigeria[b] | |
| Sweden | | | Norway[b] | |
| Switzerland | | | Philippines[b] | |
| Turkey | | | Poland | |
| United Kingdom | | | Portugal[b] | |
| Uruguay | | | Romania[c] | |
| Venezuela | | | Singapore[b] | |
| | | | South Africa[a] | |
| | | | Spain[b] | |
| | | | Sweden | |
| | | | Switzerland[b] | |
| | | | Turkey[c] | |
| | | | United Kingdom[b] | |
| | | | United States[b] | |
| | | | Uruguay[b] | |
| | | | Venezuela[b] | |

*Source*: Institute of International Bankers (2002).
[a]With limits.
[b]Through subsidiaries or affiliates only.
[c]Brokerage or agency only.
[d]Pensions only.
[e]See Note 7 of this chapter.

### Other intergovernmental organizations in financial services

A few other regional economic associations and regulatory organizations exist. For instance, the **International Network of Pensions Regulators and Supervisors** [www.bis.org/publ/joint01.htm], created in 2000, provides a forum for policy dialog and cooperation on regulatory, supervisory and financial issues related to pensions.

The **Financial Stability Forum** (FSF) [www.fsforum.org], assembled in 1999, promotes global financial stability through the exchange of information and international cooperation in financial services supervision and surveillance. This forum holds meetings on a regular basis for national authorities in charge of financial stability in key international financial centers and financial institutions, sector-specific international groupings of regulators and supervisors, and committees of central bank experts. Through this coordination, the FSF hopes to promote global financial stability, improve the functions of financial markets, and reduce systemic risk in the markets. The FSF encourages the adoption of its 12 core economic and financial standards, which are internationally accepted.

The **Islamic Financial Services Board** [www.ifsb.org] is an association of central banks responsible for the regulation and supervision of the Islamic financial services sector, including Islamic law abiding insurance operations. Created in 2002, it aims to set and disseminate best practices standards and core principles for regulation and supervision consistent with Islamic financial principles, for voluntary adoption by member countries. It cooperates with other standard-setting organizations in the areas of monetary and financial stability.

Finally, **the Financial-Sector Assessment Program** [www.imf.org/external/NP/fsap/fsap.asp], a joint activity of the World Bank and the IMF, seeks to promote the soundness of financial systems in member countries. Supported by experts from a range of national agencies and standard-setting bodies, the program seeks to identify the strengths and vulnerabilities of the financial services systems by country, to determine how key sources of risk are being managed, to ascertain the financial services sector's developmental and technical assistance needs, and to help prioritize policy responses in the country.

## STRUCTURE OF REGULATORY AUTHORITIES

The majority of countries regulate financial intermediaries on a functional basis; that is, banking and insurance (and often securities also) oversights are separate, with each industry having its own regulator. Several countries with functional regulation have established a lead regulator with respect to financial conglomerates, often based on its principal activity. However, this does not mean that the lead regulator usurps the power of other regulators.

An important recent trend is implementation of consolidated financial services regulation. For example, the Global Survey 2003 by the Institute of International Bankers shows that all countries except for Israel maintain consolidated supervisory approaches that apply to bank subsidiaries and affiliates of financial groups. See Table 8.2 for the list of countries.

## GOVERNMENTAL ACTIONS AFFECTING FINANCIAL SERVICES REGULATION

The Asian and other financial crises of the late 1990s brought forceful attention to how inadequate financial services regulation adversely affects national economies as well as

**Table 8.2** Regulation of Financial Conglomerates (2006)

| *Consolidated Supervision Applied to Bank Subsidiaries and Affiliates of Domestic and Non-domestic Financial Groups* | *Consolidated Supervision Applied to Bank Subsidiaries and Affiliates of Domestic Financial Groups But Not to Bank Subsidiaries and Affiliates or Unincorporated Branches/Agencies and Affiliates of Non-domestic Financial Groups* | *Consolidated Supervision is Not Applied to Either Domestic or Non-domestic Financial Groups* |
|---|---|---|
| *And to Unincorporated Branches/Agencies and Affiliates of Non-domestic Financial Groups* | *But Not to Unincorporated Branches/Agencies and Affiliates of Non-domestic Financial Groups* | |
| Argentina | Czech Republic | Chile |
| Brazil | Denmark[n] | |
| Canada[a] | Germany | |
| France | Norway | |
| Indonesia | Turkey | |
| Ireland | | |
| Italy | | |
| Japan | | |
| Luxembourg | | |
| The Netherlands | | |
| Panama | | |
| Philippines | | |
| South Africa[b] | | |
| Spain[c] | | |
| Sweden[d] | | |
| Switzerland[e] | | |
| United States[f] | | |
| Australia | | |
| Austria[g] | | |
| Bahrain | | |
| Belgium | | |
| Bermuda[h] | | |
| Cayman Islands[i] | | |
| Finland | | |
| Hong Kong[j] | | |
| Korea[k] | | |
| Latvia | | |
| Poland | | |
| Romania[l] | | |
| Singapore[m] | | |
| United Kingdom | | |

*Source:* Global Survey 2006, Institute of International Bankers

[a] While the Office of the Superintendent of Financial Institutions oversees the operations at the federal level, certain entities within a financial group (e.g. securities and insurance companies) also may be subject to supervision by provincial agencies, such as the Ontario Securities Commission.

[b] Consolidated supervision extends to all the companies in a banking group, including the controlling 191

company, its subsidiaries, joint ventures and companies in which the controlling company or its subsidiaries have a direct or indirect participation.

c As far as subsidiaries, affiliates or branches of non-domestic banks are concerned, consolidated supervision refers to their respective "Spanish sub-groups."

d Regarding affiliates of banks within the EEA, the Swedish Financial Supervisory Authority has a shared responsibility with the home country supervisor. After notification to the Swedish supervisor a home country supervisor may conduct an on-site exam at an affiliate location in Sweden.

e Swiss Banking law requires the Swiss Federal Banking Commission (SFBC) to exercise consolidated supervision over bank subsidiaries and affiliates of domestic financial groups. Bank subsidiaries and affiliates of non-domestic financial groups and unincorporated branches/agencies of non-domestic financial groups are only allowed in Switzerland if they are subject to consolidated supervision by their home country banking authority.

f Under the *Gramm-Leach-Bliley Act* of 1999 as well as the *International Banking Act* of 1978 the U.S. Federal Reserve Board does make determinations regarding the capital strength of the non-domestic banking organization that seeks to become a "financial holding company" or engage in other nonbanking activities permissible for bank holding companies.

g Within the European Union (EEA countries) reliance is placed on home country control; non-E.U. countries: the Austrian Banking Act stipulates that a non-E.U. non-domestic branch is treated in principle in the same way as an independent credit institution is treated. Thus, the Austrian branch is obliged to fulfill the Austrian regulatory and supervisory provisions independently. The situation of the entire bank will not be taken into account. However, legally the branch is not deemed to be independent.

h Bermuda does not license branches of overseas banks. Consolidated supervision is applied to the licensed entity and to any subsidiaries or affiliates.

i The Cayman Islands Monetary Authority (CIMA) supervises locally incorporated authorized institutions on a consolidated basis, covering their subsidiaries as well as local and overseas branches. CIMA will also require that branches of foreign incorporated banks are under adequate consolidated supervision in their home country. This is one of the minimum authorization criteria that will be assessed at the time of authorization and on an on-going basis thereafter.

j The Hong Kong Monetary Authority (HKMA) supervises locally incorporated, authorized institutions on a consolidated basis, covering their subsidiaries as well as those local and overseas branches. The prudential requirements and supervisory approach applied to branches of foreign incorporated banks are broadly the same as those for authorized institutions incorporated in Hong Kong. The HKMA will also require that branches of foreign incorporated banks are under adequate consolidated supervision in their home country. This is one of the minimum authorization criteria that will be assessed at the time of authorization and on an on-going basis thereafter.

k As far as subsidiaries, affiliates or branches of non-domestic banks are concerned, consolidated supervision refers to their respective Korean sub-groups.

l The National Bank of Romania supervises locally incorporated authorized institutions on a consolidated basis, covering their subsidiaries as well as local and overseas branches. The NBR will also require that branches of foreign incorporated banks are under adequate consolidated supervision in their home country. This is one of the minimum authorization criteria that will be assessed at the time of authorization and on an on-going basis thereafter. After the accession date, within the E.U., reliance will be placed on home country control.

m The Monetary Authority of Singapore (MAS) supervises Singapore-incorporated banks on a consolidated basis, taking into account the operations of their domestic and overseas branches and subsidiaries. MAS does not supervise on a consolidated basis unincorporated branches, agencies and affiliates of non-domestic financial groups but takes into account, among other things, the adequacy of consolidated supervision exercised by parent supervisors for the foreign banks' operations in Singapore and overseas in considering applications made under our licensing and regulatory processes.

n If the parent company is located abroad, only the subgroup is encompassed by the consolidated supervision.

to the need for better international regulatory coordination and cooperation. Since then, financial services regulation has become less diverse, with the major intergovernmental organizations involved in financial services regulation playing more active and constructive roles. While these actions have not, for the most part, been directed toward integration, they nonetheless have provided impetus for this result through coordinated efforts to address cross-industry financial issues.

Other governmental actions are also affecting financial services regulation. For example, the trend toward allowing mutual insurers and banks to convert to shareholder-owned firms opens up new opportunities for financial conglomeration. Demutualization has been particularly important in Australia, Canada, South Africa, the U.K. and the U.S.

Privatization of banks and insurance firms in several countries similarly created opportunities. Privatizations have occurred, for instance, in Belgium, the Czech Republic, Finland, France, India, Israel, Norway, Peru, Poland, Turkey, the Baltic counties and Venezuela.

Significant combinations of banks and insurance firms occurred within the past few years in Denmark, Norway, Switzerland and the U.S., while consolidation of domestic banks, insurers and securities firms continues in many countries. Foreign financial institutions have been given new authority to develop or expand their presence in many markets, including China and India, during the past decade.

## CONCLUSION AND FUTURE PROSPECTS

As this and the preceding chapters make clear, government has an appropriate and critical role in societal risk management. For purposes of private-sector financial security, this role has evolved primarily from imperfections in competitive financial markets. It is important to note, however, that these market failures are not indictments of the market; rather, it is a simple statement of its limitations and an economic rationale for the circumstances when government intervention can be desirable.

Of course, as noted, just as there are market failures, so too are government failures. Not all government interventions are directed toward rectifying market failures and, even among those that are so aimed, not all are effective. Like the market, government actions also should be assessed through an economic lens.

We are observing a new disclosure-based financial regulatory model evolving internationally.[8] In this model, risk-based prudential regulation is increasingly supplemented by new rules requiring broad disclosures of a company's finances, risks and strategies to customers, investors, counterparties and the public at large. Introduction of the model is requiring integrated international approaches to accounting standards, securities regulation and financial institution regulation (designed to protect policyholders and bank depositors). Under this model, securities regulators, auditors and rating agencies become important enforcers of rules. Their activities supplement or, in some cases, substitute for measures taken by insurance and bank regulators. This new model poses especially significant challenges for insurers because of the role that uncertain assumptions about future claim obligations play in the insurer financial reporting process. It poses similar but less severe problems for banks.

Evidence of this evolving new model includes the following:

• expanded regulation of financial reporting in the U.S. capital markets and more aggressive enforcement;

- attempts to develop a common set of international accounting standards, particularly for financial services firms;
- the use of disclosure requirements to serve objectives of solvency regulation in Basel II and the draft Solvency II regulations to be applied to E.U. insurers;
- attempts by international organizations of central banks as well as insurance, securities and banking regulators to develop a unified approach to global financial regulation and to integrate accounting regulation into the same framework.

As with the evolving international accounting standard, political support also exists for common international financial regulation in areas for which such would be feasible. Concern persists that a failure to do so allows firms to undertake regulatory arbitrage and even hide profits and evade taxes. This effort, however, is proving to be a challenge, particularly in insurance and securities, both because of complexity and political clout.

## DISCUSSION QUESTIONS

1. Explain carefully why government regulation of private-sector financial service firms is considered necessary.
2. Debate the following proposition: "government regulation of insurance premium rates is justified."
3. What are the essential differences between government supervision of banks and of insurers? Why do these differences exist?
4. Examine the structure of financial regulation in your home country and compare it with the structure in another economy. Do you find any significant differences in the structures or in the accompanying regulatory objectives? Elaborate your findings.
5. Offer your answers to the questions posed in Note 2 of this chapter.

## NOTES

1. All data on size and domicile of financial intermediaries are taken from *Fortune* (2005).
2. Could there be a "chicken and egg" problem here? Could regulation that shields consumers from the consequences of their mistakes or from failing to become better informed about the quality of financial intermediaries result in their expecting government protection? Is it possible that the market might devise its own means of minimizing the effects of mistakes and providing consumers with adequate information were government intervention at a lesser level?
3. Of course, government itself hinders competition when it creates or preserves market power, as when, in the past, it limited the interest rates that banks could pay and prohibited them from marketing their services nationwide.
4. As already discussed, any payment to a factor of production in excess of the minimum required to bring forth or retain its service is referred to as economic rent. Economic rent can be thought of as excess profits.
5. The **Bank of International Settlements** (BIS) [www.bis.org] was established in 1930 (after World War I) initially to take over the functions performed by the Agent General for Repatriation in Berlin, Germany. Its role has changed now to promote cooperation among central banks and other agencies responsible for monetary and financial stability.

The other three key BIS committees, in addition to the Basel Committee, are the Markets Committee (established in 1962), the Committee on the Global Financial System (1971) and the Committee on Payment and Settlement Systems (1990).

6. Within the U.S., the *Financial Services Modernization Act*, enacted only in 1999, repealed decades-old restrictions on affiliations among banks, securities firms and insurers. It allowed creation of financial holding companies and authorized them to engage in a broad range of financial activities. The act makes clear that the Federal Reserve Board is the holding company supervisor. Otherwise, regulation is on a functional basis – meaning that commercial banking, investment banking and insurance activities continue to be regulated as before.

7. The Chinese government recently decided to permit cross-industrial ownership and business within the financial services market.

8. This discussion draws heavily from Gora (2004), pp. 9–12.

## REFERENCES

Becker, G. (1983). "A Theory of Competition among Pressure Groups for Political Influence." *Quarterly Journal of Economics*, 98 (3): 371–400.

*Fortune* (2005). "The Global 500."

Gora, J.C. (2004). *Insurer Transparency in an Era of Aggressive Financial Disclosure Regulation*. Atlanta, GA: LOMA.

Global Survey (2003). Institute of International Bankers.

International Banking (2006). *Source*: A Survey of International Banking (2006) appearing at www.economist.com/surveys/displaystory.cfm?story_id=6908488.

Meier, K.J. (1988). *The Political Economy of Regulation: The Case of Insurance*. Albany: State University of New York Press.

Peltzman, S. (1976). "Toward a More General Theory of Regulation." *Journal of Law and Economics*, 19 (2): 211–240.

Stigler, G.J. (1971). "The Theory of Economic Regulation." *Bell Journal of Economics*, 2 (Spring): 3–21.

White, L.J. (1996). "Competition versus Harmonization: An Overview of International Regulation of Financial Services," in Claude E. Barfield, ed., *International Financial Markets: Harmonization versus Competition*. Washington, DC: AEI Press.

# Chapter 9

# Public-Sector Economic Security

## INTRODUCTION

The previous chapter explored societal risk management from the perspective of government's role in ensuring the smooth functioning of private-sector financial service providers. This chapter examines why and how government itself provides certain economic security services.[1]

Governments play an important role in providing economic security to families and individuals and sometimes also to businesses. They do this because society desires certain types or amounts of economic security that government believes private financial institutions cannot or will not provide.

## WHY PRIVATE MARKETS FAIL TO PROVIDE SOME FINANCIAL SERVICES

Private markets do not always provide financial products in quantities or at prices that society may desire. Indeed, for many risky situations, the private market provides no financial solutions. Thus, virtually no private insurance exists against the financial consequences of unemployment. Individuals with no income and no assets generally cannot secure credit cards, insurance, investments, mutual funds or virtually any other private-sector financial service.

Similarly, insurers sell comparatively little individual health insurance, disability income insurance or life insurance to those in poor health. Banks are reluctant to loan money to individuals who habitually default on loans. No financial intermediary will insure a family's investment portfolio against losses, home against a decline in market value, or computer against obsolescence. Additionally, no private insurer will cover business losses resulting from a nuclear explosion, and few are keen to sell terrorism insurance.

In each of the above and many other instances, the failure of the private market to provide the service stems from either (1) financial intermediaries refusing to offer an otherwise demanded service or (2) prices being so high that no or only a modest market evolves. These results occur for one or more of four reasons:

- Financial intermediaries cannot adequately address the information problems that they encounter.
- Positive externalities accompany the purchase.
- Buyers have insufficient income.
- Risk aversion is insufficient to motivate individuals to pay high loadings.

## Information Problems

We know that financial markets are characterized by adverse selection and moral hazard problems, as discussed in Chapters 2, 8 and 19. While some financial institutions can provide desired products even in the face of these problems, their solutions do not always work or at least work very well. For example, the private market offers very few individual life annuities that provide higher monthly payments to annuitants who are in poor health – because of concerns about adverse selection.

Where the usual techniques for dealing with these information problems do not work well or at all, the private sector offers no solutions or offers them only at very high prices. Thus, adverse selection and moral hazard problems result in some consumers being unable to secure the financial security services that they may desire. As with other market imperfections, however, the question is: does the failure provide an economic rationale for government offering or facilitating the service? In the absence of positive externalities, the answer is "no." We now take up the issue of these externalities.

## Prices Fail to Capture Positive Externalities

To the extent that society receives positive spillovers from someone having acquired additional security, the price will be too high because it reflects only private producers' marginal costs of production and fails to credit against those costs the marginal societal benefits. For example, individuals who pay for vaccinations against contracting the flu not only reduce their chances of catching the flu, they also reduce the chances for other people by virtue of their being less likely to transmit it to anyone else. Flu vaccinations also increase worker productivity directly through better health and indirectly by reducing the need for family members to forego participation in the work force because having to attend to sick family members.

As with all activities and products that exhibit positive externalities, individuals will consume too little (in society's view) if they must pay the full private cost. Subsidizing the private costs of such activities and products lowers their effective prices to be closer to the (lower) social cost, thereby encouraging more consumption. Economic security services that exhibit positive externalities are no different in this respect.

Consider government insurance against losses from acts of terrorism. Proponents of substantial government involvement in this market contend that terrorism insurance carries two categories of external benefits to society:

- *Pre-loss benefits*: Businesses that carry terrorism insurance might be less likely to have to forego otherwise beneficial activities than businesses without terrorism insurance (e.g., construction projects).

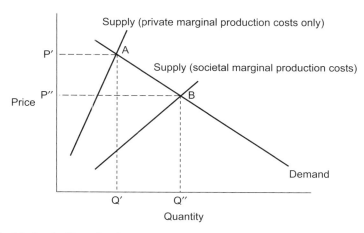

**Figure 9.1**   The Market for Terrorism Insurance

- *Post-loss benefits*: Insured businesses suffering losses from terrorism events might be less likely to become financially distressed or fail, thus preserving jobs and minimizing destabilizing economic effects.

Figure 9.1 illustrates how we conceptualize such external benefits. The supply curve incorporating only insurers' marginal costs of production shows that prices for terrorism insurance are necessarily high, at P′, and the quantity sold comparatively small, at Q′. This means that little terrorism insurance will be purchased. If we include the above spillover benefits as an offset to insurers' private costs of production, the production costs from society's point of view are lower. As a result, the price is lower, at P″, and the amount sold higher, at Q″ – thereby realizing an overall societal welfare gain equal to the area enclosed by P′ABP″.

The next question facing policymakers who believe such social benefits exist is how to lower the supply curve.[2] Options include, among others, government selling the insurance for the desired price, P″, or subsidizing private insurers' pricing, thereby lowering the price to P″.

This type of analysis is applicable to any other financial security service that carries positive externalities. Such arguments have been used to justify government providing flood insurance, nuclear power insurance and a host of other programs. Note that these externalities, attach to individuals or businesses with particular exposures and not to all of them. In other words, they carry positive externalities, but the externalities are not widespread across society; that is, they not have public good characteristics. Consequently, in most instances, the purchase of the financial service is made optional with the affected person. For example, the purchase of government-backed flood insurance is optional with the individual (although it may be required by a mortgagee).

Social insurance is also a response to this type of market imperfection (and to social equity or fairness issues). However, unlike optional government-backed financial services, the positive externalities attached to social insurance are judged to be pervasive throughout society; in other words, they are perceived as public goods. As such, and because of information asymmetry problems (see below), its purchase may be mandatory.

Society may find the private market's failure to capture positive externalities to be unacceptable. Additionally, a market economy promises efficiency and enhanced consumer choice and value, not necessarily "fairness" and equality. Societies vary in the extent to which they tolerate inequality, but most are uncomfortable with gross inequality, particularly when it is caused by conditions outside the individual's control.

Thus, if society concludes that families with young children should receive minimum levels of income if the breadwinner dies – because of either positive externalities (survivors have less incentive to resort to criminal activities) or altruistic concerns – this result can be accomplished by requiring everyone to participate in a government insurance program. If participation is mandatory and the insurance pool must accept all such individuals, contributions to the pool need not reflect each insured's expected loss potential. Government simply mandates participation and requires contributions based on whatever criteria it deems appropriate. Insureds cannot exercise discretion as to whether they participate in the pool nor can they influence the premium they pay by altering their loss characteristics. Of course, this is precisely what happens with social insurance.

Risk-based pricing and underwriting are unnecessary for social insurance. There need be no relationship between a given individual's contributions and his or her expected benefit payments. Indeed, one of the purposes of social insurance is to redistribute income from the relatively wealthy in a society to the less wealthy. A voluntary insurance arrangement could not accomplish this goal because participation by the wealthy could not be assured. In fact, we could be almost certain that such an arrangement would fail (except for any charitable motivation – which ordinarily is realized through charitable contributions and good works rather than through an insurance mechanism).[3]

In a voluntary insurance market, if some insureds pay premiums that are insufficient to cover adequately the expected value of their losses (and insurer expenses), other insureds must make good the deficit. In other words, insureds with low loss propensities would be subsidizing those with higher loss propensities. When we are dealing with hundreds and thousands of other insureds, each of whom is anonymous to us, we are not keen on voluntarily and knowingly to subsidize any of them. Indeed, it is *we* who would want a subsidy if we could get it. Human nature being what it is, we are content to accept a subsidy from anonymous people (i.e., paying a price below the cost of production), but we are much less likely to want voluntarily to provide one to anonymous people (i.e., purposefully paying a price greater than the cost of production).

Of course, insureds who suffer losses always receive a "subsidy" from those who do not. However, this type of *ex post* subsidy is fair, in the absence of a moral hazard problem and assuming fair pricing, because its occurrence is random. Each insured's likelihood of receiving this loss-payment subsidy from the insurance pool *is* the likelihood of his or her suffering a loss. This being true, contributions (premiums) from pool participants (insureds) should *logically* vary from participant to participant to reflect each participant's likelihood of collecting; otherwise, those participants who have a small likelihood of collecting from the pool might refuse to participate. This same problem does not occur with mandatory insurance programs, of course, because government has the power to require participation even with actuarially unfair contributions.

Where administrative, financing or marketing economies of scale exist, a large, mandatory program will have market power and may be able to exploit this fact and achieve savings that private insurers may be unable to attain. Government may exploit economies of scale either by creating regulated private monopolies or administering a public insurance program.

Figure 9.2 illustrates the effects of providing economic security coverages through a mandated government system. If individuals' consumption of certain economic security products carries pervasive positive externalities for society (i.e., it is a public good), individuals' consumption of those coverages in a private market will be less than society

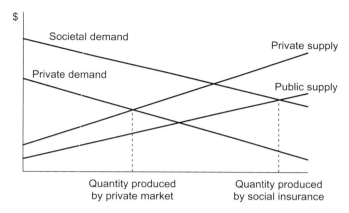

**Figure 9.2**    The Economics of Social Insurance

desires. In Figure 9.2, society demands more economic security at every price than do individuals. As suggested above, governments attempt to resolve this issue, in part, by increasing the demand for those coverages by making participation compulsory.

Also, as private insurers face adverse selection and moral hazard, they will supply less than optimal coverage. By reducing or eliminating individual risk selection, government alleviates the problem of adverse selection. Moral hazard, however, remains an issue in social benefit programs. As increased consumption of certain covered services is often a goal, moral hazard is tolerated or even encouraged in ways that a private market could not permit.

Governments, thereby, can supply more of these coverages at any given price, as shown by the public supply curve in Figure 9.2. As a result, the quantity demanded and supplied at each price is increased, yielding greater consumption of the goods and services society values, as illustrated by the new equilibrium.

## Insufficient Buyer Income

Another reason that the private sector might fail to provide financial security can be insufficient buyer income. Many individuals' and families' incomes are insufficient to pay both for life's necessities that provide immediate utility and for financial security services that provide future utility. All income is required for a hand-to-mouth existence. Stated differently, the interest rate necessary to induce a poor person to forego current consumption for future consumption is exceptionally high, maybe even infinite. No amount of additional food ("interest") tomorrow will cause a starving person to forego food today.

Most of us would not advocate government providing a subsidy or giving money to people to purchase digital cameras, sports utility vehicles or bottles of *Dom Perignon* champagne simply because they cannot afford them (not that we wouldn't accept them!). The same economic logic applies to all purchases that do not carry positive externalities. In other words, in the absence of positive externalities, insufficient income in itself provides no *economic justification* for government becoming a provider of financial security services any more than insufficient income provides a justification for government providing any other product or service. Of course, some economic security services do carry positive externalities. Additionally, irrespective of the existence of such externalities, societies often choose to provide security services for non-economic reasons such as out of compassion or concerns about fairness.[4]

## Insufficient Buyer Risk Aversion

Even when individuals have sufficient income to afford certain financial services, they may consider the price to be too high relative to the perceived benefits of the services. This condition is common in financial services, especially in insurance markets. After all, financial intermediation is not frictionless. Intermediaries incur expenses and other costs that must be paid by customers if the intermediaries are to survive. These costs – called loadings in insurance – may be high for several reasons. Below, we use insurance to illustrate the more common reasons.

### Low-severity or high-frequency exposures

Insurance is usually unavailable for loss events that exhibit low severity or high frequency. In each instance, risk aversion is insufficient to motivate individuals to pay the high loadings that insurers would require to underwrite the risk. Thus, insurers do not sell policies covering low-severity losses, such as a policy insuring this textbook against theft.[5] Who would pay a premium of $100 to insure an item worth $100 against a single loss (and the premium could be that high because of insurer loadings for its fixed costs, including underwriting and marketing expenses)?

Similarly, insurers do not generally sell policies covering high frequency events. Many such events (e.g., food spoilage) are also low-severity events. Others may be high severity, such as individuals with chronic conditions that require high recurring healthcare expenditures. Even if private insurers would issue individual health insurance policies to such persons, the premiums would be exceptionally high because of the expected high claims costs and the loadings necessary to cover correspondingly high claims administrative costs. The result could be a premium higher than the potential losses, making the insurance economically infeasible.

Again, in the absence of positive externalities, high-severity events occurring frequently provide no *economic* justification for government becoming a provider of the financial security service. If I choose to build my house on a cliff, overlooking the Pacific Ocean, that is known for regular landslides, I am likely to find insurance for damage to my house caused by landslides to be exceptionally expensive, if available at all. Should other taxpayers be required to subsidize my premium or to give money to pay my high premiums? My decision to build in a high-risk area is a private choice that carries both private benefits (beautiful view) and private costs. Presumably, society does not benefit from my having a beautiful view nor should it subsidize me.

Low-severity events are unlikely to be associated with externalities. High-severity and high-frequency events, such as healthcare for the elderly, may have associated externalities that justify government providing or subsidizing the security service. Note, however, that it is the externality, not the frequency or severity of the event itself, that justifies government intervention.

### Correlated exposures

Loadings can be high if exposure units are not independent. Lack of independence can cause a private financial services market to fail, as discussed in Chapter 19 as regards insurances.[6] Catastrophic exposures such as economic depressions, systemic risks, earthquakes, floods, nuclear liabilities and wars each fail the independence test. With correlated exposures, the probability that actual losses will exceed expected losses is higher than is the situation with uncorrelated exposures. This situation means that financial intermediaries must hold more capital than otherwise for a given level of financial solidity. Higher capital means greater costs that translate into higher loadings or simple refusal to offer financial services.

### Exposure ambiguity

Other exposures for which loadings can be high are those exhibiting **ambiguity**, meaning that underlying pricing data are lacking or believed unreliable. Terrorism risk is a good example. Unlike the situation with most other extreme events, virtually no statistically useful data exist for insurers to build and test models for acts of terrorism. As a consequence, the perceived risks by insurers in writing terrorism insurance was – and still is – high, requiring them to maintain higher than typical capital levels for a given solvency objective. In the presence of ambiguity, insurers (and other financial intermediaries) either will impose substantial loadings to compensate them for the additional risk or they will not offer the demanded service. Buyer risk aversion is often insufficient to push the demand curve into equilibrium with supply. Indeed, for risk neutral buyers, such as many businesses, loadings of any type will result in no market.

In sum, in the absence of positive externalities associated with the financial services, neither lack of independence nor ambiguity justifies government intervention. Yes, prices might be quite high and the financial service purchased substantially reduced, or none may be available at all. This situation is economically no different than that in which businesses have found themselves when their input costs rise dramatically or input data are unavailable.

## SELECTED PUBLIC-BASED ECONOMIC SECURITY SERVICES

The precise mix of public-based economic security is determined by each country's concern about externalities (even if this precise term is not used to describe spillover effects) and its national values, level of economic development, culture and history. This section highlights selected public economic security programs.

### Social Insurance

The most important government-provided economic security services in most countries are those provided under social insurance programs. Social insurance not only provides income security for individuals but is also an important public policy instrument that influences the macroeconomic health of a country and redistributes income to better achieve social equity. Not surprisingly, social insurance programs represent a significant percentage of the GDP for many economies. Typical social insurance program benefits include those for retirement, death, disability, health, unemployment and workers' injuries.

The first social insurance program was introduced in Germany in 1889 by its Chancellor, Otto von Bismarck. Generally such employment-based programs to which workers, employer and the government contributed, benefits relate directly to contributions. The concept of wealth redistribution through social insurance programs was introduced much later by William Beveridge. In his 1942 report to the British government, he outlined principles for social insurance that included universal (i.e., not employment based) coverage, unification of separate programs under a single administration, and financing primarily through progressive taxation. His principles moved social insurance away from a private insurance model and emphasized social equity as a goal. Most countries' social insurance programs today combine features of both the Bismarck and Beveridge principles.

### Definition of social insurance

The term social insurance has many definitions.[7] Some analysts limit social insurance programs to those government programs that are employment based, while others include a wider range of public and private insurance programs. For our purposes, we define **social insurance** as a government-sponsored economic security program that insures individuals and families against interruption or loss of earning power or health and which possesses three characteristics:

* Economic security is provided for well-defined loss exposures.
* Participation is compulsory for the target population.
* Contributions usually are not adjusted for probability of loss.

The programs typically require all workers to participate and provide benefits as well to workers' family members who are not employed. Contributions required of participants vary by income, not by individual risk characteristics. Given compulsory participation and contributions unrelated to risk, redistribution of income automatically occurs. In the case of retirement income security, this redistribution occurs both within and between generations.

A few countries have **universal programs** that are flat-rate cash benefit programs for citizens and residents with sufficient time in residency. The benefit payments are without consideration of income, employment or other means tests. Governments finance these programs from general revenues.

Under universal systems, governments usually do not require a minimum period of covered employment or contributions. However, most of these systems prescribe a minimum period of prior residence. In Canada, for example, age 65 and 10 years of residence after age 18 are required to receive the full universal old-age pension. These restrictions presumably are imposed because such systems are largely financed from general revenues.

The scope of universal programs varies from country to country. The program may include old-age pensions for qualified residents after a certain age as well as disability benefits for physically challenged workers. Most universal social security systems have a second-tier, earnings-related program, financed in part by contributions by employers and the working population.

### Social insurance programs worldwide

The number of social insurance programs globally has grown significantly since 1940. The International Social Security Administration (ISSA) reports that almost all of its member countries have at least one type of social insurance program. As shown in Tables 9.1 and 9.2, old-age programs and work-injury programs are the most common types. The growth in the number and variety of social insurance programs reflects general worldwide economic growth since the early 1950s.

### Funding social insurance programs

Social insurance programs are funded through three main sources: (1) taxes paid by participant workers, (2) taxes paid by employers, and (3) government contributions. About one-half

**Table 9.1**    Number of Countries with Social Insurance Programs by Type of Program (Trend)

| Type of Program | 1940 | 1958 | 1977 | 1989 | 1995 | 2003–2005[a] |
|---|---|---|---|---|---|---|
| Any type of program | 57 | 80 | 129 | 145 | 165 | 173 |
| Old age, disability, survivor | 33 | 58 | 114 | 135 | 158 | 171 |
| Sickness and maternity | 24 | 59 | 72 | 84 | 105 | 150 |
| Work injury | 57 | 77 | 129 | 136 | 159 | 168 |
| Unemployment | 21 | 26 | 38 | 40 | 63 | 81 |
| Family allowance | 7 | 38 | 65 | 63 | 81 | 99 |
| Total | 199 | 338 | 547 | 603 | 731 | 842 |

[a]Different data years and see also Table 9.2 by region.
*Source*: Social Security Administration (2005).

**Table 9.2**    Comparison of Social Insurance Programs by Region and Type: 2003–2005

| Type of Program (Data Year) | Africa (2005) | Asia (2004) | Americas (2003) | Europe (2004) | Total |
|---|---|---|---|---|---|
| Any type of program | 44 | 48 | 37 | 44 | 173 |
| Old age, disability, survivor | 43 | 47 | 37 | 44 | 171 |
| Sickness and maternity | 34 | 35 | 37 | 44 | 150 |
| Work injury | 44 | 44 | 36 | 44 | 168 |
| Unemployment | 7 | 19 | 11 | 44 | 81 |
| Family allowance | 26 | 17 | 13 | 43 | 99 |
| Total | 198 | 210 | 171 | 263 | 842 |

*Source*: Social Security Administration (2005).

of the programs worldwide derive their funds from all three sources, and almost all other programs – except for universal systems – from both employer and employee contributions.

### Contributions

Required contributions are closely related to worker earnings. The government or program administrator usually applies a percentage to wages, subject to a certain maximum amount, for the calculation of the contribution amount. In some countries, the government applies the same percentage for the contributions by both the employer and employees. In many others, the employer pays a larger share. Revenue from payroll taxes is almost always earmarked to fund benefits.

The government's contribution may be derived from general revenues or, less frequently, from special earmarked or excise taxes (e.g., a tax on tobacco, gasoline or alcoholic beverages). The contribution may be used in different ways. In Japan, Korea and Saudi Arabia, it defrays some of the administrative costs. In Austria, Bulgaria, the Czech Republic, Egypt, Italy and Lithuania, it covers deficits. In Australia, Bangladesh, Canada and South Africa, it finances the entire program. Several countries reduce or, in some cases, eliminate contributions for the lowest-paid earners, with their benefits financed entirely from general revenues or by the employer. General revenue financing as the sole source of financing is found in some universal systems.

Social insurance programs are often financed in a manner that redistributes income from one generation to another or from one income group to another or both. This redistribution is an important characteristic of many countries' social insurance programs, especially those providing retirement income security.

For administrative purposes, many countries assess a single overall contribution rate covering several contingencies. Not only pensions, but other social security programs (e.g., sickness, work injury, unemployment and survivor benefits) may also be financed from this contribution. Some countries (e.g., Bulgaria, China, Finland, France and Peru), maintain dual or multiple assessment systems. Table 9.3 shows contribution rates for selected countries.

**Table 9.3**  Contribution Rates for Old Age, Disability and Survivors' Programs in Selected Countries (2003) (As a Percentage of Earnings)

| Country | Contribution Rates | | |
| --- | --- | --- | --- |
| | *Employee* | *Employer* | *Government* |
| Algeria | 5.5% | 8% | None |
| Argentina | Up to 11% | Up to 21% | Contribution through general revenues, investment income and earmarked taxes |
| Australia | None | None | Total cost from general revenue |
| Austria | 10.25% up to €3,450 per month | 12.55% up to €3,450 per month | Any deficits and the cost of care benefit and income-tested allowance |
| Azerbaijan | 2% | Up to 27% | Subsidies as needed for social insurance and total cost for social pension |
| Bangladesh | None | None | Total cost |
| Belgium | 7.5% | 8.86% of payroll | Annual subsidies |
| Bolivia | 10% | 2% | Social insurance and social assistance pensions |
| Brazil | Up to 11% | 20% | Earmarked taxes |
| Bulgaria | 21% for social insurance plus 0.75% for mandatory individual account | 5% for social insurance plus 2.25% for mandatory individual account | Any deficit in the social insurance system |
| Canada | None | None | Total cost |
| Chile | 10% | Almost nil | Cost of the guaranteed minimum pension |
| China | None for basic pension and 8% for mandatory individual account | Up to 20% for basic pension and 3% for mandatory individual account | Variable subsidies |
| Czech Republic | 6.5% | 21.5% | Any deficit in the social insurance system |
| Egypt | Up to 13% | Up to 17% | 1% of payroll plus any deficit |
| Ethiopia | 4% | 6% | None |
| Finland | None for universal pension and 4.6% for earnings-related pensions | Up to 7.8% for universal pension and an average of 21% for earnings-related pensions | Government covers 26% of universal pension cost |

(Continued)

**Table 9.3**    (*Continued*)

| Country | Contribution Rates | | |
|---|---|---|---|
| | *Employee* | *Employer* | *Government* |
| France | 6.55% of insurable earnings for old age plus 0.1% for survivors | 8.2% of insurable earnings for old age plus 1.6% for survivors | Variable subsidies |
| Germany | 9.75% in general | 9.75–12% | Subsidy for the cost of benefits not covered by contributions |
| India | 12% to provident fund only | Up to 16.05 for various schemes | 1.16% for pension scheme only |
| Italy | 8.89% | 23.81% | Full cost of income-tested allowances and any overall deficits |
| Japan | 6.79% of basic monthly earnings and salary bonuses, according to 30 wage classes | 6.79% of basic monthly earnings and salary bonuses before tax, according to 30 wage classes | Administration cost for national pension and employee's pension plus one-third of cost of benefits for national pension |
| Korea | 4.5% of standard monthly earnings, according to 45 wage levels | 4.5% of standard monthly earnings, according to 45 wage levels | Basically part of administration cost |
| Lithuania | 2.5% | 23.4% | Any deficits |
| Luxembourg | 8% | 8% | 8% |
| Libya | 3.75% | 10.5% | 0.75% of covered earnings |
| Mexico | 1.75% | 4.9% | 10.14% of the total employer contributions for old-age plus a flat rate to finance guaranteed pension |
| Nigeria | 3.5% | 6.5% | None |
| Peru | 13% for social insurance plus 8% for private insurance | None | Finances guaranteed minimum pension |
| Portugal | 11% | 23.75% | Subsidy for social pension |
| Russia | None | Up to 35.6% | Pension costs for government personnel and special groups |
| Saudi Arabia | 9% | 9% | Cost of administration plus some subsidy |
| South Africa | None | None | Total cost |
| Sri Lanka | 8% | 12% | None |
| Sweden | 7% | 10.21% of insurable earnings for old age plus 1.7% for survivors | Total cost of guarantee pension and permanent disability benefits |
| Taiwan | 1.1% | 3.85% | 0.55% |
| U.K. | Up to 11% | 12.8% | Total cost of means-tested allowances and other noncontributory benefits |
| U.S. | 6.2% | 6.2% | Total cost of means-tested allowances |
| Vietnam | 5% | 10% | None |

*Source*: Social Security Administration (2005).

*Fully funded versus pay-as-you-go funding*

The fund for retirement income benefits can be generated through a fully funded approach or a pay-as-you-go (paygo) approach. A **fully funded approach** means that enough funds are secured presently to pay for the accrued benefits for current participants. Most private pension systems are fully funded in that they fund individual retirement benefits through contributions made over the working life of the insureds.

A **paygo** approach means that benefits for current recipients are paid from the contributions made by the currently working population. Almost all OECD countries have paygo retirement income security plans.

Politically, the paygo system of financing retirement benefits is the easier of the two funding approaches to implement. It places the least burden on the initial generation of workers (and voters). Under a paygo system, the program's initial contributions cover the cost of providing benefits to current retirees only. In contrast, contributions during the implementation period of a fully funded system would be higher because workers would be funding not only their own retirement benefits but also those of current retirees who had contributed little or nothing.

If the distribution of the population between workers and retirees remains roughly constant, the paygo system does not necessarily result in a transfer of income between generations when viewed over the lifetime of the individual. Worker contributions fund retirees' income over the working life of individuals. As these former workers (contributors) retire, they begin to receive benefits funded by the workers who replace them. When populations or economic conditions change, however, the paygo system may result in intergenerational transfers.

In most countries, demographic changes have placed serious strains on paygo social insurance programs providing retirement income. Indeed, the number of workers relative to the number of retirees has been declining worldwide, as discussed in Chapter 7. As a result, many countries face long-term financing challenges. Options for rectifying the problems are, however, limited. Benefits may be reduced, contributions increased, or some combination of these two enacted.

In some countries, such as Canada, Japan, Sweden and the U.S., the social security programs are accumulating reserves in anticipation of increased benefit payments. Even in these countries, the reserves plus future contributions are inadequate to finance the benefits currently promised to future retirees. Figure 9.3 shows the extent of the problem facing several governments. The figure shows the net present value of public pension liabilities until 2070 for selected countries, expressed as a percentage of 1994 GDP of each country, where:

Net present value = (Current reserves + Present value of future contributions)
− Present value of future promised benefits

Other countries have taken steps to reduce the amount of benefits paid in retirement (e.g., Germany) or have changed the way retirement income benefits are funded (e.g., Argentina and Chile). Australia's social security schemes are primarily economic-needs tested (except for the blind), which means that benefits are tied to assets or income of the beneficiary. Australia also permits voluntary participation in occupational pension (superannuation) schemes.

### Social insurance benefits

We now explore the nature and extent of benefits provided through social insurance programs worldwide. The discussion in this section deals with (1) retirement income including survivor benefits, (2) health insurance, and (3) unemployment insurance.

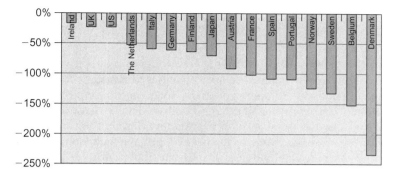

**Figure 9.3**  Public Pension Liabilities in Selected Countries (Net Present Value, Percent of 1994 GDP).
*Source*: OECD

## Retirement income

Old age is ordinarily a period of low or reduced income and of increased health risk. Historically, care for the elderly was provided by extended families. In many developing countries and closed societies, this practice is still observed. With industrialization and urbanization, life expectancy increases and the ability of families to care for their elderly reduced. See Insight 9.1.

Support for the elderly has been a prime focus of social insurance. There are three basic reasons for providing retirement income through a social insurance mechanism:

- Individuals may not have the information needed to prepare adequately for retirement. They tend to discount their future consumption needs in favor of current consumption.
- There are economies of scale in funding retirement benefits. Larger, professionally invested funds are more likely to yield greater retirement benefits than individual savings.
- The elderly's consumption is likely to have external benefits to society.

The first two rationales for providing retirement income through a social insurance mechanism are important only if the elderly's consumption has external benefits. If society values the elderly's consumption, then the individual's failure to save adequately for retirement – because of lack of income, information or willingness – must be addressed. However, merely mandating that individuals save for retirement – by regulation or by taxation – may not provide adequate retirement income if the savings do not yield a sufficient return. In many countries, an adequate return is assured through payroll taxes.

## Scope of coverage

Originally, employment-related programs for retirement benefits were available only to government employees and the military. As the programs evolved, benefits were extended to employees in selected industries such as mining, railways, banking and maritime activities. The risk involved in an occupation, the strategic importance of certain occupations to economic growth, and the economic and political strength of trade unions influenced decisions about what sectors were covered.

Gradually, coverage was extended first to private-sector workers in urban areas and then to virtually all wage earners and salaried employees. Today, OECD member states as well as many developing countries administer retirement income programs for the entire population.

---

### INSIGHT 9.1: SOCIAL INSURANCE AND FAMILY SIZE ─────

Social security programs have reduced the need for families to provide support to aged individuals. Family size in many developed countries is at historic lows and is routinely lower than that found in developing countries. Social insurance programs reduce some of the economic reasons for having large families. The costs of having children are only partially offset by social insurance programs (through lower healthcare costs), while these programs replace one of the benefits of having children – income security in the event of disability and old age. This is one explanation for lower birth rates in developed countries.

Smaller families may have fewer resources to care for disabled or elderly individuals. The presence of a social insurance program providing income security benefits has paradoxically increased the need for such a program by reducing the resources families can provide to aged individuals.

---

In some developing countries, coverage is limited to wage and salary workers in urban areas and perhaps in selected provinces. Some governments still maintain separate systems for government and military personnel.

Most social insurance programs initially excluded from coverage agricultural workers and the self-employed due mainly to administrative difficulty. Also commonly excluded for the same reason were family workers, domestics and day workers. In recent years, the trend has been to cover these groups under separate funds or to bring them under the general system. Even the non-employed may now be covered. In the U.K., the non-employed are defined as persons not currently in the labor force but making voluntary contributions at a specified level, thus maintaining their rights to a pension.

*Plan design and reform*
Rational design of a national pension policy begins by agreeing on objectives and then proceeds to an analysis of the instruments available to achieve them. Broadly, the objectives of all pension systems are to (1) provide economic security against destitution in old age, (2) smooth the distribution of consumption spending over a lifetime, and (3) provide for life's requirements for those with exceptional longevity.

In seeking to accomplish these objectives, national pension systems have evolved in three distinct tiers that highlight key public policy choices:

- The *first tier* is intended primarily to provide poverty relief, normally in a public system funded on a paygo basis participation with mandatory.
- The *second tier* provides for consumption smoothing over each person's lifetime. It can be publicly or privately managed and either paygo or fully funded.
- The *third tier* is private, funded and voluntary.

In the U.S., for example, the first tier is found in the Social Security retirement benefit that is weighted in favor of lower income workers. The second tier occurs mainly in the form of employer-sponsored retirement plans that are privately managed and intended to be fully funded. The third tier is found in individual retirement funding via Individual Retirement Accounts (IRAs), individual annuities and other personal retirement savings.

Many countries rely on voluntary private retirement pensions to supplement public programs. Some countries make participation in private pensions mandatory. For example, France has an employment-based public social security plan *and* requires all workers to participate in private employment-based pension plans. Under this bipartite basis, both the employer and the employee contribute, and the French government offers various subsidies. In 1981, Chile moved to a system in which most pension income comes from private pension funds with the government guarantees the cost of minimum pensions.

Japan has long maintained a two-tier social insurance plan. The first tier – the National Pension – is universal, provides a minimum set of benefits to all retired workers and is financed through general tax revenues. Residents between the ages 20 and 59 are the main population subject to participation in this program. In the second tier, benefits are earnings related and are available through the employee's pension programs (i.e., Employees' Pension Insurance) or other employment-related programs. Like Japan, many countries have mixed approaches (e.g., Korea and the U.K.).

Whether public pension systems should be redesigned to accomplish their policy goals remains a challenging question. The IMF has set out the prerequisites for their success and policy choices that governments face (Barr, 2002):

- All pension systems, no matter how financed, require strong and effective government to succeed. Fundamentally, government must be capable of managing the economy effectively to facilitate the growth of output. If pension systems are public, government must inspire confidence that promises will be kept. If pension systems are private, government must sustain a regulatory environment that ensures high fiduciary standards and transparency in private capital markets. This last item requires constant government vigilance, as the U.S. learned from the collapse of the energy giant Enron in 2001.

- The much-debated choice between government paygo and (private or public) funded schemes is of secondary importance to the government's ability to manage the economy effectively, to promote adequate output growth, and to sustain a stable foundation for whatever pension system is adopted. Whatever the political arguments, the economic welfare gains from one approach versus the other are vague. Both paygo and funded programs are simply different ways for organizing claims on future economic output.

- Within the limits of national economic and government capacity, countries have a wide range of choice over pension design. No one approach will prove superior.

*Benefit qualification*

Governments commonly impose two eligibility requirements for participants to receive old-age benefits: (1) attainment of a specified age and (2) completion of a specified period of contributions or covered employment. Old-age benefits generally become payable between ages 60 and 65. In some countries, length-of-service benefits are payable at any age after a certain period of employment, most commonly between 30 and 40 years.

The age at which benefits first become payable was a major policy issue in the 1970s and 1980s. There was public pressure to lower the age limits in some countries. Despite the pressure, several countries have increased their age limits due to budgetary constraints. The

U.S., for example, is gradually increasing the pensionable age from age 65 to age 67 during the years 2000–2027.

Many programs have the same pensionable age for women as for men. Others permit women, despite their typical longer life expectancy, to draw a full pension at an earlier age than men. The differential is usually about 5 years. The global trend is toward equalizing the retirement age for men and women.

*Nature of benefits*

Some countries provide for a fixed benefit amount weakly related to prior earnings. In most countries, however, retirement benefits are wage-related and based also on formulas. For example, some provide an amount equaling a percentage of average earnings of the recipient (e.g., 50 percent) once he or she has met the eligibility requirements. The amount may not rise even with additional years of service.

A more common practice is providing a basic rate (e.g., 30 percent) of average earnings, plus an increment of 1 or 2 percent of earnings for each year of service or for each year in excess of a minimum number of years for qualification. Several countries, including the U.S., have a weighted benefit formula, which returns a larger percentage of earnings to lower income workers than to higher income workers.

Typical retirement benefit programs contain provisions regarding minimum and maximum benefits. Governments set minimum benefits at the levels that would help the beneficiaries maintain a minimum standard of living. However, even in many developed economies, not to mention the majority of developing countries, this objective has not been fully achieved.

The programs may add supplements to the basic benefit for non-working spouse and dependent children. For example, the spouse's supplement may be set at 50 percent or more of the basic benefit. Commonly, the spouse's benefit is available once the spouse has reached a specified age (e.g., age 62) or when he or she becomes disabled before reaching the age.[8]

Concerning maximum benefits, many programs establish a ceiling on the earnings taken into account in the benefit computation. This can result in potentially qualified beneficiaries receiving smaller or no retirement benefits while they continue to earn income above the threshold. Another popular instrument is setting the maximum cash benefit amount or linking the maximum to a stipulated percentage of average earnings before retirement (e.g., 80 percent). A maximum also can be used to limit total benefits, including those of survivors and dependents, of a family in the interest of the financial stability of the program.

*Survivor benefits*

Most social insurance programs provide for some type of payment to dependents – spouse and dependent children under a certain age – of deceased workers. Known commonly as survivor benefit programs, they are patterned closely after their counterpart retirement income benefit programs. They generally extend coverage to the same population groups as for retirement income benefits. Thus, only covered workers are likely the target population with wage-based systems, whereas a universal system is commonly extended to all qualifying citizens and residents.

Funding for survivor benefits ordinarily follows that for retirement income benefits. With wage-based plans, payroll taxes usually provide the funding.

For survivors to be eligible for benefits, most programs require that the deceased worker be a pensioner at death or have completed a minimum period of covered employment or contribution. This period is often the same as that for the disability benefit (see below). The surviving spouse and children often must meet certain additional conditions, such as age requirements.

Periodic benefits for survivors of covered persons or pensioners are provided under most systems, although a few pay lump-sum benefits only. Survivor benefits under most programs are a percentage of the benefits being paid to the deceased at death or the benefits to which the insured would have been entitled if the insured had attained a pensionable age or become disabled at that time.

Survivor benefits are paid to some categories of widows under nearly all programs. The amount of a widow's benefit most frequently ranges from 50 to 75 percent of the deceased worker's benefits or in some cases 100 percent as in the U.S. In some countries, lifetime benefits are payable to every widow whose husband fulfills the necessary qualifying period. More commonly, the provision of widows' benefits is confined, except possibly for a brief period, to those having young children in their care, those above a specified age or those who are disabled.

The age limits for children's benefits are often the same as for children's allowances through retirement income or disability income benefit programs. Many countries fix a somewhat higher limit for children who are attending school (up to college in selected countries), undergoing an apprenticeship, or are incapacitated. In a large number of countries, the age limit is removed for disabled orphans.

Benefits are payable under a number of programs to certain widowers of insured workers or pensioners. A widower usually must have been financially dependent on his wife and either disabled or old enough to receive an old-age benefit at her death. A widower's benefit is usually computed in the same way as a widow's benefit.

### Health insurance

A variety of ways exists to help individuals or society as a whole to finance healthcare-related expenditures. Healthcare services may be funded by the government, the employer or the individual. They may be financed through general tax revenues, payroll taxes or private insurance premiums. Medical care may be provided by health professionals who are employees of the state or are private contractors. Services may be guaranteed free-of-charge to everyone as in full national health insurance schemes or to particular sub-groups of individuals only, such as the poor or the elderly, under various welfare programs.

The healthcare delivery and financing systems reflect the cultural, economic and political character of the nation. It points to the difficult choices made in how to allocate scarce healthcare resources across the population. Most industrialized countries place great value on equal access to healthcare across individuals, even if it means that some must wait for or be denied certain specialized medical services. The systems provide basic universal coverage to all, although certain high technology procedures and treatments may not be as readily available. In contrast, the U.S., which does not have a national healthcare program, provides nearly instantaneous access to state-of-the-art technology for those who are well insured, while those with no medical insurance find expensive treatments less accessible. As discussed in Chapter 11, the culture in the U.S. places relatively less value on social equity and relatively greater value on private-market solutions to financing healthcare.

Some nations devote significantly more of their national income to healthcare services than do others. For example, in 2003, the average percentage of GDP devoted to healthcare

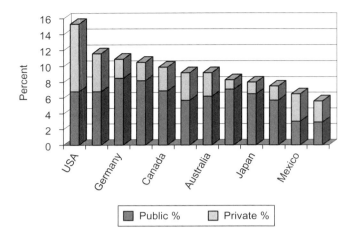

**Figure 9.4**    Healthcare Expenditures among OECD Countries (2003). *Source*: OECD

among 22 OECD countries was about 8 percent. However, as Figure 9.4 shows, spending in 2004 ranged from more than 15 percent of GDP in the U.S. to somewhat more than 5 percent in Mexico.

A global overview of healthcare financing systems offers an opportunity to compare a variety of approaches to healthcare financing and to examine whether financing alternatives affect the quality and price of healthcare. We begin by examining the economics of healthcare. Next, we describe the major types of healthcare financing systems worldwide. Public-sector provision of medical services as well as private-sector provision of medical insurance is explored, paying particular attention to the role of government, employers, and providers (e.g., physicians and hospitals). We then summarize reform initiatives, noting trends worldwide. Finally, we examine the effect of healthcare financing systems on the overall health of nations.

*The economics of healthcare*

In a perfectly competitive market, buyers have access to full information about the quality and price of goods and services traded. In the market, buyers, not sellers, determine the demand for goods and services. Demand for normal goods or services decreases with an increase in price, all else being equal. Further, price rationing occurs, since buyers base purchasing decisions on the relative quality and price of the good as well as on their willingness and ability to pay. For sellers, the market has no barriers to entry. Neither do they incur costs to exit the market.

The healthcare market differs markedly from the perfectly competitive ideal market, with innumerable market imperfections. Research suggests the following as key causes of market imperfections in the healthcare industry: (1) difficulty in measuring marginal benefit of additional medical service on health, (2) presence of information asymmetries, including adverse selection, (3) problems of moral hazard, (4) demand for services induced by suppliers, and (5) barriers to market entry.

*Marginal benefit of medical care*    In the healthcare market, buyers cannot purchase health per se but consume medical services to improve or maintain health. Medical services can improve health, but the marginal benefit of medical services on health is difficult to measure. Basic or preventive medical services, such as vaccinations, provide a much greater marginal benefit to society than do more expensive, technologically intensive interventions. Once vaccinations and basic health services are provided, overall health is positively affected more by factors such as diet, exercise and personal habits than by high technology medical procedures. Consequently, it is difficult for a society to define the optimal amount of medical care that should be provided.

*Information asymmetries*    Substantial information imbalances exist in the purchase and delivery of healthcare. We examine these imbalances between buyers and sellers with respect to the price of medical services, and between insurers and insureds.

- *Buyers and sellers*: Information asymmetry exists between buyers and sellers in the healthcare market. In general, providers are well informed about the services they deliver, but consumers are rarely well informed about the medical services they consume. Of course, consumers can become better informed, but it can be costly for physicians and hospitals to provide full information to consumers. Physicians may provide only what they consider to be essential information relative to a particular medical treatment. Even when information on alternative treatments is available such that consumers can shop for the treatment methods of their choice, consumers often find it difficult to understand and evaluate alternatives. Evaluating alternatives includes consideration of service quality (measured by criteria such as the success rate of the treatment), the degree of invasiveness of the procedure, and the length of recovery period. In addition, gathering and analyzing information often occur when the buyer is ill, further putting the consumer at an informational disadvantage.

- *Price of medical services*: Information asymmetries exist with respect to the price of medical services. In most industrialized countries, consumers have limited incentives to be informed about the price of medical services when a third party, whether public or private, pays for most medical services. Even when consumers attempt to price services, it is often difficult to determine in advance the total cost of services. In some cases, physicians themselves do not have incentives to be well informed about price if their income is unaffected by the quantity or quality of services delivered as where physicians are salaried. In other systems, consumers must first secure the service price from the provider and then contact the insurer to ascertain how much of the charge is covered by insurance, a two-stage process that is burdensome. Information asymmetries, associated with understanding the nature of the medical treatment and comparing prices of alternative treatments, constrain price rationing and efficient purchase of healthcare. In such a healthcare market, consumers cannot easily make price-quality tradeoffs based on full information.

- *Insurers and insureds*: Information asymmetries exist between insureds and insurers as well. Insureds have more information about their individual health status than do insurers. This informational disadvantage to insurers may result in adverse selection. Adverse selection occurs when individuals with higher than average health risk seek insurance and insurers, being unaware of their risk levels, fail to charge adequate premiums. When risks are pooled, adverse selection results in individuals with lower risks subsidizing those with higher risks in the pool. Ultimately low-risk individuals buy less than full insurance or leave the insurance pool to seek insurance at a lower cost.

Most industrialized countries mandate universal health insurance coverage to avoid adverse selection problems. Universal coverage funded through income taxation implies cross subsidization across income levels and between health states. Many believe that healthcare programs with such cross subsidization are preferable to having a large proportions of citizens with limited or no access to healthcare.

*Moral hazard*   Third-party payment for healthcare services not only reduces incentives for consumers to seek price information, but also increases the potential for moral hazard, another information asymmetry. Suppose a healthcare market where insureds receive free care or pay an amount significantly less than full market price (e.g., paying only for deductibles or coinsurance) for medical services. In such a market, consumers may demand more services than they otherwise would, as a unit increase in demand effectively decreases the marginal price they pay, all else being equal.

Further, consumer behavior may change since insureds do not bear the full cost of medical care. For example, insureds may be less careful about their health or wellbeing, or engage in activities that can compromise their health status. This moral hazard problem inflates demand for medical services, relative to the demand for services when buyers pay the full price. Extreme abuses of third-party payment systems can be medical fraud.

*Supplier-induced demand*   In the healthcare market, the provider of medical services not only supplies medical services to consumers, but also advises them on what to demand. Unlike a perfectly competitive market, demand and supply in the healthcare market are not independent in determining the price or quantity of services produced. In extreme cases, medical providers have recommended use of unnecessary services that benefit the providers financially. This potential for supplier-induced demand, compounded with other information and price distortions, increases the demand for medical services in systems in which providers have an economic incentive to over-serve customers.

*Barriers to entry*   Healthcare markets have barriers to entry. Providers must meet stringent capital, licensing, and other regulatory requirements that limit the number of market entrants. Hospitals require large capital expenditures for facilities and equipment. Physicians are required to obtain medical degrees, licenses, specialist certifications and continuing education to practice medicine. Barriers to entry contribute to monopoly power among providers that, in some healthcare systems, increase prices and lower the quality of services provided. Not surprisingly, hospitals and healthcare providers in the U.S. continue to grow bigger through various forms of corporate restructuring and via merger and acquisition.

*Other considerations*   Clearly, the above economic characteristics of the healthcare market underlie most cost control problems that challenge nations today, regardless of their types of healthcare financing systems. In addition, three other characteristics of the market – cultural beliefs, growth of medical technology, and medical malpractice costs – can affect the financing and delivery of healthcare in a nation.

- *Cultural beliefs*: Across cultures, many people believe that access to medical care is a universal right rather than a privilege for those who can afford care. For those who see healthcare as a right, comparison of a perfectly competitive market with the healthcare market may seem inappropriate or even offensive. They believe everyone is entitled to all services equally. However, as medical service is costly, some tradeoffs are inevitable and some form of rationing occurs. For example, the poor or the unemployed may be uninsured, waiting times to receive care may be long (so that rationing through one's price of time occurs), or access to state-of-the-art technology or certain procedures may be restricted. Cultural beliefs about the nature of healthcare – whether it is a right, a privilege or something falling on a continuum between the two – are important factors shaping national healthcare financing systems.

- *Growth of medical technology*: The healthcare market is characterized by rapid and continuing advances in medical technology (e.g., genetic engineering, nanoengineering and standing MRI). Initial capital expenditures and maintenance of medical equipment are quite costly. Over time, the price of new technology declines but, in the medical industry, the constant invention of new technology and the capital expenditures required by providers to remain up-to-date are especially pronounced. The high cost of healthcare is due in part to the cost of this new technology.

  Cost benefit analysis of medical technology can be difficult. Estimating the benefits requires not only consideration of factors such as improved morbidity and mortality rates, decreased lengths of hospitalization, and decreased recovery times. It also requires estimation of the economic value of human life. Cultural beliefs on prolonging life and quality of life affect the analysis. Despite these difficulties, by most estimates, the aggregate benefits of the development and use of rapidly advancing medical technology far outweigh the costs.

- *Medical malpractice costs*: In selected countries, particularly in the U.S., medical malpractice suits are a factor in rising healthcare costs. Patients have become increasingly likely to resolve disappointment with treatment outcomes through litigation. Malpractice settlements, on the one hand, can be an inefficient way to compensate victims as they also include payments for pain and suffering as well as attorney fees and other transaction costs. On the other hand, the increased incidence of medical malpractice claims causes insurance costs to rise, which are ultimately passed on to insureds.

  The increased willingness to sue is driven in part by a change in patient-physician relationships. Traditionally, a family practitioner has treated a broad range of medical needs over an extended time, fostering a relationship of trust between physician and patient. Increasingly, specialists outnumber general practitioners, and patients are less likely to know these specialist providers and vice versa. When treatment fails or even when unrealistic expectations are not met, patients are more likely to sue the healthcare provider. The litigious nature of the U.S. culture reinforces this avenue of conflict resolution.

  Physicians may practice defensive medicine in an effort to avoid medical malpractice liability. They order tests and procedures that may not be strictly necessary in an effort to reduce their liability in case of suit by establishing that they have performed all reasonable precautions. These additional diagnostics and treatments drive up the total cost of healthcare.

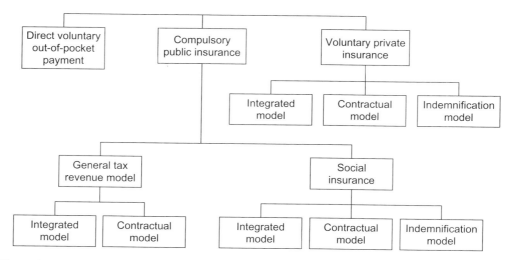

**Figure 9.5**    Worldwide Healthcare Financing Systems

*Healthcare systems worldwide*
The level of healthcare services provided within a country corresponds to the stage of economic development in the country. Typically, developed countries have modern healthcare services available to most of the population. Developing countries tend to provide a higher level of medical service to urban residents and significantly fewer services to the rural population. It is particularly so in countries where the economy is agriculture based. For countries with economies rooted in subsistence agriculture, healthcare systems are extremely limited. A final group of countries is those for which the economy is based primarily on subsistence agriculture but the land is rich in natural resources. These nations, primarily in the Middle East, typically provide modern healthcare services throughout the country.

Across these stages of economic development, the methods by which health services are financed vary greatly. As depicted in Figure 9.5, the delivery systems can be classified broadly into three groups: (1) direct, voluntary out-of-pocket payment, (2) compulsory public insurance, and (3) voluntary private insurance.[9]

Across all systems, some healthcare is paid for voluntarily and directly by patients – the **direct voluntary out-of-pocket system** with no third-party payers. Beyond these payments, more complex types of financing schemes exist. Here we classify healthcare systems, first, by the extent of public involvement in financing healthcare and, second, by the mechanism used to pay for services.

Even with a classification scheme, it is impossible to categorize most countries under a single financing system. For example, a country may finance hospitals differently from the way it finances physician services. A country may finance services for certain portions of the population differently from the way it finances services for other portions.

*Compulsory public insurance model*    As shown in Figure 9.5, there are two big branches under the compulsory public insurance model. One is the **general revenue tax model** under which the government finances healthcare from general tax revenues. This model can be further segmented into the integrated model and the contractual model. This system's strength is in providing universal coverage; that is, care is provided to everyone without regard to employment status or other eligibility criteria. Table 9.4 lists sample countries that primarily

**Table 9.4**  Percentage of Health Expenditure Attributable to Public Funds (2003)

| | Public Health Expenditure as a Percentage of Total HealthCare | Public System Coverage as a Percentage of the Population | Eligibility for Public Coverage |
|---|---|---|---|
| Australia | 68.9 | 100 | All permanent residents are eligible for Medicare (the tax-financed public health insurance system). Eligible persons must enroll with Medicare before benefits can be paid. |
| Austria | 69.4 | 99 | Almost all labor force participants and retirees are covered by a compulsory statutory health insurance. Social assistance claimants and prisoners receive health benefits and services from the state authorities. 1% of the population is without coverage. |
| Canada | 70.9 | 100 | All population is eligible to public coverage financed by federal and provincial taxation. |
| Czech Republic | 91.4 | 100 | All permanent residents are eligible to statutory health insurance coverage. |
| Denmark | 82.5 | 100 | All population is eligible to public coverage financed by state, county and municipal taxation. |
| France | 75.8 | 99.9 | The social security system provides coverage to all legal residents. 1% of the population is covered through the *Couverture Maladie Universal* |
| Germany[a] | 75 | 90.9 | All employed people and their dependents are covered by statutory health insurance coverage. This does not include self-employed individuals and civil servants. Employees with an income above an income threshold can opt out of the social sickness fund system. Fulfilling certain requirements, social security insureds can choose to "stay in" the public system on a voluntary basis even if they are allowed to opt out of the system. Self-employed may also join on a voluntary basis. |
| Japan | 78.3 | 100 | All population is covered by a statutory social health insurance system. |
| Korea | 44.4 | 100 | All population is covered by a statutory social health insurance system. |
| Luxembourg | 87.8 | 99 | All population is covered by a statutory social health insurance system, apart from civil servants. |

(Continued)

**Table 9.4**   (Continued)

| | *Public Health Expenditure as a Percentage of Total Healthcare* | *Public System Coverage as a Percentage of the Population* | *Eligibility for Public Coverage* |
|---|---|---|---|
| Mexico[b] | 47.9 | 45–55 | Public social security schemes cover all the population working in the private formal sector and government workers (i.e., excluding independent self-employed workers), informal sector workers and unemployed people. From 2004, the System of Social Protection in Health offers a new public health insurance scheme that has been implemented to provide voluntary public health insurance to the population previously excluded from social security. |
| Portugal | 68.5 | 100 | All population is covered by the National Health Service system, financed by general taxation. |
| Spain | 71.7 | 99.8 | Almost all the population is covered by the National Heath System, financed by general taxation. Civil servants and their dependents are covered through a special scheme. A minor group of self-employed liberal professionals and employers are uncovered. |
| Switzerland[c] | 55.6 | 100 | All permanent residents are mandated to purchase basic health insurance. |
| U.K. | 80.9 | 100 | All U.K. residents are covered by the National Health Service system, financed by general taxation. |
| U.S. | 44.2 | 24.7 | Individuals eligible to public programs include the above 65 and severely disabled (Medicare), poor or near poor (Medicaid), and poor children (SCHIP). Eligibility thresholds to Medicaid are set by states. |

[a]The data refer to supplementary private health insurance (PHI) policies purchased by individuals who belong to the social health insurance system. Some of the individuals with primary PHI are also covered by supplementary PHI, which are sometimes packaged with primary PHI policies.

[b]These coverage figures relate to social security schemes, which include workers in the private formal sector and civil servants. Public health expenditure as a percentage of the total health expenditure includes all public health spending; that is, both social security spending and other public spending, such as resources used to finance healthcare provision for the uninsured population through the states' health services. Estimates vary depending on the source used; population survey data report lower figures, official administrative data report higher figures but no roster of individuals covered by the social security system is available.

[c]Data on PHI refer only to voluntary PHI coverage. Mandatory health insurance covering the entire population is reported in OECD Health Data as public coverage, although it is a borderline case.

*Source*: Sakamaki et al. (2004).

use the general tax revenue model. Within this type of system, payment for services may be handled in two ways: providers may be employees of the state (an integrated model) or have contracts with the state (a contractual model).

- In a **tax-funded integrated model**, physicians are government employees and hospitals are owned by the government. The system is integrated because the insurer-and-provider (i.e., the government) functions as one entity. Physicians are paid mainly a fixed salary, regardless of the number of patients treated or the number of services rendered. Hospitals are funded by global budgets, where a prepaid annual fee is given to the hospital to provide patient care and receive fixed payments regardless of services delivered. Patients receive healthcare free of charge and are not subject to cost sharing requirements; that is, they do not pay deductibles, coinsurance or any fixed fee for services. Patients are assigned to physicians, clinics or hospitals, and have little choice about the healthcare that they receive.

  A tax-funded integrated system may reduce administrative costs and avoids transaction costs associated with third party payers (e.g., verification of payments for services). However, it provides little or no economic incentive to providers to maintain or enhance service quality, as they are not paid for delivering more or better care. Providers have little incentive to reduce the unit cost of services, as salaries and global budgets are awarded based on what they spent in the prior year. Often, patients wait longer to receive medical services relative to waiting times in other financing systems (Danzon, 1993).

- A **tax-funded contractual model** secures medical services for citizens through government contracts with public or private providers (e.g., Canada). The patients pay little or none of the direct cost for services. The contract may be paid on a fee-for-service basis; that is, the provider receives a fee for each service rendered. Thus, supplier-induced demand may increase overall system costs unless controls, such as patient cost sharing through deductibles and coinsurance, are in place. However, patient cost sharing is objectionable in some cultures, especially where medical care is viewed as a right.

  Contracts may also be arranged using **capitation fee payment** in which prepaid, fixed amounts (capitation fees) are given to the provider for caring for the patient for a set time period, regardless of the intensity or extent of the services needed by the patient in the upcoming year. Capitation fee arrangements provide an economic incentive for physicians to deliver only necessary services, thus reducing the potential for supplier-induced demand. In countries with a contractual model, the provider must ensure that a reasonable quality of care is delivered; otherwise, poor preventive care or treatment at the onset of illness could result in a higher cost to the provider.

The **social insurance model**, the second branch of the compulsory public income model, integrates both the public and the private sectors. Under the typical model, employers and employees are required by law to pay a mandatory payroll tax to insurers that in turn negotiate with physician groups to provide medical care for insureds. In addition, the government sets up a national unemployment fund or a pension fund to provide healthcare coverages to the unemployed the retired and others not actively employed. With this model, healthcare production resources are largely owned privately. There are controls, however, over price and operations, and some hospitals may be owned by the state.

Within a social insurance system, three methods of payment for services may be used. The integrated method and contractual method are similar to those described with the general tax revenue-funded system, except that funding comes from payroll taxes rather than general revenues. Italy and Spain, for example, use the social insurance integrated approach to financing. Germany and France use the social insurance contracting model to a large degree. Here again, contracting may be on a fee-for-service or capitated basis.

The **indemnification model** reimburses patients for services for which they have already paid the provider. Drawbacks to this approach include higher administrative costs of processing and paying claims as well as supplier-induced healthcare demand. This system is not widely used, but is used to a degree in Belgium and France.

*Voluntary private insurance model*    In the voluntary private insurance model, health services are financed and provided through voluntary participation in a private insurance system. Most private health insurance is obtained through employment, and employers usually pay all or a portion of the insurance premium. However, unlike the social insurance model, employment-related coverage is not compulsory. Smaller employers, thus, are less likely to offer medical insurance benefits due to the relatively greater cost. Individuals not receiving employer-sponsored insurance may purchase coverage on their own in the individual medical expense insurance market. They face the risk that insurance may be unavailable due to poor health or high cost.

The voluntary private system exhibits three methods for paying providers: (1) an integrated model, (2) a contractual model and (3) an indemnification model.

- The **private voluntary integrated model** unifies the insurer-and-provider function within the private sector. An example of this model is the staff-model health maintenance organization (HMO) in the U.S. The HMO offers a comprehensive range of medical services – including preventive care – to members on a prepaid basis.

  With the staff-model HMO, physicians are employees of the HMO and subscribers are treated in an HMO-owned hospital. Subscribers have a limited choice of providers and little or no cost sharing is required. As with the public model, the private integrated model allows administrative savings and sets up economic incentives to providers to deliver minimum services. In the private integrated model, however, efficiency and service quality can be enhanced, because HMOs compete for customers in the private voluntary market.

- The **private voluntary contractual model** is similar to the public contractual model except that coverage is not compulsory. An example is the individual-practice-association HMO, where the HMO, acting as insurer, negotiates contracts with private independent physicians to provide care for the HMO subscribers. This model is found in the U.S. and also is used to a limited degree in other countries such as Brazil and Spain. Another example is the **preferred provider organization** (PPO), which is a group of providers that contract with employers, insurers or other organizations to provide medical services to their employees, insureds and members at a discounted rate.

- The **private voluntary indemnification model** is similar to the public model in that patients pay for services and are reimbursed by a third party. This fee-for-service arrangement is inflationary, and patient cost sharing is commonly used for cost control. This approach is used in the U.S. and also is found in the private sectors of the Netherlands and the U.K.

*Healthcare financing reform initiatives*

Most industrialized countries are introducing reforms to their healthcare markets in hopes of controlling spiraling costs and improving efficiency. Previous macroeconomic reform measures such as budgetary caps met with limited success, and consequently reforms today are microeconomic in nature. Microeconomic reforms attempt to enhance the quality of service delivery (e.g., decreasing waiting times and increasing provider choice) while containing costs. Some of these initiatives are summarized below.

- *Increased use of the public contractual model*: There is a move away from use of the public integrated model toward use of the public contractual model. Contracts contain incentives for providers to improve efficiency, whereas integrated models provide incentives to providers to over-service patients.

- *Greater use of third-party payers*: Another key component in healthcare financing reform is allowing third-party payers to exercise more control in negotiating contracts or fees with providers. Here, payers take on the role of purchasing agents for patients, using their clout to control medical costs. Payers can be effective as they have access to medical service price information and bargaining power that individual patients and small groups do not.

  In addition, purchasers monitor contracts and review the quality and quantity of services delivered. Reform initiatives allow purchasers to put pressure on medical providers to improve services without raising costs. Providers are more likely to respond to quality complaints of large purchasers rather than to individuals of small groups of patients, as purchasers control payment of providers.

- *Greater independence of hospital management*: A key element in microeconomic market reform is allowing for greater independence of hospital management in the identification of potential efficiency gains in operations. Previously, centralized policy and decision-making prevented individual hospitals from seeking quality enhancing, lower cost methods and treatment alternatives for patient care. Allowing hospitals to position themselves better in the market is expected ultimately to benefit both patients and payers.

- *Enhanced use of managed care and cost sharing*: These two final components to healthcare reform appear to be successful in enhancing microeconomic efficiency. Managed care techniques are being introduced in public and private models in developing and developed countries. Managed care requires coordination among providers of patient care to reduce over-utilization of services. It provides economic incentives to providers, payers and patients so that only necessary, quality care is delivered. In some cases, this leads to reduced patient choice of providers, but the trend today toward managed care suggests that the efficiency gains are probably sufficient to outweigh this constraint.

  Patient cost sharing is common in the U.S. but has not been widely accepted in many other countries. Many cultures believe medical services should be widely available at little or no cost to patients. However, with aging populations, increased demand for healthcare, and larger budget deficits that make payment for care more burdensome, the need to increase healthcare financing efficiency becomes more pressing. Consequently, many reform initiatives include some patient cost sharing to reduce demand for health services, notably those that are discretionary or unnecessary. The drawback to patient cost sharing is that it disproportionately affects low-income individuals and may hinder the use of even necessary services. Thus, many countries choose to limit patient cost sharing to ambulatory and pharmaceutical care or make special provision for the chronically ill to ensure sufficient access to necessary medical services.

In summary, reform initiatives tend to place stronger emphasis on the role of the medical service purchaser – the third-party payer. The purchaser is in the best position to monitor and negotiate contracts and can more readily improve quality and reduce costs for patient care. To improve efficiency further, purchasers and providers receive economic incentives to provide quality care at minimum cost through managed care contracts. Patient cost sharing provides economic incentives to patients to use care efficiently as well.

*Relationship between spending and health outcomes*
The amount that nations spend on healthcare varies significantly. Across countries, many different financing systems are used. However, the differences in spending levels are not attributable to the type of financing system used (i.e., general tax revenues, social insurance or private voluntary insurance) nor to the method of payment (i.e., fee-for-service, contracts or patient indemnity). Instead, the prime determinant of differences in national spending for healthcare is national per capita income. Nations with higher per capita incomes generally spend more on health. In fact, per capita income accounts for so much of the difference in levels of spending that little other systematic variation remains to be explained. No single financing system emerges as the dominant model with respect to spending levels.

Similarly, the general health of populations varies across countries. However, this variation is again explained primarily by differences in income level. We do not know precisely how income affects health outcomes as measured by national life expectancy and infant mortality rates. A positive relationship between income and medical spending is expected, as is a positive relationship between education and income. Isolating the effects of these variables on health is difficult. In addition, income positively affects consumption of other products, some of which can improve health and others of which can harm health (e.g., rich, high cholesterol foods). Although it is not clear precisely how income affects health, the trend is clear: across most nations per capita income is the primary explanatory variable for differences in health outcomes. Not surprisingly, nations with higher per capita incomes have longer life expectancy and lower infant mortality rates.

There are notable exceptions. For example, China, Sri Lanka and Vietnam have very low per capita incomes, yet have life expectancies at birth of approximately 70 years. This may be explained by good community health programs and a greater level of education for women (who often have responsibility for maintaining the family's health). In contrast, higher income countries such as Libya, Oman and Saudi Arabia have life expectancies that are five to 10 years lower.

Another exception of note is the U.S. Given its high per capita income, the U.S. infant mortality rate is greater than expected. As noted earlier, critics point to the lack of universal health coverage as a possible explanation.

Global comparisons of spending and health outcomes do not reveal a dominant or best healthcare financing system with respect to the cost of the system or the health of the population. The major determinant of cost and overall health is the per capita income of the country. The value of system comparison then is not to identify one best solution but to identify alternative ways to improve specific healthcare service goals while controlling costs. For example, changes might be implemented to improve provider productivity, reduce patient waiting times, or discourage unnecessary visits by patients to ambulatory care facilities. The hybrid nature of most national systems is consistent with adaptation to improve the efficiency of the financing system and to improve health outcomes.

Even if one system emerged as the most efficient, adoption across countries would be limited. Systems are shaped by the economic and political character of the country as well as by its history and values. A system that works well for one country might not fit the culture of another. However, some of the lessons on improving efficiency within a system are transferable from one country to another. This is reflected in the convergence across systems in the types of healthcare reforms. Consequently, interest in the collection and sharing of international healthcare financing data is unlikely to diminish as countries worldwide face the challenge of achieving high quality, affordable healthcare for all.

*Disability income*

Social insurance programs typically also provide benefits for disabled individuals. Most programs are structured such that those who participate in the retirement income plan also participate in the disability income plan. Funding ordinarily follows that of retirement income benefit funding. Thus, with wage-based plans, the worker may be assessed a percentage of covered wages and, with universal plans, benefits usually are funded from general revenues. In most countries (e.g., France and Germany), short-term disability benefits are funded through contributions for health insurance. As such, short-term disability usually is tied to the country's health insurance program.

The principal requirements for receiving a disability benefit are (1) loss of productive capacity and (2) fulfilment of a minimum period of work or contributions. The maximum benefit amount in some countries is two-thirds of the pre-disability wage, subject to a community-adjusted ceiling. In other cases, the benefit amount varies from one-third to one-half or even as high as 100 percent of the pre-disability wage. Table 9.5 offers a summary of eligibility and benefits for permanently disabled persons in selected countries.

The qualifying period for a disability benefit is usually shorter than for an old age, retirement income benefit. Periods of three to five years of contributions or covered employment are most common. Entitlement to disability benefits usually is subject to minimum and maximum age limitations (e.g., the teens and the normal retirement age). Benefit qualification in some countries, particularly those with a universal program (e.g., Australia), is economic-needs tested.

Under most programs, provisions for persons who are permanently disabled due to non-occupational causes are similar to those for retirement. A single basic formula usually applies for total disability as for old age, where a cash amount is frequently expressed as a percentage of average earnings. Increments and dependents' supplements are generally identical under the total disability and old-age programs. For the totally disabled, a constant-attendance supplement – most often 50 percent of the benefit – may be paid to those who need help on a daily basis. Partial disability benefits, if payable, are usually reduced, in terms of average earnings, according to a fixed scale. The system also may provide rehabilitation and training. Some countries provide higher benefits for workers in arduous or dangerous employment.

A relatively short waiting period (e.g., 2–7 days) is imposed under most short-term disability programs. A waiting period reduces administrative and benefit costs by excluding many claims for short illnesses or injuries during which income loss is relatively small.

Workers ordinarily may receive short-term benefits for up to 26 weeks. In some instances, benefits may be drawn for considerably longer or even for an unlimited duration.

**Table 9.5**    Permanent Disability Eligibility and Benefits in Selected Countries

| Country | Eligibility and Benefits |
|---|---|
| Brazil | *Disability pension (social insurance)*: 100% of indexed earnings in the 36 months prior to disability.<br>*Disability assistance (means-tested)*: Average pension equals the minimum wage. |
| Canada | *Earnings-related disability pension*: A basic monthly benefit plus 75% of earnings-related retirement pension. |
| China | *Basic pension insurance*: Benefits for persons with total incapacity for work and not eligible for early retirement. |
| Czech Republic | Flat rate basic amount plus earnings-related pension. |
| France | 50% of average earnings (30% for partial disability) in the highest paid 10 years if incapable of any professional activity, subject to monthly maximum. |
| India | *Provident fund*: A lump-sum equaling total contribution by the employee and the employer plus interest.<br>*Pension scheme*: Monthly benefits based on the member's pensionable salary or a lump-sum equaling total contributions by the employee and the employer plus interest. |
| Japan | *National pension program (disability)*: Bimonthly payments based on the class of disability plus dependent supplements.<br>*Employees' pension insurance (disability)*: Bimonthly payments of a percentage of the old-age pension in each class of disability plus dependent supplements.<br>*Disability grant*: A lump-sum payment of 200% of the old-age pension. |
| Russia | *Disability labor pension*: Benefits based on the assessed degree of disability for all employed persons.<br>*State disability pension*: Benefits for persons under age 20 who became disabled due to illness, work injury or military service-related injury. |
| South Africa | *Disability grant (means-tested)*: Monthly benefits with 200% payment of benefits to married couples. |
| U.K. | *Disability living allowance (noncontributory, no means test)*: Weekly benefits. |
| U.S. | *Disability pension*: Benefit, subject to a maximum, based on covered earnings averaged over the period after 1950 (or age 21, if later) and indexed for past wage inflation, up to the year of disability, excluding up to 5 years of the lowest earnings. |

*Source*: Social Security Administration (2005).

In most countries the maximum period of benefit payment for short-term disability marks the beginning of eligibility for long-term disability coverage.

### Occupational-injury benefits

Occupational-injury benefit programs – i.e., workers' (workmen's) compensation programs – are the oldest, most widespread type of social insurance. They are designed to promote recovery of workers from injury or illness for their prompt return to work or to offer economic aid to the immediate family members (spouse and children) of deceased workers.

### Program structure and funding

Occupational-injury systems come in two varieties: (1) social insurance systems utilizing a public fund and (2) various forms of private or semiprivate arrangements required by law.

Most countries maintain work-injury programs that do not share a direct link with other social security programs. In some other countries, workers' compensation benefits are available under special provisions of the country's social security programs.

In Italy, Japan and some other countries, the government covers program administration costs or extends a subsidy. In most other countries, the employer is responsible for the full cost of occupational-injury programs. This policy reflects the traditional view that employers should be liable for payment of compensation when their employees suffer work injuries. Hence, work-injury benefits are financed primarily by compulsory employer contributions or payroll taxes. Exceptions are found where certain elements of the work-injury program are meshed with one or more of the other branches of the social insurance system. In such cases, financing often involves contributions from employees, employers and the government. Another exception occurs in countries that provide medical treatment for work-related illnesses under their ordinary public medical care programs.

With public programs, employer contributions are commonly expressed as a percentage of payroll, where the percentage varies based on the degree of risk in the area of business. Contributions vary widely across countries as well. The contribution rate in Germany, for example, is 1.33 percent of payroll, while it may be up to 16 percent for some workers in Italy.

With private insurance, premiums usually vary according to past loss experience of the employer as well as the industry into which the employer's business is classified. Under this type of experience-based premium rating, the cost of insurance can vary widely. For that reason, experience rating has been eliminated in some countries, notably Norway and Sweden, and all employers within the country, regardless of type of business, contribute at the same rate.

In countries with a public fund, employers may be allowed the option of insuring with either the public fund or a private insurance carrier. Self-insurance also is permitted in some jurisdictions, even in jurisdictions with a public fund only.

The state governments of the U.S. offer examples to illustrate the diversity of market operations. Six of the U.S. states offer occupational-injury benefits through monopolistic state funds. No private workers' compensation market exists in those states. In 13 other states, the state government runs a public fund in competition with private insurance companies. In the remaining states, only private firms offer workers' compensation insurance.

Almost all U.S. states permit self-insurance by individual employers, and 35 states also permit group self-insurance. Alabama even permits group self-insurance by employers in different industries. Only two states – North Dakota and Wyoming, which operate monopolistic state funds – do not allow any form of self-insurance of occupational-injury risk.

*Occupational-injury benefits*
Occupational-injury benefit programs provide two types of benefits. The first is medical benefits. Some governments take a position that all "necessary" medical services – unless specifically excluded in the law – must be available to qualified employees, while others maintain a list of covered medical services. In some countries, the costs for a rehabilitation program or alternative medical treatment (e.g., acupuncture) are sometimes considered as part of necessary medical services. Typical worker's compensation programs, especially those programs not intermingled with the country's social insurance programs, cover all medical expenses. Qualified employees are not responsible for deductibles or coinsurance.

The second occupational-injury benefit is income replacement. Table 9.6 provides an overview of injury benefits in selected countries.

**Table 9.6**    Occupational-Injury Coverages and Benefits in Selected Countries

| Country | Covered Persons | Type of Program | Financing | Disability Benefits |
|---|---|---|---|---|
| Australia | Employed persons | Compulsory coverage with public and private insurers | Employer contributions | Generally 95% of earnings for minimum of 26 weeks for temporary disability; permanent disability benefits covered under the Old Aged program |
| Bolivia | All workers | Social insurance system | Employer contribution of 2% of payroll | Cash payment for sickness and maternity for temporary disability; a minimum of 70% of average wage during the last 5 years of permanent total disability |
| Egypt | All workers, unless excluded, over age 18 in the private sector or age 16 in the public sector | Social insurance system | Employer contribution of up to 3% of payroll | 100% of earnings for temporary disability; 80% of average earnings during the last year for permanent total disability |
| Italy | Manual workers, non-manual employees in dangerous work, the self-employed in agriculture, domestic workers, company managers, contract workers and professional sportsmen | Social insurance system | Employer contribution of 0.5–16% of payroll, plus government's subsidy for administrative costs | 60–75% of daily average wage for temporary disability; a lump-sum for lower assessed degree of disability or pension for higher degree for permanent disability |
| Japan | Employees of all firms in industry and commerce plus voluntary coverage for employers in specific categories | Compulsory government program | Employer contributions between 0.55% and 13.5% of payroll depending on 3-year accident rate plus government subsidy | 60% of average daily wage for temporary disability; 40–100% of daily wage depending on degree of disability for permanent disability |
| U.S. | All employees unless specifically excluded | Compulsory through insurance or self-insurance | Employer contributions | In most states, 66.6% of earnings, subject to the maximum in the state |

*Source*: Social Security Administration (2005).

To minimize moral hazard and costs, most programs do not offer full indemnification of wages. Hence, compensation is stated commonly as a percentage of the (average) wage prior to disability, a stated monetary ceiling, or both. Compensation varies according to the degree of disability as follows:

- **Temporarily disability** benefits usually are payable from the start of incapacity after the passage of a short waiting period. Benefits normally continue for a limited period depending on the duration of incapacity. When the incapacity lasts longer, the temporary disability benefit may be replaced by a permanent disability benefit.

- Generally, a **permanent total disability** benefit becomes payable immediately after the temporary disability benefit ceases, based on a medical evaluation that the worker's incapacity is both permanent and total. Under most programs, the permanent total disability benefit is payable for life, unless the worker's condition changes. A minority of programs pays only a lump-sum grant equaling several years' wages. The permanent total disability benefit usually amounts to two-thirds to three-fourths of the worker's average earnings before injury.

- Still another form of cash, work-injury benefit is that for **permanent partial disability**, payable when a worker loses partial working or earnings capacity because of work-related injury or sickness. It usually equals a portion of the full benefit corresponding to the percentage loss of capacity. Alternatively, permanent partial disability benefits may be paid in the form of a lump-sum grant.

Most work-injury programs also provide benefits to survivors. These benefits are customarily payable to a widow, regardless of her age, until her death or remarriage; to a disabled widower; and to dependent children below specified ages. Survivor benefits are computed as percentages of the worker's average earnings immediately before death or of the benefit payable (or potentially payable) at death. Most systems also pay a funeral grant equivalent to a fixed sum or percentage of the deceased worker's earnings.

In developed countries, employment has shifted from the manufacturing to the service sector. As a result, claims associated with industrial injury and illness have decreased. This decrease has been countered by the growth in the number of recognized occupational diseases due to a greater understanding of the origins of certain diseases.

## Unemployment insurance

**Unemployment insurance** provides for the payment of periodic cash income to workers during periods of involuntary unemployment. The risk of involuntary unemployment is commonly considered as a social risk for which a private insurance market is unlikely. Private firms would face unmanageable adverse selection and moral hazard if they attempted or were required to offer unemployment insurance.

These programs have several objectives, each of which has public good aspects to:

- provide periodic cash income to workers during temporary periods of involuntary unemployment;
- help stabilize the economy during recessionary periods;
- encourage employers to stabilize employment;
- help the unemployed find jobs.

**Table 9.7**    Unemployment Insurance Programs in Selected Countries

| Country | Covered Persons | Financing | Benefits |
|---|---|---|---|
| Australia | Gainfully employed persons | Government from general revenues | Monthly benefits based on means test as well as allowance group (youth allowance, new-start allowance, middle age allowance and partner allowance) |
| Bolivia | All workers | Employer contribution | Family allowance, housing allowance, prenatal grant, birth grant and nursing allowance in a lump-sum or monthly payments |
| Egypt | Employed persons unless excluded | Employer contribution of 2% of payroll plus government cover of deficit | 60% of last monthly wage for up to 28 weeks |
| Italy | Employed persons, including home workers, apprentices and trainees | 3.25% of covered earnings by the employee, 3.25% of covered earnings by the employer, plus government loans or subsidy for deficit | Up to 67% of net earnings up to 960 calendar days; benefits based on means test and whether allowance is also available |
| Japan | Employees younger than age 65 | 0.7–0.8% of earnings by the employee, up to 1.25% by the employer, plus up to 33% of the cost of benefits and subsidy by government | 50–80% of daily average wage for previous 6 months for up to 150 days (plus up to 210 days in case of economic recession); several additional allowances (e.g., old worker allowance and new born child allowance) |
| U.S. | Most employees working 20 weeks or more in a year | Employer contribution of 6.2% in combination of federally and state taxable payrolls plus government cover of administration costs | About 50% of earnings (depending on the state of residence) typically for up to 26 weeks |

*Source*: Social Security Administration (2005).

Of course, unemployment insurance programs are not perfect, owing in part to the extreme difficulty and costs to monitor the behavior of each unemployed. Unemployment insurance carries moral hazard problems because the unemployed who are receiving benefits have less incentive to seek or accept new jobs. The more generous the duration or the level of unemployment insurance benefits, the greater the moral hazard.

*Program structure and funding*
Table 9.7 provides an overview of unemployment insurance programs in selected countries. The programs exist mainly in industrialized countries. Most are compulsory and fairly broad

in scope. Some unemployment programs are economic-needs tested (e.g., Australia and New Zealand). Some offer scheduled payments of benefits, and others provide lump-sum grants payable either by a government agency or by the employer. In selected countries, employers are required to pay lump-sum severance indemnities to discharged workers.

About one-half of the compulsory unemployment programs cover the majority of employed persons, regardless of industry. Coverage in other programs is limited to workers in secondary and tertiary industries. A few programs exclude salaried employees earning more than a specified amount.

Some countries rely on voluntary programs with no government mandate. These voluntary insurance systems – or unemployment funds – are typically limited to industries or firms with strong union presences. Membership in these funds is usually compulsory for union members in a covered industry and may be open on a voluntary basis to nonunion employees. The voluntary insurance systems of Denmark and Sweden cover about one-half and two-thirds, respectively, of all employees.

Contribution solely by employers is the typical method governments use to finance unemployment insurance. The contribution usually is expressed as a fixed percentage of the covered payroll. In Egypt, Italy and Japan, employees also contribute to the fund. Governments in selected countries cover fund's administration costs plus a loan guarantee or subsidy for fund deficits. In countries with means-tested unemployment assistance programs, the programs are financed entirely by the governments, with no employer or employee contribution.

*Unemployment insurance benefits*
To become entitled to unemployment benefits, a worker ordinarily must have completed a minimum period of service in a covered employment and must be involuntarily unemployed. The most common qualifying period is 6 months of service within the year before unemployment began.

Nearly all unemployment insurance programs require that applicants be capable of and available for work. An unemployed worker, therefore, is usually ineligible for the benefits when incapacitated (as he can get similar benefits under occupational-injury or disability programs) or if otherwise unable to accept a job offer. Usually, the unemployed worker must register for work at an employment office in the community and report regularly to that office. An unemployed worker who refuses an offer of a suitable job without good cause may have benefits suspended temporarily or permanently.

The amount of unemployment benefits usually is a percentage of the average wage during a recent period. A system of wage classes rather than a single fixed percentage is sometimes used. The basic rate of unemployment benefits is frequently between 40 and 75 percent of average earnings, subject to a maximum limit. Flat-rate amounts are sometimes payable instead of graduated benefits varying with past wages. These amounts customarily differ only according to the family status or, occasionally, the age of the worker. For example, the U.K. pays flat-rate unemployment benefits for up to 6 months. In some countries, such as Italy and Japan, supplements for spouse and children are usually added to the basic benefit of the unemployed worker.

Unemployment benefits become payable only after a waiting period. This provision reduces both program benefit payouts and the administrative burden of dealing with a large number of small claims. Most waiting periods are between three and seven days. Most countries place a limit on the period during which unemployment benefits may be continuously drawn. This limit varies from several weeks to a much longer period. Some countries permit extension of the benefit period to a much longer period when the country suffers from an economic recession (e.g., Japan and the U.S.).

Several countries maintain unemployment assistance or similar means-tested programs supplementing regular unemployment insurance. Thus, unemployed workers who exhaust the right to ordinary benefits often continue to receive some assistance, provided their means or incomes are below specified levels in those countries.

## Mandatory Savings Programs

Some governments, especially in Latin America and Asia, require employees to contribute toward their own personal retirement savings programs. These programs substitute for or complement paygo types of social insurance systems. In some countries, the savings are entirely through mandatory contributions by employees only (automatic withholding from wages) and, in others, through major contributions by employees with additional (or matching) contributions by employers.

Unlike the general account systems under typical social insurance programs, mandatory private savings programs maintain individual accounts. Thus, there is little or no income redistribution among participants. In that sense, such programs do not meet our definition of social insurance, although they clearly exhibit important elements. Of course, under the individual account system, the worker pays administrative fees for the management of the account. The account holder often may purchase separate disability and survivors' insurance coverages.

One of the oldest mandatory savings programs is the **provident funds** that are compulsory savings programs for retirement income security and are fully funded systems with no element of income redistribution. In some programs, the participant may make early withdrawals for plan qualified uses of the account fund (e.g., purchase of house and educational expenses for dependent children) as long as a sufficient fund for retirement benefits remains. The retirement benefit is payable at retirement, often in a lump-sum or on the onset of other specified events such as disability. Table 9.8 highlights selected countries' provident funds.

## Economic-Needs-tested Programs

An **economic-needs-tested** (or **means-tested**) **program** benchmarks each applicant's resources to formula-based standards for subsistence need estimation and offers benefits only to applicants who satisfy the test. The benefits are also known as social pensions or equalization payments. Prior financial contribution by the applicant is not an element of the test. Neither is it a funding resource of the program. Traditionally financed primarily from general revenues, economic-needs-tested programs are under the administration of local governments in many countries.

Different countries have different tests. However, they commonly take into consideration the net wealth and current income of the applicant and the family, health condition and age of the breadwinner, family size, and place of living. For example, an applicant who has failed to meet the minimum annual income threshold and possesses a net wealth less than a stipulated amount may pass the economic-needs test to receive some cash and food benefits. If the applicant also has a qualified dependent, the size of benefits may increase.

When the benefit availability is subject to an economic-needs test and if the program does not require contributions by the beneficiary, the program is a social assistance (welfare) program intended to alleviate poverty. It is not insurance. As mentioned, a true social

**Table 9.8**    Provident Funds in Selected Countries

| Country | Covered Persons | Contribution by Employee | Contribution by Employer | Remarks |
|---|---|---|---|---|
| Brunei | All employees up to age 55 plus the self-employed | 5% | 5% | Lump-sum payment of the total contributions by the employee and the employer plus interest |
| Fiji | Employed workers between age 15 and 55 | 8% | 8% | |
| Hong Kong | Basically all employers working more than 60 days a year | 5% plus additional voluntary contributions | 5% plus additional voluntary contributions | Mandatory occupational scheme in conjunction with other social security programs |
| India | Employees including part-time and daily wage workers | 12% | 3.67% | In conjunction with voluntary social insurance schemes |
| Indonesia | Employees of firms with 10 or more workers or greater than 1 million rupiah wage bill | 2.0% | 3.7% | Lump-sum payment of the total contributions by the employee and the employer plus interest |
| Kenya | Employed persons | 5.0% | 5.0% | Lump-sum payment of the total contributions by the employee and the employer plus interest |
| Malaysia | Private-sector employees and non-pensionable public-sector employees | 11% | 12% | Employees' Provident Fund (EPF) permits purchase of investment funds, financing home purchase or educational costs and withdrawal for critical illness |
| Singapore | Employees earning S$50 per month or more | Up to 20.0% | 13% | Contributions allocated to ordinary account for cash accumulation, drawdown account to finance home purchase or educational cost, and special account |

*Source*: Social Security Administration (2005).

insurance program requires contributions and makes the benefit available to all eligible participants regardless of their individual wealth status.

# THE FUTURE OF SOCIAL INSURANCE

Rising healthcare costs, low birth rates, increasing life expectancy, paygo public pension systems preservation of economic security through equitable financing approaches, all pose challenges to social insurance programs in many countries. Some countries face the unpleasant choice of reducing benefits, increasing participant contributions or a combination of both if they are to achieve fiscal soundness of their programs. Political and popular resistance, coupled with weak macroeconomic performance, has so far limited policymakers' abilities to enact meaningful reforms in many countries.

The irony of social insurance programs is that, on the one hand, their success has led to a healthier, longer living population. As the time people spend in retirement increases, so do their needs for retirement income and healthcare services. On the other hand, when these benefits are funded by active workers under paygo funding approaches, the burden on active workers increases. While the rationale for creating social insurance programs has not changed, the cost of maintaining them is projected to increase dramatically in coming decades.

## Transition into Fully Funded Programs

Several reforms in social insurance programs worldwide have been cited as examples for other countries to emulate. A major element of many of these reforms is the suggestion to move from paygo to fully funded systems. A fully funded system, once fully implemented, places a lower burden on current workers. A major hurdle is the cost burden of transitioning from the paygo to the funded system. The benefits promised to current retirees or those close to retirement must be paid at the same time that money is set aside to fund current workers' retirement benefits. The transformation costs can strain a country's fiscal system.

A fully funded retirement income system may increase a country's savings rate, whereas a paygo system may reduce the need for individuals to save for retirement. In other words, a paygo system may mean that savings that were once intended to fund an individual's retirement can be used for present consumption. In contrast, a fully funded system replaces individual savings with group savings. On a theoretical level, a nation's savings rate remains unchanged if individual savings are entirely replaced by social savings. On another theoretical level, introduction of a fully funded system should induce a higher savings rate than the rate under a paygo system. Empirical evidence in this regard is limited. For example, Chile, which moved away from a paygo system to a pre-funded system in 1981, observed a rise in savings rate after the reform. However, it is difficult to determine whether the social insurance system or the fiscal discipline necessary to fund the transition led to increased savings.[10]

## Privatization of Social Insurance Programs

Prefunding social insurance programs creates large pools of funds that must be invested. The investment decisions for those funds potentially could have large effects on a nation's economy. It has been suggested that the most efficient way to allocate those funds is to leave the investment decisions in the hands of private individuals. For example, in Chile, dozens of private pension fund management firms exist into which workers can choose to invest their retirement savings. But what obligation will or should the government have if funds prove inadequate? Conversely, one of the rationales for social insurance programs is that individuals may lack the information or expertise necessary to make those investment decisions.

Japan and the U.K. allow for partial privatization. Known as **pay or play** in the pension world, this "contracting out" provision permits firms either to contribute to a mandatory government program (pay) or to reduce the contribution by establishing and operating firms' own benefit plans (play).

"Pay or play" is a way for firms voluntarily to privatize government benefit programs. Such a policy differs from the pension system in Chile where privatization is mandatory for all new workers. Japan's "pay or play" system, in effect since 1966, expands the range of choice open to the private sector while assuring adequate retirement income. While there is strict regulatory oversight of the firms that contract out of the government plan, they benefit by being able to invest the programs' assets in the private sector, ideally leading to lower overall costs. These programs suffer from adverse selection in that those who are least expensive to cover are most likely to contract out of the government plan, but this effect is reduced somewhat by the inability of firms to move in and out of the government plan.

Privatization of social insurance programs not only requires high transition costs but also redistributes the costs and benefits of those programs. One of the rationales for social insurance programs is that private markets will undersupply the amount of insurance coverage desired by society. Privatizing these programs either allows some individuals to garner higher benefits than others or requires increased regulation to prevent uneven benefits. In either case, the cost of administering such a program will increase.

Demographic changes and technological innovation will result in tremendous changes in the provision of both public and private insurance in the coming decades, as discussed more fully in Chapter 7. Social insurance programs are likely to be one of the most important domestic political issues worldwide in the early decades of the 21st century.

## DISCUSSION QUESTIONS

1. Does flood insurance qualify as a social insurance program? Justify your answer.
2. In the section on "Low-Severity or High-Frequency Exposures," the authors discussed several types of loss exposures for which private insurance is unsuitable. What are the characteristics of exposures that insurers are willing to cover? (You may refer to Chapter 19 for a related discussion.)
3. Provide a rationale for instituting a paygo social insurance program.
4. Discuss the implications of a successful social insurance program on a country's finances.
5. Compare public and private programs for providing retirement income. Who benefits under each type of program?

## NOTES

1. This chapter draws from Custer (1998) and Doerpinghaus (1998).
2. Of course, the economist will want to know precisely where these curves fall and whether there is, in fact, a divergence between private and social costs – a challenging task.
3. This distinction between voluntary private insurance markets and mandatory social insurance is crucial to understanding why risk-based pricing and underwriting are necessary in private insurance markets and not for social insurance and why private markets can fail if the pool (insurer) is prohibited from pricing for risk.
4. "Feeling badly" about someone starving or doing without other of life's necessities is itself a negative externality that charity or welfare can eliminate.

5.  The textbook may be insured under a policy that aggregates coverage for many personal effects, such as a homeowner's (householder's) policy.

6.  Many correlated exposures can be insured in the private market through reliance on reinsurance that spreads exposures internationally. See Chapter 24. In addition, insurers can diversify such exposures by combining them with other exposures that are uncorrelated with the exposures. For example, in insuring against flood in the U.S. state of Missouri, an insurer could simultaneously sell insurance against fire losses in the state of New York, thus diversifying its portfolio. Finally, if markets were more efficient, insurers could sell the correlated exposures in the capital market by issuing securities, the investment results of which were dependent on the portfolio's loss experience.

7.  This section draws heavily from Social Security Administration (2005).

8.  This supplemental benefit is different from the survivor benefits discussed in the next section.

9.  This discussion draws from Docteur and Oxley (2003), Evans (1981), Sakamaki et al. (2004), and Swiss Re (1993).

10. For example, the Chilean government found that not only the cost of transition but also economic and political stability were key factors for the successful introduction of a new social insurance program (Kritzer, 2001/2002).

# REFERENCES

Barr, N. (2002). "The Pension Puzzle: Prerequisites and Policy Choices in Pension Design." IMF Economic Issues 29. Washington, D.C.: IMF.

Custer, W.S. (1998). "Social Insurance," Chapter 21, in H.D. Skipper, ed., *International Risk and Insurance: An Environmental-Managerial Approach*. Boston, MA: Irwin/McGraw-Hill.

Danzon, Pactricia, M. (1993). "The Hidden Costs of Budget-Constrained Health Insurance Systems," in Robert B. Helms, eds. *American Health Policy: Critical Issues for Reform*. Washington, D.C. The American Enterprise Institute Press, pp. 256–292.

Docteur, E. and Oxley, H. (2003). *Healthcare Systems: Lessons from the Reform Experience*. Paris: OECD.

Doerpinghaus, H.I. (1998). "Health Care Financing," Chapter 22 in H.D. Skipper, ed., *International Risk and Insurance: An Environmental-Managerial Approach*. Boston, MA: Irwin/McGraw-Hill.

Evans, R.G. (1981). "Incomplete Vertical Integration: The Distinctive Structure of the Health-Care Industry," in J. Van der Gaag and M. Perlman, eds., *Health, Economics, and Health Economics*. Amsterdam: North-Holland.

Kritzer, B. (2001/2002). "Social Security Reform in Central and Eastern Europe: Variations on Latin American Theme," *Social Security Bulletin* 64, 16–32.

Social Security Administration (2005). *Social Security Programs Throughout the World – 2003*. Washington, DC: Social Security Administration.

Sakamaki, H., Ikezaki, S. Yamazaki, M. and Hayamizu, K. (2004). "SHA-Based Health Accounts in 13 OECD Countries: Country Studies Japan, National Health Accounts 2000," *OECD Health Technical Paper 6*, Paris: OECD.

Swiss Re (1993). "Health Care in 8 countries: Growth in Expenditure a Problem for Social Insurance Systems and Private Insurers," *Sigma*. Zurich: Swiss Re.

# Chapter 10

# The Legal Environment

## INTRODUCTION

Most states define the supreme power to govern through a formal constitution or group of legal documents that create, distribute and limit legislative, executive and judicial powers. As nation states are formed and reformed periodically, governing documents often combine authentic reflections of national aspirations with principles borrowed eclectically from classical governments, ancient philosophers and other modern nation states.

Legal authority also is found in intergovernmental agreements, including those governing multilateral organizations as well as international treaties and conventions. Intergovernmental agreements require signatory nations voluntarily to cede some sovereignty to the new institution. So long as the participating nations perceive the agreement to be in their long-term interests, the agreement will be honored.

Risk managers and insurance professionals attempt to measure the loss exposures of their firms and clients within the frameworks of national laws and intergovernmental agreements. The tension between national and intergovernmental authority can be expected to reflect the conflict between tradition and custom on the one hand and commercial uniformity and expediency on the other. As communications, trade and wealth minimize the effects of national borders, some observers believe that national legal authority will progressively defer to intergovernmental authority.

Thus, diverse legal systems can pose significant challenges for businesses, and an understanding of the legal environment internationally is essential for those involved in risk management.[1] This chapter explores several elements of this environment. While we attempt to suggest something of the great variety of law and its foundation internationally, our main emphasis is on the U.S., E.U. and Japan.

## MAJOR LEGAL SYSTEMS OF THE WORLD

Each country has a set of laws that govern its people. A country's laws are strongly influenced by the culture and tradition of local society. Cultural differences help explain why the role of law is viewed differently throughout the world. To understand these differences, it is helpful to categorize legal systems into major groupings. Most studies of comparative

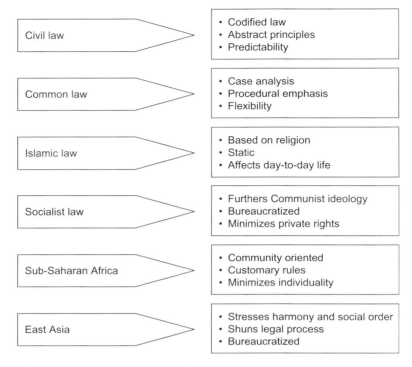

**Figure 10.1**    The Major Legal Systems of the World

law place countries within the following legal families: civil law, common law, Islamic law, socialist law, sub-Saharan Africa and East Asia, as shown in Figure 10.1.

## Civil Law and Common Law

Most developed market economies rely on either civil law or common law to determine the legal framework of societal rights. Some countries amalgamate traditional and religious heritages with the civil and common law legal model. As well documented, **civil law** is a systematic collection of laws, rules and regulations that a government enacts to differentiate its laws from the "law of nature" or general principles of international law. **Common law** derives its authority from secular courts recognizing traditional usages and customs, especially the unwritten law of England.

### Civil law

The legislative body of civil law nations establishes a code of official civil and criminal enactments. Derived from ancient Roman law (Code of Justinian, 543 AD), civil law codes describe and limit individual rights with respect to contracts (including business relationships), torts and statutes. Legislative bodies revise civil codes periodically, usually adding greater specificity. The judiciary interprets the code, with the assistance of legal counsel, by applying the statutory rules to the facts presented. The French Code Napoleon (*Code*

*Napoléon*), effective in 1804, codified rules concerning civil procedure, criminal procedure, penal law, slavery in the colonies, and commercial transactions. The French Code and the German Civil Code of 1896 provided legislative models for most modern civil codes.

Western European nations as well as most African, Asian, and South American countries follow a civil law tradition. Russia and several other Eastern European countries recently adopted civil law codes. The civil law also provides an important framework for the Islamic, Socialist, Sub-Saharan and East Asian legal systems discussed below.

### *Common law*

In common law countries, the courts look into a collection of judge-made principles that reflect usages and customs embodied in court decisions handed down from antiquity. Many countries today that once constituted the British Empire have incorporated England's common law traditions into their own laws. Central to the common law, judges have the power to make new law when the legislature has not addressed a specific issue through statute. The **Doctrine of *Stare Decisis*** ("to stand on decided cases") embodies the policy of successive courts to respect **precedents** (previous court-decided decisions), unless strong considerations of public policy compel reversal. The ability of common law courts to reject outmoded or unreasonable legal principles, while generally following precedents, promotes the litigation process as a flexible institutional alternative to the legislative process or executive order.

Common law countries provide varying degrees of autonomy to the judiciary. In the U.K., for example, courts – established by acts of Parliament – must accept the laws that Parliament enacts without regard to the constitutional principles of the Magna Carta (1215) that limit governmental authority. In the U.S., in contrast, an independent judiciary has the power to interpret the U.S. Constitution as invalidating any part of a statute that it judges to be unconstitutional. The Cayman Islands, a self-governing British territory, models its substantive law and judicial procedure after English common law, but its legislature may enact statutes that either modify or are in derogation of the English common law.

The distinction between civil law and common law systems provides a valuable framework for understanding a nation's legal infrastructure. Civil law nations expect their legislatures to codify laws that anticipate contingencies. Common law nations expect their courts to make case-by-case decisions that together comprise the law of contracts and torts. In modern times, these distinctions have blurred to some degree. Even the most rigorous civil law nation cannot codify every contingency. Even deep-seated common law nations may limit the judiciary's power in circumstances where full access to common law courts may hamper judicial system effectiveness. Table 10.1 lists several civil and common law countries.

## Islamic Law

Today, one in four world citizens is a Muslim. Islam is the principal religion of numerous countries in the Middle East, North Africa and Southeast Asia. The Qur'an (or Koran) is the ultimate source of all Islamic principles and is supplemented by the Sunnah or the tradition – decisions and sayings – of Muhammad. The principles in these two sources can be broadly classified into protection of human life, intellect, property, honor and conscience. The Qur'an and the Sunnah also provide the basis for the *Shariah* – a collection of "truths" by Islamic scholars of moral, ethical and legal standards by which Muslims must abide.

**Table 10.1**   Representative Civil and Common Law Nations

| Civil Law Nations | | Common Law Nations |
| --- | --- | --- |
| Argentina | Korea | Australia |
| Austria | Mexico | Bangladesh |
| Belgium | The Netherlands | Canada (other provinces) |
| Brazil | Poland | Ghana |
| Bulgaria | Russia | India |
| Canada (Quebec) | Sweden | Ireland |
| Chile | Taiwan | Israel |
| China | Thailand | Jamaica |
| Egypt | Tunisia | Kenya |
| Finland | Venezuela | Malaysia |
| France | Vietnam | Nigeria |
| Germany | | Pakistan |
| Greece | | Singapore |
| Indonesia | | United Kingdom |
| Italy | | United States |
| Japan | | Zambia |

Despite the introduction of new interpretation of permitted activities by scholars, the fundamentals of the Islamic legal system are unchanging. For example, the Qur'an recognizes the validity of contracts and encourages the parties to provide written evidence of the agreement. It promotes sharing profits at a predetermined ratio but does not permit interest charges.

The contract and tort law of an Islamic state is instructive for the international student. In Saudi Arabia, for example, contract disputes are resolved in *Shariah* courts or through arbitration by Islamic scholars if the disputes are commercial in nature and both parties agree on this resolution alternative. The injured party may seek rescission or damages. However, consequential damages, including lost profits, are generally not recognized under *Shariah* law. In bodily injury cases, damages are established by reference to the *Shariah* or "blood money" rules set out by Muhammad.

In that the law of Islam is set in 7th century history and not subject to modification, some observers consider it at odds with today's much more economic activity-based society. Some leaders of Arab peninsula states and other Muslim populous countries (e.g., Indonesia, Malaysia and Turkey) advocate a more flexible interpretation of Islamic law, but religious and political leaders of Iran, Libya, Saudi Arabia and other fundamentalist states remain committed to the traditional Islamic model. It should be noted that even Libya has adopted a civil code that governs commercial transactions to the extent that they do not conflict with Islamic law. The Islamic legal system presents many potential pitfalls for business persons accustomed to secular, civil code legal systems.

## Socialist Law

The dissolution of the Soviet Union and political changes in Eastern Europe in the late 20th century have diminished the role of socialist law in international business. Most of the former socialist states were originally civil law countries and have reinstituted civil codes as their principal legal framework. Although the form of these new commercial codes appears familiar to most international business persons, in reality many transactions are somewhat influenced by the socialist bureaucratic practices of the past decades.

Today, the primary socialist systems exist in China, Cuba, North Korea and Vietnam. In that the state owns all or most private property under socialist systems, the private law governing business transactions is naturally limited. Along with a renewed interest in international trade from these nations has come a willingness to modify their socialist legal systems to accommodate capitalistic needs of outside investors and traders (e.g., China and Vietnam). In socialist countries, the government often insists on a joint venture role with the outside investor.

## Laws in Sub-Saharan Africa

The nations of sub-Saharan Africa have a long tradition of unwritten customs that focus primarily on resolving disputes among tribal families and individuals. In that the culture places a premium on peaceful dispute resolution, tribal judges often assume the role of arbitrator or mediator.

As former colonies, most of these nations have adopted civil codes or common law practices from their 20th century colonial experiences. However, not all laws are actively enforced. In analyzing the limits of formal law to address regional environmental concerns effectively, Ogolla (1995), a UN official in Nairobi, observed:

> Prohibition as a juridical technique may reach its limits in cases where a resource is scarce or where there is intense pressure to satisfy basic needs. The increasing systematic encroachment into vital biodiversity habitats in most African countries notwithstanding, prohibition is clear evidence that its limits as a regulatory tool have been reached.

Under Western jurisprudence, laws that are neither enforceable nor enforced fail to meet the basic definition of law. The business person operating in this sub-Saharan African region should be particularly mindful of the differences between law as written and law as practiced.

## Laws in East Asia

As with sub-Saharan Africa, the traditions and cultures in East Asian countries (e.g., China, Japan, Korea and Taiwan) stress social order and harmony. Use of a formal legal system by individuals and businesses is viewed as disruptive to the societal goal of harmony. Much of the contemporary hostility to the legal system traces its roots to the ancient Chinese philosopher Confucius (551–479 BC). The Confucian ideal of the family as the model for society, with the father and village leader evoking absolute loyalty from the children and villagers, remains evident today in Far Eastern societies. Respected governmental bureaucrats provide guidance and leadership to businesses in much the same way as kings did in former times (and in many regions still do). Consequently, conciliation is much preferred to litigation and disagreements are typically resolved by governmental officials in a manner that maintains group harmony. Nonetheless, changes are being made in the region, as we discuss throughout this book.

Examining Japan as an example, one can find that its legal system is reflective of the intersection of Eastern and Western jurisprudence and culture. As a result of Japan's extensive trade with the West in the 19th century, it adopted many formal trappings of the European civil code. The Japanese Civil Code of 1898 and Commercial Code of 1899 were modeled extensively after the 1896 German Civil Code. However, these codes reflected the paternalistic nature of the Japanese government and depended upon the Confucian ideal of the family-group for carrying out the Western-based codes in daily life.

The U.S. instituted widespread change in the formal institutions of the Japanese government at the conclusion of World War II. The Japanese Constitution of 1947 introduced an independent judiciary and established a democratically elected parliamentary style government. Along with government "by the people," the new constitution established the U.S. concepts of due process and equal protection to empower the individual.

Despite these important Western influences on the formal legal system of Japan, the commercial codes are primarily interpreted and enforced through administrative regulations enacted by highly respected career bureaucrats in the various ministries of government. Often, the ministries give informal administrative guidance to business. Understanding the "unwritten law" provided by ministry bureaucrats is critical to the success of businesses operating in Japan.

In the event of business disputes, parties in Japan are hesitant to resort to litigation. The Confucian influence seeks alternatives to open conflict. In addition, formal and informal barriers to litigation exist in Japan. Until recently, the governmental Legal Training and Research Institute that trains all lawyers and judges, admitted only a few hundred law students each year.[2] Another practical barrier to litigation is the Japanese rule requiring the losing party to pay legal fees and costs of the winning party.

While the civil codes governing contract law in Japan and several other East Asian nations are similar to those of Western nations, Japanese culture causes parties to view the essence of contracts differently from Westerners. While Westerners view contracts as defining rights and obligations, the Eastern business executive is more likely to view the contract as a general expression of the business relationship, subject to modification as needed to reflect the realities of the ongoing business. The underlying expectation of the Japanese executive is that differences arise during the course of performing the contract may be resolved by mutual agreement, without assessing blame to either party. Westerners who successfully conduct business in East Asia understand that the spirit of the business relationship, not the letter of the law, drives the transaction.

## SUBSTANTIVE AND PROCEDURAL LAW

Risk managers and insurance professionals cannot assess corporate exposure to liability without some understanding of the controlling substantive and procedural law. Generally, **substantive law** defines, creates and regulates rights. **Procedural law** prescribes methods of enforcement of rights or obtaining redress for their violation. For example, aspects of the law of contracts that defines terms (e.g., offer and acceptance), creates rights (e.g., the measure of damages if a breach occurs) and establishes bases for avoidance (e.g., fraud and misrepresentation) are substantive in nature. On the other hand, those aspects of the law that express methods of enforcement (by framing the method to file lawsuits) are procedural in nature.

### Substantive Developments

Civil law is traditionally divided into two broad substantive categories: (1) tort and (2) contract. In general, recovery in tort is sought to compensate for damage suffered, where liability is based on the wrongdoer's socially unreasonable conduct. Damages for breach of contract are sought when a party fails to perform any promise that forms the whole or part of an agreement. A third branch of substantive law – the regulatory process – is covered in Chapters 8 and 24.

Insurance coverage and prospective tort damages can vary considerably by jurisdiction. As a result, head office risk managers must do more than maintain contact with their country managers and insurance brokers: prudent managers also should grasp the significance of legal, political, social and economic changes in each jurisdiction in which they do business.

The task of understanding international trends in tort and contract law is challenging. Countries represent an amalgam of local and national laws, all of which are steeped in unwritten customs and practices. National obligations flowing from membership in intergovernmental agencies and from international treaties and trade agreements also must be considered.

In response to the diverse legal systems, parties to international commercial activities have adopted common understandings of substantive law and procedure. For example, the most common business transaction is the buying and selling of goods. If the parties reside in countries that are signatories to the **UN Convention on Contracts for the International Sale of Goods** (CISG), the rules of the convention apply to the formation of the contract and the rights and obligations of the contracting parties, absent an express agreement in the contract to be bound by the laws of a particular nation. Although some goods and service contracts are not covered by CISG, the treaty brings a level of stability to international business transactions.

## Procedural Developments

International contracting parties often insert arbitration clauses that subject the parties to international arbitral tribunals such as the International Chamber of Commerce or the UN Commission on International Trade Law (UNCITRAL). The UNCITRAL rules are recognized in arbitrations worldwide. Such international arbitration regimes have specific procedures designed to make arbitration speedy and effective and to bypass the court system entirely.

Likewise, more than 100 countries have signed the **UN Convention on the Recognition and Enforcement of Foreign Arbitral Awards**. Known in short as the **New York Convention**, it provides a procedural mechanism to enforce international contracts that contain arbitration clauses for conflict resolution. It permits parties holding arbitral awards to seek enforcement of the award in the signatories' national courts. Because the award is enforceable in most countries, each party to the arbitration has a vested interest in respecting the arbitral process.

International trade also is influenced by governmental actions and "commercial diplomacy." In recent years, international trade policy has become subject to numerous trade agreements having the force of law. For example, the **Generalized System of Preferences**, a multinational agreement, is a program designed to promote developing countries' export potentials. Similarly, regional arrangements (e.g., NAFTA and the E.U. itself) and global agreements (e.g., GATT, the GATs) have proven to be bedrocks for the expansion of world trade.

# TORT LAW VARIATIONS INTERNATIONALLY ───────────

With the preceding background, we now examine some of the ways that legal systems compensate individuals for losses caused by other persons. Although most nations address the risks posed by modern society in similar ways, some interesting variations exist. As the financial stakes are high, an understanding of tort law and its application internationally in product liability, workers' compensation and automobile liability is important.

## The Law of Torts

A **tort** is a civil wrong resulting in injury to a person or damage to property. Torts are typically categorized as (1) intentional, (2) negligence or (3) strict liability.

- An **intentional tort** is the actual or implied intent to harm another person or his (her) property. Examples of intentional torts include assault, trespass on the property of another, and nuisance (interference with the use and enjoyment of property). Polluting the water of a downstream landowner could constitute a nuisance.

- The tort of **negligence** does not require intent to harm but merely conduct that involves an unreasonable risk of causing injury to another person or damage to another's property. The required standard of care is what a reasonable person of ordinary prudence would have done in the circumstances. For example, negligence occurs when an automobile is driven at an excessive speed and injures an occupant in another vehicle.

- A third type of tort found in some jurisdictions is **strict liability** – liability regardless of fault. The U.S. is the most prominent jurisdiction adopting strict liability torts, but the concept exists among European countries as well. Strict liability is typically imposed on product liability cases and activities involving ultra-hazardous operations. Some courts have held that disposal of hazardous environmental waste constitutes ultra-hazardous activity and place responsibility for damages on the waste handler without regard to fault.

Tort costs vary widely internationally. As Figure 10.2 shows, the U.S. tort system appears to be the world's most expensive, accounting for 2.2 percent of GDP in 2003 for an annual average growth rate of 9.6 percent between 1950 and 2004.[3] Although the costs are relatively lower in other developed economies, we cannot ignore the fact that average torts costs continue to rise in those and many other economies. This development invariably reflects changes within legal systems and can have a profound effect on risk management.

Of course, nations do not rely exclusively upon the tort system to assist the injured. By blending indemnification aspects of insurance within the legal infrastructure, those injured by industrial or automobile accidents or by product defects are compensated without regard to the fault or culpability of the party causing the injury. In addition, national laws may impose fines and criminal liability on corporations with unsafe products and work places.

## Product Liability

**Product liability** is the legal liability of the manufacturer (and sometimes the distributor or seller) for a product that causes injury to the purchaser or user. Until the early 20th century, courts applied principles of *caveat emptor* ("let the buyer beware") – a warning that parties bargain fairly yet need not voluntarily disclose all relevant information to each other – and privity of contract. The former principle transfers the responsibility of safe use of products from the manufacturer to the consumer. The latter principle requires that even when a consumer suffers an economic loss from using a product, he or she must prove the presence of a direct contractual relationship between him or her and the manufacturer. Under these stringent common law principles, product liability risk was not a significant corporate risk management issue.

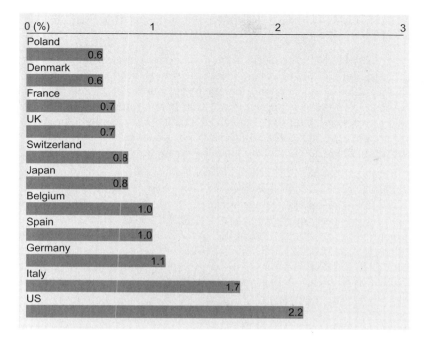

**Figure 10.2**   Tort Costs as a Percentage of GDP for Selected Countries (2003). *Source*: Towers Perrin-Tillinghast (2006). U.S. Tort Costs and Cross-Border Perspectives: 2005 Updates

## *The legal basis for lawsuits*

In today's legal environment, we not only impose on manufacturers a duty to produce goods free of harmful substances or inherent defects but also impose on them financial responsibility for breach of the duty. Product liability claims can now be based on (1) tort law (negligence), (2) strict liability or (3) contractual liability (breach of warranty), as outlined below:

- *Tort law*: Under tort law, the cause of loss can be a design defect, a marketing defect, or a manufacturing defect. A **design defect** is a flaw inherent in the design of a product. It was intended according to the product design (e.g., three-wheeled lorries are less stable than are four-wheeled versions). Hence, the defect existed before the product was manufactured. A **manufacturing defect** is a defect that the manufacturer did not intend or plan; that is a mistake in the manufacturing process (e.g., joists connected by an undetected broken bolt). A **marketing defect**, also known as a **warning defect**, flows from the way a product is sold or advertised. For example, inadequate instructions or lack of warnings can be the actual cause of loss.

- *Strict liability*: The claimant of a product liability case may be able to rely on strict liability to prevail, in the sense that he or she need only prove the proximate causal relationship between the economic loss suffered and the product defectiveness. The manufacturer can be held liable for damages even if it took all care for the production, distribution and sale of its products. It can be liable when the use involves an unreasonable risk of harm even when the product is used for the purpose for which it was manufactured. For this reason, product liability is often known as "liability without fault." This strict liability concept can also apply to the distributor or seller.

*   *Contractual liability*: Manufacturers often make representations or promises concerning the nature, quality and use of their products. Even without the presence of an express warranty, manufacturers are bound legally by an implied warranty of merchantability or fitness of the product for the use for which it was intended. For example, the U.S. **Uniform Commercial Code** (UCC) states that goods are merchantable if they "are fit for the ordinary purposes for which such goods are used." Any breach of either an express or implied warranty can be a basis for a product liability lawsuit.

Jurisdictions that have adopted product liability laws place the burden squarely on the manufacturer to show that the injured person misused the product, or otherwise it will be held responsible. The rationale behind the policy is twofold. First, the rule has a deterrent effect on the manufacturer so that safer products will be built. Second, the costs of consumer injury should be borne by the product-consuming public and not just the injured party. The tort defenses of product abuse or misuse by the consumer, assumption of risk and comparative fault are typically available as defense mechanisms for the manufacturer, the distributor or the seller in product liability cases.

## *Product safety*

A globalized economy connotes international trade of goods and services. Firms selling their goods and services in other nations must, therefore, understand not only the possible liability attaching to the production, distribution and sales of their products in their home countries but also such liability in every other country in which they operate or their products are sold.

Firms willing to adopt product safety management may find the standards set by the International Organization for Standardization (ISO) useful. The ISO has introduced a many industry operational standards. These standards, such as the ISO 9000 series, are highly specific to an industry. They contain precise technical specifications, rules and guidelines by which engineers must abide for fit and proper production of the firm's products. Many of the standards are localized as well.

Firms can use the ISO standards – international as well as localized – to assess their production or service qualities. Benchmarking their standards with ISO's, they can achieve or excel beyond an "acceptable" level of production quality in their industry. Successful benchmarking evidences that a firm has met, among others, the "state of art" at the time of production. Failure to meet such a standard can result in liability when a customer has suffered from a design defect, manufacturing defect or marketing defect of the product.

## *Product liability regulation*

Managing product liability risk differs from managing most other risks. Beatty et al. (2005) summarize the difference as follows:

> Product liability exposure arises from the firm's choice of products and markets; choices that are fundamental to the firm's business strategy and that are costly to alter. Firms are unlikely to be naturally hedged by cash flows with respect to product liability risk. Cash flows will likely be negatively correlated with product liability claims since product liability claims reduce product demand and increase costs through legal expenses and claims payments.

Despite the growing importance, however, no strong harmonization efforts can be found regarding laws and regulations governing product liability globally. Instead, efforts tend to be country specific or, at most, region specific. We discuss several key markets in this section, beginning with the U.S.

*Product liability in the U.S.*

Product liability in the U.S. is of great interest to both domestic and foreign manufacturers whose products are sold there. That the country accounts for some 17 percent of the world's imports, speaks eloquently to the exposure that non-U.S. firms have to the U.S. legal environment. More importantly, neither U.S. nor foreign manufacturers can rely on a single, comprehensive national product liability law except for elements of the *Consumer Product Safety Act* (CPSA) and in some instances for the *Model Uniform Products Liability Act*. Rather, they must look to the laws of each individual state.

This model act is purely advisory in the sense that individual U.S. states may voluntarily refer to it in the development of their own laws. In fact, several U.S. courts have held foreign standards inadmissible, although we have seen deviations from this stringent legal application in recent years (e.g., U.S. Federal Rule of Evidence 703).[4] By contrast, the CPSA addresses risks of injury associated with consumer products. The law authorizes the agency to create safety standards, order recalls of products, and ban unsafe products.

Broadly speaking, U.S. tort principles assign liability to manufacturers, suppliers and their agents for injuries by consumers and users resulting from the use of their products that are defective or when the use itself involves an unreasonable risk of harm. Product liability complaints also can be based on other causes of action, including breach of a contractual warranty of fitness or quality. A strict liability principle has been adopted or approved in nearly all U.S. jurisdictions as a matter of common law or by statute. As mentioned, to prevail under a strict liability cause of action, the injured party need only show that the product caused harm. The plaintiff need not prove that the manufacturer was negligent.

Firms domiciled, operating or selling products in the U.S. have an assortment of legal defenses. Nevertheless, product liability judgments often favor plaintiffs and may include substantial awards for both economic and non-economic damages. An injured U.S. plaintiff also can win **punitive damages** – damages intended to punish the negligent party – if a jury believes that the manufacturer was reckless or willful in its negligent behavior.

Although the policy goals of product liability have merit, implementing the policy in the U.S. has come at a high price. New approaches have evolved, as Insight 10.1 highlights. Most observers of the U.S. tort system, however, attribute its high cost, relative to that of other industrialized nations, to the jury system of determining liability and damages. The U.S. is unique among developed nations in its reliance on the jury system. A **jury** is a body of citizens, usually numbering 6–12, who are chosen at random to serve as decision makers in both civil and criminal cases. All parties in litigation have a constitutional right to a jury trial in the U.S. While this constitutional right may be waived by consent of all the parties in litigation, most injured parties do not believe it is in their best interest to waive a jury trial. Accordingly, most tort-based trials in the U.S. are heard by juries. U.S. business interests generally believe that juries are often sympathetic to plaintiffs' claims and may be unduly influenced to find wrongdoing by their sympathy for the injured plaintiff. Not surprisingly, many contracts in the U.S. contain express waivers of jury trials and mandatory arbitration as the forum for resolving disputes.

INSIGHT 10.1: MASS TORT CLASS ACTIONS IN
THE U.S.

As international interdependency grows, legal concepts based on differing cultural,
economic and political systems will continue to evolve. Consider the mass tort class
action, a U.S. procedural innovation that may be adopted in other countries. A **class
action** is a procedure enacted to provide a means for a large group of injured persons to sue wrongdoers without identifying every group member in the lawsuit. The
potential for massive damage awards is heightened through the use of this technique.
As a result, many class action settlements are negotiated.

U.S. courts have approved settlements of mass tort class action lawsuits involving asbestos-related diseases, breast implants and other product liability actions that
restrict the rights of any future claimants to sue manufacturers or suppliers. Recent
asbestos class action settlements establish a schedule of benefits and an administrative procedure for compensating class members who meet certain asbestos exposure
and medical eligibility criteria set by medical boards. Claimants who dispute the
scheduled compensation or assert extraordinary claims must take their cases before
an independent panel. Litigation and punitive damage awards, however, are virtually
foreclosed.

The advent of mass tort class actions has led the U.S. legal infrastructure to be
besieged by political and institutional demands. Lobbyists for insurers and corporations pressure U.S. state and federal legislatures to curtail "excessive" damage
awards. At the same time, some observers believe that asbestos and other mass torts
threaten to overload the entire justice system. In the past two decades or so, attempts
have been made to reform the U.S. tort system at both the state and federal levels.
Limited reform has occurred at the federal level with more substantive reform at the
state level. U.S.-type mass tort actions are beginning to appear elsewhere.

Product liability actions, subject to the statutory and common law of each U.S. state, have
developed inconsistent substantive laws and procedural rules. In reaction, about one-half of
the U.S. state legislatures have enacted tort reform laws. Some laws place an upper limit
on product liability awards for non-economic damages (e.g., US$1 million) and punitive
damages (e.g., two or three times economic damages). Tort reformers support laws that:

- codify a presumption of safety if a product meets the safety standards applicable at the time
  it is produced;
- require plaintiffs to prove conduct resulting in punitive damages by "clear and convincing"
  evidence;
- compel plaintiffs to obtain "Certificates of Merit" from experts verifying that the actions
  are not frivolous.

As noted above, however, the jury system is constitutionally protected and there has
been no movement toward amending state or federal constitutions to alter the right to trial
by jury.

*Product liability in the E.U.*

The E.U. **Products Liability Directive** is the basis of civil and criminal liability within E.U. member states for damages caused by defective products to individuals. Introduced in 1985, this directive employs a strict liability concept. Before the directive, member states had their own laws that were not in sync. For example, plaintiffs bore the burden of proof in tort in Greece, Italy, Portugal and Spain. A presumption of liability shifted the burden of proof to the defendant in Germany, Denmark, Ireland, the Netherlands and the U.K. Absolute liability could be imposed in Belgium, France and Luxembourg.

The Products Liability Directive seeks to harmonize national rules. It sets out a general duty of product safety and unambiguously requires the manufacturer to establish safety as a high priority when designing, manufacturing and distributing products. The directive not only affects manufacturers and suppliers, but importers and any persons or entities using trade names or trademarks also are affected by the directive. According to the directive, a product is defective when it "does not provide the safety which a person is entitled to expect" or the legally responsible party (e.g., a producer) fails to offer proper instructions or warn of any hazards from reasonably expected use of the product. At the same time, the directive proposes member states to adopt statutes of limitation and repose. The statute of limitation bars a person from bringing a claim after three years has elapsed since he or she discovered the damage. The statute of repose protects the accused when a claim is brought 10 years after the product was first marketed. This rather broad E.U. directive is accompanied by a number of product-specific and industry-specific directives such as the Machinery Safety Directive and the Electromagnetic Compatibility Directive.

Another landmark law in the E.U. is the **General Product Safety Directive**. First introduced in 1992, it defines a "safe product" and provides a matrix for assessing safety. The E.U. revised this directive in 2001 in part to incorporate notification requirements concerning product safety, to impose post-sale safety management obligations on manufacturers and distributors, and to give member states the power to intervene when unsafe products are found in the local market including the power to recall such products as and when necessary.[5] In 2005, the U.K. adopted the revised General Product Safety Directive as the country's own product liability and consumer safety law.

The U.S. CPSA is closely related to this directive. Table 10.2 summarizes key differences in consumer safety-related acts of the U.S. and the E.U.

*Product liability in Japan*

Attitudes in Japan toward compensation for loss cannot be separated from its history and culture that support institutional authority. Uniformity and conformity were and to a great extent remain public virtues that have been transferred over time from the imperial government to large conglomerates. For example, the post-war establishment of a new constitution that placed national power in a central government and ended the Emperor's deification has created a legal infrastructure closely tied to Japan's major industries.

The close relationship between government and industry in Japan partially explains its low level of product liability litigation. Until recent time, typical cases were settled out of court or ended in failure for the plaintiff, in part because the local legal system did not include any pre-trial discovery process and in part because litigants had to rely upon the country's civil code predicated on proving negligence or contractual liability. Put differently, litigants were required to submit proof of a defect in a specific product, negligence by the

**Table 10.2**  Comparison of Consumer Safety Acts of the United States and the European Union

| Area of Regulation | United States | European Union |
|---|---|---|
| Who to notify | Consumer Product Safety Commission (CPSC). | Competent regulatory authorities in E.U. member states as well as several non-E.U. countries in Europe. |
| What to notify | Product failing to meet an applicable safety standard, posing a substantial product hazard to consumers, or creating an unreasonable risk of serious injury or death. | Product posing risks that are incompatible with the general safety requirement, wherein a "safe product" is a "product which, under normal or reasonably foreseeable conditions of use . . . does not present any risk or only the minimum risks compatible with the products use, considered to be acceptable and consistent with a high level of protection." |
| When to notify | Immediately (within 24 hours) when a manufacturer, distributor, or retailer has "information that reasonably supports the conclusion" (can be extended up to 10 days when information is not clearly reportable). | Immediately (within 3–10 days whether or not investigation is complete) when a producer or distributor knows or ought to know that it has placed on the market a product that is not a "safe product." |
| Confidentiality | Notification and ensuring correspondence are confidential (at least during the CPSC investigation). | Public disclosure of the notification about unsafe product unless specifically protected by the E.U. General Products Safety Directive. |

*Sources*: U.S. CPSA and the E.U. General Products Safety Directive.

manufacturer, resultant damage and a causal relationship between the defendant and the damage.

Changes were made in its product liability law, effective in 1995. The law defines "liable manufacturers" and employs the principle of strict liability. Consumers can now ask certain specialized facilities to conduct investigations to determine the causes of accidents possibly involving defective products. However, the new law exempts manufacturers from legal responsibility if they can prove that a potentially dangerous defect was unforeseeable based on the principle that the product was manufactured with those technological and other capabilities that were the accepted "state of the art" at the time of manufacture or sell.

Japan's law is modeled after the E.U. Products Liability Directive. However, it is broader than the E.U. directive, as it applies to damages to corporate entities in addition to individuals. It differs from the E.U. directive by making the test of defect an ordinary safety procedure rather than the consumer expectation. The law is inapplicable to suppliers not representing themselves as manufacturers. Potential liability is unlimited in the law but manufacturers are not liable for damage to the product itself where only the product is damaged.

The Japanese legal system prohibits U.S.-type **contingency fees** system (where attorneys are compensated as a percentage of successful lawsuits) and bars plaintiffs from seeking punitive damages. As a result, plaintiffs in Japan depend greatly on the country's extensive alternative dispute resolution system. The system often provides prompt and less expensive settlements. Under the law, for example, regional prefectural government committees serve with other local officials as intermediaries in product liability disputes. Alternatively, disputes may continue to be resolved at Consumer Life Centers that are located throughout the country.

From a cultural standpoint, the Japanese have discouraged lawsuits for personal damages, perhaps because many Japanese consider court appearances shameful exercises that heap scorn upon the litigant and his or her family (Berat, 1992). The Japanese judiciary's primary function is to encourage conciliation, harmony and compromise. Private conciliation cases, *chotei*, where parties may be represented by attorneys, are encouraged. The conciliation committee of the *chotei* devises appropriate settlements with several alternatives. Subsequent hearings persuade the parties to make concessions and reach mutually agreeable solutions that become binding and enforceable.

Even in this relatively favorable environment, Japanese manufacturers are now attuned more than ever to the product liability. There has been an increasing emphasis on safety-oriented product design as well as on warnings and instructions related to product use. Interestingly, some contend that warning labels in Japan are frequently vague and only slightly cautionary, as manufacturers feared that strong language would insult their consumers.

## Automobile Liability

Perhaps every country has laws establishing liability for road accidents and specifying whether the purchase of automobile liability (third-party motor) insurance is required and, if so, in what minimum amounts. Such laws prescribe the party responsible for paying damages as a result of the negligent operation or use of a vehicle. Vehicle owners often also can be held responsible for the harm to others caused by the negligent operation of their vehicles by someone to whom they have given permission to use their vehicle.

### Variations internationally

Most countries mandate that motor vehicle owners must maintain liability insurance in connection with their ownership and use of their automobile. Other approaches that are found around the world are intended to encourage the purchase of such insurance. The U.S. has examples of virtually all approaches practiced worldwide. Insight 10.2 offers a brief history of the approaches.

In most countries, vehicle owners purchase automobile liability (third-party motor) insurance as evidence that they comply with legal requirements. Private nonlife insurance firms are primary suppliers of the coverage worldwide.

Differences exist worldwide in coverage scope and limits. As illustrated in Table 10.3, insurers in several countries must offer unlimited liability coverage for bodily injury, thus permitting a complete transfer of liability from automobile owners and users to insurance companies. Some countries also require unlimited or exceptionally high property damage liability limits as well. Insight 10.3 offers a summary of automobile liability insurance law in Japan.

In Canada and the U.S., only policies with limited liability coverage are available, and motorists are required by law to maintain the minimum liability limits set by the state or

## INSIGHT 10.2: DEVELOPMENT OF AUTOMOBILE INSURANCE IN THE UNITED STATES

*Financial responsibility laws*: Legislative attempts were first made in the mid-1920s to deal with the problems of harm resulting from the negligent operation of automobiles. The financial responsibility law in the state of Connecticut offers an example. It empowered the insurance commissioner to suspend the registration of the vehicle of a **tortfeasor** (person committing a tort) until any judgment against the person was satisfied. All U.S. states now have some form of financial responsibility law.

*Compulsory insurance laws*: The state of Massachusetts introduced a compulsory liability insurance law in 1925. The law required motor vehicle owners to provide for proof of insurance at the time of vehicle registration. Most U.S. states now have similar laws.

*Security-type laws*: In 1937, the state of New Hampshire introduced the first security-type law. Such laws prescribed that the at-fault motorist could face loss of his or her driver's license and vehicle registration suspension until the motorist not only satisfied the judgment but also provided for "security and proof" of future responsibility (most often via insurance) following an accident.

None of these laws has been proven perfect. Some motorists allow their policies to lapse for non-payment of premiums. Others simply ignore the law, owning or operating unlicensed or uninsured vehicles.

*Source*: LexisNexis (2005).

**Table 10.3**   Comparison of Automobile Liability Coverage Limits Internationally

| Country | BI | PD |
|---|---|---|
| Belgium | Unlimited | €1.25 million (fire, explosion, and nuclear only) |
| Finland | Unlimited | €3.36 million |
| France | Unlimited | €100 million per policy |
| Germany | €50 million per accident (BI and PD combined) per policy | |
| Iran | Unlimited | IRR 2 million |
| Ireland | Unlimited | €0.115 million |
| Israel | Unlimited | Not required |
| Italy | €50 million per accident (BI and PD combined) per policy | |
| Japan | Unlimited subject to up to ¥40 million under CALI | Not required by CALI |
| Luxembourg | Unlimited | €1.25 million (fire, explosion, and nuclear only) |
| Denmark | DK50 million | DK10 million (index adjusted) |
| Malaysia | Unlimited | RM3 million for commercial risks |
| Morocco | Unlimited | MAD1 million (fire, explosion, and nuclear only) |
| Slovakia | Unlimited | Unlimited |
| Switzerland | CHF100 million per accident (BI and PD combined) per policy | |
| Tunisia | Unlimited | Unlimited |
| United Kingdom | Unlimited | £20 million |
| United States | Varies by state, often US$10,000–$50,000 as minimum | Varies by state, often US$10,000–$50,000 as minimum |

BI: bodily injury; PD: property damage; CALI: compulsory automobile liability insurance.
*Sources*: Guy Carpenter (2003) and Nonlife Insurance Institute of Japan (2005).

---

**INSIGHT 10.3: AUTOMOBILE LIABILITY INSURANCE IN JAPAN**

In 1955, Japan adopted the legal concept of negligence in lieu of the formerly used concept of "responsibility for no fault," mainly to strengthen claimants' rights. Under the rules, damages may be claimed if the victim can prove that injury or death was caused by a traffic accident. The accused is then responsible for the tort claim unless he or she can establish that neither the policyholder nor the driver was negligent, that there was malice or negligence on the part of the victim, or that there was no structural defect or malfunction of the policyholder's automobile. This law has resulted in two separate automobile insurance systems in Japan: compulsory automobile liability insurance (CALI) and voluntary insurance.

Motorists in Japan must maintain a CALI policy that offers insurance coverage of ¥40 million. Under the law, automobile insurers are required to accept all compulsory insurance applications unless the applicant meets one of the "justifiable reasons" for refusal, as stipulated in the law (e.g., non-disclosure or misrepresentation). Insurers are not permitted to cancel CALI policies for reasons other than non-payment of premiums.

The voluntary insurance market provides excess coverage over the CALI limit for bodily injury as well as liability coverage for property damage. Insurers in the voluntary market also offer coverage against accidents caused by uninsured automobiles or self-sustained accidents. Insurance limits are commonly set by type of loss such as death, injury, permanent disability, or property damage. There are no per occurrence or aggregate limits.

The claimant in an automobile liability dispute is a third party under the insurance contract and can file a claim directly with the insurer. In the case of an increase or decrease in the risk during the insurance period, the insurance contract is deemed to have been altered. Once aware of a risk increase, the policyholder must give notice to the insurer without delay. If an accident occurs after an increase in the risk and the policyholder failed to give notice, the insurer must pay the loss but has a claim against the policyholder for the amount paid. When a change in risk is reported, the insurer may be entitled to additional premiums.

---

provincial government. As a result, insureds in Canada and the U.S. are responsible for any uncovered, at-fault financial losses above the limit of insurance.

In countries with limited coverage, the liability limit may be expressed in a **single limit** or **split limits**. For example, insurers in Canada – except those in the provinces of Newfoundland and Labrador – are required to offer a single limit ranging from C$200,000 (most provinces) to C$500,000 (Nova Scotia) for third-party liability. Canadian insureds thus may file a claim for up to the coverage limit for bodily injury only (whether it is for one victim or multiple victims), property damages only or a combination of both, as long as the total liability claim is within the coverage limit.[6] Similar legal applications are found in Germany, Italy, and Switzerland.

The E.U. adopted the ***Fifth Motor Insurance Directive*** in 2005. The directive requires member states to impose – after a transitional period of five years – a split minimum limit of

---

### INSIGHT 10.4: AUTOMOBILE LIABILITY IN THE U.K.

Plaintiffs must prove negligence to recover judgments for automobile liability. When a lawsuit is commenced, the plaintiff may be required to post-security for the defendant's costs, including attorneys' fees, which ultimately inure to the prevailing party. In the court's discretion, a party who engages in "wasteful" litigation tactics may be obliged to pay the other party's costs and attorneys' fees.

U.K. common law courts appear to have full control over automobile litigation, demonstrating that a nation's legal infrastructure can maintain a functioning system without major statutory limitations. Even when Parliament established a loser-pays rule and security requirements for litigants, it provided for the courts to use their discretion and let the tort system function with a minimum of legislative interference.

Under the U.K. *Road Traffic Act* of 1988, all motorists must insure against liability for death, bodily injury and damage to property caused by the use of a vehicle in the U.K. or in any E.U. member state. The insurance policy must provide coverage for the cost of emergency medical treatment. The insurer must satisfy any judgment obtained against the insured and may not rely upon any specifications or conditions. Victims of uninsured drivers may recover damages from the Motor Insurers Bureau.

---

€1 million per victim or €5 million for all bodily injuries per accident and €1 million for property damages per accident. The minimum amounts of insurance will then be adjusted annually according to the European Index of Consumer Prices. In contrast, the U.S. limits are not indexed and can only be changed through amendment to the governing act. Insight 10.4 offers a summary of automobile liability in the U.K.

### Automobile liability insurance issues

Automobile liability insurance is a major line of business in perhaps all countries. It also is one of the most highly regulated lines, with governments routinely limiting insurers' abilities to decline coverage applications and barring insurers from charging rates that they believe appropriate for the risk; that is, rate suppression is common.

From the viewpoint of a vehicle owner or user, management of the automobile liability risk is closely related to the financial protection needs of the owner, incentives for loss control activities, types of coverages available and their limits in the traditional insurance market, and whether the government permits the owner to engage in a risk financing activity other than purchase of insurance. In the remaining part of this section, we discuss three issues critical to the successful operation of an automobile liability system.

### Uninsured and underinsured motorists

Despite the compulsory nature of automobile liability insurance in most countries, some motorists still assume the risk of driving without insurance. The percentage of uninsured motorists is estimated at around 10 percent in several developed countries and much higher in some developing economies and in countries without stringent enforcement measures.

In countries with limited liability coverage, many motorists choose to purchase the minimum required coverages. Such a behavioral pattern does not necessarily become a public concern in countries (e.g., several E.U. states) where the minimum coverage is high. Conversely, it can be a serious public issue when the government sets comparatively low limits. For example, the state of New York requires a minimum liability cover of only US$10,000 for property damage, whereas the average price for newly purchased vehicles remains above US$20,000 in the state. This discrepancy has resulted in numerous cases of **underinsurance** where victims are not compensated fully for their costs. When the liable motorist has insufficient financial resources to compensate the victim, the victim can be forced to absorb the uncovered amount of loss *unless* another compensation scheme is in place in the market.

Uninsured or underinsured automobile insurance coverage is such a scheme, found in several countries. It compensates the victims of automobile accidents – through the victim's own insurance – when the liable party has no or insufficient insurance coverage. It also may compensate victims when the liable third party cannot be easily identified (e.g., hit-and-run victims). Uninsured and underinsured coverages in most U.S. states, which are commonly sold as a package, provide coverage only for economic damages such as bodily injury or property damage and not for non-economic damages such as pain and suffering.

The compulsory nature of automobile liability insurance also calls for a scheme ensuring that insurance is available to motorists and, according to many persons, is also affordable. An issue for many countries is finding a solution to the problems of coverage availability and affordability. As private insurers are the main supplier of automobile liability insurance in most countries, they must make a sufficient profit (or at least not too large a loss in any type of insurance) to remain in business. Certain high-risk motorists can find themselves in an untenable situation. They wish to comply with the law but cannot locate an insurer willing to insure them or afford the premium quoted. Without an appropriate scheme in place, they may opt to use their vehicle without insurance.

*Assigned risk plans*

As a solution to the problem of coverage availability and affordability, many countries have introduced **assigned risk plans** which are arrangements for assigning "unwanted" insureds to a servicing insurer so as to guarantee coverage and commonly at subsidized premium rates. For example, under the assigned risk plan of the U.S. state of New York, an applicant who cannot find an insurer willing to accept him or her may apply for coverage through the plan, which then assigns the applicant to one of the servicing carriers – licensed insurance firms in the state.

Servicing carriers charge such motorists premiums according to the assigned risk plan rate schedule. The plan rates are commonly higher than the rates in the standard market but not necessarily so high as the rates that those non-standard motorists would be charged without the plan. All insurers licensed to sell automobile insurance business in the market are required to subsidize the premium deficiency from the assigned risk plan operations. Whether they can transfer any of the subsidy to their other insureds (standard risks) depends on the stringency of the rate regulation in the jurisdiction. All else being equal, the more stringent is the rate or underwriting regulation in a jurisdiction, the greater the percentage of motorists likely to have to resort to the assigned risk plan.

**Residual markets**, **high-risk insurance markets**, **joint underwriting associations (JUAs)** and **automobile reinsurance pools** are similar to assigned risk plans. A major difference among these plans is the way they are administered. For example, a plan can be administered by an association of insurers in a market or by a government agency. These schemes function as insurers of last resort for high-risk motorists. The hope is that motorists securing insurance from these schemes will remain accident free for a certain period so that they can eventually find coverages in the standard market.

### No-fault insurance

**No-fault insurance** pays the expenses of persons injured in automobile accidents regardless of who was at fault. With this coverage, each injured motorist (and his or her passengers) may seek compensation from the motorist's own insurer. The typical no-fault insurance plan limits the compensation to medical expenses, loss of earnings and other reasonable expenses to the injuries sustained. Variations, of course, exist worldwide.

No-fault insurance was intended to speed claims' settlements, with prompt handling of small claims, particularly for bodily injuries. It can result in lower costs of automobile insurance as fewer disputes are brought to court.[7] In the U.S., no-fault benefits are usually primary to health insurance, meaning that a person's own health insurance steps in only when the no-fault benefits are exhausted.

Thus, no-fault insurance is a variation of first-party automobile insurance coverage.[8] No-fault insurance plans can be classified into one of three categories: pure, add-on and modified. A **pure no-fault insurance plan** replaces the tort system completely, thus making the plan the only source of recovery. Only a few jurisdictions are known to have pure no-fault plans (e.g., New Zealand as well as selected provinces in Australia and Canada).

Add-on no-fault and modified no-fault plans are found in many jurisdictions worldwide. An **add-on no-fault insurance plan** prohibits the injured person from collecting twice for the same injury, such as could otherwise occur if a medical injury could be paid by the no-fault insurance and the person's health insurance. This plan leaves the tort system intact. Similarly, a **modified no-fault insurance plan** permits recovery of economic (and non-economic) losses through the tort system only when the victim suffers a loss greater than some threshold set in the no-fault compensation statute. The threshold can be expressed by the type of injury – known as a verbal threshold – or in an amount – known as a monetary threshold. Serious injuries therefore are excluded from most no-fault insurance statutes.

## Corporate Governance Liability

Several governments have enacted revised corporate governance requirements during the past decade. The most important internationally arguably is that enacted in the U.S. in 2002 – the *Sarbanes-Oxley Act* – following the massive failure of one of the world's and U.S.'s largest businesses, Enron Corporation, because of executive malfeasance and inattention by its board of directors. Other notable corporate bankruptcies and debacles followed, each involving a failure of corporate governance.

Section 302 of the *Sarbanes-Oxley Act* requires publicly traded U.S. firms to create, implement, and maintain effective, transparent internal risk-management controls. Compliance requires regulated firms to implement broad and in-depth corporate governance policies that are intended to ensure that both senior executives and the board of directors are aware of any potential difficulties. Companies are to test their internal control systems continuously and compliance must be certified by the U.S. Securities and Exchange Commission

---

**INSIGHT 10.5: CEO AND CFO CERTIFICATIONS OF FINANCIAL INFORMATION UNDER THE U.S. *SARBANES-OXLEY ACT***

The act prescribes that the chief executive officers and chief financial officers of publicly traded U.S. firms must provide the SEC with their "personal" certification of financial information. The certification must contain the following statements:

- They have read the report.
- The report fairly presents the firm's financial condition and results of operations.
- To their knowledge, the report contains no untrue statements or omissions of material fact that would make the statements misleading.
- They are responsible for and have evaluated the firm's disclosure controls and procedures and internal controls over financial reporting.

---

(SEC). Insight 10.5 outlines key provisions of the act with regard to certifications required by senior officers.

The U.S. Accounting Standards Financial Board (FASB) also issues several rules related to this compliance requirement. Thus, noncompliance with Section 302 of the *Sarbanes-Oxley Act* alone can lead to allegations that the firm as well as its directors and officers has failed to meet the required standards.

Many countries have similar requirements, although the question arises as to "what are the standards?" Internationally, of course, there is no universal definition, as standards will vary from jurisdiction to jurisdiction. For example, in the U.S. in 2005, a court ruled in litigation involving the Walt Disney Company that directors and officers are fiduciaries and, as such, must exercise due care, manifest their loyalty to shareholders by maximizing their investment values and make decisions in good faith and untainted by self-interest. The court further elaborated fiduciary duty as follows:

- *Business judgment rule*: Directors and officers are presumed to act on an informed basis and in the honest belief that their actions are taken in the best interest of the firm. This presumption applies even in the absence of evidence of fraud, bad faith or self-dealing. Similarly, decisions of the board of directors need to be attributed to rational business purposes.

- *Fiduciary duty of due care*: A director or officer must use the amount of care that ordinarily careful and prudent men and women would use in similar circumstances. All material information reasonably available in making key business decisions must be carefully considered. This duty of due care puts an emphasis on whether the officer makes decisions in good faith to advance the interest of the firm and less emphasis on whether the outcome of the action was acceptable or egregious.

- *Fiduciary duty of loyalty*: Directors and officers must not use their positions of trust to further their own personal interests.

The above definition of fiduciary duty clearly indicates the rising importance of self-regulation; that is, good corporate governance. One requisite for good corporate governance is an independent board of directors. The directors must not only be independent "in affili-ation" with the firm, but also be "independent-minded in their oversight" of the financial reporting and operations of the firm.

## Environmental Risks and the Law

As noted in Chapter 6, environmental problems have provoked urgent warnings from sci-entists during recent years. Although these concerns have been reported to varying degrees for the past 50 years, governmental intervention has had a much shorter life. In the late 1960s, the UN General Assembly attempted to focus global attention on the problems of pollution by proposing a world conference on the environment. This produced the 1972 UN Conference of the Human Environment, held in Stockholm, Sweden. This 1972 con-ference produced the first international consensus on the magnitude and scope of the global environmental challenge and thus is regarded as the incubator for contemporary environ-mental political action.

The 1997 *Kyoto Protocol* to the UN *Framework Convention on Climate Change* went into effect in 2005. More than 150 nations that are signatory members of the protocol are required to control or reduce emission of carbon dioxide and other greenhouse gases by 2012. The requirements range from 0 percent reductions for Russia, to 6–8 percent reduc-tions for E.U. member states, Japan, the U.S. and some other countries, to an 8–10 percent increase for Australia and Iceland. Notably, Australia and the U.S., which belong to Annex II of developed economies that pay for costs of developing countries, are original signatory countries but have not ratified the treaty, thus calling into question its ultimate effectiveness to curb global warming as the U.S. is the world's largest emitter of such gases.

Significantly, both Kyoto and the Stockholm declarations acknowledged that developing countries' environmental concerns were different from those of developed nations and that developing countries had the need to continue to develop within a framework of respect for the environment. While developed nations are primarily concerned with pollution resulting from development, developing nations must by necessity focus first on the environmen-tal problems stemming from poverty and lack of economic development. The notion first articulated in Stockholm that economic development can coexist with environmental pro-tection is now known as **sustainable development**.

The UN has remained active in pursuit of environmental improvements through the United Nations Environment Program that has served as a catalyst for research, technology and education. This has led to several multilateral environmental treaties and statements. The 1992 Rio Declaration on Environment and Development was a product of UN persistence. The environmental components of current multinational agreements such as the GATT, NAFTA, and the E.U. can be traced to the ground-breaking work of the UN Stockholm Conference.

### Environmental law in the U.S.

The U.S. has adopted the **"polluter pays" principle** in its environmental legislation, which establishes environmental norms and requires any polluting party violating these norms to pay for any resultant cleanup. Also, a significant penalty can be imposed by the gov-ernment, in the form of monetary damages, criminal sanctions or both. The primary stat-utes in force today are the *Clean Air Act* (CAA) of 1970 (air quality), the *Clean Water Act* of 1987 (water quality) and the *Comprehensive Environmental Response, Compensation and Liability Act* of 1980 (CERCLA) (hazardous waste). Although the statutes have been amended recently to reflect changes in technology, the legal framework has remained essentially intact.

With passage of the *National Environmental Policy Act* (NEPA) in 1970 and creation of the Environmental Protection Agency (EPA) the same year, the U.S. government became actively involved in the regulation of environmental matters. NEPA requires federal agencies to consider the environmental consequences of all major federal actions and to prepare a formal environmental impact statement (EIS) reflecting any adverse environmental effects of the proposed action, alternatives to the action, the relationship between short-term uses of the environment and long-term productivity, and any irretrievable commitments of resources that the proposed action would involve. The EIS is available for public review. Typically, representatives of pro-environmental groups carefully monitor these EISs and share their implications with the news media and public officials.

The EPA is charged with protecting human health by safeguarding the natural environment: air, water, and land. Our discussion centers on the EPA's activities in the major areas of environmental concern.

## Air and radiation

The 1970's CAA prompted improvement in air quality. The 1990 CAA Amendments address air and radiation and other chronic air quality problems in a different way. Innovations in this law include programs based on cooperation between government and industry as well as pollution prevention incentives based on market forces. The EPA is charged with enforcing the CAA.

## Water

Although the vast majority of the earth's surface is covered with water, the oceans and seas are salty. Only 3 percent of the world's water is fresh – and two-thirds of that is ice! This tiny fraction of fresh water sustains a multitude of life forms (including our own), provides much drinking water, provides numerous forms of recreation, and is vital to agricultural and many industrial operations.

Ground water resources, in particular, are extremely valuable. More than 95 percent of the population gets their household water from underground sources. Ground water also is used for about half of all agricultural irrigation and one-third of industrial water needs. In many places, this vital resource is already contaminated or threatened. Some 38 percent of fresh-water ecosystems in the U.S. are not fit to swim in or fish. Even more than surface waters, ground water resources are often taken for granted because they are not visible.

Activities to protect ground water are guided by several different federal and state laws. Among the most important has been the Clean Water Act. Some states have comprehensive ground water protection statutes, but all states have some authority to protect ground water under solid and hazardous waste laws, public health laws, and energy extraction laws. Regulatory authority and information about ground water quantity and quality vary among state agencies, but usually reside in natural resources, environmental protection, or public health agencies.

## Pesticides

Few chemicals have had as much effect or been the subject of as much controversy in recent decades as pesticides. Pesticides are used on food, crops, lawns and golf courses; in schools as well as in the home and other buildings; and to disinfect swimming pools and hospital equipment. Because of their wide application, the EPA "registers" (licenses) thousands of pesticide products in the U.S. No pesticide may legally be sold or used unless the chemical's label bears an EPA registration number.

The EPA is charged with ensuring that pesticides will not present unreasonable risks to people, wildlife, fish and plants, including endangered species. Under the 1947 *Federal Insecticide, Fungicide and Rodenticide Act* (FIFRA) and amendments effective in 2002, the chemical's benefits must outweigh the risks. FIFRA gives the EPA the authority to limit the amount of pesticide applied, restrict the frequency or location of application, or require the use of specially trained, certified applicators. The EPA also can suspend or cancel the registration if later information shows that use of the pesticide poses unacceptable health effects.

### Wastes

Hazardous wastes include chemicals that are corrosive, flammable, reactive or toxic. Hazardous wastes may be byproducts of manufacturing processes or discarded consumer products, such as household cleaning fluids, paints, and batteries. Once generated, hazardous wastes require proper storage, treatment and disposal. If a business exceeds standards set by the EPA, administrative action is taken against the polluter. With serious violations, courts are authorized to impose penalties of US$25,000–50,000 per day of violation, sentence liable individuals to jail terms of one or more years, and even close the violator's business operation.

Most states have received authority from the EPA to regulate and enforce laws controlling hazardous waste storage, treatment and disposal. The EPA oversees activities in those states that do not have this authority. Some sites have abandoned hazardous wastes for which ownership is unclear or unknown. In these situations, control and cleanup is possible through the CERCLA. Under this act, the EPA has the authority to clean up the worst hazardous waste sites using money from a trust fund supported primarily from a tax on chemical feed stocks used by manufacturers. Those sites have been placed on the EPA's National Priorities List.

CERCLA provides that the present owner of land can be held liable for the cleanup costs of hazardous waste located on the property, even if the waste was dumped on the land by a previous landowner or tenant. Thus, CERCLA has created a form of strict liability for property owners in the U.S. Hence, the prudent risk manager need conduct an environmental audit to determine the presence of potential hazardous wastes before committing to purchase or finance industrial property.

The *Superfund Amendments and Reauthorization Act* (SARA) of 1986 provides for public participation in selecting the appropriate remedies for site contamination problems. The EPA assigns staff to each superfund site to work with the local community to reach decisions related to site cleanup activities. The EPA is required to make site-related information accessible to the public.

Today, the standard U.S. liability insurance policy expressly excludes cleanup costs associated with hazardous waste. For policies issued before the mid-1980s, the exclusion is not as clearly drafted. Litigation over the extent of environmental coverage available under the "sudden and accidental" provisions of general liability policies has been hotly contested in almost every state court system. Most courts have sided with insurers that hazardous waste dumping is not included within the policy coverage, although a minority of U.S. state courts have decided to the contrary.

## *Environmental law in the E.U.*

The E.U. has generally followed the "precautionary principle" as manifested in the E.U. Treaty that "in cases where scientific uncertainty exists but preliminary scientific evaluation gives reasonable grounds for concern about potential adverse effects on the environment or health, even if the risk is not proved, action to avert it should be considered." Borrowed from German law (*Vorsorge*), this civil law principle ordinarily ensures a higher standard of care than that required by the principles of due care and prudence. In 1977, a European Community Policy Statement (Objective 17) expressed adoption of the "polluter pays" principle, that is; "the cost of preventing and eliminating nuisances must, as a matter of principle, be borne by the polluter."

The E.U. also has adopted a series of directives: the 1967 directive on classification of dangerous substances, the 1970 directive for measures to fight air pollution from vehicles, the first European Environmental Action Program of 1973–1976, 1980 directive on minimum standards for drinking water, and 1985 directive on environmental impact assessment.

Under the terms of the 1987 Single European Act, the environment is given a high priority in the E.U. policy scheme such that the E.U. promotes "a sustainable and non-inflationary growth of the EC respecting the environment." In 1992, E.U. member states adopted the Maastricht Treaty that all E.U. policies and activities must take account of the environment. Additionally, the E.U. has committed itself to reduce emission of carbon dioxide and other greenhouse gases by 8 percent of its 1990 level by the year 2012. In 2002, the E.U. introduced its Sixth Environment Action Program (6EAP) dealing with several strategic issues for the period of 2002–2012.

The E.U. adopted in 2001 a directive dealing with water policy which aims: to establish an E.U. framework for the protection of inland surface waters, transitional waters, coastal waters, and groundwater; to prevent and reduce pollution; to promote sustainable use of water; to improve aquatic ecosystems; and to mitigate the effects of floods and draughts. By 2010, member states are required to ensure that their water pricing policies provide users with adequate incentives to use water resources efficiently.

The E.U. launched the "Clean Air for Europe" (CAFE) in 2002, a program of technical analysis of significant negative effects of air pollution on human health and the environment. It also adopted the Thematic Strategy on Air Pollution in 2005, which aims by 2020 to reduce the number of premature deaths from air-pollution-related diseases by almost 40 percent from the 2000 level. Such a reduction is expected to give the E.U. a medical cost benefit of about €42 billion per year. The E.U. Council adopted CAFÉ at 6EAP.

The E.U. uses its comprehensive regulatory framework, administered by the European Food Safety Authority, to assess pesticide risk and examine ingredients of plant production products (PPPs) before they are placed on the market. It also has set maximum residue limits for about 150 PPPs at the E.U. level and similar limits for any other unharmonized products at the member state level. Even so, E.U. directives do not fully address the actual use phase of the pesticide's life cycle such as temporary storage of pesticides and the application itself. The E.U. has proposed implementation of the Integrated Pest Management program that, among other things, would establish crop-specific standards. Once passed, the program would become mandatory in 2014 and integrate existing regulations on pesticides.

The E.U. has since 1975 developed waste legislation in three stages: the first dealing with the general regulatory framework as well as waste oils and titanium dioxide, the second setting standards for landfills and incinerators, and the third putting in place the necessary organization to expedite the recycling of several priority waste flows (e.g., packaging and end-of-life vehicles). With the Waste Framework Directives effective in 2006, the E.U. attempts to harmonize existing waste regulation for "the protection of human health and the environment against harmful effects caused by the collection, transport, treatment, storage and tipping of waste." The directive also requires member states to take measures to encourage the recovery of waste by means of recycling, reuse, or reclamation and by using it as a source of energy.

In sum, the E.U. has established standards for acceptable levels of air pollution, water pollution and hazardous waste disposal. These standards are expressed in terms of technical directives that give member states some flexibility in meeting the standards.

### Environmental law in Japan

An unwanted byproduct of Japan's aggressive post-war economic recovery in the 1950s and 1960s was significant industrial pollution and harm to its citizens. Many Japanese, consequently, have suffered from four pollution-related inflictions: *Itai-Itai* (caused by cadmium released from mining operations into rivers) in 1950, *Minamata* (caused by organic mercury waste released into rivers) in 1956, *Niigata-Minamata* (marine life contaminated with organic mercury) in 1964, and *Yakkaichi* (release of sulfur dioxide and nitrogen dioxide from industrial complexes). Primarily as a consequence of a series of citizens' pollution trial victories against industrial polluters in the early 1970s, the government of Japan created the Environmental Agency in 1971 and was forced to address the impact of unregulated industrial growth on its citizens.

It enacted the Basic Environment Law in 1993 which prescribes the responsibilities of the government, the corporation and the citizen. An integral part of the law is the Basic Environment Plan. Based on the law, the Environmental Agency (now the Ministry of Environment) has established quality standards for water (including groundwater), air, soil and noise. The Environmental Impact Assessment Law went into effect in 1997.

Japan today enforces a wide spectrum of environmental laws and regulations dealing with air and water pollution and hazardous waste. As a relatively small, yet highly developed economy, land use planning by the government enjoys a high priority in Japan. In keeping with the East Asia model of dispute avoidance, Japan has developed the widespread use of administrative guidance by both local and national government officials to develop "pollution control agreements." These agreements typically set out with great specificity emission standards as well as monitoring and reporting requirements. The pollution control agreements are neither based on legal requirements of Japanese law nor legally enforceable but occupy a central part of the environmental control process through voluntary agreement.

Japan has developed an extensive network of pollution monitoring stations. Japan's industrial companies desire to avoid a loss of face through a failure to meet their voluntary standards, thus providing an effective enforcement mechanism. Once again, we see that a national culture can influence the legal process to a greater extent than the formal legal procedures.

## INTERNATIONAL VARIATIONS IN CONTRACT LAW

Differences over the enforceability, formation, interpretation and performance of contracts generate controversy, litigation and legal thought. The law of contracts has rich, diverse roots in the English common law, Roman law as well as the legal traditions of many Muslim, Asian and African societies. It is beyond the scope of this chapter to do more than acknowledge that each society's enforcement of certain promises between private parties has been central to the development of that nation's economy. Today, thousands of free-market lawyers, legislators and entrepreneurs are scattered throughout the world, developing the legal concept of private ownership of property that gives rise to executory, enforceable contracts.

## Performance and Contract Negotiations

While contracts are central to business transactions in every economy and culture, their interpretation varies widely. In the event of breach of contract, common law countries typically provide for monetary damages, measured as the differences between the value of the performance actually received and the value contracted for. In contrast, civil law systems have traditionally denied monetary awards unless the breaching party was guilty of substantial fault or fraud. In lieu of monetary damages, civil law countries permit the buyer of a product or service unilaterally to reduce the price it pays to offset damages caused by the seller. To support the concept of reduction in price, civil law courts often grant decrees of **specific performance** to force sellers to deliver conforming goods or services and buyers to pay the contract price.

Another civil law remedy, although not widely available in common law countries, is the German concept of *Nachfrist* **notice** – a procedure that permits a party additional time to perform contractual obligations if notice of the delay is given. During this extension, the other party is barred from pursuing legal action. If the seller of the product or service fails to fully perform by the end of the extended time period, the non-breaching party can declare it void and cancel the contract.

The framework of contract law in civil law countries encourages the parties to work through their differences and to use the courts only as a last recourse. Contract law in common law countries is less concerned with performance and more focused on obtaining damages for non-performance through the court systems.

The legal significance of pre-contractual negotiations can vary greatly among countries. Common law countries generally follow the concept of *caveat emptor*. Rooted in Roman antiquity, it generally applies in pre-contractual negotiations as a warning that the other party may bargain fairly yet not disclose information that may cause the unwary to be misled.

In contract negotiations, the parties and their lawyers often develop a formal contract through several informal meetings as well as drafts of contracts circulated on various aspects of the contractual relationship. The courts in most common law countries, including the U.S. and the U.K., will not impose any pre-contractual liability stemming from the negotiations, based on the doctrine of "freedom of negotiation." Thus, unless a party intentionally misleads another, so as to give rise to tortuous conduct, courts generally refuse to find pre-contractual liability arising from failed negotiations.

## Fault in Negotiating

*Caveat emptor* may conflict with civil law notions of fair dealing and *culpa in contrahendo* ("fault in negotiating"). Many civil law countries impose an overall duty to negotiate in good faith once a legally relevant relationship has come into existence. For example, German Civil Law has imposed a duty to disclose essential information for more than a century.

In 1861, the German jurist, von Jhering, advanced the thesis that "damages should be recoverable against the party whose blameworthy conduct during negotiations for a contract brought about its invalidity or prevented its perfection" (Kessler and Fine, 1964). Taken from the German common law, this doctrine was codified in the German Civil Code and later engrafted into the civil law codes of several other countries.

By illustration, suppose a seller arranges with a prospective purchaser for an inspection of a commercial property site. The purchaser assembles staff from around the globe to join the inspection team, and lawyers are asked to begin due diligence inquiries for the purchase. At the same time, the seller has been negotiating with a third party. Without notice to the prospective purchaser, the property is sold, and the purchaser, having assembled staff and background information about the property, makes the trip in vain. In many civil law countries, the doctrine of *culpa in contrahendo* would impose liability on the party who failed to discharge his or her duty to inform. In most common law countries, while the seller's acts might be ethically defective, the prospective purchaser would be left with no recourse at law as no contractual relationship existed.

## CHOICE OF LAW AND FREE TRADE

Growth in free trade rests in part upon contractual stability. Most international contracts provide either for a certain nation's law to apply (i.e., a **choice of law provision**) or for an arbitral procedure to control dispute resolution. In that way, the parties can be better assured that national differences related to civil codes and common law traditions will be orderly resolved. Multinational corporations thus need to be aware that legal systems reflect cultural differences and that careful planning is required to minimize the effects of these differences to ongoing business relationships.

Risk can be comprehensively studied within its legal context. The legal environment for risk and insurance internationally seems destined to become more rather than less important with continuing globalization. An understanding of legal differences and their motivations will be important to successful international risk management. An understanding also should prove increasingly useful to policymakers as they consider how best to structure or modify legal systems that maintain order and define property rights.

## DISCUSSION QUESTIONS

1. What is the fundamental difference between civil law and common law?
2. Why are tort costs in the U.S. (as a percentage of GDP) significantly higher than in the other industrialized nations of the world?
3. Give several reasons why manufacturers of products sold in Japan have had little need for product liability insurance in the past. What effect on product liability insurance demand would you expect a high export volume to have?
4. Distinguish between the contract concepts of "*caveat emptor*" and "*culpa in contrahendo*." Do you believe that these concepts also should apply to contracts of financial services (e.g., insurance) (a) between individuals and insurers and (b) between large corporations as insureds and insurance companies?
5. Do you agree or disagree with the following proposition: "With increasing globalization, national legal systems will converge." Explain your reasoning.

# NOTES

1. This chapter draws from Tract et al. (1998).
2. With the introduction of the graduate law school system followed by government approval of almost 100 law schools, the institute expects to train a much greater pool of new lawyers and judges.
3. The annual average growth rate of GDP in the U.S. was 7.1 percent during the same period (Towers Perrin-Tillinghast, 2006).
4. Refer, for example, to cases such as *Garmon versus Cincinnati, Inc.* (1993) and *Hurt versus Coyne Cylinder Company* (1992).
5. The revised directive continues to define "producers" so as not to include "manufacturers, distributors, and sellers" that are not established within the E.U. market. Nevertheless, it contains several provisions that directly or indirectly affect the way non-E.U. producers conduct business in the E.U. markets.
6. Minor variations exist. In Manitoba, for example, the payment for property damage may be capped at C$20,000 when a claim involving bodily injury and property damage reaches the liability limit of C$200,000.
7. An important factor in the U.S. that resulted in the introduction of no-fault insurance was the increasing number of civil suits and subsequent long delays in court decisions.
8. For this reason, some professionals also call it "reverse liability." Personal injury protection (PIP) is another term referring to no-fault insurance in some jurisdictions.

# REFERENCES

Beatly, A., Gron, A. and Jorgensen, B. (2005). "Corporate Risk Management: Evidence from Product Liability." *Journal of Financial Intermediation*, 14: 152–178.

Berat, L. (1992). "The Role of Conciliation in the Japanese Legal System." *American University Journal of International Law and Policy*, 8: 125–154.

Guy Carpenter (2003). *Casualty Specialty Update* (September). New York: Marsh & McLennan.

Kessler, Friedrich and Edith Fine (1964). "Culpa in Contrahendo, Bargaining in Good Faith, and Freedom of Contract: A Comparative Study," Harrard Law Review, Vol. 77.

LexisNexis (2005). "No Fault and Uninsured Motorists," in *No-Fault and Uninsured Motorist Automobile Insurance*, Vol. 1. Newark, NJ: Mattew Bender & Company.

Nonlife Insurance Institute of Japan (2005). *Automobile Insurance in Japan*. Tokyo: Nonlife Insurance Institute of Japan.

Objective 17 (1977). "Restatement of the Objectives and Principles of a Community Environment Policy." *Official Journal of the European Communities* (C139).

Ogolla, B.D. (1995). "Environmental Law in Africa: Status and Trends." *International Business Lawyer*, October: 412–478.

Tract, M.M., Tenney, J.P. and Oakley III, E.F. (1998). "The Legal Environment for Risk and Insurance," Chapter 9, in H.D. Skipper, ed., *International Risk and Insurance: An Environmental–Managerial Approach*. Boston, MA: McGraw-Hill.

Towers Perrin Tilling hast (2006). *U.S. Tort Costs and Cross-Border perspectives: 2005 Updates*. New York: Towers Perrin Tinninghast.

# Chapter 11

# Sociocultural Effects on Risk Management

As Chapter 2 made clear, analysis of attitudes toward risks is a key element in modern risk management. We use various statistical, financial and other scientific approaches to better understand risk. However, humans manage risks in countless ways that have little to do with formal risk management approaches and institutions. Customary behaviors, societal values, and human beliefs greatly affect the way we view and manage risks. These behaviors, values, and beliefs flow from culture. This chapter examines risk management in a sociocultural context, with particular reference to informal means of treating risk.[1]

## THE INTERSECTION OF CULTURE AND RISK MANAGEMENT

Culture has a profound, if little acknowledged and often poorly understood, affect on risk perceptions and, therefore, on how families, groups and entire societies manage the risks that they face. This section examines the intersection between culture and risk management by highlighting how the common elements that define a culture mitigate or otherwise affect risk.

### The Nature of Culture

We understand our own culture only in comparison with other cultures. **Culture** may be defined as the customary ways of thinking and behaving of a particular population or society (Ember and Ember, 1996). Culture refers to knowledge and values shared within a society. It offers a mental map for appropriate behavior within a society. Indeed, one cannot truly understand a part of society or culture without reference to the whole.

Whenever people share common values, beliefs, history and a similar view of the outside world and their place within that world, the group makes up a distinct culture. We learn culture through the process of **socialization** by which we indoctrinate children with their group's culture. In this way, a society's culture is conveyed from one generation to the next. This socialization process shapes every human's emotions, opinions and actions.

Simultaneously, nothing humans do or think is free of cultural influences. Culture is dynamic and ever changing.

Culture has both visible and invisible dimensions. The visible aspects are obvious. They include things such as food, music, literature, ways of greeting and saying goodbye, customs and rituals.

The invisible dimensions are equally important, but more difficult to discern. For example, consider how different peoples view time. A recent harmful event is more likely to influence the risk perception of individuals than one that occurred long ago. Some cultures even discourage discussions of past harmful events, with the idea that people can more quickly forget them. In other cultures, such past trials are kept alive through stories and second-guessing. In this way, culture helps shape the society's risk perceptions from a time standpoint.

## Gender

Sex is an individual's biological maleness or femaleness. The cultural role that societies attach to each sex is known as **gender**. The ability to give birth is a sexual trait of females. A "mothering" or nurturing behavior is a female gender role. Gender roles are diverse cross-culturally.

Most societies exhibit a **gender hierarchy**, which means that *traits* associated with males – although not necessarily male – are valued over *traits* associated with females. To succeed in U.S. business, for example, women often believe that they must adopt a more direct means of communication because directness in speech, associated with maleness, is considered superior. Gender hierarchy is often associated with patriarchy, a situation in which men control political and social power. Most societies are patriarchal.

Gender roles can play an important part in risk perception and management. In several Asian countries (e.g., Japan and Korea), household finances have traditionally been the female's responsibility. If the household is to purchase insurance, the agent must convince the female of its merit. In many African societies, the husband has sole responsibility to provide for the family. Therefore, it would be disconcerting to all household members if the wife were to purchase life insurance naming the husband or children as beneficiaries. This would be interpreted as a reversal of roles and an admission of the man's inability to perform his expected role in the family.

## Language and Communication

Individuals transmit information and share their ideas, hopes, aspirations and experiences through language. It negotiates relationships. Haviland (1990) defines **language** as a system of communication using sounds put together according to a set of rules. Of the 6,800 languages spoken in the world, only 2,200 have writing systems; none relies on more than 50 sounds.

Table 11.1 shows that more individuals speak Chinese – Mandarin, Cantonese and scores of other dialects – than any other languages worldwide, with English being the second most common. English, however, is the official language of more countries (58) than any other languages, with French second (32). Also, English is the most common business language worldwide, with it often being the *lingua franca* – a language used for communication not native to any of the speakers.

**Table 11.1**   World's Major Languages

| Language | Speakers (in Millions) | Official Language in | Official Language of the United Nations? |
|---|---|---|---|
| Chinese | 1,200+ | China, Taiwan, Singapore | Yes |
| English | 500+ | 58 countries | Yes |
| Hindi | 430+ | India | |
| Spanish | 300+ | 21 countries | Yes |
| Malay-Indonesian | 300+ | Malaysia, Indonesia | |
| Arabic | 250+ | 25 countries | |
| Portuguese | 170+ | 7 countries | |
| Russian | 130+ | Russia and Belarus | Yes |
| Japanese | 125+ | Japan | |
| Bengali | 120+ | Bangladesh | |
| German | 115+ | 6 European countries (Germany, Austria, Switzerland, Luxembourg, Liechtenstein and Belgium) | |
| French | 80+ | 32 countries | Yes |

*Source*: Various (2004).

## Language and misunderstandings

Opportunities abound for cross-cultural miscommunication and, thereby, misunderstandings that can have substantial adverse operational risk effects. Translations from one language to another sometimes are direct and positive, and sometimes not. PepsiCo did not understand why its "7-Up" brand soft drink did not sell in Shanghai until someone discovered that, in the local dialect, the phrase meant "death by drinking." After disappointing sales results, Chevrolet changed the name of its Nova automobile in Latin America after it discovered Nova means "no go" (*no va*) when pronounced in Spanish.

Some societies (e.g., the U.S.) value directness ("say what you mean") in language, whereas others consider such directness crude and insensitive (e.g., France, Japan, Korea, Singapore and Taiwan). Identical words in different languages often have completely different meanings (e.g., *gift* in German means poison). Even identical words in a single language spoken by different societies may have different meanings. For example, English can be classified into almost 20 versions including Australian English, American English, British English, Canadian English, Jamaican English and South African English. Indeed, two Australians might carry on a conversation using sports and warfare terminology, slang, idioms and acronyms, and persons from another English-speaking society might not understand them. Written languages also reveal how members position themselves within the society. By way of illustration, postal addresses in many Asian cultures are written in this order: country, province city, street, last name and first name whereas in North America, addresses are written in the reverse order.

## Indirect communication

Communication also occurs through paralanguage and kinesics. Haviland (1990) defines **paralanguage** as the system of extra linguistic noises that accompany language, such as voice qualities (e.g., pitch, rhythm and loudness) and vocalizations (e.g., laughing and crying). **Kinesics**, commonly known as "body language," is the system of postures, facial expressions and body motions that convey messages. Paralanguage and kinesics often convey stronger messages than the language that they accompany.

Great similarities and differences exist worldwide in indirect communication. The facial expressions of crying, laughing, smiling and anger are similar worldwide. Leg crossing is acceptable in North America but offensive in many Arab cultures. The "okay" sign made with thumb and index finger forming a circle is positive in much of Europe and North America but obscene in many Latin American countries.

Observable differences are a result of sociocultural patterns. Interpretation is even more complex. Speaking of death is avoided in many cultures, especially Asian and African societies, thus requiring use of euphemisms. To speak of the possibility of death is to increase its likelihood in those societies. For example, an African insurance agent might say, "Let us assume that your enemy dies at an early age," to explain the benefit of life insurance. In several Asian countries, the savings aspects of life insurance are emphasized over the death-protection component in part for the same reason.

## Ethnocentrism and Cultural Relativism

**Cultural relativism** holds that each culture should be examined using its own standards and value system, not that of the observer. The opposite view, held within the internal value system of all cultures, is **ethnocentrism** – the view that one's own culture is superior to others and one judges other cultures by the standards of one's own. Every human is ethnocentric to some degree. The greater a person's international exposure, the less ethnocentric he or she is likely to be. Ethnocentrism is powerful, having been implicated in activities as diverse as ethnic conflict, war, consumer choice and voting (Axelrod and Hammond, 2003).

Both cultural relativism and ethnocentrism represent extreme viewpoints. Generally, cultural relativism is preferable. This generalization is not invariably true, especially for decisions involving negative externalities. For example, a high level of environmental pollution may be acceptable in a society, but most observers would argue that global firms should not plead cultural relativism to justify polluting a society's rivers. In the absence of ethical dilemmas such as this, cultural relativism ("when in Rome, do as the Romans do") is usually the preferred protocol in business and other activities.

Some nations' business communities seem to have more cross-cultural sensitivity than others. U.S. citizens are often accused of being particularly ethnocentric. This ethnocentrism may be interpreted as rudeness. As Maddox (1993) observed: "[U.S. citizens] have traditionally exhibited a stubbornly simple strategy when traveling abroad. That strategy is to go anywhere and act as if they are at home. . . . Americans tend to believe that everybody is like them." Insight 11.1 highlights how ethnocentrism can be costly.

Ethnocentrism can lead to failure in cross-cultural communication and business. Multinational firms contend that they cannot practice complete cultural relativism in all operations. If each foreign unit of a firm operated autonomously, it would forego economies of scale that flow from a unified international operation. Also, it presumably would forego certain other economic efficiencies because of the difficulty in adopting innovative managerial, marketing, product development and other approaches that flow from international operations. From a business point of view, attempts at complete adaptation could prove as costly as a failure to adapt.

---

### INSIGHT 11.1: ETHNOCENTRISM CAN BE COSTLY ───────

An American firm was attempting to reach an acceptable price for its products with a large Japanese buyer. After a lengthy and very thorough sales presentation, the American concluded by offering what he felt was a fair price. The Japanese buyers followed with silence. After several moments, the American anticipating rejection, said that he could perhaps cut the price a little more, and offered a second price. More silence followed. Exasperated, the visiting businessman said that he could make a final offer of his very lowest price. After a brief silence, the Japanese agreed to accept the price. One of the Japanese buyers later related that the first price offered was within an acceptable range for them. It was, however, their custom to consider the proposal silently before reaching and announcing their decision. The American businessman, automatically responding in a manner appropriate for his own culture, believed that silence meant an unacceptable price had been tendered and countered. . . . Believing that the Japanese were like him, the Americans were much less successful than they could have been.
*Source*: Maddox (1993).

---

## Morals and Ethics

Every culture seeks to maintain order and resolve conflicts through codes of social behavior. Some codes are in writing and set out broad ethical and moral standards of behavior (e.g., the Bible), while others are more detailed (e.g., the Qur'an). Such codes are subject to varying interpretations across cultures and over time. Other codes are unwritten. Both written and unwritten codes are part of each person's socialization.

Knowledge of cross-cultural variations in moral and ethical precepts is fundamental to international understanding, especially in business in general and risk management in particular. **Morals** are concerned with what individuals ought to do, with that which is fundamentally right and wrong in the society. It is a normative concept. **Ethics** are the rules that guide behavior and flow from adherence to moral precepts. It is a positive concept. Hence, ethics is the practice of morals. "Ethical behavior" represents behavior close to the moral norm; "unethical behavior" is far removed. Sound corporate governance and ethical guidelines represent businesses attempt to achieve the moral norm.

Philosophers and theologians have evolved many moral and ethical theories, two main schools of which predominate. **Moral relativists** claim that no universal standard of right or wrong exists. The customs, practices and mores of each social group are the appropriate criteria for judging right and wrong for members of that group. **Moral absolutists**, by contrast, argue for the existence of a single universal moral standard for judging ethical behavior. This view holds that what is good in one setting cannot be bad in another.

Internal conflict arises when individuals are placed in situations where a group's morals differ from their own. The greater the cultural distance between one group and another, the greater the likelihood for conflict. Such situations are not uncommon in international business.

Moral relativism and absolutism represent extreme viewpoints. A multinational corporation (MNC) adhering to moral relativist precepts might conclude that employee safety or environmental standards compatible with local requirements were ethical, even if inferior to the more rigorous standards of its home country. By contrast, moral absolutists presumably would be prone to adopt universal employee safety and environmental standards. Such behavior could be beneficial or could result in inferior safety and environmental practices. However, the moral absolutist's ethnocentric approach might result in a loss of business as locals perceived it as promoting unacceptable morals.

The United Nations Conference on Trade and Development (UNCTAD), in its *World Investment Report* (2004), notes that ". . . many services are embedded in the social, cultural and political fabric of societies. . . ." Thus, the challenge facing MNCs is how to be culturally sensitive without using cultural relativism as a crutch for inferior treatment of employees and the environment in the countries of operation. Many MNCs have been criticized for their ethnocentric tendencies flowing from heavy reliance on central office directives. Understandably, MNCs wish to maintain a unified corporate identity built on their own corporate culture. However, by drawing on more globally diverse experiences, these internal norms may come closer to matching external public expectations regarding how corporations should behave in local markets.

The UNCTAD further observes that no single social contract defines comprehensively social responsibilities of global firms. However, societal expectations do extend to MNCs' conduct outside the boundary of a single society. A variety of international guidelines promote standards of good corporate conduct. Examples of relevant intergovernmental instruments are the International Labor Organization's *Tripartite Declaration of Principles Concerning Multinational Enterprises and Social Policy* (1977) and the OECD *Guidelines for Multinational Enterprises* (2000).

Let us discuss this issue using an example – the payment of bribes. In several societies, bribes are the means of ensuring that work is done and may be needed to secure government permissions (see Insight 11.2). If bribes are part of a culture's way of doing business, should a global firm that finds such payments inconsistent with its own values nonetheless make them; that is, should the firm adopt a cultural relativist approach? Although no universal answer exists, we know that bribing can be a negative externality. As a means to discourage bribery, the OECD adopted the *Convention on Combating Bribery of Foreign Public Officials in International Business Transactions* in 1997 (see Insight 11.3).

# CULTURE AND INFORMAL RISK MANAGEMENT ARRANGEMENTS

What shapes risk and security perception in society depends on the degree of certainty that attaches to the means by which individuals and families obtain life's necessities. Throughout history and across sociocultural systems, humans always have sought ways of coping with uncertainty. In the great majority of countries, formal private and public risk management mechanisms – including insurance – have evolved in response to this need for security. Several chapters of this book document these formal means. The focus here is primarily on the less formal means.

## INSIGHT 11.2: BRIBES AND REBATES AS PRICE ADJUSTMENT MECHANISMS

Bribes ("facilitation payments") are sometimes a market's response to forced under-pricing. Thus, if government employee wages are below their market value (the price of labor), citizens may consider an *ex gratia* payment to the government employee by those seeking the employee's approval or service (e.g., water service connection or the granting of a business license) as an appropriate means by which the underpaid civil servant receives compensation closer to his or her true market value. Similarly, government-mandated underpricing of loans (i.e., below market interest rates), insurance or other financial services can result in the applicant being expected to somehow make good the difference between the market and actual prices through special "under-the-table" (also called "gray income" or "red envelope") payments or through the purchase of other services whose actual prices may be above market.

In the other direction, **rebates** – payments by the seller to the buyer to induce purchase – are often the market's response to forced overpricing. Thus, if governments mandate the use of excessive, fixed insurance prices, the policy creates incentives for buyers and sellers to lower prices. In many societies, the seller (often through the agent or broker) accomplishes price lowering by illegally rebating part of the premium to the customer. Countries that allow markets to set prices generally experience lower incidences of bribery and rebates.

## INSIGHT 11.3: OECD CONVENTION ON COMBATING BRIBERY OF FOREIGN PUBLIC OFFICIALS IN INTERNATIONAL BUSINESS TRANSACTIONS

Adopted in 1997, this version of the convention declared offering and giving bribes to foreign officials a criminal act. However, it did not deal with bribery of private sector persons or political party representatives. Neither did it criminalize acts of soliciting or receiving bribes. The revised version of the convention (adopted in 2001) attempts to correct these loopholes. All OECD member countries, which account for more than 70 percent of global exports and more than 90 percent of foreign direct investments, participate in the convention.

Prior to the adoption of the convention, the U.S. was the only country with a strong anti-corruption law through its *Foreign Corruption Practices Act*. This law prohibits U.S. corporations from paying bribes to win business. Violation of the law can result in multimillion dollar fines. The U.S. government revised the act and introduced the *International Anti-Bribery and Fair Competition Act* of 1998 mainly to accommodate the OECD convention.

## Making a Living

Obviously, what one does to make a living is fundamental to the security of his or her family. Other things being the same, the higher and more secure the income (whether in the form of money earnings or implicit income), the greater is family security. People can collect that which they need from nature, they can produce them, or they can obtain them from others. We cover each below.

### *Foraging*

Foraging has been the subsistence pattern for the vast majority of the time humans have existed. By relying on hunting, fishing and gathering, and by being highly mobile, adherents diversify their principal loss exposure (i.e., famine). They accumulate little material wealth because of their need to be highly mobile and because of a strong emphasis on family and social life. So loss or destruction of any material items becomes correspondingly less important. As collected food is usually a communal good, the group provides help to those unable to take care of themselves.

### *Production*

With the development of knowledge, humans began to produce goods. **Production** refers to the use of labor, technology and some combination of land, raw materials and capital to produce the goods and services that a society wants. Production methods range from simple to complex in terms of the technology used. Production processes can be classified into:

- **Horticulture**, the simplest form of food production, involves the planting of food using simple tools and human labor. Horticulture usually provides a less secure means of subsistence than foraging, as the food sources are more susceptible to droughts, flooding and other natural calamities. Nonetheless, it allows for greater material accumulation.

- **Pastoralism** is a nomadic subsistence pattern based on herding animals. Some risk diversification is achieved through a willingness to move homes and herds in search of more favorable conditions for animals. Some nomadic ethnic groups still can be found in Africa, Asia and Latin America.

- **Agriculture** is the systematic, large-scale production of food through use of the plow. By revolutionizing agricultural production, the plow altered societies worldwide. It allowed economies of scale in food production, resulting in greater surpluses for exchange and accumulation. It ushered in greater demand for material goods and services. Economists contend that the production of goods and services has grown in importance and with it have arisen ever larger mining, manufacturing and commercial enterprises. Business and employment specialization become even more important, thus rendering individuals more reliant on trade to obtain the necessities that they and their families no longer produce themselves. However, specialization implies vulnerability as well.

- **Industrialization** is the production of goods and services via manufacturing. With industrialization comes urbanization. Villages become towns, and towns become cities. Urbanization brings a new social order. The predominant economic and social security formerly provided by family, friends and acquaintances is supplanted to varying degrees by formal public and private arrangements. Industrialization created a need for greater financial self-reliance. Greater formality, clear and enforceable rules and bureaucracy follow. Simultaneously, the adverse consequences of damage to or the destruction of property or the loss of one's health, job or life are often magnified.

### *Distribution*

**Distribution** refers to the ways that a society allocates its goods and services. Models of distribution can be broadly classified into (1) market exchange, (2) reciprocity and (3) redistribution. Each of these is discussed below.

#### *Market exchange*

The underlying philosophy of **market exchange** is that the forces of supply and demand set the conditions of exchange (either through barter or explicit prices) of goods and services. In a predominantly market economy, individuals and families obtain formal economic security mostly from government and specialized suppliers such as insurers, pension funds, banks and the like. Market forces set the price.

#### *Reciprocity*

All societies practice reciprocity. **Reciprocity** is the mutual exchange of goods or services usually as gifts. Reciprocity can be balanced, generalized or negative. **Balanced reciprocity** involves the immediate giving and receiving of goods or services of approximately equal value.

   **Generalized reciprocity** involves the giving and receiving of goods or services where neither the timing nor the value of the exchange is specified. Generalized reciprocity is perhaps the oldest form of risk sharing. A common practice in many countries is to offer household goods, services or shelter to family members or friends whose house is destroyed – for they would do the same were the circumstances reversed. We can think of cooperative and mutual insurance organizations as formalized mechanisms for generalized reciprocity.

   **Negative reciprocity** occurs when the giver attempts to obtain an advantage from an exchange. This advantage may flow from withholding key information about the exchanged items, such as that which occurs with deception, guile and even cheating. Extreme forms include stealing, raiding and appropriation.

#### *Redistribution*

**Redistribution** involves a particular individual or group collecting goods (assets) from selected members of society and redistributing them to other members. Wage earners of the same household may pool their earnings to be redistributed among family members. In pre-state societies (and in many societies today), the chief or other group leader would perform this function. In most contemporary societies, governments perform this redistribution function through the tax system. Redistribution in this sense can be a formalized means of providing for the less fortunate in a society.

## Groups and Social Organization

Cooperation has been and remains fundamental to human survival and prosperity.[2] The organization of groups is basic to effective cooperation. The group may be a family, a clan or a multibillion dollar corporation. Groups have been the primary source of physical, emotional and economic security since the beginning of humankind. We discuss two of the basic forms: (1) households and (2) marriages.

### *Households*

The building block of all human societies is the **household**, defined by Haviland (1990) as ". . . the basic residential unit within which economic production, consumption, inheritance, child rearing and shelter are organized and carried out. . . ." Families form the core of most households worldwide. The nuclear family, consisting of husband, wife and dependent children, is perhaps the most familiar. In an earlier, more agrarian era in Western societies and several areas still in Asia, Africa and Latin America, the **extended family** – consisting of two or more nuclear families plus grandparents and possibly aunts, uncles and cousins – lived and worked together. The extended family is a logical means of providing for the essentials of life and for taking care of the elderly and the incapacitated. Having many children could guarantee necessary labor for the maintenance of family as well as comfort in one's old age.

With industrialization, however, family units became smaller. Whether nuclear or extended, families remain the most fundamental source of physical, emotional and economic security in societies worldwide.

### *Marriages*

Marriage is common in all societies, although with substantial variations in form. Marriage gives each partner access to the labor and labor products of the other, thus enhancing family security. The marriage form determines who has rights to any offspring and how property is distributed. Marriage outside one's own society is sometimes a means of garnering support from another kin group, for example, by adding security against famine, natural disaster or attack. In some societies, remarriage serves as a type of social security. Thus, in societies following the **levirate** custom, if a husband dies leaving a wife and children, a brother of the deceased man may be expected to marry the widow to provide security for her and her children.

In many societies, one or more economic transactions may accompany marriage. The most common such transaction worldwide, and especially prevalent in Africa, Oceania, and South Asia, is **bride price** (or **bride wealth**) wherein the groom or his kin makes a gift of money or goods to the bride's kin. Besides having important symbolic value, bride price can serve as a type of security for the bride. Where the marriage fails through no fault of hers and her kin do not return the bride price, the female may have some additional economic security.

Another economic transaction sometimes accompanying marriage is the **dowry** – payment by the bride's parents of her share of the property that she would have otherwise received on her parents' deaths. Also having potentially important symbolic value, the dowry helps ensure the wife of support in widowhood or after divorce, thus serving as a source of economic security. Both bride price and dowry practices are sometimes abused and can be controversial.

## The Maintenance of Order

Humans require order in their lives. We exhibit a powerful psychological drive to reduce uncertainty and eliminate ambiguity. The creation and interaction of groups inevitably lead to conflicts. Every society, therefore, creates political organizations for resolving conflicts to prevent the breakdown of social order. Religion and magic serve similar functions.

### Political organization

All societies exhibit some form of **political organization** – the means by which a society maintains social order. The forms range from the informal, decentralized approaches followed by bands, tribes and chiefdoms to the formal, centralized approaches characterized by states. All political organizations exercise social control through negative and positive sanctions.

**Positive sanctions** are incentives for social conformity, such as awards, titles and other forms of public recognition. **Negative sanctions** are threats of punishment for failure to follow society's norms, such as fines, imprisonment, corporal punishment and ostracism. The sanctions may be formal or informal. The law is the most commonly recognized formal, negative sanction.

Although anthropologists do not all agree as to the definition of law, they do generally agree that law serves three functions (Haviland, 1990):

- It defines relationships among members of a society, thereby dictating proper behavior under different circumstances.
- It allocates authority to employ coercion in the enforcement of sanctions.
- It redefines social relations and aids its own efficient operation by ensuring room for change.

Modern states distinguish offenses against the state (crimes) from those against a person (torts and contract breaches). Many societies consider all offenses personal. Legal disputes are settled through negotiation and adjudication. Whereas all societies use negotiation, not all use adjudication to the same extent as do Western societies, as discussed in Chapter 10.

Political organizations seek to regulate relations with other political organizations. They resort to force from time to time to resolve disputes between themselves. Historically, an increased likelihood of warfare is associated with increasing centralization of control, as observed in authoritarian governments. Democracies have been less likely to initiate warfare between themselves to resolve disputes.

### Belief systems

Belief systems vary enormously worldwide. Yet, religion is found in all cultures, and magic plays an important role in many. Ember and Ember (1996) define **religion** "as any set of attitudes, beliefs and practices pertaining to supernatural power, whether that power be forces, gods, spirits, ghosts or demons." **Magic** differs from religion in that its adherents believe that they can compel supernatural forces to act in some predictable way. Figure 11.1 shows the distribution of religions by the number of professed adherents worldwide. Almost one-third of the world's population is Christian, with Muslims second at 21 percent and Hindus third at 14 percent.

Most social scientists believe that humans create religions in response to certain universal needs or conditions. Belief systems serve both social and psychological needs. As a social instrument, religion provides society with foundational values and reinforces group norms. It prescribes negative sanctions for inappropriate behavior. As such, religion helps maintain social order.

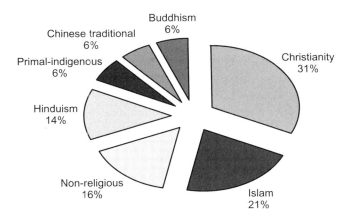

**Figure 11.1**   Major Religions by Number of Adherents. *Source*: © 2005 www.adherents.com

---

## INSIGHT 11.4: VOODOO OR INSURANCE?

Perhaps the most important belief militating against modern insurance in Africa is voodoo, according to Akhigbe (1996). Whereas insurance seeks to indemnify insureds for losses, voodoo claims to prevent the loss event or assist in finding lost items. For example, by allowing a native doctor to pray over your new car and implanting some objects in it, would-be thieves could be transfixed to the car if they attempted to steal it. If you failed originally to seek such protection before they stole your car, a visit to the oracle could help you discover who the thief is and sometimes where the stolen property is located. Why purchase insurance?
*Source*: Akhigbe (1996).

---

As a psychological tool, belief systems explain the unknown and make it understandable. They provide a means of dealing with crises when all temporal explanations fail. Belief systems can have a profound impact on individual risk perception and the means of dealing with it. For example, many conservative and fundamentalist Christian, Buddhist, Hindu and Muslim groups view life in fatalist terms; harmful events are "the will of God." People holding such views may take fewer risk management precautions. Insight 11.5 highlight selected aspects.

Many religions admonish their adherents that they are to assist the less fortunate in society. Indeed, numerous charitable organizations were founded on this principle, which are informal security arrangements.

## Buffering Mechanisms

Many societies continue to rely heavily on informal **buffering mechanisms** – practices designed to reduce consumption or income variability. Buffering mechanisms reduce uncertainty.

## INSIGHT 11.5: THE RELATIONSHIP BETWEEN DEATH AND MONEY

With agricultural and other pre-industrial societies, the economic consequences of the death of a family member were often less urgent than in industrialized societies. The family still had its land, the extended family ensured adequate security, and voluntary or reciprocal associations provided assistance. With industrialization came new death-related businesses. Simple "last requests" and traditional family distribution gave way to highly formalized systems of wills and estate planning.

While industrialization meant that families could enjoy greater income, it also made them more vulnerable because of the disability, unemployment or death of the primary income earner. A secure income stream – money – became more important. Life and health insurance became part of the general movement to formalize the management of death.

Sociology has been criticized for perpetuating a secular and rational image of money without paying due attention to its symbolic and sacred functions. In most societies today, money has both a practical and symbolic relationship with death. The widespread practice of spending large sums of money at times of death testifies to the existence of a powerful and legitimate symbolic association between money and death.

The abhorrence of pauper burials in many societies is another indicator of money's importance at the time of death. It explains, for instance, the popularity of industrial life insurance in the late 19th century in the U.S. and other Western countries.

This dual relationship between money and death – actual and symbolic – is essential to the understanding of the development of life insurance. Its intimacy with death has made life insurance vulnerable to objections based on magical and religious grounds. Many see speculating with the solemn event of death to be a degrading sacrilegious wager, which God would resent and punish as crime. By insuring his life, a man was not only "betting against his God" but, even worse, usurping His divine functions of protection. Because the ultimate function of life insurance is to compensate the widow and orphans for the loss of a husband and father, critics object that this turned man's sacred life into an "article of merchandise."

In many societies, a secret fear is the relationship between insuring ones life and losing ones life. The fear of precipitating death was once among the most common objections to the purchase of life insurance. It remains so in many societies today. Thus, because of its involvement with death, life insurance has been tied to religion, magic and superstition.

*Source*: Adapted from Zelizer (1979), pp. 43–73.

Indeed, the World Bank (1994) estimates that 60 percent of the world's work force and 70 percent of elderly persons rely on them exclusively. Buffering mechanisms differ enormously worldwide, but fall into one of four categories: (1) mobility, (2) diversification, (3) storage and (4) distribution.

Mobility is the simplest mechanism. We observed it with foraging groups that could easily relocate if food were scarce.

Diversification involves a broadening of the subsistence base. Farmers practice diversification when they rotate their crops, plant a greater variety of crops, or disperse their crops geographically. Diversification also occurs when farming households have a member employed in steady wage employment or when a child marries and moves into a geographically remote family. Not relying solely on wages for household support (e.g., growing one's own food) and diversifying the household's economic activities are other examples of income smoothing activity.

Storage can smooth income and consumption. In an economic sense, retirement saving is a contemporary example of storage. Almost all societies practice physical or financial storage or both. Credit – negative storage – is important worldwide as a buffering mechanism. Informal credit arrangements include loans from friends, relatives, community members, individual moneylenders and informal banks.

Finally, distribution – market exchange, reciprocity and redistribution – offers common buffering mechanisms. In time of need, a household might exchange its services or material goods for food or needed services. Reciprocity is a time-honored, universal means of dealing with security. Some researchers suggest that reciprocity lies at the core of the origins of human culture.

Redistribution is common, especially in Africa, Asia and Latin America. Parental support of young children is, of course, an example of redistribution but also is a type of storage in that investment in a child's education can ultimately benefit the aged parent. Indeed, in Hindu, Muslim and many other religions, children are responsible for supporting their elderly parents. Thus, three-quarters of the old in most Asian developing countries live with their children (World Bank, 1994). Rotating savings and credit associations, common in countries with underdeveloped financial systems, are contemporary examples of redistribution or balanced reciprocity over time (see Insight 11.6).

## Evaluation of Informal Insurance Systems

Informal insurance arrangements remain the mainstay in most developing countries and are important in developed countries. Informal arrangements function by pooling work opportunities, income and risk of all members of the extended family or group and by solving the information problems that plague more formal systems.

Informal insurance arrangements offer several potential advantages over formal ones. They reduce adverse selection and moral hazard problems. For example, market-based formal insurance arrangements require voluntary participation. These arrangements can break down or impose high costs on insureds because of adverse selection and moral hazard. Under informal insurance arrangements, participants (e.g., family members) often have little choice as to whether they will opt in (or out) of the arrangement, thus minimizing the adverse selection problem. Moral hazard is less of a problem as, for example, knowledgeable relatives can easily distinguish whether an illness, disability or any other adverse outcome is real or feigned. By pooling their risks, families can adjust to unforeseen outcomes in flexible ways, in contrast to formal arrangements in which every contingency cannot be anticipated.

Informal arrangements also can realize cost savings compared with formal ones. Disabled or elderly members usually can perform some light, but useful, household activities such as cooking and taking care of young children. Their contribution frees other members to undertake more demanding tasks. Also, because the care of the elderly or the disabled is

## INSIGHT 11.6: ROTATING SAVINGS AND CREDIT ASSOCIATIONS

A rotating savings and credit association (ROSCA) is "an association formed by a core of participants who agree to make regular contributions to a fund given, in whole or in part, to each contributor in rotation" (Ardener, 1964). ROSCAs are found on every continent and are particularly important in many Asian and African developing economies including *Chit Funds* in India, *Susu* in Ghana and Gambia, and *tontines* in Senegal. ROSCAs are also found in economically developed Asian countries. *Hui* in Taiwan and *Kye* in Korea are two such examples.

ROSCAs are based on mutual trust among participants where members contribute an agreed-upon amount to a central fund. At a predetermined time (e.g., on the first of each month), the fund balance is given to a member. All members replenish the fund during the next period, with another member receiving the balance. The process continues until each member has received the fund balance. As such, ROSCAs are not formal financial institutions and may last through only a single cycle.

ROSCAs assist in small-scale capital formation, usually to purchase durable goods. The order in which the fund balance is distributed may be determined by the group itself, by the organizer, by criteria such as age or seniority, or by random drawing. In many ROSCAs, order is determined or at least influenced by need. Some associations allocate the fund by auction. Thus, the pot may go to the member who pledges to make the highest contributions during the next period or who agrees to make the highest one-time side payments to other ROSCA members. Another approach is to grant the fund to the member who is willing to accept the lowest amount from the fund. With each auction approach, members who are willing to delay their accepting the fund, in effect, receive interest. With many associations, a member who urgently needs cash may pledge his or her right to the fund to another to secure a loan.

ROSCAs work because of the enormous public pressure that exists on all members to meet their obligations. ROSCAs are a type of informal insurance arrangement when the order of allocation is determined on compassionate grounds or on bidding. They represent an almost universal, simple means of accumulating savings and providing a measure of economic security. Akhigbe (1996) observed that competition from ROSCAs is one reason for the low sales of life insurance in Africa.

within the household, caretakers often can undertake other activities, thus reducing the opportunity costs of care.

Disadvantages also exist. A very harmful event for which a person (family) is in need of assistance can afflict the entire family (village). This can leave no one capable of rendering the needed assistance. In other words, risk pooling can break down because of a lack of independence. Another disadvantage is that certain cultural or legal norms can render some members of society particularly vulnerable under informal arrangements. With the demise of the extended family as a major source of security in many countries, the elderly may enjoy less support from their families. Women, in particular, are vulnerable to income insecurity in many cultures, as Insight 11.7 highlights.

## INSIGHT 11.7: INDIA: AN EXAMPLE OF WOMEN'S VULNERABILITY IN INFORMAL SYSTEMS

Throughout South Asia (mainly Bangladesh, India, Nepal Pakistan and Sri Lanka), most old women are widows, and widows are among the poorest of the poor. Informal systems of providing for the old afford little protection for these women. In India, for example, households headed by widows are by far the poorest group, with an average expenditure per person of 70 percent below the national average. Five cultural or legal constraints on widows foster this result:

- their inability to return to the parental home;
- restrictions on remarriage;
- the division of labor by gender, which limits women's opportunities for self-employment and confines them almost entirely to agricultural wage labor;
- restrictions on inheritance, which is patrilineal;
- lack of access to credit.

Despite laws to the contrary, a widow with living sons is rarely able to inherit anything – purportedly to keep her from abandoning her children to marry again. Yet, without inheritance or other property, she lacks the collateral to obtain loans, self-employment is largely infeasible, and the possibility of extreme poverty looms large. Support from sons is the primary means of support.

*Source*: The World Bank (1994), p. 53.

Informal risk-sharing practices seem to be sustainable only in societies where (1) financial institutions and markets are not fully developed or widely accessible and (2) private property rights, especially regarding contracts, are not fully developed and formalized. Indeed, informal insurance arrangements are second-best to formal arrangements. Divergence found from the first-best solution "will be larger in many situations where insurance is badly needed, such as at dates when incomes are generally low, or those at which a few incomes are available, generating high current inequality" (Coate and Ravallion, 1993).

Other research findings are consistent with this theme. For example, one study found that Indian wheat farmers could substantially increase average profits by increasing fertilizer applications but, to hedge against investment losses if their crops failed, they applied less fertilizer than needed (Bliss and Stern, 1982). In another study, Binswanger and Rosenzweig (1993) found that, as a rural environment became riskier, farm households shifted production to more conservative but less profitable modes. Their study findings show that the median household profit reduction was 15 percent and that the bottom quartile saw profits fall by 35 percent while the wealthiest witnessed a negligible effect.

Overall efficiency of informal arrangements suffers compared with formal arrangements. Recall, however, that formal arrangements require a more complete market – that is, developed risk markets and private property law – to function efficiently. Many markets are incomplete. Moreover, while formal arrangements may have efficiency advantages over informal ones (because of scale, scope, and other efficiencies), they seem to fare worse in solving enforcement and information problems. Without informal arrangements, income and consumption smoothing might not take place at all. Evidence from developing countries suggests that households that cannot smooth consumption and income through informal insurance arrangements have suffered from poorer health, higher mortality rates and lower levels of education. It is for these reasons that the World Bank has urged governments to assess carefully when, where and in what form to introduce mandatory formal programs and to adopt measures to maintain – rather than to crowd out – informal systems that may still be functioning reasonably well.

# MICROFINANCE

Most citizens of developed countries take for granted that they can readily secure a panoply of quality financial services – from mortgages, consumer loans, time deposits, mutual funds, and insurance to capital for business funding. These services are more or less priced appropriately, are convenient and are widely available.

## Why the Poor are Badly Served

By contrast, if one is financially poor and lives in a least developing country, his or her access to formal financial services is limited if not completely nonexistent. True, the poor have access formal risk management arrangements, but they suffer various deficiencies, not the least of which is their lack of depth and breadth of services offered.

The causes of the poor not having access to a broad range of financial services are manifold. Certainly, people with little money do not make attractive clients to the typical financial institution. Other, more fundamental reasons also contribute to this failure. Insight 11.8 offers *The Economist*'s summary of these problems.

## Evolving Financial Services Infrastructure

With improvements in technology, more innovation and stronger commitments to find market solutions as well as realization that a substantial pentup demand exists, microfinance is proving to be an important vehicle for servicing the financial service needs of the poor. No consensus exists as to what constitutes microfinance. For discussion purposes, we define **microfinance** as the provision of one or more financial services in small amounts to individuals who have few financial resources and who might otherwise not have access to such services. Microfinance is found most prominently in the provision of credit, but the savings function is evolving rapidly, as is the remittance of funds. We also are witnessing the evolution of microinsurance, although at a modest level to date.

Unsurprisingly, the poor – just like the rich – highly value safe places to keep their money and ways of dealing with risks that they face. Consequently, demand for the services of microfinance institutions is said to be outpacing the growth of more mainstream financial institutions, although collectively the stock of funds involved remains modest by comparison. No one knows how many such institutions exist worldwide, in part because of the problem of definition but also because most such facilities are not and do not wish to be registered with state financial services regulators. For example, according to The Economist (2005), Indonesia claims to have more than 600,000 microfinance institutions of which

INSIGHT 11.8: WHY ARE THE POOR SO BADLY SERVED? ─────

The easy answer, that people who have little money do not make suitable clients for sophisticated financial services, is at most a half-truth. A better explanation is that the poor have been hurt by massive market and regulatory failure. Fortunately that failure can be, and increasingly is being, remedied.

In most developing countries, the barriers to providing financial services for the masses are all too clear. Inflation tends to be high and volatile; government is often incompetent; and the necessary legal framework for financial services is often missing. Property laws can make it impossible for poor borrowers to use assets such as their home as collateral for loans.

Governments in developing countries often impose caps on the interest rates charged on loans for the poor. Despite their popular appeal, such caps undermine the profitability of lending and thus reduce the supply of loans. Incomplete and erratic regulation of financial institutions has also undermined the confidence of the poor in the financial services that are available. When they can find an institution that will accept their tiny deposits, it often lacks the sort of government deposit insurance that is routine in rich countries, so when a bank goes under, savers suffer.

Corruption is also commonplace in many developing countries. A recent study by the World Bank found that in two poor states in India where the financial system is largely controlled by the government, borrowers paid bribes to officials amounting to between 8 and 42 percent of the value of their loans. Corruption raises the cost of every financial transaction, allows undesirable transactions to take place and undermines consumer confidence in the financial system. This, and the related curse of cronyism, explains why access to financial services in countries where the state has control over the financial sector is poorer than where it does not.

But not all the blame goes to poor-country governments. Financial services firms too have failed to do enough to deal with the lack of the sort of data (e.g., about a client's financial history) that are taken for granted in rich-country financial systems, and to find ways of reaping economies of scale. Many have simply dismissed the possibility that serving the poor might be a viable business.

*Source*: *The Economist* (2005), pp. 3–4.

only one-in-ten is recognized by the regulatory authorities. Countries from Bangladesh to Uganda also claim to be home to thousands of such institutions.

## How Microfinance Institutions Operate

*Monte de Piedad* is a pawn shop in Mexico City, established in 1775[3]. According to *The Economist* (2005), it is the oldest financial institution in the Americas. Pawn shops – not always viewed in a favorable light by many individuals, especially the better off financially – have long played a vital financial role in the lives of the less fortunate. They transform physical assets into cash, usually at a time of financial distress for the individual.

Their services, however, suffer three limitations that severely limit their effectiveness toward becoming engines for economic development and betterment. First, they loan money only to those with physical assets. Second, the value of posted collateral determines the amount of the loan, not the worthiness of a business venture. Third, because the collateral is illquid and cannot be made so without selling it, pawn shops cannot turn around and use it – as can financial intermediaries in connection with their financial instruments – to fund business ventures.

Two noteworthy attempts have been made to find alternatives to assist the poor and less fortunate. Many developing countries created state banks, particularly to provide finance to the rural poor. As *The Economist* (2005) observed: "these have mostly been a disaster." The other attempt has proven far more durable. It involves certain organizations offering uncollateralised loans to very poor borrowers in developing countries. One of the first such ventures, by Opportunity International, a nonprofit organization, was started by a businessman in 1971 in Colombia. He was interested to trying to contribute toward irradication of povety at the "grass roots" level. In 1973, another nonprofit organization, ACCION International, made the first of what it called "micro" loans.

Grameen Bank, started in 1976, has become exceptionally successful in offering what it termed "microcredit" to women in small groups. Indeed, so impressive has been the goods works of its founder, Bangladeshi Muhammad Yunus, and the bank that they were awarded the Nobel Peace Prize in 2006 for their efforts toward aiding economic and social development.

With such loans, periods are relatively short such as 12 months or 24 months. The loan is commonly for the recipient to undertake an entrepreneurial project so that he or she can generate wealth and eventually become independent of the microfinancing service. Microfinancing contracts exhibit two unique characteristics. First, micro-loans are uncollateralized, and the borrowers' desire to maintain access to future loans lowers loan default rates. Second, in case of group loans, all participants of the group are jointly liable, and all can be considered in default when any part of the group loan is not repaid.

In the case of Grameen Bank, to qualify customers had to be extremely poor. Of course, such persons are highly unlikely to have much by way of collateral or a credit history – common conditions for larger financial instructions to make loans. To overcome these deficiencies, groupings of borrowers were formed, with members required to monitor each other at weekly meetings. This approach reduced the moral hazard and adverse selection potentials, in the same way that other informal security arrangements do so among families or small community security services. Once loans were repaid, more could be borrowed.

The model is not without its problems. For one, businesses of the individuals in the group grow at different rates and require different amounts of capital. If one owns a fast growing business, the group arrangement might constrain growth prospects. If one owns a slow growing business, the group arrangement might saddle him or her with debts that are larger than the person needs or can use. Also, the requirement to meet regularly proves burdensome. Finally, as group members developed their own credit history, they no longer required the collective guarantee of the group. The result has been a trend toward microfinance institutions offering uncollateralized loans to individuals, not through the group arrangement.

## The Future of Microfinance

To date, results have been encouraging. Many observers have bemoaned the fact that most microfinance institutions seemed to require subsidies from non-profit organizations to be operationally sustainable. They note that microfinance will never extend broadly if it has to rely on charity for its success. It must offer a sustainable profit motive to be successful.

Recently, for-profit institutions have emerged, which are proving capable of sustaining themselves. Additionally, local banks that formerly ignored this market, such as Ecuador's Bank Pichincha and India's ICICI, have entered the market. *The Economist* (2005) notes "even more strikingly, some of the world's biggest and wealthiest banks, including Citigroup, Deutsche Bank, Commerzbank, HSBC, ING and ABN Amro, are dipping their toes into the water."

# RISK PERCEPTION THEORIES AND FORMAL INSURANCE

It is perhaps trite to state that individuals' values and beliefs affect their attitudes about and behavior toward insurance. As suggested earlier, formal and informal insurance arrangements evolve consistent with a society's values and beliefs.

Insurance is an intangible product. People and businesses purchase insurance because they are convinced that some risk warrants foregoing money today for the promise of an uncertain future payment. Insurance is purchased both because the buyer is convinced of the need to purchase it and because the buyer believes that the risk bearer is trustworthy and will be around if a covered loss occurs. Insurance is purchased because it reduces or eliminates uncertainty and, as indicated earlier, humans seem to need to reduce uncertainty. These highly complex dimensions of the insurance purchase naturally vary from culture to culture and from person to person within a given culture.

In this section, we explore the interaction between the psychological and anthropological views of risk and insurance. We build on the discussion in Chapter 4.[5]

## Psychological Risk Perception and Insurance

Economic theory postulates risk aversion. Risk aversion in turn explains why individuals are willing to pay more than the actuarially fair price (i.e., expected value of loss) for insurance. In contrast to psychology, economics has little to say, however, about the components of risk aversion.

Insurers base their premiums on their estimates of the probability and severity of losses, while taking into consideration market conditions and likely overall loss variability. Potential consumers, by contrast, consider these two factors, whether weakly or not, plus a host of others – all influenced by their worldviews that reinforce their cultural biases.

Figure 11.2 illustrates individual risk perceptions following the psychological approach. It provides guidance as to the types of risk for which individuals are more likely to seek loss control, insurance or other risk management techniques.

Consumers consider not only the probability and amount of loss, but also the space and time dimensions, the *catastrophic potential*, and the degree of *personal concern*. As we discussed in Chapter 4, the kind of risk is vitally important in shaping risk perception. *Natural* risks are more acceptable than *technological* risks. We underestimate risks that we *voluntarily* assume and are *controllable*. The importance of risks that are *imposed*, are *uncontrollable*, and carry *unknown* effects is overstated. Hence, individuals tend to underestimate the adverse effects of smoking (voluntary, controllable and known) and overestimate the risk of flying in an airplane (Werner, 1994).

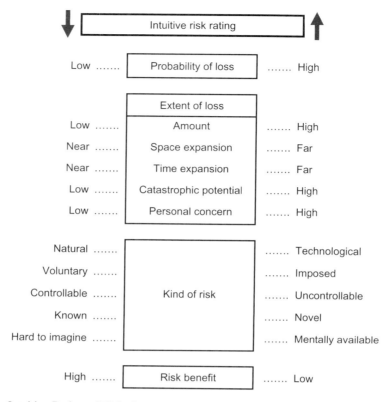

**Figure 11.2**   Intuitive Rating of Risk. *Source*: Werner (1994). Reprinted with permission by the Geneva Association

According to the findings of the psychological risk perception theory, individuals would be more likely to suffer dread and fear of the unknown as we move from the left to the right of Figure 11.2. Individuals are more likely to take ameliorating action (e.g., purchasing insurance) as we move from the left to the right.

## Cultural Risk Perception and Insurance

The anthropological theory of risk perception is, of course, more relevant for decision-making at the group level, including nation-states. Anglo countries such as Australia, Canada, New Zealand, the U.K. and the U.S. tend to be more individualistic, whereas Denmark, Finland, the Netherlands, Norway and Sweden tend to value solidarity more. We also noted that Austria, Germany, Italy and Switzerland are more individualists whereas Belgium, France and Spain "take a middle position." Low-group countries would depend more on the market to deal with risk. High-group countries would expect government to have a larger role in the provision of economic security.

Individuals and businesses in societies that place a greater emphasis on solidarity are less likely to seek legal redress for perceived wrongs. A strong sense of group argues for negotiated, rather than adjudicated solutions and for less need for detailed written contracts such as we find in Japan. The opposite would apply to more individualist societies such as the U.S.

Increasing wealth of a country is associated with movement toward low group. Also, we would expect privatization efforts to appeal more to individualistic social patterns.

Finally, Hofstede (1995) asserts that, with respect to financing the costs of natural disasters, the mutual form of insurance organization would be more readily considered in countries with a collectivist view. Similarly, the notion of compulsory insurance would be more readily accepted in such countries.

## CONCLUSION

Perhaps, most people worldwide believe that the world is getting riskier. Douglas and Wildavsky (1982) have observed that Americans are afraid of "[n]othing much . . . except the food they eat, the water they drink, the air they breathe, the land they live on, and the energy they use." Despite increases in life expectancy, better health and healthcare, decreasing rates of industrial accidents, lower transportation accident rates and a host of other data indicating enhanced safety, the perception is that life is getting riskier. The U.S. is probably one of the most risk conscious cultures in history. The psychological and anthropological theories of risk perception give insight into this paradox.

Nonetheless, our understanding of the impact of culture on risk perception, decision-making and insurance remains rudimentary. Economics provides a robust theory that informs each of these areas, but, until recently, economists rarely have taken note of the theories and research of the other social sciences and vice versa. No doubt, the risk problems that each social science chooses to explore are themselves defined and dissected with the discipline's cultural biases and are themselves structured to support that discipline's "way of life." This state of affairs is unfortunate because the issues confronting contemporary humans present a potential for harm unparalleled in human history: environmental pollution; the possibilities of nuclear, chemical or biological accidents or warfare; global warming; and other potential disasters.

Political trends globally show that governments are allowing greater freedom in individual decision-making and relying more on markets to allocate societal resources. Economists applaud these moves as providing the possibility of greater consumer choice and freedom, thus offering the possibility of enhancing social welfare. Freedom of choice is a basic tenet of a free society, provided that choice does not impose significant costs on others. Increasingly, however, individual and business choices carry externalities whose potential for widespread harm is unprecedented. In such situations, complete freedom of choice must give way to higher-order concerns. Decisions about appropriate public policy responses cannot be left to atomized individuals and businesses or to the experts only. The social sciences offer potentially great assistance in satisfactorily resolving these issues.

## DISCUSSION QUESTIONS

1.  "Bribes are always inappropriate." Do you agree or disagree? Justify your answer.
2.  Why is an understanding of how individuals perceive risk important? To whom is it important?
3.  Why is an understanding of how groups perceive risk important? To whom is it important?

4. Locate at least three sentences or concepts found in this book that suggest an ethnocentric orientation by the authors. How would you change the presentation to be less ethnocentric?
5. Would you expect to find differences in the demand for life insurance between societies that are primarily individualist versus egalitarian? What about between individualists versus hierarchists? Explain your rationale.

## NOTES

1. This chapter draws from Skipper and Skipper (1998).
2. This section draws from Haviland (1990), Chapters 8–11.
3. This discussion draws heavily from *The Economist* (2005), pp. 4–6.
4. The Grameen Bank and its founder, Muhamad Yunus, were jointly awarded the Nobel Peace Prize in 2006.
5. We omit discussion of the interaction between the economic views of risk and insurance, as this was covered in detail in Chapter 2.
6. This discussion draws heavily from The Economist (2005), pp. 4-6.

## REFERENCES

Ardener, S. (1964). "The Comparative Study of Rotating Credit Associations." *Journal of the Royal Anthropological Institute of Great Britain and Ireland*. 94(2), 201–229.

Akhigbe, A. (1996). "The Effect of African Culture on the Demand for Insurance." Unpublished.

Axelrod, R. and Hammond, R. (2003). "The Evolution of Ethnocentric Behavior." *Midwest Political Science Convention*, April 3–16, Chicago, IL.

Binswanger, H. and Rosenzweig, M. (1993). "Wealth, Weather Risk and the Composition and Profitability of Agricultural Investments." *Economic Journal*, 103: 56–78.

Bliss, C.J. and Stern, N.H. (1982). *Palanpur: The Economy of an Indian Village*. Oxford: Clarendon Press.

Coate, S. and Ravallion, M. (1993). "Reciprocity without Commitment: Characterization and Performance of Informal Insurance Arrangement." *Journal of Development Economics*, 40: 1–24.

Douglas, M. and Wildavsky, A. (1982). *Risk and Culture: An Essay on the Selection of Technological and Environmental Dangers*. Berkeley, CA: University of California Press.

*The Economist* (2005). "The Hidden Wealth of the Poor: A Survey of Microfinance." *The Economist*, 377 (November 5): 3–6.

Ember, C.R. and Ember, M. (1996). *Cultural Anthropology*, 8th edn. Upper Saddle River, NJ: Prentice Hall.

Haviland, W.A. (1990). *Cultural Anthropology*, 6th edn. Fort Worth, TX: Holt, Rinehart and Winston.

Hofstede, G. (1995). "Insurance as a Product of National Values." *The Geneva Papers on Risk and Insurance*, 20: 423–429.

Maddox, R.C. (1993). *Cross-Cultural Problems in International Business*. Westport, CT: Quorum Books.

Skipper, H.D. and Skipper, T. (1998). "The Sociocultural Environment for Risk and Insurance," Chapter 6, in H.D. Skipper, ed., *International Risk and Insurance: An Environmental-Managerial Approach*. Boston, MA: Irwin/McGraw-Hill.

Werner, U. (1994). "Aspects of Multicultural Marketing of Insurance Companies." *The Geneva Papers on Risk and Insurance*, 19: 196–214.

The World Bank (1994). *Averting the Old Age Crisis*. Washington, DC: World Bank.

Zelizer, V.A.R. (1979). *Morals and Markets: The Development of Life Insurance in the United States*. New York: Columbia University Press.

# Part III

# Enterprise Risk Management in a Global Economy

# Chapter 12

# Enterprise Risk Management

This chapter begins the third major section of this book, which covers enterprise risk management (ERM) for multinational corporations (MNCs). While aimed at MNCs, the great bulk of the discussion in this part is equally relevant for purely national corporations and for other entities such as government agencies, non-profit organizations and other business forms. This chapter introduces ERM concepts and practices. Following chapters delve more deeply into several aspects of risk management that we believe are proving increasingly relevant.

## INTRODUCTION

Even with scores of mergers and acquisitions, some 38,000 MNCs internationally control 270,000 foreign affiliates. More than 90 percent of the MNCs are based in developed countries, and about two-fifths of the affiliates are found in developing countries.

The risks that these large and other smaller global firms face in the international market are more diverse and volatile than in the local market. They must manage financial, operational and strategic risks in the local market as well as in every foreign market in which they operate. They must manage risks arising from inter-country transactions such as foreign exchange risk and political risk. They cannot afford to ignore cross-border differences in social, cultural and legal environments. MNCs also must manage risks arising from the strategic decision-making process. Some decisions are consciously made; others are made by omission. Ideally, an organized approach to risk-related decision-making is followed. The risk management process provides such an approach.[1]

A well-designed risk management approach should establish parameters on the MNC's exposure to uncertainty and enhance its economic value. For this, the firm should examine each source of significant risk in isolation, followed by evaluation of all of those risks collectively, for their effects on firm value as well as for the choice and implementation of appropriate risk management techniques.

This chapter focuses on how firms manage risk in an international setting. We take a holistic or enterprise-wide approach to the subject. We define enterprise risk management (ERM) as the process by which an entity identifies, assesses and implements decisions about the collective risks that can affect enterprise value.[2] This definition differs from that followed by most organizations for almost the entirety of the 20th century through the inclusion of the word "collective."

Despite the development of ERM in the past decade, not all have a clear understanding of it. What are the specific risks to which attention should be directed? What are the means to quantify them, if at all? At what level of the entity should the matter be administered? Is there a universal ERM approach that can be easily adopted? What are the benefits and costs of ERM? We attempt to answer these questions.

# THE EVOLUTION OF ENTERPRISE RISK MANAGEMENT

The term risk management relating to business risks seems to have first appeared in the 1950s. However, not until the 1970s did non-financial businesses begin to practice risk management in a meaningful, albeit segmented, way although the term itself was little used. It was also during this period that the Professional Insurance Buyers Association (U.S.) was renamed to the Risk and Insurance Management Society (RIMS) to reflect its members' broadening range of responsibilities. Even then, dedicated corporate risk management departments were still more than a decade away from becoming common, and, of greater importance, risk managers were overwhelmingly concerned with hazard risks and the purchase of insurance. Financial risk management – such as existed among non-financial firms – was the purview of the treasury operation, perhaps shared with the firm's commodity traders. Risks associated with the firm's production processes were managed by operational managers, and personnel risks were managed by human resources. Little consideration was given to how disparate risks related to each other, not to mention to overall firm value.

An increasingly menacing political environment internationally in the late 1970s and 1980s focused MNCs' attention on political risks and how best to manage them. Toward the end of the 1980s, MNCs and large national corporations in Europe and North America began creating dedicated risk management departments. Nevertheless, the "silo" mentality and approach to managing risks remained entrenched, with most efforts still dedicated to insurable risks only.

In the 1990s, managers of MNCs increasingly were feeling pressures from shareholders and other stakeholders to do more than buying insurance against uncertain loss events and to determine what risks were inherent in the firm's core competencies and what were the best means of managing them to enhance enterprise value. At the same time, the production process itself became more efficient but riskier both at the firm and industry levels because of tighter inventory management, outsourcing, greater dependence on technology, more frequent involvements in cross-border transactions and other supply-chain management innovations. The issue of how simultaneously to operate more efficiently and minimize disruptions while ensuring high quality became more critical than ever.

Managers have since been under pressure to gain a sophisticated understanding of the risks that their firms face. The pressure, along with other factors intrinsic or extrinsic to firm operations, has created the demand for more and better risk information as well as risk management techniques. Indeed, it seemed that risks were everywhere and every decision should embed its risk management analysis. Additionally, the potential for corporate catastrophe in the form of reputational and other losses became much better appreciated, resulting in a greater focus on crisis management. By the close of the 1990s, risk management had come to be more closely associated with the collective management of financial, operational and strategic risks.

An appreciation began to dawn that risks cannot be easily isolated (and therefore separately managed) from one another. Interactions were pervasive, yet formerly these interactions were largely ignored. Risk management had moved from a cost center to a profit center in that the questions that boards asked managers were less on "how can we lower the cost of insurance" to "how can we holistically manage the corporation's risks such that the overall risk profile is better positioned for maximizing firm value."

At about this same time, several highly publicized corporate malfeasance scandals shook public confidence in corporations themselves, especially in securities markets, and regulatory vigilance. In response, laws were enacted in the U.S. and elsewhere, the effects of which were to force corporations to have stronger corporate governance procedures in place. These requirements provided fuel to the ERM fire.

With risk management being elevated in the corporate hierarchy as its importance became better appreciated, a new type of risk manager was needed – one whose span of control matched the now wider scope of risk management. The creation of the position of chief risk officer (CRO) in 1993 by a division of General Electric was the first such high-level executive position dedicated exclusively to corporate risk management. The CRO position differs from that of traditional risk managers in two key respects. First, the CRO is a senior executive position whereas risk manager positions have not been, historically reporting to the chief financial officer (CFO) or someone on the CFO's staff. Second, the CRO position has responsibility for a broad range of corporate risks whereas risk manager positions historically have been responsible primarily for hazard risks and sometimes elements of personnel risks. The CRO concept aligns with the ERM concept in that the CRO is ordinarily responsible for the firm's entire risk portfolio.

Most corporations still have no CRO position. This is changing, especially for MNCs and other large corporations. CROs are most commonly found in financial services companies, particularly banks and insurers, as well as in the energy sector. They are less common in other sectors.

Figure 12.1 illustrates how risk management has evolved. In terms of types of risks, risk managers formerly focused (some still do) on managing hazard risks only, which is only one type of operational risk, as we covered in Chapter 1. As they gained knowledge

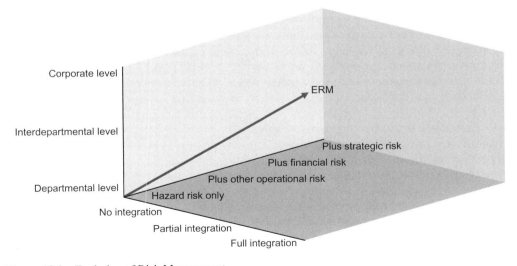

**Figure 12.1**  Evolution of Risk Management

and experience, more operational risks fell under their responsibility, followed later by the management of financial and even some strategic risks. This expansion of risk scope meant corporate risk management activity moved away from a silo approach to a full integration approach. In turn, this deeper integration meant more involvement by senior management.

This evolution to ERM was possible because of improvements in communication and information technologies and because a wide-ranging set of financial instruments and financial markets had evolved over the past decade. Additionally, the advent of sophisticated and low-cost legal and accounting systems as well as a stronger international infrastructure facilitated this evolution.

# RISK MANAGEMENT FUNDAMENTALS

To derive an optimal risk management program, managers should understand how uncertainty surrounding expected future cash flows affects firm value. As discussed in Chapter 2, corporations manage risks because of managerial self-interest, to minimize taxes, to avoid the costs associated with financial distress and because of capital market imperfections. Of course, as with other projects whose net present values are positive, risk management activities are logically undertaken when their net present values are positive as well. Except for managerial self-interest, effective risk management for these reasons can increase shareholder value.

## The Purpose of Risk Management

Risk management is most often associated with attempts to manage those risks that entail the possibility of economic harm. From a financial viewpoint, "harm" is a reduction in the economic value of a firm, which can be expressed as the value today of the firm's expected future cash flows, including its present assets. The value today of the firm is derived by taking the present (discounted) value of the difference between expected future cash inflows and outflows. We discount future cash flows because money has time value; that is, we prefer money today to the same amount of money next year. After all, if we invested the money today, we (hopefully!) would have more next year. Thus, the purpose of corporate risk management is *to contribute to the maximization of the economic value of the firm where value is defined as the discounted value of expected future cash flows.*

Risk management contributes to economic value by reducing economic harm. Economic harm can arise in four ways:

• a reduction in the value of existing wealth;
• an increase in future expenditures;
• a reduction in future income;
• an increase in the discount rate.

Existing wealth is reduced, for example, if a firm's business premises is destroyed by fire. The fire damage may necessitate the business leasing temporary replacement facilities, leading to increased future expenditures. Sales may be lost because of the fire as customers switch to other suppliers, leading to a reduction in future income. We can identify scores of other events that potentially could cause economic harm to the business enterprise. A law suit, rising interest rates causing the firm to pay more for its debt, poor overall economic conditions depressing demand for the firm's products, a hostile takeover attempt by a competitor or an unexpected action by a foreign government such as nationalization, confiscation or expropriation of the firm's assets are a few examples.

The fourth bulleted item deserves more comment. We understand from finance that the value of a business is the discounted value of expected future cash flows, but what is the appropriate discount rate? The higher the rate, of course, the lower the present value. We know and have observed that business cash flows can be quite volatile. Revenues can be less than expected or expenditures greater than expected.

In general, the greater the volatility of a firm's cash flows, the greater the return expected by its owners and those others with a stake in the firm. The stakeholders expect compensation for taking on more risk. For example, if a business is financially shaky, shareholders expect higher returns to compensate them for the risk of the firm becoming bankrupt. Creditors demand higher interest rates, employees want higher wages and customers must be offered lower prices to induce them to purchase products from a firm that might not survive – particularly if the firm produces relatively expensive products with long expected lives such as household appliances, automobiles and life insurance. Stated differently but equivalently, the more volatile its cash flows, the higher the discount rate that will be applied to future cash flows.

As noted in Chapter 2, the value of a corporation whose shares are traded on an organized securities exchange is the share price times the number of shares outstanding – called its **market capitalization**. In a perfect economic world, the net present value of the firm's cash flows precisely equals the corporation's market capitalization. No economic model of a firm's present and future cash flows, however, is likely to coincide exactly with its value as implied by its stock price. Nonetheless, because the stock price *is* the actual value of the business, many corporations assess their risk management programs (and other major activities) based on their expected affect on share price. Of course, share price subsumes all four cash flow elements mentioned above.

When it comes to managing a firm, the manager ideally should identify all opportunities and threats, quantify and prioritize them with respect to potential economic benefits or harm, and find means to manage them collectively and effectively to enhance firm value. The manager should be indifferent whether a risk is financial, operational or strategic. This collective management approach is a departure from the individual opportunity or risk-specific approach commonly used in the past (and still used by many) in the corporate world.

## The Goals of Risk Management

ERM deals with all risks critical to the maintenance and enhancement of firm value. ERM seeks to address all of a firm's risks within an organized, integrated and coherent framework. Collectively, these risks should be thought of as a portfolio. The overriding goal of ERM is to maximize the value of the firm by ensuring that this risk portfolio is aligned with the firm's risk appetite. A firm can alter its risk portfolio in three ways: (1) modify its operations, (2) adjust its capital structure, or (3) employ targeted financial instruments. Just because the firm can reduce its overall risk level through one or more of these mechanisms does not necessarily mean that it should strive to do so. It would do so only if that risk level is assessed to be excessive. Conversely, avoiding all risks (e.g., projects) merely because of the presence of some cash flow volatility could stifle the source of value creation for and by the firm.

The Committee of Sponsoring Organizations of the Treadway Commission (COSO), a U.S. non-profit organization, suggests that an effective ERM approach should be oriented toward several sub-goals:

- ensure that the firm's risk appetite is aligned with its overall strategy;
- enhance risk response decisions by providing the risk manager with the means to manage multiple and cross-enterprise risks and tools to control or finance the risks;
- reduce operational surprises and losses by enhancing the firm's capability to identify potential events and ensure adequate responses;
- identify and act on (new) business opportunities from successfully managing risks;
- allow management effectively to assess the firm's capital needs and improve capital allocation.

Findings from several studies support the importance of these sub-goals. For example, a survey of 416 major U.S. and European firms by CFO Research Services (2002) revealed that respondents employed ERM to improve their responses to all risks, better allocate capital, gain competitive advantage, reduce earnings volatility, and lower their cost of risk transfer. The respondents also expressed interest in quantifying their exposures to credit risk, business interruption, interest rate risk, management liability, employee turnover and product liability, among others. Many of them also have implemented a system to quantify these risks.

A survey of 339 financial institutions worldwide by SAS (2006) found that banks, investment companies and insurers focus their ERM efforts on improving performance management, pricing of products, client selection, loss management and allocation of economic capital. The study also found a common interest among the respondents in managing reputational risk and achieving stronger compliance with regulation – a unique interest among financial institutions as they are highly regulated. With ERM in place, the majority of those institutions (72 percent) expected a reduction of economic capital to support their exposure to credit, operational and market risks. By contrast, 10 percent of the institutions expected no change in economic capital and 18 percent an increase in the capital.

Figure 12.2 is a stylistic illustration of what firms hope to achieve with ERM. By managing all risks collectively, they expect cash flow improvements, particularly as relates to

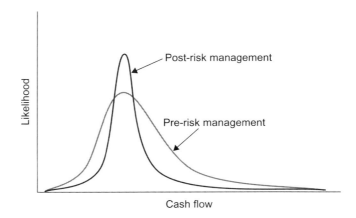

**Figure 12.2**    Impact of Risk Management on Cash Flow Volatility

achieving less volatility by reducing the weights on the tails of the cash flow distribution (Gorvett and Nambiar, 2006).

Management of a risk portfolio is more complicated than the sum of the firm's management activities of each risk separately, because risks interact with each other. Hence, the manager should have not only a sound understanding of the risk of each element in the portfolio but, if possible, also of the interactions between all major risks. Further, a successful ERM program requires coordination of risk management efforts by all functional areas as well as the deep involvement and commitment of senior officers and members of the board.

## THE ERM FRAMEWORK

No two ERM approaches will be identical. Every ERM program is and should be custom-made, reflecting the firm's profit goals, existing risk portfolio and risk appetite. Of course, a firm considering an ERM program may refer to standards set by reliable organizations. Three such sets are commonly used.

### The COSO ERM Framework

The ERM framework developed by COSO consists of eight components: internal environment analysis, objective setting, event identification, risk assessment, risk response, control activities, information and communication, and monitoring. Of these, internal environment analysis is the foundation of all other components. It involves an examination of the firm's ethical values, competence, human resources development, management style and corporate hierarchy. It is expected that senior management and board members set the firm's risk culture (the set of shared attitudes) and risk appetite (a guidepost in strategy setting).

Immediately following the environment analysis is setting objectives. These should be aligned with the firm's mission and risk appetite. Following logically thereafter are event identification and assessment (evaluation) then development of financial and other responses, including loss control. In selecting among the various risk management tools, COSO emphasizes that some level of residual risk will persist because of both limited resources and inherent limitations in the art and practice of risk management. It also stresses that all material information generated by the ERM program should be communicated in a manner that enables all parties involved to carry out their duties.

### The Australian/New Zealand Standard

Several public and private organizations in Australia and New Zealand created a joint committee to introduce risk management standards for the two countries. First published in 1995 (and revised in 1999 and 2004), the *Australian/New Zealand Standard: Risk Management* – also known as *AS/NZS 4360* – has been approved by the Council of Standards in both countries and adopted by organizations in numerous countries. Like the COSO ERM Framework, AS/NZS 4360 offers a generic guide for managing risk.

It consists of seven steps: communicate and consult, establish the context, identify risks, analyze risks, evaluate risks, treat risks, and monitor and review. The process emphasizes the importance of establishing effective communications and consultations with all stakeholders (internal and external) as appropriate and at each stage of the process. It stresses the importance of defining the relationship between the organization and external environments (e.g., social, political, regulatory, economic and market environments), understanding the organization (e.g., corporate culture and organizational structure), defining the risk management context (e.g., the roles and responsibilities of various parts of the organization and relationships among risk management activities), and risk criteria.

The framework also stresses the importance of embedding risk management in all of the organization's activities so that it is "relevant, effective, efficient and sustained." As and when necessary, a risk management activity can be project or department-specific. However, the activity should be consistent with the organization's risk management strategy and supported by senior management.

### The U.K. Risk Management Standard

Three U.K. institutes – the Institute of Risk Management (IRM), the Association of Insurance and Risk Managers (AIRMIC) and the Association of Local Authority Risk Mangers (ALARM) – issued a risk management standard in 2002. The IRM–AIRMIC–ALARM standard recognizes that risk management is a central part of an organization's strategic management. As such, it should be integrated into the organization's culture and led by the most senior management.

This version of a risk management framework is no different in principle from those of COSO and AS/NZS 4360. Nevertheless, the U.K. standard adds two distinctive features. It offers specifics as to the duties of the board and senior management, business units and individuals for risk reporting and communication. It also offers a basis with which a corporation develops its own risk map (discussed later).

## THE RISK MANAGEMENT PROCESS

We now explore the risk management process in more detail. We first offer an overview that builds on the preceding three frameworks. Next, we delve more deeply into environmental analysis, risk analysis, risk response and risk administration.

### Overview

Figure 12.3 offers a schematic illustration of the risk management process. It builds on the above three international frameworks and the generally accepted risk management process (see Chapter 1). The reader will want to refer to it as he or she goes through this overview discussion.

Goal setting is critical in ERM. Senior management and members of the board should set the broad objectives of the ERM program and a time frame for their realization. COSO advises that the objectives can be strategic (high-level goal setting), be operational (addressing effectiveness and efficiency in operations), set reporting standards (addressing effectiveness in disseminating financial and non-financial information internally and externally) or relate to compliance with applicable laws and regulations. The operational nature of the goal setting process also means that the firm should establish a risk policy dealing in general terms with the objectives of risk management and the locus of responsibility.

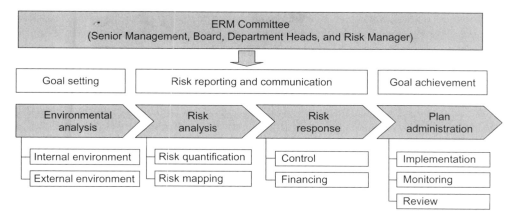

**Figure 12.3**   ERM Framework

To enhance the effectiveness of communication, a firm should consider establishing an ERM committee headed by senior management. The goals as well as the risk policy should then be communicated unambiguously to all relevant managers and other key personnel.

Equally critical and often preceding goal setting is an analysis of the internal and external environments. The external analysis is intended to identify opportunities and threats – social, political, regulatory, economic and market – that can affect firm value. The internal analysis is intended to provide a better understanding of the firm's position relative to its competitors and its strengths and weaknesses.

Opportunities may come in various forms and shapes, as do risks. To identify them, a firm may use existing data sources such as internal, industry and government publications; conduct surveys of key stakeholders (including employees and external parties); or hold brainstorming sessions. An MNC also should obtain industry and market data in each country of operation.

The risk analysis step involves measuring the probability that a given event will occur and, if it does, its impact on firm value. This step distinguishes ERM from traditional risk management. Not all events can be easily quantified. For example, the 2002 CFO Research Services study showed that only a small fraction of respondent firms attempted to quantify system interruption, political, employee relations or product recall risks. This contrasts with the attempt by most respondents to quantify credit, business interruption and interest rate risks.

Next, the ERM committee or risk manager considers how to utilize risk control and financing tools to minimize the chances that loss events have an unacceptable impact on firm value. Control tools include avoiding risks that could cause devastating economic harm and enhanced loss mitigation efforts for those unavoidable risks. Risk financing deals with how to finance losses that do occur. A firm may finance losses from internal or external funds. Nonetheless, some residual risk will remain – after all, risk is inherent in profit-seeking ventures.

Initial and continuing effective communication among all relevant parties is essential. The communication can be vertical (from senior management to functional managers and vice versa) or horizontal (between managers holding similar levels of authority and responsibility).

Finally, the plan should be fully implemented then regularly monitored and periodically evaluated. For this, the firm may adopt an ongoing monitoring system (to evaluate normal, recurring events), a separate monitoring system (to evaluate the outcome after the occurrence of an event) or both. When a deficiency – a condition representing a potential or real shortcoming or an opportunity for increasing the likelihood of the firm achieving its ERM objectives – is present, the firm should be able to identify it and take timely action.

A successful ERM program might result in a reduction in uncertainty (e.g., cash flow volatility), but not necessarily so, but it most assuredly enhances shareholder value. ERM is affected by the decisions of all persons involved and, in turn, affects their actions (and financial wellbeing).

## Environmental Analysis

As noted above, a critical part of any ERM framework is the analysis of both the internal and external environments facing the organization. We cover both below.

### *The Internal Environment*

Corporations rely on numerous techniques to assist them in conducting an internal analysis of their risks that could materially affect firm value. Financial statements are traditionally a key source for prompting consideration of the internal environment. The value of the firm's physical facilities, amounts owed to it by customers, its vehicles, its financial assets and virtually all other *present* tangible and intangible assets should be reflected in some way on the asset side of the firm's balance sheet. All assets are subject to loss of value from operational, financial and strategic risks. The liability side will help identify those to whom the firm owes money because they are suppliers or formal debt holders as well as the extent of equity underpinning the firm's operations. Between the two sides of the balance sheet, the firm's overall financial leverage reveals itself – a vitally important element of the firm's current risk profile.

The firm's income and cash flow statements also provide a wealth of risk identification information. Embedded in these figures are the sources of the firm's revenues and expenditures as well as the sources and uses of all funds. Cash flow forecasts provide essential information as to the expected value of *future* earnings, which are also assets of the firm. The present value of these future net cash inflows often greatly exceed the firm's net worth as shown its balance sheet. Of course, future revenues can decrease and expenditures can increase for innumerable reasons, from customers deserting the firm's products because they failed to live up to their expectations, resulting in lower revenues, to fire causing an increase in operational expenses because of a necessity to ensure the continuity of production.

Other methods used to identify risks include examination of production operations, questionnaires, brainstorming sessions with key personnel, scenario planning and any other method that the risk manager believes will uncover exposures that could affect firm value. Whatever methods are used, risks ordinarily will be categorized in some way for the purpose of facilitating risk responses and assigning responsibility for their management. Below we rely on the operational and financial categories to highlight some of the types of risks that often warrant the attention. As strategic categories of risk relate more to the external environment, this category is discussed in that section, below.

*Operational risks*

As we noted in Chapter 1, operational risks arise from the activities and operations of the firm. It includes risks such as those that arise from human errors, system failures, inadequate procedures and controls as well as management miscalculations. These risks are largely internal to the firm and, hence, are usually subject to control. Exceptions exist to this generalization, such as the risks associated with natural catastrophes and some human-made catastrophes, although even here the firm can take actions to control the severity of such events. Some generic aspects of operations subject to risk are as follows:

- *Earnings* can be affected by a host of risks. Thus, expenses can increase because of increases in the costs of inputs, such as electricity, raw materials, wages, fuel, components and the like. Lawsuits increase costs, whether successful or not. Also, revenues can fall because the firm's products become obsolete, supply is interrupted because of strikes or damage to production facilities, product recalls (which also increase expenses), loss of reputation and many other reasons.

- *Assets* can be damaged, destroyed and stolen, and some become obsolete over time. Damage or destruction can result from failure to maintain equipment adequately, fire, flood, sabotage, improper usage and so forth. Theft by employees and others of both tangible and intangible corporate assets is an increasing problem. Damage to physical assets often causes business interruption that leads to lower revenues, increased expenses or both. Insight 12.1 offers a cautionary tale in this respect. Information technology risks are among the most important within this category, for systems can be damaged not only by physical events but also through hacking and other nefarious tactics. We take up this important topic in Chapter 18. Other emerging technological risks that may be less apparent at present also should be identified, a few of which are discussed also in Chapter 18.

- *Employees* suffer accidents both at work and elsewhere, they sometimes resign or are fired, they occasionally go on strike, some die, some get sick, and some are the object of kidnappings and ransom. Employees also can steal from their employers. These and other personnel and fidelity risks can have a profound effect on firm value and should be appropriately managed. We examine some of the more important aspects of personnel risk management in Chapter 16 and fidelity and related risks in Chapter 21.

- *Legal liability* is a major concern for businesses in several countries, especially in North America. Defective products can precipitate not only lawsuits but also costly recalls and damage corporate brands as well. Corporations increasingly are concerned as well about liability arising from employment practices considered unacceptable such as allegations of unfair dismissal and discrimination based on age, gender or disability, and retaliation. Liability can arise directly from the negligence or the intentional acts of officers, rank and file employees and the board of directors. Liability for directors and officers (D&O) is particularly worrisome in some countries with new corporate governance requirements. A report by National Economic Research Associates (2005) offers some insight about U.S. D&O litigation trends. It reports that the mean settlement value in D&O liability cases has gradually risen from less than US$9 million in the mid-1990s to more than US$20 million in the middle of the first decade of this century.[1] Table 12.1 shows the top 10 class action settlements in the U.S.

## INSIGHT 12.1: THE SMALL FIRE THAT COSTS US$2.0 BILLION

Ericsson, a major Swedish company, has a storied history in the field of telecommunications dating back to 1876. By the early 20th century, Ericsson dominated the world market in manual telephone exchange equipment. It lagged in the introduction of automated equipment, so lost market share as the century progressed. However, by the 1990s, it again reined supreme in installed cellular telephone systems, with worldwide market shares approaching 40 percent.

In March 2000, lightning started a small fire in the New Mexico chip making plant owned by the Dutch firm Philips that made chips for Ericsson and Nokia mobile phones. The fire lasted only 10 minutes but wreaked havoc to the ultra-clean environment that chip making requires.

According to Sheffi (2005), the way that Nokia and Ericsson responded illustrates important risk management cultural differences. Ericsson was unable to locate substitute suppliers and ended up reporting a $2.34 billion loss in its mobile phone division that year. More importantly, the firm lost and never regained its position as industry leader. Nokia was proactive in pressuring Philips to locate substitute suppliers immediately. Nokia personnel quickly referred the problem to senior executives who ensured that production was not materially interrupted. Ericsson was slow to refer the problem to senior management, assuming that the disruption would not last long. This difference in culture led to Ericsson's lack of focus on the items over which it thought it had no control and made it vulnerable to any disruption.

**Table 12.1**   Top 10 Class Action Settlements in the U.S. (as of 2006)

| Rank | Defendant Firm | Maximum Asserted Value[a] (US$ millions) | Percentage of Total "Mega-settlements"[b] |
|---|---|---|---|
| 1 | Enron | $7,160 | 21.12% |
| 2 | WorldCom | $6,156 | 18.16% |
| 3 | Cendant[c] | $3,528 | 10.41% |
| 4 | AOL Time Warner | $2,500 | 7.37% |
| 5 | Nortel Networks | $2,473 | 7.30% |
| 6 | Royal Ahold | $1,091 | 3.22% |
| 7 | IPO Allocation Litigation | $1,000 | 2.95% |
| 8 | McKesson HBOC | $960 | 2.83% |
| 9 | Lucent Technologies | $673 | 2.19% |
| 10 | Bristol-Myers Squibb[d] | $574 | 1.69% |
|  | All Other Mega-settlements | $7,786 | 22.97% |

[a]Settlement values may include securities as well as cash. Securities are valued as of the highest value asserted by any party in a court filing. Settlements include proceeds from all sources. Not all settlements have received final court approval. Settlement values in some cases may still increase as additional defendants settle individual claims.
[b]Minimum case settlement of $100 million.
[c]Includes settlements in the PRIDES and common stock litigation.
[d]Includes the pending $185 million settlement of the 2000 lawsuit against Bristol Myers, the $300 million settlement of the 2002 lawsuit against Bristol Myers, and the $89 million settlement of four lawsuits filed by shareholders who decided to opt out of the $300 million settlement.
*Source*: Stanford Law School Securities Class Action Clearinghouse (2006).

- *Political risks* are especially relevant for MNCs. Host and home country governmental actions can profoundly affect firm value, even to the point of destroying it, as when a government confiscates property without proper compensation. Because of the special relevance of this topic to MNCs, we devote Chapter 17 to it.

Organizational risks are subject to management through altering operations, changing the business financial structure and targeted financial instruments, depending on the characteristics of the specific risk. For example, sales operations can be altered via diversification – such as expanding into new geographic markets – thus reducing operational risk from this source. Financial structure can be changed, for example, by seeking financing for a foreign subsidiary's operations from within its host country, thereby lessening the chances of adverse host government actions. Finally, insurance is available for several of the hazard risks emanating from operations.

### Financial risks

Recall from Chapter 1 that financial risks arise from ownership or use of financial instruments. Financial risks arise from many sources, including interest rate changes, foreign currency transactions, extensions of credit, issuance of stock, use of derivatives and innumerable others. Here we offer short summaries of many common financial risks to sensitize us to the broad range of such exposures.

- **Currency** or **foreign exchange rate risk** exists whenever a firm has operational cash flows denominated in a foreign currency. For example, if a French aircraft manufacturer agrees to accept payment in one year in Korean won for aircraft that it sold to Korean Airlines, the manufacturer runs the risk that the won will depreciate in value relative to the euro such that the manufacturer's actual (converted) payment received is reduced. Conversely, Korean Airlines runs the risk of having to pay more if the won appreciates.

- **Interest rate risk** is the possibility of a loss from an adverse movement in interest rates. Thus, the value of an organization's assets can decrease or liabilities can increase because of interest rate movements. For example, if a corporation finances its operations by issuing bonds and, market interest rates fall, the market value of its bonds (liabilities) will increase, other things being the same.

- **Input price risk** is the possibility that the price of an organization's production inputs will increase. This risk often is labeled more narrowly as **commodity price risk** to denote the risk associated with increases in the price of commodities – such as oil, electricity, salt and copper – that an organization uses in production. For example, a candy manufacturer runs the risk of an increase in the price of sugar.

- **Output price risk** is the possibility that the price realized by an organization for its production outputs will decrease. The more a firm's output is commodity-like in a competitive market, the less control the firm has over the price that it charges for its goods or services. Thus, a molybdenum mining operation runs the risk of a fall in molybdenum's market price that results in lower revenues than otherwise.

- **Credit** or **counterparty risk** is the possibility that the other party to an agreement will default on payment or otherwise not meet its obligations. Thus, all businesses that extend credit to their customers run a counterparty risk.

Many financial risks are amenable to management through targeted financial instruments – specifically derivative contracts, as we discuss in Chapter 14. Additionally, some financial risks can be reduced through operational changes, such as extending credit only to customers with excellent credit ratings. (Of course, sales may suffer, so a cost-benefit analysis is called for.)

## *External environment*

Threats and opportunities external to the organization fall overwhelmingly into the strategic risk category – risks that cannot be directly controlled by the firm. We introduced many of the more important strategic risks in Part II of this book, so our treatment here is limited.

Strategic risks stem from macroeconomic and other primarily external influences and trends. Such risks are not amenable to hedging through targeted financial instruments. They also are less likely to be considered the proper subject of changes in operations, unless the firm alters its strategic direction by altering that which is its business core. While these risks are not directly controllable, actions can be taken to plan for and often to mitigate their adverse potential.

Responsibility for managing strategic risks usually rests at the highest levels of the organization for they have the potential to expose the enterprise to substantial shocks, even to the point of financial failure. Examples of strategic risk exposures include the firm's reputation, adverse economic conditions, changing investor and customer perceptions and expectations, new "brand-killer products" and all other risks that are "out there" but not subject to precise quantification.

In some instances, what seems to be purely an operational risk issue can escalate into a disastrous reputational problem. Royal Dutch/Shell's seemingly straightforward plan to dispose of the Brent Spar offshore platform at sea in 1995 offers a prime example (see Insight 15.5 in Chapter 15).

## *Risk quantification*

After a risk environmental analysis comes risk quantification. Ideally, all risks would be quantified, but some risks do not lend themselves to quantification. We discuss analysis of both risks that lend themselves to quantification and those that do so less well.

### *Analysis of quantitative risks*

Advancements in statistical and financial theory and application, coupled with those in information technology, have facilitated the quantification of more risks than ever. Long before these latest advancements, statistical analysis, decision tree analysis and a host of other techniques were being employed to provide insight into how best to manage risks. Indeed, risk assessment based on expected values has been the foundation for pricing hazard risks by insurance companies for decades. Net present value (NPV) and internal rate of return (IRR) analyses are two additional time-honored finance techniques for evaluation of risky projects.

The capital asset pricing model (CAPM) is another familiar method. It can provide insight to the organization to determine, the required rate of return for a non-diversifiable, systematic risk that might be added to an existing well-diversified risk portfolio. In other words, the required return of the risk can be linked to its contribution to the risk portfolio.

The typical CAPM describes the relationship between risk and expected return in the pricing of a risky project and can be presented as:

$$r_a = r_f + \beta_a(r_m - r_f),$$

where ra denotes the price of the project, $r_f$ a risk-free rate (e.g., government bond rate), $\beta_a$ a relative measure of the project, and $r_m$ an expected market return. The first part of the equation ($r_f$) simply reflects the time value of money (thus a systematic risk), and the second part ($\beta_a(r_m - r_f)$) reflects the nonsystematic risk of the project – the average risk premium of similar projects ($r_m - r_f$) multiplied by the weight of risk volatility of the specific project ($\beta_a$). The sum of it ($r_a$) is what the firm expects to generate from accepting the project. The firm would decide to accept, revise or reject the project based on the outcome of this CAPM analysis.

Value at risk (VaR) is another tool to measure the likelihood that the loss of a given portfolio of assets or liabilities exceeds some threshold based on normal market conditions. The measurement is static in that the likelihood is based on a fixed time period (e.g., one day) with a confidence level of the analyst's choice (e.g., 99 percent). The difference between the expected loss and the actual loss over a certain period represents the volatility of the portfolio, thus *value at risk*. For example, suppose that an E.U. firm holds a portfolio of assets in U.S. dollars, which is exposed to a possible decrease in value by US$1 million or less with a 99 percent degree of confidence for any one trading day. Thus, the portfolio's VaR is such that the firm expects a decrease in value by US$1 million or less in 99 of 100 trading days. Stated differently, there is a 1 percent probability that the loss could be more than US$1 million during one trading day. The portfolio VaR is based on the current composition of assets, thus reflecting the portfolio risk in the current composition. When considering a merger between two asset (or liability) portfolios, the risk manager should examine whether the merger will generate a diversification effect or result in an increase of VaR of the merged portfolio.

*Analysis of qualitative risks*

The quantification of some risks falls within the realm of pure guesswork. For example, consider reputational risk. A major corporation can have its reputation damaged or destroyed from many causes, including a product recall, environmental pullution, liability lawsuits, gross misconduct by a senior officer and regulatory noncompliance, among others. The sheer diversity in the sources of this potential implies that perhaps no single quantitative mathodology would be universally applicable. For the management of reputational and other qualitative risks researchers and industry experts often recommend qualitative approaches.

Subjective risks of the type represented by reputational risk are often good candidates for scenario planning. As we discuss in more detail in Chapter 15, scenario planning involves the use of various "what if" scenarios that are intended to assist the firm in recognizing and ultimately in dealing with loss possibilities that often are less evident through other assessment approaches.

Brainstorming is another approach. By calling upon the intellects of, for example, ERM committee members, the firm often can analyze available data and derive some types of measurements for qualitative risks. To avoid possible dominance of an opinion leader in the brainstorming process, the firm may use a Delphi analysis – a structured process for collecting

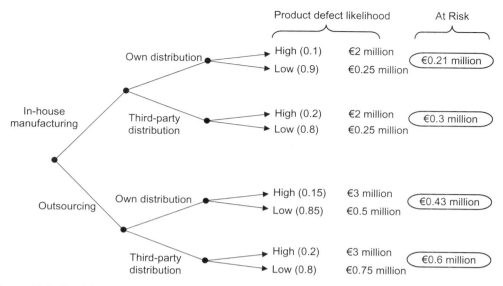

**Figure 12.4**   Decision Tree Analysis for a Product Recall Risk

and refining knowledge from a group via a series of questionnaire-feedback-comment loops until a consensus (e.g., risk valuation) is reached. One key advantage of this analysis over the brainstorming process is that ideas and comments can be submitted to the committee anonymously, thus reducing the influence of any one committee member.

An ERM committee also may use decision tree analysis, a mapping of observations of a risk using a series of factors to reach a meaningful conclusion about the value of the risk. Figure 12.4 illustrates a product recall risk evaluation using this analysis. Based on the first set of choices (in-house manufacturing or outsourcing) and the subsequent choice (own distribution or third-party distribution), the committee estimates the amount of product recall risk for each branch.

Decision tree analysis is a descriptive means for calculating conditional probabilities. It is simple to use and may require little data preparation. Indeed, it can reveal statistically reliable assessment results, as illustrated in Figure 12.4, if the analysis is supported by actual data or simulation results.

Other approaches such as CART, HAZOP and PERT can be useful. Classification And Regression Trees (CART) is a method that combines both classification tree analysis and regression analysis. The typical CART comprises "classification trees" where each tree represents a critical, risk analysis issue. For example, an analyst sets the maximum capital outlay, say, $10 million, for any new project. If a new project requires a greater capital infusion, the firm decides not to consider it or to branch the tree out to an alternative. If otherwise, the analyst asks whether the volatility of cash flow for the project will be within the tolerance level set by the firm. If the project meets this criterion, the analyst continues to examine the feasibility of the project using the remaining risk analysis questions. By doing so, the analyst can complete all the branches to identify the best tree branch (i.e., the level of risk) reflecting the internal and external constraints the firms. When available, the analyst supports each decision with statistical findings.

The Hazard and Operability (HAZOP) method allows the analyst to uncover potential problems related to a risk (e.g., a market expansion project) by asking a set of questions for

**Table 12.2**   IRM-AIRMIC-ALARM Approach of Risk Prioritization

|  |  | Financial Impact (Shareholder Concern) | | |
|---|---|---|---|---|
|  |  | *Significant (Impact* ⩾$5 million) | *Moderate (Impact* $1–5 million) | *Low (Impact* <$1 million) |
| Probability | High (⩾10%) |  |  |  |
| of Occurrence | Medium (1–10%) |  |  |  |
| (per year) | Low (<1%) |  |  |  |

each of the systematically arranged action flows. For example, suppose a firm investigates the feasibility of selling its products on foreign soil via a branch operation. The firm realizes that it may be forced to deviate from its choice of operation due to changes in certain internal and external factors. Using this method, the firm can examine all potential outcomes in each step of the branch operation project – such as possible deviations from the expected flow of export activity; causes and consequences of the deviations; actions to take or decision not to take; and when an action is to be taken, choices of risk control tools to minimize the deviations.

Program and Evaluation Review Technique (PERT) is a method with which the analyst examines possible combinations of actions from start to finish to identify the most efficient way to accomplish a given project. This technique also can help a firm to find an alternative route when the initially chosen path faces an impasse. Advances in information technology also have made available various artificial intelligence techniques.

*Risk mapping*

An important ERM element is prioritizing identified risks, thus making clear to all parties involved which risks must be managed first, followed by the management of the next risk and the next in the priority order. Upon completion of the analysis process, the firm should be able to quantify all risks identified objectively (e.g., using statistical or financial tools) or subjectively (e.g., using HAZOP or experience-based judgment). The firm then ranks the risks in the order of priority (i.e., the potential impact of each risk on firm value). At the bottom of the priority list are risks that are trivial, requiring no immediate action. At the top are those risks that are critical, needing the urgent and timely attention of management. Other risks fall in the middle.

Two effectively identical approaches to prioritizations of risks are illustrated in Table 12.2. The IRM-AIRMIC-ALARM approach prioritizes risks based on their individual impact on firm value and probability of occurrence. The risk manager may extend this approach even to rank events within each cell (e.g., significant and highly probable) to identify those warranting immediate action.

The other approach – **risk mapping** – involves the graphical positioning of events in terms of financial impact and probability. As depicted in Figure 12.5, all identified and assessed risks are positioned strategically on the map and the action status of each risk is color-coded. For example, a dark oval indicates immediate opportunity or threat (e.g., a significant, sudden change in input or output price), thus requiring close management attention, while a white oval denotes a potential opportunity or threat that is being developed but with the amount of information not warranting any immediate action (e.g., discussion of changes in foreign-ownership share of local firms).

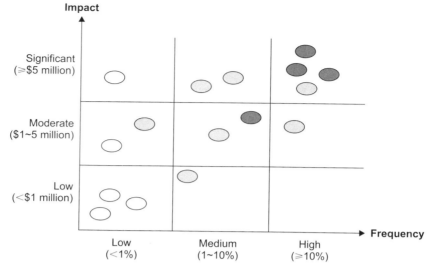

**Figure 12.5**   Risk Map

   The risk map helps the firm prioritize risks based not only on the severity-frequency analysis but also on the the timeliness of decision in managing each risk. The map would, for example, help all members of the ERM committee identify where the risks under their portfolios stand in the entire scheme.

   Risk mapping is dynamic in that the current risk ranking can be compared to rankings from previous periods and also revised from one period to the next as the firm completes selected risk management activities or as new risks are identified. The rankings can be adjusted according to changes in the environment. For instance, a new corporate governance act, an economic recession, an acquisition of a new business or spin-out of an existing business can result in what formerly was a minor risk that was managed at the departmental level becoming a critical one to be managed at the corporate level. Such revisions or adjustments are necessary for the firm to achieve the ultimate goal of ERM; enhancement of firm value.

   The organization should periodically review the appropriateness of previous risk management decisions for each risk and over time. For example, is the management of reputational risk still perceived as critical? If so, at what level should it be managed – corporate, departmental or other? Similar questions should be posed for all other risks. Figure 12.6 depicts a year-to-year comparison of risk management activities where the sample risk, formerly perceived as significant, has become critical. The numbers in the figure indicate the level within the firm at which the risk should be managed, with five being the highest. For example, the firm handles matters related to communicating the management of the sample  risk at or near the top management level in 2006, as compared to at the middle management level in 2005.

## Risk Response

After analysing risks, the firm may decide to undertake additional risk control activities aimed at mitigating losses through avoidance, loss prevention or loss reduction. It will decide that some potential losses cannot or should not be avoided or prevented completely, so risk financing alternatives should be considered.[3] The risk control and financing decisions are

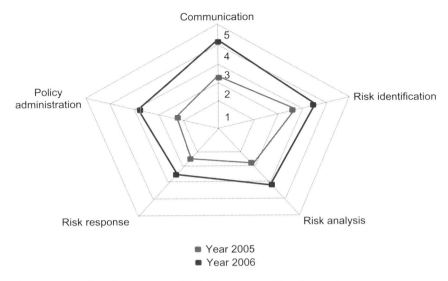

**Figure 12.6**    Year-to-Year Comparison of Risk Management Development

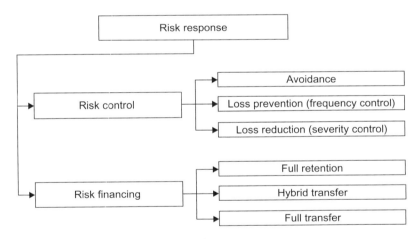

**Figure 12.7**    Risk Control and Financing Alternatives

closely related. Indeed, from an economic perspective, they can be substitutes for each other in the sense that higher costs of one (e.g., insurance) can lead to an increase in demand for the other (e.g., loss reduction activities).[4] An effective risk control program is the foundation on which organizations typically build their risk financing programs. Figure 12.7 illustrates these two classes of risk responses and the available generic options for dealing with them.

*Risk control techniques*

Risk control focuses on reducing the level of risky activity to that which is economically justified. Firms also control risk by adopting internal techniques such as asset diversification and information dissemination.

Risk control encompasses all organizational activities that seek to minimize losses by reducing loss frequency, loss severity or both. As mentioned, they include the following three measures:

• *Avoidance* eliminates what otherwise is an exposure to a loss by not engaging in the activity that gives rise to the exposure. While effective, it usually is used only where retention would be imprudent and when other control or financing methods are ineffective or too costly.

• *Loss prevention* measures focus on lowering the frequency of loss-causing events. Loss prevention measures are pre-loss activities.

• *Loss reduction* activities aim to reduce the severity of losses that do occur. They are usually planned and implemented prior to a loss event. Loss reduction activities do not prevent losses but limit their negative impact on the firm.

   Crisis risk management is an example of a loss reduction activity. Geographic diversification is another loss reduction measure. For example, an MNC may locate its production operations in many countries. This spreading practice reduces the firm's loss concentration potential, because international loss exposures are less likely to be correlated with each other.[5]

When loss events are eliminated or reduced in frequency or when severity reduction measures are in place, loss potential is reduced. For example, a litigious culture represents a hazard, because it increases the likelihood of liability payments. Having experienced legal counsel is one way to control the risk. Lack of organized public fire protection increases the likelihood of a severe fire. Establishment of in-house fire protection services is a way of overcoming this loss control deficiency. In each instance, however, benefits should be weighed against costs. After all, each risk management undertaking should be evaluated as the corporation would any other project. Insight 12.2 offers a simple example of a cost-benefit analysis.

Insight 12.2 suggests that the loss control project will add value to the firm. What is not known from the simple example is whether the firm faces a financing or other constraint that could cause this project not to be financed. As we discuss in a later section, the firm ideally will have a process that allows it to estimate the effect of each potential event and project on firm value.

### Risk-related management standards

A development that continues to influence loss control activities of corporations is the creation of international quality and environmental standards. These standards, by providing a common international frame of reference, are proving helpful in risk analysis. The following section discusses the programs of the International Organization for Standardization (ISO), one of the most important developments in this area, and the influence of the United Nations Conference on Environment and Development (UNCED).

### International organization for standardization
As introduced in Chapter 10, the ISO [www.iso.org], a Swiss-based non-profit organization, has developed a series of standards that can be used to assess quality in manufacturing

---

INSIGHT 12.2: COST-BENEFIT ANALYSIS ————————————

A corporation is considering whether to purchase and install loss control equipment costing $10,000,000. The expenditure is economically viable if the present value of the future annual benefits (cash inflows), discounted at the firm's cost of capital, exceeds the cash outflows. Consider these expected cash flows:

| *Initial Cash Outflow*: | Cost of loss control measure | $10,000,000 |
| *Annual Net Cash Flow*: | Savings in annual insurance premiums | 1,900,000 |
| | Annual maintenance costs | (400,000) |
| | Reduction in uninsured costs | 500,000 |
| | Annual net cash flow | $2,000,000 |

If the equipment has an expected useful life of 10 years and the firm's cost of capital is 10 percent, the present value of the $2,000,000 positive cash flow for 10 years at 10 percent is $12,289,000. Thus, the present value of future benefits is greater than the present value of the expenditure so the expenditure should be considered.

---

and services organizations. National delegations of experts from business, government and other relevant organizations participate in the development of ISO standards.

Most ISO standards are specific to an industry. They contain precise technical specifications, rules and guidelines that are to be observed if an organization is to gain (and retain) ISO certification for fit-and-proper production of its products and services. Two important generic sets of standards are ISO 9000 and 14000. Each series constitutes management system standards applicable to both public and private-sector organizations. These standards provide a common global frame of reference in risk analysis and control. We cover both series below.

*The ISO 9000 series*    ISO 9000 represents a global consensus on good management practices (e.g., customer focus, leadership and system approach to management and mutually beneficial supplier relationships). ISO 9000 is the generic term for a series of ISO-sponsored standards that specify the quality systems of manufacturing and service organizations. Derived from the British standards and similar to the European and U.S. standards, ISO 9000 was adopted in 1987.

Organizations wishing to maintain a system for ensuring output quality may apply for ISO 9001 : 2000 certification, which replaced the previous segmented certification processes of ISO 9001, 9002 and 9003. ISO 9000 certification is a tangible expression of a firm's commitment to quality that is internationally understood and accepted. Registration to this standard is becoming a requirement for companies in many markets to obtain customer acceptance and to maintain a competitive position. Some customers require certification to ISO standards for suppliers as well. Even in the early 1990s, several E.U. countries began to issue regulations in specific product categories that embodied ISO 9000 stipulations as an option for compliance.

ISO 9000 certification is carried out by independent accreditation organizations called registrars. The registrar reviews the applicant facility's quality management program to ensure that it meets the standard and audits the organization's processes to evaluation whether the quality management system is in place and effective. The certifying body conducts unannounced audits annually of the certification holders.

*The ISO 14000 series*    Environmental standards and practices vary enormously worldwide. Some governments have established rigorous regulatory programs with severe penalties for violation, while others have no regulation at all. Increasingly, international firms have taken a more active role in environmental management issues. In fact, many companies and trade associations have recognized this need and have been active in the creation of common, internationally accepted environmental management standards. ISO 14000 sets a standard by which businesses can become certified as environmentally responsible.

ISO 14000 addresses (1) what an organization should do to minimize harmful effects on the environment caused by its activities and (2) whether it achieves continual improvement of its environmental safety performance. The idea for this series was discussed at a UNCED meeting in Rio de Janeiro, Brazil in 1992. ISO 14000, which became available in 1996, is patterned after the British and European environmental standards. The two key standards in this series are ISO 14001 and 14004.

- **ISO 14001** deals with environment management system requirements. The requirements are generic but sufficient enough to provide a framework for an overall, strategic approach to each member organization's environmental policy, plans and actions.

- **ISO 14004** provides guidelines on the elements as well as implementation of an environmental management system. It also deals with implementation of the system.

ISO 14000 outlines the steps an entity should follow in adopting a basic, responsible environmental management system. Although it is intended to be voluntary, some government agencies (e.g., U.S. Department of Energy) mandate registration by regulated entities to this standard, just as some governments did when ISO 9000 was released. Some observers believe that entities that fail to implement an effective environmental management system will not be able to compete in the global market.

*Agenda 21*
Agenda 21 was initially adopted at the above UNCED meeting in 1992 and was reaffirmed at the World Summit on Sustainable Development in Johannesburg, South Africa in 2002. Also called the Rio Principles, Agenda 21 was the background for the birth of the ISO 14000 series. Agenda 21 sets out 32 principles with which global firms ideally should comply. Below is a summary of the key principles:

- *Global corporate environmental management*: This set of nine principles offers the basis for organizations adopting global environmental management standards, strengthening partnerships with other firms and organizations for information sharing and reporting annually on their environmental records and on their use of energy and natural resources.

- *Environmentally sound production and consumption patterns*: The nine principles in this category deal with implementation of environmentally friendly strategies and processes, initiating research and development of environmentally sound technologies, and offering training programs for the private sector and other groups in developing countries.

- *Risk and hazard minimizations*: This set comprises 10 principles related to corporations' phasing out processes that pose environmental risk, modifying their processes to reflect local ecological conditions, and providing data for risk assessment research. Organizations also are urged to develop on-premises emergency response plans, to be transparent in their operations and to apply a "responsible care" approach to chemical products.

- *Full cost environmental accounting*: The four principles here call mainly for development of concepts and methodologies for the internalization of environmental costs into accounting principle mechanisms. They also call for the private sector to work with governments to identify a mix of economic instruments and normative measures such as laws and standards.

- *International environmental support activities*. The final two principles deal with development of an international code of principles for the management of trade in chemicals. They also seek full participation of activities related to Agenda 21.

Compliance with the above principles unsurprisingly varies from country to country and from organization to organization. Table 12.3 offers a summary of the compliance status of selected business groupings.

## Risk financing

Organizations can finance their losses using internal or external resources. Financing internally is often called risk retention. External financing commonly involves risk transfer via insurance, non-insurance contracts or financial instruments. Here we offer an overview of these two classifications of risk financing: internal and external loss financing. Because of their importance to risk management, we devote a chapter to each of them, immediately following this chapter.

### Internal loss financing

**Internal loss financing** or **retention** is a risk financing technique in which the organization relies on internal financial resources to cover its losses. Ideally, organizations follow a systematic and structured funding approach. Retention is used when the financial consequences of an adverse event are negligible because of the low-frequency, low-severity nature of the loss exposure. Firms also finance losses internally if they can be predicted with relatively high accuracy, because they occur with sufficient frequency as to be treated as simply another cost of doing business.

Companies retain exposures when transfer is considered too expensive (e.g., insurance premiums are too high) or because no other feasible risk control or financing options exist. For example, insurance for product recall risk for automobile manufacturers and for research and development (R&D) exposures of pharmaceutical companies is rarely available. Even when available, they commonly command premiums considered to be exorbitantly high. Instead of purchasing insurance, those firms may retain the risk individually or collectively using a risk pooling mechanism (e.g., group self-insurance). Occasionally, organizations retain losses because they unwittingly failed to identify the exposure in the first instance.

**Table 12.3**  Agenda 21 Compliance Status for Selected Business Groupings

| | | Banks | Canadian Chemical Producers' Association | American Chemistry Council | International Chamber of Commerce | International Council on Metals and Mining | Japan Federation of Economic Associations (Keidanren) | World Travel and Tourism Council |
|---|---|---|---|---|---|---|---|---|
| • Encourage establishment of worldwide corporate policies on sustainable development | | | | | | | | |
| | 1992 | ● | ◐ | ○ | ◐ | ● | ★ | ◐ |
| | 2002 | ● | ● | ● | ◐ | ● | ★ | ● |
| • Report annually on their environmental record as well as on their use of energy and natural resources | | | | | | | | |
| | 1992 | ◐ | ◐ | ◐ | ◐ | ◐ | ○ | ○ |
| | 2002 | ◐ | ★ | ★ | ◐ | ◐ | ★ | ○ |
| • Arrange for environmentally sound technologies to be available to affiliates in developing countries | | | | | | | | |
| | 1992 | ○ | ○ | ○ | ◐ | ○ | ★ | ○ |
| | 2002 | ○ | ○ | ○ | ● | ● | ★ | ● |
| • Make available to governments the information necessary to maintain inventories of hazardous wastes, treatment/disposal sites, contaminated sites that require rehabilitation and information on exposure and risks | | | | | | | | |
| | 1992 | ○ | ◐ | ○ | ○ | ○ | ○ | ○ |
| | 2002 | ○ | ● | ● | ○ | ● | ○ | ○ |
| • Work toward the development and implementation of concepts and methodologies for the internalization of environmental costs into accounting and pricing mechanisms | | | | | | | | |
| | 1992 | ○ | ○ | ○ | ○ | ○ | ○ | ○ |
| | 2002 | ○ | ○ | ○ | ○ | ○ | ◐ | ○ |

★ = Exceeds Agenda 21 recommendation.
● = Full conformity.
◐ = Partial conformity.
○ = No conformity.
*Source*: UNCED (2003).

Retention often is the most cost effective financing approach and is selected because the firm believes that it will be able to exercise greater administrative and loss control than could an insurer. Retention could encourage better loss control efforts, for example, when the head office allocates retained losses to profit centers that have failed to control their losses reasonably.

Also, the firm may want greater flexibility in cash flow management with internal financing. For example, it may charge less severe retained losses as expenses against current income, while earmarking specific assets or securing a credit line to pay for larger losses. Generally, the larger the potential loss being funded internally, the greater the need to establish a formal financing method with a dedicated fund. A captive insurance company is such a highly structured, internal financing technique.

Severity of loss is relative rather than absolute. A potential loss considered of low severity to a large, well-financed firm could be viewed as severe to a smaller, under-financed organization. A similar observation can be made about frequency. Hence, what to retain and how much to retain is closely related to the loss bearing capacity of each firm. We take up this important topic in Chapter 13.

*External loss financing*

Organizations routinely transfer the economic consequences of adverse events to other parties in three ways. First, what we define as **contractual transfer** occurs as a part of and incidental to a commercial transaction whose primary purpose is something other than risk transfer, as with a sales contract or lease agreement. With contractual transfer, the firm expects the other party to pay any losses directly.

Second, organizations also transfer risk by purchasing derivatives that hedge specific potential causes of mainly financial losses such as currency exchange rate risk and interest rate risk. Third, they transfer risk by purchasing **insurance** contracts that agree to indemnify the organization if it suffers a loss because of a range of hazard events such as damage caused by fire or from liability arising from tortuous acts of employees. With both of these targeted financial instruments, the organization expects capital infusion if a covered loss occurs. We discuss each of these three methods below.

*Contractual transfer*

Also called **non-insurance transfer**, contractual transfer is common in commercial transactions.[6] Examples are hold harmless and indemnification provisions in leases and sales contracts. A **hold harmless agreement** is the contractual assumption by one party of the liability exposure of another. They are pervasive in lease agreements, typically requiring the tenant to hold the landlord harmless for bodily injury or property damage experienced by others while on the leased premises. Such provisions also are common in managed care contracts (whereby the health maintenance organization and contracting physicians agree not to hold the other liable for any malpractice or corporate malfeasance) and in sales contracts. Thus, a Swiss manufacturer may add a clause in a sales contract making the buyer responsible for loss during shipment.

**Indemnification agreements** provide that certain unanticipated costs or losses arising under a contract and incurred by one party to the transaction are reimbursable by the other. Such provisions are similar to and often are included with hold harmless provisions.

In these situations, risk is being managed by contractually shifting the financial consequences of loss to others. Organizations (and individuals) accepting such provisions should be aware of them and treat the resulting loss exposure as they would any other.

*Hedging*

In the broadest sense, **hedging** can be thought of as any financial activity that protects against a decline in future cash flows.[7] Hedging is commonly accomplished through the purchase of derivatives. A **derivative** is a security whose characteristics and value are a function of the characteristics and values of other securities. As with other financial instruments, derivatives trade in financial markets, both on organized exchanges and between individual buyers and sellers. As discussed in Chapter 14, the most important derivatives are forwards, futures, options and swaps.

For example, a manufacturer that relies heavily on petroleum may be concerned that a new oil shock could cause a substantial increase in costs. It could hedge against this possibility in a number of ways including buying a futures contract or options. A **forward contract** specifies the terms, conditions and price at which a future transaction will take place. Thus, the manufacturer could enter into such a contract through a bank under which the future price of oil could be guaranteed for some time period.

Alternatively, it could purchase an option on oil. An **option** is a financial instrument that gives its holder the right (but not the obligation) to purchase, by some specified future date, a commodity at a price that is set now. Of course, the manufacturer incurs additional costs to hedge the risk. It must pay a premium to buy the option but with no assurance that it will be exercised.

*Insurance*

Insurance is a principal source of external loss financing and is critical in most risk financing programs. It is particularly important in managing high-severity loss exposures, for they are often beyond the risk-bearing capacity of the organization. We know that MNCs utilize various internal and external loss financing arrangements. While statistics on the extent to which MNCs insure versus retain international exposures are unavailable, they are believed to rely heavily on insurance.

Why might a company use insurance to a greater extent in managing its international exposures than its domestic exposures? The answer may lie in the greater information asymmetries associated with international exposures such as difficulty of gathering reliable local data and unfamiliarity with environments in which they operate. The risk manager simply may be unable to obtain as complete or reliable information about some of the MNC's foreign exposures as might be available on home country exposures. Additionally, international insurers often offer real service efficiencies in pricing, loss control, underwriting, claims management and other ancillary areas (see Chapter 19) in comparison to the MNC providing equivalent services itself.

When insurance is purchased, some combination of host and home country insurance typically is arranged. One possibility is to purchase insurance in the host country through a locally admitted insurer. Another method is to purchase insurance for the exposure in the MNC's home country. Finally, instead of using these extreme approaches, many MNCs use combinations of admitted and non-admitted insurance. We describe each approach in detail in Chapter 14. A detailed description of insurance arrangements and markets internationally is found in Part IV of this book.

## Plan Administration

The ever-increasing role of international business activities and the growing interdependency of the flow of commerce between countries highlight the critical importance of having in place a well-designed and articulated international risk management program. This closing section extends the ERM process to plan administration which, as illustrated in Figure 12.3, encompasses plan implementation, monitoring and review.

## *Implementation*

Most MNCs start as domestic businesses and expand their operations internationally. Similarly, the risk management program starts as a domestic program and must expand with the organization. The typical risk management program evolves over time as the international operations of a company spread to additional countries and grow in size. Thus, we should not ordinarily think of the plan implementation step as initiating a completely new risk management program. Rather, it is more likely to represent either minor or major modifications of an existing program, with the modification having been generated from a review and evaluation of that program. The implementation stage for a large corporation often is led by the firm's CRO or risk manager.

### *The implementation process*

Implementing an international risk management program follows the same process as managing purely domestic risks.[8] Of course, the process is more involved with international exposures. The CRO or risk manager need to deal with corporate administrators, brokers, service providers and insurers in many countries. To reduce this administrative complexity, many risk managers deal with specialized international brokerage and consulting networks.

Of course, the assessment of corporate risks will already have been made and risk response techniques (control and financing) considered. The challenge in the implementation stage centers on development of the firm's risk/return profile that includes a determination as to how each identified risk affects that profile and, therefore, firm value.

Recall that businesses can alter their risk profiles by changing operations, altering their capital structure and using targeted financial instruments. The risk control step addresses issues associated with changes in operations and capital structure that can enhance firm value. For example, a corporation competing in a highly volatile field, such as technology, may elect operational activities that allow it greater flexibility in worker management. It may choose to rely heavily on temporary workers or outsourcing. In this way, operational leverage is lower as it avoids the higher fixed costs of a permanent workforce. Flexibility is high as it can more easily and quickly respond to new market and regulatory conditions that affect its production and the demand for its products. Of course, such an approach also comes at a cost. Workers may be less motivated and productive than would a permanent workforce and employment relations may be more strained.

The techniques for addressing operational risks generally are universal in concept but differ substantially in their application internationally. Environmental factors such as climatic conditions can vary from extreme to mild affecting almost every aspect of operations. Employee attitudes about work and the perception of the employer's commitment to employees can be enormously important in maintaining good employment relations and, therefore, smooth production operations. Managerial and technical capabilities vary greatly worldwide, as does construction quality. Health, safety and environmental issues similarly vary as does local regulation. Because of these types of differences, operational risk control programs can differ greatly by geographic region.

The firm's risk profile also can be altered by altering its capital structure. A well-known technique for doing so is to alter the firm's debt/equity ratio. The higher the ratio, other things being the same, the greater the likelihood of financial distress. Businesses for which costs of financial distress are high (e.g., large financial services firms and MNCs with widely dispersed operations) would, therefore, be expected to rely relatively more on equity than would other firms. Debt service costs are lower with lower debt, meaning that the lower financial leverage results in lower fixed financial obligations. After all, whether a corporation pays equity holders (i.e., dividends) is optional, but paying debt holders is not optional.

Finally, as discussed earlier, the use of targeted financial instruments such as derivatives and insurance are common techniques for altering a firm's risk profile. Organizations typically rely on these instruments in case operational or capital structure changes are not feasible because they are too expensive, not desirable (e.g., they constitute core activities) or impossible to implement.

A danger of targeted financial instruments stems from their limited applicability. They hedge specific risks only meaning that they provide cash inflows only as a byproduct of those risks. As such, they are by nature isolated unless explicitly considered within an ERM framework.

*Modeling firm value*

With knowledge of the firm's aggregate risks and the costs associated with the various ways of managing those risks, managers or, ideally, an ERM committee should then calculate the risk management strategy that maximizes firm value subject to an acceptable risk profile. To do so, a model of firm value should be built. This model should incorporate members' knowledge of the economics underlying the firm and its competitive environment as well as their or management's beliefs of the ways that risk affects firm value. By varying the inputs to the model, the changes in firm value can be observed when various risks are hedged or not. In this way, the firm can determine its optimal level of total risk the configuration of risk constituting this level of risk (i.e., risks to be retained, transferred or avoided) and the best means to achieve the desired risk profile.

Thus, the model should provide managers with a good sense of the extent to which a firm's portfolio of risks provides risk reduction through diversification of uncorrelated risks. For example, a business that chooses to use multiple suppliers located in areas remote from each other and under different ownership has greater expectation that a disruption at one supplier will have no affect on other suppliers as compared to having suppliers located close to each other or under a single corporate structure.

Uncorrelated risks provide risk reduction second only to negatively correlated risks, and the model should aid understanding here as well. While perhaps not so common, negatively correlated risks exist in all firms, although most firms probably have yet to identify them as such and, therefore, are not fully benefiting from their risk reduction effects. Negatively correlated risks often are referred to as **natural hedges**. For example, some years ago a telephone company discovered that it had a natural hedge in "connection" with earthquake damage to its transmission lines and cables. An earthquake severely damaged the company's infrastructure. However, telephone traffic increased dramatically because of victims and concerned friends and relatives placing more telephone calls. The increased earnings from this increased traffic largely offset the losses to its infrastructure.

The model also should help highlight those exposures whose correlations are positive, meaning that their combined effect on increasing firm-level risk is greater than such effects from otherwise similar uncorrelated exposures. For example, a corporation in the business of manufacturing gas-guzzling sports utility vehicles and inefficient airplanes likely would find a positive correlation between demand for the products. As fuel costs decrease, both products may well experience an increase in demand. As fuel costs increase, the opposite would be expected.

Of course, creating such a valuation model is no easy task. It requires extensive knowledge about the demand for the firm's products and the nature of competition in the industry. Some of the information and data needed to construct and to validate the model may not be readily available or easily quantifiable. The challenges in dealing with qualitative risks were discussed earlier, but they too must be accommodated in the model. Other information will be available only with time as managers begin to understand the importance of model inputs. Constant refinement is essential.

### Monitoring

If the world were static and nothing changed, the risk management plan would not change. Alas, such is not the real world! It is necessary to monitor the plan to ensure that it remains both effective and relevant. The great effort required to build a valuation model of the firm facilitates this process, as the model's constant refinement should provide valuable feedback to those in charge of the firm's risk management program.

Corporations involved in international commerce often follow one of two quite different approaches in structuring their operations, either decentralized or centralized. Their risk management programs typically are aligned with this overall corporate structure. Monitoring (and other administration) of risk management programs for corporations involved in international activities usually follows a decentralized or centralized approach.

#### Decentralized risk management program

A **decentralized risk management program** relies heavily on local operations or subsidiaries to make their own risk management decisions. This type of program commonly is found during an overseas expansion phase. A decentralized program offers several benefits. Local office accountability is enhanced, and local management may show a strong interest in managing risk. Relying on local outside firms, including insurers, for risk management services can help establish stronger ties with the local government and integrate more effectively with the local business community and economy. Further, all contracts, including commercial transactions and insurance are issued in compliance with local regulations. Premiums paid locally usually are tax deductible. Claims are handled locally, thus minimizing foreign exchange rate risk.

Concerns also exist. The MNC has a strong economic interest in the outcome of local operations but exercises little control over local risk management activities under this program. The firm hopes that the loss exposures in each local office are self-contained and will not affect the continuity of the firm's global operation. Nevertheless, it bears the risk of financial devastation from large losses in local operations or from possible delays in the settlement of local claims. Moreover, there can be a lack of coordination between the corporate and local offices, thus thwarting ERM efforts.

Even so, from a corporate perspective, risk control is usually the responsibility of local management. A corporate subsidiary's profitability will be influenced by how effectively risks are controlled. However, to the extent that the subsidiary's operations are an integral

## INSIGHT 12.3: BHOPAL: AN INTERNATIONAL LOSS CONTROL FAILURE

On the night of December 3, 1984 at a plant operated by Union Carbide in the Indian city of Bhopal, methyl isocyanate (MIC) poured out of a storage tank. MIC, used in pesticide production, is toxic. The MIC facility was adjacent to a residential area comprised of a series of shanty towns. It spread downwind over the city and, being heavier than air, remained close to the ground. Thousands of people were killed and hundreds of thousands more were injured. Victims continue to suffer serious health problems today.

The immediate cause of the accident was the chemical reaction created by the seepage of water into the MIC storage tank. The result of this accident was then exacerbated by the failure of safety and containment measures in the plant. Outside the plant, a lack of awareness and emergency preparedness by the public and public safety agencies added to the magnitude of the disaster. Safety standards and maintenance at the plant were inadequate. Some of the failures that occurred included monitoring equipment that was unreliable, safety devices that were not operational or shut off, gas suppression equipment that was inadequate and an alarm system failure. While safety equipment and design contributed to the loss, the real cause of this accident was management's failure to create and enforce appropriate safety standards.

---

part of a global supply chain, the full effects of poor loss control might not be felt by the subsidiary. For the MNC, loss control methods successfully used in one location may be transferable to others. This type of internal learning can be most beneficial and effective. However, successful loss control initiatives may not be implemented universally, as the Bhopal disaster summarized in Insight 12.3 highlights.

### Centralized risk management program

A **centralized risk management program** is one in which the corporate office exerts primary control over the risk management activities of remote operations and subsidiaries. This approach is arguably more consistent with an ERM framework, although a decentralized program can operate in this way as well. To the extent that the MNC is centralized, corporate-wide risk control standards may be established. For example, an international chain of hotels adopted a policy of having sprinkler systems in all of its hotels, regardless of whether required by local laws. For highly decentralized organizations, corporate-wide loss control standards become more difficult to implement.

Centralized programs offer several other benefits. It provides an MNC with uniform approaches to risk, allowing stronger coordination internationally. Target financial instruments, such as insurance, also should be more consistent because the MNC is more likely to have relied on an integrated insurance program, thus allowing service worldwide.

Several issues typically attach to a centralized program. The possibility exists of conflict between corporate and local offices over local autonomy, but this is no different from that which can exist in all other relations between such offices. Similar resistance can be observed when an MNC acquires a new foreign firm or merges with a foreign entity. Local operations can hinder a centralized program's effectiveness by being less forthcoming than desired with needed data and other information. Open and earlier communication between the corporate and local offices can minimize these conflicts, although it is said that MNCs sometimes fail in this respect.

Cost-of-risk allocations among subsidiaries can be another issue. Managers of the subsidiary may feel that they are being treated unfairly in terms of the assignment by the corporate risk manager of their allocation of such group costs. Also, there is always the risk that the corporate office may fail to respond on a timely basis to changes in local conditions and the need for changes in the risk management program.

### Review

The monitoring process should provide the basis for regular program reviews. Formal reviews also may be appropriate when the firm's risk profile changes because of new or additional operations, such as occurs through mergers and acquisitions. Of course, changes in the environment in which the company operates can necessitate reviews, as when new laws or regulations affect the firm's potential liabilities or responsibilities.

## CONCLUSIONS

ERM continues to gain adherents and support at the highest corporate levels. The increasing use of CROs attests to its relevance and value. As trade barriers fall, more firms expand internationally and with such expansion is a concomitant increase in the demand for more effective and efficient management of attendant risks.

MNCs' organizational structures and operational philosophies, rather than external considerations, increasingly will determine whether their risk management programs are centralized or decentralized. A challenge common to all firms operating globally will be how to reduce loss potential through risk control and financing activities. Environmental, language and cultural differences create many obstacles to effective loss control programs. The creation of international standards, such as the ISO standards, will help establish a framework for risk assessment and management.

## DISCUSSION QUESTIONS

1. Find a definition of risk management from a reliable source and compare it with the definition of ERM in this book.
2. Why is it important to have an effective communication channel involving (the most) senior management in ERM?
3. What similarities and differences can you find from the three risk management standards discussed in this book – the COSO framework, Australian/New Zealand standard, and the U.K. risk management standards?
4. Other than the risks discussed in this book, identify and discuss one risk that firms can easily quantify and another that cannot be objectively quantified.
5. Identify a representative MNC in your home country:
   (a) Classify its risks into financial, operational and strategic.

(b) Which risks, in your view, could cause (i) a significant reduction in the value of the existing wealth of the firm, (ii) an increase in future expenditures, and (iii) a reduction in future income?

(c) Attempt to create a risk map using the identified risks.

6. If the MNC that you identified has a risk management program, find out whether it is an ERM program? If not, what should the MNC do to have a true ERM program?

7. The degree to which international risk management programs are centralized or decentralized increasingly will be patterned after the basic organizational structure and operating philosophy of the firm, rather than by external constraints. What are the external constraints?

## NOTES

1. While the focus of this section is on business risk management, the same principles apply to individuals and societies.
2. Other terms used to describe the same concept include "strategic risk management," "holistic risk management," and "integrated risk management."
3. This and the following section on risk financing draw in part from Gaunt (1998).
4. See "Substitutes for Insurance" in Chapter 19 for further discussion.
5. Of course, we assume that cost, revenue, and operational efficiencies remain constant.
6. Technically, insurance and derivative contracts are "contractual transfer" as well, but for presentation purposes we treat them separately.
7. In this broad sense, insurance is a hedging instrument, but for presentation purposes we treat it separately.
8. This and the following section draw section draws from Meulbroek (2002).

## REFERENCES

Gaunt, L.D. (1998). "Risk Management," in H.D. Skipper, ed., *International Risk and Insurance: An Environmental-Managerial Approach.* Boston, MA: Irwin/McGraw-Hill.

Gorvett, R. and Nambiar, V. (2006). "Setting Up the Risk Management Office," *Enterprise Risk Management Symposium*, April 23–26, Chicago, IL.{AQ2}

The Institute of Risk Management (IRM), ALARM, and the Association of Insurance and Risk Managers (AIRMIC) (2002). *A Risk Management Standard.* London: IRM, ALARM and AIRMIC.

Meulbroek, L. (2002). "The Promise and Challenge of Integrated Risk Management." *Risk Management and Insurance Review*, 5 (1): 55–66.

SAS (2006). *Enterprise Risk Management in the Financial Services Industry.* Cary, NC: SAS.

Sheffi, Y. (2005). *The Resilient Enterprise: Overcoming Vulnerability for Competitive Advantage.* Cambridge, MA: MIT Press.

Stanford Law School Securities Class Action Clearinghouse (2006). *Top 10 Mega Settlements: Settlements of Post-Reform Act Securities Class Action Lawsuits in Excess of $100 Million* online at securities.stanford.edu/top_ten_list.html

# Chapter 13

# Internal Loss Financing Arrangements

## INTRODUCTION

As we know from the preceding chapter, risk response techniques can be broadly classified into risk control and risk financing. Control techniques focus on loss mitigation through avoidance, loss prevention and reduction. Financing techniques are intended to minimize the adverse financial impact of losses on the firm. They can be external or internal to the firm. Insurance is a common source of external financing, as are derivatives, both discussed in the chapter.

Internal financing can be arranged in several ways but all are either unplanned or planned. **Unplanned internal loss financing** occurs when no external financing source exists and the firm is unaware of the loss exposure. Obviously, effectively risk management seeks to avoid this circumstance. **Planned internal loss financing** occurs when the firm is aware of a loss exposure and takes affirmative steps to plan for its internal financing.

Planned internal loss financing takes one of two forms: formal or informal. **Formal internal loss financing** exists when the firm establishes a dedicated program explicitly to finance losses internally. Such programs themselves typically take one of two forms: self-insurance or use of captive insurance. **Self-insurance** is a planned, formal internal loss financing program whereby the self-insured borrows insurance techniques to price retained risks. **Captive insurance** is the transfer of risk to an insurer whose operations are controlled in whole or in part by the insured organization and whose business is confined exclusively or partly to providing insurance to the organization. In addition, organizations increasingly are utilizing innovative risk financing tools that sometimes include an insurance element, a financial markets element or both. These approaches, together with captive insurance are often called alternative risk transfer (ART) techniques, in contrast with insurance.

It follows that **informal internal loss financing** exists when the firm makes no special arrangements to finance losses internally, as when the amounts involved are comparatively small (e.g., employee pilferage). Our focus in this chapter is on the two formal internal financing arrangements.[1]

We first begin with an explanation as to why some corporations opt for internal financing. We then discuss self-insurance, followed by a parallel discussion of captives then a short discussion of recent innovative retention techniques.

## MOTIVATIONS FOR INTERNAL LOSS FINANCING ─────────

In theory, we expect widely held corporations to be risk neutral and to manage their risks accordingly. By this logic, corporations would not purchase insurance whose premiums were loaded for an insurer's expenses, profits, etc.[2] In other words, the use of internal funds to finance losses should be the corporate loss financing "default option." In this sense, to speak of motivations for internal loss financing by corporations carries no theoretical logic, for losses are indistinguishable for any other costs of doing business and should be financed through the firm's cash flows in the same way that other costs are financed. Even so, we should be clear about the practical benefits to corporations in electing formal internal loss financing.

Corporations typically elect formal internal loss financing arrangements for one or more of the following reasons:

- allows stronger control of the firm's risk management program;
- lowers the firm's cost of risk;
- allows for better cash flow management;
- enhances returns on investments.

### Stronger Control of Risk Management Program

As we know, insurance sometimes gives rise to moral hazard problems. Internal loss financing should reduce motivation for moral hazard as the corporation – not the insurer – captures the benefits of its loss mitigation efforts. This concept means that the firm should have a stronger motivation to undertake loss prevention and reduction efforts.

A formal internal financing program can facilitate the implementation of effective internal risk control activities by offering financial incentives to subsidiaries, divisions, or departments for favorable loss records and attention to loss mitigation. For example, Y-Mutual Insurance Ltd. is a Bermuda-based reinsurance captive owned by 110 corporate YMCAs in North America. YMCA Services Corporation manages the captive program and a wide array of risks for the corporate members. The corporation has developed an innovative risk management program for participating members. It trains active and retired YMCA executives to make annual risk reviews of all members. Their knowledge of operations and their credibility with their peers have helped this program produce a steady reduction in loss ratios. The members have been rewarded with over US$13 millions in dividends.

Internal financing programs carry other potential benefits to a firm's risk management programs, especially when the firm has decided to finance the residual risk above its retention level to insurance companies:

- *Bargaining tool.* Such programs may increase the firm's negotiating strengths with insurers, thereby gaining cost and coverage benefits not otherwise offered. They also sometimes permit buyers to obtain higher limits for excess insurance otherwise unavailable in the insurance market. Professional liability insurance with a high deductible is an example.

- *Broader and more uniform coverage.* Many insurance programs suffer from arguments between insureds and insurers about contract wording, coverage scope, or claims amount. Lawsuits sometimes result to settle disputes of extreme differences in opinions. Internal loss financing programs permit the firm to cover a wider range of exposures, adapted to the specific and changing needs of the firm. With self-insurance or a captive, no concern arises as to whether one party is attempting to take unfair advantage of the other.

Especially with a captive insurer, risk managers also can create uniformity in insurance programs. Examples abound. Nuclear Electric Insurance Ltd., a Bermuda captive of nuclear electric utilities firms, has for many years offered coverages not otherwise available in the insurance market. Many U.S. hospitals and physicians faced with the loss of medical malpractice insurance in the mid-1970s formed their own group and association captives – most within the U.S. They have been successful and remain key players in the U.S. medical malpractice insurance market. Global accounting firms use captives to underwrite most of their required accountants' professional liability insurance. The Oil Insurance Ltd. is another example. Formed in 1972 in Bermuda with 16 members, it has now grown to 85 members from all continents. Its capital of US$1.7 billion and assets of US$3.7 billion help support insurance covering assets for property, well control, and pollution exposures.

- *Coverage availability and affordability*. Various economic, market and political factors sometimes cause some insurance coverages to be unavailable or unaffordable. Coverage may become unavailable when problems of moral hazard are prominent, the insurance market is subject to severe price suppression, the risk is catastrophic and beyond the underwriting capacity of the insurance market, or an insured fails to meet insurer's underwriting standards. Coverage may become unaffordable when insurers cannot contain skyrocketing claims or when an insured faces a substantial rise in renewal premiums after experiencing a large loss. Formal internal loss financing can be an alternative to insurance for entities subject to these conditions.

## Lowers Firm's Cost of Risk

Use of formal internal loss arrangements may reduce a firm's cost of risk. Cost of risk is the sum of a firm's risk financing costs, risk control expenses, retained losses, and related administrative expenses. A reduction of risk financing cost through insurance can be expected when the insurer fails to control adverse selection. Lowering risk control expenses and the need for capital reserves to cover retained losses can be expected when a firm has strong incentives to engage in loss control activities. As noted earlier, internal risk financing also eliminates problems of moral hazard. More specifically, such a program can lower costs as follows:

- *Lower administrative expenses*. Internal programs can reduce or eliminate many costs associated with insurance. Agency commissions, premium taxes, insurer profit, guaranty fund contributions, and other costs often can be reduced or eliminated. In particular, Insurance carries loadings companies commonly ranging from 20 to 30 percent of the total premium in most lines. For example, U.S. industry data for all stock insurance companies indicates an expense ratio of 24.7 percent for 2004. As an example of lower costs, Oil Insurance Ltd. [www.oil.bm], a Bermudan group captive for North American and European oil companies, reports an expense ratio of less than 3 percent. Many captives operate at expense ratios of less than 10 percent.

- *Avoid subsidizing others*. The class rating approach in insurance – where the premium rate is based on the average loss of the risk class – often involves premium subsidy by low-risk insureds in the class. Premium subsidies can be especially significant in the compulsory lines of insurance (e.g., workers' compensation and automobile liability insurance). Corporations that finance their losses internally effectively are on an individual rating approach and can avoid such subsidies. Of course, the opposite can occur; that is, a high-risk firm may be enjoying a subsidy from purchasing insurance.

- *Provide access to reinsurance.* Reinsurance rates generally are lower than direct insurance rates. Years ago, corporate insurance buyers could gain direct access to reinsurance markets only through captives. While the application of this condition is less stringent in today's markets, some reinsurers still will deal only with other insurers, thus necessitating creation of a captive to access such reinsurers' capacity. As many reinsurers offer low-expense coverages, large line capacity, and long-term relationships, this can provide a further motivation for captive creation.

- *Gain tax advantages.* While it always has been a canon of captive creation that they should not be formed solely for perceived tax advantages, disregarding them is foolish. A prudent corporation will recognize and take tax advantages as they are offered. A captive, if recognized by the tax authority as an insurance company, has the advantage of taking a tax deduction not only for paid losses and expenses but also for reported and incurred-but-not-reported (IBNR) loss reserves. These reserves can be substantial with long-tail liability insurance. Further, certain local, state, provincial, and national transactional taxes may apply to insurance premiums. Income taxes may also apply. Captives might be able to engage in tax arbitrage to reduce corporate taxes, thus lowering the firm's overall cost of risk. Internal financing through self-insurance generally cannot take deductions for such reserves; the firm can recognize it only after an actual loss has been sustained.

## Better Cash Flow Control

Insurers generally expect payments of premiums annually and in advance. While the insurance market has created some plans that reduce these cash flow disadvantages (e.g., retrospective rating plans), formal internal loss financing programs can offer any payment plan beneficial to the firm. On the one hand, this option, coupled with loss payment flexibility, potentially can help the firm reduce its cash flow volatility and by that enhance firm value. On the other hand, sight should not be lost of the possibility of an unexpectedly large retained loss occurring at an inopportune time thus causing a cash flow strain for the firm.

## Capture Investment Income

Insurers must hold reserves to back their reported and IBNR reserves. Assets backing these reserves generate investment income that generally accrues to insurers. Captives and funded self-insurance programs earn similar investment income, but the income remains with the firm.

Liability losses are sometimes considered to be especially amenable to internal financing. On the one hand, they have proven to be notoriously difficult to estimate because of the vagaries of some countries' tort systems, notably that of the U.S., and because full settlement can take years. On the other hand, the so-called long-tail nature of such claims gives self-insured entities more time to generate funds to cover claims and to realize more substantial investment income. Of course, the self-insured firm also runs the risk of being hit with a massive tort claim that could cause disruption and possibly bankruptcy.

If a captive is domiciled in a jurisdiction offering favorable tax benefits for the investment income, the parent company enjoys those benefits as well. If permitted by the tax authorities of the parent's home country, some of this income can accumulate on a tax-deferred basis.

Captives in less restrictive domiciles are generally free to invest and can create an investment portfolio comprising securities traded locally and globally. As special purpose insurers, captives can be aggressive in their investments if they so choose. The history of captives, however, shows that most captives are extremely conservative with investments, choosing only the safest and most liquid securities. Some jurisdictions permit captives to lend to their owner(s) a portion of invested capital. If the owner has a higher internal return on capital than the investment returns available to the captive, this arbitrage possibility can be advantageous.

## Avoid Inefficiencies with Traditional Insurance

Some of the inefficiencies with commercial insurance were highlighted above, such as high administrative costs and subsidization across insureds. Other inefficiencies that have been emphasized include the fact that the insured runs a counterparty risk in purchasing insurance, as the insurer could prove unable to delivery on its promises for various reasons. After all, some insurers become insolvent.

Additionally, because of adverse selection problems with commercial insurance, the "good" risks subsidize the "poor" risks. To the extent that an MNC falls into the "good" category and the insurer's underwriting is unable to make fine distinctions in insureds' risk profiles, the good MNC may be subsidizing others.

The other information asymmetry of concern is moral hazard. The company that intends to finance its loss exposures internally should not have a moral hazard problem and, therefore, avoids contributing to a pool whose rates include a charge for claims arising from moral hazard.

Finally, for large corporations, the question is sometimes asked: Why should we rely on the financial security of another corporation that is much smaller in size and perhaps less secure than we are? Indeed, the capacity of all of the *world's* nonlife insurers and reinsurers is tiny in comparison to the capacity of any one of the world's major stock markets. Is it not better, therefore, to rely on the market for any needed additional internal risk-bearing capacity – through issuance of more stock – and avoid insurance altogether? (the reader may note that as we explore in Chapter 18, almost all large (not to mention small) corporations purchase insurance for *bona fide* reasons.)

# SELF-INSURANCE

Many corporations rely on self-insurance. Where permitted, workers' compensation and group healthcare expenses are commonly self-insured. Additionally, numerous non-profit organizations such as hospitals, educational institutions, and government agencies rely on self-insurance. A firm might establish an **individual self-insurance plan** – a special retention plan solely for the firm – or participate in a **group self-insurance plan** – a special retention plan where two or more entities, often in the same industry, pool their capital to cover a common loss exposure (e.g., workers' compensation).

## Risk Analysis

As the term implies, the self-insured firm borrows several key techniques used by insurers. It analyzes the characteristics of any risks that it might retain, including estimations of expected losses based on its own past experience as well as the industry experience. As alluded to above, it might have additional motivation toward loss mitigation. Like an insurer, it also sets aside reserves to fund future claims and incurs administrative cost to maintain the program. In effect, the firm assumes the role of an insurer.

Self-insurance is not a solution to every risk. All businesses and individuals should retain exposures that exhibit both low frequency and severity. Exposures reasonably expected to exhibit high frequency and low severity also are prime candidates for self-insurance. A formal self-insurance program (and a captive program) ideally should have a large number of exposure units. Large corporations usually can meet this condition for self-insured healthcare or workers' compensation plans for which the exposure units are qualified employees (small to mid-sized entities also usually can meet this condition if they can pool their loss exposures).

A firm may use the industry loss experience as a reference for its estimation of future losses. However, its loss estimation analysis should rely primarily on its own experience. This means that the richer its own loss data in terms of duration and units, the more reliable is its estimation of future losses likely to be.

A self-insured firm still faces the problem of possible correlation among loss exposures. This possibility exists because all exposures belong to the firm. An extreme loss – not necessarily a catastrophic loss – can threaten the soundness of the self-insurance program. Self-insured firms limit such exposures by setting an appropriate upper limit for that portion of exposures to be financed internally then purchasing excess insurance from the commercial insurance market. In fact, self-insured firms are required to purchase excess insurance in some jurisdictions.

### *Reliability analysis*

Any loss estimation results should be statistically significant before they can be applied to a practical situation. Loss estimation analyses for self-insurance are no exceptions to this rule. One of the challenges to a firm considering self-insurance is whether it has a sufficiently large number of exposure units (Williams et al., 1998). Consider a case where a manufacturer examines its exposure to workplace injuries. The firm estimates that the number of injuries has been 10 percent of the number of employee years, where an employee year is one employee working for one year. The firm is willing to self-insure these injuries, if a minimum of 95 percent of the injuries does not exceed 125 percent of the expected value, or:

   95% limit $=$ 125% of expected value

The firm wants to know the number of full-time employees necessary for this program to meet this objective. Workplace injuries commonly follow a pattern typified by a Poisson distribution. Thus, the problem can be stated as follows:

$$m + 1.645\sqrt{m} = 1.25m$$

where $m$ is the expected number of injuries and $\sqrt{m}$ is its standard deviation. The central limit theorem allows us to approximate a Poisson distribution via a normal distribution with a mean of $m$ and a standard deviation of $\sqrt{m}$ .[3] Using a 95 percent confidence interval (equivalent to 1.645 standard deviations) and solving for $m$ yields:

$$m = \left(\frac{1.645}{0.25}\right)^2 \approx 43.3.$$

Thus, 43.3 is the expected number of injuries, which is 10 percent of the number of employee years. The approximate number of employee years – the number of full-time employees during a year – for this self-insurance program is 433.

A perhaps obvious shortcoming of the above case is that we have constructed it in isolation from other risks. In other words, it is only the first step in the ERM quantification process and this type of information is an example of that which should now be fed into the firm's valuation model.

### Setting self-insurance reserves

Maintaining financial solvency is not less critical to a self-insurance program as to an insurance company. Financial solvency requires a self-insured firm not only to set aside a sufficient amount of capital at the beginning of the program to cover future losses but also to make periodic adjustments of reserves as loss experience develops.

In the previous section, we examined how statistics plays a role in estimating the minimum number of exposure units. In this section, we use a simplified case to explore how a self-insured firm manages its loss reserves.[4] Suppose that a hospital has self-insured its professional liability risk since January 1, 2002. On August 1, 2006, the risk manager examines the need for a further financial contribution to the hospital's reserves for future claims payments.

To conduct her analysis, the risk manager relies on data from previous years' losses. Relevant data are given in Table 13.1. As the analysis is intended to provide an estimate of the adequacy of *today's* reserves, it is necessary to adjust all past losses to reflect changes that have taken place from then until today. These changes fall into three categories for our purposes, each of which adjusts past data to the present:

- *Loss development factors* adjust the values recorded for losses in past years to reflect the facts that (a) estimates for incurred but not fully settled losses will be incorrect to some degree and (b) some losses might have been incurred during past years but not yet reported.

- *Exposure factors* adjust the losses that have already been adjusted for development to reflect any change in the exposure base; e.g., an increase in the number of exposure units.

- *Trending factors* adjust the losses that have already been adjusted for both development and exposure changes to reflect economic, legal, demographic and other relevant environmental factors that affect past losses; e.g., a change in liability laws.

The hospital risk manager decides that the average number of hospital visits (both inpatient and outpatient) is a good measure of its exposure to losses. These are shown for each relevant year as "exposure units" in the table. Each year's losses are shown in the next column. They are recorded on an incurred basis, meaning that the figures reflect both amounts that were actually paid during that year for claims filed during that year plus estimated additional amounts to be paid in the future for claims already filed in that year. Not all reported claims

**Table 13.1**    Estimation of Loss Reserves for Self-Insured Hospital Liability Risks

| Year | Exposure Units | Incurred Losses[b] (a) | Loss Development Factor (b) | Ultimate Loss (c) = (a) × (b) | Exposure Factor (d) | Adjusted Ultimate Loss (e) = (c) × (d) | Trending Factor (f) | Final Ultimate Loss (g) = (e) × (f) |
|---|---|---|---|---|---|---|---|---|
| 2003 | 500 | $400,000 | 1.5 | $600,000 | 1.300 | $780,000 | 1.464 | $1,141,910 |
| 2004 | 550 | $200,000 | 2.0 | $400,000 | 1.182 | $472,800 | 1.331 | $629,297 |
| 2005 | 600 | $200,000 | 3.0 | $600,000 | 1.083 | $649,800 | 1.210 | $786,358 |
| 2006 | 625 | Incomplete | | | | | | |
| 2007 | 650[a] | Unavailable | | | | | | |
| Total | | | | $1,600,000 | | | | |
| Average | | | | | | | | $852,492 |

[a]Estimated.
[b]As of August 1, 2006.

are finalized in the year they were incurred. The claims data are not complete for 2006 and unavailable for 2007.

Next the risk manager applies loss development factors to each year's incurred losses. A factor of 1.0 indicates that all losses have fully developed for the period, and a factor of 3.0 indicates that ultimate losses for the period are estimated to be three times the losses incurred at the time of the analysis. The more recent a year, the greater the development factor for that year, other things being equal. Column (c) shows the estimated ultimate losses as the product of each year's loss development factor and incurred losses. For example, the analysis suggests that the 2005 incurred losses of $200,000 will eventually grow to become $600,000 after all 2005 losses are settled in the future.

Column (d) shows each year's exposure factors, which are calculated as the ratio of the exposure units for 2007 to each year's exposure units. For example, for 2003, the exposure factor is 1.3 (650 ÷ 500). Column (e), the product of the values in columns (c) and (d), then gives the adjusted ultimate loss for each year.

Finally, adjusted ultimate losses are further adjusted for trending factors, shown in column (f), revealing the final ultimate losses in column (g). The trending factors reflect the risk manager's belief that losses will have increased by an average of 10 percent annually, calculated as follows:

$$Final\ Ultimate\ Loss_{year\ t} = (1 + 0.1)^{(2007 - year\ t)} \times Ultimate\ Loss_{year\ t}$$

The average of the three year's final ultimate losses is $852,492. This, then, is the expected losses for the hospital for 2007. Were this a very large hospital with thousands of exposure units of data, the calculation might be completed at this point. However, the risk manager knows that the number of her hospital's exposure units is not so great as to be completely credible on its own. Hence, she takes a blend of her own experience and that of the industry as a whole.

The risk manager learns that the expected loss per exposure of the hospital industry is $2,000. Thus, a typical hospital with 650 exposure units is likely to experience losses of $1,300,000 during 2007. The difference between the hospital's expected losses and the industry's expected losses offers a range between the hospital's expected and actual losses. Using a credibility factor of 0.45, she estimates that expected losses of the hospital for 2007 is:

($1,300,000 × (1 − 0.45)) × ($852,479 × 0.45) = $1,098,621

In other words, we estimate that $1,098,621 – to be discounted for investment income that it will generate – is the additional amount that the hospital needs to set aside to its existing reserve for its professional liability self-insurance program.

## Use of Self-Insurance

Self-insurance can be a cost-effective alternative to commercial insurance. Self-insuring a risk may, however, increase the insolvency risk of the firm, for it is solely responsible for all losses it has retained. Given that little or no risk pooling occurs with self-insurance, the probability of insolvency can be higher than that of the insurer. Therefore, governments internationally tend to discourage – if not prohibit – self-insurance insurance compulsory covers such as automobile liability and workers' compensation insurance.[5]

Self-insurance is probably a better choice for liability than for property risk loss exposures. The reasons are twofold. First, as noted earlier, the long-tail nature of liability claims offers self-insured entities more time to accumulate funds and generate investment income. Second, as liability claims tend to be more volatile than property claims, commercial insurers often add a risk surcharge to base premiums. Self-insured entities also can reduce the total cost of risk by actively implementing loss mitigation programs along with their self-insurance programs.

Below are summaries of the most common uses of self-insurance in the U.S.:

- *Commercial liability risks.* When the U.S. insurance market goes through what is said to be a "hard" phase – meaning that prices are high and availability limited – self-insurance can be a good alternative to insurance. The candidate risks are commercial general liability and automobile liability. Product liability and professional liability exposures also can be retained through self-insurance. A firm may establish a self-insurance program for a single type of risk or multiple risks. For example, the University of California, comprising 10 campuses with 160,000 faculty and staff, maintains a self-insurance program covering losses up to US$750,000 per occurrence of general liability, automobile liability or employment practices liability.

- *Group healthcare plan.* Insurance programs are generally subject to state regulation in the U.S. However, the *Employee Retirement Income Security Act* (ERISA) permits employers to opt to self-insure their employee benefit programs.[6] This provision offers some flexibility in benefit design (as long as the program meets minimum federal standards) and uniformity in programs for large employers and those operating in many states. Today, about 50 million employees in the U.S. receive healthcare benefits through self-insured plans.

- *Workers' compensation benefits.* As discussed earlier, employers in most countries generally are required to make available medical and wage indemnity benefits to their qualified employees who suffer workplace injuries or illnesses. Often, provision for benefits can be made through either insurance or self-insurance. All U.S. states except for North Dakota and Wyoming permit self-insurance.

  In Wisconsin, the first U.S. state to adopt a workers' compensation law, only corporations, limited liability companies and limited liability partnerships may self-insure their programs. The state requires an applicant to submit a copy of the resolution adopted by the firm's board of directors or a person with the authority to establish the program,

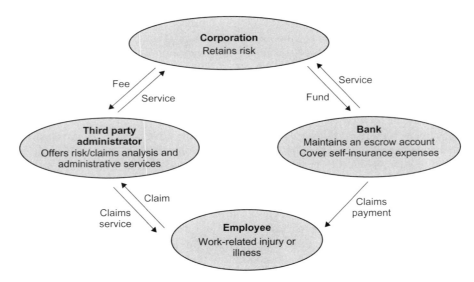

**Figure 13.1**   Self-Insurance Through a Third Party Administrator

five years' audited financial statements, acceptance of certain safety and health standards at the workplace, a report of proposed claims administration and financial security (e.g., bond) of US$500,000 or more. In addition, the state requires the applicant
to secure excess insurance from a licensed insurer in the state. Other U.S. state and
Canadian provincial governments requirements are similar.

## Third Party Administrators

A **third party administrator** (TPA) is a private company that offers services to businesses
and other entities for the establishment and maintenance of self-insurance programs. Services
usually include pricing and reserve setting, managing claims, investment management, and
assisting in regulatory compliance among others. When required by law or asked by the client, the TPA arranges excess insurance with a commercial insurer.

Figure 13.1 depicts a simplified version of a TPA arrangement for workers' compensation. In the figure, the employer-corporation hires a TPA to administer its self-insurance
program. The TPA conducts an analysis of the risk and loss profiles to estimate the necessary size of the loss reserve, and it helps the firm acquire approval for the program from the
government. Based on the TPA's recommendation, the employer opens an escrow account
with a bank and makes an initial deposit. Under this escrow arrangement, the money in the
account is available only for the maintenance of the program. For example, an employee
suffering from a work-related injury or illness files a claim with the TPA. Using the money
in the escrow account, the TPA arranges for necessary medical services and wage indemnification for the term of the employee's disability. The employer is responsible for maintaining a minimum balance in the escrow account. The TPA reviews the self-insurance
program periodically or when necessary so that the program remains financially solvent.

A TPA can be a consulting firm, an insurer or an insurance brokerage firm. Use of TPA services is not required by law. Several self-insured entities, particularly large ones, rely on their
own risk management or human resources staff to administer their self-insurance programs.

**Table 13.2**   Distribution of Risk Financing Premiums Internationally (2001)

| Direct Risk Financing Premiums | Total Commercial Lines | Largest 2,500 Corporations' Premiums | |
|---|---|---|---|
| | US$ billion | US$ billion | Percent of Total |
| Traditional insurance | 370 | 49 | 13 |
| Captive insurance | 38 | 31 | 80 |
| Self-insurance[a] | 49 | 22 | 45 |
| Total | 457 | 102 | 22 |

[a]Self-insurance includes other risk financial alternatives permitted in the U.S.
*Source*: Swiss Re (2003).

## The Future of Self-Insurance

Table 13.2, used also for in the captive discussion in the next section, indicates that many large corporations internationally rely on self-insurance. Greatest reliance is found in North America. Whether self-insurance can emerge as a viable risk financing alternative in regions outside North America remains an unanswered question to both regulators and private and public entities.

The widespread use of self-insurance requires regulatory confidence and managerial integrity. The government should enact and enforce well-structured guidelines that, not only promote self-insurance, but also can be used to monitor sound operations of self-insurance programs. The entities using self-insurance must be able to maintain the operational and financial integrity of their programs. A failure by the regulator or the firm can cause harm to the claimants, who will then be forced to seek financial compensations through the legal system.

Even in countries that permit self-insurance, governments are reluctant to allow qualified entities to finance their entire risks through self-insurance. Such reluctance is evident when corporations wish to self-insure workers' compensation liability or automobile liability, because the government has a duty to make available the same quality benefits to the claimants regardless whether they seek compensation through insurance or self-insurance. The fact that self-insured entities are required to purchase excess insurance for workers' compensation and automobile liability risks implies that governments have greater confidence in insurance than in self-insurance.

Entities considering self-insurance must note the difficulty of changing their risk financing approaches from self-insurance to insurance. Such a change requires them to set aside a fund sufficient to cover their claims obligations for all unsettled claims including estimated claims to be filed in the future. Further, firms with poor loss experience in recent years can be subject to stringent underwriting and a relatively high cost of insurance.

## CAPTIVE INSURANCE COMPANIES

Corporations not in the insurance business may finance their loss exposures through captive insurance companies, the oldest and most common form of ART. We noted earlier that captive insurance involves the transfer of risk to an affiliated insurance company. Most captives are small and managed by firms specializing in captive management. Despite their simple structure, captives can offer several significant benefits.

## Background

Captives are not new to risk management and insurance professionals. We can find examples even in the mid-19th century when selected firms, frustrated with coverage availability and cost, decided to create their own facilities. American ship owners, dissatisfied with marine insurance from Lloyd's of London, formed Atlantic Mutual in the 1840s. In 1845, warehouse owners in London, unable to obtain desired coverage, created the Royal Insurance Company. Yet, these and other establishments were rather isolated instances.

Not until the 1960s did several pioneers flight the resistance of established commercial insurers and persuade many U.S. corporations to create their own insurers. By the 1970s, most major insurance brokerage firms had set up their own captive management facilities in Bermuda and elsewhere. The captive movement has since gathered momentum. The hardening insurance market in the late 1990s and early 2000s, especially in medical malpractice and professional liability lines, kindled a rapid growth of the captive insurance market internationally.

Captive insurance has become a significant market force internationally, fueling a dramatic growth in the use of alternative risk financing techniques by commercial entities. Today, more than 90 percent of the top 500 U.S. firms own a captive. Numerous large firms in Sweden and the U.K. use captive insurance. Similar trends are observed in France, Germany and Japan. Indeed, large corporations are the major users of captive insurance. Swiss Re (2003) reports that, in 2001, the premiums paid by 2,500 of the world's largest firms accounted for 13 percent of the global commercial insurance market, but their share of the captive insurance market was 80 percent. Sixty percent of captive insurance premiums originate from the U.S. Table 13.2 shows that distribution of nonlife premiums by risk financing technique internationally as well as the shares of those 2,500 corporations.

Captive insurance use is not limited to the private sector. Various government entities also use this arrangement. For example, the U.S. Federal Emergency Management Agency (FEMA) created a captive insurer in New York. This firm, using US$1 billion from the Disaster Relief Fund as the seed money, provides FEMA with coverage for its environmental, remedial and other liability loss exposures arising from cleaning up the former World Trade Center. The Metropolitan Transportation Authority of New York City, operator of the public transportation system in the city, also created a captive insurer, the first mutual transportation insurance company, to finance part of its loss exposures.

Captive insurers domesticate throughout the world, primarily in jurisdictions noted for less restrictive regulation than those found in most developed market-economy countries. Those domiciles often have special legislation for captive establishment (e.g., with low initial capital requirements and concessionary tax benefits) and sound economic infrastructure (e.g., developed capital markets and strong human resources).

Captives exert a disproportionate influence on the commercial insurance market. They lead a global movement by commercial entities that seek more rational and efficient means of financing risk. Kloman and Rosenbaum (1982) noted that the development of captive operations even in the early 1980s was a result of relentless pressure by the growing ranks of sophisticated risk managers and corporate officers to dissect and examine every element of typical insurance transactions. Many observers contend that several large global firms have simply outgrown the risk financing capabilities of the traditional insurance market, supplementing the shortage of insurance supply with captive and other alternative financing arrangements.

Captives also are a result of the growing instability and unpredictability of modern economic activities. In this uncertain environment, corporate managers seek arrangements that

**Table 13.3**  Number of Captives by Domicile (2005)

| Domicile | Number of Captives |
|---|---|
| Bermuda | 987[a] |
| Cayman Islands | 733 |
| Vermont (U.S.) | 542 |
| British Virgin Islands | 383[a] |
| Guernsey | 382 |
| Barbados | 301[a] |
| Luxembourg | 208 |
| Dublin | 207 |
| Tucks and Caicos Islands | 166[b] |
| Isle of Man | 165 |
| Hawaii (U.S.) | 158 |
| South Carolina (U.S.) | 122 |
| Singapore | 60 |
| District of Columbia (U.S.) | 59 |
| Nevada (U.S.) | 58 |
| Arizona (U.S.) | 53 |
| Switzerland | 48 |
| New York (U.S.) | 33 |
| Labuan (Malaysia) | 28 |
| Bahamas | 22 |
| Other | 1,154 |
| Total | 4,882 |

[a]Estimate by *Business Insurance.*
[b]Excludes credit life insurers.
[c]Includes pure captives only in Gibraltar.
*Source*: Business Insurance (2006a). Reprinted with permission.

give them more reliable means of funding for the unexpected. Captive insurance as a contingency reserve has been a driving force behind the movement.

The first reliable survey of captives globally was made in 1974, when *Risk Management Reports* provided a list of 316 captive insurance firms. The number has since grown significantly. Table 13.3 lists almost 4,900 captives, most of which operate in 40 domiciles in North America, Europe and Asia. Bermuda accounts for one-fifth of all captives, primarily because of its early start as a domicile (1960s) and continued revision of its regulatory framework to remain positioned in the forefront of the movement. Nevertheless, its market share, in terms of the number of captives incorporated, continues to shrink as other jurisdictions (particularly, several U.S. states in recent years) emerge as new homes for captives.

Captive markets generated an estimated annual premium of US$50 billion in 2004. The majority of the firms are owned by single parents, which are commonly large.

## Classification of Captive Insurance Companies

A captive insurer is a closely held corporation whose insurance business is supplied primarily by its owner(s) and in which the owners are the principal beneficiaries. Captives differ from other insurers in at least in two aspects.

- *Ownership and management control.* A captive is owned by a corporation not in the insurance business. The owner has direct influence over its captive operations including underwriting, claims management and investment decisions. This active participation of the insured-owner differentiates captives from public mutual insurance firms, owners of which play no or only a limited role in management.

- *Scope of operation.* The business of a captive is confined primarily or exclusively to the risks of its owners. In fact, the majority of captives underwrite only the exposures of their owner-insureds. This limited scope of operation differentiates captives from traditional stock insurance companies that underwrite risks for the general public and whose writings of its parent firm business, if any, is incidental.

Captives are not uniform. Some are owned by a single firm and others by a group of firms. Some operate in the domiciliary countries of their owners, and others offshore. Some captives insure their owner(s) directly, while others accept risks through fronting insurers. Some businesses operate their own captives, while others use captives owned by other firms or participate other arrangements. We examine each of these structures below.

## Single-parent and group captives

Captives can be classified broadly into single-parent and group captives. A **single-parent captive** is an insurance company owned by one entity. For example, a corporation may create its own subsidiary captive – therefore becoming the principal insured of the captive – to meet the insurance needs of the corporation and its subsidiaries. Some decentralized corporations operate single-parent captives effectively as mutuals, more for the benefit of their insured operating units than for the ultimate owner. Single-parent captives account for about 70 percent of captives internationally. Figure 13.2 illustrates a typical single-parent captive arrangement. Formation of a single-parent captive is permitted in all captive domiciles.

A **group** or **association captive** is an insurance company owned by and providing coverage for two or more unrelated entities. Organizations using these captives typically exhibit these traits:

- *Entities sharing common needs.* The captive owners typically share a common risk financing need and are in the same industry or government sector (e.g., municipal governments). Group captives providing coverage for non-homogeneous risks also exist.

- *Capital constraint.* Some firms often are reluctant to make a capital commitment necessary to create and operate a single-parent captive. Two or more such firms may pool their financial and personnel resources to create and operate a group captive.

- *Business volume constraint.* Two or more firms that do not have sufficiently large loss exposures often consider a group captive, through which they can finance their risks together.

About 30 percent of captives worldwide are group captives. Figure 13.3 illustrates a typical group captive arrangement.

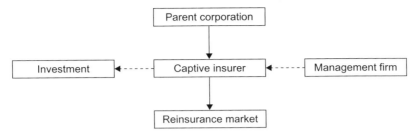

**Figure 13.2**  Typical Single-Parent Captive Arrangement

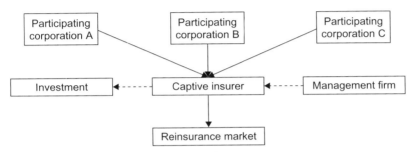

**Figure 13.3**  Typical Association Captive Arrangement

## *Rent-a-captives and protected cell companies*

Establishing and operating a captive can be costly, thus leaving this risk financing tech-nique typically unavailable to medium- and small-sized firms. Use of a rent-a-captive can be a solution for such firms. Even large firms that are reluctant to make a capital commit-ment to create their own captives may consider using a rent-a-captive. A **rent-a-captive** is a captive owned and operated by an unrelated firm with which an entity places its insur-ance. In effect, in a rent-a-captive, an insured entity leases the capital of an existing captive so that the firm can fund some of its risks more efficiently. Rent-a-captives usually are off-shore firms created by insurance brokerage firms or institutional investors.

A typical rent-a-captive arrangement requires the insured firm not only to be responsible for the underwriting results of its own risks but also participate in the ultimate operating results (e.g., investment performance) of the sponsoring captive and of other renters of the captive. As a result, the insured firm faces potentially high collateralization and usage costs in addition to counterparty risk. While often easier to initiate than a pure captive – particu-larly regarding capital and management requirements – rent-a-captive arrangements gener-ally remain short-term solutions.

**Protected cell companies** (PCCs), also known as **sponsored captives**, are captive insur-ance operations established within an existing captive owned and operated by an unrelated firm. The set-up procedure is similar to that of a single-parent captive except for regulatory approval. The sponsoring captive is subject to regulatory compliance of all of its operations including sponsored PCCs.

The operations of PCCs are shielded from the other operations of the sponsoring captive. This can be a significant benefit when compared to use of a rent-a-captive, operations of which are separate from the sponsoring firm only at the underwriting level. Risk financing through a PCC is permitted in selected captive domiciles.

## Risk Retention Groups

A **risk retention group** (RRG) is a type of U.S. group captive created under special U.S. law to underwrite certain of its members' liability exposures. To address the U.S. liability insurance crises during the late 1970s and mid-1980s, the U.S. government enacted the *Product Liability Risk Retention Act* of 1981 and the *Liability Risk Retention Act* of 1986. The former act paved the way for the creation of RRGs for product liability insurance coverage, and the latter expanded RRGs' business scope to other liability coverages with a specific exception of workers' compensation coverage. RRGs are different from typical insurance firms insurers in that they need to be licensed in a single state only – by default, their domiciliary state – but can operate in all U.S. states. Like many other captives, risk retentions groups purchase reinsurance.

Nearly 180 RRGs were operating in 2004, a significant drop from 794 in 2000.[7] They wrote premiums more than US$2 billion in 2004. The reasons for the decline of the RRG market include the restriction of business to liability lines and the unavailability of state insurance guarantee benefits to their insureds. The U.S. Government Accountability Office (2005) also pointed out that a lack of uniform accounting standards, non-uniformity in RRG management standards across U.S. states, and unavailability of state guaranty protection to RRG members hinder sound development of RRGs.

Reciprocal RRGs are found in some domiciles. A reciprocal risk retention group is an RRG operating as a reciprocal which is an unincorporated association of entities that exchange insurance liability with each other through an attorney-in-fact that manages the reciprocal. Profits and losses arising from operations are allocated to each member's notional account. This individual account system offers reciprocal RRGs some flexibility in accepting new members.

## Use of a Captive as a Risk Financing Technique

Captive insurance is not a guarantee of risk financing success. Even with the potential benefits noted earlier, captives may not enjoy a competitive advantage over commercial insurers. Greater risk diversification, economies of scale and scope and a host of other reasons as outlined earlier may argue for risk financing via insurance over captives. In addition, captives themselves carry some potential disadvantages that should be weighed as carefully as the advantages.

### *Capital commitment and expenses*

From the initial feasibility study to formation and operation, a captive costs money. Preliminary studies for regulatory compliance only can cost from US$10,000 for a small single-parent captive to a considerably larger amount for a group captive. Similarly, management fees can be substantial. Some captives depend on fronting – having the parent corporation's (and its subsidiaries') insurance place first with a licensed, direct and unaffiliated insurer which

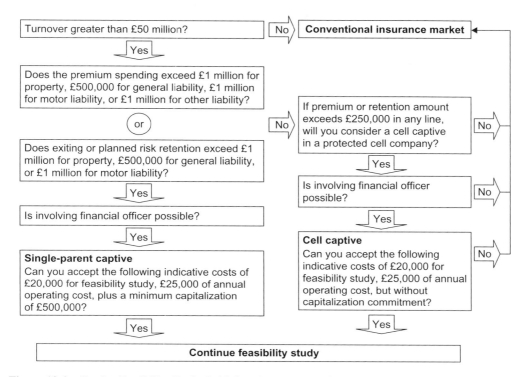

**Figure 13.4**  Captive Feasibility Study Guideline. *Source:* Aon Dimensions (January 2003)

then cedes the business to the captive. Most captives incur a fronting fee of less than 10 percent of their premium receipts. However, depending on the scope of service and types of risks, the fee can be 20 percent or more of the premium.[8] Figure 13.4 offers a captive feasibility study guideline suggested by Aon.

As pointed out in Table 13.4, captives are subject to initial capital requirements. The amounts vary depending on the place of domicile, line of business or both. For example, firms wishing to establish a captive in the Isle of Man must have at least £500,000 to write life business, £150,000 for nonlife business or £100,000 for reinsurance. The amount rises to €1.2 million in Luxembourg for any captive operation. Most captives are formed with capital and surplus greater than minimum requirements.

In most domiciles, captives are subject additionally to solvency requirements as shown in Table 13.1. Retained risk in terms of premiums and reserves generally dictate the required size of capital and surplus captives must maintain to be in compliance with the local authority. In jurisdictions that use solvency margin approaches for on-going capital calculation in insurance operations, the regulators tend to apply a lower threshold, thus a lower net worth requirement, to captives than to typical insurance firms.

### Risk of adverse results

When a captive retains most of the risks, it is, in effect, a sophisticated self-insurance fund. Simply creating a captive offers only partial insulation to the parent company against unusual losses. This holds even if we assume that expected losses are jointly funded internally

**Table 13.4** Captive Insurer Capital, Operational Regulations and Taxations for Selected Domiciles (2006)

| Domicile | Capital Regulation | Premium to Surplus Regulation | Taxes |
|---|---|---|---|
| Bahamas | $200,000 or at discretion of regulator | 5-to-1 premiums to surplus limitation | None |
| Bermuda | $120,000 for Class 1 (single parent); $250,000 for Class 2 (group and association captives deriving no more than 20% of net premiums from unrelated firms); and $1 million for Class 3 (more than 20% from unrelated firms) | 20% below $6 million; 10% for Class 1 and 2; 15% for Class 3 | Company tax – minimum of US$3,635 for Class 1 and $5,610 for Class 2 and 3 |
| Dublin | Minimum share capital of €635,000 | Determined by review of business plan | 2% on nonlife premiums; corporate tax of 12.5% |
| Hawaii | Minimum requirements vary by type of captive; additional requirement on a case-by-case basis | Varies by case | 0.25% on first US$25 million in premium; 0.15% on the next $25 million; 0.05% thereafter |
| Isle of Man | £500,000 for long term; £150,000 for general; £100,000 for reinsurance; £50,000 for restricted | Restricted business – £50,000 plus 10% of net written premium (NPW); general business – £150,000 plus 15%; long-term business – £500,000 or its variation; reinsurance – £100,000 | Standard tax of 15%; Isle of Man firms operating internationally may elect 1–35% taxation; insurers including may elect to pay a 0% tax rate |
| Luxembourg | €1.2 million | 10% for nonlife; 2% for life | Varies |
| Singapore | S$400,000 | Assets equal liabilities for risks outside Singapore; otherwise, the highest of S$400,000, 20% of previous year's net premiums, or 20% of that year's loss reserve | Corporate tax is 20%; captives may apply for a 10% concessionary tax rate on offshore business |
| Vermont | US$250,000 for single parent; $250,000 for industrial insured or sponsored; $750,000 for association captives; $1 million for RRGs | None | Insurance premium – US$7,500 minimum annual premium tax; 0.38% on first $20 million of direct written premium, 0.285% on next $20 million, 0.19% on next $20 million, 0.072% thereafter; 0.214% on first $20 million reinsurance premium; 0.143% on next $20 million; 0.048 on next $20 million; 0.024% thereafter |

*Source:* Business Insurance (2006b). Reprinted with permission.

by the parent company and in the captive. Thus, a firm should conduct and regularly update feasibility studies with projections for heavy loss scenarios of its captive insurance program. Of course, reinsurance for the captive can mitigate adverse loss experience.

Owners of group captives should model the possibility of accumulation risks – those events or lawsuits that can occur to insureds simultaneously. For example, all asbestos manufacturer-members of a group captive may fall within a class action suit.

### The captive as a distraction

One of the more insidious potential disadvantages from having a captive insurance program is that the firm's risk managers and finance staff can become entranced with the mechanics of the captive insurance program, thereby distracting them from their essential roles in risk assessment and risk control. In the words of Rudyard Kipling, they become enthralled in "playing the great game" to the exclusion of risk management responsibilities. The risk manager who becomes CEO or a director of a captive may become more interested in the ego boost of his or her new position than in prudent risk management duties.

## Captive Operational Issues

When considering establishment of a captive, the firm must consider whether the captive will directly insure the firm or reinsure it through a fronting arrangement. The firm should select a captive domicile with the most favorable regulatory, tax and infrastructure. The captive may then underwrite any risks for which its parent needs coverage or selected risks only.

### Underwriting

Captive insurers generally direct their underwriting toward nonlife risks. Many captives – called protection and indemnity (P&I) clubs – specialize in writing liability insurance for ship owners. Other captives underwrite high hazard risks not generally covered in the insurance market, such as political risk, gradual environmental pollution, and D&O liability.

Some captive domiciles permit captives to mix life and nonlife business within a single firm. Owners have only infrequently considered life and health insurance though a single captive because of the limited or non-existent cost advantage or because of legal and tax constraints (e.g., the U.S. *Employee Retirement Income Security Act*).

### Direct insurance and reinsurance

Use of captive as a direct writer can be useful when the parent company faces difficulty in placing risks in the local insurance market or when it wants to control the transaction costs in risk financing through insurance as well as reinsurance. Direct writing captives tend to retain only a small portion of the original risks and depend heavily on reinsurance. The majority of captives are direct writers.

Local statutes may dictate whether a captive insurer can underwrite insurance directly. In the U.S., many types of foreign and domestic property, marine and liability premiums can flow directly to a captive, whether domiciled onshore or offshore. Workers' compensation and automobile liability insurance, however, may be written only with locally admitted insurers. Elsewhere, similar restrictions may exist on direct underwriting, as in Brazil where local insurance must be placed with domestic insurers and reinsurance must flow to the state reinsurance facility.[9] Direct operations, however, are the least costly and most efficient for captive insurers. This fact is one reason why many firms with European operations elect an Irish domicile and thereby secure the right to underwrite commercial insurance directly throughout the E.U.

### Captive reinsurance and fronting arrangements

A captive reinsurer can assume the risks of the parent company through one or more fronting insurers. As introduced earlier, **fronting** is a contractual arrangement between a locally licensed direct insurer – termed as **fronting company** – and a foreign insurer under which the direct insurer agrees to accept the local risks of the foreign insurer and reinsure most of those risks with the foreign insurer. In the special case of captives, the foreign insurer is a captive and the business of the captive is that of the captive's parent firm. Under this arrangement, the policy is issued locally – thus minimizing conflicts with the local regulatory authority – but the actual coverage comes from the captive. Fronting insurers commonly receive a fee plus reimbursement of all the expenses they incur for underwriting and other coverage-related services.

For example, suppose that a French MNC would like to consolidate liability loss exposures in all of its countries of operation using its captive. It can accomplish this objective by maintaining a fronting arrangement between the captive and a licensed insurer in each of its countries of operation. Under this arrangement, the captive functions as a reinsurer. The captive reinsurer may be a single-parent captive, a rent-a-captive or a PCC. See Figure 13.5 for an illustration of use of a captive in a fronting arrangement.

Corporations use fronting when:

*   local regulations prohibit the use of foreign, unlicensed insurers;
*   the corporation needs certificates of insurance, services, or claims handling from local insurers;
*   the number and dispersion of the owner's offices or subsidiaries make it more practical to use an insurer with numerous locations and branches at the localities of the risks.

This approach can be costly, as the fronting insurer charges a fee, incurs usual underwriting expenses, and is subject to premium taxation, licensing fees, and guaranty fund assessment (where applicable). When the cost for the operation of the captive itself is combined with fronting fees, we can conclude that fronting arrangement is suitable primarily for relatively large companies.

### Captive management

Captives can be managed by their own staffs or by special captive management firms. Slightly more than one-half of captives are self-managed. Several large international insurance and insurance brokerage companies offer captive management services through subsidiaries. Several of them generate substantial income from their management firms and expect additional insurance business (e.g., sales or placement of excess insurance coverage) from the parent. As shown in Table 13.5, the 10 largest firms managed 3,466 captives in 2005.

These management firms interface with regulators, provide services related to captive operations (e.g., underwriting, reinsurance, claims and accounting), offer coordination with investment firms and prepare locally required financial reports. Some provide actuarial

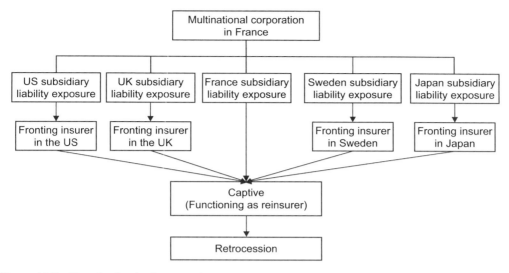

**Figure 13.5**    Use of a Captive in a Fronting Arrangement

**Table 13.5**    Ten Largest Captive Insurance Management Firms Worldwide (Ranked by the Number of Captives under Management, 2005)

| Rank | Firm Name | Domiciliary City/Country | Captives Under Management | Total Staff |
|---|---|---|---|---|
| 1 | Aon Insurance Managers | Dublin, Ireland | 1,267 | 442 |
| 2 | Marsh Captive Management Services | Bermuda | 1,103 | 446 |
| 3 | Willis Management | Burlington, Vermont (U.S.) | 240 | 109 |
| 4 | International Advisory Services | Bermuda | 183 | 108 |
| 5 | USA Risk group | Montpelier, Vermont (U.S.) | 177 | 43 |
| 6 | HSBC Insurance Management | London | 146 | 54 |
| 7 | AIG Insurance Management Services | New York City | 98 | 59 |
| 8 | Beecher Carlson Holdings | Atlanta, Georgia (U.S.) | 93 | 61 |
| 9 | Quest Management Services | Bermuda | 80 | 15 |
| 10 | Global Captive Management | Cayman Islands | 79 | 17 |

*Source*: Business Insurance (2006a).

services, although most contract this work out to independent consultants. As a captive grows, however, it usually hires its own full-time management for both cost and control reasons.

### *Selection of a captive domicile*

The owners of captives seek domiciles in which regulations are adapted to their interests and in which taxation is reasonable. The initial rush of captives offshore in the early 1960s was attributed to the absence of U.S. federal income tax policies for offshore operations (see

---

## INSIGHT 13.1: CONSIDERATIONS IN SELECTING A CAPTIVE DOMICILE

In choosing a captive domicile, management should examine many issues, among the most important are the following:

- quality of regulation and supervision;
- investment restrictions;
- minimum capitalization requirements;
- premium and other taxes and expenses;
- underwriting restrictions and reserve requirements;
- reinsurance restrictions;
- reporting requirements;
- tax relationship of domicile with home country of owner(s);
- currency stability and convertibility;
- quality of local infrastructure;
- political and economic stability;
- quality and ease of transportation and communications.

---

the next section). For similar reasons, U.K. and other European captives were established in havens such as Guernsey, Isle of Man and Luxembourg. In the 1980s and early 1990s, the U.S. states of Vermont and Hawaii created favorable climates for captives, drawing some back to the U.S. Despite regulatory and tax changes, U.S. firms still seem to prefer domiciles such as Bermuda and the Cayman Islands. Similarly, captives owned by Asian corporations are found primarily in Hong Kong, Malaysia and Singapore.

Dozens of considerations will enter the decision about where to establish a captive. We note the more important ones in Insight 13.1. For example, many medical malpractice captives were domiciled in the Cayman Islands because of the government's early willingness to attract them, favorable regulations and a continued responsive infrastructure to the need. Geographic proximity to the head office or executives is another key factor affecting the choice of captive domicile.

### The tax situation

Any captive, wherever domiciled, is subject to local, state, provincial or national transactional taxes. These taxes may be avoided sometimes and modified or deferred in others. Tax policy in many countries seems to favor insurance over alternative risk financing arrangements, a testimony to the force of the status quo and the lobbying power of established financial interests. It is critical that a captive meet the conditions set by the tax authority if it is to be taxed as an insurer.

### Background

A key goal for the parent of a captive is the allowance of a tax deduction for the premiums it pays to the captive. A further goal is tax deduction for the reserves established by the captive.

Captive owners agree that captives, like other corporations, should pay their fair share of taxes. Their focus is on the ability to defer other taxes so that their captives can better serve their role as a contingency reserve fund.

From its inception, the captive movement in the U.S. has been a target of the U.S. tax authority – the Internal Revenue Service (IRS) and state insurance regulators. Tax authorities of other countries, such as Revenue Canada and the Inland Revenue of the U.K., have been more lenient. In early 1996, the Australian Federal Court ruled in favor of the tax deductibility of premiums paid to Australian captives. Tax authorities in most countries, however, seem to be following the U.S. lead on tax treatment of captives. Consequently, the U.S. tax situation is of widespread interest.

U.S. tax legislation in 1962 created an opportunity for U.S.-domiciled corporations to create captives outside the country, to which premiums paid by the parent would be tax deductible and which in turn would not be subject to U.S. corporate income tax until and unless surplus funds were repatriated. By 1972, the IRS took the position that premiums paid to certain captives would be disallowed. Its argument centered on its **economic family theory** that viewed the parent and the captive as a single economic unit. Under this logic, actual risk shifting could not occur with single-parent captives, thus making risk shifting a necessary condition for tax deductibility of premiums. Five years later, the IRS set forth explicit guidelines for risk shifting and risk distribution to single-parent captives and embarked on a challenge to captive premium deductibility.

Throughout the 1970s and 1980s, corporations faced deductibility disallowance for premiums paid to captives. When they appealed to the courts, they invariably lost. A major change occurred in 1989 in the *Humana* case in which the tax court ruled that premiums paid by subsidiaries (brother-sister) within a holding company structure to a captive owned by the parent company were properly tax deductible, although premiums for risks of the parent remained non-deductible.[10] That case was effectively reaffirmed in 1993 in *Malone & Hydel*.[11] Group or association captives have generally been permitted tax deductibility of premiums paid to them, as long as they met certain control criteria, risk shifting and distribution guidelines.

### Conditions for tax deductibility of premiums

Today, the tax situation is clearer than in times past, although interpretation issues remain. In the U.S., for example, premiums paid to a captive by its parent will generally be tax deductible to the parent if the following conditions are met (Westover, 2002):

- *The captive assumes underwriting risk.* An element of underwriting risk transfer from the parent company to the captive must be present. Any arrangement that technically eliminates this transfer element (e.g., an automatic return of underwriting profit to the parent) may cause the captive not to be recognized as an insurer. This results in the non-deductibility of premiums paid by the parent.

- *Risk distribution is present.* The tax authority (e.g., the U.S.) requires that the insurance transaction via a captive must involve not only a transfer of risk but also a redistribution of risks for the purpose of tax deductibility. A single-parent captive thus faces difficulty in meeting this condition, unless it assumes a sufficiently large number of risks from unrelated firms. Tax authorities hold apparently differing views as to what constitutes a reasonable degree of pooling (i.e., the minimum number of risks). However, the premiums paid by subsidiaries of the parent company, which are legally independent of the parent, may be treated as deductible business expenses by the subsidiaries.

- *The captive operates according to accepted industry practices.* This condition requires the captive to have the minimum required legal structure of an insurance company, issue policies as a genuine insurer, and underwrite risks and handle claims as a typical insurer in the insurance market. It also implies that the captive must meet the minimum initial and ongoing solvency standards and other requirements imposed by the local regulatory authority.

Captives and their owners have two continuing tax problems. First is their need to convince tax authorities and accountants around the world of the economic desirability of permitting tax deductibility for premiums paid by the parent companies to single-parent and group captives, just as they would be for premiums paid to any commercial insurers. Second, the parents of captives face questions involving the taxation of their captives' net income. Some tax authorities impute this income back to the parent irrespective of whether dividends are declared and distributed. Taxation of net income can be considered part of the broader transfer pricing issue, one that plagues multinational taxpayers.

### Corporate governance

All captive insurers, wherever located and in whatever form, face increasing pressure to have appropriate corporate governance structures in place. Among those captives facing the greatest pressure are those domiciled offshore and those owned by publicly held corporations. Group captives also need to adopt corporate governance structures, but coordination among the parent companies is a challenge.

The corporate governance standards of a captive should deal with the following issues, which are stipulated in the *Sarbanes-Oxley Act* of the U.S. as well:

- The captive must be managed based on a well-established code of ethics. The code governs the scope of responsibilities and authority of the board and its members.
- The board of the captive bears the responsibility for overseeing sound captive operations.
- The board bears the responsibility for financial reporting according to the laws governing the captive. The responsibility includes appointment of an auditor or an auditing committee as well as oversight of the auditing process.

## OTHER ART TECHNIQUES

As noted in the introduction, corporations increasingly are using innovative financing techniques. The evolution of these techniques has been motivated by the inefficiencies with traditional insurance of the types identified earlier and the need for a wider scope of risk transfer and retention as corporations seek new means of financing loss exposures. In this section we introduce two comparatively new ART techniques: (1) contingent capital and (2) reverse convertible debt. Other ART products that combine traditional insurance with coverage for non-insurable exposures are introduced in the next chapter.

### Contingent Capital

A post-loss financing agreement, a contingent capital contract provides that capital will be infused into the corporation to fund a non-insured loss on terms agreed to before the defined event occurs. The capital might be a loan or new equity.

An instrument of this type is the catastrophe equity put option (cat e-put) designed by insurance broker Aon. As discussed more fully in the next chapter, is the contractual right to sell something to the other party on terms and at a price agreed to in advance. With this arrangement, the corporation issues a put option to sell its own shares to a counterparty at an agreed upon price if some specified hazard loss occurs. A cat e-put avoids the problem of the firm possibly having to raise new equity after some major loss when its share price is likely depressed.

## Reverse Convertible Debt

A recent innovation is reverse convertible debt (RCD). As issued by the Dutch financial services group ING, for example, an RCD alters the firm's capital structure to reduce financial leverage at a time when some major hazard event has occurred that might otherwise result in an increase the firm's overall risk profile. Under the typical RCD arrangement, debt is converted to equity at the firm's option, ordinarily when share price has fallen because of some major loss event. In this way, leverage is automatically reduced.

# CONCLUSION

Self-insurance, captives and other ART techniques seem likely to continue to play an increasingly important role in risk financing internationally. Liberalization, deregulation and the continued globalization of business seem likely to stimulate further such use. As global changes and communications affect all forms of risk financing, the larger, more sophisticated corporations will rely more on formal internal loss financing arrangements as they seek alternatives to external risk transfer. The rate of growth of these internal loss financing arrangements likely will be fastest in Europe, Asia and Latin America – the regions where they are less popular because of entrenched, although weakening, established insurance interests. In North America, growth in the number of captives will probably slow as their assets continue to grow, as existing captives are more imaginatively employed. Self-insurance arrangements in North America seem likely to grow both because of a more reasoned application of enterprise risk management by organizations and because of insurers devising more imaginative combinations of risk transfer and retention products.

Captives are now found throughout the world, from Bermuda to Singapore and from Vermont to Luxembourg. Their owners range from the major MNCs such as CRA and BHP (Australia), Fletcher Challenge (New Zealand), BMW (Germany), ABB (Switzerland), Guinness and British Petroleum (U.K.), and Mobil Oil and Union Carbide (U.S.) to groups of organizations that have realized the financial benefits of sharing risk. With advancements in information technology, we are beginning to see **virtual captive insurers** – captives with minimum in-house operations (e.g., program management, underwriting and auditing) and cost efficient outsourcing (e.g., actuarial, accounting and marketing). Government Entities Mutual [www.gemre.com] is an example.

## DISCUSSION QUESTIONS

1. Other than the involvement of a third party, can we argue that self-insurance and traditional insurance are virtually identical? What bases of arguments for or against this statement can you provide?
2. Do you believe it is necessary for very large, well diversified MNCs to purchase excess insurance over their self-insurance limits? Explain.
3. Why might a widely held corporation utilize a captive even though it would not purchase commercial insurance if it had no captive?
4. What types of exposures might a firm specifically want to avoid writing in its captive and why?
5. Do tax laws in your country discriminate for or against captives or are they neutral toward them vis-à-vis commercial insurers? Vis-à-vis non-captive self-retention?

## NOTES

1. This chapter draws in parts from Kloman (1998).
2. We know that corporations do routinely purchase commercial insurance. Chapter 2 explained the economic logic for why corporations engage in risk management. These reasons apply equally to the purchase of insurance – a risk management tool. Corporations have additional possible motives for purchasing insurance that are explored in Chapter 19.
3. The central limit theorem states that when the sample size is sufficiently large (e.g., the number of injuries) in each sample group, the averages of each sample group tend to be normally distributed.
4. This example and discussion is based on Math and Youngerman (1992).
5. Unsurprisingly, governments are supported in this position by the insurance industry lobby.
6. U.S. employers that self-insure their employee benefit programs are also subject to the provisions of the *Health Insurance Portability and Accountability Act* of 1996. This act guarantees health insurance coverage for workers (and their families) when they change or lose jobs.
7. Hikes in premium rates and reduced availability for medical malpractice coverage caused a sudden rise in the formation of RRGs in the early 2000s

(Cutts, 2004). The number of RRGs continued to rise in 2005.
8. A May 2003 survey by the Captive Insurance Companies Association and the Vermont Captive Insurance Associations, both of the U.S., reports that 23.9 percent of the respondents believed that fronting fees were high and 65.2 percent found them to be reasonable. Some 26.1 percent and 58.7 percent of the respondents said that fronting services were excellent and moderate, respectively (Captive Insurance Company Reports, 2003).
9. The Brazilian government is expected to relax this restriction in the near future.
10. *Humana Inc. versus Commissioner*, 881 F2d 247 (6th Cir 1989) affirming in part and reversing in part, 88TC (1987).
11. *Malone & Hyde Inc. versus Commissioner*, 66 T.C.M. (CCH) 1551 (1993). In 1995, a U.S. appeals court ruled against *Malone & Hyde*, but only because it had executed hold harmless agreements with a fronting insurer and because the captive was undercapitalized. The Court seemed to have affirmed, at least by implication, the analytical framework created by *Humana*.

## REFERENCES

Government Accountability Office (2005). *Risk Retention Groups: Common Regulatory Standards and Greater Member Protection Are Needed.* Washington, DC: U.S. Government.

Cutts, K. (2004). "Soaring RRG Formations Continue into 2004." *National Underwriter: Property-Casualty/Risk & Benefits Management Edition* (January 26): 28.

Kloman, H.F. and Rosenbaum, H.D. (1982). "The Captive Insurance Phenomenon: A Cautionary Tale?" *The Geneva Papers on Risk and Insurance*, No. 23, April.

Kloman, H.F. (1998). "Captive Insurance Companies," in H.D. Skipper, Jr. ed. *International Risk and Insurance: An Environmental-Managerial Approach*. Boston: Irwin/McGraw-Hill.

Math, S. and Youngerman, H. (1992). "A Look Inside the Actuarial Black Box." *Healthcare Financial Management*, 46 (December): 36–39.

"Fronting Arrangements Continue to Disappoint." *Captive Insurance Company Reports* (July 2003): 6–7.

"Self-Insurance & Captive Management." *Business Insurance* (March 6, 2006a): 11–12.

"Directory of World Captive Domiciles." *Business Insurance* (March 6, 2006b): 30–35.

Swiss Re (2003). *Reinsurance: A Systematic Risk?* Zurich: Swiss Re.

Westover, K. (2002). *Captives and the Management of Risk*. Dallas: International Risk Management Institute.

Williams, A., Smith, M. and Young, P. (1998). *Risk Management and Insurance*, 8th edn. New York: McGraw Hill/Irwin.

# Chapter 14

# External Loss Financing Arrangements

## INTRODUCTION

Chapter 12 emphasized the necessity for organizations to arrange financing for some types of loss exposures, either from internal or external funds. Chapter 13 introduced various aspects of internal loss financing. This chapter focuses on external loss financing arrangement, except for contractual transfer.

We first introduce the targeted financial instruments that are commonly used to hedge risks. As defined in Chapter 12, *hedging* is any financial activity that protects against a decline in future cash flows and is commonly accomplished through the purchase of derivatives. Recall that a *derivative* is a security whose characteristics and value are a function of the characteristics and values of other securities. The security from which the derivative is *derived* is called the **underlying security** or simply the **underlying**. The most important derivatives are forwards, futures, options and swaps, each of which is introduced in this chapter.

Insurance, of course, is a risk financing instrument that organizations commonly use to manage their hazard risk exposures. Given that key aspects of corporate insurance are explored in later chapters of this part as well as in Part IV of the book, we limit our discussion of insurance here to certain liability insurance contracts and global insurancce programs.

## RISK FINANCING THROUGH DERIVATIVES

As with other financial instruments, derivatives trade in financial markets, whether on organized exchanges or between individual buyers and sellers.[1] Various types of markets exist, perhaps the most familiar being **barter markets** (the exchange of non-standardized goods or services not involving currency) and **cash-and-carry markets** (goods and services are purchased with cash and taken away). The main financial markets are spot markets. A **spot market** is one in which standardized goods are exchanged via currency transactions taking place in the present. Markets for forwards, futures and options are similar to spot markets except that delivery takes place at some future point.

## Forwards and Futures

A **forward contract** specifies that terms on which a future transaction will take place. The contract specifies the price and delivery date of the underlying. Forward contracts are flexible, and the parties can specify the quantity and quality of the asset as well as other details such as place of delivery. Forward markets arise when traders have special needs, and others are willing to meet them for a price. Forward contracts are written on commodities, financial assets such as stocks, bonds, capital market indices and currency exchange rates. They usually are personal contracts and thus are customized to the needs of each party. As such, they are not easily transferred to other parties. Forward contracting is perhaps most commonly recognized in real estate markets where buyers and sellers specify a particular property, sales date and sales price in the contract.

Traders in the forward market must honor the contract, regardless of the outcome. This gives rise to a potential problem of credit risk, as forwards are not regulated. Therefore, for the market to function, each trader must be assured that his or her *counterparty* – the other party to the contract – will perform on the contract instead of default.

Like a forward contract, a **futures contract** is for the future purchase and sale of goods or services. Futures differ from forwards, however, in several ways. Futures are regulated, liquid and traded on organized exchanges, which attract many traders. They contain standard contract terms and cannot be customized to individual needs. Forward and future contracts differ also in how they deal with credit risk.

Futures are dominant in government bond and other markets where many traders need to manage interest rate risk or are willing to speculate on it. Currency markets support both forwards and futures contracts because some traders can use relatively inexpensive standardized futures while others have specific needs with regard to currency type, amount and maturity date.

### *The basics*

We now examine the basics of forwards and futures trading. As both contracts deal with future delivery or receipt of goods or services, we can consider a single model for both. Additionally, both forwards and futures trading may be contrasted with spot market trading.

In the spot market, buyers and sellers know the price of each unit of the spot or underlying security. We denote the price in today's spot market as $S_t$, and the price in the spot market in the future as $S(T)$.

In a forward market, contracts are made for future delivery or receipt of goods. That is, both parties in a forward contract agree now, at time $t$, to trade the asset at future time $T$ (where $t < T$) at a price of $F(t, T)$. Assume that, as date $T$ approaches, the actual price of the underlying asset becomes $S(T)$. At date $T$, the buyer under the forward contract must pay $F(t, T)$ for the asset, even if the market price is less than the contract price; that is, $S(T) < F(t, T)$. Conversely, the seller under the forward contract must deliver the asset at time $T$ for $F(t, T)$, even if the market price is greater. We summarize below the relationship between price and date in the spot contract and the forward contract:

|  | *Present* | *Future* |
|---|---|---|
| Time | $T$ | $T$ |
| Spot contract price | $S_t$ | $S(T)$ |
| Forward contract price |  | $F(t, T)$ |

If a contract is held to maturity, the buyer pays cash of $F(t, T)$ and takes delivery of the underlying that has a market value of $S(T)$ at time $T$. If $S(T)$ is greater than $F(t, T)$, the buyer immediately sells the underlying for $S(T)$ and generates a gain of $S(T) - F(t, T)$. The seller realizes a gain of $F(t, T) - S(T)$ if the execution price $F(t, T)$ is greater than the spot price $S(T)$, because the seller receives a cash payment greater than the value of the underlying.

Traders in the forward market can open new contracts at any time, regardless of their current holdings of forwards or spot assets. In other words, instead of holding a forward contract to maturity, a party in a forward contract may offset his or her original position with another contract. For illustration, suppose a buyer has an obligation to purchase an underlying asset at price $F(t, T)$. At any moment between the contract purchase date $(t)$ and the contract expiry date $(T)$, the buyer can enter into another contract to sell the same underlying asset at a new price, $F(u, T)$, where $u$ denotes the time the buyer purchases the new contract $(t < u < T)$. From the opening of this new contract, the trader effectively has no further obligation under the original contract because the requirements to deliver the asset under the terms of the sell contract exactly meet the requirements to accept delivery under the buy contract. This procedure is called **closing out** the position.

The price for this new forward contract, $F(u, T)$, could be different from the price for the original obligation, $F(t, T)$. The net effect on the trader with an original obligation to buy at $F(t, T)$ and a close out position to sell at $F(u, T)$ is:

$$\underbrace{[S(T) - F(t, T)]}_{As\ a\ buyer} - \underbrace{[F(u, T) - S(T)]}_{As\ a\ seller} = F(u, T) - F(t, T) \tag{14.1}$$

The gain occurs on date $T$ for forward traders and on date $u$ for future traders due to marking to market, as explained below.

### *Marking to market in futures contracts*

Counterparty risks are managed differently in derivative markets. In the currency market, for example, a trader may enter into a forward contract with a bank functioning as the dealer. That is, the bank is the other party of the contract and stands behind the forward contract. As the default risk of the bank is relatively low, it usually is the bank that requires the trader for a credit history or a deposit of assets with the bank to back the forward contract.

When it comes to contractual arrangements through a broker, thus relying also on trading via an organized exchange, the market depends on a different risk management technique. Under this type of arrangement, the exchange stands behind the contracts, and a trader's default on its obligations become the exchange's own liability.[2] To manage this risk, the exchange imposes a condition that the value of each futures account must be **marked to market** each trading day, meaning that the value of each contract is adjusted to reflect that day's market value of the underlying. The mechanism requires a daily settlement of gain or loss. Marking to market is not done with forward contracts.

For a better understanding of this credit risk management technique, consider a buyer and a seller who enter into a contract for a 90-day government bond with a face value of 1,000,000 and that the contract opens at a price of $F(t, T) = 990,000$. This means that at date $t$, the buyer and the seller agree that 990,000 will be a fair price for buying or selling a 90-day bond at future date $T$. No cash is exchanged at $t$, although the exchange may require a deposit of both the buyer and the seller to their accounts held by the exchange.

Let us further suppose that only three trading days exist: the contract date, date $u$, and the expiry date, where $t < u < T$. Suppose also that at the close of trading on date $u$, the market consensus of the bond price at time $T$ has changed to $F(u, T) = 992,000$. The price increase favors the buyer, as he or she can buy later at date $T$ a bond for 990,000 for a potential gain of 2,000. The seller's position has deteriorated by an equivalent amount.

To this point, the example applies equally to forward and future traders. The futures exchange, however, requires marking to market; that is, the seller actually pays 2,000 at $u$, which is simultaneously credited to the buyer's account. After this settlement, the futures price for the buyer and the seller adjusts to the new price such that, at the end of day $u$, they have an obligation to trade at 992,000 at time $T$ rather than 990,000, because they have already realized part of the transaction. The buyer has 2,000 more cash and the seller has 2,000 less cash in their accounts.

Ignoring interest earning on the account values, the net effect of marking to market on the transaction is nil. However, the exchange has at risk the amount of price movement during each trading day, so the exchange protects itself by requiring traders to maintain a margin of cash in their accounts adequate to cover the price movement for a single day. If traders (in this example, the seller) do not have an adequate margin after the 2,000 deduction, the exchange closes the trader's position. In this way, marking to the market price practically eliminates future default risk.

To continue the example, assume now that the spot price at date $T$ of the futures is $S_T = 991,000$. The buyer must then pay 992,000 (the value to which its futures contracts was reset on day $u$) for a bond worth only 991,000. The buyer loses 1,000. Therefore, the net effect from date $t$ on the buyer is a gain of 1,000 (2,000 − 1,000). Similarly, the net effect on the seller is a loss of 1,000 (−2,000 + 1,000).

We note two important things. First, the exchange has no counterparty risk as long as it pairs up the buyer and the seller each day, and they maintain adequate margins. Second, the cash flows of forwards and futures differ as to timing but have the same total effect on traders' accounts (exclusive of interest). The following table illustrates this:

| | Trading Days | | | Sum of |
| --- | --- | --- | --- | --- |
| | $t$ | $u$ | $T$ | Cash Flows |
| $F(s, T)$ | 990,000 | 992,000 | 991,000 | |
| Forwards' cash flow | 0 | 0 | 1,000 | 1,000 |
| Futures' cash flow | 0 | 2,000 | −1,000 | 1,000 |

## Options

Forward and future markets offer traders a way to manage risk unavailable in the spot market. For example, a firm planning to sell stocks can hedge against a market price decline by selling stock index futures. The futures contract locks in a price for the stock, avoiding adverse consequences of a price decline, but it also prevents the firm from taking advantage of a price increase.

Options work differently. **Options** give its holder the right (but not the obligation) to buy (or sell) assets at a specific price – called the **strike** or **exercise price** – during a specified period. Like futures contracts, options provide hedgers with protection against an unfavorable price movement. Unlike futures contracts, options allow for the benefit of a price increase. By paying an up-front premium to the other trader, the option owner obtains this more favorable outcome. The owner's loss is limited to the price of the option.

   Option contracts appear in many areas of finance. Organized markets offer standard-ized contracts. The Chicago Board Options Exchange offers options on stocks. Commodity exchanges around the world offer options on real assets such as wheat, corn and oil. Over-the-counter (OTC) markets as well as exchanges provide options on bonds and currency exchange rates. Customized option contracts occur in other important financial settings, such as performance options, which are sometimes part of a corporate manager's or a professional baseball player's compensation. Customized options are also written on real estate, jet airliners and other expensive real assets to facilitate transfer of ownership. Other business contracts such as insurance policies, lease agreements and employment contracts typically have embedded options. The option contracts traded in organized markets are eas-ier to evaluate than customized options, because they are standardized and the markets are more efficient.

## *The basics*

Option contracts can be broadly grouped according to the position of the option holder – call versus put options. A **call option** gives its holder the right to purchase an asset (e.g., shares of stock) at a specified price before a specified date. A **put option** gives its holder the right to sell an asset at a fixed price during the option term.

   Like investors in other areas, option holders attempt to maximize gains from taking a call or put position. Consider a holder of a put option. If the market value (denoted by $S$) of the asset on which the option is written is less than the exercise price (denoted by $X$), the holder will exercise the right to sell the asset at $X$ and obtain it at the spot price of $S$. The hold-er's gain is $(X - S)$. The holder will not exercise the option when the spot price is greater than the exercise price. Therefore, the exercise value of a put option can be shown as:

$$(X - S)^+ = \begin{cases} X - S & \text{if } X > S \\ 0 & \text{if } X \le S \end{cases} \tag{14.2}$$

where the plus symbol on $(X - S)$ suggests the excess, if any, of the exercise price over the spot price. The expression is often written in a short form as:

$$\text{Max}(X - S, 0) = (X - S)^+ \tag{14.3}$$

Likewise, the gain, if any, of a call option holder can be expressed in a short form as:

$$\text{Max}(S - X, 0) = (S - X)^+ \tag{14.4}$$

   For example, consider a call option contact to buy bonds at a price of 70. The contract opens at time $t$ and matures at time $T$. The strike price 70 is analogous to the price $F(t, T)$ on a similar futures contract. The strike price remains unchanged throughout the contractual period. The difference is that the long (sell) position gain on the futures is $S(T) - F(t, T) = S(T) - 70$, whereas the option holder will exercise the right to buy the underlying asset only if the spot market price at time $T$ is greater than 70.

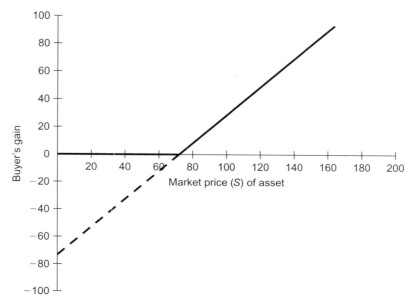

**Figure 14.1**  Option and Futures Contract Payoffs

Figure 14.1 shows the exercise value of a call option as a function of the closing price. This figure also depicts the key difference between future (and forward) contracts and options. The gain on the futures and options contracts is the same over the range of prices that are favorable to the buyer (prices in excess of 70). That is, if $S(u) > X$ at time $u$ (where $t < u < T$), the holder of the sell right can gain $S(u) - X$ by buying the underlying asset under the terms of the option and immediately selling it in the spot market. If the price $S(u)$ is below $X$ (prices less than 70), the holder will not exercise the option, because its exercise value is zero. Its intrinsic value is also zero at time $u$, but the market value of the option is positive because of a possibility that the market price rises above the exercise price until time $T$ reaches. (The option premium in this example is five.)

In the above example, the option holder's right increases in market value as the bond price rises. For example, a change in the bond price from 70 to 80 increases the exercise value to the holder from 0 to 10. If $S(T) \leqslant 70$, however, the option holder will not exercise his or her right and will allow the option to expire. Thus, the option holder's loss is limited to the price of the option. To secure this right, the option holder pays the other party in the contract the option's price – known as **premium** – at the time the holder obtains the right. The right to buy or sell under the terms of the option expires when the holder exercises the option. In contrast, no monetary consideration is exchanged at the time a futures contract is drawn.

Option contracts can be classified according to the time of the exercise right. **European (style) options** can be exercised only on the contract expiration date. **American (style) options** can be exercised at any time from the date of purchase until contract expiry. For two otherwise identical contracts, the American option is worth at least as much as the European option, because the former includes all the rights of the European option. Exchange-traded stock options are American style. So are most options traded on U.S. exchanges.

An option is analogous to a fire insurance contact written on a building. The insurer accepts a premium at time $t$ in exchange for the promise to indemnify the insured for fire damage $S(u)$ at time $u$ (where $u \leqslant T$) in excess of a deductible $X$ if the fire occurs no later than $T$. That is, if fire occurs no later than $T$, the insured receives a claims payment of $(S(u) - X)^{+}$.

The analogy is useful, but not perfect. It is useful because it illustrates the mathematical similarity of options to insurance. It is not perfect for at least two reasons. First, the fire insurance contract is personal, and the insured cannot transfer rights granted under the insurance policy to a third party. In contrast, option rights are easily traded in exchanges, and the value of options depends on this trading. Second, the fire insurance policy may not expire when the insurer pays fire damage, but exchange-traded options expire when exercised.

### *Option prices*

The most important contribution to option pricing theory or practice is the formula developed by Black and Scholes (1973) and the hedging techniques that underlie it. Merton (1973) contributed substantially to the development of this theory. The Black-Scholes model is frequently used to price options and to spot arbitrage opportunities in the securities market.

The model is based on several assumptions.[3] It assumes that default-free borrowing and investing at a known constant rate (denoted $r$) are available to all traders, that traders pay no transaction fees or taxes and that no arbitrage opportunities exist in or across the asset and option markets. Short selling and borrowing are allowed in the model. Securities can be traded in any quantity, including fractional amounts, and the number of stocks can be any real number, positive or negative.

The Black-Scholes formula assumes that the spot price follows a geometric Brownian motion. This can be described more formally as an assumption: the continuously compounded annual return $R(t, T)$ of the spot asset over the period $(t, T)$, defined by:

$$R(t, T) = \frac{1}{T - t} \log\left(\frac{S_T}{S_t}\right) \tag{14.5}$$

is normally distributed with mean $\mu$ and variance $\sigma^2$, where $\mu$ and $\sigma$ are constants. Also the stock's returns over disjoint time intervals are statistically independent.

As the stock price and return are related by the equation such that:

$$S_T = S_t e^{(T - t)R(t, T)} \tag{14.6}$$

we can conclude that the distribution of the return determines the distribution of prices. We in turn can estimate this distribution by observing price movements, calculating actual returns, and using the sample mean and variance as estimators for $\mu$ and $\sigma$. When the values of $\mu$ and $\sigma$ are based on actual price movements, we refer to the price distribution as the physical distribution. This so-called random walk model is often associated with stock price movements.

## Arbitrage

**Arbitrage** is the possibility of making a riskless gain with no chance of loss. Consider the practical possibilities of arbitrage based on the so-called **January effect**. Observers of the U.S. stock markets have long noticed that during the last days of each year and the beginning of the following year, stocks of small firms exhibit higher returns than stocks of large firms. Suppose now that an investor sells short the stock of a large firm in December for $10,000. Investors sell **short** when they sell assets that they do not own, borrowing them from a broker temporarily. Of course, the short seller ultimately must buy the stock and return it to the broker, hoping that the later purchase price is lower than the price at which he or she realized in selling the shares.[4] Short sellers hope to gain from a decrease in the price of the shares.

The investor uses the cash to purchase $10,000 worth of stock in a small firm. Assume the January effect occurs again, and the large-firm stock has risen 1 percent and the small-firm stock 1.2 percent. In January, the investor sells the small-firm stock for $10,120, and closes out the short position in the large-firm stock by buying it for $10,100. The investor is left – assuming no transaction costs – with a $20 trading profit.

This is only an apparent arbitrage. Even if it always has worked in the past, it is not certain to work in the future. A true arbitrage always works with certainty; that is, a no-risk money machine. For example, consider two investment opportunities $A$ and $B$ that do not pay dividends or coupons during a period $(t, T)$, where $t < T$. $A_t$ and $B_t$ are the current prices of these investments, and $A_T$ and $B_T$ the market values at time $T$. These future values are random as viewed from time $t$, but suppose that we are sure that $B_T$ will exceed $A_T$. If the price $A_t$ is higher than $B_t$, an arbitrage could be constructed as follows. An investor sells $A$ now (getting $A_t$ as cash) while incurring an obligation to pay $A_T$ at time $T$. As $B_t$ is less than $A_t$, the trader can buy $B$ with the cash from selling $A$ and is left with a positive amount, $A_t - B_t$. The benefit from buying $B$ is $B_T$ at time $T$, which is adequate to cover the trader's liability to pay $A_T$. This is a true arbitrage because the trader has a sure profit, $A_t - B_t$ now and no liability to pay in the future as $B_T - A_T = 0$.

Thus, we can conclude that in a market with no arbitrage, if the probability of $B_T > A_T$ is one, then $B_t$ is greater than or equal to $A_t$. Extending this conclusion, we know that in a market that admits no arbitrage, two assets (or securities, portfolios, liabilities and so forth) with identical cash flows in the future have the same prices today. This is sometimes called the **law of one price**. This simple idea has powerful consequences. The notion of arbitrage, or lack of it, is one of the most important concepts in finance.

An efficient market does not allow arbitrage because investors in the market respond instantaneously to any arbitrage opportunities, thus quickly eliminating such opportunities. Are the well-established stock and derivatives markets around the world so efficient that no arbitrage opportunities exist? The financial theory literature generally assumes that markets are efficient for two reasons.[5] First, no simple way exists to allow for individual or firm-specific behavioral differences. For example, we do not know how to include psychological differences of investors. Second, the efficient market assumptions yield results that often work well. Common sense also tells us that, with easy access to markets and well-informed traders, little arbitrage opportunities should exist.

The presence of some persistent anomalies seems to indicate a lack of efficiency and the possibility of arbitrage profits. The January effect discussed earlier is a rough example. Researchers also have found anomalies in the way that investors react to earnings announcements, initial public offerings and acquisitions.

## Swaps

A **swap** is the exchange of one security for another. Swaps are popular with traders in interest rates and currency rates. We discuss both below.

### *Currency swaps*

Suppose that two firms, one British and one Indian, can borrow in their own country or that of the other.[6] The British firm needs to finance a project in India for which it needs financing in Indian rupees. Similarly, the Indian firm needs British pound financing for its British project. Assume that each firm can borrow domestically at a lower rate than it can borrow in a foreign market, because it is easier to enforce a loan agreement domestically or because the firm has established a credit record at home but not abroad.

Suppose further that lenders offer 10-year bonds issued at face value with the following annual coupon rates:

| Country | British Borrower (%) | Indian Borrower (%) |
|---|---|---|
| United Kingdom | 9.0 | 11.0 |
| India | 12.0 | 10.0 |

Each firm has an advantage borrowing domestically. If they can engage in a currency swap, they can lower their cost of borrowing. For instance, the British firm borrows £100,000 at a coupon of 9 percent per year and immediately loans £100,000 to the Indian firm. The Indian firm's own cost is 11 percent for pounds, so it will gladly pay 9 percent. In turn, the Indian firm borrows 8.5 million rupees, the current equivalent of £100,000 pounds, at 10 percent per year, and immediately loans the entire amount to the British firm. Ten years later when the loans mature, the firms simply return each other's principals. The Indian firm returns the £100,000 to the British firm, and the British firm pays off the pound-denominated debt. Similarly, the British firm returns the 8.5 million rupees, and the Indian firm pays off the rupee-denominated debt. The net result is that each firm obtained its foreign financing at a better rate than it could using its own line of credit domestically.

A currency swap defines the cash flows between two firms subject to the agreement. The firms take care of their own domestic borrowing, if needed. The swap agreement specifies the initial exchange of principal amounts, the coupon rates and the final return of principal amounts. In the example, both firms pay fixed rates. In fact, the rates they charge each other need not be the rates they pay. In other words, the Indian firm could charge the British firm 11 percent, and the British firm would still accept it because the loan is still below its own cost of borrowing.

A swap also can be arranged such that one party pays a floating rate. For example, the pound-denominated debt may carry a floating interest rate. In this case, the swap would specify that the British firm pay fixed-rupee coupons and receive floating-rupee coupons from the Indian firm. The parties in a currency swap settle their interests due in each scheduled settlement (payment) date.

A swap is a financial application of the principle of comparative advantage. Firms gain by specializing in the production of goods or services for which they have the lowest opportunity cost, and exchange them for desired goods or services for which they have a high opportunity cost.

### Interest rate swaps

A second popular type of swap, called an interest rate swap, also is widely used, especially by financial intermediaries. These swaps are similar to currency swaps, but the investment principals on both sides of the swap are in the same currency. Typically, one party pays a fixed rate of interest on the principal, and the other party pays a floating rate of interest on the principal. Unlike currency swaps, these payments are exchanged on a net basis; that is, one party that owes the greater of the two interests calculated on the settlement date pays the other party the difference.

The predecessor to the modern swap product involved actual exchanges of principals, but these exchanges of principals exposed both parties to greater default risk than does the modern practice of dispensing with exchanges of principals. Further, the principals on both sides of the swap are the same amount and in the same currency, and, hence, they always net to zero. As a result, the principals are not exchanged in interest rate swaps.

The markets in currency and interest rate swaps are made by dealers such as commercial banks, investment banks and insurance firms, among others. The markets are OTC markets, but several major futures exchanges offer services to facilitate the markets, including collateral depositories that have some of the characteristics of clearing houses.

## Managing Financial Risk: Two Examples

We now offer two examples of firms managing two types of financial risk. The first is an MNC that desires to hedge it foreign exchange (FX) exposure. The second is an energy company that wishes to hedge against loss of revenues because of too warm winter.

### Example 1: FX risk

Currency futures developed in the 1970s as a means of managing exposures arising from changes in currency exchange rates. Exchanges in the world's major financial centers offer currency futures and options. For example, the Chicago Mercantile Exchange (CME) makes available futures on exchange rates between U.S. dollars and the euro as well as the currencies of Australia, Brazil, Canada, Japan, Mexico, New Zealand, Russia, South Africa, Switzerland and the U.K. It also places futures between the euro and currencies of Japan, Switzerland and the U.K.

In addition to exchanges, many banks deal in currency forward contracts. As with the exchange-traded futures discussed earlier, currency futures traded on exchanges require marking to market. Forward contracts are not marked to market so they carry default risk. The banks in the forward market are solid financially, so little default risk exists when dealing with them. Banks dealing with their customers must consider their customer's credit worthiness.

The currency futures and forward markets are well integrated and huge with a large number of sophisticated traders. This suggests that currency market prices adjust quickly and arbitrage opportunities are rare. Several currency relations follow from the no arbitrage assumption. Accordingly, if $S_{a,b}$ denotes the rate of exchange for converting one unit of currency $b$ to units of currency $a$, then the no arbitrage currency exchange relation is:

$$S_{a,b} \times S_{b,c} = S_{a,c} \qquad (14.7)$$

for any three currencies ($a$, $b$, and $c$) under the no arbitrage theory. See Appendix 14A for the proof.

Suppose that an Australian MNC borrows US$90 million from a U.S. pension trust. In return, the MNC promises to repay US$100 million in one year. One year later, it will have to buy US$100 million to meet its investment contract obligation. To lock in the rate of exchange – thereby hedging the exposure – it opens a forward contract with a bank. The MNC and the bank agree that one year from now, the corporation will buy US$100 million at a rate of A$1.35 per U.S. dollar. This is the forward price: $F(t, T) = 1.35$. The MNC will have to honor the terms of the forward contract, buying at 1.35, even if the market price of U.S. dollars turns out to be less one year later. If, for example, the market price is 1.30, the MNC pays A$135 million for US$100 million with a market value of only A$130. The MNC loses A$5 million. If the price moves up to 1.40, the bank must deliver US$100 million, with a market value of A$140 million, in exchange for A$135 million. The bank loses A$5 million.

The forward contract handles the downside risk but, as we saw before, the forward also eliminates the benefit of a favorable price movement. Options can handle the unfavorable risk without eliminating the benefit of a favorable price movement.

Currency options, in both European and American styles, are widely available in numerous exchanges. For an option on futures, an exchange first has to offer futures on the currency rate. The option on futures contract allows the option owner to open a futures contract at the option's exercise price. The day the owner exercises the option, he or she becomes a futures trader and must mark to market. Of course, the futures position can be closed out the same day that the option is exercised. This allows futures options to be used in the same way as options written directly on the rate. The options on futures are more complex, and the American exercise feature makes them much harder to evaluate (Stoll and Whalley, 1993). See Appendix 14B for an example of pricing a currency option.

### Example 2: weather risk

Weather is purely external to any organization. It is largely localized to a region, with forecasts still problematical. Weather affects everyone and perhaps all businesses. It has an enormous effect on business revenues and profits. For example, an estimated 30 percent of U.S. economic activity is believed affected directly by weather. Numerous affected industries come quickly to mind: agriculture, beverage, construction, energy, hospitality, retailing, transportation, utilities and others. Thus, an unusually warm winter with reduced snowfall could result in reduced revenues for ski resorts as skiers and riders stay away. Utility and energy companies could similarly suffer reduced revenues because less heat was needed to warm homes and buildings. Conversely, an exceptionally cold summer might discourage people from traveling to beach resorts, leaving many hotel rooms and airline seats vacant.

Of course, insurance is available for many weather-related losses, especially natural catastrophes. Such protection, when effected, indemnifies only if a weather event causes direct physical damage and the resulting (consequential) loss of business income as well as extra expenses. However, traditional insurance does nothing to replace lost revenues resulting from weather merely being hotter or colder than normal, being wetter or dryer than normal or being more or less windy than normal.

Corporations that are exposed to weather-related risk may consider weather derivatives. The first transaction of a weather derivative took place in 1997. With this sale, the notion that weather could be a tradable commodity took concrete shape. With such instruments, weather as measured in various ways (e.g., by temperature, precipitation and wind speed) for each instrument is indexed in terms of monthly or seasonal averages and a value attached to each unit of the index. Deviations from the index then become the basis for payment to the holder if the derivative is in the money. The underlying is the index rather than more traditional stocks, stock indices, currencies, interest rates or commodities.

In 1999, the CME introduced exchange-traded weather futures and options, thus bringing standardization and the other benefits of exchange trading as discussed earlier, such as settlement in cash. The CME now trades temperature-based weather derivative contracts for 18 U.S. cities, nine European cities and two Japanese cities. Recent additions to the CME offerings track frost days in the Netherlands and snowfall in Boston and New York.

The mechanics are as follows. For the winter months, indexes of heating-degree-day (HDD) values are provided for the cities covered by CME's products. For the U.S., indexes are calculated as the differences between 65°F and each city's average daily temperature for those days for which energy is used for heating (i.e., the months of November through March as one winter season).[7] Similar contracts are available for the summer season (May through September), based on indexes of cooling-degree-day (CDD) values, representing the difference between 65°F and the average daily temperature for those days for which energy is used for air conditioning. HDD values above 65°F are zero and CDD values below 65°F are zero on the theory that heating is not needed for temperatures above 65°F nor air conditioning needed for temperature below 65°F. Each city's average daily temperature is the simple average of each day's high and low temperatures.

Thus, summing each day's HDD in the winter season or CDD in the summer season yields the value of the corresponding monthly or seasonal index. For example, assume that Atlanta recorded 10 days in March 2007 with the following HDD values: 21, 22, 14, 25, 20, 21, 25, 12, 29 and 20. Conversely, in other days of the month, the average daily temperature was above 65°F, thus yielding a zero HDD value. The HDD index for the month thus becomes 209 – the sum of the individual days' values. The minimum tick fluctuation at the CME is "one-degree-day index point" with a value of US$20. Thus, the March index for Atlanta would settle for US$4,180 (US$20 × 209).

Let us now examine how a manufacturer can use weather derivatives. Suppose that a European energy company is concerned that global warming may cause an abnormally warm winter this year for its major client city, resulting in substantially reduced revenues because its customers will need less home heating, penalizing earnings per share for the entire year. From past data, its CRO has estimated that it will suffer a revenue decline of €10,000 for each degree when the actual daily winter temperature falls above the long-term average daily temperature, say 18°C, for the 150-day period of November through March. Based on discussion with the CFO, the CRO also has learned that the company has a capital cushion to withstand up to 1,000 HDD values for the winter.

To hedge this financial risk, the CRO may recommend that the company purchase a weather put option with a right to exercise it once the accumulated HDD values exceed a certain threshold set by the firm. For example, suppose that the firm secures an option right at a premium of €5 million and with the option threshold at 500 HDD values. During the contract period, the firm will then exercise its option once the HDD index passes 500 points, thus generating an option benefit of €10,000 per one-degree-day index point. If the HDD index passes 1,000 (the break-even point based on the option premium) during the season, the firm will generate income from this contract.

One can construct numerous other cases. The CME reports more than 630,000 weather contracts with a notional value of US$22 billion traded through September 2005. Insurers, reinsurers, banks and energy companies in France, Japan, Switzerland and the U.S. are the commonly known participants in the weather derivatives market. With the recent increase in the concern about global warming, the market is expected to continue its growth.

Not surprisingly, several insurance companies offer weather insurance, probably with their own exposure hedged by their purchase of weather derivatives. For example, municipal governments and commercial property owners may purchase so-called "snow insurance" that promises a fixed compensation (e.g., $10,000) per centimeter of snow exceeding a total accumulation set in the policy (e.g., 50 centimeters). Imagine the potential benefit of such insurance to New York City that spends on average of US$1 million per inch of snow removal. The average annual snowfall is 25–35 inches (63–89 centimeters). Of course, ski resort operators may consider snow insurance for the opposite reason – to protect them from the increase in the cost for artificial snow generation in warm winter.

# RISK FINANCING THROUGH INSURANCE

As noted, MNCs are believed to rely heavily on insurance, not necessarily because such global firms lack the capacity to retain most of their loss exposures, but often for servicing efficiency and knowledge that an international insurer and brokers can bring to corporate risk management. Corporations also may purchase insurance for matters related to managerial self-interest, taxation, financial distress and capital market imperfections, which we discussed in Chapter 2. Issues and solutions related to specific needs for insurance to manage personnel, property and liability risks are discussed throughout this book.

In this section, we first examine two major, developing liability risks: director's and officer's (D&O) liability and employment practices liability (EPL). Next, we discuss how MNCs manage their local and foreign loss exposures using an international insurance program as an extension of the international risk management program discussed in Chapter 12.

## Liability Insurance for MNCs

When using insurance to manage liability risks, both purely domestic companies (including even small business owners) and MNCs need to examine the sources of liability. The most common sources of liability arise from ownership or use of business premises and business activities. Insight 14.1 provides an overview of the liability that can be associated with a firm's premises and its operations.

Managing legal liability can be especially complicated for firms operating in multiple jurisdictions. The legal environments differ from one jurisdiction to another as do the magnitude and scope of the economic consequences. In some countries, the term liability is interpreted broadly, and any persons or entities that believe that they are victims of a wrongdoing by another can bring a legal action. Under the contingency fee system found in the U.S., individuals may file cases in civil court at little or no cost to themselves, as plaintiffs compensate their lawyers only if they prevail. Consumerism continues to develop in many countries, thus increasing the likelihood of class actions. Insight 14.2 offers further observations on trends in liability worldwide.

---

### INSIGHT 14.1: GENERAL BUSINESS LIABILITY ──────────

Businesses are responsible for the health and safety of their employees and customers and sometimes their vendors, visitors, and even strangers. This so-called general (public) liability deals primarily with managing premises and operational liability loss exposures. That is, owners and those using business premises have a duty to make the premises and their operations safe to third parties. The third party can be a guest, licensee or trespasser. A **guest** is a person entering the premises primarily to benefit the property owner or user. Business clients and shoppers – irrespective of whether they actually purchase a product or service from the business – are commonly classified as guests. A **licensee** is a visitor entering the premises primarily to conduct his or her own business such as a delivery person. A **trespasser** is a person entering the premises with no apparent reason to be there and without explicit or implied permission from the owner or user.

Courts in many countries award up to three types of monetary damages to successful plaintiffs because of tortuous acts of others. **Economic damages** result directly from an injury, such as lost wages, medical expenses and repair or replacement of damaged property. **Non-economic damages** (also called **special damages**) result from the consequences of economic damages such as awards because of the pain and suffering of the injured person or the loss that a spouse feels from the death of his or her spouse. **Punitive damages** are court-imposed financial penalties arising from tortuous acts that are determined to be especially egregious, ordinarily because of a tortfeasor's intentional or willful act. They are intended to punish the tortfeasor.

---

Managing liability risks is a global phenomenon. Swiss Re (2004) reports that liability claims in the largest 10 nonlife insurance markets worldwide reached US$84 billion in 2002, of which US$67 billion was from the U.S. market alone. It also reports long-term growth of liability claims at 1.5–2 times faster than that of GDP. In the U.S., liability claims account for 2.2 percent of GDP, making the country's liability system twice as expensive as those of other developed countries. This U.S. liability environment can affect non-U.S. corporations that export goods and services to or have a physical presence (e.g., offices and plants) in the U.S. The most problematic lines of business are EPL, D&O liability, product liability, medical malpractice and other errors and omissions (E&O) liability. The first two are especially relevant to MNCs so we explore them in more detail below.

Chapter 10 deals with major systems of law, tort law and contract law globally. That discussion is directly applicable to MNCs' management of their liability risks and provides background for this section.

#### Employment practices liability insurance

Governments globally continue to introduce new regulatory and remedial measures dealing with various types of employee discrimination. As a result, we observe a rise in the number of claims where employers are alleged to have wrongfully terminated employment or failed to ensure that procedures were in place and enforced to protect employees against various offensive actions. These changes in the legal environment, and employee attitudes as well,

---

### INSIGHT 14.2: THE CHANGING LIABILITY LANDSCAPE ————

The issue of past, current and potential liabilities has occupied the boards of directors of large companies for decades. This landscape of liability – therefore the risks for companies and to shareholder value – is changing rapidly.

First, the meaning of legal liability itself is undergoing a period of significant change. The causes of action, standards of evidence, and procedural rules that courts either tolerate or require are all shifting to describe a new legal landscape in which business must now operate.

Second, business is vulnerable to new and more aggressive forms of legal activism. This reflects three trends: the shift by non-governmental organizations away from attacking to exploiting legislation; the emergence, particularly in North America, of a highly profitable class actions industry; and the arrival of a new generation of lawyers, many of whom put correcting social and environmental injustice ahead of salary and career development.

Third, there is an accelerating shift in societal values and expectations and a corresponding mistrust of industry that feeds a demand for greater corporate accountability whether through new standards of governance, new disclosure requirements, or accounting rules.

Finally, a progressive internalization of social and environmental costs is bringing business into the firing line of liability for its past and future activities. This will not only bring huge costs to business for its on-going trading, but might also render companies vulnerable to legal action for past and future impacts resulting from corporate actions which are perceived to be irresponsible.

*Source*: Swiss Re (2004).

---

drove commercial insurers to shift coverage for such claims from general liability insurance to EPL insurance, with broader coverage and higher limits.

*Trends in employment practice liability*

As noted in Chapter 12, EPL allegations can arise from unfair dismissal; discrimination based on age, gender or disability; and retaliation (e.g., penalizing a "whistle blower" – a person who tells of a wrongdoing). Employment-related misrepresentation (e.g., an employer providing a baseless evaluation about its former employee to his or her prospective employer) as well as libel (written defamation), slander (spoken defamation) and emotional distress also can be the basis of EPL claims in some jurisdictions. The recent lawsuits against Wal-Mart for gender discrimination in personnel actions and for underpaying illegal aliens for custodial work are well-publicized EPL examples.

Employers manage EPL risks in various ways, the most effective being establishment of employment practices guidelines that are widely communicated, clear and rigorously enforced. Insight 14.3 offers several preventive measures that employers use to minimize EPL loss exposures.

INSIGHT 14.3: PREVENTIVE MEASURES TO MANAGE EPL  ⸺

Employers commonly use some or all of the following both because they represent good personnel practice and because their effective use can prevent lawsuits:

- Establish hiring practices in compliance with local laws.
- Distribute employee handbooks that clearly document the entity's employment policies and procedures without using ambiguous words or jargon.
- Provide all employees with a formal, published policy dealing with sexual harassment and discrimination. Good practice calls for regular review and revision of the policy. Most firms post all related documents.
- Conduct scrupulous annual performance reviews with interim reviews to correct unacceptable behaviors.
- Strictly follow established policy for terminating employees.
- Conduct and document exit interviews.
- Promptly investigate all allegations of harassment or discrimination.

*Source*: Jarret (2003). Reprinted with permission from Risk Management Magazine. © 2003 Risk and Insurance Management Society, Inc. All right reserved.

Employers increasingly purchase EPL insurance. This trend is particularly strong in the U.S. where employers are subject to numerous employment-related laws, including *Title VII of the Civil Rights Act* of 1964, the *Age Discrimination in Employment Act* of 1967, *Americans with Disabilities Act* of 1990, *the Civil Rights Act* of 1991, and *the Family and Medical Leave Act* of 1993. The contingency fee system and the breadth of EPL claims (e.g., to include emotional distress) provided impetus for the early development of EPL insurance in the U.S.

Jury Verdict Research (2004) reports that the median compensatory EPL award in the U.S. rose from US$93,000 in 1994 to US$250,000 in 2003. Most successful cases were of plaintiffs claiming age or disability discrimination. In comparison, Agatstein (2000) reports that unfair dismissals dominate EPL cases in many other countries. Differences in economic conditions, cultural norms (e.g., perceived role of women in the family and society), and labor unionization also affect the frequency of EPL claims and damage awards.

Punitive damage awards are no longer unique in the U.S. In Europe, the European Court of Justice has established cases permitting payments for aggravated or moral damages – similar to the concept of punitive damages in the U.S. – caused by negligent employers. This principle has been adopted by Switzerland, the U.K. and elsewhere in the E.U. (Agatstein, 2000). Limited forms of non-economic damage awards are available in some other countries.

*EPL insurance coverage*

EPL policies usually insure the corporation, its subsidiaries and their directors, officers and employees as insureds.[8] Most policies include former employees. Some policies also cover leased employees, temporary employees and volunteers, whereas some other limit the coverage to managerial or supervisory employees only. Given the importance of loss prevention measures in EPL risk management, several insurance companies offer services such as EPL risk management audit and sample employee handbooks.

EPL policies indemnify the insured up to the limit of insurance, which can be in combination of the actual claims and legal expenses. Coverage is triggered by allegations that the insured committed unfair dismissal, discrimination or retaliation, subject to the precise terms of the policy. EPL policies do not respond to general liability claims or fiduciary liability claims. Neither do they respond to work-related bodily injuries to employees. Some policies cover only claims arising in a single location, whereas others offer global coverage.

### Directors and officers liability insurance

A wrongful act – error, misstatement, misleading statement, omission or breach of duty – of a director or officer of a corporation can trigger a claim against not only the director or officer but also against the firm itself. D&O liability insurance – a type of E&O coverage – is designed to respond to this type of loss exposure. The specifics of the insurance are as follows:

- *D&O liability coverage*: This E&O coverage agrees to defend and, if necessary, to indemnify any directors and officers – broadly those responsible for tactical and strategic decision-making – of the insured entity in connection with allegations that they failed to carry out their duties according to the reasonable standards in the community or economy. Often called "Side A" coverage, this coverage will play claims on behalf of the affected directors and officers.

- *Corporate reimbursement coverage*: Often called "Side B" coverage, it agrees to indemnify the entity for the legal and other costs that it incurs in defending its directors and officers in any "threatened, pending or completed action or proceeding, whether civil, criminal, administrative or investigative" (Oshinsky and Howard, 2001). In the usual arrangement, the business will have agreed, as part of the engagement or employment contract, to cover any such costs incurred by directors and officers. In this and the above coverages, the suit is against one or more of the directors and officers, not against the entity.

- *Entity coverage*: Increasingly, directors and officers plaintiffs name the entity itself as well as its directors and officers as defendants. In response to this trend, insurance companies introduced entity coverage. This extension covers legal expenses and any resulting financial liability from cases in which a claim is made directly against the entity for a wrongful act of the entity. This endorsement eliminates the coverage gap under standard D&O insurance, which otherwise responds only to allegations of a wrongful act committed by a director or officer of the insured entity.

When entity coverage is added (commonly as an endorsement) to a typical D&O policy, the limit of this endorsement is subject to the aggregate limit of the policy itself. Thus, a concern arises that directors and officers covered by the policy could end up sharing the limit of insurance with the entity, because the addition not only broadens the coverage trigger but also the potential share of legal expenses subject to the limit. Directors and officers also face the risk of the coverage limit being drained through litigation between an officer and the entity or, if the firm were to face bankruptcy, the risk of the entire policy limit being attached by the trustee (Flinter and Trupin, 2004). D&O insurers offer a solution to these concerns with a separate limit or a restriction on the coverage limit for entity coverage.

D&O insurance policies available in most E.U. countries and Japan are similar to those in the U.S. Insurance premiums are tax deductible expenses to the corporation and are usually not considered as (imputed) income to directors.

The *Canada Business Corporations Act* explicitly permits corporations to purchase D&O insurance.[9] As a result, a corporation operating in Canada may purchase insurance to cover liability damages assessed against them and their directors and officers as well as to cover their defense costs. Coverage may be extended to liabilities arising during the bankruptcy of a corporation. Some limitations exist. For example, a Canadian firm may be barred from purchasing insurance for liability arising from a director's failure to act prudently and in good faith (unless the director participates in premium payment). Also, insurers may require insureds to assume high deductibles, a rather general trend in the midst of recent corporate governance crises worldwide.

## Insurance Programs for MNCs

MNCs ordinarily can arrange cover for their international exposures in three major ways. They can rely on admitted insurance (a decentralized approach), use nonadmitted insurance (a centralized approach), or rely on a combination of the two approaches (a global master program approach).[10]

### *Admitted insurance*

Purchasing locally admitted insurance coverage means that the MNC has purchased insurance from insurers authorized to do business in that country. The insurer issues policies that comply with local laws, and the contract is written in the language of that country. Policy servicing is by the insurer's local offices, and a local agent or broker usually is involved.

Governments often require organizations doing business in a particular country to purchase insurance from an admitted insurer, as discussed in Chapter 3. An MNC, therefore, may be required to purchase coverage from locally admitted insurers in some countries in which it operates. Even though more efficient ways of managing the exposure may exist, most MNCs place a high priority on complying with local laws. Local authorities may levy high penalties if insurance was not purchased locally as required. Additionally, business activities such as contracts, ownership of property or banking relationships may require the purchase of admitted insurance.

Purchasing coverage locally may offer advantages. The policy will be serviced locally, and local management likely will be more accustomed to the practices of the local insurer and broker. That premiums and claims will be paid in the local currency makes such transactions less complex. When losses are paid in the local currency, the effect of foreign exchange rate fluctuations is eliminated unless the foreign subsidiaries must import equipment and materials to repair or replace damaged items. Where this is a significant problem, one solution is to have policies that might be called upon to finance such losses denominated in the currency of the country from which the equipment and materials would be imported.

Premiums paid locally usually are deductible as a business expense for tax purposes. By contrast, premiums for unauthorized nonadmitted insurance may not be deductible. Additionally, by having the subsidiary pay for its insurance locally, local accountability may be enhanced. Local management might retain a stronger interest in the cost of insurance purchased and in loss control. While incurring the cost centrally, by purchasing nonadmitted insurance and then allocating that cost to the subsidiary would accomplish the same loss control objectives, the expense may not be tax deductible locally.

The local insurer and broker can provide advice and risk management services. The local insurance representatives may understand coverage nuances and local practices and be able to design more appropriate programs than could be done from another country.

Additionally, there is value in knowing that the insurance program is complying with local laws and the corporation is being a good corporate citizen. Doing business with local insurance organizations also serves to help integrate the firm with the local economy and business community.

However, purchasing local coverage can have drawbacks for the MNC. A policy written in another language may be difficult to evaluate and manage by the MNC's risk manager. The risk manager also may be unfamiliar with local insurance practices, and the terms and conditions of local contracts may not be as favorable or easily understood, resulting in non-uniform conditions and increasing the possibility of coverage gaps and underinsurance. For example, in those countries where 100 percent insurance to value (coinsurance) is required, underinsurance can subject loss settlements to penalties.

Also, local policies may be more costly. If the country has tariff rates or lacks a competitive market or underwriting sophistication, rates are likely to be higher. It may be more difficult to evaluate local insurers' financial security. The availability of meaningful solvency regulation, financial statements and insurer rating services varies widely. Uncertainty regarding the financial security of host country insurers often leads to the selection of a large multinational insurer whose security is more certain.

By buying insurance locally in each country, the corporation looses negotiation power and the spread of risk associated with centralized purchasing. Moreover, in some cases, local coverage programs can run counter to corporate policy, making corporate risk management strategy difficult to implement. This problem can be especially acute as MNCs embrace ERM. If the corporate policy is to retain significant amounts of loss through large deductibles or self-insured retentions to control premium outlays, it may face difficulty when the local market does not offer such insurance programs. In fact, business practices in many countries do not favor large retentions, and they may not be encouraged by the local insurance industry or regulator. For highly decentralized multinationals, coordinating local programs with a common risk management philosophy is difficult. However, for highly decentralized multinationals, which seems to be a growing trend, or where the risk manager does not have centralized authority, local programs are common.

### Nonadmitted insurance

Nonadmitted insurance exists when an individual or company buys insurance from an unauthorized insurer. Thus, when an MNC purchases insurance for its subsidiary from an insurer licensed in its home country but not in the subsidiary's host country, it purchases nonadmitted insurance.

The advantages of nonadmitted insurance are centralized administrative control, broader terms and conditions and possibly lower cost. The nonadmitted policy will be administered by the risk manager on a centralized basis for operations worldwide. The program would be negotiated with insurer representatives domestically, which reduces administrative and communication problems. The security of the insurer selected is more easily ascertainable than may be the case with multiple local insurers. That coverage is written in the home country language and denominated in a common currency makes nonadmitted insurance easier to administer at the corporate level. For example, a U.S. risk manager may be accustomed to all-risks coverage, coverage extensions or conditions that may be unavailable in some countries or be strictly controlled by regulatory authorities. The uniformity of coverage design simplifies administration and provides assurance that the unique exposures of the corporation are treated similarly. The premium rate for nonadmitted coverage may be lower than for local admitted policies. This may be due to rate regulation or the existence of tariff rates locally and the leverage of buying a consolidated coverage.

The nonadmitted policy premium will be payable in the home country currency, as will losses. A single currency eliminates the risk of exchange rate fluctuations on loss payments. The MNC can then decide whether to reinvest those loss recoveries in its subsidiary. As the nonadmitted policy would be administered in the home country, any coverage disputes would be subject to the home country legal system and courts.

Nonadmitted programs may have serious disadvantages. Claims settlement can become more complicated without local coverage and the assistance of local insurer representatives. This is particularly true with liability claims. Additionally, just as the risk manager might want to purchase nonadmitted insurance because of his or her uncertainty with local coverage, local management may not understand the nonadmitted coverage and buy their own coverage to be sure they are protected. In practice, nonadmitted coverage is more likely to be used where the exposures or the availability of local coverage is limited, or as explained below, in conjunction with local coverages.

### *Global master program*

The third approach is for the MNC to use a combination of admitted and nonadmitted coverages. MNCs with highly decentralized operations, including risk management operations, often allow subsidiaries to manage all of their risks, including insurance purchase, as they wish. In such situations, different insurers are used in each country, so program coordination becomes more difficult. Two solutions to this fragmentation problem are fronting and a global master program. As we have already discussed fronting arrangement in Chapter 13, we focus on the global master program.

MNCs often use one international insurer and its network of subsidiaries, affiliates or both to structure their insurance programs in this way. The insurer is commonly known as the master policy insurer or lead insurer. Those subsidiaries or affiliates are admitted in the countries of operation, thus issuing admitted contracts and providing claims and other policy-related services. It also is possible to coordinate a global master program through an international insurance broker. In this case, the broker assumes primary responsibility for selecting and arranging insurance coverages and services.

In designing the program, local conditions determine the scope of local coverage. Thus, minimum amounts may be purchased if tariff rates are high and coverage restricted. Where pricing and terms and conditions are flexible, purchasing locally the broadest coverage available will be more appropriate. A broad admitted contract may provide the greatest tax benefit and local accountability, and its premium may more accurately reflect local experience.

To supplement the local policies, the MNC purchases an excess policy providing broad additional coverage from the lead insurer. This policy is called the master contract and is nonadmitted in the countries where the subsidiaries operate. The effect is to upgrade the coverage of local primary policies to a uniform, worldwide standard created by the master contract. The master contract contains (1) difference-in-conditions (DIC) and (2) difference-in-limits (DIL) clauses that, while not standardized, provide coverage (1) against additional perils with fewer restrictions and (2) with higher limits, respectively.

With this arrangement, premium savings can be realized by minimizing duplicate coverage and consolidated purchasing. Risk management goals are more likely realized through such a centralized approach. The lead insurer can better coordinate the program with its subsidiaries/affiliates internationally. Ideally, the controlling home country insurer considers the program comprising the master policy and local policies as a single portfolio of risks and underwrites the program centrally. Centralized underwriting involves considering the exposures, loss experience and pricing in the aggregate. The lead insurer is expected to provide direction in claims administration and other services, such as loss control. Of course, the combined approach requires more cooperation from local management.

This process sometimes can work even in strictly regulated markets. Centralized underwriting and pricing is facilitated when the local insurer acts as a fronting insurer; that is, the insurer fronts the coverage to (reinsurers with) the master contract insurer. The master contract insurer even can be a captive of the MNC. This approach, of course, is subject to any local reinsurance restrictions.

The emphasis, up to this point, has been on the foreign exposures of MNCs. MNCs often treat their domestic exposures separately from foreign exposures for several reasons. U.S. MNCs usually have separate policies covering their U.S. exposures, as an attempt not to expose either the domestic or foreign insurance to difficulties in the other. For a similar reason, many non-U.S. MNCs do not want to expose their global programs to what many consider a hostile U.S. liability environment. Some insurers do not want to write a global program with a high concentration of U.S. liability exposures.

A complete separation of the domestic program from the foreign program, however, may expose the MNC to another issue. For example, when the MNC's international operations are interdependent, a disruption in one facility can interrupt others, thus potentially creating a gap in coverage when the policies in other countries do not respond. By more fully integrating the foreign and domestic exposures in a global master program, questions of coverage are further minimized. Figure 14.2 shows a full extension of the program integrating both domestic and international insurance needs.

Figure 14.2 shows that an MNC purchases its own property and liability insurance coverages from the master policy insurer. This insurer, through its subsidiaries/affiliates, provides admitted insurance to the MNC's subsidiaries located in other countries. Local subsidiaries/affiliates of the insurer work with the subsidiaries of the MNC in each country to place risks locally when required by law and to provide additional insurance coverage services when such a placement is more cost effective. Risks that are not covered locally due to the limit of coverage amount, scope or both but that the MNC has decided to finance through insurance are then covered under the master policy issued by the lead insurer. The lead insurer also covers the MNC's exposures in the home country using separate property and liability insurance policies subject to the terms and conditions of the entire global program. The figure also shows two types of upper-layer excess insurance. The umbrella insurance is to protect the MNC from excess losses in selected lines of liability insurance. The whole account insurance protects the firm from excess losses in the entire portfolio of insurance policies.

With this integrated approach, the MNC's can reduce potential coverage gaps. Consistency of liability limits also can be achieved whether a legal action is brought in the MNC's

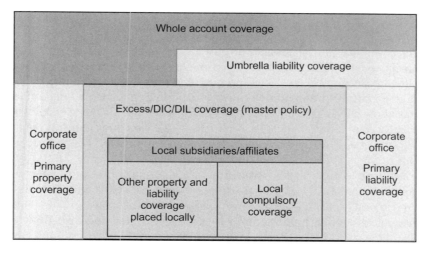

**Figure 14.2**    Illustration of a Fully Integrated Controlled Master Program for MNCs. *Source*: Kwon and Sarma (2004)

home country for operations in a foreign country and vice versa. For example, if a franchisee in Cameroon of a French multinational hotel has a serious liability claim, but the suit is brought in France, the higher limit normally carried in France would be available on a worldwide basis. An additional advantage of a global program is that worldwide rates, terms and conditions are negotiated to reflect the global size and experience of the MNC, thus the firm gaining great economies of scale and scope in external risk financing through insurance.

Because global programs require more central control, the risk manager has additional opportunities to implement a consistent global ERM strategy. For example, the global program can use additional risk financing options that incorporate incentives for loss control through cost allocation. Thus, a global program might allow for various deductible levels to offer local managers more decision authority. If local managers are more comfortable with low deductibles, they may be allowed to buy down the deductible for an increased premium. Funding the higher premium provides an incentive to reduce losses and use higher deductibles.

Full integration of local and foreign exposures, however, does not mean that it is without any shortcomings. The MNC may face an undesired counterparty risk in concentrating its insurance purchases in a single insurer. To avoid this, the MNC may demand that the global insurer spread the MNC's risk using various reinsurance arrangements. Few insurers have the ability to write global programs. Global programs seem to be best suited to organizations with centralized organizational structures and highly integrated worldwide operations, such as high technology MNCs.

## INTEGRATED LOSS FINANCING ARRANGEMENTS

Over the past decade, insurers and brokers have introduced risk financing arrangement that combine elements of both financial and hazard risk protection. We introduce two such products below.

## Integrated Multi-line/Multi-year Financial Products

A multi-line insurance policy is one that provides coverage over multiple lines of insurance, where lines are different classes of insurance, such as property insurance, liability insurance, fidelity insurance, etc. The most common forms of nonlife insurance sold today are multi-line contracts. A corporation may be interested in having a single financial contract that provides coverage for a range of hazard risks and financial risks with a single deductible and policy limit applicable to all losses and over time. Such a contract differs from a traditional multi-line umbrella policy (as shown in Figure 14.2) with separate limits and deductibles for each line of insurance coverage.

An extension of a multi-line insurance policy is a multi-line/multi-year policy. This extended insurance policy not only covers multiple lines but also offers the insured a single contract covering multiple years (e.g., three years) subject to renewal.

Such integrated contracts ordinarily will experience less loss volatility over time. Additionally, there should be less chance of over-insurance. One can envision this approach being expanded to include a broader range of loss exposures. The more exposures included, the closer such a contract is aligned to the ERM concept, as it takes a holistic approach to loss payouts.

## Multi-trigger financial products

Shareholders do not much care whether earnings per share are eroded by insurable or uninsurable losses. They care about total losses. With multi-trigger products, claims are paid only if, in addition to an insurance event ("first trigger") during the contract period, a non-insurance event ("second trigger") also occurs.

For example, assume that an oil company can sustain a $10 million loss internally from either some hazard event, say a fire, or lower oil prices, but it cannot finance both from internal funds during the same year. The solution is to design a multi-trigger product whose retention (deductible) is ordinarily $10 million unless the price of oil falls below some agreed upon level. If it does, reductions in the retention automatically kick in as the price of oil drops below the threshold set in the insurance policy.

Insurers offer other types multi-trigger coverage. Suppose, for example, that an MNC can sustain a fire loss to one of its plants *or* a loss resulting from a deep depreciation of its local currency against that of the export country but not both for a given year. An international insurer may customize a policy such that the insurer indemnifies the MNC for both fire damage and currency exchange loss provided that (1) both events occur during the same policy year (usually one year) and (2) the traditionally insurable loss (e.g., fire) is the first trigger. Given that the probability of the MNC experiencing both losses is lower that the probability of any one of the two events, the premium will be lower than otherwise. Such a contract is probably more consistent with ERM programs where the MNCs use internal risk financing arrangements as primary and wish to limit their loss exposures resulting from a series of disastrous events in any given year.

## CONCLUSION

Financial market derivatives – futures, forwards, options and swaps – are important tools for managing an organization's financial risks. Also, MNCs can use various insurance programs to better manage their risks. The larger an MNC becomes, the more challenges it encounters in attempting to arrange an insurance program comprising admitted insurance or nonadmitted insurance alone. Not surprisingly, the majority of large MNCs use an integrated approach that permits recognition of differences in regulations and insurance market capacities in the countries of operation. The discussion of global insurance programs – one focusing on foreign exposures only and the other integrating both local and foreign exposures – offers such a view.

Note also that the boundary between pure financial risk financing tools and traditional insurance tools is blurring, as financial institutions continue to introduce new tools that better meet the risk management needs of their clients. For example, the development of weather derivatives offered insurance companies an opportunity to design snow insurance contracts. The expansion of traditional umbrella liability insurance coverage has resulted in multi-line coverage with a single limit and a single deductible. Multi-line/multi-year coverage is another example, not to mention multi-trigger insurance policies. From the discussion of internal financial tools in Chapter 13, it is clear that MNCs also use both internal and external financing tools to design truly integrated risk management programs. Use of captives to consolidate risks in different countries and to transfer the consolidated risk to the reinsurance market using a multi-line/multi-year contract is an example.

Indeed, we should remind ourselves that all risks ideally should be considered collectively. What is important are the correlations among the firm's various risks not just the risks themselves.

Many firms expanding internationally are not large. These companies will need substantial support for their risk management activities. Comprehensive insurance products are being developed to meet this need. Even large MNCs are heavily dependent on the networks created by insurers and brokers for the coordination of international operations. Their effectiveness will continue to develop. Much of this development will depend on improved information systems and communications. To the extent that cross-border trade continues to be liberalized, truly international risk management programs can be expected to evolve.

## DISCUSSION QUESTIONS

1. What are the common methods to control or finance loss exposures? Why would a typical MNC consider control methods before financing methods? What role does insurance play in managing the exposures?
2. Describe two important distinctions between forward and future contracts.
3. Describe the corporate liability environment in your country? Are there new laws governing how corporations should handle employment-related issues such as age and gender discrimination or what is defined as "unlawful discharge from employment" in your country? If so, what changes can you identify that have been taken by corporations in response to such new laws?
4. A multi-trigger policy contains a condition that the traditionally insurable loss event (e.g., fire) must be the first trigger, followed by, say, a financial loss?
   (a) What adverse effect would the insurance market experience in offering policies with a financial loss as a first trigger?
   (b) Based on the second example in the multi-trigger coverage, explain the reason why the insurance premium for this multi-trigger policy would be much, if not significantly, lower than the premium for a single-event coverage?

## NOTES

1. This section draws from Cox (1998).
2. The exchange can also fail, perhaps though some natural or man-made catastrophe, but the probability is exceedingly low.
3. Many formulas analogous to the Black-Scholes formula have been developed (e.g., Gerber and Shiu, 1994). These models share the same assumptions for the Black-Scholes except commonly for different distribution assumptions.
4. Short selling is the opposite of **going long** – meaning that the investor buys the asset in hopes of realizing a gain because its price increases in the future.
5. Elton and Gruber (1995) discuss the evidence on efficiency in detail.

6. This illustration is drawn from Marshall and Kapner (1990).
7. Europe and Japan use 18°C.
8. When the coverage is extended to subsidiaries, the policy defines what constitutes a subsidiary; for example, a firm for which the insured corporation holds majority voting rights, owns more than 50 percent of the capital or can appoint or remove the majority of the its board of directors.
9. The validity of this insurance has been questioned in Quebec, Canada.
10. This section draws in parts from Gaunt (1998).

## APPENDIX 14A: PROOF OF CURRENCY RELATIONS

To examine currency relations with respect to interest rates, consider two countries: $d$ (domestic) and $f$ (foreign). Let $S_t$ denote the rate of exchange for converting one unit of $f$ to currency units of $d$ at time $t$. In other words, $S_t$ is a price index – the price of a foreign currency unit in terms of domestic currency. Let $r_d$ and $r_f$ denote the risk-free bond rates for period $(t, T)$ for domestic and foreign. Now consider two strategies of investing U.S. dollars over the period. The first strategy is at $t$ to buy the foreign currency to purchase foreign bonds and later at $T$ to sell the bonds to buy back U.S. dollars. This strategy, on the one hand, allows the investor to generate risk-free return based on the foreign currency during the period. On the other hand, it exposes the investor to exchange rate risk that $S_{d,f}$ at $T$ might not be as favorable as at $t$.

Another strategy, use of a forward contract, can remove this uncertainty. Suppose that the forward contract requires delivery of 100 units of foreign currency for a price of $[100 \times F(t, T)]$ domestic units. To meet this obligation, an investor can purchase, using currency $f$, risk-free bonds of the foreign country for an amount, denoted by $X$, that will accumulate to provide a fund for delivery of the 100 units the contract. The initial investment $X$ can be found using:

$$Xe^{(T-r)r_f} = 100 \tag{14.8}$$

or its transformed form

$$X = 100e^{-(T-r)r_f}$$

Because $X$ is in foreign currency, the investor needs to convert $Y$ units of domestic currency to $X$ units of foreign currency such that:

$$Y = XS_t \tag{14.9}$$

Investing $Y$ using this strategy – converting from domestic to foreign, buying risk-free foreign bonds and opening a forward contract, and converting at maturity from foreign to domestic under the forward contractual terms – provides a risk-free return of $[100 \times F(t, T)]$ units of domestic currency at time $T$. The value of $Y$ is completely determined by market values at $t$:

$$Y = S_t X = S_t 100 e^{-(T-t)r_f} \tag{14.10}$$

How does this compare to domestic investing? The results must be the same or there is an arbitrage. Domestic investing requires investing $100 \times F(t, T) e^{-(T-t)r_d}$ at time $t$ to accumulate the same value. Therefore, from the no arbitrage condition, the following currency relation can be drawn:

$$100 \times S_t e^{-(T-r)r_f} = 100 \times F(t, T) e^{-(T-r)r_d} \tag{14.11}$$

This is the interest rate parity relation. It is usually written as follows:

$$F(t, T) = S_t e^{-(T-r)(r_d - f_f)} \tag{14.12}$$

# APPENDIX 14B: PRICING CURRENCY OPTIONS

Consider again the investment contract in this chapter where the Australian MNC accepts US$90 million now and promises to return the U.S. trust fund US$100 million in one year. Suppose that the MNC's bank offers a customized OTC option on the exchange rate. This company can then modify the Black–Scholes formula to assess the option price. For example, the option price $p$ at $t$ of a European call option on a currency rate with maturity $T$ and exercise price $X$ is given by:

$$p = S e^{-\tau r_f} N(d) - X e^{-\tau r_d} N(d - \sigma \sqrt{\tau}) \tag{14.13}$$

where

$r_d$ = the domestic risk-free interest rate;
$r_f$ = the foreign risk-free interest rate;
$\tau$ = the time remaining to maturity, that is $\tau = (T - t)$;
$X$ = the exercise price;
$S$ = the current price of the foreign currency ($S = S_t$);
$\sigma$ = the volatility of the foreign currency price;
$d$ is given by:

$$d = \frac{1}{\sigma \sqrt{\tau}} \left[ log \left( \frac{S}{X} \right) + \tau (r_d - r_f + 0.5\sigma^2) \right]$$

The symbol in equation (14.3) denotes the cumulative standard normal probability distribution. The volatility is the variance of the random variable:

$$R(t, T) = \frac{1}{T - t} \ln \left( \frac{S_T}{S_t} \right) \tag{14.14}$$

which is the annualized rate of return over the interval $(t, T)$ obtained by buying Australian currency at the beginning of the period and selling it at the end.

The economic parameters may be estimated from standard data available in the financial press. For example, consider that on the date of investment contract, the risk-free rates are 4.25 percent in Australia and 4.85 percent in the U.S., and the spot exchange rate is US$1.00 = A$1.3734. The MNC specifies $\tau = 1$. With this assumption, all of the elements of the formula are known except the volatility $\sigma$. This volatility can be estimated using a series of past values of the exchange rate; that is, $S_i$ observed at time $t_i$. From calculating the return $R_i$ over each interval using equation (14.14), the MNC can thus obtain a sample variance, which can be used as an estimate of the volatility:

$$\sigma = \sqrt{\frac{1}{k}\sum_{i=1}^{k} R_i^2 - \left(\frac{1}{k}\sum_{i=1}^{k} R_i^2\right)^2} \tag{14.15}$$

Suppose $\sigma = 0.25$. The price now follows from the option formula: $r_d = 4.85\%$, $r_f = 4.25$, $\tau = 1$, $X = 1.35$, $S = 1.3734$, and $\sigma = 0.25$.

Equation (14.13) gives a price of 0.067 Australian dollars. An option to buy US$100 million, accordingly, would cost A$6.7 million. The assumptions underlying the model are not realized in practice, so we cannot expect this figure to be precise. It is a good starting point, giving a check on the price the bank will quote. The Australian MNC would pay about A$7 million for the right to buy US$100 million on the date of investment contract at a price of A$1.35. If the market rate turns out to be less than A$1.35, the MNC will simply buy U.S. dollars in the currency market. If the price is above A$1.35, it will exercise its option to buy the U.S. dollars from the bank at A$1.35. The MNC locks in the price without giving up the potential benefit of a price decline, at a cost of about A$7 million.

# REFERENCES

Agatstein, R. (2000). "Employment Practices Liability Insurance: Its Development and Evolution on a Global Basis." *PLUS Symposium – EPLI*, April 26, New York.

Black, F. and Scholes, M. (1973). "The Pricing of Options and Corporate Liabilities." *Journal of Political Economy*, 81: 673–684.

Cox, S.H. (1998). "Insurance Risk from a Financial Perspectives in H.D. Skipper, Jr. ed. *International Risk and Insurance: An Environmental-Managerial Approach*. Boston: Irwin/McGraw-Hill.

Elton, E.J. and Gruber, M.J. (1995). *Modern Portfolio Theory and Investment Analysis*. New York: John Wiley & Sons, Inc.

Flitner, A. and Tropin, J.(2004) *Commercial Insurance* Malvern: American Institute for CPCU/11A

Gaunt, L.D. (1998). "Risk Management," in H.D. Skipper, ed., *International Risk and Insurance: An Environmental–Managerial Approach*. Boston, MA: Irwin/McGraw-Hill.

Gerber, H.U. and Shiu, E. (1994). "Actuarial Approach to Option Pricing." *Transactions of the Society of Actuaries*, XLIV: 99–140.

Jarret, J. (2003). "Reducing Employment Practices Liability." *Risk Management*, 50 (September): 20–25.

Jury Verdict Research (2004). *Practice Liability: Jury Award Trends and Statistics*. Horsham, PA: LRP Publications.

Kwon, W.J. and Sarma, H. (2004). "An Integrated Master Insurance Program for Global Firms." *CPCU Journal*, January: 1–18.

Marshall, J.F. and Kapner, K.R. (1990). *Understanding Swap Finance*. Cincinnati, OH: South-Western Publishing Co.

Merton, R.C. (1973). "Theory of Rational Option Pricing." *Bell Journal of Economics and Management Science*, 4: 141–183.

Stoll, H.R. and Whalley, R.E. (1993). *Futures and Options Theory and Applications*. Cincinnati, OH: South-Western Publishing Co.

Swiss Re (2004). *The Changing Landscape of Liability: A Director's Guide to Trends in Corporate Environmental, Social and Economic Liability*.

# Chapter 15

# Risk Management for Catastrophes

## INTRODUCTION

With the preceding chapters as a basis, we now begin a more focused exploration of risk management. We do this by highlighting some of the more compelling potential loss exposures that confront corporations in general, with particular references to those facing MNCs. This chapter examines key aspects of managing risks that hold a catastrophic potential for the corporation.[1]

Our emphasis is on corporate risk management with respect to natural and human-made catastrophes. We do not explore in any depth the catastrophic potential that torts in general and mass torts in particular hold for businesses, as they were covered in Chapters 10 and 12. We build from the essential background provided in Chapters 5 and 6. We also explore how other, purely internal operational (nonsystematic) risks can have catastrophic effects on the firm, even to the point of causing financial failure. Because of the unique nature of such risks, we rely heavily on *Insights* to provide real-world context and illustrations. We structure the chapter around the three steps of the risk management process: (1) risk analysis, (2) risk control and (3) risk financing.

## RISK ANALYSIS

The processes by which a firm conducts analysis for events that hold a catastrophic potential are largely identical to those for non-catastrophic event, with three exceptions. First, risk managers whose firms are exposed to natural (and human-made) catastrophes devote greater time and effort to exploring the susceptibility of the firm's physical structure to damage. Second, such corporations commonly rely more heavily on modeling to estimate the probable effects of natural catastrophes on their businesses. Third, they find that scenario planning can play a significant role in helping them to broaden and deepen their thinking about possible adverse events and the environment. We, therefore, explore each of these here. In addition, because of the unique aspects of terrorism risk analysis, we discuss it as a separate item.

## Susceptibility to Damage

The susceptibility to damage of an organization's physical property determines the extent to which it would suffer damage were it to be hit by a significant natural or human-made event. With certain types of perils, the design and quality of construction features of property can be a major determinant of damage. The age of property can be a factor, with older structures often sustaining more significant damage in catastrophic events. Finally, the infrastructure in the affected community can be important in determining the size of a loss.

### *Design features and construction quality*

Architects and engineers consider the physical environment when designing structures. For example, brittle forms of structural design would be incompatible with an area where earthquake or volcanic activity is prevalent. Unfortunately, almost all existing structures, even in economically advanced countries, fail to conform to this general rule. In some instances, existing structures can be retrofitted to correct deficiencies. In many cases, however, design defects cannot be easily corrected. When catastrophic damages occur, these defective properties often become the focal points of property loss.

Closely related to building design is the quality of construction. In the aftermath of major property disasters, it becomes clear that the appropriateness and quality of construction figure prominently in structural integrity. Construction can run the gamut from bamboo huts to steel reinforced concrete behemoths. Obviously, poor-quality construction is no match for earthquake, windstorm, or flood or against even a low-level explosion. This has been a particularly difficult issue in many developing economies where enforcement of building codes is often lax. Even the best quality construction may not be enough to withstand the effects of significant catastrophic perils.

The tradeoff between cost and quality often tips in favor of economy in many construction decisions. The development of new structural components may actually reduce structural integrity of a building. These new components are often light, easy to install and cost-effective, yet some of them may provide less resistance to major structural stress and damage.

Not only natural catastrophes cause severe property damages, the nefarious activities of terrorists or disgruntled employees also can cause similar damage. Risk managers and engineers increasingly focus on the ability of high-rise buildings to withstand the impact of significant external physical distress and still maintain structural integrity to allow safe exits of building occupants. The 1995 collapse of a federal building in Oklahoma City, U.S., and the fall of the World Trade Center towers in New York City in 2001 brought attention to the risk of progressive collapse – "the spread of an initial local failure from element to element that eventually results in the collapse of an entire structure or a disproportionately large part of it" (The American Society of Civil Engineering, 2002).

### *Age of structures*

The age of structures is another factor to consider. Old urban areas seem to become target risks for catastrophic events. The design, quality of construction and general condition may be inferior to contemporary construction. In most instances, not much can be done to improve the situation. Urban renewal can be a slow and incomplete answer to the problem.

In some cases, major loss events trigger the reconstruction that is necessary to improve the overall condition of the structures in many old urban areas. Sad to say, such were the situations with the Great Hanshin (Kobe) Earthquake in Japan in 1995 and Hurricane Katrina in 2005 in the U.S.

### Infrastructure

The final factor in determining susceptibility to damage is the transportation and communications' capabilities of the affected area after a major event. Can the necessary equipment, personnel and building materials get to the affected area? Are the roads and rail systems functioning to permit such movement? Do adequate communications networks exist to coordinate damage assessment, recovery and rebuilding?

These infrastructure issues are critical to a prompt and orderly recovery process. A large loss in a relatively remote area poses significant problems, as was the case with the 2005 Kashmir earthquake that killed almost 100,000 in Pakistan. Effective communication can be cut off or greatly hindered for days, even in developed countries, as was the situation in New Orleans after Hurricane Katrina. Accessibility, normally difficult, can become next to impossible.

Obviously, this leads to frustration in the recovery process. Pakistan experienced weeks of delay in securing adequate food, water and other basic necessities for their earthquake victims. The U.S. experienced days of delay in getting to the stranded people in New Orleans after hurricane Katrina. Recent winter storms in Europe; typhoons in China, Japan, Korea and Taiwan; and earthquakes in Japan, Taiwan and the U.S. have caused enormous communications problems. Telephone lines were severely damaged and cellular capability was negated by downed cell towers. This resulted in confusion for days until temporary communications capabilities were restored.

## Catastrophe Modeling

The key to effectively managing the risk of the physical environment is a thorough assessment of the risk to determine the appropriate risk control and financing responses. Risk assessment requires both curiosity and imagination to appreciate fully the myriad loss potentials associated with the physical environment.

For many years, insurance firms – insurers, reinsurers and intermediaries alike – have been involved in the assessment of loss potentials from various perils. For the most part, this risk assessment has been done on a site-specific basis; that is, information regarding the physical characteristics of the particular property was coupled with hazard information (e.g., use and maintenance of building and distance from fire protection condition of adjoining building structures) to determine the insurability of the property. While a site assessment may be helpful as part of the underwriting process, risk managers should examine risk assessment from a macro perspective. Risk modeling offers this possibility.

**Catastrophic (cat) modeling** involves the use of computer-assisted mathematical techniques to estimate possible losses associated with catastrophic events, using site and specific property characteristics (the so-called "exposure data"). The intent of cat modeling is to lead to a greater understanding of the potential impact of catastrophic events on the firm (or region). Models are used primarily for natural catastrophes ("nat cats") including hurricanes, earthquakes, storms, flood and brush fires. Some models have been developed

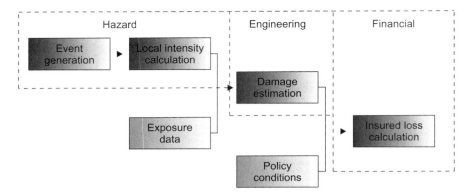

**Figure 15.1**    Natural Catastrophe Risk Modeling. *Source*: AIR Worldwide Corporation (2006) [www.air-worldwide.com/_public/html/catmodeling.asp] © AIR Worldwide Corporation

for terrorism as well, although critics observe that such intentional, human-caused disasters make them ill-suited to modeling.

Cat models are widely used by insurers and reinsurers to estimate their insured exposures in cities and regions. Insurer models and those developed by specialized modeling firms also are used by risk managers. These models often are exceptionally complex, relying on combinations of meteorology, seismology, engineering and actuarial science.

Scientists have put considerable effort into the assessment of natural hazards and the development of models over the past 20 years or so. Development of geographic information systems and advances in information technology have also fostered growth of this field. Researchers share the view that the key purpose of risk modeling is risk reduction before as well as after the catastrophe.

Figure 15.1 depicts a nat cat model developed by AIR Worldwide Corporation. It shows three modeling stages: hazard assessment, engineering and loss estimation.[2]

- *Hazard assessment* requires completion of two steps: event generation and local intensity calculation (physical model). The event generation step determines the frequency, severity, and other characteristics of potential catastrophic events by geographic location. It requires an analysis of historical data and an understanding of region-specific features – seismotectonic, geological, topographic or atmospheric – that may influence the likelihood of catastrophic events in the future. It also requires use of a parametric or a dynamic approach to develop a probability distribution as well as to test goodness-of-fit and robustness of the physical model.

   The second step involves estimation of local intensity. The magnitude of the event, distance from the source of the event and an array of local conditions affect the intensity at each locality.

- By superimposing the intensity of each simulated event onto a database of properties, the model attempts to estimate damages in the locality (i.e., *engineering*). At this stage, the AIR Worldwide model employs damageability relationships between the response of buildings (e.g., structural and nonstructural components and building contents) and the intensity to which it is exposed. The AIR damageability relationships vary according to construction class and occupancy.

- *Loss calculation* is the last stage, in which the model calculates insured losses by applying the specific insurance policy conditions to the total damage estimates. Examples of the policy conditions may include coverage limits and sublimits, loss triggers, deductibles, coinsurance and endorsements to the policy.

Development of a cat risk model is very complex, requiring detailed and up-to-date historical databases. The statistical approaches and assumptions differ from model to model as well. No model is perfect, with their being refined constantly. For example, even though the size and impact of Hurricane Katrina would have been modeled, it is doubtful that any model had correctly included the costs and burdens imposed on business and citizens created by the inept governmental response.

Models remain simplified representations of incredibly complex real-world phenomena and have been calibrated based on imperfect and incomplete information. Moreover, underlying probabilities shift over time, because of both poorly understood natural forces and human activity, such as global warming, which is difficult to simulate mathematically. Even so, progress is being made with these models already having proved their worth by helping us better to understand the potential impact of catastrophic events on firm operations and helping individuals, businesses and governments be better prepared to minimize economic losses before and after such events. With the furtherance of information technology and data standardization, models will be improved even more.

## Scenario Planning

Modeling relies on an extrapolation of past trends into the future, using the latest data, information and techniques to estimate likely effects. This technique can provide useful and often reliable results for short run planning in comparatively stable environments and for events that have been observed with at least reasonably frequent in the past. While these conditions generally apply with natural catastrophes, they are less applicable to human-made catastrophes that may involve one-of-a-kind events. Scenario planning has proven to be a useful risk management tool for such rare events, both in assessment and control.

**Scenario planning** is a strategic planning method in which analysts generate *simulation games* that are used by management to consider and develop plans to deal with alternative futures. These games are built by combining the relevant facts that their framers can reasonably muster about the future with relevant societal trends. Thus, a team likely would rely on the types of information presented in Part II of this book to construct exploratory scenarios that seek to set out the possible contours of unknown futures. The combinations of fact and possible societal trends are called *scenarios*. They typically include plausible but unexpected situations or problems that exist in some form today. This approach can be quite useful in teasing out risks that otherwise might be inconceivable.

To be truly instructive in a risk management context, scenarios should bring forth decisions by those who are ultimately responsible for making them. The decision-makers will interpret facts in different ways, based on their own worldviews, biases, psychological attitudes and other influences on their risk perceptions, as discussed in Chapters 2 and 11. Thus, scenario planning subsumes elements that are difficult and often impossible to formalize, let alone quantify.

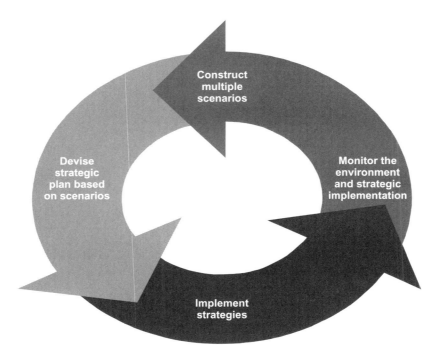

**Figure 15.2**    Closed Strategic Management Loop

The intent is to cause decision-makers to realize that they consciously or unconsciously likely have a preconceived notion of what the future will hold – what in scenario planning terminology is called an "official future." This realization is accomplished often by engaging them in lengthy interviews in which a series of abstract questions might be asked. The responses are then categorized in some way and presented back to the decision-makers, with the idea that some type of collective decisions ultimately will be developed for each scenario, with no decision necessarily reflecting any one person's original opinions.

A good strategy is one that proves viable under all scenarios and can be adjusted for extreme conditions. It includes a set of indicators that help identify which scenario seems to be evolving. Ideally, scenarios are the foundation of a closed strategic risk management loop, as illustrated in Figure 15.2. Scenarios help to envision alternative future environments. They do not include predictions of the future. Rather, they suggest the possible general shape of potential futures.

A risk management plan derived from these visions and from an organization's current situation describes how goals can be achieved. The implementation for this strategy and the evolution of the external environment must be monitored constantly and can then be used for reviewing or revising the underlying strategic scenarios. Insight 15.1 highlights how the legendary scenario planning of Royal Dutch/Shell was prescient in its risk management.

Various exploratory scenarios should be created to address important potential strategic risks and other issues of importance to the organization. One of the most interesting examples of how scenario planning might have helped a corporation avoid making what seems in hindsight to have been an incredibly poor decision is provided courtesy of AT&T

INSIGHT 15.1: SCENARIO PLANNING AT ROYAL DUTCH/
SHELL

The first company to successfully integrate scenarios into its strategic management process was the Royal Dutch/Shell group. Traditionally, Shell was an engineering-oriented company, and this was reflected in its management processes. From 1955 to 1965, Shell's planning became more financially oriented. By that time, Shell had an elaborate planning and forecasting system in place that covered its entire value chain: from exploration and drilling to the sale at the gas station. The first year of each planning cycle was planned in detail, with the others more broadly based. The oil business, however, must manage long-term investments, so at the end of the 1960s, Shell's planning department set up a study to examine the company's position in the year 2000.

Common belief was that the price of oil would remain stable. Shell's planners challenged this idea. They carefully considered how a potentially volatile political situation in the Middle East could affect oil. They developed several scenarios, one of which explored how a political crisis could lead to significantly higher prices. Their scenario also included the consequences of these rising oil prices and the changes in consumer behavior. Only a few years later, reality caught up. In the aftermath of the 1973 Yom Kippur War, the world faced its first oil crises. Anticipating developments of this sort and preparing the company by employing scenarios for planning purposes was one of the driving forces that propelled Shell into a leading position in the oil industry.

History was to repeat itself several years later, but in the opposite direction as oil prices fell. The experts were convinced that the price of oil would continue to rise. Shell considered the possibility of falling prices. By analyzing the divergent political agendas of its member states, Shell anticipated a weakening of the Organization of Petroleum Exporting Countries (OPEC) and a resulting erosion of the oil price. Shell was well positioned when prices did fall, as its strategy was built on several different scenarios.

Of course, oil prices were to rise again at the beginning of the 21st century, as OPEC regained some cohesion. What would you guess is the likelihood that Shell had a scenario for this result as well?

*Source*: Thinking Out of the Box: Scenario Planning, pp. 10–11.

through its decision to turn down a free offer to take control of the Internet. Insight 15.2 provides background.

## Terrorism Risk Analysis

Because of a heightened interest in the management of the terrorism risk and its catastrophic potential for harm to major corporations, we focus specifically on this peril in this chapter. We summarize the process that the U.S. Federal Emergency Management Agency (FEMA) proposes for the protection of business assets against terror threats.[3]

---

### INSIGHT 15.2: AT&T AND THE INTERNET: COULD SCENARIO PLANNING HAVE HELPED?

In the late 1980s, AT&T was the biggest U.S. long-distance telephone company. The National Science Foundation, wanting to withdraw from its role of administering the Internet, offered to transfer the entire operation to AT&T at no charge. AT&T, thus, could have had a free monopoly on what was to become perhaps the most important communication media in contemporary times. AT&T declined the offer. How did this happen?

According to Schwartz (2000), the answer can be found in the mental maps of top AT&T executives at the time. They saw the incredible virtues of the efficient, reliable centrally switched telephone network that they had designed and built. Their technical experts reinforced this view. After all, the "packet switching" inherent in the Internet's operation was largely unproven, and management saw little demand for its services.

Schwartz contends that had AT&T's decision-makers considered alternative scenarios (futures), they might have reached a different decision. First, early reports and discussions, admittedly controversial, were already available at the time to the effect that the Internet could restructure telephony. What if AT&T had constructed a scenario around the views of those who believed it could do so, rather than implicitly embracing its "official future" view?

Second, what if AT&T had included in a scenario the early work on development of business-to-business electronic commerce? According to Schwartz, it required no great leap to project efficiency improvements that were to prove real.

---

### *Protection priority*

Of course, as with other significant loss exposures, the firm identifies the business assets and their values that need to be protected. These assets include critical components (e.g., people, function and facilities), critical information systems and data, life safety systems and data, and security systems. FEMA recommends that such assets be classified as following:

- *High priority*: Loss or damage of the asset would bring grave consequences. Examples are loss of life, severe injuries and loss of primary services.
- *Medium priority*: Loss or damage of the asset would bring moderate to serious consequences. Examples are injuries and impairment of core functions and processes.
- *Low priority*: Loss or damage of the asset would bring minor consequences. An example is a slight and temporary impact on core processes and functions.

### *Hazard and vulnerability assessment*

The firm should next identify, define and quantify the threat or hazard. The threat can be from a person or a group of persons who have expressed the intent to harm and are capable of taking hostile action. It is a continual process and consists of the following elements:

- *Defining threats*: This involves information analysis of terrorist existence, capability, history, intention and targeting. National security advisory systems, such as those in the U.S. and the U.K., can be the basis for this analysis.

- *Identifying likely threat event profile and tactics*: This involves evaluation of attack intention, hazard profiling and expected effect of an attack on assets or the firm. For example, a firm may evaluate the threat of biological agents (e.g., anthrax, brucellosis and toxins), potential application modes (e.g., use of aerosol generators), hazard duration, extent of static and dynamic effects of the hazard and mitigating and exacerbating conditions (e.g., altitude of release).

- *Assignment of a threat rating*: Finally, the firm assigns a threat rating (e.g., high, medium or low threat) to each hazard it has evaluated. Firms should be concerned with high threat ratings in the near term and medium ratings over time.

There should follow a vulnerability assessment based on the findings of the preceding two steps. Here the firm evaluates weaknesses of its facilities according to the identified threats and hazards and obtains a basis for determining mitigation measures. Vulnerability ratings may range from low to high based on facility inspections, document review, and organization and management process review.

# RISK CONTROL

As we discussed in the preceding chapters, organizations engage in various risk controls techniques, either intentionally or otherwise. These techniques fall into two categories: loss prevention and loss reduction. We cover both categories here with particular reference to the risks associated with the physical environment with regard to loss prevention and crisis management with regard to loss reduction. In each instance, the objective is loss mitigation in which attempts are made to reduce the magnitudes of losses. The best that society can do is to plan for these events so that we minimize the loss of life and damage to property through use of several techniques simultaneously.

Loss prevention and reduction efforts are relevant in managing the terrorism risk as well. As acts of terrorism affect society and the economy, government and private business should coordinate risk management efforts to protect all societal members. Therefore, terrorism risk management includes security checks at ports of entry, protecting infrastructure and key properties, terrorist databases and intergovernmental coordination of intelligence efforts.

## Loss Prevention

Loss prevention activities as an integral part of catastrophe risk control programs can be grouped broadly into (1) land use restrictions, (2) building codes and (3) disaster planning. We discuss each of the activities below.

### *Land use restrictions*

Land use restrictions are probably the most effective form of loss mitigation with respect to natural catastrophes. They can limit large concentrations of people and property value in hazard-prone areas. They are, however, usually the most difficult to implement.

Restrictive zoning proposals often provoke enormous political pressure against them. For example, many people like to live right on the beach. Land use restrictions requiring buildings to be at a minimum distance from the ocean may be viewed as excessive and contrary to the rights of property owners. Developers want to maximize property value per square meter of beachfront property. Zoning attempts to balance the rights of property owners with reasonable protection of people and property. Sometimes zoning provisions are compromised by economic pressure or when the enforcement of restrictive zoning is lacking, resulting in new construction that is clearly exposed to the forces of nature.

### Building codes

Closely associated with land use restrictions are guidelines regarding design and construction. Architects, engineers and contractors in areas exposed to catastrophic perils generally are aware of necessary design and construction requirements, as discussed earlier.

Unfortunately, building codes are not always fully enforced. For example, it was thought that southern Florida had the most stringent building codes within the U.S. The effects of Hurricane Andrew in 1992 revealed, however, that 25 percent of the insured losses were attributable to construction that failed to meet the region's building code. The superior performance of fully engineered, wind-resistant buildings along the hurricane's path reinforces the notion that proper construction can serve to greatly mitigate losses associated with catastrophic events.

Adoption and implementation of rigorous building codes can reduce human casualty and property losses in catastrophe-prone areas. When the codes are standardized in a country or between neighboring countries, we can expect additional benefits of lower cost risk financing and faster loss recovery.

In the U.S., for instance, the Institute for Business and Home Safety has created the Building Code Effectiveness Grading Schedule that the Insurance Services Office uses to evaluate communities on their effectiveness on code enforcement. However, not all U.S. states – including some natural catastrophe-prone states – mandate building codes that cover all buildings or occupancy classifications.

Several countries have undertaken efforts toward standardization. The European Union continues its effort to introduce the European Standard (EN), *Eurocodes* – a set of 58 standards in 10 codes containing methods to assess the mechanical resistance of building structures and parts.[4] These EN standards also are used to check the conformity in building and civil engineering works with the essential requirements stipulated of the *Construction Product Directive*.

### Disaster planning

Disaster planning is key to loss mitigation. Proper disaster planning encompasses a public and private sector joint venture, with government establishing the general framework for the plan. The public sector needs to provide the leadership in emergency management, communications and transportation, but failures in this regard are not uncommon. These observations are as relevant for human-made catastrophes such as terrorist acts as they are for natural catastrophes.

For example, in its report on Hurricane Katrina, the U.S. congressional committee appointed to investigate the preparation and response to the hurricane observed that all Americans should be disturbed by the national, state and local governments' responses. The committee stated that citizens were let down, not because of some individual's failure of initiative, but because of organizational and societal failures of initiative. Its report documented these failures:

- tardy and ineffective execution of the National Response Plan;
- an under-trained and under-staffed FEMA;
- a Catastrophic Incident Annex that was never invoked and doubt that it would have done the job anyway;
- a perplexing inability to learn from Hurricane Pam – an exercise conducted in 2004 to help officials develop joint response plans to a simulated strong category 3 hurricane hitting New Orleans;
- levees not built to withstand the most severe hurricanes;
- an incomplete evacuation that led to deaths and tremendous suffering;
- a complete breakdown in communications that paralyzed command and control and made situational awareness murky at best;
- the failure of state and local officials to maintain law and order;
- haphazard and incomplete emergency shelter and housing plans;
- an overwhelmed FEMA logistics and contracting system that could not support the effective provision of urgently needed supplies.

The committee continued (*A Failure of Initiative*, 2006):

> We are left scratching our heads at the range of inefficiency and ineffectiveness that characterized government behavior right before and after this storm. But passivity did the most damage. The failure of initiative cost lives, prolonged suffering, and left all Americans justifiably concerned our government is no better prepared to protect its people than it was before 9/11, even if we are.

The committee made many recommendations for change, many of which, as this book was going to print, had not been implemented.

The private sector also must do its part in disaster planning. Any business with a major facility in a catastrophic-prone area must be ready to respond to any catastrophic event. Insurers and reinsurers often provide expert advice in this respect. Prompt action is necessary to minimize human suffering, damage to property and interruption of operations. An effective disaster plan can reduce the firm's legal liability exposure as well. Disaster planning starts with conservation efforts to mitigate damage to property. Prompt detection of damage is crucial to minimizing loss. Emergency action may be necessary to reduce further damage. The disaster plan should include a framework for repairing the damage. In some instances, loss of use can be much greater than the direct damage to property. Prompt action can shorten the restoration period thereby reducing the loss of use exposure.

*Fortune* (2005) highlighted how several large businesses, because of their careful risk control planning, were able to reopen quickly after Hurricane Katrina and help both themselves and those most in need to their products and services. Insight 15.3 highlights Home Depot's reactions to the hurricane.

Disaster plans need to take into account timescales, both in terms of the likely duration of emergency conditions and the time span over which emergency assistance is likely to be needed. Emergency planning needs to be integrated with plans for rehabilitation and

---

### INSIGHT 15.3: RISK CONTROL AT HOME DEPOT: THE CASE OF HURRICANE KATRINA

As residents along the shattered U.S. Gulf Coast returned to what was left of their homes and businesses after Hurricane Katrina's visit, many found their way to the big concrete boxes with the battered orange signs. Home Depot stores were among the first to reopen in the storm's wake, offering rebuilding supplies plus the even more precious commodities of electricity and normalcy.

This was no accident. Home Depot had started mobilizing four days before Katrina slammed into the coast. Two days before landfall, maintenance teams battened down stores in the hurricane's projected path, while electrical generators and hundreds of extra workers were moved into place along both sides of its path. At the company's hurricane center in Atlanta, staff from different divisions – maintenance, human resources, logistics – worked 18 hours a day to cut through logjams and get things where they needed to be.

A day after the storm, all but 10 of the company's 33 stores in Katrina's impact zone were open. Within a week, it was down to just four closed stores (of nine total) in metropolitan New Orleans.

Other big businesses would tell similar stories. They prepared well, they responded quickly, and they did so because Katrina was exactly the kind of event for which well run corporations prepare themselves. Home Depot even reorganized geographically in 2005 to match its divisions with the main disasters with which they must deal.

*Source*: Fox, J. and Boorstin, J. (2005, p. 51).

---

long-term development. The full environmental impact of disasters may not become evident until long after the emergency phase (in which basic humanitarian needs are met) is over and media interest in the disaster situation has waned. Environmental assessments during the emergency phase can help integrate these concerns into longer-term rehabilitation plans.

The "Environmental Integration Manual" of the E.U. offers a good example of management plans and strategy in case of a catastrophic event. They are as follows:[5]

- Environmental considerations need to be integrated into disaster management plans. This requires coordination among the various actors concerned with what can be quite separate tasks.

- Emergency responses should be based on a needs assessment and incorporate environmental considerations. Disaster management plans should make provision for guidance, training and research into post-disaster environmental assessment. Environmental assessment techniques have been developed as planning tools, so there remains a need to develop specific post-disaster assessment methods.

With respect to the terrorism threat in particular, firms employ several loss prevention measures. Thus, firms make facilities (assets) inaccessible to potential terrorists. Highly visible security systems and fencing are two examples of deterrence. Firms also share intelligence and security service systems with each other to detect threats. Another tactic is to make the firm's facilities appear of little or no value from the perspective of terrorists.

Of course, the firm should conduct a cost-benefit analysis of each mitigation option. While conducting the analysis, it may consider the availability of other risk management options, in particular, risk financing through insurance.

## Loss Reduction

Of course, not all harmful events can be prevented. In such instances, firms should have considered the steps to be taken to mitigate further loss, as we discuss in Chapter 12. The typical catastrophic situation, however, requires a deeper and broader approach to loss mitigation, which often is called **crisis management** – the process of identifying those situations that constitute a crisis, having an organized response to the crisis and ultimately resolving the crisis.

That crisis management is important to corporations has been recognized for many years. Many risk managers consider the 1982 Tylenol case to have been a watershed event in the evolution of crisis management. Insight 15.4 summarizes this famous case.

### *The process*

How firms respond to a crisis obviously determines how quickly they recover, if at all. Crisis management plans often are developed as the end product of cat modeling or scenario planning. While many firms have the expertise in house to handle the process, many rely on outside consultants to develop desired structure, especially when a crisis strikes.

A suggested approach to the overall process of crisis management is as follows:

- Engage appropriate employees to consider the range of possible crises to which the organization could be subjected.
- Develop responses for each identified crisis, including a master plan that is clear to and known by all relevant employees.
- Assign clear recovery responsibilities to individuals across the entire organization.
- Speak with one voice and through one high-level person, ideally the CEO.
- Keep employees, customers, other stakeholders and the public well informed by honestly and openly sharing the nature of the difficulty and what the organization is doing about it.

### *The Importance of effective crisis management*

For some firms, reputation and brand are said to represent more than 60 percent of their market value. All crises damage a firm's reputation, at least initially. Corporate leaders increasingly recognize these facts, yet too often seem to remain deaf to the need for what Anderson (2005) defines as **sustainability risk management** – the application of risk management by corporations and government to alter, change and adjust risk control systems through innovation and creativity to produce sustainable natural systems.

Not all crises can be anticipated, and the unanticipated crisis usually is the most challenging to manage. A crisis might arise that involves no damage to property or individuals, but results from seemingly rational, common actions taken (or not) by the organization. These crises often are of the sustainable risk variety. Insight 15.5 offers a famous example.

INSIGHT 15.4: EFFECTIVE CRISIS MANAGEMENT: THE TYLENOL CASE

Early in the morning of September 29, 1982, a 12-year-old girl from a Chicago, Illinois suburb took an extra strength Tylenol capsule for her pain. She died shortly thereafter. By October 1, another six persons throughout the Chicago region also had died from taking Tylenol capsules.

Investigators quickly discovered the Tylenol link. Someone had added cyanide to the capsules, and issued warnings to residents in the area. Police eliminated the possibility that the tampering had occurred during the manufacturing process as the bottles had come from different factories and all deaths were in the Chicago area. Rather they concluded that someone had taken packages of Tylenol from various stores, replaced the contents of the capsules with cyanide, then placed them on the shelves of five stores in the Chicago area. At that time, so-called tamper-resistant packaging was unknown. The perpetrator was never found.

Johnson & Johnson (J&J) halted production of Tylenol, issued nationwide warnings not to consume any type of Tylenol products and recalled an estimated 31 million bottles of the pain reliever with a retail value of approximately US$100 million. J&J offered to exchange all Tylenol capsules already purchased by the public with solid tablets. Of course, the event had significant immediate negative repercussions for J&J: its share price fell and the market share of Tylenol dropped from 35 to 8 percent.

Within two months, J&J had reintroduced its capsules but in triple-sealed packages designed to reveal whether tampering had occurred. Within a few months, Tylenol had regained its market dominant position. J&J's prompt, aggressive and open reactions to the incident drew praise from the press and the risk management community.

This tragedy is recognized in the risk management and insurance community as a defining event. It put crisis management on the corporate map. A major corporation has demonstrated the enormous importance of sound crisis management; of not panicking, of moving quickly to address the problem and, importantly, of being and being perceived as open and honest with the affected public. Also, the event caused the pharmaceutical industry to move away from use of capsules that were easy to contaminate and to introduce tamper-resistant packaging. Finally, the event was the impetus for the introduction by AIG of insurance specifically for malicious product tampering.

We have tangible evidence of the enormous importance that attaches to how well an organization manages its crisis. Studies by Knight and Pretty (1996, 2001 and 2005) have examined the impact on shareholder value of corporate catastrophes, of reputation crises and of events involving mass fatalities.

*Corporate catastrophes and shareholder value*

Knight and Pretty's first study examined the effect on share price of corporate catastrophes. They found that companies affected by catastrophes fall into two relatively distinct

## INSIGHT 15.5: BOYCOTT AS A CATASTROPHE: THE BRENT SPAR INCIDENT

Brent Spar was a massive floating oil storage and tanker loading facility located in the North Sea and operated by Shell Oil. It was constructed in 1976 and, by 1991, was considered of no value. Shell explored several options for disposing of the facility, ultimately deciding in 1994 that the best was to sink it in the deep waters of the North Atlanta. This option was both less costly (at £17–20 million) than on-shore dismantling (at £41 million) and potentially safer, with less likelihood of harming the environment, according to Shell. The facility was known to contain various pollutants, but Shell's analysis suggested that the effects of their being released into the deep sea would be quite localized. Shell believed that deep-sea disposal was acceptable to the U.K. and other regional authorities as well as to the public.

Greenpeace disagreed, arguing that we had too little understanding of the long-term effects of such deep-sea disposal and that the precedent set could lead to further deep-sea dumping of contaminated structures. It also contended that Shell was using scientific arguments to disguise its true motivation for deep-sea disposal – to save money.

Greenpeace decided to conduct an energetic media campaign to mobilize public opinion against deep-sea disposal. On April 30, 1995, it transported activists by helicopter onto the deck of the Brent Spar as it was being towed. Ultimately, some two dozen activists, photographers and journalists were involved directly, with their employing video cameras and satellite broadcasting to link directly with the major European news outlets. The result was widespread, often real-time coverage of the event throughout Europe.

Greenpeace urged a boycott of Shell Oil and its services and products. The boycott gathered momentum throughout much of northern Europe, with the result that sales fell in some countries by 30 percent, resulting in losses in the millions of pounds, substantial damage to the corporation's reputation, and a meaningful drop in its share price.

At an emergency meeting of its board on June 20, 1995, Shell reversed its position of deep-sea disposal in favor of the on-land option. Brent Spar has since been dismantled and its steel recycled.

Anderson (2005) says that the Brent Spar incident offers lessons in the importance of sustainability risk management for other corporations. First, even if a well-reasoned and well-meaning internal scientific assessment supports a particular environmental decision, the general public may not agree, as it may react at a more basic and fundamental level. (We have but to reflect on the psychological theory of risk, especially as relates to the unknown and dread to understand this position – see Chapters 2 and 11.) Corporations ignore these effects at their peril.

Second, modern communication systems and the Internet enable environmental and other advocacy groups to transfer key information to great numbers of the public at very little cost. In the past, a deep-sea disposal of Brent Spar may have attracted little attention.

Third, businesses can suffer massive losses from boycotts. Shell lost hundreds of millions. These were uninsurable losses. The event damaged Shell's environmental reputation.

To its credit, this and another incident, according to Anderson, provided a catalyst for Shell becoming one of the two principal sustainability leaders in the petroleum industry. He says that Shell and BP are leaders in developing clean renewable energy alternatives.

groups: recoverers and non-recoverers where these terms refer exclusively to the effects of the catastrophe on the firm's share price. With each group, the initial loss of stock value was about 5 percent on average for the recoverers and 11 percent for the non-recoverers. After the 50th trading day, results were even more revealing, with recoverers having positive returns of 5 percent and non-recoverers stuck at the loss of 11 percent (Knight and Pretty, 2000).

Recall from Chapter 12 that a firm's stock price is the market's per share estimate of the present value of the firm's future net cash flows. Thus, a decline in share price represents the market's expectation that the firm suffers a long-term decrease in revenues or increase in expenses. The researchers found that the difference in recoverers and non-recoverers was due more to the way that senior management, and particularly the CEO, handled the disaster than to the direct financial consequences of the loss (Knight and Pretty, 2005).

*Reputation crises and shareholder value*

A major corporation's reputation often is a key driver of overall corporate value, as alluded to above. In some instances, the hit to a firm's reputation can lead to its complete financial failure. Insight 15.6 highlights one of the largest corporate failures in this respect.

Knight and Pretty's second study (2001) centered on such reputation crises, irrespective of any underlying physical loss. The results were consistent with their first study in terms of the corporations exposed to a reputation crisis falling into two relatively distinct groups: recoverers and non-recoverers, again depending largely on the ability of senior management to deal effectively with the aftermath. The authors noted the considerable power of signaling (see Chapter 11) in markets as investors adjust their views of management and, therefore, of future cash flows of the affected firms.

Figure 15.3 gives a reproduction of their findings for one calendar year following the crises (261 trading days). Note that the value differential between the recoverers and non-recoverers at the end of one year is 25 percent.

*Mass fatality events and shareholder value*

Their final study (2005) examined the impact on share prices of mass fatality events – incidents that produce more fatalities than can be handled using local resources and incidents that had the potential to become such events. The authors examined corporations in aviation disasters, fire and explosion disasters, terrorism attacks and the 2004 tsunami in the Indian Ocean. Again, corporations segregated themselves into the two distinct categories. Figure 15.4 gives the average share value movements for both groups.

INSIGHT 15.6: REPUTATION LOSS AS A CATASTROPHE: THE ANDERSEN DEBACLE

For decades, Andersen LLP was the world's leading accounting firm. Its practices set the standard for the field, and its ethics were considered to be impeccable. In less than a year, however, reputation damage because of allegations of poor practice in connection with its work for the disgraced executives of Enron had destroyed the firm.

Anderson (2005) offers insight into this failure. First, he notes that Andersen LLP lost sight of the fact that it was an independent auditing firm on which many stakeholders relied, including consumers, employees, investors, lenders and regulators. That independence was compromised when Andersen auditors became too cozy with Enron management. The large fees that Andersen LLP was collecting from Enron through both its consulting and auditing practices set up a classic conflict of interest. A tough auditing stance may have compromised the consulting business, but protecting the consulting business compromised its auditing standards.

The practices that Andersen LLP followed at Enron were used by the auditing company at numerous other firms and produced similar problems, indicating that their strategy had systemic characteristics and that the Enron case had not been an isolated event. That Andersen LLP shredded tons of documents gave the appearance that it had something to hide. The public outrage and resulting damage to reputation was particularly acute as so many innocent parties, such as employees and small investors, were harmed.

The Andersen/Enron case also demonstrates that insurance will not save the firm or its top management in this type of catastrophic event. While Andersen LLP had errors and omissions liability insurance, the limits proved inadequate, with the result that partners' equity positions was called upon to meet additional claims.

No one would have predicted that a firm of Andersen's size and reputation could have effectively been forced out of business in such a short time period. Had Andersen executives been aware of the enormity and swiftness of these consequences, they almost certainly would have changed their business practices to reduce the risks.

A striking difference between the two figures is the relative differential after one year. Whereas the difference is 25 percent for the reputation study, the difference here is double that percentage, suggesting that the ability to manage well a mass casualty event is even more impressive to investors, and the *inability* to manage such events is even more disappointing than in less tragic crises.

The researchers again find that the key determinant of value recovery relates to the ability of senior management to demonstrate strong leadership and to communicate at all times with honesty and transparency. For mass fatality events in particular, the sensitivity and compassion with which the CEO responds to affected families as well as the logistical care and efficiency with which the response teams carry out their work becomes paramount.

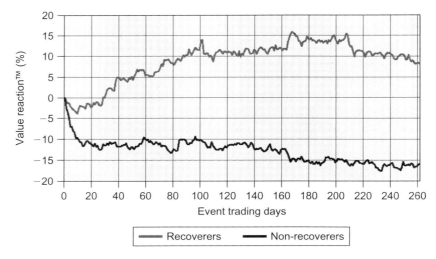

**Figure 15.3**    Reaction of Share Prices to Reputation Crisis. *Source*: Knight and Pretty, 2005, p. 5) (© 2006 Oxford Metrica

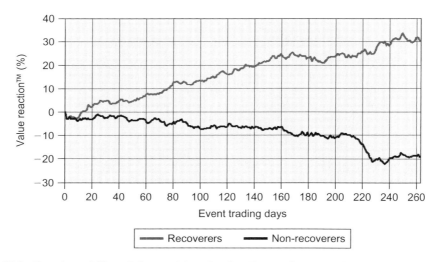

**Figure 15.4**    Reaction of Share Prices to Mass Fatality Events. *Source*: Knight and Pretty, 2005, p. 7 (© 2006 Oxford Metrica)

# RISK FINANCING

Risk financing through insurance has long been a technique for spreading the financial impact among a group, thereby reducing the cash flow volatility for individual insured firms. Creditors often require property owners to protect collateral property with property insurance. Retention in its various forms also can be an effective risk financing technique. We discuss both the techniques in this section.

## Retention

As chapter 13 made clear, retention is recommended when insurance is unavailable or unaffordable or when property owners have the capability of financing losses internally. Retention is often used along with other risk financing options. For example, large commercial entities may choose to retain a significant portion of their property loss potential, with excess property insurance responding to larger losses beyond some retention. Generally, such entities are financially capable of absorbing a sizeable portion of property loss without a material impact on their financial strength.

The problems with retention are vividly demonstrated when a catastrophe occurs. Catastrophic losses in some developing countries can have a devastating impact on their citizens and businesses. No private insurance mechanism provides indemnification. In many cases, there is no public sector safety net to offer food and shelter. Often the victims are left to the caring of the international community and charitable organizations to provide for their basic needs.

In developed countries, the degree of suffering ordinarily is not as great, yet enormous loss is felt by those directly affected by the catastrophic event. The rebuilding process may be delayed or forgone due to the lack of insurance or private financing. In some cases, emergency funding is provided by local or national governments to cope with immediate needs. This form of funding creates a risk-spreading mechanism through the public sector as society subsidizes the losses of those in catastrophe-prone areas.

## Insurance

Risk financing capacity for catastrophic loss exposures remains a major concern for the insurance industry internationally, with estimates of worst-case scenarios in major metropolitan areas threatening the entire capital base of the industry. Some interesting developments have taken place recently that attempt to deal with this capacity concern, as we highlight briefly below and in more detail in Chapters 17 and 18.

Insurance policies often exclude coverage for many catastrophic events. Nuclear-related events are not covered in most nonlife insurance policies. Nor is damage from flood covered in standard insurance policies in many countries. Earth movement from earthquake and volcanic eruption is a covered peril by standard policies in most countries. Terrorist acts are excluded in many markets, although various government or private pools or reinsurance have eased availability in some markets.

### Catastrophe reinsurance

Catastrophe reinsurance provides that the reinsurer will indemnify the ceding company above its retention for an accumulation of losses over some period. The catastrophe may be an event causing two or more losses during a period (e.g., 72 hours). Catastrophe reinsurance differs from pure catastrophe coverage in that it is often a risk-financing and loss-sharing arrangement between insurance firms. Both parties of the contract may be able to use their capital in a more efficient way.

The market has witnessed a steady rise in the demand for catastrophe reinsurance after a series of natural and human-made catastrophes in the 1990s and early 2000s. With technical advances in risk modeling, reinsurers have been able to have more accurate loss projections, which have mostly aided the growth in catastrophe reinsurance supply. Several reinsurers that specialize in catastrophe reinsurance are domiciled in the Caribbean. The London market also has been active in catastrophe reinsurance.

## *Private risk pools*

A risk pool is created when a group of firms invest collectively to provide insurance capacity against a specified risk. Examples include pools for non-standard drivers in automobile insurance and pools for employers with poor loss experience in workers' compensation. Corporations also have formed risk pools to provide capacity that is not available in the traditional insurance market. Marsh & McLennan, a global insurance brokerage, orchestrated the creation of ACE and XL Insurance Company as buyer-driven risk pools to provide high coverage limits not available in the traditional insurance market.

An examination of how risk pools operate in the nuclear power field will be instructive. Nuclear facilities are highly protected risks and increasingly run by private firms. Their liability exposures for bodily injury and property damage are extremely high. This creates a concern about the financial capability of any party that would ultimately be responsible for the damages resulting from a massive nuclear event.

The World Nuclear Association takes the position that nuclear power plant operators are absolutely liable (i.e., regardless of fault) for any damages but their liability should be limited to an amount set by international conventions or by national legislation. E.U. member states and Canada comply with international conventions such as the International Atomic Energy Agency's *Vienna Convention on Civil Liability for Nuclear Damage* of 1963 (amended in 1997) and the OECD's *Paris Convention on Third Party Liability in the Field of Nuclear Energy* of 1960 (amended in 2004).[6] Other countries, including China, Japan, Russia and the U.S., apply their own national standards.

For instance, the U.S. introduced the Price-Anderson Act in 1957 to promote private investment in commercial nuclear power. For this, the act placed a cap on the total liability that a nuclear power plant operator would face in the event of a catastrophic accident. This attracted the attention of the private insurance sector, and groups of insurance firms began to pool their financial resources and created nuclear risk pools. American Nuclear Insurers (ANI), which include Lloyd's of London syndicates as participating members, is an examples. Insight 15.7 summarizes three types of insurance protection offered by members of the ANI.

## *Government risk pools*

The pooling mechanism is not limited to the private sector. Governmental pooling entities have been created in the catastrophic risk insurance markets that were inadequately addressed in the private sector. In the U.S., several states have formed risk pools for windstorm and earthquake risks.

In California, a pooling mechanism combines the capital resources of insurance, reinsurance and borrowed funds. The California Earthquake Authority (CEA) is a privately financed, state-administered entity established in 1996 in response to the problem of unavailability of homeowner's insurance, particularly after the 1994 Northridge earthquake in that state. With the creation of the CEA, earthquake insurance has become available from private insurers participating in the CEA program. It is now the world's largest writer of residential earthquake insurance (see Figure 15.5).

Other countries and U.S. states have various forms of pooling and reinsurance facilities that address catastrophic exposures. In most instances, they relate to individual and family insurance needs and not to that of corporations, especially large ones. Where relevant, these are covered in Chapter 23.

## INSIGHT 15.7: NUCLEAR INSURANCE COVERAGE

Typical nuclear insurance policies offered by members of the American Nuclear Insurers (ANI) comply with the federal Price-Anderson Act requirements. The insured may purchase one or more of the following policies:

- *Facility form (liability) policy*, the primary coverage, is purchased by all commercial nuclear power plant operators in the U.S. This insurance covers bodily injury and property damage liability (for up to US$300 million) when the injury or damage is caused by nuclear materials at the insured premises. With minor exceptions, the policy does not indemnify the insured for own property damage. Neither does it respond to environmental cleanup costs arising from government decrees unless the cost results from an "Extraordinary Nuclear Clearance" as defined by the U.S. Nuclear Regulatory Commission or a "transportation incident" as defined in the policy.

- *Secondary financial protection policy* offers an excess coverage over the facility form coverage. The limit of insurance depends on the "retro premiums" actually collected by the ANI from participating insureds.

- *Master worker policy* covers radiation tort claims of nuclear workers employed at the insured facilities for up to the industry aggregate limit of US$300 million.

- *Suppliers and transporters policy*, purchased by companies that provide products or services to operators of nuclear facilities in the U.S., offers an excess coverage over the operator's facility form limit and up to US$300 million per occurrence.

*Source*: U.S. Nuclear Regulatory Commission (www.nic.gov)

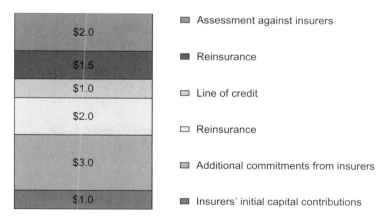

**Figure 15.5**    The Capacity of CEA (in US$ Billion). *Source*: CEA, www.earthquakeauthority.com

### *Terrorism risk pools and other arrangements*

One important, evolving area in which pools are playing an expanding role is in supporting the market for terrorism coverage. Some pools emerged even before the September 11, 2001 attacks. In each instance, the government is deeply involved in developing the program or in assisting the local industry in developing one. In selected countries, the government functions as the insurer of last resort. In others, government assumes the role of reinsurer or retrocessionaire. Table 15.1 offers a summary of some of the world's major programs.

## Catastrophic Risk Securitization

An insurance company exposed to catastrophic losses can purchase catastrophe options as a hedge against losses. To the extent that the index is proportional to the insurer's own losses, a rising index offsets the insurer's rising losses. The seller of a catastrophe option

**Table 15.1**    Terrorism Insurance in Selected Countries (2006)

| Country | Pool | Operations | Government Funding/Support |
|---|---|---|---|
| Australia | Australian Reinsurance Pool Corporation (ARPC) created in 2003 as reinsurer. | Levels above A$10.3 billion (the government will decide whether to go pro rata). | Backed by a commercial line of credit underwritten by the state with government indemnity of A$9 billion. |
| | Cash pool of A$300 million funded by premiums. | No per policy limit. Compulsory for commercial property (not compulsory for insurers to reinsure through ARPC). | |
| Austria | *Osterreichischer VersicherUngspool zur Deckung von Terrorisiken* (Terrorpool Austria) created in 2002 as a mixed risk sharing and reinsurance pool. Members' share of the pool prorated to their market share in property insurance. | Annual aggregate of €200 million; initial premium covering up to €5 million per policyholder; coverage for property insurance for industrial, commercial, and private lines. Non-compulsory coverage. | No government funding or support. |
| France | *Gestion de L'assurance et de la Reassurance ds Rsques Attentats* (GAREAT) – Large Risk scheme introduced in 2002 and Mass Risk scheme in 2005, both as primary/reinsurance pool. | Unlimited guarantee of the government above a certain threshold. | Acting as reinsurer of last resort through *Caisse Centrale de Reassurance* (CCR) for support at levels above €2.269 billion (for 100% market share). |

(Continued)

**Table 15.1**    (Continued)

| Country | Pool | Operations | Government Funding/Support |
|---------|------|-----------|---------------------------|
| | Insurers' retention of share of €340 million + 9% coinsurance of the next €1.929 billion. | 100% coverage per risk. Compulsory insurance; the Mass Risks scheme does not include the unlimited guarantee of the state, which is negotiated by each insurance company directly with CCR; underlying cover through GAREAT is not compulsory. | |
| Germany | Extremus created in 2002 to cover terrorism risks as insurer | Maximum (first loss) aggregate limit of indemnity of €1.5 billion per insurer per year, subject to annual aggregate of €10 billion by Extremus. | Damages from €2 billion up to €10 billion. |
| | The shareholders of Extremus (German insurers and reinsurers) and the international reinsurance market provide the capacity for the first €2 billion. | Coverage limited to original property policies with a limit above €25 million. | |
| Israel | The Property and Tax Compensation Fund Law (PTCF) created in 1961 as insurer. | Non-compulsory insurance. No program cap. | Fully responsible. |
| | Entirely government compensation scheme. | No limit for property but household contents for up to €20,000. Free coverage for any Israeli resident. | |
| The Netherlands | *Nederlandse Herverzekeringsmaatschappij voor Terrorismeschaden* (NHT) created in 2003 as reinsurer. Participating primary insurers provide first €400 million in the aggregate. | Annual aggregate of €1 billion, pro rata at levels >€1 billion. Property/business interruption risk limited to €75 million per location per year. Non-compulsory insurance. | Top layer of €50 million (i.e., in excess of €950 million). |
| Spain | *Consorcio de Compensacion de Seguros* (CCS) created in 1941 to cover any violent action to destabilize the political system or cause fear and insecurity within the groups of people targeted; | Not limited or conditioned to a certain number of losses or to any specific amount of loss. | Supported by an unlimited state warranty. |

(Continued)

**Table 15.1**    (Continued)

| Country | Pool | Operations | Government Funding/Support |
|---|---|---|---|
| | functions as primary insurer/reinsurer. No insurer's share required. | Compulsory. | |
| South Africa | South African Special Risks Insurance Association (SASRIA) established in 1979 as reinsurer. | Program guarantee of ZAR1 billion | Government stop loss coverage of ZAR1 billion in excess of reserves and reinsurances. |
| | Insurers' share of ZAR5 million. | ZAR300 million per insurer per year. Non-compulsory insurance. | |
| United Kingdom | Pool Re created in 1993 as reinsurer. | No program or per policy cap. | Reinsurer of last resort for an unlimited coverage. |
| | Absolute terrorism exclusions are applied to all commercial property policies. Pool Re member insurers offer full value terrorism coverage for risks in selected lines in England, Scotland and Wales only. | Members of Pool Re required to offer coverage when requested by insureds (mainly commercial property owners) | |
| United States | Terrorism Risk and Insurance Act (TRIA), introduced in 2002 for three years and extended through 2007 as the government acting as reinsurer. | TRIA protection of up to annual limit of US$100 billion; pro rata at levels >US$100 billion. | For 2007, 85% of losses covered once deductible is reached. |
| | Amount below deductible + coinsurance of 10% in 2006 and 15% in 2007. | Where required, insurers must make the coverage option available. | |

*Source*: Guy Carpenter (2006).

contract places money at risk, anticipating a profit if the option contract expires with the index below the strike price. The seller's money acts in much the same way as capital for the insurer, thereby spreading the risk of catastrophe losses to other segments of the economy.

*Catastrophe bonds* – also known as *cat bonds*, *event bonds*, *disaster bonds*, or *Act of God bonds* – are placed by insurance firms to finance catastrophic risks through capital markets. Cat bonds are commonly placed privately. Access to the bond funds is contingent upon the insurer exceeding a certain level of catastrophic losses in a defined period. For example, an insurer may issue a $500 million cat bond, to which the insurer will have access only if its loss exceeds $1 billion from a single catastrophic event within 2 years from the date of bond issuance.

At present, these non-traditional financing techniques have been used only by insurers and reinsurers. They are of interest catastrophic risk management because they may point the way for non-insurance firms to address their cat risks, perhaps with the aid of brokers and insurers.

## CONCLUSION

The physical environment, on the one hand, represents a source of great value to individuals, to society and to the economy. On the other hand, numerous perils pose a significant threat, even to human survival. Catastrophic loss-causing events are particularly challenging for risk managers, insurance companies and governments. By definition, their potential for wreaking havoc is great, and the exposure is not easily diversified.

An understanding of the nature of such events is essential to loss mitigation and, with respect to technical disasters, their prevention. Many of the world's most populous and developed urban areas are in close proximity to damage from earthquakes, storms and flooding. Unfortunately, this trend continues as people's movement and property investment seem to be focused on the naturally hazardous regions of the globe – coastal areas. This trend argues for more appropriate risk pricing and against subsidization to encourage appropriate behavior.

Managing catastrophe risk involves risk analysis, control and financing. Cat risk analysis is more complex than analysis of less hazardous events. Cat modeling and scenario planning are important tools in this analysis. Loss mitigation includes a role for the public and private sectors. The public sector should improve and enforce meaningful land use restrictions and building codes. Property owners need to consider retrofitting existing structures to mitigate loss potential and the design and construction specifications of new structures. Private insurers can provide premium incentives for such actions. Crisis management has an especially critical role in managing catastrophic risk exposures. Finally, disaster planning is essential for both business and government.

The financing of risk runs the gamut from retention to transfer. For many exposures, retention the only choice. For others, either government or private insurance may be available, if costly. Catastrophe reinsurance and risk securitization continue to develop, although they remain available only in selected countries (e.g., E.U. member states, Japan, the U.S. and recently Taiwan). All of these developments suggest that humans *should* be better able to manage catastrophic risks. Technological advances coupled with changing expectations regarding safety imply that we will probably face new risks, particularly human-made ones, losses from which may not be realized for decades to come.

## DISCUSSION QUESTIONS

1.  Older facilities often are more susceptible to damage than newer ones. Explain why this is so and make a case for why the government should not require that the owners of such older facilities to upgrade them to contemporary structural standards?
2.  Loss mitigation is a fundamental factor in better managing the physical environment risk. What aspects of loss mitigation do you believe offer the most promise for the future? Explain.

3. Develop at least two "alternative futures" for how risk management might change for operators of nuclear power plants.
4. If sound crisis management is as important as suggested in this chapter, why do major corporations seem to accord it so little attention?
5. We have described terrorism risk pools in selected countries.
   (a) Find the reasons why some governments listed in the table acted upon creation of a terrorism insurance scheme before September 11, 2001.
   (b) Do you find any other governments offering similar programs? (Hint: Examine Brazil, Finland, Hong Kong and Japan for possible programs.)

# NOTES

1. This chapter draws in part from Feldhaus (1998).
2. This section draws heavily from AIR Modeling by AIR Worldwide Corporation as of October 2004 and as of October 2006.
3. The discussion draws heavily from FEMA (2003a, b).
4. The E.U., via Eurocode Experts [www.eurocodes.co.uk], plans to publish the 58 parts of the 10 Eurocodes by 2007, which will then replace national codes from 2008 to 2010. The codes are mandatory for European public works and set to be the *de facto* standards for the private sector.
5. Adapted from "Environmental Integration" of the European Commission (2004) available at europa.eu.int/comm/development/body/theme/environment
6. The 1997 revision of the Vienna Convention includes an increase of the operator's liability at not less than 300 million Special Drawing Rights (approximately US$400 million).

# REFERENCES

AIR Worldwide Corporation (2004, 2006). *AIR Modeling Technology.* Available at www.air-worldwide.com/_public/html/modeltech.asp

The American Society of Civil Engineering (2002). *Minimum Design Loads for Buildings and Other Structures* (ASCE 7-02), Reston, Virginia, VA: ASCE.

Anderson, D.R. (2005). *Corporate Survival: The Critical Importance of Sustainability Risk Management.* New York: Universe, Inc.

*A Failure of Initiative* (2006). Final Report of the Select Bipartisan Committee to Investigate the Preparation for and Response to Hurricane Katrina. Available at www.gpoacess.gov/congress/index.html

Federal Emergency Management Agency (2003a). *Insurance, Finance and Regulation Primer for Terrorism Risk Management in Building.* Washington, DC: Federal Emergency Management Agency.

Federal Emergency Management Agency (2003b). *Reference Manual to Mitigate Potential Terrorist Attacks Against Buildings.* Washington, DC: Federal Emergency Management Agency.

Feldhaus, W.R. (1998). "The Physical Environment for Risk and Insurance," in H.D. Skipper, Jr. ed., *International Risk and Insurance: An Environmental-Managerial Approach.* Boston, MA: Irwin/McGraw-Hill.

Fox, J. and Boorstin, J. (2005). "A Medication on Risk." *Fortune,* 152 (October 3): 50–62.

Guy Carpenter (2006). *The World Catastrophe Reinsurance Market,* New York: Guy Carpenter.

Knight, R.F. and Pretty, D.J. (1996). *The Impact of Catastrophes on Shareholder Value.* Templeton College, University of Oxford, commissioned by Sedgwick.

Knight, R.F. and Pretty, D.J. (2000). "Survey – Mastering Risk 9: Day of Judgment: Catastrophe and the Share Price." *Financial Times* (June 20).

Knight, R.F. and Pretty, D.J. (2001). *Reputational Value: The Case of Corporate Catastrophes.* Oxford: Metrica.

Knight, R.F. and Pretty, D.J. (2005). *Protecting Value in the Face of Mass Fatality Events.* Oxford: Metrica.

Schwartz, P. (2000). "Survey – Mastering Risk 2: The Official Future, Self-Delusion and the Value of Scenarios." *The Financial Times* (May 2).

*Thinking Out of the Box: Scenario Planning* (no date). Emap Finance and Zurich Financial Services (no place).

# Chapter 16

# Personnel Risk Management

The multinational firm has an obvious and compelling interest in hiring and retaining quality, dedicated employees by offering competitive compensation, including employee benefits. It has an equally compelling interest in minimizing disruption, taking a hit to its reputation or incurring financial setbacks because of its employees engaging in improper behavior or being kidnapped, killed or injured. We use the term **personnel risk management** to subsume both employee benefits and employee behavior and safety.

## EMPLOYEE BENEFITS

**Employee benefits** consist of all forms of employer-provided compensation, exclusive of direct wages and salaries.[1] This section's primary focus is on benefit programs that are voluntary in nature and offered to large segments of a firm's workforce and to which the firm makes a significant monetary contribution toward the program's cost. Customs and practices regarding the provision of voluntary employee benefit plans vary from country to country. Figure 16.1 shows the more common types of government-mandated and private employee benefit plans internationally and perquisites.

Government-mandated social insurance programs are discussed in this chapter only peripherally as they relate to the types and design of voluntary benefit programs offered by a firm. We provide extensive treatment of social insurance programs in Chapter 9.

Many corporations have extensive operations internationally, having attained success through organic growth, acquisitions, joint venture agreements, marketing arrangements or direct entry into foreign markets. Expansion of a firm's operations internationally adds to the complexity of designing and administering employee benefit plans. Each nation's rules and regulations must be respected by the MNC. Local customs, traditional benefit design and the availability of adequate insurance coverage in each local market also must be considered. Even purely national firms can benefit from understanding employee benefit practices of other nations.

Economic expansion and the substantial growth in salaries, particularly for executives and managers for whom social insurance benefits are often modest compared to their compensation, have contributed to the increasing popularity of voluntary employee benefit plans in many countries. In most developed countries with aging populations, the discussion about

| Common types of government-mandated employee benefit plans | • Death (survivor's) benefits to widows/widowers and children<br>• Disability benefits<br>• Retirement benefits<br>• Occupational accident and sickness benefits<br>• Termination/severance allowances<br>• Unemployment benefits<br>• Family/child allowances |
| --- | --- |
| Common types of voluntary (private) employee benefit plans | • Life insurance (and other death) benefits<br>• Sick leave and other short-term disability income benefits<br>• Long-term disability income benefits<br>• Basic or supplemental medical expense benefits<br>• Basic or supplemental retirement benefits (pension and profit-sharing)<br>• Payments for time not worked, including vacations, holidays, and rest periods<br>• Termination/severance benefits |
| Perquisites | • Club membership<br>• Company-provided car (for personal and business use)<br>• Personal driver and servants<br>• Company-provided or subsidized housing<br>• Low rate or interest-free loans<br>• Tax and financial planning services |

**Figure 16.1**   Commonly Observed Employee Benefit Plans and Perquisites Worldwide

privatization of social insurance programs has heightened further the interest in these plans. In addition, in countries with national healthcare programs, employer-provided supplemental medical benefits have enjoyed increasing popularity.

Generally, firms should strive to ensure consistency of treatment among employees. However, firms make a clear distinction between employee benefits that they provide to a broadly defined segment of the company's workforce and **perquisites** that are special employer-financed services limited to a select group of executives and key managers. Customs and practices regarding the use and role of perquisites vary from country to country. In some countries (e.g., the U.S.), the custom is to offer relatively few perquisites while in others (e.g., India), they constitute an important part of employee compensation. For example, a Towers Perrin study (2005–2006) found that CEOs in India receive about 30 percent of the total compensation in the form of perquisites, whereas those in France, Germany and Singapore receive mainly basic compensation and variable remuneration.

## Rationales for Employee Benefit Plans

Several business and economic reasons underlie the establishment of employee benefit plans. Some arguments are theory based while others are practical. The six rationales described in this section have played important roles in most countries where expansive employee benefit programs exist. Other factors also play an important role in the growth and development of employee benefits worldwide. These factors assume greater or lesser importance depending on the individual country under consideration.

## Lifetime utility maximization

Employees may have a preference for substituting current wages for future retirement benefits, when income otherwise might be expected to be lower, so as to achieve a smoother income/consumption stream over their entire life cycle. This preference is consistent with life cycle utility maximization models. Such models assert that individuals can be expected to maximize their utility (see Chapter 2) over their lifetimes; that is, to arrange their affairs as best they can to derive maximum enjoyment (and minimum discomfort) throughout their lives.[2]

A managerial version of lifetime utility maximization is the **deferred wage theory** that holds that retirement benefits can be thought of as the employee agreeing to defer some current wages in favor of payments during retirement years. Strict adherence to the deferred wage theory implies that certain design features, such as full and immediate vesting of employer contributions, are present in the pension plan.

## Meeting the competition

Although largely self-evident, it warrants stating that businesses offer employee benefit plans to meet competition for employees. In countries where labor is scarce, at least as to the type and quality needed, firms offering attractive benefit packages often are at a competitive advantage in attracting quality labor. Other firms may have to offer similar benefit packages simply to retain their pool of employee talent.

## Improved employee productivity

Some employers believe that employee morale is enhanced when workers are assured of reasonable levels of retirement income. This in turn may contribute to greater employee efficiency, reduced turnover and increased productivity. Also, workforce morale can be boosted when employees have assurances that they and their dependents will be financially protected if they die or become disabled. The presence of employer-provided medical benefits also may reduce turnover, thereby contributing to increased productivity. Further, certain retirement income programs – those in which employer contributions are tied directly to profitability – may greatly improve employee productivity as increased employee productivity translates into higher profits, which leads to larger employer contributions to the programs and greater benefits at retirement.

The principal-agent literature suggests a relationship between deferred wage payments (such as pensions) and productivity. Specifically, a wage deferral should create an incentive for employees to work diligently, at least during the vesting period, to avoid being fired for being non-productive and to assure that they will receive the wages that have been deferred (Hutchens, 1986). Although Hutchens develops his theory in terms of an implicit contract, it can be argued that the existence of pension plans and vesting provisions are explicit or formal versions of Hutchens' implicit contracts.

## Efficiency of the group mechanism

Employee benefit plans frequently utilize a group funding mechanism, such as group insurance. Even when individual contracts are used or when the employee benefit plan is funded on a pay-as-you-go basis, certain cost efficiencies generally exist when individuals have access to death benefits, health, accident and sickness benefits, and retirement income at their place of employment. These cost efficiencies will be great for large firms and may be minimal or non-existent for firms below a specific size (e.g., 10 employees).

Those cost efficiencies observed when employers use insurance as a group funding mechanism can be summarized as follows:

- *Marketing efficiencies*: The marketing of insurance coverage to many individuals through a single entity, such as an employer, provides cost savings over marketing directly to the individuals. When writing group insurance, insurers typically incur lower marketing expenses (e.g., sales commission rates) due to the larger volume of coverage or the employer buying more than one product (e.g., life insurance and disability insurance).

- *Administrative efficiencies*: Lower per-unit, administration costs typically are present in employee benefit plans, in comparison with the purchase of individual coverage. Instead of issuing separate insurance policies to each covered employee, insurers commonly use a single master contract to effect coverage, resulting in significant cost savings. Employee contributions under contributory plans generally are collected via payroll deduction and remitted directly to the insurer or other funding mechanism, thus providing significant cost savings over other methods of premium collection. Further, employers frequently play a role in enrolling employees in the group benefit plan and may perform other administrative tasks typically done by an insurer in individual insurance sales.

- *Underwriting efficiencies*: Not only insurers but also covered employees benefit from streamlined underwriting procedures under group insurance. Little or no underwriting of individual employees (and their dependents) occurs in groups of medium to large size. Instead of determining the health status of individual employees and their dependents, insurers are most interested in the insurability of the group itself. Insurability primarily depends on the predictability of the group's claims experience that, in turn, depends mainly on firm size.

  Efficiencies also are possible through a reduction in adverse selection. It is believed that the group health insurance market is more resistant to adverse selection than is the individual health insurance market because coverage in group insurance typically is incidental to the employment relationship (Browne, 1992).

The marketing, administrative and underwriting cost efficiencies embodied in the group mechanism should translate into lower costs for economic security provided through employee benefit plans than the costs through the purchase of individual insurance or other arrangements. This, in itself, is a valuable *benefit* of employee benefit plans even when employees are required to pay part or even all of the cost of the coverage.

### External pressures

In many countries, organized labor has played an influential role in the development and expansion of employee benefits. Evidence exists that unionism has a substantial impact on total expenditures for employee benefit plans as well as the percentage of total employee compensation allocated to employee benefits. In addition, the influence of organized labor typically extends beyond any specific benefit programs established as a direct result of collective bargaining negotiations between the employer and the union. For example, employers commonly provide their nonunion employees with at least the equivalent benefits provided to union members under any collective bargaining agreement. In addition, firms may decide to offer or expand employee benefit plans in an attempt to dissuade employees from joining a labor union. Although empirical studies focus mostly on the impact of unions on the wages of nonunion employees, a simple extension of economic theory supports the expectation of the same type of impact of unionism on the provision of employee benefits for nonunion workers.

Besides pressure from organized labor, firms often are subject to two types of government pressures. First, the state may mandate that employers offer certain types of benefits to their employees. Common government-mandated benefits include workers' compensation, unemployment insurance, healthcare, family leave and retirement benefits. Second, in an attempt to dissuade governments from adopting further mandates, employers may decide voluntarily to offer one or more employee benefit plans.

### Tax advantages

In countries that base their tax collections on the income of individuals and corporations, certain tax advantages may result from the establishment of employee benefit plans. Two primary advantages are (1) current deductibility of employer or employee contributions used to fund plan benefits and (2) deferral or complete avoidance of the taxation of benefits received by plan participants and their beneficiaries.

In addition, it is common for payroll taxes (for unemployment insurance and other social security programs) to be applied only to money wages, with employee benefits exempted from such taxes. Thus, an increase in total compensation in the form of greater benefits is less expensive to the employer than the cost of a comparable increase in money wages. The specific tax treatment accorded employee benefit programs varies widely, depending on the country and the specific type of employee benefit plan.

## Designing Employee Benefit Plans

Most experts recommend that employers apply a total compensation approach to the design of their employee benefit plans. In addition, employers should make an active determination as to whether they should follow a traditional, defined benefit (DB) approach to their employee benefit programs or adopt a defined contribution (DC) approach.

### Total compensation approach

An employee's **total compensation (remuneration)** consists of all forms of *direct* (base pay, bonuses, etc.) and *indirect* (employee benefits and perquisites) compensation provided by the employer. A total compensation approach to employee benefit plan design recognizes the importance of employee benefits in the total compensation and the existence of distinct tradeoffs between benefits and wages. It further recognizes that total compensation and its various components should reflect overall firm objectives, competitive market forces, and the needs and desires of employees.

In some countries, base pay forms only a small part of total compensation for managers and executives, while short and long-term incentives (e.g., bonuses, profit sharing and stock options), benefits (e.g., retirement, life insurance, disability income, medical/dental coverage and vacation) and perquisites (e.g., company cars, country club memberships and loans) constitute a large percentage of key employees' total compensation. Understandably, firms throughout the world are increasingly adopting an approach to compensation and benefits management that addresses simultaneously base and variable pay (including both short and long-term incentives), government-mandated employee benefits, voluntary employer-provided benefits and perquisites.

The need for a total compensation approach to wage and benefit design takes on greater importance as benefit costs escalate, becoming a larger component of total compensation. Through an integrated approach, organizations are better able to ascertain total compensation expenditures and how these expenditures should be allocated between direct wages (including incentive compensation) and various benefit programs to deliver maximum worth to employees at the lowest cost to the organization. The specific allocation of total compensation between cash payments and employee benefits (including perquisites) should consider both individual need for the benefit and any differences in the tax treatment between direct pay and employee benefits.

Using a total compensation approach to benefit plan design can be a difficult process and an impossible task in some instances. Additional data must be compiled in determining both the cost to the employer and the perceived value to employees of specific benefit programs. Cash equivalents need to be determined for each benefit and each perquisite if a total compensation approach is to be successful.

### Defined benefit versus defined contribution

In designing an employee benefit program, employers examine the benefits and costs of a defined (or fixed) benefit and a defined contribution plan design approach. Under the traditional **defined benefit (DB) approach**, the employer determines the benefit amounts to be provided. Although some benefit amounts commonly vary by salary level, for the most part, all employees covered by the plan(s) are provided with the same fixed or predetermined, set of benefits, irrespective of differing ages, family composition and overall needs.

In some countries, most notably the U.S. and Canada, many employers have adopted a **defined contribution (DC) approach** to plan design, wherein the employer contribution amounts rather than the benefits are fixed. Under so-called **flexible benefit** (or simply **flex**) **plans**, the employer determines how much it will spend overall on employee benefit plans, and the total funds are spread over all covered employees according to some predetermined allocation method such as a fixed amount or a fixed percentage of pay. Employees are then able to apply their individual contribution allocations to the purchase of specific benefits from a wide array of benefits offered by the employer. For this reason, the flexible benefit plan is sometimes called a **cafeteria benefit plan**. Through this process, individual employees should be able to satisfy their benefit needs (and the needs of their families) better than that which occurs under the DB approach.

A potential disadvantage of flex plans is the possibility that employees may make unwise choices. This risk can be reduced through proper education of employees and by including in the plan certain restrictions on employee choice. Quite commonly, flex plans include a required core of benefits such as vacation and holidays, life insurance, medical expense and disability.

Employers can enjoy several advantages through the adoption of a DC approach. Most importantly, they can fix the firm's total benefit costs as a percentage of the payroll. Under the DB approach, employer costs usually escalate over time, even when expressed as a percentage of payroll, as healthcare costs increase and new benefits are likely added. Under the DC or flex approach, the employer may choose to set the firm's costs as a fixed percentage of payroll (e.g., 30 percent). Additional costs in excess of wage increases, attributable to inflation or to the addition of new benefits, are to be absorbed within this set percentage through reductions in the levels of one or more existing benefits.

DC and flexible benefit plans often receive little support from labor unions. They generally prefer the traditional, DB approach to plan design, whereby they can bargain for more coverage under existing benefit programs (i.e., higher limits and greater breadth of covered expenses), for additional employee benefits to be offered or for both. In contrast, firms and their owners generally prefer the greater cash flow certainty associated with DC plans. The reasons are obvious. With DC programs, the employer does not incur salary inflation risk, longevity risk (i.e., employees collecting benefits for longer periods than originally projected because of increased longevity) or the possibility of under-funding the plan. In fact, a motivation for General Motors Corporation's (U.S.) significant reduction in its workforce in 2005 was to reduce the financing burden of its DB programs.

A disadvantage of flex plans to employers is that these plans generally entail greater administration costs when they provide many choices and options. However, information technology frequently is able to reduce these extra costs. In addition, flexible benefit plans should provide a more efficient allocation of resources through the expenditure of employer funds on benefits that have the greatest perceived need as determined by individual employees. Under the traditional DB approach to plan design, employees often are provided with one or more benefits or more coverage of a particular benefit than they want or need.

## International Variations in Employee Benefit Plans

As described earlier, the underlying rationale for the development and expansion of employee benefit programs is essentially the same worldwide. Together, government-mandated and voluntary employer-provided benefit plans typically address the usual personal risks of death, disability, accident and sickness, and retirement. Nonetheless, considerable variation exists in the major types of employee benefit plans worldwide because of economic and cultural differences; diversity in tax laws, local labor markets, and employer attitudes toward their employees; and a myriad of other factors.

Great differences also exist across national boundaries in the extent to which specific employee benefits are mandated by government. In several Western European countries (e.g., France and Italy), governments require employers to offer a fairly broad collection of employee benefits which then form part of the country's approach to providing social security. In these instances, only limited private-sector markets may exist for supplemental, voluntary employee benefit plans. By contrast, in the U.S. and in many Pacific-Rim countries, government-mandated benefit programs are less expansive. In these countries, employee benefit plans usually are offered at the employer's discretion, without any legal requirement to do so.

In many developing countries, relatively small percentages of the total workforce are covered by employee benefit plans, whether voluntary or government mandated. A more agrarian, less industrialized economy, the presence of relatively few large firms, and a less wealthy nation in general are significant contributing factors to a less developed system of social insurance and employee benefit schemes.

### Pension schemes worldwide

As noted in Chapter 9, social insurance programs internationally vary in many respects as they relate to retirement income. In addition, some countries permit employers to contract out a portion of social insurance retirement benefits by providing employees with equal or greater benefits from a voluntary employer-provided benefit so long as certain conditions are met. The major components of social security programs and the overall level of government-provided retirement benefits should be factored into the design of voluntary employer-provided pension plans for the firm to achieve a predetermined goal as to the combined level of desired income replacement.

*Pensionable ages*

The **pensionable age** (also called **normal pension age**, **normal retirement age** and **pension eligibility age**) is the age at which covered participants are eligible to receive *unreduced* retirement benefits. For most OECD countries, the age in their social insurance schemes that allow unreduced benefits is 65. Denmark, Iceland, Norway and the U.S. are exceptions, with normal pension ages being 67. Several countries' retirement ages are lower, with 60-year-olds usually qualifying to retire at full benefit in France, the Slovak Republic, Korea and Turkey. Commonly, voluntary employer-designed retirement plans incorporate a normal pension age that is the same as the pension age for full social security benefits. A significant worldwide trend, however, is toward increasing this age, at least in social insurance schemes.

In addition, **gradual** or **phased retirement**, where individuals move to a part-time employment status before retiring fully, is being strongly encouraged, commensurate with the increase in normal retirement age. Gradual retirement may become a necessity in the future in developed countries faced with aging populations and threats to the financial security of their social insurance (retirement) schemes. Indeed, part-time earnings, resulting from some employment activity beyond the pension entitlement age, seems likely to become so significant in some countries as to constitute a fourth pillar underpinning old age financial security (in addition to social insurance, employee benefit plans and individual savings for retirement).

Some countries employ different pensionable ages for men and women. Generally, when sex-distinct pensionable ages are used, the pensionable age for women is lower (usually by three to five years) than that for men. The trend is away from using pensionable ages differentiated by sex. However, lower social security pensionable ages still apply to women today in many countries, including Argentina, Austria, Colombia, Czech Republic, Poland, Pakistan and the U.K.

*Types of pension plans*

As discussed, employers tend to adopt either a DB or DC approach to overall benefit plan design. However, many use the other approach in isolation to design the retirement plan component of the entire benefits package. We summarize below the characteristics of DC and DB retirement plans as well as the pros and cons of each as perceived by employees and employers.

- *DB retirement plans*: Under these plans, the benefit may be expressed as (1) a flat amount per year of service (e.g., a monthly retirement benefit of $25 for each year of service times the number of years of service) or (2) a total amount for an aggregated period of service (e.g., a monthly benefit of $500 after 20 years of service). Alternatively, the benefit formula can be expressed as (1) a percentage of the employee's average wages (e.g., 1.0 percent) multiplied by years of service or (2) a percentage of average wages (e.g., 50 percent) for a certain period of service. Average wages can be determined over the employee's entire work period with the employer (so-called career-average plans) or over a relatively shorter period of five or 10 years immediately pre-ceding retirement (final-average or final-pay plans).

*   *DC retirement plans*: By contrast, under a DC retirement plan, the employer (and fre-quently employees) contributes to a fund that, through investment earnings and addi-tional contributions, increases over time. At retirement, the employee is entitled to a benefit equal to the lump-sum amount in the fund or a stream of annuity income ben-efits purchased with the lump sum.

Whether an employer should adopt a DB or DC plan should be a function of relative plan costs (including administration costs), employer/employee risk sharing objectives, age mix of the workforce as well as the employer's objectives in employee recruitment and reten-tion. In general, younger employees are attracted more to DC plans, while older employees prefer the predetermined benefit amounts under DB plans. Thus, the attractiveness of the employer's retirement plan will, to a large degree, be determined by the age mix of the employee population.

Fundamentally different employer/employee risk sharing is embodied within DB and DC plans. Under DB plans, employers promise a specific benefit at retirement and, as a result, must make the necessary contributions to fund the promised benefits. *Employers* bear the investment risk under DB plans. If the earnings on the invested plan assets are relatively high, the otherwise required employer contributions in the future will be reduced. Conversely, if investment earnings are low, employers will have to make greater contribu-tions. By contrast, *employees* bear the investment risk under DC retirement plans. Larger (smaller) investment earnings translate into larger (smaller) fund balances and thereby to larger (smaller) lump-sum or annuity payments at retirement.

Although total plan administration costs may be comparable for DB and DC plans, the major expenditure categories are usually quite different. Specifically, DB plans gener-ally entail larger actuarial fees related to the determination of periodic funding amounts. DC plans typically incur larger record-keeping costs associated with contributions and investment earnings that are allocated to individual employee accounts. With the advances in informational technology, administrative costs have been reduced significantly.

*Retirement plan variations worldwide*

To provide a better understanding of the variations in retirement plans worldwide, we examine retirement plans in selected countries representing different geographic regions and differing levels of economic development. Table 16.1 displays selected characteristics of pension and severance plans in seven countries. Similar tables, using the same seven countries, are presented later showing international variations in the provision of healthcare financing, life insurance and disability benefits.

For most of the countries included in Table 16.1, employers provide both pension and lump-sum severance payments, either because both are required by the government, or it is their customary practice to do so. Although severance plans typically are designed as a retirement-type benefit, they frequently provide lump-sum payments upon any severance of employment. Lump-sum severance payments range from 3 to 40 times monthly salary. Towers Perrin (2005–2006) reports that, of 26 countries surveyed, only firms in Germany pay no severance payments to top executives or manufacturing employees. By contrast,

**Table 16.1**   Overview of Retirement Plans (Pension and Severance) in Selected Countries

| Country | Benefits Provided |
| --- | --- |
| Brazil | Severance plans and a type of profit sharing plan are mandatory. Severance plans resemble a DC retirement plan with an 8 percent annual employer contribution. Private pension plans are increasingly found. |
| Germany | Employers are permitted to establish tax-deductible book reserves, without establishing a separate trust for pension schemes. Separate trusts and insured schemes also are common. |
| Japan | Lump-sum severance plans are universal using tax-deductible book reserves as the funding mechanism. Separate pension trusts are allowable only for employers with more than 100 employees. Insured pension schemes are available for smaller employers. Pension trusts are subject to an annual tax of approximately 1.2 percent on the assets. Employers with 500 or more employees may partially contract out of government-provided pensions. |
| Korea | Recently introduced changes permit existing severance plans are defined as DB plans. DC plans are also introduced. The DB plans permit employees to receive severance payments after a minimum period of service. Both the employer and the employee may make contributions to such plans. |
| Norway | Pension schemes are common only in medium and large companies. The plans are commonly DB arrangements. |
| Thailand | Employer-sponsored pension plans are not mandatory, but some employers offer a type of matching savings program. Employees must contribute at least 3 percent of salary. Employers contribute at least as much as do the employees and may contribute up to a tax-deductible limit of 15 percent. Invested assets are not in an irrevocable trust, thereby allowing the employer to capture some of the investment income for the company. This is equivalent to the book reserve method in other countries. |
| United Kingdom | A wide range of DC and DB plans is available. If the benefits provided are substantial, the employer can contract out of the government-provided pension benefits. Lump-sum payments at retirement are common, resulting in many arrangements that mimic the severance plans found in other countries. The U.K. is one of only a few countries that does not require a minimum recognition of accrued liabilities through separate funding or book reserves. |
| United States | A wide variety of DB and DC plans using tax-exempt trusts or insurance contracts is used. Non-tax-deductible book reserves, with no separate funding, are common for benefits provided to executives. Mandatory employee contributions are allowable but are not common. When employee contributions are mandatory or otherwise allowed, their tax status is dependent on the particular type of plan established by the employer. |

*Source*: John Hancock Financial Services (2005).

departing employees receive a government-mandated severance payment of 150–300 percent of basic annual salary in Korea and 250–300 percent in Spain. Firms in Italy and Japan tend to pay voluntarily 50–150 percent of annual basic salaries to departing employees. Argentina, Belgium, Canada and South Africa practice a combination of government-mandated and voluntary payments to affected employees.

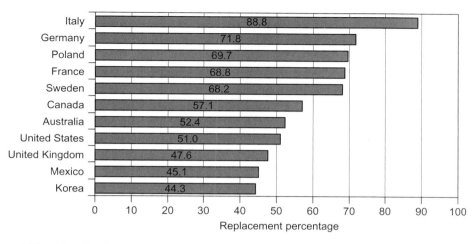

**Figure 16.2**   After-Tax Replacement Ratios of Public Pensions in Selected OECD Countries (Middle-Income Males at Age 65 or Older). *Source*: Jackson and Howe, 2003

Some countries (e.g., the U.S.) emphasize pension plans. Other countries (e.g., Brazil) emphasize lump-sum severance benefits, with the other form of retirement benefit virtually non-existent.

Favorable tax treatment usually is accorded pension schemes. Frequently, employer contributions are tax deductible. In addition, earnings on pension assets often incur no current income or other taxation. Retirement benefits generally are subject to taxation, however, with some countries giving preferential tax treatment to either periodic income or lump-sum retirement benefits. Unlike the U.S., with its extensive collection of nondiscrimination requirements, most other countries permit pension plan designs that favor highly paid employees. Some countries permit both *pre-tax* and *after-tax* employee contributions, and some (e.g., Thailand) mandate employee contributions to the plan. Many countries permit the establishment of tax-deductible book reserves whereby pension liabilities are recognized on the sponsoring company's financial statements, but specific assets are not required to be set aside or transferred to an irrevocable trust or held under contract by an insurer, although the latter are commonly used funding vehicles.

*Income replacement at retirement*

The income replaced for retirees by public pensions naturally influences the income that retirees seek to secure from other sources, including private-sector pensions. Figure 16.2 presents retirement income replacement ratios – the ratio of retirement income to pre-retirement income – for selected OECD countries for middle-income males, aged 65 and greater. The figure shows relatively higher after-tax replacement ratios in European countries (e.g., Italy, Germany and Poland) than those in North American or the Asia-Pacific region.

Figure 16.3 gives the percentage breakdown by major source of total income for males, age 65 and greater in selected OECD countries. This figure shows clearly that private pensions are less important in some countries, including Italy, Germany and France, than in others.

In general, we observe that the higher the pre-retirement income replaced by public pensions, the less important are private pensions. With continuing retrenchment of public pensions in many developed countries, we can anticipate growth in private pensions.

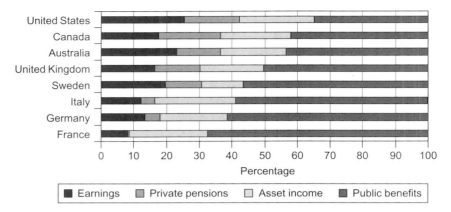

**Figure 16.3**  After-Tax Income by Source as Percent of Total Income in Selected OECD Countries (Middle-Income Males at Age 65 or Older). *Source*: Jackson and Howe, 2003

*Mandatory inflation adjustments*

Although inflationary pressures differ considerably from one economy to another, inflation and its erosive effects on retirement benefits is a concern worldwide. In response to this issue, some countries prescribe mandatory indexing of retirement benefit payments. Germany, the Netherlands and the U.K., among other countries, follow this practice.

*Cutbacks in government pension schemes*

As discussed in Chapters 7 and 9, many countries are examining ways to reduce their public pension benefits and shift retirement benefit costs to the private sector. This is especially true in countries with aging populations where there will be fewer workers in the future to contribute to the cost of pay-as-you-go public benefits for an increasing population of retirees. Given these and related concerns, we expect governments to liberalize their regulation and taxation of voluntary employee benefit plans to encourage the private sector to expand its role in the provision of retirement income and other economic security benefits.

The aging population trend is not universal with some countries experiencing growth in their younger population. For example, the age 0–14 cohorts of Africa (all regions) and parts of the Asia-Pacific region are expected to remain at or above 20 percent of total population in the year 2050. By contrast, this age cohort in developed economies is projected to shrink to 15.7 percent by the same year.

Reductions in government-provided pension schemes should be of particular importance to employers that link their retirement benefits directly to the pension benefits provided under the social insurance scheme. If the employer-provided retirement benefits are offset directly by government pension benefits – for example, the private plan benefit is reduced by 50 percent of the government benefits payable – then the employer's pension costs will increase as countries reduce government-provided retirement benefits. In these instances, many employers likely will move away from the offset approach, thereby decoupling the employer-provided retirement benefit from the government benefit. The design of the voluntary employer plan still can recognize the new social insurance benefits without linking its retirement benefits directly to the government-provided benefit and automatically committing the employer plan to pick up the net difference as government benefits are cut.

**Table 16.2**  Overview of Healthcare Benefits in Selected Counties

| Country | Benefits Provided |
| --- | --- |
| Brazil | Basic healthcare benefits are provided by the government. Supplemental coverages are growing in importance and typically is provided through prepaid groups (clinics, cooperatives, and PPOs), with insured plans growing in popularity. |
| Germany | Universal, comprehensive healthcare benefits are provided by the government. High-wage earners may opt out and select private insurance (employer must pay one-half of the insurance premiums) and/or may be provided supplementary insurance for high-quality care (e.g., private accommodations). |
| Japan | Universal, comprehensive healthcare benefits are provided by the government. Employers with more than 700 employees may opt out and form their own private health insurance society. |
| Korea | Universal, comprehensive healthcare benefits are mandated by the government and are provided through either government facilities or government-authorized healthcare groups ("societies"). The government plan includes co-payments and deductibles that may be financed through private insurance. |
| Norway | Universal, comprehensive healthcare benefits are provided by the government. Private plans are essentially non-existent. |
| Thailand | Comprehensive healthcare benefits are provided by the government, although coverage is not universal. Employers commonly sponsor insured plans that cover basic healthcare. Employees do not contribute to the basic coverage but often purchase supplemental coverage through the same contracts. |
| United Kingdom | Universal, comprehensive healthcare benefits are provided by the government. Redundant insured plans provided by employers are growing in popularity because of improved service of the private sector the government system. |
| United States | A wide variety of private-sector arrangements is offered by employers, with the government generally providing coverage only for the elderly and the poor. Employer plans range from basic to comprehensive coverage (major medical coverage). Employees typically share in the costs. The working population without employer-provided coverage (mostly employees in small firms, temporary workers and the self-employed) may purchase insurance from private insurers or may be without any healthcare insurance. |

*Source*: John Hancock Financial Services (2005).

### *Healthcare plans worldwide*

*Worldwide variations in healthcare plans*

Benefits under the U.S. national health insurance program, Medicare, are limited to individuals age 65 and over and to a few under-age-65 population subsets. By contrast, most other developed countries have some type of broad national health insurance scheme for individuals of all ages, as discussed in Chapter 9. In these countries, however, employers commonly offer supplemental medical expense plans to provide employees with higher quality medical care than that available from national health insurance providers or to provide another perquisite to executives and key managers.

Table 16.2 contains an overview of government and employer-provided healthcare benefits in seven countries. For purposes of this discussion, **basic healthcare benefits** consist

of a basic level of medical treatment typically including emergency care, outpatient services, and some hospitalization and extended care coverage possibly through a set of scheduled payments. **Supplemental healthcare benefits** provide coverage for additional medical
treatment beyond basic medical care, although this coverage frequently is not as comprehensive as that contained in major medical coverage common to the U.S.

Employer contributions to national health insurance schemes and to private health insurance plans typically are a tax-deductible business expense. Deductibility of employee contributions varies by country. For example, Brazil and Norway do not permit employees to
take tax deductions for their contributions to health insurance plans. By contrast, Japan
grants employees tax deductions. In the U.S., the tax-deductibility of employee contributions is dependent on the type of arrangement set up by the employer and, to a lesser extent
usually, the employee's own personal circumstances.

Many national health insurance systems allow either the employer (i.e., all employees)
or an employee to avoid participating in the government scheme when equivalent, private insurance coverage is purchased. The specific requirements that must be met in these
instances vary from one country to the next.

*Containing escalating healthcare plan costs*

Rising healthcare costs are a global phenomenon, constituting a major problem in both
social insurance and private-sector health plans, especially in developed countries. Although
healthcare costs as a percentage of GDP remain in single digits for most countries, such
costs now amount to 15 percent of GDP in the U.S., with the percentage continuing to rise.
Many governments are exploring the possibility of shifting more medical expense costs to
employers and individuals. Increasing attention is being given to extending the privatization concept beyond unfunded public DB pensions and into the healthcare arena.

On average, older persons use more healthcare services than do younger individuals. Considering that many developed countries are confronted with an aging population,
rising healthcare costs will continue to be a major problem in many of the countries, for
both government-sponsored and private-sector employee benefit plans, as discussed in
Chapter 9.

Employers will continue to look for ways to restrain anticipated healthcare cost
increases. U.S. firms, which have experienced significant increases in employee healthcare
costs, have adopted several measures to address this problem. Most notably, many U.S.
firms have implemented some or all of the following programs in an attempt to stem rising
medical claims: (1) managed care programs, (2) flexible benefit plans and (3) wellness programs. These U.S. managed care programs are discussed here because of the considerable
worldwide interest in the possibility of transporting these techniques to other countries to
help control their rising healthcare costs.

*Managed care programs*
Managed care means a coordinated medical treatment approach emphasizing controls
designed to provide high quality service and contain costs. It may be limited to the implementation of claims utilization review techniques, second surgery opinions, pre-admission
(to a hospital) testing and similar cost-saving devices within a traditional indemnity health
insurance plan.[3] More dramatically, it may involve the offering of preferred provider organizations (PPOs) or health maintenance organizations (HMOs) as options to employees in

lieu of more traditional healthcare financing arrangements. Many variations of PPOs and HMOs exist. The basic characteristics of each follow:

- A **preferred provider organization** consists of a network of healthcare providers, which may include hospitals, physicians and pharmacies. PPOs usually are presented as an option to employees in lieu of a traditional medical expense indemnity plan. Incentives such as lower or no deductibles and higher reimbursement rates (e.g., 90 percent instead of 70 or 80 percent) are generally offered to employees as inducements to use network providers. Typically, the providers in the PPO network agree to discount the fees charged PPO patients in return for an anticipated increase in the demand for their professional services due to the network's contracts with employers (and their insurers).

- A **health maintenance organization** is a type of managed care organization that functions as both the financier and provider of healthcare. In other words, an HMO recruits members (commonly through their employers) from whom they collect premiums and to whom the HMO provides medical services. In addition, HMOs commonly emphasize preventive and comprehensive medical care as compared to indemnity plans. Some HMOs use their own facilities and medical staff to offer medical services. Other HMOs look like PPO and offer medical services using networks of external providers such as hospitals, physicians and pharmacies. Under traditional HMO plans, participants and their dependents who have chosen HMO coverage generally must use HMO-approved providers for the cost of medical care to be covered.

Changes over time in the basic structure and operation of PPOs and HMOs have made it sometimes difficult to tell them apart. An example of this is the **point-of-service plan** under which covered employees and their dependents can use HMO network providers or out-of-network providers but with different deductibles and reimbursement rates depending on which provider is selected.

*Flexible benefit plans*
Although offering a variety of designs, the common feature in flexible benefit plans is that employees are given a choice among several benefit options. If more of one benefit is desired, then the employee may be required to accept less of another benefit, thus creating tradeoffs among different benefits. To illustrate, if an employee wants more healthcare coverage (e.g., a lower deductible or a higher maximum), the employee may have to accept a smaller disability income benefit (e.g., a longer waiting period or a shorter maximum benefit period).

As discussed, flexible benefit approaches are used frequently by employers in the U.S. and Canada. Although many underlying reasons exist for the adoption of such a program, in many instances, the employer adopts a flex plan in an attempt to control rising healthcare costs. With a flex plan, employees are provided with a specified amount of flexible-spending money that can be used to purchase items from a menu (cafeteria) of benefits. Employers hope that employees and their beneficiaries have a better appreciation of employee benefits, the varying costs of different benefits and, specifically, a better recognition of the factors that affect health plan costs. In this way, flex plans can have a mitigating effect on rising healthcare costs. Flexible benefit plans probably will continue to emerge internationally as a technique to address workforce diversity and as a method to manage and control employee benefit costs.

**Table 16.3**  Overview of Group Life Insurance in Selected Countries

| Country | Benefits Provided |
|---|---|
| Brazil | Death benefits equal to 1.5–2 times annual salary are typical. |
| Germany | The government provides substantial survivor benefits to married male employees. Therefore, it is customary to provide group life insurance only to females and unmarried males. |
| Japan | Death benefits equalling two times annual salary are customarily provided in MNCs. |
| Korea | Group life insurance is provided at a variety of benefit levels. |
| Norway | Group life insurance is common, typically equal to one to two times annual salary. |
| Thailand | Death benefits, if provided, are set typically at one to four times salary. |
| United Kingdom | Group life insurance is commonly provided equal to two to three times annual salary. |
| United States | Death benefits equalling one to two times annual salary are common. |

*Sources*: John Hancock Financial Services (2005).

*Wellness programs*

**Wellness programs** are programs designed to improve the health and wellbeing of a firm's employees. Wellness programs can range from simple employee awareness activities (e.g., newsletters, no-smoking days) to extensive risk appraisals of an employee's wellbeing. Increasingly, they are perceived as important prescriptions for controlling rising health benefit costs worldwide.

Several countries offer examples of documented savings from wellness programs – as much as three to five times their costs. Wellness programs possess great potential for mitigating somewhat the increasingly higher healthcare costs experienced by many employers. Although many MNCs have implemented wellness programs only with respect to their domestic operations, this situation is likely to change as foreign employment becomes a larger component of the total worldwide workforce for multinationals. The extent to which managed care approaches, flexible benefit plans and wellness programs can be effective in controlling employer healthcare costs in other countries – with different cultures, different work and lifestyle habits, different tax systems, and differences in the mix of government-sponsored/employer-sponsored healthcare benefits – remains to be seen.

### Group life insurance programs worldwide

Employer-provided death benefits are common in most countries worldwide, although the method through which they are provided varies. Table 16.3 presents selected features of employer-provided death benefit programs in seven countries representing different geographic regions throughout the world.

Group life insurance is used to fund employer-provided death benefits in many countries. In addition, death benefits frequently are included in pension schemes. In countries where group life insurance is common, the death benefits range from one to four times annual salary. Employer contributions toward the cost of group life insurance often do not create any income tax liability to employees, within limits. Insurance coverage limits generally are expressed either as a multiple of salary or a flat amount.

**Table 16.4**   Overview of Short- and Long-term Disability Plans in Selected Countries

| Country | Benefits Provided |
| --- | --- |
| Brazil | Only short-term disability plans are provided by employers, supplementing government-provided short-term benefits. |
| Germany | Short-term disability plans are not provided by employers due to government-provided benefits. Long-term disability benefits are common in pension schemes, in lieu of group disability insurance plans. |
| Japan | Only short-term disability plans are provided by employers. Long-term disability benefits are provided through a government program. |
| Korea | Employer-provided disability plans are uncommon due to substantial government-provided benefits. |
| Norway | Short-term disability plans are not established by employers due to the existence of government-provided benefits. Long-term disability benefits are provided through pension schemes rather than through group insurance plans. |
| Thailand | The only employer-provided disability benefits are through disability riders attached to group life insurance contracts. |
| United Kingdom | Short-term disability benefits are frequently provided by employers. Long-term disability benefits are common only for certain classes of employees at large firms. |
| United States | Employers frequently provide short-term and long-term disability benefits, although not universally. |

*Sources*: John Hancock Financial Services (2005).

### Disability benefit plans worldwide

Table 16.4 contains a brief overview of employer-provided disability income benefit programs typically found in the seven countries for which pension, healthcare and life insurance benefits have been examined. In general, disability income benefits are found less frequently than pension and life insurance benefits. Plans providing short-term benefits (e.g., for three to six months) are more common than long-term benefit plans, and these benefits often are tied with severance benefits or to government-provided disability benefits. In some countries, it is customary to include long-term disability benefits in pension schemes (e.g., Germany and Norway) or in group life insurance contracts (e.g., Thailand) in lieu of separate disability insurance contracts.

## Special Issues Facing MNCs

Several special benefit (and compensation) issues face MNCs. They include the previously discussed total compensation approach to benefit design and multinational pooling arrangements.

### Total compensation

Both purely national and multinational organizations generally should adopt an integrated, total compensation approach to compensation and benefits management. The total compensation approach, however, assumes its greatest significance in the international arena because of the widely varying mixes of the components of total remuneration from one country to the next. Differing tax systems, local customs and cultures, and varying living costs, collectively, argue for varying levels of total compensation and, of equal or greater significance, differing packages of wages, benefits and perquisites.

The direct or indirect substitution of wages, employee benefits and perquisites holds great significance for companies that employ local nationals, headquarters-country expatriates and third-country nationals (TCNs) in various operations worldwide. Traditionally, MNCs compensated their employees throughout the world according to the compensation practices of the employees' home countries. Local nationals were compensated according to competitive wage and benefit practices in the local economy. Headquarters-country expatriates received a level of compensation designed to preserve the expatriate's standard of living in his or her home country. TCNs typically were provided with a wage and benefits package determined under a home-country or a headquarters-country approach, depending on the employee's status within the firm and the organization's own philosophy. Consequently, under the traditional approach, wide variations could exist in total compensation earned by local nationals, expatriates and TCNs even though they possessed comparable skills and performed similar jobs at the same performance level.

As MNCs have evolved from country-specific organizations with international operations to global organizations less tied to the business practices and the corporate culture in the headquarters' countries, they search and compete for talent in a global marketplace to fill their most important international positions. In doing so, many of these firms are moving away from local-country compensation practices to designing pay structures that provide greater fairness for all employees concerned. As to the benefits component of total compensation, benefit types and amounts for executives and key managers still tend to be tied to local-country practices, but specific decisions are made within the broader context of an overall company-wide benefit strategy to assure fairness in the system.

The process of compiling data on specific employee benefits is more complex for organizations with international operations. Both the perceived value of certain types of employee benefits and the costs of those benefits are likely to vary considerably from country to country. Using a total compensation approach may be impossible in instances when data are not readily available and the daunting task of measuring every component of compensation is too costly and too time-consuming.

### *Multinational pooling*

Multinational pooling is a method whereby an MNC participates in a global insurance arrangement to finance the costs of its worldwide benefit programs, thus enjoying economies of scale and scope and participating in favorable claims experience. As an alternative to the use of separate group insurance contracts in each local market with its own regulatory and rating laws, a multinational pooling arrangement entails the purchase of insurance through a network of insurers offering employee benefit coverages in various countries. See Figure 16.4, at least 15 multinational pooling networks exist.

When a firm uses a multinational pooling arrangement, it insures a portion or all of its employee benefits worldwide with local insurer affiliates of the network. The network is used to provide insurance coverage under a single master contract for employee benefit plans covering employees of subsidiary or related firms in one or more international locations.[4]

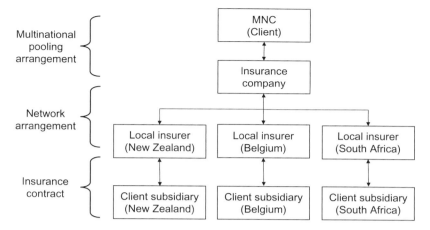

**Figure 16.4**   Multinational Pooling of Employee Benefit Programs. Adapted from Swiss Re (2006) Swiss Life, www.swisslife-network.com

When compared to separate local programs, multinational pooling can offer several advantages to the MNC, including the following:

- Total insurance costs are reduced, including lower administrative and risk charges, through economies of scale and scope generated from the worldwide aggregation of all insured employees and all benefit plans (e.g., life, medical and disability).

- Favorable claims experience in some local markets can be used to offset unfavorable claims experience in other markets, and the MNC shares in the realized savings via an international dividend when the aggregated claims experience is favorable.

- The administration and management of geographically dispersed employee benefit plans are made simpler through combined financial reporting and communication with a single insurer that coordinates the network. Less time and effort are required to put in place (and service) the insurance coverage of the MNC's worldwide subsidiaries because of the network's established relationships with local insurers.

- Excessive margins inherent in cartel and tariff-premium markets can be overcome through the international dividend calculation.

- An MNC may use a traditional or create its own captive, whichever is the more cost effective.

As depicted in Figure 16.4, a typical multinational pooling arrangement involves two agreements. *First*, a master contract is made between the client MNC and the insurer that sponsors or coordinates the network. This agreement calls for the pooling of premiums, claims and other costs among all local insurance contracts in determining whether an international dividend (or premium refund) is payable to the MNC. A typical dividend formula aggregates the paid premiums under all local contracts, credits investment income, and adds the reserves at the beginning of the year. From this amount, aggregated claims, risk charges, expenses (including commissions and taxes), dividends payable to local subsidiaries and yearend reserve amounts are subtracted to determine the amount of any international dividend payable. International dividends can be 10–20 percent or more of paid premiums.

*Second*, local subsidiaries of the MNC enter into an agreement with local insurer affiliates of the pooling network. The insurance coverage at each location is determined by this agreement and will be unaffected by the terms of the master contract. The local contract must comply with local laws and government requirements. It may provide for the payment of a local dividend when premium income exceeds claims, administration expenses and other insurer costs.

Within the E.U., the Single Market Program can lead to a situation where a particular multinational pooling network competes with itself, depending on how the pooling network is structured.[5] Cross-selling should present minimal problems in those networks where the coordinating insurer has branch offices (or subsidiary operations) in various locations within the E.U. By contrast, in networks comprised of independent local (insurer) affiliates, multiple network insurers may find themselves in direct competition with each other.

Although E.U. regulatory harmonization has been achieved in some financial services areas, as discussed in Chapter 3, other important areas (e.g., tax and contract law) remain subject to varying national standards. Many observers believe that protectionist regulation prominent in many E.U. countries decreases the attractiveness of employee benefit coverages purchased through a single European insurer and, simultaneously, provides a competitive edge to multinational pooling networks.

### An international employee benefit program

Without question, it is of utmost importance that MNCs, as with all other firms, establish sound policy statements and objectives describing the firm's compensation philosophy and where employee benefits fit into this structure. It also is imperative that the MNC's employee benefits program and the individual benefit plan components be designed in ways that are consistent with and contribute toward the achievement of the firm's overall business goals and strategies at an affordable cost.[6] Several other characteristics of a sound international employee benefits program exist, and they are included in Insight 16.1.

# RISK MANAGEMENT FOR INTERNATIONAL EMPLOYEES

All corporations seek to protect personnel from harm, but those firms engaged in international activities face greater challenges in doing so.[7] Certainly they wish to minimize work-related injury and disease, and most countries have occupational health and safety standards as well as mandate payments for occupation-related injury or disease. Important and obvious elements of general personnel risk management will be built around these standards and requirements. However, a somewhat different set of risk management considerations apply to employees who live in or travel to regions that might pose special risks to them and, therefore, the firm.

## Definitions and Nature of the Concerned Risks

Kidnapping, terrorism and extortion pose risks for all businesses everywhere and are not unique to MNCs. Nonetheless, MNCs' employees – especially those perceived by the bad

INSIGHT 16.1: DESIRABLE CHARACTERISTICS OF AN
INTERNATIONAL EMPLOYEE BENEFITS PROGRAM

In design an employee benefit plan for an MNC, consideration should be given to
innumerable factors that do not typically arise with a purely national firm. The design
should:

- Be sufficiently flexible to permit different lines of business or operations in various parts of the world to offer amounts and types of benefits reflective of differing employee needs and total compensation structures.
- Be responsive to diverse cultural, economic and political issues in the country
  markets in which the firm operates.
- Be flexible, responsive, fair and equitable to a changing workforce composition –
  one that recognizes work place diversity, the growing numbers of single parents,
  two-income families and permanent part-time employment.
- Be responsive to other societal changes, including an aging population and
  address resulting changes in benefit needs (e.g., retiree medical, long-term care,
  and employee leaves to care for aged parents).
- Be consistent with employee recruitment and retention objectives and adaptable
  to evolving technology, need for employees with new, updated job skills, and the
  disappearance of the career employee.
- Enhance employee morale and be a source of employee motivation which contribute to increased firm profitability.
- Take full advantage of tax incentives and cost efficiencies associated with particular benefit options and be responsive to changes in tax and benefits legislation and
  to new developments in employee benefits.
- Include a strong and effective communications program that ensures employee/
  beneficiary understanding and appreciation of the value and worth of employer-
  provided benefits.

guys to be of greatest value to the firm – have proven attractive targets, and these employees usually are the most vulnerable outside the MNC's headquarters country.

**Kidnapping** is the abduction and detention, usually by unlawful force and sometimes by
fraud, of an individual. The purpose of the kidnapping most commonly is to secure the payment of a ransom in exchange for the promised release of the victim. An estimated 10,000–
25,000 kidnappings occur globally per year, although specialists contend the actual number
is far higher. Most kidnappings occur in Latin America, particularly in Brazil, Colombia,
Ecuador, Guatemala, Mexico and Venezuela. Kidnappings also occur frequently in other
countries, including the former Soviet Union republics, Iraq, India, the Philippines and the
U.S.[8] One insurer in this market estimates that 67 percent of victims are released with a
ransom paid, 15 percent are released without a ransom payment, 7 percent are rescued, and
10 percent are murdered.

As Chapter 6 explained, **Terrorism** is an act of violence or threat of violence against individuals or property committed by one or more individuals acting on behalf of an organization for the purpose of influencing government policy or actions to advance a political, religious or ideological cause. While this definition necessarily extends to property, our concern in this chapter is with the portion dealing with individuals in general and employees specifically. Of course, kidnapping is a tool of terrorist, but the objective of terrorism usually is to alter government policy, not necessarily to secure a ransom. Conversely, terrorists may have no interest whatsoever in kidnapping, instead focusing on injuring or killing individuals.

**Extortion** is the use of force or intimidation to obtain money or other property from someone. Extortion demands typically relate to threats that individuals or property will be harmed if the money demanded is not paid. Our concern here, of course, is with the reference to individuals and not property, although similar risk management approaches apply to both.

Each of these three exposures involves the threat of harm. A related exposure, **detention**, is the temporary custody of an individual for lawful purposes. The detention usually is by law enforcement officials because of a belief that the individual committed a crime. Our concern does not extend to legitimate detention of an employee who did commit a crime. Rather, we are concerned about detention when the employee did not commit the crime alleged.

We are in the midst of a period of unprecedented global economic integration. The breakdown of the rigid bipolarity of the cold war years, however, has rendered many parts of the world unstable. Perversely, the waning of authoritarian rule in many countries has triggered an unprecedented increase in crime, including kidnappings and extortions. For MNCs, enormous opportunities are tempered by appreciable risks.

## Risk Management

The first step in managing these risks is to become knowledgeable about their nature and magnitude in areas in which the company operates or expects its employees to conduct business. Of particular concern to MNCs at the time of this writing are:

- leftist guerrillas who kidnap foreign corporate employees in Colombia and in neighboring Ecuador and Venezuela;
- criminal gangs that target executives in Brazil, Guatemala, Mexico and elsewhere in Latin America;
- aggressive, organized-crime groups that run protection rackets in Russia, and vendors, distributors and joint venture partners who threaten and even employ violence to resolve business disputes in the absence of an effective judicial system;
- Islamic zealots who target foreigners and foreign business interests as part of their terrorist activities.

Fortunately for corporate decision-makers obliged to deal with these threats, they are by no means random. Indeed, the security firms that specialize in advising MNCs on these risks contend that most violence-prone groups operate in a reasonably predictable manner, which makes it possible to assess risks with a fair degree of accuracy. One such security firm analyzes terrorism and political stability-related developments in some 90 countries on a continuing basis and provides Internet-based analysis to its client companies.

In short, the risks of kidnapping, terrorism, extortion and political instability are facts of life for companies operating abroad. Well-managed corporations respond by:

*   carefully analyzing risks and weighing them against potential rewards of a particular project;
*   fully informing employees of the hazards they face;
*   supplying the wherewithal to enhance their safety – through training, technical means such as armored cars and, in some cases, even protective details;
*   planning the company's response in the event of an event.

## Crisis Management Plan

The first step in the crisis management process is the development of a plan to ensure an efficient response to a kidnapping, extortion or related event. The company's core crisis management team should consist of at least three individuals: (1) the ultimate decision maker – the CEO or his or her designee; (2) the coordinator, often the corporate security director, risk manager or chief of international operations; and (3) the corporate general counsel. The team also might include a finance officer (to arrange for the ransom), a human resources specialist (to oversee the care of a hostage's family) and a public relations specialist (to handle press inquiries).

Crisis management teams usually work in tandem with specialized security firms that are prepared to execute the recovery of a kidnap victim or other required response. In a hostage recovery, specialists should be ready to recommend and implement a negotiating strategy, interface with authorities, counsel and comfort the victim's family, protect the ransom sum, and undertake, or at least supervise, its delivery.

Even the best plans are useless if managers are unaware of their existence or of their particular roles and responsibilities in the event of a crisis. Key executives must be made familiar with the process of recovering kidnap victims and managing the related threats, from the development of an effective corporate notification process, to negotiating strategies, to difficulties in dealing with local police services. Ideally, this training should be undertaken by the same specialists who would execute the crisis management plan.

## Loss Prevention

While responsible MNCs will prepare for the worst possible scenario, the primary objective of any strategy for dealing with terrorism, kidnapping and political instability risks is *avoidance*. Employees should be fully informed of the hazards they face in particular assignments and be provided with training and technology that will help them protect themselves from those hazards. Students of terrorism are struck time and again by terrorists' propensity to sniff out and attack easier targets. Defensive programs cannot guarantee immunity from terrorism, but their absence over a prolonged period of time in a high-risk area almost always assures trouble.

Training should involve employees and, when appropriate, family members. It may require no more than a few hours, surely no more than several days, to make an executive a harder kidnap target; not only more elusive, but also sensitive to the danger signals that often precede kidnappings and other assaults. As a last line of defense, it also is possible to train those who may be taken hostage to conduct themselves while under hostile control in ways that maximize their chances for survival.

INSIGHT 16.2: KIDNAPPING AND TERRORISM SURVIVAL GUIDE

Individuals who have been kidnapped or otherwise held hostage should do their best to take the following advice into consideration during their captivity:

- Avoid resistance and sudden or threatening movements. Do not struggle or try to escape unless you are certain of being successful.
- Make a concerted effort to relax. Prepare yourself mentally, physically, and emotionally for the possibility of a long ordeal.
- Try to remain inconspicuous and avoid direct eye contact and the appearance of observing your captors' actions.
- Avoid alcoholic beverages. Consume little food and drink.
- Consciously put yourself in a mode of passive cooperation. Talk normally. Do not complain, avoid belligerency and comply with all orders and instructions.
- If questioned, keep your answers short. Don't volunteer information or make unnecessary overtures.
- Don't try to be a hero, endangering yourself and others.
- Maintain your sense of personal dignity and gradually increase your requests for personal comforts. Make these requests in a reasonable, low-key manner.
- If you are involved in a lengthier, drawn-out situation, try to establish a rapport with your captors, avoiding political discussions or other confrontational subjects.
- Establish a daily program of mental and physical activity. Don't be afraid to ask for anything you need or want – medicines, books, pencils, papers.
- Eat what they give you, even if it does not look or taste appetizing. A loss of appetite and weight is normal.
- Think positively. Avoid a sense of despair. Rely on your inner resources. Remember that you are a valuable commodity to your captors. It is important to them to keep you alive and well.

*Source*: U.S. Department of State [travel.state.gov/travel/tips/safety/safety_1747.html].

Of course, the first and best protection is to avoid travel to or living in unsafe areas where there has been a persistent record of terrorist attacks, kidnapping or extortion. The vast majority of countries have good records of maintaining public order and protecting residents and visitors within their borders from such events. If travel to or residence in areas known to be unsafe is required, the training referenced above becomes essential.[9]

## Loss Control

Normally, the most dangerous phases of a hijacking or hostage situations are the beginning and, if there is a rescue attempt, the end. At the outset, the terrorists or other criminals typically are tense, high-strung and may behave irrationally. It is extremely important for the victim to remain calm and alert and manage his or her own behavior to minimize further aggravating the situation. Insight 16.2 offers the recommendations of the U.S. Department of State on how best to accomplish this goal.

Besides the desired behavior of the victim, the successful resolution of a crisis requires the cooperative efforts of the field manager faced with the emergency, the company's crisis management team and its security consultant. All need to act swiftly and with a clear understanding of the procedures that need to be followed.

The first hours following a kidnapping are critical to successful resolution. Actions taken, such as the notification of a particular police agency, cannot be undone. Decisions should be made, not by a field manager, but by core members of the crisis management team in consultation with a specialty security firm.

Such firms are prepared to handle virtually all the aspects of a recovery process, including negotiating directly with the kidnappers, dealing with the police, and converting, protecting and even delivering ransom funds. Those who kidnap corporate employees do so mainly for financial reasons. The primary objective of most corporations is to obtain the safe release of the hostage in the least possible time. Thus, most firms are willing to pay a ransom to this end.

At the same time, most MNCs recognize a responsibility to pay as little as possible to the kidnappers, be they terrorist or common criminals, and certainly no more than is customarily paid for a hostage in the country in question. Police services are adamant that corporations pay as little as possible. They rightfully recoil at the very thought of rewarding evildoers and, in the case of guerrillas, are especially sensitive about companies, in effect, financing revolution.

Companies are more likely to fall victim to bodily injury or property damage extortions (wherein recompense is demanded for not harming a person or property, such as a computer database) than to kidnappings or terrorism. One advantage in extortion cases is that the person or property threatened is under corporate control, and steps normally may be taken to protect the person or property.

## Insurance

Corporations (and individuals) purchase kidnap/ransom and extortion insurance policies. Lloyds of London, AIG, Liberty Mutual and Chubb are well-known insurers offering these policies. *The Economist* (2006) reports that about 60 percent of the largest firms in the U.S. have kidnap/ransom insurance policies, and this insurance globally generates an annual premium of around US$250 million.

This insurance is considered controversial in many markets as there is concern that its existence might encourage the very nefarious events against which it insures. As a practical matter, policies routinely prohibit insureds from disclosing the existence of the insurance. As discussed more fully below, one of the most important aspects of this insurance is the promise to provide advice and services if an event occurs.

### *Direct payments*

The primary feature of such policies is that they provide reimbursement for monies (or the monetary value of other consideration) surrendered, as either a ransom payment or an extortion payment, as a result of a threat made against an insured. While policies can be written in the name of an individual or a family, most policies are purchased by commercial enterprises looking to cover all employees, not just senior management. The coverage extends to all relatives and guests of covered persons, even if no demand is made against the employer/insured.

What follows is an overview of the key coverage elements of today's kidnap/ransom and extortion policies and what coverage is likely to cost. The extortion coverage section addresses threats of harm to individuals and threats of damage to property. Generally, there are no restrictions regarding the perils in the extortion property damage provisions. Thus, if a threat is made against an insured person or entity to destroy or contaminate insured property or products, extortion property damage coverage is triggered.

Detention claims can arise from some peculiar situations in which travelers can find themselves entangled. One such incident involved an American executive on a business trip to Guatemala. Before embarking on his trip home, the executive discovered that the weight of his baggage exceeded the limit allotted to each passenger. He asked a female passenger carrying one small bag if she would be good enough to check one of his luggage pieces. She agreed. Unbeknownst to the executive, she was a drug courier. Both were arrested by drug officials at the departure gate. The executive, guilty of no wrongdoing, spent a few unpleasant nights in a Guatemalan jail. Fortunately, his company, when informed of the incident, immediately contacted the response team on retainer to his company's insurance carrier. That team, with local assistance, was able to sort out the situation and secure the man's release.

While fear of kidnap and extortion has traditionally been the primary reason for the coverage's purchase, detentions at the hands of terrorists or over-zealous government officials are a growing concern of MNCs. Detention coverage provides for reimbursement of not only the salary of the victims, but also any reasonable expenses incurred in negotiating the release of the victims.

### Consequential loss payments

The financial loss an insured may suffer due to kidnappings, extortions and detentions can go far beyond out-of-pocket ransom payments and negotiation expenses. Commercial enterprises can incur staggering costs not only in terms of damage control expenses but also lost earnings due to operation shutdowns necessitated by kidnappings or extortions. Significant costs also can be incurred if an insured chooses to redirect the efforts of internal staff toward resolving the situation. For the victims, the financial upheaval can be just as devastating, if their personal affairs go unattended for months (or even years) as a result of involuntary confinement. The second element of kidnap/ransom and extortion insurance policy addresses the myriad of indirect expenses that may follow in the wake of a covered incident.

Such policies cover lost revenues associated with the disruption of business operations because of a kidnap, extortion or detention. They also provide reimbursement for legal expenses, judgments and settlements as well as for medical/psychiatric expenses arising out of incidents covered by the policies. Consider the executive who is kidnapped and who, upon his release, brings suit against his employer, alleging that the company exercised something less than "due diligence and dispatch" in securing her release. There also are instances in which lengthy convalescences are required to help kidnap or detention victims recover from the physical and emotional trauma of their ordeals.

What have been highlighted thus far are coverages that address the most severe loss exposures. However, kidnap/ransom and extortion policies provide coverage for a variety of additional expenses as well. These include:

• rewards paid to informants for information that leads to the arrest and conviction of parties responsible for a loss covered by the policy;

- travel and accommodation expenses incurred by the insured in investigating or paying a covered loss;
- salaries of kidnap or detention victims;
- salaries for persons newly hired to conduct the duties of kidnap or detention victims during the period of their confinement;
- personal financial losses suffered by an individual due to that person's inability to attend to personal financial affairs during the period of their confinement;
- reasonable costs incurred by the insured for wages of its salaried employees specifically assigned to assist in the negotiation of any loss covered by the policy;
- fees of security guards hired to protect threatened persons or property;

These may appear insignificant but, when aggregated, may lead to serious financial setbacks. Kidnap/ransom and extortion policies also can include accidental death and dismemberment coverage for losses arising out of covered incidents – for example, death or dismemberment at the hands of captors.

## Crisis assistance

For many insurance buyers, the most critical element of kidnap/ransom and extortion insurance is the crisis response service available in the event of a covered incident; that is, the hostage negotiation professionals to whom policyholders are, quite literally, entrusting their lives. The major kidnap/ransom insurers have on retainer a firm that specializes in hostage/extortion negotiation and offers consulting services across a broad range of topics relating to investigation, executive protection and internal security. Access to these highly specialized and well-trained teams is available on a 24-hour basis anywhere in the world should the need arise. The knowledge that expert negotiators are close at hand to deal with possibly life-threatening situations provides many insurance buyers with an added measure of security. In some cases, these services are the primary reason they purchase the coverage.

## Pricing

As is true in all insurance lines, kidnap/ransom and extortion pricing is a function of exposure and limits. In this world of underwriting, exposure is in part measured by individual risk characteristics, such as type of operation, company profile, size (in terms of turnover and headcount), global positioning, global travel patterns of covered persons and, of course, loss history. Another important element in underwriters' perception of exposure is the risk inherent in the countries in which the firm operates and to which staff is sent. A single-location bank in a rural setting in the U.K. or the U.S. will pay significantly less for kidnap/ransom coverage than a comparably sized oil company building a pipeline in rural Russia. In considering these two enterprises at opposite ends of the risk spectrum, the sheer number of possible combinations of risk characteristics and the fluidity of global risk exposures, it is easy to understand why kidnap/ransom and extortion coverage does not readily lend itself to "box rating," with predetermined rates applied to static exposure bases. While most underwriters operate within certain pricing parameters, individual judgment and individual underwriting aptitudes and inclinations play a key role in the assessment of risk, the formulation of terms and pricing.

## CONCLUSION

Personnel risk management lies at the heart of every organization, irrespective of whether it is labeled as such. Employers have strong economic and public relations incentives both to hire and retain first-rate employees and to ensure their safety. This chapter has explored how employers seek to accomplish both results.

As we look to the future, the aging populations of most developed market-economy countries will put incredible strains on all government-provided economic security systems. Greater reliance inevitably will fall on individuals and families to provide for themselves. At the same time, we can reasonably anticipate that governments and employees will apply steadily increasing pressure on employers to step into the void created by governmental withdrawal.

This trend suggests that employee benefits will become relatively more important in the future than they have been in the past. Simultaneously, the globalization of national economies causes businesses to do all within their power to hold the line on all costs, including employee benefit costs. This trend suggests that firms will be less inclined to fill the governmental void. The net result of these two trends is, of course, not completely clear. If history is any indicator, we would be unsurprised to witness more governmental tax and other incentives as well as mandates for employers to provide ever more generous benefit packages to their employees.

The situation for developing countries might be somewhat different. Many have relatively young populations. Many also are experiencing rapid economic growth, sparked by higher education levels and lower costs of production. In many countries, employer-provided benefit packages are modest, at best. In developing countries with a tradition of relatively little governmental involvement in individual economic security – as found in many Asian markets – we anticipate increasing expectations that businesses should provide ever more generous benefit packages to complement economic development.

By contrast, in developing countries with a tradition of greater governmental involvement, such as found in many African, Latin American and some Asian markets, employer/public blends of economic security can be expected to emerge. We could anticipate, however, a relatively greater emphasis on employers than on the government, given the worldwide trend toward embracing the market-economy model, even in formerly socialist countries.

At the same time, MNCs can be expected to continue to grow in importance worldwide. With this growth and with the internationalization of markets, the total compensation approach will gain popularity. They neither will want to nor can they offer greatly different benefit packages among their key employees internationally. Of course, local practices will continue to dominate benefit packages for rank and file employees of MNCs.

During the 21st century, we envision an increasing role in virtually all countries for employer-provided economic security. Cost-effective programs that are sufficiently flexible to address both varying employee needs and changing employer objectives will dominate employee benefit plan design in an increasingly global marketplace.

Simultaneously, MNCs face a myriad of challenges as they seek means of effectively and efficiently minimizing harm to all employees, but especially to those most likely to be targets of terrorism and other criminal activities. We can expect this element of personnel risk management to remain somewhat "below the radar screen" of rank-and-file employees and, indeed, most businesses, although placing employees in harm's way – as is the situation in Iraq, for example – also might become more commonplace in the future.

# DISCUSSION QUESTIONS

1. How will changing employment patterns, changing demographics and movement to a global marketplace affect employee benefit plan design in your country in the future? Has the government in your country introduced new laws related to this issue? If not, is it considering such a measure in the near future?
2. What are the primary factors that account for the cross-country differences in voluntary employer-sponsored benefit programs?
3. What unique or special issues/problems do MNCs face in the provision of employee benefits? How are MNCs addressing these issues today?
4. Why is it envisioned that employer-provided economic security will assume an increasing role in virtually all countries?
5. Should we expect greater uniformity worldwide in the types of employee benefit programs offered and the way in which they are provided? Why or why not?
6. Identify a large MNC in your home country and examine (a) the scope of employee benefits and (b) the approach (DB, DC or hybrid) it uses to offer the benefits.
7. Briefly describe the structure of (a) healthcare programs and (b) employee retirement programs in your country.
8. Why do kidnap/ransom and extortion insurance policies prohibit the insured from disclosing the existence of the insurance?
9. How do MNCs' personnel risks differ from those of purely national corporations?

# NOTES

1. This section is based in part on Palmer (1998) and Doerpinghaus (1998).
2. Black and Skipper (2000), pp. 17–22, summarizes this and related theories.
3. Claims utilization review techniques include prior authorization for non-emergency hospital admissions, concurrent review of the plan of medical treatment during hospitalization, discharge planning (e.g., planning for continued non-hospitalization treatment), and post-claim review.
4. Refer to the discussion of the global insurance program in Chapter 14.
5. This material is based on Luck (1992), pp. 15 and 20.
6. This section draws partly from Rotello (1993).
7. This section draws heavily from *Managing Terrorism Risks* (2005) and *Kidnap/Ransom and Extortion Insurance* (2005).
8. Based on 1993–2001 data quoted in Merkling and Davis (2001).
9. The MNC's headquarters country, via its Department of State (Internal Affairs) usually offers suggestions for loss prevention in such situations and encourages its citizens to register with the Department if travel or residence is required.

# REFERENCES

Black Jr., K. and Skipper Jr. H.D. (2000). *Life and Health Insurance*, 13th edn. New York: Prentice-Hall, Inc.

Browne, M.I. (1992). "Evidence of Adverse Selection in the Individual Health Insurance Market." *The Journal of Risk and Insurance*, 59: 13–33.

*The Economist* (2006). "Kidnap Insurance: A King's Ransom." 380 (August 24): 64.

Doerpinghaus, H. (1998). "Health Care Financing," Chapter 22 in H.D. Skipper Jr., ed., *International Risk and Insurance: An Environmental-Managerial Approach*. Boston, MA: Irwin/McGraw-Hill.

Hutchens, Robert (1986). "Delayed Payment Contracts and a Firm's Propersity to Hire Older Workers," *Journal of Labor Economics*, 4(4): 439–457.

International Benefit Guildlines (2005), International Benefit Guidelines (1995). William M. Mercer Limited.

Jackson, R. and Howe, N. (2003). *The 2003 Aging Vulnerability Index*. Washington, DC: CSIS and Watson Wyatt at www.csis.org/gai/aging_index.pdf

John Hancock Financial Services (2005). *International Group Program (IGP) Country Profiles*. Boston, MA: John Hancock Financial Services.

*Kidnap/Ransom and Extortion Insurance* (2005) at libertymutual.com.

Luck, L. (1992). "Multinational Pooling." *Benefits Quarterly*, 8 (4): 15–20. *Managing Terrorism Risks* (2005) at chubb.com.

Merkling, S. and Davis, E. (2001). "Kidnap & Ransom Insurance: A Rapidly Growing Benefit." *Compensation and Benefit Review*, 33 (November/December): 40–45.

Palmer, B.A. (1998). "Employee Benefits," Chapter 27, in H.D. Skipper Jr., ed., *International Risk and Insurance: An Environmental-Managerial Approach*. Boston, MA: Irwin/McGraw-Hill.

Rotello, P.A. (1993). "Developing an Integrated Retirement Plan Strategy, or Does the Shoe Still Fit?" *Benefits Quarterly*, 9 (4): 61–65.

Swiss Re (2006). *Multinational Pooling Creates Added Value*, at www.swisslife-network.com

Towers Perrin (2005–2006). *Managing Global Pay and Benefits*, at www.towersperrin.com

# Chapter 17

# Political Risk Management

## INTRODUCTION

All businesses face the risk that governments may take actions that reduce the firm's value. For the great majority of businesses worldwide, this risk stems from possible actions by the government where their businesses are located. The MNC in particular faces the daunting task of having to understand, anticipate and deal with risks from many, possibly dozens of governments, any one of which could harm the firm. Indeed, all firms that conduct business on foreign soil must manage attendant risks on that soil. Therein lies the importance of political risk management.

What is the perception by executives of larges businesses as to the gravity of the political risk exposures of their firms? To a survey by Aon Corporation (2001), 86 percent of Fortune 1000 companies responded that political risk posed a moderate to great threat to their firms. More than one-third of respondents experienced currency inconvertibility and repatriation restrictions, one-fourth suffered losses from trade restrictions (e.g., embargos) and 18 percent were the subject of expropriations.

Although much has been written about political risk insurance coverage available from both public and private insurers, relatively little has been written about the application of risk management techniques to political risks. Yet, the basic process used to understand and manage other risks should be applied to political risks as well.

This chapter explores the risks associated with governmental actions that diminish firm value.[1] Our focus is on MNCs primarily, although the concepts apply equally to purely national enterprises. We begin our examination by reviewing the various modes of foreign market entry. We then define political risk and explore its elements. Next we apply the risk management process to political risks. The chapter concludes with an overview of political risk insurance coverages in selected countries and of how political risk is underwritten and priced.

## MODES OF FOREIGN MARKET ENTRY

Firms enter foreign markets through a variety of techniques. Each of these entry modes carries with it certain risks and returns. Many risks are financial and managerial, while others are political. As discussed in earlier chapters, businesses conduct international trade in two broad ways, either cross-border or via establishment. Cross-border trade is synonymous with exports. Establishment is most commonly through joint ventures or subsidiaries/branches. Each of these three modes (exporting, joint venture and subsidiary/branch), along with their political risk implications, is discussed below.

## Exporting

Exporting through an export management company (a firm in the home country that purchases products domestically and exports them to other countries) represents one end of the export continuum. In this case, the producing firm incurs little political risk. However, it loses all managerial control of the product in the foreign market and, potentially, control over the brand name.

Typically, as firms gain more experience in foreign markets, they move from passive exporting to actively entering export markets using the resources of the firm itself. It may form an export or international department to trade directly with foreign partners. Financial returns are potentially increased as is managerial control, but the firm's exposure to a variety of risks likewise increases.

## Joint Venture

The next step along the typical foreign market entry mode continuum occurs when the firm engages in foreign direct investment (FDI). FDI exists when a firm from one country acquires financial assets in another country with the intention of actively managing those assets. A common form of FDI is a joint venture. In the international market, typical joint ventures are formed between a home-country firm (the firm making the FDI) and a host-country firm (a firm located in the country where the investment is made) or government agency.

The use of joint ventures may allow foreign firms to enter markets that they otherwise might not be able to enter. For example, joint ventures with the Chinese government were, for many years, the only way for foreign firms to enter China. Joint venture with a local firm still is the only way for international insurers to enter the Indian market. A home-country firm may believe that risks are reduced by having a knowledgeable host-country partner, but it must be remembered that the home-country firm now has financial assets that are exposed in the foreign country.

## Wholly Owned Subsidiary or Branch

A firm has the greatest exposure when it enters a foreign market using a wholly owned subsidiary or branch. Managerial control and potential financial returns are greatest under these circumstances. Usually, only the most experienced MNCs enter foreign markets using this mode of entry. Creating a subsidiary or branch requires not only FDI (i.e., financial resources) but also substantial managerial talent and experience – additional risk that the foreign firm assumes.

As firms expand internationally and move along the continuum of increasing participation and commitment to foreign markets, they become more visible to host-country consumers and governments. Where modest import levels of a commodity product may go virtually unnoticed, foreign acquisition of a prominent domestic company may even evoke public outrage and government action. Even in countries that welcome FDI, acquisition of highly visible assets can bring about unintended consequences. For example U.S. public ire was drawn and political action threatened when Japanese firms began to acquire "trophy" U.S. real estate such as Rockefeller Center in New York City.

# NATURE OF POLITICAL RISK

## Defining Political Risk

Broadly defined, **political risk** is any governmental action that diminishes the value of a firm operating within the political boundaries or influence of that government. Many authors extend the definition to include any action by governments that differentiate between foreign and domestic firms or a threat that may affect the feasibility of foreign operations.

Political risk arises from governmental action and is thus distinct from terrorism risk (even though some political state may be connected with the act), kidnap or ransom. It also is different from sovereign risk that government may default its debt repayment obligations. Credit risks arising from global operations also are distinct from political risk, except credit risk that arises from currency inconvertibility.

Most often we think of political risk in terms of adverse actions taken by a host-country government. In fact, home-country government also can affect the value of firms of its own country that operate in foreign markets. In a dispute with then Panamanian leader, Manual Noriega, the U.S. government forbade U.S. firms from paying taxes to Panama. The Panamanian government considered these taxes to be payment for services and utilities, such as water and electricity. The subsequent shutoff of utilities brought local production by U.S.-owned firms in Panama to a halt.

Of course, governments can take a broad spectrum of actions, ranging from those of little more than nuisance value to expropriation of a firm's assets. Foreign firms may encounter difficulty in importing products or components into the host country, whereas domestic firms may experience little trouble clearing customs. For many years, some Latin American countries were known to have a "special duty" for "rich" U.S. firms. Also in Latin America, changes of government often led to the confiscation or expropriation of foreign firms' assets, as was the case in Chile in 1975 and, more recently in Venezuela in 2006 and 2007.

## The Changing Political Risk Landscape

The political risk map has changed over time. Minor (2003) contends that the map prior to 1985 was covered mainly by confiscation and nationalization of foreign assets by then newly independent countries. For instance, the exile of the Shah of Iran in 1979 led to the nationalization of foreign assets and contract defaults by the Iranian government. The 1973 oil embargo and nationalization of foreign-held oil concessions by Arab oil-exporting countries following the Yom Kippur War is another example. The domestic insurance industry often was a nationalization target in many developing countries.

Since the end of the Cold War in the 1980s, global firms have faced different types of political risks. Some governments have used economic reasons to justify expropriation of foreign firms' assets. Insight 17.1 presents such a case. In several instances, it was not the new head of state but local government officials who caused loss to foreign firms. Ethnic and religious tensions have caused political instability on numerous occasions as well.

---

## INSIGHT 17.1: BELCO PETROLEUM CORPORATION

The change in the nature of the (political) risk can be seen in an expropriation in the mid-1980s of Belco Petroleum Corporation's Peruvian operations. Belco maintained offshore production until 1985, when its license to operate offshore rigs was revoked after a dispute over taxes with the Garcia government. Essentially, the Peruvian government imposed retroactive punitive taxes on the company, which it refused to pay.

This was one of the largest political insurance claims the market had seen at the time (US$230 million). It illustrates the changing pretenses used by host governments for expropriating foreign-owned assets. While the newly elected Garcia government was certainly considered to be left-leaning, unlike the actions taken by leftist regimes during the 1970s, this was not a declared nationalization. Rather it was dressed up to look like an economic (or commercial) issue.

The Garcia government claimed that the decision to impose retroactive taxes and (eventually) revoke Belco's operating license was a legitimate response to years of collusion between the company and self-interested Peruvian presidents. The strong public protest that followed the Garcia government's attempt to nationalize the banking sector in 1987, however, suggests even more strongly that in Peru (as elsewhere in the developing world) the nationalizations of the 1970s were going out of vogue.

*Source*: Minor (2003). Reprinted with permission from Risk Management Magazine. © 2003 Risk and Insurance Management Society, Inc. All rights reserved.

---

## Elements of Political Risk

Nationalization, confiscation and expropriation represent the most severe governmental actions against foreign firms. Foreign governments also may repudiate contracts with firms or impose restrictions on currency convertibility. Each is defined and covered briefly below:

- **Nationalization** is government takeover of a firm's assets with compensation. Frequently when firms are nationalized, the compensation provided by the government does not adequately reflect the on-going value of the firm.

- Confiscation and expropriation are the taking of the firm's assets without compensation. Specifically, **confiscation** is the taking of property without compensation by government, which is usually the result of commission of a crime associated with the property. For example, using a rented vehicle to distribute illegal drugs, even though unknown to the vehicle owner, may result in confiscation of the vehicle. **Expropriation** is governmental taking of property without compensation as in eminent domain.

- Firms that build infrastructure projects and so-called turnkey facilities on foreign soil and firms with government agencies as joint-venture partners occasionally find themselves at odds with host-country governments. Generally, these disputes are not about governmental taking of assets but more likely involve a dispute about payment for performance. The government may **repudiate the contract** – refuse to honor the contract – because of real or imagined non-performance, or performance of the contract may be impossible (**contract frustration**) because of conditions beyond the firm's control. In many instances, payments have been made up to the point of the dispute. Governments sometimes renege on contracts for financial reasons.

- As global trade grows, more of the world's currencies are becoming convertible. Nevertheless, some governments still believe that convertibility restrictions generally and, more importantly, the rate at which currency is converted are important economic tools. **Currency inconvertibility** occurs when a country refuses to allow foreign firms to convert local currency to the home-country currency (e.g., for repatriating profits) or when they force foreign firms to convert currency at less than market rates.

Political risk arises from other sources as well. Political instability, war and an unfair regulatory environment are some of the examples:

- *Political instability*: A decentralized government system can be a source of political risk. As local governments gain in political power relative to the central government, they may make decisions at odds with central government policy. As an example, Wilkin and Minor (2001) noted that foreign firms could face the risk in China that provincial governments would fail to enforce the agreements that the firms had negotiated with the central government.

- *War*: War clearly represents a potential threat to the assets of foreign firms. Over the years, numerous cases have been brought before courts – local and international – in an attempt to define war. The narrowest definition of war refers to hostile contention by means of armed forces carried out between nations. Many commentators broaden the definition to include civil war and armed insurrection.

  Most insurers, however, exclude or intend to exclude common domestic conflicts, riot and civil commotion. Herein lies a potentially contentious issue. When does "civil commotion" become "civil war?" "Armed insurrection" also may be subject to dispute. In many countries, unions are political parties or at least are active politically.[2] The term "insurrection," in addition to referring to an uprising, also may refer to any resistance to the lawful authority of the state.

- *Unfair regulatory environment*: Finally, firms operating in other countries can be discriminated against in a variety of ways. These include various national treatment inconsistencies (see Chapter 3) such as discriminatory capital requirements, differing tax structures and limitations on access to necessary materials, components or distribution systems. One point of contention in global trade has been the right of foreign firms to bid on host-government contracts (i.e., government procurement).

Political risks generally exhibit one or a combination of the above traits. Firms consider a variety of approaches to managing political risk, irrespective of whether they purchase insurance against such risks.

## RISK ANALYSIS

To prevent, control and manage losses resulting from adverse political events, the MNC needs first to identify and map the sources of political risk. It then strives to measure its exposure.

**Table 17.1**   Public Information Sources of Country Study

| Source | URL |
|---|---|
| *Country study* | |
| Business Environment Risk Intelligence | www.beri.com |
| Political Risk Services – Coplin-O'Leary Rating System | www.prsonline.com |
| Control Risks Information Services | www.crg.com |
| Economist – Economist Intelligence Unit | www.economist.com/countries |
| EmbassyWorld | www.embassyworld.com |
| Euromoney | www.euromoney.com |
| European Union – Eurostat | www.eurostat.com |
| International Country Risk Guide | www.icrgonline.com |
| U.S. Library of Congress – Country Studies | lcweb2.loc.gov/frd/cs/cshome.html |
| World Trade Organization – Member and Observer Information | www.wto.org/english/thewto_e/whatis_e/tif_e/org6_e.htm |
| *Sovereign risk* | |
| Fitch – IBCA | www.fitchibca.com |
| Institutional Investor | www.institutionalinvestor.com |
| Moody's Investor Services | www.moodys.com |
| Standard and Poor's – Rating Group | www.standardandpoors.com |
| Transparency International | www.transparency.org |

## Identification

Risk identification requires both a firm and country-specific examination. Thus, a firm considering expansion into another country should first consider whether it has the expertise and financial capacity to do so. If it considers exporting only, it needs to know whether its products are in compliance with the host-country's quality standards. If it considers creating a subsidiary in another country, the task is more demanding. It must conduct a thorough study, not only of the country's sociocultural environment, but also of its legal, political and taxation situation, including identifying any conflicts between the home country and the host country.

A study of the host country should include its history, government, legal structure, demography (including ethnic and religious composition), and economic and financial market infrastructure. For the study of government, the MNC should examine how the government came to power (including how power is transferred), political influence leaders, key governmental ministries and agencies, main participants in the political process (including whether any large groups are disenfranchised), and the organization of the political structure.

The firm can use data and information available from intergovernmental and governmental agencies as well as several reliable private entities. For example, the World Trade Organization provides trade policy reviews for its member states and observers. The U.S. Central Intelligence Agency annually publishes the *World Fact Book* that contains key governmental, demographic and economic statistics by country. These and other sources are listed in Table 17.1. The firm should take careful note that political analysts sometime disagree in drawing conclusions about countries.

Also, embassies and consulates regularly file reports of host governments with their ministries of foreign affairs. Those reports are shared with other governmental ministries and agencies in the home country. The government may maintain a country desk within a ministry or agency wherein country-specific information is available to local firms and citizens.

While analysis is readily available at the national level, public information concerning political subdivisions such as provincial, state and municipal governments is less likely to be available. These political subdivisions may become particularly important where potential environmental concerns exist. These smaller entities also may offer economic inducements or tax incentives that, if withdrawn, could have significant financial effects. Areas such as special economic zones in China, the *Maquiladora* zone in Mexico, the Labuan area in Malaysia, free trade zones in Dubai, UAE, and many free trade zones worldwide offer attractive economic incentives.

Finally, identifying experienced personnel within the firm is important. A relatively large multinational enterprise may have an international risk manager at the corporate office, field managers on assignment in foreign affiliates and subsidiaries, and information specialists at the corporate office who monitor political activities. These specialists can help the firm assess the impact of political risk on the corporate level, as an event that may have little consequence for one subsidiary may mean substantial risk for another.

## Measurement

Political risk measurement aims to estimate the likelihood of a foreign government taking an action adverse to the firm's interests and its effects on the firm. Predicting political outcomes remains an inexact science. However, it does not mean that we rely only on intuition and experience. Research and scientific tools have been developed that can assist in the measurement process. Market research, political polling and attitude surveys are increasingly used to examine preferences of local consumers toward products, brand names and corporate images of foreign firms. These tools also are used to assess the mood of the electorate on a variety of issues.

Many developing countries have already undergone rapid political and economic changes (e.g., Commonwealth of Independent States member states in Europe and the emerging democracies in Africa, Asia and the Americas), rendering country analysis more reliable. In numerous other countries, however, information is less readily available.

One of the most difficult tasks in political risk assessment is predicting the timing of an adverse event. It may be relatively easy to predict that a particular disenfranchised group in a certain country will attempt to seize power in the future, but the precise time frame and the means of action may not be known – even by the group itself. Even though timing may be vague, the fact that issues of concern to a particular group and political movement in a particular direction can be understood with reasonable clarity is still valuable information to the MNC.

Rating agencies are common sources of information about countries' political risk profiles. Several rating agencies are included in Table 17.1. We summarize below the rating approaches of two agencies:

• *Political Risk Services (PRS)*: Also known as the Coplin-O'Leary System, the PRS system forecasts country risk in two stages. First, it identifies the three most likely future regime scenarios over two time periods: 18 months and five years. It then assigns a probability to each scenario over each time period. There are 12 risk components for the 18-month model – turmoil, restrictions on equity, restrictions on local operations, taxation discrimination, repatriation restriction, exchange control, tariff barrier, other important barriers, payment delay, expansionary economic policy, labor cost and foreign debt. For the five-year model, this Washington, DC firm uses turmoil, investment restriction, restriction on foreign trade, domestic economic problem and international economic problem as risk factors.

- *Business Environment Risk Intelligence (BERI)*: A U.S. firm, BERI provides risk ratings for more than 140 countries. Its rating system permits comparisons between countries for the past and the present as well as for one and five-year forecast periods. Two survey-based indices – operations risk index and political risk index – and computer-simulated remittance and repatriation factors are the key components for this analysis. It uses, among others, political factors (e.g., coercive measures to maintain regime), social conditions (e.g., population, income distribution), economic data (e.g., inflation, balance of payments and economic growth), repatriation and remittance of capital, foreign loan structure and terms and technocratic competence for the measurement.

Despite the differences in their research assumptions and analytical approaches, the major rating agencies share some commonalities. First, they examine key demographic, social, economic and political factors for their analyses. Second, they tend to use both quantitative and qualitative methodologies to draw risk ratings. Finally, they tend to focus on debt repayment capability of the issuer, whether it is the government or a non-sovereign entity.

# RISK CONTROL

Two general strategies exist for political risk management. An **integrative strategy** relies on tactics designed to make the firm part of the social and economic fabric of the host country, thus making it difficult to single out the foreign firm for differential treatment. A **defensive strategy** relies on tactics designed to reduce dependence on local economic elements within the host country, such as tax abatements, local suppliers, etc., thus minimizing exit costs should the firm be forced to leave. The following is a summary of integrative and defensive approaches in political risk management based on work of Punnett and Ricks (1992).

## Integrative Strategy

The tactics for implementation of an integrative risk control strategy to political risk can be considered as falling into two categories: managerial and financial.

### *Managerial Tactics*

In general, managerial tactics are designed to increase communication and strengthen the relationship between the firm and the host-country government. Tactics might include the following:

- Develop channels of communication with the host-country government so that both parties are aware of the other's concerns before they become public issues.
- Develop and implement good pre-departure training so that home-country nationals assigned to the host country are familiar with host-country culture, customs and managerial styles.
- Maximize localization in a positive way wherever possible including hiring and promoting host-country nationals to positions of authority.

- Structure contracts and agreements in ways that can be renegotiated if they are perceived by the host-country government to be unfair or burdensome.
- Provide assistance, expertise and capital for projects of local public importance (e.g., education and other types of infrastructure).

### Financial tactics

Integrative financial tactics likewise involve actions that can strengthen the bond to the host country. Host-country governments are likely to be less suspicious of foreign firms if the firms have an attitude of openness and fair dealing. Working with local firms helps to convey this attitude. Some integrative financial tactics include the following:

- Establish joint ventures with host-country firms. This may increase influence over the host-country government and may help local citizens feel more a part of the firm.
- Be sensitive to pricing issues. The host government needs to be assured that inter-affiliate pricing is being done fairly and at arm's length.
- Establish a policy of fair, accurate and transparent financial reporting. The firm should demonstrate to the host government that it has nothing to hide.

## Defensive Strategy

A defensive strategy toward political risk control relies on tactics designed to reduce dependence on local economic elements within the host country, thus minimizing exit costs should the firm be forced to leave.

### Managerial tactics

Defensive managerial strategies involve tactics that convey to the host-country government that the foreign firm could easily shift its operations to another country or that interference with operations would be more costly than allowing the firm to continue operations without concession to the host government. In general, defensive tactics are designed to separate the firm from close interaction with the host government or firms within the host country. Some defensive managerial tactics include the following:

- Select joint-venture partners from outside the host country. When a local operation involves multiple partners from differing countries, the host government may be reluctant to offend multiple governments.
- Minimize the use of host-country nationals in important positions. This assures that home-country nationals remain in control of both operations and sensitive information.
- Source key components from outside the host country. Should the firm be taken over, this minimizes the ability of new managers to continue production.
- To the greatest extent possible, maintain control over transportation and distribution channels so that they cannot be transferred with the sale or takeover of the firm. This would cause new managers to have to replace these valuable assets, costing time as well as money.
- Use and enforce intellectual property rights such as copyrights, patents and trademarks. Global organizations such as the World Intellectual Property Organization can assist in influencing host-country governments to respect these rights.

## *Financial tactics*

Financial tactics that are defensive in nature, unlike defensive managerial tactics, tend to rely more on host-country governments and institutions. The defensive nature of this activity results from the fact that interference with the foreign firm would result in financially punishing the host-country government or its financial market. The following are possible defensive financial tactics:

- Source both equity and debt financing to the greatest extent possible from within the host country. By doing this, the government may be reluctant to take action which would negatively affect its own citizens, banks or other institutions.
- Obtain host government guarantees wherever possible. If the government fails to honor its guarantees, other FDI may be discouraged.
- Minimize local retained earnings. This minimizes liquid assets in the host country, making a takeover less attractive.

What strategy and combination of tactics should a firm employ? The answer depends on the particular host government under consideration, the firm's ability to predict major political risk developments in the host country, and the firm's ability to carry out a particular strategy. Most MNCs use a mixture of integrative and defensive approaches.


# FINANCING THE POLITICAL RISK EXPOSURE ——————

## Retention

The choice of risk financing techniques also depends on the firm's characteristics. Truly global firms have a portfolio of markets in which they operate, allowing them to diversify political risk and rely more on retention. Such firms have the capacity through geographic diversification to avoid endue concentration of exposure in any one market. By contrast, less-diversified firms are more subject to political events in individual countries and are more likely to turn to insurance for risk financing.


## Insurance

As international trade and investment grew in importance during the past three decades, more governments concluded that they should provide some form of protection for their countries' MNCs to further encourage trade and investment, especially with developing countries. Stated in economic terms, they believed that providing such coverage offered positive externalities for the economy. Several countries have some form of government agency to provide political risk insurance. Several intergovernmental agencies and private firms also provide selected forms of risk financing. We discuss selected financing means below.


### *Insurance via intergovernmental agencies*

Several intergovernmental agencies provide political risk insurance. We discuss only a few, but their fundamental orientations differ little.

*The Multilateral Investment Guarantee Agency*

Discussions concerning a multilateral political risk market were held as early as the 1950s, prompted in part by expropriations following the Cuban revolution. Not until 1985, however, did the World Bank establish the Multilateral Investment Guarantee Agency (MIGA), the first truly global agency issuing political risk policies. In 1988, capital subscriptions enabled it to become a World Bank affiliate.

Although affiliated with the World Bank, MIGA is legally and financially independent of it. Membership is open to all members of the World Bank and Switzerland. When an investor applies for coverage from MIGA, it checks whether both the host-country and home-country governments for the investment project are MIGA members. Membership status of both governments is necessary, because MIGA seeks approval of the host country to provide the insurance. This arrangement also places some psychological pressure on the host-country government to honor any contracts into which it may have entered. MIGA then enters into a study process during which risks are analyzed and coverages are decided upon.

MIGA provides political insurance coverages (i.e., investment guarantees) to eligible investors for qualified investments in member developing countries. The four types of investment guarantees offered by MIGA are as follows:

- *Expropriation*: The policy covers loss of the insured investment resulting from expropriation, confiscation or nationalization by the host government. It also covers loss resulting from "creeping" expropriation – a series of acts that have an expropriatory effect over time – and from "partial" expropriation like confiscation of funds. Coverage is not extended to *bona fide* or nondiscriminatory measures that the host government exercises.

- *Contract repudiation*: MIGA covers loss of firm value (up to the insured amount) arising from the host government's breach or repudiation of a contract with the insured.

- *War and civil disturbance*: Policies cover property damages and disappearance of tangible assets caused by war, civil disturbance, revolution, insurrection, *coup d'état*, sabotage and terrorism in the host country. Consequential business interruption (income loss) coverage for up to 12 months also is available from MIGA.

- *Currency inconvertibility*: MIGA indemnifies the insured for losses resulting from fund transfer restrictions imposed by the host government. It also covers excessive delays in acquiring foreign exchange caused by the host government, adverse changes in exchange control laws and deterioration in the local foreign exchange market. MIGA does not cover mere devaluation of local currency.

A qualified investor may choose any combination of the four types of coverages. MIGA covers up to 90 percent of an equity investment and up to 95 percent of debt. The coverage typically is available for up to 15 years and, in selected cases, for up to 20 years for an investment amount commonly up to US$200 million. MIGA calculates premiums based on both country risk and project risk. An insured may cancel the coverage after three years. MIGA may not cancel the coverage.

In addition to functioning as a direct insurer, MIGA is authorized to act as a reinsurer to government agencies and private insurance entities. MIGA also provides coverage for service firms and service contracts as well as for medium and long-term loans made by financial institutions. Since its establishment, MIGA has issued nearly 850 investment guarantees in 92 developing economies (as of January 2007). Forty-five percent of the total guarantees (US$16 billion) are shared by economies in Europe, 25 percent by countries in Latin America and the Caribbean, and 17 percent by sub-Saharan African countries.

### World Bank Guarantee Program

The World Bank offers guarantees of partial recovery of private debts that a government fails to honor. The World Bank guarantees are available to all countries that have borrowing privileges from its two banking arms – the International Bank for Reconstruction and Development (IBRD) and the International Development Association (IDA). These guarantees can be summarized as follows:

- *Partial risk guarantee* covers the risk that a government or its agency fails to perform its obligations to a private project.
- *Partial credit guarantee* provides protection against all risks related to financing of debt for a public investment.
- *Policy-based guarantees* provide payment guarantee of the principal and interest to private market investors who purchase debt issuance (e.g., bonds) issued by IBRD member countries to fund certain qualified projects. The qualification criteria include a satisfactory social, structural and macroeconomic policy framework.

The World Bank Guarantee Program is different from the MIGA program in at least two aspects. First, the World Bank does not cover equity investments, whereas MIGA covers both debt and equity investments. Second, the World Bank covers specifically defined events for each project, whereas MIGA offers protection against a broader range of risks.

### Other intergovernmental agency programs

Quite a few regional public-sector political risk underwriters target investment in specific areas. The Inter-Arab Investment Guarantee Corporation provides two financial guarantee schemes – the Arab Investment Guarantee Scheme and the Export Credit Guarantee Scheme – to its member countries. The scope of risks covered by the corporation is similar to that of MIGA.

The Asia Development Bank offers two guarantee programs. Its "partial credit guarantees" cover a specified portion of commercial debts provided by co-financiers of Asia Development Bank-assisted projects or programs. The bank's political risk guarantees cover the lower of up to US$150 million or 50 percent of the project cost. In Africa, the African Development Bank, along with 53 African and 24 non-African member countries and *la Banque de Développement des Etats de l'Afrique Centrale* (Bank of Development of Central Africa) offer similar services to member countries. Table 17.2 lists these and other agencies.

### Insurance via government agencies

Political risk insurance, particularly for risks arising from export, may be available from the government itself, a quasi-governmental agency or a private insurance firm supported by the government. These political risk insurance providers may also offer investment fund guarantee services to qualified firms. Table 17.3 offers a fuller list of national agencies. There follows a discussion of four countries' agencies.

**Table 17.2**   Multilateral Export Credit Agencies Internationally

| Region | Bank Name | URL |
| --- | --- | --- |
| Africa | African Export-Import Bank (Afreximbank) | www.afreximbank.com |
| Arabian countries | Arab Investment Guarantee Corporation | www.iaigc.org |
| Andean countries | *Corporación Andina de Fomento* (CAF) | www.caf.com |
| Asian countries | Asian Development Bank (ADB) | www.adb.org |
| Central Africa | *La Banque de Développement des Etats de l'Afrique Centrale* | |
| Central/Eastern Europe | *European Bank for Reconstruction and Development* (EBRD) | www.ebrd.com |
| Latin America | Inter-American Development Bank (IADB) | www.iadb.org |
| Islamic countries | Islamic Corporation for the Insurance of Investment and Export Credit (ICIEC)[a] | www.iciec.com |
| Global | *Multilateral Investment Guarantee Agency* (MIGA) [b] | www.miga.org |
| Global | World Bank Guarantee Program | www.worldbank.org |

[a] Part of Islamic Development Bank.
[b] Part of the World Bank.

**Table 17.3**   National Export-Import Banks

| Country | Bank Name | URL |
| --- | --- | --- |
| Austria | *Oesterreichische Kontrollbank Aktiengesellschaft* (OeKB) | www.oekb.at |
| Australia | Export Finance and Insurance Corporation (EFIC) | www.efic.gov.au |
| Belgium | *Office National du Ducroire/Nationale Delcrederedienst* (ONDD) | www.ducroire.be |
| Brazil | *Seguradora Brasileira De Crédito À Exportação* | www.sbce.com.br |
| Canada | Export Development Canada (EDC) | www.edc.ca |
| Czech | Export Guarantee and Insurance Corporation (EGAP) | www.egap.cz |
| Republic | Czech Export Bank | www.ceb.cz |
| Croatia | Croatian Bank for Reconstruction and Development | www.hbor.hr/eng/ |
| Denmark | *Eksport Kredit Fonden* (EKF) | www.ekf.dk |
| Finland | *Finnvera Oyi* | www.finnvera.fn |
| | FIDE Ltd. | www.fide.fn |
| France | *Compagnie française d'Assurance pour le commerce extérieur* (COFACE) | www.coface.fr |
| | *Banque Française du Commerce Extérieur* (BFCE) | www.dree.org |
| Germany | *Euler Hermes* | www.hermes-kredit.com |
| Greece | Export Credit Insurance Organization | www.oaep.gr |
| Hungary | Hungarian Export Credit Insurance (MEHIB) | www.mehib.hu |
| | Hungarian Export-Import Bank | www.eximbank.hu |
| India | Export-Import Bank of India | www.eximbankindia.com |
| Iran | Export Guarantee Fund of Iran | www.iran-export.com exporter/company/egfi/ |
| Italy | *Sezione Speciale per l'Assicurazione del Credito all'Esportazione* (SACE) | www.isace.it |

(Continued)

**Table 17.3**   (Continued)

| Country | Bank Name | URL |
|---|---|---|
| Japan | Japan Bank of International Corporation (JBIC) | www.jbic.go.jp |
|  | Nippon Export and Investment Insurance (NEXI) | www.nexi.go.jp |
| Jordan | Jordan Loan Guarantee Corporation | ww.jlgc.com |
| Korea | Korea Export Insurance Corporation | www.keic.or.kr |
|  | The Export-Import Bank of Korea (KEXIM) | www.koreaexim.go.kr |
| Luxembourg | *Office du Ducroire* (ODD) | www.ducroire.lu |
| The Netherlands | *Atradius* | www.atradius.com |
| New Zealand | Export Credit Office (ECO) | www.nzeco.govt.nz |
| Norway | *Garanti-Instituttet for Eksportkreditt* (GIEK) | www.giek.no |
| Malaysia | Malaysia Export Credit Insurance Berhad | www.mecib.com.my |
| Mexico | *Banco National de Comercio Exterior* | www.bancomext.com |
| Philippines | Philippine Export-Import Credit Agency | zeus.philexim.gov.ph |
| Slovene | Slovene Export Corporation | www.sid.si |
| Poland | *Korporacja Ubezpieczén Kredytów* (KUKE) | www.kuke.com.pl |
| Portugal | *Companhia de Seguro de Créditos* | www.cosec.pt |
| Saudi Arabia | Islamic Corporation for the Insurance of Investment and Export Credit (ICIEC) | www.iciec.org |
| Singapore | ECICS Credit Insurance Ltd. | www.ecics.com.sg |
| Slovak Republic | *Eximbanka SR* | www.eximbanka.sk |
| Slovenia | Slovene Export Corporation | www.sid.si |
| South Africa | Credit Guarantee Insurance Corporation | www.creditguarantee.co.za |
| Spain | *Compania Espanola de Seguros de Credito a la Exportacion* | www.cesce.es |
| Sweden | *Exportkreditnämnden* (EKN) | www.ekn.se |
| Switzerland | Export Risk Guarantee (ERG) | www.swiss-erg.com |
| Turkey | Export Credit Bank of Turkey (Türk Eximbank) | www.eximbank.gov.tr |
| United Kingdom | Export Credits Guarantee Department (ECGD) | www.ecgd.gov.uk |
| United States | Export-Import Bank of the U.S. (ExImBank) | www.exim.gov |
|  | U.S. Overseas Private Insurance Corporation (OPIC) | www.opic.gov |

*The United States*

The U.S. government supports two entities that provide political risk cover for U.S. businesses: the Export-Import Bank (Ex-Im Bank) and the Overseas Private Insurance Corporation (OPIC).

*The Export-Import Bank*

The Ex-Im Bank of the United States was founded in 1934 as a U.S. banking corporation and operates as an independent agency of the U.S. government. The bank, however, is subject to U.S. foreign policy guidelines. As such, the bank is prohibited from providing financial assistance, including insurance, to either the public sector or the private sector in selected countries (e.g., a complete ban applicable to 22 countries as of 2006), unless the U.S. President certifies that it is in the interest of the U.S. to do so.

   The Ex-Im Bank provides insurance coverages for export credit risk. The credit risk policies cover losses that result from bankruptcies, insolvencies, credit report delays, default and fraud. The bank offers four types of policies tailored to the needs of exporters. Two policy forms are of particular interest. One is a policy designed especially for firms new to exporting. The second is a policy designed to meet the needs of service firms such as architectural, engineering and contracting companies. The bank calculates premiums based in part on territory (country of import), payment terms (length of payment) and obligator–guarantor classification.

The Ex-Im Bank also offers political risk policies. Indeed, the bank became successful in part by offering a policy that combines credit risk and political risk. The first of two options is the multi-buyer or master policy that provides blanket coverage of as much as 90 percent of the gross invoice amount. Longer-term political risks can be covered for as much as 100 percent of the invoice value. The second option covers both credit and political risks up to 95 percent of value. Coverage as high as 98 percent can be obtained for certain agricultural products. This difference in limits is the result of historical efforts to promote certain agricultural products such as corn and wheat. Political risk perils and coverage provisions are similar to those contained in OPIC policies described next.

### Overseas Private Insurance Corporation

The *Economic Cooperation Act* of 1948 provided domestic multinational enterprises with political risk coverage. The coverage from the government was limited initially to the risk of currency inconvertibility and almost exclusively to risks in Europe. Later, perils such as insurrection and war risk were added. The *Foreign Assistance Act* in 1969 relocated control for these activities to a newly created entity, the OPIC. OPIC began operations in 1971.

OPIC provides investment and insurance services exclusively to U.S. firms. Its insurance covers currency inconvertibility; nationalization, expropriation and confiscation by foreign governments; and political violence (e.g., war, revolution, insurrection, politically motivated civil strife, terrorism and sabotage) in more than 150 developing countries. It extends coverage for equity investments, parent company and third-party loans and loan guaranties, technical assistance agreements, cross-border leases and other forms of investment exposure. Coverage also is available to contractors, exporters and financial institutions.

Insurance premiums are based on a variety of considerations including the country where the investment is made, experience of the applicant firm in foreign markets and size of the operation. Premiums generally are established by a rate schedule with little flexibility in pricing. Rates are not influenced by supply and demand as in private-sector markets. OPIC covers up to US$250 million per project for up to 20 years. OPIC insurance is backed by the full faith and credit of the U.S. government (OPIC, 2005).

OPIC, and other public-sector insurers for that matter, are subject to the influence and policies of the home-country government. Insureds are subject to strict eligibility requirements. Projects located in countries with whom the U.S. government has some dispute may be ineligible for coverage. One positive aspect of this influence, however, is that projects in areas where the U.S. is trying to foster economic development may see rates discounted to encourage U.S. investment.

### United Kingdom

The U.K., one of the first countries to establish a public-sector political risk agency, insures both political risk and credit risk through the Export Credits Guarantee Department (ECGD). ECGD, established in 1919, offers three insurance covers:

- The *export insurance policy* insures both credit and direct investment against political loss exposures for U.K. exports of goods and services to developing countries, thus complementing similar private-sector insurance. This policy covers up to 95 percent of insured loss. Covered perils are purchaser insolvency or failure to meet its contractual obligations; currency inconvertibility; contract repudiation by a foreign government; and administrative and legislative measures by host-country governments.

- The *bond insurance policy* provides excess insurance against any bonding liabilities of insured U.K. exporters or investors. Covered perils are unfair calls or calls made due to a political event (e.g., contract repudiation, war or civil disturbance) for advance payment guarantees, performance bonds, on-demand bonds and counter-guarantees and counter-indemnities. This policy covers 100 percent of the insured loss.

- *Tender to contract and forward exchange supplement* covers the risk of adverse exchange rate movements to U.K. firms that tender payment using a foreign currency.

*France*

Two French agencies are potential sources of political and credit risk coverage: the *Banque Française du Commerce Extérieur* (BFCE) and *Compagnie Française d'Assurance pour le Commerce Extérieur* (COFACE). BFCE is designed to cover risks important to the French economy, especially in former French colonies, whereas COFACE, established in 1946, is designed more to serve the needs of French exporters.

Political risk insurance can be extended to countries outside the French sphere of influence based on individual application. COFACE offers four types of coverages: political risk insurance, credit insurance, investment insurance and foreign exchange insurance.

*Japan*

In 1999, the Japanese government established the Japan Bank for International Cooperation (JBIC) through a merger of the Ex-Im Bank of Japan and the Overseas Economic Cooperation Fund. JBIC's operations can be classified into two broad areas. First, its International Financial Operations offers export and import loans (including uncollateralized) to Japanese firms, whether they operate within Japan or abroad. Second, the Overseas Economic Cooperation Operations extends loans to foreign governments for qualified social and economic projects. In this regard, JBIC functions more as a loan-financier than as a risk-financier. JBIC also may provide debt repayment guarantee of bonds issued by foreign governments and placed in private markets.

Japan also has Nippon Export and Investment Insurance (NEXI). Established in 2001, NEXI took over underwriting foreign trade risks from the Ministry of Economy, Trade and Industry. The government reinsures risks accepted by NEXI. Political risk insurance is an integral part of the Japanese approach to expanding international trade. Eligible projects include those that are new or are an expansion of an existing project as well as those that foster Japanese economic policies.

### Insurance via private-sector markets

The pace of international trade and investment has increased dramatically. This rapid growth has strained the capacity of private insurers. New insurers are entering the political risk market, although it remains largely the purview of firms familiar with the specialized realm of international insurance in other areas.

Several insurers offer political risk insurance. Lloyd's of London comes to mind as having both the financial capacity and experience in specialized international risks to underwrite this coverage. Since the early 1970s, Lloyd's has provided political risk insurance through both direct coverage and reinsurance. True to its reputation, Lloyd's offers broad policies covering all of the usual political risk perils, including land-based war risk coverage that is rare in private markets. Lloyd's also offers export credit insurance.

The U.S. private market for political risk insurance began to develop in the early 1970s, although much more slowly and with much less overall capacity than that found in the U.K. The most aggressive political risk writer in the U.S. is American International Group (AIG), which began writing this coverage in 1974.

Additional insurers writing this cover include *Atradius* (Germany), Cox (U.K.), Chubb (U.S.), *Pohjola* (Finland), *Seguradora Brasileira de Credito à Exportação* (Brazil), Skandia (Sweden) and Zurich Insurance (Switzerland). Exporters Insurance (Bermuda), a group captive with 114 members from 23 countries and in 26 industries, also underwrites political risks.

### Differences between public and private-sector insurance

Public and private-sector insurers view political risks differently. Public insurers must consider their governments' policy objectives (e.g., encouraging exports), the need to support friendly governments and the wish to encourage economic development in particular areas of the world. Private insurers are in the business to make a profit while avoiding undue risk. These differences manifest themselves in different approaches to underwriting and pricing.

Unlike public-sector agencies, private market providers need not follow the guidelines and dictates of governments. These providers are perceived as being more flexible, being able to provide broader coverage and willing to insure risks in areas prohibited to public-sector providers. Their coverages are more expensive and may be available for much shorter terms than those offered by government agencies. Private insurers typically issue policies with one- or three-year terms subject to renewal.

In general, public-sector insurers rely more on published rate schedules than do private insurers, which rely more on judgment rating. This difference evolved in part from a need by public-sector insurers to be perceived as treating all applicants equally and because of the desire of governments to encourage certain types of investment. Whether through published rate schedules or through individual judgment rating, political risk insurers still examine certain key factors to determine premiums.

Geographic area or country of investment or import is a major underwriting factor. With public insurers, government policy toward a particular country or region heavily influences pricing and coverage availability. For private insurers, much more than for public-sector insurers, demand for coverage and the amount of coverage already provided in a particular country are key factors. In areas of high demand, prices are driven up because private insurers are willing to put only limited amounts of capital at risk. As private insurers rely on individual underwriters to set prices (judgment rating), they are more responsive to marketplace pressures. Fluctuations in demand due to political events, such as coups, elections, regional conflicts, changes of government and changes in social policy are reflected more quickly in the rates of private insurers.

Traditional actuarial methods based on probabilities are less applicable to this class of insurance. Hence, private insurers use portfolio management and diversification to assure a spread of risks, both in terms of coverage provided and geographic area. Other factors in underwriting and rating political risk insurance include the size of the investment, the experience of the applicant firm in international markets, the level of deductible and loss participation in the risk, the quality of the firm's risk management, forecasts of political risk and country risk within the region.

## THE IMPORTANCE OF MONITORING

Whatever combination of approaches and techniques firms take to address political risk, they should carefully monitor the effectiveness of their political risk management programs, including the environment in the country of operation. Circumstances that create political risk in one country may create it in another. Marketing practices that are effective in a developed country may provoke suspicion and controversy in a developing country. Managerial practices that are effective in the home country may precipitate labor unrest in a host country. Data concerning the political risk management practices of the firm should be centralized so that managers throughout the corporation can benefit from others' experiences and assist in developing consistent risk management philosophy and practice.

## POLITICAL CONSIDERATIONS IN EMERGING MARKETS

Following the movement toward democratization and liberalization worldwide, especially in Asia, Latin America and Eastern Europe, global firms continue to increase investment and trade in these regions. Major infrastructure projects, many funded by intergovernmental institutions, are being undertaken. Many other projects, especially in the form of joint ventures with indigenous firms, including former state-owned firms, also are being consummated, albeit on a smaller scale.

Western governments are abetting investment in friendly markets in a variety of ways. MNCs that fear being left out of big emerging markets such as China, India, Eastern Europe and Latin America are seeking methods of entry. The result is a rush to enter these markets, which strains political risk insurance capacity and, in some cases, reflects a lack of careful risk management.

Although expropriations and nationalizations have been less frequent recently, political tensions that may take many years to resolve themselves still simmer. Conflicts of varying degrees exist in some former states of the Soviet Union, in South and Southeast Asia, and in sub-Saharan Africa. Recent political events in Latin American countries portend increased political risk. While governments of developed economies wish to encourage investment in these countries, they have been slow to provide political risk coverage through their respective public-sector insurers. Thus, insuring expansion in these countries has been left largely to the private sector. Private markets, however, have seen capacity strained by rapidly increasing investment in these geographic areas.

Because of potential restrictions in political risk market capacity and availability, firms must pay increasing attention to risk management considerations when entering these markets. Projects that involve investment in infrastructure are particularly sensitive. In some cases, firms are becoming involved in projects that, in the past, have been almost exclusively the purview of the state, such as building and then operating toll roads.

Wells and Gleason (1995) offer advice for minimizing political risks of infrastructure projects. These strategies are largely integrative in their approach. They advise choosing projects carefully and avoiding highly visible and potentially sensitive ones, such as operating a highway. Firms increase risk when they fail to add increased capacity in response to increasing demand. Firms also increase risk when they sell services or products whose prices might rise. This can occur particularly when private firms acquire formerly state-run utilities, which often have been operating with subsidized rates.

Wells and Gleason advise firms to seek local partners or pursue a strategy of diversification by involving partners from several other nations. They caution firms to be sensitive to environmental issues, even though the country in which they are operating may not yet have a strong environmental movement. Finally, they advise firms involved in infrastructure projects to seek innovative agreements. In the extractive industries, separating work contracts and service contracts separates the issue of ownership from the issue of control and earnings. Other potential risk reducing solutions include production-sharing agreements, advance scheduling of changes in major components of the agreement, build-own-transfer agreements and other agreements that eventually return control of resources to the host country.

## CONCLUSION

With increasing globalization, a corresponding increasing need exists to manage the accompanying political risks effectively and efficiently. As corporations gain experience in entering other countries' markets, risk management techniques will continue to be refined and applied with greater efficacy. This fact will not eliminate the need for political risk insurance. Due to their flexibility and ability to tailor contracts to conform to other forms of international insurance, private market providers will remain important sources of coverage. Of great concern to MNCs is the increasing spread of terrorism. Terrorism is not traditionally considered part of political risk insurance, although global risk managers increasingly consider the potential for terrorist threats when designing international coverages.

Increasing globalization of business will bring with it increased risk in particular sectors. Yet, this same globalization also provides opportunities for risk reduction through diversification, both economic and geographic. Because the fundamental economic consideration in pricing political risk is diversification, not an actuarial measure of central tendency, the very expansion that creates the risk also facilitates insuring it. As in addressing any risk, the firm that is best able to apply appropriate risk management techniques will enjoy the lowest cost of risk and the greatest competitive advantage.

## DISCUSSION QUESTIONS

1.  With increasing internationalization of national economies, would you expect political risk exposures to grow or diminish in importance? Justify your answer.
2.  Could political risk exposures of MNCs might be hedged in the capital market? Speculate as to how this might be accomplished.
3.  An entire national economy can be exposed to political risks in the sense that the actions of other governments can diminish its collective "value." How should governments apply sound risk management principles to such exposures? Do government considerations in this respect differ fundamentally from those of firms? Explain.

4.  Can governmental political risk exposures justify the creation, maintenance and protection of a domestically owned insurance industry? Justify your response.
5.  We discussed two strategies for political risk management: an integrative strategy and a defensive strategy. Pick a country (or a political environment) for which an MNC might use an integrative strategy. Pick another country (or an environment) for which an MNC might use an integrative strategy. Support your choice for each with logical explanation. Would your choices of countries, tactics or both change depending on the nature of business? Explain.

# NOTES

1.  This chapter draws from Schroath (1998).
2.  Although strikes, even violent strikes, may occur and result in injuries and damages, they generally are not thought of as political risk.

# REFERENCES

Aon Corporation (2001). *Aon Survey: Majority of Fortune 1000 Firms Feels More Vulnerable to Political Risks Than Other Types of Losses*, Press Release (August 7) at www.aon.com/about/news/press_release/pr_006A1A3C.jsp.

Minor, J. (2003). "Mapping the New Political Risk." *Risk Management*, 50 (March): 16–21.

Overseas Private Insurance Corporation (2005). *OPIC Program Handbook*. Washington, DC: Overseas Private Insurance Corporation.

Punnett, B.J. and Ricks, D.A. (1992). *International Business*. Boston: PWS-Kent Publishing Company.

Schroath, F. (1998). "The Political Environment for Risk and Insurance", in H.D. Skipper, Jr. ed., *International Risk and Insurance: An Environmental-Managerial Approach*. Boston: Irwin/McGraw-Hill.

Wells, L.T. and Gleason, E.S. (1995). "Is Foreign Infrastructure Investment Still Risky?" *Harvard Business Review* (September–October): 44–55.

Wilkin, S. and J. Minor (2001). "Managing Today's Political Risks." *The Risk Management Letter*, 22 (no paging). Also online at www.riskcenter.com.tr/risknews/subat/aon_political_risks_today.pdf

# Chapter 18

# Intellectual Property and Technology Risk Management

## INTRODUCTION

Ongoing technological change presents both new risks and new ways to manage the old as well as the new risks. Effective management of many contemporary technological risks has become a survival issue for many firms. An entire industry has developed worldwide to manage these risks. In addition, a thesis has been cogently advanced that the true dividing line between modern and ancient times is risk and our understanding of it. Insight 18.1 explains its author's thesis.

This chapter addresses key practical and strategic implications of various technological innovations and deals with their potential for creating and exposing firms to new and unaccustomed risks.[1] It also discusses their expected impact on the management of risks for corporations. Thus, we first examine the importance and risk management implications of intellectual property in the modern economy. This section is followed by a study of the revolution in information technology and related risks.

Next, we consider a modern revolution in biotechnology, emphasizing particularly the advancement in the genetic sciences typified by the human genome project. They create new risks and liabilities for firms and societies involved in their development.

Finally, we consider advances in environmental sciences and our developing ability to detect chemical and biological hazards at successively smaller dose levels. Of particular interest are nanotechnology and attendant risks. This expanding knowledge base not only has implications for manufacturing, regulation, insurance indemnification and international politics, but also raises the potential for creating environmental catastrophes of an unparalleled scale and scope.

## INTELLECTUAL PROPERTY RISK

Over the past few decades, knowledge, ideas, innovation and creativity – so-called intellectual property – have become recognized as being at least as important as land, labor, capital and equipment in business. Indeed, we hear regularly that we are in a *knowledge economy*. Businesses and individuals have every expectation that their ideas and innovations will be

INSIGHT 18.1: RISK AS THE DIVIDING LINE BETWEEN
THE PAST AND THE PRESENT

What is it that distinguishes the thousands of years of history from what we think of as modern times? The answer goes way beyond the progress of science, technology, capitalism, and democracy.

The distant past was studded with brilliant scientists, mathematicians, inventors, technologists, and political philosophers. Hundreds of years before the birth of Christ, the skies had been mapped, the great libraries of Alexandria built, and Euclid's geometry taught. Demand for technological innovation in warfare was as insatiable then as it is today. Coal, oil, iron, and copper have been at the service of human beings for millennia, and travel and communication mark the very beginning of recorded civilization.

The revolutionary idea that defines the boundary between modern times and the past is the mastery of risk: the notion that the future is more than a whim of the gods and that men and women are not passive before nature. Until human beings discovered a way to cross that boundary, the future was a mirror of the past or the murky domain of oracles and soothsayers who held a monopoly over knowledge of anticipated events. . . .

[There was] a group of thinkers whose remarkable vision revealed how to put the future at the service of the present. By showing how to understand risk, measure it, weigh its consequences, they converted risk-taking into one of the prime categories that drives modern Western society. Like Prometheus, they defied the gods and probed the darkness in search of the light that converted the future from an enemy into an opportunity. The transformation in attitudes toward risk management unleashed by their achievements has channeled the human passion for games and wagering into economic growth, improved quality of life, and technological progress.

*Source*: Bernstein (1996).

valued and, in some instances, afforded legal protection to prevent others from expropriating them for their private gain.

## Definition and Scope

Broadly defined, **intellectual property** stems from a branch of property law that confers ownership rights to one's intangible innovations and creativity. The ownership right may accrue to individuals because of their literary, artistic or scientific works or performances and to organizations because of their creativity and inventions in any field of human endeavor, including industrial designs, scientific discoveries, trademarks, service marks and commercial names, designations, and protection against unfair competition.

Intellectual property rights attaching to patents, trademarks, designs and logos often are referred to as **industrial property**. Other examples include protected trade secrets, sensitive

## INSIGHT 18.2: CATEGORIES AND DEFINITIONS OF INTELLECTUAL PROPERTIES

A **patent** is an exclusive right granted for an invention, which is a product or a process that provides a new way of doing something or offers a new technical solution to a problem. A patent gives the holder an exclusive right to commercially exploit the invention for a limited period, generally 20 years.

- A **trademark** or **brand name** is a distinctive sign that identifies certain goods or services as those produced or provided by a specific person or enterprise. Trademark gives the holder the right to prevent others from selling works that appear to be made by the holder. The period of protection for a trademark varies, but can generally be renewed indefinitely.

- An **industrial design** – or simply a design – is the ornamental or aesthetic aspect of an article produced by industry or handicraft. Registration and renewals provide protection for up to 15 years.

- **Copyright** describes the rights given to the creator for his or her literary or artistic works (including computer software). Related rights are granted to performing artists, producers of sound recordings and broadcasting organizations in their radio and television programs. Copyright gives the holder an exclusive right to control reproduction and modification of the creative endeavor for a certain time period.

- A **geographical indication** is a sign used on goods that have a specific geographical origin and often possess qualities or a reputation that are due to that place of origin and so use is constrained by law.

- **Trade secrets** are protected information that generally is not known among or readily accessible to persons who normally deal with the kind of information in question, has commercial value because it is secret, and has been subject to reasonable steps to keep it secret by the person lawfully in control of the information.

*Source*: World Intellectual Property Organization [www.wipo.int].

proprietary information (e.g., customer database, financial information for internal uses only, pricing information and future business plans) and business know-how – a unique, value-added style of conducting business. Insight 18.2 shows the main categories and definitions of intellectual property.

In today's global economy, the protection of intellectual property has become increasingly difficult, as clever individuals in remote areas can take advantage of technology to infringe on other's rights with virtual impunity. Indeed, a survey reported in *Harvard Business Review* (Kramer et al., 2005) revealed that one of the two major concerns that corporations expect to evolve over time is "... the potential failure of the global intellectual-property-rights system." Already, the E.U. claims that counterfeiting and piracy is an "international phenomenon with considerable economic and social repercussions." It estimated that these illegal activities accounts for 5–7 percent of global trade and lead to 200,000 job losses a year worldwide.

## Intellectual Property Law

Governments have adopted laws to protect intellectual property, particularly industrial property, for two related reasons. First, the laws are said to offer a statutory expression to the moral and economic rights of creators in their creations. Second, they are said to promote creativity as well as the dissemination and application of the results, while facilitating fair trade.

Consider the writer who works for years to produce her great novel. If anyone who wishes could freely copy the book and sell it, the author likely would have far less motivation to devote so much of her life to writing the book in the first place, for others may be profiting from her work at her expense. In economic terms, others would enjoy a free ride, so suppliers will provide less of the good. The World Intellectual Property Organization (WIPO) (2004) notes the importance of protecting these types of rights:

> Accessible, sufficient and adequately funded arrangements for the protection of rights are crucial in any worthwhile intellectual property system. There is no point in establishing a detailed and comprehensive system for protecting intellectual property rights and disseminating information concerning them, if it is not possible for the right-owners to enforce their rights effectively. . . . They must be able to take action against infringers in order to prevent further infringement and recover the losses incurred from any actual infringement. . . . All intellectual property systems need to be underpinned by a strong judicial system for dealing with both civil and criminal offenses. . . .

### World Intellectual Property Organization

WIPO [www.wipo.int] is a specialized agency of the United Nations. It is charged with developing a balanced and accessible international intellectual property system that is intended to reward creativity, stimulate innovation and contribute to economic development while safeguarding the public interest. It was established through the WIPO Convention in 1967 with a mandate from its member states to promote the protection of intellectual property worldwide through cooperation among states and in collaboration with other international organizations. Its headquarters are in Geneva, Switzerland and it has 184 member states.

WIPO is responsible for the administration of 24 international treaties including the *Paris Convention for the Protection of Industrial Property* (1883), the *Patent Law Treaty* (2000), the *WIPO Copyright Treaty* (1996) and *the Convention Relating to the Distribution of Programme-Carrying Signals Transmitted by Satellite* (1974). Two of these treaties are jointly administered with other international organizations, the WTO, and International Union for the Protection of New Varieties of Plants. WIPO also offers assistance to developing countries for their compliance with the Agreement on Trade-Related Aspects of Intellectual Property Rights (TRIPS) administered by the WTO.

### The Paris Convention

The first substantial motivation for a formalized system of protection of intellectual property dates from 1873. Austria and Hungary were hosting an international exhibition at which they experienced low participation by foreigners who feared inadequate legal protections for their exhibits. The Austrian and Hungarian governments spurred the efforts that led to the creation in 1883 of an international treaty, commonly called the Paris Convention, that protected industrial property. The convention was revised several times, the latest in 1979. Some 170 countries are today contracting parties, making it one of the world's most widely subscribed treaties. The U.K. joined the convention in 1884, the U.S. in 1887, Japan in 1899, China in 1985 and India in 1998.

The key principles found in the Paris Convention dealing specifically with industrial property can be divided into the following categories (WIPO, 2004):

- *National treatment*: The member country must grant the same protection to nationals of other member countries as it does to its own nationals. This principle extends to the nationals of non-member countries if they are domiciled or have a "real and effective" commercial or industrial establishment in a member country.

- *The right of priority*: When an owner of an industrial property right files an application for protection of the right in one member country followed by the same application in other member countries within a specified period (e.g., 6 months), all later applications are deemed to have been filed on the date of the first application. This principle has the effect of ensuring that the intellectual property is protected in multiple jurisdictions from the earliest filing. Additionally, the application is protected against any laws, new or revised, that would reduce the patentability or value of the invention.

- *Independence of patents*: This principle holds that the grant of a patent for an intellectual property in one member country does not oblige other member countries to grant a patent for the same property. It also applies in the other direction: a member country cannot refuse or invalidate a patent application or terminate a patent because another country refused, invalidated or terminated it.

- *Unfair competition*: Member countries must provide persons entitled to benefits under the Convention effective protection against unfair competition. The Convention defines "unfair competition" as "acts of competition which are contrary to honest practices in industrial or commercial matters." Creating confusion by any means about the intellectual property or to the commercial activity of the right owner is an example.

### U.S. Traffic Act of 1930

Section 337 of the *U.S. Traffic Act* of 1930, administered by the U.S. International Trade Commission, provides the legal bases regarding unfair competition involving intellectual property as well as unfair acts of importation to or sales of articles in the U.S. On finding a violation of the statute, the commission may impose several remedies. It may ban entry of the articles into the country from the date of its remedy order. It may issue a "temporary exclusion order" that temporarily halts entry of articles to the U.S. during the period of investigation. The commission may issue a "cease and desist order" that in effect requires the respondent to make a change in an illegal action or conduct (e.g., ceasing a market practice). Finally, if the respondent fails to abide by a cease and desist order, the commission may bring a civil action seeking a monetary sanction, issue an exclusion order to ban the articles in the U.S. or issue a consent order to settle the dispute between the complaint and the respondent.

Before deciding which remedy to use, the commission must consider the potential impact of the relief on the public interest. When a remedy is necessary, it may take one or more of the above regulatory measures.

The key U.S. law for the protection of *copyright* is the *Copyright Act* of 1976 and subsequent amendments. This law is supplemented by others including the *Intellectual Property Protection and Courts Amendments Act* of 2004 and the *Copyright Royalty and Distribution Reform Act* of 2004.

### The European Union

The E.U. acknowledges the importance of harmonization of intellectual property laws in part to remove barriers to competition as well as to free trade in goods and services among member states. The E.U.'s initial attention to the protection of industrial property was given to trademarks. It laid out the conditions for registration of national trademarks that each member country adopted. With the adoption of the *Regulation on the Community Trademark* in 1993 (amended in 2004), the holder of a community trademark benefits from a single set of rules of protection and can market its products in all E.U. member countries under that trademark.

The E.U. adopted the *Munich Convention on the European Patent* in 1973, the *Luxembourg Convention* in 1975 (amended in 1989), and a regulation in 2000 based on a 1997 "Green Paper" to have in place an E.U. community patent system. It has taken similar measures for other types of intellectual property (e.g., E.U.-wide community design and community patent). Protection and regulation of copyrights in the E.U. is based on the two WIPO treaties – the Copyright Treaty and the Performances and Phonograms Treaty.

The E.U. presented two "Green Papers" on how to fight against counterfeiting and piracy in the single market in 1998 and 2000. These papers led to the introduction of the *Directive on the Enforcement of Intellectual Property Rights* in 2004.

## Intellectual Property Risk Management

A rise in the value of intellectual property rights has driven intellectual property litigation. A 2001 survey by the American Intellectual Property Law Association (Gauntlett, 2005) reveals a median legal cost of US$0.4 million for copyright lawsuits, US$0.5 million for trademark lawsuits, and US$1.5 million for patent lawsuits for cases filed in the U.S. These estimates indicate a significant rise in legal costs when compared to the association's survey in 1995 – US$0.2 million for copyright lawsuits, US$0.25 million for trademark lawsuits, and US$1.0 million for patent lawsuits.

Intellectual property risk management can be examined from two perspectives. First, firms should have programs in place to protect their intellectual property rights from unauthorized or illegal users. Second, they also should have in place systems that ensure that they do not infringe, even accidentally, on the intellectual property rights of others. Protection of privacy, including that of customers, is equally important.

### Risk assessment and control

To control their intellectual property loss exposures, firms its develop their own procedures and educate employees on the importance of complying with the procedures. The procedures should explain how to document the development of intellectual property assets, search for patents before release of new products and timely register the new products with legal authorities. Firms also may require certain employees to enter into confidentiality agreements.

For internal evaluation of the intellectual property procedure, Gauntlett (2005) recommends a close investigation of the following key areas.

- *Right to use and patent screening*: A firm may use a "right to use" opinion to examine whether it can market a new design without exposing itself to liability for infringement of an existing product. When such a potential exists, the firm may consider acquiring a license from the owner of the intellectual property right. The firm should update the "right to use" opinion periodically to identify any new issues or developments. The firm should have a formal internal search policy administered by trained personnel.

- *Past or pending claims or willful actions*: A firm should maintain, respond to and track all contracts and documents in an organized and timely manner. This procedure includes obtaining opinion letters and, when available, other supporting opinions such as an opinion of invalidity and good faith "design around" advice.

- *Contributory and induced infringement*: A firm may supply its products to another firm that uses them as parts for a complete product. If the latter firm infringes the intellectual property right owned by a third firm, the former firm can be exposed to a contributory or induced infringement claim. A **contributory infringement** exists when an intellectual property (e.g., patent) owner proves that:

1. a direct infringement of the property exists;
2. if not an infringement of the entire item, the portion infringed upon is a material component of the protected item;
3. the seller knew that the portion was made for use in an infringement of the patent;
4. the portion is not a staple article of commerce suitable for another substantial non-infringing use.

Besides an **induced infringement** exists when an intellectual property owner proves that the supplier knowingly aided and abetted another firm's infringement of the intellectual property right. Not surprisingly, directors and officers, particularly those of publicly held firms, who are found to have participated in or approved an act that led to an infringement of another firm's right can be held liable for compensatory damages.

One approach to control the risk (or to protect its own right) is establishing a document retention policy from the initial stage of a new product design. At minimum, it should retain key documents based on the law-prescribed ownership protection period, which can last for 20 years from the date of application. A firm also may use a patent portfolio to shield itself against infringement claims. For example, cross-licensing agreements, where both parties affirm joint uses of their own intellectual properties, can minimize disputes between joint users.

### Risk financing

As with other insurable exposures, corporations have essentially two financing options. They can retain the exposure internally or transfer it to an insurer. Retention is a viable option for the corporation with strong internal controls, diversified portfolios of products and services that have minimal commonalities (or products and services of the type not subject to intellectual property protection), and the financial capacity to meet any legal expenses and adverse judgments.

It is not uncommon, however, for firms to insurer this peril. Several insurers offer intellectual property insurance. The policies are not standardized, with variations in scope of coverage. Some policies cover a particular type of intellectual property (even to the point of listing the specific properties listed in the policy), while others cover all intellectual properties (e.g., patents, trademarks, copyrights, trade secrets and cross-licensing agreements). Some insurers limit coverage to a specific territory (e.g., a Lloyd's policy for the U.K. and other European countries only), while others offer worldwide coverage. Common exclusions include willful or intentional infringement by the insured, litigation initiated by the insured and litigation pending or occurring prior to the purchase of coverage.

Insurers make underwriting and pricing decisions based on the requested insurance limit, the size and strength of an intellectual property portfolio, desired coverage territory, the insured's retention, and the quality of the firm's risk assessment. Large firms in biotechnology, medical equipment, information technology, medicinal science, manufacturing, robotics and business design are usual buyers of the insurance.

The mainstream policies also commonly cover the cost of any legal defense. Some insurers offer offensive coverage. Also known as enforcement or abatement coverage, **offensive coverage** indemnifies the insured for legal expenses to prosecute an infringer. However, the coverage is limited to the insured's litigation expenses associated with infringement on the intellectual properties scheduled in the policy. The policy requires the insured to seek the insurer's prior approval before commencing litigation. The insurance company may share in recoveries up to specified limits; for example, US$1 million (Gauntlett, 2005).

## INFORMATION TECHNOLOGY RISK

The noted futurist Alvin Toffler speaks of civilization advancing in three major waves. He designates the first wave as the development of agriculture that allowed people to stop having to follow the food supply and thus enabled them to gather into cities and create civilizations. He cites the industrial revolution as bringing about the second wave, instrumentally transforming civilization into an industrialized society. With the third wave, information technology (IT) transforms the global economy much as the changes wrought by the agricultural and industrial revolutions did.

In this wave, we depend on our senses, intellect and memories rather than our physical strength. Work can be done at the office, at home or on the road. Bill Gates, founder of Microsoft, contends that technological changes in information sharing will profoundly affect society globally at every socioeconomic level. He envisions a world in which communication is instantaneous and in which multimedia information is available in all countries and to all individuals regardless of socioeconomic condition. New digital telecommunications technologies will quickly, inexpensively, and effortlessly transmit large quantities of data and information throughout the world via the Internet, Digital Multimedia Broadcasting (DMB) and other networks. This process multiplies our data gathering and information processing ability and will continue to revolutionize the way in which firms and governments operate.

While the IT revolution has brought and continues to bring impressive improvement in business and personal life, it also has created and will continue to create new risks. Many are and will be obvious, but many others less so. The Year 2000 (Y2K) issue is instructive in this regard. Insight 18.3 reminds us of the world's state of mind at that time and highlights how IT itself can give rise to global systemic risk.

### Risk Assessment

In the past, natural hazards were the principal hazards faced by humans and societies. With the development of modern technology, firms can control their loss exposures with higher levels of confidence, and insurers can pool natural risks and diversify their risk pools more effectively than ever.

Hazards arising from technology seem to have replaced their natural counterparts. As technological systems become more complex, the ability to predict untoward events

INSIGHT 18.3: SMART OR SIMPLY LUCKY? THE DAY THAT THE
WORLD (ALMOST) STOOD STILL ⎯⎯⎯⎯⎯⎯⎯⎯⎯⎯⎯⎯⎯⎯

During the latter half of the 20th century, hundreds of thousands of computers were
programmed with only two digits to denote the year. During the 1990s, companies
and governments worldwide became widely aware of this fact and realized that they
did not know how their computers which controlled billions of transactions and
processes would respond at midnight on December 31, 1999. Predictions of massive worldwide computer failures were commonplace. Electrical power, telephone
and other utilities would fail. Airplanes would fall from the air. Transportation would
be paralyzed, and on and on. Anarchy would ensue. Thousands of governments and
companies spent billions to rectify the problems, but most did nothing.

   As the fateful date approached in the U.S., sales of guns, ammunition, non-perish-
able foods, batteries, bottled water, gasoline-powered electrical generators and other
"survival goods" soared. At midnight, millions held their collective breaths. Nothing
happened – as least for the overwhelming majority of people worldwide. The
entire world sighed in relief. Humanity had missed a possible global catastrophe –
or had it? Did the world community overreact or was the risk successfully contained through voluntary and government-mandated Y2K compliance policies with
respect to critical infrastructure and key corporations? We cannot answer the question. However, we do know that the cost to thousands of public and private entities
was enormous. Had society never known of an electronic box called a computer, we
never would have had the risk and never would have even thought about the day that
the world almost stood still.

becomes less certain as their complexity increases and the problems of criticality become
more evident. Low probability, high severity events are the mainstay of complex technological systems. As we discuss in Chapter 6, highly interactive, tightly coupled, high-risk
technological systems have increased the potential for catastrophic events. Research suggests that such post-industrial risks can be managed most effectively by management teams
whose members are characterized by a higher level of functional heterogeneity, higher
education levels, shorter organizational tenures and greater tenure diversity. Such staffing
creates an atmosphere that is more likely to promote complex thinking and better decision-
making. Even so, firms with such risks seem to continue their reliance on engineers and
other technical specialists for risk control.

   We summarize below some of the hazards that seem to be most prominent with IT risks.
These include computer fraud, damage to systems and records, and privacy concerns.

### Computer fraud

The recognition and integration of organizational factors and state-of-the-art security cannot provide protection for every exposure corporations face. Encrypting devices can be broken and signatures forged. Evidence of electronic fraud such as identity theft, credit card
abuse and unauthorized bank transactions abound. Figure 18.1, reproduced from the annual

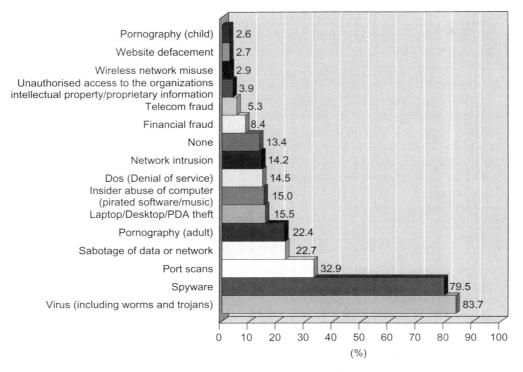

**Figure 18.1**   Proportion of Organizations Reporting a Computer Security Incident. *Source:* 2005 FBI Computer Crime Survey (www.fbi.gov/publications/ccs2005.pdf), p. 6.

*FBI Computer Crime Survey* (2005), shows the proportions of U.S. government and corporate respondents that experienced some type of attempted computer security beech during the prior 12 months, by type of attempt. The average organization reported several different types of incidents (2.75), and the vast majority (87 percent) reported at least one incident.

Figure 18.2 suggests that almost all firms (98 percent) reported employing at least some type security technology. Interestingly, having more security measures did not mean a reduction in attacks. In fact a significantly positive correlation existed between the number of security measures employed and the number of "denial of service" attacks. According to the FBI, organizations that are attractive targets of attacks are also most likely to both experience attack attempts and employ more aggressive computer security measures. Also, organizations employing more technologies are likely more aware of computer security incidents aimed at their organizations.

Finally, the FBI made a gross estimate as to the cost to the U.S. economy of all such incidents, using what they state are conservative figures. Ignoring the cost of staff, technology, time and software employed to prevent such incidents, the bureau estimated other costs to be at least US$67.2 billion per year or approximately 0.5 percent of the entire U.S. GDP.

Table 18.1 offers a listing of the top 10 Internet-based frauds in the U.S., by category. While the average dollar amounts of loss might not be considered to be large, the aggregate amounts are enormous.

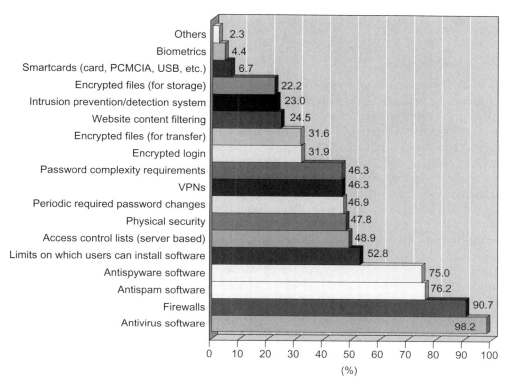

**Figure 18.2**  Security Technologies Employed by Organizations. *Source*: 2005 FBI Computer Crime Survey (www.fbi.gov/publications/ccs2005.pdf), p. 5.

**Table 18.1**  Top 10 Internet-based Frauds in the U.S.

| Category | Percent of Complaints | Average Loss (U.S. dollars) |
|---|---|---|
| **Auctions** (goods never delivered or presented) | 51% | $765 |
| **General merchandise** (sales not through auction but goods never delivered or presented) | 20% | $846 |
| **Nigerian money offers** (false promises of riches if people makes advance transfers to culprits' bank accounts) | 8% | $2,649 |
| **Phising** (e-mails pretending to be from a well-known source, e.g., bank, asking to confirm personal information) | 5% | $182 |
| **Information/adult services** (cost and terms of services misrepresented or not disclosed) | 3% | $241 |
| **Counterfeit checks** (consumers having paid with phony checks for work or goods sold, or instructed to wire money back) | 3% | $5,201 |
| **Lotteries** (requests for payment to claim lottery winnings or to get help win, often by foreign bogus lottery clubs) | 3% | $2,225 |
| **Computer equipment/software** (non-auction sales of equipment or software never delivered or misrepresented) | 1% | $1,401 |
| **Fake escrow services** (crooks directing buyers or sellers to phony escrow services, and pocketing money or getting goods free) | 1% | $2,585 |
| **Internet access services** (cost of Internet access and other services misrepresented or services never provided) | 1% | $1,187 |

*Source*: National Internet Fraud Watch Information Center [www.fraud.org].

### Systems and records

The risk of corporate liability for its employees' negligence or maliciousness can take on new scope and scale when computers and other IT systems are involved. Many firms now impose restrictions on employees' downloading software into company computers because the employee may inadvertently install a worm – a program that reproduces itself, resulting in a slow down of the affected computer system – or potentially devastating computer virus. A virus program could destroy the company's data records and computer system.

Interestingly, one of the main sources of damage to systems as well as damage and theft of electronic records is from employees. A surprisingly large proportion of damage occurs purposefully. Moreover, it appears that proprietary information theft is heavily under-reported, because organizations have no way of knowing of such thefts, do not know how to quantify the loss, or prefer to avoid admitting their security breaches for public relations reasons. The issue is not limited to the private sector. For example, the U.S. Department of Veterans Affairs in 2006 lost a database containing unencrypted personal records of 26.5 million military veterans and their spouses, as a result of a break-in at its analyst's home. It postponed a public announcement of the incident for two weeks. As an interim measure to mitigate any damages to the affected veterans, the government agency decided to offer a credit rating monitoring service. Fortunately, the database was recovered intact, likely saving millions in expenses of taxpayer money.

### Invasion of privacy

IT opens a new door for possible invasions of privacy. Who should have access to the information gathered about employees, customers, investors and others and under what conditions? Collected data may completely describe the consumption and lifestyle behaviors of individuals who may prefer to keep such information private. For example, credit card information on purchases can be cross-referenced with telephone, medical, educational, insurance, tax and police records to generate a quite exacting (and perhaps invasive) profile of a person's life. While these data profiling abilities enhance firms' target marketing abilities, they also expose the information holder to potential invasion-of-privacy lawsuits.

Governments regulate the privacy rights of individuals vis-à-vis government agencies. In a growing number of countries, governments also have enacted laws regulating the circumstances under which private-sector organizations collect, disseminate, and use personally identifiable information. For example, corporations in the U.S. are required to comply with the *Financial Services Modernization Act* and the *Fair Credit Reporting Act*. These laws require firms, unless exempted, to offer an "opt out" choice to their clients with regard to sharing personally identifiable information. If a client chooses to opt out, the firm cannot contact the client to generate additional business, share the client's creditworthiness with its affiliates, or disclose the client's personally identifiable information with non-affiliated individuals or firms. Residents in the U.S. also may register with a federal system to block unsolicited correspondence (including phone calls) from telemarketers.

## Regulation of IT Risk

Governments work to address threats to computer crime. For example, representatives of 29 countries – including Canada, Japan and the U.S. – signed the *Council of Europe Cybercrime Convention* in 2001. The convention deals with substantive and procedural cybercrime law.

The substantive section defines the following activities as criminal: illegal access, illegal interception, data interference, system interference, misuse of devices, computer-related forgery, computer-related fraud, child pornography and offences related to copyright. The procedural law section covers law enforcement issues, including measures to be taken against the crimes and offenses, search and seizure of stored computer data, collection of real time computer traffic, and preservation of stored data. The convention also contains provisions concerning intergovernmental cooperation in the fight against cybercrime. Despite it being the first multi-governmental instrument related to cybercrime, some argue that the convention falls short of addressing privacy protection as well as restrictions on government use of powers.

The Asia-Pacific Economic Cooperation (APEC), which represents more than 60 percent of world's Internet users, also decided in 2002 (reaffirmed in 2004) to adopt cyber-security regulatory measures, which follow the Council of Europe Cybercrime Convention. The African Union, in particular its African Commission on Human and Peoples' Rights, adopted in 2002 a Declaration of Principles on Freedom of Expression in Africa, which deals in part with cybercrime as well as criminal and economic measures.

Separately, the OECD (2002) issued a non-binding guideline for the security of information systems and networks. Although the guideline is subject to further review, it proposes nine principles that each member state should adopt to promote a culture of security. The principles are:

- *Awareness*: Participants should be aware of the need for security of information systems and networks and what they can do to enhance security. They also should be aware of the potential harm to others arising from interconnectivity and interdependency.

- *Responsibility*: All participants, including policymakers and program designers, are responsible for the security of information systems and networks.

- *Response*: Participants should act in a timely and cooperative manner to prevent, detect and respond to security incidents. Where permissible, this may involve cross-border information sharing and cooperation.

- *Ethical standards and conducts*: Participants should respect the legitimate interests of others.

- *Democracy*: The security of information systems and networks should be compatible with essential values (e.g., freedom to exchange ideas, free flow of information, and confidentiality of information and communication) of a democratic society.

- *Risk assessment*: Participants should conduct risk assessments, to include identification of key internal and external factors (e.g., technology, physical and human factors, policies, and third-party services).

- *Security design and implementation*: Participants should incorporate security as an essential element of information systems and networks. Participants should focus on the design and adoption of safeguards and solutions to manage potential harm from identified threats and vulnerabilities.

- *Security management*: Participants should adopt a comprehensive approach to security management. The approach should include forward-looking responses to emerging threats, detection and response to incidents, review and audit.

- *Reassessment*: Participants should review and reassess the security of information systems and networks and make appropriate modifications to security policies, practices, measures and procedures.

Individual governments also have enacted laws in an effort to minimize nefarious activity. The U.S. seems to be most active in this regard. It introduced the *National Information Infrastructure Protection Act* of 1996, the *Digital Millennium Copyright Act* of 1998, the *Computer Fraud and Abuse Act* (amended in 2001), the *Homeland Security Act* of 2002 (amendment to Section 225 known as the *Cyber Security Enhancement Act*), the *Internet Spyware Prevention Act* of 2004, and a series of sections in the Federal Criminal Code.

## Risk Control and Financing

A Global Security Survey (Deloitte Touche Tohmasu, 2005) reports that 35 percent of the survey respondents – mainly financial institutions – experienced internal attacks within the previous 12 months (in comparison to 14 percent in the 2004 survey). The survey concludes: "internal information security attacks are outgrowing external attacks at the world's largest financial institutions."

Not many firms seem to have proper IT risk management measures in place. A global information security survey by Ernst and Young (2004) of 1,233 organizations in 51 countries found that a "lack of security awareness by users" was reported as the top obstacle to effective information security management. Only 11 percent deemed that government regulations were highly effective in "improving their information security posture" or in "reducing data protection risks." Nonetheless, only 20 percent of the respondents strongly believed that information security should be a CEO-level priority.

### Liability issues

From a risk management perspective, liability issues associated with electronic communication rank high. Governments internationally continue to introduce new laws dealing with liability arising from owning, sharing or using IT. For example, with electronic communication such as e-mail and Internet Related Chat (IRC), the boundaries between the paper and cyber world become blurred. Would an imprudent e-mail or IRC message be considered slander (spoken) and libel (written)?

A potentially damaging area of liability exposure for firms relative to e-mail concerns employment practices liability (e.g., harassment, unfair discrimination or invasion of privacy). E-mail messages can be retrieved from a computer system long after the user has disposed of the message. Attorneys subpoena electronic files and computer records to search for incriminating messages long forgotten. Disgruntled employees can send internal company data outside the firm, and management can suffer the adverse consequences.

For IT liability risk management, corporations should, at minimum, install firewalls, use passwords to control system access and use the highest level of encryption standards for electronic communication. It needs to identify and evaluate its IT loss exposures. This step includes creation of a priority list based on the opinions provided by IT personnel and senior members of management. The chief risk officer should run vulnerability tests based on a list of priorities to identify the systems in need of additional protective measures. The next step is to select and implement appropriate risk management techniques. The last step is to monitor the techniques for revision or updates regularly and as and when necessary. Insight 18.4 offers an example checklist for IT risk management for financial institutions.

Vicarious liability is another corporate concern. A firm can be exposed to vicarious liability if an employee negligently damaged the intellectual property of a third party while providing services for or acting on behalf of the firm. Although not crystal clear in legal application, a firm can be sued for allowing a disgruntled employee to send malicious files to innocent

---

## INSIGHT 18.4: IT RISK MANAGEMENT CHECKLIST

*Cyber risk needs*

- Does your financial institution employ a chief information security officer?
- Is a network security audit performed by a third-party security expert at least annually?
- Does your institution install firewalls and use passwords to control system access? Does it have a corporate policy governing password usage? If so, how is the policy enforced?
- Does your institution utilize an intrusion detection system (IDS)? Does someone monitor IDS reports? Is the IDS continuously updated to keep pace with technological changes and new types of computer abuse?
- Does your institution use anti-viral software? Is the software continuously updated?
- Who is responsible for identifying and continuously patching known software vulnerabilities?
- Does your institution use the highest level of encryption standards for private and confidential information that is collected, stored, and transmitted over a network?
- Who is responsible for monitoring the content of your institution's website to detect any unauthorized changes?
- Are breaches in security reported to the appropriate law enforcement officials?

*Invasion of privacy and identity theft*

- Does your financial institution collect personal information from website visitors, either through online forms or cookies?
- Does your financial institution collect and store confidential customer information on its website?
- (Compliance with U.S. regulation) Do you comply with the *Health Insurance Portability and Accountability Act* (HIPAA) and the *Gramm-Leach-Bliley Act* with respect to the protection of confidential information?
- (Compliance with U.S. regulation) If your institution collects information from children on its website, does it comply with the *Children's Online Privacy Protection Act* (COPPA)?
- Are visitors notified that your institution is collecting information and the reasons for doing so? Are visitors given the opportunity to opt-in or opt-out of this data collection activity?
- Does your institution have a privacy policy that has been reviewed by legal counsel? Is the policy conspicuous on its website? Does your institution adhere to its policy?

*Source*: PriceWaterHouse Coopers (2001) © All rights reserved by Chubb Insurance.

third parties. Plagiarism from web pages and other electronic sources poses further risks to firms whose employees use the Internet for research and distribution of material. Finally, a firm can be held liable for harassment if an employee downloads an item from the Internet and sends it to a coworker who finds it offensive.

Liability also can arise from defamation caused by Internet users. For example, Prodigy Communications Inc. (now SBC Prodigy) was sued in 1995 by Stratton Oakmont, Inc. that asserted that an anonymous posting made available via the Internet service provider was slanderous. The company asked Prodigy to furnish the names of the posters, claiming that Prodigy was liable for information posted through it. Prodigy argued that it was merely a conduit to the Internet and should be no more responsible for the conduct of transmission of information than telephone companies would for conversations made between phone users or newspaper companies for the words printed in the editorials. A similar argument prevailed in an earlier case with a similar nature, *Chubby versus CompuServe*, in which the defendant won.

In the case of *Stratton Oakmont versus Prodigy*, however, a U.S. state court ruled that Prodigy was *de facto* a publisher – rather than merely a distributor – because it exercised some control of its bulletin boards by using software that censored messages containing swear words and racial epithets. Ultimately, Stratton Oakmont, Inc. dropped its lawsuit after receiving an apology from Prodigy.

### *Insurance*

Risk financing via insurance is available for the IT loss exposure. Commercial property insurance provides for indemnification of both direct property loss and indirect loss of income exposures. However, the coverage is limited primarily to tangible property, and many policies define "electronic data" as intangible property. The coverage for loss of income and continuing expenses – commonly part of business property insurance in the U.S. or a stand-alone policy in the U.K. – is of little help here, because payment is triggered only when the income loss and expenses follow a direct damage to insured property.

Equipment breakdown insurance, formerly known as boiler and machinery insurance, also is available. These policies cover not only traditionally defined equipment (e.g., boilers, pressure vessels, elevators and production equipment) but also electric and electronic equipment (e.g., computer technology, communication systems, security systems, inventory control systems and data restoration). However, they too insure against only those losses resulting directly from an insured property damage event and subsequent loss of business income and continuing expenses. Further, equipment breakdown insurance often excludes from the definition of accident any defect, programming error, computer virus and other conditions within or involving data or media of any kind.

Some larger corporations find fidelity (bond) insurance useful for their needs. This insurance indemnifies the insured for the direct loss of money, securities or property stolen by an employee. However, fidelity insurance typically excludes coverage for loss of proprietary information and covers only direct, not indirect, losses.

Many corporations purchase broad, IT-specific insurance. These policies respond directly to many of the direct and indirect property and liability loss exposures discussed above. Typical policies provide coverage for the following:

- *Property insurance*: It covers the cost of damages to the insured's computer system including websites. The damage may be caused by fraudulent use of an encrypted electronic signature, digital signature or similar products. The insurer may even indemnify the insured for payments that the insured makes under coercion to hackers, provided the insured acted reasonably to prevent loss and secured the insurer's approval before payment. Coverage for business income loss also is available.

- *Liability insurance*: This insurance covers the insured's legal expenses and any amounts due to third parties arising from the contents of the insured's e-mail system, websites and intranet (including the domain name, hyperlinks, and marketing and advertising on the website). It also may indemnify the insured for liability resulting from alterations or additions by a hacker. Other covered causes of loss include breach of data protection or privacy laws and negligent transmission of contaminated software.

- *Exclusions*: Excluded from coverage are infringement of any intellectual property right, defamatory statements on the insured's website or in e-mails and breach of privacy rights. Neither does the typical insurance cover any virus or worm generated by the insured or automatically disseminated on a national or global scale unless a hacker has specifically targeted the insured. The usual exclusions found in other insurance policies (e.g., war, terrorism and nuclear risks) also apply to this insurance.

As insurers only recently began offering specific IT insurance, the scope and limits of coverage vary widely. One unresolved issue in IT liability – thus, a likely insurance issue – is losses resulting from an artificial intelligence system error, such as could result with expert systems and robotics that perform tasks independent of human operation.

## BIOTECHNOLOGY RISK: THE HUMAN GENOME PROJECT

The 21st century will be no less dramatically transformed by the biotechnology revolution as it has been by the IT revolution. Biotechnology creates new industries and products and simultaneously creates new risks. Biotechnology is a broad subject encompassing pharmaceutical advancements, medical innovations, mechanical organ manufacturing and a wide variety of biologically related technological advancements. In this section, we focus on a single but important biotechnological area of advancement, namely genetics.

A cornerstone of modern genetic research is the Human Genome Project, begun in 1990 with participation of geneticists from the China, France, Germany, Japan, the U.K. and the U.S. (A **genome** is a complete set of genetic information, including DNA and RNA, of an organism.) The purposes of the project are:

- identification of all the approximately 20,000–25,000 genes in human DNA;
- completion of **sequencing** – the process of determining the exact order of the 3 billion chemical building blocks – of human DNA;
- storing the information in databases and improving tools for data analysis;
- transfer of related technologies to the private sector;
- addressing the ethical, legal and social issues that may arise from the project.

A so-called "rough draft" of the genome was finished in 2000, well ahead of schedule due to strong international cooperation, advances in the field of genomics and enormous advances in computing technology. The initial part of the project (high-quality reference sequencing) was completed in 2003, five years earlier than originally projected. In 2006, the sequence of the last and most complex human chromosome was published, another important step in completion of the project.

The project continues, now jointly with the private sector. Questions remaining under investigation include what accounts for the differences between individuals and races, what is the role of "junk DNA" (portions of the DNA sequence for which no function has been identified and which constitute 98.5 percent of the human genome) and understanding how the genome evolves.

## Potential Benefits

The potential benefits of the project are multifold. With a better understanding about the effects of generic variations on individuals, scientists and medical professional anticipate finding revolutionary ways to diagnose, treat or prevent scores of disorders that afflict humans. Knowledge about nonhuman organisms' DNA sequences helps us understand their natural capabilities that we can apply to solve challenges in healthcare and environment remediation. Imagine a future in which a physician can correct a faulty genetic sequence by inserting the desired DNA (e.g., cultured using the DNA of a bacterium) into the body. The bacterium reproduces itself, yielding more of the desired gene having a correct genetic sequence, and eventually repairing the genetic defect in the human body.

The U.S. Department of Energy, a leading agency of the project, reports current and potential applications of genome research findings, including the following:

- *Molecular medicine*: Technology and resources promoted by the project help scientists widen the spectrum of biological research and clinical medicine. Researchers now have access to information related to dozens of genetic conditions (e.g., myotonic dystrophy and Alzheimer's disease). Advances in molecular medicine may lead to earlier detection of genetic predispositions to disease and design of custom-made drugs for gene therapy and control.

- *Energy and environmental applications*: A spin-off of the project is the Microbial Genome Program, also known as Genomics. Begun in 1994, the program focuses on sequencing the genomes of bacteria useful in energy production, environmental remediation, and global climate change mitigation. A deeper knowledge about biomanufacturing, microbial systems that function in extreme environments and organisms that can metabolize waste materials will assist in the development of biofuels, invention of monitoring techniques to detect pollutants, sequestration of carbon monoxide and creation of a healthier bio-environment. Microbial genomics also can help researchers better understand the relationship between pathogenic microbes and diseases.

- *DNA forensics*: Forensic scientists collect data about 10 DNA regions, which vary from individual to individual, to create DNA profiles of individuals. There is an extremely low probability that another individual has the identical DNA profile for a particular set of regions. Also known as DNA fingerprints, these profiles can help identify catastrophe victims, solve crimes and match organ donors with recipients in transplant programs.

- *Agriculture, livestock breeding and bioprocessing*: Scientists may be able to use findings from the project to create more disease-resistant plants and animals, thus increasing agricultural productivity and reducing the cost of food. Genetically modified organisms can probably be more nutritious, generate less waste or be used to cleanup the environment.

- *Risk assessment*: Genetic differences make some people more susceptible and others more resistant to exposure to toxic agents. Fuller knowledge about the human genome can help us to understand the impact of those agents on humans (particularly related to cancer risk) and reduce the likelihood of inheritable mutations.

The benefits of genetic research indeed appear tremendous, extending both the length and quality of human life and curing deadly diseases. Not surprisingly, many countries have established national human genome research programs, including Australia, Brazil, Canada, China, Israel, Japan, Korea, Mexico, Russia and the U.S. The E.U. itself as well as its member countries – Denmark, France, Germany, Italy, the Netherlands, Sweden and the U.K. – also maintain large programs. The Human Genome Organization [www.hugo-international.org] helps to coordinate international collaboration in the genome project.

## Legal and Ethical Issues

Despite the potentially boundless benefits of genome research programs to society, we are running headlong into equally monumental legal, ethical and moral issues. Especially affected by these issues are the firms that in one manner or another have or might have reason to use genetic test information, such as employers, self-funded benefit plans, pension funds and insurers. (A further critical issue in genetics relates to the possibility of unknown adverse effects on the ecosystem and on human health and safety. These issues are explored in Chapter 6.)

During the two previous decades alone, more than 30 infectious diseases – including acquired immune deficiency syndrome (AIDS), Ebola, hantavirus, severe acute respiratory syndrome (SARS), and hepatitis C and E – have been identified in humans. Thousands of diseases are linked to specific sites on specific chromosomes, leading the way to potential detection of diseases – or perhaps even the propensity toward a disease – long before symptoms become apparent. It may be years, however, before this knowledge can be utilized to find a cure for the disease. During this interval, the knowledge is available but controls on usage are not fully developed.

The Human Genome Project sets aside a significant share of its funds to study the ethical, legal and social issues. Insight 18.5 highlights the range of issues being investigated.

Privacy and confidentiality of genetic information are a major concern. In response to this concern, the U.S. issued an executive order in 2000 to which all federal agencies must comply. The order prohibits obtaining or disclosing genetic information about current or prospective civil servants, except when it is necessary to provide medical treatment to the employee, ensure health and safety at the workplace, or provide occupation and health researchers to data.

Who else should be allowed access to personal genetic information – insurers, employers or any organizations having an economic interest of the person? Is it acceptable for insurance companies to use the information to deny, limit or cancel health insurance? May employers use the information about existing employees or to vet employment applications? Is it possible that the information could be used to promote individual interests over social welfare, such as provision of a minimum floor of economic security for citizens? Indeed, use of genetic information by government agencies could be as extensive as imaginable.

No specific U.S. federal law addresses limits on the use of genetic information in the private sector. Nevertheless, several existing laws are relevant to the issue. For example, Title VII of the *Civil Rights Act* of 1964, which prohibits discrimination on the basis of race, color, religion, sex or national origin, can be used to forbid use of genetic information to screen applicants at the workplace.

The *Americans with Disabilities Act* of 1990 prohibits discrimination at the workplace based on disability, including symptomatic genetic disability. It does not, however, protect individuals against discrimination on the basis of an unexpressed genetic condition. Neither

# INSIGHT 18.5: ETHICAL, LEGAL AND SOCIAL ISSUES IN THE HUMAN GENOME PROJECT

*Fairness in the use of genetic information.* Who should have access to personal genetic information – insurance companies, employers, courts, schools, adoption agencies and the military, among others? How will it be used?

- *Privacy and confidentiality of genetic information.* Who should own and control genetic information?

- *Psychological impact and stigmatization.* How does personal genetic information affect an individual and society's perceptions of that individual? How does genomic information affect members of minority communities?

- *Reproductive issues.* These issues include adequate informed consent for complex and potentially controversial procedures, use of genetic information in reproductive decision-making, and reproductive rights. Do healthcare personnel properly counsel parents about the risks and limitations of genetic technology? How reliable and useful is fetal genetic testing? What are the larger societal issues raised by new reproductive technologies?

- *Clinical issues.* These issues include the education of physicians and other healthcare service providers, patients and the general public in genetic capabilities, scientific limitations and social risks; and implementation of standards and quality-control measures in testing procedures. How will genetic tests be evaluated and regulated for accuracy, reliability and utility? How do we prepare healthcare professionals for the new genetics? How do we prepare the public to make informed choices? How do we as a society balance current scientific limitations and social risk with long-term benefits?

- *Uncertainties.* Uncertainties are associated with gene tests for susceptibilities and complex conditions (e.g., heart disease) linked to multiple genes and gene-environment interactions. Should testing be performed when no treatment is available? Should parents have the right to have their minor children tested for adult-onset diseases? Are genetic tests reliable and interpretable by the medical community?

- *Conceptual and philosophical implications.* This concern is related to human responsibility, freewill versus genetic determinism, and concepts of health and disease. Do people's genes make them behave in a particular way? Can people always control their behavior? What is considered acceptable diversity? Where is the line between medical treatment and enhancement?

- *Health and environmental issues.* This concern is related to genetically modified foods and microbes, as discussed in Chapter 6. Are genetically modified foods and other products safe to humans and the environment? How will these technologies affect developing nations' dependence on the West?

- *Commercialization of products.* We are concerned about intellectual property rights and accessibility of data and materials. Who owns genes and other pieces of DNA? Will patenting DNA sequences limit their accessibility and development into useful products?

*Source*: Human Genome Project Information (2007).

does it protect employees from requirements to provide job-related, business-necessary medical information.

The *Health Insurance Portability and Accountability Act* (HIPAA) applies to commercial group health insurance provided by employers. HIPAA explicitly prohibits the use of genetic information in group health insurance plans as a basis for determining coverage eligibility or pricing. It also states that, without a current diagnosis of illness, genetic information is not considered a pre-existing condition.

The E.U. has taken a similar approach by adopting a series of directives that, in the aggregate, ban discrimination in employment on the basis of gender, race, ethnic origin, age or disability. Like other E.U. member states, the U.K. is in the process of adopting these directives.

## Employers and Genetic Information

Employers, insurers, pension plans and other entities have a motivation to secure and use genetic test information. Other things being the same, employers want to hire individuals whom they believe will take the fewest number of days off because of sickness. Genetic tests can provide employers with some information about which employees might fall into the more and less costly groups. Employer-sponsored and union-sponsored pension plans and healthcare and disability income benefit plans likewise can benefit from knowledge about the likely evolution of their members' health. Again, genetic testing information can shed light on this.

Insurers, particularly those in the life, health and disability insurance business, benefit through more refined pricing and underwriting if they know more about the likely future evolution of the health status of individuals requesting insurance coverage. Indeed, any corporation, government agency or other entity whose cash flows are influenced by the cost of individuals' healthcare will have some motivation to secure and use genetic testing information. Of course, motivation does not necessarily translate into action, but establishing corporate and governmental policy and practice while ignoring these inherent motivations would be foolish.

Our concern here relates to corporations as employers and how they manage resulting risks. Will they be permitted to test employees and, if so, who will have access to the information and how will the results be used? Some employers already no longer hire individuals who smoke, even though such smoking is not done at work. The analogy to workers who have genetic predisposition is apparent. As a case in point, a recent breakthrough in genetic testing identified a gene responsible for colon cancer propensity. Should the employer be permitted to test for this gene and make hiring decisions based on it? With differing national laws, MNCs may be able to use this information in some countries but not others.

Protecting the confidentiality of such information and ensuing its proper use are obvious risk control issues. Adequate control systems will be essential as will consideration as to how possible adverse liability developments be financed.

A lack of attention to these considerations by employers will pass the decision-making to politicians and activists who may not understand the role of information in risk decisions. Employers, insurers, regulators, politicians, judges and others should identify and resolve the many ethical, moral and legal issues posed by the new genetic information explosion.

# NANOTECHNOLOGY RISK

A nanometer is one billionth of a meter.[2] Nanotechnology, the technology of the tiny, is leading another revolution. Application of the technology can be segmented into the following three approaches:[3]

* *Top-down approaches*: Bulk materials are reduced in size to produce nanoparticles. The particles can then be systematically inserted into larger structures or used as an admixture to other materials.

* *Bottom-up approaches*: Large structures are built up molecule by molecule or allowed to grow through self-assembly.

* *Self-assembly approaches*: Parts or components extemporaneously assemble, usually by moving in a solution or gas phase, until stable structures of minimum energy (e.g., a living cell) are reached.

The idea of building machines on a nanoscale began in the 1980s, but it was not until recent years that the idea became practical. Nanomaterials now used commercially include carbon tubes; calcium, silver, or zinc-based materials; and proteins. For example, a cosmetics company adds tiny zinc oxide particles to ultraviolet (UV) protection cream. A manufacturer uses organic light emitting diode display technology to improve the quality of its digital cameras.

Nanotechnology or more precisely molecular nanotechnology (MTN) makes it possible to alter the properties of materials and products without altering their chemical compositions (Cappello, 2005). The Center for Responsible Nanotechnology expects that, in 20 years or so, MTN will ensure that high-quality products are available at low cost to both the rich and the poor, mitigate environmental degradation by using less land, labor and materials (e.g., energy and water) for production, and reduce pollution. It predicts improvement in medical treatments and disease prevention, wide use of precision surgical equipment, and further advances in pharmaceutical science. Many governments and industries welcome the opportunities and are assisting in the research efforts. Governments' investments globally in this area are expected to exceed US$1 trillion by 2015 (Roco, 2003).

## Risk Assessment and Control

Yet we still have very limited knowledge about nanotechnology. The technology remains in its infancy, with many expressing fear about the risks that accompany this new technology.

Being tiny is not, in itself, a cause for concern. Rather, concern stems from the properties that accompany this smallness: that is, substantially enhanced mobility and reactivity. These properties mean that the effects of nanoparticles cannot be deduced by examining the known effects of their larger counterparts. Risks exist in four areas: health, environment, manufacturing and society.

* Health issues arise from the properties of nanoparticles that create uncertainty about how they are likely to behave on entering the human body. They can enter the body by being inhaled, swallowed or absorbed through skin. Concerns exist specifically about their effects on the cells that destroy foreign matter and on the body's biological processes.

* Environmental issues arise because of uncertainty about possible adverse effects of nanoparticles on the environment. Concern accompanies the fact that scientists are unsure

whether certain nanoparticles might be biodegradable. If they are not, scientists are unsure how they can be removed from the soil, air and water, as suitable filters do not exist.

- Manufacturing issues stem from uncertainty about the effects on the workers of firms that use nanoparticles in manufacturing and that conduct nanotechnological research. The only seemingly existing relevant national standards touching on this concern are those relating to worker exposure to dusts, yet these seem largely irrelevant to nanoparticles.

- Societal issues stem from the above three issues, but two truly globally catastrophic scenarios relating to nanotechnology have been hypothesized. Each stems from concerns about the self-assembly approaches, and each hypothesizes scenarios in which tiny self-replicating critters capable of functioning autonomously in the natural environment quickly convert the natural environment (biomass) into replicas of themselves (nano-mass) on a global basis.

    1. In the first, called the "grey goo problem," the earth's surface is transformed into a "grey goo" (intended purely as a useful metafor) by self-replicating nanorobots run amok. Drexler (1986) summarizes:

        "Plants" with "leaves" no more efficient than today's solar cells could out-compete real plants, crowding the biosphere with an inedible foliage. Tough omnivorous "bacteria" could out-compete real bacteria: they could spread like blowing pollen, replicate swiftly, and reduce the biosphere to dust in a matter of days. Dangerous replicators could easily be too tough, small, and rapidly spreading to stop – at least if we make no preparation. We have trouble enough controlling viruses and fruit flies. . . .

        The gray goo threat makes one thing perfectly clear: we cannot afford certain kinds of accidents with replicating assemblers. . . . Gray goo would surely be a depressing ending to our human adventure on Earth, far worse than mere fire or ice, and one that could stem from a simple laboratory accident.

    2. The second scenario, called the "green goo problem," is a variation of the first scenario. Here, instead of malicious nanorobots, self-replicating organisms built using nanotechnology are the culprits (Freitas, 2000). The outcome, unfortunately, is the same – no more humans (or other life as we know it).

Critics have identified other concerns that overlap with the above four areas. For example, the potential military uses of nanotechnology, including altering members of the military via nanotechnical improvements and employing nanosurveillance, cause many grave concerns.

Other issues parallel many of those in the biotech evolution. Who will own and control nanotechnological innovations and inventions? Nanotechnology involves molecular manipulation. Can matter be patented? Already hundreds of nano-related patents have been granted, and the number of patent requests grows each year. Still other issues lurk. How widely will the technology be available? Could society be disrupted by the availability of unethical nanotechnology-based products? How best to regulate the ownership or distribution of nanotechnology as well as nanoproducts?

Loss control related to nanotechnology risk is not well developed, especially at the workplace. The National Institute for Occupational Safety and Health (U.S.), in conjunction with other government agencies and private institutions, investigates the behavior and health risks of ultrafine and nanoparticles. The American National Standards Institute and ASTM International offer a series of fora for coordination of nanotechnology standards at the international level.

**Table 18.2**   Nanotechnology Risk versus Asbestos Risk

| Aspect | Nanotechnology | Asbestos |
|---|---|---|
| Manufacturer known | √ | √ |
| Defined substance | No | √ |
| Worldwide dissemination | √ | √ |
| Wide range of use | √ | √ |
| Acutely toxic | No | No |
| Persistent | In some cases | √ |
| Long-term effect | Conceivable | √ |
| Risks | Unknown | cancer |
| Claims series potential | √ | √ |
| Loss accumulation potential | √ | √ |
| Agent analytically available | √ | √ |

*Source*: Swiss Re (2004).

The International Dialogue on Responsible Research and Development of Nanotechnology, held in 2004, was probably the first meeting dealing with intergovernmental coordination of nanotechnology risk management and regulation issues. However, no national or international level regulation of nanotechnology is known at the time this book was going to press. For example, the U.S. Federal Drug Administration (FDA) applies its standard regulatory approach to nanotechnology regulation; that is, it regulates on a product-by-product basis and such products fall into three categories – pre-market approval, pre-market acceptance and post-market surveillance (FDA, 2007).

## Risk Financing

In the absence of standardization of nanotechnology and nano-manufacturing and more and deeper research, it is impossible to measure a cause-and-effect relationship between the release of nanoparticles and damage to humankind. However, nanotechnology development might be outpacing the ability of insurers to respond reasonably and responsibly. Indeed, Swiss Re (2004) commented as follows:

> [T]he insurance industry is concerned, not as much because experience shows that new technological developments tend to give rise to new loss scenarios, as because the extent of those potential claims can either be difficult or impossible to access correctly. . . . The situation is different [from previous technological changes, to which the industry successfully responded] in relation to developments that in terms of risk are *revolutionary* . . . [which] come into two different forms: firstly, potential risks related to events attributable to the cause, and, secondly, those whose casualty merely cannot be excluded, i.e., the so-called *phantom risks* [a phenomenon which is perceived by the population as a threat, although no scientifically demonstrated causal connection can be established].

As the provider of both financial and psychological security to families and executives, the insurance industry must examine carefully the possibilities for adverse developments arising from this technology. As an analogy, Swiss Re (2004) uses the benefits and costs of asbestos. For decades, asbestos was a popular fire-resistant and durable substance. Businesses worldwide manufactured products containing asbestos in innovative ways, which was initially considered as an excellent construction material. Even children's nightclothes included asbestos fibers, for the noble reason that they were less susceptible to catching on fire.

Today, asbestos is recognized worldwide as an extremely hazardous material that causes cancer. Use of products containing asbestos is now banned worldwide, and lawsuits from its former use have bankrupted hundreds of firms. However, the world had to wait for almost a century for the introduction of internationally accepted asbestos standards.

As noted earlier, scientists have identified several aspects of nanotechnology that cause concern. Table 18.2 offers a comparison of the nanotechnology and asbestos risks. It may take decades until we learn whether nanotechnology poses real or phantom risks.

# TECHNOLOGY AND THE ENVIRONMENT

The development of virtually any product or technology, no matter how beneficial, produces waste or pollution as side effects. Computer chip manufacturing produces hazardous metal and acid contaminants. Biohazards and radioactive hazards can result from biotechnology developments, and medicine and electricity generation use nuclear materials. As society creates more advanced technology, it may produce more deadly byproducts as a natural side effect. Such byproducts can threaten not only the financial survival of the manufacturers, distributors and sellers, but also affect the health of society.

## Risk Assessment and Control

At the time of a technological advancement, the risks associated with its advancement often are unrecognized. Asbestos was noted above. Fluorocarbons are another, which manufacturers used as a raw material, refrigerant and solvent. Use of this chemical is now banned in most countries, as chlorofluorocarbons (CFCs) and their variations are known to deplete the earth's protective ozone layer and cause skin cancer. For 40 years from the late 1930s, farmers used Diethylstilbestrol, a synthetic nonsteroid with the properties of estrogen, to increase livestock and poultry productivity. As it causes more harm than benefits, use of it was banned in 1979. Dichloro-diphenyl-trichloroethane (DDT), thought to be a miracle pesticide, was sprayed liberally on standing water to kill mosquitoes – unknowingly poisoning more than insects.

Consider the extent of the pollution that already exists. The Superfund program (U.S.) lists almost 1,300 sites on its National Priority List. This program, administered by the U.S. Environmental Protection Agency (EPA), spent more than US$530 million for waste cleanup, construction and post-construction, and related activities in 2006. The EPA estimates that the U.S. has some 680,000 underground storage tanks that store petroleum or hazardous substances. Release of the stored contents can adversely affect human health and damage the environment.

### The costs

For an individual firm involved in developing or using technology, the cost of cleaning up resulting pollution and compensation to third parties for damages can be enormous. Just a single incident, the 1989 Exxon Valdez oil spill in Alaska, U.S., led to more than US$2 billion in cleanup costs for Exxon and its insurance companies. Asbestos-related liability claims are expected to reach US$75 billion in the U.S. alone. Few corporations can sustain losses of this magnitude.

Yet the problems of the developed world pale in comparison to those of other regions, particularly those of Central and Eastern Europe (CEE) after decades of environmental abuse by their governments and government-owned businesses anxious to meet production quotas yet not held responsible for environmental degradation. Cleanup costs will easily top hundreds of billions of Euro. The existence of such an enormous pool of environmental liabilities has created major challenges for the CEE nations and for the E.U.

The existing pollution problem is compounded by the fact that extensive pollution continues to be created. As discussed in Chapters 4 and 6, regulation and other governmental actions can address ongoing pollution problems. Still, society faces the problem of cleaning up existing pollution and allocating the costs of such efforts. Today's estimated costs for technology-based pollution may grow even larger in the future, because procedures currently considered as environmentally safe may yet prove to be inadequate or dangerous.

### Who is liable?

The pollution liability problem can be split into two segments: liability for cleanup of existing pollution due to past technological advances and liability for preventing or controlling new pollution from new advances. In each case, society faces the difficult decision of determining who should be held responsible for cleaning up this "trash from technology."

Only near the end of the 20th century did growing environmental concerns fuel a dramatic increase in environmental regulation and legislation. As we discuss in Chapter 10, laws in the U.S., Europe and elsewhere specify clearly that any firm involved in the production, handling or disposal of hazardous substances is liable for any remediation costs. The laws allow governments to sue one or more of the offending firms severally or jointly. In general, the environmental laws hold businesses strictly liable.

National and international attention focuses in part on the deleterious cross-national and cross-regional effects of pollution that have resulted from technological advancements. The *Single European Act* of 1985 made environmental protection an official responsibility of the European Economic Council. The *Montreal Protocol* called for the reduction of substances feared to deplete the ozone layer. The *Kyoto Protocol* was even more specific.

While stricter regulation and a more vigorous liability system within a particular country may reduce pollution within that country, it may perversely create an incentive to locate the industry in other countries with less stringent regulations. Of course, pollution continues to deteriorate the global ecosphere and respects no national boundaries. Thus, costly regulation may put technology firms in some countries at a competitive disadvantage, while in the long-term global problems of pollution management are ignored or ineffectively addressed.

## Risk Financing

Despite numerous efforts made by the private and public sectors, no comprehensive method for financing the cleanup of environmental pollution exists. Until such time as they evolve, corporations in general and MNCs in particular must be prepared to deal with the financial consequences of environmental accidents as well as environmental problems that were not foreseen.

In the absence of environmental insurance, corporations will have retained the financial consequences of such exposures. This strategy may be financially astute, as we have discussed earlier with other technological risks. Indeed, for some types of environmental impairments, the corporation may have no other effective choice.

A wide array of environmental liability insurance coverage is generally available internationally. Frequently termed as environmental impairment liability or pollution legal liability insurance, these policies protect insureds against the financial consequences of pollution. They commonly include coverages for claims by third parties for bodily injury or property damage, cleanup costs and legal defense costs (including government-ordered investigation costs).

It is true that traditional insurance arrangements, particularly environmental pollution liability coverages, offer a means to smooth the capital burdens of corporations responsible for the cleanup of hazardous wastes and environmental pollution. However, the coverage is usually limited in amount and to losses resulting from unknown pre-existing conditions or new conditions. Moreover, private insurance schemes are not designed to protect corporations against environmental calamities. The reader may apply some of the risk financing solutions discussed in Chapters 13 and 14.

## CONCLUSION

The ability to identify, measure and cope with new risks has aided the growth of technology. Conversely, advances in technology will continue to not only revolutionize the way that business is conducted but also transform the risk management function. Improved data-warehousing, management and mining facilities will allow for more rapid and exact analyses of risks and their implications, providing an improved ability to identify and assess risks and to monitor and control overall risk management costs. Risk managers will have immediate access to data and experts hitherto unavailable. Electronic communication, the Human Genome Project and nanotechnology will link all areas of the globe providing a new global economy and marketplace for goods and services. The hoped-for effect will be to move the world toward the economists' idealized purely competitive market with all the accompanying rewards and challenges.

These advances are a double-edged sword, simultaneously creating new potential liabilities and new facilities for multi-billion dollar risks, IT crimes, mega-scale physical damages and liabilities and other risky endeavors. Ethical, legal and regulatory pitfalls abound as we move into this new technological era. We shall, indeed, as in the Chinese curse, "live in interesting times" for the foreseeable future.

## DISCUSSION QUESTIONS

1. Develop a risk and risk management scenario for some comparatively new yet still infant technology.
2. Should genetic testing be used for insurance classification purposes? What are the arguments pro and con?
3. Which solutions for dealing with environmental hazards make the most economic sense for Eastern Europe? Why? Do they differ from those that you might suggest for a developing country in Africa? Why?
4. What do you consider to be the greatest risks that electronic technology creates? What steps would you recommend to control or finance these risks?

## NOTES

1. This chapter draws in part from Brockett (1998).
2. By way of comparison, the diameter of human hair is about 80,000 nanometers.

3. This discussion draws in part from Cappello (2005) and Swiss Re (2004).

## REFERENCES

Bernstein, P.L. (1996). *Against the Gods: The Remarkable Story of Risk*. New York: John Wiley and Sons.

Brockett, P.L. (1998). "Technological Change and Its Impact on Risk Creation and Management," in H.D. Skipper Jr., ed., *International Risk and Insurance: An Environmental-Managerial Approach*. Boston: Irwin/McGraw-Hill.

Cappello, J. (2005). *Overview of Nanotechnology: Risks, Initiatives and Standardization* (online article), the American Society of Safety Engineers at www.asse.org/nantecharticle.htm.

Deloitte Touche Tohmasu (2005). *2005 Global Security Survey*. London: Deloitte Touche Tohmasu.

Drexler, K.E. (1986). *Engines of Creation: The Coming Era of Nanotechnology*. New York: Anchor Press/Doubleday.

Ernst and Young (2004). *A Global Information Security Survey 2004*. New York: Ernst & Young.

*FBI Computer Crime Survey* (2005). U.S. Federal Bureau of Investigation at www.fbi.gov/publications/ccs2005.pdf

Federal Drug Administration (2007). *FDA Regulation of Nanotechnology Products* at www.fda.gov/nanotechnology/regulation.html.

Freitas Jr., R.A. (2000). *Some Limits to Global Ecophagy by Biovorous Nanoreplicators, with Public Policy Recommendations*. Richardson, TX: Zyvex LLC.

Gauntlett, D. (2005). *Insurance Coverage of Intellectual Property Assets*. New York: Aspen Publishers.

Human Genome Project Information (2007) at www.ornl.gov/sci/techresources/Human_Genome/home.shtml.

Kramer, R.M., Kirby, J., Bower, J. and other (2005). "Breaking Through Ideas for 2005." *Harvard Business Review*, 83 February: 17–54.

Organization for Economic Cooperation and Development (OECD) (2002). *OECD Guidelines for the Security of Information Systems and Networks: Toward a Culture of Society*. Paris: OECD.

PriceWaterHouseCoopers (2001). *Chubb Cyberrisk Handbook: Guidelines for Risk Management*. Warren, U.S.: Chubb Group of Insurance Companies.

Roco, M.C. (2003). "Broader Societal Issues of Nanotechnology," *Journal of Nanoparticle Research*, 5: 181–189.

Swiss Re (2004). *Nanotechnology: Small Matter, Many Unknowns*. Zurich: Swiss Re.

World Intellectual Property Organization (2004). *WIPO Intellectual Property Handbook: Policy, Law and Use*. Geneva: WIPO Publication.

# Part IV

# Insurance in a Global Economy

# Chapter 19

# The Economic Foundations of Insurance

As discussed earlier, insurance occupies a key role in risk financing for individuals, families, organizations and governments. This chapter begins Part IV of this book, whose chapters comprise an analysis of insurance in both its microeconomic and its practical context. We begin by building on the materials on risk perception presented in Chapter 2 through an expansion of the economic analysis of insurance demand and supply. This expansion permits a deeper understanding of the challenges that insurance buyers and sellers face, from both theoretical and practical viewpoints.[1]

## EXPECTED UTILITY AND THE DEMAND FOR INSURANCE

In Chapter 2, we assumed that insurance was available to risk-averse individuals at the actuarially fair premium rate; that is, the expected value of projected insurance losses without any provision for expenses, taxes or profits. In reality, insurers rarely offer coverage at this rate. They need to cover their expenses and make a profit if they are to remain in business. In addition, insurers face problems of moral hazard and adverse selection that complicate the simple situation depicted with Maria in Chapter 2. Finally, while we understand that corporations might buy insurance as part of their risk management strategy as set out in that chapter, are there other reasons why we observe the pervasive purchase of insurance by corporations?

### Insurance Demand with Premium Loadings

Like other firms, insurers incur operating expenses. They incur underwriting expenses (e.g., medical examination fees in life insurance and property survey costs in nonlife insurance), pay commissions to sales representatives and incur claims investigation expenses. They incur policy maintenance costs (e.g., billing and IT expenses) and other overhead expenses and pay taxes, licenses and other fees. They hope to generate profits. These additional outlays are generically termed **premium loadings**, or the amount added to the actuarially fair premium intended to cover the insurer's underwriting, claims and other expenses plus taxes

## INSIGHT 19.1: DIFFERENT MEANINGS OF "PREMIUMS"

An insurance **premium** is the amount paid by one party (usually the insured) as a consideration for insurance provided by another party (the insurer). While this definition is useful, especially from a legal point of view, more technical and precise variations are necessary for insurance professionals, regulators and accountants.

Thus, the term **written premiums** is a measure the premiums paid by insureds and received by an insurer within a specific time period (usually a calendar year). Ordinarily, portions of these premiums are for coverage that extends beyond the measurement period. For example, suppose an insurer receives a payment of $600 on September 1, 2006 for a one-year insurance policy effective on that date. The written premium is $600 for 2006. However, only one-third of coverage was provided in 2006, with two-thirds provided in 2007. Thus, only one-third of the premium paid was *earned* during 2006. The accounting treatment for this transaction is for the insurer to record the entire $600 written premium as an asset on September 1, but it must show an offsetting liability – called an **unearned premium reserve** – for the *pro rata* share of the written premium applicable to the period for which coverage has yet to be provided. So, in our example, on December 31, 2006 the insurer would show an unearned premium reserve for two-thirds of the premium or $400.

Insurers receive premiums for direct business and for reinsurance sold (assumed). They pay premiums for reinsurance purchased (ceded). Premiums received from direct business are called **direct premiums**. The term **net premium** is used to denote the difference between (1) premiums received for direct business and reinsurance assumed and (2) premiums paid for reinsurance purchased. Related terms whose meanings will be apparent are **direct premiums earned** (or **written**) and **net premiums earned** (or **written**).

and profits. The sum of the actuarially fair premium and premium loadings is known as the **gross premium** – the premium that the insurer actually charges. The percentage of such loadings varies depending, among others, on the line of insurance business, local law governing insurance pricing and the prevailing competitiveness in the insurance market. Other permatations of the term premiums are useful, as Insight 19.1 shows.

We now examine how premium loadings affect insurance demand. We begin by continuing the illustrative example of Maria from Chapter 2. Recall that she could purchase $150,000 of earthquake insurance from XYZ Insurance Company for an actuarially fair premium of $15,000 per year.

We now assume that XYZ Insurance Company adds a 50 percent loading to cover its costs and provide a profit. The new insurance premium now becomes $22,500 ($15,000 × 150 percent). If Maria purchases insurance, her final wealth would be $177,500 ($200,000 − $22,500). Her utility associated with this level of wealth ($EU_{Loaded\ premium}$), shown in Figure 19.1, is still higher than the expected utility of no insurance ($EU_{No\ insurance}$). Thus, even with this premium loading, Maria would still be better off with insurance.

Higher premium loadings will cause a decline in Maria's expected utility with insurance. As the loading rises, her utility with insurance at one point will be the same as her utility

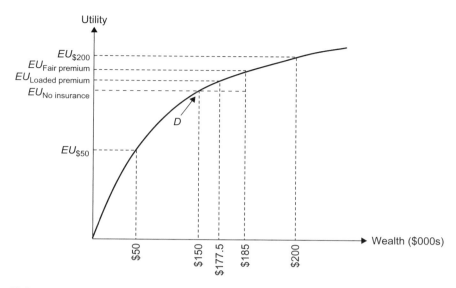

**Figure 19.1**    Maria's Expected Utility with Insurance: Premium with Loadings

from retaining the risk. This point of indifference is labeled *D* in Figure 19.1. By drawing a ray to the x-axis from this point, we can determine exactly how low Maria is willing to permit her wealth to decline (from $200,000) to completely transfer the earthquake loss exposure. The figure shows that she would pay a premium of up to $50,000. We define the **risk premium** as the maximum amount an individual is willing to pay above the actuarially fair premium. Maria's risk premium in this example is $35,000 ($50,000 − $15,000).

Using this expected utility analysis, we have shown that the premium an insurer can charge is bound to be no greater than the sum of the expected value of the loss and the person's risk premium. Of course, each person's attitude toward risk affects the risk premium the person is willing to pay. Risk premiums also can differ as an individual's wealth level changes. Risk attitude and wealth, along with other factors we examine throughout this book, affect the demand for insurance.

## Insurance Demand in Markets with Moral Hazard

The mere existence of insurance can have unintended consequences. One of the more troubling aspects is moral hazard. As discussed in Chapter 2, it is the propensity of individuals to alter their behavior when risk is transferred to a third party. There are two types of moral hazard: ex-ante and ex-post. The difference between them relates to the timing of actions by insureds in relation to their determination of suffering losses:

- **Ex-ante moral hazard** is the effect insurance can have on insureds' incentive to prevent losses. For example, individuals with no automobile insurance may drive more carefully than those with insurance because insureds know that any losses suffered in an accident can be recovered under the policy. Similarly, employees covered under workers' compensation policies may be less careful than those not covered. With insurance, they no longer bear the full financial consequences from an accident. In extreme instances, the presence of insurance may entice insureds to commit **insurance fraud** – the intentional causing of losses to collect insurance proceeds illegally. Fraud is an important issue in every insurance market, particularly in countries with a wide variety of insurance products.

• **Ex-post moral hazard** is about the effect that insurance can have on the insured's incentive to minimize further losses after a loss has occurred. For example, a person who suffers an insured loss may expend little or no effort to minimize further damage. An unemployed person collecting unemployment insurance may expend less effort to find a job than an otherwise identically situated person not receiving unemployment insurance benefits. Thus, the presence of insurance can alter insureds' attitude in preventing losses or in mitigating their wealth from further losses.

### The effect of moral hazard on insurance demand

Consider the effect moral hazard can have on insurance markets. Suppose Andrew, a risk-averse salesperson, has €12,000 in cash and owns a compact car worth €4,000. An accident would result in the total loss of his automobile. The probability of Andrew having an accident depends on how carefully he drives. When he drives fast, thus less carefully, the probability of an accident is 50 percent. When he drives slowly, the probability of an accident is only 20 percent. Andrew estimates that he incurs additional expenses of €1,000 per year from driving slowly because of the additional travel time required to complete his job.

Assume Andrew's utility function is the square root of his wealth. Using the expected utility rule, we can predict how Andrew will drive. His expected utility of being careful, $EU_{\text{Careful}}$, is:

$$EU_{\text{Careful}} = 0.8 \times U(16,000 - 1,000) + 0.2 \times U(16,000 - 1,000 - 4,000)$$
$$= 0.8 \times \sqrt{15,000} + 0.2 \times \sqrt{11,000} = 118.96$$

Similarly, his expected utility from not being careful, $EU_{\text{Fast}}$, is:

$$EU_{\text{Fast}} = 0.5 \times U(16,000) + 0.5 \times U(16,000 - 4,000)$$
$$= 0.5 \times \sqrt{16,000} + 0.5 \times \sqrt{12,000} = 118.02$$

His expected utility from driving carefully is greater than his expected utility of not being careful. Therefore, Andrew, a risk-averse person, will rationally choose to drive carefully although he incurs additional expenses of €1,000 per year.

Now assume that Ecu Insurance Company offers Andrew *full* insurance at the actuarially fair premium. Determining the premium is not an easy task in this scenario. If the insurer assumes that Andrew chooses to be careful even with insurance, the actuarially fair premium would be €800 (0.2 × €4,000). If, however, it assumes he chooses to be less careful and thus drives fast, the actuarially fair premium would be €2,000 (0.5 × €4,000).[2]

Which rate should the insurer charge? To answer this question, consider the incentives that Andrew has to be careful. With full insurance, he will be reimbursed for the full value of his car lost in an accident. If he purchases the insurance for €800, would he still be willing to incur expenses of €1,000 per year from driving carefully? He would not, because the benefit accrues to the insurer, not to him. Knowing that Andrew has no economic incentive to drive carefully, the insurer would logically assume that Andrew will be careless and charge him a premium reflecting the associated expected losses, which is €4,000. Therefore, Andrew's expected utility of purchasing full insurance at this premium rate is:

$$EU_{Insurance} = U(16,000 - 2,000) = \sqrt{14,000} = 118.32$$

We now can rank the expected utilities that Andrew would have based on his driving behavior and coverage availability:

| Andrew's Choice | Expected Utility |
|---|---|
| Drive carefully without insurance ($EU_{Careful}$) | 118.96 |
| Drive fast with insurance ($EU_{Insurance}$) | 118.32 |
| Drive fast without insurance ($EU_{Fast}$) | 118.02 |

This summary table shows that the expected utility with insurance priced on the assumption that Andrew would not be careful ($EU_{Insurance}$) is greater than the expected utility from driving fast and without insurance ($EU_{Fast}$). However, $EU_{Insurance}$ is less than $EU_{Careful}$, the expected utility when he chooses to be careful and not purchase insurance. This implies that Andrew would choose to retain the risk and drive carefully instead of purchasing insurance priced at the actuarially fair rate.[3]

### Insurer responses to moral hazard

What ameliorating actions can insurers take in markets with moral hazard? Recall that the reason for the existence of moral hazard is that the presence of risk transfer to the insurer shifts the benefits of being careful from the insured to the insurer, while the insured still retains the additional cost of being careful. To overcome this problem, insurers try to make the marginal benefit of being careful or the marginal cost of being careless or both positive.

One way to manage problems of moral hazard is to include a deductible or coinsurance provision in the insurance contract such that the insured is partially responsible for the loss consequences. Such a sharing mechanism makes insureds' marginal cost of being careful positive thus giving insureds economic incentives to manage their risks. (Insight 19.2 explains how deductibles and coinsurance clauses work.)

Another way is to reward insureds who undertake loss preventing activities. For example, retrospective and experience rating plans reward insureds with favorable loss experience with lower premiums. Under a **retrospective rating** plan, the insurer charges its insured an initial premium and audits the actual loss experience of the insured at the end of the coverage period to make premium adjustments. In an **experience rating** plan, the premium for the current period is determined based in part on the insured's average loss experience for the most recent coverage periods (e.g., three policy years preceding the renewal period), usually adjusted for the industry-wide experience. Both methods reward insureds for taking care and therefore producing fewer or less severe losses.

As we noted in Chapter 9, the moral hazard potential can be so severe for some loss exposures that private insurers will not offer any coverage against such losses. Several moral hazard potential exists whenever insureds control outcomes. Examples are abundant. If an investor were guaranteed the principal of an investment by way of insurance, the investor

## INSIGHT 19.2: DEDUCTIBLES AND COINSURANCE

In selected lines of insurance, insurers often include cost-sharing provisions in their contracts, most commonly deductibles and coinsurance. As illustrated in the left-most figure below, a (straight) **deductible** is a predetermined fixed amount of loss that the insured is required to bear. Suppose Jennifer's automobile insurance policy carries a deductible of $500 for damage to her vehicle. (This coverage is known as "collision and other-than-collision coverage" in the U.S.) Under this deductible provision, her insurer indemnifies her for qualified claims in excess of the first $500 of each loss. Deductibles benefit both the insurer and the insured. The insurer benefits from paying fewer small claims. The insured benefits from reduction in premium. Imagine the cost for handling 10,000 cases of 1-dollar claims!

Other types of deductibles exist. In a policy with a **franchise deductible**, the insurer promises to indemnify the insured for the full amount of loss – as if there were no deductible – if the loss exceeds the stipulated deductible amount. An **aggregate deductible** is an arrangement where the insured retains all losses, regardless of the number of losses, so long as the aggregate sum of the losses is within the amount of deductible; afterward, the insurer no longer applies any deductible and indemnifies the insured fully. Large corporations often purchase insurance policies with large aggregate deductibles (e.g., $1 million). Those corporations frequently employ programs similar to self-insurance to manage the retained portion of the risks.

As depicted in the middle figure below, **coinsurance** provides that the insurer and the insured share in the loss by a predetermined percentage. For example, a 90/10 coinsurance provision in a health insurance contract requires the insured to bear 10 percent of medical expenses. If an insurance policy carries both deductible and coinsurance, the insurer first applies the deductible to the total amount of loss and indemnifies its share of the remaining loss amount according to the applicable coinsurance percentage. Some contracts include a **stop loss provision**, shown in the right-most figure below, under which the insured's maximum out-of-pocket loss is capped at a predetermined amount, such as $5,000. (See Insight 22.1 for use of the term "coinsurance" in other ways.)

These loss-sharing provisions make the marginal benefit of being careful positive, thus giving the insured an economic incentive to control losses.

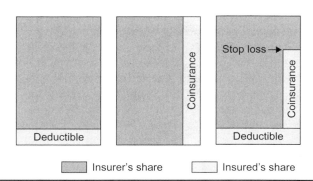

would always put the money in the riskiest areas. If a business owner were protected by insurance for any loss of income, the owner would try every means to generate maximum income. Due to the presence of extremely high levels of moral hazard in these and other situations, insurers consider such exposures as uninsurable. If, however, the element of control by the insured is removed or significantly reduced, insurance can be made available. For example, business income loss (business interruption) insurance reimburses the insured for a loss of income only if the loss results from an event over which the insured has no control, such as damage to insured property from a fire (not intentionally set by the insured!).

## Insurance Demand in Markets with Adverse Selection

An important assumption in the competitive model is that buyers and sellers have complete knowledge. In fact, however, potential insurance buyers often have more information about their own loss propensities than do insurers. This information asymmetry can affect insurance markets. As we learned in Chapter 2, the tendency of purchasers to use their superior knowledge to secure insurance at lower prices than actuarially justified is known as adverse selection.

Adverse selection leads to situations where the insurer may be unable to determine the appropriate premium for every type of individual. For example, individuals who know they might be sick are more likely to seek health insurance. Skilled physicians are less likely to experience medical malpractice claims than unskilled physicians. If an insurer can accurately distinguish between the two, it can charge appropriate premiums. Problems arise when insurers cannot so distinguish.

In the typical insurance market, insurers often possess limited information about their prospective insureds and price risks based on that limited information. Insurers price risks based on an economically reasonable amount of information from cost-effective sources. Examples of the sources include the insurance application (proposal) form, site survey report and other supporting documents such as financial statements, past loss experience of the insured, and industry loss data, analyses, and forecasts.

### *The effect of adverse selection on insurance markets*

This section examines the effect of adverse selection on insurance markets. Suppose two Japanese, risk-averse individuals have the same utility function (the square root of wealth). Each has initial wealth of ¥125,000 and faces a chance of suffering a ¥100,000 loss if they develop cancer within the coming year. One person is at "low-risk," with a 25 percent chance of developing cancer. The other person is at "high-risk," with a 75 percent chance of loss.

Let us further assume that both persons consider purchasing cancer insurance from Byorin Insurance Company. We know from the Bernoulli Principle that each person is financially better off from purchasing insurance if full coverage is available at the actuarially fair rate. Thus, for the low-risk person, the expected utility of insuring at this rate ($EU_{\text{Insurance}}^{\text{Low}}$) is greater than the expected utility of retaining the risk ($EU_{\text{No Insurance}}^{\text{Low}}$), as proved as follows:

$$EU_{\text{Insurance}}^{\text{Low}} = U(125{,}000 - 25{,}000) = \sqrt{100{,}000} = 316.23$$

$$EU_{\text{No Insurance}}^{\text{Low}} = 0.25 \times U(25{,}000) + 0.75 \times U(125{,}000)$$
$$= 0.25 \times \sqrt{25{,}000} + 0.75 \times \sqrt{75{,}000} = 244.92$$

Likewise, for the high-risk person, the expected utility of insuring the risk ($EU_{\text{Insurance}}^{\text{High}}$) is greater than the expected utility of retaining it ($EU_{\text{Insurance}}^{\text{High}}$):

$$EU_{\text{Insurance}}^{\text{High}} = U(125{,}000 - 75{,}000) = \sqrt{50{,}000} = 223.61$$

$$EU_{\text{No Insurance}}^{\text{High}} = 0.27 \times U(25{,}000) + 0.25 \times U(125{,}000)$$
$$= 0.75 \times \sqrt{25{,}000} + 0.25 \times \sqrt{75{,}000} = 187.05$$

If Byorin Insurance prices each person based on the actuarially fair premium, it breaks even. If, however, the insurer were unable to distinguish the high-risk from the low-risk person, what premium would it charge to break even? For the sake of simplicity, let us assume that only these two individuals purchase this insurance and that the insurer charges each person the same **fair pooled premium** – the premium based on the average loss expectation of the insureds in the risk pool. The fair pooled premium in this case is ¥50,000 [(¥75,000 + ¥25,000) ÷ 2].

In deciding whether to purchase insurance, both persons determine their expected utility with insurance based on the fair pooled premium and compare it with their expected utility with no insurance. As both individuals have the same initial wealth and both pay the same premium to transfer their risks, each will have the same expected utility with insurance at the pooled premium, as follows:

$$EU_{\text{Insurance}}^{\text{Pool}} = U(125{,}000 - 50{,}000) = \sqrt{75{,}000} = 273.86$$

Will both persons opt to transfer their risks to the insurer? The high-risk individual will be delighted to purchase insurance, because the premium is less than the expected loss. However, the low-risk individual, who would be forced to subsidize the high-risk person, will enjoy a higher expected utility without the insurance. Therefore, she will rationally decide to forego the policy.

What effect do these actions have on the insurance market? Recall that the pooled premium is devised assuming both individuals purchase insurance. Nevertheless, we have just observed that, in the presence of this information asymmetry, the only persons likely to purchase insurance at a pooled premium are high-risk individuals. More importantly, in a market where only pooled premiums are used, low-risk persons would tend toward not purchasing insurance and, thereby, suffer a loss in utility – a deadweight loss – from not being able to obtain insurance at actuarially fair rates.

### Insurer responses to adverse selection

Two approaches can help insurers mitigate problems of adverse selection. One approach is to elicit more information about applicants, while maintaining well-segmented risk classes. Collecting sufficient information about prospective insureds should permit the insurance company underwriters a more accurate risk classification. This is the function of underwriting, but it also is costly.

The second approach is to design insurance contracts that encourage insureds with differing risk types to self-select into the most appropriate risk class. For example, suppose Byorin Insurance Company in the above scenario offers two contracts of identical benefits with the following two options:

- *Contract 1*: Full insurance at a premium of ¥75,000.
- *Contract 2*: Insurance with a ¥60,000 deductible at a premium of ¥25,000.

**Table 19.1**  Expected Utility for High- and Low-Risk Individuals with Different Contracts

| Contract Type | Expected Utility | |
|---|---|---|
| | Low risk | High risk |
| No Insurance | 244.92 | 187.05 |
| Contract 1: ¥75,000 with no deductible | 233.61 | **233.61** |
| Contract 2: ¥25,000 with ¥60,000 deductible | **287.17** | 229.06 |

*Note:* The expected utilities of contract 2 for the low- and high-risk persons are calculated as follows:

$$EU_{\text{Deductible}}^{\text{Low}} = 0.25 \times \sqrt{125,000 - 25,000 - 60,000} + 0.75 \times \sqrt{125,000 - 25,000}$$
$$= 287.17$$
$$EU_{\text{Deductible}}^{\text{High}} = 0.75 \times \sqrt{125,000 - 25,000 - 60,000} + 0.25 \times \sqrt{125,000 - 25,000}$$
$$= 229.06$$

Note that the premium for contract 1 is the actuarially fair premium for the high-risk person ($0.75 \times ¥100,000 + 0.25 \times ¥0$). The premium for contract 2 is based on the actuarially fair premium for the low-risk person ($0.25 \times ¥100,000 + 0.75 \times ¥0$) plus an additional potential outlay (deductible) of ¥60,000.

Again assume a utility function of the square root of wealth. Table 19.1 shows the expected utility for the high and low-risk persons for each contract. The high-risk person would prefer contract 1 to no insurance, which is consistent with the Bernoulli Principle. The high-risk person also prefers contract 1 to contract 2, knowing that contract 2 is less desirable because of the greater probability that she must pay the deductible. Therefore, although contract 2 is less expensive, the high-risk person still prefers the higher-priced, no-deductible contract, by which this individual's risk type is revealed.

The low-risk person prefers a full insurance contract priced at his or her actuarially fair premium, with expected utility of 316.23, but it is unavailable. Thus, the low-risk individual would pick the second best option, contract 2. In purchasing insurance at a premium of ¥25,000, the low-risk person bears a deadweight loss, which is 29.06 units of utility ($316.23 - 287.17$) in this example.

## Substitutes for Insurance

To this point we have considered only how an insurance contract could be used by risk-averse individuals to transfer risk. Individuals, of course, can undertake other risk-mitigating activities to reduce either the probability of a loss or its size.

The availability and the price of these alternatives can affect an individual's (and corporation's) demand for insurance. The alternatives to insurance are two types of loss mitigation activities, as discussed earlier in this book. The first is loss reduction, which reduces the size or severity of potential losses. The second is loss prevention, which reduces the probability or frequency of losses. For example, the installation of a burglar alarm should reduce the probability of someone gaining illegal access to one's home or business and therefore is an investment in loss prevention. The installation of a sprinkler system can reduce the damage caused by fires and is an investment in loss reduction.[4]

Loss reduction has been shown in the theoretical literature to be a substitute for insurance. Two goods are **substitutes** when an increase (decrease) in the price of one of the goods raises (lowers) the demand for the other. Higher insurance prices tend to decrease the amount of market insurance purchased by risk-averse individuals and increase the amount of loss reduction "bought." Likewise, higher prices of loss reduction induce risk-averse individuals to demand less of it and more market insurance.

The results for loss prevention yield different predictions. Several authors have shown that loss prevention and market insurance are complements, not substitutes. Two goods are **complements** when an increase (decrease) in the price of one of the goods lowers (raises) the demand for both. The reason for this rather counterintuitive result is because an investment in loss prevention may actually raise the amount of risk that a risk-averse person faces and therefore raises the demand for market insurance.

## Why Corporations Purchase Insurance

The previous sections highlighted that risk-averse individuals, faced with risky situations, will pay more than the expected value of the loss to transfer the exposure to another party. The same analysis applies to corporations except that managers of widely held corporations are usually assumed to make decisions as if they are risk neutral, as discussed in Chapter 2.

Given that insurance is rarely available at the actuarially fair rate, the question arises as to why such corporations purchase commercial insurance. The reasons given in Chapter 2 for why corporations manage risk apply equally to the purchase of insurance – which, of course, is a risk management tool. The reader will recall that the four rationales offered were (1) managerial self-interest, (2) corporate taxation, (3) cost of financial distress and (4) capital market imperfections.

Insurance is equally relevant to each of the above rationales, but corporations have additional possible motives for purchasing insurance that may not be relevant in the context of corporations employing other risk management tools. They include the following:

- Insurers may offer real service efficiencies.
- Regulated industries have a higher demand for insurance.
- The purchase of some types of insurance is required by government.

Each of these is discussed briefly below.

### *Insurers may offer real service efficiencies*

Insurance provides more than loss reimbursement. For example, liability insurance commonly guarantees to provide a legal defense when the insured is sued. Insurance companies have expertise in loss analysis claims investigation and settlement, investment and in numerous other administrative activities dealing with hazard risks.

Risk management services are provided as part of certain commercial insurance contracts. During the underwriting phase, inspections may be undertaken to assess loss potential and to offer loss control advice. Corporations that self-insure might not have the experience or knowledge necessary to reduce these loss costs, or they may have to retain consultants to obtain it. In addition, insurance companies have a direct economic incentive to reduce or prevent losses. Because insurance companies bear at least some, if not all, of the risk of losses, they have a strong incentive to reduce loss costs. This may explain why insurance companies, and not just loss reduction consultants, are used by corporations for these risk management services.

### *Regulated industries have a higher demand for insurance*

Although the trend internationally is toward deregulation, many industries (e.g., telecommunications and public utilities) remain subject to close regulatory oversight, including with respect to the rates charged to customers. During the rate-setting process, the regulated company submits estimates of its expected costs, including any loss costs. Because insurance companies specialize in estimating loss distributions, many regulated companies find it easier to purchase insurance directly rather than defend their own loss estimates that the regulators may feel are suspect.

Also, any premium loadings are just another cost to be included in the rate filing. These loadings presumably can be passed directly to customers.

### *Compulsory insurance laws*

Corporations in many countries are required to purchase certain types of insurance, usually liability coverages. Such compulsory insurance laws effectively create a further demand for corporate insurance. Table 19.2 illustrates some types of corporate insurance whose purchase is compulsory in selected countries.

## INSURANCE SUPPLY: CHARACTERISTICS OF IDEAL INSURABLE EXPOSURES

We have seen how the transfer of an uncertain loss possibility from a risk-averse individual to another party by using an insurance contract can increase the expected utility of the individual. We also have seen how this willingness to transfer risk is limited; that is, risk-averse individuals will not rationally purchase insurance if the price of the policy exceeds their risk premium plus the expected value of the loss. In this section, we investigate how insurance companies can offer insurance at a price that consumers are willing to pay and examine the ideal characteristics of an insurable risk.

Insurers are in the business of assuming risks transferred by others. However, they do not accept all risks that individuals and corporations wish to transfer. A risk *should* meet several requirements for it to be considered insurable in the private market. The word "should" is emphasized because probably no exposures covered by insurers meet all requirements perfectly. Generally, the more remote a given exposure class is from the requirements, the less likely it is insurable in the private market. The requirements for ideal insurable exposures include:

- presence of numerous independent and identically distributed (IID) units;
- unintentional losses;
- easily determinable losses as to time, amount, and type;
- economically feasible premium.

### Numerous IID Exposure Units

An **exposure unit** can be thought of roughly as the person, place, or thing exposed to the possibility of loss. It refers to the number of lives covered in life and health insurance, number of planes in aviation insurance, number of buildings and cars in property insurance,

**Table 19.2**   Selected Compulsory Insurance Laws by Country

| | Automobile Third Party | Workers' Compensation | Other (Selected) |
|---|---|---|---|
| Argentina | √ | √ | Fire insurance (selected) |
| Belgium | √ | | Liability arising from fire and explosion in public buildings |
| Canada | √ | √ | |
| China | √ | | Nuclear liability |
| Denmark | √ | √ | Third-party aircraft<br>Medical malpractice (selected)<br>Liability for nuclear installations |
| France | √ | √ | Risks relating to construction, other people's welfare and use of aircrafts<br>Major risk relating to the nuclear industry and oil transport<br>Professional indemnity risk |
| Germany | √ | √ | Oil pollution from ships |
| Greece | √ | √ | Hail or frost damage to crops<br>Aviation liability<br>Oil pollution from ships |
| India | √ | √ | Professional indemnity by insurance brokers |
| Japan | Bodily injury only | | Liability for nuclear risks<br>Liability for maritime oil pollution |
| Korea | √ | | Fire insurance (selected)<br>Atomic energy risk |
| Malaysia | √ | √ | Professional indemnity by insurance brokers |
| Peru | | √ | Life insurance for private-sector employees<br>Aviation liability |
| Romania | √ | | Professional indemnity (selected)<br>Aviation liability<br>Nuclear liability |
| Saudi Arabia | √ | | Health insurance for expatriates |
| South Africa | √ | √ | Third party for commercial flight operators |
| United Kingdom | √ | Employer's liability | Third party (selected)<br>Professional indemnity (selected) |
| United States | √ | √ | Aviation liability |

*Source*: Lloyd's of London (2006) – Country Guide (www.lloyds.com/Lloyds_Worldwide/Country_guides).

and types of occupations in liability insurance. The number of exposure units may be different from the number of insurance policies. For example, an automobile insurance policy may cover more than one vehicle. Individuals, especially those in economically developed markets, tend to maintain more than one life insurance policy. Similar exposure units are grouped to form **insurance pools** that are also called **risk classes** in many lines of insurance.

Each exposure unit in an insurance pool represents a possible liability for the insurance company. In the ideal case, these exposure units should be IID. The terms "independent" and "identically distributed" are statistical terms used to describe the properties of random variables in relation to each another.

### Independent exposure units

Two random variables (e.g., exposures units) are **independent** if the occurrence of an event affecting one of the variables has no affect on the other variable. For example, two automobiles traveling on different highways in different countries would be considered independent of one another. The driver of the first car can do nothing to affect the probability that the second car will have an accident. As another example, suppose that one car is towing another car. If the towing car veers off the road and suffers a loss, the other car also would be damaged. Here, the two random variables representing the loss amounts attributable to the two automobiles would not be independent. For the same reason, catastrophe risks violate this most fundamental requirement of insurance.

The independence property is important because it affects how well insurers can diversify the systematic risk of their insurance pools. Ordinarily insurers are able to diversify risk by forming large pools of exposure units that are statistically independent of one another thereby lowering the average risk per exposure unit in the pool. However, when the exposure units in insurance pools are all subject to the possibility of suffering losses due to a single catastrophic event, they are no longer statistically independent. In this case, the exposure units are interdependent or correlated. When risks are correlated, diversification across exposure units is severely weakened and the resulting negative effect on insurance markets can be dramatic.

### Identically distributed exposure units

Random variables are **identically distributed** if the probability distributions of two random variables prescribe the same probability to each potential occurrence. When this occurs, the expected values and the variances of the distributions are equal. This condition is important because it allows insurers to charge each potential insured the same premium. Note that implicit in this condition is that insurers possess the same loss likelihood information as do their insureds; i.e., there is no adverse selection.

In reality, however, not many exposure units are truly identically distributed, and insurers may group similar exposure units into a class and charge pooled premiums. We have already studied how charging pooled premiums can lead to problems in insurance markets. Further, two identically distributed exposure units are not always independent.

### The law of large numbers

Let us investigate here the effect of pooling a number of IID risks. For this, we need the expected value of the risks and the dispersion (riskiness) of distributions. Two measures of dispersions – variance and standard deviation – can be useful for the latter purpose.

**Table 19.3**   Summary Statistics of John's Investment Options

| Option | Expected Value | Variance | Standard Deviation |
|---|---|---|---|
| Option 1: Put money in a safe | $10,000 | $0 | $0 |
| Option 2: Invest in CD | $10,700 | $0 | $0 |
| Option 3: Invest in mutual fund | $10,750 | $5,062,500 | $2,250 |

*Note*: The variance of option 3 is calculated as follows:

$$V = 0.5 \times (\$13,000 - \$10,750)^2 + 0.5(\$8,500 - \$10,750)^2 = \$5,062,500$$

### Measures of dispersion

As a measure of dispersion, **variance** shows the extent to which a random variable is dispersed about its expected value. It predicts how far any given outcome from a distribution can deviate from the expected value. Variance equals the sum of the squared deviations around the expected value for each outcome, each weighted by its probability of occurrence. Using mathematical notation, the variance ($V$) of a random variable $X$ which contains $i$ possible outcomes can be expressed as:

$$V = \sum_i p_i(X_i - EV)^2 \tag{19.1}$$

The standard deviation is a second measure of dispersion often used to describe the riskiness of a particular distribution. The **standard deviation** is the square root of the variance, that is $\sqrt{\text{variance}}$. This measure of dispersion is useful as it is denominated in the same units as the expected value.

To illustrate the relationship between the expected value and the variance (and standard deviation) of a random variable, consider the Chapter 2 problem that John faced. Recall that his three investment options were to (1) keep his money in a safe, (2) invest in a risk-free certificate of deposit, or (3) invest in a risky mutual fund. Table 19.3 summarizes the expected value, variance, and standard deviation of each of these options.

The variance and standard deviation of options 1 and 2 are zero because no outcome can deviate from the expected outcome. They are risk free. Option 3, however, is risky and therefore the variance and standard deviation are positive.

### Effects of pooling IID exposures units

Suppose that Fireproof Insurance Company has identified many ($N$) homes that are IID and pooled them into a single risk class. To estimate its liability from providing fire insurance coverage for these homes, the insurer is interested in four statistics:

- the total amount of losses expected to be paid during the year;
- the standard deviation of the total loss distribution (to understand the riskiness inherent in providing this insurance);
- the average loss (to determine the premium to be charged);
- the standard deviation of the average loss distribution (to determine the risk each exposure unit contributes to the risk class).

Let us denote $L_j$ a random variable that describes the amount of loss that the $j$th exposure unit of a risk class suffers during a particular coverage period. Then, $L$, the total claim payments made during the policy year, is equal to:

$$L = L_1 + L_2 + \cdots + L_N = \sum_{j=1}^{N} L_j$$

The average loss per exposure unit in the risk class, denoted as $\bar{L}$ in this example, equals:

$$\bar{L} = \frac{L_1 + L_2 + \cdots + L_N}{N} = \frac{\sum_{j=1}^{N} L_j}{N}$$

The distribution of the total loss payments of the insurer during the policy year is called either the **total loss distribution** or the **aggregate loss distribution**. $\bar{L}$ denotes the average loss and can be used to construct the **average loss distribution**.

Both $L$ and $\bar{L}$ are random variables. We could calculate the expected value and standard deviation of these two random variables using the earlier equations, but this could be quite difficult because these equations require knowledge of the probability associated with each possible outcome of the random variable. However, with the assumption that all exposure units in our insurance pool are IID, we can determine the expected value and the standard deviation of the total and average loss distributions using some simple formulas.

Suppose the expected value and the variance of each random variable, $L_j$, equals $\mu$ and $\sigma^2$, respectively. The expected value of the total loss distribution thus is:

$$
\begin{aligned}
EV(L) &= EV\left(\sum_{j=1}^{N} L_j\right) \\
&= EV(L_1) + EV(L_2) + \cdots + EV(L_N) \\
&= \mu_1 + \mu_2 + \cdots + \mu_N = N_\mu
\end{aligned}
\tag{19.2}
$$

In other words, the expected value of the sum of IID random variables equals the number of random variables multiplied by the expected value of one of the random variables. For example, if an insurer's expected loss from a householder's policy is $10,000, then the total loss the insurer could expect from a risk class containing 100 houses is $1,000,000 (100 × $10,000).

The variance of the total loss distribution, $V(L)$, is:

$$
\begin{aligned}
V(L) &= V\left(\sum_{j=1}^{N} L_j\right) \\
&= \sum_{j=1}^{N} V(L_j) \\
&= \sigma_1^2 + \sigma_2^2 + \cdots + \sigma_N^2 \\
&= N\sigma^2
\end{aligned}
\tag{19.3}
$$

In words, the total variance of a risk class (pool) containing $N$ IID exposure units equals the variance of one of the exposure units multiplied by $N$.

The expected value of the average loss distribution shows how much each exposure unit in the risk class contributes to the total expected losses of the class. The expected value of the average loss distribution is:

$$
\begin{aligned}
EV(\bar{L}) &= EV\left[\frac{\sum_{j=1}^{N} L_j}{N}\right] \\
&= \frac{1}{N} \times \left[EV(L_1) + EV(L_2) + \cdots + EV(L_N)\right] \\
&= \frac{1}{N}(\mu + \mu + \cdots + \mu) \\
&= \frac{1}{N}(N\mu) \\
&= \mu
\end{aligned}
\tag{19.4}
$$

The expected value of the average loss distribution is, quite simply, the average loss of one of the exposure units. That is, each exposure unit's expected contribution to the overall expected liability of the insurance pool is its expected value.

The variance of the average loss distribution shows how much each exposure unit in the pool contributes to the overall risk inherent in insuring $N$ exposure units. The variance of the average loss distribution is:

$$
\begin{aligned}
V(\bar{L}) &= V\left(\frac{\sum_{j=1}^{N} L_j}{N}\right) \\
&= \frac{1}{N^2} V\left(\sum_{j=1}^{N} L_j\right) \\
&= \frac{1}{N^2}(\sigma_1^2 + \sigma_2^2 + \cdots + \sigma_N^2) \\
&= \frac{1}{N^2}(N\sigma^2) \\
&= \frac{\sigma^2}{N}
\end{aligned}
\tag{19.5}
$$

The standard deviation of the average loss distribution, therefore, is:

$$
SD(A) = \frac{\sigma}{\sqrt{N}}
\tag{19.6}
$$

Equation (19.6) shows the contribution to the overall riskiness of a *risk class* that each IID exposure unit makes is not equal to the riskiness of the individual exposure. Rather, it equals the riskiness of its own losses divided by the square root of the number of exposure units in the risk class. This relationship, known as the **law of large numbers**, states that

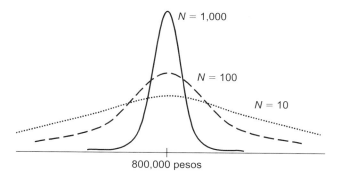

**Figure 19.2**    Average Loss Distribution of an Insurance Pool with Different Numbers of Exposure Units

the average loss for a pool of IID risks tends to fall closer and closer to the true expected value of losses the more exposure units are added to the pool. It is the reason that insurance pools have a comparative advantage in spreading risk compared with individuals trying to manage risks on their own.

We can see this result easily with a simple example. Suppose Independencia Insurance Company pools a risk class of $N$ IID fishing boats, each with an expected loss of 800,000 pesos and a standard deviation of 40,000 pesos. Figure 19.2 shows the effect on the distribution of the average loss as more IID exposure units (boats) are added to the risk class. As the number of boats increases, the probability that the average loss will equal the (true) expected loss becomes greater. In fact, as $N$ becomes very large, the risk per exposure unit becomes arbitrarily close to zero.

We have seen how the law of large numbers allows insurers to pool IID exposures which effectively lowers the average risk contribution in the pool. Pooling IID exposures has a second effect that gives pools a comparative advantage in managing losses. This effect, known as **pooling of resources**, provides that the larger the number of exposure units in an insurance pool, the greater the likelihood that the insurer will have sufficient funds to pay all claims that arise during the coverage period.

To show this effect, consider the following example.[5] Assume an insurer has established an insurance pool of IID exposures that are binomially distributed (i.e., only two possible outcomes exist) with an accident probability, $p$, of 0.2 and the probability of not having an accident of 0.8 (1.0 − 0.2). In the event of a loss, the insured suffers a £5,000 loss. Finally, assume the insurer charges a 40 percent loading, making a gross premium of £1,400 [1.40 × (0.2 × 5,000 + 0.8 × 0)].

Figure 19.3 shows the probability of ruin for the insurance pool as a function of the number of exposure units in the pool. **Ruin** occurs when total insured losses exceed total premiums paid into the pool.

The figure shows that, with only one exposure unit in the pool, the probability of ruin equals 0.20, which is exactly the probability of the insured suffering a loss. The reason for this result is that the pool contains only £1,400 and, if the insured suffers a loss, the loss will be £5,000 thereby bankrupting the pool. When a second exposure unit is added to the pool (shown as "2" on the left-most vertical line), pool resources increase to £2,800, but the probability of ruin actually increases.

Of course, the pool cannot pay a full claim until its resources are greater than £5,000. This occurs when the fourth exposure unit is added to the pool and can be seen in Figure

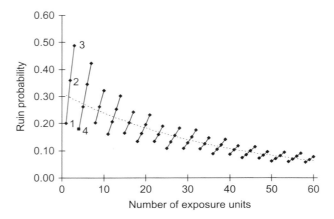

**Figure 19.3**   Probability of Ruin and the Pooling of Recourses Effect

19.3 by the discontinuity of the graph between the third (shown as "3") and fourth ("4" on the second line) exposure units. This pattern continues until the positive effect of adding additional resources to the pool overwhelms the negative effect of adding an additional exposure unit to the pool. The ruin probability becomes closer and closer to zero as the number of exposure units in the pool becomes very large.

## Accidental Losses

The second ideal prerequisite for exposures to be considered insurable is that losses should be accidental or unintentional. We made this point earlier in the context of moral hazard, as when the insured has some control over either the probability of a loss occurring or its severity. Additionally, from a societal viewpoint, it clearly is not good public policy to allow policyholders to collect insurance proceeds for internationally causing losses. Finally, some losses occur naturally over time, such as wear and tear to a person's property. As these losses are certain to happen, it is usually less expensive to budget for possible repair or replacement of the property than to purchase insurance.

## Determinable Losses

Third, whenever a claim is filed, the details of the insured loss – time, place, and amount – must be verified and the payment amount agreed upon by the insured and the insurer. Any costs incurred by the insured, such as time away from work, during this claims adjusting process lowers the expected utility of insuring. Likewise, any direct costs incurred by the insurer during the claims adjusting process will be passed onto future insureds as higher premium loadings. Therefore, the costs of verifying loss details should be relatively low for insurance to be offered at an economically feasible premium.

## Economically Feasible Premiums

We discussed earlier that, on the one hand, rational risk-averse individuals will pay a maximum premium equal to the expected value of the loss plus the risk premium. On the other hand, the owners of private insurance companies require that insurance rates be enough to give them a competitive return on their investments. These two offsetting influences define the range of economically feasible premiums.

Many factors can affect this range. For example, the degree of competition in the insurance market, the threat of new entrants, and the price and/or threat of alternative products and substitutes all have a direct effect on the insurer's ability to set prices. Likewise the bargaining power of customers, the degree to which they face risks and their attitudes toward risk affect customers' abilities to define the upper limit of the range of feasible premiums.

# CONCLUSION

This chapter examined the most important theoretical principles underlying the economics of risk and insurance in private markets. The reader should understand that the treatment is necessarily shallow given space limitations and relative to the hundreds of scholarly articles and dozens of books written on the subject's various dimensions. Nonetheless, our conceptual and applied economic knowledge continues to expand as researchers and practitioners increasingly take holistic, innovative approaches to managing risk.

# DISCUSSION QUESTIONS

1.  Hannah owns a home worth US$50,000, which is subject to the risk of fire. The probability of a fire is 25 percent and the amount of damage due to the fire would be US$40,000. Assume Hannah's utility function is the square root of wealth. Hannah has been offered full insurance at a cost of US$13,000. Will she buy the insurance? Why or why not? Use the figure below to answer the question.

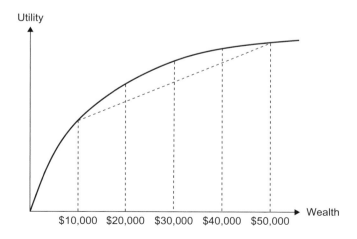

2.    A frequency distribution shows the number of accidents that an insurer can expect from each exposure unit in its insurance pool during the year. Use the information provided below to answer the following questions:

| Number of Accidents | Number of Exposure Units |
|---|---|
| 0 | 32,567 |
| 1 | 1,986 |
| 2 | 57 |
| 3 | 3 |

(a)  Calculate the expected number of accidents a single exposure unit could expect during the next year.
(b)  Calculate the standard deviation of the number of accidents a single exposure unit could expect during the next year.
(c)  Calculate the standard deviation of the number of accidents.

3.    Consider the following lotteries, $x$, $y$ and $z$:

| $x$ | $p(x)$ | $y$ | $p(y)$ | $z$ | $p(z)$ |
|---|---|---|---|---|---|
| 0 | 0.50 | −5 | 0.10 | 0 | 0.70 |
| +10 | 0.50 | +2 | 0.60 | +9 | 0.25 |
| | | 15 | 0.30 | +100 | 0.05 |

(a)  Calculate the expected value of each gamble.
(b)  Assuming a risk-averter's utility function of wealth is:
$U(w) = w - 0.02w^2$
       Calculate the expected utility of each gamble for a person who has an initial wealth level of 10. Which gamble does this person prefer? Why?

# NOTES

1.  This chapter draws from Phillips (1998).
2.  This example assumes that the insured cannot cost-lessly signal that he will choose to drive carefully when he purchases insurance. However, the literature suggests that insureds can signal their levels of care over time, and insurers can then reward (punish) those insureds who behave carefully (carelessly), for instance, by lowering (raising) their renewal premiums.
3.  Is this a violation of the Bernoulli Principle (see Chapter 2)? Not directly, but an implicit assumption underlying the principle is violated. The Bernoulli Principle assumes that the weights used to calculate the actuarially fair premium and the expected utility are identical. In the presence of moral hazard, however, the weights differ. Therefore, in the presence of moral hazard, the Bernoulli Principle does not apply.
4.  The economic literature uses different terms for these two loss mitigation strategies. Loss reduction is called *self-insurance*, and loss prevention is called *self-protection*. To avoid confusion and to make the research compatible with widely accepted corporate and insurance terminology, we have chosen to follow industry practice in terminology.
5.  This example is drawn from Smith and Kane (1994).

# REFERENCES

Lloyd's of London (2006). *Lloyd's Worldwide – Country Guide* at www.lloyds.com/Lloyds_Worldwide/Country_guides.

Phillips, R.D. (1998). "The Economics of Risk and Insurance: A Conceptual Discussion," Chapter 2, in H.D. Skipper, Jr., ed., *International Risk and Insurance: An Environmental-Managerial Approach.* Boston, MA: Irwin/McGraw-Hill.

Smith, M.L. and Kane, S.A. (1994). "The Law of Large Numbers and the Strength of Insurance," in S.G. Gustavson and Harrington, S.E., eds., *Insurance, Risk Management, and Public Policy: Essays in Memory of Robert I. Mehr.* Boston, MA: Kluwer Academic Press.

# Chapter 20

# The Nature and Importance of Insurance

This chapter provides an overview of insurance internationally, including a discussion of the insurance production process.[1] It also sketches the international dimensions of the subject and examines the factors that determine national insurance market structure. Finally, it explores the role of insurance in economic growth.

## THE INSURANCE PRODUCTION PROCESS

An understanding of the insurance production process is helpful to appreciating the role of insurance internationally and also to distinguishing aspects that are largely domestic from those that are not. The production of insurance services – as with other financial services – relies heavily on financial and human capital. Financial capital underpins all operations. The most important functional operations in the production process include pricing and product development, underwriting, claims handling, distribution and investment management. Figure 20.1 illustrates the functioning of and important relationships in this process.

### The Role of Capital and Surplus

Financial capital provides the insurance company with a cushion against the possibility that actual losses, expenses or investment results deviate negatively from assumptions implicit in the insurer's pricing. Insurance policies are contingent claim contracts that rely on pricing inversion, meaning that the product is priced before actual production costs are known. Therefore, insurers must provide a margin for unfavorable pricing deviations if the market is to perceive that they can meet their obligations. Insurers, in effect, can borrow additional capital, thus increasing capacity, through the purchase of reinsurance. Overall, the greater an insurer's capital compared with its premium writings and liabilities – that is, the less its financial leverage – the greater the perceived security and the more favorable its reception among informed buyers and their representatives.

Herein lies the most significant consumer problem in insurance. Consumers pay now for the promise of future payment under contractually defined conditions. Yet what assurance

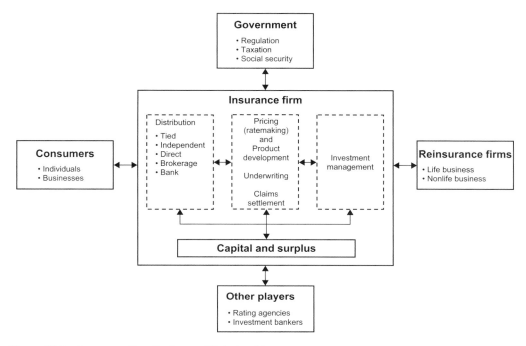

**Figure 20.1**   Insurance Functioning and Relationships

does the buyer have that the insurer will be able to pay? A strong capital position is desirable, but how does the consumer know what is "strong?"

Like others, an insurer's net worth – the sum of its capital and surplus – is the simple difference between its assets and liabilities. Even if the consumer determines what a strong capital position is, can the consumer be assured that the firm's apparent capital position is not inflated through asset overvaluation or liability undervaluation? This lemons (information asymmetry) problem can be magnified with foreign insurers. A foreign insurer's balance sheet may be prepared using its domiciliary country's accounting standards and asset and liability valuation methods that likely differ from the permitted standards and methods of the host country. As such, neither the assets nor the liabilities as shown on their balance sheets are strictly comparable with those of domestic insurers. The buyer, therefore, has even less basis for confidence. Harmonization of the standards and valuation methods in insurance is one of the important objectives that the International Accounting Standard Board hopes to achieve.

## Pricing and Product Development

Pricing, also known as ratemaking, is one of the principal technical elements of insurance operations. Insurance pricing is an important part of the discipline of **actuarial science**, which is the application of mathematical and statistical tools to risky events. **Actuaries** determine insurance prices (premium rates and reserves) using their best estimates as to future losses and expenses with an eye toward competitiveness. Given time lags between the receipt of premiums and claims payments, they calculate the competitive premium rate using the present value of expected losses and loadings. Other things being equal, the greater the average period between premium receipt and loss payout, the greater the influence of investment returns in setting premium rates. Thus, investment results are exceedingly important in life insurance and in the long-tailed nonlife lines (lines with long claim payout periods such as medical malpractice and environmental pollution liability insurance).

To the extent that an insurer includes a liberal discount factor (i.e., a high investment return) into its rates, its exposure to pricing errors – and possible insolvency – is heightened. Accurate insurance pricing requires knowledge of local loss characteristics but usually does not require a local presence of the insurer.

Product innovation and price competitiveness are often understandably crucial determinants of success, especially for new entrants. In many, particularly developing 'countries the government historically has not encouraged product innovation and price competition. New companies are discouraged from entering the market, or, if they enter, they have found themselves at a competitive disadvantage compared with entrenched companies. Thus, national treatment in the context of a restrictive regulatory regime does not necessarily provide effective market access. (As discussed in Chapter 3, national treatment means that governments accord foreign companies treatment no less favorable than that accorded domestic companies.)

## Underwriting

**Underwriters** are skilled practitioners who determine whether to issue insurance (called **selection**) and, if so, at what price and on what terms and conditions (called **classification**). This can be a complex process, depending on the type of client and scope of coverage. On simple cases (e.g., individual life insurance, personal automobile insurance and homeowner's insurance), the process is often automated. On complex cases, an underwriter may work with an actuary.

The underwriter must assemble information about the applicant (or the insured in the case of policy renewal) and the subject of insurance in order to assess the loss potential. For large or unusual risks as well as global insurance programs, the underwriting process can be quite complex. It requires knowledge of local conditions and the local environment. If continuous monitoring and local knowledge acquisition is necessary, as is usually desirable in the personal lines of insurance, a local presence may be competitively necessary. For complex risks, underwriters ordinarily can secure needed selection and classification information from local sources (e.g., engineers and surveyors) and through brokers.

## Claims Settlement

The expertise required of **claims personnel** – those who investigate, negotiate and settle claims – varies directly with the nature of the loss. Claims under life insurance policies typically can be settled easily. The beneficiary completes a simple claim form and sends a copy of the insured's death certificate to the insurer. A local presence of the insurance company is not required. Health insurance claims can range from simple to complex, depending on the nature of the policy and the health conditions of the claimants.

In lines of insurance where losses require on-site examination (e.g., property insurance), some type of local presence is typically necessary. It may be especially so when the insurer wishes to develop a reputation for efficient, quick service. For these types of cases, the insurer may send its own employee-investigator or hire an independent claim adjustor.

Indeed, a growing number of companies specialize in offering claims investigation services for insurance companies. Such decentralization (outsourcing) of the insurance production cycle is becoming increasingly common.

With other large, complex losses (e.g., loss of a freighter or an airplane crash), claims settlement may take months or even years. Those claims often require technical and legal investigation as well as keen negotiation skills. A local presence is required but usually during settlement only.

Claims personnel, sometimes with the assistance of an actuary, estimate amounts to be established as balance sheet liabilities (reserves) for unpaid nonlife claims. In life insurance, liabilities for future claims are called variously **policy reserves, mathematical reserves** or **technical provisions**. They are typically established by the actuarial department based on mathematical formulae, mortality tables, morbidity tables and assumptions as to future investment earnings. The investment manager may participate in this process. A local presence is not required with either nonlife or life insurance reserve setting.

**Contract situs** – the jurisdiction whose law applies to contract creation, interpretation and enforcement – is one of principal consumer protection issues within the insurance pricing, underwriting and claim settlement process. In cases involving domestic insurers, including subsidiaries of foreign insurers, the insurer and the insured reside in the same jurisdiction and, conflicts of law do not arise. The national treatment standard suffices. The same logic generally applies also to agencies and branches. For cross-border business, the question of whose law applies – home or host country – is potentially quite important. For commercial insurance and reinsurance, the parties typically agree as to contract situs. Such an approach is reasonable with informed parties in other insurance contracts.

Less informed customers who have taken the initiative in seeking cross-border insurance have placed themselves within the insurer's jurisdiction and, in effect, must be considered to have forfeited any *home*-country protection. When the foreign insurer solicits such customers, a different situation arises. Home-country rules arguably should apply.

## Distribution

Insurers distribute (sell) insurance in four ways: (1) direct response, (2) agents, (3) brokers or (4) other financial institutions. Many insurers distribute products using a single channel only. Others use one or several channels.

- *Direct response system.* Some companies sell insurance products directly to customers via the Internet, mail, telephone solicitation, newspaper advertisements or other direct means. They distribute products without the use of intermediaries. The volume of insurance business through such direct solicitation is relatively small. However, with the rapid development of information technology, the volume is growing in some markets – particularly in selected Asian and European countries.

  Where employed, direct response commonly involves relatively simple, commodity-like insurance products. Examples are term life insurance, homeowner's insurance, and personal automobile insurance policies.

- *Distribution through agents.* The great majority of life and nonlife insurance worldwide is sold through agents. An **agent**, a legal representative of an insurer, is authorized to sell the insurer's products and represent the insurer in this process. Of course, an agent is not a risk-bearing entity but only an intermediary. An agent may be authorized by the insurer to handle limited underwriting and claim settlements.

Two broad types of agents are found internationally. **Captive agents** – also called as **exclusive** or **tied agents** – distribute exclusively for an insurance company (and its affiliates). **Independent agents** represent many insurers.

- *Distribution through brokers.* A **broker**, a legal representative of an insurance purchaser, represents the interests of the insured and, with regard to reinsurance, the cedant. It helps its clients with loss control and policy design activities and places risks with qualified insurers (reinsurers) that best meet the insurance (reinsurance) needs of its clients. Brokers are expected to be knowledgeable about insurance products and markets and tend to work with large clients. In the primary insurance market, brokers reinforce product and price competition by rectifying, to some extent, the information imbalance between the buyer and the seller. For competitive reasons, a local distribution network is essential for international brokerage firms. Like agents, brokers are not risk-bearing entities.

- *Distribution through other financial institutions.* Banks and some other depository institutions are important insurance outlets in some markets. In the majority of instances, banks serve as agents for either an affiliated insurer or an insurer with whom the bank has a special arrangement. In no OECD country are banks broadly permitted directly to underwrite insurance, although most countries permit them to do so through holding company arrangements (e.g., Japan and the U.S.). Banks have been most successful in selling simple, commodity-type insurance products in personal lines. We explore this topic in more depth in Chapter 25.

An insurer's success ties directly to the success of its distribution system. Insurance distribution channels are vitally important to new entrants – both foreign and domestic. For this reason, we give an overview of prominent insurance distribution channels in the U.S., Europe and Asia below.

Each of the four distribution channels discussed above is found in the U.S. Generally, the exclusive agency system has been most successful in the nonlife personal lines and, to a lesser extent, with some life insurers. Most life and nonlife insurance is sold in the U.S. through thousands of independent agents and brokers. Except for annuities, banks are not yet major insurance distributors in the U.S. Selected insurers use employees to market their products.

Within the E.U., distribution concerns are said to be driving the restructuring of insurance markets, especially concerning bank and insurer linkages. Besides bank/insurer linkages as distribution channels, distribution methods differ from country to country throughout Europe. Overall, brokers and independent agents predominate in northern European countries, especially in the Netherlands and the U.K. Tied agents predominate in the south, including in Austria, France, Germany, Italy, Spain and Switzerland. The lack of major independent agent and broker networks in some European countries serves as a structural barrier to entry for *de novo* insurance operations.

In Asia, the majority of insurers distribute their products through tied agents. Only a few insurers use independent agency systems, and insurance brokerage is a relatively new concept in most Asian countries. In the Far Eastern countries (China, Japan, Korea and Taiwan), most life and nonlife insurance is sold by thousands of part-time, tied agents. Many of them sell policies to their relatives, friends and customers. As a result, new entrants to some markets are met with substantial distribution impediments. In recent years, however, several insurance companies have begun using highly educated, full-time employees to sell insurance as part of their financial planning services. Cancer insurance also is frequently solicited via infomercials in Japan and Korea. *Bancassurance* also is strongly promoted in several Asian countries (e.g., Korea and Malaysia).

Consumer protection concerns attach to insurer marketing efforts. Where distribution is via local establishment, such as an agency, branch or subsidiary, local regulation and a national treatment standard are sufficient. Cross-border distribution, however, may not ensure local consumers adequate protection against marketing abuses.

As with questions of contract situs concerning claims settlement, the issue of adequate consumer protection from marketing abuses may warrant little government concern as respects reinsurance or commercial insurance lines. In contrast, individuals are vulnerable to abuses, and a mechanism to ensure *host*-country protection may be warranted in a liberalized insurance world.

## Investment Management

Insurers, especially life insurers, manage significant investment portfolios. They are key institutional investors in capital markets worldwide. Insurers have strong incentives to maximize investment returns, as this can be a major factor in determining product competitiveness and profitability. Investment management requires decisions on investment quality and quantity, including asset-liability matching and diversification. A poorly diversified or low-quality portfolio can lead to financial difficulties and even failure.

Regulators and supervisors are greatly concerned about maintaining financial soundness of insurers and the industry, thus paying close attention to the composition and management of invested assets of insurance companies. We explore this topic in Chapter 21.

Nothing inherent in the investment management function requires a local presence, although knowledge of local investment conditions obviously is required. For instance, one large U.S. insurer monitors much of its American pension clients' funds through operations in the Republic of Ireland. Nevertheless, foreign investments can exacerbate the buyer's (and the regulator's) problem of information asymmetry, because judging the quality of such investments can be difficult. As such, national insurance regulation typically places severe limits on foreign investments by domestic insurers. Such limitations find less justification with the increasing globalization of securities markets.

A related but different concern arises with cross-border insurance trade. Unlike the situation with locally established subsidiaries of foreign companies whose assets typically must be maintained locally, the assets backing cross-border insurance liabilities are not ordinarily maintained in the host country. If a foreign insurer in cross-border business fails to meet its obligations, the host-country insureds could be at a legal, not to mention a practical, disadvantage compared with the insureds (and creditors) in the home country in attaching the insurer's assets. Hence, the resolution of this issue is essential if cross-border insurance is to grow.

# OVERVIEW OF INSURANCE WORLDWIDE

Insurance markets vary enormously in size and structure. The size of a country's insurance market depends greatly on the size of its economy. Innumerable factors influence its structure, the most important of which we discuss in this chapter.

506    Chapter 20: The Nature and Importance of Insurance

## Insurance Companies Worldwide

National insurance markets differ markedly. In a few, state-owned monopolies remain the sole suppliers, although the trend is away from such. Some developing countries still deny foreign-controlled insurers effective market access. Most OECD country markets exhibit a blend of domestic and foreign companies, with domestic-controlled undertakings commonly dominating. Some markets are quite concentrated, while others are not.

### World's most important insurance companies

Table 20.1 lists the world's 10 largest life insurers nonlife insurers and reinsurers and their countries of domicile. The U.K. claims three of the world's largest life insurers, followed by France and Japan each with two. European and U.S. insurers dominate the nonlife list, with Allianz being the world's largest nonlife insurer in 2005.

Most large insurers write the great majority of their business within their domestic markets. For example, not many life insurance companies are truly international and capable of servicing their clients worldwide. However, reinsurers differ in terms of the scope of business and the ability to serve their client insurers internationally.

As previewed in Chapter 2 and discussed in detail in Chapter 23, reinsurers are vitally important links in the insurance supply chain. Almost all insurers (and reinsurers themselves) purchase reinsurance to avoid undue concentrations of loss exposures and for other reasons. Four of the largest reinsurance groups are European, including the world's largest, Munich Reinsurance Group. The U.S. and Bermuda each is home to three.

### Nature of insurance companies

We can classify insurance companies by the nature of their (1) ownership structure, (2) place of domicile and (3) licensing status.

#### Ownership structure

The two most prevalent forms of ownership structures of insurance companies worldwide are stocks and mutuals. **Stock insurers** are owned by shareholders, with profits accruing to them. **Mutual insurers** have no shareholders, being controlled by and profits flowing to policyholders. The stock insurer form predominates in most lines and markets worldwide. Mutuals control important market shares, particularly in life insurance in Japan, the U.K. and the U.S.

Mutual insurers can be further divided into assessment mutuals and non-assessment mutuals. An **assessment mutual** is a mutual insurer that can assess its policyholders additional premiums, in proportion to the size of the insured exposure, for any operating losses incurred during a year. A **non-assessment mutual** is a mutual insurer that cannot assess its policyholders any additional premiums for losses. It may absorb the losses using any capital reserves from previous years or charge policyholders higher renewal premiums.

Most mutuals are non-assessment mutuals. Assessment mutuals are chiefly in commercial lines of insurance. A well-known form of assessment mutual is Protection and Indemnity (P&I) clubs.

#### Licensing status

Insurers can be classified based on their licensing status. Thus, an **admitted insurer** is an insurer that is licensed to sell insurance within the jurisdiction. By contrast, a **nonadmitted**

**Table 20.1**    World's Largest Life Nonlife and Reinsurance Companies (2005)

| | Life Insurance | Revenue (US$ million)[a] | Country |
|---|---|---|---|
| 1 | ING Group | $138,235 | The Netherlands |
| 2 | AXA | 129,839 | France |
| 3 | Assicurazioni Generali | 101,404 | Italy |
| 4 | Aviva | 92,579 | U.K. |
| 5 | Prudential | 74,745 | U.K. |
| 6 | Nippon Life Insurance | 61,158 | Japan |
| 7 | Legal & General Group | 56,385 | U.K. |
| 8 | CNP Assurances | 48,745 | France |
| 9 | MetLife | 46,983 | USA |
| 10 | Dai-ichi Mutual Life Insurance | 44,598 | Japan |

| | Nonlife Insurance | Revenue (US$ million)[a] | Country |
|---|---|---|---|
| 1 | Allianz | $121,406 | Germany |
| 2 | American International Group | 108,905 | USA |
| 3 | Berkshire Hathaway | 81,663 | USA |
| 4 | Zurich Financial Services | 67,186 | Switzerland |
| 5 | Munich Reinsurance Group | 60,256 | Germany |
| 6 | State Farm Insurance Companies | 59,224 | USA |
| 7 | Allstate Insurance Companies | 35,383 | USA |
| 8 | Millea Holdings | 30,030 | Japan |
| 9 | Swiss Reinsurance | 28,093 | Switzerland |
| 10 | Hartford Financial Services | 27,083 | USA |

| | Reinsurance | Net Premiums Written (US$ million) | Country |
|---|---|---|---|
| 1 | Munich Re | $22,603 | Germany |
| 2 | Swiss Re[d] | 21,204 | Switzerland |
| 3 | Berkshire Hathaway Re | 10,041 | USA |
| 4 | Hannover Re | 6,697 | Germany |
| 5 | GE Insurance Solutions[d] | 6,557 | USA |
| 6 | Lloyd's | 7,653 | U.K. |
| 7 | XL Re | 5,013 | Bermuda |
| 8 | Everest Re | 3,972 | Bermuda |
| 9 | Reinsurance Group of America | 3,893 | USA |
| 10 | Partner Re | 3,616 | Bermuda |

[a] Revenues include premium and annuity income, investment income and capital gains or losses but excludes deposits; includes consolidated subsidiaries, excludes excise taxes.
[b] Lloyd's is a marketplace for a number of syndicates.
[c] See also Table 23.5.
[d] Swiss Re acquired GE Insurance Solutions in 2006.
*Source*: Insurance Information Institute (III).

**insurer** is an insurer doing cross-border trade and not licensed to do business within the jurisdiction.

Most admitted companies are licensed to do business in a single class of insurance only. Thus, most life insurers worldwide sell life insurance products only, and most nonlife insurers sell nonlife insurance products only. Health insurance often can be sold by both life and nonlife insurers.

An insurer holding a license for one class of insurance (e.g., life) is commonly permitted to do business in other classes (e.g., nonlife) though a subsidiary. In a number of countries (e.g., Austria, Belgium, Czech Republic, Greece, Italy, Luxembourg, Malaysia, Mexico, Portugal, Singapore, Sri Lanka, Spain, Turkey and the U.K.), insurers may operate as **composite insurers** – insurance companies selling both life and nonlife insurance.

*Place of domicile*

The third criterion we can use to group insurance companies is the place of domicile. National insurance markets typically are composed of some combination of domestic and foreign insurers (or at least foreign-owned insurers). A **domestic insurer** is one domiciled (incorporated) in the concerned country or jurisdiction. Except in the U.S., a **foreign insurer** refers to one domiciled in another country. An insurer's country of domicile is its **home country**. The country in which an insurer conducts business as a foreign insurer is its **host country**.

In the U.S. terminology, a **domestic insurer** is one domiciled in the same state in which it sells insurance. A **foreign insurer** is one domiciled in a U.S. state different (e.g., Georgia) from that in which it sells insurance (e.g., New York). An **alien insurer** is one (incorporated) domiciled in a country other than the U.S. and, thus, is equivalent to a foreign insurer in other countries. The reason for these distinctions in the U.S. is because insurance is regulated by each individual state and not at the national level.

## Insurance Premiums Internationally

The most commonly accepted measure of insurance market size is gross direct written premiums.[2] Globally, gross direct written premiums totaled more than US$3,426 billion in 2005, having experienced a real average annual growth rate of about 5.0 percent over the preceding 10 years. The South and East Asian, Eastern European and Latin American developing countries have experienced particularly strong growth in recent years. Insurance premium growth in emerging markets has been roughly double that of the advanced economies over the preceding two decades, although advanced economies continue to dominate premium writings worldwide.

### Life and nonlife insurance sectors

The life sector accounts for about 58 percent of world direct premiums, with 42 percent from the nonlife sector.[3] Considerable regional diversity exists in the balance between the life and nonlife sectors, as Figure 20.2 suggests. The high proportion of life business for Africa is distorted because of the large South African insurance market, which, in total, accounts for 80 percent of African premiums written, with more than four-fifths of this proportion being life premiums. The high Asian propensity to save via life insurance is revealed. Conversely, the adverse effects of past high inflation rates and political instability have historically depressed Latin American life premium growth, with the situation having changed dramatically for several countries recently.

The life and nonlife sectors continue to evolve quite differently. Growth in life insurance premiums written worldwide continues to be good, driven by increasing life expectancy

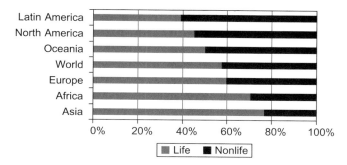

**Figure 20.2**    Share of Life and Nonlife Insurance Premiums Worldwide (2005). *Source*: Swiss Re (2006)

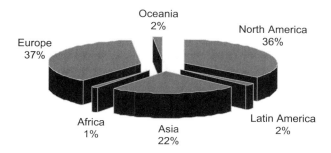

**Figure 20.3**    Distribution of Insurance Premiums by Region (2005). *Source*: Swiss Re (2006)

and governments having to reduce the generosity of social insurance programs in the face of fiscal imbalances. The effects are to substitute private insurance for government insurance, increasing demand for the products sold by life insurers. Thus, the demand for products to protect against the longevity risk, such as annuities and other pension products, has been growing stronger. Favorable stock market results in some countries have further enhanced demand for variable (unit-linked) policies. Conversely, the elimination of tax favoritism in some markets, notably Germany and Russia, penalized growth. Finally, in some countries, a growing loan market has promoted stronger sales of mortgage-related life insurance policies.

   The nonlife sector overall internationally has experienced relatively little growth over the past few years, although several individual markets have witnessed robust growth. In general, we observe that emerging markets have experienced and are expected to continue to experience more rapid nonlife premiums growth than the more mature developed countries' nonlife markets.

### Distribution of premiums worldwide

Figure 20.3 shows the regional distribution of insurance premiums worldwide. Europe was the world's largest insurance market in 2005, accounting for 37.6 percent of total direct premiums written, followed by North America with a 35.7 percent share. Asia's share followed at 22.2 percent, having fallen absolutely and relatively over the past several years because of the difficulties experienced in the Japanese market. Additionally, year-to-year results are distorted because of currency fluctuations. The OECD countries accounted for

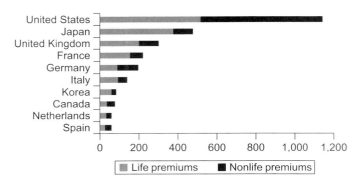

**Figure 20.4**   World's 10 Largest Insurance Markets (2005) ($U.S. billion). *Source*: Swiss Re (2006)

90.8 percent of worldwide insurance premiums written in 2005, with the G7 countries alone having a 74.7 percent world share.

The world's 10 largest national markets are shown in Figure 20.4. The U.S. is the largest, followed by Japan, with the U.K., France and Germany closely bunched thereafter. Note the relatively high share of life business in Japan, France and Korea. The high share for the two Asian countries is attributable to a high propensity to save, favorable tax treatment and less developed capital markets. The high French share is attributable to favorable taxation and to successful *bancassurance* sales.

### The Relative importance of insurance in national economies

Two measures are used traditionally to show the relative importance of insurance within national economies. **Insurance density** indicates the average annual per capita premium within a country. Values are usually converted from national currency to U.S. dollars. As such, currency fluctuations affect comparisons, and this fact can lead to distortions, especially over time. Even so, this measure is a useful indicator of the importance of insurance purchases within national economies.

The other measure, **insurance penetration**, is the ratio of yearly direct premiums written to GDP.[4] It shows roughly the relative importance of insurance within national economies and is unaffected by currency fluctuations. Even so, it does not give a complete picture as it ignores differences in insurance price levels, national product mixes, and other market variations.

Figure 20.5 shows the 10 countries with the highest insurance density for 2005, along with the OECD and E.U. averages. As can be seen, the Swiss per capita expenditure – all in U.S. dollars – of $4,654 is easily the world's highest, with Japan ($3,584), the U.K. ($2,859), the U.S. ($2,723), and The Netherlands ($2,360) following. The OECD average for 2005 was $2,606. The average for the then 25 E.U. member states was $2,460. Note the substantial variations between expenditures for life and nonlife insurance. By contrast, the ASEAN average (not shown in the table) was $60 (inclusive of $39 for life insurance). Low densities are also found in most countries in Africa and Latin America.

Figure 20.6 shows the 10 countries with the highest insurance penetration for 2005. Penetration was highest in Taiwan (14.11 percent), followed by South Africa (13.87 percent) and the U.K. (12.45 percent). The OECD ratio was 8.68 percent with the E.U. at 8.37 percent. Note that the high overall penetration figures are driven by high life insurance

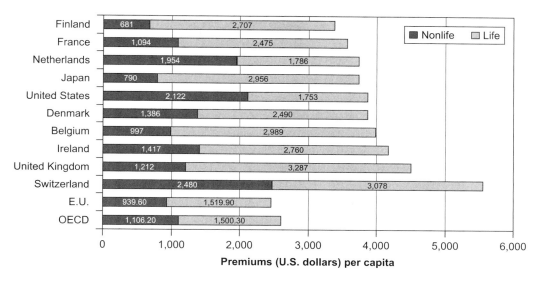

**Figure 20.5**   Ten Countries with Highest Insurance Density (2005). *Source*: Swiss Re (2006)

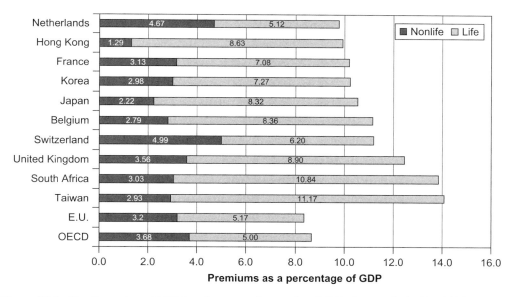

**Figure 20.6**   Ten Countries with Highest Insurance Penetration (2005). *Source*: Swiss Re (2006)

penetration. In part, this reflects the retreat in social insurance generosity plus favorable tax treatment of life insurance and, for Taiwan, South Africa and Korea, also less developed financial markets (i.e., fewer savings options). More information on insurance within individual national markets is given in Chapters 21 and 22.

# THE INTERNATIONAL DIMENSIONS OF INSURANCE SUPPLY

With the increasing globalization of business comes a corresponding increase in size, concentration, and complexity of the risks of MNCs as well as of many purely domestic firms. This requires a mustering of global insurance capacity, for no single market can provide all the needed coverages for personnel, property and liability loss exposures arising from oil refineries, tankers, offshore rigs, satellites, jumbo jets, environmental impairment and scores of other exposures. An international spread is essential if such large risks are to be financed. Also, the only effective means of achieving additional growth for many insurance companies is through international expansion, as their domestic markets – particularly those in many developed countries – may be saturated.

National markets can benefit from a greater international presence as well. They benefit from the increase of domestic market capacity (insurance supply), thereby enhancing competition and providing better consumer value and choice in the market. As with other international operations, knowledge sharing can bring innovative products, production and underwriting techniques, and claims-settling practices. With increasing competition and innovation in insurance, the international competitiveness of domestic firms that purchase insurance is enhanced. Foreign interests can deliver insurance services through either cross-border trade or establishment.

## Cross-Border Insurance Trade

As mentioned in Chapter 1, cross-border insurance trade exists when the buyer purchases (imports) insurance from a firm domiciled in another country. Cross-border insurance trade can take several forms.

- **Pure cross-border insurance trade** exists when the resultant insurance contract is entered into because of solicitations by a foreign insurer. Solicitations may be via direct response or through intermediaries. Pure cross-border insurance typically involves large risks. Not surprisingly, much reinsurance is marketed in this way.

- **Own-initiative cross-border insurance trade** means that the insured initiated the transaction with a foreign insurer. Where permitted, many corporations often seek insurance abroad trying to secure coverage with more favorable terms, conditions or prices than those available locally. Small firms and individuals less frequently will do so. We should make a distinction here between such own-initiative insurance in which the insured has no relationship with the insurer and where the insured owns the foreign insurer (i.e., a captive insurer).

- **Consumption-abroad cross-border insurance trade** occurs when an insured enters into an insurance contract with a local insurer in the country in which the insured is temporarily residing or visiting. For example, travelers may purchase a short-term automobile insurance for rental car. We should note a distinction between such purchases intended to provide coverage only during the length of stay and insurance intended for longer-term coverage.

- As defined in Chapter 14, **difference-in-conditions (DIC)** and **difference-in-limits (DIL)** insurance trade exists when a global firm purchases DIC or DIL coverage as part of its global risk management program. Such policies, usually written in the MNC's home country, may involve coinsurance with foreign or other domestic insurers. As discussed in Chapter 12, coverage may extend to personnel, property and liability exposures of the parent and its foreign affiliates. Affiliates often purchase underlying insurance locally, with the master (excess) insurance contract providing DIL or DIC coverage.

- **Excess and surplus (E&S) insurance**, a hybrid form of cross-border insurance trade, is found in the U.S. It occurs when an insured, denied desired coverage by licensed insurers, places the risk with a nonadmitted insurer. Most U.S. jurisdictions otherwise prohibit such cross-border insurance, even when placed with a U.S. insurer domiciled in another state. Such insurance is placed through specialty domestic E&S brokers. The use by the regulator of white lists (any insurer on the list is acceptable) and black lists (any insurer on the list is unacceptable) is common. This arrangement is not pure nonadmitted insurance as the E&S insurer is licensed in some U.S. jurisdiction.

## Establishment Insurance Trade

Delivery via **establishment insurance trade** exists when the buyer engages in insurance transactions with a domestic, foreign-owned entity. The entity may be an (1) agency, (2) branch, (3) subsidiary or (4) representative office.

- **Agency** exists when a domestic agent represents a foreign insurer for the purposes of making sales and sometimes limited underwriting and claims settlement. As discussed, the agent is not a risk-bearing entity. Neither does it hold nor manage any insurer premiums. Premiums must be forwarded to the insurer and payments to claimants must come from funds held by the insurer in its home country. This form of establishment closely resembles cross-border trade with the principal regulatory responsibility resting with the home-country supervisor, except for marketing practices.

- **Branches** represent more substantial forms of establishment, in that assets to back local reserves for insurance liabilities are usually maintained in the host country. Governments often require local deposits from the foreign insurer equal the minimum capital and surplus requirements applicable to domestic insurers. Nonetheless, branches are not separate corporations but a part of the home-country insurer. As such, branches are subject to dual regulatory oversight.

- **Subsidiaries** are companies owned and established by another company either by purchasing a local firm or incorporating a new company. Thus, the local subsidiary of a foreign insurer is a domestic corporation. It must meet the local minimum capital and surplus requirements and is fully subject to other laws and regulations in the country of operation.

- **Representative offices** conduct market research for, promote the interests of, and sometimes service the local clients of the foreign insurer owner. The representative office neither bears risk nor sells insurance. Within OECD countries, its establishment requires host-country regulatory notification but not approval. In some countries (e.g., China and Vietnam), foreign insurers seeking entry to the market are required to maintain one or more representative offices in the country for a certain minimum period (e.g., two years in the case of China).

**Table 20.2**   Market Share of Foreign-Owned Insurers in Selected Emerging Markets

| Region/Country | Life (%) | Nonlife (%) | Region/Country | Life (%) | Nonlife (%) |
|---|---|---|---|---|---|
| *Asia* | | | *Eastern Europe* | | |
| China | 2 | 1 | Czech Republic | 81 | 89 |
| Hong Kong | 87 | 74 | Hungary | 85 | 89 |
| India* | 0 | 0 | Poland | 52 | 41 |
| Indonesia | 48 | 25 | Slovakia | 97 | 96 |
| Malaysia | 81 | 25 | Slovenia | 17 | 2 |
| Philippines | 61 | 29 | | | |
| Singapore | 58 | 53 | *Africa* | | |
| Taiwan | 33 | 12 | Egypt | 11 | 10 |
| Thailand | 41 | 7 | Morocco | 52 | 28 |
| Vietnam | 56 | 6 | South Africa | 0 | 14 |
| *Latin America* | | | *Middle East* | | |
| Argentina | 53 | 35 | Iran | 0 | 0 |
| Brazil | 32 | 43 | Kuwait | 14 | 14 |
| Chile | 62 | 63 | Lebanon | ≥64 | ≥35 |
| Colombia | 38 | 46 | Turkey | 12 | 7 |
| Mexico | 75 | 58 | | | |
| Venezuela | 39 | 50 | | | |

*Foreign insurance companies are those with a foreign majority ownership stake. Under this definition, India, which does not allow majority ownership by foreign firms, shows zero percent in foreign market share.
*Source*: Swiss Re (2004).

Foreign insurance companies' success within a market varies with the market's structure. Traditionally, they have been most successful in the complex lines, such as reinsurance, large commercial insurance, and marine, aviation and transport (MAT) insurance. Their typical large size, geographic spread of risk, in-depth knowledge of complex risks and management efficiency have enabled them to compete successfully with local firms. Conversely, domestic insurers dominate, with important exceptions, in the less complex personal lines and life insurance. The main reason for this situation relates to restrictive regulation as well as the high information and distribution costs associated with a large number of small risks.

The extent of foreign presence within domestic insurance markets varies greatly worldwide, from nil within closed markets to 100 percent in a few small markets. Table 20.2 shows foreign presence within the life and nonlife insurance markets for selected emerging markets, where the share represents the percentage of market premiums generated by companies whose majority ownership stake is controlled by foreign partners. Shares vary not only from country to country (e.g., Slovakia and China) but also between life and nonlife insurance within many countries (e.g., Thailand and Vietnam).

# THE ROLE OF INSURANCE IN ECONOMIC GROWTH

As suggested in Chapter 2, insurance offers many benefits to risk-averse individuals and executives, including an elusive but important "peace of mind." In fact, insurance offers more tangible benefits. It underpins numerous private undertakings.

This section explores the question as to how insurance supports economic growth. We first examine the relationship between private insurance and property rights, for private financial services can flourish only where such rights are well developed and impartially enforced. We then examine the relationship between financial and economic development. Finally, we explore the theoretical benefits and costs of insurance to national economies.

## Property Rights and Economic Development

Countries that provide their citizens with stronger property rights experience greater economic growth, *ceteris paribus*. Private property rights include (1) the right to own and alienate real and personal property, (2) the right to contract and (3) the right to be compensated for damage resulting from the tortuous conduct of others. Hence, government's responsibility is to establish a system to protect property rights and resolve-related disputes (e.g., through a court system). Without a well-defined system of private property rights and a means to enforce these rights, markets do not function well. Markets are, after all, simply means of exchanging property rights.

Similarly, private financial services will not flourish unless individuals' ownership interests in property are well defined and protected. Thus, legal environments that provide strong investor protections are associated with great reliance on financial intermediation and economic growth.[5] Additionally, Levine et al. (2000) note that countries with stronger creditor rights and law enforcement and more transparent financial information tend to have more highly developed financial intermediaries. Certain governmental action can diminish the value of such ownership interests. For example, if individuals know or expect government to indemnify them for earthquake, flood and other catastrophic losses, they have less incentive to provide for their own protection through the purchase of private insurance. Likewise, if government makes available generous retirement, disability and other personal benefits, individuals have less incentive to provide for themselves.

Usually, any action that diminishes the value of one's ownership interest in private property hinders private financial services development. More subtle are indirect government actions that diminish value such as a failure to control inflation (which diminishes the value of savings), high income tax rates (which diminish the value of earnings), substantial trade restrictions (which diminish purchasing power) and poor fiscal policy leading to currency devaluation (which diminishes purchasing power).

Private property rights, however, are restrictive by their nature. Without some restraints, their complete exercise could actually interfere with the efficient functioning of markets. The prohibitions on monopolies that are common worldwide are restraints on private property rights. Insider trading prohibitions restrict one's use of private information. Property rights are not unlimited.

## Financial Development and Economic Growth

As financial intermediaries, insurance companies perform the same types of functions and provide similar generic benefits to a national economy as other financial intermediaries. At the same time, their role in individual and corporate risk management means that their contributions to economic development will not precisely overlap with those of other financial intermediaries.

Financial services generally and insurance in particular are of primordial importance to economic development.[6] At first, however, economists considered that economic growth was driven mainly by labor and capital inputs. When it was found that these two factors alone left much of economic growth unexplained, economists added technology to their equations, thereby increasing their explanatory power but with troubling gaps remaining.

Some of these gaps, so it turns out, can be explained by endogenous growth theory that investment and growth of one sector of an economy can provide positive externalities to other sectors. Several researchers have demonstrated that financial services offer the possibility of providing such externalities, thereby enhancing economic growth.[7] Thus, nonlife insurance, life insurance and banking are all shown to be important predictors of economic productivity. Additionally, evidence exists of synergies among financial intermediaries. Each sector fuels economic growth independently, but they collectively provide greater growth impetus than suggested by merely summing their component contributions.

Thus, the more developed and efficient a country's financial market, the greater will be its contribution to economic prosperity. It is for this reason that governments should foster greater competition among financial service providers, while ensuring that the market is regulated appropriately and is financially sound.

## The Benefits of Insurance in Economic Growth

It is wrong to view insurance as a simple pass-through mechanism for diversifying risk under which the unfortunate few who suffer losses are indemnified from the funds the insurer collects from many insureds.[8] Laudable though it is, this function masks other fundamental contributions that insurance makes to prosperity. That is, insurance:

- promote financial stability;
- substitutes for and complements government security programs;
- facilitates trade and commerce;
- helps mobilize savings;
- enables risk to be managed more efficiently;
- encourages loss mitigation;
- fosters a more efficient capital allocation.

Countries that are best at harnessing these contributions give their citizens and businesses greater economic opportunities. We examine each of the contributions below.

### *Promotes financial stability*

Insurance helps stabilize the financial situation of individuals, families and organizations. It accomplishes this task by indemnifying those who suffer loss or harm. Without insurance, individuals and families could become financially destitute and forced to seek assistance from relatives, friends or the government. Businesses that incur significant uninsured losses may suffer major financial reverses or even fail. Besides the loss in value of the owners' stake in the business occasioned by an uninsured loss, the firm's future contribution to the economy is reduced or foregone. Employees lose jobs, suppliers lose business, customers forgo the opportunity to buy from the firm, and government loses tax revenues. The stability provided by insurance encourages individuals and firms to invest and create wealth.

### *Substitutes for and complements government security programs*

Insurance, especially life insurance, can substitute for government security programs. Private insurance also complements public security programs. It, thus, can relieve pressure on social insurance systems, preserving government resources for essential social security and other worthwhile purposes and allowing individuals to tailor their security programs to their own preferences. Studies have confirmed that greater private expenditures on life insurance are associated with a reduction in government expenditures on social insurance programs. This substitution role is especially important because of the growing financial challenges faced by national social insurance systems.

### Facilitates trade and commerce

As discussed in Chapters 2 and 19, large businesses whose ownership interests are widely dispersed conceptually have little need to purchase insurance. Of course, not all businesses are large, and ownership is not always widely dispersed even in large firms. Yet, even most large, broadly owned firms purchase insurance.

Further, many products and services are produced and sold only if adequate liability insurance is available to cover any claims for negligence. Insurance coverage may be a condition for engaging in a particular activity, for example, operation of an airplane. Because of the high risk of new business failure, venture capitalists often make funds available only if tangible assets and the entrepreneurs' lives are adequately insured. Entrepreneurs are more likely to create and expand their business ventures if they can secure adequate insurance protection. Insurance underpins much of the world's trade, commerce and entrepreneurial activity.

These facts are unsurprising. Modern economies are built on specialization and its inherent productivity improvements. Greater trade and commercial specialization demand, in turn, greater financial specialization and flexibility. Without a wide insurance product choice and continuing service and pricing innovations, insurance inadequacies could stifle both trade and commerce.

Insurance also underpins business activity by enhancing the creditworthiness of customers. Thus, banks and other creditors typically insist that loan collateral be insured or they will not make the loan (or charge for risk through a higher interest rate). They also may require the purchase of life insurance on the principal wage earner's life for personal loans or on the lives of key employees for business loans. In these ways insurance serves as a "lubricant of commerce."

### Helps mobilize savings

The general financial services literature emphasizes the important role of savings in economic growth. Savings can be either financial or non-financial. Non-financial savings take the form of real assets such as land, jewelry, buildings, etc. Financial savings are held in financial assets such as savings accounts, bonds, shares, annuities and life insurance policies. Generally, the more economically developed a country, the greater the proportion of its total wealth in financial savings. This result is consistent with the view that financial development and overall economic development move in tandem.

#### Insurers and financial intermediation

Insurers, especially life insurers, offer the same advantages as other financial intermediaries in channeling savings into domestic investment. Studies have shown that, on average, countries that save more tend to grow faster.[9] Indeed, insurers play an important role in channeling savings into domestic investment. Insurers enhance financial system efficiency in three ways. First, as financial intermediaries, insurers reduce transaction costs associated with bringing together savers and borrowers. Thousands of individuals each pay relatively small life insurance premiums, part of which typically represents savings. The insurers invest these amassed funds as loans to businesses and other ventures. In performing this intermediation function, direct lending and investing by individual policyholders, which would be exceptionally time-consuming and costly, is avoided.

Second, insurers create liquidity. They borrow short term and lend long term. "Borrowing" for insurers means that they use funds entrusted to them by their policyholders to make loans and other investments. Both life and nonlife insurers stand ready to provide policyholders (and third party beneficiaries) with instant liquidity if a covered event occurs. Additionally, life insurers stand ready to provide policyholders with some or all of the savings accumulated within their policies.

The creation of liquidity allows policyholders to have immediate access to loss payments and savings while borrowers need not repay their loans immediately. If all individuals instead undertook direct lending, they likely would find unacceptable the proportion of their personal wealth held in long-term, illiquid assets. Insurers and other financial intermediaries, thereby, reduce the illiquidity inherent in direct lending.

Third, insurers facilitate economies of scale in investment. Some investment projects are quite large, thus requiring correspondingly large amounts of financing. Such large projects often enjoy economies of scale, promote specialization and stimulate technological innovations and therefore can be particularly important to economic growth. By amassing large sums from thousands of smaller premium payers, insurers can often meet the financing needs of such large projects, thereby aiding growth by enlarging the set of feasible investment projects and encouraging economic efficiency.

*Financial intermediaries versus financial markets*

In general, the more developed a country's financial system, the greater the reliance on markets and the less the reliance on intermediaries. Indeed, financial intermediaries would not exist if these three conditions were met: (1) the users and providers of funds had complete information about each other, (2) the borrowing/lending functions were frictionless and (3) monitoring was costless. In such an idealized world, all risks could be exchanged at little or no transactions costs in financial markets in which both buyers and sellers possessed all the information they needed about possible future "states of the world." The closer a financial market comes to achieving these three ideals, the more complete it is and the more important will be the financial market compared with financial intermediaries, *ceteris paribus*. (For this reason, many clever people are working diligently to lower information, transaction and monitoring costs in insurance with the goal of utilizing the financial market to cover some insurance risks.)

Financial markets are more sophisticated in developed countries and, therefore, are of greater importance in such countries than in emerging economies. Even so, financial intermediaries in all countries are more likely to be providers of investment funds than are financial markets. Only firms of a certain minimum size typically can tap into securities markets. Comparatively few such companies exist in emerging markets. Because of this fact and because financial markets are less incomplete in developed countries, one would expect financial intermediaries, such as insurers, to play a relatively greater role in investment finance in emerging markets than in developed countries.

*Insurers versus other financial intermediaries*

A well-developed financial system will have a myriad of financial institutions and instruments. The greater the variety, *ceteris paribus*, the more efficient the system and the greater its contribution to economic growth.

Contractual savings institutions, such as life insurers and private pension funds, can be especially important financial intermediaries in emerging markets. In contrast with commercial banks, which often specialize in collecting short-term deposits and extending short-term credit, contractual saving institutions usually take a longer-term view. Their longer-term liabilities and stable cash flows are ideal sources of long-term finance for government and business.

## Enables risk to be managed more efficiently

Financial systems and intermediaries price risk and provide for risk transformation, pooling and reduction. The better is a financial system in providing these various risk management services, the greater the saving and investment stimulation and the more efficiently are resources allocated.

### Risk pricing

A competitive market's success depends on pricing. Price is the basis for allocating society's limited resources, thereby ensuring that they are used for maximum societal benefit. The pricing of risk is fundamental to all financial intermediaries and is no less important to their resource allocation than to any other supplier of goods or services.

Insurers price risk at two levels. First, through their insurance activities, insurers evaluate the loss potential of businesses, persons and property for which they might provide insurance. The greater the expected loss potential, the higher the price. In evaluating loss potential, insurers attempt to quantify the consequences of insureds' risk-causing and risk-reduction activities and, thus, cause them to deal with risk more rationally. Investors in projects judged too risky for insurance at any price are put on notice and should rationally expect returns commensurate with the high risk. When governments interfere with accurate insurance pricing, they distort the allocation of insurance and therefore other resources.

Second, through their investment activities, insurers evaluate the creditworthiness of those to whom they extend loans and the likely business success of those in which they invest. By these activities, business owners, potential investors, customers, creditors, employees, and other stakeholders can be better informed about the firm's overall risk characteristics and thereby make better decisions.

### Risk transformation

Insurance permits businesses and individuals to transform their risk exposures to suit their own needs better. Many property, liability, loss of income and other risk exposures can be transferred to an insurer for a price and, in the process, the insured's risk profile changed. Moreover, life insurers, by tailoring contracts to the needs of different clients, help individuals and businesses transform the characteristics of their savings to the liquidity, security and other risk profile desired. Moral hazard and adverse selection problems arise for insurers in this risk transformation process, as discussed in Chapters 3 and 19.

*Risk pooling and reduction*

Risk pooling and reduction lie at the heart of the insurance mechanism and, as with risk pricing, occur at two levels. First, in aggregating many individual risk exposures, insurers rely on the law of large numbers to permit them to make reasonably accurate estimates as to the pool's overall losses. Of course, they cannot predict which insureds will have losses, but they do not require this for the scheme to function efficiently.

Overall, the larger the number of insureds, the more stable and predictable will be the insurer's loss experience, as explained in Chapter 19. This fact leads to a reduction in expected loss volatility and, by that, permits the supplier to charge a lower price for its risk transfer services and potentially to maintain more stable premium income.

Second, insurers also benefit from pooling through their investment activities. In providing funds to a broad range of enterprises and individuals, insurers diversify their investment portfolios. The default or bankruptcy of a few borrowers is likely to be offset by many sound investments. The more stable and predictable an insurer's investment experience, the less it can charge for loans.

## Encourages loss mitigation

Insurance companies worldwide have economic incentives to help insureds prevent and reduce losses. Moreover, their detailed statistical and other knowledge about loss-causing events, activities and processes affords them a competitive advantage over other companies in loss assessment and control. If pricing is tied to loss experience, insureds have economic incentives to control losses.

Insurers support many loss control programs, typical of which are fire prevention; occupational health and safety; industrial loss prevention; reduction in automobile property damage, theft and injury; and literally dozens of other loss control activities and programs. These activities and programs reduce both direct and indirect losses to businesses and individuals and complement good risk management. Society as a whole benefits from the reduction of such losses.

Of course, not all losses can or should be prevented. The costs of loss mitigation activities must always be weighed against its direct and indirect benefits.

## Fosters a more efficient capital allocation

Insurers gather substantial information to conduct their evaluations of firms, projects and managers both in deciding whether (and at what price) to issue insurance and in their roles as lenders and investors. While individual savers and investors may not have time, resources or ability to undertake this information gathering and processing, insurers have an advantage in this regard and are better at allocating financial capital and insurance risk bearing capacity. Insurers will choose to insure and to provide funds to the most attractive companies, projects and managers.

Because insurers have a continuing interest in the companies, projects and managers to whom they provide financial capital or risk bearing capacity, they have an incentive to monitor them to reduce the chances that they engage in unacceptable risk-increasing behavior. Insurers thus encourage them to act in the best interests of their various stakeholders (customers, stockholders, creditors, etc.). In other words, insurers and other financial intermediaries can help resolve a principal-agent problem. By doing so, insurers tangibly signal

the market's approval of promising, well-managed firms and foster a more efficient allocation of scarce financial capital and risk bearing capacity. National financial systems that
impose minimum constraints on insurers' abilities to gather and evaluate information in this
way should realize a more efficient allocation of capital and therefore stronger economic
growth.[10]

## The costs of insurance to society

Although insurance offers great social and economic benefits, it also entails societal costs.
First, insurers incur sales, servicing, administration and investment management expenses.
These expenses are an indispensable part of doing business, but increase the cost of insurance. The higher are such expenses, the less efficient are insurers, other things being the
same, and the less insurance will be sold.

Second, the existence of insurance encourages moral hazard. Moral hazard can manifest
itself in mere carelessness, with attendant higher losses than otherwise. Some individuals
deliberately destroy or damage property to collect insurance proceeds. From 5 to 15 percent of all nonlife claims are believed to be fraudulent in Germany, Spain, Italy, Austria,
Finland and the U.S. Each year, some insureds are murdered for life insurance proceeds.[11]
All such behavior causes premiums to be higher than they would be otherwise, represents a deadweight loss to society, can lead to disruptions in otherwise well-functioning
markets, and truly is a societal cost of insurance.

# DETERMINANTS OF INSURANCE MARKET STRUCTURE

National insurance markets have evolved to suit each country's particular environment. The
interaction of supply and demand forces determines market structures. Price and innumerable economic, social and cultural factors influence the demand for insurance. Insurance
supply is molded by price and, to a great degree, by a market's risk-bearing capacity and
government regulation.

Some influences are logically predictable. For example, we would expect comparatively
lower demand for insurance in the least developed countries, with the demand increasing with economic development. Similarly, we would expect developed market-economy
countries, which rely more on private sector operations, to exhibit a correspondingly higher
demand for private insurance.

## Price

Of course, price is determined by the interaction of the forces of demand and supply.
From the insurer's perspective, its prices are influenced by its cost structures, by the competitiveness of the particular line of insurance, and by government tax and other policy.
Unfortunately, what constitutes the price of insurance is not so easy to define, so researchers have used proxies for price that, while not completely satisfactory, nonetheless allow us
to gain insight into the effect of price on quantity demanded.

**Table 20.3**   Price and Income Elasticities for Selected Insurance Lines

|  | Price Elasticity | Income (GDP) Elasticity |
|---|---|---|
| Germany | | |
|    Industrial Fire | −0.2 to −0.3 | 1.5–2.0 |
| Chile | | |
|    Fire | −0.9 to −1.2 | 3.0 to 4.0 |
|    Earthquake | −1.0 | 3.0 |
|    Marine | −1.0 | 2.0 to 2.5 |
|    Motor | −0.8 | 2.8 |
| Japan | | |
|    Fire | −1.0 | 1.7 |
| United States | | |
|    Group Life | −0.7 | 2.0 to 2.5 |

*Source*: Swiss Re (1993).

To explore the effect of price on insurance consumption, we need to understand **price elasticity** of demand which is the percentage change in demand for a good or service that results from a given percentage change in price; in formula format:

$$\text{Price elasticity} = \frac{\Delta Q}{Q} \div \frac{\Delta P}{P}$$

In theory, price elasticity can range from zero (perfectly inelastic) to minus infinity. In practice, price elasticities typically range from zero to about minus two. Of course, price elasticities ordinarily carry a negative sign as the quantity demanded can be expected to decrease (increase) as prices increase (decrease). A price elasticity of −1.0, therefore, means that a given change in price can be expected to evoke a precisely proportionate negative change in quantity demanded; thus, a 1.0 percent price increase (decrease) should lead to a 1.0 percent decrease (increase) in quantity demanded.

In life insurance, one researcher (Babbel, 1985) calculated the price elasticity of whole life insurance policies issued in the U.S., using various price measures. Under this study, new sales were negatively related to prices, as expected, with elasticities ranging from −0.32 to −0.92, depending on policy type and the price measure used. Another study, using a different approach, estimated an elasticity of −0.24 (Browne and Kim, 1993). A study that examined the price elasticity of group life insurance demand in the U.S. found it to be −0.7; meaning that a 10 percent increase (decrease) in price could be expected to cause a 7 percent decrease (increase) in quantity ($1,000 face amount units) demanded (Swiss Re, 1993).

Results of a study that explores the effects of price changes on insurance demand by insurance type across countries are shown in Table 20.3. As the authors point out, we should not view the elasticities as precise values, but as indicative of an order of magnitude. We observe that, based on this methodology, price has an important effect on nonlife insurance demand. For some lines in some countries, it has a substantial effect.

In examining the nature of retail nonlife insurance purchases, we observe that personal automobile, homeowner's and other retail lines of insurance tend overwhelmingly to be purchased from domestic firms. The same is true of retail life insurance. The typical purchaser of retail insurance seems to reveal a preference for better known, locally regulated companies (Browne et al., 2000). In this sense, well-known firms should enjoy a competitive advantage over less-known new entrants.

In large part, this revealed preference for local firms may be government driven. Personal automobile liability insurance is compulsory in most countries worldwide, and domestic laws typically limit the purchase of compulsory insurance to locally licensed companies. The logic for this requirement is that such insurance, being closely related to public policy and the protection of innocent third parties, requires the utmost in government scrutiny – which cannot be adequately achieved with unlicensed companies, especially when they do not hold any of their assets locally.

The typical corporate insurance consumer is better informed than the typical retail consumer and can better protect its own interest. As such, demand for at least some types of corporate insurance is often less domestically oriented if foreign insurers have reasonable market access (Browne et al., 2000). Also, large commercial and industrial companies have more options than do individuals. If insurers fail to offer terms or prices that these companies believe they need and warrant, they may form their own captive insurer. They thereby gain access to the wholesale insurance market (reinsurance) and exercise greater control over cash flow and insurance coverage.

## Economic Factors

Numerous economic factors influence insurance consumption. Among those found to be the most consistently important is the level of a country's economic development. We discuss below these factors in terms of income and inflation.

### *Income*

The level of an economy's income seems to be the most important factor in explaining the level of insurance consumption.[12] The higher an economy's income, other things being equal, the more it spends on all types of insurance. Also, at the microeconomic level, the higher a household's income, the greater the insurance consumption.

If we assume that countries follow a similar development path, a reasonable conclusion from the studies is that the income elasticity of insurance premiums is greater than 1.0 (see Table 20.3). The **income elasticity of insurance premiums** tells us the relative change in insurance premiums written for a given change in national income. An interesting finding by Ward and Zurbruegg (2000) is that life insurance consumption in Asia is three times more sensitive to changes in income than in OECD countries.

Studies suggest that the elasticity itself varies with level of income.[13] Figure 20.7 provides a conceptual way of visualizing this relationship. Thus, for the least developed countries, the ratio of premiums written to GDP is fairly low. For mid-income countries, the ratio begins to rise rapidly; that is, the income elasticity is higher. For economically advanced economies, the ratio of premiums to GDP seems to flatten out (and therefore, the elasticity declines relative to mid-income countries) as consumers presumably have need for only so much insurance and, at higher incomes, have many more alternatives to insurance, including retention.

### *Inflation*

Inflation rates influence insurance consumption. Inflation has long been considered as detrimental to life insurance supply and demand, and studies confirm this intuition.[14] In

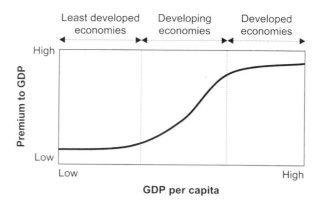

**Figure 20.7**  Stylized Relationship between Insurance and Economic Development

times of high inflation and significant economic volatility, consumers seek shorter-term, more liquid investments and avoid longer-term, fixed commitments. Traditional cash-value insurance products have been perceived as long-term, fixed commitments, and, therefore, demand for them shrinks during inflationary or volatile times.

Another interesting finding of the Ward and Zurbruegg (2000) study is that inflation's affect seems to vary by region. They show that inflation's affect is about 2½ times more important to life insurance demand in Asian economies than in OECD economies.

## Demographic Factors

Changes in demographics affect insurance consumption. For example, the age of first marriage, for both men and women, is increasing in many countries, while the years of higher education lengthen. Married couples that have children – and many choose not to do so – are having fewer of them. Dual-income families are more common, as are single-parent families. The fitness trend results in healthier insureds, but also sometimes in a perception of less need for life and health insurance. These and other demographic trends should be expected to affect insurance demand.

### Aging populations

That much of the world's population is aging is well recognized, as discussed in Chapter 7. As a consequence, increasing proportions of individuals in many societies are elderly, with prospects for even greater population aging in the future. Increasing life expectancy is predicted to translate into a greater demand for savings-based life insurance products as well as for long-term care insurance. Moreover, longer life is hypothesized to translate into lower priced, death-based life insurance, which should stimulate sales to the segment of populations needing such coverage. Research results are generally consistent with these expectations.[15]

### Education

The educational level of a population or of a household is believed by many to affect insurance consumption. The expectation is that the more educated or literate a population or household the greater the likelihood of understanding the need for insurance. However, research findings are inconsistent, with some supporting and others not supporting this view.

### Household structure

The structure of households continues to evolve worldwide. The nuclear family accounts for a declining majority of households in most developed countries. Research findings suggest, unsurprisingly, that life insurance demand increases as the number of young children in the household increases, other things being the same.[16]

### Industrialization and urbanization

By revolutionizing agricultural production, the plow altered societies worldwide. The production of goods and services thus grew in importance and with it arose ever-larger mining, manufacturing and commercial enterprises. Business and employment specialization became more important, thus rendering individuals more reliant on trade to obtain that which they and their families no longer produced themselves. However, specialization implies vulnerability.

Industrialization brings urbanization which in turn brings about a new social order where the predominant economic and social security formerly provided by family, friends and acquaintances is replaced to varying degrees by formal public and private arrangements and a necessity for greater financial self-reliance. Research has documented the positive relationship between industrialization and urbanization and insurance consumption.

## Social Factors

Cultural perceptions of the role of insurance products can vary substantially, as noted in Chapter 11. In many countries, especially in Asia, life products are sought primarily as savings instruments, and this is consistent with a high cultural propensity to save. In other countries, especially those that are predominantly Muslim, insurance is sometimes viewed as inappropriate because of religious beliefs (although products and insurer operations can be made to comport fully with these beliefs). Research has documented less insurance of all types is consumed in countries that are predominantly Muslim.[17]

In some cultures and with certain relationships (e.g., as between close friends), it might be socially unacceptable to refuse the offer to purchase insurance, because saying no is considered impolite. Too often, in such circumstances, the policy is purchased, but is terminated shortly thereafter. This has been a particularly difficult issue in Korea, for example.

## Political and Legal Factors

Research has established that improvements in a country's political environment enhance insurance demand. Conversely, an unstable political environment depresses insurance demand. Such an environment means that private property rights, human rights or both, including due process, are less secure. Therefore, the non-insurance-related decisions made by public policymakers – regulatory agencies, the courts, the legislature and others – have a profound impact on all financial services, including insurance.

Governments make decisions that directly affect insurance demand and supply. As expected, research has established an inverse relationship between private insurance consumption and the generosity of public economic security services; that is, the more important is public economic security sources, the less important are private-sector sources, other things being the same. Governments also determine what insurance products can be sold, who can sell them and how they can be sold. Indeed, government often spurs insurance demand by making the purchase of some types compulsory or affording tax concessions to the purchase of some types of insurance.

Thus, insurance regulators worldwide typically determine whether a given insurance product can be sold within their jurisdiction through a policy review and approval process. Similarly, tax laws and the premium approval process greatly influence product design, availability and value. For example, most countries' laws permit a tax-deferred accumulation of interest on life product cash values. Repeal of this benefit would undoubtedly decrease the attractiveness of cash-value insurance policies.

Other aspects of the legal environment seem to have a profound affect on insurance. Ward and Zurbruegg's (2000) study showed that an improvement in legal systems had a significant and positive affect on life insurance demand, with a 10 percent improvement in the functioning of the system generating a 5½ percent increase in life insurance demand. Interestingly, they found no significant affect for the OECD countries, likely because their legal systems are mature and do not vary significantly. Esho et al. (2004) show a strong positive relationship between the protection of property rights and nonlife insurance demand.

### Globalization

The continuing globalization of financial services adds a new dimension to insurance consumption, especially for markets that have been highly restrictive regarding new entrants. Countries can no longer view themselves as isolated economic islands.

With increasing internationalization can come increased capital from abroad, product and marketing innovations, and different ways of managing companies. Increased capital strengthens the financial capacity of insurance companies and can result in more competition and therefore consumption. Product and marketing innovations and different management styles can lead to greater consumer choice and value. The trend toward greater market internationalization almost certainly affects insurance consumption, although to date, research on this issue is sparse and somewhat inconclusive.[18]

## CONCLUSION

This chapter has set out key functional areas of insurance operations, provided an overview of the importance of insurance worldwide, examined the determinants of insurance market structures and explored how insurance promotes national economic growth. Clearly, however, our knowledge of these aspects remains basic. Hence, a deeper understanding of the determinants of market structure could aid insurance and reinsurance companies in their expansion efforts, national governments in deciding how best to foster insurance markets for the greatest benefit for citizens, and, of course, consumers themselves.

## DISCUSSION QUESTIONS

1.  For what reasons might two countries with roughly equivalent levels of per capita incomes exhibit vastly different insurance density and penetration figures?

2. With a few important exceptions, U.S. insurers seem to have less interest in international expansion than do many European insurers. Suggest some historical, cultural and other reasons that might explain this situation.

3. The life cycle hypothesis discussed in Chapter 2 suggests that individuals' savings decisions are influenced by their location within their life cycle. Thus, during pre-adult years, we are net dissavers. During our early working years, we save some but usually to acquire durables. During our later working years, we tend to focus much more intensely on saving for retirement. During retirement, we tend to draw down savings.

   (a) Of what benefit might this hypothesis be to a life insurer contemplating expansion into other markets?

   (b) Of what benefit might this hypothesis be to a government thinking about how to encourage personal saving for retirement?

4. What specific economic, social, demographic and political factors do you find have affected consumption of (a) life insurance and (b) nonlife insurance in your country? Do you also find globalization of financial systems in general and insurance in particular has affected insurance consumption in the country? Justify your answer..

## NOTES

1. This chapter draws from Skipper (1998), Chapters 4 and 5.
2. All international insurance premium data are from Swiss Re (2006).
3. The data source follows the European convention of including health and accident premiums in the nonlife category.
4. The ratio does not measure the contribution of insurance to GDP as it includes the pure intermediation function of claims and related payments.
5. La Porta et al. (1997, 2000) and Levine (1998, 1999).
6. For example, Webb (2000) investigated the mechanisms by which insurance and banking jointly stimulate economic growth.
7. See Hussels, Ward and Zurbruegg (2005) for a discussion.
8. This section draws on Levine (1996).
9. Of course, this finding does not suggest that every country with a high savings rate will have a high growth rate. Countries whose financial systems are inefficient are less likely to achieve high growth rates even with high savings rates.

10. This statement is not intended to suggest that all limitations on insurers' information gathering and evaluation are inappropriate. For example, government may conclude that certain types of information (e.g., religion or race) should not be collected because of concerns about unfair discrimination.
11. The purpose of underwriting individually issued life insurance policies is to discourage and detect moral hazard and adverse selection. Legal requirements that the applicant have an insurable interest in the life of the proposed insured also are intended to minimize adverse selection (e.g., murder) by the beneficiary, but neither approach can be totally successful.
12. See Hussels et al. (2005) for discussion of the studies.
13. Enz (2000) and Ward and Zurbruegg (2000).
14. See Hussels et al. (2005) for discussion of the studies.
15. Ibid.
16. Ibid.
17. Ibid.
18. See Ma and Pope (2003) and Browne et al. (2000).

## REFERENCES

Babbel, D. (1985). "The Price Elasticity of Demand for Whole Life Insurance," *Journal of Finance*, 40 (1): 225–239.

Browne, M., Chung, J.W. and Frees, E. (2000). "International Property-Liability Insurance Consumption," *Journal of Risk and Insurance*, 67: 73–90.

Browne, M.J. and Kim, K. (1993). "An International Analysis of Life Insurance Demand," *Journal of Risk and Insurance*, 60: 616–634.

Enz, R. (2000). "The S Curve Relations Between Percapita Income and Insurance Penetration," *Geneva Papers on Risk and Insurance: Issues and Practice*, 25: 396–406.

Esho, N., Kirievsky, A., Ward, D. and Zurbruegg, R. (2004). "Law and the Determinants of Property-Casualty Insurance," *Journal of Risk and Insurance*, 71: 265–283.

Hussels, S., Ward, D. and Zurbruegg, R. (2005). "Stimulating the Demand for Insurance," *Risk Management and Insurance Review*, 8: 257–278.

Insurance Information Institute (III) (2006). *The Financial Services Fact Book*. New York: III.

La Porta, R., Lopez-de-Silanes, F., Shleifer, A. and Vishney, R. (1997). "Legal Determinants of External Finance," *Journal of Finance*, 52: 1131–1150.

La Porta, R., Lopez-de-Silanes, F., Shleifer, A. and Vishney, R. (2000). "Investor Protection and Corporate Governance," *Journal of Financial Economics*, 58: 3–27.

Levine, R. (1996). "Foreign Banks, Financial Development, and Economic Growth," in C.E. Barfield, ed., *International Financial Markets*. Washington, DC: The AEI Press.

Levine, R. (1998). "The Legal Environment, Banks, and Long-Run Economic Growth," *Journal of Money, Credit and Banking*, 30: 596–620.

Levine, R. (1999). "Law, Finance, and Economic Growth," *Journal of Financial Intermediation*, 8: 8–35.

Levine, R., Loayza, N. and Beck, T. (2000). "Financial Intermediation and Growth: Causality and Causes," *Journal of Monetary Economics*, 46: 31–77.

Ma, Y.L. and Pope, N. (2003). "Determinants of International Insurers' Participation in Foreign Nonlife Markets," *Journal of Risk and Insurance*, 70: 235–248.

Skipper, H.D. (1998). "Risk Management and Insurance in Economic Development" and "The Structure of Insurance Markets Worldwide," in H.D. Skipper, ed., *International Risk and Insurance: An Environmental-Managerial Approach.* Boston, MA: Irwin/McGrew-Hill.

Swiss Re (1993). "The Effects of Price Adjustment on Insurance Demand," *Sigma*, Zurich: Swiss Re.

Swiss Re (2004). "Exploiting the Growth potential of Emerging Insurance Markets," Sigma, Zurich: Swiss Re.

Swiss Re (2006). "World Insurance in 2005," *Sigma.* Zurich: Swiss Re.

Ward, D. and Zurbruegg, R. (2000). "Does Insurance Promote Economic Growth? Evidence from OECD Countries," *Journal of Risk and Insurance*, 67: 489–507.

Webb, I.P. (2000). *The Effect of Banking and Insurance on the Growth of Capital and Output*, Unpublished Ph.D. dissertation, Georgia State University.

# Chapter 21

# Life Insurance

## INTRODUCTION

The risk transfer aspect of life insurance dates back more than 2,500 years to Greek societies and, more recently, to 16th century England. At that time, individuals served as insurers, so the guaranty was no better than the individual's financial solidity. Life insurance involving a contract to pay money to a beneficiary on the death of the insured has, by comparison, existed for but a brief period.

The emergence of corporate firms in the U.K. in the late 17th and early 18th centuries coupled with the availability of adequate mortality statistics and the development of sound actuarial principles marked the birth of modern life insurance. The introduction of the agency system of marketing using commissioned salespersons gave further impetus to life insurance growth. Today, life insurance companies are found in every country and the products provided by these companies are important sources of national economic security.

This chapter begins a two-chapter examination of insurance policies and markets. Here we introduce the various products sold by life insurers internationally and examine the importance of life insurance in selected countries. The following chapter on nonlife insurance parallels this one.

## POLICIES SOLD BY LIFE INSURANCE COMPANIES

Life insurance is purchased by either individuals or organizations.[1] As noted in Chapter 1, if purchased by individuals, we refer to it as *personal insurance*.[2] If purchased by organizations, we refer to it as *commercial insurance* or, if related exclusively to a group such as employees or society members, as *group insurance*.[3] Personal insurance sales dominate group insurance sales in most markets worldwide.

As we know, insurance companies sell policies whose payments are *contingent* on the happening of some event. Historically, policies sold by life insurers involved only **life contingencies**, meaning that payments to policyholders or their beneficiaries are determined by whether insureds are alive or dead. **Mortality tables** show yearly probabilities of death by age (and sometimes by other variables) and are necessary for pricing these policies.

Life insurance companies also sell policies whose payments are *contingent* on whether insureds become incapacitated, sick or injured. **Morbidity tables** show yearly or other probabilities and durations of incapacity, sickness or injury by age (or age brackets) and are necessary for pricing these policies.

Typical policies sold by life insurance companies worldwide can be classified as being either mortality based or morbidity based, depending on their underlying statistical source. Recall from Chapter 1 that we classified the life branch as selling insurance to cover (1) death, (2) living to a certain age, (3) incapacity and (4) injury or disease. We can see that the first two classifications are mortality based and the last two are morbidity based.

Definitions within the life branch are not always consistent internationally. Thus, in some countries, such as Canada, the U.S. and several Asian countries, life insurance includes both mortality and morbidity-based insurance whether issued to an individual or organization. In other countries, including throughout Europe, morbidity-based insurance typically falls within the nonlife branch. We follow the former convention in this book.

## Mortality-Based Insurance Policies

Mortality-based insurance policies fall into two classes. Policies that pay a benefit if the insured dies during the policy term are commonly labeled as *life insurance policies* or *life assurance policies*. The latter term is commonly used in the U.K. and other Commonwealth countries. Policies that pay a benefit if the insured survives for a prescribed time or to a certain age are commonly labeled *annuities* (or *pensions*) or *endowments*.[4] As endowments usually pay a death benefit, they are commonly considered a life insurance policies, and our discussion follows this tradition.

This terminology is potentially a bit confusing as the branch of private insurance called *life insurance* includes not just *life insurance policies*, but also annuities and endowments as well as the morbidity-based policies discussed in the next section. Similarly, *life insurance companies* are insurers that may write any mortality or morbidity-based policy.

### Life insurance policies

Life insurance policies pay a death benefit as a stated sum of money – called the **face amount** or **sum assured** – on the death of the insured. The **insured** is the individual whose death triggers payment of the face amount. The person who applies for the policy is the **applicant**. In most instances, the applicant is also the proposed insured, but sometimes the applicant is someone else, as when a parent applies for a policy on a child's life. In these and other such circumstances, the policyowner is someone other than the insured. The **policyowner** or **policyholder** is the person who can exercise all policy rights and with whom the insurer deals. The applicant names someone – the **beneficiary** – to receive the face amount on the death of the insured. Of course, premiums must be paid for the policy to become effective and remain in force.

Insurance companies determine whether to issue the requested insurance policy based on an application submitted to the company – typically by an insurance agent – and sometimes based also on results of a physical examination, laboratory tests and other information. The

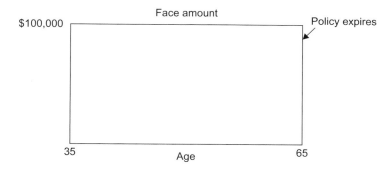

**Figure 21.1**    Illustration of Term-to-Age 65 Life Insurance Policy

application contains questions relating to insurability. Besides trying to determine the proposed insured's health status, the underwriter also wants to be satisfied that the amount of insurance requested bears a reasonable relationship to the economic loss that the beneficiary would suffer on the insured's death. A prime concern of the underwriter is detecting adverse selection and avoiding the creation of moral hazard.

Literally thousands of different life insurance policies exist. Luckily, all life insurance policies are one of two generic types: (1) term life insurance or (2) cash value life insurance.

### Term life insurance

**Term life insurance** pays the policy face amount if the insured dies during the policy term, which is usually a specified number of years, such as 10 or 20 years, or to a specified age, such as age 65. If the insured lives to the set term, the policy **expires**, meaning that it terminates without any payment. Figure 21.1 illustrates a term-to-age 65 policy. Under this $100,000 term life policy, the insurer will pay $100,000 to the beneficiary only if the insured dies before age 65. Nothing is paid if the insured survives the policy term.

Term life insurance usually provides either a level or decreasing death benefit. Premiums either increase with age or remain level. Term policies with level death benefits and increasing premiums are commonly referred to being renewable, a term synonymous with increasing premium. Thus, **yearly renewable term** (YRT) – also called **annual renewable term** – and **5-year renewable term** policies provide term insurance whose premiums increase yearly and at 5-year increments, respectively. Insurers often offer renewable term policies of other durations, such as 3, 6 or 10 years.

Some term life insurance policies have the same premiums each year. Such level-premium term contracts may be written for a set number of years or to cover the typical working lifetime. Contracts of the first type include **10-** and **20-year** (level-premium) **term** policies that sometimes can be renewed for another term. Contracts of the second type, providing essentially the same protection but not renewable, are **life-expectancy term** and **term-to-age 65** (or to other ages). Insurers also sell term life insurance policies whose face amount decreases over time. Such policies are commonly used to pay off a loan balance on the death of the debtor/insured, be it in connection with a mortgage loan or a business or personal loan.

Term insurance policies may include a **conversion** feature that allows the policyowner to exchange the term policy for a cash value insurance contract (see below), without having to prove good health. Some term policies include a **reentry provision** that affords the policyowner the possibility of paying a lower premium than otherwise if the insured can demonstrate periodically that he or she meets continuing insurability criteria. For example, one company's policy provides that every 5 years, insureds who can demonstrate continued insurability can enjoy much lower premiums than those who do not. The reentry feature, in effect, encourages insureds to self-declare their expected mortality status, thus making for more refined risk classification.

Initial premium rates per unit of coverage are lower for term life insurance than for other life products issued on the same basis. Premiums, however, can escalate rapidly with policy duration. Term product prices are more easily compared than are prices of other life products, as term policies are usually structurally simpler than other policies. Term products usually have no cash values (i.e., internal savings – see below) and often no dividends (see below), thus permitting policy price comparisons on the basis of premiums alone. As a consequence, buyers suffer fewer information problems with term insurance, thus rendering the term life insurance market more price competitive.

Some proponents of term insurance argue for its use to the virtual exclusion of cash value insurance, with others advocating the opposite viewpoint. Term insurance can be useful for persons with low incomes and high insurance needs (a situation that occurs often because of family obligations). Good risk management principles suggest that the family unit should be protected against catastrophic losses. Also, term life insurance is well suited for ensuring that mortgage and other loans are paid off on the debtor/insured's death and as a vehicle for ensuring that education or other desired funds will be available if death were to cut short the period needed for the provider/insured to save the needed funds. Term insurance is also a natural for all situations that call for temporary income protection needs.

### Cash value life insurance

**Cash value life insurance** policies combine term insurance and internal savings – called the **cash value** – within the same contract; that is, they accumulate funds that are available to the policyowner, much as with a savings account with a bank. Thousands of variations of cash value policies exist, consistent with insurers' product differentiation strategies to gain market power. To aggravate an already tough lemons problem for the customer, terminology is not always standard. We can, however, take a shortcut through this maze. Virtually every cash value policy sold falls into one of three categories, even if the insurer does not label the policy as such. The three categories are (1) universal life insurance, (2) whole life insurance and (3) endowment insurance.

All cash value policies operate in essentially in the same way. They can be considered as a combination of YRT insurance and a savings account, such that the combination always precisely equals the policy face amount. Thus, for policies with level face amounts, the amount of term insurance purchased each year changes by precisely the same amount but in the opposite direction as the cash value changes. The difference between the policy face amount and the cash value is called the **net amount at risk** (NAR). This concept is illustrated in Figure 21.2 that shows a cash value life policy whose cash value increases each year and, therefore, whose NAR decreases each year.

Two types of charges are assessed annually under all cash value policies. First, a charge is assessed to pay for the policy's internal term insurance – the NAR. Each year's charge is the product of the NAR and the YRT insurance rate (called the **cost of insurance** rate

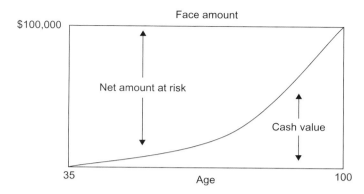

**Figure 21.2**   Illustration of Whole Life Insurance Policy

or **COI** rate). COI rates are a set of internal YRT rates that increase with age. Second, a charge is assessed to cover the insurer's loadings.

Cash value policies typically contain guaranteed maximum COI and loading charges, even if not explicitly stated in the policy. Most insurers assess COI charges at less than the maximum permitted. As with other savings media, interest is credited yearly or more frequently to the cash value. In most policies, a minimum interest rate is guaranteed to be credited but the insurer commonly credits a higher rate.

The gross premium paid by policyholders for some life insurance policies are calculated using the maximum COI and loading charges and minimum guaranteed interest rates. In other words, the premiums are set conservatively. Because of conservative pricing, the policies as a group are expected to experience (1) lower mortality rates, (2) higher investment earnings and (3) lower expenses than those built into policy pricing. The excess amounts from these expected favorable deviations of actual experience from that assumed in pricing can be returned to policyholders. If this surplus is returned in the form of **dividends** (also called **bonuses**), the policies are classified as **participating (par)** or as being **with bonus** – meaning that they participate in the insurer's surplus resulting from favorable past experience.

**Nonparticipating (nonpar)** or **without bonus** policies originally differed from par policies in that they (1) did not pay dividends and (2) all policy elements (premiums, cash values and death benefits) were fixed at issuance and never changed. Today, many nonpar policies provide some means of allowing policy elements to change in accordance with the insurer's operating results – in much the same way that par policies allow participation in the insurer's results.[5]

*Universal life insurance*
**Universal life (UL)** policies are flexible-premium, adjustable death benefit contracts whose cash values and durations depend on the premiums paid into them. After deciding on the policy face amount, the applicant pays a premium of at least a certain minimum amount to get the policy started. Thereafter, the policyowner pays as little or as much as he or she wishes into the policy.[6] The more that is paid into the policy, the greater is the internal savings.

The applicant selects one of two patterns for the NAR. Under the so-called Option A pattern, the face amount remains level. The NAR, therefore, varies inversely with the cash value. Under the Option B pattern, the NAR remains level. The face amount, therefore, varies directly with the cash value. The pure insurance amount (NAR) can be adjusted upward or downward over time, to meet the changing needs of the policyowner, but increases require evidence of insurability satisfactory to the insurer.

The policy's first-year cash value (savings) is derived from the amount remaining after deducting charges for COI and loadings from whatever premium the policyholder decides to pay at policy inception. UL policies set out the maximum charges that can be assessed each year, but insurers usually charge less than the maximum permitted. The insurer credits interest to this difference to yield the cash value at the end of the year. UL policies guarantee to credit a minimum interest rate (e.g., 3–4 percent), but insurers usually credit higher rates. UL policies are **transparent**, meaning that their internal operations, interest rates and charges for COI and loadings are disclosed each year to the policyowner.

UL is not a generic type of insurance. Rather, it mimics generic insurance types based on the policyowner's choices of premium payments. As the policyholder, not the insurer, determines the magnitude of the premium payment, the policyholder also determines the magnitude and rate of the cash value buildup in the policy and the generic type. A UL policy *will* be either term life insurance, whole life insurance (see below) or endowment insurance (see below), depending on the premiums paid. The policyholder's actions determine the type, but this too can change with time. Because of this premium flexibility, policyholders effectively design their own policies to reflect their own needs and financial circumstances.

It is not unusual for the loading charges in the early policy years to be less than the insurer's actual expenses, taxes and desired profit. Insurers take one or both of two design approaches to recover expenses, taxes and profits not explicitly included in the loadings. *First*, universal life policies usually carry a **back-end load**, often called a **surrender charge**, which ordinarily is a graded penalty applied against the cash value if the policy is terminated (surrendered) within a few years of issue (such as 7 years). *Second*, insurers usually build margins into the COI charges and interest credits. In this way, the policyholder is less aware of the actual magnitude of expenses, taxes and profits implicit in the policy.

An increasingly popular type of UL insurance is **variable universal life** (VUL) or **unit-linked UL** which combines the flexibility and transparency of a universal life policy with the investment flexibility and risk of a mutual fund (unit trust). With VUL policies, the assets backing the policyholder's cash values usually are held in accounts separate from the insurer's general asset account. These separate accounts are effectively mutual funds in which policyholders typically are permitted to invest in bonds and common stocks and other riskier investments than those available through the insurer's general investment portfolio.

The VUL policy cash value is linked directly to the account's investment experience and risk. If the account earns 15 percent, the VUL policy is credited with 15 percent, less some charges to cover the insurer's guarantees. If the account loses 15 percent, the policyholder suffers a corresponding loss. Most VUL policies contain no interest guarantees.

Unlike other policyholders, those owning VUL policies ordinarily can exercise control over the assets backing their policies. Often, they may select from a menu of separate accounts in which to have their funds invested. They also may change funds as they wish, thus altering the risk/return profile of their policies. The assumption of investment risk by the policyholder in VUL is a feature not found in universal or whole life insurance where the risk is borne by the insurance company.

### Whole life insurance
**Whole life insurance** pays the policy face amount whenever the insured dies and, therefore, is life insurance intended to remain in effect for the insured's entire (whole) lifetime. Unlike

universal life policies, premiums for whole life insurance policies (1) are directly related to the amount of insurance purchased, (2) must be paid when due or the policy will terminate, and (3) are calculated to ensure that the policy will remain in effect for the entire lifetime of the insured, which often is assumed to be age 100. If the insured does not die during the policy term and lives to the terminal age underlying policy pricing, the face amount is paid as if the insured had died. With some whole life policies – called **ordinary life** or **level-premium whole life** – uniform premiums are assumed to be paid over the insured's life-time. The necessary annual premium to fund the policy equals the level amount that would have to be paid into a UL policy over the policy term (i.e., to age 100) to cause its cash value to equal the face amount at age 100, using the guaranteed interest rate and guaranteed COI and loading charges.

Other whole life policies – called **limited-payment whole life** – provide that premiums will be paid over some period shorter than the insured's entire lifetime, such as to age 65 or for a set period such as 10 years. The necessary annual premium to fund the policy equals the level amount that would have to be paid into a UL policy over the premium-paying period to cause its cash value to equal the face amount at age 100, using the guaranteed interest rate and COI and loading charges. Naturally, the shorter the premium-paying period, the higher must be each year's premium. The higher is each year's premium, the greater will be the cash value, other things being the same. In turn, the lower will be the policy's internal COI charges. Of course, the policy remains in effect after all premiums have been paid – it is said to be **paid up**. Thus, the lowest premium level-premium whole life policy (and the lowest cash values) is ordinary life. The highest premium whole life policy (and the highest cash values) is **single-premium whole life insurance** under which only a single (large) premium payment is made at policy inception.

Whole life policies often participate in the insurer's experience; that is, they are participating. Unlike universal life policies, however, the values used by the insurer for each of the three policy components – lower mortality rates, higher investment earnings and lower expenses than assumed for pricing – typically are not disclosed to the policyholder. Rather, these excess amounts are combined and made available to the policyholder as a dividend.

Nonpar whole life usually allows policy elements to change in accordance with the insurer's operating results – in ways similar to that of par policies. A common such policy is **current assumption whole life** (CAWL), also called **interest sensitive whole life** and **fixed-premium universal life**. It usually operates identically to universal life policies except that premiums are set by the insurer.

Whole life insurance can be purchased as **variable (unit-linked) whole life**, meaning that, as with VUL, the assets backing the policyholder's cash values are held in accounts separate from the insurer's general investments. Unlike VUL, however, typically (1) the premiums for variable whole life policies are fixed, (2) the policy is guaranteed to remain in effect for the whole of the insured's life (assuming premiums are paid when due) even if the separate account investment returns are not as high as those used to calculate premiums, and (3) not only the cash value, but also the face amount varies with the performance of the underlying assets.

The above forms of whole life insurance involve one insured only. A policy can insure two or more lives. Thus, with so-called **first-to-die** (also called **joint**) **life insurance**, the face amount is paid on the first death of either of two insureds. This policy is commonly purchased by married couples. **Second-to-die** (also called **survivor**) **life insurance** also insures two lives but pays the face amount only after the second insured dies. This policy is commonly purchased to fund estate tax obligations.

*Endowment insurance*

With **endowment insurance**, the insurer makes two mutually exclusive promises: to pay the face amount if the insured (1) dies during the policy period or (2) survives to the end of the period. The first promise is identical to that made under a term policy. The second promise introduces a new concept, the pure endowment. A **pure endowment** promises to pay a maturity amount only if the insured lives to the end of a specified period, with nothing paid on earlier death. Pure endowment insurance is not commonly sold as a separate contract but rather often is embedded within policies that provide other benefits. Thus, to provide a death benefit during the endowment period, only term insurance for the same period need be added to the pure endowment. It can be seen that these two elements – level-premium term insurance and pure endowment – together meet the two promises made under endowment insurance.

Many endowment policies are for set durations of 2–30 or more years, and others mature at certain ages, such as at ages 60, 65, or 70. Premiums often are due throughout the term, although limited-payment plans, such as an endowment at age 65 paid up in 20 years, have been available.

## Annuities

Life insurance has as its principal mission the creation of a fund. An annuity's function is the systematic liquidation of a fund. Most annuities sold by life insurers are also accumulation instruments, but this is the mechanism for developing the fund to be liquidated. The purpose of most annuities is to protect against the possibility of outliving one's income – just the opposite of life insurance.

Technically, an **annuity** is any series of periodic payments. An **annuity contract** promises to make a series of payments through systematic liquidation of principal and interest for a fixed period or over a person's lifetime. The person who receives the periodic payment is called the **annuitant**. A **life annuity**, also called a **pure life annuity**, is the generic term for any annuity whose payments are contingent on whether the annuitant is alive. Thus, a **whole life annuity** is a life annuity payable for the whole of the annuitant's life, irrespective of how long that may be. In contrast, an **annuity certain** makes payments for a set period of time that is unrelated to whether the annuitant is alive. A **temporary life annuity** is a life annuity payable for the earlier of a fixed period (e.g., 20 years) or until the death of the annuitant.

Each payment under a life annuity is a combination of principal and interest income and a survivorship element. Although not completely accurate, we can view the operation of an annuity as follows: if a person dies precisely at his or her life expectancy, he or she would have neither gained nor lost through utilizing a life annuity contract. Those annuitants who die before attaining their life expectancies would not have received payments equal to their contributions (plus foregone interest), with the difference between that which they contributed to the insurance pool and that which they received being used to provide continuing income to those who outlive their life expectancies. As no one knows into which category he or she will fall, the arrangement is equitable and succeeds through the operation of the law of large numbers.

*Classification of annuities*

Annuities may be classified in numerous ways. We classify them as shown schematically in Figure 21.3.

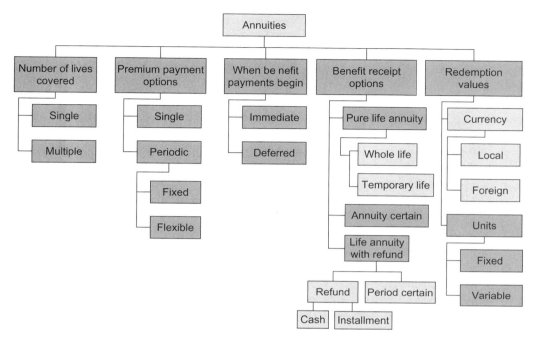

**Figure 21.3**   Classification of Annuities. *Source*: Black and Skipper (2000)

Thus, annuities are classified based on whether their payments are determined on a single life or multiple lives. Most annuities are issued on a single life, but annuities covering two or more lives are popular, especially in husband/wife situations. For example, the **joint and last-survivor annuity** provides income payments for as long as *either* of two persons lives. As this annuity provides for payment until the last death, it will pay to a later date, on average, than a single-life annuity and, therefore, is more expensive than single-life annuity forms. A modified form provides that the income will be reduced following the death of the first annuitant to two-thirds or one-half of the original income. Naturally, for a given principal, the modified form provides more income initially because of the later reduction.

Annuities may be purchased with single or periodic premiums. Thus, some single-life annuities are purchased by beneficiaries of life insurance policies from the payment of the policy's face amount. Other single-premium payments are accumulated through savings, inheritance, or other means.

Annuities also may be classified as to whether income payments are deferred or immediate. An **immediate annuity** is an annuity purchased with a single premium with the first benefit payment due (almost) immediately. A **deferred annuity** is an annuity purchased with either a single premium or periodic premiums with the first benefit payment typically made only after several years have passed.

Insurers offer a variety of options as to how annuity proceeds can be distributed. Most insurers also include a provision in their contracts to the effect that they will provide any other payment option that is mutually agreed upon by the insurer and the contract owner.

Annuity benefits can be expressed in different currencies and in fixed or variable units. Fixed annuities are much like bank savings accounts. The insurer guarantees to credit a

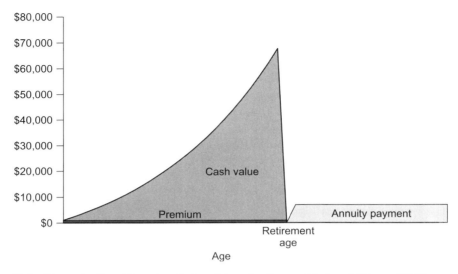

**Figure 21.4**   Illustrative Level-Premium Deferred Annuity *Source*: Black and Skipper (2000)

minimum interest rate during the accumulation period to the cash value, but usually credits a higher rate. In addition, a minimum annuity payout is guaranteed.

Variable annuities are similar to mutual funds. With a **variable (unit-linked) annuity**, cash values and benefit payments vary directly with the experience of assets designated to back the contract. Assets backing variable annuities, as with those backing variable life policies, are typically maintained in separate accounts, and the variable annuity values directly reflect the account's investment results. Most variable annuities do not contain interest guarantees. The contract owner typically bears the investment risk and receives the return actually earned on invested assets, less charges assessed by the insurance company. No minimum cash value is guaranteed either.

*Nature of insurance company's obligations*

Most annuities have an accumulation and a liquidation phase. The **accumulation period** is that time period during which annuity fund values accumulate, commonly prior to retirement. The **liquidation period** is that time period during which annuity fund values are paid to annuitant(s). The retirement income amount provided by an annuity depends on the accumulated cash value, the annuitant's sex (where permitted) and age, and the payout option selected.

Figure 21.4 shows a hypothetical deferred annuity on which level premiums are paid throughout the accumulation period. For simplicity, we assume a constant interest rate. The retirement age is shown separating the liquidation and accumulation periods. At retirement age, the annuitant has several options as to how to utilize the cash value, including taking the entire amount as a single sum payment. If an annuity option is elected, the right to the cash value vanishes, replaced by a guarantee of income. The insurer's obligations differ between the accumulation and liquidation periods.

During the accumulation period, the insurer usually is obligated to return all or a portion of the annuity cash value if the purchaser dies or voluntarily terminates the contract. Otherwise, values accumulate in accordance with contract terms. The fund necessary to provide a certain income beginning at a set age is the same, other things equal, irrespective of how the funds were accumulated. Consequently, the following discussion of the nature of the insurer's obligation during the liquidation period is applicable to both immediate and deferred annuities and to both fixed and variable annuities. The nature of the obligation for annuities certain and pure life annuities was explained above, so the focus here is on modified forms of payouts.

As most persons seem to oppose placing a substantial sum of money into a contract that promises little or no return if they should die shortly after income payments commence, companies permit annuitants various so-called refund options if death occurs shortly after annuity payments have begun. Not all of the purchase price of refund annuities is used to provide income payments, because the insurer applies part of the purchase price to meet the cost of guaranteeing a minimum amount of benefits, irrespective of whether the annuitant lives to receive them. Thus, for a given premium outlay, a smaller periodic income payment will be available under a refund life annuity than under an otherwise identical pure life annuity.

One class of life annuities with refund features, often named **life annuity certain and continuous** or **life annuity with installments certain**, calls for a guaranteed number of monthly (or annual) payments to be made whether the annuitant lives or dies, with payments to continue for the whole of the annuitant's life if he or she should live beyond the guarantee period. Contracts are usually written with payments guaranteed for 5, 10, 15 or 20 years. Of course, the longer the guarantee period, the smaller the income payments, other things being the same. These refund life annuities are a combination of (1) an annuity certain for the length of the guarantee period plus (2) a pure whole life deferred annuity thereafter.

Two other forms of annuities promise to "return" all or a portion of the purchase price. The first form, the **installment refund annuity**, promises that, if the annuitant dies before receiving income installments at least equaling the purchase price, the payments will be continued to a beneficiary until this amount has been paid. The second form, the **cash refund annuity**, promises to pay in a lump sum to the beneficiary this difference.

As with other annuities, the owner of a variable annuity may select from the above optional modes of payment. However, instead of providing for the payment each month of a fixed number of *currency* units, such as ten, a variable annuity provides for the payment each month or year of the current value of a fixed number of *annuity* units. The amount of each payment depends on the value of the annuity unit when the payment is made. The valuation assigned to a unit depends on the investment results of the separate account. For example, if an annuitant were entitled to a payment of 100 annuity units each month and the dollar values of annuity units for three consecutive months were $10.20, $9.90 and $10.10, the annuitant would receive an income for these months of $1,020, $990 and $1,010.

## Types of annuity contracts

As with life insurance, only a limited number of generic annuity contracts exists, although individual insurer variations are great. Three categories of annuities are discussed below: (1) flexible-premium deferred annuities (FPDAs), (2) single-premium deferred annuities (SPDAs) and (3) single-premium immediate annuities (SPIAs).

## Flexible-premium deferred annuity

The FPDA permits annuitants to pay premiums whenever and in whatever amount they wish (subject to a nominal minimum). An FPDA can be thought of as a UL policy with no NAR. At some future time designated by the annuitant, the cash value can be applied to supply an income in accordance with the liquidation options discussed above. FPDA contracts typically have either front-end or back-end (surrender charges) loads or both, as with the cash value products discussed earlier. Surrender charges usually are stated as a percentage of the total accumulation value and decrease with duration.

Fixed-value FPDA contracts typically guarantee a minimum interest rate – often in the 3.0–4.0 percent range, depending on economic conditions at the time of issuance, but usually credit higher rates. Although the guaranteed rate seems low, the guarantee could easily span three or more decades. Variable FPDAs usually contain no interest rate guarantee. The interest credited to the cash value varies directly with the return earned on the assets backing the annuity. The majority of variable annuities are FPDAs.

*Single-premium deferred annuity*

The name of the SPDA is truly descriptive, as it is a *deferred annuity* contract purchased with a *single premium*. The annuity may be of the traditional, guaranteed interest variety or variable. As with the FPDA, a minimum stated rate of interest is guaranteed with a fixed-value SPDA for the duration of the contract, with most insurers crediting rates above that guaranteed. The rate is subject to change by the insurer, just as with the FPDA. SPDAs commonly carry no identifiable front-end loads but have graded surrender charges akin to the FPDA. Many variations exist but two will give an idea of the flexibility in design:

- The **equity-indexed annuity** (EIA) – also called simply **indexed annuity** – is a non-variable annuity contract whose interest crediting mechanism is tied directly to some external index, such as the Standard & Poor's 500 Index. EIAs contain elements of both fixed-value and variable annuities but which are not found in either. *First*, they offer a minimum guaranteed interest rate – typically 3.0 percent. This provides a downside guarantee. *Second*, they offer the potential for stock-market-like gains by tying the current crediting rate to equity indexes, thus providing upside participation. Most EIAs are issued as SPDAs, although flexible-premium varieties are emerging. Most carry a maturity date of from 5 to 10 years from issuance. The EIA is appealing to consumers because they gain upside participation with downside protection. Simultaneously, they cause some concern. The guarantees carry a cost, and owners do not participate fully in the index. The variety of ways for calculating the equity return means that consumers might be confused and possibly even misled.

- The **market-value annuity** (MVA) – also referred to as a **market-value adjusted annuity** – permits contract owners to lock in a guaranteed interest rate over a specified period, typically from 3 to 10 years. If kept until maturity, its value reaches the amount guaranteed at issue. However, early withdrawals typically incur surrender charges and market-value adjustments can increase or decrease the cash value depending on market conditions at withdrawal.

*Single-premium immediate annuity*

The SPIA provides that payments to the annuitant commence immediately after the insurer has received a single-premium payment. As with other annuity contract forms, the SPIA may have traditional guarantees or follow the variable format. SPIAs are often used by those who have large sums of money and desire to have the fund liquidated for retirement income purposes.

A contemporary use of SPIAs has evolved from liability insurers' efforts to minimize their loss payouts. A **structured settlement annuity** (SSA) is an SPIA contract issued by a life insurer whereby the plaintiff (the injured party) receives periodic payments on behalf of the defendant via the SSA. Typically, the defendant and the plaintiff, together with their attorneys and a structured settlement specialist, negotiate a settlement package intended to compensate the plaintiff for his or her losses, including future earnings. The periodic payments are funded through an SSA purchased by the defendant or the liability insurer from a life insurer that guarantees to make the agreed-upon payments, usually for the life of the injured person (or a designated beneficiary).

## Morbidity-Based Insurance Policies

Individuals face three broad categories of potential economic losses associated with the health risk. First, they can incur medical expenses when injured or sick. Second, they may incur expenses to provide long-term care (LTC) if mental or physical illness, injury or old-age frailty prevents them from engaging in the activities of daily living. Third, poor health or incapacity also can be so debilitating as to prevent employment, which means a reduction or even elimination of income. Health insurance, LTC insurance and disability income insurance policies, respectively, are designed to meet each of the three loss exposures.

### *Health insurance policies*

Healthcare expenses are most commonly financed by government programs and employers and from personal financial resources, as we discuss in Chapters 9 and 16. In many markets, individuals and families purchase individually issued health insurance policies, because no other third-party financing source is available or to augment or replace governmental or employer-provided coverage considered too limiting or too expensive. Individuals in a few markets can secure individual coverage from managed care organizations such as health maintenance organizations, preferred provider organizations and point-of-service plans, but most such coverage is employer based. These are covered in Chapter 16, so are not discussed further here.

Numerous commercial insurers write some form of health insurance in many markets. These stock and mutual corporations are organized as life, nonlife or health insurance companies and may provide coverage for medical expenses or for LTC or disability. These insurers often sell both basic and comprehensive health insurance on both a group and individual basis, with the former being more common.

The coverage under individually issued health insurance policies may parallel that available through group health insurance as discussed in Chapter 16. It may cover inpatient and outpatient hospital services, physician and diagnostic services as well as specialty services such as physical therapy and radiology and prescription drugs. More commonly, however, it is more restrictive and, depending on the market, such policies often are more expensive in comparison to employer-provided and subsidized health insurance. Deductibles and other copayments often are higher with individual policies than under group insurance. Our focus in this section is on individual health insurance provided by commercial insurers.

In addition to hospital-surgical and major medical insurance policies, insurers offer several special individual policies. These include (1) supplemental health insurance, (2) hospital confinement indemnity and (3) specified-disease policies:

- As its name indicates, **supplemental health insurance** provides coverage that augments the benefits provided by governmental or employer-sponsored health insurance. These policies may extend indemnification to areas not covered by the primary health insurance, provide additional indemnification limits, extend the duration of covered confinement in a hospital or other healthcare facility or cover the use of private healthcare specialists.

- In contrast with basic hospital expense insurance that is provided on a indemnity basis, **hospital confinement indemnity** insurance pays a fixed sum for each day of hospital confinement typically for up to one year, usually irrespective of other health insurance coverage.

- So-called **dread disease insurance** is individual coverage that can pay a variety of benefits up to substantial maximums solely for the treatment of diseases named in the policy, most typically cancer and heart disease. Benefits usually are paid as scheduled amounts for designated events, such as hospital confinement, or for specific medical procedures, such as chemotherapy. Because the insurance pays only for medical expenses associated with a single devastating disease, the scope of this coverage is quite limited.

Individual health insurance policies can be issued on a guaranteed or non-guaranteed renewable basis. With **guaranteed renewable health insurance policies**, the insured has the contractual right to continue the policy by the timely payment of premiums usually to a specified age, such as 65, but the magnitude of future premiums usually is not guaranteed. With **non-guaranteed renewable health insurance policies**, the insurer may unilaterally refuse to renew the policy, sometimes subject to restrictions.

### Long-term care insurance policies

The second major type of health risk faced by individuals and families stems from the possibility of becoming unable fully to care for oneself. Most often, such incapacity is associated with the aging process.

LTC needs can be met through the care rendered by family members or friends, typically at no charge, or by professionals and trained assistants for a fee. If the care requires paid professionals or assistants, which increasingly is the situation, their charges must be financed either through (1) the individual's or family's existing wealth or future income (retention) or (2) external sources (transfer).

In most countries, substantial portions or the totality of such care is provided by family members or financed through the individual's or family's resources. The common external sources of LTC financing include government, group plans and individual insurance policies issued by commercial insurers. Coverage through the first two sources is common in many markets, although benefits may be limited. Government funding of LTC expenses accounts for the great majority of coverage in developed countries. Coverage under individually issued policies, while not widespread in any market, is growing in many of them.

Private LTC insurance pays for services when the insured is unable to perform certain activities of daily living without assistance, such as bathing, eating, dressing, toileting and transferring from and to bed. These policies also may pay benefits when the insured requires supervision due to a cognitive impairment such as Alzheimer's disease.

LTC insurance in some markets covers only skilled care in a nursing home following a period of hospitalization. Generally, however, coverage extends to an array of services that promote independent living, including personal care, assisted living, care management, support for family caregivers, home modifications, homemaker services and hospice care, in addition to institutional care.

Coverage varies from market to market and also based on how benefits are paid. Some policies pay a fixed daily benefit, usually for nursing home confinement. Others pay a fixed daily benefit regardless of whether the insured incurs LTC expenses, provided eligibility requirements are met. Still others reimburse for incurred expenses, up to the policy daily maximum.

Insureds under individually issued policies may select from an array of options, including the length of the benefit period, which ranges from one to five years or to lifetime. They also must select the maximum daily benefit (e.g., in the U.S., $40–250 per day) and length of the elimination (waiting) period before benefits become payable (e.g., 0–365 days). Of course, the greater the benefit the higher the premium, and the longer the elimination period the lower the premium, other things being the same. Other options may be available, such as inflation protection and funding for different levels of care.

Individual LTC policies may be offered on a guaranteed renewable basis, the same as with health insurance policies. Applications for individual LTC insurance are carefully underwritten by the insurer. LTC benefits are sometimes available as a rider to a life insurance policy.

### Disability income insurance policies

Disability can seriously affect a worker's and a family's lifestyle and savings plans. For example, the U.S. Department of Housing and Urban Development estimates that 46 percent of foreclosures on home mortgage loans are caused by disability versus only 2 percent caused by death. The need for external sources of disability income typically declines with age, ideally disappearing at retirement when adequate non-employment income should be sufficient to maintain the individual or family. During the working years, most individuals require substantial external coverage.

The three major sources of external finance for the disability exposure – ignoring family and friends – are government, group plans and individual disability income insurance policies. The most common external sources of disability income in developed countries are social insurance programs. Additionally, many employers provide disability income benefits to employees who are unable to work because of sickness and injury, often funded via group insurance policies purchased from commercial insurers. Insurers also sell individual disability income insurance policies, although group coverages typically predominate.

Disability income insurance policies are designed to provide monthly benefits to replace lost income when the insured is disabled as the result of sickness or injury. Policies sold to individuals may be issued on a guaranteed renewable basis, with some policies issued on a basis that not only guarantees the insured the right to continue the policy but also guarantees future premiums.

Three basic components establish the premium and define the payment of benefits under disability income policies: the elimination period, the benefit amount and the benefit period. As with LTC policies, the elimination (waiting) period is the time at the onset of disability during which no benefits are paid. Elimination periods typically range from seven to 365 days, with three months being common for individually issued policies and seven days being the most common for employer-provided short-term disability income coverage.

The benefit amount is typically stated in terms of a fixed monthly sum. The insurance usually is written on a valued basis, which means that it is presumed to equal the actual monetary loss sustained by the insured. The amount often is not adjusted as the insured's earnings change, even if earnings fall substantially. Additionally many policies make no distinction between occupational and non-occupational disabilities – paying for each – and pay the benefit amount irrespective of any other sources of disability income. Insurers limit the amount of insurance that they will sell to an insured such that disability income from all likely sources would replace a maximum proportion (e.g., 60–80 percent) of gross wages.

The benefit period is the longest period for which benefits will be paid. This period usually is the same for disability resulting from sickness and accident, but sometimes it is longer for accidents. Typical benefit periods are two or five years or to age 65.

An important component in social insurance, group insurance and individual disability income insurance is the definition of disability. Because of the complexity of defining a disability in specific medical terms, insurers generally define it in terms of sickness or injury limiting one's ability to work. Two definitions are common:

- The so-called **any occupation definition of disability** states that insureds will be deemed to be totally disabled only if sickness or injury prevents them from performing the major duties of any occupation. This definition, common also in social insurance plans, means that the insured will *not* be considered disabled if she or he can engage in any gainful employment – making it difficult for many to qualify for benefits. Sometimes, disability income plans modify this conservative definition by a stipulation that the occupation must be one for which the insured is reasonably suited by reason of education, training or experience. This latter addition is common in some group and individual disability income plans.

- The **own occupation definition of disability** states that insureds will be deemed to be totally disabled if sickness or injury prevents them from performing the major duties of their own occupations. This liberal definition in less frequently encountered, although some individual policies offer it.

Individual disability income policies sold by commercial insurers may include various supplemental benefits, some of which are as follows:

- *Residual disability benefits* that provide a reduced monthly benefit in proportion to the insured's loss of income when the insured has returned to work at reduced earnings.

- *Partial disability benefits* that provide a reduced monthly benefit of a set percentage of the full benefit (e.g., 50 percent) payable for a limited period, such as six months, when the insured has returned to work on a limited basis after a period of compensable total disability.

- *Inflation protection benefits* that provide for adjustments of benefits each year during a long-term claim to reflect changes in the cost of living.

- *Provisions for increased benefit amounts* that allow the insured to purchase additional disability income insurance in future years without having to offer evidence of insurability.

## SELECTED LIFE INSURANCE MARKETS INTERNATIONALLY

We now provide an overview of several life insurance markets worldwide, focusing on the products and systems of distribution as well as key issues in many of the markets.[7]

**Figure 21.5**   Premium Income of U.S. Life Insurers (2004) *Source*: ACLI, 2005.

Inevitably, we cannot examine even most markets but have selected those that either represent important proportions of life insurance internationally or offer the promise of strong growth. Because international premium data on morbidity-based insurance are either unavailable or exhibit inconsistencies, we are unable to provide premium data on them equivalent to those which we provide on mortality-based products sold worldwide.[8]

## Life Insurance Markets in the Americas

The life insurance markets of North America and Latin America and the Caribbean collective account for about 29 percent of total world life insurance premiums. The U.S. is easily the largest market in the Americas, but several others are growing more rapidly than the U.S. market.

### The United States

The first U.S. life insurance company was established in 1759. Almost 250 years later, almost 1,200 life companies generated a premium volume in 2005 of some US$517 billion, making the U.S. the world's largest life insurance market.[9] Figure 21.5 shows the latest distribution of premium income for U.S. life insurers. As can be seen, annuities account for 51 percent of sales, with morbidity-based products and life insurance of roughly equal proportions. Premium growth has been stagnant in recent years. Because savings products are less profitable for insurers than traditional products and because insurers increasingly compete with banks and mutual funds for consumers' savings, the industry has been under increasing pressure to operate more efficiently and reduce expenses. Another outgrowth of this change has been industry consolidation through mergers and acquisitions, with the number of insurers having fallen by almost one-half from a high of 2,343 in 1988.

Because of the large size of the market, most U.S. insurers historically saw ample opportunities at home. However, the slowing growth rate of the industry in the last decade combined with the profitability problems experienced by some life insurers led to a reassessment of international opportunities. International interest by U.S. insurers has increased dramatically.

Among the reasons given by U.S. insurers seeking to enter foreign markets are (1) the sense that the U.S. market is mature, (2) the attractive growth rates existing in various overseas markets, (3) the search for more profitable business and (4) increasing competition in U.S. market. In addition, about 10 percent of life insurers in the U.S. are controlled by owners from other countries such as Canada, France, the Netherlands, Switzerland and the U.K. (ACLI, 2005).

*Products and distribution systems*

Until the late 1970s, most life insurance sold in the U.S. could be characterized as either whole life or term life insurance. The past three decades witnessed an explosion of new products and innovative product features. Many new products transfer more of the investment risk to policyholders, while at the same time giving policyholders the opportunity for better rates of return and enhanced flexibility. Other product features offer enhanced guarantees to policyholders.

The distribution systems used by life insurance companies in the U.S. also are in a state of flux. Agents and brokers still account for almost 90 percent of life insurance sales, although the share of annuity sales by securities firms and banks exceeds annuity sales by agents and brokers. Also, companies are experimenting with alternate distribution systems because of the high costs and low productivity associated with agent distribution.

*Market issues*

The U.S. life insurance industry faces a myriad of compelling issues. Competition among financial institutions has never been fiercer. Pressures to strengthen corporate risk management continue to grow, as insurers seek competitive advantages and regulators push for stronger financial monitoring. Below, we touch on a few of the key issues:

- *Financial modernization*: As discussed in Chapter 8, the 1999 enactment of what has become know as the *Gramm-Leach-Bliley Act* dramatically reduced restrictions on U.S. financial institution integration. For almost seven decades prior thereto, banks were restricted in offering securities, investment and insurance products, and vice versa.

    The law was intended to modernize U.S. financial services and their regulation by establishing clearer lines of regulatory authority, enhancing consumer choice and value by allowing each financial sector to offer products of the others, reducing litigation and facilitating more consistent regulation. Many observers expected massive merger and acquisition activity that would lead to large, dominant financial conglomerates ultimately offering the full spectrum of financial services and products. To date, we have not seen this result, although several large life insurer mergers and acquisitions have taken place. For example, Manulife Financial Corporation merged with John Hancock Financial Services (a deal worth US$11 billion) in 2004. MetLife bought Travelers Insurance Company, Travelers Life and Annuity, and Citi Insurance International from Citigroup for a total price of US$11.8 billion in 2005. Lincoln National merged with Jefferson-Pilot (a deal worth US$7.3 billion) in 2006.[10] The market share of annuity and life insurance policy sales by banks continues to grow.

- *Regulatory concerns*: The 1945 *McCarran-Ferguson Act* decreed that the U.S. insurance industry was to be regulated at the state rather than the federal level. However, several insurers, various U.S. government officials and consumerists advocate the creation of federal regulation. They argue that neither U.S. insurers' nor consumers' interests are well served by a fragmented state-by-state approach to supervision and that a competitive, globalized financial services market would benefit from a more cohesive regulatory approach. Prospects for change appear greater today than at past, as increasing numbers of large insurers support change.

- *Health insurance reform*: The U.S. healthcare system has been plagued by rising costs for more than two decades. As we note in Chapter 9, the U.S. spends more on healthcare than any other nation, devoting more than 1/7th of its entire national output to it, with the proportion forecast to grow. At the same time, some 45 million U.S. inhabitants have no health insurance coverage.

Proposals to change the system abound, including, at one time, a single payer system akin to Canada's system, a managed competition plan where the federal government would work with insurance companies on provision of healthcare benefits, as well as others. To date, all proposals have failed to gain Congressional approval and no major overhaul of the system appears imminent. However, insurers have made a significant move toward managed care and away from traditional indemnity coverage in an effort to control costs. With the aging of the U.S. population and therefore ever more citizens qualifying for publicly financed healthcare (Medicare), the fiscal burden on the U.S. government could become a major impediment to strong U.S. economic growth.

- *Emphasis on financial stability*: During the late 1980s and 1990s, the U.S. witnessed several well-publicized life insurer insolvencies. As a result of adverse publicity, many insurers bolstered their financial positions and emphasized their financial stability. A company's financial stability is now a selling factor that is, for many consumers, as important as policy cost. The effect has been a so-called "flight to quality," with buyers having moved to life insurers that have top ratings and unimpeachable financial strength.

- *Implementation of risk-based capital (RBC)*: The same series of events mentioned above was a factor in influencing regulators to pursue the idea of RBC. Conceptually, RBC requirements rely primarily on an assessment of a life insurer's investment, pricing and underwriting riskiness. The greater an insurer's riskiness, the greater the amount of capital required. Critics express concern that the formula places too much emphasis on the short term (which they view as inappropriate given the long-term nature of many life insurance obligations), results are too easily manipulated and results are poor at discerning financially sound from unsound companies.

## Canada

The Canadian and U.S. life insurance industries are closely intertwined, with much cross-border business. Total Canadian life premium volume in 2005 was US$34 billion, generated by 105 companies – the number of insurers down from earlier times because mainly of consolidation. Despite similarities with the U.S., the Canadian life insurance industry differs in important ways from its neighbor, including that Canadian life insurers may be subject to federal regulation or provincial regulation, depending on their charter and how they conduct their business. About 90 percent of Canadian insurers are federally regulated.

Canadian life insurance companies have long been major players in the U.S. market as well as in the Caribbean and the Pacific Rim. In 2005, life and health premium volume written by subsidiaries and branches of Canadian life insurers – mostly excluded from the above national figure – totaled some C$72 billion.

### Products and distribution systems

Canada has experienced strong growth in the annuity and morbidity-based insurance sectors, with their accounting for 42 and 35 percent, respectively, of total life insurer income in 2004 (CLHIA, 2005). The life insurance share continues to decline, down to 23 percent in 2004. The group annuity business has witnessed especially strong growth recently.

About 60 percent of life insurance premium income in Canada is generated by full-time career agents. Brokers account for about one-third of income, independent marketing organizations for 4 percent and multi-line agents for 3 percent. Brokers and independent marketers are taking market share from career agents.

*Market issues*

Similar to the U.S., events of the preceding three decades have precipitated unprecedented change:

- *Solvency crisis*: In the early 1990s, several major Canadian life insurance companies (*Confederation Life, Les Coopérants* and *Sovereign*) became insolvent. CompCorp (a guaranty fund set up under the auspices of the Canadian Life and Health Insurance Association) was established as a means to minimize insolvencies and to make good the losses of policyholders of insolvent companies. The failure of Confederation Life in particular was a major blow to the prestige of the Canadian life insurance industry, which enjoyed the reputation of being solid and fiscally conservative.

- *Entry of banks into market*: Canada possesses a strong national banking system where a handful of banks controls the vast majority of the business. The federal government in Ottawa introduced regulatory reform for the financial services industry in the early 1990s. Thus, the Canadian life insurance market was gradually opened to banks, although the legislation permitted banks to own insurers but prohibited banks from using their customer lists for marketing insurance – a major handicap. Nevertheless, Canadian banks have become formidable competitors because of their large size which affords them economies of scale. It has been difficult for life insurers to reduce their expense ratios to those of the banks, and therefore life insurers have lost market share.

- *Québec Sovereignty issue*: From time to time, the issue of relative rights and balance of power between the province of Québec and the rest of Canada flares anew. When this happens, the political crisis leaves open the possibility that Québec may secede from Canada. Because most Canadian insurers operate in Québec, this continuing uncertainty makes long range planning difficult. The uncertainty also affects the ability of Canadian financial institutions to raise money, as international financial managers have assigned extra risk to Canadian investments.

### Latin America

In a global comparison, Latin America remains relatively small, with premiums for the entire region accounting only for somewhat more than 1 percent of the world share. When we exclude its three major markets (Brazil, Mexico and Chile), the region's share in 2005 falls to 0.14 percent. Nonetheless, the region's average annual growth rate in life premiums over the past decade or so has been a robust 12 percent.

While many countries in this region have had life insurance companies since the turn of the 20th century, rampant inflation and government instability historically had combined to impair the industry's growth. However, the moves toward market economies in leading countries such as Argentina, Brazil, Chile, Colombia and Mexico has brought economic growth and at least some measure of relative financial stability. Since the liberalization of

Chile's insurance market in 1980 and the privatization of its pension schemes, there also has been a trend in the other more advanced economies in the region to open their insurance markets. These markets have attracted much attention from international insurers interested in expansion because of the high growth rate potential in such an underinsured region.

Life insurance premium growth during 2005 was slightly negative for the entire region due to changes in pension fund legislation in Chile and Colombia, tax changes in Mexico and general declines in the pension business in several other countries. Expectation was that strong premium growth would resume for 2006, perhaps approaching the 10-year average rate of 12 percent.

*Products and distribution systems*

A wide variety of life insurance products and distribution systems exists in Latin America. For example, ALICO (an AIG subsidiary) operates in many countries in the region and sells a full range of life and health insurance products. Chile is ALICO's largest Latin American income contributor. Many U.S.-based life insurers active in Latin America offer dollar-denominated policies targeted to wealthy clients. Brazil has a rapidly emerging life insurance market, with the restructuring of its social security system continuing to result in sales of more savings products.

Traditionally, most life insurance distribution in the region has been through career agents. In recent years, independent agents, brokers, marketing firms and international brokers have appeared. Distribution practices vary widely. For example, in Honduras and El Salvador, career agents predominate, whereas in Panama and Ecuador, independent agents and brokers are the most effective distribution channels. *Bancassurance* has grown rapidly in the region, with banks in many markets now controlling significant market shares. For example, in Brazil, banks (e.g. Banco do Brasil, Bradesco and Itall) control about 70 percent of insurance sales in terms of premiums. Life insurers are heavily involved in the pension business in many countries in the region, as the countries increasingly have adopted pension systems akin to that of Chile which relies on mandatory savings via private-sector financial institutions.

*Market issues*

Although Latin America presents many attractive growth opportunities, it also involves risks. We touch on two issues:

- *Regional trade agreements*: The trade pacts discussed in Chapter 3, particularly NAFTA and MERCOSUR and discussions of broader trade pacts, continue to have a major impact on the life insurance industry in each participating country. As new foreign companies enter these markets, governments are being forced to update their regulatory structures. Domestic insurers find themselves in a market with much stronger competition, with a shortage of trained personnel. Failures of any life insurance company ventures could have substantial negative effects in a region where life insurers are not widely known and do not enjoy great prestige.

- *Economic and political stability*: Most Latin American countries moving toward market economies remain early in that process, and political parties in many oppose reforms. Major changes in governing parties could lead to a loss of investor confidence in the country and a withdrawal of foreign capital that could weaken fragile economic reforms.

## European Life Insurance Markets

Products characterized as life insurance in many European countries would not meet the usual definition of life insurance in many other countries, such as the U.S., because many are pure investment/savings products with little or no mortality risk. This fact inflates premium volume in Europe vis-à-vis other regions, as the premiums for these products are actually capital transfers invested at interest.

Total life insurance premium volume for Europe in 2005 was US$769 billion, which represented approximately 39 percent of worldwide life premiums. The U.K. and France lead the region in terms of total life premium volume; Switzerland and the U.K. in terms of per capita premium; and Belgium, Finland, France, Switzerland and the U.K. in terms of life insurance density. Other important markets include Italy, Germany, the Netherlands and Spain. With the expansion of the E.U. from 15 to 25 countries in 2004 and to 27 countries in 2007, the E.U.'s importance both in Europe and the world stage has increased.

Among the non-E.U. markets in Europe, the largest in life premium volume easily is Switzerland, at US$22.7 billion, making the small country of 7.3 million citizens the world's 16th largest life insurance market. It achieves this status by virtue of its citizens spending more per capita on life insurance (at US$3,078 in 2005) than all countries except the U.K. (at US$3,287). The Swiss market is sophisticated, offering a full range of products and distribution channels.

Western European insurers are among the largest and most international of life insurers. Among the advantages European insurers enjoy internationally are their experiences with other cultures and ways of doing business, language skills and ability to access substantial capital. As life insurance becomes increasingly global, a more competitive European life insurance business should work to their advantage.

Under the E.U. law, a life insurer domiciled in one E.U. country has the right to sell life insurance in any other E.U. country. However, because of major country-to-country differences in matters such as types of products that may be sold, legal aspects of insurance, life insurance taxation and social security systems, important barriers persist within the E.U. Some companies are proponents of regulatory harmonization, while others (that may enjoy an advantageous regulatory structure in their country of origin) are less enthusiastic. Given these differences, it is misleading to contend that a pan-European life insurance industry, as such, exists.

The *bancassurance* movement, particularly when it involves over-the-counter sales, continues to increase cost pressures on traditional insurers in many European countries. For example, banks are the main distribution channels in France (over 60 percent of the market share), in Italy (60 percent) and in Spain (70 percent). Banks also generate 25 percent of life business in Germany. As *bancassurance* becomes more widely accepted, it will be increasingly difficult for conventional insurers to support costly agency distribution systems and overhead.

### The United Kingdom

By most measures, the U.K. has the largest life insurance market in Europe, with 2005 premium income of about US$200 billion. Towers Perrin (2005) reports that foreign premiums written by U.K. insurance companies account for about 20 percent of the premiums. Life insurance and pension funds traditionally have been the preferred savings vehicles for the British, contributing to the major growth of the market. About 160 insurers, including 45 composite insurers, operated there in 2004. Barkley's Global Investors, a pension management firm, is the leader in the U.K. life insurance market. Standard Life, Prudential (U.K.) and Norwich Union Life lead the pure life insurance sector. GE Frankona, Munich Re (U.K.), Swiss Re (Life and Health), Hanover Life Re (U.K.) and Scottish Re dominate the U.K. life reinsurance market. They assume about 98 percent life risks, about £1.2 billion, reinsured in the country.

The U.K. life insurance business can be segmented into three sectors:

- Life insurance comprising basic life insurance and annuities, pension business, individual savings account business, overseas life insurance business, and basic life reinsurance business.
- Other long-term business such as permanent health insurance and pension fund management activity.
- Other than long-term business.

In 2003, U.K. insurers sold about 3.8 million new life insurance policies to individuals or about 60 percent of new policies sold in the country. In terms of premiums, however, life insurance policies accounted for only 28.6 percent of the total premiums in the market. Unit-linked policies are among the most popular.

Annuities, including single-premium unit-linked annuities, remain popular as retirement income supplements. Conventional endowment contracts make up a major portion of in-force life insurance in the U.K. These policies usually are issued on a with-profits (participating) basis and often are used to pay mortgage loans at maturity. Many mortgage banks permit "interest only" payments until maturity. Term insurance, while still a minority, continues to gain market share.

Bonuses are a key feature of many U.K. life insurance policies. **Reversionary bonuses** are paid-up additional life insurance expressed as a percentage of either the original or current benefit amount. This percentage often is the same over a broad group of policies. By contrast, **terminal bonuses** are used to distribute unrealized capital gains to policyholders on the insured's death or at policy maturity. Terminal bonuses often represent a substantial percentage of the ultimate benefit. Insight 21.1 illustrates the functioning of U.K. bonus plans.

In the late 1980s, the government introduced **Personal Equity Plans** (**PEPs**) as a means to increase consumer savings. PEPs permit investments in unit trusts (mutual funds). Dividend income and capital gains from PEPs are tax free. PEPs compete with traditional endowment policies in the area of mortgages. The government also introduced in 1988 new provisions of the *Social Security Act* under which workers may opt out of State Earnings Related Pension Schemes (SERPS) sponsored by employers and invest their funds in private plans. As a result, personal pensions became a high growth area for life insurers. Effective 2006, new tax laws establish a lifetime limit of £1.5 million on fund balances. This law is expected to have a substantial impact on pension contributions.

*Bancassurance*, which first appeared in the U.K. in the 1970s, has not made significant inroads into the life insurance market, with about 18 percent of new premiums written. Banks, sometimes in alliance with life insurers, have developed several simple life insurance products and sell them through their branches at attractive rates. Those attractive rates are possible in part by banks' lower overhead and distribution costs.

Distribution channels in the U.K. have been in flux since the late 1980s because of regulatory changes. The implementation of the *Financial Services Act* of 1986 resulted in a clear distinction between independent financial advisors (IFAs) and appointed and

---

### INSIGHT 21.1: HOW BONUSES WORK IN THE UNITED KINGDOM

Assume an endowment policy with a guaranteed sum assured of £10,000 and 5 years to maturity. The policyholder thus expects at least £10,000 payable on death or at the policy's maturity date. If the policy is with profits, the insurer declares a reversionary bonus at the end of each year. If this bonus is 5 percent, the guaranteed sum assured will have increased to £12,763 at the end of 5 years, as these bonuses are usually calculated on a compound basis.

If the policy also has a terminal bonus feature, the insurer will pay the bonus as a percentage of the sum of the original sum assured and reversionary bonuses. This percentage is often quite high. For example, if the terminal bonus were 100 percent, the policyholder would receive the £12,763 (the original sum plus reversionary bonuses) and a terminal bonus of £12,763, for a total payout of £25,526. Bonuses obviously are a major factor in the purchase of life insurance policies in the U.K.

*Source*: Popplewell (1992).

---

company representatives. IFAs, including insurance brokers, banks, building societies, lawyers and accountants, are required by law to survey the market to find the best products to meet their clients' needs. Appointed and company representatives include tied agents, home service employees and other types of company agents. They are limited to selling products of the company with which they are affiliated.

The role of independent brokers in the U.K. has traditionally been stronger than in other European countries, but they also are beginning to lose market share to banks and building societies. The traditional tied agent sales force has declined in relative importance. Most insurers have switched to IFAs. Premium volume via direct marketing comprises about 5 percent of the life insurance sector. By contrast, IFAs generate about 63 percent of regular premium businesses and about 70 percent of single-premium businesses.

The U.K. has had its problems. Selling scandals involving PEPs and other products have weakened consumer confidence in the life insurance industry. The regulatory landscape seems to change frequently, complicating insurer management and sales. Finally, poor stock market returns in the early 2000s penalized unit-linked and other product returns.

### *France*

With one of the largest and most highly developed life insurance industries in the world, France ranks fourth in terms of premium volume at US$154 billion in 2005, behind the U.S., Japan and the U.K. The life and health insurance market accounts for about 70 percent of the total French insurance market. *Caisse Nationale de Prévoyance* (CNP), AXA, Predica, BNP Parabas Assurance and Generali are leading life insurance writers in France. The combined premiums of these top five companies were more than 50 percent of the premiums written in 2003.

Life insurers in France offer a variety of products. These include term life insurance (*assurances en cas de décès*), endowment insurance (*assurances en cas de vie*), accident and health insurance (*assurance en cas de maladie ou d'accident*) and credit insurance (*assurance emprunteur*). Some French insurance products are unique. For example, the **capital redemption bond** (*bon de capitalization*) is a cash value contract that guarantees a fixed, lump-sum benefit at maturity. Unlike typical life insurance, no insured is designated.

France continues to enjoy spectacular growth of endowment insurance. The *Fédération Française des Sociétés d'Assurances* (FFSA) reports that euro-based endowment insurance and unit-linked endowment insurance contributed 67 percent and 14 percent, respectively, to the premiums written in France in 2002. Most of the endowment policies were purchased by individuals. By contrast, the share of term life insurance remains relatively low at 6 percent. The FFSA also reports life insurance accounts for one-third of household financial assets in France.

French life insurance distribution systems have changed markedly, particularly in terms of the *bancassurance* share of the market. In 2004, 62 percent of life policies were written by *bancassurance* companies – banks, the Post Office and the Treasury Office – compared with only 19 percent in 1983. CNP has long held the right to distribute its products through the Post Office and Treasury Office branches. This strategy has proven successful. *Bancassurance* insurers such as Prédica (subsidiary of the large French bank *Crédit Agricole*) and SOGECAP (subsidiary of the large French bank *Société Générale*) are both among the largest life insurers in France.

This unusual dominance of *bancassurance* in insurance marketing was fueled by the advantageous tax treatment accorded life insurance products in France. Other legal changes fostering growth was the elimination in 1990 of premium taxes for most individual life insurance contracts and the introduction of new individual pension plans in 2004 that allowed citizens to make tax-free contributions to individual accounts up to a defined limit.

Marketing through salaried sales associates generated 16 percent of life insurance premiums in France in 2003, a slight decrease from the previous year. General agents and brokers are not major players for the distribution of life and health insurance products in France.

### Germany

Life insurance premium volume in Germany was about US$90.2 billion in 2005. It is the fourth largest European market in premium volume. Its European rank drops to 12th using the insurance penetration ratio as a basis and 13th when measured on a premium per capita basis. The largest five life insurers – Allianz, Hamburg-Mannheimer, Aschener und Munchener, R&V and Deutsche Herold – are locally incorporated stock companies. Their aggregate market share was 33 percent in 2005 (Towers Perrin, 2005).

Annuities and endowment insurance are the most popular products in Germany. They account for 38 percent and 23 percent, respectively, of premiums written. Unit-linked products are somewhat popular, although their market share fell in the difficult 2001–2003 stock market period. Recent figures suggest a return to growth. The share of term life insurance remains low at 5 percent. Group life insurance is increasingly popular.

In terms of product features, policy dividend treatment in Germany is similar to that of the U.K. and includes automatic increases in policy face amounts. This extremely popular feature is found in more than two-thirds of existing policies in Germany.

Tied agents are the main distribution channels in Germany, accounting for about 35 percent of the premium volume. Independent agents and brokers together claim a 25 percent market share. The share by banks is about 25 percent. Interestingly, tied-pyramid sales forces claim a share of 6 percent.

With recent income tax reform, changes in insurance consumption in Germany are anticipated. The government no longer permits deduction of insurance premiums by individuals from taxable income. For all endowment policies purchased in 2005 and later, capital gains embedded in maturity benefits are taxable in the year of payment.[11] Capital gains embedded in annuity benefits also are subject to income tax at the year of receipt according to the *Ertragsanteil* (earnings proportion) table (Towers Perrin, 2005). At the same time, recently introduced individual and occupational pension products that enjoy tax preferences are expected to enhance life insurer premium income.

## Russia

The largest European market by population is Russia, with some 145 million inhabitants. This great population may be contrasted with Russia's comparatively modest life insurance premium volume of US$904 million or only about US$6 per head for 2005. These figures represent a three-quarters decrease from their 2004 counterparts, caused by the elimination of salary schemes involving the purchase of life insurance to avoid paying taxes on wages. These financial schemes dominated the Russian life insurance industry.

We also must realize that prior to 1990, Russia had a monopolistic market with no laws governing insurance supervision, including licensing or insurance contracts or sales. The newly formed Russian Union of Insurers provided some regulatory guidance, a variation of which passed the Russian Parliament in 1992, but this was later supplanted by presidential decrees in 1993. Today, Russia has both an insurance code and an insurance inspectorate.

After moving away from state monopoly – *Gostra* (or its descendent, *Rosgosstrakh*) for local business and *Ingostra* for international business – to a competitive market, Russia is now a home of about 1,500 life and nonlife insurance companies, 700 brokerages and more than 50,000 tied agents. The Russian life insurance market grew by an average of 23 percent per annum between 1998 and 2004, largely because of the above salary scheme. While Russia has constructed a rudimentary legal framework for free-market insurance activities, compliance remains problematic. Another challenge is defining what legally constitutes an insurance company and what legal ownership forms it may take, two items on which Russian legislators continue to work.

## Other European markets

Life insurance markets continue to mature in Eastern and Central European countries. With the continued deregulation and liberalization of the region, most countries abolished state monopolies and invited foreign insurers to enter their markets. Such moves have been, to some extent, in line with their expectation to join the E.U. Some already achieved this goal and became E.U. members in 2004 – the Czech Republic, Estonia, Hungary, Latvia, Lithuania, Malta, Poland, Slovenia and Slovakia. Bulgaria and Romania joined the E.U. in 2007. Additionally, Croatia, Turkey and the Former Yugoslav Republic of Macedonia seek approval for their entry applications.

Hungary, the Czech Republic and Poland appear to be the strongest new E.U. life insurance markets. Relatively large populations, a strong propensity to save and sound economic growth in recent years in these countries have enhanced life insurance demand. Workers previously protected by state pension schemes now worry about the effects of inflation on their benefits. These factors coupled with private pension reforms have further enhanced interest in private life insurance. The Czech Republic and Hungary registered life insurance premiums of US$1.9 billion and US$1.5 billion, respectively, in 2005. Poland established a new regulatory framework in 1990. With a population of almost 40 million, it generated life insurance premiums of US$3.9 billion in 2005. Successful life products in the Polish market include whole life, endowment and unit-linked insurance.

## Market issues

E.U. life insurance markets are becoming more competitive and, with the continuing push by the European Commission, promise to become both more harmonized and still more competitive in the future. Even so, several important issues are yet to be fully resolved. We discuss some of these issues below:

- *E.U. harmonization*: It remains to be seen what form harmonization ultimately will take. Under the *Third Life Insurance Directive*, strict regulatory regimes in E.U. countries may no longer hinder competition from insurers domiciled in other E.U. countries. Still, important questions related to taxation, pension policy, competition policy and contract law remain to be addressed before a true single market can be achieved.

- *Introduction of International Financial Reporting Standards (IFRS)*: The E.U. and most other major markets (e.g., Australia, China, Japan and Switzerland) are moving toward compliance with the IFRS of the International Accounting Standards Board (IASB). This attempt to harmonize financial accounting rules internationally promises profound changes within many markets and with many insurers. The E.U. decision to require its member states to abandon their national accounting standards in favor of IFRS effective 2005 has been the focus of great discussion and concern.

    The IFRS requires changes in the way assets and liabilities are valued; from historical or book cost to fair value. Consequently, many insurers' balance sheets will look different and take on the appearance of being more volatile as assets and liabilities are required to be adjusted to better reflect underlying economic reality. The introduction of IFRS is especially important to life insurers, given their long-duration liabilities and corresponding assets. The effects could be that they (1) favor investment in bonds over equities, (2) take on less risk by reducing their writing of long-duration contracts and (3) place greater reliance on reinsurance and/or other risk-shifting techniques as a risk management tool.

- *Bancassurance movement*: The *bancassurance* movement continues to increase cost pressures on traditional insurers. As *bancassurance* becomes even more widely accepted, it will be increasingly difficult for conventional insurers to support costly agency distribution systems and overhead. Consolidation will likely occur in countries with strong *bancassurance* movements unless insurers can find a way to compete effectively against these low-cost providers.

- *Direct response marketing*: Direct response marketing has gained momentum in Europe, especially in the nonlife personal lines. As direct insurers become more adept, their life insurance business should grow. Direct insurance companies frequently benefit from an even lower cost structure than that of the *bancassurance* companies. Once again, conventional insurers fear losing market share to these low-cost providers. The direct insurance movement also may hold risks for *bancassurance* firms, as the direct insurance products are likely to be similar to those of many *bancassurance* firms.

• *Recession and unemployment*: Europe continues to experience major unemployment problems, particularly among the youth. The high costs of various European social insurance programs, coupled with difficulty in terminating redundant employees, have resulted in the reluctance of potential employers to hire new people. Over staffing results in high overhead costs for all employers, including established insurers. It is difficult for firms to undertake staff reengineering projects, hence hindering established insurers vis-à-vis new entrants.

   During the early part of the 21st century, investment returns fell throughout most of the E.U. Because E.U. life insurers tended to invest heavily in equities, they suffered substantial capital reductions and ratings downgrades. Meeting their policy guarantees often proved challenging as well. Consequently, life insurers began readjusting their investment portfolios away for equities toward fixed income instruments such as bonds and mortgages and also began offering products with fewer long-term guarantees. Today, with the market having turned around, insurers seem largely to have weathered the storm and have much stronger internal risk management programs in place.

• *The evolving pension and health market*: One result of the turmoil being experienced by many European governments as they struggle with policy decisions about how best to address the long-term costs of financing their generous health and welfare programs has been the realization by many consumers that they need supplemental insurance. Given the aging population in Europe and the inability of governments to continue current levels of funding for these programs, benefit reductions in some form seem all but certain. This challenge offers a major market opportunity for private insurers that provide supplemental health insurance and pensions.

## Life Insurance Markets in the Asia-Pacific Region

To many observers, the Asia-Pacific region offers the world's greatest life insurance potential. Japan was for years the global leader in life insurance premium volume. Life insurance also figures prominently in the financial markets of Australia, Hong Kong, Korea, New Zealand, Singapore and Taiwan, to name the markets with per capita premium volumes of greater than US$1,000 in the region.

   As other markets in the region have been deregulated and opened to international competition, they have seen significant premium increases, brought about because of competition that brings innovative products, distribution and management processes. Two of the most promising markets, China and India, have yet to fully liberalize, but both seem committed to this path longer term – with the promise of enormous markets.

   Countries in the Asia-Pacific region display immense diversity in level of economic and political development, ethnicity, culture and religion. Some are developed (e.g. Australia, Hong Kong, Japan, Korea, New Zealand, Singapore and Taiwan), some developing (e.g., Brunei, Malaysia and Thailand), and others among the least developed (e.g., Bangladesh, Cambodia, Laos, Myanmar and Nepal).

   In most developing countries in the region, simple term and whole life insurance products are sold, but their consumption, as measured by per capita premium, remains low. Life insurance other than personal accident insurance is virtually unavailable in Cambodia. Neither is life insurance popular in Laos as it is commonly believed that insurance is "tantamount to calling down misfortune to one's head" (Laos Ministry of Finance, 1999).

   In economically affluent countries, life insurance products with strong savings elements predominate. For example, Taiwanese parents often purchase an endowment policy for which maturity is synchronized with the year that their child enters college or the year they plan to use the insurance benefit as a down payment for home purchase. In Hong Kong, Malaysia and Singapore, individuals use their cash balances in the national mandatory savings schemes to purchase single-premium annuities to secure their retirement. The result is relatively high life insurance penetration ratios in those countries.

## *Japan*

The Japanese life insurance market is the world's second largest after the U.S. in terms of premium volume. The 2005 premium volume of US$376 billion accounted for 19 percent of life premiums written globally. Japan's insurance density of US$2,956 ranks as the world's fourth largest after the U.K., Switzerland and Belgium. Forty life insurance companies – including seven mutuals – operate in Japan.

For many years, Japan's life insurance market was the world's largest. However, the malaise of the Japanese economy during the 1990s and early 2000s took its toll on life insurers' premium income as policyholders sought alternative savings vehicles to insurance. Insurers experienced financial instability because of a so-called "negative spread" (investment yields below those guaranteed in policies). As an attempt to revive the market, the government began to liberalize the market. It allowed new entrants, imposed fewer restrictions on product development and pricing, promoted competition, and introduced other measures unfamiliar to Japanese life insurers.

The reforms caused changes in market behavior. In the past, for example, agent commissions were set by the Ministry of Finance, and agents would never leave their company for another. Only exclusive agents were permitted in the market. Product and dividend rates were set by the ministry, so all insurers offered basically the same products. The chief means by which they differentiated themselves and attained greater market share was either better agent recruiting or more convenient office networks, in addition to advertising. These practices have now fallen into disfavor but their effects remain: real life premium volume has fallen an average of 1 percent annually over the preceding decade.

The government introduced several other reform measures. The *Insurance Business Law* revised in 1996 permits demutualization and entry of life insurers into the nonlife business through subsidiaries and vice versa. The government lifted the ban of insurance holding companies in 1997, removed fire walls within the financial services sector in 1998, permitted insurance companies to enter the so-called "third sector" (the segment of the insurance business having an exclusive right to develop and sell certain morbidity-based products) in 2001 and made it possible for insurers to act as agents for other financial institutions in 2003. The government also partially lifted the ban on over-the-counter sales of long-term fire insurance products, credit life insurance and overseas travel insurance in 2001. Two years later, the government also permitted banks to market individual annuity as well as *Zaikai* savings and personal accident insurance products.

## *Products and distribution systems*

Until the mid-1960s, pure endowments were popular.[12] With rapid economic growth and the attendant movement away from the traditional extended family, Japanese began to purchase more death-protection products. In the 1970s, the market was dominated by endowment insurance with a term life rider. The 1980s witnessed a shift from endowment insurance with term rider to whole life insurance, particularly after a reduction of premium rates in 1985. Not surprisingly, annuities, LTC and health insurance have witnessed strong growth

## INSIGHT 21.2: SELECTED LIFE INSURANCE PRODUCTS IN JAPAN

The following are major life insurance products for individuals sold in Japan:

- *Term insurance with survival benefits*: Term policy payable at death within a specified period and also pays survival benefits at the end of every specified period. Purchased mainly by young people and women.

- *Whole life with term insurance rider*: A whole life policy combined with a term rider that pays, for example, 10 times the amount payable at death when death occurs during the premium-paying period.

- *Endowment with term insurance rider*: An endowment policy combined with a term rider that pays, for example, 10 times the amount payable at maturity when death occurs prior to maturity.

- *Juvenile insurance*: Policy payable not only at maturity, but it also pays a stipulated amount of congratulatory benefits at the insured child's entrance to school. Purchased to prepare for the expenses of the child's education, marriage, and independence.

- *Savings insurance*: Policy payable at maturity or at prior death. Serves mainly as a short-term savings plan.

- *Individual annuity*: Annuity purchased as a means to secure income during retirement. A stipulated annual income becomes payable from a predetermined age. Two types are available. One is either whole life or term annuity payable only during the beneficiary's lifetime. The other is payable during a specified period regardless of the beneficiary's death.

- *Variable life insurance*: A variable policy whose maturity benefit and surrender value vary according to the performance of an underlying separate account, except the guaranteed basic portion of the death benefits. Endowment type with maturity and whole life type with death protection for whole life are available.

- *Sickness/medical insurance*: Medical insurance and living benefits are available. Medical insurance is purchased to cover the expenses from hospitalization and surgical operations caused by sickness or injury. With living benefit insurance, a death benefit is payable prior to death if the insured develops any of the three killer geriatric diseases.

- *Disability income protection insurance*: A policy that provides both death protection and benefits if the insured becomes unable to work due to sickness or injury.

- *Nursing care insurance*: A long-term care policy whose benefits are payable if the insured becomes demented or bed-ridden and the condition persists for a specified period.

*Source*: Adopted from the English version of "Life Insurance Business in Japan," published by the Life Insurance Association of Japan (2003).

in recent years, as the population continues to age and fewer children are available to take care of elderly parents. See Insight 21.2 for a description of selected life insurance products available in Japan.

In terms of policies in force at yearend 2004, individual and group insurance (including annuity) accounted for 75 percent of the market. In terms of premiums written during the same year, however, individual insurance and annuity accounted for 90 percent of the market. Of all major lines of business, only individual annuity continues to grow in terms of new business. Individual insurance remains relatively unchanged, and group insurance and reinsurance continue to shrink. Traditional life insurance products, particularly term life, whole life (with or without a term rider), adjustable interest rate whole life and endowment insurance remain popular in Japan.

Distribution in Japan remains dominated by the industry's large network of part-time, female agents. In 2006, some 260,000 agents were associated with sales branches of life insurers throughout the country. These operating units, which report to local branch offices, handle sales, premium collection and policyholder service. The sales agents are required to be exclusive agents and generally transact business through house calls. During the past decade or so, the number of financial planners offering life insurance products as part of their services has risen. Many of them are employed by non-insurance financial institutions and by foreign-owned life insurers.

*Market issues*

The life insurance market in Japan continues to address several issues. We summarize some below:

- *Role of non-conventional life insurers*: Two major life insurance suppliers in Japan are the Postal Insurance Service and Japan Agricultural Cooperative Insurance. The former, better known as *Kampo*, is the largest insurer and drew premium income of ¥12,191 billion in 2003. Japan Agricultural Cooperative Insurance, run by *Zenkyoren* (National Mutual Insurance Federation of Agricultural Cooperatives), generated premium income, including income from the nonlife insurance business, of ¥5,587 billion. By contrast, the aggregate premium income of the five largest life insurance companies – Nippon Life, Dai-ichi, Meiji Yasuda, Sumitomo and ALICO Japan – was ¥15,876 billion in 2003 (Towers Perrin, 2005). With the passage of postal laws in 2005, the government plans to restructure its postal agency as a holding company for privatization in 2007. Two of its subsidiaries – one for the postal savings business and the other for the life insurance business – are scheduled to be sold off by 2017.

- *Mega mergers and acquisitions*: Already large life insurance companies have become even larger through a series of mergers and acquisitions since the late 1990s. In 2004 alone, Meiji Yasuda Life was born through the merger of Meiji Life and Yasuda Life; T&D Holdings emerged from consolidating the businesses of Daido Life (demutualized in 2002), Taiyo Life (demutualized in 2002) and T&D Financial Life; the Millea Group acquired Skandia Life and renamed it as Tokio Marine & Nichido Financial Life; and Prudential (U.S.) acquired Aoba Life. These mergers and acquisitions likely guarantee the dominance of a few large life insurers in Japan.

- *Fallout from the bubble economy*: The steep decline in the value of Japanese equities and real estate holdings in the 1990s, as the so-called "bubble economy" came to an end, has had a continuing impact on Japanese life insurance companies. Most Japanese insurers remain solvent, but virtually every Japanese insurer suffered heavy losses in their stock and real estate portfolios. A contributing factor in these problems has been the tendency of the Ministry of Finance to "encourage" life insurers to invest in segments of the Japanese market that the ministry believed were weak and in need of bolstering.

- *Aging population*: The Japanese enjoy the world's greatest life expectancy, and Japan is probably the world's oldest country in terms of population age. While population aging should offer the promise of additional demand for savings, LTC and health products offered by life insurers, it also raises potentially troubling questions longer term about the fiscal impact that, in turn, affects the level of economic prosperity. Japan is also among the countries with the world's lowest birth rates. The population is projected to continue to decline for years to come.

- *"Westernization" of the younger generation*: Some part of the historical success of Japan's life insurance industry must be attributed to the social and cultural norms that have helped Japan to have one of the world's highest savings rates. However, as the Japanese culture is more influenced by the West, many traditional Japanese social mores have begun to erode. The younger generation of Japanese has consumer spending habits that are often more akin to those of their American peers than to those of their parents, with a concomitant reduction in savings. This shift in cultural norms could have profound implications for the financial services sector which will have to adapt to an environment where purchasing life insurance is no longer an automatic decision for many consumers.

Japanese life insurers have substantial presences in other countries, but mostly as investors. Japanese insurers are much less involved in overseas expansion than their European and North American counterparts. Indeed, while no Japanese insurer can be said to have a truly global life insurance business, Nippon Life has embarked on a modest program of expansion within Asia, already being licensed in China, the Philippines and Thailand and is studying the markets in Malaysia and India.

### Korea

The Korean life insurance market is the world's seventh largest, with total premiums written of US$59 billion in 2005. Its penetration ratio of 7.27 percent is 8th highest in the world, and its per capita consumption of US$1,211 ranked at 18th worldwide in 2005. The penetration ratio was much higher before the economy suffered from the Asian economic crisis in the late 1990s (e.g., 11.63 percent in 1997, the world's second highest at the time). The Korean economy has recovered from the crisis, with strong growth in life insurance premium income recently. Nevertheless, continuing low interest rates make life insurance products less attractive than formerly.

The Korean life insurance market has undergone several changes. With a revision of the *Insurance Business Act* in 2003, life insurers began to offer investment insurance products (e.g., variable life), participate, albeit on a limited basis, in indemnity insurance and offer their products jointly with banking institutions. Sales of life insurance products as part of long-term financial planning services also are observed. Critical illness insurance including cancer insurance has grown in popularity recently.

The Korea Life Insurance Association (2006) reports that endowment and death-protection life insurance accounted for 97 percent of individual life insurance sales. Variable life, introduced in 1999, accounts for less than 1 percent of market share in terms of new businesses sold as of 2006. Life insurers in Korea generate almost 50 percent of their premiums from selling savings-oriented products.

A chronic problem of policy lapses and surrenders remains as a key issue in the market. In 2005, the industry experienced lapses and surrenders amounting to 4 percent of business in force but 42 percent on new business (KLIA, 2006).

Life insurance products are sold through mostly part-time, female agents who comprise more than 80 percent of the 125,000 insurance agents. As a result, new business per agent remains relatively low in terms of premiums. Recently, the number of male agents as well as full-time agents has been growing.

The Korean government actively promotes *bancassurance* and has been expanding the scope of products in several phases permitting sales of savings-type, credit products since August 2003, exclusively protection-type "third insurance" covering (post) illness and injury risks since April 2005, "third insurance with cash value at maturity" since October 2006 and automobile and other protection-type products from April 2008. The government expects *bancassurance* to capture more than 50 percent of life insurance and 36 percent of non-life sales (FSS Korea, 2006). Banks, through strategic alliances with life and nonlife insurers, dominate this market (capturing over 90 percent of the *bancassurance* market share in terms of earned premiums), although security firms and credit card companies also offer *bancassurance* products. The Korea Life Insurance Association (2005) reports that, as of 2004, 14 of the countries' 23 life insurers were using *bancassurance* channels along with their traditional agency-based sales forces.

Government policy prohibits life insurers within large conglomerates from acquiring or establishing banking operations, thus hindering Korea's largest life insurers from taking full advantage of *bancassurance* operations. By contrast, the large Korean banks can benefit fully from such operations.

Life insurance companies in Korea also face competition with nonlife insurers. A law enacted in 2005 permits nonlife insurers to sell individual pension products. This law is in addition to an existing one that permits nonlife insurers to sell selected life insurance products, provided the length of insurance protection is not for the whole of life. Another key issue in the life market is when and under what terms several large life insurance cmpanies will conduct their initial public offerings.

## Taiwan

The fourth largest life insurance market in Asia (after Japan, Korea and China) in terms of premium volume, Taiwan has a strong life insurance industry and the world's highest life insurance penetration at 11.17 percent (2005). The 2005 life premium volume in Taiwan was US$38.8 billion. Taiwan began to open its market to foreign insurance companies in the mid-1990s and recently embarked on stronger deregulation, especially as to investments and product design and pricing flexibility. As of 2006, 30 life insurance companies – including eight foreign companies – operated in Taiwan, with the three largest life insurers – Cathay Life, Shin Kong and Nan Shan – maintaining their 80 percent combined market share. Taiwan has been a low interest environment, with the result that life insurers have had to manage through the same type of "negative spread" issue as in Japan.

Unit-linked life and annuity products have shown strong recent sales, although traditional products such as whole life and endowment have the largest proportions of in-force business. Taiwan uses distribution systems found in established life insurance markets, with the brokerage channel and *bancassurance* growing rapidly (holding 13 percent of market share in 2005). As is the case in other Asian countries, many of Taiwan's life insurance agents are part time.

## *China*

With a population of 1.3 billion, the Peoples Republic of China is the life insurance market with the greatest growth potential in the world, according to many observers. Indeed, a well-known consulting firm recently predicted that the market would be the world's largest by the year 2025. China's moves toward a market-oriented economy have attracted enormous interest from overseas insurers. Starting from essentially no life insurance in force during the 1980s, China's life insurance premium growth has averaged 24 percent per year for more than a decade. Such rapid growth is attributable to several forces, including starting from a low base, a high savings propensity among Chinese citizens, comparatively low rates on bank savings, a paucity of other investment vehicles and limited public retirement schemes.

China began allowing foreign insurer participation in its market only during the 1990s. Except for AIG, which was granted a full license in 1992, all foreign insurers have been required either to form 50/50 joint ventures with large local businesses or to take no more than a 25 percent ownership stake in a Chinese insurer. To date, more than 20 joint ventures operate.

The market is dominated by three large, established Chinese life insurers: China Life Insurance Company, Ping An Insurance and China Pacific Life. New companies have a small, but rapidly growing market share. Because established insurers are said to lack some state-of-the-art operations and have low agent sales rates, they are considered vulnerable to the new competitors. Additionally, their agents are said to offer poor service and sometimes misleading advice. Foreign insurers are said to offer strong brands, provide better service and employ more professional agents.

Distribution in China is via exclusive agents. A full portfolio of whole life, term, endowment, annuity and special savings products is offered by most companies. Variable life also is found in China. *Bancassurance* is promising.

Hong Kong, a special administrative region of China as of 1997, has a sophisticated, well-developed life insurance market. All traditional products (whole life, endowment and term) are available, but endowment and whole life hold the largest market shares. The career agent/branch office system dominates in terms of distribution, although brokerage is attracting interest. Direct response marketing is becoming more common, as is distribution through banks.

## *India*

India is the world's second largest country as measured by population, with projections for it to surpass China within the next two decades. Some observers expect India to become one of the world's largest life insurance markets in the future. Annual life premium growth averaged about 13 percent over the preceding decade and is expected to achieve even stronger growth as new competitors vie for the business of more than 200 million middle and high-income Indians who previously were underserved.

Less than a decade ago, India's life insurance market was composed of a single, monopoly insurer, the Life Insurance Corporation (LIC) of India. As of 1999, new insurers were allowed, but foreigners can own no more than 26 percent of any new Indian life insurer. Today, 16 life insurers, mostly created jointly with large international life insurers, contest in an increasingly competitive market. Their market share based on new business has grown to 20 percent in terms of first-year premium, from a base of zero in 1999.

Premium volume in India was US$20.1 billion in 2005, although life insurance penetration was only 2.53 percent. Products in India are mostly traditional whole life and endowment with some term insurance. Variable policies are now permitted, with such products gaining rapid acceptance in the market. Whereas formerly the regulatory authority allowed distribution via exclusive agents only, new channels are now allowed, including brokers and *bancassurance.*

For the year ending 2005, premium income from renewal policies accounted for 68.4 percent of life business, followed by new policies (19.1 percent) and single-premium policies (12.5 percent). Increasingly popular unit-linked insurance (32.5 percent increase in premiums from 2004) contribute to the growth in the market. LIC continues to dominate the market, generating 79 percent of life insurance premiums written and 91.5 percent of policies sold. Nevertheless, its market share continues to shrink.[13]

## Australia

The Australian life insurance market, with 35 companies generating US$27.6 billion in premium (2005), is one of the world's most sophisticated. Australia, along with its partner, New Zealand, underwent significant deregulation some years ago. Today, both markets are incredibly competitive and are subject to strict disclosure requirements and strong consumer protection, solvency, and actuarial standards.

The market is dominated by several large companies, with the top three accounting for two-thirds of new business premiums. The top three companies – Australian Mutual Provident (AMP), National Australia and ING (Australia) – accounted for 65 percent of total life premiums written in 2005. Traditional and investment-linked products are sold, with 80 percent on a single-premium basis. Easily the largest product sales occur in the pension (or **superannuation**, the term used in Australia and elsewhere) area, which accounted for 88 percent of premiums written in 2005 (APRA, 2006). Bank-owned life insurers accounted for 38 percent of new premiums written in 2005, and foreign-owned insurers wrote another 28 percent. With the recent introduction of higher capital requirements and the elimination of life insurance tax preferences in 2005, unit-linked business could suffer.

## Southeast Asian Nations

The Association of Southeast Asian Nations (ASEAN) region (comprising Brunei, Indonesia, Malaysia, Philippines, Singapore, Thailand and Vietnam) has been one of the most dynamic in the recent decades. Total ASEAN life premium volume in 2005 was US$19.2 billion, with an overall life insurance penetration ratio of 2.22, which varied from a low of 0.82 percent in Indonesia to a high of 6.00 percent in Singapore. The economies and life insurance industries within ASEAN are at different growth stages, with Singapore being the most advanced.

ASEAN life products are mainly traditional whole life and endowment but with unit-linked and annuity business growing rapidly in a few markets. Endowment policy sales are decreasing in proportion to other types of insurance. Distribution systems in the ASEAN region rely almost exclusively on face-to-face selling by part-time, male and female captive (tied) agents. Group representative offices are established in some countries.

Because of the high growth potential for life insurance, most of these countries have attracted significant foreign direct investment. Indeed, numerous foreign life insurers, including those from Australia, Canada, Europe the U.S., and recently other Asian countries, are attracted to the region because of its growth potential. These new entrants bring different approaches to the business in terms of distribution, product design, management style and technology.

In some ASEAN countries, insurance regulations are not well established; thus, regulations may change dramatically from one political administration to the next. Items such as reserve limits, investment policy limits, and limits on overseas control of domestic companies can pose difficulties for foreign insurers entering these markets. For example, Indonesia's dual market entry and capital regulation – being more stringent for foreign companies – places a difficult burden on new market entrants.[14]

The image of the life insurance industry is mixed in the ASEAN region. Some cultural groups oppose the idea of life insurance as they perceive it to conflict with their religious beliefs and family norms. Another image problem results from the lack of professionalism shown by some insurance salespeople. These image problems hinder market development.

The rapid pace of change in the ASEAN region affects the life insurance industry as well. Some countries face shortages of qualified labor. Rapid urbanization and social change are disrupting cultural norms that have been in place for centuries. For local insurers accustomed to a more stable environment, new entrants precipitate an avalanche of change.

## African Life Insurance Markets

Most life insurance markets of African countries have long been hampered by political and economic turmoil, resulting in the some of the world's lowest life insurance penetration ratios. African life insurance figures are dominated by South Africa. It accounts for more than 90 percent of the region's total life insurance volume. In countries with a measure of stability, life insurance has become important, particularly in Namibia, Mauritius and Botswana. The large Egyptian market has recently recorded the continent's most impressive life premium growth rates, averaging around 30 percent for each of the previous three years.

The South African life insurance market has the world's second highest life insurance penetration at 10.84 percent (2005). The industry is concentrated, with several large companies – Old Mutual, Sanlam, Momentum, Liberty and Invested Assurance – controlling most of the market. South African insurers sell a mix of individual and group products, including term and whole life, health, pension and annuity products. Single-premium policies formerly were quite popular, but the growing South African stock market has given impetus to variable products. Banks, offshore financial services companies, unit trusts and other structured product providers also are involved in insurance. Distribution is usually through field offices, brokers and captive agents.

# CONCLUSION

Life insurance companies are important financial intermediaries in developed and emerging economies. While wide variations exist from country to country in approach to such issues as foreign insurers in the marketplace, regulation, products for savings versus products for risk, and distribution systems, numerous similarities exist between markets at similar stages of development. As the industry grows internationally, both insurers and consumers will benefit from the sharing of new ideas and from the efficiencies that global competition will bring.

Life insurers are major sources of long-term investment funds. These investments can contribute to a country's economic development. The establishment of a secure and growing life insurance market is often a primary objective of emerging market-economy countries.

The pace of global change in life insurance is accelerating. The life insurance industry's products and methods of operating changed little from the beginning of the 20th century until the 1970s. However, competition from other financial services providers, a constantly changing regulatory structure and cost pressures in the past and even today have resulted in dramatic upheavals in the industry. As traditional life insurers struggled to cope with the new environment, an unprecedented wave of product innovation and business process improvement (reengineering) coincided with the increasing globalization of the industry. As a result, the industry has become much more dynamic and competitive. Insurers are pursuing widely differing strategies to try to succeed in this new environment.

Mergers, acquisitions, strategic alliances, and new entrants are changing the face of the industry. Prior to the 1980s, it was unusual for life insurance companies to acquire other life insurers or financial institutions. In recent decades, we have witnessed an enormous increase both in merger and acquisition activity among domestic life insurers as well as in cross-border alliances, acquisitions, and joint ventures involving partner companies from different countries. In addition, many life insurers acquired or entered alliances with banks, securities brokers and nonlife insurance companies. A related phenomenon has been **demutualization**, whereby mutual insurance companies change their corporate form to become stock companies in an effort to position themselves to attract more capital in part to fund acquisition activity, new market entry, or new product development.

With aging populations in many countries, life insurance companies are positioned to garner substantial consumer savings. Simultaneously, competition promises to become more severe, both within the life insurance industry and across financial service sectors.

Much of the success of life insurers in many markets has been due to tax preferences accorded government for their products. These preferences continue to be reduced or even eliminated, as governments seek to establish a "level playing field." Additionally, with increased consumer protection and mandatory disclosure, including of agent commissions, we can expect the character of markets to evolve, perhaps along the lines that we observe in Australia. Each of these matters will create both opportunities and challenges for life insurance companies within the domestic market and globally.

# DISCUSSION QUESTIONS

1. As the ASEAN insurance industry grows, we can expect continuing tensions between ASEAN countries with a well-developed market economy and those with more restrictive regimes. What advice would you give to an ASEAN insurance company that wishes to operate throughout the region?

2. Many U.S. life insurers have been reluctant to enter international markets. Why have they been reluctant historically to do so? Why do you believe U.S. insurers have begun to increase their international activities? Do you believe they will succeed? Why or why not?

3. In Europe, the direct marketing and *bancassurance* movements have gained enormous momentum. In many other countries, insurance is still sold through personal contact with an agent. What do you see as the strengths and weaknesses from the consumer's point of view of these three different strategies for selling life insurance?

# NOTES

1. This section is based in part on Black and Skipper (2000).
2. In Canada, the U.S., and many other countries, the term **ordinary insurance** is most commonly used in lieu of personal insurance. We use the latter term as being more descriptive.
3. Not covered in this book is **credit life insurance,** which is life insurance sold by and payable to credit-granting institutions insuring their borrowers' lives for the amounts of their indebtednesses. A variation is **credit health insurance**. The amount sold internationally is small in most markets.
4. In some markets, annuities and pension-related products are classified separately from life insurance policies.
5. Participating life insurance historically has been associated closely with mutual (i.e., policyholder-owned) insurance companies and nonpar has been associated closely with stock (i.e., stockholder-owned) insurers. In fact, most par insurance is still sold by mutuals and most nonpar by stocks, although each may sell the other form as well.
6. Tax law in some countries, such as the U.S. and Germany, effectively places an upper bound on the maximum premium that can be paid. Also, if the policyholder chooses to pay a premium, insurers typically insist on some minimum amount, such as US$25.
7. This section draws in part from McGreevy (1998).
8. Unless indicated otherwise, all national life insurance premium data are from Swiss Re (2006).
9. The 1,200 figure is the number of individually incorporated companies and not the number of life insurance company groups. Many groups have five or more affiliated companies. Additionally, the total premium figure does not include premiums paid to the more than 600 organizations that are not regulated as traditional insurance companies that write various types of healthcare coverage.
10. A. M. Best (2006).
11. Only 50 percent of the capital gains are taxable if, at policy maturity, the policyholder is at least 60 years old and the policy has been in force for 12 years or longer.
12. This section draws in part from LIAJ (2006).
13. IRDA (2006).
14. See Kwon (2002).

# REFERENCES

ACLI (American Council of Life Insurers) (2005). *Life Insurers Fact Book*. Washington, DC: American Council of Life Insurers.

Best, A.M. (2006). "Healthy Shrinkage." *Best's Review* (October): 48–52.

Black Jr., K. and Skipper, H.D. (2000). *Life and Health Insurance*, 13th edn. Upper Saddle River, NJ: Prentice Hall.

CLHIA (Canadian Life and Health Insurance Association) (2005). *Key Statistics 2005* at www.clhia.ca/download/KeyStats2005.pdf.

Financial Supervisory Commission (FSS Korea) (2006). *Press Release: Introduction of "Third Insurance" with Cash Value and Bancassurance Supervision (September 19)*. Seoul: FSS Korea.

Insurance Regulatory and Supervisory Authority (IRDA) (2006). *Annual Report 2004–2005*. New Delhi: IRDA.

Korea Life Insurance Association (KLIA) (2005). *Life Insurance Business in Korea: 2004/2005 Annual Report*. Seoul: KLIA.

Korea Life Insurance Association (KLIA) (2006). *Key Statistics 2006 (June)* at www.klia.or.kr/eng/statistics/stat_01.asp.

Kwon, W.J. (2002). "Free Trade in Services: Emerging Insurance Markets in Asia," *The Geneva Papers on Risk and Insurance – Issues and Practice*, 27 (October): 638–668. Laos Ministry of Finance (1999). "Country Note: Laos," in *Insurance Regulation and Supervision in Asia* (OECD: Paris), Singapore.

Life Insurance Association of Japan (LIAJ) (2003). *Life Insurance Business in Japan 2002/2003*. Tokyo: LIAJ.

Life Insurance Association of Japan (LIAJ) (2006). *Life Insurance Business in Japan 2004/2005*. Tokyo: LIAJ.

McGreevy, B.K. (1998). "Life and Health Insurance," in H.D. Skipper, Jr., ed., *International Risk and Insurance: An Environmental-Managerial Approach*. Boston, MA: Irwin/McGraw-Hill.

Popplewell, K. (1992). *Life Assurance*. London: Chartered Insurance Institute.

Swiss Re (2006). "World Insurance in 2006," *Sigma*. Zurich: Swiss Re.

Towers Perrin (2005). *Insurance Pocket Book 2005*. Oxfordshire, U.K.: Towers Perrin.

# Chapter 22

# Nonlife Insurance

## INTRODUCTION

Forms on risk transfer involving transported good can be traced back almost 4,000 years to the Chinese and the Babylonians. For example, the Babylonians around 1750 BC developed a system under which merchants who wished to finance their Mediterranean shipments through loans could pay a sum – a "premium" of the loan amount plus normal interest – to secure the lender's guarantee that the loan would be cancelled if the shipment was lost at sea or stolen.

The first distinct nonlife insurance policy seems to have originated in Genoa, Italy in the 14th century. The Great Fire of London in 1666, however, is said to have been the impetus for the creation of nonlife insurance as we know it today, with the creation in 1680 of the first nonlife insurance company, The Fire Office. Eight years later, Lloyd's of London came into existence.

This chapter completes the two-chapter sequence on insurance policies and insurance markets worldwide by focusing on the nonlife insurance sector. Paralleling our discussion in the preceding chapter, here we first provide an overview of the more common types of nonlife insurance policies sold worldwide. We follow this overview with information on selected nonlife insurance markets internationally. We close the chapter with a discussion of some of the issues confronting nonlife insurers.

## POLICIES SOLD BY NONLIFE INSURANCE COMPANIES

As we noted in Chapter 1, *nonlife insurance* is generally synonymous with the more descriptive terms *property and liability (P&L) insurance* and *property and casualty (P&C) insurance*. *General insurance* is also used in many markets. Chapter 1 also noted that insurance can be classified in several ways. Table 22.1 offers the OECD's classification scheme that relies on the object of insurance. This classification has the advantage of highlighting the many forms of nonlife insurance.

For present purposes, however, we opt for two other classifications. First, recall that we can classify insurance based on the purchaser. Thus, *personal insurance* is any insurance

**Table 22.1**   OECD Classification of Nonlife Insurance

| Category | Product Type |
|---|---|
| Motor Vehicle | • *Land Vehicles* (other than railway rolling stock) covering all damage to or loss of: land motor vehicles or land vehicles other than motor vehicles<br>• *Motor Vehicle Liability* covering all liability arising out of the use of motor vehicles operating on land (including carrier's liability) |
| Marine, Aviation and Transportation (MAT) | • *Railway Rolling Stock and Other Transport* covering all damage to or loss of railway rolling stock<br>• *Aircraft* covering all damage to or loss of aircraft<br>• *Ships* (sea, lake, and river and canal vessels) covering all damage to or loss of: river and canal vessels, lake vessels, and sea vessels<br>• *Aircraft Liability* covering all liability arising out of the use of aircraft (including carrier's liability)<br>• *Liability for Ships* (sea, lake, and river and canal vessels) covering all liability arising out of the use of ships, vessels, or boats on the sea, lakes, rivers, or canals (including carrier's liability) |
| Freight | • *Goods in Transit* (including merchandise, baggage and all other goods) covering all damage to or loss of goods in transit or baggage, irrespective of the form of transport |
| Fire and Other Property Damage | • *Fire and Natural Forces* covering all damage or loss of property due to fire, explosion, storm, natural forces other than storm, nuclear energy or land subsidence (excluded is property included in land vehicle, railway rolling stock and other transport, aircraft, ships and goods in transit)<br>• *Other Damage to Property* covering all damage or loss of property (other than property included in land vehicle, railway rolling stock and other transport, aircraft, ships and goods in transit) due to hail or frost, and any event such as theft, other than those mentioned under fire and natural forces |
| Pecuniary Loss | • *Credit* covering insolvency (general), export credit, installment credit, mortgages and agricultural credit<br>• *Surety*<br>• *Miscellaneous Financial Loss* covering employment risk, insufficiency of income (general), bad weather, loss of benefits, continuing general expenses, unforeseen trading expenses, indirect trading losses other than those mentioned above, other financial loss (non-trading), and other forms of financial loss |
| General Liability | • *General Liability* covering all liability other than those forms mentioned under motor vehicle liability, aircraft liability and liability for ships |
| Accident and Sickness | • *Accident* (including industrial injury and occupational diseases) covering: fixed pecuniary benefits, benefits in the nature of indemnity or injury to passengers |
| Other Nonlife Insurance | • *Legal Expenses* covering legal expenses and costs of litigation<br>• *Assistance*<br>• *Miscellaneous* |
| Treaty Reinsurance | • *Treaty Reinsurance* |

*Source*: OECD (2003).

purchased for individual or family needs, as opposed to business needs. *Commercial insurance* is any insurance purchased primarily for business or other organizational needs. Second, we can classify nonlife insurance based on its two broad categories: *property insurance* and *liability insurance*. We rely on both classifications in this section, organizing our presentation around the latter classification.

## Property Insurance Policies

Property insurance is the oldest form of insurance and the most widely sold form of nonlife insurance internationally. While property is the object of such insurance, legally the property itself is not insured – rather the owner of the property is insured based on his, her or its ownership interest in the property. This distinction is important because, among other reasons, it effectively prohibits anyone from insuring someone else's property for purposes of collecting insurance proceeds – an obvious moral hazard.

### Common aspects of property insurance policies

Property insurance policies are available to cover innumerable types of property and to cover them in different ways. This section provides an overview of the key aspects of such policies.

#### Nature of property and property losses

The term **property**, as used in the law, refers not to the object itself, but to the rights of possession, control and disposition. Ownership rights associated with land and objects permanently attached to land, such as buildings and factories, are referred to as **real property** or **immovable property**. Ownership rights in movable property, such as motor vehicles, money, aircraft, computers and ships are classified as **personal property** or **movable property**. Property insurance is available for both immovable and movable property, although not all such properties.

Personal property can be either tangible or intangible. **Tangible property** is physical property, whereas **intangible property** does not have a physical nature. Examples of intangible property include copyrights, patents and trade names. Such intangible property can be difficult to evaluate. Stock certificates, certificates of deposit and insurance policies are also examples of intangible property. These pieces of paper that establish one's ownership rights have no value in themselves but can represent assets of substantial value. Property insurance is generally available for both types of personal property, although as might be suspected, the moral hazard element is often more pronounced with intangible than with tangible personal property.

Two types of losses are associated with property damage: direct and consequential. **Direct property losses** are reductions in property values caused by a loss event and are the most obvious types of losses for property owners. The loss may be partial or total. **Consequential property losses** – also called **indirect property losses** – are reductions in income or increases in expenses that result from (are a consequence of) direct losses. Most direct loss is accompanied by loss of use that adds to the financial impact of the loss event, and sometimes this loss can be greater than the actual direct loss to the property.

#### Nature of covered perils

No property insurance policy promises to cover losses from all possible perils. While policies can be highly tailored to meet the needs of large customers, all policies limit their coverage through one of two general approaches: by inclusion or exclusion. First, policies that provide indemnification to the insured only if the cause of loss is one specifically "named as covered" in the policy are called **named-peril policies**. Coverage under named-peril policies is, thus, by *inclusion*. For example, if flood is *not* in the list of covered perils (a common omission from named-peril policies), no coverage is provided for damage caused by a flood.

Second, policies that provide indemnification to the insured for all causes of loss except those explicitly excluded by the policy are called **all-risks policies**. Coverage under all-risk policies is by *exclusion*. For example, if flood is *not* listed in the exclusions, damage to the covered property caused by flood would be covered. All-risks coverage is almost always broader and more expensive than named-peril coverage, other things being equal.

How insurers use the above two approaches naturally varies from country to country as well as from insurer to insurer. In general, however, coverage often is one of three generic types: basic form, broad from or special form:

* *Basic form policies* usually provide named-peril coverage for damage to covered property resulting from the most common perils such as fire lightning, windstorm, riot and civil commotion (commonly not including terrorism). Such policies typically are the most restrictive but also the least costly.

* *Broad form policies* often provide named-peril coverage for damage to covered property resulting from the basic perils but add others such as water damage (but not resulting from a flood), sinkhole collapse, weight of snow, ice or sleet and sprinkler leakage. Such policies offer coverage broader than the basic policy form but are more expensive.

* *Special form policies* provide all-risks coverage for damage to covered property resulting from any cause not specifically excluded by the policy such as flood, earth movement, war and warlike operations, and vermin. Such policies offer the broadest coverage but are the most expensive.

### Nature of indemnification

Property insurance policies typically promise to indemnify the insured for damage to covered property on one of two bases: actual cash value (ACV) or replacement cost. **ACV** is the cost presently (not original purchase price) to replace or repair damaged property less the value of physical depreciation and obsolescence. **Replacement cost** (also called **reinstatement value**) is the cost at the time of loss to replace destroyed or severely damaged property with the same or like-kind new property or the cost to repair damaged property, in each instance without deduction for any depreciation or obsolescence in property value.

ACV settlements obviously are less generous than replacement cost settlements. In effect, replacement cost settlements allow the insured to gain "new for old." It, thereby, carries a greater moral hazard potential than ACV settlements, but insurers believe that they minimize this potential by insisting that the property actually be replaced or repaired, as opposed to their paying the insured the equivalent amount in cash. If a cash settlement is preferred by the insured, the insurer's payment ordinarily is limited to an ACV basis. Of course, exceptions exist to this generalization of payment methods.[1] Property insurance coverage on immovables is more likely to be indemnified on a replacement cost basis than is coverage on movables.

Indemnification under consequential insurance coverage usually is on the basis of the **economic** or **use value** of property that reflects the lost utility associated with damaged property. Thus, a retail business whose premises are damaged by a fire may lose sales revenue because customers cannot purchase their goods. Insurance covering this loss would ordinarily be settled based on some measure of this lost revenue (e.g., as shown in financial statements).

Indemnification for inventory sometimes is based on its market value. **Market value** is the price prevailing in the market for the goods in the firm's inventory.

Of course, property insurance policies ordinarily carry deductibles. Many of them also contain a "coinsurance provision" to encourage insureds not to underinsure their properties. See Insight 22.1 for this and other uses of the term coinsurance.

### Pricing property insurance

Commercial insurers are free to use their own mix of underwriting factors (unless prohibited by law) to price property risks in most countries. Moreover, no two insurers would have identical risk and loss portfolios. This can result in a wide range of premiums quoted by insurers for the same risk. Nonetheless, several common underwriting factors are used in property insurance. Those factors can be classified into two groups: (1) characteristics of the covered property itself and (2) scope of insurance requested.

Thus, insurers use construction type (e.g., masonry or steel), occupancy (e.g., residential, office or warehouse), protection (e.g., security and surveillance systems), exposure (e.g., hazards posed by surrounding properties) and location (e.g., distance from the nearest fire department). These factors, along with the property value, are used to derive an expected loss profile for the property (i.e., a base premium). Second, the base premium is adjusted according mainly to the limit of insurance, covered causes of loss, deductible, coinsurance percentage and other optional coverages (e.g., flood, earth movement and terrorism endorsements) each insured elects.

### Types of policies

Property insurance policies are issued for personal and commercial purposes. Some policies cover only direct destruction and damage to property while others cover both direct and indirect losses. The focus of this section is on these policies. We should note, however, that many policies – called **package policies** or sometimes **multi-line policies** – cover both direct and indirect property exposures plus financial obligations and legal expenses arising from the insured's legal liability for injuries to others or damage to their property. Three of these liability policies are introduced in a later section. We summarize below some policies that emphasize property insurance and that either are common internationally or illustrate the breadth of coverage available:

- *Fire insurance policies* are named-peril contracts that agree to indemnify the insured if covered property is destroyed or damaged because of fire or lightning. Fire insurance policies are sold for residential and commercial purposes and cover both immovable and movable property. Because they cover only two perils, these policies are no longer very popular in most markets, particularly in developed economies. Often, however, these policies are endorsed to cover other named perils.

---

### INSIGHT 22.1: DIFFERENT POLICIES, DIFFERENT MEANINGS OF COINSURANCE

Due in part to differences in insurance (and reinsurance) practices worldwide, we end up using "coinsurance" in various ways. We here offer a summary of such uses:

- As described in Chapter 19, coinsurance often refers to a contract provision wherein the insurer and the insured share in a loss by a predetermined percentage (e.g., 10 percent of the loss borne by the insured). We observe such use in selected health insurance, property insurance, and liability insurance policies.
- In business income (interruption) insurance, coinsurance may refer to the period of insurance protection from the date of loss until recovery (e.g., 100 percent meaning 12 months).
- Coinsurance also is used to mean insurers sharing jointly to provide coverage for a risk or policy. For example, four property insurers might each write 25 percent of a large, highly protected risk. The term "jointly" here means that they are all primary insurers; conversely, none functions as a reinsurer of others in the contract.
- In reinsurance (see Chapter 23), coinsurance can be used to mean the share of the reinsured loss borne by the primary insurer. For example, a catastrophic excess-of-loss reinsurer may require the insurer to share 5 percent of the reinsured loss. A similar practice is found in stop loss excess-of-loss reinsurance.
- When used as part of the "coinsurance (penalty) provision" in property insurance, coinsurance refers to the percentage of property value insurers encourage the insured to purchase as the policy limit, a failure to do so resulting in a reduction in claims payment. The clause provides that any covered loss will be indemnified in full up to the policy limit *provided* the limit selected is at least equal to the product of the property value times the stipulated coinsurance percentage. For example, if the coinsurance percentage is 80 percent and the property value (on an ACV or replacement cost basis, depending on the policy) is $100,000, the policy limit should be at least $80,000 to avoid a penalty. If the insured elected a policy limit of $60,000, any claim would be paid in the ratio of 60:80 or 75 percent, thus resulting in a 25 percent penalty. Had the insured elected a policy limit of $80,000 or higher, any claim would be paid in full, up to the policy limit. The higher the required percentage, the lower the premium rate per unit of coverage, other things being the same. Common percentages used for this coinsurance provision are 80, 90 and 100 percent.

- *Commercial property insurance policies* insure businesses against both direct and indirect property losses. These policies often target large businesses. (For small and mid-sized businesses, insurers tend to offer a package policy covering both property and liability risks.) Coverage usually is provided for the most common types of movable and immovable business property, including buildings, inventory, fixtures, furniture, computers, etc. Indirect coverage can include a variety of consequential losses. The policy often can be tailored more specifically to the insured's needs by the addition of various optional coverages to insure against, for example, (1) physical loss or damage to computer hardware, loss of data and computer software, (2) loss of valuable papers, (3) damage to contractor equipment and tools and (4) damage or destruction to property in transit.

- *Consequential loss insurance*, also known as *business income (interruption) insurance*, is to indemnify the insured for specific indirect losses – additional expenses and loss of income – that result from the insured incurring a loss of or damage to the covered property *directly* by an insured peril. The coverage, available in this form only for commercial purposes, may be a stand-alone policy or offered as part of a broader policy.

- *Industrial all-risk insurance policies*, also called *special risk insurance policies*, are all-risk contracts that typically provide liberal coverage to a broad array of high-value movable and immovable properties, with loss settlement made on a replacement cost basis except for inventory that may be settled on a market value basis. These policies are commonly sold to large industrial and commercial enterprises. Indirect losses are often covered under the policies as well.

- *Contractors' all-risk (CAR) insurance policies*, also called *builders all-risk policies*, are all-risk contracts that insure contractors against physical loss or damage to works, plant, equipment and materials during the course of construction. CAR insurance usually is combined with liability insurance.

- *Boiler and machinery insurance*, also known as *equipment breakdown insurance* and *engineering risks insurance*, covers the direct physical losses resulting from an explosion of most types of boilers and pressure vessels and from mechanical breakdown. Such coverage ordinarily is excluded from other property policies. It also covers electronic equipment breakdown, loss of records and, more recently, losses resulting from communication or computer virus infiltration to information technology systems. This type of policy can be extended to cover damage to the insured's surrounding property, business interruption (including expediting expenses incurred to speed replacements and repairs) and third-party liability. Of particular value is the loss control service that accompanies this insurance that can result in sound loss control recommendations that can help insureds ensure efficient operation and longer equipment life.

It has been estimated that 20 percent of U.S. business failures are caused by employee dishonesty. Businesses also sometimes fail or suffer major setbacks because of other criminal acts committed against them, such as fraud, forgery and burglary. Fidelity/crime insurance is designed to respond to these and other criminal acts. **Fidelity/crime insurance policies** are named-peril contracts that agree to indemnify the insured for loss of money, securities and inventory from a criminal act. These policies are available for commercial purposes (although limited coverage may be included in some personal property insurance policies) and can be structured to provide a range of coverages, including against the following perils:[2]

- *Computer fraud*: Use of a computer to steal property.

- *Employee dishonesty*: A criminal act committed by an employee acting alone or in collusion with others. Coverage insures against loss of money, securities and other property. Two forms are generally available: the blanket form and the scheduled form. The blanket form provides coverage for dishonest acts of all employees and provides a single limit per loss. The scheduled form provides coverage only for the dishonest acts of employees specifically listed in the policy. A separate limit applies for each listed employee.

- *Extortion*: The surrender of property because of the threat of bodily harm to someone being held captive. This form applies to money, securities and other property. Extortion coverage also may be available as part of "kidnap/transom and insurance" coverage.

- *Forgery or alteration*: **Forgery** is the generation of a document or signature that is not genuine. **Alteration** is the changing of a document in a way neither authorized nor intended. This form covers loss caused by the forgery or alteration of a check or other instruments drawn against the insured's accounts.

- *Theft and robbery*: **Theft** is the unlawful taking of property. **Robbery** is the taking of property from a person by threat of bodily injury. This form provides coverage for on-premises theft of property other than money and securities and off-premises robbery of property other than money and securities while the insured property is in the care, control and custody of a messenger. By contrast, disappearance is the loss of property from an unknown cause, and destruction is the complete loss of property.

Several forms of insurance in addition to fidelity/crime and money insurance cover movable property only. We can divide these policies into two categories: self-propelled property and property being transported. **Self-propelled property** includes motor vehicles, ships and aircraft:

- *Insurance for motor vehicles*: Motor vehicle owners, individuals and businesses alike, purchase insurance covering the direct loss of or damage to their vehicles. Coverage may be available separately or combined for damage caused by a collision – a named peril – and damage caused by all causes except collision (i.e., all-risks coverage). Policies also may provide consequential coverage in the form of extra expense of renting a replacement vehicle temporarily. When purchased, this insurance is commonly combined with automobile liability insurance (discussed later) into a single package policy. Small motorized vehicles not licensed for public roads sometimes are covered under commercial property (or homeowner's) insurance policies.

- *Insurance for ships*: More commonly known as **hull insurance**, this broad, named-peril insurance is to indemnify the insured shipowner for damage to the structure of the vessel (hull) and its machinery, equipment caused by maritime perils which include perils of the sea such as heavy weather, stranding and collision and similar perils. Liability flowing from collision with another ship or object and from wreck removal because of waterway blockage are commonly included. For commercial vessels, policy wording usually aligns with international conventions. For pleasure craft, coverage can vary from liability only to comprehensive first-party coverage. When the term **marine insurance** is used, the policy provides both hull insurance and insurance on the vessel's cargo (see below).

- *Insurance for aircraft*: Called **aircraft hull insurance**, this all-risk policy agrees to indemnify the insured aircraft owner for damage to the aircraft itself and its equipment as well as its cargo if included in the policy, whether the aircraft is on ground or in flight. Commonly, liability arising from property damage and injury to passengers and others is combined with this coverage into a packaged policy.

**Property being transported** includes any property being moved by rail, parcel post, land, sea or air. Coverage is usually restricted to direct damage to or loss of the property. Common forms of insurance follow:

- *Cargo insurance*: This segment of a marine insurance policy is used for all forms of cargo being moved by conventional means; that is by ship, aircraft or land vehicle.[3] Cargo insurance applies from the departure port to the final destination and may include temporary stopovers. Coverage varies from "total loss only" to all-risks, depending on the insured's preference and the insurer's underwriting judgment.

- *Insurance for transportable property*: Properties subject to this type of insurance include items worn (e.g., jewellery), carried from place to place (e.g., traveller's baggage) or temporarily removed (e.g., office equipment). The coverage for temporary removal of property is limited to a small percentage of the total amount of insurance and is intended to insure circumstances as removal for cleaning or repair or property left at a place of work away from the insured premises. These coverages are commonly included in other property insurance policies.

## Liability Insurance Policies

Liability insurance promises to pay damages for which an insured is legally liable because of the insured's negligent or other tortuous actions. Recall from Chapter 10 that *torts* are civil (as opposed to criminal) wrongs for which an individual or organization can be held liable and are typically categorized as (1) intentional, (2) negligence or (3) strict liability. Liability insurance policies typically provide coverage for negligence and strict liability and sometimes for selected intentional torts.

Damages are measured in monetary terms under tort law and most commonly result from negligence on the part of the insured that resulted in bodily injury and damage to property. Liability insurance policies pay for such damages on behalf of the insured up to the policy limit and often also agree to cover the costs of the insured's legal defence. It is not unusual to find a condition in liability policies that the insurer may settle a claim against the insured without the insured's approval. This right of settlement typically is not applicable in professional (including director's and officer's) liability and product liability cases.

Liability insurance policies are available worldwide to cover either personal or commercial losses. Rarely does a liability policy provide extensive coverage for both categories of loss exposures however. Some of the more common liability policies are as follows:

- *General (public) liability insurance policies* provide all-risks coverage for either individuals or organizations for their tortuous actions. Exclusions apply, such as liability arising from the operation of motor vehicles, aircraft and large sea-going vessels – as those liability risks are covered commonly by specific policies such as automobile and commercial air carrier passenger liability insurance – and from illegal activities. Many intentional torts are ordinarily excluded.

- *Automobile (motor) liability insurance policies* cover insureds' legal liability to third party for bodily injury or property damage arising from the negligent operation of an automobile. This insurance is compulsory in most countries for automobile owners and users.

- *Product liability insurance policies* agree to pay claims on behalf of the insured made by third parties for bodily injury or damage to property for which the insured is legally liable.

- *Workers' (workmen's) compensation policies* provide legally required coverages in connection with worker injuries, sicknesses and death. **Employer's liability insurance** is similar to workers' compensation insurance in scope but differs in that it agrees to pay on behalf of the employer only those claims resulting from lawsuits brought by injured employees who assert employer negligence as the cause of their injuries or illness.

- *Professional liability insurance policies*, also known generically as **errors and omissions (E&O) insurance**, agree to pay claims on behalf on the insured for his or her professional negligence. These policies are commonly purchased to cover liability of healthcare professionals, directors and officers, and other professionals resulting from their professional negligence.

## Package Insurance Policies

As noted earlier, insurers commonly include both property and liability insurance within a single policy rather than issuing two or more separate policies. Several of the coverages discussed above can fall into this category. Specific examples are homeowner's (householder's) insurance, businessowner's insurance and commercial multiperil policies that are more or less standardized in each local market:

- *Homeowner's insurance*, also known as *householder's insurance* or *household insurance*, provides both direct and indirect property insurance as well as general liability insurance for residential property owners. These policies commonly cover loss of or damage to the residence and its contents, consequential expenses while the property is being repaired and general liability of the insured as a property owner. Coverage for contents only is also available to property renters in many countries. Policies are often available on a named peril (basic and broad form) or all-risks basis.

- *Businessowner's insurance* provides both direct and indirect property insurance as well as general liability insurance for owners of businesses. These policies commonly cover loss of or damage to the business premises and its contents, indemnify the insured for consequential expenses following a direct property loss, and agree to pay any judgments against the insured because of business-related tortuous actions. This comprehensive policy is commonly sold to small and mid-size businesses. Policies are available on a named-peril and all-risks basis depending on the market in which they are sold.

- *Commercial multiperil insurance policies* are package policies covering both the property and general liability loss exposures of large businesses. Often, these policies are endorsed to provide additional coverages, such as crime, boiler and machinery risk, and others.

## SELECTED NONLIFE INSURANCE MARKETS INTERNATIONALLY

The world's total nonlife insurance premium volume in 2005 exceeded US$1,452 billion.[4] Nonlife premium growth varies greatly over time and between markets. Nonlife insurance premium growth continues robust in many markets, particularly in several developing economies.[5] As with life insurance, China and India in particular are believed to offer enormous nonlife potential. Additionally, several Latin American and Eastern European markets hold great promise. In this section, we examine the main nonlife insurance markets by region, paralleling the treatment in Chapter 21. We begin with the Americas, move to Europe, then to the Asia-Pacific region and close with Africa.

## Nonlife Insurance Markets in the Americas

The North American nonlife markets dominate the markets of the Americas in terms of premium volume, with the U.S. being especially prominent, reflecting its economic size and maturity. Indeed, the U.S. nonlife market is the world's largest, accounting for 43.1 percent of global premiums written in 2005.

### *The United States*

Unsurprisingly, the U.S. market ranks second in per capita expenditures (US$2,122) and first on premiums as a percentage of GDP (5.01 percent – the penetration ratio). These rankings are all consistent with expectations for two reasons. First, recall that these premium data include health insurance premiums, and the U.S. per capita spending for *private* health insurance is among the world's highest. Second, U.S. businesses and families spend more on liability insurance than do the citizens of any other country, because of litigiousness in the U.S.

Understanding the U.S. nonlife insurance market is important for several reasons. First, it has been the world's largest nonlife market for decades. Second, the market remains highly competitive, a phenomenon that has encouraged much experimentation in product development, methods of distribution and general business practices. This learning laboratory environment has been useful to regulators and insurers in other nonlife insurance markets, because, based on their review of changes in the U.S. market, they can often anticipate changes in their own markets and assess their appropriateness for local conditions. Finally, the size and complexity of many U.S. risks demand the capacity and expertise of the global insurance and reinsurance markets. Many non-U.S. firms have a history of providing services to the U.S. nonlife insurance market.

Real U.S. premium growth in commercial lines was either negative or flat throughout the 1990s and into the very early 2000s. This poor growth rate is attributable to the fact that the U.S. nonlife market is mature and highly competitive as well as to the widespread use of various alternative risk financing techniques by commercial enterprises. These techniques comprise an estimated 30 percent of the U.S. commercial insurance market. After the events of September 11, 2001, direct insurers and reinsurers raised their premium rates and tightened their underwriting. As a result, the market experienced more rapid premium growth and an increase in underwriting capacity during 2002–2006 – the capacity becoming over US$400 billion at the beginning of 2007.

The personal lines segment of the U.S. market has experienced modest real premium growth over the past decade or so. With fewer non-traditional risk transfer options, individuals and small businesses remain largely bound to property and liability insurance to cover their loss exposures.

More than 2,500 nonlife insurance companies compete in the U.S., resulting in a relatively low market concentration. About 800 or so insurers are independent; that is, unaffiliated with other insurers. Most of the other insurers are under common ownership and management through some 250 insurance groups and holding company arrangements.

**Table 22.2**    Distribution of Premiums by Line in the United States (2005)

| Lines of Insurance | Premiums (US$ Million)[a] | Market Share (%) |
|---|---|---|
| Private passenger automobile | 159,567 | 37.3 |
| Homeowner's multiple peril | 53,013 | 12.4 |
| Workers' compensation | 39,734 | 9.3 |
| Other liabilities | 39,103 | 9.1 |
| Commercial multiple peril | 29,668 | 6.9 |
| Commercial automobile | 26,778 | 6.3 |
| Medical malpractice | 9,734 | 2.3 |
| Accident and health | 9,577 | 2.2 |
| Inland marine | 8,246 | 1.9 |
| Product liability | 3,561 | 0.8 |
| Ocean marine | 2,946 | 0.7 |
| Other lines | 47,453 | 10.8 |

[a]Rounded.

*Source*: Insurance Information Institute (2006a) using NAIC Annual Statement Database.

### Products and distribution systems

Virtually any type of nonlife insurance is available in the U.S. Even so, as Table 22.2 shows, the U.S. market is dominated by personal and commercial automobile insurance, which accounted for 49.7 percent of premiums written in 2005. Homeowner's insurance, workers' compensation, other liabilities (including general and E&O liabilities for commercial insureds) and commercial multiperil coverage for small to mid-sized businesses also share significant portions of the U.S. market.

U.S. nonlife insurers use multiple distribution channels to reach their customers. The traditional marketing approach in the U.S. is the agency system. Some insurers, such as State Farm and Allstate, rely primarily on exclusive agents. Other insurers market some or all of their business through independent agents who represent several insurers. A few insurers rely exclusively on direct response marketing. The direct response market share is expected to increase in the future.

Brokers also figure prominently in the U.S. market. Brokers in the U.S. have been most successful as regional or national insurance intermediaries, usually targeting medium and large commercial insurance buyers. Independent agents and brokers control most commercial nonlife insurance, while captive agents control most personal nonlife insurance.

### Market issues

Besides the issues relevant to nonlife insurance markets worldwide (and discussed at the end of this chapter), several issues relate particularly to the U.S. market and are summarized as follows:

- *State regulation*: U.S. insurance regulation is state based, with differences in each of the regulatory jurisdictions. The National Association of Insurance Commissioners (NAIC), a trade association of the state insurance regulators, continues to strive toward uniformity in regulation but notable differences persist. A major issue in nonlife insurance is rate regulation. Many states require regulatory approval prior to insurers implementing rate changes. This process can lead to delay or outright rejection of needed rate changes, causing deteriorating underwriting results and coverage availability problems, especially at times of catastrophic events.

Licensure by states is another pressing issue. To conduct business nationally, an insurer must qualify for a license from each of the 50 states – an expensive and time-consuming process. It also must comply with 50 separate sets of regulations. Large insurance groups sometimes create subsidiaries for operations in selected states that impose stringent rate or other regulation. If U.S. insurance were subject to federal regulation, the number of insurance companies almost certainly would be less. This state-based regulatory structure has impeded some foreign companies from entering the U.S. insurance market, a problem repeatedly emphasized by the E.U.

- *Market consolidation*: In part because of its fragmented regulatory structure, the U.S. insurance market has long had a surprisingly large number of relatively small insurers. In many instances, these small insurers were created to focus on the insurance needs of niche markets. Low state capitalization requirements facilitated their creation. The imposition of RBC requirements has not been kind to small insurers, having triggered numerous mergers and acquisitions. Mega-scale mergers and acquisitions also have been observed in the market. The Berkshire Hathaway Group now holds 100 percent ownership of GEICO. In 2003, St. Paul Companies merged with Travelers Property Casualty Corporation (a deal valued at US$16 billion), and American International Group acquired GE's U.S. auto business (US$2.1 billion). Within the nonlife sector only, there were 48 mergers and acquisitions with an aggregate transaction value of US$10.4 billion, a substantial increase from 22 transactions in 2005 with an aggregate transaction value of US$500 million from the previous year.[6]

- *Loss reserve adequacy*: Those interested in assessing the financial position of nonlife insurers are concerned about a lack of precision in their establishing loss reserves. This concern is exacerbated by the dynamics of the U.S. tort environment and its impact on actual claims. The long-tail liability lines – those whose payments may extend over many years – are especially difficult from a pricing and reserving perspective.

Compounding this loss-reserving problem is the potential impact of asbestos and environmental (pollution) liability on U.S. nonlife insurance business. Numerous mass-tort actions for alleged damages caused by asbestos and environmental contamination have rocked the market, especially for companies with significant premium writings in commercial lines. Disputes often have arisen as to the insurance coverage provided for losses involving repeated exposure over time. In many instances, the courts have found coverage to apply, resulting in significant claims for a largely unrecognized and unreserved loss exposure. Some insurers have begun to establish liabilities for these obligations, but common wisdom suggests that current-reserving levels do not reflect the true obligation.

- *Impact of catastrophes*: Chapters 5 and 6 discuss the impact of catastrophes particularly relevant to the U.S. Nonlife insurance market performance was significantly affected by natural catastrophes in the early 1990s and again in 2004 and 2005. Between these years, of course, the terrorist attacks in 2001 contributed further to poor results. With global warming, prospects for more devastating catastrophes and their attendant negative impact on the nonlife insurance market in the U.S. and internationally through reinsurance can be anticipated. In fact, most reinsurers have increased prices and insisted on higher retentions by ceding companies in recent years – especially after 9/11 – although they may ease or even reverse their positions as the market becomes soft. While this move allows insurers to keep a greater share of premium, it exposes their balance sheets to more significant hits from catastrophic events. Not surprisingly, insurance companies, both in the U.S. and elsewhere, have embarked on creative risk financing techniques to cope with this problem.

## Canada

The nonlife insurance market in Canada shares some similarities with the U.S. market. The market is competitive and is served by more than 200 insurance companies whose aggregate premium writing exceeds US$44.2 in billion, making it the world's 7th largest nonlife market in 2005. Per capita nonlife premiums amount to US$1,377 (7th ranked) and penetration is 3.92 percent of GDP (6th ranked). It has attracted numerous foreign interests, particularly U.S. and U.K. and other European insurance groups. Foreign-owned insurers account for about two-thirds of premiums written in Canada.

As noted earlier, Canada maintains a dual regulatory system. The federal agency, the OSFI, supervises federally chartered – multi-province operating – insurers and branches of foreign companies. Provincial agencies oversee operational and financial soundness of locally incorporated insurers that in the aggregate comprise about one-fifth of all nonlife companies in Canada. The federal government imposes regulatory requirements in the areas of financial reporting, minimum capital, investment constraints and solvency criteria. Provincial governments deal with issues such as solvency of provincially incorporated companies, form regulation, licensing of agents and brokers and other matters relating to policy-holders and claimants.

Nonlife insurance accounts for 36 percent of the Canadian insurance market. By line, automobile insurance generated 49.3 percent of net nonlife premiums written, followed by personal property (15.3 percent), commercial property (14.4 percent) and liability (13.1 percent) in 2004. The compulsory component of automobile insurance is available from only state-owned insurers in some provinces (e.g., both bodily injury and property damage liability in British Columbia, Manitoba and Saskatchewan).

The agency form of distribution dominates the Canadian nonlife insurance market. Agents and brokers account for about two-thirds of premiums written. Direct writers and other forms of distribution make up the remaining share. The Canadian government continues to regulate rating of automobile insurance premiums. The OSFI reports that, despite recent improvements in the nonlife insurance and reinsurance markets, the market "remains inherently volatile" as increased profitability could lead to more competition and less stringent underwriting practices.[7]

## Latin America

Latin American (and the Caribbean) markets consist of two broad groups of economies. The first group comprises the Cayman Islands, Barbados, Bahamas, Trinidad and Tobago, and other island countries in the Caribbean that are home to a number of large insurers and reinsurers as well as thousands of captive insurance companies. Other countries in the region are mainly developing economies. Among them, only Argentina, Brazil, Chile, Colombia, Mexico and Venezuela each generated more than US$1 billion of nonlife insurance premiums. Although the region has more than 550 million inhabitants, in the aggregate it accounted for only 2.43 percent to global nonlife premiums.

Overall, Latin American experienced a real growth of nonlife premiums of 4.6 percent for 2005, down from 6.5 percent for 2004. Venezuela at 22.7 percent and Brazil at 6.0 percent were the fastest growing markets. Mexico's growth was relatively flat, owning to fewer major construction projects in 2005.

While penetration ratios are low, this fact signals a high growth potential. Growth, however, is predicated on reasonable economic and political stability and a robust financial infrastructure. Economic crises in the region have led to the collapse of several nonlife insurers in the past, which does not give confidence to consumers. Additionally, many Latin American insurers have comparatively high expenses, making their products less attractive.

Traditional insurance intermediaries (brokers and agents) and employees of insurance companies dominate Latin American distribution channels. Recently, several insurance companies introduced new marketing channels, including telemarketing and *bancassurance*, especially in Brazil and Chile. Internet-based marketing activities are also observed in Argentina, Brazil and Chile.

Most nonlife insurance companies now face competition of a formerly unknown intensity. Many Latin American governments have privatized insurers and opened their markets to foreign interests. Rigid rate and form regulation that simplified insurer management and reduced competition has been replaced with more open competition.

The challenge for insurers that operated under the old regimes is how to compete in these new markets. Many traditional products with coverage limitations and few options no longer satisfy the demands of the market. New products are being developed to meet these changing needs. Pricing decisions made in a competitive atmosphere often are more a function of competitor's prices than actuarial considerations. With increasing bilateral (e.g., U.S. and Colombia) and multilateral (NAFTA and Free Trade Agreement of the Americas (FTAA)) trade agreements and more regional arrangements such as MERCOSUR (*Mercado Comun del Cono Sur*), future competition promises to be even more vigorous.

## European Nonlife Insurance Markets

Europe is the world's second largest regional nonlife insurance market at 35.7 percent. The market consists of the "big three" markets of Germany, the U.K. and France, followed by a second tier group that includes Italy, Spain, the Netherlands, Switzerland, Russia and Belgium. Other countries account for less than a 1 percent share of the world market.

Most European countries have a rich history and tradition that are reflected in their insurance markets. For example, structure and order are very much a part of the German tradition. These characteristics can be seen in the German insurance market. The U.K. has a long history of international exploration and trade. This penchant is certainly evident in its nonlife insurance industry that has been a world leader in MAT insurance.

The role of European insurance companies in the global market has gained more attention with the creation of a single E.U. market. Nonetheless, E.U. member states retain much authority in insurance taxation and regulation, as alluded to in the preceding chapter. The *Third Generation Directives* prohibit national requirements for the prior approval of rates and forms except for compulsory insurance. Member states still can require rates and technical reserves to be based on local actuarial requirements. The directives also leave authority and responsibility for sales and market conduct practices, contract law and taxing of policies to the member state in which the sale takes place. As the E.U. has expanded beyond 15 members, questions of control and effectiveness have arisen. Insurance taxation and contract law differences seem likely to persist, giving rise to conflicts.

*Bancassurance* has been primarily a life insurance phenomenon in Europe. Even so, a question remains whether the traditional stand-alone nonlife insurers can compete with the *bancassurance* giants. Another clear trend in Europe is the success of direct marketing schemes in the mass risks market. Telemarketing of motor and household insurance in the U.K. has been a success in a relatively short period. Several direct marketers have claimed a rising share of the U.K. mass risks market. This phenomenon has not gone unnoticed in continental Europe, with growing direct marketing efforts in France, German and Spain.

### Germany

The reunification of Germany merged two quite different nonlife insurance markets into a single entity that represents 7.4 percent of the world market share in 2005. West Germany had a well-developed private insurance industry, while East Germany utilized a public sector approach to nonlife insurance. When the barriers between these two entities fell, West German insurers were quick to stake their claim in the new market. Some foreign insurers also entered the market. However, the unified German market remains dominated by German insurers. In 2002, the government merged all then sector-specific regulatory bodies into *Bundesanstalt für Finanzdienstleistungsaufsicht* (the Federal Financial Supervisory Authority or BaFin), which supervises, among others, 233 nonlife insurers and 47 reinsurers: of which, 64 were from other E.U. countries.

The German nonlife insurance market is the world's second largest market at US$107 billion in premiums written by 250 companies in 2005. The insurance density of US$1,268 ranks 10th worldwide, and insurance penetration of 3.73 percent ranks 7th. These premium figures do not include workers' compensation business, because the Germany government – like others in Europe – includes workers' compensation insurance as part of its highly developed social welfare system. Nonlife insurance represents about 54 percent of the total insurance business in the country. Motor insurance is the largest nonlife segment (41 percent of market share) followed by property insurance (25 percent) and general liability insurance (11 percent). Germany is home to the world's largest nonlife insurer, Allianz, and the world's largest reinsurer, Munich Re.

Insurance distribution in Germany is dominated by exclusive agents. Many large commercial insurers in Germany have established their own brokerage operations. The importance of independent brokers in the commercial insurance market is far less than that seen in other developed countries. A few insurers market mass risks coverage on a direct basis. An interesting feature of the German market is the long-term relationship between the insurance buyer and the seller. Guaranteed renewal features are common in many nonlife insurance contracts. One-year policies were often replaced by policies with 5- or 10-year policy periods. With greater competition from other E.U. insurers, these long-term commitments are seen less frequently.

### The United Kingdom

The nonlife insurance market in the U.K. has a rich tradition and continues to play a prominent role in the world insurance market. Because of this important role both historically and presently, we focus particular attention to the core aspects of its worldwide presence via what is called the London Market.

**Table 22.3** Nonlife Insurance in the United Kingdom: 1999–2003 (Current £ Million)

| Segment | 1999 | 2000 | 2001 | 2002 | 2003 |
|---|---|---|---|---|---|
| Domestic business | 22,032 | 23,310 | 26,387 | 28,486 | 29,712 |
| Overseas business | 12,840 | 14,954 | 12,981 | 11,658 | 10,224 |
| Total | 34,872 | 38,264 | 38,368 | 40,144 | 39,936 |

*Source*: Towers Perrin (2005). Insurance Pocket Book 2005.

*Market overview*

Insurers in the country generate business from accepting domestic risks as well as overseas risks. Table 22.3 shows nonlife insurance business in the U.K. between 1999 and 2003. The U.K. is the world's third largest nonlife insurance market after the U.S. and Germany. The U.K. market ranks second worldwide to Switzerland (at US$2,480) in nonlife premiums per capita, at US$1,312, and second to the U.S. in nonlife insurance penetration at 3.55 percent.

As of March 2006, 886 insurers were licensed to do business in nonlife insurance in the U.K., of which 836 (including 412 U.K. incorporated companies) were solely in the nonlife business and 50 (including 22 U.K. incorporated companies) in both the life and the non-life business. The U.K. domestic nonlife market is dominated by a few large insurers such as Royal & Sun Alliance, CGU International Insurance, Zurich (U.K.) and AXA Insurance. The prevailing regulatory system is characterized by freedom with publicity. As such, the environment is comparatively free of government intervention. Barriers to market entry are low. *The Insurance Companies Act* of 1982 permits freedom of rate and form for insurers. Regulation is focused primarily on solvency and corporate governance.

Foreign-owned companies generated about 40 percent of premiums written in the U.K., an increase from about 25 percent in the early 1990s. Major lines of business are motor insurance (21.9 percent of market share in 2003), property insurance (18.2 percent) and MAT insurance (13.6 percent).[8] Brokers accounted for the largest proportion of premiums at 36 percent, followed by company employees at 24 percent and both tied and independent agents at 23 percent.

*The London Market*

The London Market is an international insurance center that specializes in large accounts and target risks such as MAT and hard-to-place business. It comprises insurance and rein-surance companies and Lloyd's syndicates that accept risks through accredited brokers. An accredited London broker places a risk with a member of the International Underwriting Association of London (IUA) or with a Lloyd's syndicate. The IUA [www.iua.co.uk] and Lloyd's of London [www.Lloyds.com] have jointly introduced the London Market Principles to create a combined back office bureau and to standardize London Market slips (application forms), among other aspects.

The London Market is a **subscription market** in that the coverage needs are often satisfied by a group of insurers or reinsurers on a collective basis. Insurance brokers play a crucial role in the placement of risks. Usually a broker approaches a prominent underwriter to act as the lead underwriter for the transaction. The lead underwriter, generally a respected expert in the particular line of insurance, accepts a certain share of the risk and, thereby, sets the coverage

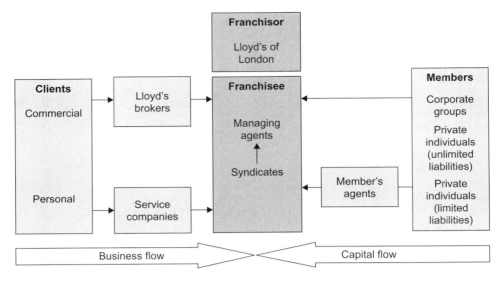

**Figure 22.1**   Insurance Transactions at Lloyd's of London. *Source*: Lloyd's of London [www.Lloyds.com]

terms, conditions and price. Once this initial step is accomplished, the broker proceeds to other underwriters for their participation until the required limits are fully subscribed.

*Lloyd's of London*
Much has been written about Lloyd's of London, a unique insurance marketplace with a history dating back to 1688. Accredited Lloyd's brokers are the access point to Lloyd's underwriters. They place risks with 46 managing agents who operate 64 syndicates. At Lloyd's, **syndicates** are the underwriting entities and represent investors referred to as **names** or **underwriting members**. Lloyd's provides other services for its operating syndicates, such as engineering and claims services. Lloyd's syndicates are active in commercial insurance and personal motor vehicle insurance. Figure 22.1 illustrates business and capital flows within the Lloyd's structure.

Lloyd's syndicates generated about one-half of their business from direct insurance for risks situated mainly in North America (the U.S. in particular) and Europe (the U.K. in particular). Fifteen percent of Lloyd's business originates from Asia, Latin America, the Caribbean and Africa. Lloyd's generated gross written premiums of £15 billion (or net-of-reinsurance premiums of £11.8 billion) in 2005.

For many years, Lloyd's enjoyed a formidable worldwide reputation for its creativity and unquestioned financial strength. In the early 1990s, however, this reputation was severely tested by global market conditions and several major events. A sluggish demand for nonlife insurance worldwide coupled with excess capacity resulted in downward pressure on rates. Several large natural disasters (including earthquakes and hurricanes in the U.S.) resulted in large losses for several syndicates. Numerous retrocessions of non-marine excess reinsurance resulted in an unsafe interdependency among Lloyd's names. The whole structure almost collapsed when a chain of catastrophes caused a so-called excess-of-loss reinsurance market spiral. Lloyd's continues its adverse loss experience arising from U.S. asbestos and environmental liability claims.

These compounding problems resulted in significant losses for many syndicates and their members who then faced unlimited liability with regard to their participation in syndicates. These unexpected developments and associated financial losses caused great concern globally about Lloyd's financial security. Subsequently, Lloyd's initiated a reconstruction plan to regain its reputation and financial strength. The outcome of the plan can be summarized as follows:

- *Limited liability corporate and individual members*: Lloyd's revised its membership qualifications to permit corporate capital with limited liability. This fundamental change in Lloyd's membership has had a major impact on restoring Lloyd's capacity to £15 billion. (**Underwriting capacity** refers to the maximum amount of insurance that can be safely written by the firm, expressed commonly in terms of premiums. The capacity is determined mainly by the company's capital and surplus.) Lloyd's reports 714 corporate members and 1.497 individual members.[9]

- *Equitas*: In 1996, Lloyd's established Equitas – technically a reinsurance company – to assume run-offs of Lloyd's nonlife liabilities written until 1992. Equitas had settled more than US$23 billion in asbestos claims through early 2004. This amount included US$472 million with Honeywell in April 2003 and US$575 million with Halliburton a year later.

In 2003, Lloyd's of London adopted a franchise model to change its role from a regulating body to a commercially managing entity. The key activities of Lloyd's under this model include capital management, risk management and franchise performance assessment. Specifically, it uses Lloyd's Risk Based Capital model to determine capital adequacy for its members. It applies Lloyd's Realistic Disaster Scenarios at the syndicate level as well as at the market level to access Lloyd's ability to manage catastrophe risks. The Financial Services Authority (FSA) of the U.K. regulates the Lloyd's market.

### International Underwriting Association of London

Relatively new in the global market, the IUA was formed in 1998 as a result of a merger of two major associations in the London Market: the London International Insurance and Reinsurance Market Association (LIRMA) and the Institute of London Underwriters (ILU). The IUA had 43 ordinary member companies, 32 associate members and 12 affiliates in 2004. It generated premiums exceeding £5.5 billion – including £1.28 billion of marine insurance premiums – in 2003. The IUA does not regulate members.

### Protection and indemnity clubs

Protection and indemnity (P&I) insurance comprehensively covers shipowners and charterers against third-party liabilities arising in their commercial operations. P&I insurance is provided by so-called P&I clubs – the first of which was created by British shipowners in the 18th century – that are assessable mutual insurance associations owned by their shipowner/insureds. Members can be assessed additional premiums at the end of each operating year to cover losses.

The insurance covers liability arising from such perils as cargo damage, pollution, death, injury or illness of passengers or crew, damage to docks and other installations, and a great breadth of other possibilities. This insurance runs parallel to the hull and machinery insurance cover on vessels, but the latter insurance often can be extended to provide only limited liability coverage, such as that arising from collisions.

P&I coverage commonly falls into three categories: (1) P&I insurance, (2) freight, demurrage and defense (FDD) costs and (3) insurance for charterers' risks. FDD costs are the legal costs that a shipowner might incur in connection with liability claims. Charterers' risks are those arising from the failure of a charterer to perform as agreed, such as not unloading a ship within the agree-upon time frame.

The 13 P&I clubs that are members of the International Group of P&I Clubs [www.igpandi.org] collectively provide P&I insurance for some 90 percent of the world's ocean-going shipping. Their member clubs are now located in Bermuda, Japan, Luxembourg, Norway, Sweden and the U.S. in addition to its birthplace, the U.K.

### *France*

France is the fifth largest nonlife insurance market globally, at US$68.2 billion, which was 4.7 percent of the world nonlife market for 2005. It is the third largest in Europe. Of a total of 470 insurers, the largest domestic nonlife writers are AXA and Groupama. AXA, whose main source of revenue derives from the life business, is the world's second largest insurance group based on total revenues. (The ING Group of the Netherlands in the largest.) The top 10 nonlife insurance writers account for 71.5 percent of the French nonlife insurance market. Some 25 reinsurance companies operate in France, the largest being Scor Re.

The two leading nonlife insurance distribution channels at 35 percent market share each are company employees and agents (both tied and independent). Brokers account for 18 percent of premiums written, with banks and others claiming the remaining 12 percent market share. *Bancassurance* has not met with the same success in nonlife as in life activity. This difference is said to be attributable to the fact that life insurance savings products more closely align with other savings products sold by banks and to the willingness of customers to keep privileged relationships with their agents or brokers who often are able to offer greater convenience. Brokers are strong in commercial lines and tied agents in personal lines. Distribution by mutual insurers through non-commissioned sales offices plays an important role in motor insurance and householder's insurance in France.

Motor insurance is the largest line of nonlife insurance, with 32.5 percent of the market in 2003. Accident and health premiums are next at 24.2 percent, followed closely by property insurance writings at 23.2 percent. Liability (10.2 percent), MAT (2.0 percent) and miscellaneous lines (8.8 percent) account for the remaining portions.

## Nonlife Insurance Markets in the Asia-Pacific Region

Asia is home to the world's fastest growing economies. This economic growth has resulted in a corresponding expansion of nonlife insurance in numerous countries. Japan, Korea and Taiwan have established insurance markets, with China growing rapidly, followed by India. Japan's nonlife market is the world's fourth largest in premium volume. Hong Kong and Singapore function as regional hubs for insurance, reinsurance and captive insurance transactions.

In Southeast Asia, we can find economically advanced countries as well as countries where the populaces struggle with burning poverty. With an exception of Brunei, Malaysia,

Singapore and Thailand, ASEAN countries GDP per capita are less than US$5,000 (purchasing power parity adjusted). This implies that insurance industries in these countries are yet to fully develop, and insurance consumption remains low. Nevertheless, signs of governmental moves toward more liberal trade in insurance services are increasingly observed in the region. Also, Indonesia, Malaysia and Singapore promote Islamic principle-based takaful insurance.

The Middle Eastern markets are probably the least developed in Asia. The only country with what can be considered a broadly thriving nonlife insurance market is Israel. Use of insurance is limited to selected commercial insureds in other countries that are basically Islamic. With the introduction of takaful insurance and the creation of the Islamic Financial Services Board in 2002, a gradual growth of the nonlife insurance business is expected in the Middle East.

The Asian region is known for its concentration of people and property. Large urban property accumulations exist in almost every market. These concentrations are exposed to several catastrophic perils such as earthquake, flood and volcanic activity. Unfortunately, the nonlife insurance markets in the region are sometimes ill-equipped to deal with major property disasters. High levels of underinsurance compound the problem, putting pressure on the public sector for the financing of catastrophic losses. The Indian Ocean tsunami disaster in 2004 vividly demonstrated this problem. The low levels of property insurance protection compared to actual damage resulted in excessive hardship for the affected people and businesses. The delays associated with the recovery process are indicative of catastrophe areas with a low level of private insurance protection.

Asian markets are changing and receive close attention from multinational insurance groups. Because of its large economy, Japan hosts many insurers from such groups. The continued introduction of a market economy and the liberalization of the market following its accession to the WTO, coupled with the sheer size of its population, have brought much attention to China by foreign groups. The same can be said of India, which began partially to open to foreign insurers in 1999. We further explore the markets in Japan, China, India and Australia in this section.

## Japan

Japan is home to the world's fourth largest nonlife insurance market with US$101 billion of premiums written in 2005. This accounts for 6.9 percent of the world market share. Nonlife insurance density stands at US$790, which ranks 20th worldwide. Insurance penetration is similarly low for an economy of its size, at 2.22 percent. Interestingly, the nonlife sector is but 21 percent of Japan's total premium volume, as the local market is heavily skewed toward the life business.

### Products and distribution systems

Compulsory automobile liability insurance (CALI) and voluntary automobile insurance (functioning as excess insurance to CALI) account for 54 percent of the nonlife insurance business in Japan for the year ending March 2006.[10] Fire (17.3 percent) and personal accident (16.0 percent) are two other major lines. Other liability lines – so-called "miscellaneous lines" in Japan – in the aggregate share 9.2 percent of the market, within which general liability and workers' compensation are most popular.[11] Japan is home to 28 domestic insurers and reinsurers (including four foreign owned) and 22 foreign insurers and reinsurers operating through branches or agencies.

Japanese insurance companies are known for offering **maturity-refund policies** that have a savings element built into the products. Holders of these policies are entitled to a refund of, say, 10 percent of the amount of insurance or the amount of premiums paid over a 10-year period. In addition, dividends may be paid based on the actual yield on the premiums paid. If, however, a claim above the threshold set by the insurer occurs during this period, the insured will not receive the maturity refund. This savings feature creates somewhat of a distortion when comparing Japanese nonlife premiums with those of other countries. Maturity-refund policies are found in fire, automobile, personal accident and selected miscellaneous casualty lines (e.g., workers' compensation).[12] From an actuarial viewpoint, maturity-refund policies carry higher premiums than policies without a refund. The share of maturity-refund policies continues to decline. About 13 percent of direct premiums written in 2005 were from maturity-refund policies, a decline from about 30 percent in 1994.

Nonlife insurance products in Japan are distributed by agency, brokerage and direct distribution systems. The agency system – comprising mainly female exclusive agents working part time – generates about 93 percent of direct premiums. Almost 1.9 million agents in Japan solicit insurance contracts, accept applications, receive premiums and accept notifications of insurance claims. The brokerage system, introduced in 1996, generated only 0.2 percent of direct premiums in 2005–2006. About 40 brokerage companies operate in Japan. Direct distribution, which includes marketing approaches through mass media as well as the *chokuhan-shain* system where staff members of insurance companies market products, contributes about 7 percent of the direct business in Japan. Insurance sales through the Internet also are observed in the nonlife insurance market.

*Market issues*

Despite the opening of the market in the early 1970s, the Japanese government was criticized for offering little opportunity for foreign insurers to participate in Japan's prosperous economy. The government also was criticized for protecting local insurers from bankruptcy. Political and economic pressure, especially from the U.S., encouraged a more open market and transparency in regulation. The Japanese government responded to this request by introducing a new insurance act followed by a Japanese Financial Reform Plan (known as Japanese Big Bang) in 1996. These measures facilitated eventual deregulation of rates and products, permitted holding company structures for insurance distribution by banks and other financial institutions and created the Financial Services Agency (FSA) of Japan in charge of supervision of all financial institutions. The Nonlife Insurance Policyholders Protection Corporation of Japan also was created in 1998. Its main function is taking over and settling claims of insolvent nonlife insurers using financial contributions from member insurance companies.

The government continued insurance market reforms into the 2000s. As a result, life and nonlife insurance companies are now permitted to sell each other's products, banks can own insurance subsidiaries and sell selected insurance products, life and nonlife insurance companies may sell third sector products (e.g., critical illness insurance and cancer insurance) and the CALI Government Reinsurance Scheme was abolished in 2002.

In spite of implementation of these measures, the nonlife insurance market in Japan is dominated by a few large locally owned companies, namely, Mitsui Sumitomo, Millea Holdings, Sompo Japan Insurance and Meiji Yasuda Life General. These insurers have

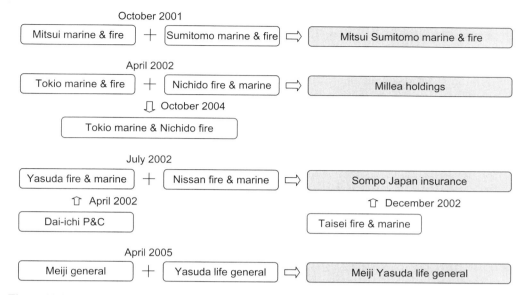

October 2001

Mitsui marine & fire + Sumitomo marine & fire ⟹ Mitsui Sumitomo marine & fire

April 2002

Tokio marine & fire + Nichido fire & marine ⟹ Millea holdings

⇩ October 2004

Tokio marine & Nichido fire

July 2002

Yasuda fire & marine + Nissan fire & marine ⟹ Sompo Japan insurance

⇧ April 2002                              ⇧ December 2002

Dai-ichi P&C                              Taisei fire & marine

April 2005

Meiji general + Yasuda life general ⟹ Meiji Yasuda life general

**Figure 22.2**   Mergers of Insurance Firms in Japan (*Source*: Japan General Insurance Association (2006a))

**Table 22.4**   Nonlife Insurance Market Share in Japan (Fiscal Year Ending March 2005) (¥ Million)

| Insurance Line | Total Direct Premiums | Direct Premiums by Foreign Insurers | Foreign Insurer Market Share |
|---|---|---|---|
| Fire | 1,463,668 | 46,973 | 3.21% |
| Voluntary Automobile | 3,503,607 | 117,084 | 3.34% |
| Personal Accident | 1,478,875 | 169,763 | 11.48% |
| Miscellaneous Casualty | 784,794 | 41,624 | 5.30% |
| Marine and Inland Transit | 269,116 | 7,814 | 2.90% |
| Compulsory Automobile Liability | 1,189,010 | 6,272 | Almost nil |
| Total | 8,689,120 | 356,008 | 4.10% |

*Source*: General Insurance Association of Japan (2006b).

become larger – in terms of capital and underwriting capacity – after a series of mergers in the 2000s (see Figure 22.2) and maintain a strong hold on insurance agencies. This market environment, coupled with certain Japanese cultural propensities, including loyalty to Japanese products and companies, has created a market not easily penetrated by new companies, whether local or foreign. Not surprisingly, the share of the market serviced by foreign insurers remains around 4 percent. The only line with a significant foreign presence is the so-called third sector where foreign companies offer personal accident coverages. See Table 22.4 for the distribution of insurance business by line and market shares of foreign insurers in Japan.[13]

Management of catastrophic loss exposures is another critical issue in Japan. The country is exposed to the risks of earthquake, typhoon and flood. The Great Hanshin-Awaji earthquake in 1995 caused 6,434 deaths and destruction or damage of 250,000 properties.

Metropolitan cities such as Tokyo and Osaka continue to experience earthquakes of vary-ing magnitudes. Earthquake risk in Tokyo has been securitized through several catastrophe bond arrangements in capital markets worldwide.

Government-sponsored insurance for household losses caused by earthquake, vol-canic eruption and tsunami are available in Japan. The amount of insurance is usually set between 30 and 50 percent of the amount of property (fire) insurance subject to a maximum of ¥50 million for dwelling structures and ¥10 million for personal property. The coverage is written directly by licensed insurers and the Toa Re in Japan. The Japan Earthquake Reinsurance Corporation – the only earthquake reinsurer in Japan and jointly owned by selected local insurers – assumes liability of up to ¥75 billion per year and shares excess losses with others insurers and the Japanese government. The total market capacity for earthquake risk in Japan is ¥4,500 billion (including the government's share of up to ¥3,753 billion) per year.

### China

The People's Republic of China is still a communist party led, socialist state. However, the government implemented extensive economic reforms after adopting its "Open Door Policy" in 1978 and a series of subsequent market-oriented policies for economic development. Nowadays, a relatively large number of domestic and foreign financial institutions, including insurers, operate in the country.

Insurance business was vigorous in major cities in China, especially in Shanghai, in the early 20th century. However, this private-sector-driven insurance model became incom-patible with China's centralized, state-owned economic system. The industry was reborn in the late 1970s. At that initial stage, insurance was available only through the People's Insurance Company of China (PICC), a state-owned monopoly. PICC's monopoly ended in 1985 with the creation of five additional national insurance companies, including Ping An Insurance Company and China Pacific Insurance Company as well as four regional insurers. These national insurers were affiliated to the PICC, and the regional companies remained small.

Foreign insurers were not permitted until 1992. American International Assurance, a unit of American International Group (originally incorporated in Shanghai and redomesticated to the U.S.), was the first foreign insurer to be admitted in 1992, followed by Tokyo Fire and Marine Insurance Company in 1994. As of December 2006, 13 foreign insurers were competing with 22 local insurers in the nonlife insurance market. The China Insurance Regulatory Commission (CIRC), created in 1998, regulates the insurance industry.

With market-oriented economic policies, the Chinese insurance market has grown remark-ably. In 2005, nonlife premiums amounted to US$20.5 billion. Motor insurance is the largest line with a two-thirds market share. The PICC and its subsidiaries generate about 70 percent of the nonlife premiums in China. Insurers depend heavily on agents for distribution.

The nonlife insurance market grew an average at 10.8 percent per annum between 1993 and 2003 (Swiss Re, 2004). Nevertheless, per capita nonlife premiums remain low at about US$16 in 2005. The nonlife penetration ratio was 0.92 percent of GDP. Despite low insur-ance consumption and penetration, the growth rate in China signals a great potential – especially after China's entrance into the WTO in 2001.

Since the introduction of the Insurance Law in 1995 (amended in 2003), the Chinese gov-ernment has further reformed regulation. For example, dating from accession to the WTO, the government no longer uses an economic needs test, thus technically setting no quantitative limits on the number of insurer licenses issued. A holder of a direct insurance license may engage in the reinsurance business upon securing approval of the CIRC, but no direct insurers are allowed to hold licensure for both life and nonlife insurance.[14] The insurance law sets the minimum registered capital for an insurance company at 200 million yuan (renminbi) – a significant reduction from 500 million yuan stipulated in the 1995 law. A licensed insurer must maintain a minimum solvency margin commensurate with the size of its business. Despite a series of regulatory reforms, regulation lacks transparency in administration.

## *India*

India is growing fast not only in population but also in terms of its potential influence globally.[15] Its population is expected to exceed that of China by 2025, and its economy is projected to become the world's third largest as measured by purchasing power parities by then. The Indian government is adopting a market economy approach, having introduced several reform measures in an effort to revive the economy. As a result, the Indian insurance market is partially open and is being deregulated.[16]

India's nonlife market is the world's 27th largest at US$4.8 billion for 2005. Insurance penetration is a low 0.61 percent, with a comparably low per capita nonlife expenditure of US$4.40. While these figures are quite low, growth has been and promises to remain robust, thus suggesting increasing density and penetration. For example, overall inflation-adjusted nonlife premium growth was 11.5 percent for 2005. What is more revealing is that premium growth for the private-sector nonlife insurers was an amazing 55 percent against a 4.8 percent growth for the public-sector companies.

To promote insurance, the government, based in large part on the 1993 report of the so-called Malhotra Committee, decided to open the market. As the first step in the process, it created a new insurance regulator, the Insurance Regulatory and Development Authority (IRDA), in 1999. The IRDA issued its first license in 2000 to the nonlife insurer Royal Sundaram Alliance. Today, 15 nonlife insurers compete for business, eight of which are private-sector ventures and six remain public-sector companies.

A newly licensed insurance company must be an Indian domiciled company with an initial paid-up capital of at least 1 billion rupees for direct insurance or 2 billion rupees for the reinsurance business. Composite insurers are not permitted. A foreign insurer's equity ownership in an Indian joint venture insurer is limited to a maximum of 26 percent. The local partner can be any qualified entity (examples include the State Bank of India, the Industrial Credit Investment Corporation of India, HDFC and Vysya Bank). Branches and wholly owned subsidiaries of foreign insurers are not admitted to the Indian insurance market.

Every insurer in India must maintain a required minimum solvency margin. In nonlife insurance, the minimum solvency margin is the greatest of (1) 500 million rupees (1 billion rupees for nonlife reinsurers), (2) 20 percent of premium income (net-of-reinsurance), or (3) 30 percent of incurred losses (net-of-reinsurance claims). Additionally, all nonlife insurers must make a deposit with the Reserve Bank of India of cash or approved securities equivalent to 3 percent – subject to maximum 100 million rupees – of its total gross premiums written in India in any financial year. Reinsurers are subject to a flat deposit of 200 million rupees.

The investment guidelines and conditions in India give insurers and reinsurers little flexibility in deciding where to invest their assets. An insurer must invest no less than 20 percent of its invested assets in central government securities and no less than 30 percent in state and other approved securities. It also must invest no less than 10 percent of its assets in the infrastructure and social sectors. The guidelines additionally state that every insurer must maintain a proper balance between the investments made in infrastructure and investments in the social sector.

An objective of reinsurance in India is to maximize retention within the country. Three specific rules relate to this purpose. First, insurers in India are advised to maintain the maximum possible retention commensurate with their individual strength and business volume. Second, a compulsory cession of 20 percent of each Indian risk must be ceded to the Indian state reinsurer (the General Insurance Corporation (GIC)) before placing any part of the risk with another reinsurer – a rule likely to disappear after India's accession to the WTO. Finally, the GIC assists nonlife insurers in organizing domestic pools for reinsurance surpluses in fire, marine hull and other nonlife classes.

Although fewer lines of insurance are subject to price regulation, the IRDA is still expected to influence premium rates as well as the terms and conditions of nonlife insurance policies. Whether it can directly control such areas, however, remains unclear because the Insurance Act of 1938 gives the Tariff Advisory Committee the power to "control and regulate the rates, advantages, terms and conditions that may be offered by insurers in respect of nonlife insurance business." The IRDA is examining the issue of rate deregulation, beginning with automobile insurance business.

The market generated 19 percent of premiums in fire insurance, 7 percent in marine insurance and the balance in other lines of business, the shares of the first two continuing to decline as insurers introduce new products (e.g., mutual fund package policy and third-party liability and asset cover). Public insurers – particularly, National Insurance, New India Insurance, Oriental Insurance and United Insurance – dominate the market, in the aggregate holding a 75 percent market share in terms of premiums or 89 percent in terms of new policies issued during 2004–2005.[17]


## *Australia*

Australia is home to a sophisticated nonlife market composed of 112 insurers and 21 reinsurers (as of December 2005). Although sparsely populated comparatively, Australia's market ranks as the world's 10th largest at US$24.3 billion. Nonlife insurance penetration of 3.09 percent ranks 12th worldwide, while an insurance density of US$1,203 ranks 13th.

As noted in the preceding chapter, an integrated Australian Prudential Regulatory Authority (APRA) has authority over deposit taking institutions, pension funds and life and general insurers. The *Financial Services Reform Act* established higher consumer protection standards, among other things. Insurers express concern that, while they support the objectives of the law, they fear consumers are being overloaded with information, the effect of which can be to frustrate the laws original purpose. Activities of APRA to reform the nonlife insurance industry include strengthening the prudential framework, liability valuation, capital adequacy and insurer risk management.

In terms of gross premiums written, domestic motor vehicle insurance holds the largest share at 21.7 percent, followed by householder's insurance (14.5 percent), fire and allied insurance (12.2 percent) and commercial third-party motor vehicle (10.6 percent). Sales of reinsurance outside Australia accounts for 23.6 percent of the market. Lloyd's of London is active in the Australian nonlife insurance market, generating A$1.5 billion of premiums during 2003–2005. The states of New South Wales and Western Austria lead the market, generating 53.8 percent of nonlife insurance premiums.[18]

## African Nonlife Insurance Markets

Africa represents perhaps the most challenging region of the world. Numerous economic, social and political problems in multiple parts of the continent threaten the very survival of many of its people. It is understandable, given these circumstances, that formal insurance has yet to play a major role in most countries, particularly in the nations in central Africa. Indeed, the total 2005 nonlife premiums volume of all of the continent's 54 countries is only US$12.2 billion or about US$13.50 per capita, but even these numbers overstate the size of the typical African market because of the influence of the large South African nonlife market on these data.

The insurance market in South Africa is undoubtedly the most developed in the continent. The market has been greatly influenced by Dutch and English insurers. This large market generated nonlife insurance premiums of US$7.3 billion in 2005 or 3.03 percent of GDP, which ranks as the world's 13th highest nonlife insurance penetration. More than 150 insurers and 10 reinsurers operate in South Africa.

The trading activities in northern Africa have resulted in active insurance markets in Morocco, Egypt and Tunisia, each with about 20 insurance companies. Other African countries with active insurance markets are Nigeria with 112 insurers and four reinsurers, and Kenya with 40 insurers and four reinsurers.

Eastern Africa and parts of southern Africa are situated in earthquake zones. Floods, landslides and severe draughts are perennial problems in most parts of Africa. Cyclones hit the coasts of South Africa and its neighboring countries. Despite the presence of these threats, insurers play a very limited role in these markets. In those small, underdeveloped markets, any large loss can be catastrophic, causing severe market distortion.

Two fires in Ethiopia in 1991, for instance, cost the local insurance industry US$47 million which was greater than the total premium income or the aggregate of authorized capital of all insurance companies for that year. The bomb blasts – terrorist attacks – in Kenya and Tanzania in 1999 resulted in an economic loss estimated at US$500 million, 250 human fatalities and thousands of injuries. For the year 2005, Swiss Re (2006) reports 41 catastrophes in Africa, which in the aggregate caused 1,581 deaths (in comparison to 2,666 in 2004) and US$49 million in comparison (US$577 million in 2004) of property losses. Only a fraction of these economic losses was covered by insurance. Hence, a critical issue in most African countries is how to foster vigorous insurance markets with larger capacities and wider arrays of products. Achieving political and economic stability remains the critical, underlying issue in many African countries.

Many governments in Africa still impose compulsory reinsurance sessions, as discussed in the following chapter. Some countries also subject local firms to compulsory reinsurance cessions – 5 percent of all reinsurance treaty business – to the African Reinsurance Corporation, a regional reinsurance pool [www.africa-re.com] established in 1976. Forty-one companies in Africa participate in the pool. Angola, Ethiopia, South Africa, Tunisia, Uganda and Zimbabwe do not require compulsory cessions. It is generally accepted that compulsory cessions hinder the orderly development of national insurance markets.

# NONLIFE INSURANCE ISSUES

The demand for nonlife insurance as well as the nature and structure of the markets created to satisfy this demand often can be explained by assessing the stage of economic development, the social and cultural fabric of the people and the political history and philosophy of the country and its region. While the world's nonlife insurance markets differ in many respects, some global trends can be expected to affect all markets. We highlight three trends.

## Liberalization and Deregulation

Nonlife insurance competition is increasing worldwide in both developing and developed markets, as governments embrace the philosophy that increased competition enhances social welfare and that increased competition is best achieved by liberal, open and appropriately supervised markets. In most developed markets, competition in some lines (e.g., homeowner's insurance, automobile insurance and general liability insurance) remains strong. The E.U. single market program continues to bring competitive benefits to Europe. New marketing arrangements (e.g., Internet-based marketing and *bancassurance*) have fostered growth in several markets.

Many developing nations are encountering the challenges of more open competition. The orderly structure of closed and strictly regulated markets is being replaced by new market entrants and deregulation. This has meant facing the complexities of new product development, competitive market pricing, and enhancing quality of service.

The most far-reaching changes are taking place in countries that historically have limited competition. Numerous developing economies – notably Eastern European economies, China and India – that limited nonlife insurance supply to public entities have privatized or otherwise allowed private insurers into their markets. Other markets, with traditions of form restrictions and tariff rating, now permit competition in both form and rate. Some countries with significant barriers to entry to foreign insurers have eased these restrictions. Infusion of new capacity by domestic private and foreign entities has been a significant factor in the growth of those countries' markets. Convergence in financial services and the development of securitization techniques also have increased the underwriting capacity in numerous countries. These changes have created numerous opportunities and challenges for insurers dealing with the dynamics of competitive markets.

## Coping with Catastrophes

Natural and human-made catastrophes can have a significant impact on nonlife insurance markets globally. In some markets, property insurance covers damage caused by catastrophic perils such as earthquake, severe windstorm, flood and volcanic activity. Insurance coverages for human-made catastrophe risks also are available, albeit limited, in selected developed markets and in the global reinsurance market.

The frequency and severity of catastrophic losses continue to rise worldwide. As a result, the mere presence of catastrophe risk exposures can leave a market with a fear of a financial ruin. Nonlife insurers depend greatly on catastrophe reinsurance to spread the loss to a broader risk-bearing base, especially those in developing countries. However, catastrophe reinsurance is unavailable in some markets or available only at a price that insurers consider prohibitive. This trend has exacerbated the catastrophe problem for the private insurance sector as well as for the public sector.

The nonlife insurance markets in the developed countries face a different set of challenges. One is coping with the financial consequences of catastrophes. The accumulation of significant property values in many of the potentially high-risk areas of the world has greatly exacerbated the catastrophe exposure. Can the private insurance sector fully satisfy the demand for property insurance protection? Is some type of joint arrangement between the private and public sectors needed to cope with this catastrophe potential, as many observers contend?

## Solvency

Insurance markets being privatized, deregulated and liberalized arguably face an increased risk of insurer insolvency. Insurance regulators in these markets are challenged to cope with this risk. Insolvency risk does not disappear when the market becomes competitive. To the contrary, it becomes a more critical issue for regulators, as they must encourage more competitive markets but such markets inevitably carry the risk that competitors will become insolvent. Insurer insolvency is an unavoidable derivative of competition.

Generally, insurer insolvency risk is greater in competitive markets than in strictly controlled markets, as alluded to earlier. With nonlife insurance, however, some insurance lines are highly volatile and notoriously difficult to price such that both insurer financial soundness and marketplace competitiveness can be assured. Maintaining financial solvency is thus a common concern of every regulator and, of course, every insurance firm.

## DISCUSSION QUESTIONS

1.  This chapter discussed several key issues that affect nonlife insurance operations on a global basis. How do these issues interact with each other and how could they affect the way that corporations manage their risks?
2.  Compare the nonlife liability insurance markets in developed countries and developing countries with respect to the following:
    (a) types of insurance products;
    (b) growth rates;
    (c) regulatory environments.
3.  Distribution systems are a key component of any nonlife insurance market.
    (a) Compare the distribution systems used in two countries of your choice or in the U.S. with those of Japan.
    (b) In your opinion, will nonlife insurance be transacted using the "information highway"? Explain your position.
4.  Privatization and deregulation are "mega-trends" in many of the nonlife insurance markets in the developing world. Discuss the challenges facing insurance executives of established domestic insurers in those markets.

## NOTES

1.  Of course, exceptions to this generalization of payment methods exist. Moreover, some property insurance policies – called valued policies – provide for payment of a fixed amount agreed to by the insured and the insurer at the time the policy is issued. Policies of this type are commonly used for insuring objects whose value is subjective, such as works of art.

2.  Hill & Usher Insurance & Surety (n.d.).
3.  To be specific, cargo transported by ship often is called ocean marine cargo, whereas cargo transported by land vehicle is called inland marine cargo.
4.  Unless indicated otherwise, all premium data are from Swiss Re (2006) and Towers Perrin (2005). Recall that Swiss Re follows the European convention of treating premiums for health and accident

insurance as nonlife insurance. Thus, the nonlife premium figures include more than property and liability insurance premiums only.

5. This section draws in parts from Feldhaus (1998).
6. Insurance Information Institute (2006b).
7. OSFI (2006).
8. In the U.K., non-comprehensive motor vehicle insurance covers third-party liability as well as loss of insured vehicle by theft or fire. Comprehensive insurance covers other perils.
9. Investment by individuals with limited liability is available in two syndicates only.
10. See Insight 10.3 for a description of the automobile insurance market in Japan.
11. General Insurance Association of Japan (2006).
12. "Miscellaneous casualty line" in Japan is broad in scope and includes all liability lines except automobile liability insurance.
13. Note that the share of foreign insurers is based on March 2005 data.
14. This regulation resulted in restructuring of the PICC – then a composite insurer – as a holding company for the newly created China Life Insurance Company, the People's Insurance Company of China (for nonlife business) and China Reinsurance Company.

15. This discussion draws heavily from Kwon (2002).
16. It would be more accurate to state that the market has *reopened* to the private sector. In 1956, the then socialist government nationalized then merged the more than 200 foreign and locally owned life insurers into the newly created Life Insurance Corporation (LIC) of India. In 1972, it completed its drive toward a state-controlled market with the nationalization of 100 or so foreign and domestic nonlife insurers to create four new subsidiaries of the state-owned General Insurance Corporation (GIC) of India. Each subsidiary held a monopoly in a region of India. Formerly, the private insurers provided insurance primarily to the urban   sector and to organized trades and industries. In instituting its monopolistic policy, the government claimed that insurance was a social device that should be available to everyone and the industry should be free of profit motives. Insurance growth, thereafter, was stifled.
17. IRDA (2006).
18. APRA (2006).

# REFERENCES

Australian Prudential Regulatory Authority (APRA) (2006). *APRA Annual Report 2005*. Sydney: APRA.

Feldhaus, W.R. (1998). "Nonlife Insurance," in H.D. Skipper Jr., ed., *International Risk and Insurance: An Environmental/Managerial Approach*. Boston, MA: Irwin/McGraw-Hill.

Hill & Usher Insurance & Surety (n.d.). Available at www.hillusher.com/define/insurance/Glossary/cr2.htm.

General Insurance Association of Japan (2006a). *Fact Book 2004–2005*. Tokyo: General Insurance Association of Japan.

General Insurance Association of Japan (2006b). *2005 Statistics*. Available at www.sonpo.or.jp/e/statistics/index.html.

Insurance Information Institute (2006a). *Property/Casualty Insurance by Line*. Available at www.financialservicesfacts.org/financial/.

Insurance Information Institute (2006b). *Financial Services Fact Book*. New York: Insurance Information Institute.

Insurance Regulatory and Supervisory Authority (IRDA) (2006). *Annual Report 2004–2005*. New Delhi: IRDA.

Kwon, W.J. (2002b). *The Insurance Markets of South Asia*. Washington, DC: International Insurance Foundation.

Office of the Superintendent of Financial Institutions Canada (OSFI) (2006). *2006–2007 to 2007–2008: Reports on Plans and Priorities*. Ottawa: Ministry of Finance.

Organization for Economic Co-operation and Development (OECD) (2003). *Insurance Statistics Yearbook 1994–2001*. Paris: OECD.

Swiss Re (2004). "World Insurance in 2003." *Sigma*. Zurich: Swiss Re.

Swiss Re (2006). "World Insurance in 2006," *Sigma*. Zurich: Swiss Re.

Towers Perrin (2005). *Insurance Pocket Book 2005*. Oxfordshire: Towers Perrin.

# Chapter 23

# Reinsurance

## INTRODUCTION

Insurance companies provide risk financing services through pooling large numbers of similar risks. Their underwriting capacity is, however, subject to numerous internal (e.g., capital, underwriting expertise and line of business) and external (e.g., regulatory, economic and market conditions) constraints. To increase their capacity and to manage their risk portfolios more efficiently, insurers frequently rely on reinsurance.[1] Recall from Chapter 1 that *reinsurance* is insurance purchased by primary insurers to hedge their own portfolios of insured risks. It involves financing by the insurer of part of a risk, a policy or a portfolio of risks by means of a contract with another insurance company, called variously the *reinsurer*, *reinsurance company* or *assuming company*. The insurer is also termed the *cedant*, the *ceding company* or the *reinsured*. The amount of risk not reinsured and retained by the *cedant* is known as the **retention** and the amount transferred as the **cession**.

The reinsurance contract is between the primary insurer and the reinsurer. Ordinarily, the original insured must look solely to the direct insurer for payments. The original insured has no *privy of contract* with the reinsurer. Thus, if an insurer fails to meet its claims obligations, its insureds and claimants, in principle, cannot seek recoveries from its reinsurers. Exceptions exist. For example, a large corporate insured may demand inclusion of provision – a so-called **cut-through provision** – in the insurance contract that gives the insured a right to seek claims payment directly from the reinsurer on the insurer's failure to meet its obligations fully or on time. Of course, the reinsurer must agree on inclusion of this provision before the original insurance contract is finalized.

Originally, the sharing of risk between underwriters was accomplished through coinsurance wherein direct insurance coverage was provided by more than one insurer.[2] Coinsurance is used extensively in the London market and in many other countries, but less so in the U.S.

Before the development of a separate reinsurance business in the mid-19th century, underwriters also would share risk through **reciprocity agreements** wherein insurers would reciprocate in the sharing of each other's risks, with each insurer transferring a portion of its portfolio of risks to another insurer and vice versa. This was a method of gaining geographic distribution of exposures to loss. Reciprocity still exists in many markets, most commonly between reinsurers.

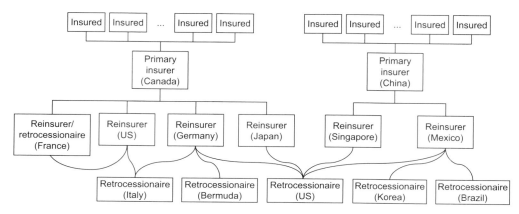

**Figure 23.1**    Worldwide Risk Sharing

Direct insurers purchase reinsurance to hedge themselves against volatilities in their insurance portfolios, to minimize undue potential loss concentrations, to secure greater underwriting capacity, to stabilize overall financial results and to take advantage of special expertise of reinsurance companies. Reinsurance typically involves large exposures to loss, often those with a catastrophic loss potential. In this chapter, we describe the fundamentals of reinsurance contracts and operations, portray the role of reinsurance internationally, and summarize reinsurance market issues.

## WORLDWIDE RISK SHARING

Reinsurance is vital to the smooth functioning of insurance markets internationally, with virtually every insurer worldwide relying on it. Due to the large size of some loss exposures, primary insurers find it necessary to share these exposures with reinsurers that can then, if necessary, distribute the risk internationally. Purchasing reinsurance from several international reinsurers is not uncommon for a primary insurer.

As a means of risk management, reinsurers typically seek their own reinsurance. The term **retrocession** is used to describe the purchase of reinsurance by reinsurers, thus distinguishing this type of reinsurance from that purchased by primary insurers. The party accepting the retrocession is termed a **retrocessionaire**, although no companies are known to specialize in the retrocession business alone. Through multiple reinsurance cessions and retrocessions, large loss exposures can be spread among dozens of insurers and reinsurers worldwide.

Figure 23.1 provides an illustration of the global nature of reinsurance. It shows relationships among primary insurers, reinsurers, and retrocessionaires. In the figure, two insurers, one Canadian and one Chinese, cede part of their risks to various reinsurers. The Canadian insurer has agreements with four international reinsurers and the Chinese insurer has two similar agreements. Each of the reinsurers maintains multiple retrocession agreements. With this web of arrangements, the financial impact of a large loss – whether it results from a single loss or an accumulation of smaller losses – on a primary insurer and its reinsurers can be spread internationally. Note in Figure 23.1 that the reinsurer in France functions both as a reinsurer for the Canadian insurer and as a retrocessionaire for the U.S. reinsurer.

# REINSURANCE DEMAND

Recall from Chapter 2 that finance theory holds that widely held corporations generally can be thought of as being risk neutral. Thus, such corporations would not ordinarily be expected to purchase insurance. By this logic, insurance companies would not purchase reinsurance or retrocession.

We know, however, that non-insurance corporations purchase insurance and that insurers purchase reinsurance. Chapter 19 explained why corporations might purchase insurance. In concept, we would expect insurers to purchase reinsurance for essentially the same reasons. Thus, Mayers and Smith (1990) find that reinsurance demand is influenced by the insurer's ownership structure, the cost of financial distress, capital market imperfections, real service efficiencies, and the structure of tax codes. Lewis and Murdock (1996) further describe the influence of an insurer's desire to reduce volatility in earnings and compliance with regulatory constraints on the demand for reinsurance. We summarize each of these rationales below:

- *Ownership structure*: Finance theory indicates that reinsurance would be redundant for diversified, widely held firms. In fact, many insurers are neither diversified nor widely held. For these insurers, reinsurance allows diversification of their loss exposures beyond their internal risk pools. Insurers with more concentrated ownership are more likely to reinsure than those with less concentrated ownership, all others being equal. To achieve more optimal risk diversification, closely held stock insurers, small mutuals, reciprocals and captives have an incentive to reinsure.

- *Cost of financial distress*: As noted in Chapter 2, financial distress can impose additional costs on the firm, such as additional borrowing and regulator-imposed examination and auditing costs. Insurers may purchase reinsurance to reduce the likelihood of financial distress because doing so reduces attendant costs. Also, policyholders presumably will be willing to pay more for policies from insurers whose probability of default is lower. Therefore, insurers have incentives to reduce their default risk with reinsurance.

- *Capital market imperfections*: Insurers facing large potential losses will not be as attractive to potential investors as those facing smaller potential losses. For example, consider an insurer that could experience a large loss that would reduce the value of both the firm's equity and its outstanding policies. Because loss payments would accrue primarily to policyholders who have a prior claim on the firm's assets, the equity holders face an investment disincentive. If the insurer purchases reinsurance to cover such large losses, the investment disincentive would be reduced. This problem is more severe for firms with smaller capitalization and more volatile cash flows.

- *Real service efficiencies*: Reinsurers with broad exposure bases may have real efficiencies in risk diversification associated with low probability events. They often operate in multiple jurisdictions and possess specialized ratemaking, underwriting and claims management expertise. They can assist insurers in entering new markets and exiting markets by sharing insurers' books of business for particular lines of business or territories. In one or more of these dimensions, direct insurers may gain from working with reinsurers.

- *Reduction of tax liability*: The purchase of reinsurance can reduce the direct insurer's expected tax liability by reducing the volatility of taxable income. This incentive can be particularly strong for insurers or product lines with high-income volatility and for firms that are not members of a group. For group-affiliated insurers, reinsurance might be used to transfer earnings within the group, thus minimizing group taxes. This can be particularly important where insurer income is taxed differently across countries, because taxes affect underwriting capacity. For example, the underwriting capacity of local insurers in high-tax domiciles can be augmented by the opportunity for them to cede risks to reinsurers operating in low-tax domiciles, as the latter will be willing to assume more risk. This may explain why large reinsurers tend to be located in certain countries (e.g., Switzerland and Germany).

- *Volatility control*: Hoerger et al. (1990) and Garven (1990) show that a positive relationship exists between the level of risk by line of insurance and the demand for reinsurance. Indeed, reinsurance can reduce the variance of retained losses by line. Effective use of reinsurance also can provide an insurer with more predictable cash flows and less earnings volatility.

- *Regulatory constraints*: Regulation, along with industry practice, often limits insurers' financial leverage, typically measured as the ratio of net premiums written to surplus. By purchasing reinsurance, an insurer can reduce its leverage. All other factors being constant, the higher the leverage, the greater the demand for reinsurance. For example, reinsurance allows insurers to use ceding commissions (discussed later) paid by the reinsurer to increase underwriting capacity by more than would otherwise be possible with a given amount of capital.

# REINSURANCE FUNDAMENTALS AND OPERATIONS

In this section, we introduce several aspects of reinsurance fundamentals and operations. We begin by identifying the types of reinsurers and the channels by which reinsurance is sold. Next, we examine the types of reinsurance contracts and the forms of reinsurance covered by them. We close this section with a brief discussion of reinsurance program, retention and ceding commissions.

## Types of Reinsurers

Reinsurance is available from (1) professional reinsurers, (2) reinsurance departments of primary insurers, (3) pools and (4) Lloyd's associations. A primary insurer may place its risk with a **professional reinsurer** – an insurance company that specializes in writing reinsurance and does not normally assume risks as a direct insurer (although it may do so through its insurance subsidiary).

Insurance laws generally permit direct insurers to sell reinsurance in the lines of direct business for which they are licensed. Accepting reinsurance can help them diversify their risks. It also is an additional business opportunity. The share of the reinsurance market held by primary insurers has traditionally been less than that of professional reinsurers.

Pools – also sometimes called associations – are mechanisms for sharing risks among their members. A **pool** is an arrangement where member firms jointly accept risks in a line of business. Pools may be formed by primary insurers or by reinsurers. Pools provide a means to write larger limits of insurance than a single reinsurer may want to assume. Examples are the Africa Oil and Energy Pool and the Arab Fire, Marine and Aviation Pools.

Pools are sometimes used to provide insurance (or reinsurance) for risks that primary insurers do not wish to retain. Thus, in some jurisdictions, insurers selling automobile liability or workers' compensation insurance may redirect all risks that they do not wish to retain to a pool created by law or voluntarily to underwrite such risks. The pool or a member insurer functioning as a servicing carrier issues policies and provides claims and other administrative services. The operating results of the pool are then shared by all member insurers, commonly according to their share of premiums in the standard market.[3]

Finally, several Lloyd's of London syndicates accept reinsurance. A significant inter-syndicate reinsurance business also is conducted at Lloyd's. Other Lloyd's associations include Lloyd's of Asia and Lloyd's of Japan.

## Reinsurance Distribution Systems

Reinsurance is sold by brokers and directly by reinsurance companies. Reinsurers selling directly to primary insurers are called **direct writing reinsurers**. They use their employees to solicit business and help client insurers design reinsurance programs. Although the majority of reinsurers obtain business through brokers, some of the largest and most secure reinsurers write directly.

**Reinsurance brokerage (broking) firms** represent primary insurers wishing to place business with one or more reinsurers. The intermediary usually can access many reinsurance markets throughout the world to which an insurer alone may have difficulty gaining access. This and other expertise of the intermediary can benefit the insurer by being able to secure reinsurance under favorable terms and conditions. An intermediary may place risk with a large reinsurer or multiple reinsurers, depending on how the reinsurance program is structured. Reinsurance brokers often are experienced in designing such programs, another potential benefit to the cedant.

When the placement involves several reinsurers, the intermediary usually identifies a lead reinsurer. After evaluating the a proposal – also known as a **slip** – provided by the intermediary on behalf of the client insurer, the lead reinsurer – also termed **lead** or **leading underwriter** – may decide to underwrite the risk. It normally assumes the largest percentage of the ceded risk, the balance to be shared by other follower reinsurers. Some markets (e.g., the London market) have a strong "lead-follower" system, whereas in other markets (e.g., the U.S.) reinsurers are more inclined to evaluate proposals independently.

In selected cases, brokers are given in-principle approval to accept certain risks on behalf of their reinsurers. Under this arrangement, known as the **broker's cover**, the reinsurer is contractually bound to accept all risks that the intermediary accepts from ceding companies.

The intermediary usually receives broking commissions – commonly stated in the slip as a percentage of reinsurance premium – from the reinsurer. The size of commission depends in part on the nature of the contract (facultative or treaty) and how the risk or loss is shared (proportional versus excess-of-loss (XL)) between the insurer and the reinsurer(s). The broker customarily helps the insurer and the reinsurer settle their accounts – premiums, commissions, losses and so forth.

Reinsurance intermediaries offer one additional service. They monitor the financial and operational soundness of the reinsurers with whom they place business. Small and new insurers tend to depend heavily on the judgment of brokers in selecting reinsurers.

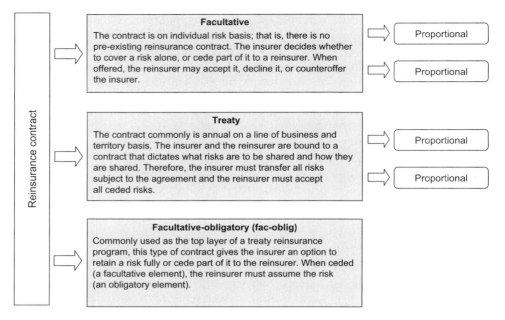

**Figure 23.2**   Classification of Reinsurance Contracts *Source*: Kwon (1999)

## Types and Nature of Reinsurance Contracts

Reinsurance contracts are not standardized, and contractual terms and conditions can vary widely from line to line and from market to market. Nonetheless, reinsurance contracts can be classified as being either facultative or treaty agreements. Figure 23.2 summarizes this classification.

### Facultative reinsurance

With **facultative reinsurance**, the insurer negotiates a separate reinsurance agreement for each policy that it wishes to reinsure. For example, suppose an insurer is considering a large risk (policy) for which it has insufficient underwriting capacity. The insurer may seek a reinsurer or group of reinsurers that are willing to assume part of the risk. For another risk, the insurer repeats the same process. In this way, the insurer is placing risks or policies individually (i.e., facultatively).

In this oldest form of reinsurance, the primary insurer decides how much of each risk to retain and thus how much to cede and to whom to cede it. The insurer is free to decide whether to retain a risk fully or to cede part or all of it. Likewise, the reinsurer is under no obligation to accept any incoming risk. It can decline it or counteroffer a modified contract.

Facultative reinsurance is commonly sought when the insurer is in the process of underwriting a risk or has just accepted it. The insurer may consider a facultative arrangement when it has no treaty arrangement for a line of business or territory, when a certain risk is excluded from or not fully reinsured by existing treaties or when an existing treaty's capacity is exhausted. Facultative reinsurance enables small and new insurers to write large risks beyond their individual underwriting capacity. Facultative reinsurance also helps insurers maintain balanced risk and loss portfolios under treaty arrangements.

Disadvantages exist with facultative reinsurance. It is not always available. Finding a willing reinsurer can be time consuming and result in high administrative expenses or low ceding commissions (see below). The insurer must disclose competitive information (e.g., premium rates) to all reinsurers to which it wishes to cede risk. In "hard" insurance markets or with difficult-to-place lines, primary insurers may end up with higher premium outflows than in soft markets or stable lines of business, respectively from placing risks facultatively.

### Treaty reinsurance

**Treaty reinsurance** refers to reinsurance agreements under which the insurer agrees to cede and the reinsurer agrees to assume all risks written by the insurer that come within the terms of the treaty. For example, they may agree to share risks proportionally – up to S$1 million per risk – written by the insurer for residential property risks situated in Brunei, Malaysia and Singapore for one year, subject to renewal. A treaty is formal and binds both parties. It *automatically* applies to the entire portfolio of risks covered by the treaty unless specifically excluded. A treaty usually notes the maximum size of risk, the reinsurance limit and the business territory to which it applies. Reinsurance treaties are written on a continuous or term basis. A continuous contract continues indefinitely but generally with a notice period (e.g., 90 days) whereby either party can inform the other of its intent to cancel or amend the treaty. With this type of arrangement, insurers and reinsurers build a long-term relationship. A term agreement has a built-in expiration date.

With treaty reinsurance, the primary insurer enjoys an automatic increase in underwriting capacity and, often, technical assistance from the reinsurer. Because risks are not individually ceded, the insurer can benefit from low administration costs and earn favorable ceding commissions. However, the insurer is not likely to be free to change its underwriting policy or retention limits. Such changes often are subject to the reinsurer's consent.

A hybrid type of reinsurance contract, known as the **facultative-obligatory (fac-oblig) treaty**, gives the insurer an option as to what risks it cedes (a facultative element). The reinsurer is then bound to accept all reinsured risks (a treaty element) that fall within the terms of agreement. This arrangement can expose the reinsurer to adverse selection. Not surprisingly, a high degree of trust must exist before a reinsurer agrees on this hybrid contract. When ceding a risk, the insurer must provide full details of the risk to the reinsurer. Facultative-obligatory reinsurance can be used as a top layer in a treaty reinsurance program, thus providing some catastrophe loss protection for the cedant.

## Forms of Reinsurance

Reinsurance can be either proportional or non-proportional (excess-of-loss of XL). Each may be written on a treaty or facultative basis. These two forms of reinsurance differ in the way that the insurer and the reinsurer share the amount of insurance, premiums and losses. Figure 23.3 summarizes these types of reinsurance, plus financial reinsurance, which are covered later in this section.

### Proportional reinsurance

With **proportional reinsurance**, also called **pro-rata reinsurance**, the reinsurer takes a stated share of each risk that the insurer writes and shares in the premium and losses in that

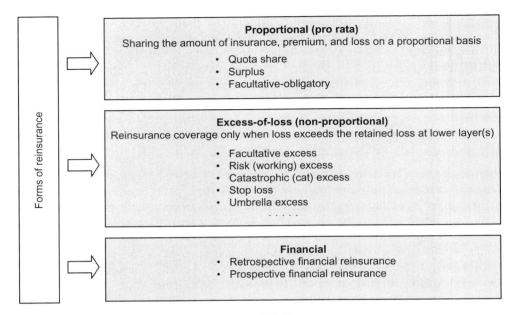

**Figure 23.3**   Forms of Reinsurance. *Source*: Kwon (1999)

same proportion. The sharing proportion can be the same for all sizes and types of risks or vary with the size and type.

Proportional reinsurance is more widely used in property than in liability lines. It is of two types: quota share and surplus share, each discussed below.

*Quota share reinsurance*

Reinsurance that stipulates a fixed ratio for the sharing of *all* risks and thus attached premiums and losses in that same ratio is called **quota share (QS) reinsurance**. The contract usually states a maximum amount above which the reinsurer is unwilling to be committed on any one risk. For example, a quota share treaty might provide that the insurer must cede and the reinsurer must accept 75 percent of all risks falling within the treaty, to a maximum of $500,000 per risk. Table 23.1 offers an example.

An insurer uses quota share reinsurance for various reasons, including to

- support a new line of business for which it has insufficient experience or lacks reliable statistics;
- finance growth by reducing its unearned premium reserve by the amount of premiums ceded;
- benefit from the reinsurer's expertise;
- increase its capacity to write policies with higher limits.

Insurers often use more than one reinsurer in quota share arrangements (e.g., two reinsurers each sharing 30 percent of the risk and the cedant retaining the remaining 40 percent).

A drawback with this arrangement stems from the requirement that the insurer must cede all risks falling under the treaty to the reinsurer. This leads to forwarding premiums even for small risks that the insurer alone could underwrite.

**Table 23.1** An Example of Quota Share Treaty Reinsurance

| *Quota Share Treaty Reinsurance – 75% Cession with a Reinsurance Limit of $500,000 per Risk* | | | | | | | | |
| --- | --- | --- | --- | --- | --- | --- | --- | --- |
| *Original Risk* | | | *Insurer's Share* | | | *Reinsurer's Share* | | |
| *Risk* | *Premium* | *Loss* | *Risk* | *Premium* | *Loss* | *Risk* | *Premium* | *Loss* |
| 50,000 | 100 | 4,000 | 12,500 (25%) | 25 (25%) | 1,000 (25%) | 37,500 (75%) | 75 (75%) | 3,000 (75%) |
| 100,000 | 160 | No loss | 25,000 (25%) | 40 (25%) | N/A | 75,000 (75%) | 120 (75%) | N/A |
| 500,000 | 500 | 5,000 | 125,000 (25%) | 125 (25%) | 1,250 (25%) | 375,000 (75%) | 375 (75%) | 3.750 (75%) |

*Surplus reinsurance*

With **surplus reinsurance**, the insurer determines how much it can retain per risk for every risk in a portfolio (e.g., commercial property risks in Madrid, Spain) and locates one or more reinsurers willing to offer additional capacity. The cedant's retention is called a **line**, and any risk falling within that line is the exclusive responsibility of the direct insurer. The reinsurance coverage on any ceded risk is expressed as a multiple of the line. Thus, a four-line surplus treaty means that the maximum reinsurance on any risk is 4 times the amount of the insurer's retention. All premiums and losses above the insurer's retention and up to the reinsurance limit are pro rated. Hence, the higher the retention, the greater the share of risk retained and the lower the reinsurance premium outlay.

As the cedant decides its retention for each risk, the proportionate sharing varies with each risk. Surplus reinsurance differs in this respect as, with quota share reinsurance, the percentage sharing is fixed for all risks.

Table 23.2 illustrates the operation of surplus reinsurance. It shows the insurer elects a retention of $100,000. Thus, the first risk ($50,000) is not shared with the reinsurer. When the insurance amount exceeds the retention, the excess is automatically ceded to the reinsurer, and the reinsurer is bound to accept it up to the treaty limit (4 times the retention in the table). This results in 60-percent cession for the second risk ($250,000) and 80-percent cession for the third risk ($500,000).

As with quota share reinsurance, the cedant under surplus reinsurance does not provide the reinsurer with details of risks or claims except when the amount exceeds a threshold defined in the contract. The insurer may stack surplus treaties. Further, it can share the retention with a quota share reinsurer.

Figure 23.4 shows a treaty reinsurance program under which the insurer constructs a $2.0 million capacity. On the lowest layer, the insurer shares $100,000 retention with a quota share reinsurer. It also has secured two surplus reinsurers that offer a combined limit of $900,000. Finally, it adds a $1.0 million facultative-obligatory contract on top of the second surplus reinsurer.

A surplus treaty provides the insurer with substantial automatic reinsurance capacity. It allows the insurer fully to retain small risks, thus helping it stabilize its risk and loss portfolios. It can help the insurer build surplus, thus providing additional capacity to write larger lines while minimizing the insurer's exposure to large losses and catastrophic events. When deciding the number of layers and the lines for each surplus (and facultative-obligatory)

**Table 23.2**   An Example of Surplus Share Treaty Reinsurance

*Surplus Treaty Reinsurance – Four Lines with the Insurer's Retention of $100,000 per Risk*

| Original Risk | | | Insurer's Share | | | Reinsurer's Share | | |
|---|---|---|---|---|---|---|---|---|
| *Risk* | *Premium* | *Loss* | *Risk* | *Premium* | *Loss* | *Risk* | *Premium* | *Loss* |
| 50,000 | 100 | 4,000 | 50,000 (100%) | 100 (100%) | 4,000 (100%) | 0 (0%) | 0 (0%) | 0 (0%) |
| 250,000 | 500 | 50,000 | 100,000 (40%) | 200 (40%) | 20,000 (40%) | 150,000 (60%) | 300 (60%) | 30,000 (60%) |
| 500,000 | 1,000 | 5,000 | 100,000 (20%) | 200 (20%) | 1,000 (20%) | 400,000 (80%) | 800 (80%) | 4,000 (80%) |

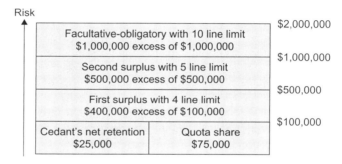

**Figure 23.4**   Illustrative Proportional Treaty Reinsurance Program with $2 Million Risk Capacity

treaty, insurers consider several factors, such as their own underwriting capacity, each reinsurer's capacity and financial stability and the size of ceding commissions.

Surplus treaties are commonly of one year's duration and are renewable subject to annual review by both parties. This form of reinsurance also is frequently used when two insurers agree on a reciprocal arrangement.

Insurers also use proportional arrangements to cede a risk facultatively. As in treaty reinsurance, the reinsurer's share of the risk is expressed as either fixed percentage in a quota share contract or can vary with the size of the insurer's retention and the reinsurance limit in a surplus contract. Each risk in Tables 23.1 and 23.2 can be viewed as an example of facultatively arranged proportional reinsurance. In all cases, the reinsurer's share of premium and loss is directly proportional to its share of the risk.

### Excess-of-loss reinsurance

**Excess-of-loss reinsurance, also known as non-proportional or XL reinsurance**, provides that the reinsurer indemnifies the cedant only for losses in excess of the cedant's retention of *loss*, subject to the reinsurance limit. For example, a contract stating "$3 million xs $1 million" affords the insurer reinsurance recovery up to $3 million when a loss subject to the agreement exceeds $1 million.

XL reinsurance is more of a loss financing arrangement than a risk sharing arrangement. The attached premium varies depending on the severity and frequency of claims subject to the contract, thus resulting in a nonlinear (i.e., non-proportional) relationship between the premium and the loss. XL reinsurance is more common in liability than in property reinsurance.

XL reinsurance can be purchased to provide indemnification for a wide range of circumstances. Some of the more common are listed below:

- **Facultative XL reinsurance also known as per risk** (or **policy**) **XL reinsurance**, it is designed to cover the losses of an individual risk or policy over the cedant's loss retention. Facultative XL reinsurance tends to grow, albeit not necessarily proportionally, along with the rise in large risks (e.g., hazardous, complex, and highly protected risks) that can pose significant loss exposures to insurers. Captive insurers often depend on facultative XL reinsurance.

- **Risk (working) XL reinsurance** is a type of treaty under which the reinsurer indemnifies the insurer for any losses, subject to the reinsurance limit, in excess of the insurer's retention for *each* risk falling under the treaty. For example, the reinsurer agrees to indemnify up to $500,000 for each loss in excess of the insurer's retention of $100,000 per loss and per risk. Working XL reinsurance can be an effective means of stabilizing an insurer's loss experience. By setting low retentions, XL reinsurance is triggered for many losses. It functions similarly to surplus reinsurance but with a sharing of losses, not risks. When entering into risk XL arrangements, reinsurers often set not only their maximum obligations per loss but also their aggregate coverage for the entire coverage period.

- Reinsurance limit in typical XL reinsurance is based on the insurer's own retention. **Common account XL reinsurance** protects the combined exposure of the insurer and its quota share reinsurer. (Common account XL reinsurance is not feasible when the initial reinsurance is surplus share because of the difficulty in determining the share of that reinsurer's premium.)

- Also known as **per occurrence XL reinsurance**, catastrophe (cat) XL reinsurance protects the cedant against adverse loss experience resulting from an accumulation of losses from a single, major natural or human-made disaster. The reinsurance will indemnify the insurer only when there are two or more losses per event and when the accumulation of losses paid by the cedant, less other reinsurance payments, exceeds the cat reinsurance threshold. An **hours clause** is commonly included in cat XL reinsurance contracts to clarify what constitutes an occurrence. For example, a 72-hour clause treats as a single claim all losses arising from an event during any 72-hour period chosen by the cedant. Coinsurance by the cedant (e.g., 5 percent) may apply for the loss above the threshold.

- In stop loss reinsurance, the reinsurer indemnifies the insurer once the insurer's loss ratio in a line of business exceeds a percentage stipulated in the contract. It can be an effective risk management tool when an insurer desires to shield itself from wide fluctuations in loss ratios in a given line. Unlike other types of reinsurance, the reinsurer does not set the upper limit of reinsurance but requires the insurer to share in all losses falling into the stop loss reinsurance. This coinsurance often is defined as a percentage (e.g., 10 percent) or as a fixed amount.

- Similar to stop loss reinsurance, **aggregate XL reinsurance** indemnifies the insurer once the insurer incurs losses in excess of a stipulated amount. For example, a reinsurer may promise to cover losses up to $10 million in excess of the insurer's retention of $50 million in a line of business. (Compare this with working and stop loss XL reinsurance!)

- **Umbrella XL reinsurance** is designed to indemnify the insurer in case it experiences a run of losses in two or more lines of business in the same class (e.g., all liability lines). It can be effective when an insurer wants protection against a chain of losses affecting multiple lines of insurance simultaneously. Umbrella reinsurance coverage is triggered when the reinsurance limit in any line subject to the contract has been exhausted. **Whole account XL reinsurance**, broader in scope, indemnifies the insurer for a run of losses in the aggregate from all lines in which it operates. Pricing of these coverages can be complicated, thus making markets for these two types of reinsurance limited.

Insurers often design XL reinsurance programs in layers. Figure 23.5 offers an example. Note that the layers are in terms of losses not risk (policy limits) as in Figure 23.4 for proportional reinsurance programs.

XL property reinsurance often includes a **reinstatement provision** that allows the insurer to restore (reinstate) the reinsurance limit to the original level after collecting part or all of the original limit. For example, if an insurer has a cat XL reinsurance contract with two reinstatements, it can recover losses from the reinsurer up to 3 times – once from the initial limit and twice from exercising the reinstatement option – during the coverage period. Some reinsurers offer reinstatement benefits at no identifiable additional premium (often for the first reinstatement), while others charge it for every reinstatement. Reinstatement premiums generally are pro rated to the amount to be reinstated or the remaining coverage period or both.

### Reinsurance program design

When designing a reinsurance program, insurers consider several factors, including risk and loss portfolios over several years (past and projected), types of reinsurance contracts, apportionment of risks or losses by layer, availability of reinsurers specializing in each type of reinsurance and their ancillary services, prevailing conditions in the reinsurance market and in the economy, profitability (including the size of ceding and other commissions from reinsurers) and, importantly, the insurer's own capacity to retain losses (i.e., setting retentions). Figures 23.4 and 23.5 offered a simplified version of reinsurance programs.

Retention can be based on per loss, per event, aggregate of all losses in a line as well as the entire loss the insurer can bear for each operating period. By setting retention at an optimal level, the insurer can effectively transfer the burden of rising claims to reinsurers and stabilize its loss experience. Thus, the size and form of retention affect claims experience and the insurer's profitability. Setting proper retentions is especially critical for newly incorporated and rapidly expanding insurers.

Insurers usually incur substantial expenses to market their products and underwrite risks, whereas reinsurers incur relatively small front-end expenses for these activities. Thus, as noted earlier, reinsurers often compensate cedants for a share of their expenses. This compensation is generally termed as **ceding commissions**. Several types of ceding commissions exist.

In proportional reinsurance, especially in quota share and first surplus arrangements, the commission is likely based on a fixed or sliding-scale percent of the reinsurance premium.

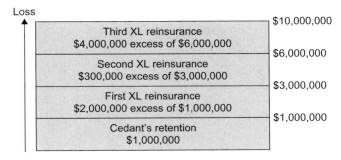

**Figure 23.5** An Illustrative XL Reinsurance Program with $10 Million of Total Loss Coverage

In higher layers of proportional reinsurance (e.g., fac-oblig) or XL reinsurance, reinsurers may pay little or no commissions on a fixed term. They instead may offer a **profit commission**, which is based on the reinsurer's operating experience – for one year or as an average of multiple years – for the cedant's book of business.

Today, how to arrange ceding commissions is a critical element in contract negotiations in the reinsurance market. For example, insurers usually ask for higher ceding and profit commissions in soft markets. Reinsurers usually offer lower commissions when in hard markets.

Ceding commissions provide financial relief to or increase the underwriting capacity of the insurer, as the commissions often are treated as fully earned by the insurer. The following case illustrates use of a ceding commission.[4] Suppose an insurer pays a 20-percent commission to its agents and incurs underwriting expenses of 10 percent of the premium. It has a 50-percent quota share treaty reinsurance agreement with a 30-percent ceding commission. Suppose also that the insurer has accepted a risk for a premium of $5,000, thus the reinsurer assuming 50 percent of the risk along with one-half of the premium. The resulting financial statuses based on traditional statutory accounting conventions that require the immediate write-off of expenses can be summarized as follows:

|  | Insurer ($) | Reinsurer ($) |
|---|---|---|
| Gross premium | 5,000 | |
| Ceded premium | (2,500) | 2,500 |
| Less expenses: | | |
| Agents' Commissions (20%) | (1,000) | |
| Underwriting (10%) | (500) | |
| Premium retained | 1,000 | 2,500 |

The summary shows that, after deducting commissions and underwriting expenses, the insurer ends up with retained funds of $1,000 while being responsible for 50 percent of the risk. This mismatching of expenses and revenues can cause difficulty to newly incorporated insurers, small insurers and insurers expanding rapidly. By including a 30 percent ceding commission, the insurer can recover one-half of its production and underwriting costs. The insurer now has 50 percent of the premium – net of expenses – for the risk it has retained. So does the reinsurer:

|  | Insurer ($) | Reinsurer ($) |
|---|---|---|
| Premium retained | 1,000 | 2,500 |
| Ceding commission<br>(30% of $2,500) | 750 | (750) |
| Net effect | 1,750 | 1,750 |

### Financial reinsurance

The discussion above focused on traditional reinsurance products whereby the reinsurer assumes the risk that losses and expenses under the contract will be greater than expected (i.e., what is referred to as **underwriting** or **pricing risk**). The reinsurer also makes assumptions regarding when reinsured losses will be paid. If losses are paid more quickly than expected, the reinsurer loses cash flow with a resulting loss of investment income. The possibility of a loss of investment income because funds are not held for as long as have been anticipated is called the **timing risk**. The reinsurer also must assume *investment risk* that the actual investment performance will be poorer than expected.

With traditional reinsurance products, the reinsurer assumes all three risks. For a contract to be viewed as insurance or reinsurance for income tax purposes, tax authorities generally require the transfer of a significant share of pricing risk, as contrasted with investment or timing risk. Conversely, they commonly refuse to recognize as insurance a contract with no or only slight risk transfer.

**Financial reinsurance** differs from traditional reinsurance in that it explicitly considers the investment and timing risks and may provide little or no pricing risk transfer. Financial reinsurance can be broadly divided into retrospective financial reinsurance (relatively old) and prospective financial reinsurance (relatively new).

### Retrospective financial reinsurance

Historically, financial reinsurance took the form of **retrospective reinsurance** that covers an insurer's past loss experience. Losses subject to the reinsurance agreement have already occurred but not yet been reported or settled. Hence, retrospective financial reinsurance helps insurers transfer existing loss exposures to reinsurers. Two of these products are (1) time and distance contracts and (2) loss portfolio transfers.

### Time and distance contracts
The functioning of a time and distance contract can be illustrated as follows.[5] Suppose that an insurer in need of surplus relief – a situation where it needs to increase surplus or decrease liabilities – is considering the transfer of €1 million (non-discounted) of its loss liabilities to a reinsurer. If the insurer assumes that losses are to be paid out evenly (€200,000 per annum) each year over a 5-year period and that the investment return on assets backing the reserves is 5 percent per annum, it would need only €865,895 (net present value) to meet

its insurance obligations. Assume that the law requires the insurer to maintain undiscounted loss reserves, even though it may wish otherwise.

If the insurer could transfer the entirety of this liability to a reinsurer, it could reduce its liabilities by €1 million. If the insurer could further make the transfer by paying the reinsurer the discounted value of these liabilities, in this instance, €865,895, it could increase its surplus position by €134,105 (€1,000,000 − €865,895), ignoring all transaction costs. Reinsurance of this type is termed time and distance reinsurance.

Under this time and distance contract, the reinsurer assumes the investment risk – the risk that it fails to earn 5 percent. This is so because the reinsurer would pay the insurer, according to the schedule, that provided for losses of up to €200,000 per year for five years. The reinsurer realizes an underwriting gain if aggregate, actual losses of the insurer are less than €1 million but incurs no underwriting loss even when losses exceed this amount, because €1 million is the limit of reinsurance.

This product was developed to increase surplus through the immediate recognition of the future investment income on the loss reserves of the insurer. It is important to note that the cedant is able to increase its surplus because of the country's accounting convention of not permitting the discounting of loss reserves. Were the insurer permitted to discount these reserves, this reinsurance contract would afford little value to the insurer. As more countries permit such discounting, the rationale for using time and distance contracts is reduced. In the U.S., regulators objected to these contracts and they are no longer recognized as reinsurance.

*Loss portfolio transfer*

**Loss portfolio transfer (LPT)** involves an insurer ceding all of its liabilities on a portfolio of policies to a reinsurer. By not having a fixed schedule of payments, it transfers the timing risk to the reinsurer. In some agreements, it also transfers part of the underwriting risk because the reinsurer assumes the risk of an increase in loss reserves. Recently adopted accounting rules have limited its use in the U.S.

The above example of time and distance reinsurance also can be used to illustrate LPT reinsurance. That is, if the contract is to transfer the loss *reserve* of €1 million to the reinsurer, it becomes an LPT contract and the reinsurer becomes responsible for the payment of all claims associated with the portfolio of losses. Unlike time and distance reinsurance, LPT reinsurance does not have a fixed schedule of payments by the reinsurer, thus exposing it to timing risk in addition to investment risk. The reinsurer also assumes the underwriting risk that the actual losses would be greater than expected.

LPT reinsurance is limited in its use. It is often used by an insurer ceasing operations entirely or in a line of business or territory. LPT is also used when an insurer wants to liquidate its liabilities as a condition for a merger or acquisition. Under these circumstances, the business is said to be in "run-off."

*Prospective financial reinsurance*

Today, the primary focus of financial reinsurance is on **prospective reinsurance** – the transfer of risk on current and future exposures to another party, not necessarily a reinsurer. Some contracts are multi-year arrangements where the insurer pays premiums over several years and the reinsurer promises to cover losses subject to the reinsurance limit. The example in Insight 23.1 illustrates the structure of financial reinsurance for a product liability insurance policy issued to a manufacturing firm.

---

**INSIGHT 23.1: AN EXAMPLE OF PROSPECTIVE FINANCIAL REINSURANCE FOR PRODUCT LIABILITY** ————————

- Coverage period      3 years
- Annual premium      $2 million
- Reinsurance limit      $5 million excess of $2 million per loss, subject to the aggregate limit of $20 million for the entire period
- Profit sharing      Return of 90% of the difference between premiums plus interest and reinsurance claims payment

---

Financial reinsurance arrangements usually have one or more of the following characteristics, as exhibited in the above example:

- *Lengthy coverage period*: They are flexible in the length and scope of coverage, and each contract is designed to meet the insurance or reinsurance need of the client. The contract is for a long term to smooth year-to-year loss results. Most contracts have a term of two or three years.

- *Finite term of contract (non-renewability)*: Regardless of the differences in coverage periods, financial reinsurance arrangements, particularly finite reinsurance (and insurance), are not renewable (hence, "finite"). Renewal of the coverage literally means writing a new contract.

- *Explicit profit sharing agreement*: If loss experience is favorable, a profit sharing refund is made to the cedant (e.g., 90 percent of the excess of premium and interest over losses indemnified). Premiums and interest are credited to an account from which losses are paid.

- *Limit on coverage*: As with typical reinsurance contracts, the assuming company's exposure to loss is limited in financial reinsurance (e.g., $5 million per loss and $20 million in the aggregate). The aggregate limit is commonly for the entire contract period.

Financial reinsurers assume mainly timing and investment risk, and limit underwriting risk by imposing per loss and aggregate limits. Elliot et al. (2005) describe this aspect as follows:

> Finite risk [re]insurance differs from guaranteed cost insurance because a large part of the insured's premium under a finite risk insurance agreement creates a fund for the [re]insured's own losses, and the remaining amount of the premium is used to transfer a limited portion of risk of loss to the [re]insurer.

Other types of financial reinsurance arrangements exist. For example, an insurer, with help from a reinsurer, may offer a "multi-year, multi-trigger" contract that provides coverage only when the insured suffers from a traditional insurable loss (e.g., fire in the assembly plant) during a year followed by a speculative loss (e.g., loss of income due to unfavorable foreign exchange rates) in the same year and that this year-based protection is guaranteed

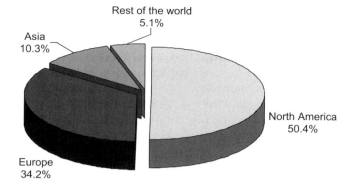

**Figure 23.6**   Distribution of Reinsurance Premiums Globally (2005). *Source*: Datamonitor, 2005

**Table 23.3**   Cession Rates by Region (1998)

|  | Life Industry (%) | Nonlife Industry (%) |
| --- | --- | --- |
| North America | 1.6 | 12.6 |
| Latin America | 4.6 | 15.1 |
| Western Europe | 2.2 | 14.6 |
| Asia | 0.8 | 29.2 |
| Rest of the World | Nil | 26.1 |
| World Total | 1.5 | 14.0 |

*Source*: Swiss Re (2004a).

for multiple years. Securitization of insurance risks through catastrophic bonds or contingent capital arrangements is another example of prospective financial reinsurance. The reader may refer to the discussion of integrated loss financing arrangements in Chapter 14.

## REINSURANCE MARKETS

Reinsurance is the most international aspect of the insurance business. Datamonitor (2003, 2006) reports that global reinsurance premiums grew from US$97 billion in 1997 to US$214 billion in 2005 and that the nonlife reinsurance sector generated 83.4 percent of the premiums written in 2005. As with their direct insurance markets, North America – including Bermuda – and Western Europe are the major reinsurance markets. Emerging markets are more consumers of reinsurance than suppliers. Their role as suppliers is, however, growing. As Figure 23.6 shows, North America accounted for 50.4 percent of global premium writings and Europe 34.2 percent in 2005.

The contribution of reinsurance to the world's insurance markets can be measured in terms of **cession rates** – reinsurance premiums divided by direct insurance premiums. Swiss Re (2004a) used its 1998 data to examine the rates by region and by branch. As summarized in Table 23.3, the study shows significantly higher cession rates in the nonlife branch in all regions – a finding similar to the result based on 2003 data.[6]

Several other aspects of reinsurance markets are interesting. Western European insurers use proportional reinsurance (e.g., quota share) more frequently than do North American insurers (Swiss Re, 1998). In particular, German reinsurance demand largely takes the form of proportional reinsurance with low retention rates, thereby resulting in German insurers ceding relatively more premiums to their reinsurers and so showing a relative larger reinsurance demand as measured by premiums.

Retention rates vary by line of business, market concentration and regulatory rigidity. Retention ratios tend to be low in countries with low market concentration (i.e., a large number of small insurers dominating the market). This explains why cession rates are high in Western Europe where about 5,000 nonlife insurers operate. Many of them are too small to handle alone MAT and other large property and liability risks. In contrast, high retention rates in the U.S. and Canada are influenced by a preference toward XL reinsurance in contrast to the European propensity to rely on proportional reinsurance all other things being constant.

In the personal and small commercial insurance lines, insurers write a large number of policies with modest coverage limits. The business volume enables them to predict losses relatively accurately. With modest coverage limits, they are less likely to be exposed to extremely large claims. Hence, insurers in these lines of business demand less reinsurance. Conversely, insurers dealing with large commercial accounts, and thus facing narrow spread of risks and large loss potentials, demand more reinsurance, all other things being constant.

The cost of providing the pure risk protection component in life insurance contracts is relatively small in comparison to the savings component. Thus, reliance on reinsurance to hedge the protection component is correspondingly small in comparison with the pure risk component in nonlife contracts (see Table 23.3). Conversely, life insurers with a greater proportion of business in mortality or morbidity-based lines are likely to demand more life reinsurance than those with a greater proportion of business in savings-oriented products. When measured based on risk premiums only, however, life insurers spend more than 10 percent of the risk premiums for reinsurance and life *reinsurers* spend about 20 percent of their premium receipts for retrocessions – a result similar to that of the global nonlife insurance market.

## Dominance of Large International Reinsurers

Large international, professional companies dominate reinsurance markets globally. A review of Table 23.4 highlights this fact. Eight of the 10 largest reinsurers are domiciled in Europe, with the remaining two in the U.S. Reinsurers in Bermuda are relatively new but play an increasingly important role in the global market, already occupying eight of the top 25 positions. These new reinsurers have substantially enhanced worldwide reinsurance capacity, particularly in the property catastrophe market. The market attracted large amounts of capital after investment bankers, brokerage firms and new insurance companies saw opportunities to benefit from a worldwide shortage of property catastrophe capacity, particularly for U.S. insurers.

Table 23.4 also shows that the aggregate net reinsurance premiums written in 2005 by the 25 largest reinsurers exceeded US$135 billion, a significant increase from US$60 billion in 1995. Policyholders' surplus of these reinsurers was US$237 billion in 2005, a substantial increase from US$65.6 billion in 1995, owing in part to several mega M&As in recent years.

## Reinsurance in Emerging Markets

Reinsurance is critical to building a domestic insurance industry. Domestic insurers in most developing countries, due mainly to low levels of capitalization, have low capacity

**Table 23.4**   The 25 Largest Reinsurers (2005) (US$ Millions)[a]

| Rank[b] | Group Name | Prior Rankings[b] | | | Premiums ($) | | Surplus ($) |
|---|---|---|---|---|---|---|---|
| | | 2004 | 2003 | 2002 | Gross | Net | |
| 1 | Munich Re (Germany) | 1 | 1 | 1 | 30,558 | 26,408 | 26,445 |
| 2 | Swiss Re (Switzerland) | 2 | 2 | 2 | 28,047 | 25,789 | 16,950 |
| 3 | Berkshire Hathaway Re Group (U.S.) | 4 | 3 | 3 | 13,085 | 11,816 | 64,099 |
| 4 | Hanover Re (Germany) | 3 | 4 | 5 | 13,053 | 10,129 | 4,219 |
| 5 | Lloyd's of London (U.K.) | 5 | 5 | 6 | 11,883 | 7,654 | 26,242 |
| 6 | GE Global (U.S.) | 6 | 6 | 4 | 9,631 | 8,173 | 9,415 |
| 7 | XL Capital (Bermuda) | 9 | 9 | 11 | 4,764 | 4,149 | 7,812 |
| 8 | Everest Re (Barbados) | 8 | 13 | 15 | 4,704 | 4,531 | 3,713 |
| 9 | Transatlantic Re (U.S.) | 12 | 11 | 13 | 4,141 | 3,749 | 2,587 |
| 10 | PartnerRe (Bermuda) | 13 | 14 | 14 | 3,888 | 3,853 | 3,352 |
| 11 | Converium Re (Switzerland)[c] | 11 | 10 | 10 | 3,841 | 3,553 | 1,720 |
| 12 | RGA (U.S.) | 15 | 15 | 17 | 3,649 | 3,347 | 2,279 |
| 13 | SCOR Re (France)[c] | 7 | 7 | 8 | 3,449 | 3,298 | 2,056 |
| 14 | London Reinsurance (Canada) | 14 | 12 | 12 | 3,068 | 2,757 | 3,724 |
| 15 | Odyssey Re/Fairfax (U.S.) | 16 | 16 | 24 | 2,657 | 2,363 | 1,586 |
| 16 | Korean Re (Korea)[d] | 17 | 18 | 21 | 2,209 | 1,523 | 401 |
| 17 | ING (Netherlands)[c] | 19 | 17 | 19 | 2,037 | – | 38,310 |
| 18 | White Mountains Re (Bermuda) | 26 | 29 | 34 | 1,993 | 1,246 | 3,884 |
| 19 | Ace (Bermuda) | 23 | 28 | 31 | 1,795 | 1,745 | 9,836 |
| 20 | Caisse Centrale de Re (France) | 24 | 27 | 30 | 1,784 | 1,719 | 1,224 |
| 21 | Endurance Specialty (Bermuda) | 21 | 33 | – | 1,711 | 1,697 | 1,863 |
| 22 | Platinum Underwriters (Bermuda) | 31 | 21 | – | 1,660 | 1,646 | 1,133 |
| 23 | Arch Re (Bermuda) | 20 | 32 | – | 1,658 | 1,588 | 2,242 |
| 24 | QBE (Australia) | 18 | 23 | 25 | 1,600 | 1,306 | 3,495 |
| 25 | Alea (Bermuda) | 29 | 30 | – | 1,583 | 1,338 | 706 |
| | **Total** | **N/A** | **N/A** | **N/A** | **99,901** | **135,377** | **237,239** |

[a]The premium information in this table is not consistent with that in Table 20.1, due likely to differences in data collection methods.
[b]Rankings are based on gross premium written in prior year.
[c]Operations were materially curtailed in 2005.
[d]Yearend is March 2005.
*Source*: Group of Thirty (2006).

and retentions and a correspondingly high demand for reinsurance. Undercapitalized insurers face extreme difficulty in increasing their retentions without rending themselves less sound financially. Less retention results in slower asset growth and therefore less investment income to absorb fluctuations in losses and to support further growth.

Insuring industrial infrastructure necessitates technical expertise. Historically, large global reinsurers have provided risks assessment and underwriting services necessary for local insurers – sometimes state-owned firms – to facilitate their acceptance of large and complex risks, which are then heavily reinsured by the global reinsurers. These conditions plus low capitalization of the majority of insurers in developing economies have led to a dependency on reinsurance supplied by foreign reinsurers.

**Table 23.5**    Examples of Compulsory Cessions in African Developing Countries (2005)

| Country | Reinsurer | Cession Percentage |
|---|---|---|
| Cameroon | CICA Re and Africa Re | 10% |
| Egypt | Egypt Re | 50% (life); 10% (nonlife) |
| Ghana | Ghana Re | 20% except life |
| Kenya[a] | Zep Re[b] and Africa Re | 15% including 5% to Africa Re |
| Morocco | Société Centrale de Réassurance and Africa Re | 15% including 5% to Africa Re |
| Sudan | National reinsurers, Zep Re, and Africa Re | 65% including 50% to national firms |
| Tanzania | Zep Re and Africa Re | 15% including 5% to Africa Re |
| Togo | CICA Re and Africa Re | 20% including 5% to Africa Re |
| Zimbabwe | Zep Re and Africa Re | 15% including 5% to Africa Re |

[a]Until 2005, insurers in Kenya was also subject to a 18% mandatory cession to Kenya Re.
[b]Zep Re is also known as PTA Re.
*Source*: African Insurance Organization (2005).

Most insurers in developing countries have proportional treaties as the basis of their reinsurance programs. As discussed, this form of reinsurance permits small, undercapitalized insurers to accept more risks than they could otherwise. Facultative reinsurance is used in the traditional way to supplement treaties for large loss exposures.

Fronting is common in developing countries. Recall from Chapter 13 that with fronting, the insurer acts more as an insurance service provider than a risk-bearing insurer. Fronting insurers can come to rely on ceding commissions without developing national retention capacity and underwriting expertise necessary for the development of a viable domestic insurance industry.

### Compulsory placement of reinsurance

The mechanism by which reinsurance is placed in the international market often is specified by local laws. In some countries (largely in Africa), all reinsurance must be placed through national reinsurance companies, although the trend is to abandon such practices. With such compulsory cessions, the governments believe that they can increase domestic retention capacity by (1) diversifying the pools of risks from individual insurers to the national reinsurer and (2) permitting more favorable terms and prices when the national reinsurer retrocedes risks internationally. Additionally, special skills, which domestic insurers lack, may be available by maintaining retrocession with large international reinsurers. For example, the *Instituto de Resseguros do Brasil* (IRB), being the national and exclusive reinsurer in Brazil until 1996, attracted great attention and thus services of large global reinsurers.[7] Table 23.5 provides examples of compulsory proportional cessions in selected countries in Africa. For domestic reinsurers in numerous developing countries, compulsory and voluntary cessions by domestic insurers are their primary sources of business.

In addition to compulsory cessions to domestic reinsurers, some governments impose obligations for domestic insurers to cede business to regional reinsurers. African Re [www.africa-re.com], a regional reinsurance pool, for example, receives 5 percent of the business by insurers in member countries. Although inactive now, Asian Re formerly received 5 percent of the business by insurers in its member countries in Southeast Asia. Moreover, some governments require that a certain percentage of domestic business be retained in the local market or at least first offered locally before going to the international market.

A significant portion of the business ceded to reinsurers through mandatory cessions is often retroceded back to the ceding companies. This can benefit the domestic market if the retrocessions result in greater individual insurer risk diversification. The retrocessions, however, can result in an unhealthy concentration of risk within the domestic market.

Compulsory cessions usually harm markets relying on them. Regulators and insurers now know that the resultant concentration of insured exposures usually fails to diversify risks and exposes the industry to catastrophic loss potential. Domestic insurers too often fail to develop desired expertise, instead relying on ceding commissions for large portions of their income. Many countries have instituted reforms. Korea eliminated compulsory cessions to Korean Re, and China is eliminating compulsory cessions to the PICC in accordance with its WTO commitments. In Latin America (e.g., Argentina, Chile and Peru) and in Africa (e.g., Ethiopia and Tunisia) many domestic insurers are no longer required place business with the national reinsurer. Colombia no longer requires that business be placed in the local market. In contrast, Nepal does not even permit cross border reinsurance. Access to the local market is not permitted in North Korea and several other markets throughout the world.

### *Demand and supply of reinsurance in developing countries*

Improving retention capacity has been a common goal of developing economies, which necessitates the presence of financially stronger insurers. This can be achieved through M&As and higher capitalization requirements. A smaller number of larger companies can result in a higher national retention.

Insurers in developing countries sometimes accept reinsurance to improve their spread of risks or to utilize available capacity. Such insurers can sometimes negotiate a reciprocal exchange of business with their foreign reinsurers if the insurers have favorable operating results. With reciprocity, the insurer cedes business to the reinsurer and, in turn, receives reinsurance from it.

In general, business from many developing countries is considered desirable by international reinsurers. One reason for this is that many markets allow high premium rates because of a lack of competition. High rates at the primary level means more profitable business for both the direct insurer and thus its reinsurer. With the worldwide deregulation and liberalization trends, such opportunities are becoming rarer and many of those markets are embracing competition. Of course, rate inadequacy would have a negative impact on the reinsurance market.

International reinsurers wish to diversify their portfolios. The markets of developing countries sometimes offer an attractive alternative to the markets found in some developed countries, such as the U.S., with its long-tail liability exposures.

International reinsurers are an important resource for insurance companies of developing countries. They provide financial support and technical expertise and assistance. Purchasing reinsurance from financially secure reinsurers should always be a primary objective of ceding companies. In general, security concerns result in preference for the prominent, financially strong international reinsurers.

**Table 23.6**   Some Regulatory Developments in Reinsurance

| Regulation | Geographic Application | Purpose | Effective Date |
|---|---|---|---|
| IAIS Standard on Supervision of Reinsurers | Global | Lays down supervisory standards for reinsurance globally | 2003 |
| Financial Groups Directive | E.U. | Introduces a financial regime for international financial conglomerates to enable regulation on a whole-group basis in lieu of piecemeal in each country of operation | 2005 |
| International Financial Reporting Standards | Global | Introduces international accounting standards | Phase I in 2005 with full implementation expected in 2007 |
| Reinsurance Directive | E.U. | Introduces fast-track adoption of regulation for European reinsurers | 2008 |
| Solvency II | E.U. | Creates a consistent, risk-based insurance solvency system, that is compatible with international developments in supervision and financial reporting | 2011 |

*Source*: Global Reinsurance Highlights (2004). With permission by Standard & Poors.

## REINSURANCE REGULATION

We noted that reinsurance is subject to less stringent regulation than is direct insurance. Even so, it is of critical concern to regulators because of its importance to the stability and growth of insurance markets. Further, the reinsurance market internationally is dominated by a relatively small number of very large reinsurers. The markets of most countries host both a much smaller number of and smaller-sized domestic reinsurers. Thus, the deterioration of financial strength of just one large international reinsurer could lead to systemic problems for insurance companies in multiple domestic markets.

Current initiatives in reinsurance regulation are largely the domain of advanced economies and intergovernmental organizations. These include the E.U., the U.K., the U.S. and the International Association of Insurance Supervisors (IAIS). Table 23.6 summarizes some key initiatives, emphasizing those of the IAIS and the E.U.

For example, the IAIS introduced *Standard on Supervision of Reinsurers* in 2003. This standard prescribes that the home-country supervisor is responsible for effective supervision of its reinsurers for both domestic and foreign operations. To comply, insurance supervisors in member countries are advised to establish minimum licensing and financial security requirements for reinsurers. The standard also includes an IAIS position that "it is the responsibility of the ceding insurer to evaluate the security of proposed reinsurers and the duty of that ceding insurer's supervisor to ensure that the evaluation is adequate." The two principles introduced in the standard are as follows:

*Principle One.* Regulation and supervision of reinsurers' technical provisions (loss reserving), investments and liquidity, capital requirements and policies and procedures to ensure effective corporate governance should reflect the characteristics of its business and be supplemented by systems for exchanging information among supervisors.

*Principle Two.* Except as stated in Principle One, regulation and supervision of the legal forms, licensing and the possibility of withdrawing the license, fit-and-proper testing, changes in control, group relations, supervision of the entire business, on-site inspections, sanctions, internal controls and audit, and accounting rules applicable to reinsurers should be the same as those for primary insurers.

These guidelines are more or less in line with IAIS core principles issued in 2003 as well as the principles governing direct life and nonlife insurance supervision.

Until recently, the E.U. had no standardized, prudential requirements dealing specifically with reinsurance. At one extreme (and even today in some countries), reinsurers were subject to the same regulation applicable to insurers (e.g., Denmark, Finland, Luxembourg, Portugal and the U.K.). At the other extreme, no supervision of reinsurance operations existed in several countries (e.g., Belgium, Greece and Ireland). In the middle, regulators in Austria, Italy, Spain and Sweden were said to exercise relatively more stringent regulation than those in France, Germany and the Netherlands. No regulatory solvency margin requirements for reinsurers existed in Austria, Belgium, France, Germany, Greece, Ireland, Italy, and the Netherlands.

To minimize differences in reinsurance regulation among member states, the European Parliament approved the *Reinsurance Directive* in 2005. Member states were given two years to comply with the directive. Key features are as follows:

- *Supervisory power*: The directive lays down supervisory powers to be in place in cases in which (1) a reinsurer's financial strength deteriorates, (2) "no adequate technical provisions" are found, or (3) "insufficient solvency [regulation]" exists. However, the financial supervision of the reinsurer remains the sole responsibility of its home state.

- *Single licensing*: All reinsurers must be authorized in their home states. Those duly authorized are then permitted to carry out their businesses in all other member states.

- *Solvency provision*: The solvency provisions, which apply primarily to nonlife reinsurance, require companies to maintain a minimum guarantee fund of not less than €3 million. For captive reinsurers, the amount may be reduced to €1 million. If an insurer conducts both life and nonlife reinsurance, the total required for solvency margins must be covered separately by the life fund and the nonlife fund.

## CONCLUSIONS

Standard and Poor's characterizes the recent reinsurance market as "stable" (meaning that it does not expect significant changes in the market) and exhibiting "greater transparency" (meaning improved corporate governance, greater professionalism, better discipline, transparent accounting, etc.). Nevertheless, several challenges remain.

First, the U.S. liability environment remains a major concern of insurance and reinsurance companies worldwide. Some reinsurers limit coverages for U.S. liability losses, recognizing the seeming open-endedness of some claims. Nonetheless, foreign reinsurers cannot afford completely to ignore the U.S. market, as it remains the world's largest reinsurance buyer.

Second, as discussed in Chapter 5, catastrophe losses have been increasing since 1970. Earthquakes, tropical cyclones, floods and winter storms continue to devastate vulnerable regions worldwide. As we noted, the number of tropical storms in the Atlantic Ocean in 2005 set records. The ever-rising growth of population and concentration of wealth in coastal areas and metropolitan cities worldwide will likely make future losses even more costly, and reinsurers always take the brunt of such losses. More extensive use of catastrophe modeling technology is expected to help insurers and reinsurers sharpen their underwriting capacity, smooth their cash flows, and reduce pricing volatility (Guy Carpenter, 2005).

Third, the development of various types of financial reinsurance programs, on the one hand, increasingly is helping corporations with hard-to-place, large risks to secure risk financing from the capital markets. On the other hand, it also requires prudence by all involved parties and transparency in transactions because of the strong profit sharing but small actual risk transfer inherent in many of the contracts. Otherwise, the purpose for entering into a financial reinsurance transaction can be questioned by government authorities and other stakeholders. Several cases highlight these difficulties, an especially public one involving AIG where the company attempted to enhance its loss reserves by disguising receipt of a US$500 million loan from General Re, as a financial reinsurance contract.[8]

Finally, competition is strong in most segments of the reinsurance market. The catastrophes in the early 2000s – particularly the 9/11 attacks – significantly reduced the capacity of the global insurance and reinsurance industry, thus triggering premium rate increases worldwide during the following years. With fewer major human-made catastrophes and natural calamities – other than the 2005 hurricane season in North America – in developed economies, the global insurance industry has had an opportunity to strengthen its financial position. Further, with a series of M&As in insurance (e.g., Swiss Re's purchase of GE Risk Solutions in 2006), the market seems likely to continue to be dominated by large international reinsurers. In the traditional reinsurance market, excess capacity can reduce the prospects for improved pricing in insurance markets, and intense competition will make it increasingly difficult for small and medium-sized regional reinsurers to generate business.

Competition is likely to continue to increase from non-traditional sources as well. Catastrophe futures and options, bonds, and other innovative insurance-linked derivative products have not yet made a big impact but are expected to grow in importance. Additionally, new capital market products are being used by primary insurers, such as catastrophe-triggered surplus notes and other forms of securitization. The larger insurers and reinsurers are involved in developing these capital market products. They are expected to exercise a higher level of prudence in contractual arrangements and transparency in accounting transactions.

Reinsurer security has become a critical factor for insurers. Reinsurers with larger capital bases have a better chance of surviving both the impact of catastrophes and competitive forces in the marketplace. Conversely, less capitalized reinsurers will incur more difficulty absorbing adverse loss development and the possible impact of increased environmental claims. Competing on a global basis demands a large surplus.

Catastrophic loss exposures, consolidation and capitalization issues as well as competition in the market continue to shape the reinsurance business. While we can reasonably expect further success in efforts to develop innovative means of dealing with catastrophic exposures, the need for traditional reinsurance seems likely to remain strong for years to come. Worldwide deregulation and liberalization will continue to provide great opportunities for reinsurers but, at the same time, will continue to put ever greater pressure on margins.

## DISCUSSION QUESTIONS

1.  What advantages and disadvantages would an insurance company expect from ceding its risks (a) facultatively or (b) using a treaty?
2.  Describe how premiums and losses are shared in (a) surplus treaty reinsurance and (b) working XL reinsurance.
3.  What effect would you expect from continuing consolidation in the reinsurance market? Discuss its impact on competition, capacity and reinsurance market security.
4.  An author cited in this chapter wrote "reinsurance can be viewed as both a leverage and a risk management mechanism." Explain.
5.  What are the reasons that some governments offer for subjecting domestic nonlife insurance companies to compulsory cessions to a national or regional reinsurance company? In those countries, why do you believe the cession commonly applies to treaty reinsurance only?
6.  In view of the trends in the reinsurance *market*, what is their likely impact on reinsurance *distribution* systems.
7.  Why are the world's largest reinsurance firms located in Europe?

## NOTES

1.  This chapter draws in part from Gaunt (1998).
2.  Refer to Insight 21.1 for other definitions of coinsurance.
3.  The pool as well as the markets to which insurers can direct risks that they do not wish to accept (e.g., assigned risk plans, joint underwriting associations) are collectively known as the **residual market**, as compared to the **standard market** – risks underwritten at will by insurers.
4.  This illustration is drawn from Feldhaus (1996).

5.  The discussion in this section is based in part on Bunner (1995).
6.  Swiss Re (2004) shows a global cession rate of 1.9 percent for life and 13.7 percent for nonlife in 2003.
7.  The national firm is now known as IRB-Brasil Re. The majority of its shares are owned by the government and several member insurers in Brazil.
8.  See Brady and Vickers (2005) for a fuller description of the transaction.

## REFERENCES

African Insurance Organization (2005). Available at www. africaninsurance.org/english/resources/index.htm.

Brady, D. and Vickers, M. (2005). "AIG: What Went Wrong." *Business Week* (April 18): 32–25.

Bunner, B.A. (1995). "Financial Reinsurance: New Products for a New Environment," Reinsurance Fundamentals and New Challenges. New York: Insurance Information Institute Press.

Datamonitor (2003 and 2006). *Global Reinsurance: Industry Profile*. New York: Datamonitor USA.

Elliot, M., George, H. and James, B. (2005). *Risk Financing*. Malvern, PA: Insurance Institute of America.

Feldhaus, W. (1996). "Reinsurance and Surplus Lines." *Surplus Lines Insurance: Principles and Issues*. Malvern, PA: Insurance Institute of America.

Garven, J. (1990). "The Demand for Reinsurance: Theory and Empirical Tests." Working Paper.

Gaunt, L. (1998). "The Role, Importance and Functioning of Reinsurance," Chapter 23, in H.D. Skipper, ed., *International Risk and Insurance: An Environmental–Managerial Approach*. Boston, MA: Irwin/McGraw-Hill.

Group of Thirty (2006). *Reinsurance and International Financial Markets*. Washington, DC: The Group of Thirty.

Guy Carpenter & Company (2005). *The World Catastrophe Reinsurance Market*. New York: Marsh & McLennan Companies.

Hoerger, T., Sloan, F. and Hassan, M. (1990). "Loss Volatility, Bankruptcy, and the Demand for Reinsurance." *Journal of Risk and Insurance*, 57: 221–245.

Kwon, W.J. (1999). *Risk Management and Insurance in Singapore*. Singapore: Singapore College of Insurance.

Lewis, C.M. and Murdock, K.C. (1996). "The Role of Government Contracts in Discretionary Reinsurance Markets for Natural Disasters." *Journal of Risk and Insurance*, 63: 573–577.

Mayers, D. and Smith Jr., C.W. (1990). "On the Corporate Demand for Insurance: Evidence from the Reinsurance Market." *Journal of Business*, 63: 19–40.

Standard & Poor's (2004). *Global Reinsurance Highlights*. London: Reactions.

Swiss Re (1998). "The Global Reinsurance Market in the Midst of Consolidation," *Sigma*. Zurich: Swiss Re.

Swiss Re (2004). *Understanding Reinsurance: How Reinsurers Create Value and Manage Risk*. Zurich: Swiss Re.

# Chapter 24

# Regulation and Taxation in Insurance Markets

## INTRODUCTION

In a non-technical sense, insurance is purchased in good faith. Consumers implicitly rely on the integrity of the insurers with which they deal. The complex nature of this future-deliverable affords the easy potential for customer abuse. The mission of insurance is security. Thus, if the suppliers of security are themselves perceived as insecure, the insurance system could easily break down. Private insurance cannot flourish without public confidence that it will function as promised. Government's duty is to ensure that this confidence is neither misplaced nor undermined.

Government intervention into insurance markets is universal and profound.[1] As discussed in Chapter 8, the most common rationale for intervention is, in economic terms, to rectify market failures. Governments also require revenues to provide services to the public. Taxation and regulation in the financial services industry are two sides of the same coin. We explore both in this chapter.

## INSURANCE REGULATION

Insurance regulation internationally generally seeks to ensure that *quality, fairly priced* products are *available* from *reliable* insurers. Arguably, a competitive market should be able largely to ensure that the *quality, fairly priced* and *available* goals are attained. Government intervention usually is most evident and needed to ensure that insurers are *reliable*. In many developing countries, an additionally stated goal is the promotion of the domestic insurance industry and ensuring that the national insurance industry contributes to overall economic development.

Every country has insurance laws and regulations that determine who may sell and underwrite insurance and the circumstances under which they may do so. Minimum reserve, asset quality and quantity, and capital requirements are usually laid down. Special accounting standards often are mandated. In many countries, prices and policy conditions are regulated.

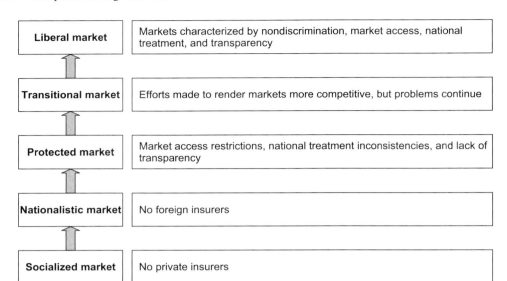

**Figure 24.1**  Evolving International Insurance Markets

Regulation varies from "light" to "heavy" worldwide. Thus, for example, the U.K., Chile, Hong Kong and the Netherlands generally rely more on market forces to ensure a viable insurance market, with regulation principally relating to solvency (prudential) matters. At the other extreme, Japan, Korea and Switzerland as well as the majority of developing countries have historically practiced intensive regulation, focusing not only on insurer prudential matters but also on product pricing and content and on market stability. The Canadian and U.S. regulatory styles fall between the two extremes.

The section begins with an overview of worldwide liberalization trends. We then discuss the mechanisms and philosophies of insurance regulation as well as common regulatory areas.

## Insurance Regulatory Trends Worldwide

The two philosophical extremes of capitalism and socialism dominated 20th century economic thought. During the late 1980s and the decade of the 1990s, however, countries worldwide began moving toward more liberal (i.e., freer) markets and away from more circumscribed markets. They embraced the capitalist model as offering greater opportunity for enhancing overall consumer welfare. We have seen this same trend in insurance markets worldwide. Figure 24.1 illustrates these market trends.

Countries have moved from more to less restrictive insurance markets. They have increasingly embraced competition and eschewed special interest regulation. Consequently, insurance markets today look quite different from what they did just 25 years earlier. The great majority of the world's largest 50 insurance markets are more liberal today than in 1990, many substantially so. The 150 or so other, smaller insurance markets generally are less liberal than the top 50, but many of these have undertaken substantial liberalization efforts recently.

## Mechanisms of Insurance Regulation

Government regulatory (and tax) policy and practice regarding insurance typically take place at three levels: (1) legislative, (2) judicial and (3) executive.[2] We discuss each level below.

### *Legislative*

First, the legislative body (e.g., congress or parliament) enacts laws to establish the country's broad legal framework for insurance, including the general standards and scope of responsibilities of the administrative agency charged with enforcement of the insurance laws. Each country's insurance laws and regulations differ in nature and scope. However, each commonly includes most or all of the following areas:

- formation and licensing of insurers;
- licensing of agents and brokers;
- filing and approval of insurance rates;
- filing and approval of proposal material and policy forms;
- unauthorized insurance and unfair-trade practices;
- insurer financial reporting, examination and other financial requirements;
- rehabilitation and liquidation of insurers;
- guaranty funds;
- insurance product and company taxation.

### *Judiciary*

Courts are the second mechanism of government oversight. The judiciary has a three-fold role in insurance oversight. First, it resolves disputes between insurers and policyholders. Second, it enforces insurance laws through orders supporting the insurance supervisor and by assessing civil and sometimes criminal penalties against those who violate insurance law. Finally, insurers and intermediaries occasionally resort to the courts seeking to overturn arbitrary or unconstitutional statutes, administrative regulation and orders promulgated by regulators.

### *Executive*

The third area of government oversight falls under the state's executive branch. Because of the many complexities in the insurance business, policymakers commonly delegate this authority to a ministerial department of the government. The ministry – commonly of finance, industry or commerce – has broad administrative, quasi-legislative and quasi-judicial powers.

In Canada, for example, regulatory oversight responsibilities are split between the federal and provincial governments, with the latter being charged primarily with policyholder protection matters. In the U.S., regulation resides primarily at the individual state level. No U.S. federal agency has broad responsibilities for insurance regulation, although issue of federal regulation continues to be debated.

In most countries, a special department or subordinate institution of the relevant ministry carries out insurance regulatory oversight. The department can be explicitly for insurance regulation and supervision (e.g., *Office de Contrôle des Assurances* of Belgium, *Superintendencia de Seguros de la Nacion* in Argentina, and the Insurance Board in Nepal), part of a larger institution that also oversees banking (e.g., *Superintendencia de*

*Banca y Seguros del Peru*) or part of the bigger financial supervisory agency (e.g., Financial Services Authority of the U.K., Australian Prudential Regulatory Authority, and Financial Services Agency of Japan). In some other countries, such as India, the body responsible for insurance regulation is a quasi-independent authority, not housed in any ministry.

The person responsible for insurance supervision commonly holds a title of commissioner, superintendent, supervisor or director. The position holder is responsible for administering the insurance laws and regulations governing insurance activities in the domestic market and supporting policy decisions made at the ministerial level. The position is usually appointive.

A formal advisory body assists regulatory authorities in most countries (but not typically in the U.S.). Commonly, this body is composed of representatives of insurance companies, consumer groups, insurance experts and others with an interest in insurance. The number of members varies from 5 to 60, depending on the country. The body advises the supervisory authority on important decisions. In some countries, the regulator must consult the advisory body before taking certain actions.

The regulatory situation in the E.U. is unique. One of the principal means of establishing minimum regulatory harmonization among the 27 E.U. member countries is through directives, as discussed in Chapter 3.

## Approaches to Regulation

We can classify all areas of insurance regulation in every market as being ex-ante, ex-post, or some combination of the two. **Ex-ante regulation** seeks to prevent any offensive activity from occurring by proscribing or regulating it before-the-fact. **Ex-post regulation** calls for government intervention into the market, if at all, only after an offensive activity has occurred. Any redress is remedial thus after-the-fact.

In all insurance markets, for example, insurers must secure a license before they can sell insurance. In many insurance markets, premium rates and policy wordings are subject to regulatory approval before insurers use them. These are examples of ex-ante regulation. In many other markets, insurers may set their own rates. They are subject to regulatory review, if at all, only if they are deemed excessive, too low or inequitable. This is an example of ex-post regulation.

Although not completely accurate, in general, the more an economy relies on market forces, the less the reliance on ex-ante regulatory techniques. Conversely, the less the reliance on market forces, the greater the belief in ex-ante regulatory techniques. In theory, government policymakers should use ex-ante regulation to prevent harm if the cost of prevention is less than the harm caused by a failure to take preventive action. The optimal regulatory response should examine the costs and benefits of both approaches and select that which is more effective.

## Areas of Regulation

Because insurers are important financial intermediaries selling promises of future delivery, they are subject to regulation in every market. While no two nations' laws are identical, regulation is typically designed to address five key questions:

- Who should be permitted access into the market?
- How to balance the benefits of competition against the need to protect consumers?

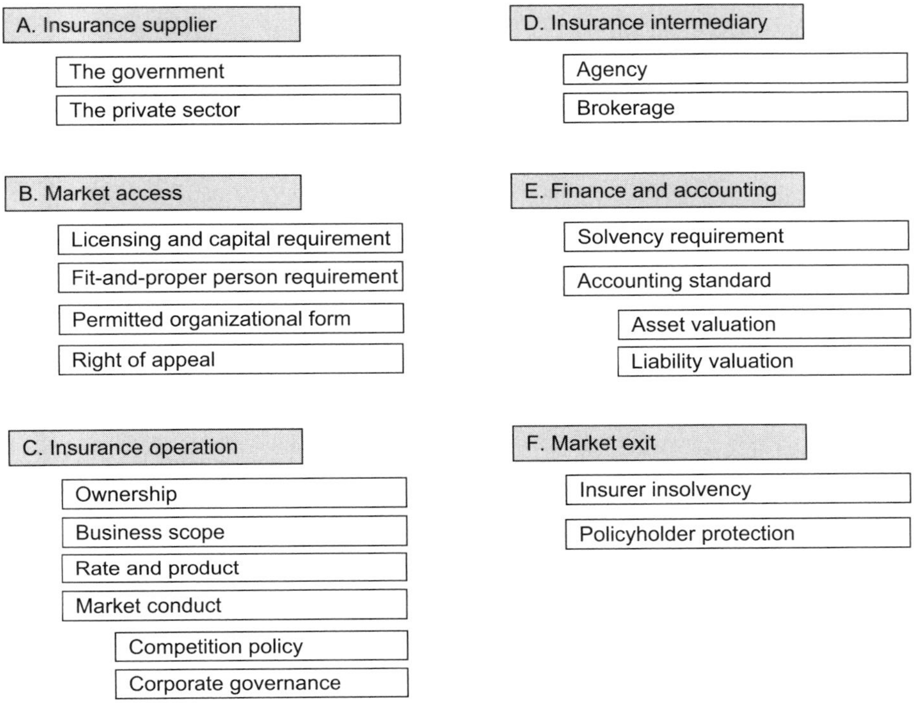

| A. Insurance supplier | | D. Insurance intermediary | |
|---|---|---|---|
| The government | | Agency | |
| The private sector | | Brokerage | |

| B. Market access | | E. Finance and accounting | |
|---|---|---|---|
| Licensing and capital requirement | | Solvency requirement | |
| Fit-and-proper person requirement | | Accounting standard | |
| Permitted organizational form | | Asset valuation | |
| Right of appeal | | Liability valuation | |

| C. Insurance operation | | F. Market exit | |
|---|---|---|---|
| Ownership | | Insurer insolvency | |
| Business scope | | Policyholder protection | |
| Rate and product | | | |
| Market conduct | | | |
| Competition policy | | | |
| Corporate governance | | | |

**Figure 24.2**   Areas of Insurance Regulation

- What is the best approach to detecting insurer solvency?
- What is the appropriate response to insurers in financial difficulty?
- What protections should be accorded insureds of insolvent insurers?

See also Figure 24.2 showing the areas of insurance regulation.

### *Controlling access to the market*

The first question by logic is: who should the government allow into the market. The answer to this question hinges on the philosophy of the government relative to its role as a source of economic security in the nation.

#### *The role of government as a supplier of insurance*

A baseline issue for every government is determining the role of the public sector vis-à-vis the private sector in the provision of economic security, as we discuss in Chapter 8. If the response is that government should be the sole insurance provider, as it has been and remains in some markets, other regulatory issues become moot.

The majority of countries today subscribe to the philosophy that government should serve as a supplier of insurance only where some overriding social issue demands it or where the market has failed to respond adequately to some perceived need and no market-based solution seems feasible. This philosophy underpins most social insurance schemes.

**Table 24.1**    Monopolistic Insurance Markets (2005)

| Region | Selected Countries |
|---|---|
| Africa | Algeria, Angola, Benin, Cape Verde, Congo, Ethiopia, Guinea-Bissau, Libya, Mauritania, Mozambique, Seychelles, Somalia, Swaziland, Tanzania, Zaire |
| Asia – Southeast and East | Afghanistan, Bhutan, Cambodia, Laos, North Korea |
| Asia – Middle East | Iran, Iraq, Syria |
| Central and Latin America | Costa Rica, Cuba |

These programs typically provide basic retirement, disability, survivor and unemployment benefits. Most also provide both occupational and non-occupational health benefits, as discussed in Chapter 8.

In other instances, government provides insurance when policymakers have determined that the private insurance mechanism has failed to respond adequately to a perceived need for insurance. The private insurance market often fails to provide needed insurance services when the associated risk is not easily diversifiable – that is, the independence criterion of the law of large numbers is not met – or when the private sector avoids business in lines where considerable problems of adverse selection exist. Examples worldwide include crop insurance, flood insurance, earthquake insurance, nuclear liability insurance and expropriation insurance.

Although the trend globally is toward placing greater reliance on competitive insurance markets, governments still dominate several national markets. Table 24.1 lists the countries in which the government has a monopoly in supplying what in most other countries is private insurance.

Twenty years ago, more than double the number of countries shown in Table 24.1 had monopolistic insurance markets. Every insurance market in Eastern Europe was then monopolistic, the most important of which was Russia. The motivations for a country to create a totally monopolistic insurance market relate almost exclusively to the government's political philosophy. As noted earlier, countries continue to move toward more competitive markets, privatizing formerly monopolistic and non-monopolistic state-owned insurers and reinsurers. **Privatization** is the process of allowing the private sector to provide services formerly provided by government or of converting a government-owned asset to private ownership. Of course, privatization alone does not ensure a competitive market or define the regulatory scheme. It merely shifts services or ownership from the public to the private sector. Private sector providers or owners could, in theory, maintain the monopoly.

Simultaneously, many countries have liberalized or are considering liberalizing their markets, thus permitting competition. Liberalization need not involve full privatization. A state can liberalize its insurance market and maintain ownership of its former monopolistic insurer. China and India, two of the most important developing markets, are both in various stages of liberalization. Nearly all economies in transition and several other countries such as Indonesia, Egypt and Nicaragua have already privatized and liberalized their insurance markets.

### Licensing requirements

After resolving the issue of government's role as an insurance supplier, it is next necessary to determine who should be allowed to enter a country's insurance market and on what terms. This decision embodies both market access and national treatment issues.

The most effective and efficient means of reducing the chances that citizens might purchase insurance from financially insecure insurers is to bar their entry into the market in the first instance. In countries permitting new entries, whether an insurer can enter the market is determined by the country's authorization requirements. These requirements begin with the requirements to secure a license to do business in the jurisdiction.

Licensing is the most important and powerful means of controlling access to a country's insurance market. Licensing provides regulators with leverage to compel insurers to comply with national laws. Without licensing, insurance buyers cannot be protected fully and competition could be distorted. Licensing requirements establish minimum acceptable standards for insurer financial strength and, as discussed in the next section, for the quality of persons seeking to manage insurance firms. To promote sound insurance operation, the government must carefully balance competing public policy interests. Standards set too stringently limit market access and impede competition, thereby reducing consumer choice and value. Standards set too liberally can permit financially unsound insurers or ethically unfit persons to prey on unsophisticated consumers through the inherent complexities of insurance.

*Admitted insurers*    In perhaps all jurisdictions, applicants wishing to establish an insurance company in the jurisdiction must secure a license, thereby becoming an *admitted* or *authorized insurer* (see Chapter 20). Already established insurers wishing to conduct new business within a jurisdiction also usually must secure a license. An unlicensed insurer is termed as *nonadmitted* or *unauthorized*. Traditionally, cross-border supply and consumption of insurance have been prohibited in many countries. In those countries, only licensed insurers may offer insurance products, citizens may purchase insurance only from admitted insurers, and intermediaries may not place risks with unauthorized insurers. In many cases, advertising restrictions apply to unlicensed insurers.

Brazil, Colombia, Venezuela and most other Latin American countries prohibit nonadmitted insurance. Most African countries have similar prohibitions. China, India, Indonesia, Japan, Korea, the Philippines, Taiwan, Thailand and most other Asian countries similarly restrict the sale by and purchase from nonadmitted companies. Important exceptions are Hong Kong, Malaysia and Singapore. Canada, Mexico and the U.S. prohibit nonadmitted insurance. Consumers within the E.U. may purchase insurance from E.U. insurers in other member states, and E.U. insurers may solicit insurance in all E.U. countries. In the U.K., particularly in the London market, placement of risk with unlicensed insurers is permitted in all except the compulsory lines of insurance. In most states, agents and brokers may place personal insurance only with admitted insurers.

Indeed, most countries historically have prohibited their citizens from purchasing insurance from nonadmitted insurers, although the trend is toward permitting such consumer-initiated purchases. If buyers purchase insurance from an unlicensed insurer, however, certain tax concessions and regulatory protections, such as guaranty fund cover, may be unavailable. Even liberal regulatory regimes restrict the purchase of compulsory insurances (e.g., automobile liability) to admitted insurers.

Nonadmitted reinsurers often can operate freely although direct insurers ceding business to nonadmitted reinsurers may be subject to more stringent accounting regulations. Also, a liberalization trend in direct insurance is evident in some commercial insurance markets. Even where purchase from or sale by nonadmitted insurers is prohibited, most countries allow such purchase where needed commercial coverage is unavailable locally. The excess-surplus line of insurance in the U.S. (see Chapter 20) is an example in this regard.

*The licensing process*   To obtain a license, insurance applicants universally must meet government-prescribed minimum financial requirements. These requirements typically include a minimum paid-in capital amount (or initial fund for mutual insurers) and, with some countries (e.g., Canada, Germany, Switzerland and the U.S.), amounts greater than the prescribed minimum capital to serve as an initial working capital fund.

In most countries, insurers seeking authorization are requested to submit their proposed business operation plan. The regulator assesses the plan's economic soundness as part of the admission process. This process may range from vigorous and probing (as in Germany and Switzerland) to a lesser review (as in the U.S.).

Insurance laws typically require officers, board members and incorporators of proposed insurance companies to meet certain residency or citizenship requirements. Some countries (e.g., Singapore and the U.K.) focus particular attention on the professional qualifications of the company's executives, the theory being that good people make for good companies. The regulator usually is charged with investigating the experience and character of those seeking a license and may deny a license if circumstances warrant. Poor management and decision-making have caused the failure of several insurance firms. History evidences that some regulators have been criticized for failing to identify unscrupulous individuals and prevent their becoming involved in insurance. If the applicant company is foreign, the local regulator may seek information, confidentially or otherwise, from the applicant's home-country regulator.

Finally, as part of the licensing process, the regulator may investigate the extent to which the applicant is committed to the national market. Some regulators express concern that some insurers (particularly some U.S. firms) take such a short-term view of profitability that they too quickly exit a market if the expected profitability fails to materialize soon. Such actions can create market disruptions that regulators wish to avoid.

In many countries, insurers exiting a market are required to give adequate notice to their policyholders, submit a plan detailing how they will satisfy claims and other incurred obligations, and work closely with the regulator until the exit process is complete. All of these requirements are designed to reduce market disruption. Reasonable market exit rules protect consumers and insurers there for long term. Some U.S. states have been accused of attempting to extract unreasonable concessions from insurers seeking to withdraw from certain lines or from the state. Harrington (1992) notes that exit restrictions may be used to enforce cross subsidies or extract economic rents in the insurance market.

*Nondiscrimination and national treatment*   As discussed in Chapter 3, countries increasingly are adopting a nondiscrimination standard for granting market access. Recall that *nondiscrimination* (or *most-favored-nation*) *treatment* means that no country's firms obtain better market access than any other country's firms, thereby making licensing requirements for foreign insurers, whatever their home country, essentially equivalent. Further, *national treatment*, toward which most OECD countries are moving, means that foreign entrants into a market are accorded treatment no less favorable than that accorded domestic companies. Thus, licensing (and other) requirements generally are applied nondiscriminatorily as between a state's *domestic* insurers owned by nationals and those owned by foreigners (i.e., national treatment) and domestic insurers and *foreign* insurers (i.e., most-favored-nation treatment).

Many developing countries still discriminate against establishment by foreign insurers. Some countries are reluctant to license new insurers no matter their nationality. The stated reason for this position is that the market does not require additional capacity or that the government wishes to avoid excessive competition. In practice, such restrictions often persist because established insurers wish to avoid further competition.

Foreign insurers seeking admission into a market usually must prove that they are lawfully organized and licensed in their home jurisdiction. Several jurisdictions (e.g., Canada, China, Iceland, India, Japan, Korea, Norway, Switzerland, Taiwan and several U.S. states) admit foreign insurers only if they have operated successfully in another jurisdiction for a specified time, often 3–5 years.

Insurers that choose to operate through a branch often are required to establish a trusted asset account equaling a domestic insurer's minimum required capital and surplus or to the insurer's liabilities in the country of operation. They also may be subject to larger deposit requirements. Without such requirements, regulators are concerned that foreign branches could too easily avoid meeting their obligations.

National insurance oversight generally differentiates between licensing requirements for direct insurers and reinsurers. Most countries require licenses for domestic reinsurers but not for foreign reinsurers. Most countries, therefore, do not directly regulate reinsurance except if the reinsurer is licensed, in which case regulation often parallels that of direct insurers. Indirect reinsurer regulation may occur through the state disallowing direct insurers' reserve credit for reinsurance placed with unauthorized reinsurers or with reinsurers not on a white list. As direct insurers are generally sophisticated buyers of insurance, the need to protect their interests through government regulation is less than that required for individual consumers. Uncollectible reinsurance, however, has been a major contributor to some direct insurer insolvencies in the past.

### Permitted organizational forms

Ideally, insurance laws should be simple and economically neutral as between organizational forms. Simplicity argues for avoiding artificial distinctions among otherwise similar firms. Economic neutrality argues for treating organizationally different insurers in a way that does not advantage one form over others. The law should not, however, attempt to make all organizational forms equal because a natural economic advantage may exist for one form over another (e.g., stock over mutual), and regulation should not attempt to equalize this natural advantage.

Insurance laws stipulate permissible organizational forms. Stock and mutual corporations are the most common forms worldwide and seem to be permitted in all non-monopolistic jurisdictions. Many other organizational forms are also found: unincorporated mutuals, fraternal benefit societies, cooperative insurers, reciprocals, non-profit service plans and health maintenance organizations. These other forms typically are permitted under special insurance laws. Japan, Singapore, the U.S. and, of course, the U.K. permit the creation of Lloyd's associations (e.g., Lloyd's of London and Lloyd's of Japan). Most countries that permit foreign insurers into their markets apply a national treatment standard regarding legal form.

### Ownership restrictions

In the absence of national security or other overriding public policy concerns, the competitive market model requires no restrictions on insurer ownership. Several developing countries, however, prohibit foreign ownership of domestic insurers or require certain minimum ownership rights to be held by nationals. Such restrictions can limit market access and curtail competitiveness. The country may, thereby, be denied additional financial intermediation services, which can penalize economic growth and technology transfer that liberal markets enjoy. In addition, citizens may be denied innovative products and product pricing that additional competition might bring.

About one-half of the U.S. states in some way prohibit authorization of government-owned insurers. Such ownership restrictions, dating from the 1950s, arose from apprehension about socialism. Today, their common concern is about government-owned insurers' ability to compete unfairly (e.g., through predatory pricing) because of the government's taxing authority. Many commentators question the relevance or usefulness of such prohibitions.

Countries generally permit banks to own insurers and vice versa. Nevertheless, concerns are expressed about competitive fairness and about the possibility of an insolvent bank contributing to the insolvency of an affiliate insurer and vice versa. These and other issues are discussed in Chapter 25.

### Restrictions on business scope

Typical insurance laws restrict the scope of an insurer's operations in various ways, including:

- *Restriction to the conduct of insurance business*: Governments generally hold that, for prudential reasons, insurance enterprises themselves should be limited to the business of insurance. With appropriate regulatory safeguards in place, however, governments seem content to permit insurers to own non-insurer enterprises and to be included within a holding company structure.

- *Separation of classes of insurance business*: The essential risk transfer, pooling, diversification and financial intermediation functions common to all insurance provide an economic rationale for permitting the use of composite insurers. Recall that composite insurers are authorized to underwrite both life and nonlife insurance within the same corporation.

In countries that permit composite insurance operations, internal safeguards and asset, liability and surplus separation requirements are set out. Regulatory simplicity, the ease with which separate corporate entities can be formed and combined within a holding company structure, and prudential considerations flowing from different insurer risk profiles are offered as reasons justifying prohibitions on composite insurers. Composite insurers exist in most European countries, although not in Scandinavia, and selected Commonwealth member states. By contrast, many developed economies (e.g., Japan and the U.S.) and numerous developing countries prohibit composite insurers. Korea is considering permitting composite insurers.

Health insurance is treated as part of life insurance in some countries and nonlife insurance in others. Many governments permit both life and nonlife insurers to offer health insurance.

### Rights of appeal

In most developed economies, an applicant denied an insurance business license has a right to appeal the denial. The appeal may be to a court (as in Finland, Germany, Switzerland and the U.S.), to an administrative tribunal (as in Australia), or to a government ministry (as in Japan).

## Balancing competition against consumer protection

After establishing rules determining who will be permitted to compete within their insurance markets, policymakers decide how best to balance the benefits of competition against the need to protect insurance consumers. Generally, this relates to the following four areas: (1) rate and product regulation, (2) financial regulation, (3) intermediary regulation and (4) competition policy regulation.

### Rate and product regulation

If it exists at all, rate regulation should strive to ensure that rates are not (1) excessive, (2) unfairly discriminatory or (3) inadequate. Regulation of policy terms and conditions is intended to reduce the likelihood that insurers take unfair advantage of insureds via the insurance contract itself. Inadequate competition within a market or lines of insurance can lead to excessive and sometimes inequitable rates as well as to unfair policy terms and conditions. Rate and policy form regulation – for example, *le contrôle matériel* (France and other French-speaking states) or *materielle Staatsaufsicht* (German-speaking nations) – is common worldwide.

A variety of rate regulation practices is found internationally. Governments or governmental-sanctioned cartels set prices in some markets. In other markets, governments or rating bureaus set rate ceilings or rate increase limits. This occurs where policymakers contend that price competition is insufficient to avoid rate excessiveness. Various forms of ex-ante (prior approval) and ex-post (subsequent disapproval) rate regulation exist. We highlight the five most common forms of rate regulation below:

- The most rigid practice of rate regulation can be found in **tariff markets** where the government or a government-sanctioned rating bureau sets premium rates or where licensed insurers must subscribe to the rate schedules set by an industry association. Many developing countries have tariff markets.

- In a market subject to a **prior approval** system, insurers cannot use proposed rate schedules until the rates are officially approved by the regulator. This form of ex-ante rate regulation is more common in personal lines than commercial lines of insurance. In countries where a deemer provision or equivalent exits, insurers may use new rate schedules if the regulator fails to respond to the approval request within a time period stipulated in the law.

- In some markets, governments set acceptable rate ceilings or rate increase limits (i.e., **flexi-rates**). This occurs where policymakers contend that price competition is insufficient to avoid rate excessiveness but desire to provide insurers with some flexibility in setting rates.

- Regulators use ex-post approaches in other markets. In markets subject to **file-and-use** regulation, insurers file new or revised rate schedules and can use them immediately. Similarly, insurers subject to **use-and-file** systems may use new rate schedules but must file the rates within a specified period. In these countries, regulators reserve the right to order an insurer to cease using a filed rate schedule if the regulator determines the schedule to be inconsistent with sound public policy.

- Finally, some countries have either no rating laws or permit "open competition" in selected lines. Insurers operating in jurisdictions with no rate regulation need not file anything with the regulator who has no authority over the rates charged. Insurers subject to open competition regulation do not file rates but, if requested, must provide the regulator with the data supporting their rates. Regulators do so if they believe that the rates do not comply with statutory guidelines. The *E.U. Framework Directive* has created a single insurance market in which ex-ante rate regulation is largely abandoned, although joint loss data may still be used and regulators retain broad rate oversight authority.

Stringency of rate regulation often differs among classes and types of insurance. Most commercial lines of insurance and reinsurance are free from rate regulation. By contrast, those lines closely identified with social policy (e.g., workers' compensation and automobile liability) are generally subjected to greater rate and policy oversight. Perhaps the line experiencing the most intensive rate regulation – and often unreasonable rate suppression – internationally is automobile liability insurance. Even today, some governments, including those of developed economies, maintain bureau-mandated premium rate schedules for that compulsory line of insurance.

Direct rate regulation in life insurance is the exception worldwide. Through mandated reserve requirements, however, life insurers often are subject to a type of indirect rate control. In some jurisdictions, some components of life insurance pricing (e.g., interest rates and expense ratios) are subject to control, thus potentially precluding meaningful price competition.

### Financial regulation

The requirements to obtain a license were discussed earlier. Consumer protection concerns, however, drive governments to insist on certain continuing levels of insurer financial solidity. Thus, insurance regulators are charged with overseeing the continuing viability of insurers in the market through **financial regulation** – also referred to as **prudential regulation** (U.K. and Commonwealth countries), as *le contrôle financier* (France and its former colonies) and as *Finanzaufsicht* (Austria and Germany).

Generally, more restrictive financial regulation is associated with more secure insurers. E.U. member states, Switzerland, Japan and many other countries that historically practiced strict solvency regulation have rarely seen domestic insurers in financial difficulty. Nevertheless, extensive restrictions stifle competition and innovation and, thereby, can lower consumer value and choice. It is the government's difficult task to balance these competing public interests.

Interestingly, the more competitive a market, the more important is prudential regulation. In a market where prices and other market elements are strictly regulated, insolvencies are less likely. With deregulation, insurers may price products more closely, occasionally even charging inadequate rates in an effort to gain market share. The insurance regulator in a deregulated market faces more complex regulatory issues than its counterpart in a strictly regulated market. Thus, it is arguably more important for regulators to maintain vigilant oversight of insurer solvency in a competitive market than in a restrictive one. The following discussion highlights the means by which governments seek to accomplish this task.

### Ongoing capital requirements

If one aspect of solvency regulation must be singled out as the most critical, it surely would be an insurer's relative net worth or capital position – the excess of assets over liabilities.

To gauge an insurer's capital, therefore, one must properly assess asset values and liability obligations. The terms **surplus**, **capital and surplus**, **policyholders' surplus** and **shareholder funds** are used synonymously with capital.

Within the E.U. (and many other countries), minimum ongoing capital and surplus requirements – called **solvency margins** – are set out as the relationship between surplus and premiums written (life and nonlife) and an claims incurred (nonlife) or mathematical reserves (life).[3] For nonlife insurance, minimum capital must equal at least 18 percent of premiums written (with adjustments for reinsurance) or 26 percent of the average net claims paid over the preceding 3–7 years (with adjustments for reinsurance), whichever is the greater. This procedure is, on the one hand, explicit recognition that insurer financial resources should increase with increases in business written. On the other hand, the requirements fail to consider other explicit risks inherent in insurance operations. To correct the problems related to this solvency margin approach – retrospectively termed as **Solvency I** – the E.U. has been developing a new approach since 2001. Known as **Solvency II**, it adopts a risk-based approach that relies on risk management-based supervision akin to that adopted for banks via the Basel II requirements.

Regulators in the U.S. have been using RBC models that are vastly different from earlier, fixed-capital approaches or informal premiums-to-surplus ratio approaches on which state regulators relied to monitor insurer financial condition. In the RBC models, minimum acceptable capital for business continuation of an insurer is directly related to the size and riskiness of the firm's underwriting (technical) and investment (non-technical) operations. Several other countries have developed (e.g., Singapore and Taiwan) or are developing their own RBC models. Insight 24.1 sketches how U.S. RBC requirements are determined and used.

The solvency margin regulation in Japan seems to resemble the U.S. RBC approach. The solvency margin ratio for nonlife insurance, for example, is expressed as the ratio of "total solvency margin" to "capital cushion representing the risks which may exceed the insurer's usual estimates" or:

$$\text{Solvency margin ratio} = \frac{\text{Total of solvency margin}}{0.5\left(\sqrt{A^2 + (B^2 + C^2)^2} + D + E\right)}$$

where $A$ denotes ordinary insurance risks, $B$ represents assumed interest rate risks, $C$ is for asset management risks, $D$ is an estimate of major catastrophe risks and $E$ is the sum of business management risks.

### Asset limitations and valuation

To assure solidity and investment diversification, governments generally establish quantitative and qualitative asset standards. Insurers are, thereby, prohibited or discouraged from undertaking what are considered imprudent investments. Assets backing policyholder liabilities are routinely subject to more restrictive provisions than are assets backing capital or unassigned liabilities.

Countries follow different approaches to investment regulation. Some are rigid in their approaches (e.g., China and India), setting out in detail how insurers and reinsurers should apportion their investments. Others follow more liberal, "prudent investment" approaches that allow insurers greater flexibility, subject to certain guiding principles. Whatever the

INSIGHT 24.1: RISK-BASED CAPITAL REQUIREMENTS IN THE
UNITED STATES

The NAIC developed the RBC standards in an attempt to judge better the adequacy
of each insurer's capital. The NAIC approach relies on a formula to derive the
implied capital (authorized control level, ACL) needed by an insurer to be able safely
to carry the risk inherent in its assets (particularly investment volatility), liabilities
(particularly loss reserves), premium writings, lines of business (e.g., property versus
liability), diversification of risk portfolio, reinsurance quality and several other
financial and nonfinancial aspects of insurance operations. The riskier the element,
the larger the weighing factor and, hence, the larger total adjusted capital (TAC)
the insurer needs to support the risky activity. TAC is the insurer's statutory capital
with adjustments for voluntary reserves and other items more properly classified as
surplus.

Whether the regulator intervenes with the management of an insurer – known as
the ACL – depends on the ratio of TAC to RBC. Insurers with ratios above 200 percent generally warrant no special regulatory attention. Insurers with ratios between
200 and 150 percent are required to submit an RBC plan to their home states detailing corrective actions proposed to be taken. Ratios between 150 and 100 percent
require submission of an RBC plan and, after examination or analysis by the regulator, an order by the regulator specifying corrective action to be taken. Ratios between
100 and 70 percent can lead to regulatory seizure, with ratios below 70 requiring
seizure of the insurer.

actual nature of investment restrictions, common elements exist in countries' investment
laws and regulations:

- *Authorized (admitted) investments*: The typical classes of investments permitted to back
  policyholder liabilities include government-backed securities, corporate bonds, mortgage and other loans, common and preferred stock, deposits and real estate. Limitations
  ordinarily apply as to quality and quantity for each asset category. Investments in foreign securities or other assets often are severely limited, if not prohibited all together.
  An approach followed in a few countries (e.g., Canada) that is gaining interest is to permit insurers broad investment discretion, subject to a "prudent investment" rule. This
  rule sets out general guidelines for acceptable investments.

- *Diversification*: Laws typically require investment diversification. This diversification
  may be stated generally or, more commonly, quantitative criteria are laid down. The
  criteria, where they exist, prohibit insurers from excessive investments in a single asset
  category, in a particular investment market or in a single investment. For example, the
  E.U. limits investments that are not traded on a regulated market to 10 percent of total
  reserves and limits unsecured loans to 5 percent of reserves. The E.U. also generally
  limits investments in the shares or bonds of or loans to a single entity. The E.U. directives as well as the laws of many other countries apply such limits exclusively to investments backing policyholder reserves and not to investments backing insurer capital. Most

countries apply the same criteria to life and nonlife insurers, although several countries (e.g., Canada, Ireland, Japan and several U.S. states) establish different criteria.

- *Currency matching (congruence)*: Insurers typically are required to match their liabilities denominated in one currency with assets denominated or realizable in the same currency.

- *Localization*: Insurance laws typically require that assets be located in the insurer's domiciliary jurisdiction. This requirement reduces the chances of the regulator and policyholders being unable to attach insurer assets in the event of insurer financial difficulty.

*Liability regulation*
Life insurer policy reserves ordinarily are estimated through mathematical formulae whereas nonlife insurer reserves are subject to less precise estimation methods. The methods and assumptions used to derive life insurer technical (mathematical) reserves may be prescribed in great detail (Germany, Portugal and the U.S.) or the regulator may rely on an actuarial valuation (Canada, Ireland and the U.K.). The requirements typically result in a conservative assessment (i.e., overstatement) of insurers' liabilities.

National laws are more general for nonlife insurers' reserves. They routinely require insurers to establish a liability, called unearned premium reserves (as discussed in Insight 19.1), to recognize that portion of paid premiums for which coverage has yet to be provided. The reserves may be prescribed in some detail and calculated as a pro rata share on a gross premium basis (Japan and the U.S.) or on premiums net of acquisition expenses (Belgium, Denmark and Germany).

Appropriate loss reserve establishment has been a regulatory challenge. Detailed reporting schedules may be required (as in the U.S.), or reporting may be more general. The discounting of loss reserves is not, in general, practiced. Some countries make no provisions for claims incurred but not reported (IBNR), covered losses that have yet to be reported to the insurer.

*Accounting standards*
If an assessment of an insurer's financial solidity is to be meaningful, insurers must follow similar procedures, for the terms "assets" and "liabilities" have meaning only in relation to some accounting convention. As a prerequisite to the establishment of acceptable levels of insurer financial solidity, governments therefore decide the basis on which insurers will be permitted or required to value their assets and liabilities. In some jurisdictions, this basis is one created by regulatory authorities and required of all licensed insurers. In other jurisdictions, it is one generally agreed upon and, in effect, enforced by the accounting profession with regulatory oversight. International variations in accounting are great. These variations reflect differences in traditions, culture, the way insurance is transacted and the purposes for which accounting statements are used.

Accounting standards extend not only to insurers' balance sheets (hence to assets and liability valuation) but also to insurers' income statements (profit and loss accounts) and other financial statements. Differences arise in recording underwriting results and investment results as well as in the mechanism for recognizing realized and unrealized capital gains and losses.

While a wide variety of accounting practices exists internationally, most are based on one or both of the following two accounting principles:

- *Statutory accounting principles (SAP)* are detailed accounting conventions that insurers are required to follow in preparing their financial statements for insurance regulatory oversight purposes. The emphasis is on insurer solvency; therefore, the conventions generally are conservative.

• *Generally accepted accounting principles (GAAP)* are less detailed accounting conventions that are supposed to reflect a firm's going concern value, meaning that the values posted for assets and liabilities are intended to be more accurate reflections of their current market value. GAAP typically results in a less conservative view of the firm's operations.

Several international organizations and the accounting standard-setting bodies of the major economies have been working since the late 1990s through the International Accounting Standards Board (IASB) to develop a set of acceptable international accounting standards for insurance (as well as for all other financial institutions) that all relevant countries might adopt. The goal is to have the standards in place not later than 2007. The purpose is to allow stakeholders to have more meaningful comparisons of financial institutions internationally and to ease the burden on multinational financial institutions in the preparation and reporting of their financial results.

The IASB seeks the admirable goal of having financial statements better reflect corporations' true economic value; that is, closing the gap between a firm's net worth as shown on its balance sheet and its economic worth as assessed by the market through it overall market capitalization. This ambitious goal has led to several concerns by insurance executives regarding certain IASB proposals, including the appropriate treatment of insurance contracts versus other, closely related financial instruments and how to fairly value insurers' liabilities for which no organized market exists for their trading and, therefore, for deriving the true economic value. Also, that insurers might be able to change their accounting for some contracts over time has caused concern.

The E.U. has announced that publicly held financial institutions domiciled in E.U. member states are to use the IASB accounting conventions in reporting their 2007 results. Already, E.U. companies were required to report their 2005 results and thereafter following some of the proposed asset valuation standards.

*Intermediary regulation*

Insurance intermediaries, agents and brokers, are found in every insurance market. Most insurance worldwide is sold through them. Because individuals and businesses rely on the advice as well as risk management and insurance services of such intermediaries, they should be knowledgeable, trustworthy advisors. For this reason, most governments prohibit the sale of insurance, directly by en employee or through an intermediary, by anyone who is not licensed (or registered).

As markets become more competitive, a greater variety of products and services evolves, and products and pricing become more complex. These conditions suggest that the services of knowledgeable intermediaries are often more important in highly competitive than in more restrictive markets in which policy form and rate regulation as well as financial regulation allow for little differentiation among sellers and their products.

To qualify for an intermediary license, individuals typically must establish that they have not engaged in fraudulent or criminal activities, meet residency requirements and pass a qualifying examination or examinations. Certain minimum experience in the insurance business or a deposit of capital is required in some countries. To protect consumers from financial difficulty arising from errors or omissions in the services offered by insurance intermediaries, governments increasingly require agents and brokers to purchase professional liability insurance coverage. Some governments also apply the principle of imputed liability, thus holding insurers responsible for the unprofessional acts of their agents. U.S. E&S (excess and surplus) brokers can additionally be held financially responsible when the insurers with which they place risks become insolvent.

Once an intermediary is licensed, either the insurance regulator or a self-regulatory body exercises ongoing intermediary oversight. Some countries (e.g., Argentina, Brazil, Colombia and India) limit or set the commission rates that can be paid to intermediaries. Sanctions usually exist for actions such as misrepresentation of policy terms and benefits, misappropriation of funds and other forms of malpractice. A particularly acute problem in some developing countries is the misappropriation of premiums by ill-minded intermediaries.

The issue of appropriate life insurance intermediary oversight is especially critical in some markets. Consumers in the U.K. and the U.S., in particular, have experienced difficulties in connection with life insurance marketing practices. In the U.K., these difficulties have led to especially stringent intermediary oversight and disclosure requirements.

Intermediaries in a competitive market, by definition, face competition among themselves, from direct insurers and other financial services providers (e.g., banks). This strong competition sometimes tempts salespeople to try to gain a competitive edge over their rivals by misrepresenting or omitting key information about the quality or characteristics of the products they sell, the companies they represent or other elements of the purchase. Hence, as markets become more competitive through less intrusive regulation, policymakers increasingly realize the need for more carefully crafted, clearer market conduct regulation and greater vigilance in oversight of insurance distribution whether by intermediaries, banks, or direct marketing operations. In line with this philosophy, Singapore introduced the *Financial Advisors Act* in 2002. The act all entities, including insurance intermediaries, that offer financial advisory services.

### Competition policy regulation

Policymakers lay down rules by which competition in markets is to be conducted.[4] With the increasing globalization of financial services, competition regulation is assuming greater prominence in insurance regulation. **Competition policy**, also known as **antitrust regulation**, constitutes a nation's laws and regulations that govern private producers' behavior and the market structure within which interactions between producers take place. Competition regulation addresses anti-competitive practices of individual firms as well as both horizontal and vertical competition-reducing arrangements between firms. It also includes measures governments use to assess market competitiveness, including those related to privatization and deregulation of the market. Sometimes it extends to government actions taken in accordance with regional or international agreements.

Regulation related to competition policy can be distinguished philosophically from traditional forms of regulation by the continuity of contact between the regulator and the regulated. With traditional regulation, the relationship is continuing. With competition policy regulation, contact is episodic and, for many firms, non-existent.

### Typical elements of competition law

Competition policy in its modern form is a North American invention, first arising in Canada in 1889 then in the U.S. in 1890. These first laws were reactions to the large "trust" forms of organizations that wielded substantial market power. Competition policy evolved more slowly in other parts of the world, generally appearing in market-economy countries

---

INSIGHT 24.2: THE LAW OF LARGE NUMBERS AS AN ENTRY
BARRIER

Insurance functions because of the law of large numbers. Because many insurers are
small, their loss experience predictability may be subject to great fluctuation. This fact
may put them at a significant competitive disadvantage compared with larger insurers,
as they should charge a higher price given their comparatively riskier portfolios. When
they fail to do so, rational investors will not supply the needed capital. Reinsurance can
mitigate this additional risk to an extent (see Chapter 23), but reinsurance comes at a
price and, like the insurer, the reinsurer needs to make a profit.

The law of large numbers serves as an economic barrier to entry for new and small
insurers. In recognition of this fact, most governments permit industry cooperation in
the collection and distribution of loss information for ratemaking purposes, provided
subscribers do not use the information so that collusion is the effective result.

---

during the latter half of the 20th century, with some countries enacting meaningful laws
only within the past two decades.

National laws and regulations typically address competition related to three board areas:
(1) collusive practices, (2) mergers or acquisitions and (3) abuse of dominant position.

*Collusive practices*    Collusive practices can take three forms: (1) horizontal, (2) vertical and
(3) conglomerate. **Horizontal collusion** occurs when two or more firms undertake competition-reducing activities in the same market. The most common form of horizontal collusion
in insurance internationally probably occurs in insurance pricing. Cartel pricing represents
the most obvious price collusion arrangement. "Advisory rates" offered by a rating bureau or
an insurance association can become the market rate. Nonetheless, some forms of collective
activity may be desirable to allow a more competitive market, as discussed in Insight 24.2.

Even more subtle is horizontal collusion that appears as consortiums, syndicates, cooperatives, joint ventures and strategic alliances. Many such cooperative arrangements serve legitimate marketplace needs and do not restrain competition. Others may be purposely designed
to avoid competition. The challenge for regulators is to distinguish between the two.

**Vertical collusion** occurs when two or more firms on different functional levels undertake activities to reduce competition. Common forms of vertical collusion in insurance
internationally can occur in distribution arrangements (e.g., agreements by distributors not
to rebate commissions where otherwise legal) and between insurers and reinsurers (e.g.,
arrangements in which direct insurers must follow the reinsurer's pricing lead). These and
other types of activities typically are subject to competition regulatory requirements.

**Conglomerate collusion** occurs when a conglomerate or a related group of firms
restrains competition by virtue of cooperative arrangements in different markets or in different sectors of markets. Ordinarily, conglomerates, in themselves, seldom restrict competition because their activities do not compete with each other. The potential for competition
restriction, nonetheless, exists, especially with increasing financial services integration and
the formation of financial service conglomerates. For example, concern exists about tie-in
sales with *bancassurance*.

*Mergers and acquisitions*    Insurance regulators often are charged with determining whether a proposed merger or acquisition tends to create market power. The merger of two large insurers, reinsurers or brokerage firms might result in a new firm whose market power is so great as to reduce competition. Merger and acquisition regulation is designed to prevent such outcomes. As with collusion, the possibility exists for horizontal, vertical and conglomerate market concentration.

*Abuse of dominant position*    National laws and regulations also are designed to discourage major market suppliers from using their dominant positions to restrain competition. The objective is to prevent exclusionary or exploitative practices. Attempts by insurers, reinsurers or intermediaries to impose unfairly high prices or unreasonably disadvantageous policy or purchasing conditions could constitute abuse.[5] Similarly, unfair discrimination or tie-in sales arrangements are offensive.

The potential for abuse of dominant position is greater the more concentrated is an insurance, reinsurance or intermediary market. The relevant market may be a particular line of business or territory. The narrower the scope of the relevant market, the greater the possibility of achieving a market-dominant position.

*International legal norms*
A distinguishing characteristic of competition laws is their broad formulation and brevity. As a result, regulators and the courts worldwide enjoy a wide margin of discretion in their application.

Countries usually take a pragmatic position to enforcement. While their purposes are solidly grounded in economics, competition laws and their interpretation have evolved from real problems revealed in the functioning of markets. Thus, the usual position is that anti-competitive behavior is permitted provided that the positive economic effects seem to dominate the negative effects. Hence, bureau data gathering and distribution (as described in Insight 24.2) and form promulgation may be permitted although such actions are cooperative.

The effectiveness of competition regulation depends on both the law itself and the stringency of its enforcement. U.S. competition law is noted to be the most constraining internationally and the most vigorously enforced. By contrast, Japanese law is perhaps equally strict – being patterned after U.S. law – but lightly enforced.

Competition law in the E.U. and the U.S. cannot be evaded by initiating the anti-competitive behavior outside the relevant territories. Both E.U. and U.S. authorities look more into the effects of such behavior on their markets (the so-called **effects doctrine**) than to where the offensive actions themselves take place. Thus, the U.S. Department of Justice will challenge the conduct of a business operating outside the U.S. if it believes its conduct harms U.S. exports or affects a market in the U.S. An action by the Justice Department requires the conduct to have violated U.S. antitrust laws had it occurred in the U.S. and for it to have a direct, substantial and foreseeable effect on U.S. commerce. The U.S. is noted for the vigorous extraterritorial application of its law, much to the chagrin of other jurisdictions that consider U.S. actions infringements in their internal affairs.

Competition laws and provisions are structured around the principle of prohibition or the principle of abuse. Under the **principle of prohibition**, enumerated behavior is deemed anti-competitive and automatically illegal; that is, it is illegal per se. Use of this principle is another example of ex-ante regulation.

Under the **principle of abuse**, an inquiry into the economic effects of the alleged offensive behavior is required. Only with an ex-post finding of damaging effects can the activity be declared illegal. Switzerland and the U.K. rely on the principle of abuse.

U.S. competition regulation is stringent, in part, because it relies on the prohibition principle and, more importantly, because sanctions for violations can involve criminal prosecution.[6] Most other countries rely on fines. E.U. competition law also is based on the principle of prohibition and has been the cause of substantial ratcheting up of member country laws and enforcement.

Within the E.U., mergers and other concentration activities must be pre-notified to the European Commission. However, the European Commission has issued block exemptions with respect to certain otherwise offensive behaviors. These cover the development of common pure premiums (i.e., premiums without loadings), the elaboration of common standard policy provisions, common coverage (e.g., coinsurance or reinsurance pools) for certain risks and common rules for testing and acceptance of security devices. These block exemptions contain many conditions. For example, pure premiums can be advisory only. Numerous policy provisions are prohibited. Common coverage is permitted only if the carriers have certain low market shares.

Competition law can be expected to gain in importance as markets liberalize and deregulate. Because of differences in laws and enforcement, national competition policy itself is becoming an important trade issue. One has but to consider the conflicts between the U.S. and Japan concerning the way Japanese businesses operate, especially regarding the perceived trade restricting activities of its *keiretsu* (cross shareholding or horizontal or vertical linkage of major industrial, post-World War II Japanese firms) to appreciate the increasing importance of this type of government regulation.

## Detecting insurer financial difficulty

After deciding whom to admit into the market and establishing a balance between the adverse consequences of imperfect competition and of imperfect regulation, governments create a solvency surveillance and enforcement system. Solvency surveillance typically takes place through three formal mechanisms: (1) reporting requirements, (2) financial examination and (3) oversight by the professions.

### Reporting requirements

Reporting requirements generally are the core of insurer solvency surveillance. The great majority of countries require all licensed insurers yearly (or more frequently) to file detailed financial statements. These statements, prepared according to local accounting conventions, contain the insurer's balance sheet, income statement, and other prescribed statements, notes and exhibits. Detailed guidelines specifying precisely how the information is to be prepared and presented are typically set forth.

The E.U. requires that all member states prepare their balance sheets and income statements in the same format (although not necessarily using the same valuation standards). In addition, companies are required annually to file a report describing the development of their business, their present situation and future trends of possible importance.

Regulators typically conduct financial analyses of insurers, based mainly on the reported information. The analysis usually involves calculation of ratios and use of other financial tools to assess capital adequacy, underwriting leverage, asset quality and liquidity, and cash flow.

Statistical, financial and various other methods (e.g., financial stress tests) may be employed to identify insurers that require special regulatory attention. No completely satisfactory methods exist, although the E.U. Solvency II efforts are considered promising by many observers.

### On-site financial examinations

On-site financial examinations (inspections) are relied upon by all OECD member countries and probably most other countries. The insurance regulator typically is required to conduct such examinations at some stated interval, such as every three to five years. Some countries carry out examinations on a case-by-case basis, or as when the regulator suspects possible financial irregularity or difficulty because an insurer fails to meet some regulatory test.

Regulators judge on-site financial examinations to be one of their most useful surveillance tools. However, the intensity and quality of examinations vary widely. They typically involve a verification of selected or all information reported in the annual statement filings. Some countries carry out examinations only to seek clarification on specific matters of concern.

### Professional oversight

Greater reliance on the professions is an obvious, efficient and effective means of discouraging inappropriate insurer behavior and of revealing it if it occurs. Insurance regulators routinely rely on the accounting and actuarial professions for additional solvency surveillance. Thus, actuarial opinions regarding the adequacy of an insurer's ratemaking and reserves often are required, and insurers' financial statements are typically required to be audited annually by an independent accountant and the results provided to regulators. With the development of more stringent corporate governance rules lately, insurers increasingly also conduct their own internal risk management assessments using audits and examinations, particularly at the prompting of the firm's board of directors.

In addition, regulators rely on informal communication channels to gather information of possible insurer wrongdoing or difficulty. The IAIS is one mechanism for information sharing among the world's regulators.

## Responding to insurers in financial difficulty

An objective of insurance regulation should be to establish proper incentives for efficient and safe insurer operation and institute safeguards to keep the number of insurer insolvencies to an acceptable minimum. Within a competitive marketplace, some insurer financial difficulties and failures are inevitable. A marketplace with no insurance failures is likely one in which insurance is expensive and consumer choices limited.

After identifying an insurer as financially (or operationally) troubled through surveillance mechanisms discussed in the preceding section, regulators have four options: (1) informal actions, (2) formal actions, (3) rehabilitation and (4) liquidation. In each case, the question that policymakers should address is: what authority should the regulator have compared with the regulated firm. Regulatory actions taken precipitously might needlessly harm insurers, assuring their demise because of adverse publicity. Delayed regulatory action can lead to greater consumer (and possibly taxpayer) loss. We discuss below the four regulatory options.

### Informal actions

A regulator's typical first responses to a troubled company are informal. The regulator may attempt to work with company management to identify and deal with the sources of difficulty.

The success of such actions is dependent on the voluntary cooperation of the insurer, on its financial condition and on the good will of other firms in the market or the coercive power of the regulator. In many countries, a friendly merger or acquisition is a common response.

### Formal actions

Governments use formal actions against financially troubled licensed insurers. The nature of any formal action varies from country to country, but ordinarily might consist of written directives requiring the distressed insurers, among other things, to (1) obtain state approval before undertaking certain transactions, (2) limit or cease its new business writings, (3) infuse capital or (4) cease certain business practices. Failure of an insurer to rectify the identified problem leads to more drastic action.

In some OECD countries, the regulator may publish its recommendations or orders in newspapers and in its official journal when an insurer fails to comply with them, thereby alerting the public to the insurer's shortcomings. Other countries (e.g., Australia) grant the regulator the right to dismiss company executives, actuaries and auditors in serious cases. The most severe measure is suspension or revocation of the insurer's authority to write certain classes of insurance or of the entire license. Such actions are typically subject to judicial or other review.

The situation can be a bit more complex within the E.U. when an insurer conducts cross-border business in another E.U. member state and the host-country regulator determines that the insurer has violated its national laws or regulations. When it happens, the host-country regulator must first request the insurer to remedy the irregularity. If that fails, the regulator must inform the insurer's home-country regulator of the deficiency and the failure of the insurer to rectify it. The home-country regulator is then to take appropriate regulatory action against the insurer but based on the home country's laws and regulations. If this action fails to achieve the desired result, the host country can, if necessary, prohibit the foreign insurer from writing insurance in the host country.

### Rehabilitation

Regulators usually have the authority to assume control of financially troubled domestic insurers with the hope of their **rehabilitation**; that is, actions to return the insurer to the marketplace as an independent, fully functioning insurer. The action may require a court order, although in some states the regulator may assume control of an insurer without a prior order if the regulator has determined such action is urgent and necessary to preserve assets. Regulators may use the rehabilitation process to arrange a merger or acquisition.[7]

### Liquidation

The final option for insurance regulators in dealing with financially troubled domestic insurers is **liquidation**; that is, the winding up of the company's entire business. A liquidator is appointed either by the insurance regulator or, more frequently, by a court. The liquidator musters the assets of the company and prepares for their distribution to policyholders, to creditors, and possibly to shareholders. Policyholders usually enjoy preferential rights, although this is not true for all jurisdictions. Also, policyholders in some lines of insurance (e.g., life insurance or other third-party claimants) may enjoy preference over other policyholders. Insurance guaranty funds may be activated (see the next section).

### *Protecting insureds of an insolvent insurer*

Policymakers in market economies must decide what protections they should afford insureds of insolvent insurers. One response might be that they should provide no protections. In a spirit of true *laissez-faire* economics, insured individuals and businesses should bear the full responsibility of their poor purchase decisions, so goes the argument. In this way, the marketplace itself eventually would evolve solutions to the problem of how insureds can meaningfully assess insurer solidity.

Even if this view were correct, few policymakers seem willing to test the theory fully. Consequently, many countries have some mechanism to guarantee insurance benefits. Several have insolvency guaranty associations or funds. Some insolvency mechanisms are advanced-funded through assessments of authorized insurers (e.g., U.S. state of New York), while others rely on post-insolvency assessments of authorized insurers (e.g., all other U.S. states). Funds may involve modest (as in the E.U.) or generous (as in the U.S.) indemnity limits. The insured may be fully indemnified to a maximum amount (the U.S.) or some loss-sharing by the insured may be included (the U.K.). The fund may be government run (some E.U. countries) or operated and financed by the insurance industry (e.g., Canada and Japan).

Guaranty funds diminish market discipline to some degree by creating moral hazard. If consumers are aware that they will be made whole if there were an insolvency, they have less incentive to investigate and monitor solvency. This assertion is more relevant for informed buyers than for less informed individuals. This fact explains why guaranty fund benefits often are not available to commercial insureds. Also, if no distinction for insurer financial solidity is made in the guaranty fund assessment mechanism, the opportunity for moral hazard by firms is enhanced, thus further weakening market discipline.

Policymakers are aware of this difficulty, and researchers have proposed alternatives to the flat-assessment approach. Although details vary, such alternative approaches rely on some type of assessment method that takes into consideration the likelihood of insurer financial distress.

# TAXATION IN INSURANCE

This section explores insurance taxation by, first, presenting certain principles of taxation. Insurance taxation ideally should be consistent with these principles. We next discuss taxation of insurance companies and policyholders internationally.

## Principles of Taxation

An understanding of taxation principles is important if one is properly to assess governmental tax policy regarding insurance consumers and companies. Here we cover the general purposes of taxation, desirable traits of tax policy and systems of taxation.

### *General purposes of taxation*

We can identify three general purposes of tax systems: (1) to raise revenue, (2) to promote economic goals and (3) to promote social goals. That governments intend taxation *to raise revenue* needs little explanation. Governments require revenues to provide the services demanded of them by their citizens. Taxation is the most important and a universal means of obtaining this needed revenue.

Governments often design tax systems also *to promote economic goals*, although this purpose is usually subservient to the revenue-raising objective. The economic goals may be national, or they may relate to some specific industry or even to individual economic activity. Thus, governments attempt to stimulate overall national economic activity through tax decreases and, at other times, attempt to retard excessive growth through tax increases. Certain industries may enjoy tax concessions because government wants to stimulate productive activity of those industries. Indeed, some governments have provided significant tax concessions to stimulate research and development by businesses.

Many countries impose high tariffs on imported manufactured goods in the stated belief that they are promoting economic goals. The stated goal may be to discourage the outflow of foreign exchange reserves or to shelter a domestic industry from the fullness of foreign competition. Of course, tariffs also raise revenue for the government (see Chapter 3).

Policymakers also design tax systems *to promote social goals*. Examples can be found in virtually every tax system. These social goals relate either to discouraging or to encouraging certain behavior. The typically heavy taxation imposed on tobacco and alcohol products reflects not only a desire to raise revenue from the sale of such products but also an attempt by government to discourage their use or to impose a type of social levy for the perceived harm that their use causes society. Taxes on pollution, theoretically, could serve the same purpose.

Governments often permit tax deductions and credits to encourage certain activities. Tax rates, deductions, exemptions and credits are the tax-related tools that policymakers use to craft a tax system to promote specific economic and social goals.

### *Desirable traits of tax policy*

Ideally, a tax policy is one that possesses the following traits: (1) equity, (2) neutrality and (3) simplicity. We discuss each trait briefly.

**Equity** in taxation (also called **vertical equity**) means that each taxpayer should contribute his, her or its fair share in taxes. Determining the fair share is the difficult part for tax planners. Most countries have adopted some measure of "ability to pay" as a test of fair share and assume that those with greater ability should pay higher taxes.

A tax system or provision should possess **economic neutrality** (also called **horizontal equity**) meaning that governments should tax economically equivalent entities, products and services equivalently. In the absence of the tax system serving economic or social goals, the system should minimize interference with the economic decisions of individuals, businesses and other taxpaying entities. Thus, lacking overriding social or economic goals, the tax system (1) should avoid benefiting one industry compared with others; (2) within a single industry (e.g., financial services), should accord no advantage to one set of competitors over others; and (3) within a given firm, should not influence the firm's choice of production inputs or product outputs.

The principle underlying the economic neutrality concept is that social welfare is enhanced if resources flow to their highest-valued uses. An ideal tax system minimally distorts this flow. Its adverse incentive effects should be low. In practice, however, tax systems always affect individual and business decision-making. Incentives (and disincentives) are natural byproducts, but policymakers should strive to understand and minimize these effects.

A tax system can be considered to be **simple** if it is not complex administratively, its costs of collection are low, it is not easily evaded and taxpayers can comply with the law without undue expenditure of time and money. Implicit within this trait is that the tax system is appropriate for the country's level of development and the sophistication of its administrative apparatus. This trait often conflicts with equity and neutrality. How these conflicts are resolved depends on the country's economic circumstances and conditions at the time the tax system is implemented. A tax system not attuned to its environment is an invitation to inefficiency.

### Systems of taxation

Tax systems evolve over time and vary from country to country. Nevertheless, we can identify several common elements of the systems, of which three are fundamental: (1) tax bases, (2) tax exemptions, deductions and credits and (3) tax rates.

A tax system must begin with a tax base. According to fiscal experts, the broader the tax base, the better. Common tax bases are the taxpaying entity's income, consumption and wealth.

Tax exemptions, deductions and credits are the most important mechanisms for modifying a tax system to accomplish social and, to a large extent, economic goals. Without appropriate use of these items, a tax system cannot be fine tuned to target specific behaviors.

The tax rates that government chooses to apply to taxable income determine the relative tax on taxpayers. Other things being equal, the higher the marginal tax rate, the greater the impact that the tax rate itself has on economic behavior, as individuals and businesses undertake activities to minimize the tax's effects. Consequently, economists advocate low marginal tax rates.

## Life Insurance Taxation

Life insurance products enjoy favorable taxation in most countries. Life insurers also enjoy favorable taxation in many countries, although, as discussed below, premium taxation can result in heavy tax burdens. We provide an overview of taxation of life insurance consumers and companies.

### Life insurance consumers

Many countries provide tax concessions concerning the purchase, ownership or execution of life insurance policies. The extent and nature of these concessions vary from minor, and designed to simplify tax administration, to substantial, and designed to encourage life insurance purchase and maintenance. We structure the following examination of life product tax treatment around policy cash flow components: (1) premiums, (2) living benefits and (3) death benefits.

#### Premiums

Many countries provide tax relief to policyholders for premiums paid for qualifying life insurance policies. This relief is granted only for policies meeting prescribed parameters and may take the form of a tax credit or tax deduction. Governments intend such tax concessions to encourage the purchase of life insurance.

**Table 24.2**   Tax Relief on Life Insurance Premiums in Selected OECD Countries

*Some tax relief on premiums paid for qualifying, individually issued life insurance products*

| | | |
|---|---|---|
| Austria | Ireland | Portugal |
| Belgium | Italy | Spain |
| Denmark | Japan | Sweden |
| France | Luxembourg | Switzerland |
| Germany | The Netherlands | Turkey |
| Greece | Norway | |

*No tax relief on premiums paid for individually issued life insurance products*

| | | |
|---|---|---|
| Australia | Iceland | United States |
| Canada | New Zealand | |
| Finland | United Kingdom | |

Table 24.2 shows selected OECD countries that provide some form of tax-based premium relief for qualifying life insurance policies issued to individuals (as opposed to employers). Some OECD countries (Australia, Canada, Finland, Iceland, New Zealand, the U.K. and the U.S.) make no provision for general relief, whereas other OECD countries provide relief for some types of life insurance policies.

Where granted, tax concessions usually apply to policies whose exclusive or predominant purpose is to provide living benefits (e.g., endowments and annuities). Less commonly, governments extend concessions to policies whose purposes are exclusively or predominantly to provide death benefits. Governments frequently deny tax concessions when citizens purchase otherwise qualifying policies from unlicensed insurance firms.

The tax treatment of premiums paid by employers on employee life and health insurance is important. The general rule internationally is that employer contributions for qualified employee benefit plans are tax deductible by the employer. Contributions often are not taxable to the employee, although this treatment varies by country. Many countries include employer-paid premiums in employee income. In several countries, certain types of employee contributions are tax deductible to the employee, especially when such contributions are compulsory.

### Living benefits

Living benefit payouts or accruals can be classified broadly into three categories. The first category comprises dividends (bonuses) under participating (with profits) contracts. The second category includes policy cash values and maturity amounts. Payouts under annuity contracts form the third category. In most countries, these types of payments exceed death-related payouts by life insurers.

### Dividends

As described in Chapter 21, life insurance policy dividends, at least in the early years of a policy, represent largely a return to the policyholder of a deliberate premium overcharge. In later policy years, dividends may be composed mostly of excess interest earnings and other favorable experience deviations. The general rule worldwide is that dividends are not considered as taxable income. Countries follow this practice because dividends are chiefly a return to the policyholder of his or her own funds and because of the complexity entailed in any attempt to identify the excess investment income component within dividends.

*Cash values*

Countries generally do not directly tax interest credited on policy cash values – the so-called "inside interest build-up." When taxed, the build-up is considered as part of benefits (e.g., Spain and Switzerland). Finland and Luxembourg exempt build-ups from income taxation. Laws in Canada, Germany and the U.S. prescribe that certain policies with high cash values in relation to the policy's death benefit or with unacceptably short durations may provoke taxation of the inside interest build-up.

One explanation for the generally favorable tax treatment of the inside interest build-up relates to the complexity involved in trying to do otherwise. Rather than attempt to tax policyholders on interest earnings within the policy, governments commonly adopt a measure of gain that is administratively simple and that reduces policyholder confusion and displeasure. It involves taxing policyholders only on policy maturity or surrender. At that time, tax is due only to the extent that the benefits received (the maturity amount or the cash value received plus the sum of dividends received) exceed the sum of the premiums paid under the policy. This difference, if positive, might be subject to income tax. Some countries do not tax even this gain. If the difference is negative, governments deem that no taxable event occurred, so no deduction is permitted against taxable income.

*Annuities*

Payments under annuity contracts are the third category of living benefits. The inside interest build-up of annuities during their accumulation period usually receives the same tax treatment as that of other life insurance products. Most countries seem to tax annuity payouts to some degree. In a few countries, a prescribed, fixed portion of each payment is subject to tax. Most countries prescribe various mechanisms by which the excess of payments received over premiums paid is taxed, usually on some type of pro rata basis over the annuity payout period.

*Death proceeds*

Most countries exempt death proceeds paid under qualifying life insurance policies from income taxation. Germany and the U.S. tax a portion of death proceeds under certain high cash value policies.

A cash value policy's death proceeds can be viewed as comprised partly of the cash value. As noted above, the interest component of the cash value typically would not have been taxed during the insured's lifetime. As it is not taxed on death, it can escape income taxation all together.

Governments commonly levy estate duties (taxes), measured on the deceased person's net wealth – assets minus liabilities. In most countries, life insurance death proceeds are subject to estate duties. In most of these instances, however, governments make provision for special circumstances that can result in proceeds being excluded, in whole or in part, from assessment. For example, death proceeds escape estate duties in the Netherlands if the beneficiary was responsible for premium payments. In the U.K., proceeds are estate-duty exempt if the benefits are held in trust for other beneficiaries. In the U.S. and other countries, death proceeds are excludable if the insured did not own the policy and proceeds were not payable to or for the direct benefit of the insured's estate. Some countries (e.g., Belgium, France, Germany, Italy, Ireland, Japan and Luxembourg) exclude proceeds from death duties, wholly or partially, if the beneficiary falls within certain classes of persons (e.g., a spouse or a direct relative).

## *Life insurance companies*

This section presents an overview of life insurer taxation. Such taxation is commonly of two types: (1) premium taxation and (2) net income or value added taxation.

### *Premium taxation*

Several OECD countries and perhaps most developing countries levy taxes on insurers' premium revenues. Premium taxes are the most common, but some countries levy stamp duties and other assessments. Life insurers are responsible for tax collection and payment in the great majority of countries. However, when the insured places life insurance with an unauthorized insurer, he or she may be responsible for tax payment.

Even when insurers are responsible for payment, such taxation is closely related to policyholder taxation, as insurers commonly add premium taxes to premium loading. Thus, premium taxation can affect price and the relative attractiveness of life insurance products.

Under the typical premium tax structure, the tax base is the simple total of the insurer's premium revenue, with certain adjustments. Premiums received for risks assumed through reinsurance usually are excluded from the tax base, because the ceding companies that originally sold the insurance already paid tax on their direct premiums. Also, most jurisdictions permit a deduction from the tax base for dividends paid to policyholders. The premium tax base may include premiums received for personal accident and health insurance, but more commonly governments tax them separately. Insurers' investment income is excluded from the tax base, and no deductions are permitted for expenses, claim payments or reserves.

Most countries do not levy premium taxes on annuity considerations. Even those countries that tax annuity considerations typically exempt contributions to qualified retirement annuity plans or tax them at a lower rate. Personal accident and health insurance premiums often are subjected to premium taxation or other premium-based assessments. Canada and the U.S. levy premium taxes for these insurance lines at the provincial and state level, respectively.

### *Income taxation and value added taxation*

Generally, governments tax life insurers on some variation of net income or value added and sometimes both. Value added taxation (VAT) seeks to tax companies on the basis of the value added by each of them in the production process. VAT is used in some markets in Europe and is gaining exposure in Latin America, although, as applied to life insurance, both theoretical and practical problems persist. With regard to net income taxation of life insurers, in the past, several countries based life insurer taxation on their investment income only, but the trend is toward using total income – that is, the sum of premium income, investment gain and other income – as the tax base. Determining life insurer profit is a challenge because of the differences in timing between premium payments and claim payments.

When using total income, governments permit several deductions in deriving taxable income. In addition to claims payments, other deductions typically include increases in policy reserves, acquisition and administrative expenses, policy dividends paid and premiums paid on ceded reinsurance. Governments may permit other deductions, and special rules may exist for loss carryovers and (domestic and foreign) branch income.

# Nonlife Insurance Taxation

The taxation of nonlife insurance is less complex than that found with life insurance. The difference is because most life insurance products sold worldwide involve an element of savings and most nonlife insurance products do not.

## Nonlife insurance consumers

The general rule internationally seems to be that premiums paid by individuals for personal nonlife insurance policies are not deductible from income for tax purposes. Exceptions exist. Germany permits a deduction for personal liability insurance premium payments. Luxembourg permits a similar deduction for premiums paid for certain liability insurance products. Premium payments by businesses to purchase compulsory insurance (e.g., workers' compensation and unemployment insurance) are commonly tax deductible. Payments by individuals to purchase insurance to cover professional or business pursuits (e.g., rental property) are generally treated as business expenses and thus deductible.

The general rule internationally for benefits received under personal nonlife insurance policies seems to be that they are received tax free. However, several governments levy taxes on liability claims payments made to the injured party (or his or her dependents) in compensation for loss of professional earnings. For benefits received by a business, the situation is often more complex. In many countries, such benefits are tax free. Other countries tax any financial gain from the benefit payment.

## Nonlife insurance companies

Nonlife insurers are subject to income taxation or VAT as well as to various forms of premium-based taxation. The discussion below highlights these two modes of taxation.

### Premium taxation

It appears that countries are less reluctant to impose premium taxation in nonlife insurance than in life insurance. Moreover, tax rates with nonlife insurance are generally higher. Of those countries that levy nonlife premium taxes, rates range from less than 1 percent (Japan) to a high of 50 percent (automobile liability insurance in Denmark). Most countries apply uniform tax rates to all nonlife lines. In selected countries, the rates vary by line of business (e.g., 1–4 percent in the U.S.).

Some governments levy other premium-based taxes that can greatly increase the effective tax in nonlife insurance. Examples of these less obvious but no less important forms of premium-based taxes are provided in Table 24.3.

Premium-based taxation is to be paid irrespective of insurer profitability. Although the rates are low in some countries, the taxation applies to a large tax base – typically gross premiums written minus reinsurance assumed. The effective tax on insurers and ultimately on policyholders can, therefore, be astoundingly high. These taxes, included in the premiums charged, raise insurance prices and thus depress nonlife insurance demand. To the extent that competing non-insurance techniques of dealing with risk escape such taxation, the competitive environment is biased against insurance.

**Table 24.3**    Examples of Other Premium-Based Taxes on Nonlife Insurance

| Category | Country | Charges |
| --- | --- | --- |
| Fire brigade taxes (levied on fire insurance premiums) | Australia | 8% in fire insurance |
| | Germany | Up to 8% in fire and business interruption insurance, insurance for nuclear installations, property all risks and householders' insurance |
| | Portugal | Up to 13% in fire insurance, householders' insurance, motor insurance, and insurance for goods in transit |
| | Spain | Up to 5% in nonlife insurance |
| | United Kingdom | £35 per £1 million of gross value of goods insured by fire insurance |
| | United States | 1–2% in selected states |
| Other indirect taxes (levied on certain nonlife lines) | Belgium | Up to 17.5% in motor insurance; 6.5% in fire insurance |
| | France | 15% of special contribution of motor liability insureds (as a social security budgetary resources) |
| | Hungary | 1% in most nonlife insurance |
| | Italy | Up to 15% in motor insurance for various parafiscal taxes; 1% in fire and theft insurance |
| | Spain | 5% in compulsory travel insurance for fund for the insurance of extraordinary risks |
| | United States | Up to 2% in selected states |

*Source*: Comité Européen des Assurances (2004).

*Income taxation and value added taxation*

Governments usually tax nonlife insurance companies as other corporations. The basis for taxation is value added or net income and sometimes both. Net income is revenues less deductions. Premiums earned and investment income (including realized capital gains) are the chief revenue sources. Insurer expenses (including commissions to agents), claims payments and increases in loss reserves are the main deductions.

The great majority of countries seem to allow deductions for claims reported but unpaid and certain other reserves. For instance, most of them permit a deduction for claims IBNR. IBNR claims deductions can be particularly important in some markets, such as the U.S., and for some insurers, such as reinsurers, where liability business constitutes a significant portion of insurers' business. Some countries permit tax deductions for general contingency or catastrophe reserves, although the trend is toward their elimination.

The tax rates in most countries are the same as those applicable to other corporations and as for life insurers. Exceptions to this generalization apply with mutual insurers in some countries. A few countries tax them (or some of their insurance lines) on a more favorable basis than that applicable to other corporations (e.g., France, New Zealand, Spain, and the U.K.).

# CONCLUSION

This chapter has highlighted variations in insurance regulatory and tax philosophy and practice internationally. These variations reflect different traditions, cultures and political and economic systems.

At this stage of our knowledge about the effects of regulation on markets and product value, we cannot with much certainty assert which approaches are preferred to others. We can, however, observe that some approaches deviate more substantially from the competitive model and interfere with business and individual decision-making more than others. In the absence of a compelling case that stricter and more intensive regulation results in greater consumer welfare than a lighter approach, less rather than more government intervention into insurance markets becomes the default position. This general principle is of only limited help as governments and markets struggle with the issue of the optimal nature and degree of regulation.

# DISCUSSION QUESTIONS

1. "The influence of interest rates on the trend in insolvency is not clear *a priori*, however, as two opposite effects exist. On the one hand, assets lose value when interest rates rise, which means that solvency is reduced. If a company in this situation is forced to dispose of assets in order to pay claims, it can get into payment difficulties. On the other hand, high interest rates also mean high current income from investments. High interest rates when a contact is arranged make it possible to reduce prices (this is known as "cash flow underwriting"). If interest rates fall and current investment income declines, the overall result deteriorates and the risk of insolvency increases (Swiss Re, 1995)."

   Discuss which of these two effects you believe would be the more important. Why?
2. In the U.K. and Germany, no more than 10 percent of the earnings attributable to a stock life insurer's participating (with bonuses) business may be distributed to shareholders. France limits such distributions to 15 percent of investment gains and 10 percent of all other gains. Italy limits distributions to 20 percent of investment gains. By contrast, the Netherlands and most states in the U.S. have no similar restrictions:
   (a)  What public policy arguments support limitations on such distributions?
   (b)  Why do believe that the Netherlands and many other countries have not such limitations?
3. Signatory countries to the GATS bind themselves to the fair-trade principles of market access, nondiscrimination, national treatment and transparency. GATS's purpose is to create a more liberal market in trade in services in general and in financial services, including insurance, in particular. A provision within the agreement reads as follows (Annex to Financial Services, Article 2a):

   > [member countries] shall not be prevented from taking measures for prudential reasons, including for the protection of policyholders . . . or to ensure the integrity and stability of the financial system.

   (a)  What is your interpretation of this provision?
   (b)  Do you believe that this provision is justifiable in view of a competitive insurance market internationally? Why or why not?
   (c)  The provision is quite general. Could you imagine that some countries might try to place a conservative interpretation of this provision and, if so, what measures might they take that you would believe to be inconsistent with the spirit of the provision?

    (d) Could insurance be the cause of a country's financial system loosing its integrity and stability? If so, how? Justify your answer.
4. Explain why insurance is regulated.
5. Examine the insurance act in your country to answer the following:
    (a) What is the relationship between the insurance regulator and the government?
    (b) Summarize the key provisions related to licensing insurers, reinsurers and insurance intermediaries. Does the act include a "fit-and-proper person" provision or equivalent?
    (c) What information are insurance companies required to submit to the regulator?
    (d) Do you find any sections relating to anti-competitive practices in the insurance industry?
    (e) What are the steps that the regulator is empowered to take against insurance companies experiencing extreme financial or operational difficulty?
6. Analyze the premium tax using the desirable traits of tax systems.
7. Economies in transition have expressed interest in the possibility of stimulating the purchase of life insurance through tax concessions to its purchase.
    a. Why might such countries want to promote the purchase of life insurance?
    b. Would you expect such tax concessions to lead to increased sales of life insurance? Why?
    c. What effect might such tax concessions have on savings through other financial intermediaries and through government?

## NOTES

1. This chapter draws from Skipper (1998), Chapters 11 and 12.
2. This section draws, in part, from Black and Skipper (2000) and Angerer (1993).
3. The concept of a solvency margin was first introduced in 1946 in the U.K. It provided that total assets for a nonlife insurer should exceed total liabilities by 20 percent of the premiums written. This approach was adopted in many other countries, including Australia, Malaysia, Singapore and Thailand, to name but a few.
4. This section draws, in part, from Angerer (1993) and Swiss Re (1992).
5. Many are aware of the 2004 investigation by the state of New York of the alleged bid rigging activities and market placement agreements by the world largest brokerage firm, Marsh & McLennan and its business partners including AIG, ACE and Zurich America.
6. U.S. insurers and reinsurers are exempted from much of U.S. *federal* but not individual *state* competition law by the McCarran-Ferguson Act.
7. Many U.S. and probably other nations' regulators use rehabilitation less because they believe recovery is likely than as an intermediate step before moving insurers into liquidation, so as to reduce publicity and a possible mass withdrawal of business.

## REFERENCES

Angerer, A. (1993). "Insurance Supervision in OECD Member Countries," *Policy Issues in Insurance*. Paris: OECD.

Black Jr., K. and Skipper Jr., H.D. (2000). *Life and Health Insurance*, 13th edn. Englewood Cliffs, NJ: Prentice Hall.

CEA (Comité Européen des Assurances) (2004). *Indirect Taxation of Insurance Contracts in Europe*. Paris: CEA.

Harrington, S.E. (1992). "Presidential Address: Rate Suppression." *Journal of Risk and Insurance*, 59:185–202.

Skipper, H.D. (1998). *International Risk and Insurance: An Environmental-Managerial Approach*. Boston, MA: Irwin/McGraw-Hill.

Swiss Re (1992), "Competition Law – Increasing Significance for the Insurance Sector," *Sigma*. Zurich: Swiss Re (1995). "Development of Insolvencies and the Importance of Security in the Insurance Industry." *Sigma*. Zurich: Swiss Re.

# Chapter 25

# Financial Services Integration

## INTRODUCTION

Historically, insurance organizations sold insurance, banks stuck to traditional banking services, and securities firms dealt with stocks, bonds and related advice and instruments. Within the past several years, however, we have been witnessing a trend toward financial services integration – also known as convergence – whereby actors in one financial sector have sought to enter other financial sectors.[1]

This chapter summarizes and synthesizes the current knowledge and opinions on these and related issues. We begin with a discussion of the many meanings ascribed to the phrase "financial services integration." We then offer a summary of the existing economic literature on the subject and of the key issues that managers of integrated companies face. To provide context, there follows an overview of financial services integration in selected countries. Next we attempt to classify and summarize the numerous public policy concerns that have been raised with integration. The chapter closes with some speculations about the future of financial services integration.

## MEANINGS AND FORMS OF INTEGRATION

As discussed in Chapter 8, insurance companies, depository institutions and securities firms comprise the three major classes of financial intermediaries. More specialized intermediaries include mutual funds and pension funds. In many markets, other specialized intermediaries such as finance companies, real estate investment trusts and mortgage companies exist. While intermediaries compete in asset management and risk management, all specialize.

### The Meaning of Financial Services Integration

The term financial services integration is subject to multiple meanings, and we need to be clear about how it is used. Additionally, because firms offering integrated financial services can be structured in multiple ways, we should understand these different structural possibilities.

**Financial services integration** occurs when a financial service traditionally associated with one of the three main financial sectors is produced or distributed by companies in another financial sector. It occurs at one of three levels: (1) supplier, (2) product or (3) advice. Terms such as *bancassurance, allfinanz,* universal banks and financial conglomerates are all used to convey some notion of integration at the supplier level. Terminology, however, is not yet standard, so these terms carry different meanings for different people and markets:

- The French term ***bancassurance*** commonly refers to banks selling insurance products and usually vice versa. Occasionally, the term ***assurfinance*** is used to signify banking products being marketed through traditional insurance distribution channels. *Bancassurance* is likely the best known form of integration. It is commonly found in at least four forms: (1) distribution agreements, (2) buying or creating an insurance agency, (3) joint ventures and (4) strategic alliances or joint marketing arrangements.

- The German term ***allfinanz*** usually is synonymous with *bancassurance*. However, it sometimes suggests integration via distribution across all three major financial services industries, as does *bancassurance* at times.

- **Universal banks** are most commonly thought of as a financial institution that combines production and distribution of commercial and investment banking within a single firm. Universal banks usually are thought of as representing a greater degree of integration. Some universal banks distribute insurance but through a separate subsidiary.[2]

- As noted in Chapter 8, a *financial conglomerate* is commonly defined as any group of companies under common management control whose predominant activities are to provide significant services in two or more of the three major financial services sectors. The definition of a financial conglomerate within the E.U.'s conglomerate directive requires the conglomerate to include an insurance firm and at least one financial intermediary from another financial sector.

The degree of integration may range from shallow to deep. Consider two groups of companies that are identical from a legal point of view. Each group is composed of a non-operating holding company that owns a bank and an insurer. In one group, the bank and insurance firm are managed as separate profit centers, with no effort made to integrate overall management and operations. Activities are aligned precisely with legal form. The other group has global control functions allowing management and operations at the group level. Activities align with target markets, not legal form. Profit centers cut across sectoral lines.

In this scenario, both groups, which are *de facto* conglomerates, might sell the same portfolio of products. Hence, this dimension of production is indistinguishable. They are, however, managed quite differently. The latter group is more integrated, expecting that economies can be secured through operational integration.

A conglomerate that is predominantly commercially or industrially oriented and has a financial services subsidiary (other than a captive insurer) does not meet the definition of financial conglomerate. Such a conglomerate headed by an unregulated non-financial company with a regulated financial services entity in the vertical corporate structure is commonly referred to as a **mixed conglomerate**.

The other two types of financial services integration occur through product integration or advisory integration. When permitted, financial services firms in one sector may create and sell products containing elements that have traditionally been associated with products of another financial services sector. This is known as **product integration**. Unit-linked annuities and variable life insurance, for example, combine elements of insurance and securities. Securitization of banks' asset cash flows – for example, mortgages, credit card balances and other debt portfolios – combines key elements of securities and banking. Alternative risk transfer techniques such as catastrophe options, bonds and equity puts; standby letters of credit (contingency capital); and finite insurance and reinsurance are other examples. Money market mutual funds, offered by securities firms, are effectively demand deposit accounts. This product convergence trend can be expected to be an important force toward operational integration of financial services.

   **Advisory integration** of financial services occurs at the level of the advisor, without necessarily any supply-side integration or even cooperation. Accountants, attorneys, risk management consultants, insurance intermediaries, brokers, financial planners and other personal and corporate advisors often effectively integrate financial services for their clients. They may sell products themselves, or direct the client's purchasing behavior based on an integrated financial or risk management plan. Integration also occurs when employers or affinity groups offer a range of financial products to employees or group members, as, for example, when an employer offers a cafeteria of employee benefits that may be self-funded or funded through an insurance firm or another financial intermediary.

   For purposes of this chapter, we focus on integration at the supplier level. Thus, product and advisory integration receive scant attention here, although we recognize the importance of this type of integration.

## Structures for Delivering Integrated Financial Services

Integrated financial services may be delivered through several structural forms. We adopt the scheme that Saunders and Walter (1994) used and classify the structural forms into the following five groups:

- *Full integration*: The most fully integrated operational form is one wherein all financial services are produced (underwritten) within and distributed by a single corporation, and all activities are supported by a single capital base. Figure 25.1 illustrates this form. Full integration, which probably exists presently only in theory, provides a schema for thinking about the issues associated with regulation and management of financial conglomerates that, while separate sectorally for legal and regulatory purposes, may be operationally integrated. Full integration could represent a future structure of large financial services firms.

- *Universal bank (German variant)*: German universal banks, a step removed from the fully integrated firm above, represent the next structural form of integration. As illustrated in Figure 25.2, universal banks combine commercial and investment banking within a single corporation but conduct other financial services activities through separately capitalized subsidiaries owned by the bank. The German *grossbanken* ("big banks") – for example, Deutsche Bank, Dresdner Bank and Commerzbank – are organized in this way. Large Swiss banks also are structured in this fashion, as are many other continental European financial institutions.

- *Bank or insurer parent*: The third structural variation of financial conglomerates is one in which the parent company is a bank or an insurance firm. The parent firm thus produces financial services for its sector and owns one or more separately capitalized

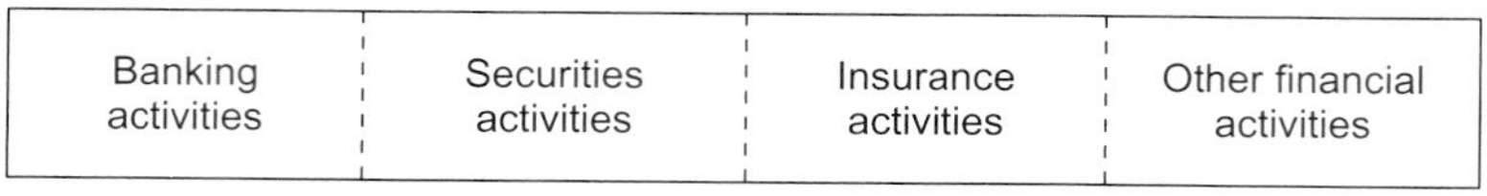

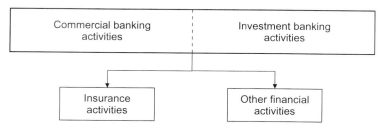

**Figure 25.1**    Full Financial Services Integration

**Figure 25.2**    Partial Financial Services Integration (Universal Bank, German Variant)

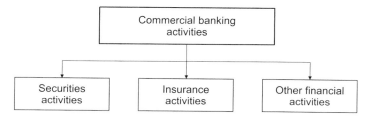

**Figure 25.3**    Financial Services Integration via Bank Ownership

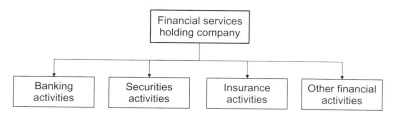

**Figure 25.4**    Integrated Financial Services via a Holding Company

subsidiaries that produce other financial services. Figure 25.3 illustrates this approach, with the bank as the parent. This structure is common in the U.K., with Barclays and Lloyds TBS being examples.

- *Holding company arrangement*: The fourth form of financial conglomerate is via a holding company arrangement. Typically, a non-operational holding company owns all or most of the shares in separately incorporated and capitalized sectoral subsidiaries. Figure 25.4 illustrates this form. This arrangement is the evolving model for the U.S.

- *Joint venture and other arrangements*: Another form through which integrated financial services are provided involves joint venture and other similar arrangements between unaffiliated financial services companies. In such structures, two financial intermediaries – such as a bank and an insurance firm – form a joint venture firm, strategic alliance, joint marketing arrangement or other formal arrangement through which one or both firms' products are sold. Joint venture arrangements in which insurance companies enter with banking institutions are popular in China (life insurance), India and Korea.

A myriad of factors influences the structure adopted in delivering integrated financial services. The historical context of a country's financial services market and its legal and regulatory environments are critically important. Issues such as market power, economies of scale and scope, operating efficiencies and how best to address conflicts of interest can be equally influential factors.

# THE ECONOMICS OF INTEGRATION

We now explore our existing understanding of the economics of integration. Integration is economically logical if it results in greater value. One means of viewing this issue is to consider stock market reactions to the announcement of cross-industry mergers and acquisitions. A positive reaction suggests an expectation of enhanced profitability.

In a study of 54 merger and acquisition deals covering 14 European banking markets, the researchers (Cybo-Ottone and Murgia, 2000) find positive gains in shareholder value in the case of average domestic bank-to-bank mergers and in bank-insurer deals but not in bank expansion into investment banking. In another study centered on the announcement of the Citicorp/Travelers merger, Carow (2001) finds that large banks and life insurers had significant share price increases, suggesting a market expectation of additional profitability accruing to these companies.[3] However, small banks, health insurers and nonlife insurers did not have such increases.

Another means of examining the economics of financial services integration is to conduct studies on the companies themselves. With this approach, we hypothesize that higher profits could flow from a reduction in operating costs, an increase in revenues or any combination that yields increased firm value (e.g., revenues increasing more rapidly than costs).

The above observations imply that the effects of financial services integration can be examined based on the following three analyses:

- cost effects;
- revenue effects;
- profit efficiency.

## Cost Effect Analysis

Financial services conglomerates could enjoy cost advantages through realizing (1) economies of scale, (2) economies of scope in production or (3) operational efficiencies.

### *Economies of scale*

**Economies of scale** exist if the average cost of production falls with increasing output, holding product mix constant. Economies of scale, in themselves, would not seem to justify the formation of multi-sectoral financial companies, although they may justify existing conglomerates growing larger. Studies provide some evidence for scale economies from the 1980s and the early 1990s for financial conglomerates, but not for very large institutions. For example, a study of the world's largest banks, including several universal banks, found economies of scale only in the middle range of big banks (Saunders and Walter, 1994). Growing from US$1 billion to $10 billion in assets seems to gain scale, but growing from US$10 billion to $100 billion seems to gain little.[4]

Other work suggests that a historically more favorable European regulatory environment may contribute to the different results for European financial services companies. For example, Vander Vennet (2002) finds that a large sample of European universal banks and other financial conglomerates enjoyed neither scale benefits nor disadvantages. This finding suggests that the minimum efficient scale for such financial institutions, as least in Europe, has increased since the earlier studies and that diseconomies of scale pose few problems to further growth.

### *Economies of scope in production*

**Economies of scope in production** exist if multiple products can be produced at less cost than the sum of the costs of producing each separately. Economies of scope could be important in financial services integration because of the ability to share overhead, technology and other fixed costs across a range of products. For instance, the fixed costs of managing a client relationship would seem to lend themselves to sharing across a broad range of financial services (Herring and Santomero, 1990).

Scope economies could come about from:

- investment operations (having a single investment unit for all industries of operation);
- information technology (having customer databases consolidated and available for multiple uses including data mining);
- distribution (using distribution channels established for one sector to sell products of another sector);
- reputation (the good reputation of one firm – for example, a bank – enhancing the sale of other conglomerate products).

As with studies on economies of scale, most scope studies are on U.S. single-sector financial services companies, finding that, where they exist, they are exhausted at fairly low levels of output. However, most studies were conducted over periods during which they were undergoing great change, perhaps incurring substantial sunk costs that may have distorted results.

Diseconomies of scope are not unlikely. Financial conglomerates are large companies with substantial bureaucracies. They may suffer from inertia and an inability to respond quickly to changing markets or customer demand. They may lack creativity, experience "turf" battles, realize internal compensation conflicts that erode synergy, and suffer from serious internal cultural differences across industries that inhibit cooperation and coordination necessary for synergy (Walter, 1997).

Also, not all customers will want to purchase financial products from a single conglomerate. They may be concerned about being treated impersonally, about a large firm not passing lower costs of operation to its smaller customers, about having their financial purchases concentrated within a single group (and foregoing diversification) or about use of personally identifiable information within the conglomerate family to the customer's detriment.

## *Operational efficiencies*

Economies of scale and scope are static efficiency concepts, with studies focusing on size and product mix cost effects for a given time frame. *Dynamic efficiency*, involving product and process innovations and other operational efficiencies (also called X-efficiencies), can be even more important. Financial conglomerates might have an informational advantage over specialized firms in that they can more quickly develop products in response to changing technological or market conditions, especially products carrying attributes of multiple sectors. Indeed, several studies have found that technical inefficiencies (excess use of inputs) and allocative inefficiencies (suboptimal input mix) are large and dominate scale and scope economies.[5]

Considerable effort has gone into the measurement of X-efficiency of financial institutions. From a survey of 130 studies on efficiency that covered 21 countries and used various efficiency and measurement methods, it appears that the average unit costs in banking range from 20 to 25 percent above the costs of best practice firms (Berger and Humphery, 1997). Understandably, comparatively few efficiency studies have been conducted of financial conglomerates. One such study (Vander Vennet, 2002) suggests that universal banks enjoyed significantly higher average levels of operational efficiency than specialized banks and that this finding is most pronounced for other-than-German universal banks.

## Revenue Effect Analysis

Two aspects of financial services integration could give rise to important revenue effects which are given below.

## *Economies of scope in consumption*

Integration may enhance the earnings potential of a financial conglomerate through distribution of a greater product – so-called **economies of scope in consumption** (i.e., demand-side economies of scope). They could follow from the cross-marketing of investment, savings, credit and insurance products. Many financial products are complements: mortgage loans and mortgage protection life insurance policies; automobile loans and automobile insurance; and wrap accounts and investment products. Customers could realize lower search, information, monitoring and transaction costs by purchasing products from a conglomerate than by purchasing the same array of products from specialty companies. Private banking always has been designed to exploit such economies.

These economies may not entail lower priced products. In fact, if such consumption economies exist, customers presumably would be willing to pay more for products offered in this convenient way and the resulting costs may actually be higher, but presumably revenues would be higher still. Evidence of such economies exists, although the literature is thin.[6]

## *Market power*

Large size can convey *market power* – the ability to affect price. It can result from concerted practices among competitors that restrain competition, such as market sharing arrangements, pricing collusion or exclusive dealings. It also can evolve through predatory pricing.

Market power also can arise from size alone if barriers to entry are great. In fact, regulation can be the source of market power for incumbent companies, as when government creates unreasonable barriers to entry for new competitors or mandates price controls (as in mandating interest rates on demand deposits or premiums for insurance policies). Until the 1990s, for example, many countries strictly limited access to their financial services markets, especially by foreign companies, and sheltered highly concentrated markets. Government-sanctioned market power flows naturally in such markets.

When barriers to entry exist in a country and its financial services market tends toward oligopoly, financial conglomerates may be able to charge higher prices, at least to some market segments, than they would in a more competitive, less concentrated market. In exercising their market power, such conglomerates would enhance their revenue (or at least profit) stream.

With the deregulation and liberalization trend worldwide, such markets seem likely to be the exception rather than the norm even in developing economies. With fewer barriers to entry, more competitive markets with fewer opportunities to gain market power should evolve.

## Profit Efficiency Analysis

A conglomerate could incur greater costs (resulting in cost inefficiency) yet realize greater revenues (from revenue efficiency) such that net profits increased. The reverse is also possible. Both cost and revenue effects are factored in measuring profit efficiency.

Studies of profit efficiency tend to be sector specific. One study on conglomerates, Vander Vennet (2002) finds that European universal banks (except for those in Germany) were more profit efficient than non-universal banks. The author suggests that the trend toward cross-financial services specialization could lead to a more efficient banking system.

## Relationship between Effects and Operational Structure

If integration yields positive microeconomic cost effects, one would expect that conglomerates move toward production and operational integration. Back-office operations such as investment, accounting, information technology, risk management and the like would more likely be the basis for realizing economic gains. Synergies would likely relate to both the corporate and retail markets.

If integration yields positive microeconomic revenue effects, one would expect to find financial services integration more toward distribution. It may be that little or nothing is gained by production and operational integration. In such instances, *bancassurance* or similar arrangements, with or without affiliation, would be sufficient. Synergies would likely relate more to the retail than to the corporate market.

# MANAGEMENT ISSUES IN INTEGRATION

The preceding discussion highlighted several challenges associated with financial services integration but did so in the terminology of the economist. This section translates some of those economic concepts into practical management concerns. They are shown in Figure 25.5 and discussed below.

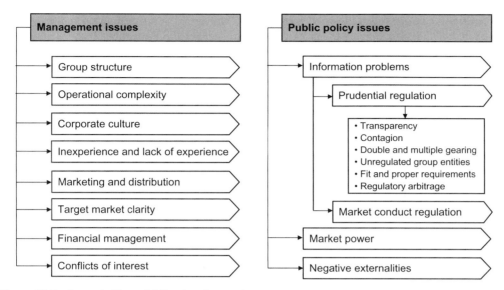

**Figure 25.5**    Issues in Financial Services Integration

## Group Structure

After establishing the group's mission and strategy, management must decide on the most desirable operational structure. We can distinguish between *de jure* (law-based) and *de facto* (fact-based) structures. The formal structure of a group of companies must comply with legal requirements (e.g., conducting insurance operations through an insurance subsidiary). However, this need not necessarily dictate the operational structure. In fact, adopting the legal structure as the operational basis could fail to capture hoped-for economies, as alluded to earlier.

Group structure decisions also relate to whether the necessary manufacturing platforms for financial services will be acquired or created *de novo*. Such decisions need not be the same from market to market or from one period to the next. In general, organic (greenfield) growth of the platform leads to fewer cultural difficulties and allows operations to be oriented quickly and efficiently toward the group's mission.

On the one hand, many observers believe that organic growth has been more successful than growth through acquisition. On the other hand, organic growth means that the group needs time to be a major player within a country's financial services market. If, as many financial conglomerates believe, being among the five or so largest financial institutions in the market is important for operational efficiency and profitability, organic growth may not be the best choice. This is especially true in mature markets where consolidation has already been well under way and opportunities for acquisitions abound. As such, organic growth tends to be more common in emerging markets than in mature markets.

## Operational Complexity

Integrated financial services companies are complex operations. This observation seems especially relevant when integration is accomplished via merger or acquisition. Such complexity is not associated solely with consolidation. It has been observed that long-established European universal banks consistently subsidize unprofitable activities, seem reluctant to outsource nonessential operations and rarely excel or become innovative in any one sector. Many are said to operate with a "silo" mentality. These observations may explain why these European banks achieve a lower return on equity than U.S. commercial banks. Some observers even contend that no European investment banks are capable of competing with large U.S. institutions (Kraus, 1998) such as Morgan Stanley, Goldman Sachs, Bankers Trust or JPMorgan Chase.

The problem of complexity seems largely to be ignored at present. As reported in *European Banker* (1999), it is as if consolidation and being big were not just necessary but sufficient conditions for success in financial services. Again, if the professional press is accurate, this seems particularly true for Europe's universal banks. From examining annual reports of Europe's 50 largest banks, Lafferty Business Research finds only one bank that questioned whether merger and consolidation were the appropriate answers to the advent of the European Monetary Union. Banco Popular, perhaps prophetically, was quoted in *European Banker* (1999) as follows:

> It is, to say the least, surprising that there should be such widespread and critical [sic] acceptance of this need, with no precise distinction between types of business and without meticulous analysis of the many drawbacks that these processes may involve and of the problematic nature of their purported advantages.

## Corporate Cultures

Corporate cultures vary across firms and across industries. They can lead to potentially crippling management problems. The investment bank corporate culture is one of entrepreneurship, market risk taking and incentive compensation. The commercial banking culture is one of relationship building, credit risk taking, stability and compensation schemes less related to performance. The insurance culture is bi-polar. Life insurance is associated with aggressiveness, marketing innovation, consultative selling and incentive compensation. The nonlife insurance culture falls between that of life insurance and commercial banking. Nonlife products are largely demand-pull, not demand-push products like life insurance.

These cultural differences pose challenges for management of financial conglomerates, especially those resulting from merger and acquisition. For instance, a frequently reported difficulty with *bancassurance* is indifference by bank employees to insurance. They treat such products as sidelines or as too complex to sell within the traditional banking relationship. Indeed, one-half of all mergers and acquisitions are unsuccessful, with the most frequently cited reason for failure being cultural differences (Tuohy, 1999). Cultural differences seem less of an obstacle when integration is organic.

Another dimension of corporate culture seems to be related to national differences in management dedication to shareholder value. This is a principal-agent agency problem. In a study touching on this issue, it was found that European banks clustered around two distinct business approaches: (1) focused banks and (2) universal banks (*European Banker*, 1999).

Focused banks operate within a culture of shareholder value, use internationally accepted accounting principles and have a sharper focus on retail banking operations. Universal banks, in contrast, operate within a managerial culture, follow inferior accounting practices that prevent shareholders from gaining an accurate picture of the business, and believe in universal banking as a concept. Lafferty Business Research finds that the boundary between the two groups is blurred, in constant movement and rapidly losing its geographic consistency.

---

INSIGHT 25.1: *BANCASSURANCE* COMPROMISE IN ING ─────────

The situation of ING – the first large-scale merger of a bank and an insurer – offers an example. ING was formed in 1991 by the merger of the insurance group Nationale-Nederlanden (NN) and the banking group NMB-Postbank which was itself a result of a 1989 merger between two important Dutch banks. At the time, NN was the largest insurance group and NMB-Postbank was the third largest banking group in the Netherlands.

   In announcing the merger, NN indicated that it would design special insurance products to be sold through Postbank. Such products would compete with and be less expensive than those sold by NN's army of independent agents, which accounted for some 85 percent of NN's sales. Their agents promised a boycott. Only after agreeing to limit Postbank distribution to very simple products, such as travel accident insurance and certain types of annuities, was the boycott canceled (Van den Berghe and Verweire, 1998). The channel conflict for ING has since eased but remains a challenge for the group in the Dutch market, arguably causing the group to forgo some demand-side economies of scope.

---

## Inexperience and Lack of Expertise

Inexperience in managing an integrated financial services group can pose vexing problems at the early stage of integration. This issue is particularly relevant in markets where financial services integration was unprecedented because of either market philosophy or regulatory prohibitions, such as in the U.S. and Eastern Europe. Financial conglomerates from other countries, particularly from Western Europe, may have a competitive advantage over domestic financial institutions in such markets.

   Joint ventures and strategic alliances between domestic and experienced foreign companies may prove most appealing to both domestic and foreign entrants. Although foreign financial conglomerates have greater knowledge and insights into how to make integration work, local companies have a competitive advantage in understanding the local culture and in local relationships. For example, in the Indian insurance market (see Chapters 21 and 22), we find a number of insurers where a local non-insurance Indian firm jointly partners with a foreign insurance firm, such as ING Vysya (insurer-bank) and ICICI Prudential (insurer-investment firm) in the life business and IFFCO-Tokyo (bank-insurer) and Royal Sundaram (insurer-investment) in the nonlife business.

## Marketing and Distribution

Distribution issues can be among the most challenging for management of integrated financial institutions, especially those groups created via merger and acquisition. The concern, of course, is that marketing intermediaries, especially agents and brokers that have been the primary distribution outlet for one of the formerly independent institutions, face the possibility of disintermediation by new channels, such as a bank branches, direct response or the Internet. The situation of ING, the first large-scale merger of a bank and an insurer, offers an example (see Insight 25.1).

Channel conflict, however, seems to be less of a management challenge for *de novo* operations. The creation of Deutsche Lebensversicherungs AG by Deutsche Bank and the creation of Predica by Credit Agricole are good examples of this. Similarly, consolidation occurring between affiliated companies such as integration of direct writers seems to reduce potential channel conflict. Integration of distribution channels between USAA Life and USAA (U.S.) and between Maybank Life and Maybank (Malaysia) are two examples. Also, channel conflict can be less of a managerial challenge in countries with less mature financial services markets.

Marketing issues are associated largely with demand-side economies of scope. As such, they usually are of greater concern with *bancassurance* integration than others, especially those related to investment, risk management and other back-office integration possibilities. As described above, exceptions exist.

## Target Market Clarity

Management must be clear about the group's target market. History is littered with attempts at financial services integration that were unsuccessful largely because of ambiguity in this regard. When Prudential (U.S.) acquired Bache in 1981, it was expected that Prudential (with its largely blue collar, lower middle-income target market) and Bache (with its largely white collar, upper-income target market) would cross-market each other's products. That the experiment failed is unsurprising, in retrospect.

To date, most success in financial services integration has been in the retail market. Within the retail sector, greatest success has been with middle and lower-income markets. The affluent market seems largely to be the province of financial planners and independent agents and brokers. For instance, it was predicted several years ago that *bancassurers* would capture one-third of the U.K. life insurance market. Their share today is still about 10 percent. Independent financial advisors, by contrast, now dominate the market in terms of premium revenue. These advisors have expanded their own product offerings; in effect, offering integration at the advisory level and blunting bank distribution.

In selecting the target market, management must determine the classes of products to be offered. The emphasis can be on the retail market, the corporate market or both. Different demographic, economic and geographic emphasis must be taken with each broad market segment.

Management also should decide which asset accumulation, debt management and asset protection products to manufacture and through which channels to distribute them. In this connection, an issue confronting all financial conglomerates is the extent to which it is better to manufacture the desired product or to market other institutions' products through their distribution channels.

Management of some financial conglomerates is seemingly concerned that some financial products carry the potential of creating diseconomies of scope. Nonlife insurance is perhaps the most commonly discussed product line in this regard. An insightful story is that of a superb banking customer taking her entire account elsewhere because the group's insurer denied automobile insurance to her 17-year old son who had two speeding tickets. What is the anticipated effect on a good securities customer of being dissatisfied with a property insurance claim settlement? The divestiture by Citigroup of its Travelers (nonlife) insurance subsidiary in 2002 – after only three years as a Citicorp subsidiary – speaks directly to this point. Many conglomerates have chosen to avoid the manufacture of nonlife insurance for reasons of this type, with some not even making it available via marketing arrangements.

## Financial Management Issues

Financial management is a core competency for financial institutions and conglomerates interested in manufacturing their own products and services. Two areas of financial management seem to be particularly important:

- *Enterprise risk management*: Only in the past 10 years or so have risk management issues been addressed in anything resembling an integrated way by financial institutions (see Chapter 12). Integrated risk management activities, however, have been observed chiefly within individual companies, not across companies within a group, with some notable exceptions. It is in part because of the differences in product lines and in industries within the financial services industry. Pricing risk, credit risk, market risk, operating risk and many other risks vary greatly from product to product and from sector to sector. For example, interest rate risk for a securities firm ordinarily is far less important than it is for a life insurer.

  A challenge for risk management of financial conglomerates is, first, to understand the risk profile of the group as a whole rather than its parts in isolation. Second, management must develop risk management policies and techniques appropriate for the entirety of the group. If synergies are to be realized through integration, one would fully expect them to arise, among other places, through a holistic approach to measuring and managing risk.

- *Performance appraisal*: Insurers, banks and securities firms have used different performance appraisal techniques. Banks historically have focused on interest spread, with return on equity of more recent importance. Life insurers increasingly use embedded value analysis – the value inherent in the insurer's existing and future business. Nonlife insurers use combined and operating ratios and return on equity. How are these diverse techniques to be reconciled, if at all, for the benefit of management and ultimately shareholders? This issue of how best to appraise the financial performance of the entire group is equally important in financial conglomerate operation.

## Conflicts of Interest

The potential for internal conflicts of interest between services providers and their clients is endemic to financial services integration. Conflicts of interest exist when incentives within a group do not align with customers' best interests. In this regard, Walter (1997) groups major conflicts of interest into five categories:

- *Salesperson's stake*: When one financial institution within a conglomerate has the power to sell affiliates' products, salespeople and managers of the institution may be less likely to offer objective product advice to customers. Rather, they will have a stake in pushing the conglomerate's products, possibly to the disadvantage of customers.

- *Stuffing fiduciary accounts*: When a financial institution that offers a client firm an underwriting service for its initial public offering expects a difficulty in placing the securities, the institution may attempt to minimize its loss by stuffing the unwanted securities into other accounts that its investment department manages and over which it has discretionary authority.

• *Bankruptcy risk transfer*: When a financial conglomerate, through its banking arm, for example, offers commercial loan and insurance services, the conglomerate may be able to secure private information that the bankruptcy risk of a client firm has increased. It may have an incentive to induce the client firm to issue bonds or equities – underwritten by the securities subsidiary of the conglomerate – to an unsuspecting public. Proceeds could be used to reduce the bank loan. This undesirable conduct effectively transfers the credit (loan default) risk of the banking arm to outside the group, while earning fees and generating underwriting spreads.

• *Tie-in sales*: A conglomerate could make available below-market loans to selected clients of its banking arm on the condition that those client firms use the proceeds to purchase products sold by other subsidiaries of the conglomerate, such as securities or life insurance.

• *Internal information transfer*: One unit of the conglomerate may secure material, private information about a customer that enables other units to charge higher prices than otherwise to that customer. (The result also could be lower prices.) For example, in underwriting a life insurance policy, the insurance arm of a group might discover that the proposed insured had a substantial health problem. Information about this problem might influence a reverse mortgage loan decision by the group's bank. Irrespective of whether the customer might suffer harm, the important issue of the extent to which he or she should be able to control the flow of personally identifiable information within a financial conglomerate remains an important public policy and corporate governance concern.

Incentive conflicts can be managed through regulation or by finding a market solution – rearranging the incentives to be more compatible with the desired result. Most universal banking systems are said to rely on market incentives. The U.S. historically has relied more heavily on regulation, including "firewalls" between activities potentially giving rise to incentive conflicts.

From a myopic management approach, building internal firewalls or creating other substantial limitations on information sharing within the group can be self-defeating. Preventing or mitigating the adverse effects of internal conflicts of interest is expensive. Training and monitoring systems are costly. However, reduction, if not elimination, of such conflicts is fundamental for the long-term survival of financial conglomerates and to the soundness of a financial system.

Management of reputational risk is an increasing concern. Conglomerates seek to instill a sense of professionalism and ethical conduct within salespeople and employees. Training, close supervision and internal monitoring are essential. Further, the group's reputation and competition act as disciplinary mechanisms. **Franchise** (a firm's market reputation) greatly affects **goodwill** (the value of future business) of the firm, as the accounting, market conduct and trading scandals in the late 1990s and the early 2000s demonstrated.

## PUBLIC POLICY CONCERNS IN INTEGRATION

Many observers and policymakers express concern about certain aspects of financial services integration.[7] The question is whether new or additional regulation is needed to protect consumers or the financial services system.

In considering this question, we should remind ourselves that financial services regulators are concerned primarily with three broad categories of market imperfections:

- *Information problems*: Government intervention is potentially justified to minimize the chances of consumers being harmed because of incomplete or misleading marketing or solvency problems.

- *Market power*: Firms seek to create market power and thus enhance profitability.

- *Negative externalities*: The question here is "will financial conglomeration increase the likelihood of cascading failures or runs".

The public policy question hence is whether financial conglomerates pose a greater risk to financial stability than do solo institutions. If they do, their failure could not only create greater harm to the real economy but also impose greater costs on taxpayers.

## Regulatory Interventions

As noted earlier, government regulation of financial intermediaries is justified when market imperfections could cause substantial economic harm to consumers or the economy and, importantly, government intervention can ameliorate the harm. Governments are not always capable of ameliorating harm.

As with insurance regulation, regulatory intervention regarding conglomerates falls into three categories: (1) prudential, (2) market conduct and (3) competition policy. *Prudential regulation* concerns the financial condition of the financial intermediary. Prudential regulation evolved primarily because of information problems and negative externalities (especially for banking). *Market conduct regulation* addresses the behavior of the financial intermediary and its agents in connection with the marketing of its products and services. Market conduct regulation evolved primarily because of information problems. *Competition policy (antitrust) regulation* concerns actions of financial intermediaries that have the effect of substantially lessening competition. It evolved because of market power concerns. Among these three categories of regulatory interventions, prudential regulation has been and remains the most critical element in government oversight of financial intermediaries.

In considering public policy issues that have arisen in connection with financial services integration, our focus is on only those public policy issues that arise from integration, not on issues of the type ordinarily dealt with by sectoral regulation alone.[8] The discussion is framed around the three classes of market imperfections and associated typical regulatory responses. Also see Figure 25.5 provided earlier in this chapter.

## Information Problems

This area addresses potential information problems that could accompany integration. The problems are clustered around prudential and market conduct regulation. As will be seen, prudential issues dominate.

### Issues in prudential regulation

At least six prudential issues can be identified as flowing from financial services integration. These issues are discussed below as if they were distinct from each other, for ease of exposition. Of course, they relate to each other, often intimately so. They include: (1) transparency,

(2) contagion, (3) double and multiple gearing, (4) unregulated group entities, (5) fit and proper requirements and (6) regulatory arbitrage.

### Transparency

Overarching all public policy concerns about financial services integration is the issue of group transparency. **Transparency** is about the extent to which accurate, complete, timely and relevant information about the financial group is readily available to regulators. Transparency also is sometimes considered as encompassing the availability of such information to other interested parties, such as customers (especially corporate customers), investors, rating agencies, marketing intermediaries and the general public. This form of transparency often is termed **disclosure**.

Transparency relates mainly, but not exclusively, to prudential concerns. Using the narrower definition, regulators are concerned about the possibility of opaque management, ownership and legal structures. If supervisors do not fully understand these structures, they may be unable to assess properly either the totality of the risks faced by the financial conglomerate or the risk that non-regulated members of the group may pose to the regulated members.

The structures of financial conglomerates vary greatly because of cultural, historic, tax, legal and regulatory considerations. Complexity is multiplied with such groups. Regulators are concerned that they be able to understand fully the lines of accountability relevant to their tasks. Large international financial conglomerates can be particularly complex, making effective regulation more difficult, especially with multiple national and international regulators. There is concern that some groups may choose complex structures to make their operations opaque in order to avoid or impede effective regulation. To avoid these problems, regulators must have the power to secure needed information from the group itself and from other regulators.

### Contagion

Contagion entails the risk that financial distress encountered by one unit in a financial conglomerate could have adverse effects on the financial stability of the group as a whole or possibly on the entire market in which the constituent parts operate (i.e., negative externalities). Hence, close monitoring of the relationships among entities in the group is of paramount importance. Adequate transparency minimizes the risk of contagion.

The Tripartite Group (1995) identified two types of contagion. The first is psychological in that the market effectively transfers problems associated with one part of a conglomerate to other parts. The financial difficulties of an insurer within the group may be perceived as threatening to the financial performance of the bank, for example, irrespective of whether the perception comports with reality.

The second type relates to intra-group exposures – direct or indirect claims of units within a conglomerate that are held by other conglomerate units. Some such exposures include:

- credit extensions or lines of credit between affiliates;
- cross-shareholdings;
- intra-group trading in securities;
- insurance or other risk management services provided by one unit for another;
- intra-group guarantees and commitments.

Intra-group exposures can have implications for both liquidity and group solvency. An example is a life insurer placing its premiums on deposit with its parent bank, a practice that might not be obvious to regulators. The Tripartite Group emphasized the importance that regulators be aware of all intra-group exposures and their specific purposes. In countries without a unified supervisory structure, close coordination among sectoral regulators is essential, especially when uncertainties arise. Each sectoral regulator should ensure that the pattern of activity and aggregate exposure between the regulated entity for which it is responsible and its affiliated companies do not pose contagion risk of any significance. Otherwise, the failure of an affiliated firm could undermine the regulated entity. The Tripartite Group admonished regulators to ensure that the capital of the regulated entity is increased or its activities limited if the risk that affiliated companies pose to the regulated entity appears to be unacceptable.

### Double and multiple gearing

**Double gearing**, also called **double leverage**, occurs whenever one entity holds regulatory capital issued by another entity within the same group, and the issuer is allowed to count the capital in its own balance sheet.[9] **Multiple gearing** (leverage) occurs when the subsidiary firm in the previous instance itself sends regulatory capital downstream to a third-tier affiliate. Double and multiple gearing are special classes of intra-group exposures and ordinarily are associated with the parent firm downstreaming capital to subsidiaries. The flow can be reversed or can be by a sister affiliate.

The principal issue concerning double and multiple gearing is less the ownership structure flowing from it and more the proper assessment of a financial conglomerate's consolidated capital. With double and multiple gearing, group capital derived directly from each entity's solo capital would be overstated. Consequently, assessments of group capital should exclude intra-group holdings of regulatory capital. For the most part, capital derived only from external sources provides support for the group.

The Joint Forum notes three methodologies – each for dominant holding, influential holding and other holding – used for adjusting financial data for double and multiple gearing.[10] These methodologies also accommodate the important issue of capital adequacy assessment for groups containing subsidiaries that are not wholly owned by the group.

### Unregulated group entities

Additional information problems stemming from financial services integration can occur when the group contains an unregulated entity; that is, one not subject to oversight by any financial services regulator. One such issue is excessive leveraging (Joint Forum, 1999 and 2001). **Excessive leveraging**, another class of intra-group exposure, can occur when an unregulated parent issues debt or other instruments not acceptable as regulatory capital in a downstream entity and downstreams the proceeds to a subsidiary firm in the form of equity or other regulatory capital. The subsidiary's effective leverage may be greater than appears on a solo basis. Such leverage is not inherently unsafe but can become so if undue stress is placed on the regulated subsidiary because of the parent's obligation to service the debt.

With an unregulated holding company, an assessment of group-wide capital adequacy should encompass the effect of the holding company's structure. Regulators should, therefore, obtain information about the holding company's ability to service all external debts.

Excessive leveraging as well as double and multiple gearing also can occur when the unregulated entity is an intermediate holding company. The group-wide capital assessment should eliminate the effect of such holding companies. Such intermediate holding companies typically are non-trading entities whose only assets are their investments in subsidiaries or that provide services to other companies.

Finally, some unregulated group entities conduct activities similar to those of regulated companies – for example, leasing, factoring and reinsurance. In such instances, a comparable or notional capital proxy may be estimated by applying to the unregulated entity the capital requirements of the most analogous regulated industry. Unregulated non-financial entities normally would be excluded from the assessment of the group.

### Fit and proper requirements

The probity and competence of the top management of insurance companies, banks and securities firms are critical to the achievement of regulatory objectives, particularly as relates to prudential aspects (Joint Forum, 1999). An effective and comprehensive supervisory regime should include controls designed to encourage the continued satisfaction of the fitness, propriety or other qualification tests of supervisors and to allow supervisory intervention where necessary. The application of such tests for managers, directors and key shareholders is a common regulatory mechanism to ensure that the institutions are operated in a sound and prudent manner.

The organizational and managerial structure of financial conglomerates adds complexity for supervisors seeking to ensure the fitness, propriety and other qualifications of the top management of regulated entities. The management of such entities can be influenced by individuals who may not be managers or directors of the regulated entities themselves. Thus, managers and directors of unregulated entities, such as those within an unregulated upstream holding company, can exercise a material influence over many aspects of the regulated entities' business (e.g., retired board chairperson with a significant ownership share). They also can play a key role in controlling risks in the various entities of the group.

Additionally, for regional and international financial conglomerates, issues of supervisory jurisdiction arise. A supervisor's reach may not extend beyond the national boundary. This raises the issue of the sharing of information among supervisors with respect to individuals (and companies, see below).

To address these concerns, the Joint Forum (1999) recommended that qualification tests should be applied to managers and directors of other entities in a conglomerate if they exercise a material or controlling influence on the operation of regulated entities. Tests should apply as well to individuals holding substantial ownership or being able to exercise material influence on regulated entities within the conglomerate.

### Regulatory arbitrage

Financial conglomerates should be expected to undertake their activities in ways that minimize their regulatory burdens and taxes. Of course, tax treatment, accounting standards, investment restrictions, capital adequacy requirements and other elements of regulation differ between types of financial intermediaries and across countries. To the extent that industry-specific regulations and taxation differ, arbitrage possibilities are created.

For example, regulations typically limit the maximum exposure that credit institutions may undertake with respect to a single client or group of related clients. In the E.U., loans or other exposures to a single client may not exceed 25 percent of a bank's free capital. In contrast, limitations on insurers' counterparty exposures generally are unrelated to their capital. Therefore, it is possible for an insurer's exposure to a single client to exceed 100 percent of its capital. Even in countries that subject all major types of financial intermediaries to capital-related limitations (e.g., the U.S.), they are rarely the same across different types of intermediaries. Similar examples are found with capital requirements in connection with other investments and products.

Arbitrage possibilities influence decisions about the structure of the group. If the parent firm is a regulated financial institution, as is common with banks in the U.K., the group itself could be subject to regulations applicable to that institution. The parent is fully subject to regulatory oversight. If the parent firm is an unregulated entity, many of its activities could pass outside regulatory scrutiny.

With continued globalization and convergence of financial services, the material differences in sector-specific and cross-country regulation will gradually disappear, as governments individually and collectively converge toward more common approaches.[11] In the interim, however, arbitrage is possible. In some instances, it may result in no meaningful weakening of regulation; in others, the opposite. The Tripartite Group (1995) believed that regulatory arbitrage in relation to core activities in most jurisdictions was rare. That there is scope for arbitrage, however, suggests that it must be considered carefully. The suggested solutions to this issue are to move toward consolidated financial regulation where such differences are eliminated, or to ensure that regulators cooperate fully with each other to identify and, if necessary, address such instances collectively.

### Issues in market conduct regulation

Market conduct regulation is the other major regulatory category intended primarily to address information problems. The information asymmetry problems here are conflicts of interest (i.e., agency problems). Concern has been expressed that conflicts of interest within integrated financial services groups might lead to deficiencies in market conduct. These conflicts of interest were discussed above in connection with management issues in financial conglomeration. Additionally, there may be greater scope for churning of a customer's investments within a conglomerate structure.

As between commercial and investment banking activities, most authorities seem to doubt the importance of such conflicts of interest. Many authorities note that financial services companies have strong reputational incentives to address these potential problems internally. As between insurance and banking activities, the same reputational incentives should apply. Besides, there have been comparatively few instances of bank/insurance tie-in sales.

To the extent that proper private incentives and appropriate management control are insufficient to address conflicts of interest, a regulatory response may be called for. Already, most potential conflicts are illegal.

## Market Power

The second major classification of market imperfections addressed by regulation is market power. Market power could, in theory, arise from size alone if barriers to entry are great. It also could evolve through predatory pricing.

An established, large conglomerate could sell at less than the cost of production if it wished to drive out smaller competitors or to discourage new entrants. As a practical matter, this option seems remote, provided there are not substantial barriers to entry. For every large national or multinational financial conglomerate that might attempt such practices, there are several others with the financial capacity to weather the storm. Existing competition law would seem to be sufficient, if enforced reasonably, to prohibit or punish concerted anti-competitive behavior by conglomerates. An exception could occur if the collusion occurred outside of a national market but with respect to that national market, such as by large international financial conglomerates.

## Negative Externalities

The third major classification of market imperfection addressed by financial services regulation is negative externalities. The principal negative externality is systemic risk, most commonly associated with commercial banking. The public policy question is whether financial service conglomerates pose a greater risk to system-wide financial stability than do solo institutions. If they do, as discussed earlier, their failure could both create greater harm to the real economy and impose greater costs on taxpayers.

### *Are financial conglomerates riskier?*

In an examination of the studies on the effects on risk and return of combining banking and non-bank financial activities, Kwan and Laderman (1999) conclude that both securities activities and insurance (agency and underwriting) generally are riskier and more profitable than banking. The literature suggests that such activities provide diversification benefits, with the result that they offer the potential to reduce bankruptcy risk.[12]

A much discussed issue is whether restrictions on commercial banks engaging in securities, insurance and real estate render national financial systems less efficient but more stable, as many policymakers have contended. Researchers have found no reliable statistical relationship between integration restrictiveness and level of economic development.[13] Interestingly, restrictions on banks' engaging in securities activities are associated with higher interest rate margins and greater likelihood of suffering a financial crisis, thus suggesting that integration at this level promotes efficiency and financial stability.

Hence, it appears that financial services integration could lead to a reduction in systemic risk. This hoped-for benefit, however, might not materialize if the smaller likelihood of failure (because of diversification) is accompanied by a much higher severity associated with those failures that do occur. That is, if financial services companies are larger because of integration (a likely result), their now-less-frequent failure might cause greater harm to the financial system. In turn, government authorities presumably would be more likely to take a "too-big-to-fail" (TBTF) position.

The TBTF policy creates substantial moral hazard problems. If customers (depositors, policyowners, creditors, etc.) believe that they will be made whole financially were the financial institution to fail, they have much less incentive to monitor the institution or to cease doing business with it even if it takes on more risk. In turn, managers, with shareholder approval, might take on greater risk than they would otherwise. Thus, it is possible that large financial conglomerates, contrary to research findings, could be riskier even in the face of diversification benefits. This increased riskiness would have stemmed, however, from an increase in the risk appetite of managers and shareholders, or brought about because of a TBTF policy of government or other reasons.

### *Safety net issues*

Governments build safety nets into financial services systems to minimize systemic risk. The safety net includes deposit insurance, guaranty funds, the discount window and payment system guarantees. Does financial service integration pose additional burdens on the safety net, with resultant taxpayer exposure?

As with a TBTF policy, safety nets create problems of moral hazard. Customer incentives to monitor the condition of financial institutions with which they do business is diminished, so managers are prone to take on more risk than they otherwise would. An expansion of banking activities through integration, thus, could lead to excessive risk taking that could weaken the fabric of the financial services system.

Neither the TBTF nor the safety net issue is new. Suggested reform proposals include eliminating deposit insurance, pricing deposit insurance premiums to reflect institutional risk, limiting deposit insurance protection to "narrow banking," increasing capital requirements and enacting stricter closure rules, practicing more vigilant supervision, and imposing a program of "constructive ambiguity" onto the safety net.

These and other proposals to address the moral hazard issue seem as applicable in an integrated financial services world as in a segregated one. Supervision admittedly will be more complex as will problems of regulatory arbitrage such as moving the underwriting of products from units not within the safety net to units enjoying safety net protection. To the extent that these problems prove valid, however, they are not caused by integration but by government failure. As such, the first-best solution is governmental reform, not limitations on financial services integration.

## The Relationship Between Integration and Regulatory Structure

A final public policy concern is whether existing regulatory structures are appropriate in an integrated financial world. If financial services sectors are integrating, should supervisors do the same? The underlying issue is what regulatory structure minimizes the chances of government failure in ameliorating market imperfections and does so most efficiently.

The case for consolidated regulation is compelling. To have true consolidated regulation, it would seem that the single regulator should:

* have oversight responsibilities for all or most types of financial intermediaries, especially banks and insurers;
* work under laws that are not inconsistent across types of intermediaries;
* apply comparable (although not necessarily identical) regulation to all intermediaries and cross-sector competing products, ensuring equality of competitive opportunity between types of intermediaries.

Having a unified supervisory agency could minimize the problems of information sharing and coordination associated with sector-specific supervision, at least at the national level. In concept, it would permit a less complex approach for addressing issues such as transparency, multiple and excessive gearing, fit and proper requirements, and contagion. It would facilitate needed harmonization of accounting and capital adequacy requirements across financial intermediaries, and it should lessen opportunities for regulatory arbitrage.

It is argued, however, that existing sectoral regulatory approaches, especially when augmented by information sharing and agreement on coordination issues among the regulators, are adequate and involve less disruption. Moreover, the objectives of regulation vary by industry. Banking supervision is oriented more toward stability of the financial system as a whole, rather than the solidity of individual banks or efficiency, and relies on consolidated regulation. Securities regulation is oriented more toward consumer protection through disclosure and market efficiency than toward system stability. Insurance regulation is oriented more toward financial soundness of individual insurers and fairness, with less focus on systemic risks and efficiency. Systemic risks are not as important in insurance as they are in banking or even securities.

Additionally, arguments have been made that product differences justify solo regulatory approaches. Insurance products tend to be more complex and often involve much longer guarantees than banking and securities products. As a consequence, risk and risk management practices differ by industry, and regulatory specialization offers greater efficiency, so the argument goes.

This debate might be moot to some extent. Already many banking regulators have captured the "high ground" of consolidated regulation because of their charge to protect the financial system against systemic risk and because they already focus their regulatory efforts at the group level. Thus, so the argument goes, if a financial conglomerate contains a commercial bank, the banking supervisor should have an important voice in the supervision of the group.

No international consensus has yet emerged on this issue, although the trend is toward consolidated approaches. Some countries already have consolidated supervision, and others have recently moved in this direction. The Australian Prudential Regulatory Authority, the Financial Services Agency of Japan, the Securities and Exchange Commission of Pakistan, the Office of the Superintendent of Financial Services of Canada, the Danish Financial Supervisory Authority and the Financial Services Authority of the U.K. are some of the examples. Other countries retain sectoral regulation, although some include investment banking within the overall banking function.

According to one authority (Thompson, 1999), the case for consolidated regulation is strongest in a market that exhibits the following characteristics:

- Similar products and services are offered by different types of intermediaries in the same market segments.
- Institutions in competing sectors have similar strategies for growth and development in the domestic market, the international market or both.
- Institutions in one sector create systemic risk exposure for another industry.
- Competing sectors are at a similar and advanced stage of development.
- Institutions are combining in ways that make it difficult to distinguish a bank from an insurance firm.
- The financial services industry is pushing for reform to meet competitive pressures.

Clearly, the larger the financial services market of a country, the greater the complexity and difficulty in moving to consolidated regulation. Thus, for example, substantial regulatory change in the U.S. financial services regulatory system would seem problematical. In contrast, the more modest in size is a country's financial services sector, the easier it should be to move to consolidated approaches.

# THE FUTURE OF FINANCIAL SERVICES INTEGRATION

Services in general and financial services in particular lie at the center of all developed economies. Financial services innovation and production efficiency are essential to economic development. The question is how integrated financial services fit into this evolution and whether it poses unacceptable risk to consumers and the financial system.

Whether integration leads to economies of scale or scope or to greater efficiencies cannot be answered with confidence at this time. In one sense, the answers are irrelevant. The present pressures for integration seem strong. Financial services companies are battling for customers and understand that they must allow potential and present customers to conduct their financial affairs in ways most convenient to them. This translates into figuring out how to make available a range of financial products and services through multiple distribution channels and how to offer multiple service points. Our poor understanding of the possibilities for technology to assist them in making integration work hinders the making of sound forecasts.

With time being the currency of the future, the opportunities for economies of scope in consumption seem to loom large. Securing these economies does not require financial conglomeration, however. It requires integration only at the interface of the customer and the distributor (advisor), and that distributor can as easily be Microsoft as Citigroup representatives.

The market will determine whether financial conglomeration makes good business sense and, if so, the optimum operational structure. One can imagine different outcomes in different markets, depending on cultural, historical and economic factors, such as stage of development. Additionally, even for markets in which some financial services companies move aggressively to integrate, we will find many other companies that decide that specialization offers greater opportunities. These trends seem contradictory, but they need not be. Important market segments will prefer specialized service providers, in part because their needs will themselves be highly specialized (e.g., large businesses and wealthy individuals). Additionally, we should not be surprised to find that specialized financial institutions are able to develop a better understanding of their narrower target markets and corresponding core competencies, thus allowing them to compete effectively with conglomerates.

The globalization of business in particular and financial services specifically fosters integration. One has but to consider whether the recent U.S. reforms would have been enacted as sweeping without the compelling arguments from U.S. financial institutions that they were at a competitive disadvantage internationally under former U.S. law.

Integration seems to be further advanced in Australia and the Netherlands than other countries, with France and the U.K. not far removed. Each of these and other countries with reasonably advanced integration offer a wealth of experiences for countries that are not as far along. At the same time, care must be taken to recognize those situations or elements that do not travel well. For example, unique circumstances aiding integration in Australia, France, the Netherlands, Spain and the U.K. may not exist in other markets.

The financial services integration trend will push regulatory convergence in two dimensions. First, with integration and product convergence, those aspects of national regulation and taxation that are specific to one financial services industry or its products can be expected to cause increasing distortion. Firms will offer products and structure themselves in ways that minimize their regulatory burdens and taxes; that is, regulatory and tax arbitrage will ensure. This will continue to drive governments to seek greater horizontal equity in financial institution and product regulation as well as in taxation. In turn, this will lead to national regulatory and tax convergence. This could facilitate the move by more nations toward consolidated regulation.

Second, international differences in regulation and taxation of financial institutions and products increasingly will afford opportunities for international regulatory and tax arbitrage. This is especially true as markets continue to liberalize and as the cross-border provision of financial services grows, facilitated in part by the Internet. It is logical that companies will take advantage of these differences. Pressure will mount for governments to harmonize key elements of tax and regulation. A danger is that governments will succumb to the sirens' song of *de jure* harmonization, and harmonize the wrong things or at the wrong level, thereby stifling innovation and efficiency. In this process, the importance of meaningful accounting harmonization internationally cannot be overemphasized.

Many knowledgeable observers believe that the financial world of the future will be dominated by a dozen or so financial conglomerates. Even if accurate, those apparently oligopolistic markets can remain competitive and innovative if barriers to entry and exit remain low, especially to foreign financial service suppliers. Certainly, specialist suppliers, even if small, will provoke continuous improvement by the giants. Irrespective of which view proves correct, changing demographics and economic prosperity ensure a growing role for financial service providers and distributors.

# DISCUSSION QUESTIONS

1. If *bancassurance* becomes a globally accepted method of insurance distribution, are consumers more likely to be helped or harmed? How would your answer differ if the same question were asked about a perfectly competitive market compared with an oligopolistic market?

2. From a strictly marketing perspective, what role might culture play in the process of financial services integration? As the executive vice president of marketing for a global conglomerate, how might your overcome these challenges?

3. Speculate about the degree to which each of the following market segments would be affected (either positively or negatively) if financial services competition were dominated by financial services conglomerates: low, middle and upper income?

4. What are some of the political ramifications of financial services integration? As the financial services regulation czar for the E.U., list the three most pressing challenges you would have to overcome. How would you accomplish each?

5. Choose any two public policy issues. Argue either for integration, citing potential solutions, or against integration, citing reasons why the issue cannot be overcome?

6. If full integration were permitted tomorrow in your country, how would the financial landscape look 1, 10 and 25 years from now? What would be the impact on (a) the national economy and (b) consumers?

# NOTES

1. This chapter draws in part from Skipper (2000).
2. Some scholars, following the German model, further distinguish universal banks from other financial institutions through their holding of important equity positions and voting power in non-financial firms. Some other scholars apply a theoretical definition of a universal bank – a firm manufacturing and distributing all financial services within a single corporate structure (Saunders and Walter, 1994).
3. Travelers Property Casualty Corporation was separated from Citigroup and became a fully independent, publicly traded firm in 2002. It merged with the St. Paul Companies in 2003 to create the St. Paul Travelers Companies.
4. Berger (1999).
5. See Group of Ten (2001) for an overview of the literature.
6. Berger et al. (1993) find that gains inherent in universal banking may lie more on the revenue than the cost side. Canals (1993) finds that bank performance was improved by the increased revenues from new business units. Mutual fund activities increase bank profitability (Gallo et al., 1996). Various risk-simulation studies by Saunders and Walter (1994) suggest that combinations of banking, insurance and securities activities may lead to a more stable profit stream, as each industry's cash flows are usually imperfectly correlated.

   Boyd et al. (1993) find that simulated mergers of U.S. bank holding companies with life insurance and nonlife insurance companies may reduce risk, but that mergers with securities firms would likely increase risk. Kwan (1997) offers a reason that U.S. bank holding companies gain potential diversification benefits from having securities subsidiaries, which is the low correlation between their returns and those of the other operating units of the bank holding company. Benston (1989) reports that the

returns for combined operation of commercial and investment banking would be significantly higher, but without an increase in overall risk. Vander Vennet (2002) finds that European financial conglomerates were more revenue efficient and enjoyed higher profits than specialized financial services companies.

   Further, Walter (1997) observes that network economies – a special type of economies of scope in consumption and positive externalities – are associated with some elements of universal banking. With network economies, relationships with end users represent a network structure wherein additional client linkages add value to existing clients by increasing the feasibility or reducing the cost of accessing them. These positive externalities tend to increase with the absolute size of the network itself and are characteristics of activities such as securities clearance and settlement, global custody, funds transfer and international cash management, foreign exchange and securities dealing, and the like.
7. For an interesting analysis of unfavorable outcomes, see Wilmarth (2002).
8. Thus, we ignore the important issue of whether financial institutions should be permitted extensive equity investments in or other control of commercial businesses and vice versa, as this issue applies equally to isolated financial institutions.
9. This discussion draws from the Joint Forum (1999 and 2001), pp. 8–9.
10. See Annexes 1 and 2 in the Joint Forum (2001).
11. For a discussion of these issues, see Barfield (1996).
12. Exceptions occur in certain securities activities. According to Kwan and Laderman (1999), the literature suggests that, while securities trading tends to be more profitable and riskier than banking, it may not provide diversification benefits because of its high stand-alone risk.
13. See, for example, Barth et al. (2001).

# REFERENCES

Barfield, C.E., ed. (1996). *International Financial Markets: Harmonization versus Competition.* Washington, DC: AEI Press.
Barth, J.R., Caprio Jr., G. and Levine, R. (2001). "Banking Systems around the Globe: Do Regulation and Ownership Affect Performance and Stability?" in F.S. Mishkin, ed., *Prudential Supervision: What Works and What Doesn't.* Chicago, IL: University of Chicago Press (pp. 31–95).

Benston, G.J. (1989). "The Federal Safety Net and the Repeal of the Glass-Steagall Act's Separation of Commercial and Investment Banking." *Journal of Financial Services Research*, 2 (October): 287–306.

Berger, A.N. (1999). "The Integration of the Financial Services Industry: Where are the Efficiencies?" paper presented at the 1999 Thomas P. Bowles Symposium on Financial Services Integration. Georgia State University.

Berger, A.N. and Humphrey, D.B. (1997). "Efficiency of Financial Institutions: International Survey and Directions for Future Research." *European Journal of Operational Research*, 98: 178–212.

Berger, A.N., Hancock, D. and Humphrey, D.B. (1993). "Bank Efficiency Derived from the Profit Function."*Journal of Banking and Finance*, 17: 317–347.

Boyd, J.H., Graham, S.L. and Hewitt, R.S. (1993). "Banking Holding Company Mergers with Nonbank Financial Firms: Effects on the Risk of Failure." *Journal of Banking and Finance*, 17 (February): 43–63.

Canals, J. (1993). *Competitive Strategies in European Banking*. Oxford: Oxford University Press.

Carow, K.A. (2001). "Citicorp-Travelers Group Merger: Challenging Barriers Between Banking and Insurance." *Journal of Banking and Finance*, 25: 1553–1571.

Cybo-Ottone, A. and Murgia, M. (2000). "Mergers and Shareholder Wealth in European Banking." *Journal of Banking and Finance*, 24: 834–859.

*European Banker* (1999). "Bigger Size Fits All," January 1.

Gallo, J.G., Apilado, V.P. and Kolari, J.W. (1996). "Commercial Bank Mutual Fund Activities: Implications for Bank Risk and Profitability." *Journal of Banking and Finance*, 20 (December): 1775–1791.

Group of Ten (2001). "The Effects of Consolidation on Efficiency, Competition and Credit Flows," Chapter V, in *Report on Consolidation in the Financial Sector*.

Herring, R.J. and Santomero, A.M. (1990). "The Corporate Structure of Financial Conglomerates," *Journal of Financial Services Research*, Dec., 471–497.

Joint Forum (1999). *Supervision of Financial Conglomerates*.

Joint Forum (2001). *Risk Management Practices and Regulatory Capital*.

Kraus, J.R. (1998). "Europe's Universal Banks: Flawed Models," *American Banker*, June 8.

Kwan, S.H. (1997). "Securities Activities by Commercial Banking Firms' Section 20 Subsidiaries: Risk, Return, and Diversification Benefits."*Federal Reserve Bank of San Francisco Economic Review*, October.

Kwan, S.H. and Laderman, E.S. (1999). "On the Portfolio Effects of Financial Convergence – A Review of the Literature." *Federal Reserve Bank of San Francisco Economic Review*, January 1.

Saunders, A. and Walter, I. (1994). *Universal Banking in The United States*. New York: Oxford University Press.

Skipper Jr., H.D. (2000). "Financial Services Integration Worldwide: Promises and Pitfalls." *North American Actuarial Journal*, 4: 71–108.

Thompson, J. (1999). "Financial Services Reform: Basic Components, Position and Prognosis," presented at the *Conference on Insurance and Financial Services Regulation*, Hartford, U.S.

The Tripartite Group of Bank, Securities, and Insurance Regulators (1995). *The Supervision of Financial Conglomerates*.

Tuohy, M.R. (1999). "Financial Services: What Lies Ahead?" *Emphasis*, 3: 32.

Van den Berghe, L.A.A. and Verweire, K. (1998). *Creating the Future with All Finance and Financial Conglomerates*. Boston, MA: Kluwer Academic Publishers.

Vander Vennet, R. (2002). "Cost and Profit Efficiency in Financial Conglomerates and Universal Banks in Europe." *Journal of Money, Credit, and Banking*, 34: 254–282.

Walter, I. (1997). "Universal Banking: A Shareholder Value Perspective."*European Management Journal*, 15 (August).

Wilmarth Jr., A.E. (2002). "The Transformation of the U.S. Financial Services Industry, 1975–2000: Competition, Consolidation, and Increased Risks." *University of Illinois Law Review*, 2 (2): 215–476.

# Part V

# Conclusions

# Chapter 26

# Risk Management and Insurance in a Global Economy: A Future Perspective

## INTRODUCTION

As we noted in the conclusion of Chapter 11, despite a two-third's increase in life expectancy during the 20th century, unparalleled health and healthcare for most citizens, decreasing rates of industrial and transportation accident rates and a host of other data indicating enhanced safety, the perception is that life is getting riskier and that tomorrow's world will be more volatile than yesterday's world. Much of this perception matches objective reality. Certainly, the terrorists' attacks on September 11, 2001 fundamentally altered risk perceptions by millions of citizens throughout the world, not just in the U.S. The massive tsunami that struck in the Indian Ocean region without warning on December 26, 2004, instantly snuffing out tens-of-thousands of lives and erasing entire towns and villages, reminded the world that nature can, at any time, unleash unpredicted super-catastrophes. Hurricane Katrina, in wreaking havoc throughout the U.S. Gulf Coast and inundating the city of New Orleans on August 29, 2005, reminded the world that nature, even when predictable, could overcome human-made plans and defenses.

The opportunity for major natural and human-made catastrophes has grown with global warming, increasing industrial sophistication, the advent of genetic and other new technologies, growing coastal populations, an increasingly networked society, and greater political and social unrest. Additionally, corporate excesses and scandals have put enormous pressure on corporate executives and their boards of directors to do a much better job of identifying and managing risks. On the one hand, our perceptions are often selective, if not distorted. On the other hand, perception is the reality on which decisions are made in a world perceived as increasingly risky and volatile. In this context, risk management – especially enterprise risk management – is recognized globally as an increasingly important and vital means of enhancing and protecting shareholder value and societal welfare.

Risk management is all about trying to anticipate and deal with alternative potential futures. Our perspective in this final chapter is the future. As students of risk management, we are compelled to consider how a future world might evolve, what new risks might arise, how old ones could change and the means by which we deal with these risks. We live in a global economy that seems likely to be even more international in the future. Our intent is to help the reader reflect thoughtfully about how the world's future may evolve and how this evolution may alter risks and their management. We explore various elements of potential futures by both making predictions and offering scenarios.[1] This exploration is intended to provoke debate and analysis. We structure the examination around the environmental factors discussed throughout this text.

# ENVIRONMENTS OF THE FUTURE

The economic influence of the U.S. waned over the past 50 or so years, as its share of world output shrank from about one-half to about one-quarter today. The likely 21st century economic and political powers (e.g., China, the E.U., India, Japan, the U.S., Brazil and Russia) promise to be more diverse than those of the 19th and 20th centuries which shared many common cultural and religious elements. This diversity will manifest itself in different worldviews, including different conceptions of what constitutes a market economy and a democracy, and potentially in more miscalculations of other nations' intentions and reactions.

Important decisions in the 21st century world should take into consideration multiple interests, but prospects for this result are not encouraging as viewed from our myopic perch at the beginning of the century. The consequences could be unpleasant. In short, the world is and promises to remain a risky place.

As we explore the future, it is good to remind ourselves that whatever we believe about the future almost certainly will prove wrong to varying degrees. But what types of generic lessons can we learn from past predictions and scenarios? *The Wall Street Journal* provided five observations relevant to this chapter (Silverman, 2000):

- Present trends almost never continue. Straight-line extrapolation may be both the most common and the worst method. Trends almost always generate their own countertrends.
- Every prediction suffers from situational bias; that is, they are influenced by the times in which they are made.
- Distance and objectivity are powerful virtues. Individuals with vested interests or who are too close to events make notoriously poor predictions.
- The future is not preordained. While we can do nothing about the past, the future begins in the present.
- The exercise of making predictions and scenarios widens our horizons and deepens our capacity to imagine.

As we imagine the possible elements of future environments, we should keep these five observations uppermost in mind.

## The Economic Environment

The industrial economies of Europe and North America have dominated world production and trade for more than 150 years. The sole Asian representative, Japan, joined the club only during the latter half of the 20th century. Yet, within a single generation, several emerging economies could become important world economic powers.

Emerging economies are expected to continue to grow at a faster rate than most of the mature OECD member states. They can realize this happy result because they possess more underutilized production factors and can gain rapidly from adopting proven innovation and production practices from more economically advanced economies. Globalization and the continuing application of new technology to the various sectors of the economy facilitate financial capital mobility as well as mobility of investment, managerial and marketing expertise. These facts should translate into more competitive, vigorous, and open markets. In turn, this should mean more opportunity for all businesses, especially financial institutions, in the future.

With such rapid economic growth, demand for energy will increase markedly.[2] In particular, China's rapid growth is expected to continue to put huge strains on both world energy supplies and other raw materials. China already is the world's biggest consumer of many commodities (e.g., steel, coal and cement) and the second-biggest consumer of oil, after the U.S. Consequently, changes in Chinese demand will have a major impact on world prices. A similar impact of the global economy can be expected when other emerging markets of enormous potential (e.g., India and Russia) realize accelerated economic development.

Continuing industrialization and urbanization will increase China's and other emerging markets' demand for raw materials and fuels. Economic development is always highly energy intensive, because basic industries tend to use large quantities of energy. Moreover, as incomes rise, more households can afford cars and energy-consuming household appliances.

A risk is that oil shortages could aggravate worldwide inflation. As the OPEC's share of world production is expected to increase from its mid-1980s level of 30 percent to more than 50 percent by 2010, the world's oil supply could be even more vulnerable to adverse political developments, especially as the OPEC governments, not their private sectors, control most OPEC oil.

Westerners probably will continue to criticize their MNCs for outsourcing and placing manufacturing and other production facilities in developing countries. On the one hand, trade-induced national disruptions are essential for long-run economic transformation. On the other hand, lacking an unlikely educational leap, the world's 21st century citizens seem destined to remain poorly informed about the economics of international trade and investment, thereby allowing facile posturing by self-interested politicians and businesses to influence governmental trade policies adversely.

Even so, a networked global economy seems likely to emerge, driven by rapid and less restricted flows of information, cultural values, capital, goods and services and people accompanied by political pressures for higher living standards and an increasingly dynamic private sector. A globalized economy should be a net contributor to world political stability and economic growth.

One can imagine a scenario in which important markets become less open, political instability reigns, a pandemic occurs or property rights are massively abused. Any one of these outcomes, especially when coupled with widespread anti-globalization attitudes or increased terrorist activities, could result in much reduced economic growth.

Under the most optimistic globalized scenario, it seems likely that countries failing to adopt political and economic reforms will be left behind and face deepening economic stagnation and cultural alienation that could lead to more political instability, repression or both. Such situations offer fertile ground for political, ethnic, ideological or religious extremism, along with the violence that often accompanies it. The societal risk management challenge for the more economically advanced countries will be to minimize the chances of this unfortunate outcome materializing by encouraging greater integration of those countries into the world economy. Helping them develop and implement sound economic policies while safeguarding human and property rights can be a means to achieve this goal.

## The Financial Environment

The dynamic 21st century economic environment promises to foster an equally interesting 21st century financial environment. The efficiency of financial intermediaries and of financial markets will probably become important issues of national concern. The current efficiency lead enjoyed by the U.S. seems destined to erode, as other nations' companies and markets improve rapidly. The exceptional window of opportunity now enjoyed by U.S. and European financial services companies to export and exploit their efficiency through international expansion will not stay open forever.

Financial services integration and convergence seem destined to continue. Convergence of the insurance and the capital markets will probably continue through the provision of catastrophic loss protection and securitization of risks. We can expect increasingly creative means for financing risk via capital markets.

The remaining regulatory walls separating the various financial services sectors will continue to crumble. In many markets, banks can be expected to become even more important distribution outlets for personal insurance, especially for the middle and lower-income market segments.

## The Political and Legal Environments

Democratization is expected to continue to spread, but will it be wedded to the Western pattern? We could witness some movements oriented toward the libertarian ideal of small government and rugged individualism, others toward the predictable ideal of order and still others toward a communal ideal of universal security. At the same time, economic and political freedoms probably will expand but with occasional setbacks. It seems too hopeful to expect all experiments in democracy to succeed. The risk of trade wars and regional "hot" wars may increase. What actions or strategies should public policymakers, risk managers and financial service providers undertake in anticipation of such events?

### The role of government

Will we continue to witness increased reliance on markets and reduced reliance on governments or will the backlash against globalization succeed in reversing progress? Will a new world order prevail, led by a benevolent superpower dedicated to promoting human rights and economic development for all of the world's citizens – including the one billion who live on less than a dollar per day?

There can be no question but that the U.S. today is the world's only superpower. The U.S. leads the world in virtually all dimensions of power: military, economic, cultural and scientific. This lead is out of all proportion to its share of world population. However, these very strengths underlie increasing resentment by "most of the globe [that] perceives [the U.S.] as an arrogant, self-interested 'hyperpower' determined to preserve its lead" (Sanger, 2001).

It is perhaps good that we should be reminded of an earlier incarnation of the world that bears striking resemblance to the beginning 21st century. Insight 26.1 offers a caution.

Based on current trends (always a sure sign of danger in predictions!), a likely scenario involves national economies becoming more international. Capital and factor mobility, technology, and citizens demanding greater economic and political freedom all argue for it. Yet governments still are able to and probably will make imprudent decisions, especially regarding property rights. Moreover, the world has witnessed increased civil wars and their attendant disruptions – wars that demand attention, as Insight 26.2 highlights.

INSIGHT 26.1: A CAUTIONARY HISTORY LESSON ——————

Americans and foreigners alike usually take the United States to be invulnerable, but why should this be so? In 1900, the British Empire was the sole superpower. While it had rivals, as the U.S. does today, the conventional belief more than a century ago was that the interests of the great powers – above all, their economic interests – were so closely linked that war no longer made sense. The world at that time was considered to be even more globalized than it is today.

The 20th century began in circumstances of apparent security more reassuring than those of today. No one in 1900 could have imagined the events that only 14 years later would destroy the existing international system and unleash a wave of totalitarianism that would dominate world affairs for most of the 20th century. Responsible political and economic leaders and scholars at the time would undoubtedly have described the coming century in terms of continuing imperial rivalries within a Europe-dominated world, lasting paternalistic tutelage in Europe's colonies, solid constitutional government in Western Europe, steadily growing prosperity, increasing scientific knowledge turned to human benefit, and so on. All would have been wrong.
*Source*: Pfaff (2001).

With the technology for the creation of nuclear, biological, and chemical weapons more readily available and with the former Soviet Union's arsenal seemingly under less strict control, we cannot rule out the spread of such weapons or the know how to produce them. Additionally, states such as North Korea and Iran possessing or obtaining nuclear weapons and possibly selling or using them remains a grave concern of many analysts. Non-proliferation treaties and other agreements can help but have proven insufficient.

Terrorists or alienated individuals with chemical, biological or nuclear weapons are growing possibilities. The *Aum Shinri Kyo* cult's 1995 release of deadly sarin gas in a Tokyo subway killed 12 and sickened 5,500 individuals. Had the gas been mixed properly, it would have been far more deadly. It is said that al-Qaeda remains committed to securing such weapons. Use of such weapons of mass destruction not only could kill and maim thousands of lives but also could disrupt national or even regional economies for years.

One of the 21st century's political dangers stems less from deliberate policies of military and economic confrontations and more from policy uncertainty by governments. At least the pre-1990s Soviet/U.S. stalemate led to relatively clear policymaking by governments. Without such an overriding rallying point, future governments may be too tentative in their policy responses, as with the breakup and ensuing civil war in Yugoslavia. These and a host of other potential political uncertainties suggest that sound political risk management will be more critical in the future.

### *Internationalization of the legal environment*

The future legal environment could become less diverse with internationalization. The general growth in tort system costs worldwide probably will continue, especially as other countries incorporate elements of the U.S.-style tort system into their own systems. The internationalization of production and the increased importance of international trade to national economies could drive this increase in costs as well as a decrease in tort system

INSIGHT 26.2: THE GLOBAL MENACE OF LOCAL STRIFE  ———

A century ago most conflicts were between nations and 90 percent of casualties were soldiers. Today, almost all wars are civil, and 90 percent of the victims are civilians. Why is this happening? The most common factor among war-prone counties is their poverty. Rich countries almost never suffer civil war, and middle-income countries rarely do so. But the poorest one-sixth of humanity endures four-fifths of the world's civil wars.

The best predictors of conflict are low average incomes, low growth, and high dependence on exports of primary products such as oil or diamonds. Poor, stagnant countries are so vulnerable partly because it is easy to give a poor person a cause. But also, almost certainly, because poverty and law or negative growth are often symptoms of corrupt, incompetent government, which can provoke rebellion.

Natural resources tend to aggravate these problems. When a state has oil, its leaders can grow rich without bothering to nurture other kinds of economic activity. Corrupt leaders often cement their support base by sharing the loot with their own ethnic group, which tends to anger all the other groups.

Rebellions rarely begin as criminal business ventures, but they often mutate into them. Their leaders can grow fabulously rich. War creates a vicious circle. When rebel groups start to make money, they attract greedy leaders. At the same time, war makes it harder for peaceful people to earn a living. No one wants to build factories in war zones. People with portable skills flee, and those with money stash it offshore. Peasants find it hard to farm when rebels keep plundering their villages.

Poverty fosters war, and war impoverishes. A typical civil war leaves a country 15 percent poorer than it would otherwise have been and with perhaps 30 percent more people living in absolute poverty. The damage persists long afterward. Skills and capital continue to flee, because people do not trust the peace; half of newly peaceful countries revert to war within a decade. Infant mortality also remains high, not least because war nurtures disease.

Since places prone to civil war are poor, stagnant places, anything that promotes growth ought to help. Governments in poor countries should strive to keep corruption, inflation, and trade barriers low, while attempting to build better health, education, and legal systems.

Spending on health and education seems to provide an immediate boost to the economy of a newly peaceful nation. This is surprising. But in countries emerging from war, a new school, or clinic shows that the government is serious about peace, which buoys confidence and may encourage private investment.

*Source*: "Special Report: Civil Wars" (2003). © The Economist.

diversity. Efforts to reform tort systems to rein in costs probably will continue in some countries, as high system costs begin to impinge on the international competitiveness of domestic industries and risk taking.

At the same time, opportunities for conflicts of law, especially regarding property rights (e.g., intellectual property) could grow. Risk managers of the 21st century will experience the daunting challenge of maintaining currency and appropriate oversight during periods of great change.

## The Regulatory and Tax Environments

The mobility of people, ideas, information and financial capital means that governments *should* take more careful note of the economic consequences of their regulatory and tax decisions. Whether they do so influences their international competitiveness and, thereby, national welfare. The effects would seem to be to drive regulation and taxation toward convergence with a corresponding need for agreement on principles and, ultimately, standards.

An interesting challenge might await governments as new solvency standards and international accounting standards are adopted worldwide over the next few years, depending on their precise requirements. Consider, for example, the important "shock-absorber" role that life insurers play in national economies as they warehouse comparatively long-duration securities. In doing so, they partially insulate consumers and markets from volatility. To a considerable extent, today's solvency and accounting standards do not punish insurers' balance sheets for undertaking these functions. Likely future solvency standards and proposed fair value accounting would change this treatment and, in the process, seem likely to result in insurers shifting more risk into the market.

If this occurs, the questions for policymakers are: (1) will the financial system itself become more volatile, and, if so, what to do about it and (2) what effect would it have on consumers who may not understand that such a shift has occurred. With the latter question, one can imagine a scenario in which problems occurred that resulted in mass tort actions and/or government taking extreme protective measures such as price controls, shoring asset values, or greater forbearance.

The cost of complying with the myriad of new regulations and standards continues its steady increase in most markets worldwide. These costs have been particularly burdensome within the E.U. because of the necessity to comply with the many directives implementing the single market program and in the U.S. because of Sarbanes-Oxley and the multitude of individual states laws and regulation.[3] An obviously important question for the future is: Are there means to control these explosive costs while ensuring quality supervision?

National economic growth rates have become more synchronized during the past three decades, thanks to globalization, and can be expected to grow still closer in the future. This fact suggests that governments will be less able fully to control national economic activities in the future. Consequently, they can be expected grudgingly to recognize the need for greater cross-national regulatory cooperation and could reluctantly cede limited national sovereignty to regional and international intergovernmental arrangements. In turn, intergovernmental organizations could follow a ragged path toward greater importance in the 21st century, even in the face of recent U.S. trends to the contrary.[4]

A nation's tax system should not be the basis for allocating international risk bearing capacity. It is at present. Tax and regulatory arbitrage are problems that, in time, a liberalized international financial market should cure but not without considerable disagreement and debate. Again, intergovernmental organizations could become important venues for advancing the debate.

Deregulation probably will yield less government involvement in many aspects of financial services operations in most countries. Deregulation could permit deeper financial services integration that would call for greater integration of or at least cooperation among sectorial supervisors. Simultaneously, the trend toward enhanced and more tailored prudential regulation seems destined to continue, led by the E.U.'s Solvency II initiative. Also, governments and businesses will have to evolve new standards for dealing with innovative risk financing alternatives, the quickly approaching international accounting standards and greater financial transparency.

By nature and history, nation-states seem comfortable with the market's invisible hand only when they can control or regulate it. Although future financial markets can be expected to punish ill-advised government behavior, one would be surprised if governments make politically popular short run, but economically unwise long run, decisions. After all, the future is a constituency that casts no votes. The general good will continue to fall prey to special interests.

Nonetheless, policymakers increasingly seem to acknowledge the role of the pricing mechanism as being central to smooth functioning markets. They seem to understand more fully, for example, that when governments bar insurers from fully pricing the risk exposure in flood plains, along coasts and other disaster-prone regions or when they subsidize construction and living arrangements through insurance, reinsurance or disaster relief, they impose costs on other insureds and taxpayers. Insurance and other prices, therefore, fail to reflect the true cost of risky behavior. This fact means that individuals and businesses are more likely to locate in such risky areas, less likely to engage in loss mitigation activities and less likely to provide for their own economic security.

## The Sociocultural and Demographic Environments

One risk of globalization is a loss of cultural diversity. Will the world's citizens all drink Coca Colas, wear Levi jeans, eat Kentucky Fried Chicken, listen to British and American music and speak English? What difference does its make anyway?

At one level, the internationalization of national economies is superficial. Whether Malaysians drink Coke, guava juice or Evian has little effect on their beliefs, attitudes and behavior. This type of internationalization therefore might not lessen true diversity. At another level, however, an increasing exposure to different cultures through travel, reading, the Internet, television, multinational businesses and a host of other inputs could result in the indigenous culture becoming a corrupted version of someone else's. Again, if this happens, does it make any difference? After all, cultures have forever borrowed from each other.

Arguably, most citizens favor more rather than less cultural diversity internationally and internationalization might work against this ideal. On the other hand, some sociologists have argued that internationalization might help preserve diversity; in other words, taking pride in their own heritage in the face of ethnic homogenization, groups might make greater efforts to record, preserve and celebrate their distinctiveness. Whatever way the crosscurrents move a country's cultural ship, 21st century financial service providers and risk managers – both local and foreign – must be more sensitive to cultural issues.

### Risk perceptions

Economics offers the most fully articulated theory of individual risk perception and, through the law of large numbers, offers important mechanisms for coping with uncertainty. Neither economics nor any other social science, however, offers a fully developed, generally acceptable normative or positive theory of risk that can guide society in making some of its most critically important decisions. In particular, economists only recently have begun to provide some limited insight into activities that inspire terror, fear and distrust in the public. They still offer little insight into how individuals react to poorly understood, complex processes. Experimental evidence from psychology (and recently, its offspring, behavioral economics) suggests that the expected utility model's postulates and conclusions are especially suspect in offering insights into behavior involving disastrous outcomes of events whose probability of occurrence is either very low or very high.

We can expect 21st century social scientists to develop a deeper understanding and, perhaps, even a cohesive theory of individual and group risk perceptions. An important challenge is coping with increasing incidences of negative externalities.

### *Demographics*

Unlike the fuzzy contours of other future environments, the future demographic profile offers some clarity.[5] After all, a society's demographic profile today – especially in terms of population size, age and sex composition – profoundly affects what that society's profile will be in the future, for today's babies are tomorrow's students then workers then retirees. In turn, tomorrow's demographic profile profoundly affects that society's employment opportunities and economic growth prospects as well as its relative importance in the world as measured by its economic, political and military power.

The risks that societies – countries – face today are both numerous and potentially grave, ranging from global warming to terrorism. None, however, is as certain or as likely to have as enduring an effect as the world's forthcoming demographic changes in general and global aging in particular. For almost the entirety of human history, the elderly represented a tiny portion of the world's population – never more than 3 percent. Today, more than 15 percent of the population in industrial countries is elderly and that share is projected to reach 25 percent by 2030 and to increase still further thereafter. While the developing countries' elderly proportions are not as high, they too will increase over the next few decades.

The coming demographic transformation will affect almost every dimension of public and private life in ways that suggest that its effects will underlie the greatest risk management challenges facing nations. The enormous fiscal costs, arising from supporting the public pension and health benefits systems for the typical developed country, are the most discussed challenge. Other effects could prove of even greater importance. Population aging could cause economic growth to slow dramatically, at the same time that tomorrow's families are compelled to cope with numerous frail elders and tomorrow's businesses cope with a dearth of young consumers and less innovation. The entire international geopolitical order could be rearranged in profound ways, as the developed countries' proportion of total world output shrinks and the political and military balance of power shifts.

This century's demographic transformation results from the combination of rising longevity and falling fertility. Increasing longevity increases the relative number of elderly, and decreasing fertility rates decreases the relative number of young. Both greater longevity and falling fertility are associated with economic development. In general, increasing personal incomes mean that people have better healthcare, live in safer conditions and have fewer children because of urbanization and a lessened need for them to care elder parents. Worldwide, life expectancy at birth rose dramatically during the 20th century. Indeed, gains during the century exceeded such gains achieved over the previous 50 centuries.

Increasing incomes are associated with decreasing fertility rates, and, of course, the world is richer (and healthier) today than in the past. Worldwide fertility rates have fallen from 5.0 to 2.8 births just since the mid-1960s. Fertility rates in every developed country at that time were above the replacement rate of 2.1. Today, fertility rates are below the replacement rate in 61 countries, including throughout Western Europe and much of Asia, including China, Japan, Korea and Taiwan.

The world's two most populous countries, China and India, face especially daunting challenges. Both are aging rapidly. China is aging faster than any country in history, thanks to its one-child policy, with its fertility rate already below the replacement level. India's fertility rate is projected to fall below the replacement level by 2010. Life expectancy in each country continues to increase. An economic and political issue for both countries is whether they can grow rich before they grow old. If not, future prospects will be dimmed.

Chapter 8 gave the proportion of population at age 65 and greater in the developed and developing world for the 100-year time span 1950–2050. Recall that the proportion of elder is growing worldwide, with Germany, Italy and Japan expected to have particularly large age 65+ segments, whereas the U.K. and the U.S. will have less of a challenge in this respect.

It seems reasonable to expect birth rates to continue to be below replacement levels in Western Europe, North America and Japan. This will aggravate the financial difficulties of social security programs and probably induce an easing of the sometimes strict immigration policies of some countries. We can expect greater racial and ethnic diversity. The challenge for nations is to ensure integration of immigrants into their new societies through educational, employment, and other opportunities. Failure to do so, as we have seem recently in Europe, can lead to disaffected, alienated young men and women who are prone to anti-social activities and even terrorism.

Citizens in most countries are becoming better educated and more demanding. They are less willing to accept inferior services and products, more willing to voice their opinions and less reluctant to purchase products and services from foreign companies. These social phenomena seem unlikely to be reversed in an increasingly globalized economy. With less free time, 21st century consumers will reward businesses, including financial service providers, that emphasize convenience and high-quality service. Price can be expected to continue to be important but, except for large price differences, probably will be determinative only with commodity-like products.

## The Physical and Technological Environments

Driven by advances in agricultural technologies, world food production should be adequate to feed the world's growing population, but poor infrastructure and distribution, political instability, and chronic poverty will lead to malnourishment in parts of Sub-Saharan Africa, Southeast and South Asia, and Central and Latin America. The potential for famine will persist in countries with repressive governments or internal conflict and continuing natural disasters, as in North Korea, requiring greater international aid.

The use of genetically modified crops has great potential for meeting the nutrition needs of the poor in developing countries. Opposition in the E.U. countries and, to a lesser extent, in the U.S. clouds prospects for applying this technology widely.

A shortage of fresh water promises to be one of the world's most serious resource problems over the next few decades. This notion may seem almost absurd to many in North America and Western Europe, where fresh water is taken for granted. However, by 2015, nearly one-half of the world's population will live in countries that are "water stressed." In the developing world, 80 percent of water usage goes into agriculture, a proportion that is unsustainable. Already, the water table in northern China is falling at the rate of 5 feet per year and water tables throughout India are falling from 3 to 10 feet per year. Nearly one-half of the world's land surface consists of river basins shared by more than one country, and more than 30 countries receive more than one-third of their water from outside their borders.

Thus, control over water could come to be seen as a strategic matter, with water-rich nations exerting their influence, much as oil-rich countries did during the latter part of the 20th century. The potential for conflict and shifting national power could easily follow.

In the not-too-distant past, a smaller, less complex world meant that the effects of individual and business activities were more likely to be internalized within the decision maker, with perhaps some spillover calling for limited government attention. In this century, individuals and businesses can be expected to have even less discretion in making decisions about activities and processes involving potentially high negative spillovers, such as waste disposal, energy generation, clearing of the rain forests, genetic engineering, mining of the ocean bed and like events. Issues that involve high levels of potential worldwide negative externalities cannot be considered matters of purely national concern. Loss of the rainforests in Africa, Latin America (particularly Brazil) and Indonesia affects the entire planet's climate, not just that of the concerned states. Carbon dioxide emissions in the U.S., China and Russia erode the *world's* ozone layer.

How much should we spend to ensure a reasonably safe environment? How much is too much? At what point do marginal costs outweigh marginal benefits, and how do we measure them? Should we seek to equalize the amount spent to save lives across different ways of dying and between different countries? Would doing so penalize economic development in emerging markets unfairly, thus perhaps reducing local employment opportunities and reducing monies available for education, healthcare and other life-enriching activities? In one instance, the U.S. Environmental Protection Agency (EPA) argued for spending approximately US$ 250 million to save an estimated seven to eight lives over 13 years. Is this reasonable and who decides? (A U.S. court ruled against the EPA, noting that over the same time twice as many people would die of ingested toothpicks.)

Regrettably, as the preceding section suggests, we do not fully understand the social consequences of and have few good decision rules for activities involving high levels of negative externalities. How will this century address the prospects of technology run amok; of major biological, chemical and nuclear accidents; of new and ever more resilient strains of viruses? Even with the anthropological theory of risk perception, we do not know the extent to which such global risks are perceived similarly because of some universal human information- processing strategy or differently because of cultural influences. We can hope that this century will witness the development of a deeper understanding of this issue as a prerequisite for developing effective communication strategies between peoples of different cultures and thereby for developing successful international risk policies. Economists and other social scientists have much to contribute here, but their contributions could go unheeded unless policymakers take a long-term perspective.

While we can eagerly anticipate the development of a deeper understanding of global risk issues, we also look forward to a more intensive application of our *current* economic knowledge about disaster prevention and mitigation. Consider, for example, how today's economists would seek to reduce environmental degradation. Starting with the pricing mechanism, they would note that environmental problems are exacerbated because the market (or government) underprices environmental resources; that is, not all costs are borne by producers so their goods and services are underpriced. If full-cost pricing were followed, the offending externality would be reduced, if not eliminated.

To reduce environmental pollution, governments could bring market prices into alignment with true producer costs by imposing direct or indirect pollution taxes or using pollution credits. Although our knowledge of how best to design and implement such programs remains rudimentary, some countries have enacted such systems. They have proven exceptionally promising, and we can expect more in the future.

Economists also point out that governmental subsidies distort pricing. In the energy sector alone, the IMF noted in the mid-1990s that governmental subsidies accounted for between 20 and 25 percent of the value of fossil fuel consumption worldwide. It estimated that, if these subsidies had been eliminated, global carbon emissions would have fallen by 7 percent. Similar examples were noted with electricity generation and agricultural production. As 21st century governments continue to embrace the market-economy philosophy, we look for such subsidies to fall.

Technology has another dark side besides that which flows from non-malicious actions that have bad consequences. By concentrating risk, technology affords an attractive target for criminals, terrorists, disgruntled employees and mentally unbalanced individuals. Most of the information held by governments and the private sector is vulnerable to terrorism simply because it is computer accessible. As we have already seen, today's protective measures are not completely reliable. Vulnerability increases as technology advances. Governmental and business risk managers should carefully consider these and other non-traditional exposures.

## RISK MANAGEMENT IN A FUTURE GLOBAL SETTING

While many see no good risk management substitute for personal insurance, insurers and other financial intermediaries could devise instruments that help individuals manage their wealth and risks over their entire lifetimes in much the same way that enterprise risk management is evolving for corporations. Moreover, some scholars believe that, with increasingly sophisticated information technology, we can do a better job of harnessing the market to minimize certain individual risks. Insight 26.3 offers one expert's opinions on this possibility.

Historically, the study and practice of risk management were limited to events that could cause harm. To shareholders, however, it makes little difference whether an uninsured fire, a poor product development decision or a foreign exchange loss causes a charge to earnings. It seems logical, therefore, that operational and financial risk management will strengthen their mutual embrace with potentially profound implications for the practice, study and definition of risk management.

One can envision two polar scenarios for tomorrow's risk managers. They either evolve into the true corporate risk guardians – the chief risk officer – or they devolve into an administrative function. Whichever way this issue evolves, it seems reasonable that 21st century corporations will continue efforts to measure and manage risk in an integrated way.

In the future, with appropriate financial innovation, the firm's *total* risk profile could be measured and monitored, and risk management decisions could flow from this profile, not from its components. Such a firm's risk financing portfolio – composed on various internal and external tools – could be carefully assembled in much the same way that today's asset managers assemble investment portfolios to minimize risk. Possibly unfavorable deviations from hazard risks may be offset with possibly favorable deviations in foreign exchange or interest rate risks. An integrated risk management approach would have us consider insurance as a contingent capital mechanism.

## INSIGHT 26.3: RISK MANAGEMENT FOR THE MASSES: HOW REASONABLE?

Few people think of inequality as a risk management problem. However, in many instances, economic inequality results from events over which individuals may have little or no control, such as occurs when an economy goes into recession, and individuals lose their jobs and the values of their homes plummet. An argument can be made that society should wish to reduce inequality resulting from such random shocks, as opposed to that which flows from individual education, talent and effort.

Shiller (2003) believes that, by coupling of risk management with technology and markets, society could reduce these negative effects for individuals and families. He notes that investment banks use sophisticated financial instruments to assist their clients in hedging the downside risks accompanying currencies and commodity prices and that venture-capital firms help start-up companies by designing compensation plans that simultaneously shield employees from some of the greatest risks of such young business ventures while offering them potential rewards to simulate them to work hard. The key to their being able to structure such hedging arrangements is having sufficient information on which to base decisions. Shiller argues that these same general risk management techniques could applied more broadly, extending to all workers, as more information becomes readily available and as automation and technology reduce costs and facilitate the tailoring and delivering of risk-management contracts to specific individuals.

Shiller imagines a possible future in which our personal financial services software – aided perhaps by professionals – allows individuals to make contracts to reduce income risk. Financial swaps based on average incomes in their regions could be used. Additionally, individuals could hedge against a decline in the market value of their homes – relying on regional indices of home values – through home-equity insurance contracts.

Perhaps advances in technology and information would permit the offering of insurance with broader coverage. Consider disability income insurance which presently provides indemnification only for lost income occurring because of injury or illness. Shiller believes that the scope of such coverage could be expanded to more risks, such as employees losing their jobs because of outsourcing or new technology, through these same approaches.

Finally, this new information technology could facilitate the growth of international markets for "a complex array of aggregated risks that today are not traded at all. In the not-too-distant future, we can have what will in effect be online auctions for occupational-income indices, for gross domestic product, and for swaps between GDPs of different nations," according to Shiller. By hedging their own risk portfolios in such markets, providers of risk management services, including insurers, shoule be able to offer a wider aray or risk management services to individuals.

Also, we might see companies allocating more time and resources to monitoring strategic risks in an integrated way. Strategic risks are those over which the firm has no control, such as inflation, new laws and regulations, changing social mores and the like. In periods of rapid change, the only way to manage successfully is to remain knowledgeable about possible causes of change. Corporations manage risks that they cannot control through superior knowledge. With increasing emphasis on ethical behavior by corporations and their employees, we might also observe risk mangers assuming greater responsibility for violations of corporate ethical norms, the consequences of which can be financially devastating for the firm. Hence, it is expected that more organizations in the private and public sectors as well as individuals will adopt an integrated (enterprise) approach to risk management in the 21st century.

# INSURANCE IN A FUTURE GLOBAL SETTING

How will the various environmental factors explored throughout this book and the speculations about their future affect the future world of insurance? This section explores some of these dimensions, looking first at the private sector then at the public sector.

## The Private Insurance Sector

Emerging markets have achieved real, annualized growth rates of 10.6 and 6.9 percent for life and nonlife insurance respectively over the preceding 10 years, as against 3.4 and 2.8 percent respectively for industrialized countries (Swiss Re, 2006). As economic growth is expected to be remain strongest in East Asian, Latin American and Central and Eastern European countries, future insurance demand should be correspondingly strongest in these countries. As promising signs of political and economic stability continue to pop up in Africa, we also can look forward to larger segments of this continent finally joining the trend toward global prosperity, with accompanying insurance growth.

### Trends in insurance demand

In the more mature markets, population aging coupled with fewer dependents will likely result in a continuing decline in the demand for traditional death-based life insurance. This decline likely will be accelerated as income tax preferences accorded life insurance are eliminated in the interest of tax neutrality. Demand for death-based insurance in many developing countries, however, should be strong where rapid economic growth combines with young populations, comparatively more dependents and a decline in informal insurance arrangements.

In all markets, but especially in OECD countries, demand for "living needs" products should swell. Disability income, long-term care and supplemental health insurance as well as annuities, pension and other savings products fall into this category. This strong demand stems from a combination of aging populations, reduced reliance on family and the gradual reduction of governments and employers as sources of individual economic security.

Future demand for personal nonlife insurance seems likely to be flat in most OECD countries because of slow growing or declining populations. Running counter to the adverse effects of these demographic trends should be increasing incomes and wealth, leading to more and higher valued insurable property, especially as middle-aged and retired persons buy second homes and move to locations considered desirable, such as along coasts and mountains which often connote greater hazards and higher premiums. Additionally, even with tort reform in some developed countries, liability insurance premiums seem likely to continue their greater than GDP growth rates.

Future personal nonlife insurance demand in rapidly growing emerging markets can be expected to be robust, realizing double-digit growths as growing populations of wealthy are able to afford the premiums for their increasingly valuable housing, cars and other assets. Additionally, look for such countries to continue to import elements of U.S. tort law interpretations, resulting in more litigious societies, with correspondingly greater demands for liability insurance. Developing countries whose economic and political houses remain disorderly cannot be expected to realize meaningful nonlife insurance growth.

Demand for commercial nonlife insurance in the OECD countries, at least in its traditional form, probably will decline relatively, as corporations, especially MNCs, continue to rely on non-traditional risk financing arrangements and to exploit more effectively enterprise risk management techniques. Opportunities exist for insurers to provide consultancy and innovative products to facilitate this transition.

An exception to this negative trend of commercial insurance should be an increase in demand from the many new, small entrepreneurial enterprises. Demand for such insurance within rapidly growing emerging markets should be robust. It will remain anemic and unbalanced in unstable developing countries.

### Trends in insurance supply

Insurance supply internationally will grow along with overall increased demand, led by growth in China, India, and countries in Central and Eastern Europe (including, ultimately, Russia) and in Latin America. Financial services conglomerates, led by established European groups, could gain market shares, especially through bank distribution to middle- and lower-income groups. Banks that successfully exploit their extensive customer databases should enjoy a competitive advantage. Their historical lack of strong marketing expertise probably will evaporate. Banks generally have been ahead of insurers in their innovative use of technology and in international expansion. This gap should narrow.

The number of major insurers and reinsurers can be expected to continue to decline worldwide through consolidation. Of course, specialized niche firms should prosper provided they focus intensely on their core competencies and markets. With continued liberalization and deregulation in many developing markets, we should see not only new domestic insurance capacity via new local establishments but also new international capacity.

In reinsurance, the trend toward creation of ever larger, more sophisticated reinsurers can be expected to continue. The complex, risky world of 21st century reinsurers will demand exceptionally strong capital positions, coupled with adequate profitability and liquidity. Reinsurance capacity seems likely to be increasingly augmented, but not replaced, by financial market products.

It appears that, to date, the anticipated future negative effects of global warming have yet to be factored into insurance and, especially, reinsurance pricing, policy limits or terms, and conditions. As our understanding of the effects of global warming grows, we can expect higher premiums and possibly restricted supply of weather-related insurances. Additionally, we can expect a more vigorous catastrophe bond market and large capacity finite insurance (reinsurance) arrangements to respond to enhanced demand.

Insurers will continue to adopt more consumer-focused ways of doing business, in sharp contrast to the traditional product-focused orientation prevailing throughout almost all of the previous century. This orientation would reinforce the notion that the insurer's customers, not its agents, are the ultimate consumers – contrary to the view that has prevailed with many insurers throughout most of the 20th century.

Insurers should seek answers to several questions. What products and services do our customers want? How do they want to purchase them? How and when would they like to receive service? The answers will differ from customer to customer. However, it seems logical that customer-driven firms should be prepared to provide a broad range of custom-tailored products and services through whatever means the customer chooses (e.g., agent, electronic, bank and telephone) and to service customers according to the customer's convenience.

Financial services conglomerates and insurance companies must be well capitalized, be efficient, and maintain profitable operations to be successful. Insurance expense ratios of 25–35 percent seem unsustainable in nonlife insurance. First-year commissions of 50 percent and higher seem similarly unsustainable in life insurance. Transaction costs seem destined to fall. Lower distribution costs probably will translate into fewer but more highly qualified agents in mature markets and in greater use of bank distribution, direct response distribution (especially for commodity-like products in personal life and nonlife insurance), and non-traditional distribution channels. Costs also could be lowered through more cooperative activities such as private labeling, co-marketing and product development, outsourcing and joint ventures as companies recognize that they cannot be superior in everything.

The marketing role of information technology remains unclear but promising. Many observers doubt that most individuals or businesses will purchase financial services products, especially insurance, electronically. Others note that nay-sayers made similar observations about banking when automatic teller machines (ATMs) were first introduced. Today, one-half of all retail banking transactions in numerous countries are via ATMs, automated telephone response systems, and the Internet. Might we expect similar results from the Internet marketing of insurance? Indeed, many insurers use the Internet as a means not only to market their products but also to offer online client services and to expedite claims services.

## The Public Insurance Sector

Population aging in the OECD countries means more elderly people to support, relatively fewer workers to pay taxes and higher healthcare bills than most governments promised to fund. When these so-called invisible debt problems are combined with existing and likely future national deficits in most OECD countries, budget prospects do not look good – a situation opposite that which exists for most East Asian developing countries.

Elderly dependency ratios in the major economies have drifted modestly upward over the past four decades but will increase sharply over the next 50 years. Dependency ratios will roughly double for most industrial countries by 2030. The problem is particularly acute in Japan and in most E.U. countries, except in the U.K.

Many countries must make substantial changes in their social insurance programs, of which the most critical is the public pension program. Delay is costly. Governments must wrestle with issues of intergenerational fairness and economic development.

It seems reasonable to expect governments to adjust benefits to financially sustainable levels. Partial employment in retirement likely will be encouraged. Contribution rates in many OECD countries are already high, so attempts at substantial increases are unlikely to be sustainable politically. Moreover, higher tax rates, coupled with already high national debts, could stifle economic growth. This fact, plus certain others, argues against moving to fully funded pension schemes.

Governments likely will increase normal and early retirement ages, especially in light of increasing life expectancy. We can expect income replacement ratios to decline, either directly or indirectly, through taxation or other means. Less liberal benefit indexing formula may prove more politically feasible. In addition, trends suggest that governments will link contributions more closely to benefits by allowing tax-preferred personal investment accounts to minimize long-term government liability for pension payments. Governments certainly will continue also to encourage individuals to make greater provision for their own retirement using private market instruments.

It would be surprising were there not continued intense discussion about moving from a pay-as-you-go, defined benefit system to a fully funded, defined contribution system, especially in developing countries. For most OECD countries and many developing countries, however, a complete shift to a fully funded system seems neither politically feasible nor economically sensible.

As for healthcare financing, it seems similarly unlikely that most governments can afford to sustain high quality, fully financed public healthcare systems. Moves toward increased cost sharing by patients as well as privatization of much of the systems' operations and financing seem inevitable. In the U.S., the strong emphasis on private financing seems destined to give way to some combination of private-public financing, especially for the more than 40 million citizens without health insurance.

## CLOSING OBSERVATIONS

We proffer no conclusions here, as each chapter has offered its own. What we have discussed throughout this book indeed lets us know the growing importance of risk management and insurance in a global economy. We hope that the speculations in the preceding sections of this chapter will provoke sufficient *disagreement* as to form a basis for the reader drawing his or her own conclusions. In this closing section, we offer three general observations.

First, we might reflect seriously on comedian Woody Allen's observation that we live in a world of too many moving parts. Certainly, today's world is more complex and ambiguous than yesterday's, while it will prove less complex and ambiguous than tomorrow's. We have an official future drawn by those whose wisdom we respect. However, relatively few major predictions have proven their worth over the past several decades and centuries. We can expect the "predictions" herein to suffer a similar fate!

Something seems always to shock the system – something that was not foreseen. Who, just 15 years ago, could have predicted the abrupt end of the cold war or the growth of the Internet? The one constant, paradoxically, is change, and we are likely to witness more of it in the next 10 years than has occurred in the preceding 100.

The second observation relates to externalities, a subject that resurfaces in various guises throughout this book and chapter. With increasing economic development, the world must cope with increasing possibilities of bad things being imposed by one group on others. Global warming, the possibility of horrendous chemical or genetic accidents or attacks, systemic risks to the financial system and innumerable other potentially catastrophic events are examples of *negative* externalities that demand both national and international attention. The private sector, on its own, is unlikely to resolve these mega issues. However, the risk management process and many of its economic and financial tools can help structure the debate.

Simultaneously, we should recognize that the increasing interconnectedness of peoples means also that good things accruing to one group may benefit others. High-quality education, adequate healthcare, smaller government deficits, sound public safety and a host of other activities carry life-enriching *positive* externalities that demand both national and international attention; or rather, their absence demands our attention. Again, the private sector, left to its own devises, is unlikely to ensure a sufficient supply of such goods.

The competitive model probably will continue to be embraced as offering each country's citizens the best hope for economic prosperity and, by that, a higher quality of life. Policymakers should take care to avoid holding unreasonable expectations about what the market-economy model can accomplish. It offers much, but also has sharp edges.

Finally, it will be interesting to observe how the U.S., in particular, continues to react to the new economic and political realities of the 21st century. Already, essentially unilateral actions (e.g., the Iraqi war) and other policy decisions by the U.S. government are said to have alienated many of the world's citizens and their governments. Coupled with an expected gain in economic and political clout by other countries, will the U.S. see the world as a dangerous place and become isolationist? Will it become more aggressive or will it seek to build strong international coalitions through which it seeks to affect change? It has been said that U.S. citizens believe in the notion of **American exceptionalism** – that only good things happen to the U.S. and that it is largely inoculated from the evils of the world, such as wars on U.S. soil, etc. If this view changes, what effect might it have on the national psyche and ultimately on world trade, political and military policies?

## DISCUSSION QUESTIONS

1.  Former Harvard University Professor Robert Reich liked to ask his students which they would prefer: (1) the U.S. economy growing at 2 percent and Japan at 3 percent or (2) both countries growing at 1 percent. A clear majority routinely chose the second option.
    (a) If you are a U.S. citizen, which option would you prefer? Explain your rationale. (If you are not a U.S. citizen, substitute your home country for the U.S. and your country's major trading rival for Japan, then answer the question.)
    (b) Analyze the majority response of the Harvard students. Is it economically rational? Why or why not?
2.  Scientists examining a recently discovered meteorite believed to be from Mars concluded that it showed some elementary components necessary for life. Scientists also have, for the first time, discovered scores of planets orbiting other stars, and many believe that planets are more numerous than the stars. What economic, political, technological, religious and cultural effects do you believe that the discovery of intelligent life on other planets would have on us earthlings?
3.  About 75 percent of the world's proven oil reserves are in the Middle East. Economic prosperity now and into the near future seems inextricably tied to an ample supply of oil.
    (a) As the risk manager of a major MNC, what actions would you recommend taking to minimize any adverse effects of another oil shock on shareholder value?
    (b) As the head of a major OECD country whose economy depends on Middle East oil, what actions would you recommend that your government take to minimize any adverse effects of another oil shock on your country's economy?

# NOTES

1. This discussion draws in parts from Skipper (1998), Chapter 28 and from *Global Trends 2015: A Dialogue about the Future with Nongovernmental Experts* (2000).
2. This discussion draws from *The World Economy* (2004).
3. In addition to compliance with the shear number of directives, there is also a question whether the E.U. has abandoned its formerly liberal approach to market reform in favor of a more Germanic style of regulation. A recent E.U. decision to adopt a restrictive rather than a liberal approach to cross-border mergers is seem by some as boding ill for future general business directives, including those relating to tax harmonization.
4. A continuing weakness of most intergovernmental organizations is that economically powerful governments, unhappy with an organization's decisions, can ignore them with comparatively few short-term negative consequences to themselves but with potentially enormous debilitating effects for the organization's effectiveness.
5. This part draws partly from Jackson (2002) and Jackson and Howe (2003).

# REFERENCES

*Global Trends 2015: A Dialogue about the Future with Nongovernmental Experts* (2000). Washington, DC: National Foreign Intelligence Board.

Jackson, R. (2002). *The Global Retirement Crisis*. Washington, DC: Center for Strategic and International Studies.

Jackson, R. and Howe, N. (2003). *The 2003 Aging Vulnerability Index*. Washington, DC: Center for Strategic and International Studies.

Pfaff, W. (2001). "The Question of Hegemony." *Foreign Affairs*, 80 (January/February): 221–233.

Shiller, R. (2003). "Economic Focus: Risk Management for the Masses." *The Economist* 366 (March 22) 70–71.

Skipper, H.D. (1998). "A Future Perspective," Chapter 28, *International Risk and Insurance: An Environmental-Managerial Approach*. Boston, MA: Irwin/McGraw-Hill.

"Special Report: Civil Wars." *The Economist* 367 (May 24, 2003): 23–25.

Swiss Re (2006). "World Insurance in 2005," *Sigma*. Zurich: Swiss Re.

"The World Economy." *The Economist* (September 30, 2004).

Silverman, R.E. (2000). "The Future is now . . . ." *The Wall Street Journal* (January 1).

# Glossary of Key Terms and Acronyms

**Absolute advantage**  *See* Chapter 3; cf. **Comparative advantage** and **Opportunity cost**.

**Accumulation period**  In annuity, time period during which annuity fund values accumulate, commonly prior to retirement. *See also* Chapter 21; cf. **Liquidation period**.

**Activities of daily living**  Often in long-term care, daily activities such as bathing, eating, toileting, dressing and walking. *See also* Chapter 21.

**Actual cash value**  The cost presently (not original purchase price) to replace or repair damaged property less the value of physical depreciation and obsolescence. *See also* Chapter 22; cf. **Replacement cost**.

**Actuarial science**  *See* Chapter 20.

**Actuarially fair premium**  The expected value of the insurance benefit with no allowance for insurer loadings. (Actuaries use the term "pure premium" and "net premium" to denote the same concept.)

**Admitted insurance**  The purchase of insurance from an insurance company authorized to do business within the jurisdiction. *See also* Chapters 14 and 20; cf. **Nonadmitted insurance**.

**Admitted (authorized) insurer**  An insurer licensed or otherwise authorized to conduct business within a jurisdiction. *See also* Chapter 24.

**Adverse selection**  An asymmetric information problem in which the seller knows less than the buyer about the buyer's situation. *See also* Chapters 2 (general) and 19 (effect on insurance); cf. **Moral hazard** and **Asymmetric information**.

**Advisory integration**  Financial services integration occurring at the level of the advisor, without necessarily any supply-side integration or even cooperation. *See also* Chapter 8; cf. **Product integration**.

**Agency**  In international insurance, a domestic agent representing a foreign insurer for the purposes of making sales and sometimes limited underwriting and claims settlement. *See also* Chapter 20; cf. **Branch**, **Subsidiary** and **Representative office**.

**Agenda 21**  *See* Chapter 12.

**Aggregate deductible**  *See* Insight 19.2.

**Agriculture**  The systematic, large-scale production of food through use of the plow. *See also* Chapter 11; cf. **Production**, **Horticulture, Agriculture** and **Industrialization**.

**AIG**  American International Group (U.S.).

**Alien insurance company**  In the U.S., an insurance company domiciled (incorporated) outside the U.S. *See also* Chapter 20; cf. **Domestic insurance company** and **Foreign insurance company**.

**AIRMIC**  Association of Insurance and Risk Managers (U.K.).

**ALARM**  The Association of Local Authority Risk Managers (U.K.).

*Allfinanz*  *See* **Bancassurance**.

**All-risks insurance**  Nonlife insurance coverage that promises to indemnify the insured for losses caused by any peril not specifically excluded. *See also* Chapter 22; cf. **Named peril insurance**.

**Ambiguity**    *See* **Exposure ambiguity**.

**American (style) option**    An option that can be exercised at any time before its expiration. *See also* Chapter 14; cf. **European (style) option**.

**American exceptionalism**    The myth that only good things happen to the U.S. and that it is largely immune from the evils of the world. *See also* Chapter 26.

**Americans with Disabilities Act (ADA)**    *See* Chapter 18.

**Annuity**    (1) Any series of periodic payments. (2) A branch of life insurance where the insurer pays a series of payments through systematic liquidation of principal and interest for a fixed period or over a person's lifetime. *See also* Chapter 21 for **pure life annuity, whole life annuity, annuity certain, temporary life annuity, joint-last-survivor annuity, installment refund annuity, immediate annuity, deferred annuity** and **equity-indexed annuity, market value annuity** and **structured settlement annuity**.

**Antitrust policy**    *See* **Competition policy**. *See also* Chapter 24.

**APEC**    Asia-Pacific Economic Cooperation.

**APRA**    Australian    Prudential    Regulatory Authority.

**Arbitrage**    The possibility of making a trading gain with no chance of loss. *See also* Chapter 14; for the **January effect**.

**Association of Southeast Asian Nations (ASEAN)**    [www.aseansec.org]. *See* Chapter 1.

**Asia-Pacific    Economic    Cooperation (APEC)**    [www.apecsec.org.sg]. *See* Chapter 1.

**AS/NZS    4360**    Australian/New    Zealand Standard: Risk Management. *See* Chapter 12.

**Assigned risk plan**    In automobile (motor) insurance, an arrangement for assigning "unwanted" insureds in the standard market to the servicing carrier so as to guarantee coverage and commonly at subsidized premium rates. Similar arrangements are known as **Residual market, High-risk insurance market, Automobile reinsurance pool** and, in the U.S., **Joint underwriting association (JUA)**. *See* Chapter 10.

**Association captive**    Also called as **group** captive, a captive insurance company that represents the interests of multiple unrelated organizations that share premiums and losses. *See* Chapter 13.

**Asymmetric information**    When one party to a transaction has relevant information that the other does not have.

**Asset liquidity (risk)**    Discussed under **financial risk** in Chapter 1.

**Automobile reinsurance pool**    *See* **Assigned risk plan**.

**Avoidance**    (1) The risk control technique of not engaging in an activity to eliminate the possibility of being exposed to a loss. (2) In a contract, the right of a non-breaching party to nullify the contract.

**Back-end    load**    In    life    insurance. *See* Chapter 21.

**Balanced reciprocity**    The immediate giving and receiving of goods or services of approximately equal value. *See also* Chapter 11.

*Bancassurance*    Bank    selling    insurance products or insurer selling banking products. Also known as *allfinanz*. *See also* Chapter 25; cf. **Financial conglomerate** and **Mixed conglomerate**.

**Basel    Capital    Accord    (Basel    II)**    *See* Chapter 8.

**Basel Committee on Banking Supervision (BCBS)**    *See* Chapter 8.

**Basic healthcare benefit**    A basic level of medical treatment typically including emergency care and outpatient services and some hospitalization and extended care coverage possibly through a set of scheduled payments. *See also* Chapters 16 and 21; cf. **Supplemental healthcare benefit**.

**Beaufort scale**    A scale used to classify a storm's wind speed. *See also* Chapter 5.

**Beneficiary**    A person who is named to receive life insurance death benefits. *See also* Chapter 21; cf. **Policyholder** and **Insured**.

**Bernoulli Principle**    *See* Chapter 2.

**Biotechnology**    *See*    Chapter    18    for    risk management.

**Boiler and machinery insurance**    Also known as **equipment breakdown insurance**. *See also* Chapter 22.

**Branch**    Of an insurance company, a substantial form of foreign establishment but without incorporation. *See also* Chapter 20; cf. **Agency, Subsidiary** and **Representative office**.

**Bribe**   *See* Insight 11.2; cf. **Rebate**.

**Bride price (wealth)**   A gift of money or goods from the groom or his kin to the bride's kin. *See also* Chapter 11.

**Broker**   An insurance intermediary (individual or firm) representing the insured and assisting the client in placing risk with an insurance company with whom the broker does not have any contractual (agency) arrangement. *See also* Chapter 20; cf. **Captive agent** and **Independent agent**.

**Broker's cover**   In reinsurance, *See* Chapter 23.

**Buffering mechanisms**   Practices designed to reduce variability in consumption and in income. *See also* Chapter 11.

**Business judgment rule**   *See* Chapter 10.

**Businessowner's insurance**   *See* Chapter 22.

**Cancer insurance**   *See* **Dread disease insurance** and Chapter 21. CAPM capital asset pricing model.

**Cedant (cedent, ceding company, or reinsured)**   An insurance company that transfers part of its risks or risk portfolios to another insurance company (also known as the **assuming company** or **reinsurer**). *See also* Chapter 23.

**Cafeteria benefit plan** *See* **Flexible benefit plan**.

**Call option**   The right to purchase an asset (e.g., shares of stock) at a specified price before a specified date. *See also* Chapter 14.

**Capital**   The excess of assets over liabilities. **Surplus**, **capital and surplus**, **policyholder surplus**, and **shareholder funds** are used synonymously with capital.

**Capital asset pricing model (CAPM)**   *See* Chapter 12.

**Capitalism**   A social and economic system in which the means of production (i.e., property, including capital and land) are owned and controlled largely by private persons.

**Capital market imperfection**   *See* Chapter 2.

**Capitation (fee) payment**   Per person payments for healthcare provider services that are capped to encourage providers to deliver only necessary care. Capitation payments are made prospectively, which puts providers at risk for financing services that total more than the capitated amounts. *See also* Chapter 9.

**Captive agent**   Also known as **tied agent** or **exclusive agent**, insurance intermediary who represents a single insurance company or group only. *See also* Chapter 20; cf. **Independent agent** and **Broker**.

**Captive insurer**   A closely held insurance company that provides insurance primarily or exclusively to its owner or owners. *See also* Chapter 13 for other forms of financing programs; cf. **Association captive**, **Single-parent captive** and **Virtual captive**.

**Capture theory of regulation**   A positive economic theory that holds that regulation is "captured" by and operated for the benefit of the regulated industry. *See also* Chapter 8; cf. **Private interest theory of regulation** and **Public interest theory of regulation**.

**Cargo insurance**   *See* Chapter 22.

**Cascading failure**   A type of systemic risk under which the failure of one financial institution is the proximate cause of the failure of others. *See also* Chapter 8.

**Cash market**   *See* **Spot market**.

**Cash value life insurance**   *See* Chapters 21 (general) and 24 (taxation).

**Catastrophe**   *See* Chapters 5 (definition) and 15 (risk management, modeling and reinsurance).

**Catastrophe excess-of-loss reinsurance**   *See* Chapter 23.

**Catastrophe risk securitization**   *See* Chapter 15 for **Catastrophe bond**.

*Caveat emptor*   ("let the buyer beware")   A warning that parties bargain fairly yet need not voluntarily disclose all relevant information to each other.

**CBOT**   Chicago Board of Trade (U.S.).

**CEA**   California Earthquake Authority (U.S.) [www.earthquakeauthority.com]. *See also* Chapter 15.

**Ceding commission**   Commission paid by the reinsurer (retrocessionaire) to the primary insurer (reinsurer) to compensate the latter for production and underwriting expenses. *See also* Chapter 23; for **Profit commission**.

**Centralized risk management program**   One that relies heavily on the head (corporate) office for establishment and control of the risk management programs of local operations and subsidiaries. *See also* Chapter 12; cf. **Decentralized risk management program** and **Global insurance program**.

**Centrally planned economy**   *See* Chapter 1.

**CERCLA**   Comprehensive Environmental Response, Compensation and Liability Act of 1980 (U.S.).

**Cession**   In reinsurance, transfer of risk or loss to the reinsurer. *See also* Chapter 23; for **Cession rate**; cf. **Retention**.

**China syndrome**   A nuclear meltdown as known in North America.

**Choice of law provision**   A provision in a contract stipulating the jurisdiction whose law will apply to contract interpretation. *See also* Chapter 10.

**Chotei**   Private conciliation method in Japan at which parties may be represented by attorneys. *See also* Chapter 10.

**CIS**   Commonwealth of Independent States (former USSR states).

**Civil law**   A systematic collection of laws, rules and regulations that a nation enacts to differentiate its laws from the "law of nature" or general principles of international law. *See also* Chapter 10; cf. **Common law**.

**Claims (settlement)**   In insurance operations., *See* Chapter 20.

**Class action**   A procedure enacted to provide a means for a large group of injured persons to sue wrongdoers without identifying every group member in the lawsuit. *See also* Insight 10.1.

**Classical economy theory**   *See* Chapter 3.

**Classification And Regression Trees (CART)**   *See* Chapter 12.

**CME**   Chicago Mercantile Exchange.

**Coase's Theorem**   When property rights are unambiguous and there are no transactions costs, markets will generate efficient outcomes, even with externalities. *See also* Chapter 4.

**COFACE**   *Compagnie Francaise d'Assurance pour le Commerce Exterieur.*

**Coinsurance**   *See* Insight 19.2 and Insight 22.1 for various definitions.

**Commercial   multiperil   insurance**   *See* Chapter 22.

**Common Market for Eastern and Southern Africa (COMESA)**   [www.comesa.int]. *See* Chapter 1.

**Common law**   Law that derives its authority from secular courts recognizing traditional usages and customs, especially the unwritten law of England. *See also* Chapter 10; cf. **Civil law**.

**Comparative advantage**   *See* Chapter 3; cf. **Absolute advantage** and **Opportunity cost**.

**Complement**   In insurance economics. *See* Chapter 19; cf. **Substitute**.

**Computer fraud**   *See* Chapter 18.

**Concentration risk**   Uncertainty arising from a firm concentrating its business or property in a narrow sector or territory. *See also* Chapter 1.

**Consequential loss**   *See* **indirect loss**.

**Contingency fee**   As in the U.S., legal services system in which attorneys are compensated as a percentage of successful lawsuits.

**Contractual transfer** (of risk)   *See* Chapter 12.

**Contributory infringement**   In intellectual property. *See* Chapter 18; cf. **Induced infringement**.

**Commercial lines insurance**   Nonlife insurance for business buyers.

**Common   account   excess-of-loss   reinsurance**   *See* Chapter 23.

**Competition policy (antitrust) regulation**   A nation's laws and regulations that govern private producers' behavior and the market structure within which interactions between producers take place. *See also* Chapters 8 and 24; cf. **Market conduct regulation** and **Prudential regulation**.

**Compulsory insurance law**   *See* Chapter 19.

**Composite insurer**   An insurance company authorized to write both life and nonlife insurance.

**Confiscation**   The taking of property by government without compensation, which is usually the result of commission of a crime associated with the property. *See also* Chapter 17; for **Political risk**, **Contract frustration**, **Currency inconvertibility**, **Expropriation** and **Nationalization**.

**Conglomerate collusion**   Behavior by a conglomerate or related group of firms that restrains competition by virtue of cooperative arrangements in different markets or in different sectors of markets. *See also* Chapter 24; cf. **Horizontal collusion** and **Vertical collusion**.

**Congruence**   *See* **Currency matching**.

**Constant returns to scale**   The condition that exists when a firm's average cost remains constant with increasing output. *See also* Chapter 2.

**Consumer surplus**   The difference between (1) the amount consumers are willing to pay for the good or service and (2) the amount actually paid (i.e., the market price); cf. **Producer surplus** and **Social welfare**. *See also* Chapter 3.

**Consumption-abroad cross-border insurance trade**   *See* Chapter 20.

**Contagion**   In financial integration. *See* Chapter 25.

**Contestable Markets**   Markets with low entry and exit barriers.

**Contextualist risk theory**   The class of risk perception theories that begins with the context in which risk-based decisions are made (e.g., culture, affinity group, organization, lifestyle), drawing inferences about group and then individual risk behavior. *See also* Chapter 4; cf. **Individualist risk theory**.

**Contingent capital**   *See* Chapter 13.

**Contract frustration**   Non-performance of contract because of government action or political instability. *See also* Chapter 17; for **Political risk**, **Confiscation**, **Currency inconvertibility**, **Expropriation**, and **Nationalization**.

**Contractual liability**   *See* Chapter 10.

**Contract situs**   The jurisdiction whose law applies to contract creation, interpretation and enforcement. *See also* Chapter 20.

**Contractors' all risk (CAR) insurance policy**   Also called **builders all risk policies**. *See* Chapter 22.

**Contractual model**   A healthcare payment model in which the insurer contracts with providers (public or private) to provide medical services to patients. *See also* Chapter 9.

**Conversion**   Of a life insurance policy. *See* Chapter 21.

**Copyright**   As intellectual property. *See* Insight 18.2.

**Corporate governance**   *See* Chapter 10 (general), Chapter 13 (captive insurance), and Chapter 14 (director's and officer's liability).

**Corporate reimbursement liability insurance**   *See* Chapter 14; for **D&O liability coverage** and **Entity coverage**.

**COSO**   Committee of Sponsoring Organizations of the Treadway Commission [www.coso.org]. *See* Chapter 12.

**Cost/Benefit Analysis**   *See* Insight 12.2. Cost of insurance. See Chapter 21.

**Cost of risk**   The sum of all property-liability insurance premiums, retained losses, risk control expenses, and administrative costs.

**Counter party**   The other party to a contract.

**Counterparty (credit) risk**   *See* Discussed under **financial risk** in Chapters 1 and 12.

**Credit (counterparty) risk**   Discussed under **financial risk** in Chapters 1 and 12.

**Crisis management**   The process of identifying those situations that constitute a crisis, having an organized response to the crisis and ultimately resolving the crisis. (1) *See also* Chapter 15 (catastrophe risk management); cf. **Disaster planning** and **sustainability risk management**. (2) *See also* Chapter 16 (personnel risk management).

**Critical infrastructures**   Systems whose incapacity or destruction would have a debilitating impact on the defense or economic security of a nation. *See also* Chapter 6.

**CRO**   Chief Risk Officer.

**Cross-border trade**   In insurance. *See* Chapter 20; for **Own-initiative cross-border insurance Consumption-abroad cross-border insurance trade**, **DIC/DIL insurance trade** and **Excess and surplus insurance**.

*Culpa en contrahendo*   "Fault in negotiating."

**Cultural biases**   Culturally based rationales for different ways of behaving. *See also* Chapter 4.

**Cultural relativism**   A central anthropological tenant used in understanding other cultures, holds that each culture should be examined using its own standards and value system, not that of the observer. *See also* Chapter 11.

**Cultural risk perception**   *See* Chapter 11.

**Culture** Customary ways of thinking and behaving of a particular population or society. *See also* Chapter 11.

**Currency options** *See* Appendix 14B.

**Currency [foreign exchange (FX)] rate risk** *See* Chapter 12.

**Currency inconvertibility** Inability to covert a local current to the currency of the home country or a hard currency. *See also* Chapter 17; for **Political risk**, **Confiscation**, **Contract frustration**, **Expropriation** and **Nationalization**.

**Currency swap** *See also* **Swap** and Chapter 14.

**Currency matching** The practice of having liabilities denominated in one currency being backed (matched) with assets denominated or realizable in the same currency. Also called **congruence**. *See also* Chapter 24.

**Current assumption whole life** *See* Chapter 21.

**Cut-through provision** When added to an insurance contract, the insured's right to seek claims payment directly from the reinsurer on the insurer's failure to meet its obligations fully or on time. *See also* Chapter 23.

**Cybercrime** *See* Chapter 18.

**Cyclone** *See* Chapter 5.

**D&O insurance** *See* **Director's & Officer's (liability) insurance**.

**DB** In employee benefits, *See* **Defined benefit**.

**DC** In employee benefits, *See* **Defined contribution**.

**Decentralized risk management program** One that relies heavily on local operations or subsidiaries to make their own risk management decisions. *See also* Chapter 12; cf. **Centralized risk management program** and **Global insurance program**.

**Decision regret** A notion that we feel far worse about having made bad choices than we do about our failures to have made smart choices. *See also* Chapter 2; cf. **Mental accounting** and **Welfare effect**.

**Decreasing returns to scale** The condition that exists when a firm's average cost increases with increasing output.

**Deductible** *See* Insight 19.2 for various definitions.

**Defensive strategy** In political risk management. *See* Chapter 17; cf. **Integrative strategy**.

**Deferred annuity** An annuity whose first benefit payment is made after the passage to some time, typically several years. *See also* Chapter 21; cf. **Immediate annuity**.

**Deferred wage theory** Concept that retirement benefits can be thought of as the employee agreeing to defer some current wages in favor of payments during retirement years. *See also* Chapter 16.

**Defined benefit (DB) approach** A traditional approach to employee benefit design in which the benefits to be provided to employees are fixed with the employer determining the types and amounts of employee benefits. *See also* Chapter 16; cf. **Defined contribution approach** and **Flexible benefit approach**.

**Defined contribution (DC) approach** An approach to employee benefit design wherein the employer contribution amounts rather than the benefits are fixed. *See also* Chapter 16; cf. **Defined benefit approach** and **Flexible benefit approach**.

**Demutualization** The process by which mutual insurance companies change their corporate form to become stock companies.

**Deregulation** The process of reducing regulation to that which is minimally necessary to achieve its goal and, in the process, placing greater reliance on market forces to ensure consumer protection. *See also* Chapter 3; cf. **Liberalization** and **Privatization**.

**Derivatives** A financial market security whose characteristics and value are a function of the characteristics and values of other securities. *See also* Chapters 12 and 14.

**Detention** The temporary custody of an individual for lawful purposes. *See also* Chapter 16; cf. **Extortion**, **Kidnapping** and **Terrorism**.

**Developed market economy** *See* Chapter 1.

**Developing economy** *See* Chapter 1.

**DIC** Difference-in-conditions. *See* Chapters 14 and 20.

**DIL** Difference-in-limits. *See* Chapters 14 and 20.

**Direct response (marketing)** A type of marketing in which the insurer sells directly to customers without the use of intermediaries, by means of the Internet, mail, telephone solicitation, or other mass media.

**Direct insurer** (1) An insurance company that sells insurance directly to the general public. (2) In reinsurance, primary insurer; cf. **Reinsurer** or **Retrocessionaire**.

**Direct loss** Reduction in value (e.g., property) caused by a loss event. *See also* Chapter 22; cf. **Indirect (consequential) loss**.

**Direct voluntary out-of-pocket system** In health insurance, payment of healthcare cost with no third-party payers. *See also* Chapter 9.

**Direct writer** Insurer that markets without using intermediaries.

**Direct writing reinsurers** Those that use their own employees to market reinsurance. *See also* Chapter 23.

**(E.U.) Directive** (1) An order issued by the E.U.'s Council of Ministers that requires member countries to enact new national laws or alter existing laws to come into compliance with the directive's provisions. (2) Also known as **administrative directive**, an order issued by the regulatory authority to insurers operating within the jurisdiction.

**Director's & Officer's liability insurance** *See* Chapter 14; for **D&O liability coverage**, **Corporate reimbursement liability** and **Entity coverage**.

**Dirty bomb** Nuclear material such as waste by-products from a nuclear reactor that is wrapped or mixed with conventional explosives. *See also* Chapter 6 for discussion under terrorism.

**Disaster planning** *See* Chapter 15; also **Crisis management** and **Sustainability risk management**.

**Disability benefit plans** *See* Chapter 9 (occupational injury), Chapter 16 (employee benefits) and Chapter 21 (private disability insurance).

**Disclosure** *See* **Transparency**.

**Distribution** One of the ways that a society allocates its goods and services. *See* Chapter 11.

**Domestic insurance company** One domiciled (incorporated) in the concerned country or jurisdiction. *See also* Chapter 20; cf. **Alien insurance company** and **Foreign insurance company**.

**Double gearing** *See* Chapter 25.

**Dowry** A payment by her parents of a bride's share of the property that she would have otherwise received on her parents' death. *See also* Chapter 11.

**Dread disease insurance** Specialty insurance that pays a variety of benefits up to substantial maximums solely for the treatment of diseases named in the policy, typically including cancer and heart disease. *See also* Chapter 21.

**Dumping** Predatory pricing practiced on an international basis; that is, selling products or services at less than their cost of production to gain market share. *See also* Chapter 3.

**Dynamic (operational) efficiency** Also called **X-efficiency**, promptness in incorporating product and process innovations and other operational efficiencies into production. *See also* Chapters 3 and 25 (financial integration).

**E&O** In liability insurance, **Errors and omissions**. *See also* Chapter 22.

**Earned premium** *See* Insight 19.1; cf. **Unearned premium**.

**Earthquake** *See* Chapter 5.

**Economic damages** In court settlement. *See* Insight 14.1; cf. **Special (non-economic) damages** and **Punitive damages**.

**Economic family theory** The position of the U.S. Internal Revenue Service that a single-parent captive and its parent company are part of the same economic unit and, therefore, risk shifting cannot occur. *See also* Chapter 13.

**Economic needs-tested** (or **means-tested**) **program** A method that determines eligibility by comparing each applicant's resources to formula-based standards for subsistence need estimation and offers benefits only to the applicants who satisfy the test. *See also* Chapter 9.

**Economic neutrality** In taxation, *See* Chapter 24; cf. **(Vertical) equity**.

**Economic power theory** Deteriorating population bases mean declining economic strength, which in turn invites other countries to expand into that space. *See also* Chapter 7; cf. **Political power theory**.

**Economic rent** Any payment to a factor of production in excess of the minimum required to bring forth or retain its service. *See also* Chapter 3; cf. **Rent-seeking behavior**.

**Economic regulation** *See* Chapter 8.

**Economies of scale**   The condition that exists when a firm's output increases at a rate faster than attendant increases in its production costs. *See also* Chapters 3 (general) and 25 (financial integration).

**Economies of scope**   The condition that exists when a firm realizes efficiencies from the joint production of products. *See also* Chapter 3 (general) for discussion including **economies of scope in production** and **geography-based economies of scope** as well as Chapter 25 (financial integration).

**EEC**   (1) European Economic Community; (2) European Economic Council.

**Effects doctrine**   *See* Chapter 24.

**Embedded value analysis**   The value inherent in a life insurer's existing and future business. *See also* Chapter 25.

**Emerging market**   *See* Chapter 1 for definition and other terms/definitions.

**Employee benefits**   All forms of employer-provided compensation, exclusive of direct wages and salaries. *See also* Chapter 16.

**Employer's liability insurance**   A contract that promises to indemnify the insured/employer for injuries to employees resulting from the employer's negligence. *See also* Chapter 22; cf. **Workers' (workmen's) compensation insurance**.

**Employment practices liability (EPL)**   *See* Chapter 14.

**Endogenous growth theory**   The belief that a positive correlation exists between the *development* of productivity and economic growth. *See also* chapter 7.

**Endowment insurance**   A policy that pays the face amount if the insured (1) dies during the policy period or (2) survives to the end of the period. *See also* Chapter 21; for **Pure endowment**.

**Enterprise risk management (ERM)**   The process by which an entity identifies, assesses and implements decisions about the collective risks that can affect enterprise value. *See also* Chapters 12 (fundamentals) and 25 (financial integration).

**Entity coverage**   In D&O insurance. *See* Chapter 14; for **D&O liability coverage** and **Corporate reimbursement liability**.

**Environmental risk**   Prospects of damage to the physical environment caused by human activities. *See also* Chapter 6.

**EPA**   Environmental Protection Agency (U.S.).

**E-put**   *See* Chapter 13.

**Equipment breakdown insurance**   Also known as **boiler and machinery insurance**. *See* Chapter 22.

**Equity**   (1) The firm's own capital. (2) In taxation, also known as **vertical equity**, each taxpayer paying a fair share in taxes. *See also* Chapter 24; cf. **Economic neutrality**.

**Errors and omissions (E&O) insurance**   *See* Chapter 22.

**ERM**   Enterprise risk management.

**Ethics**   The rules that guide behavior that flow from adherence to moral precepts. *See also* Chapter 11.

**Ethnocentrism**   The view that one's own culture is superior to others, and one judges other cultures by the standards of one's own. *See also* Chapter 11.

**E.U.**   European Union [www.europa.eu].

**E.U. Directive**   *See* **Directive**.

**Eurocodes**   A set of 58 standards in 10 codes containing methods to assess the mechanical resistance of building structures and parts. *See also* Chapter 15.

**European Commission**   E.U. entity with primary responsibility for proposing and administering directives and other orders.

**European Court of Justice**   E.U.'s judicial arm responsible for adjudicating disputes between member states and between the E.U. and member states.

**European Parliament**   E.U. entity responsible for reviewing and commenting upon proposed directives.

**European (style) option**   An option that can be exercised only on the expiration date specified in the contract. *See also* Chapter 14; cf. **American (style) option**.

**Ex-ante moral hazard**   *See* Chapter 19; cf. **ex-post moral hazard**.

**Ex-ante regulation**   Government intervention to prevent any offensive activity from occurring by proscribing or regulating it before-the-fact. *See also* Chapter 24; cf. **ex-post regulation**.

**Excess and surplus (E&S) insurance**   *See* Chapter 20.

**Excess-of-loss (non-proportional) reinsurance** *See* Chapter 23.

**Exclusive agent**   *See* **captive agent**.

**Excessive leveraging**   *See* Chapter 25.

**Exercise price**   In option contracts, *See* **strike price**.

**Exercise (intrinsic) value**   The value available to the owner by exercising an option.

**Ex-Im Bank**   (1) Generically, export import bank promoting export and foreign direct investment by domestic firms and offering political insurance to those firms. (2) Export Import Bank (U.S.) [www.exim.gov]. *See also* Chapter 17 for similar banks in other countries in Table 17.3.

**Exclusive agent**   *See* **captive agent**.

**Expected utility rule**   Risk-averse individuals will select the option with the highest expected utility. *See also* Chapter 2.

**Experience rating**   Pricing plan in which the insurer relies heavily on the insured's past loss experience with industry-wide adjustment. *See also* Chapter 19; cf. **retrospective rating**.

**Ex-post moral hazard**   *See* Chapter 19; cf. **Ex-ante moral hazard**.

**Expropriation**   The taking of property by government without compensation as in eminent domain. *See also* Chapter 17; for **Political risk**, **Confiscation**, **Contract frustration**, **Currency inconvertibility** and **Nationalization**.

**Ex-post regulation**   Government intervention into the market only after an offensive activity has occurred. *See also* Chapter 24; cf. **Ex-ante regulation**.

**Exposure ambiguity**   A situation in insurance pricing where underlying pricing data are lacking or believed unreliable. *See also* Chapter 9.

**Exposure unit**   A unit for insurance purchase/pricing (e.g., an automobile, a house, $1,000 of life insurance coverage). *See also* Chapter 19; for **Independent, Identically distributed exposure units**.

**Extended family**   One or more nuclear families plus grandparents and possibly aunts, uncles and some cousins who live and work together. *See also* Chapter 11; cf. **Nuclear family**.

**Externality**   Direct and uncompensated effects of a firm's production or an individual's consumption on others, either negatively or positively. *See also* Chapters 4 and 9.

**Extortion**   The use of force or intimidation to obtain money or other property from someone. *See also* Chapter 16; cf. **Detention**, **Kidnapping** and **Terrorism** (on individual).

**Face amount**   Also known as **sum assured** in life insurance, a death benefit as a stated sum of money.

**Facultative-obligatory (fac-oblig) treaty**   *See* Chapter 23.

**Facultative reinsurance**   Contract in which the primary insurer negotiates a separate reinsurance agreement for each policy it reinsures. *See also* Chapter 23; cf. **Treaty reinsurance**.

**Fair trade principles**   *See* Chapter 3; cf. **Market access**, **Non-discrimination**, **National treatment**, **Transparency**, and **Reciprocity**.

**Fault**   Boundary between tectonic plates of the earth.

**FDI**   Foreign direct investment.

**Fee-for-service**   Payment for health-care provider services after they are rendered. *See also* Chapter 9; cf. **Managed care**.

**Fertility rate**   The average number of lifetime births per woman. *See also* Chapter 7.

**FFSA**   *Fédération Française des Sociétés d'Assurance* (France).

**Fidelity/crime insurance policy**   *See* Chapter 22.

**Fiduciary duty**   In corporate governance, *See* Chapter 10.

**File and use**   A system of insurance rate regulation in which insurers are allowed to use a proposed rate schedule after filing it with the regulator. The regulator may later disapprove the rates, but failing this, the rates are deemed to be acceptable. *See also* Chapter 24.

**Financial conglomerate**   A group of companies under common control whose exclusive or predominant activities consist of providing significant services in at least two of the three major financial sectors. *See also* Chapters 8 and 25; cf. *Bancassurance* and **Mixed conglomerate**.

**Financial distress (of a firm)**   *See* Chapter 2.

**Financial (prudential) regulation**   Regulation designed to oversee the continuing financial viability of financial intermediaries. Also referred to as *le contrôle financier* (France and its former colonies) and as *Finanzaufsicht* (Germany and Austria). *See also* Chapter 24.

**Financial reinsurance**   Differs from traditional reinsurance in that it explicitly recognizes the traditional risk components (underwriting, timing, and investment) but limits one or more of them in the agreement. *See also* Chapter 23.

**Financial responsibility law**   In automobile insurance. *See* Insight 10.2.

**Financial risk**   Risk arising from individuals' or organizations' ownership or use of financial instruments. *See also* Chapter 1.

**Financial Sector Assessment Program**   [www.imf.org/external/NP/fsap/fsap.asp] *See* Chapter 8.

**Financial Stability Forum**   [www.fsforum.org] *See* Chapter 8.

**Finite (re)insurance**   An insurance arrangement with an explicit profit-sharing between the parties where the reinsurer (insurer) offers insurance protection for a unique, large risk for multiple periods but with no renewal possible. *See also* Chapter 23.

**First Generation Insurance Directives**   A set of early E.U. insurance directives establishing common standards for the granting of authorizations and solvency margins and financial guarantee funds. cf. **Second Generation Insurance Directives** and **Third Generation Insurance Directives**.

**First-to-die (joint) life insurance**   A contract that promises to pay the face amount on the first death of two insureds. *See also* Chapter 21; cf. **Second-to-die life insurance**.

**Flexible benefit (flex) plan**   A defined contribution approach to benefit plan design wherein employees (according to their needs and wants) select the types and amounts of coverage from an array of benefits offered by the employer, subject to specific cost and other constraints. *See also* Chapter 16; cf. **Defined benefit approach** and **Defined contribution approach**.

**Fit and proper regulation (requirement)**   *See* Chapter 25.

**Flood**   Partial or complete inundation of a normally dry land area caused by an overflow of tidal, river or lake water or after a heavy rain. *See also* Chapter 5.

**Foraging**   Reliance on hunting, gathering, and foraging for food. *See also* Chapter 11.

**Foreign Direct Investment (FDI)**   Investment by foreigners in domestic businesses as in when a firm from one country acquires financial assets in another country with the intention of actively managing those assets. *See also* Chapters 1 (general) and 17 (political risk management).

**Foreign exchange (FX) risk**   *See* Chapters 12 (general) and 14 (case).

**Foreign insurance company**   An insurance company domiciled (incorporated) in another country/jurisdiction or, in the U.S., a different state. *See also* Chapter 20; cf. **Alien insurance company** and **Domestic insurance company**.

**Formal internal loss financing**   A dedicated program explicitly to finance losses internally, such as self-insurance or captive insurance. *See also* Chapter 13 for other forms of financing programs.

**Forward contract**   Specifies trading terms for a transaction to take place at a future time. *See also* Chapters 12 and 14; cf. **Options** and **Futures**.

**Forward market**   A market in which forward contracts are traded and in which no cash changes hands until contract maturity. *See also* Chapter 12.

**Franchise**   A firm's market reputation. *See also* Chapter 25; cf. **Goodwill**.

**Franchise deductible**   *See* Insight 19.2.

**Fraud**   *See* Chapters 18 (IT fraud) and 19 (in insurance).

**Free-market economy**   An economy in which no government intervention exists.

**Free rider problem**   The condition that exists with positive externalities wherein a good or service, if supplied to one person, is available to others at low or zero cost. *See also* Chapters 2 and 4.

**Free Trade Agreement of the Americas (FTAA)**   [www.ftaa-alca.org]. *See* Chapter 1.

**Fronting**   A contractual arrangement between a local direct insurer – termed as **fronting company** – and a foreign insurer under which the direct insurer agrees to accept the local risks of the foreign insurer and reinsure most of those risks with the foreign insurer. *See also* Chapter 13.

**FSA** Financial Supervisory Agency (Japan, the U.K.).

**Fully funded approach** In public pensions, having sufficient funds presently to pay accrued benefits for current participants. *See also* Chapter 9; cf. **Pay-as-you-go approach**.

**Futures** Contracts traded on organized exchanges for the future purchase and sale of goods or services. *See also* Chapters 12 and 14; cf. **Options** and **Forward contract**.

**GAAP** *See* Generally accepted accounting principles.

**GBL** **Gramm-Leach-Bliley Act**. *See* Chapter 21.

**Gee Gees** *See* Insight 5.3.

**General Agreement on Trade in Services (GATS)** *See* Chapter 1.

**General Agreement on Tariffs and Trade (GATT)** *See* Chapter 1.

**GDP** Gross domestic product.

**Gender** The cultural roles that society assigns to men and women. *See also* Chapter 11.

**Gender hierarchy** A situation in which traits associated with males, although not necessarily male, are valued over traits associated with females. *See also* Chapter 11.

**General business liability** *See* Insight 14.1.

**General insurance** Nonlife insurance; synonymous with property and liability insurance. *See also* Chapter 1.

**General tax revenue model** Healthcare financing in which services are paid by the government from general tax revenues, generally, with universal healthcare coverage. *See also* Chapter 9; cf. **Social insurance model** and **Voluntary insurance model**.

**Generalized reciprocity** The giving and receiving of goods or services where neither the timing nor the value of the exchange is specified. *See also* Chapter 11.

**Generally accepted accounting principles (GAAP)** Accounting principles prescribed by the accounting profession. *See also* Chapter 24; cf. **Statutory accounting principles**.

**Genetic engineering** *See* Chapter 6.

**Geographic indication** As intellectual property. *See* Insight 18.2.

**GIC** Guaranteed investment contract.

**Goodwill** The value of future business of the firm. *See also* Chapter 25; cf. **Franchise**.

**Government imperfection** *See* Chapter 8.

**Government procurement** Government policy requiring government agencies to buy certain goods and services from local producers. *See also* Chapter 3; cf. **Quota**, **Subsidy** and **Government procurement**.

**Gradual (phased) retirement** A process whereby individuals move to a part-time employment status before retiring fully. *See also* Chapter 16.

**Gramm-Leach-Bliley Act** *See* Chapter 21.

**Great natural disaster** As defined by the UN (and Munich Re), catastrophes of such magnitude that the affected region's capabilities to respond effectively are clearly overstretched, and supraregional or international assistance is required. *See also* Chapter 5; cf. **Catastrophe**.

**Green goo problem** In nanotechnology. *See* Chapter 18; cf. **Grey goo problem**.

**Greenhouse effect** The natural warming of the earth because of the atmosphere.

**Greenhouse Enhancing Effect** The enhancement of the greenhouse effect caused by the increase in trace gases in the earth's atmosphere.

**Grey goo problem** In nanotechnology. *See* Chapter 18; cf. **Green goo problem**.

**Grid** In the anthropological approach to risk, the degree to which individuals are constrained by internally or externally imposed classifications. *See also* Chapter 4.

*Grossbanken* Big bank (German).

**Group** In the anthropological approach to risk, the degree to which individuals are incorporated into a social unit. *See also* Chapter 4.

**Group life insurance** *See* Chapter 16.

**Group captive** *See* **Association captive**. *See also* Chapter 13.

**Hazard** A condition that increases the likelihood or severity of a loss. *See also* Chapter 1 for specific definitions; cf. **Peril**.

**Hazard and Operability (HAZOP)** *See* Chapter 12.

**Hazard risk** Uncertainty relating to losses caused by perils. *See also* Chapter 1.

**Health** A state of complete physical, mental, and social wellbeing and not merely the absence of disease or infirmity (defined in WHO's Constitution). *See also* Chapter 1.

**Health Insurance** *See* Chapter 9.

**Health maintenance organization (HMO)** A healthcare organization that provides comprehensive services to members on a prepaid, capitated basis. An HMO acts is a type of managed care organization where the *financing* of healthcare and the *delivery* of healthcare are combined into the same entity. *See also* Chapter 9; cf. **Preferred provider organization (PPO)** and **Point-of-service program**.

**Health outcomes** Measures of the overall level of health. Life expectancy and infant mortality rates are the two health outcome measures often used in cross-country comparisons of health systems. *See also* Chapter 9.

**Hedge** The use of futures or other financial instruments to protect the value of an asset portfolio. *See also* Chapters 12 and 14.

**HGP** Human Genome Project.

**High-risk insurance plan** In automobile (motor) insurance, *See also* **assigned risk plan**.

**High value (highly protected) risk** Complex and highly integrated industrial property that uses the latest technology in construction, property maintenance and production process. *See also* Chapter 1.

**Hindsight bias** Things that were not seen or understood at the time of an accident seem obvious in retrospect. *See also* Chapter 6.

**HMO** *See* **Health maintenance organization**.

**Hold harmless agreement** Contractual assumption by one party of the liability exposure of another. *See* Chapter 12; cf. **Indemnification agreement**.

**Home country** The country of domicile (incorporation); cf. **Host country**.

**Homeowner's insurance** *See* Chapter 22.

**Horizontal collusion** When two or more firms undertake competition-reducing activities in the same market. *See also* Chapter 24; cf. **Vertical collusion** and **Conglomerate collusion**.

**Horticulture** The simplest form of food production, involves the planting of food using simple tools and human labor. *See also* Chapter 11; cf. **Production**, **Pastoralism**, **Agriculture** and **Industrialization**.

**Hospital confinement indemnity insurance** Coverage paying a fixed sum for each day of hospital confinement typically for up to 1 year, usually irrespective of other health insurance coverage. *See also* Chapter 21.

**Host country** The country of operation other than the domiciliary country; cf. **Home country**.

**Householder's (household) insurance** *See* Chapter 22.

**Human Genome Project** *See* Chapter 18.

**Household** The basic residential unit within which economic production, consumption, inheritance, child rearing, and shelter are organized and carried out (Haviland, 1990).

**Hurricane** *See* Chapter 5 for discussion and also Insight 5.2 about hurricane Katrina.

**IAIS** International Association of Insurance Supervisors [www.iaisweb.org]. *See* Chapter 8.

**IBNR** See Incurred but not reported.

**IFA** Independent financial advisor (U.K.).

**IMF** *See* **International Monetary Fund** [www.imf.org]; Chapter 1.

**Immediate annuity** An annuity purchased with a single premium with the first benefit payment due (almost) immediately. *See also* Chapter 21; cf. **Deferred annuity**.

**Import substitution policy** The government promoting or protecting those local industries that compete directly with imports. *See also* Chapter 3.

**Income elasticity of insurance premiums** *See also* Chapter 20.

**Income replacement** In pension. *See* Chapter 16.

**Income taxation** *See* Chapter 24.

**Incurred but not reported (IBNR)** Claims that have been incurred during a policy period but have not been reported to the insurer.

**Indemnification agreement** A contractual agreement that certain unanticipated costs or losses arising under a contract and incurred by one party to the transaction are reimbursable by the other. *See also* Chapter 12; cf. **Hold harmless agreement**.

**Independent agent**   An insurance intermediary who represents multiple, non-affiliated insurers simultaneously. *See also* Chapter 20; cf. **Captive agent** and **Broker**.

**Indirect loss**   Reductions in value or increases in expenses that result from (are a consequence of) direct losses. *See also* Chapter 22; cf. **Direct loss**.

**Individual aging**   The maturational development of individual men and women. *See also* Chapter 7; cf. **Population aging**.

**Individualist risk theory**   The class of risk perception theories that focuses on the behavior of individuals when faced with risky conditions from which generalization about group risk behavior may be inferred. *See also* Chapter 4; cf. **Contextualist risk theory**.

**Induced infringement**   In intellectual property. *See* Chapter 18; cf. **Contributory infringement**.

**Industrial all risk insurance policies**   *See* Chapter 22.

**Industrial design**   As intellectual property. *See* Insight 18.2.

**Industrial insurance**   *See* The discussion about **commercial lines insurance** in Chapter 1.

**Industrial property**   Intellectual property rights attaching to patents, trademarks, designs and logos. *See also* Chapter 18; cf. **Intellectual property**.

**Industrialization**   The production of goods and services via manufacturing *See also* Chapter 11; cf. **Production**, **Pastoralism**, **Horticulture**, **Agriculture** and **Industrialization**.

**Infant industry argument**   A contention that government should shelter certain "infant" industries from the fullness of foreign competition until the industries are sufficiently mature to be able to compete with foreign firms on a reasonably equal basis. *See also* Chapter 3.

**Informal internal loss financing**   The making of no special arrangements to finance losses internally, as when the amounts involved are comparatively small (e.g., employee pilferage). *See also* Chapter 13 for other forms of financing programs.

**Input price risk**   The possibility that the price of an organization's production inputs will increase. *See also* Chapter 12; cf. **Output price risk**.

**Insurance**   Risk financing contractual arrangement with an insurance company.

**Insurance broker**   *See* **Broker**.

**Insurance density**   The average annual per capita premium. *See also* Chapter 20; cf. **Insurance penetration**.

**Insurance penetration**   The ratio of insurance premiums to a country's GDP. *See also* Chapter 20; cf. **Insurance density**.

**Insurance pool**   (1) A risk pooling and sharing arrangement by multiple insurers. (2) An alternative term for **risk class**. *See also* Chapter 19.

**Insurance production process**   *See also* Chapter 20.

**Insured**   (1) In nonlife insurance, the person whose loss exposure is insured. (2) In life insurance, the individual whose death triggers payment of the face amount. *See also* Chapter 21; cf. **Policyholder** and **Beneficiary**.

**Intangible personal property**   Property without tangible or physical substance, including goodwill, copyrights, patents, trademarks and licenses. *See also* Chapter 22.

**Integrated model**   Healthcare financing in which the insurer and provider are the same entity, which typically reduces administrative costs of the system. *See also* Chapter 9.

**Integrative strategy**   In political risk management. *See* Chapter 17; cf. **Defensive strategy**.

**Intellectual property**   Ownership rights to one's intangible innovations and creativity. *See* Chapter 18; cf. **Industrial property**.

**Intentional tort**   The actual or implied intent to harm other persons or their property. *See also* Chapter 10; cf. **Negligence** and **Strict liability**.

**Interest rate risk**   The possibility of a loss from an adverse movement in interest rates. *See also* Chapter 12.

**Interest rate swap**   *See* **Swap** and Chapter 14.

**Interest sensitive whole life insurance**   *See* Chapter 21.

**International Association of Insurance Super-visors (IAIS)**   [www.iaisweb.org] *See* Chapter 8.

**International insurance**  Insurance transactions, that transcend or cross-national boundaries. *See also* Chapter 1.

**International Monetary Fund (IMF)**  [www.imf.org]. *See* Chapter 1.

**International Network of Pensions Regulators and Supervisors**  [www.bis.org/publ/joint01.htm] *See* Chapter 8.

**International Organization of Securities Commissions (IOSCO)**  [www.iosco.org] *See* Chapter 8.

**International Organization for Standardization (ISO)**  [www.is.org]. *See* Chapters 10 and 21.

**International risk**  Unintended outcomes that transcend or cross national boundaries.

**International Underwriting Association of London**  [www.iua.co.uk]. *See* Chapter 22.

**Intra-group exposure**  In financial integration. *See* Chapter 25.

**Investment risk**  Possibility that investments will yield a lower return than expected.

**IRA**  Individual retirement account (U.S.).

**IRM**  Institute of Risk Management (U.K.).

**Islamic Financial Services Board**  [www.ifsb.org]. *See* Chapter 8.

**ISO**  (1) Insurance Services Office [www.iso.org]; (2) International Organization for Standardization.

**IT**  Information technology. *See* Chapter 18 for IT risk management and insurance.

**IUA**  International Underwriting Association of London [www.iua.co.uk]. *See* Chapter 22.

**Joint and last–survivor annuity**  *See* Chapter 21.

**Joint Forum (on Financial Conglomerates)**  [www.bis.org/bcbs/jointforum.htm]. *See* Chapter 8.

**Joint Underwriting Association (JUA)**  (1) In automobile (motor) insurance. (2) A risk pooling, reinsurance mechanism for nonstandard risks (U.S.). *See* **Assigned risk plan**.

**Joint venture**  A type of ownership arrangement wherein two or more firms or government establish and own another firm.

**Jury**  A body of citizens chosen at random to serve as decision makers in civil and criminal cases.

**Keiretsu**  Cross shareholding or horizontal or vertical linkages of major post-World War II Japanese industrial firms (Japan). *See also* Chapter 24.

**Kidnap/ransom insurance**  *See* Chapter 16.

**Kidnapping**  Abduction and detention, usually by unlawful force and sometimes by fraud, of an individual. *See also* Chapter 16; cf. **Detention**, **Terrorism** (on individual) and **Extortion**.

**Kinesics**  Sometimes called "body language." More specifically, the system of postures, facial expressions, and body motions that convey messages. *See also* Chapter 11; cf. **Language**, **Lingua franca** and **Paralanguage**.

**Language**  A system of communicating using sounds put together according to a set of rules. *See also* Chapter 11; cf. **Lingua franca**, **Paralanguage** and **Kinesics**.

**Large risk**  E.U. classification of risk (firm) that has met at least two of the following conditions: assets greater than €6.2 million, sales over €12.8 million, and 250 or more employees; cf. **Mass risk**.

**Lava**  Molten material that has erupted onto the surface resulting from volcanic activity; cf. **Magma**.

**Law of diminishing marginal utility**  The marginal utility of wealth decreases as wealth increases. *See also* Chapter 2.

**Law of large numbers**  *See* Chapter 19.

**Law of one price**  The idea that, in a market that admits no arbitrage, two assets (or securities, portfolios, liabilities, etc.) with identical future cash flows will have the same current price. *See also* Chapter 14.

**Lead insurer (underwriter)**  (1) Commonly in reinsurance transactions, the insurer/underwriter that establishes the terms and conditions of coverage. *See also* Chapter 23. (2) In a global insurance program, the insurer that designs the global insurance program along with its subsidiaries and affiliates operating in other countries. *See also* Chapter 14.

**Lemons problem**  An asymmetric information problem in which the buyer knows less than the seller about the seller's products.

**Levirate**  The custom under which, if a husband dies leaving a wife and children, a brother of the deceased man is expected to marry the widow to provide for her and her children. *See also* Chapter 11.

**Liability risk**    Uncertainty related to financial responsibility arising from bodily injury (including death) or loss of wealth that a person or an entity causes to others.

**Liberalization**    The process of breaking down government and artificial barriers to international trade and investment. *See also* Chapter 3; cf. **Deregulation** and **Privatization**.

**Life contingencies**    When payments to policyholders or beneficiaries are determined by whether insureds are alive or dead. *See also* Chapter 21.

**Life cycle hypothesis**    *See* Chapter 2.

**Life expectancy term life**    *See* **Term life insurance** in Chapter 21.

**LIRMA**    London Insurance and Reinsurance Market Association.

**Lingua franca**    A language used for communication but not native to any of the speakers. *See also* Chapter 11.

**Liquidation**    In regulation, the winding up of a company's business. *See also* Chapter 24; cf. **Rehabilitation**.

**Liquidation period**    In annuity, time period during which annuity fund values are paid to annuitant(s). *See also* Chapter 21; cf. **Accumulation period**.

**Lloyd's association**    Any joining together of a group of individuals in their personal capacity to provide insurance or reinsurance to others.

**Lloyd's broker**    Insurance intermediary who is the access point to the underwriting syndicates at Lloyd's of London.

**Long-term disability insurance**    Long-duration income replacement insurance for individuals who are permanently disabled. *See also* Chapter 9; cf. **Short-term disability benefits**.

**Long-tail liability insurance**    Liability insurance in which claim payments may extend over several years. *See also* Chapter 22.

**Loss development factor**    (1) The ratio of the projected, ultimate loss value to the given size of losses at the time of examination. (2) A statistical approach to measure the development of losses from initial reporting and reserving to final closure or settlement. *See also* Chapter 13 for an example in self-insurance.

**Loss exposure**    A thing or person subject to the possibility of a loss.

**Loss frequency**    The number of losses expected or that did occur during a certain period; cf. **Loss severity**.

**Loss mitigation**    The act of reducing the magnitude of a potential loss.

**Loss portfolio transfer reinsurance**    A primary insurer's transfer of a complete portfolio of policies to a reinsurer. *See also* Chapter 23.

**Loss severity**    The expected or actual average of loss expressed in monetary value; cf. **Loss frequency**.

**Lulling effect**    *See* Insight 4.2.

**Magma**    Molten material that can erupt from volcanic activity; cf. **Lava**.

**Major medical insurance**    *See* Chapter 21.

**Managed care**    A coordinated medical treatment plan emphasizing controls designed to provide high quality service and control costs. *See also* Chapter 16 for **HMO**, **PPO** and **POS**.

**Mandatory cession**    In reinsurance, the government requirement that local insurance companies transfer part of their risks to the state-owned reinsurer, commonly via proportional reinsurance. *See also* Chapter 3.

**Mandatory inflation adjustment**    In pension. *See* Chapter 16.

**Mandatory savings programs (in social insurance)**    *See* Chapter 9.

**Margin of solvency**    *See* **Solvency margin**.

**Marked to market**    The periodic restatement of an asset or contract to its market value, especially with futures contracts. *See also* Chapter 14.

**Market access (right of)**    The right of a foreign firm to enter a country's market. *See also* Chapter 3; cf. **Non-discrimination**, **National treatment**, **Transparency** and **Reciprocity**.

**Market conduct regulation**    Government prescribed rules establishing inappropriate marketing practices. *See also* Chapters 8 and 25; cf. **Competition policy (antitrust) regulation** and **Prudential regulation**.

**Market exchange**    A means of distribution whereby the forces of supply and demand set the conditions for exchange of goods and services. *See also* Chapter 11.

**Market failures**    Also called **market imperfections**, market-based situations causing an inefficient allocation of resources. *See also* Chapter 2.

**Market power**    The ability of one or a few sellers (or buyers) to influence the price of a product or service in which it is trading. *See also* Chapters 4 and 25 (financial integration).

**Market risk**    Discussed under **financial risk** in Chapter 1.

**Market value**    The price prevailing in the market. *See also* Chapter 22.

**Marketability risk**    Discussed under **financial risk** in Chapter 1.

**Mass risk**    Nonlife insurance for individuals and small businesses, as used in the E.U. *See also* Chapter 1 for discussion about **commercial lines insurance**; cf. **Large risk**.

**MAT (insurance)**    Marine, aviation and transport (insurance).

**Maturity-refund policy**    Nonlife insurance with a savings element (Japan). *See also* Chapter 22.

**Means-tested program**    *See* **Economic needs-tested program**.

**Medicaid**    U.S. healthcare financing program for the poor, financed through general tax revenues; cf. **Medicare**.

**Medicare**    U.S. healthcare financing program through its social insurance system that pays medical expenses primarily for the elderly. *See also* Chapter 16; cf. **Medicaid**.

**Mental accounting**    A notion that we tend to separate a whole into its components. *See also* Chapter 2; cf. **Decision regret** and **Welfare effect**.

**Mercantilism**    *See* Chapter 3.

**MERCOSUR** (*Mercado Comun del Cono Sur*) [www.mercosur.org.uy]. *See* Chapter 1.

**Microfinance**    The provision of one or more financial services in small amounts to individuals who have few financial resources and who might otherwise not have access to such services. *See also* Chapter 11.

**MIGA**    Multilateral Investment Guarantee Agency [www.miga.org]. *See* Chapter 17 for other organizations in Table 17.2.

**Minimum efficient scale (MES)**    The point at which a firm's long-run average costs are at a minimum.

**Mirror-image reciprocity**    One or more trading partners imposing or offering identical market access and other conditions to the other(s). *See also* Chapter 3.

**Mixed conglomerate**    One that contains one or more financial services firms but which is predominantly commercially or industrially oriented. *See also* Chapter 25; cf. **Bancassurance** and **Financial conglomerate**.

**Mixed-market economies**    Economies with some degree of central government control.

**MNC**    Multinational corporation.

**Modified Mercalli Intensity Scale**    A scale used to measure the intensity of earthquakes. *See also* Chapter 5.

**Monopolistic competition**    Markets in which a large number of firms produce similar but not identical products. *See also* Chapter 2.

**Monopoly**    A market containing only one supplier of a product or service. *See also* Chapter 2.

**Moral absolutists**    Those who believe in the existence of a single universal moral standard for judging ethical behavior. *See also* Chapter 11.

**Moral hazard**    An asymmetric information problem in which the buyer of services engages in behavior riskier than otherwise, because of the existence of the insurance. *See also* Chapter 2 (definition) and Chapter 19 (effect on insurance); cf. **Adverse selection**, **Ex-ante moral hazard** and **Ex-post moral hazard**.

**Moral relativists**    Those who believe that no universal standard of right or wrong exists. *See also* Chapter 11.

**Morals**    That which individuals should do; concerned with that which is fundamentally right and wrong. *See also* Chapter 11.

**Morbidity table**    A table showing yearly or other probabilities and durations of incapacity, sickness or injury by age (or age brackets). *See also* Chapter 21; cf. **Mortality table**.

**Mortality table**    A table showing yearly probabilities of death by age (and sometimes by other variables). *See also* Chapter 21; cf. **Morbidity table**.

**Most favored nation (MFN) treatment**    *See* **non-discrimination**.

**Multi-line/multi-year (financial) product**    *See* Chapters 14 and 23.

**Multinational pooling (of employee benefit programs)**    An international network that facilitates local provision of employee benefits for subsidiaries of multinational corporations worldwide. *See also* Chapter 16.

**Multiple gearing**    *See* Chapter 25.

**Multi-trigger (financial) product**    *See* Chapter 14.

**Mutual fund**    A pool of managed assets offering investors convenient access to the securities markets. *See also* Chapter 8.

**Mutual insurance company**    An insurance company owned by its policyholders. *See also* Chapter 20 for **Assessment mutuals** and **Non-assessment mutuals**; cf. **Stock insurance company**.

***Nachfrist* notice**    A German procedure that permits a party additional time to perform contractual obligations if notice of the delay is given. *See also* Chapter 10.

**NAFTA**    North American Free Trade Agreement    [www.nafta-sec-alena.org].    *See* Chapter 1.

**Name**    At Lloyd's, the investors. *See also* Chapter 22.

**Named-peril insurance**    In nonlife insurance, cover that promises to indemnify the insured if a loss is caused from among the perils listed. *See also* Chapter 22 for **Basic form** and **Broad form**. cf. **All-risks insurance**.

**Nanotechnology**    *See* Chapter 18 for risk management.

**National Association of Insurance Commissioners (NAIC)**    [www.naic.org] Association of U.S. state insurance regulators whose are to coordinate regulatory matters among the several states and recommend model insurance legislation, but it has no enforcement power.

**National treatment**    The fair trade principle that foreign entrants into a market are accorded treatment (e.g., regulation and taxation) no less favorable than that accorded domestic companies. *See also* Chapters 3 and 24; cf. **Market access**, **Non-discrimination**, **Transparency** and **Reciprocity**.

**Natural hedge**    *See* Chapter 12.

**Natural monopoly**    When efficiency increases (i.e., average costs decrease) over an industry's entire relevant output range, giving rise to a minimum efficient scale firm so large relative to market size that only one firm can operate efficiently. *See also* Chapter 2.

**Nationalization**    Government takeover of a firm's assets with compensation. *See also* Chapter 17; for **Political risk**, **Confiscation**, **Contract frustration**, **Currency inconvertibility** and **Expropriation**.

**Natural catastrophe**    A catastrophe caused by natural forces. *See also* Chapter 5.

**Negative externality**    When a firm's or individual's activities impose uncompensated costs on others. *See also* Chapters 9 and 25.

**Negative reciprocity**    When the giver attempts to obtain an unfair advantage from an exchange. *See also* Chapter 11.

**Negative sanctions**    The threats of punishment for failure to follow the society's norm, such as fines, imprisonment, corporal punishment, and ostracism. *See also* Chapter 11; cf. **Positive sanctions**.

**Negligence**    A tort wherein injury is caused by another's failure to exercise the degree of care required by the ordinarily prudent person. *See also* Chapter 10; cf. **Intentional tort** and **Strict liability**.

**Net amount at risk (NAR)**    In life insurance, the difference between the policy face amount and the cash value. *See also* Chapter 21.

**Newly industrialized economy**    *See* Chapter 1 for definition and other terms/definitions.

**New York Convention**    *See* **UN Convention on the Recognition and Enforcement of Foreign Arbitral Awards**.

**No-fault insurance**    Commonly in automobile insurance, coverage under which the victim seeks compensation (often for bodily injuries only) from his or her own insurance company. *See also* Chapter 10 for specific types of no-fault insurance.

**Nonadmitted insurance**    The purchase of insurance from an insurance company not authorized to do business within the jurisdiction from which the insurance is purchased. *See also* Chapters 14 and 20; cf. **Admitted insurance**.

**Nonadmitted (unauthorized) insurer**    An unlicensed or otherwise unauthorized insurer; cf. **Admitted insurer**.

**Non-discrimination (most favored nation) treatment** The fair trade principle that trade concessions, including market access, extended to one country must be extended to all trading partners. *See also* Chapters 3 and 24; cf. **Fair trade principles**, **Market access**, **National treatment**, **Transparency** and **Reciprocity**.

**Non-economic damages** In court settlement. *See* Insight 14.1; cf. **Economic damages** and **Punitive damages**.

**Non-insurance transfer** (of risk) *See* Chapter 12.

**Nonlife insurance** Insurance that covers direct and indirect losses from damage to property and from legal liability. *See also* Chapter 1.

**Non-participating (without bonus/profits) life insurance policy** *See* Chapter 21.

**Non-proportional (excess-of-loss or XL) reinsurance** A loss sharing arrangement where the reinsurer shares a specified amount of loss in excess of the loss retained by the cedant. *See also* Chapter 23; cf. **Proportional reinsurance**.

**Non-rival consumption** Where one person's consumption of the good or service does not reduce its availability to others. *See also* Chapter 2.

**Nonsystematic risk** Risk that is unique to a firm (or individual) and which, therefore, often can be controlled by the firm (or individual); cf. **Systematic risk**. Discussed under **Financial risk** in Chapter 1.

**Normal pensionable age** *See* **Pensionable age**.

**Normal retirement age (NRA)** *See* **Pensionable age.**

**Normative economics** The study of economics as it should

**North American Free Trade Agreement (NAFTA)** [www.nafta-sec-alena.org].*See* Chapter 1.

**Nuclear family** Husband, wife and dependent children living as a household. *See also* Chapter 11; cf. **extended family**.

**Nuclear insurance** *See* Chapter 15.

**Nuisance** A tort wherein one party interferes with another's use and enjoyment of his or her property. *See also* Chapter 10.

**OECD** Organization for Economic Cooperation and Development [www.oecd.org]. *See* Chapter 1.

**OEEC** Organization for European Economic Cooperation.

**Offensive coverage** Intellectual property insurance coverage indemnifying the insured for legal expenses to prosecute an infringer. *See also* Chapter 18.

**Oligopoly** A market containing few suppliers that can exercise market power (often because of entry barriers). *See also* Chapter 2.

**Operational efficiency** *See* Chapter 25.

**Operational risk** *See* Chapters 1 and 12.

**Opportunity cost** the value of the most desirable foregone alternative action. *See also* Chapters 2 and 3; cf. **Absolute advantage** and **Comparative advantage**.

**Option** A contract giving its holder the right to buy (or sell) assets at a specified price during a specified period. *See also* Chapters 12 and 14; cf. **Forwards** and **Futures**.

**Ordinary life insurance** *See* Chapter 21.

**OTC** Over-the-counter (security market).

**Output price risk** The possibility that the price realized by an organization for its production outputs will decrease. *See also* Chapter 12; cf. **Input price risk**.

**P&I** *See* Protection and indemnity (club). *See also* Chapter 22.

**Paralanguage** The system of extra linguistic noises that accompany language, such as voice qualities (e.g., pitch, rhythm, loudness) and vocalizations (e.g., laughing and crying). *See also* Chapter 11; cf. **Language, Lingua franca** and **Kinesics**.

**Pareto efficiency** A condition that society's scarce resources are allocated such that no one in society can be made better off without making someone else worse off. *See also* Chapter 2.

**Paris Convention** In intellectual property, *See* Chapter 18.

**Pastoralism** A nomadic subsistence pattern of production based on herding animals *See also* Chapter 11; cf. **Production, Horticulture, Agriculture** and **Industrialization**.

**Patent** *See* Insight 18.2.

**Pay-as-you-go approach** A funding approach such that benefits for current recipients are paid from the contributions made by the currently working population. *See also* Chapter 9; cf. **Fully funded approach**.

**PCC**    *See* Protected cell company.

**Pensionable age**    The age at which covered participants in a pension scheme are eligible to receive unreduced retirement benefits. Also known as **normal pension age**, **normal retirement age** and **pension eligibility age**. *See also* Chapter 16.

**PEPs**    Personal Equity Plans (U.K.).

**Peril**    The cause of loss; cf. **Hazard**.

**Perquisites**    Special employer-financed services available only to select executives and managers. *See also* Chapter 16.

**Personal Equity Plans (PEPs)**    Personal savings/investment plans, the income on which is tax free (U.K.). *See also* Chapter 21.

**Personal insurance**    Life and nonlife insurance for individuals and families.

**Personal lines insurance**    Property and liability insurance for individuals and families.

**Personal property**    Moveable tangible property such as machinery, equipment, hardware, inventories, as well as money, accounts and documents. *See also* Chapter 22 for **Real property**.

**Personal value function**    An individual's degree of satisfaction derived from gains and losses from some reference point. *See also* Chapter 2.

**Personal risk**    Uncertainty related to loss of health, incapacity, death, and outliving one's financial resources.

**Personnel risk**    Uncertainty related to the loss to a firm due to death, incapacity, loss of health, prospect of harm to, or unexpected departure of employees. *See also* Chapter 1 (definition) and Chapter 16 (risk management).

**PERT    Program    and    Evaluation    Review Technique**. *See* Chapter 12.

**Phased retirement**    *See* **Gradual (phased) retirement**.

**PICC**    The People's Insurance Company of China.

**Planned internal loss financing**    A program where the firm is aware of a loss exposure and takes affirmative steps to plan for its internal financing. *See also* Chapter 13 for other forms of financing programs.

**Point-of-service plan**    A managed care plan under which covered employees and their dependents can use **HMO** network providers or out-of-network providers, but with different deductibles and reimbursement rates depending on where the service is received (i.e., in-network or out-of-network); cf. **HMO** and **Preferred provider organization (PPO)**.

**Policyholder (or policyowner)**    The person who can exercise all policy rights and with whom the insurer deals. *See also* Chapter 21; cf. **Insured** and **Beneficiary** in life insurance.

**Policyholders' surplus (PHS)**    The excess of assets over liabilities. The terms **capital**, **capital and surplus**, **surplus** and **shareholder funds** are used synonymously with policyholders' surplus.

**Political organization**    The means by which a society maintains social order. *See also* Chapter 11.

**Political power theory**    Other things being equal, countries with large populations are more powerful politically than are countries with small populations. *See also* Chapter 7; cf. **Economic power theory**.

**Political risk**    Any governmental action that diminishes the value of a firm operating within the political boundaries or influence of that government. *See also* Chapter 17; for **Confiscation**, **Contract frustration**, **Currency inconvertibility**, **Expropriation** and **Nationalization**.

**Political theory of regulation**    Assertion that regulation will be shaped by a type of bargaining occurring among different interest groups within the existing political and administrative structure.

**Polluter pays principle**    The party causing pollution should pay for its cleanup. *See also* Chapter 10.

**Pollution liability**    Legal responsibility for environmental impairment.

**Pool**    A collective risk sharing mechanism in insurance or reinsurance usually targeted to a particular type of large risk or policy. *See also* Chapter 23; **Insurance pool** and **Reinsurance pool**.

**Pooling of resources**    In insurance pricing. *See* Chapter 19.

**Population aging**    The aging of a population resulting from increasing longevity and decreasing fertility rates. *See also* Chapter 7; cf. **Individual aging**.

**Positive economics**    The study of economic behavior as it is.

**Positive externality** When a firm's or individual's activities provide free benefits to others. *See also* Chapters 9 and 25.

**Positive sanctions** Incentives to social conformity, such as awards, titles, and other forms of public recognition. *See also* Chapter 11; cf. **Negative sanctions**.

**PPO** Preferred provider organization.

**Precautionary principle** The civil law concept that, where threats of serious or irreversible environmental damage exists, a lack of full scientific certainty shall not be used as a reason for postponing cost-effective measures to prevent environmental degradation. *See also* Chapter 6.

**Precedent** Previous court-decided principles.

**Predatory pricing** Lowering prices to unprofitable levels to weaken or eliminate competition with the idea of raising prices after competitors are driven from the market.

**Preferred provider organization (PPO)** An arrangement under which a group of providers contracts with employers, insurers or other organizations to provide medical services at a discounted rate; cf. **HMO** and **Point-of-service (POS) plan**.

**Premium** (1) The consideration that the insured pays for insurance. *See also* Insight 19.1 for various types and definitions of premiums. (2) The price of an option.

**Premium loading** The amount added to the actuarially fair premium intended to cover the insurer's underwriting, claims and other expenses plus taxes and profits. *See also* Chapter 19.

**Premium taxation** *See* Chapter 24.

**Price discrimination** When firms offer identical products at different prices to different groups of customers.

**Price risk** (1) Discussed under **financial risk** in Chapter 1. (2) Discussed under **financial reinsurance** in Chapter 23.

**Price takers** Buyers and sellers that are so small compared with the market that they cannot exercise any influence over price.

**Primary insurers** Insurers that sell insurance to the general public. Also known as direct insurers.

**Principal-agent problem** An asymmetric information problem in which the buyer (principal) of services knows less about its agent's actions than does the agent. *See also* Chapter 2.

**Principle of abuse** The approach to enforcement of competition policy in which an inquiry into the economic effects of the alleged offensive behavior is required to determine whether it is anticompetitive. *See also* Chapter 24.

**Principle of prohibition** The approach to enforcement of competition policy in which enumerated behavior is deemed anticompetitive and automatically illegal. *See also* Chapter 24.

**Prior approval** An insurance rate regulation system in which insurers cannot use proposed rate schedules until they are officially approved by the regulator. *See also* Chapter 24.

**Privacy right** The right of an individual to control the circumstances, quantity, and type of personally identifiable information about him or her that is disclosed to others.

**Private good** A good in which one person's consumption precludes it being consumed by another.

**Private interest theory of regulation** The positive economic theories that holds that regulation exists to promote the interests of private parties. *See also* Chapter 8; cf. **Capture theory of regulation** and **Public interest theories of regulation**.

**Privatization** The process of allowing the private sector to provide services formerly provided by government or of converting a government-owned asset to private ownership. *See also* Chapters 3 and 24; cf. **Deregulation** and **Liberalization**.

**Probability of ruin** *See* Chapter 19.

**Procedural law** The area of law prescribing methods of enforcement of rights or obtaining redress for their violation. *See also* Chapter 10; cf. **Substantive law**.

**Product integration** Financial services integration occurring when firms in one sector create and sell products containing significant elements traditionally associated with products of another sector. *See also* Chapter 8; cf. **Advisory integration**.

**Product liability** The legal liability of the manufacturer (and sometimes the seller) of a product that causes injury to the purchaser or user. *See also* Chapter 10; for **Design defect**, **Manufacturing defect** and **Marketing (warning) defect**.

**Product regulation** In insurance. *See* Chapter 24.

**Production**    The use of labor, technology and some combination of land, raw materials and capital to produce the goods and services that a society wants. *See also* Chapter 11; cf. **Horticulture**, **Pastoralism**, **Agriculture** and **Industrialization**.

**Professional liability insurance** *See* Chapter 22.

**Professional reinsurer**    An insurance company that specializes in writing reinsurance. *See also* Chapter 23.

**Program and Evaluation Review Technique (PERT)**    *See* Chapter 12.

**Property and casualty insurance**    Nonlife insurance; synonymous with property and liability insurance.

**Property and liability insurance**    Nonlife insurance; a more descriptive term used to categorize those insurance policies designed to cover damage to property and legal liability exposures.

**Property risk**    Uncertainty related to loss of wealth due to damage or destruction of property.

**Proportional reinsurance**    Reinsurance in which the insurer and reinsurer share the risk proportionally and attached premium and loss according to that proportion. *See also* Chapter 23 for **Quota share reinsurance** and **Surplus reinsurance**; cf. **Proportional reinsurance**.

**Prospective reinsurance**    *See* Chapter 23; cf. **Retrospective reinsurance**.

**Protected cell company (PCC)**    Also known as **sponsored captives**, are captive insurance operations established within an existing captive owned and operated by an unrelated firm. *See also* Chapter 13.

**Protection and Indemnity (P&I) club**    *See* Chapter 22.

**Provident fund**    A type of government-mandated pension program with an individual account system. *See also* Chapter 9.

**Prudential regulation**    Regulation focused on the financial condition of financial intermediaries. *See also* Chapter 8; cf. **Competition policy (antitrust) regulation** and **Market conduct regulation**.

**Producer surplus**    The difference between (1) the amount for which the producer is able to sell its goods or services (i.e., the market price) and (2) the amount which the producer is willing to charge; *See also* Chapter 3; cf. **Consumer surplus** and **Social welfare**.

**Product differentiation**    The strategy of imbuing products with characteristics that differentiate them from those of competitors in the minds of customers.

**Product homogeneity**    Products that are perfect substitutes in the minds of buyers.

**Production**    The use of labor, technology and some combination of land, raw materials or capital to produce the goods and services that society wants.

**Progressive liberalization**    Concept that once a reservation is removed, it cannot be reinstated, thus preventing the erection of new trade barriers; cf. **Liberalization**.

**Property right**    *See* Chapter 4.

**Prudential carve-out**    Provision in the GATS giving countries the ability to differentiate between foreign and domestic providers to protect consumers and the integrity of their financial systems. *See also* Chapter 1.

**Psychological** (or **psychometric**) **theory of risk perception**    The belief that risk is inherently subjective and is influenced by an array of social, political, cultural, psychological, and other factors. *See also* Chapter 11.

**Public goods**    Collectively consumed goods or services that carry extensive positive externalities. *See also* Chapter 4.

**Public interest theory of regulation**    The normative economic theory that asserts that regulation exists to serve the public interest. *See also* Chapter 8; cf. **Capture theory of regulation** and **Private interest theories of regulation**.

**Public liability**    *See* Insight 14.1.

**Punitive damages**    In court settlement. *See* Insight 14.1; cf. **Economic damages** and **Special (non-economic) damages**.

**Pure cross-border insurance trade**    *See* Chapter 20.

**Pure premium**    *See* Insight 19.1.

**Pure risk**    Also called **hazard risk**, where the range of outcomes involves only no loss or a loss. *See also* Chapter 1.

**Put option**    The right to sell an asset at a fixed price during the option term. *See also* Chapter 14.

**Quota**   Limitations set by the government on the quantity of goods produced or purchased, typically in international trade. *See also* Chapter 3; cf. **Tariff**, **Subsidy** and **Government procurement**.

**Quota share reinsurance**   *See* Chapter 23.

**RBC**   Risk based capital. *See* Insight 24.1; cf. **Solvency margin**.

**Reactor scram**   The sudden shutting down of a nuclear reactor usually by rapid insertion of control rods either automatically or manually. *See also* Chapter 6.

**Real property**   Land, buildings and other structures attached to land. *See also* Chapter 22; cf. **Personal property**.

**Rebate**   *See* Insight 11.2 for **Bribe**.

**Rate regulation**   In insurance. *See* Chapter 24.

**Reciprocity**   (1) The response in kind by one or more governments to trading actions taken by another government. *See also* Chapter 3; cf. **Market access**, **National treatment**, **Non-discrimination** and **Transparency**. (2) The mutual exchange of goods or services usually in the form of a gift. *See also* Chapter 11 for **Balance reciprocity**, **Generalized reciprocity** and **Negative reciprocity**. (3) Agreements among insurers to share risks by transferring portions of their portfolios to each other; cf. **Mirror-image reciprocity**. *See also* Chapters 3 and 23.

**Reciprocal risk retention group**   An RRG operating as a reciprocal which is an unincorporated association of entities that exchange insurance liability with each other through an attorney-in-fact that manages the reciprocal. *See also* Chapter 13.

**Redistribution**   A particular individual or group collecting goods (assets) from selected members of society and redistributing them. *See also* Chapter 11.

**Re-entry provision**   In life insurance. *See* Chapter 21.

**Regulatory arbitrage**   *See* Chapter 25.

**Reinsurance**   Insurance purchased by primary insurers to hedge their portfolios of insurance policies. cf. **Insurance** and **Retrocession**.

**Rehabilitation**   Regulatory actions to return a financially troubled insurer to the marketplace as an independent, fully functioning insurer. *See also* Chapter 24; cf. **Liquidation**.

**Reinstatement**   Restoring the reinsurance limit to the original level after collecting part or all of the original limit. *See also* Chapter 23.

**Reinstatement value**   *See* **Replacement cost**.

**Reliability analysis**   In self-insurance. *See* Chapter 13.

**Religion**   A set of attitudes, beliefs and practices pertaining to supernatural power. *See also* Chapter 11.

**Rent-a-captive**   An insurance company set up to insure or reinsure the risks of unrelated organizations with the express purpose of returning underwriting profit and investment income to the insureds. *See also* Chapter 13.

**Rent-seeking behavior**   To seek to influence regulation in a way that gains economic benefit for private parties. *See also* Chapter 3; cf. **Economic rent**.

**Replacement cost**   Also known as **reinstatement value**, in property insurance, the cost to replace or repair damaged property without depreciation. *See also* Chapter 22; cf. **Actual cash value**.

**Replacement rate**   The birth rate needed to maintain a stable population over time, ignoring immigration. *See also* Chapter 7.

**Representative office**   An office of a foreign company primary for market research and promotion of the interests of the company. *See also* Chapter 20; cf. **Agency**, **Branch** and **Subsidiary**.

**Reputational risk**   Uncertainty associated with an event that could damage a firm's good reputation with the result that it suffers decreased revenues, increased expenses or both.

**Reservations**   Measures taken by countries that are inconsistent with trade agreements, such as the OECD Codes. *See also* Chapter 1; cf. **Measures**.

**Residual market plan**   In automobile (motor) insurance, *See* **assigned risk plan**.

**Retaliation**   A government action that restricts access to its market in response to a trading partner's restricting access or failure to lower existing trade barriers to its market. *See also* Chapter 3.

**Retention**   (1) The internal funding of losses. (2) The amount of loss that an insurer retains when reinsuring a risk (or, a reinsurer retains when retroceding a risk). *See also* Chapter 23; cf. **Cession**.

**Retrocession** Risk transfer/sharing arrangement by which reinsurers themselves purchase reinsurance. *See also* Chapter 23.

**Retrospective rating** Pricing plan whereby the insurer makes premium adjustments at the end of each policy period based primarily on the insured's loss experience. *See also* Chapter 19; cf. **Experience rating**.

**Retrospective reinsurance** A form of financial reinsurance covering past loss experience. *See also* Chapter 23; cf. **Prospective reinsurance**.

**Reversionary bonuses** Paid-up additions expressed as a percentage of either the original or current benefit amount. *See also* Chapter 21; cf. **Terminal bonus**.

**Richter scale** A logarithmic scale that measures the magnitude of an earthquake. *See also* Chapter 5.

**Ring of Fire** *See* Chapter 5.

**Risk administration** The management of the risk assessment, risk control and risk financing activities. *See also* Chapter 12 (ERM).

**Risk assessment** The process of identifying and analyzing both the likelihood and possible severity of potential losses. *See also* Chapter 12 (ERM).

**Risk aversion** *See* Chapters 2 and 9.

**Risk-based capital** *See* Insight 24.1; cf. **Solvency margin**.

**Risk classification** In insurance underwriting. *See* Chapter 20.

**Risk control** *See* Chapter 12 (ERM).

**Risk (Working) excess-of-loss reinsurance** *See* Chapter 23.

**Risk financing** *See* Chapter 12 (ERM).

**Risk-neutral utility function** *See* Chapter 2.

**Risk mapping** *See* Chapter 12.

**Risk premium** The maximum amount an individual is willing to pay above the actuarially fair premium. *See also* Chapter 19.

**Risk retention groups (RRG)** A type of U.S. group captive created under special U.S. law to underwrite certain of its members' liability exposures. *See also* Chapter 13 for **Reciprocal risk retention group**.

**Risk selection** In insurance underwriting. *See* Chapter 20.

**RRG** *See* Risk retention group.

**RRSP** Registered Retirement Savings Plan.

**Rule of reason** *See* **Principle of prohibition**.

**Rotating savings and credit association (ROSCA)** *See* Insight 11.6.

**Run** A type of systemic risk under which many depositors (or other creditors) demand their money at once because of loss of confidence in the financial institution or system. *See also* Chapter 8.

**Safety net issues** In financial integration. *See* Chapter 25.

**Saffir-Simpson scale** *See* Table 5.2.

**SAP** *See* **Statutory Accounting Principle**.

**Sarbanes-Oxley Act** *See* Chapter 10.

**Scenario planning** A strategic planning method in which analysts generate simulation games that are used by management to consider and develop plans to deal with alternative futures. *See also* Chapter 15.

**Second-to-die (survivor) life insurance** Life insurance insuring two lives but paying the face amount only after the second insured dies. *See also* Chapter 21; cf. **First-to-die life insurance**.

**Security-type law** In automobile insurance. *See* Insight 10.2.

**Second Generation Insurance Directives** A set of E.U. directives establishing liberalization requirements in nonlife insurance, motor insurance and life insurance based on the size and status of policyholders and the degree of consumer protection needed; cf. **Third Generation Insurance Directives**.

**Securitization** The process of creating a security backed by the cash flows from a pool of assets or liabilities. *See also* Chapter 15.

**Self-insurance** A planned, formal internal financing program whereby the self-insured borrows insurance techniques to price retained risks. *See also* Chapter 13 also specific forms of self-insurance as well as other financial programs.

**SERPS** State Earnings Related Pension Schemes (U.K.).

**Shariah** A collection of "truths" by Islamic scholars of moral, ethical, and legal standards by which Muslims must abide. *See also* Chapter 10.

**Short-term disability benefits** Income replacement insurance of comparatively short duration for individuals. *See also* Chapter 9; cf. **Long-term disability benefits**.

**Signal value**  (Of an event), the perception that the event provides new information about the likelihood of similar or more destructive future mishaps. *See also* Chapter 4.

**Single-parent captive**  A captive insurer owned by one organization. *See also* Chapter 13.

**Slip**  A simplified proposal for insurance or reinsurance. *See also* Chapter 23.

**Social insurance**  A program that meets the following three criteria: income security is provided for well-defined risks; participation is compulsory for the target population; and contributions to the program are not adjusted for probability of loss. *See also* Chapter 9.

**Social insurance model**  A healthcare financing in which compulsory employment-related payroll taxes pay for healthcare services for workers and their dependents. *See also* Chapter 9; cf. **General tax revenue model** and **Voluntary insurance model**.

**Social regulation**  *See* Chapter 8.

**Social welfare**  The sum of producer surplus and consumer surplus. *See also* Chapter 3; cf. **Consumer surplus** and **Producer surplus**.

**Socialism**  A social and economic system in which the means of production are owned and controlled largely by the community as a whole and administered in its collective interest.

**Socialization**  The process by which children are inculcated with their group's culture. *See also* Chapter 11.

**Solvency margin**  Minimum ongoing capital and surplus requirements set out as the relationship between (1) surplus and (2) premiums written (life and nonlife), claims incurred (nonlife) or mathematical reserves (life insurance). *See also* Chapter 24; cf. **Risk-based capital requirement**.

**Southern Cone Common Market**  *See* **MERCOSUR**.

**Specific performance**  A legal decree that forces performance by a non-performing party to a contract. *See also* Chapter 10.

**SPV**  Special purposes vehicle (in reinsurance or risk securitization).

**Spot (cash) market**  A market in which standardized goods are exchanged via currency transactions taking place in the present. *See also* Chapter 14.

**Spread**  A portfolio of two call options in which one is to buy a call option with exercise price *a* and sell a call option with exercise price *b*.

***Stare decisis***  "To stand on decided cases"; the principle in common law legal systems that precedent will be followed.

**Statutory accounting principles (SAP)**  Accounting principles prescribed by the insurance regulator for use by insurers in preparing their financial statements for regulatory oversight purposes. *See also* Chapter 24; cf. **Generally accepted accounting principles (GAAP)**.

**Stock insurance company**  An insurance company owned by its shareholders. *See also* Chapter 20; cf. **Mutual insurance company**.

**Stop loss**  (1) In insurance. *See* Insight 19.2. (2) As a reinsurance arrangement, *See also* Chapter 23.

**Straight deductible**  *See* Insight 19.2.

**Strategic risk**  *See* Chapters 1 and 12.

**Strict liability**  Liability without having to establish negligence. *See* Chapter 10; cf. **Negligence** and **strict liability**.

**Strike (exercise) price**  The price specified in an options contract at which assets may be bought (or sold). *See also* Chapter 14.

**Subscription market**  A market in which coverage needs are often satisfied by a group of insurers or reinsurers on a collective basis. *See also* Chapter 22.

**Substantive law**  Law that creates and regulates rights. *See also* Chapter 10; cf. **Procedural law**.

**Subsidiary**  A company owned by another company either by purchasing an existing company or incorporating a new company. *See also* Chapter 20; cf. **Agency**, **Branch** and **Representative office**.

**Subsidy**  Governmental actions that lower the cost of products to individuals. *See also* Chapter 3; cf. **Quota**, **Tariff** and **Government procurement**.

**Substitute**  In insurance economics. *See* Chapter 19; cf. **Complement**.

**Sum assured**  *See* **Face amount**.

**Superannuation**  Traditional or investment-linked and pension products (Australia and elsewhere). *See also* Chapter 21.

**Superfund**   In U.S. environmental pollution risk management. *See* Chapter 10.

**Supplemental healthcare benefit**   Benefits for additional medical treatment beyond basic medical care. *See also* Chapters 16 and 21; cf. **Basic healthcare benefit**.

**Surplus**   The excess of assets over liabilities. The terms **capital**, **capital and surplus**, **policyholders' surplus** and **shareholder funds** are used synonymously with surplus.

**Surplus reinsurance**   *See* Chapter 23.

**Surrender charge**   In life insurance. *See* Chapter 21.

**Surveillance**   The regular dialogue and policy advice that the IMF offers to each of its members. *See also* Chapter 1.

**Sustainable development**   The concept first articulated at the Stockholm conference on the environment that economic development can coexist with environmental protection. *See also* Chapter 10.

**Sustainability risk management**   The application of risk management by corporations and government to alter, change and adjust risk control systems through innovation and creativity to produce sustainable natural systems. *See also* Chapter 15; cf. **Disaster planning** and **Crisis risk management**.

**Swap**   The exchange of one security for another. *See also* Chapter 14 for **Currency swap** and **Interest rate swap**.

**Syndicates**   Entities that conduct the underwriting activities for their **underwriting members**. *See also* Chapter 22 (in the London market).

**Systematic risk**   The possibility that difficulties of financial intermediaries could cause meaningful disruptions elsewhere within an economy. Discussed under **financial risk** in Chapter 1; cf. **Nonsystematic risk**.

*Takaful*   In Islam, a solidarity fund relying on a pact among participants to guarantee each other.

**Tariff**   (1) A tax levied on imported goods. *See also* Chapter 3; cf. **Quota**, **Subsidy** and **Government procurement**. (2) Government-controlled premium rates in the insurance market.

**Tariff market**   An insurance market or line of insurance in which government-sanctioned cartels or government bodies set insurance rates, acceptable ranges for rates or the permissible factors used to derive rates. *See also* Chapter 24.

**Temporary life annuity**   *See* Chapter 21.

**Term life insurance**   *See* Chapter 21 also for **Yearly (annual) renewable term**, **Life expectancy term** and **Term-to-age-65**.

**Terminal bonuses**   Distributions of unrealized capital gains to life insurance policyholders at death or policy maturity. *See also* Chapter 21; cf. **Reversionary bonus**.

**Terrorism**   An act of violence or threat of violence against individuals or property committed by one or more individuals acting on behalf of an organization for the purpose of influencing government policy or actions to advance a political, religious, or ideological cause. *See also* Chapters 6 and 9 (general) as well as Chapter 15 (risk management and pools) and Chapter 16 (personnel risk management); cf. **Detention**, **Extortion**, and **Kidnapping**.

**Third Generation Insurance Directives**   A set of E.U. directives taking the E.U. liberalization program to a higher level by establishing requirements for a single license system that allows insurers authorized by a member state where their head office is located to operate both through establishment and through freedom of services throughout the E.U.

**Third party administrator (TPA)**   A private company that offers services to businesses and other entities for the establishment and maintenance of self-insurance programs. *See also* Chapter 13.

**Tied agent**   *See* **Captive agent**.

**Timing risk**   The possibility of loss of investment income because funds are not held for as long as had been anticipated. *See also* Chapter 23.

**Tort**   A civil wrong resulting in injury to a person or property.

**Total adjusted capital (TAC)**   A capital level related to RBC regulation.

**Total compensation (remuneration)**   All forms of direct (base pay, bonuses, etc.) and indirect (employee benefits and perquisites) compensation provided by the employer. *See also* Chapter 16.

**Total compensation (remuneration) approach**   An approach to employee benefit plan design that recognizes the importance of employee benefits in total compensation and the existence of distinct tradeoffs between benefits and wages. *See also* Chapter 16.

**TPA**   *See* **Third Party Administrator**.

**Trade secret**   As intellectual property. *See* Insight 18.2.

**Trademark**   *See* Insight 18.2.

**Trade round**   Trade negotiations conducted under the auspices of the WTO or, in the past, the GATT. *See also* Chapter 3.

**Transparency**   Requirement that regulatory and other legal requirements regarding market access and domestic operation should be clearly set out and easily available. *See also* Chapters 3 and 25; cf. **Market access**, **National treatment**, **Non-discrimination** and **Reciprocity**.

**Treaty reinsurance**   Reinsurance agreements under which the primary insurer agrees to reinsure and the reinsurer agrees to accept all insurance written by the primary insurer that comes within the treaty's terms. *See also* Chapter 23; cf. **Facultative reinsurance**.

**Tropical storm**   *See* Chapter 5.

**Tsunami**   *See* Chapter 5.

**Typhoon**   *See* Chapter 5.

**UN Conference on Trade and Development (UNCTAD)**   [www.unctad.org]. *See* Chapter 1.

**UN Convention on Contracts for the International Sale of Goods (CISG)**   *See* Chapter 10.

**UN Convention on the Recognition and Enforcement of Foreign Arbitral Awards**   *See* Chapter 10.

**UNCED**   United Nations Conference on Environment and Development. *See* Chapter 12.

**Underwriting**   *See* Chapter 20.

**Underwriting capacity**   The maximum amount of insurance that can be safely written by an insurer, expressed commonly in terms of premiums. The capacity is determined mainly by the company's capital and surplus. *See also* Chapter 22.

**Underwriting members (Names)**   Individual investors in Lloyd's of London. *See also* Chapter 22.

**Underwriting risk**   Assumption of risk that losses and expenses under an insurance contract will be greater than expected. *See also* Chapter 23 for reinsurance application.

**Underinsurance**   (1) Purchase of property insurance below the limit required (or recommended) by the insurer. (2) When the available insurance limit is less than the amount of damage. *See also* Chapter 10 for **Uninsurance**.

**Unearned premium reserve**   Liability established by an insurer to recognize that portion of paid premiums for which coverage has yet to be provided. *See also* Insight 19.1 for **unearned premium** and other definitions of premium, also Chapter 24 (regulation).

**Unemployment insurance**   *See* Chapter 9.

**Universal (social insurance) program**   A social insurance program providing benefits to all citizens. *See also* Chapter 9.

**United Nations (UN)**   [www.un.org]   *See* Chapter 1.

**Unit-linked life insurance policies**   *See* Chapter 21.

**Universal bank**   *See* Chapter 25

**Universal life insurance**   *See* Chapter 21.

**Unplanned internal loss financing**   A situation in which not external financial source exists and the firm is unaware of a loss exposure. *See also* Chapter 13 for other forms of financing programs.

**Utility**   An index of satisfaction derived from economic goods. *See also* Chapter 2.

**Utility function**   Mapping of particular wealth levels to corresponding levels of satisfaction for an individual. *See also* Chapter 2.

**Value at risk (VaR)**   *See* Chapter 12.

**Variable universal life**   *See* Chapter 21.

**Vertical collusion**   When two or more firms on different functional levels undertake activities to reduce competition. *See also* Chapter 24; cf. **Horizontal collusion** and **Conglomerate collusion**.

**Victim compensation fund**   *See* Chapter 4.

**Virtual captive insurers**   Captives with minimum in-house operations (e.g., program management, underwriting, and auditing) and cost efficient outsourcing (e.g., actuarial, accounting, and marketing). *See also* Chapter 13.

**Volcano**   (1) The vents in the earth's crust through which gases, molten rock or lava and solid fragments are discharged and (2) the conical shaped mountains or hills produced by the lava and other erupted material around the vent. *See also* Chapter 5.

**Voluntary insurance model**   Where health services are financed and provided through voluntary participation in a private insurance system *See also* Chapter 9; cf. **General tax revenue model** and **Social insurance model**.

**Voodoo**   *See* Insight 11.4.

**Weather risk**   *See* Chapter 14 for a case.

**Welfare effect**   (1) The tendency to set a higher price to sell that which we already own than what we would be willing to pay to purchase the identical item if we did not own it. *See also* Chapter 2; cf. **Decision regret** and **Mental accounting**. (2) In international trade. *See* Chapter 3.

**Wellness programs**   Programs (e.g., no-smoking days, health risk appraisals) designed to improve the health and wellbeing of a firm's employees. *See also* Chapter 16.

**Whole account excess-of-loss reinsurance**   *See* Chapter 23.

**Whole life insurance**   Insurance intended for the entirely of the insured's life. Variations include limited-payment whole life, single-premium whole life, fixed-premium universal life, and variable (unit-linked) whole life. *See* Chapter 21 also for **Ordinary life insurance, current assumption whole life** and **interest sensitive whole life**.

**WIPO**   World Intellectual Property Organization [www.wipo.int]. *See* Chapter 18.

**With-profits policy**   Life insurance policy on which bonuses (dividends) are paid; also known as participating policy. *See also* Chapter 21; cf. **Non-participating (without profit) policy**.

**Working excess-of-loss reinsurance**   *See* Chapter 23.

**World Bank**   [www.worldbank.org].   *See* Chapter 1.

**World Bank Guarantee Program**   In political risk insurance, *See* Chapter 17 also for other organizations in Table 17.2.

**World Health Organization (WHO)**   [www.who.int]. *See* Chapter 1, also refer the definition of **health**.

**World Trade Organization (WTO)**   [www.wto.org]. *See* Chapter 1.

**Workers' (Workmen's) Compensation**   A strict liability insurance indemnifying the insured/employer for work-related injuries of employees regardless of who is at fault. *See also* Chapter 9 (occupational injury benefits) and Chapter 22 (general).

**Worldview**   A society's deeply held beliefs about the environment, nature, their social organizations and their values. *See also* Chapter 4.

**X-efficiency**   *See* **Dynamic efficiency**. Chapter 25.

**XL reinsurance**   *See* non-proportional reinsurance.

**Yearly renewable term life**   *See* **Term life insurance** in Chapter 21.

# Index